Management Information Systems

**Solving Business Problems
with Information Technology**

Third Edition

Gerald V. Post
University of the Pacific

David L. Anderson
Loyola University

**McGraw-Hill
Irwin**

Boston   Burr Ridge, IL   Dubuque, IA   Madison, WI   New York
San Francisco   St. Louis   Bangkok   Bogotá   Caracas   Kuala Lumpur
Lisbon   London   Madrid   Mexico City   Milan   Montreal   New Delhi
Santiago   Seoul   Singapore   Sydney   Taipei   Toronto

McGraw-Hill Higher Education

A Division of The **McGraw-Hill** *Companies*

MANAGEMENT INFORMATIONS SYSTEMS:
SOLVING BUSINESS PROBLEMS WITH INFORMATION TECHNOLOGY
Published by McGraw-Hill/Irwin, a business unit of The McGraw-Hill Companies, Inc., 1221 Avenue of the Americas, New York, NY, 10020.
Copyright © 2003, 2000, 1997 by The McGraw-Hill Companies, Inc. All rights reserved. No part of this publication may be reproduced or distributed in any form or by any means, or stored in a database or retrieval system, without the prior written consent of The McGraw-Hill Companies, Inc., including, but not limited to, in any network or other electronic storage or transmission, or broadcast for distance learning. Some ancillaries, including electronic and print components, may not be available to customers outside the United States.

This book is printed on acid-free paper.

domestic   3 4 5 6 7 8 9 0 VNH/VNH 0 9 8 7 6 5 4 3
international 1 2 3 4 5 6 7 8 9 0 VNH/VNH 0 9 8 7 6 5 4 3 2

ISBN 0-07-248942-1

Publisher: *George Werthman*
Senior sponsoring editor: *Rick Williamson*
Developmental editor: *Kelly L. Delso*
Manager, Marketing and Sales: *Paul Murphy*
Media producer: *Greg Bates*
Project manager: *Laura Griffin*
Lead production supervisor: *Heather D. Burbridge*
Senior designer: *Jennifer McQueen*
Photo research coordinator: *Judy Kausal*
Photo researcher: *Judy Mason*
Senior supplement producer: *Rose M. Range*
Senior digital content specialist: *Brian Nacik*
Cover image: *© Digital Vision*
Typeface: *10/12 Times New Roman*
Compositor: *Shepherd Incorporated*
Printer: *Von Hoffmann Press, Inc.*

Library of Congress Cataloging-in-Publication Data

Post, Gerald V.
   Management information systems : solving business problems with information
technology / Gerald V. Post, David L. Anderson.—3rd ed.
     p. cm.
   Includes bibliographical references and indexes.
   ISBN 0-07-248942-1 (alk. paper)—ISBN 0-07-119874-1 (International ed.)
   1. Management information systems. I. Anderson, David L. (David Lee), 1953- II.
Title.
   HD30.213 .P67 2003
   658.4'038—dc21

2002021268

INTERNATIONAL EDITION ISBN 0-07-119874-1
Copyright © 2003. Exclusive rights by The McGraw-Hill Companies, Inc. for manufacture and export. This book cannot be re-exported from the country to which it is sold by McGraw-Hill. The International Edition is not available in North America.

www.mhhe.com

To my parents for their support through the years.

Gerald V. Post

To my parents.

David L. Anderson

Brief Contents

Contents

Chapter 3
Networks and Telecommunications   78

Chapter 4
Security, Privacy, and Anonymity   122

Chapter 12
Systems Development 458

Chapter 13
Organizing Information System Resources 506

InformationTechnology

INFORMATION TECHNOLOGY AT MCGRAW-HILL/IRWIN

At McGraw-Hill Higher Education, we publish instructional materials for the higher education market. In order to expand the tools of higher learning, we publish everything you may need: texts, lab manuals, study guides, testing materials, software, and multimedia products—the Total Solution.

We realize that technology has created and will continue to create new mediums for professors and students to use in managing resources and communicating information to one another. McGraw-Hill/Irwin continues to provide the most flexible and complete teaching and learning tools available as well as offer solutions to the changing world of teaching and learning. McGraw-Hill/Irwin is dedicated to providing the tools for today's instructors and students, which will enable them to successfully navigate the world of Information Technology.

- **Seminar Series and Focus Groups**—McGraw-Hill/Irwin's seminar series and focus groups are offered across the country every year. At the seminar series we provide you with the latest technology products and encourage collaboration among teaching professionals. We conduct many focus groups year round where we can hear from you what we need to publish.

- **ITAP-Information Technology Advisory Panel.** This is a "super focus group," where we gather many of the country's top IT educators for three days to tell us how to publish the best IT texts possible. ITAPs are very instrumental in driving our publishing plans.

- **McGraw-Hill/Osborne**—This leading trade division of the McGraw-Hill Companies is known for its best-selling Internet titles, Harley Hahn's Internet & Web yellow pages, and the Internet Complete Reference. If we don't have it in our CIT/MIS, you can find it at Osborne. For more information, visit Osborne at www.osborne.com

- **Digital Solutions**—Whether you want to teach a class online or just post your "bricks-n-mortar" class syllabus, McGraw-Hill/Irwin is committed to publishing digital solutions. Taking your course online doesn't have to be a solitary adventure, nor does it have to be a difficult one. We offer several solutions that will allow you to enjoy all the benefits of having your course material online.

- **Packaging Options**—For more information about our discount options, contact your McGraw-Hill/Irwin Sales representative at 1-800-338-3987 or visit our website at www.mhhe.com/it.

Preface

A Tale of Two Careers

Jack Lewis had it made. Or so he thought. A number of well-timed promotions at his Midwest publishing firm, W.C. Green, Inc., had landed him comfortably in the role of marketing director of the educational book division. Unlike many of his colleagues, Jack tried to keep up with the latest changes in information technology. He entered data into spreadsheets to create color graphs for budgets and expenses. His reports were created with professionally designed word-processing templates. The dark mahogany desk, the 180 degree view of the duck pond and the $30,000 of computer hardware and software in his office were testaments to his success. Then it happened. A competitor developed an information system that used advanced technology to deliver custom books to students on demand over the Internet. Caught without a competitive marketing strategy, sales at W.C. Green dropped dramatically. Driving home after losing his job, Jack still could not figure out what went wrong.

Julie Nilar just would not quit. She too had a marketing degree like Jack, but decided not to pursue a traditional career right out of college. A nationally ranked bicycle racer, on graduating she chose to develop her cycling skills in international competition; she dreamed of being chosen for the U.S. Women's Olympic Road Team. To pay the bills, she got a part-time job as a marketing representative for Rolling Thunder Bicycles, a small Colorado mail-order service providing custom-made bicycles to a national customer base. Because international competition kept Julie away for long periods of time, she always took her laptop with her to stay in touch with the office. No stranger to information technology, one project she developed during these long absences was a powerful database application that kept track of Rolling Thunder's suppliers, customers, and their orders. This application became a powerful tool for Rolling Thunder and one which led to greatly increased productivity for the company.

MANAGERS AND INFORMATION TECHNOLOGY

As these two contrasting scenarios demonstrate, continual improvements and advances in information (IT) are encouraging even more changes in business and society. Managers and professionals who use IT not only to present and deliver information but also to solve their business problems will reap the rewards while those who do not will be left behind to ponder what went wrong.

The last few years brought exciting changes to managers, and the future promises even more. Increased competition forces organizations to cut costs and operate with fewer managers. The growth of small businesses encourages entrepreneurs to run their own businesses and consulting firms. Continual performance improvements, expanded storage capacity, increased capabilities of software, the Internet, and wireless access affect all aspects of management.

The exponential growth of the Internet is exceeding all forecasts. The Internet holds the potential to revolutionize virtually all aspects of business. Add in the capabilities of wireless access and the business world changes again. Consumers are presented with more choices and more data. Companies have more ways to track customer actions and preferences. Investors have instant access to data around the world. Managers have more ways to communicate and share ideas. Team members can share data and work together from any location.

Continual changes in IT present two challenges: learning to use it and finding new opportunities to improve management. Most students have taken a hands-on course that teaches them how to use a computer. Many expect the introductory MIS course to be more of the same—hands-on computer usage tied to specific needs. However, there are more complex and interesting problems to be solved. Managers need to apply their knowledge of IT tools to solve management problems and find new opportunities to improve their organizations. The focus of this book is to investigate the more complex question: How can we use IT to improve our performance in the business environment?

ABOUT THE BOOK

Features that Focus on Solving Problems

Each chapter contains several unique features to assist in understanding the material and in applying it to analyze and solve business problems.

- **What You Will Learn in This Chapter.** A series of questions highlight the important issues.

- **Lead Case.** An introductory, real-world case illustrates the problems explored in the chapter.

- **Overview.** A managerial perspective of the issues and solutions covered in the chapter.

- **Trends.** Sidebar boxes that present the major changes, brief history, or trends that affect the topics in the chapter.

- **Reality Bytes.** Brief applications, mini-cases, and discussions that emphasize a specific point, highlight international issues, business trends, or ethics. They also illustrate problems and solutions in the real world.

- **Chapter Summary.** A brief synopsis of the chapter highlights—useful when reviewing for exams.

- **A Manager's View.** A short summary of how the chapter relates to managers and to the overall question of how information technology can improve management.

- **Key Words.** A list of words introduced in the chapter. A full glossary is provided at the end of the text.

- **Review Questions.** Designed as a study guide for students.

- **Exercises.** Problems that apply the knowledge learned in the chapter. Many utilize common application software to illustrate the topics.

- **Additional Reading.** References for more detailed investigation of the topics.

- **Website References.** Websites that provide discussions or links to useful topics.

- **Industry-Specific Cases.** In-depth discussion of the lead case and several other companies. Each chapter highlights a specific industry and compares different approaches to the problems faced by the firms.

Chapter	Case focus: Industry
1	Fast food
2	Entrepreneurial businesses
3	Specialty retail
4	Wholesale trade
5	Retail sales
6	Airlines
7	Automobiles
8	Computer hardware
9	Franchises
10	Travel
11	Package delivery
12	Government agencies
13	Financial services
14	Health care

- **Appendix.** A hands-on application and demonstration of using various tools to help managers solve common business problems.

Goals and Philosophy

- All of the chapters emphasize the goal of understanding how information technology can be used to improve management. The focus is on understanding the benefits and costs of technology and its application.

- Emphasis is on the importance of database management systems. Increasingly, managers need to retrieve data, utilize a DBMS to investigate, analyze, and communicate.

- Emphasis is also placed on the importance of communication, teamwork, and integration of data. Understanding information technology requires more than knowledge of basic application packages. Students need to use and understand the applications of groupware technologies.

- Students increasingly want to know how technology is used to solve problems in their chosen major/functional area. Several current applications, including hands-on exercises are highlighted in Chapter 8. The applications can be expanded to even more detail depending on the background of the students.

- In-depth cases that illustrate the use of technology. By focusing each chapter on a specific industry, students can understand and evaluate a variety of approaches. Many cases illustrate companies varying over time, so students can see the changes occurring in business and understand the evolving role and importance of information technology.

- The Rolling Thunder Database, a medium-size, detailed database application of a small business, is available on disk. Specific exercises are highlighted in each chapter. The database contains data and applications suitable for operating a small (fictional) firm. It also contains data generation routines so instructors can create their own scenarios.

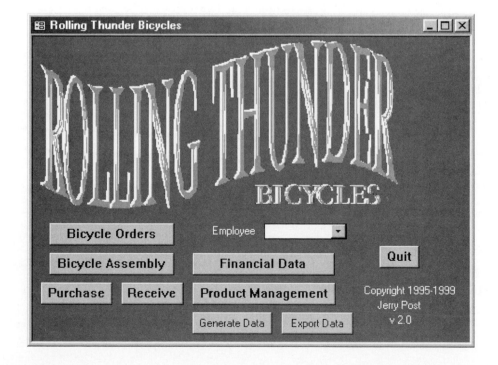

Changes to the Third Edition

1. **The Internet and e-business.** In many ways, e-business is just another aspect of MIS in business, but the Internet has brought some new technologies to managers. Consequently, a large portion of the text has been rewritten to emphasize the role and importance of the Internet in business. E-business represents more than just e-commerce. The text has also been reorganized to present topics in a sequence that is necessary for e-business. For example, the topic of networks has been moved to Chapter 3, followed by computer security issues in Chapter 4, and transactions in Chapter 5. It is relatively important to cover security issues early in the book because of the recurring importance of security in e-business.

   Chapter 11 is new and describes issues in e-business, m-commerce, and entrepreneurship. Because of the innovations in e-business, entrepreneurs create many of the businesses, so students are interested in the details of starting and growing a business. These chapters cover the issues in organizing and managing an Internet-based business.

2. **Impact on society.** Chapter 14 has an expanded discussion of how IT issues are affecting society. In particular, the role of the government in business, the Internet, privacy, and protection raise many questions. Students need to be aware of the issues to become effective citizens in the new world.

3. **Systems design.** Coverage of systems design has been consolidated into Chapter 12. The discussion has been consolidated, but it is still important. Managers need to understand the issues involved in developing systems and managing the MIS departments.

4. **New cases and Reality Bytes.** All of the chapter cases and most of the Reality Bytes examples have been replaced or rewritten.

5. **Application appendixes.** Every chapter has an application appendix that examines a hands-on topic. These appendixes provide a new level of instruction, enabling the instructor to focus on hands-on applications that are relevant to the specific chapters. Each appendix has sample applications and a set of exercises that illustrate the topic. The exercises can also be combined with the Rolling Thunder Bicycle case—providing a small, but realistic illustration of decision making and management in a real-world environment. The topics can be covered in class, in a lab, or given as assignments. PowerPoint slides and the sample application files are all available on the Instructor CD-ROM. Some of the appendixes from the second edition have been moved to the website.

Chapter	Appendix
1	Finding information
2	Displaying data
3	Creating Web pages
4	Encrypting e-mail
5	Accounting review
6	Building forms in access
7	Interactive online meetings
8	Forecasting
9	E-mail rules
10	Solving business problems and cases
11	Creating a business plan
12	Visual basic
13	Project management

Organization of the Text

The text is organized into four sections to explore answers to the question of how information technology can improve management.

- **Part One.** Information technology is used to improve business transactions and operations.

- **Part Two.** IT is fundamental to business integration.

- **Part Three.** IT plays a crucial role in analyzing situations and making decisions.

- **Part Four.** IT raises new issues and possibilities in organizing businesses and information resources, and creates new effects and changes in society.

The organization of the text is based on two features. First, each chapter emphasizes the goal of the text: applying information technology to improve management and organizations. Second, the text is organized so that it begins with concepts familiar to the students and builds on them.

Each chapter is organized in a common format: (1) the introduction ties to the goal and raises questions specific to that chapter; (2) the main discussion emphasizes the application of technology and the strengths and weaknesses of various approaches; and (3) the application of technology in various real-world organizations with end-of-chapter cases.

Organization
Part One: Business Operations
Chapter 1: Introduction
Chapter 2: Information Technology Foundations
Chapter 3: Networks and Telecommunications
Chapter 4: Security, Privacy, and Anonymity
Chapter 5: Transactions and Electronic Commerce
Part Two: Business Integration
Chapter 6: Database Management
Chapter 7: Integration of Information
Part Three: Decisions and Analysis
Chapter 8: Models and Decision Support
Chapter 9: Complex Decisions and Expert Systems
Chapter 10: Strategic Analysis
Part Four: Organizing Businesses and Systems
Chapter 11: Electronic Business and Entrepreneurship
Chapter 12: Systems Development
Chapter 13: Organizing Information System Resources
Chapter 14: Information Management and Society

Chapter 1 (Introduction) remains an introduction to MIS and provides an explanation of the goals—emphasizing the text's focus on how technology can help managers perform their jobs and improve the companies they manage.

Chapter 2 (Information Technology Foundations) reviews the basic issues in personal productivity and hardware and software. It emphasizes recent issues such as handheld PDAs and tablet computers. It also discusses issues in choosing computers used in e-business such as the importance of scalability in servers.

The network chapter is now **Chapter 3 (Networks and Telecommunicatons).** To discuss e-business and the Internet, students need to understand networks and the major structure of how the Internet works.

Chapter 4 (Security, Privacy, and Anonymity) is a new chapter that contains an expanded discussion of computer security. Security is a natural expansion of transactions. The topics are also important to understanding the technologies and business relationships of the Web.

Chapter 5 (Transactions and Electronic Commerce) raises the main issues in operations and transaction processing. In addition to the traditional issues, new sections discuss the important transaction elements that arise in e-business. It also examines risk elements and explains how e-commerce changes relationships between businesses and customers.

Chapter 6 (Database Management) is relatively unchanged and explains the importance of database systems in business. New sections illustrate the use of databases in creating interactive Web businesses.

Chapter 7 (Integration of Information) explains the importance of integrating data and systems. It contains an expanded discussion of ERP systems. It also illustrates using the Internet to integrate and share data, including a presentation of Microsoft's XP integration using SharePoint services.

Chapter 8 (Models and Decision Support) describes the methods of analyzing data and creating decision support systems. It contains an expanded discussion of data mining (and its importance in e-business), as well as a discussion of digital dashboards for constantly monitoring the health of the business.

Chapter 9 (Complex Decisions and Expert Systems) explains the increasing use of expert systems, including the importance of expert systems in e-business to provide personalized service and support.

Chapter 10 (Strategic Analysis) presents the issues in strategy, maintaining its focus on using IT to gain a competitive advantage.

Chapter 11 (Electronic Business and Entrepreneurship) is a new chapter that explores the details of e-business options and how to establish them. It covers Internet marketing as well as various methods of building and hosting e-business sites. An important aspect of the chapter is an evaluation of the dot-com failures and the lessons for future e-businesses. The entrepreneurship section summarizes the basic issues in starting a business. It also examines the role of entrepreneurship within an existing business. Both are important topics in establishing the new roles of e-business.

Chapter 12 (Systems Development) looks at systems design and various development alternatives. It examines the challenges faced in developing software and the continuing movement to commercial off-the-shelf software.

Chapter 13 (Organizing Information System Resources) looks at the issues involved in the organization and management of MIS resources. In examining MIS roles, it also presents job opportunities. The chapter discusses how wireless, intranets, and Web services are having important effects on the structure and management of IT resources.

Chapter 14 (Information Management and Society) is an expanded discussion of the impact of IT on society—particularly the effects of the Internet. It investigates the issue of privacy versus business, social, and governmental needs. It examines the potential changes in a global society that is increasingly linked online.

Instructor Resources

An Instructor CD-ROM is available to adopters and offers the following resources for course presentation and management. All the instructor supplements were created by the authors, except the test bank:

- Instructor's Manual includes answers to all end-of-chapter review questions, exercises, and teaching notes for the industry-specific cases. Teaching tips and ties to the Power-Point slides are included for each chapter.

- A test bank contains true/false, multiple choice, and short answer questions, as well as mini-cases.

- Computerized/Network Testing with Brownstone Diploma software is fully networkable for LAN test administration, but tests can also be printed for standard paper delivery or posted to a website for student access.

- Lecture notes and overheads are available as slide shows in Microsoft PowerPoint format. The slides contain all of the figures along with additional notes. The slides are organized into lectures and can be rearranged to suit individual preferences.

- Several databases and exercises are available on disk. The instructor can add new data, modify the exercises, or use them to expand on the discussion in the text.

- The Rolling Thunder database application is available in Microsoft Access format. It is a self-contained application that illustrates many of the concepts and enables students to examine any facet of operating a small company. The *Instructor's Manual* includes further guidance on how to incorporate this innovative tool into your course.

The McGraw-Hill/Irwin Information Systems Video Library contains 14 10- to 12-minute videos on numerous companies demonstrating the use of a variety of IT facets, such as intranets, multimedia, computer-based training systems, and concepts like client-server computing and business process re-engineering. It is available free to adopters.

Digital Solutions

- Website/OLC—The book's website at *www.mhhe.com/post* provides resources for instructors and students using the text. The Online Learning Center (OLC) builds on the book's pedagogy and features with self-assessment quizzes, key words, and glossary of terms, additional PowerPoint slides, and Web links.

- Pageout/Pageout Lite—our Course website Development Center, Pageout, offers a syllabus page, website address, online Learning Center content, online quizzing, gradebook, discussion forum, and student Web page creation. Pageout Lite, a scaled-down version of Pageout, offers three templates for posting your own material online and instantly converts it to HTML.

Packaging Options

McGraw-Hill/Irwin has a huge selection of IT products that can be packaged with this text to meet the needs of your course—three different application software series of manuals and CDs on the Microsoft Office suite, Internet Explorer and Netscape products, programming languages, and Internet literacy. For more about our discount options, contact your local McGraw-Hill/Irwin sales representative or visit our website at www.mhhe.com/it.

ACKNOWLEDGMENTS

Like any large project, producing a book is a team effort. In developing this book, we have had the privilege of working with dedicated professionals. The contributions of many people have resulted in an improved book and have made the process enjoyable.

First, we thank our students over the years who encouraged us to explore new technologies and to focus on how IT can benefit students, managers, and organizations. We are indebted to the reviewers listed below who offered many improvements and suggestions. Their ideas and direction substantially improved the book.

Alisa Acosta
University of Las Vegas, Nevada

Jeff Butterfield
Western Kentucky University

Jane M. Carey
Arizona State University West

Qidong Cao
Winthrop University

Chuleeporn Changchit
Texas A&M University—Corpus Christi

Thad Crews
Western Kentucky University

Pi-Sheng Deng
California State University, Stanislaus

Evan W. Duggan
The University of Alabama

Jerry Fjermestad
New Jersey Institute of Technology

Zbigniew J. Gackowski
California State University, Stanislaus

Paul Keller
University of Maryland University College

Barin Nag
Towson University

Robert D. Wilson
California State University—San Bernadino

John E. Powell
University of South Dakota

Joseph Otto
California State University

Surrender Reddy
Saginaw Valley State University

Rene Reitsma
St. Francis Xavier University

Steve Robischon
University of Idaho

Young U. Ryu
University of Texas—Dallas

Morgan Shepherd
University of Colorado, Colorado Springs

Werner Schenk
University of Rochester

Betsy Page Sigman
Georgetown University

This text has been substantially improved through the dedication and professionalism of the editors and staff at McGraw-Hill. It is a pleasure to work with people like Rick Williamson, Kelly Delso, and Laura Griffin, whose guidance, support, ideas, and answers to innumerable questions were invaluable to the project.

About the Authors

Jerry Post

University of the Pacific

Dr. Post is a professor of information systems at the University of the Pacific's School of Business. Jerry holds a Ph.D. in economics and statistics from Iowa State University. He earned his post doctorate from Indiana University's Graduate School of Business and earned a B.A. in mathematics and economics from University of Wisconsin—Eau Claire. Jerry has worked as a freelance programmer and software designer for various companies. Jerry has published numerous papers that explore security, systems development, and evaluation issues in MIS. He is also the author of *Database Management Systems: Designing and Building Business Applications.* When he is not tied to the keyboard, he can be found riding one of his bikes.

David L. Anderson

Loyola University

Dr. Anderson is an assistant professor of information systems and operations management in the Graduate School of Business at Loyola University. He received his law degree from the George Washington University in Washington, DC, and is a member of the Ohio, District of Columbia, federal, and U.S. Supreme Court Bars. David earned his MBA from the University of Michigan in Ann Arbor. He received his master of science degree in computer science from Northwestern University in Evanston, Illinois. David earned his doctorate in educational administration from Harvard University in Cambridge, Massachusetts.

David has served as a lead technology analyst at a major provider of health care insurance in the greater Chicago metropolitan area. Previous to this position, he served as a project management specialist at Hewitt Associates, a strategic technology planner at ISSC/IBM Corporation, a corporate information access planner at the Continental Bank, and a senior consultant at Andersen Consulting (now Accenture) in Chicago.

David is also the author of *Managing Information Systems: Using Cases within an Industry Context to Solve Business Problems with Information Technology* and, with James Pannabecker, *Guide to Financial Privacy: Regulatory Impact on Technology.*

Business Operations

HOW ARE INFORMATION SYSTEMS USED TO IMPROVE BUSINESS OPERATIONS?

From the very beginning, computers have helped businesses tackle basic operations—collecting data, handling transactions, and creating reports. Today, businesses and managers would find it difficult or impossible to function without information systems. Electronic business and electronic commerce go a step further and move all of the major transactions online. Supporting modern transactions and operations requires networks and increasingly complex security controls.

All managers perform tasks like writing, scheduling, calculating, and graphing. One of the most powerful uses of information systems lies in helping managers with these personal applications. Hundreds of tools exist to help managers with their daily tasks.

Networks and the Internet are critical to any business today. Networks are used to share data, support teamwork, and build relationships with customers and suppliers. They make it possible to support new forms of business and change the way firms are managed.

As more aspects of our daily lives move online, security and privacy become critical elements to everyone. Businesses have obligations to protect resources and data. These protections need to be integrated into the heart of every business technology plan. As technology becomes more widespread and integrated into more aspects of our lives, everyone needs to consider the effects of various security policies.

The heart of any company is its daily operations. Whether the company manufactures products or provides services, basic operations must be performed continuously. These operations give rise to transactions with suppliers, customers, employees, other firms, and governmental agencies. Transactions must be recorded, aggregated, and analyzed. Information systems are crucial to maintaining, searching, and analyzing transactions.

CHAPTER ONE

Introduction

What you will learn in this chapter

- What is an information system?

- How does information technology help managers?

- What is e-commerce?

- What do managers do?

- What technology and business trends are affecting organizations?

- How has technology changed the role of management?

- What types of decisions do managers face?

- How can a firm gain a competitive advantage over its rivals?

McDonald's uses a considerable amount of information technology to maintain consistency, monitor employees, and track sales.

McDonald's

McDonald's Corporation has sold billions of hamburgers. Beginning in 1955 with a single drive-in in Des Plaines, Illinois, McDonald's has grown to today's system of more than 25,000 restaurants across 115 countries. As a brand, McDonald's is synonymous with a quality product at a reasonable price. Equally important, McDonald's markets itself as more than a place to get a hamburger. Ronald McDonald, Happy Meals, the clean restaurants, and each new product or promotional theme add to the fun that brings more than 40 million customers of all ages to its restaurants around the world each day.

Eighty percent of worldwide McDonald's restaurants are franchised. Each restaurant must meet strict requirements to make it the same as all others. This ensures that each time you drive or walk into a McDonald's, no matter where you are, the Big Mac that you order will always be the same taste, size, weight, and quality. It will also be competitively priced.

Legal contracts, quality standards, and performance specifications direct the individual restaurants in the effort to keep all the food orders the same. What most individuals do not think about when they walk or drive into McDonald's is that McDonald's management information system (MIS) plays a critical role in ensuring the quality and consistency of each sandwich. McDonald's Corporation maintains a strict requirement that food be fresh and not stored more than a limited amount of time. MIS applications direct managers in the management of employees and the ordering and tracking of hamburgers, buns, potatoes, and soft drinks. Because restaurants are not consistently busy throughout the day, the MIS is called upon to assist the manager in maximizing the scheduling of individuals to cook and serve the food. The MIS further helps track restaurants' cash flow and guard against inaccuracy and waste. As McDonald's adds new products and addresses market segments more specifically targeted both ethnically and geographically, the manager must make more complex decisions about the best mix of products to prepare to serve at each meal and throughout the day.

McDonald's "Made for You" campaign uses a point of sale system to register each customer's "Made for You" order. Its "Fresh Tastes" campaign seeks to bring new and more focused products to its customers' attention. Special promotions and communitywide events add additional factors that must be added to the equation that can best be addressed through management information systems.

Overview

Richard:	Hi Ally. Welcome to the firm. We are excited about your extensive computer skills.
Ally:	Thanks, it looks like a fun company. I'm not a computer programming whiz, but I did like my MIS courses. We learned a lot about solving business problems.
Elaine:	(joking) Well, we have enough problems here to keep everyone busy for a long time.
Richard:	Ha! Ha! Elaine is joking. We do work in teams for most of our projects, so we'll start you out on two or three projects that are pretty solid. Eventually, you'll be team leader on some projects. Most of our employees have two or three main specialties, so you should start thinking about areas where you want to focus. And if you hear anything about the competition, or have any good ideas about new opportunities, let me know immediately.
Elaine:	Yes, we run an informal strategy discussion website where everyone throws in ideas and comments about customers and the competition. Except on April 1, then we all tell jokes about the managing partners.

Introduction

Welcome to the information age. Going shopping? As a consumer, you have instant access to millions of pieces of data. With a few clicks of the mouse button, you can find anything from current stock prices to video clips of current movies. You can get product descriptions, pictures, and prices from thousands of companies across the United States and around the world. Trying to sell services and products? You can purchase demographic, economic, consumer-buying-pattern, and market-analysis data. Your firm will have internal financial, marketing, production, and employee data for past years. This tremendous amount of data provides opportunities to managers and consumers who know how to obtain it and analyze it to make better decisions.

There is no question that the use of computers in business is increasing. Walk into your local bank, grocery store, or fast food restaurant and you will see that the operations depend on computers. Go into management offices and you will find computers used to analyze marketing alternatives, make financial decisions, and coordinate team members around the world.

The expanding role of technology raises some interesting questions. What exactly are computers being used for? Who decided to install them? Do computers increase productivity or are they just expensive paperweights? Are there new uses that you should be considering? Are there some tasks that should be performed by humans instead of computers? How can you deal with the flood of data that you face every day?

What Is MIS?

The first step in learning how to apply information technology to solve problems is to get a broader picture of what is meant by the term *management information system.* You probably have some experience with using computers and various software packages. Yet, computers are only one component of a management information system. A **management information system (MIS)**, or *computer information system (CIS),* consists of five related components: hardware, software, people, procedures, and collections of data. The term **information technology (IT)** represents the various types of hardware and software used in an information system, including computers and networking equipment. The goal of MIS is to enable managers to make better decisions by providing quality information.

The physical equipment used in computing is called **hardware**. The set of instructions that controls the hardware is known as **software**. In the early days of computers, the **people** directly involved in MIS tended to be programmers, design analysts, and a few external users. Today, almost everyone in the firm is involved with the information system. **Procedures** are instructions that help people use the systems. They include items such as user manuals, documentation, and procedures to ensure that backups are made regularly. **Databases** are collections of related data that can be retrieved easily and processed by the computers. As you will see in the cases throughout the book, all of these components are vital to creating an effective information system.

So what is information? One way to answer that question is to examine the use of information technology on three levels: (1) data management, (2) information systems, and (3) knowledge bases. **Data** consists of factual elements (or opinions or comments) that describe some object or event. Data can be thought of as raw numbers or text. Data management systems focus on data collection and providing basic reports. **Information** represents data that has been processed, organized, and integrated to provide more insight. Information systems are designed to help managers analyze data and make decisions. From a decision maker's standpoint, the challenge is that you might not know ahead of time which information you need, so it is hard to determine what data you need to collect. **Knowledge** represents a higher level of understanding, including rules, patterns, and decisions. Knowledge-based systems are built to automatically analyze data, identify patterns, and recommend decisions. Humans are also capable of **wisdom**, where they put knowledge, experience, and analytical skills to work to create new knowledge and adapt to changing situations. To date no computer system has attained the properties of wisdom.

To create an effective information system, you need to do more than simply purchase the various components. Quality is an important issue in business today, particularly as it relates to information systems. The quality of an information system is measured by its ability to provide exactly the information needed by managers in a timely manner. The information must be accurate and up-to-date. Users should be able to receive the information in a variety of formats: tables of data, graphs, summary statistics, or even pictures or sound. Users have different perspectives and different requirements, and a good information system must have the flexibility to present information in diverse forms for each user.

Data, Information, Knowledge, and Wisdom

Consider the case of a retail store that is trying to increase sales. Some of the data available includes sales levels for the last 36 months, advertising expenses, and customer comments from surveys.

By itself, this data may be interesting, but it must be organized and analyzed to be useful in making a decision. For example, a manager might use economic and marketing models to forecast patterns and determine relationships among various advertising expenses and sales. The resulting information (presented in equations, charts, and tables) would clarify relationships among the data and would be used to decide how to proceed.

It requires knowledge to determine how to analyze data and make decisions. Education and experience create knowledge in humans. A manager learns which data to collect, the proper models to apply, and ways to analyze results for making better decisions. In some cases, this knowledge can be transferred to specialized computer programs (expert systems).

Wisdom is more difficult to define but represents the ability to learn from experience and adapt to changing conditions. In this example, wisdom would enable a manager to spot trends, identify potential problems, and develop new techniques to analyze the data.

Why Is Information Technology Important?

Personal Productivity

An enormous amount of data is available to managers—generated internally and externally. It is impossible to deal with this volume of data without information technology. The era of "pure" managers who simply direct other people is gone. Managers today must be capable of performing the tasks within their area of expertise. For example, accounting managers still practice accounting, lawyers handle cases, and financial managers still track investments. In other words, managers do two jobs: perform basic day-to-day functions, as well as plan, organize, and communicate.

Firms are increasingly required to improve productivity, which means that each year managers must increase production without increasing the number of workers. Information technology is critical to this improvement process, enabling employees to perform more tasks, getting work done faster at lower cost.

Teamwork and Communication

It is tempting to believe that once you learn how to use a word processor, a spreadsheet program, and a Web browser, you have all the computer knowledge needed to solve business problems. In fact, these are powerful tools that will help you solve business problems that arise at a personal level. But businesses have many more levels of problems, such as data collection, departmental teamwork, information shared throughout the corporation, and uses of IT that help the business gain a competitive advantage.

You also need to understand database, groupware, and enterprise tools that give you access to data across the company and help you share it with team members around the world. Most companies are in a continual race to get products and services to customers faster than the competition. Moving communication away from paper to electronic messages and online meetings can significantly reduce the time required to coordinate a group and make decisions—speeding up the overall process.

Business Operations and Strategy

Information technology is increasingly critical to the daily operations of a business. Obviously, online businesses cannot live without technology, but neither can the local grocery store, bank, or many other businesses. Computers process sales, handle payments, and place new orders. They also analyze the sales data and help set prices and predict trends. Information technology is also used to create new products and services or to provide unique features to existing products. These new features can give your company a strategic advantage and help the company grow.

What Are e-Commerce and e-Business?

Electronic commerce, or **e-commerce** (or EC), denotes the selling of products over the Internet. These sales can be from a business to consumers (**B2C**) or from one business to another (**B2B**). For a while in 1999, some people believed that e-commerce would become the dominant form of business—where everyone bought all items over the Internet. Thousands of firms and websites were created, trying to become the dominant firm in some niche. The group was called **dot-coms** because almost all had an Internet address of something.com. Many of the firms received huge amounts of funding from venture capitalists, and experienced surprisingly high prices for their stock. Some foolish people predicted a new economic world. But beginning in mid-2000, thousands of these firms failed. Most had enormous expenses and huge losses. Many had been taking losses on every item they sold. And foolish people predicted the end of e-commerce.

E-business is a more general term that encompasses e-commerce but also includes using the Internet for other business tasks, such as teamwork, communication, and new business

Reality Bytes   **Internet Access**

According to the Census Bureau, in 2000, almost 113 million adults (56.6 percent) had Internet access from home or work. About 51 percent of all households owned computers. About one-third of the total U.S. population used e-mail. About 90 percent of school-aged children had computer access. About 65 percent of them had computers at home. Of course, wealthier families were far more likely to have computer access, where almost 90 percent of households making more than $75,000 had Internet access.

Sources: Adapted from:

http://www.census.gov/statab/freq/00s0913.txt

http://cyberatlas.internet.com/big_picture/demographics/article/0,,5901_879441,00.html

services. As Internet technologies improve, more firms are offering e-business services—such as digital maps, remote data backup, and language translation.

With the crash of the dot-coms, it is important to remember that e-commerce and e-business are increasingly valuable tools for more traditional firms. For example, when the Webvan grocery delivery company failed, a traditional giant grocery and drug retailer (Albertson's) picked up many of the customers with its online service. E-commerce and e-business have a large role to play in the future of many companies. As with any technology, you must strive to find profitable solutions. Chapter 11 discusses e-commerce and e-business in more detail. Chapter 12 explains the issues involved in becoming an entrepreneur.

What Do Managers Do?

Traditional Management and Observations

To create useful information systems, it is helpful to examine the various roles of management. Traditional concepts of management focus on organizing, planning, and control. However, when observed at their jobs, managers appear to spend most of their time in meetings, talking on the phone, reading or preparing reports, discussing projects with their colleagues, explaining procedures, and participating in other activities that are difficult to fit into the traditional framework.

Henry Mintzberg, a psychologist who studies management, classifies managerial tasks into three categories: (1) interpersonal, (2) informational, and (3) decisional. Interpersonal roles refer to teaching and leading employees. Informational tasks are based on the transfer of information throughout the organization, such as relaying information to subordinates or summarizing information for executives. Decisions involve evaluating alternatives and choosing directions that benefit the firm.

Other researchers have studied managers and developed alternative classifications. Fred Luthans uses three classifications of management activities. He indicates that approximately 50 percent of a manager's time is spent on traditional management activities (planning, organizing, etc.), 30 percent in formal communications, and 20 percent in informal networking. Formal communications include attending meetings and creating reports and memos. Informal networking consists of contacts with colleagues and workers that tend to be social in nature but often involve discussions regarding business and jobs.

Making Decisions

In many ways managers expend a lot of their effort in making decisions or contributing information so others can make decisions. When you look at courses offered for future managers, you will find a focus on administration, human behavior, quantitative modeling and problem solving, decision theory, and elements of business ethics and globalization.

Managers and professionals spend considerable time in meetings. Providing support for teamwork and group decisions is an important issue in MIS.

Typically, these courses are designed to help managers solve problems and make decisions. However, if you ask managers how much time they spend making decisions, they are likely to say that they seldom make decisions. That seems like a contradiction. If managers and executives do not make decisions, who does?

In many organizations, day-to-day decisions are embodied in the methodology, rules, or philosophy of the company. Managers are encouraged to collect data and follow the decisions that have resulted from experience. In this situation and in many others, the managers are directly involved in the decision process, even though they may not think they are making the final choice.

The broader **decision process** involves collecting data, identifying problems, and making choices. One more step is often involved: persuading others to accept a decision and implement a solution. With this broader definition, many of the tasks performed by managers are actually steps in the decision process. Meetings, phone calls, and discussions with colleagues are used to collect data, identify problems, and persuade others to choose a course of action. Each of these steps may be so gradual that the participants do not think they are actually making decisions.

Because of the subtlety of the process and the complexity of the decisions, it is often difficult to determine what information will be needed. Decisions often require creativity. Because data generally need to be collected *before* problems arise, it is challenging to design information systems to support managers and benefit the organization. One important job of management is to examine the need for information and how it can be used to solve future problems.

Business and Technology Trends

Even without the Internet, management and companies are changing. The most important change is the move away from the traditional hierarchical structure to a team-based approach. Most of today's large companies developed years ago when communications were limited and there were no computers. Most adopted a military-inspired hierarchical command structure shown in Figure 1.1. The top-level managers set policy and directed the vice presidents to carry out the mission of the company. Sales staff dealt directly with customers, collected data, and passed it to middle managers. The middle managers organized and summarized the data and passed it up the chain. Little data was shared among the middle and lower levels.

In contrast, because it is easy to share data, information technology offers the ability to alter the way companies are organized and managed. Figure 1.2 shows the new approach. This method focuses on teamwork and a shared knowledge of all relevant data. Some teams,

FIGURE 1.1

In a traditional organizational structure, lower-level managers deal with customers and collect basic data. Middle-level managers analyze the data, create reports, and make suggestions to upper-level managers. The higher-level managers make decisions and set rules to guide the other managers.

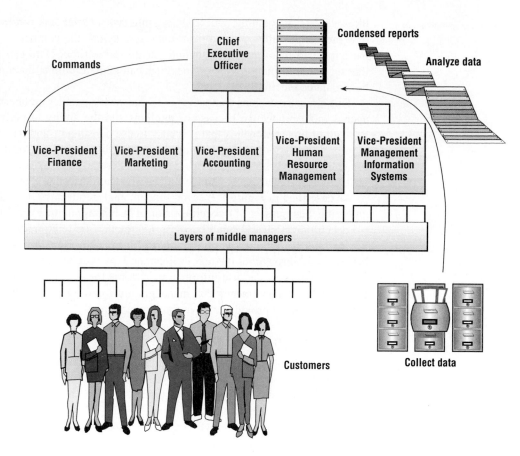

FIGURE 1.2

In the last few years, many companies have moved toward a more decentralized form of management. They have removed the middle layers of management and replaced them with smaller teams. Franchises and smaller teams have become the primary service contact with customers. Information sharing becomes crucial in this environment. Teams communicate directly and share data across the company.

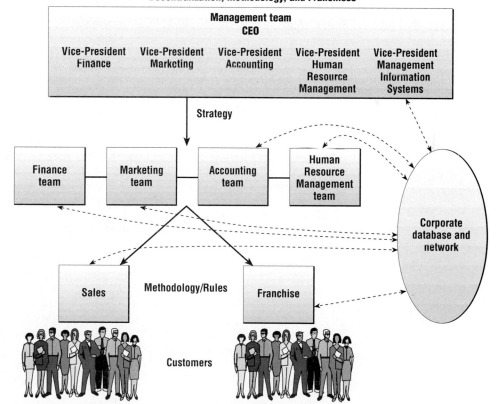

like sales and accounting, will have ongoing tasks. Other task forces will be formed to solve new problems—often created from managers across the company. Managers can expect to participate in many teams, essentially at the same time. Data can be obtained and shared through the information system, meetings can be held online, documents and comments can be circulated electronically.

This structure enables companies to be run with a smaller number of managers. Each manager is more productive because of the tools and the ability to perform many jobs. Another strength of this approach is that it is easy to use consultants and temporary workers for short-term projects. In today's legal climate, it is exceedingly difficult to fire workers, so firms often use temporary workers for individual projects. Permanent workers, supplemented with specialized temporary talent, can organize a team. The team disbands when the project is finished.

As described in Figure 1.3, seven fundamental trends have been driving the economy and changing businesses: (1) specialization, (2) management by methodology, (3) mergers, (4) decentralization and small business, (5) reliance on temporary workers, (6) internationalization, and (7) the increasing importance of service-oriented businesses. These trends will be discussed throughout the text to illustrate how they affect the use of information systems and how managers can use information systems to take advantage of these trends. Tightening job markets also means that managers must continually work on self-improvement. To survive, you must provide value to the organization.

Specialization

The basic advantages of specialization and division of labor in manufacturing were discussed by Adam Smith more than 200 years ago. The concepts are now being applied to managers. As functional areas (such as marketing or finance) become more complex, they also become more specialized. Area managers are expected to understand and use increasingly sophisticated models and tools to analyze events and make decisions. As a result, the demand for managers with specific technical skills is increasing, while the demand for general business managers is

FIGURE 1.3

Changes occurring in the business world affect the use of information technology. These trends and the implications are discussed throughout the book. Managers who understand these trends and their relationship with technology will make better decisions.

Business Trend	Implications for Technology
Specialization	• Increased demand for technical skills • Specialized MIS tools • Increased communication
Methodology and franchises	• Reduction of middle management • Increased data sharing • Increased analysis by top management • Computer support for rules • Re-engineering
Mergers	• Four or five big firms dominate most industries • Need for communication • Strategic ties to customers and suppliers
Decentralization and small business	• Communication needs • Lower cost of management tasks • Low maintenance technology
Temporary workers	• Managing through rules • Finding and evaluating workers • Coordination and control • Personal advancement through technology • Security
Internationalization	• Communication • Product design • System development and programming • Sales and marketing
Service orientation	• Management jobs are information jobs • Customer service requires better information • Speed

declining. This trend is reflected in MIS by the large number of specialized tools being created and the increased communication demands for sharing information among the specialists.

Management by Methodology and Franchises

An important result of specialization is the reduction of management tasks to smaller problems. Using specialization coupled with technology, firms have reduced many management problems to a set of rules or standard operating procedures. Day-to-day problems can be addressed with a standard methodology. For example, the manager's guidebook at Wal-Mart or at Mrs. Fields Cookies explains how to solve or prevent many common problems. These rules were created by analyzing the business setting, building models of the business, and then creating rules by anticipating decisions and problems. This approach gives less flexibility to the lower-level managers but encourages a standardized product, consistent quality, and adherence to the corporate philosophy.

Management by methodology also allows firms to reduce their number of middle managers. By anticipating common problems and decisions, there is no need to call on trained managers to solve the daily problems. Franchises like McDonald's or Mrs. Fields Cookies carry this technique one level further by making the franchisee responsible for the financial performance of individual units. The common management tasks, however, are defined by the central corporation.

Mergers

Up to the late 1800s and early 1900s, most businesses were small, having markets limited to small geographic regions. A brief history of industrial organization reveals four waves of mergers in the United States: (1) the horizontal mergers of the late 1800s epitomized by the oil and banking industries; (2) the vertical integration of the early half of the 20th century, illustrated by the oil, steel, and automobile companies; (3) conglomerate mergers of the 1950s and 1960s, in which firms like IT&T (an international telecommunications giant) acquired subsidiaries in many different industries (including a bakery!); and (4) giant horizontal mergers of the late 1990s. All of these mergers arose to take advantage of economic power, but technology made them possible. Without communication (telegraph and telephones earlier, computer networks later), firms could not grow beyond a certain size because managers could not monitor and control lower-level workers.

The mergers in the mid- to late 1990s were impressive in terms of the size of the firms and the sectors involved. The banking industry was one of the first to begin consolidation. Relaxation of federal restrictions quickly led to large regional and national banks. The telecommunications industry also experienced several changes, such as the ABC-Disney and AOL-Time/Warner merger between telecommunications and entertainment industries.

Reality Bytes   Bertelsmann

Only a few Americans know about Bertelsmann—one of the largest publishers in the world, and rapidly gaining control over many levels of distribution. A German company, Bertelsmann bought 5 percent of AOL back in 1994. It is the number one online music retailer worldwide and number two book retailer, through Barnes and Noble and CDNow. In addition, Bertelsmann owns a two-thirds stake in RTL, Europe's biggest broadcaster and the largest producer of programs for television outside of Hollywood. Depending on how you measure it, Bertelsmann is the fourth or fifth largest publisher in the world. It is the combination of control over distribution (sales) and publishing that makes Bertelsmann a dominant player. For example, book and magazine publishing houses Random House, Springer, and Gruner+Jahr are divisions of Bertelsmann. Music lovers will also recognize that Bertelsmann owns one of the largest music publishers: BMG. Through the BMG division, Bertelsmann invested $50 million in 2000 with Napster. While American-based music publishers were hammering Napster in court, BMG recognized the customer demand for a new music format and funded Napster to develop a new file-sharing system that would enable it to collect royalties on the transfers.

Sources: Adapted from Justin Fox, "Bertelsmann's Next Big Thing," *Fortune,* September 28, 2001; and www.bertelsmann.com; and Devin Leonard, "The Music Men Are Out of Tune," *Fortune,* June 11, 2001.

Telephone, Internet, and cable companies also were fertile ground for mergers, such as MCI and WorldCom or AT&T and TCI. The horizontal mergers in the petroleum, food production, automobile, and grocery industries represented major consolidations of operations as well. Some of these combinations crossed international boundaries (e.g., Daimler and Chrysler). Some of these trends were fueled by the high stock market valuations, which provided capital to the successful firms and punished the weaker ones.

One of the important keys to these mergers was the improved capability of information and communication technology. Without the IT structure, it would be exceedingly difficult to manage these combined firms. Most of the combinations also resulted in a loss of middle-management jobs. The remaining workers relied on technology to improve their productivity. The newly centralized firms also relied on communication technology to provide customer service across the country.

Decentralization and Small Business

Today, technology makes it possible to split firms into smaller managerial units that make decisions at lower levels (decentralization). In addition to faster communication, technology makes available low-cost hardware and software to each division. It is now possible to operate a company as a collection of small teams and maintain complete management statistics without the need for hundreds of bookkeepers and accountants. In the past, with limited information technology, small divisions were expensive to maintain because of the cost of collecting and processing the basic accounting and operating data.

Within a firm, operations can be decentralized into teams of workers. In this situation, departments operate relatively independently, "selling" services to other departments by competing with other teams. They often perform work for outside firms as well—essentially operating as an independent business unit within the corporation.

Decentralization and smaller businesses can eliminate layers of middle managers in an organization. One goal of decentralization is to push the decisions and the work down to the level of the customer, to provide better customer service and faster decisions. Information systems enable executives to gather and manipulate information themselves or with automated systems. As a result, there is less need for middle managers to prepare and analyze data.

Reliance on Temporary Workers

So what happens to the people who are no longer needed as middle-level managers? At various times in the past, some companies provided a form of lifetime employment for their workers. As long as workers continued to do their jobs and remained loyal to the company,

Reality Bytes **Is E-Commerce Dead?**

The goal of many early Internet firms was to be there first, develop brand recognition, then drive down operating costs by cutting out the middleman. Profits would come later, the goal was to get big fast. Most of the firms never made it to "later." Between January 2001 and September 2001, at least 435 Internet companies (47 percent of them e-commerce firms) shut down. Of the 494 Internet-related businesses that went public from 1998 to 2001, only 11 percent trade for more than their offering price, and nearly one-third go for more than 80 percent below their original price. The list includes companies that raised (and spent) tens of millions of dollars in capital. Even the well-known firms like Amazon.com are not yet profitable. Venture capital dried up, falling more than 90 percent from $843.4 million to $68.5 million from the first quarter of 2000 to first quarter 2001. But, consumer e-commerce revenues hit $44.5 billion in 2000; an increase of 66 percent from 1999 and 1.7 percent of all U.S. retail revenue. And revenue for 2001 is likely to increase another 46 percent to $65 billion. So, customers do exist, and people are beginning to accept e-commerce. Firms like Travelocity, Eddie Bauer, and Sharper Image have become profitable at e-commerce. Often by providing more information, better service, and attracting customers to stores as well as the Web. Ultimately, the key is to provide services and products that customers want—and provide them at prices that generate profits. Which is a simple statement, with difficult answers.

Source: Adapted from Susannah Patton, "What Works on the Web," *CIO Magazine,* September 15, 2001.

their jobs were secure. Even in more difficult times, when employees were laid off, they were often encouraged (through extensions of unemployment benefits) to wait until the economy improved and they could be rehired. Companies in other nations, especially Japan, had stronger commitments to workers and kept them on the payroll even in difficult times.

Today, in almost every industry and in many nations (including Japan), companies increasingly rely on a temporary workforce. Individuals are hired for specific skills and tasks. When these basic tasks are completed, the employees move on to take other jobs. Increasingly, even executives are hired because of their specific expertise. Consultants and other professionals are hired on a contract basis to solve specific problems or complete special assignments.

In many ways, it is more difficult to manage a company that relies on temporary workers. Special efforts must be made to control quality, keep employees working together, and ensuring that contract provisions are met. Technology can play an important role in these situations. It can improve communications, maintain easy (but controlled) access to data and contracts, and help to institute corporate standards. The Internet is beginning to play this management role—finding contract workers, negotiating the work, and distributing the finished products.

To individual workers, a firm's reliance on temporary workers means that to achieve a position with more responsibility and command higher rates of pay, workers will need to possess more analytic skills than other potential employees. Even as a manager, you will need your own competitive (professional) advantage. Along with additional education, your use and knowledge of technology can give you an advantage.

Internationalization

Several events of the early 1990s demonstrated the importance of international trade: closer ties forged with the European Union, creation of the North American Free Trade Area (NAFTA), and the continued relaxation of trade restrictions through the General Agreement on Tariffs and Trade (GATT) and the World Trade Organization (WTO). Although barriers to trade remain, there is no doubt that the international flow of trade and services plays an increasingly important role in many companies. Even small firms are buying supplies from overseas and selling products in foreign markets. Trade also brings more competition, which encourages firms to be more careful in making decisions.

As Figure 1.4 shows, the role of exports and imports has expanded rapidly in the United States since 1970. In European nations, international trade is even more important. Today, internationalization is a daily fact of life for workers and managers in almost every company. Even small businesses have links to firms in other nations. Many have set up their

FIGURE 1.4

By almost any statistic, in almost every nation, the level of international trade has increased dramatically during the last 20 years. International trade brings more choices, more competition, more data, more complexity, and more management challenges.

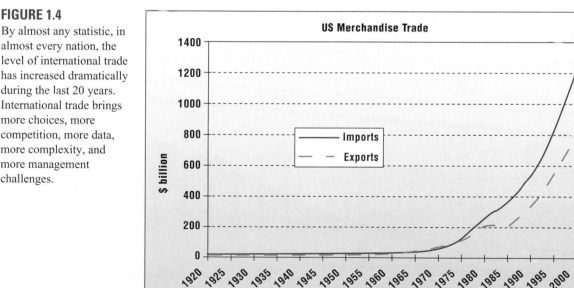

own production facilities in other nations. Much of this global expansion is supported by technology, from communication to transportation, from management to quality control.

Communication facilities are one of the most prominent uses of information technology to support the move to international operations. Communication technology is especially important for service industries such as consulting, programming, design, marketing, and banking. Several years ago, services were often considered to be nontradable goods because they tended to have high transportation costs, making them difficult to export. Today, improved communication facilities through the Internet have made certain types of services easy to export. For example, financial institutions now operate globally. Although not on the same level as banks, software development is also beginning to achieve an international presence. Some U.S. firms are turning to programmers in Ireland, India, and Taiwan. Through the use of programmers in India, for example, a U.S.-based firm can develop specifications during the day and transmit them to India. Because of the time difference, the Indian programmers work during the U.S. night and the U.S. workers receive updates and fixes the next morning.

Internationalization also plays a role in selling products. Groups of countries have different standards, regulations, and consumer preferences. Products and sales techniques that work well in one nation may not transfer to another culture. Information technology can track these differences, enabling more flexible manufacturing systems that can customize products for each market.

The increased competition created by internationalization and decentralization requires corporations to be more flexible. Flexibility is needed to adapt products to different markets, choose suppliers, adopt new production processes, find innovative financing, change marketing campaigns, and modify accounting systems. Firms that attain this flexibility can respond faster to market changes, catch opportunities unavailable to slower firms, and become more profitable.

Service-Oriented Business

Another trend facing industrialized nations is the move toward a service-oriented economy. As shown in Figure 1.5, in 1920 the U.S. census showed 29 percent of the employed were in farming. By 1990, that figure had shrunk to 3 percent. In the early 1900s, people were afraid that this trend would cause food shortages throughout the United States and the world. Improvements in technology in the form of mechanization, transportation, growing techniques, chemicals, and crop genetics proved them wrong.

A similar trend in manufacturing has produced similar consternation. Although the number of workers employed in manufacturing has varied over time, it is clear that the largest increase in jobs has been in the management, clerical, and service sectors. In 2000, 25 percent

FIGURE 1.5
Over time, Americans have moved from agricultural to manufacturing to service and management jobs. Management and service jobs are often dedicated to collecting and analyzing data. Just as the decline of workers in agriculture did not create a shortage of food, the relative decline in manufacturing did not create a shortage of products.

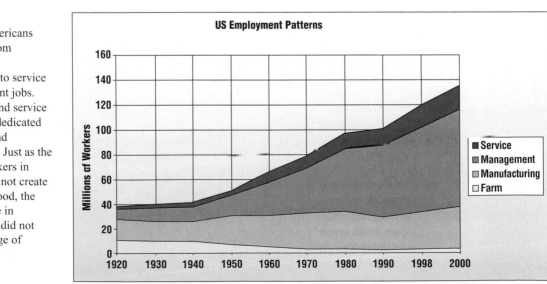

of the jobs were in manufacturing, with 73 percent in service and management jobs. The largest increase in new jobs has been in the management, clerical, and service sectors.

These trends represent changes in the U.S. economy and in demographics such as age characteristics of the population. The importance of the management, clerical, and service sectors has to be considered when we examine how MIS can benefit a firm and its workers. The goal is to gain a competitive advantage through better customer service. Even manufacturing companies are beginning to focus their efforts around the concept of providing services to the customer.

Re-Engineering: Altering the Rules

Many companies are managed by rules and procedures. It would be virtually impossible to do otherwise—the cost of an intense evaluation of every single decision would be overwhelming. Hence, upper-level managers establish procedures and rules and an organizational structure that automatically solve typical problems. More complex problems are supposed to be identified by managers and forwarded up the chain-of-command for answers.

This type of management creates a fixed approach to operations and to solving problems. However, the business environment rarely remains constant. Over time, new technologies are introduced, new competitors arrive, products change, old markets shrink, and new markets arise. At some point, firms that have been guided by relatively static methodologies find their methods no longer match the marketplace. Hence, they decide to **re-engineer** the company: beginning from scratch, they identify goals along with the most efficient means of attaining those goals, and create new processes that change the company to meet the new goals. The term *re-engineering* and its current usage were made popular in 1990 by management consultants James Champy and Michael Hammer. Many of the underlying concepts have been in use for years.

Sometimes re-engineering is undertaken by internal management as a means to improve the company. For example, in the early 1990s, Compaq Computer altered its strategy and re-engineered its operations and management to cut millions of dollars in costs and save the company. But in 2000, Dell Computer's just-in-time and made-to-order production system dominated the industry. Unable to alter the company fast enough, Compaq sought a merger with Hewlett-Packard.

Sometimes re-engineering is forced on the company when it is taken over by another corporation. In a few rare cases, managers continually evaluate the firm to make several small changes instead of relying on a major overhaul.

Re-engineering can be a highly complex process, requiring thousands of hours of time to analyze the company and its processes. In addition to the complexity, re-engineering often faces resistance because it results in a change in the organization's structure, which affects the authority and power of various managers.

Like any management technique, re-engineering is not guaranteed to work. A report by CSC Index, a major re-engineering consulting company, which surveyed 497 large companies in the United States and 124 in Europe, noted that 69 percent of the American and

Reality Bytes   Information Technology to Streamline Processes

With a slowing economy and tight budgets, it becomes even more important for firms to cut costs and maintain responsive service by improving processes. One objective is to use fewer, more skilled workers to increase productivity. Many firms can re-engineer their processes by using information technology to handle the simpler tasks and to make it easier for one person to handle more data. In one study, 85 percent of the respondents focused on the use of enterprise application software to integrate their company's data and give managers easier access to any information throughout the company. Almost two-thirds were investing in employee training to make better use of the information technology.

Source: Adapted from Jennifer Zaino, "Business Processes Meet Stumbling Blocks," *Information Week,* August 27, 2001.

75 percent of the European companies have already undertaken re-engineering projects. Several of these projects have not been successful. CSC Index notes that three factors are necessary for success: (1) overcome resistance by managers who are afraid of losing jobs or power; (2) earn strong support by upper management; and (3) aim high and go for major changes instead of small rearrangements.

Re-engineering has a close relationship with management information systems. In many cases, the new processes will rely on new computer systems to transfer and manipulate information. The important tie between re-engineering and information technology is that it is not sufficient to install new computers; the company must also re-engineer its underlying processes. A common situation occurred throughout the 1980s and 1990s when companies purchased millions of dollars of personal computers but failed to reorganize business operations to capitalize on computerization. As a result, the companies showed little or no gain in productivity from the use of the computers. For automation to be useful, managers need to understand how the computers will alter the tasks and management of the firm.

Management and Decision Levels

To understand management, re-engineering, and information systems, it helps to divide the organization into three decision levels: strategy, tactics, and operations. Each level has unique characteristics, which use different types of support from information technology. These levels were explained by Robert Anthony in 1965. In 1971, Gorry and Scott Morton added a detailed explanation of how information systems at that time could support the various levels of management. Figure 1.6 is an updated picture of the typical pyramid shape of most organizations involving operations and tactical and strategic decisions. As is typical with most management models, the various levels are not strictly delineated. Some problems will encompass all management levels of the firm. Similarly, making a change at one level may have unexpected repercussions on the other levels. Classifying a problem by its most relevant level makes it easier to concentrate on a solution. Once the primary problems are solved, the other effects are easier to handle. This text begins by discussing operations and works up to strategy. The cases in each chapter will help you identify problems at each level.

FIGURE 1.6

There are three primary levels of decisions in business. Business operations consist of tasks to keep the business operating on a day-to-day basis. Tactical decisions involve changes to the firm without altering the overall structure. Strategic decisions can alter the entire firm or even the industry. Information system tools exist to help with each type of decision.

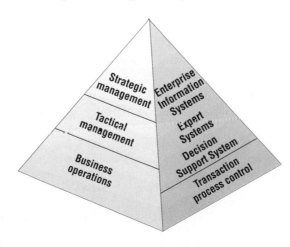

Operations

The *operations level* consists of day-to-day operations and decisions. In your first job, you will typically concentrate on the problems that arise at this level. For example, in a manufacturing firm, machine settings, worker schedules, and maintenance requirements would represent management tasks and decisions at the operational level. Information technology at this level is used to collect data and perform well-defined computations. Most of the tasks and decisions are well **structured,** in the sense that they can be defined by a set of rules or procedures. For example, a clerk at Wal-Mart follows the procedures in the guidebook to deal with typical operations. Common problems are anticipated, with actions spelled out in the guidebook.

Summarized in Figure 1.7, managers in other disciplines, such as accounting, marketing, or finance, also face operational decisions. Personal productivity tools, such as spreadsheets, word processors, and database management systems help managers collect and evaluate data they receive on a daily basis. The use of these tools is reviewed in Chapter 2.

An important task at the operations level is to collect data on transactions and operations, hence **transaction processing systems** are a crucial component of the organization's information system. The data collected form the foundation for all other information system capabilities. As discussed in Chapter 4, an important characteristic of transaction processing systems is the ability to provide data for multiple users at the same time. A special class of transaction processing software designed for factory operations is called *process control* software.

Database management systems are increasingly used to control data and build systems to share data. Their role is explained in Chapter 5. Chapter 3 shows how communication networks are used to provide access to data throughout the organization. Increasingly managers work in teams—either with workers in the same department or across departments and sometimes companies. Increasingly sophisticated software tools are being developed to help integrate data in these collaborative arrangements. These integration tools and *enterprise resource planning systems* are described in Chapter 7.

Operational decisions are often the easiest to understand. They deal with structured problems over relatively short periods of time.

Tactics

As you move up in your career to project leader or department manager, you will encounter a different level of decision making, where the types of problems will depend on your specialization, but some common features will stand out. At the *tactical level,* decisions typically involve time frames of less than a year. As shown in Figure 1.8, these decisions usually result in making relatively major changes but stay within the existing structure of the organization.

A manufacturing tactical-level decision might involve rearranging the work area, altering production schedules, changing inventory methods, or expanding quality control measures. These changes require time to implement and represent changes to the basic methods of the firm. What distinguishes them is that they can be made without altering the overall characteristics of the organization. For example, in most cases, expanding quality control measures does

FIGURE 1.7

Each functional area of management faces the three categories of decisions and problems. Only a few examples are presented here.

Sector	Operations	Tactics	Strategy
Production	• Machine settings • Worker schedules • Maintenance schedule	• Rearrange work area • Schedule new products • Change inventory method	• New factory • New products • New industry
Accounting	• Categorize assets • Assign expenses • Produce reports	• Inventory valuation • Depreciation method • Finance short/long term	• New GL system • Debt vs. equity • International taxes
Marketing	• Reward salespeople • Survey customers • Monitor promotions	• Determine pricing • Promotional campaigns • Select marketing media	• Monitor competitors • New products • New markets

FIGURE 1.8
Each decision level
affects the firm in
different ways. Each
level uses and produces
different types of
information.

Decision Level	Description	Example	Type of Information
Strategic	Competitive advantage, become a market leader Long-term outlook	New product that will change the industry	External events, rivals, sales, costs quality, trends
Tactical	Improving operations without restructuring the company	New tools to cut costs or improve efficiency	Expenses, schedules, sales, models, forecasts
Operations	Day-to-day actions to keep the company functioning	Scheduling employees, ordering supplies	Transactions, accounting, human resource management, inventory

Reality Bytes   Baxter Healthcare/American Hospital Supply

Hospitals use a large amount of routine supplies such as bandages and antiseptics. Originally, they purchased them from various suppliers, held them in inventory, and distributed them throughout the hospital as they were needed. This relationship is shown in Figure 1.9. American Hospital Supply (AHS) was one of these suppliers. To gain an advantage over their competitors, AHS created a new system and made an offer to the hospital managers. AHS placed computer terminals in hospital locations where the supplies were used (emergency, operating rooms, nursing stations, etc.). As shown in Figure 1.10 these terminals were connected to the AHS computer.

As hospital personnel removed supplies, they recorded them on the terminals. The computer kept track of the amount of supplies in each location. A list would be printed at the warehouse, and drivers delivered the necessary supplies to each location in the hospital. Monthly usage statistics were sent to the hospital.

The hospital gained because the facility did not need to maintain extra inventory, which saved money and space. Fewer hospital employees were needed, because the supplies were delivered directly to the needed locations. Additionally, the hospital received detailed usage records.

To offer this service, AHS incurred higher costs—largely the cost of creating and maintaining the information system. What did AHS gain in return? As long as it was the only company offering this service, AHS gained a competitive advantage by providing a new service. Hospitals were more likely to choose AHS over the rivals. But what would happen if a competitor created a similar system? Would the hospitals stay with AHS or switch to the rivals?

Although the answer depended on the prices, hospitals had a strong incentive to stay with AHS. They would encounter various **switching costs** if they chose another supplier. For example, daily operations would be disrupted while the system was changed. Employees would have to be retrained to use the new system. Managers who used the monthly usage reports would have to adapt to the new system. A rival would have to offer strong price advantages to overcome these costs.

Eventually, Baxter Healthcare, a large manufacturer of supplies, purchased AHS. Of course, over time Baxter had an incentive to cut its costs to maintain higher profits. In the process their delivery service might suffer. Some hospitals apparently experienced problems and returned to in-house stock rooms to eliminate shortages of basic supplies.

not require the firm to expand into new industries, build new facilities, or alter the structure of the industry. Much of the information for making tactical decisions comes from the transaction records that have been stored in the computer. Computer tools to help analyze this type of data are called **decision support systems (DSSs)** and are described in detail in Chapter 8.

Other types of problems that involve more complex models occur in business. For instance, **diagnostic situations** consist of spotting problems, searching for the cause, and implementing corrections. Examples of these situations include responding to problem reports from operations to identify the cause of the problem and potential solutions. For instance, a marketing manager might be asked to determine why the latest marketing approach did not perform as well as expected. Tactical-level decisions tend to involve specialized problems, and can often be solved with the help of an expert. Chapter 9 presents **expert systems** to make this knowledge more accessible to an organization.

FIGURE 1.9
American Hospital Supply began as an intermediary that bought various medical supplies and distributed them in bulk to hospitals. The hospital distributed supplies throughout its facility and was responsible for maintaining its own inventory.

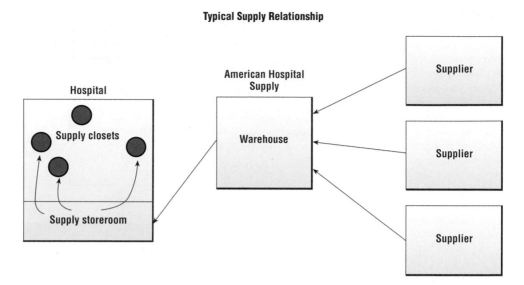

Typical Supply Relationship

FIGURE 1.10
American Hospital Supply changed the industry by providing a just-in-time inventory delivery service. Supplies then were delivered directly to where they are used within the hospital. AHS could offer this system only by maintaining a computer link between supply usage and the local warehouse. The computer data also provided summary reports to management. By purchasing AHS, Baxter Healthcare gained immediate access to that sales data.

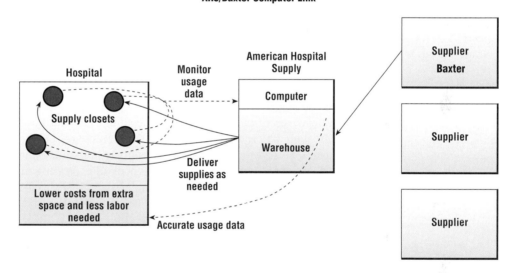

AHS/Baxter Computer Link

Strategy

The next step on the pyramid moves up the corporate ladder to executive-level decisions. Although you may never be a CEO, you might be in a position to advise upper-level management about strategic opportunities—especially in small businesses. **Strategic decisions** involve changing the overall structure of the firm to give it an advantage over the competition. They are long-term decisions and are unstructured. In other words, they are usually difficult and risky decisions. Examples of strategic decisions in the manufacturing arena include building new factories, expanding to new products or industries, or even going out of business. Strategic decisions represent an attempt to gain a competitive advantage over your rivals. Because of the complexity and unstructured nature of executives' decisions, it is difficult to determine how information systems can help at the strategic level. However, Chapter 10 explores information system techniques that firms have used to gain a competitive advantage.

FIGURE 1.11

In analyzing strategies, Michael Porter focuses on the five forces: threat of new entrants, threat of substitute products or services, bargaining power of suppliers, bargaining power of buyers, and rivalry among existing competitors. Competitive advantage can be obtained by using these forces or altering the relationships between these external agents.

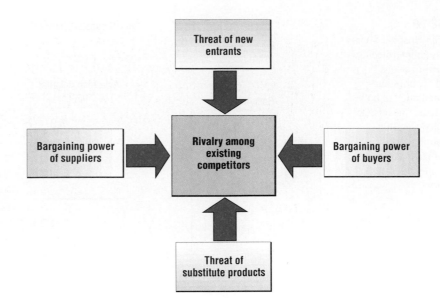

An Introduction to Strategy

Firms are constantly searching for ways to gain an advantage over their rivals. Finding these opportunities is hard: it requires extensive knowledge of the industry, and it requires creativity. Managers also have to be willing to take risks to implement strategic options. Strategic uses of IT often involve the use of new technology and development of new software. Being the first company to implement a new idea can be risky. However, it can also bring substantial rewards.

Strategic uses of IT are discussed in detail in Chapter 10 because you need to understand the technology before trying to solve difficult problems. On the other hand, to stimulate the imagination needed for creativity, it helps to begin thinking about the basic ideas right from the start. Many cases used throughout the book illustrate how firms have used technology to gain substantial advantages. These examples should help you solve other problems. If you can recognize a pattern or similarity between your problem and actions taken by other firms, the association may help you create a solution.

Michael Porter noted that often the first step in searching for competitive advantage is to focus on *external agents,* or entities that are outside the direct control of your company. Porter's Five Forces model in Figure 1.11 illustrates that typical external agents are customers, suppliers, rivals, and governments. For instance, competitive advantages can be found by producing better quality items or services at a lower cost than your rivals. Also, many firms have strengthened their positions by building closer ties with their suppliers and customers. An excellent example of this situation is provided by Baxter Healthcare, as illustrated in Figures 1.9 and 1.10. Information technology can be used to exchange information with suppliers or customers. Over time, the customers and suppliers will come to rely on this information and the capabilities you provide. Even if a competitor eventually offers similar ties, your new partners (customers and suppliers) will be reluctant to deal with a different firm because it would be difficult for them to change their systems and processes.

Summary

Information technology is altering jobs, businesses, and society. Managers who understand and use this technology will be able to improve companies and advance their personal careers. Information systems consist of hardware, software, people, procedures, and collections of data. These components work together to provide information and help managers run the firm, solve problems, and make decisions. Studying information systems will also teach you to analyze business operations and solve problems.

A Manager's View

Modern managers are also experts in their fields. You must rely on information technology to solve problems, make decisions, communicate with others, and increase your productivity. You must also be aware of the changing business and technology worlds to take advantage of trends. Managers must understand the importance of strategy and continually search for new ways to gain a competitive advantage.

The role of a manager is changing, but at a basic level all managers spend time organizing resources, planning, motivating workers, and communicating with other employees and managers. Several business trends will affect individual jobs, business operations, and society. Important trends include specialization, management by methodology and franchising, decentralization, the increased importance of small businesses, the use of temporary workers and consultants, the growing international scope of business, and the rise in service-oriented businesses. Information technology is used to support these trends and provide new management alternatives.

As is true of many problems, management and information technology can be studied by breaking them down into smaller pieces. The three basic levels to management are operations, tactics, and strategies. The operations level is concerned with day-to-day operations of the firm. Tactics involve changes and decisions that improve operations but do not require a major restructuring of the firm. Strategies are designed to give a firm a competitive advantage.

Strategy typically involves examining external forces: rivals (competitors within the industry), customers, suppliers, potential new competitors, and potential substitute products or services. Information technology can be used to strengthen links strategically between customers and suppliers. It can also be used to create new products and services and to improve the quality of the operations.

Information technology can be the foundation of a business, but it can also be expensive. It is important that the information system be designed and organized to match the needs of the firm. Designing and creating effective information systems is a complex task, and several techniques have been developed to analyze organizations and build information systems. Common techniques include the systems development life cycle, prototyping, and end-user development. Business managers need to understand the strengths and limitations of the various methodologies to ensure that companies get an information system that meets their needs.

Key Words

B2B, *6*
B2C, *6*
data, *5*
databases, *5*
decision process, *8*
decision support systems, *18*
diagnostic situations, *18*
dot-coms, *6*
e-business, *6*
e-commerce, *6*

expert systems, *18*
hardware, *5*
information, *5*
information technology (IT), *4*
knowledge, *5*
management information system (MIS), *4*
people, *5*
procedures, *5*

re-engineering, *15*
software, *5*
strategic decisions, *19*
structured decisions, *17*
switching costs, *18*
transaction processing system, *17*
wisdom, *5*

Website References

General Searches

AltaVista	**www.altavista.com**
AskJeeves	**www.ask.com**
Dogpile	**www.dogpile.com**
Go	**www.go.com**
Google	**www.google.com**
Lycos	**www.lycos.com**
Meta Crawler	**www.go2net.com**
Savvy Search	**www.savvysearch.com**
Northern Light	**www.northernlight.com**
Yahoo	**www.yahoo.com**
Web Crawler	**www.webcrawler.com**

People and Businesses

Anywho	**www.anywho.com**
SuperPages	**www.superpages.com**
Knowx	**www.knowx.com**
Switchboard	**www.switchboard.com**
Whitepages	**www.whitepages.com**
Zip2	**www.zip2.com**

Reference

Britannica (encyclopedia)	**www.britannica.com**
Encarta (encyclopedia)	**www.encarta.com**
American Heritage dictionary	**www.bartleby.com/61/**
Translation dictionaries	**www.freedict.com**
CIA World Factbook	**www.cia.gov/cia/publications/factbook/**

Additional Reading

Anthony, Robert N. *Planning and Control Systems: A Framework for Analysis.* Cambridge: Harvard University Press, 1965. [Early MIS]

Booker, Ellis. "Baxter Gets PC Smart, Ousts Dumb Terminals." *Computerworld,* April 3, 1989, p. 33. [Baxter Healthcare]

Bureau of Labor Statistics, http://www.bls.gov/webapps/legacy/cpsatab4.htm. [Summary of job statistics.]

Gorry, G.A., and M. Scott Morton. "A Framework for Management Information Systems." *Sloan Management Review,* Fall 1971, pp. 55–70. [Early MIS.]

"Health-Care Guys Can Make Good on Retail IT." *PC Week,* August 21, 1995, p. 11. [Baxter Healthcare.]

Leavitt, Harold J., and Thomas L. Whisler. "Management in the 1980s." *Harvard Business Review,* November 1958, pp. 41–48. [Prediction of decline in middle management.]

Luthans, Fred. *Organizational Behavior: A Modern Behavioral Approach to Management.* New York: McGraw-Hill, 1973. [Management.]

Mintzberg, Henry. *The Nature of Managerial Work.* Harper & Row, New York, 1973. [Management.]

Nash, Jim. "Just What the Doctor Ordered." *Computerworld,* June 1, 1992, p. 79. [Baxter Healthcare.]

Office of Trade and Economic Analysis, http://www.ita.doc.gov/td/industry/otea/usfth/aggregate/HL00t01.txt. [Summary of U.S. trade statistics.]

Porter, Michael. *Competitive Strategy: Techniques for Analyzing Industries and Competitors.* New York: Free Press, 1980. [Strategy.]

Sloan, Alfred. *Adventures of a White-Collar Man.* New York: Doubleday, 1941. [Management.]

Review Questions

1. What is the main purpose of MIS?
2. Why do students who are not MIS majors need to study MIS?
3. What are e-commerce and e-business?
4. What are the roles of managers in a modern company?
5. Describe how seven basic trends in today's business environment are related to MIS.
6. Describe the five components of a management information system.
7. How has the management structure of many businesses changed in the past decade—largely due to re-engineering?
8. Describe the three basic levels of management decisions.
9. How can an understanding of the levels of management decisions help you solve business problems?
10. How are information systems used at the various levels of business management?
11. How do you begin the search for strategic uses of information systems?

Exercises

1. Interview a local manager (or a student who has recently graduated) to discover how he or she uses computers on the job. How does the business use the Internet for e-commerce or e-business?
2. Using the resources of your library (government data, annual reports, business publications, etc.), find statistics to document at least two business trends. Draw graphs to reveal the patterns.
3. Choose one large company. Using annual reports, news articles, trade journals, and government data (e.g., 10K reports), research this company. Identify any changes that have been made in the last few years.
4. Choose a specific industry. Read news articles and trade journals to identify the major companies in that industry. Extend your research to include the primary international firms in the industry. Compare the growth rates of the two types of firms during the last five years.
5. Choose a specific industry and identify three common decisions within it. Identify one decision at each level (operations, tactical, and strategic).
6. Interview a recent graduate in your major (or a relative or friend). Find out what they do on a daily basis. Ask what his or her managers do. Do managers have operations tasks to perform as well as management duties? For instance, does a manager in an accounting firm work on tax returns?
7. As an entrepreneur, you decide to open a fast food restaurant. You can purchase a franchise from one of the established corporations (as discussed in the McDonald's case) or create your own restaurant. Compare the choices by identifying the decisions you will face with each approach. What data will you need to collect?
8. Choose a relatively large firm and research its sales to identify the items sold and the percentage of sales made over the Internet.
9. Think of a part-time job you have or have had. How does your manager break down his or her time among categories of communication, traditional management, networking, and human resource management? What issues have you felt your manager has dealt with effectively? On what issues could your manager spend time to improve?

 C01Ex10.txt

10. The data disk contains a text file for this problem. You have been hired as a consultant to a fast food store. The store manager has listed the cash received and the number of orders for each half hour of the day during one week of operations. Read the file into a spreadsheet.

a. Format the columns, then compute daily and weekly totals.

b. Create two line charts: one for cash, one for orders. Show transactions by the half hour. (There should be seven lines on each chart). Highlight the line for Saturday.

c. Create a separate schedule that shows the cumulative cash and orders through the day.

d. Draw a graph for the cumulative cash flow. Indicate on the graph when the manager should take the cash to the bank (any time the total exceeds $2,000.)

e. The manager wants an estimate of the number of workers needed at any time of the day during the week. Create a table that displays the total number of counter workers and kitchen staff needed at each half hour (two columns per day). For every 25 orders during a half hour, we need two kitchen workers. For every 15 orders during the half hour, we need one counter worker.

Rolling Thunder Database

11. Install the Rolling Thunder Bicycles database. Look through the various forms. List each of the main forms and briefly describe the purpose of the form.

12. Using the Rolling Thunder help files or the description available on the Internet site, describe the goals of the firm and outline the basic operations.

13. Using Internet sources, identify the competitors to Rolling Thunder Bicycles.

14. Using Internet, financial, and government sources, estimate the size of the market (total sales and number of bicycles) for quality bicycles.

15. Locate at least five sources for additional information about bicycles and bicycle components on the Internet. List and briefly describe the sites.

Cases

The Fast Food Industry

Introduction and Context

Fast food franchising is the fastest growing area of the restaurant industry. Franchising is a system in which a producer or marketer of a service, the franchisor, sells others, the franchisees, the right to duplicate a concept, apply the training techniques, and use the registered trade name. The franchisor promises the exclusive right to sell within a specific territory and provides sales and other support for an agreed period of time. A franchise usually includes the name, decor, menu, management system, accounting system, and, almost always, the information system. Supplies are ordered from preapproved sources according to predetermined standards. Managers often receive training at corporate-sponsored institutes.

Due to the rapid growth in franchising since the 1950s, franchised chains account for roughly 25 percent of restaurant outlets and 43 percent of industry sales. In recent years, the saturation of this marketplace has slowed new unit growth and sales. Restaurant chains that want to focus on continued high-growth and above-average sales have turned instead to the international marketplace. New domestic initiatives include operating units in nontraditional markets and dual-branding. This involves several restaurant chains or services operating in the same location or colocating with gasoline stations or department stores.

The simplest franchise type involves a contract between a supplier and a business owner. The business owner agrees to sell only one version of a particular product. For example, McDonald's sells only Coca-Cola soft drinks. Conversely, product-trade name franchising, which accounts for 52 percent of all franchise sales and 33 percent of all the franchise units in the United States, involves selling products to distributors who resell them.

The type of franchise that is growing fastest is the prototype or package franchise in which the entire mode of business operation, including the product or service, inventory system, sales and marketing methods, and record-keeping procedures are sold to the franchisee. Package franchising has grown 10 times faster than product trade-name franchising, 11.1 percent versus 1.1 percent on average per year.

Through franchising, a business can grow quickly and achieve a higher market penetration than a single-owner business. Franchisees are often entrepreneurs who lack the knowledge to start a business. Franchising provides these individuals with the tools, format, name recognition, and national advertising program to rapidly advance a business concept without developing all of the business components from scratch. Franchises reduce the risk normally associated with starting a business. Less risk is involved because the franchise has already proven to be profitable on a limited scale. Thus, the five-year survival rate for franchises is much higher than that of traditional start-up businesses (85.7 percent vs. 23 percent).

The franchiser's revenues are in the form of a start-up fee, ranging from $10,000 to $600,000 depending upon the size and market share of the franchise. This includes a license for the use of the trade name, managerial training and support, and royalties that amount to 3 to 8 percent of gross sales.

Additional initial outlays include rent, inventory, legal fees, equipment, insurance, and licenses. Collectively, these can amount to 10 times the start-up fee. In the case of McDonald's they can reach $500,000. The average initial cost of $330,000 per franchise often limits the ability of individuals to enter these business opportunities. As a result, franchisers tend to be groups of investors who enter a specific area. To increase the probability of success, franchisors often require potential franchisees to demonstrate proven experience in the particular franchise or in the segment represented.

Financial Analysis

Franchise restaurants are an $800 billion industry employing more than 8 million people. One out of every three dollars spent in the United States on food services goes to franchise restaurants. The changing lifestyle continues to provide the industry with a steady increase in revenues. This continues a decade-long trend in which the industry benefited from a strong economy. While the number of dollars spent on fast food continues to grow, industry growth as measured by the increase in the total number of domestic restaurant units has been slowing.

Stock/Investment Outlook

The growth rate for the fast food industry remains about 15 percent per year. This is reinforced by the continued trend toward two-income households. Today's working parents eat out far more often than their parents did. Increasingly, it is easier to go out to eat than to stay home and prepare a meal after a long day at work. In 1999, according to the National Restaurant Association (www.restaurant.org/research/spending.cfm), 42.1 percent of all spending on food took place away from home (in restaurants). Conversely, in 1972, only 38.2 percent of spending occurred in restaurants while 61.8 percent went to groceries. With their targeted marketing and expanded menus, the larger restaurant franchises have positioned themselves to take advantage of this social trend toward dining out.

Even with the changes in the marketplace, investment projections for the largest franchises remain optimistic. Analysts continue to project that sales for Wendy's and McDonald's will increase by 17 percent and 14 percent respectively for the next five years. Paralleling the growth in sales, however, is a concern regarding margins. While sales increase, the trend toward 99 cent specials and value meals are cutting into the overall profitability of these companies and the fast food industry.

If investors are willing to risk moving toward less proven names, there continue to be a large number of initial public offerings from small franchise chains. Of course, it is important to remember that these opportunities are increasingly present in crowded marketplaces. Investors can also expect the trend toward mergers and acquisitions to continue. Long-term, the prospects remain favorable.

Growth Potential

Growth in the entire franchise industry is expected to continue with expansion from 41 to 50 percent of all retail sales. Sales are expected to reach $2.5 trillion by the year 2010. Even though the domestic market for the fast food restaurant industry has matured and competition is tight for consumer dollars, companies are continually searching for new areas for growth. These include:

- Niche marketing in the United States
   Marketing toward children and young people
   Health-conscious and nutritionally balanced meals
   Home meal replacement (traditional family meals with the ease of fast food)

- Mergers and considerations
   Wendy's purchase of Tim Horton's, Hardees, and Roy Rogers
   Boston Market's purchase of Einstein Bros. Bagels
   McDonald's purchase of Boston Market

- Dual-branding, where several restaurants operate at the same location
   Taco Bell and KFC locations under one roof
   Dunkin' Donuts and Baskin-Robbins
   Arby's and p.t. Noodles

- Nontraditional operations
   McDonald's operations in Wal-Mart stores and gas stations
   Little Caesar's Pizza outlets in Kmart stores
   International development
   Companies such as McDonald's, KFC, and Burger King continue aggressive development of markets in Asia and South America.

- Value offerings
   Consumers want value, so prices will be kept to a minimum. Many restaurants continue to focus on combo value offerings or value menus.
   Wendy's 99¢ Value Meal
   McDonald's Combo Value Meal, which offers standard combinations of popular items at reduced prices

The growth in restaurant franchising can also be attributed to the changing age demographics. The elderly, seeking convenience, will continue to make up an increasing percentage of the population.

Competitive Structure

The fast food industry is highly competitive and very fragmented. The 10 largest chains make up approximately 15 percent of all units and account for only 23 percent of sales. McDonald's remains the industry leader with more than $15.9 billion in sales and more than 11,000 units in the United States. Burger King, Hardee's, Pizza Hut, KFC, Wendy's, and Taco Bell follow in size.

Mergers have changed the competitive structure of the industry. In 1995, Wendy's merged with Tim Horton's, Canada's largest national chain of coffee and baked goods. Subsequently, Wendy's has purchased and integrated into its chain Roy Rogers restaurants in New York, Hardees restaurants in Detroit, and Rax restaurants in Ohio and West Virginia. Wendy's currently has more than 5,000 Wendy's units and 1,300 Tim Horton's units.

Boston Market was one of the fastest-growing restaurant chains with sales of approximately $384 million in 1994. This represents an almost 150-percent increase over 1993. It also more than doubled its unit growth between 1993 and 1994, jumping from 217 units to 534 units. Boston Market focuses on homestyle entrees, vegetables, and salads. However, their rapid growth resulted in a loss of control and the firm closed many stores by the end of 1998 and was subsequently purchased by McDonald's. By 2002, most Boston Market stores were closed, but the name is used on frozen food products sold through traditional grocery chains.

A chief competitor to the franchise food industry is grocery stores. They have targeted busy students and working parents by offering more prepared foods, deli counters, and eat-in dining areas.

Technological Investment and Analysis

Technology has impacted the growth of the franchise industry. Improvements have included electronic systems, which help track inventories and sales. These systems yield more efficient operations and ease in the transmission of information between owner and franchisor. Electronic data interchange (EDI) is also being used by some franchises such as car rentals and hotels to communicate regarding reservations and customers.

Prospective franchisers can also use the Internet to find key locations for their businesses by examining demographic and market research reports rapidly and at a low cost. Constructing websites to advertise to prospective owners is another use of technology. Since starting a franchise network requires a great deal of communication comprising training and support, leaps in telecommunications technology have helped make the global exchange of information easier than ever. This development has made it even easier to monitor and enforce the uniformity of the franchisee.

The role of research and development in the fast food industry is generally limited to the test marketing of new products and improvement in food taste, calories, and consistency. Fast food companies constantly test the market acceptance of new menu items. Usually several restaurant locations serve as a test market to check the popularity of a new menu item. This type of market research helps keep the company ahead of the competition by adjusting to consumers' changing food tastes. Research also includes food science experimentation to improve the cost, taste, texture, shelf life, and fat content of menu items.

Future Recommendations

The fast food industry continues to face many new challenges. While there is plenty of room for growth in the international market, sales and margins will continue to lag in the United States. Companies will have to fight to increase or even keep their market share. In an effort to increase domestic market share, companies must focus on nontraditional markets and niche marketing. They must also focus on dual-branding. Careful focus must also be placed on delivery speed and customer service. As competition continues to tighten, mergers between companies will continue to take place.

Case: McDonald's Corporation

McDonald's has worked hard to be more than a restaurant chain. It has become a marketing icon and is part of the regular routines of millions of people. Its success is so far-reaching that it has developed its own culture and identity. Often, McDonald's represents the symbol of the success and desirability of American popular culture.

Short Description of the Company

McDonald's operates more than 29,000 restaurants in 114 countries. It has a 21 percent share of the very competitive fast food marketplace. Overseas restaurants now account for one-half of the company's profits. McDonald's plans to open 10,000 additional new restaurants by the year 2005. It has been a forerunner in the industry trend of co-branding and satellite locations.

Technology Innovations

Networks

Networks are particularly important to McDonald's because they provide a mechanism to manage the franchises spread over large geographic areas. Networks reinforce the centralization of power by enabling headquarters to communicate with the franchises. This ensures standardization and quality control through the analysis of inventories and franchises. Networks achieve these functions at a comparatively low cost and without the time constraints of more mainframe-based communications.

Smart Card Technology

Both McDonald's and Burger King are implementing credit and smart card technologies in their restaurants. The transaction costs of credit cards have changed to make the smaller, more intensive purchases more economically feasible. Smart cards further reduce transaction costs by storing the cash value of each card on a computer chip or a magnetic strip on the back of each card. Value can be added to the card through machines that accept cash or through ATM-like machines that add value by transferring funds out of a customer's bank account. Customers can use the cards, instead of cash, to make their food purchases. Corporate goals for smart card implementation include cost savings in relation to money handling, reduced shrinkage, and increased loyalty through incentives and premiums. Smart cards eliminate the need for merchants to communicate with banks for authorization of purchases.

McDonald's has implemented this technology in Europe, where smart cards are more broadly accepted. Customers at McDonald's Deutschland, Inc. restaurants pay for goods by swiping smart cards through small, countertop terminals. They add value to their smart cards by downloading money electronically from their bank accounts at touch-screen terminals in the restaurants. The terminals lead the users through the process of downloading new money to the cards.

McDonald's Deutschland continues to implement smart card technology in its restaurants. In doing so, it has obtained the terminals from Hewlett-Packard's (HP's) VeriFone. Adding value to the smart cards has sometimes proven to be difficult in Germany. According to Rolf Kreiner, senior vice president of marketing at McDonald's Deutschland, by letting customers not only buy goods but also add value to their cards, McDonald's is hoping to lead a trend toward the wide-scale acceptance of smart cards across Germany. The German smart-card payment infrastructure, known as the GeldKarte-System, has about 40 million cards in circulation. McDonald's has committed to support this approach by using VeriFone's SC552 smart-card reader, which supports GeldKarte-System cards. The system that enables users to add value to their cards will be separate from the smart-card readers and will be called VeriFone's Transaction Automation Loading and Information System (TALIS). The system enables users to add value to their cards separately from the smart-card readers. While customers wait for TALIS terminals to connect to their banks, the screens flash advertising and marketing messages.

VeriFone's TALIS touch-screen terminals are equipped for two cards, permitting consumers to "transfer" monetary value from a debit or credit card to a smart card after first tapping in a personal identification number. Once the smart card has been filled with stored value, it can then be inserted into a smart-card reader at the point of sale to make payment on goods or services.

Technologically, smart cards were designed to function in place of credit cards in the fast food environment. Historically, fast food transactions were too small and credit card transactions were too slow for this industry. The associated costs were too high in the face of small margins. Smart cards are an important step in resolving these issues; they enable restaurants to leverage their sales. Since authorization and settlement technology are rapidly improving and the costs of network connectivity are decreasing, credit card use is further enhanced.

Within the United States, McDonald's has also adopted Speedpass. Originally developed by CitiBank in conjunction with Mobil, Speedpass was implemented to enable purchasers of gasoline to quickly and efficiently select and pay for their gasoline at the pump. McDonald's has implemented this technology in their restaurants. Once the purchase selection is made and the cost of the order determined, the Speedpass "wand" is swiped across the designated area of the pump or register, and the charge is made directly to the linked credit card.

Internet Sites

McDonald's first announced a Web presence in 1994 with McDonald's interactive, an area in NEC Online on America Online. In 1995, the company developed and implemented a website called McFamily (www.mcdonalds.com). It was aimed at families, perceived by McDonald's as its most important target market. The site featured "seasonal ideas for fun family activities such as block parties, travel games, and household safety information." The Auditorium sponsors monthly guest speakers, including celebrities and parenting experts. It included a Hey Kids area which housed a gallery with McArt submitted by children with downloadable games and contests. The goal of all of these web pages is to enhance the brand image that McDonald's presented to families. McFamily included a section on helping others. This section featured information on Ronald McDonald House and other related children's charities. It also included information on McDonald's efforts to preserve the environment.

The McDonald's website cannot be used to sell food. However, it can capture revenue through the sales of merchandise related to McDonald's sponsorships. The McStuff for You section offered gear from McDonald's racing teams and the Olympic Games. The website was also used to collect customer information and profiles through online surveys.

The McFamily website was judged to be less than successful. As a result, the site was discontinued and a Ronald and Friends page introduced. This page includes games and graphics reinforcing the Ronald McDonald theme.

Data

Decision makers at McDonald's Corporation realize that consumer preference is paramount to their success. In keeping with this focus, the chain is implementing a restaurant-level planning system. Named Made for You, the system enables each restaurant to stop making sandwiches and other foods in advance. Instead, workers make sandwiches based on actual demand without sacrificing any of the efficiency.

Over 800 McDonald's restaurants have adopted the system. It consists of PC-based cash registers running inhouse software. Orders are routed to monitors at different food preparation tables to balance the workload among employees.

In McDonald's restaurants without the new system, workers must anticipate the demand for each type of sandwich in advance and place them in bins. When a customer wants a sandwich that is not premade or one with a different topping, the person at the register shouts out the order and workers move out of the assembly line to fulfill the special request. This slows the process and extends the customer's wait.

McDonald's introduced the new system in March 1998 at a meeting for its franchisees. The company is encouraging its 12,400 U.S. restaurants to incorporate the system, but the actual decision is left to each franchise. The technology greatly eases the workload. As such, it could add a percentage point to the company's profit margin since it enables the restaurant to sell more food faster, according to Douglas Christopher, a financial analyst with Crowell Weedon & Co.

Wal-Mart and McDonald's have joined together to share retail space. These two companies have been partners since 1993, placing more than 800 restaurants in Wal-Mart stores. McDonald's has taken this partnership one step further. Wal-Mart's clerks and registers sell the McDonald's food. In several test locations, when Wal-Mart shoppers pull their carts up to the checkout, there is a mat on the counter displaying McDonald's products, much like one you would see at one of the restaurants. Each product, from hamburgers to Happy Meals, has a code number that the clerk scans into the Wal-Mart system while ringing up the customers' purchases. The orders are automatically relayed from the register to the kitchen using software jointly developed by McDonald's and Wal-Mart. The food is brought to the customers as they leave the store. Since the food appears on Wal-Mart's registers and receipts, customers can pay for it with a single credit card purchase. At the end of the day, McDonald's receives an allocation of its portion of the day's purchases. This process only works in Wal-Marts with a McDonald's kitchen somewhere in the store, whether it be in a restaurant or a stand-alone counter. Based on this joint success, McDonald's hopes to continue implementing these systems as extensively as possible.

"It's an inevitable process," according to Ross Telford, vice-president of retail practice at NCR, the Dayton, Ohio-based company that supplies the point-of-sale (POS) systems. NCR helps vendors and retailers such as Wal-Mart, JC Penney, and Qantas Airways capture, process, and analyze customer data. According to Telford, individuals are starting to use one another's environments and skills to reach as many potential customers as possible.

The Wal-Mart/McDonald's partnership is part of a much larger, industrywide trend toward the cost-effective use of information at the cash register to increase profits. Known as real-time cross-marketing, the concept enables companies to use information technology to increase the number of sales from each transaction. As the buyer produces his or her checkbook or wallet, the retailer offers another product that matches the customer's original selection, or one that targets a profile of the customer's previous purchases stored in the database. Matching a customer's current or past purchases with new ones and completing the sale requires both skill and tact. The information must be found and the product must be presented so the customer does not feel as if the company is intruding. "Acquisition of detailed data is always a challenge. Even more challenging is how to use the data without being intrusive," said Steve Keller, director of general merchandising and industry marketing at NCR.

McDonald's has implemented supply-chain software to better manage its inventory. This implementation enables McDonald's to better share demand and supply information among its restaurants, suppliers, and distributors.

Questions

1. What is McDonald's strategic/future direction?

2. What are McDonald's critical success factors?

3. What are McDonald's core competencies?

4. Upon which technologies has McDonald's relied?

5. What has caused a change in the use of technology within McDonald's?

6. How has this change been implemented throughout the franchise?

7. How successful has the technological change been?

8. How has McDonald's use of technology impacted the financial performance of its stock?

Additional Reading

Davey, Tom. "Personalized Service at Lower Cost—Hotels and Restaurants Turn to Transaction Processing and Real Time Communications to Get a Strategic Edge," *InformationWeek,* September 14, 1998, p. 173.

Essick, Kristi. "Put a Big Mac on my Smart Card, Please," *Computerworld,* August 24, 1998, p. 45.

Frank, Diane. "The New ROI in Point of Sale," *Datamation,* November 1997, pp. 73–77.

Gallagher, Sean. "Getting More Miles from IT," *InformationWeek,* September 9, 1996, pp. 124–127.

"Germans to Buy Big Macs with VeriFone's Smart Cards," *Newsbytes News Network,* August 17, 1998.

"McDonald's McCyberSpace," *Electronic Market Report,* September 5, 1995, p. 4.

"McDonald's Supply Chain," *InformationWeek,* April 13, 1998, p. 30.

Nash, Kim S. "McDonald's IT Plays Catch-Up with Rivals," *Computerworld,* December 14, 1998, p. 1.

Schien, Esther. "Telecom Tango: Telecom Deregulation in Central and South America Will Encourage U.S. Business Emigration," *PC Week,* February 16, 1998, pp. 73–74.

"Smart Cards and Big Macs," *InfoWorld,* August 24, 1998, p. 51.

Case: Rainforest Café

Steven Schussler was an owner of a chain of nightclubs. He also loved exotic birds. For the benefit of his pet birds, he turned his house into a rainforest habitat. The project turned out so well that he decided to apply the rainforest idea he had developed into a rainforest-theme restaurant. Since the prototype was already in place, he could use his home to convince potential investors to commit to the project. They did. The result is the multi-outlet, multimillion-dollar enterprise known as Rainforest Café.

Short Description of the Company

"One of the hottest concepts in themed retailing, Rainforest Café integrates food, entertainment, and retail into a carefully detailed, tropical-themed fantasyland." [*Chain Store Age Executive*] Rainforest Café, Inc., owns, operates, and licenses rainforest-theme restaurants and retail stores. The first café opened in The Mall of America in October 1994. In April 1995, seven months after opening the first restaurant, the company went public. [Annual Report] In 1996, six restaurant/ retail stores opened throughout the United States. In 1997, eight more opened. Rainforest Café has licensing agreements for restaurants in Mexico, Canada, and England.

The restaurant section of the café accounts for approximately 78 percent of store sales. [Walkup] The menu is unique and always changing. Full-flavored cuisines from Mexico, Asia, the Caribbean, Italy, the American Southwest, Louisiana, and elsewhere greatly influence the dishes served.

The Rainforest Café's retail section accounts for approximately 22 percent of total sales. [Walkup] Of this amount, general merchandise accounts for 45 percent of sales and private label items account for 50 percent of sales. [Annual Report] The private label items carry margins up to 50 percent. "The biggest potential for the Rainforest Café is the licensing of eight animal characters. [*Discount Store News*] A move to push this licensing has not yet taken place.

The environmental awareness theme of the café is carried throughout the operation. The restaurant will not serve net-caught fish or beef raised on deforested land. Recycled products are used as much as possible and only organic cleaners are applied for cleaning. The café, along with many of its suppliers, donates a portion of its proceeds to environmental groups or causes. [Rubel]

Technological Investment and Analysis

Rainforest Café uses eight Profit Series POS workstations with five printers in each restaurant. Rainforest executives chose the Profit Series manufactured by HSI for a number of reasons. First, the HSI Profit Series did not require proprietary hardware. This enabled systemwide integration in existing and new restaurants alike. Rainforest executives wanted to work with a mature company like HSI, which could grow with them and meet the company's future needs. The Profit Series system was user friendly. This made training easy, lowered costs, and increased flexibility.

The point-of-sale system used by Rainforest Café simplifies the inventory tracking. The system indicates what sells the most, what needs to be ordered, when it needs to be ordered, and how much needs to be ordered, thus lowering inventory costs. This saves time and eliminates ordering mistakes that could result in running out of needed goods.

Rainforest Café also uses a computer system to calculate waiting times for tables to within seven minutes. With this knowledge, restaurant patrons can use their time more efficiently. Thus, they can be encouraged to shop or do whatever they desire while waiting for their tables. The timing system also accounts for part of the increased table turnover.

The Rainforest Café was sold to Landry's Restaurants in early 2000. The chain will continue to exist as a subsidiary of Landry's, but Landry's stock price has fallen substantially in the last few years as investors question its profitability.

Questions

1. What trends are driving the strategic direction for the Rainforest Café?

2. Upon which systems has the Rainforest Café been built and why?

3. How has Rainforest Café used its web page to present its business directives?

4. What challenges and opportunities is the industry facing?

5. How important are Rainforest Café's databases to its continued success?

Additional Reading

"Rainforest Café sells to Landry's," *City Business,* February 10, 2000.

"Rainforest Café: Welcome to the Jungle," *Chain Store Age Executive with Shopping Center Age,* March 1997, p. 94.

Rainforest Café Inc., *Corporate Report—Minnesota,* October 1995, p. 47.

"A Really Wild Place to Shop and Eat," *Discount Store News,* May 15, 1995, p. 78.

Rubel, Chad, "New Menu for Restaurants: Talking Trees and Blackjack," *Marketing News,* July 29, 1996, p. 1.

Schwartz, Mathew, "Which Way to the Web?" *Software Magazine,* September 1998, pp. 70–76.

Walkup, Carolyn, "Rainforest Café: It's a Jungle in There," *Nation's Restaurant News,* May 12, 1997, p. 129.

Case: Dave & Buster's

Dave Corriveau met James Corley in Little Rock, Arkansas. Corriveau considers himself the "fun-and-games guy." He was still quite young when he opened up his own business in Little Rock. It was a game parlor and a saloon. In 1976, he opened a larger version named Slick Willy's World of Amusements. It has been rumored that Bill Clinton was among those that frequented the place. The 10,000-square-foot business generated sales in excess of $1.2 million while Corriveau was still in his early twenties.

During the same time, Corley was a general manager for TGI Friday's in the same town. He aspired to open up his own restaurant. He liked the location in which Slick Willy's was operating, a renovated train station. Corley approached Corriveau to request financial support in opening his restaurant. Corriveau agreed, and Corley opened right next door with a walkway connecting the businesses. Corley was also in his early twenties.

The walkway between these two businesses is probably the best thing that ever happened to the two entrepreneurs. The walkway enabled customers to migrate easily between the restaurant and the game parlor and saloon. Customers who initially came to one of the establishments would end up walking to the other establishment. They came to eat something and then stayed to play a couple of games. Sometimes they came to play a couple of games and then stayed to eat. It was good business and the two owners soon realized the potential that existed for a complex that would combine both businesses under the same roof.

The Slick Willy Restaurant was sold to raise money. Corriveau and Corley then moved to Dallas. They were in Dallas a little over two years before they were able to open up their first place. In 1982, inside a 40,000-square-foot building located next to an expressway, Dave & Buster's (D&B) was born.

Technology Investment and Analysis

D&B provides a PowerCard for customers to use. The card provides convenience to the customer by taking away the burden of carrying around a bucket of coins and allows D&B to make gradual increases in the amount they can charge for a game. Previously, prices could be raised only in whole increments (one token at a time). The card has done away with that by allowing incremental increases of 0.1 through 0.9 at a time. The customer simply swipes the card through a scanning mechanism located in front of each machine, and the credit amount is automatically deducted from the card.

The system has the capability of tracking what games have been played with each card and how much has been spent. Customers can verify the amount they have on their card by using analyzer/rechargers that are located throughout the arcade area. These analyzer/rechargers also allow customers to put more money on a card without having to stand in a line. The tokens are still used for some of the ticket redemption games that involve skill activities with the tokens.

A discount on the games is offered to those who have spent over a certain amount of credits on the same card. Members can sign up for the card by filling out an application with some particular information, and they are then given a card with their name on it. The "gold" card gives the customer a 10-percent discount on the amount required to play the games.

The card offers bonuses to customers through a lottery-type system that matches the numbers on their card with a randomly drawn number by the computer. Credits are awarded accordingly to the card. The PowerCard system does have certain limitations. The card can only be used at the issuing store, the credits are nontransferable, and no cash back is allowed on any remaining credit balance of the card. Furthermore, customers can only get their bonuses if they see an attendant at one of the desks and not at the analyzer/rechargers.

Recommendation for the Future

Other PowerCard bonuses should be considered. Whereas additional game-buying power is certainly a fun incentive, it might also be useful to give incentives that customers can take home. These incentives could be like boardwalk and game prizes—stuffed toys, toy jewelry, and so on.

At the end of 2001, Dave & Buster's is a publicly traded firm with 31 locations throughout the United States. The company also signed a development and license agreement to develop five complexes in South Korea (Business Wire/Press Release).

Questions

1. What technology tools are Dave & Buster's using to keep its focus on expansion?

2. What are the technological forces that are driving this direction?

3. Why do you think Dave & Buster's would choose not to have an Internet site?

4. What challenges and opportunities is the theme-restaurant industry facing?

5. How important is data to the corporation's continued success?

6. How will the capture and maintenance of customer data impact the corporation's future?

Additional Reading

"Late Earnings Roundup: Dave & Buster's Reports Income," *Newsbytes,* September 9, 1996, p. NEW09090021.

Press Releases, *Business Wire,* December 5 and 6, 2001.

Appendix

Finding Information

Think about your education for a minute—consider all of the classes you take. Many of the classes focus on specific skills (reading, writing, arithmetic, and so on). Yet, a common thread in all of these classes is learning to find information. You learned how to use a dictionary, an encyclopedia, newspapers, the library, a phone book, maps, and so on. Now, imagine a world where all of this data is stored in digital form on computers. We are not quite there, but the Web is rapidly beginning to provide the capability of searching for virtually any information.

Computers offer several advantages for searches. They are fast, they can search full text so they rarely miss material, and the search is automatic so it is inexpensive and up to date. On the other hand, computer searches generally lack human intelligence, so the computer does not truly understand what you are searching. Consequently, the computer may not find what you really want, or the search may return thousands of responses, which makes it hard to answer your questions.

The key to becoming efficient with computer searches is to understand how the computer organizes the search. This appendix presents the basics of computer searches and gives you hints on how to find what you want. The first section lists some of the common Web search engines. The second describes the most common search methods using Boolean techniques. The third section provides some hints on how to narrow your search and find exactly what you want. The fourth section gives you ideas on where to start when you have a general topic, but do not know exactly what you want to find.

Web Search Engines

Several companies provide free search engines for use on the Web. Some popular sites are listed in Figure 1.1A. The full-text engines function by automatically scanning pages posted on the Web and building indexes of keywords. Your search looks up the keywords in the index and retrieves the Internet

FIGURE 1.1A   Web search engines. These companies use advertising revenue to cover their costs, so you can search for free.

Full-Text Web Searches	
Altavista	www.altavista.com
Dogpile	www.dogpile.com
Google	www.google.com
Lycos	www.lycos.com
NorthernLight	www.northernlight.com
Webcrawler	www.webcrawler.com
Category Searches	
Yahoo	www.yahoo.com
Encarta (encyclopedia)	encarta.msn.com
People and Business	
AnyWho	www.anywho.com
SuperPages	www.superpages.com
Switchboard	www.switchboard.com

address of the matching pages. Sometimes a page will no longer exist even though it is still in the index.

Note that each search engine has different methods for entering Boolean conditions. Some require commands to be in uppercase (e.g., AND, OR). Some use symbols (e.g., &, +). You will have to read the specific documentation for each system.

Some of the search engines (e.g., Lycos) provide a numeric rating that attempts to indicate how well the page matches your search condition. Most likely pages are listed first.

Boolean Searches

The most basic possible search is to enter a single word and tell the computer to retrieve all the information related to that one word. And every once in a while, you will have a topic where you know exactly which word to use. On the other hand, a search for the word *autarky* on Hotbot returned "only" 868 matches. Even the word *onomatopoeia* resulted in 1,791 matching pages. Both of these words describe well-defined and relatively obscure topics—yet they both returned more data than you are willing to read.

Almost every search you perform will need to use more than one word. The power of a Boolean search lies in how you combine the words. Consider a search with two words (white, knight). There are three basic options: (1) treat the words as a phrase where the document must contain exactly that phrase "white knight"; (2) return documents that contain both words in any order: white and knight; or (3) return documents that contain either word: white or knight. The first method is the most restrictive and treats the phrase as a single word. Most Web systems use the quotation marks to indicate a phrase. The second method is the most common. The computer searches for documents that contain all of the words you enter. If you do not specify the connector (and, or), most Web systems assume you want all of the words (and). The third approach can be dangerous—it widens the search. You would never use the example given here because both words are far too common, and one or the other would be found in millions of documents. Some systems support modifications of these commands. For example, you might be able to search for documents where the two words appear within *n* words of each other.

The real power of a Boolean search is that you can form complex searches using the algebra that you learned in school. Any word (or phrase) can be connected by AND, OR, or NOT. You can also group terms together by enclosing them in parentheses. Figure 1.2A uses a truth table to show the basic logic.

Consider the example shown in Figure 1.3A. Say you are going to be transferred to an office in Medellin, Colombia, for two years. You decide to search the Web to learn more about Medellin. What happens if you ask the search engine to find all references to Colombia? You will be flooded with several thousand articles containing that word. Even the city Medellin returns thousands of matches. Your next step is to narrow the search by providing a more specific topic. Say you add the word *terrorism.* Then you will get a more reasonable number of responses (430).

There is another problem, however. If you are looking for the word *terrorism,* you should include other words that refer to the same topic, such as terrorist, bombing, and kidnap. In other words, you want to search for all articles that refer to Medellin AND (terrorist OR terrorism OR bombing OR kidnap). One useful trick is to know that most search engines match parts of words. Instead of entering *terrorism* and *terrorist,* you can just enter the word *terror,* which will match both of those words. You should always use root words in your search phrases (such as *bomb* instead of *bombing*). The fourth and fifth rows in Figure 1.3A show the difference—the root words return almost twice as many matches. Your full search is given by the last condition in Figure 1.3A. Your query can include AND and OR connectors, but you should always use parentheses to indicate how the phrases should be combined.

You Know What You Are Searching for

This topic should be easy. As long as you know what you are looking for, just tell the computer and it will find it. Life, however, is rarely that easy. First, you need to be able to describe what you want in a few key words. Second, the real problem is that the authors of the Web pages and articles may not have used the same words that you choose. You need to think about which words and phrases are most likely to be used.

The first step is to write down a list of words that describe your topic. Then run some initial searches to see how many pages are returned. If the number is too large, add more search terms (connected by AND) to restrict the search. If no matches are found, delete search terms, or add new terms connected by an OR. If the initial articles do not match what you want, throw out your search words and start over.

Once you have a core group of articles, read a few of them at random and look for new search ideas. If the page contains a keyword list, consider adding some of them to your search list. When you find the results you want, save your search list. It is a good idea to keep a search journal. You might have spent several hours searching for information. Do not discard your work. Use your word processor to keep a journal. Whenever you do a search, enter the date, the search topic, the search engine, and the final search condition into the journal. If you need to find similar information again, you can save time by referring to your journal.

Consider an example. You read somewhere that ITT was involved in a corporate merger. Hilton Hotels wanted to buy out ITT to gain control of their Sheraton Hotels. ITT directors did not like the idea and sought out a third company, which purchased them, becoming what is known as a *white knight.* You want to find the name of that company. To make it more interesting, say that you are not certain about many of the details. You only remember that ITT was a participant in some corporate merger that resulted in a white knight takeover.

FIGURE 1.2A

Truth table. An AND statement is true only if both components are true. An OR statement is true if at least one of the components is true.

A	B	A and B	A or B	Not A
T	T	T	T	F
T	F	F	T	F
F	T	F	T	T
F	F	F	F	T

FIGURE 1.3A

Sample Boolean search. The number on the right is the count of the number of documents that matched the search clause. Note the use of parentheses to group terms.

Colombia	1,889,871
Medellin	37,682
Medellin AND terrorism	575
(terror OR bomb OR kidnap)	1,920,549
(terrorism OR bombing OR kidnap)	1,012,458
Medellin AND (terror OR bomb OR kidnap)	1,563
Medellin AND (terror OR bomb OR kidnap) AND American AND (dead OR death)	535

FIGURE 1.4A

Web search for ITT merger. Knowing that the merger involved a "white knight" significantly narrows the search. It is easy to scan the 26 matches to learn the details.

ITT	81,801
ITT corporate merger	908
ITT corporate merger "white knight"	26

FIGURE 1.5A

Web search for a topic. After reading some of the items from the second search, you decide to rule out some topics. Adding the word *merger* restricts the list even further. Removing some additional topics (Germany and foreign) reduces the list to a manageable number.

"white knight"	47,000
"white knight" corporate	5,060
"white knight" corporate NOT (history, Canada, India)	2,820
"white knight" corporate merger NOT (history, Canada, India)	699
"white knight" corporate merger NOT (history, Canada, India, Germany, foreign)	463

Figure 1.4A shows your search strategy and the resulting matches. Clearly, searching for ITT is too broad. If this were the only information you had, you would be better off going directly to the ITT website and seeing if they had information on a merger. But, as a second attempt, you add the words: corporate merger. You might narrow the search by requiring them to be a phrase (instead of separate words), but that might be too narrow. Once you add the "white knight" phrase, the list is narrowed considerably. It is now easy to scan the articles until you find the answer (Starwood Lodging).

You Have a Vague Idea About What You Want

How can you find something when you do not know what you want? In practice, you will often find that you want information about a topic, but you do not yet know enough to ask specific questions. Without detailed questions, a computer search would return way too much data. So, you first need to find resources that provide a general introduction to the topic and show how it is organized.

If you are really uncertain about where to begin, you should first look through the categories provided by the search engines. In particular, Yahoo uses people to categorize sites that they find. These categories are arranged hierarchically, so you can start with general topics and work down to more detail. The process is similar to looking through a table of contents for a book. The advantage of this approach is that human intelligence has already organized and sorted the basic data, making it easier for you to find information based on concepts. The drawback is that it is nowhere near as complete as the automated searches. Consequently, it makes a good starting point.

In other situations, or after your initial search, you will have a vague idea of what you want to find. You can still run searches on key words—just be prepared to receive thousands of matches. One useful technique is to select some of these matches randomly and use them to help refine your search. If the document matches what you want, look for key words and phrases that you can add to your search condition. If the document does not contain information you want, look for key words that you can tell the search engine to avoid. By continually refining your search, you should eventually get closer to the information you want.

Consider the example used in the last section, but this time assume you do not know as much information. For instance, you might start out with an interest in "white knight" takeovers. Figure 1.5A shows the progression of the search. You begin with "white knight" and get thousands of matches.

Adding the term *corporate* reduces the list considerably, and you decide to scan some of the results. You notice that many of these pages refer to topics that do not interest you—they refer to companies in Canada and India, or they refer to historical concepts (real knights). Your third pass asks the search engine to ignore pages with those references, and the list is cut in half. After a little thought, you realize that the word *corporate* by itself is insufficient—for example, you are getting matches with companies that have "white knight" in their name. Adding the word *merger* reduces the list to about 100 matches. Skimming these entries, you notice several articles on Germany; so you add "Germany" and "foreign" to the restricted list. The query now returns only 79 matches. Although that might seem like a large number of items to read, remember that you started with a vague topic. You will have to read many of these items to make a decision about what you want to learn. Once you make up your mind, you can modify your search to narrow the topic.

Interactive searching is the key to finding information. You add terms to restrict the list. You skim random articles to find new terms. Look for terms to restrict the list (add with AND), to expand the list (add with OR), or to be excluded (add with NOT). You could also use a thesaurus to find synonyms that writers might have chosen. When you find an article that interests you, use its list of keywords to find related articles.

Internet Changes that Cause Complications

While the search engines are powerful, they were designed to handle a specific type of data: static pages of text. Increasingly, companies are creating websites based on database systems. At these sites, the data is stored in a database, and specific pages are built on the fly in response to a customer query. For example, if you go to a site that sells computer products, the items are all listed in the company's database; they are therefore generally not accessible to the search engines. Hence, if you ask a search engine to find every store that sells a specific type of printer, the search engine will probably miss most of the stores. Instead, you would have to search for printer sales and hope that the company has at least a few pages that will be found by the search engines.

Exercises

1. Using Internet resources and search engines, find the name of the person who was the lead prosecutor for President Clinton's impeachment trial. [Henry Hyde]

2. Using five different search engines, search for Vizsla and report the number of pages returned by each site.

3. Find three Internet sites that provide financial and background information about companies.

4. Run the search in Figure 1.3A in two different search engines. How do they differ in syntax for entering the Boolean conditions?

5. You have been asked to start a recycling program for the toner and ink jet cartridges used in your company offices in three cities: Boston, San Francisco, and Dallas. Using the Internet, find a company that can provide these services in each of the three cities. (It would be better if the same company can be used in all three cities.)

6. You want to buy a new car (assume you have a job and money). Find two sites that provide detailed information on the car, including prices. Can you find a site that lets you buy the car over the Internet? Can you finance the vehicle over the Internet? Can you get insurance over the Web?

CHAPTER TWO

Information Technology Foundations

What you will learn in this chapter

- What is a computer?

- What types of data can a computer handle?

- What options are available, and do you need them?

- What features do computers need to perform as Internet servers or browsers?

- How can computers help you with common personal tasks?

- How can they make you more efficient?

- Can they help you make better decisions?

Small businesses increasingly rely on computers to manage firms efficiently with a minimal number of employees.

Small Business

Despite its founding in Jeff Bezos's garage, Amazon.com never fit the stereotypical Web startup of twenty-somethings in ponytails. In the late 1980s, Bezos was a systems development executive at Bankers Trust in New York. He became the bank's youngest vice president ever. Yet, when the explosive growth of the World Wide Web caught his eye, he saw an even bigger opportunity: online commerce.

Today, Bezos, as CEO of the Internet bookstore Amazon.com, is representative of a group of young entrepreneurs who are using cyberspace technology to take market share from traditional businesses with strong consumer and industrial franchises.

This type of analytical thinking is not foreign to Bezos. "I always wanted to start a business, but my wake-up call was when I found out the Internet was growing at a 2,300 percent rate," he says. "That's a market that nothing compares to. Then I sat down and made a list of 20 possible products to sell on the Web. Books were the biggest commodity."

According to Bezos, the thing about books is that there are so many of them. At any given time, there are 1.5 million English-language books in print plus another 3 million worldwide. No other consumer commodity item comes close, with music being a distant second, with about 200,000 total titles available. The largest real-world physical bookstores house only about 170,000 books. This leads to the opportunity that an online bookstore provides for an ideal electronic-commerce business.

Overview

Elaine: Hey Ally. The new software showed up. That digital video camera is awesome! But other than shots of your beach vacation, what are you going to do with it?

Ally: Come on, Elaine. We've needed this system for months. The new PC has a monster hard drive and video-editing software. Now we can make our own demos in a couple of hours instead of contracting it out and waiting for days.

FIGURE 2.1
Every manager must perform certain basic personal tasks, including searching for data, communicating, scheduling, writing, and making various computations. Several software packages have been designed to help with these basic tasks.

Richard: Check this out . . . I can mix this customer comment with this new MP3, throw in some animations from the old slide presentation, finish off with some video of our last project, and wow . . . have a demo I can take to my new client presentation this afternoon.

Elaine: Sure, but what's a keyframe, and do I really need to know the difference between D1 and D2 DV formats?! (shouting) Hey! Did anyone here ever take a video-editing course?

Ally: Relax, it's not that bad. You can drag most of the things around on the screen. We don't have to be perfect. We can turn it over to the pros later if we need a better copy. But, Richard, we might need some more money to improve the network. That file you're saving looks a little big . . .

Introduction

Why do you care how computers work? After all, it is easy to use a photocopy machine without understanding how it works. Automobiles cost more than most computers, yet you can buy an automobile without knowing the difference between a manifold and a muffler. You can also make telephone calls without understanding fiber optic cables and digital transmissions.

On the other hand, when you buy an automobile you need to decide if you want options such as power windows, a turbo charger, or a sunroof. Similarly, many options are available for telephone services. If you do not understand the options, you might not end up with the car, telephone service, photocopier, or computer that you need. Or, you could end up paying extra money for services that you will not use. To choose among the various options, you need to know a little about how computers work. Many features are particularly important when evaluating computers to use as Web servers in e-business.

Computers are typically discussed in terms of two important classifications: hardware and software. *Hardware* consists of physical items; *software* is the logical component such as a set of instructions. Of course, many functions can be provided in either software or

Trends

The first computers were simple pieces of hardware. Like all computers, they had to be programmed to produce results. Programming these machines was a time-consuming task, because all of the pieces were connected by individual wires. Programming the computer consisted of rearranging the wires to change the way the pieces were connected. As computer hardware improved, it became possible to program the processor without having to change the internal wiring. These new programs were just a list of numbers and short words that were input to the machine. These lists of commands were called *software,* because they were easier to change.

Programmers soon learned that some tasks needed to be performed for most programs. For example, almost every program needs to send data to a printer or retrieve information stored on a disk drive. It would be a waste of time if every programmer or user had to write a special program to talk to the printer. By writing these common routines only once, the other programmers could concentrate on their specific applications. As a result, every computer has a basic collection of software programs called an *operating system.* The operating system handles jobs that are common to all users and programmers. It is responsible for controlling the hardware devices, such as displays, disk drives, and printers.

As machines became faster and added new capabilities, operating systems evolved. These new capabilities have changed the way the computer is used. The early computers could only recognize individual characters and numbers, so keyboards were used to type information for the computer. Printers that could handle only characters and numbers were the only way to get output from the computer. Eventually, television screens were used for output, but most of this output remained as characters. With the introduction of microcomputers, low-cost graphics hardware allowed the video screens to display pictures that were created by the computer. Today's operating systems are graphical, which enables users to work with pictures and icons. Inputs are changing to graphics, sound, and video.

The Internet changed everything by focusing on networks and sharing data. The Web changed everything by making the browser the most important display device. Increasingly, software and data are stored on Web servers. Users rely on browsers installed on a variety of clients—from desktops to handheld computers, PDAs, and cell phones.

hardware and a computer user often cannot tell which has been used, and most often does not care. The one main difference is that it is easier to make changes to software than to hardware—especially since software patches can be transmitted across the Internet.

Types of Data

Computers are used to process five basic types of data: numbers, text, images, sound, and video. Because of limited speed and storage capacity, early computers could only handle simple text and numbers. Only recently have computers become fast enough and inexpensive enough to handle more complex sound and video data on a regular basis. As computers continue to improve, these new capabilities will alter many aspects of our jobs and society.

As always, the business challenge is using technology to add value. For example, putting music and video footage in an accounting presentation might be entertaining, but in many cases it would not add value to the presentation itself. On the other hand, holding meetings with digital video links could save money by eliminating travel for a face-to-face meeting. You need to understand the concepts and characteristics of these emerging technologies so that you understand their merits and costs and learn to identify worthwhile uses.

Object Orientation

One of the most important concepts to understand with existing computers is that all data are represented as **binary data**. Binary data may be written as a collection of ones and zeros, and the name is shortened to *bits.* A set of 8 bits is called a *byte.* Data that are not in binary form are converted during data entry with various **input** devices. **Output** devices then change this data back to a form that humans can understand. Even complex objects can be represented by binary data. Figure 2.2 illustrates the five basic data types.

Recent software development has strongly embraced the concept of *object orientation.* The designers create objects for each software package. Each object has its own *properties*

FIGURE 2.2 Five basic types of data. Because processors only deal with binary data, each format must be converted or digitized. Computer peripheral devices are used to convert the binary data back to the original format.

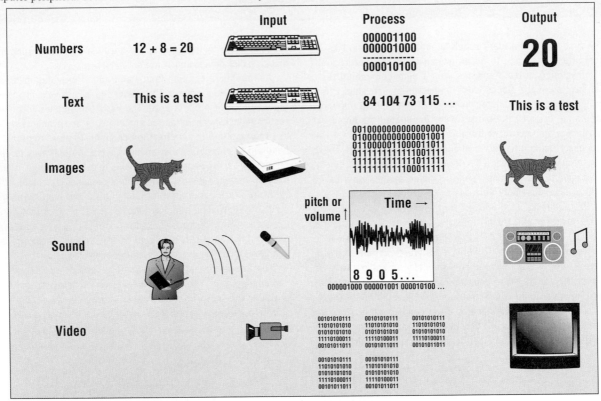

and *methods* or *functions*. Users can change properties and call the predefined functions. Although objects can become complex, most software begins with the five basic data types as fundamental objects. Software designers are beginning to standardize the properties and functions of these basic data types. Once you learn these basic features, it is easier to use software.

Each of the basic data types has its own characteristics. Numbers have a precision and usually a scaling factor. Text has a typeface and display size, as well as appearance attributes such as bold, underline, and italic. Pictures can be described by their resolution and the number of colors. Digitized sound is based on a specified sampling and playback rate, and fits into frequency and amplitude ranges. Video combines the attributes of pictures with a frames-per-second definition. Any computer program dealing with these objects must understand their basic attributes. As a manager, once you understand the attributes, it will be easier to use most new software packages.

Along with the attributes, several predefined functions can operate on each data type. Basic functions dealing with numbers include totals, calculations, and comparisons. Standard methods to manipulate text include searching, formatting, and spell-checking. Methods dealing with pictures involve artistic alterations such as color or lighting changes, rescaling, and rotation. Existing functions for sound and video are often limited to recording, playback, and compression/decompression.

Most application packages create their own objects as combinations of the basic data types. For example, graphs consist of numbers, text, and pictures. As a result, all of the attributes and functions that apply to the base types also apply to derived graph objects. Hence, graphing packages can perform calculations on numbers, select fonts for displaying text, and enable you to set colors and rotation for the graph. Other applications, such as slide shows, provide additional functions, like controls for how one slide is replaced by another (e.g., fades, dissolves, and wipes).

The point is, once you understand the properties and functions of the basic data types, you can learn how to use any new application by concentrating on the new objects, their

FIGURE 2.3

Numeric precision. If you tell a spreadsheet to display two decimal-digits, it performs the additions in the full precision of the data—and displays the data in the right column. If you really want two-digit precision, you should use the Round(x, 2) function to round off the data before adding—giving the results in the middle column.

Precision	Round Off before Add	Round Off after Add
5.563	5.56	5.56
0.354	0.35	0.35
+ 6.864	+ 6.86	+ 6.86
12.781	12.77	12.78

attributes and functions. This approach is especially true since many applications are designed and built using object-oriented methods.

Of course, the process of learning how to use new software would be much easier if software designers always chose the same set of commands to perform the same functions. Although the world does not quite work that way, you can come close by purchasing software *suites,* which are a combination of software packages sold by a single company. Commands to perform basic functions, such as setting text attributes, are the same for all the suite's applications. The suites also make it easier to exchange data between applications.

Numbers and Text

Numbers and text are still the most common types of computer data used in business—for example, each cell in a spreadsheet can display a number or text (labels). Most business reports consist of tables of numbers with supporting text.

Computers handle numbers differently than do humans. Our base 10 (decimal) numbers are first converted to base two (binary). However, some decimal numbers do not convert to an exact binary value, so you will occasionally run into round-off problems. Most of the time the computer uses enough precision to avoid problems, but if you are dealing with very large or very small numbers, the errors can accumulate.

As shown in Figure 2.3, you must be careful with round off—particularly within spreadsheets. Consider the first column of numbers with three decimal digits. What happens when the format command tells a spreadsheet to display those numbers in the third column with only two decimal places? The computer will perform the addition first, and round off the displayed result, which means the total will appear to be incorrect. If you really want only two digits of precision, you should use the Round function to convert each number before it is added, as shown in the second column. Precision of calculations is important in business. For example, the 1999 European Union standards require that all monetary conversions be computed to six digits to the right of the decimal point.

Alphabetic characters are represented internally by numbers. The simplest method is to number the characters alphabetically, so A is 65, B is 66, and so on. These numbers are then stored in binary form. Two basic complications exist. First, large IBM machines use a different numbering sequence (EBCDIC) than do most other computers (ASCII). Fortunately, most existing methods of transferring data to and from IBM machines automatically convert between these numbering schemes. The second problem is that different countries use different characters. Today's hardware and software can be configured with special character sets for each country, but it can cause problems in conversion of files between people in different nations. These problems are gradually being solved by a new standard method of encoding characters known as Unicode. **Unicode** is an international standard that defines character sets for every modern (living) language, and many extinct languages (e.g., Latin). Unicode solves most difficulties with phonetic languages such as Japanese or Chinese by using a two-byte code for every character, so it can handle up to 65,000 characters. Most recent hardware and software can handle Unicode, but if you need to use foreign-language characters, you should test the software carefully.

Figure 2.4 illustrates one of the more important properties of text: its typeface. You can choose from several thousand typefaces to achieve a desired style. Be careful with your choices. Some choices are obvious; for example, do not use a script typeface to write a business report. Also, serif fonts are typically used for printed material, and sans-serif fonts are used for very small or very large presentations. Other choices are more subtle and may

FIGURE 2.4
Typefaces fall into two main categories: serif and sans serif. Serifs are little curls and dots on the edges of letters. They make text easier to read; however, san serif typefaces are useful for overheads and signs because the added white space makes them easier to see from a distance. Ornamental typefaces can be used for headlines. Size of fonts is measured in points. Characters in a 72-point font are about 1 inch tall, and most books and newspapers use a font between 10 and 12 points.

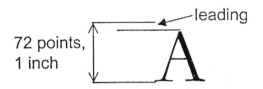

Typeface Classification

Sans serif — Arial 20 — Courier 18 (monospace)

Serif — Garamond 24 — New Century Schoolbook 16 — Times 22

Ornamental — Braggadocio 18 — Brush Script 20

72 points, 1 inch — leading — A

require the assistance of a professional designer. You will also have to choose font sizes. The basic rules of thumb are that most printed text is displayed at 10 to 12 points. It is also useful to know that letters in a 72-point font are approximately one inch tall.

Pictures

Pictures, graphics, and icons are used to display graphs and charts. Pictures are sometimes used as backgrounds or as **icons** in presentations that are used to help the audience remember certain points. In fact, almost all of the computer work that you do today is based on a graphical perspective. Video screens and printers are designed to display everything, including text, in a graphical format. The graphical foundation provides considerably more control over the presentation. For example, you can change the appearance of characters or combine figures and graphs in your reports.

Two basic ways to store images are bitmap or vector format. The easiest to visualize is bitmap (or raster or pixel) format. A **bitmap image** is converted into small dots or *pixels (picture elements)*. If the picture is in color, each dot is assigned a (binary) number to represent its color. This method is often used to display photographic pictures where subtle changes in color (such as blends) are important. Bitmap pictures are evaluated in terms of the number of colors and resolution of the picture. Resolution is often measured in *dots-per-inch (dpi)*. You will encounter certain problems with bitmap images. Consider what happens if you create a bitmap picture in a square that has 50 pixels per side. How do you make the image larger? Use larger dots? Then the lines are very rough. How can you stretch the picture into a box that is 100 by 200 pixels? Although these operations are possible, they do not usually produce good results.

Historically, each graphics software package created its own file format for saving image files. Hence, it is easy to find more than 50 different formats on one computer. These differences cause problems when you attempt to exchange files. Your colleagues might not have the same graphics software and might not be able to convert your images correctly. With the Web, it is crucial that everyone be able to read the same graphics files. Hence, two major formats are used for sharing image files: GIF and JPEG. GIF files tend to be smaller, but

FIGURE 2.5

Bitmap images are evaluated by their resolution and number of colors. Photographic quality requires 24-bit color (16.7 million colors). The Kodak Photo-CD standards define six levels of resolution, each requiring more bits of storage.

	Photo-CD Resolutions		
Image Pac	**Name**	**Resolution (v × h)**	**dpi at 3 × 5**
Base/16	Thumbnail	128 × 192	40
Base/4	Thumbnail	256 × 384	80
Base	TV	512 × 768	160
Base*4	HDTV	1024 × 1536	300
Base*16	Digital Print	2048 × 3072	600
Base*64	Pro	4096 × 6144	1200

they support only 256 colors. Hence, GIF files are often used for icons, while JPEG files are used for more realistic photographs. A third standard (PNG) began gaining acceptance in 1998. PNG files combine the advantages of both GIF and JPEG formats. However, remember that all three of these formats are bitmap formats.

When you need to change the size of pictures and keep fine lines and smooth edges, it is better to store pictures in vector format. **Vector images** consist of mathematical descriptions instead of dots. In most cases, they take up less storage space than bitmaps do. For example, a line is described by a statement such as: "line from (0,0) to (10,10) in yellow." Do not worry, you do not have to be a mathematician to use vector images. Most of the current drawing packages store their work in vector format. Web browsers are beginning to support a new Internet vector image format that provides for faster image transfers and scalable images.

In recognition of the usefulness of digital images, Kodak created a standardized system to convert photographs to digital (bitmap) form and store them on optical disks. The system is known as **Photo-CD**. Several commercial firms convert photographs to a Photo-CD format. Depending on how you want to use the pictures, you can choose among the resolutions listed in Figure 2.5. All of the resolutions use 24-bit color. Higher resolution means that fewer pictures can be stored on one compact disk (CD).

Two basic methods are used to convert pictures into a computer format. One is to use a scanner that examines a photograph and identifies the various pixel colors. The second method is to use a digital camera. The basic difference between the two methods is convenience. However, scanners currently provide better resolution (more pixels) than digital cameras do. Most scanners are capable of at least 600 dpi; whereas most digital cameras operate at about 100 dpi. If you want to display the resulting pictures on a website, 100 dpi resolution is probably acceptable. If you want to print the digital photographs, you will need 300 to 600 dpi (and sometimes higher) to get satisfactory images.

Sound

Digitized sound is increasingly important for computer users. For example, you can use music to add emphasis and entertainment to a presentation. More important, you can use your computer to send voice mail messages, and to store notes with your e-mail and documents. Tools exist to convert text to voice—so you can have your computer read your e-mail messages over the phone. Increasingly, voice input is being used both to control the computer and for dictation. Increased storage capacity and declining costs make it easier for sound to be stored in digital format.

Sound consists of two basic components: volume (amplitude) and pitch (frequency). These two values are changed over time to produce words and music. To digitize sound, volume and pitch are measured several thousand times per second. The resulting binary numbers are stored in sequence. The challenge is to sample the source often enough so no important information is lost. Synthesizers convert the sampled numbers back into music or speech and play them through amplifiers and speakers.

Most audio applications store sound by digitizing the sound waves. These files can become very large—depending on the quality. If you tell the computer to sample the sound more often, you will get a higher quality recording, but it can take considerably more storage space. For example, compared to high-quality recordings used in CDs, the MP3 standard results in a substantially smaller file with a decrease in quality that most people cannot detect. A more efficient method of storing music is to find it in the musical instrument data interchange (MIDI) format. MIDI is a method of specifying music based on the musical notation and instrument so it is substantially more efficient.

Video

The use of computerized video is still in its infancy. Several recent technological changes are lowering the cost of digitized video, which will ultimately increase its use in business. For years, people have talked about sharing video applications, but the hardware, software, and networks could not handle the data. For instance, physicians can send images to specialists for consultation. Engineers can use video transmissions to diagnose problems remotely. Managers can carry on face-to-face conversations. Computer imaging tools also make it easier for workers to create animated presentations for demonstrations or for analyzing designs and layouts.

Although it is possible to convert motion picture and television signals to binary form, the conversion results in a tremendous amount of data. The process is similar to that for single pictures, except standard movies display 24 frames (images) per second, while U.S. televisions display 30 frames per second. Perhaps you have heard of *high definition television (HDTV)*. The U.S. government, in cooperation with industry leaders, has defined standards for HDTV broadcasts in the United States; other countries use different standards. Television broadcasts are being converted to digital form for transmission. In the United States, Hughes Corporation established the first commercial digital TV broadcasts in 1994 with direct broadcast satellites to small satellite receivers with special decoders to convert the signals back to standard TV format. Much like audio CDs, HDTV provides improved quality with bigger, yet sharper pictures, less interference, and more channels. Another major advantage to digital signals is that they can be compressed, allowing broadcasters to send more channels within the same space. With digital technology, cable TV companies can broadcast 500 channels over existing connections. Major television networks began the conversion to HDTV in 1998. Traditional analog broadcasts are scheduled to cease after 20 years.

Digital video signals also enable you to alter the image. In fact, it is now common to create entire digital scenes that never existed in nature. These techniques are commonly used in marketing. They are also used by engineers to develop and market-test new products.

Size Complications

To understand the importance of the five types of data, it helps to examine the size of each type. For many years, computers predominantly handled numbers and limited text. Over time, usage has gradually changed to include images, sound, and video. The more

FIGURE 2.6

Size complications. Video is the most troublesome. Even with compression, full-screen video fills up 2 GB in 10 minutes.

Object	Raw	Compressed
Text and numbers	5 K/page	0.6 KB/page
Image (300 dpi, 24-bit color, 4 × 6 in.)	2 MB	0.5 MB
Sound (44.1 KHz stereo)	150 KB/sec	100 KB/sec
Video (NTSC 30 fps, stereo sound)	25 MB/sec	3 MB/sec

complex data types require much greater storage space, processing power, and transmission capacity.

Consider a typical single-spaced printed page. An average page might contain 5,000 characters. A 300-page book would hold about 1.5 million characters. Now, consider a picture. At 300 dots per inch, a full 8.5 by 11-inch page would require a little over a million bytes if it were scanned in black and white. A photograph in Kodak Base*16 resolution with 16 million colors (24 bits per pixel) would require 18 **megabytes** (million characters) of storage space. Fortunately, most pictures have a lot of repetitive (or empty) space, so they can be compressed. Even so, high resolution pictures often fill more than one megabyte of space. Kodak's compression technology reduces Base*16 images to 4.5 megabytes.

Sound and video require considerably more storage space. Remember that thousands of numbers are being generated every second. A typical CD holds 650 megabytes of data, which can store 72 minutes of stereo music. At lower quality, the current standard for digitizing telephone conversations generates 64 kilobits per second, almost half a megabyte per minute. Video generates approximately 3 megabytes of data every second. However, some compression systems reduce the amount of data needed to transmit video. They start with the first frame and store just the parts that change for each succeeding frame. To address this issue, Intel has a software-based technology called Indeo that compresses and decompresses video pictures in real time. It reduces a one-minute video to about 9 megabytes on average. Several other companies are producing customized processors that will convert and compress video signals faster. These techniques also provide automatic picture scaling, to let the user choose the size of the final picture—from a small window up to the full screen. Figure 2.6 summarizes the basic size characteristics for the standard data types.

Hardware Components

Certain hardware components are needed regardless of the job. The four main components are devices that handle: input, processing, output, and secondary storage. Of course, for each component, there are hundreds of options, which means you can tailor a computer to your specific job. The features and costs of each component are continually changing, so it is difficult to derive simple rules that you apply when choosing a computer for your job. However, the basic roles of the four components are likely to remain relatively constant for the next few years. One trend that you have to remember is that the hardware industry changes rapidly, especially for small systems. Most computers that you buy today will have a short economic life—perhaps only three years. At the end of that time, each component will have changed so much that typically you will want to replace the entire computer.

The relationship among the four components is summarized in Figure 2.7. Note that the process subsystem consists of **random access memory (RAM)** and at least one processor. In many ways, the **processor** is the most important component of the computer. It carries out instructions written by various programmers. It uses RAM to temporarily store instructions and data. Data and instructions that need to be stored for a longer time are transferred to *secondary storage*. The capabilities, performance, and cost of the computer are affected by each of these components.

You need know three important characteristics to evaluate each component: speed, capacity, and cost. As illustrated in Figure 2.7, each component operates at a different speed. For example, how fast can you type? If you type 60 words per minute, then the computer receives five characters in one second, or one character every two-tenths of a second.

FIGURE 2.7

Computer performance and capabilities are highly dependent on the peripheral devices. Most computers will use several devices in each of the four major categories. Technological progress in one area often results in changes to all four types of components.

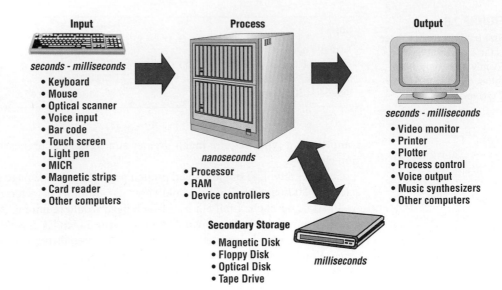

Input

seconds - milliseconds

- Keyboard
- Mouse
- Optical scanner
- Voice input
- Bar code
- Touch screen
- Light pen
- MICR
- Magnetic strips
- Card reader
- Other computers

Process

nanoseconds

- Processor
- RAM
- Device controllers

Output

seconds - milliseconds

- Video monitor
- Printer
- Plotter
- Process control
- Voice output
- Music synthesizers
- Other computers

Secondary Storage

- Magnetic Disk
- Floppy Disk
- Optical Disk
- Tape Drive

milliseconds

However, the processor runs much faster. Some processors can perform billions of operations in one second. Between each of your keystrokes, the computer processor could execute several hundred million instructions! The same concept applies to most output devices because their speed is often measured in characters per second. Speed of most secondary storage devices is measured in **milliseconds** or thousandths of a second. That is still pretty slow when compared to billionths of a second (**nanoseconds**) that measure processor speed.

Why are there secondary storage devices? Why not just store everything in high-speed RAM? The main reason is cost. Although prices vary, memory chips are under $0.50 per megabyte. Typical storage devices cost less than one cent per megabyte. Additionally, most RAM chips are dynamic—when the power is removed, the contents disappear. So you need a place to store data for longer periods of time. The primary drawback to disk drives is that data transfer is limited by the physical need to spin the disk and to move the read/write heads. Besides being slower, mechanical processes are sensitive to movement and deteriorate faster than pure electronic systems. Consequently, several manufacturers have developed static memory chips that hold data for portable devices—like Sony's memory stick.

Processors

Processors come in a wide variety of formats. Some computers use one processor that consists of a single silicon chip *(microprocessor)*. Others use several different chips to make up one processor. Still other computers use multiple processors. The critical point to remember is that each type of processor is unique. Each manufacturer creates its processor in a certain way and designs it to follow a specific set of instructions. For instance, a processor made by Intel works differently than one made by Motorola (used in Apple computers). As a result, instructions written for one processor cannot be used directly by the other processor. Note that some companies (especially in the personal computer world) produce "clones" of the leading chip manufacturer. For example, Advanced Micro Devices and Cyrix/IBM make chips that are compatible with Intel processors and can run the same programs. Conversely, when Intel develops a new chip, like the Itanium, it must be careful to provide backward compatibility, so that the millions of existing programs can continue to run on the new processors.

The Evolution of Processors

Figure 2.8 shows the approximate measure of Intel processor performance over time, measured by an index value (estimated SysMark). The exponential increase in performance arises because the industry has been able to follow Moore's Law: the number of components

Reality Bytes   Building Processors and Memory Chips

Building processors and memory chips involves growing silicon crystals and slicing them into wafers. The internal circuits are then etched onto these wafers using chemical deposition techniques. The catch is that cramming more storage on a chip requires finer and finer circuit lines. Common RAM chips in 1994 held 4 megabits of data, with leading-edge chips at 16 megabits. Because of capital costs, manufacturers will only produce new chips if they can gain four times the amount of storage.

In 2001, common processor and RAM chips were being created with lines that were 0.12 microns (about 1/200,000 of an inch) wide. A micron is one-millionth of a meter.

Using conventional laser lithography to etch patterns onto the chip becomes difficult as the lines get smaller. Conventional methods rely on a mask to cover parts of the

chip that are then exposed to laser light, which removes a photo-resistive material on the uncovered sections. The main difficulty with small sizes is that the light waves are too wide. Modern chip technology relies on ultraviolet rays because they are narrower, but they are still 0.193 microns wide. Manufacturers are experimenting with smaller wave X-rays or electron beams.

A second problem is that the etching size is coming closer to the size of a single molecule, which brings in quantum physics effects, where atoms randomly "tunnel" through barriers.

Researchers are working with new materials, and entirely new technologies, such as biocomputers, to overcome the physical limits of the existing process.

FIGURE 2.8   To assist buyers, Intel provides a measure of its own processors. The rating is an index that measures relative performance. A processor with a rating of 200 would generally be about twice as fast as a processor with a rating of 100. Of course, your other devices also influence the overall system speed, so just buying a faster processor does not guarantee that your machine will run faster.

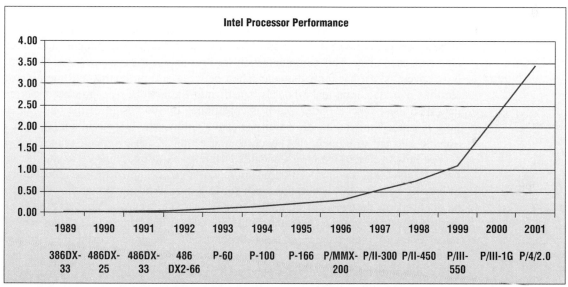

placed on a chip doubles every 18 months. But three potential problems are facing the chip industry: (1) light waves are too wide to draw increasingly smaller lines; (2) when the components shrink to the size of a couple of atoms, the electronic properties no longer behave the same (quantum effects); and (3) the power requirements and heat generation increase dramatically.

For at least two decades, the IT industry has lived with and relied on this increasing performance (and reduction in costs). Eventually, this pattern will stop—possibly within 10 or 20 years. With luck and research, the industry will develop entirely new technology that will produce even greater performance. But in any case, managers need to monitor technical developments and be prepared for substantial changes.

Reality Bytes   Heat Wave

Typically, processor performance has been increased by placing more components on a chip and by running the chips at a higher clock speed. Both of these techniques require more power and generate more heat. Today, processors generate so much heat that without complex cooling systems, the processor would quickly fry. The traditional solution was metal heat sinks, which were simply metal forms attached to the processor that draw heat away and dissipate it through fins. Eventually, fans were added directly to the heat sinks to pull the hot air away faster. But even more radical solutions will be needed. Novel Concepts, Inc. is one company working on the problem.

The IsoSkin is one technology they created. It uses a thin layer of water to pull heat away from the processor. Early supercomputers faced similar problems, and manufacturers resorted to exotic liquid nitrogen or liquid helium cooling systems, but these systems would be too expensive and impractical for desktops and laptops. But ultimately, new cooling technologies will be critical to improving the speed of new processors.

Source: Adapted from Mike Musgrove, "Processors Won't Keep Their Cool," *Washington Post,* July 19, 2001.

Random Access Memory

As processor speed has improved, RAM has become a crucial factor in system performance. Because disk drives are mechanical, they are the greatest bottleneck in a computer system. Hence, modern operating systems try to hold as much data as possible in RAM. Although RAM speeds have remained relatively constant in the last few years, RAM price has dropped substantially. In relative terms, RAM is virtually free. For a few hundred dollars, you can easily buy enough RAM to hold several applications and their data in RAM at one time.

Connections

Even if two computers have the same basic components, it is still possible for one machine to be substantially faster than the other. The reason is that the components need to exchange data with each other. This communication requires an electrical connection. Most computers have special slots that form the connection between add-on boards and the processor *bus.* Various manufacturers make boards that fit into these slots. The processor can exchange data with these other devices, but it is constrained by the design of the bus. For example, even if a processor can handle 64 bits of data at a time, the bus might not have the connections to allow it to transfer that much data at a time. Each computer manufacturer has to choose how to design the bus. Standards enable users to exchange cards and devices from one computer with another. The problem is that a bus designed for today's computers will eventually become obsolete as the processor improves. At some point, the standards need to be changed. In the personal computer market, standards for the bus have been gradually evolving. For several years, the industry has relied on an Intel-sponsored design known as *Personal Computer Interconnect (PCI)* bus. PCI was also designed to make it easier for users to set up their computers. Over time, manufacturers have increased the transfer speeds of PCI, but it is increasingly a limitation in computer performance.

One interesting connector was introduced on personal computers in 1998. Known as IEEE 1394, or *firewire,* it was originally developed to connect game machines. It can transfer data at extremely high speeds and easily connects several devices. It is gaining rapid acceptance for consumer devices such as digital video cameras. One of the strengths of firewire is that it can support external devices as easily as internal ones. Hence, it is simple to plug in additional disk drives—without opening the computer. A competing technology called fiber channel can use fiber optic cables to connect components at high speeds.

Parallel Processors

In the past, when processors were more expensive, designers used only one processor in a machine. Today, many computers contain multiple processors. Although it can be a desirable feature, you must be careful when evaluating parallel-processing machines. If a

Reality Bytes   Moore's Law

Intel cofounder Gordon Moore realized in the mid 1960s that the number of transistors on a chip (density) doubles every 18 months. That practice has held true for 40 years and is known as Moore's Law. Eventually, several major problems arise: (1) the transistors and lines get too small to create; (2) the transistors get so close together that electrons jump barriers; (3) the chips need increasing amounts of power; and (4) they generate increasing amounts of heat. In terms of size, to remain on target, by 2014, the half-pitch must be reduced from 130 nanometers (billionths of a meter) to 35 nanometers; and experts currently do not know how to reduce the size to the 60 nanometers needed by 2003. Researchers believe it is possible, but note that with conventional silicon, they will eventually be dealing with gate sizes only three atoms wide.

Source: Adapted from Dennis Normile and Robert F. Service, "The End—Not Here Yet, but Coming Soon," *Science,* August 3, 2001, p. 787.

FIGURE 2.9

Some computations must be performed in sequence, so there is little to be gained with multiple parallel processors. In this example, the second computation (yyy) must wait for the first one to finish.

$$
\begin{array}{cc}
23 & \text{xx} \\
+54 & +92 \\
\hline
\text{xx} & \text{yyy}
\end{array}
$$

computer has four processors, it is tempting to say that the machine is four times faster than a computer with only one processor. Indeed, many computer companies advertise their computers this way.

Can a computer with four processors really do your job four times faster? The answer is that it depends on your job. Consider an example. A computer with two processors has to add two sets of numbers together. Each processor works on one pair of numbers and finishes in half the time of a single processor. Now, the same two computers have to work the problem in Figure 2.9.

Notice that the second calculation depends on the outcome of the first one. The second one cannot be computed until the first one is finished. Even if we assign one processor to each calculation, the parallel-processing machine will take just as long as the single processor.

A parallel-processing computer is faster than a single processor only when the job can be split into several independent pieces or there are several jobs and each processor can be assigned to different jobs. There is one more problem: The computer has to spend some time assigning jobs and collecting the results. For a small number of processors, this may not be a major problem. However, some companies are selling computers that contain as many as 32,000 separate processors. Seymour Cray, of Cray Computer Corporation, in 1994 indicated that by 1999 he wanted to produce a machine with 32 million processors, capable of performing 1 quadrillion (billion, million) operations per second. Two important questions should leap into your mind at this point: (1) For what types of jobs would these massively parallel computers be useful? and (2) How much will the computer cost? Although there are many interesting uses for supercomputers, companies are increasingly faced with the question of determining how much value such expensive machines could contribute.

Massively parallel machines can include thousands of processors. They are used for some highly specialized applications. For example, governments use them to break codes; physicists use them to simulate large-scale events such as nuclear explosions and weather patterns; computer artists use them at special-effects studios, such as Industrial Light & Magic to create movies.

Input

Because of the variety of data types, many input devices are available. The purpose of an input device is to convert data into electronic binary form. Keyboards are the most common method of entering new text and data. Note that you can purchase different types of keyboards to suit individual users. For example, some keyboards enable you to change the layout of the keys. Keyboards have their own feel; some individuals prefer sensitive keys requiring a light touch, others like stiffer keys to support their hands.

Ergonomics is the study of how machines can be made to fit humans better. One of the main conclusions of this research in the computer area is that individuals need to be able to adjust input (and output) devices to their own preference. Forcing people to adapt to rigid devices can lead to complaints and even physical injuries. Since the mid-1980s, many workers have encountered a disabling condition known as *repetitive stress injury,* which some people claim results from extended use of tools that do not physically match the worker.

Although there is limited scientific study of these injuries and causes, some people have found relief after ergonomic changes to their work environment. Complaints typically involve back pain, eye strain, headaches, arm and shoulder pain, and finger or wrist pain due to carpal tunnel syndrome. Common ergonomic suggestions include adjustable chairs, foot rests, arm rests, adjustable keyboards, high-resolution low-flicker monitors, and improved lighting.

Of course, all of these adjustments cost money—especially if they are added as an afterthought. The key to the problem is to evaluate individual requirements and adjust the environment *before* installing computers.

Pointing Devices

With the increased use of graphics and pictures, it is common for computers to use pointing devices for input. A mouse is the most popular device in use today, although light pens, touch screens, and digitizer tablets are heavily used in some applications. Touch screens are commonly used for displays that involve customers or other atypical computer users. Many tourist bureaus, hotels, and shopping areas use computer displays with touch screens to give directions to visitors. Besides the fingerprints, the biggest problem with touch screens is that the tip of your finger is often too large to be a useful pointer. For more detailed use, an engineer who is designing a wiring diagram for an automobile would use a digitizer tablet with a special pen to draw fine lines and select individual points that are close together.

Scanners

When you are dealing with pictures, it is often helpful to have a scanner convert a paper-based image into digital (bitmap) form. For certain types of images (line-drawings and text), vector tracing software can convert the bitmap image into vector form.

The quality of a scanner is measured by the number of pixels per inch that it can distinguish as well as the number of colors. Most scanners can read at least 600 dots per inch. More dots mean you get finer lines and sharper pictures.

Scanners also can be used to input text and data into a computer. The scanner first converts the page into a picture of dots. Then **optical character recognition (OCR)** software examines the picture and looks for text. The software checks each line and deciphers one character at a time. Although OCR software is improving, it is not 100-percent accurate. Some systems automatically look up each word in a dictionary to spot conversion errors and improve accuracy. Even then, users report about a 95 percent accuracy rate—which is highly dependent on the quality of the original document.

Pen-Based Systems

A new category of computers is being created. Some handheld, notebook-size computers use a pen as the primary input device. The pen is used to point to objects on the screen, make changes to documents, and even write notes. In some cases, the machines can convert handwriting to computer text—much like OCR converts typed papers. Of course, deciphering individual handwriting is much more difficult than reading typed characters, and the accuracy of data can be limited. Despite the hype about potential applications for traveling managers (and salespeople), the first versions of pen-based computers did not sell well. As processors, storage, and display technology and telecommunications improve, we will probably see more acceptance of pen-based handheld computers.

Sound

Sound is initially captured with a microphone that converts sound pressure waves into electrical signals. A *sampler* then converts these signals into numeric data that can be stored on the computer. Musical **synthesizer** technology is used to convert the numbers back to electrical signals that can be heard with speakers. Sound boards can be purchased for personal computers that contain both the sampler and synthesizer technology. Digital sound conversion occurs on almost every long distance telephone call you make. Your voice is converted to 1s and 0s to be sent across fiber-optic telephone lines.

Speech Recognition

As long as computers have existed, individuals have dreamed of being able to talk to them and have their words translated into text. Today, computers can digitize and record speech, and they can convert spoken words into computer text. Some problems still exist, and the systems need to be trained to a specific user. Common problems include the use of homonyms, variations in speech patterns or dialects, and the effects of punctuation on meaning.

Initially, speech recognition systems were adopted by occupations that require note taking along with two hands to do the job. Quality control inspectors and surgeons use them regularly. As performance continues to improve, we will see an expanded use of speech recognition systems among all users. Ultimately, speech recognition will be a key element in dealing with computers. Keyboards do not work well in a wireless environment. They are too large to be portable and hard to use.

Video Capture

As technology improves, companies are increasingly adding video clips to presentations. Probably the most common use of video is for computer-based training (CBT). Users interact with scenarios described in video clips to solve problems or learn new techniques. Digital video transmissions are also being used for communication.

Because computer monitors and television sets are loosely based on the same technology, it would seem easy to merge the two. However, computer monitors deal with different types of video signals. Computers need special video boards to convert and display TV signals on the computer monitor. These cards accept standard coaxial video output from a VCR, camcorder, and television receiver. Not only can the signal be displayed on a monitor but it can also be converted to digital form and saved or replayed.

Digital video offers substantial improvements over traditional video signals. But several nations have different standards for digital video, and the signals are not directly compatible with computer formats. So, you will continue to need conversion devices.

Output

Most people are interested in two types of output: video and paper copy. Video output is created by a video card and displayed on a monitor. The quality is measured by the **resolution**, which is number of pixels and colors it can display. Resolution is established by the video card, but higher resolutions require larger, more sophisticated (and more expensive)

Reality Bytes — Electronic Paper (E Ink)

Researchers at E Ink and Gyricon Media have been working on a new display device they are calling electronic paper. Essentially it is a paper-like sheet consisting of thousands of devices that can display white or black when electrically charged. The device is similar in concept to traditional LCD displays, but Russ Wilcox of E Ink notes that "It's five times brighter, it uses 99 percent less power, it's more portable, has a bigger screen, and a long battery life. It's thinner and lighter, has a higher resolution, and gives workers more freedom." Gyricon's SmartPaper has been used in tests at retail stores. The display device is used to create shelf signs. The signs, and item prices, can be changed instantly from the main computer.

Source: Adapted from Jim Battey, "Electronic Paper Gets Its Bearing," *Infoworld,* April 16, 2001.

FIGURE 2.10

Common video resolutions. Note that higher-resolution video cards require larger monitors. Current video cards also contain features to increase the speed of 3-D imaging. Monitor size is viewable space measured in inches along the diagonal.

Video	# Colors	Resolution	Monitor
VGA	256	640 × 480	10 in.
SVGA	65K	800 × 600	12 in.
XGA	16.7M	1024 × 768	14 in.
Super XGA	16.7M	1280 × 1024	16 in.
No name	16.7M–4B	1600 × 1280	20 in.

monitors. Common personal computers today can support 1,024 horizontal and 768 vertical dots at 16 million colors, which requires a video card with 2 megabytes of memory. Some video cards support as many as 2 billion colors. This level of color is called **true color**, because it exceeds the range of colors that can be distinguished by the human eye. True color requires 32 bits (4 bytes) per pixel to attain this level of color. Computer projection systems used for meetings and presentations use high-intensity light to project an image onto a screen. In addition to resolution, they are evaluated by the intensity of the light, measured in lumens.

High-resolution screens with multiple colors can display beautiful pictures and excellent quality text. As indicated in Figure 2.10, they do have some drawbacks, however. They are relatively expensive, especially because large-screen monitors (19 inches or more) are often needed to display text in a legible size. Because high-resolution true-color screens require over 15 times more data than the older video boards, the higher-resolution boards can also be slower. Manufacturers have compensated by building special hardware and software to accelerate them. Accelerators for 3-D imaging are particularly useful for intensive graphics.

Most of the existing video screens are designed to display images at an effective resolution of about 100 dots (or pixels) per inch. Researchers and manufacturers are developing new computers that will use displays of 200 dots per inch or higher. These higher resolutions will produce crisper text and better images—making it easier for people to read the screens. One company is even working on electronic paper that looks much like a typical sheet of paper but can display (and erase) digital images.

The other common output device is the printer. Printers come in many different forms. The most common formats are laser and ink jet, where the output is created by printing dots on the page. Common resolutions include 300 and 600 dpi, and 1,200 dpi lasers are available. In contrast, standard typesetters, such as those that are used to print books, operate at resolutions of at least 2,400 dots per inch. Again, higher-resolution devices are more expensive. Also, the increased amount of data being displayed takes longer to print (for the first copy).

Laser printers operate much like photocopiers. In fact, newer copiers include hardware to connect to a local network so the departmental copier can function as a high-speed printer. From your desktop, you can tell the printer to make multiple copies and collate and staple them—at speeds of over 70 pages per minute.

FIGURE 2.11 Printer evaluations. Printers are evaluated in terms of initial cost, cost per page, resolution, and speed. There are many types of printers, led by laser, ink jets, and dot matrix printers. Prices vary depending largely on speed and resolution. Technological changes are leading to new varieties of printers that can produce full color at a cost of around 5 to 10 cents per page.

Printer	Initial Cost (dollars)	Cost per Page (cents)	Quality (dots/inch)	Speed (pages/min.)
Laser: B&W	400–70,000	0.6–3	300–1,200	4–8–17–100+
Laser: Color	2000+	5–75	300–1,200	0.5–8
Ink jet: B&W	100–500	5–50	300–600	0.25–7
Ink jet: Color	200–2,000	25–150	300–720	0.1–4

FIGURE 2.12 Disk drives are evaluated in terms of capacity, speed, initial cost, and cost per megabyte—especially for removable media. Many drives are available in each category so a range is displayed for each feature. Note there has been a strong downward trend in hard drive costs in the last few years.

Drive	Capacity (megabytes)	Speed (milliseconds)	Initial Cost (dollars)	Cost/MByte (dollars)
Magnetic hard	40,000–100,000	9–15	200–2,000	0.02–0.15+
Removable hard	100–1,500	12–20	200–400	0.05–0.20
Floppy	1–120	80–200	50–100	0.02–0.35
Solid State/RAM	4–1,000	0.00006–0.006	50+	25.00–100.00
Tape	250–2,000	sequential	300–5,000+	0.04–0.15
CD-ROM	650	100	50–150	0.001
DVD	8,000	150	75–200	0.004

As noted in Figure 2.11, the initial cost is usually only a minor component of a printer's price. It is more important that you look at the cost per page—particularly for color copies.

Secondary Storage

Except for prices (declining) and capacity (increasing), typical secondary storage devices have changed little during the last few years. Secondary storage is needed to hold data and programs for longer periods. Secondary storage is evaluated by three attributes: capacity, speed, and price. The values for different types of storage are summarized in Figure 2.12.

The device most commonly used today is the magnetic hard drive. *Magnetic hard drives* consist of rigid platters that store data with magnetic particles. Data is accessed by spinning the platters and moving drive heads across the platters to access various tracks. Hard drives come in a variety of sizes, ranging from 2 to 15 gigabytes (billions of bytes). One thousand gigabytes are called a *terabyte* (trillion bytes). Drive prices have dropped to less than a half-cent per megabyte. **Access speed** is the time needed for the drive to move to a particular location and begin transferring data. Typical access speed is around 9 milliseconds. Faster drives and drives that use more powerful connections, like SCSI and firewire, are more expensive.

With the increasing importance of data, companies are searching for ways to prevent loss of data by providing continuous backups. One straightforward method is to install an extra disk drive and keep duplicate copies of all files on this *mirror drive*. If something goes wrong with one of the drives, users simply switch to the other drive. A second method of protecting data is known as a **redundant array of independent drives (RAID)**. Instead of containing one large drive, this system consists of several smaller drives. Large files are split into pieces stored on several different physical drives. At the same time, the pieces can be duplicated and stored in more than one location. In addition to the duplication, RAID systems provide faster access to the data, because each of the drives can be searching through its part of the file at the same time.

On personal machines, even if you do not want to spend the money for a RAID solution, it can be a good idea to buy two hard drives instead of one large drive. Particularly for data-intensive applications like video editing, it is wise to put the operating system and application software on one drive and place the data files on the second drive. Two drives are better than one because the computer can retrieve the data simultaneously from both drives. In fact, video and large database applications often benefit from using three drives: one for the system, one for the main data, and one to hold temporary files. Putting everything on one drive forces the computer to trade between tasks and wait for the single drive to spin to the proper location.

On personal computers, another common storage device is the floppy disk drive. These use thin, removable disks to store data. They operate similarly to magnetic hard drives but are much slower. Typical capacity is around 1.5 megabytes per disk, which costs less than 5 cents per megabyte when bought in quantity. However, the access speed is around 100 milliseconds, or 10 times slower than hard drives.

Magnetic tapes are also used to store data. Their biggest drawback is that they can only store and retrieve data sequentially. That means you have to search the tape from the beginning to find any data. A single tape can hold a gigabyte of data at a cost of 4 to 10 cents per megabyte. Because of these two features, tapes are most commonly used to hold backup data.

With the increased use of images, sound, and video, there is a need for substantially greater storage capacity for data files. Optical disks have provided substantial capacity at relatively low costs. The optical (or magneto-optical) disk drive uses a laser light to read data stored on the disk. There are three basic forms of optical drives: CD-ROM, CD-R (recordable), and erasable. **CD-ROM** stands for *compact disk-read only memory,* the format used to store music CDs. The ROM portion of the name means that you only can read data from the disk. A special machine is required to store data on a CD-ROM. One side of a CD can hold 650 megabytes of data and costs less than a dollar to produce in quantity. The biggest drawback is that a fast access speed is 200 milliseconds (one-fifth of a second). Hence, it could take a full second to find five different pieces of data. CD-ROMs are most useful for storing large quantities of data that will not change. CDs are available that contain text, pictures, sound, and video for an entire encyclopedia.

Manufacturers have tried to improve the access speeds on CDs, but they are limited by the existing standards. In the 1980s, to ensure compatibility, the major manufacturers agreed on how data would be stored on CDs. As part of this process, they decided to maintain compatibility with audio CDs, so that computer-based CD readers could also play musical selections. Although this decision helped create multimedia applications, it currently limits the speed of CDs. To meet the standards, the CD must spin at a predetermined speed. This spin rate is a major factor in determining access times, because data can only be found and retrieved when it is spun under the read head. A common method to speed up CDs is to build in two spin rates: the standard speed to read the data and a faster rate (two, three, or four times faster) to search the CD indexes.

CD-R drives enable users to record data onto a CD-ROM disk. These drives can only write data once—the data cannot be erased. They use a special disk that can be read by standard CD-ROM drives. The process can take an hour or more to record data. Hence, a CD-R drive is useful for making one or two copies of data. To create multiple copies of a CD for distribution, it is better to pay a company to create a standard CD-ROM.

It is possible to purchase a CD-erasable drive, which enables you to create and change data on the disk. However, the **DVD (digital video disk or digital versatile disk)** is a significantly better technology. DVD was created to distribute digitized video. Compared to CD, the strengths of DVD are: (1) increased capacity; (2) significantly faster access speeds; (3) standards for audio, video, and computer data; and (4) the ability to record data. The standards are evolving, but a double-sided DVD should hold at least 6GB of data. Some manufacturers are beginning to ship recordable DVDs, but many of them cannot write data in a form that is readable by standard DVD players. Although the technology exists to make compatible DVD recorders, the movie studios (including Sony) are afraid of consumer devices that can make exact copies of DVD movies.

The biggest drawback to all forms of disk drives is that they are sensitive mechanical components. They can be damaged if dropped, they wear out with use, and there are physical limits to how fast they can store and retrieve data.

Due to speed constraints and the declining costs of memory chips, some applications are beginning to use memory chips as secondary storage. Although the cost can be as high as $30 per megabyte, data can be stored and retrieved a thousand times faster. One increasingly common version is the PCMCIA (Personal Computer Memory Card International Association) card that is used with laptop and notebook computers. PCMCIA cards are about the size of a thick credit card, ranging from 3-mm to 16-mm thick. The cards can hold 20 megabytes of data in a type of memory chip that does not lose its contents when the power is turned off.

Operating Systems

Computers follow instructions called software that are written by programmers. Every computer needs one special type of software known as the *operating system.* The **operating system** is software that is responsible for communication among the hardware components. The operating system is also a primary factor in determining how the user deals with the machine.

Historically, each computer manufacturer created its own operating system tailored for that specific hardware. Proprietary operating systems caused many problems; in particular, changing vendors typically required purchasing new application software. AT&T researchers began to solve this problem when they created a hardware-independent operating system. It is known as *UNIX* and was designed to work with computers from many different manufacturers. However, UNIX is not a complete standard, and application software must generally be rewritten before it can function on different computers.

Today, fewer operating system choices exist. Personal computers generally run a version of Microsoft Windows. However, a version of UNIX is available for personal computers. AT&T essentially released the source code to UNIX to the public. Linus Torvalds used the code to create an inexpensive and relatively popular version for personal computers. His base versions are called Linux. Apple Computer also adopted the UNIX foundation with its OS X operating system. Most midrange computers and many servers also run an operating system derived from UNIX. Notably, both Sun (Solaris) and IBM (AIX and Linux) focus on UNIX versions for their servers. IBM also continues to support some older, proprietary operating systems. For servers and midrange systems, you still typically use the operating system provided by the hardware manufacturer.

Computers in e-Business

The Internet and the Web changed computing and business in several ways. Beyond the issues of connectivity, the key feature of the Web was the introduction and acceptance of the browser. To see its importance, you need simply look at the Microsoft antitrust case—where the integrated browser played a critical role. The reason the browser is so important is that it has become the standard display mechanism. Increasingly, applications are being built that

As technology continues to improve, major computer manufacturers vie for the top performance numbers. Shortly after Sun announced a new high-end Sun Fire 15K server, IBM unveiled its new Unix-based p690. Based on IBM's Power4 microprocessor, IBM's senior vice president of the server group, William Zeitler, says "We committed to deliver the world's best Unix product." Prices depend on the number of processors and amount of memory, so they range between $450,000 and $1.8 million. The high-end servers are often used to handle large databases and Web sites. Scientists and engineers also use them for complex computations. IBM claims that the new systems are half the price of Sun's 16-processor server and run twice as fast. Systems from both companies can be scaled up with many more processors. But the advantage of using fewer processors to attain the same speed is that some software vendors charge licensing fees based on the number of processors in the machine. In 2000, the high-end Unix market was divided into Sun at 47 percent, IBM at 19 percent, and HP at 12 percent.

Source: Adapted from William M. Bulkeley, "IBM Unveils High-End Computer Server, Stepping Up Its Battle with Competitors," *The Wall Street Journal,* October 4, 2001.

rely on the services of the browser. When the browser becomes the most important display device, then nothing else matters. For example, developers no longer care what type of computer you use: IBM or Apple; desktop, laptop, handheld **personal digital assistant (PDA)**, or cell phone. As long as your equipment supports the major browser standards, you will be able to use the applications.

What Is a Browser?

At heart, browsers are simply software display devices. They read incoming files, recognize the data type, and display the data as instructed. The data could be text, images, sound, or even video. However, the sound and video are usually handled by an add-in component for the browser because standards are still evolving.

To add more interactivity, browsers also have an internal programming language. Developers can include program code that gives detailed instructions to the browser and reacts to changes users make. For example, when users move the cursor, the code can highlight an object on the browser. Browser code is also used to check user data. This code runs entirely on the local machine, but can send data in batches to the Web server.

The beauty of the browser approach is that it standardizes the way data is displayed, so that everyone is free to choose any hardware and software platform they prefer. Since browsers are relatively easy to implement and do not require huge amounts of hardware, they can be built into smaller, portable devices. Combined with the wireless Internet possibilities, these new devices have the ability to change the business world.

What Is a Server?

So you want to run a website? Being a participant in the Internet and running a browser is one thing. Running a Web server is completely different. Establishing an e-business requires that you either run a server or pay someone to run it for you, so you should understand some of the main issues in Web servers.

Technically, almost any reasonably up-to-date PC can function as a Web server. A Web server is essentially a piece of software that monitors the full-time Internet connection and delivers the requested pages. But to perform e-business tasks, the server also needs to evaluate programmed Web code and interact with a database.

In most cases, the primary issue with Web servers is scalability. The goal is to build a server inexpensively enough to make the application profitable, yet capable of expanding to handle increased demands of the future. It does not take much hardware to handle a simple website. Even a laptop can be used—but do not expect it to handle many simultaneous hits or complex database processing.

In terms of hardware, the primary characteristics that you want in a Web server are: (1) scalability, (2) easy backup, and (3) easy maintenance. One solution to all of these problems is splitting the major computer components into separate pieces. For example, server farms use multiple small computers instead of one large machine. A server area network (SAN) can be built using fiber channel connections to a set of external disk drives. If a processor or disk drive needs to be replaced, it can be hot-swapped—each individual component can be shut down and replaced without shutting down the rest of the system. Similarly, new processors and drives can be added without disrupting the others—and the system automatically identifies the changes and uses the hardware. These types of systems provide a relatively inexpensive solution to the three goals. But managing the system requires a sophisticated operating system and Web server software.

Application Software

The main reason for buying a computer is its application software. It is good software that makes your job easier. Regardless of your job, you will always perform certain tasks. As a manager and decision maker, you first have to gather data (research). Then you analyze the data and determine alternatives (involving calculations). Next you will make decisions and implement them (requiring writing, communication, and organizing resources). Each of these tasks can be supported by computer resources. The trick is to use the appropriate tools for each task. The objective is to use the tools to make you more productive in your job.

The catch is that productivity is a slippery problem in business—especially with respect to computer tools. One measure of productivity involves efficiency: Can you perform tasks faster? A second, more complicated measure of productivity involves effectiveness: Can you make better decisions? Early uses of computers focused on improving efficiency by automating manual tasks. The tools were often justified on the basis of decreased labor costs. Today, managerial uses often focus on effectiveness, which is harder to measure.

An important concept to remember with application software is that it was created by teams of designers and programmers. In the "old" days, when software was custom-written for specific companies and users, users could tell the designers how the software should behave. Today, we are moving rapidly to off-the-shelf software that is created to support the needs of millions of different users. In creating the software, designers had to make thousands of decisions about what the software should do and how it should appear. Sometimes their final choices might seem strange, and software does not always work the way you might prefer. Some issues can be resolved by customizing the software to your particular situation. Other times, just remember that you acquired the software for a tiny fraction of the price you would have paid for custom software.

Research: Databases

Almost any job involves workers searching for information. This search could involve any of the five basic types of data. Computers have made it substantially easier to find, compare, and retrieve data. Two important strengths of a *database management system (DBMS)* are the ease of sharing data and the ability to search for data by any criteria. In terms of productivity, a DBMS can make you both more efficient and improve your decisions. It improves efficiency by providing easier and faster data retrieval. By providing more complete access to data, a DBMS helps ensure that your decision incorporates all relevant data.

One complication with research is that you must first determine where the information is located. It could be located on your personal computer, the group's networked server, the company's central computers, a computer run by the government, or one purchased from another company. Unless all of these databases are connected, you must first determine which database to search. Chapter 5 focuses on the use of database management systems. Most DBMSs can handle numbers and simple text well. Only recently have they begun to tackle large text files, pictures, sound, and video. Internet search engines help you do research, but they only support data stored in one format.

Analysis: Calculations

Almost everyone performs computations in a job. Although simple calculators are useful, they have some drawbacks. For example, it is difficult to go back and change a number entered previously. Also, calculators cannot save much data, and it is hard to print out the results. Finally, because of their small screens, they can display only a few numbers at a time. Spreadsheets were initially designed to overcome these limitations. These features are designed to make you more efficient at making calculations.

Most people find spreadsheets useful because their disciplines began with models on paper that used columns and rows of numbers. For instance, most accounting systems and financial models were designed for ledgers in this way. Whenever software mimics the way you already work, it is easier to learn.

Spreadsheets have many additional features. Graphs can be created with a couple of mouse clicks. Most packages enable users to modify the graphs by adding text, arrows, and pictures. Spreadsheets also perform various statistical and mathematical analyses. You can perform basic matrix operations such as multiplication and inversion. Statistics capabilities include multiple regression to examine the relationships among different variables. Linear programming can be used to search for optimum solutions to problems. These additional features are designed to help you make better decisions by providing more powerful decision-evaluation tools.

Communication: Writing

The primary gain from word processing is increased efficiency. Word processors improve communication by making it easier to revise text, find writing errors, and produce legible reports. Word processors today also include a spell-checker, a thesaurus, and a grammar-checker. Although they are not the same as having a human editor correct your writing, they are all useful tools for writers. Grammar checkers use standard measures to estimate the reading difficulty level of your writing. For instance, if you write an employee policy manual, you want to make sure that an average employee can understand it. Most word processors also have outline tools that help you organize your thoughts and rearrange a document, improving the communication.

The proliferation of word processors creates additional advantages. At some point, a company finds that almost all of its reports, data, and graphs are being created and stored on the computer. If this transition is handled carefully, managers can use the computer to search

---

Reality Bytes | International Notations

Most applications today have the ability to use characters that are not found in the U.S. alphabet. For instance, in France or Mexico, you might need to use an acute mark (é). However, different software packages handle the characters differently, so you might have trouble converting a document from one word processor to another or to a different computer. For example, if a French subsidiary is using *WordPerfect* and the Canadian headquarters is using *Microsoft Word,* they can both print reports using the special characters. However, the document might change when the Canadian users attempt to retrieve a French document electronically.

Additionally, if you work for an international organization, remember that people in different countries write dates differently. For example, 5/10/93 means May 10, 1993, in the

United States but would be interpreted as October 5, 1993, in Europe. Most word processors enable you to choose how automatic dates should be displayed.

Numbers are also handled differently in European nations. The use of commas (,) and points (.) is reversed from the U.S. version where commas separate thousands and the decimal point delineates the fractional component. (126,843.57 in the U.S. should be denoted as 126.843,57 in Europe.)

You also need to be careful with currencies in spreadsheets. When you transfer documents to other languages or fonts, be sure to check any currency symbols. A few systems will automatically change the symbol to the local units (e.g., change $ to £) but unless the numbers are converted by exchange rates, these changes would be incorrect.

for any prior reports or data. It also becomes easier to send reports and notes to other managers. It sounds as though companies would use less paper and rely on electronic transmissions. Most organizations have not made it to this stage yet, and some people believe we never will. In fact, the use of personal computers has dramatically increased the usage of paper by U.S. companies.

Software companies have continued to add features to their products. The biggest trend in word processors is the addition of desktop publishing features. **Desktop publishing (DTP)** provides more control over the final print. For example, you can choose a typeface to convey a certain image. You can include graphics images, tables, special characters, equations, and borders. You can automatically build an index and a table of contents. One problem that some companies have experienced with desktop publishing is that it appears to decrease the efficiency of employees. It takes employees longer to create reports because they spend more time experimenting with layouts and presentation. The trade-off is that the reports now contain more information or communicate it better so that the effectiveness has improved and managers can make better decisions. Be careful when you communicate with documents that will be transferred to other nations. Even if the language is the same, some systems will replace characters with the local alphabet—which can be a major problem with currency signs.

One interesting impact of low-cost computers is that it is increasingly difficult to evaluate organizations by the quality of their publications. Even small groups can afford to produce high-quality reports and brochures. In the past, people tended to dismiss poorly typed and handwritten papers because they obviously came from small organizations. Now, one person can produce a report that looks like it came from a major organization.

Communication: Presentation and Graphics

In many cases, the difference between a good report and an outstanding report is the presence and quality of the artwork. Graphs and pictures are used to communicate information and feelings. Charts and graphs are easy to create, store, and modify using graphics software. Even if you are not an artist, you can buy **clip art** that was created by someone else and use it in your reports or charts. By using existing art libraries, reports and presentations can be created in a few hours. In the past, reports and presentations took days or weeks to finish by a staff of artists. By improving the appearance, a well-designed graphic can also improve communication and decision making.

To create or modify your artwork, you need a graphics package and an input device such as a mouse that enable you to draw on the computer screen. Most commercial artists use scanners so they can draw the original on paper and convert it to computer form. The digitized form enables you to make very precise changes, since you can *zoom* into a specific area. Zooming is helpful if you need to force lines to meet exactly or you want to make changes to small items, such as eyelashes on a person.

Color often presents problems to computer artists. Colors on display screens are usually different from those generated by the printer. If you are serious about exact color matching, the Pantone® color standard is supported by some printers (especially those used by commercial printshops), graphics software, and even some monitors. By choosing colors according to these definitions, you are assured of getting the precise color on the final copy. Some software packages also support color separation. In modern four-color presses, color is created based on four different masks [cyan (blue), magenta (red), yellow, and key (black)—abbreviated CMYK]. Other colors are created by blending portions of these colors, as controlled by the masks. Software that supports color separation can use a special machine to print the separate masks, which go directly to a commercial printing press.

Although you do not have to be an artist to incorporate artwork into your reports and documents, you do need an element of artistic sensibility. The goal is to use art to enhance your presentation, not clutter it. Knowing what looks good and using restraint are signs of artistic talent. Remember that faster does not always mean better. Use some of the time savings to put more thought into your presentations.

Reality Bytes   **Personal Digital Assistants**

Personal digital assistants (PDAs) are popular, but not completely accepted. The original PDAs have somewhat limited capabilities—largely used as personal organizers to hold contact lists, schedules, and simple notes. As technology improves, the PDAs are beginning to include Internet browsers, e-mail, and even cell-phone capabilities. In the second quarter of 2001, 2.796 million PDAs were shipped worldwide, with 1.273 million of those in the United States. Both numbers represent a decline in sales from the first quarter of the year. Palm sales were leading with 898,000 total shipments. Compaq Computer Corp. was second with 450,000 devices. The Palm devices run the custom Palm operating system. The Compaq machines run Windows CE, enabling them to handle many common software applications. Many of the PDA vendors are rapidly adding wireless connections making it possible to connect to the Internet and corporate networks.

Source: Adapted from Ecomworld.com, "E-mail is set to energize the corporate PDA sector," August 10, 2001. [http://www.ecomworld.com/search/author/article.cfm?ContentId=1573]

Communication: Voice and Mail

All jobs require communication—with co-workers, managers, and customers or clients. Word processors help with reports and memos, but much of our communication is less formal. Everyone is familiar with answering machines for telephones. Businesses have taken this concept a step further by using voice mail systems. **Voice mail** systems record messages much like an answering machine, but they store the messages in digital form on computers. They usually give the caller control over where the message is sent. Most people in the United States have dealt with systems that direct you to press buttons on the telephone to make choices. Some voice mail systems enable you to send the same message to several people. Some systems also enable you to skip messages or fast forward to the end.

Networked computers can be used to send messages directly to other users. These **electronic mail (e-mail)** systems are typically used to send written notices to various people. They can be used to send pictures, facsimiles (faxes), or even voice messages if the computers have sound boards and speakers. The basic problem with any communication system is that sooner or later it becomes cluttered with junk mail. One of the advantages of text e-mail is that the recipient can have the computer scan the messages to search for items that are important or interesting. With the appropriate *mail filters,* junk mail can be discarded automatically. Messages also can be retrieved and stored for future reference or forwarded to other people.

Organizing Resources: Calendars and Schedules

An important task of managers is to organize company resources so that they are used most effectively. An important function is scheduling workers. Schedules involving line workers entail making sure that there are enough employees to get the job done, but no extra employees. Schedules involving managers typically involve meetings and require trade-offs between competing demands for a manager's time. Several software tools are available to improve both types of scheduling and make more efficient use of the human resources.

Most managers spend a considerable amount of time in meetings. In fact, it becomes difficult to keep track of appointments, set up new meetings, and reschedule meetings. The process is even more difficult when some participants are traveling or are based in another city or country.

Several software packages store appointments and schedules on electronic calendars. Electronic calendar and scheduling software enables data to be shared with other people. For instance, each person in a department would use the electronic calendar to keep track of his or her personal, departmental, and corporate appointments. To schedule a meeting with departmental members, the manager selects an approximate time, specifies the priority of the meeting, and fills in the participants, location, and subject information. The calendar software then searches each personal calendar for the best time for the meeting. It overrides lower-priority meetings and places the complete notice on each person's calendar in a matter of seconds. Employees have to check their calendars periodically to see whether meetings have been added or changed.

The Paperless Office?

You might think that with increased use of electronic data, there would be less need for paper. So far, the opposite has happened. According to *The Economist,* in the 1990s in Britain the use of paper increased by 65 percent over 10 years. From 1993 to 1998, despite the growth in use of personal computers and the Internet, paper usage increased by 13 percent. Worldwide, paper use doubled from 1982 to 1998. Some people might argue that electronic capabilities helped hold down the increased use of paper, but there is little evidence to support this claim.

Why would the use of paper increase? First, corporate information systems and the Internet have made it easier to create and distribute information. Second, the current electronic displays are generally not as readable or as portable as paper copies. Consequently, people retrieve the data they want and print it out.

Today, electronic displays are approaching the point where they might eventually be able to replace paper copies. Screen resolution has been a big factor in readability. Conventional monitors operate at about 100-dpi resolution. Newer technologies will produce 200-dpi resolutions, which will produce good quality text at traditional book sizes. Portability is also improving, although battery life is still an important issue.

There are still unresolved issues about future compatibility. Properly cared for, paper documents will last for decades. While electronic data can survive for years on CDs or DVDs, the hardware and software to read them may disappear in a short time.

Summary

One of the original purposes of computers was to make it easier to perform basic tasks. Over time, as computers have become more powerful, they have come to support increasingly complex tasks. Today, in addition to increasing efficiency, computers can help you make better decisions. One major change is in the type of data routinely processed. The five major types of data are: numbers, text, images, sound, and video. To handle more sophisticated data and more difficult tasks, computer hardware and software have grown increasingly complex.

To choose a computer that best meets your needs, you must evaluate the four basic hardware components: input, processor, output, and secondary storage devices. Each component is measured by slightly different characteristics. Input devices are selected based on the specific task (such as a keyboard for typing, mouse for pointing, or a microphone for voice input). Processors are often selected based on speed and price. Output device quality is appraised by resolution and color capabilities as well as initial and ongoing costs. Secondary storage is evaluated based on speed, capacity, and price.

Although computer hardware and software are becoming more complex, operating systems are being improved to make them easier to use. Through graphical user interfaces and standardized menus, operating systems make it easier to use common applications. When choosing an operating system, you should also evaluate its ability to run several applications at once (**multitasking**).

Application software is the primary source of improved productivity. Packages exist to assist in research, analysis, communication, and organizing resources. Database management systems are used for research and data sharing. Spreadsheets and other analytical tools assist in calculations. Word processors, desktop publishing, drawing packages, voice mail, and e-mail are used for communication. Electronic calendars and scheduling software are used to help organize human resources. There are hundreds of other software applications for specific tasks, but most people begin with these basic tools.

A Manager's View

Many tools available for personal computers will help you in your daily tasks. Every manager needs to write reports and memos. Most also deal with numbers on a regular basis. Calendars, schedules, and personal notes are used by most executives. Contact managers and phone lists are particularly important for sales managers.

You need to know how to use all of these tools. You also need to keep up with changes in the industry. Many times in your career, you will need to purchase computer hardware and software. You can make better decisions if you understand the technology and trends.

Key Words

access speed, *53*
binary data, *39*
bitmap image, *42*
CD-ROM, *54*
clip art, *59*
desktop publishing, *59*
digital video/versatile disk (DVD), *54*
electronic mail (e-mail), *60*
ergonomics, *50*
icons, *42*
input, *39*

megabyte, *45*
milliseconds, *46*
multitasking, *61*
nanoseconds, *46*
operating system, *55*
optical character recognition (OCR), *50*
output, *39*
personal digital assistant (PDA), *56*
Photo-CD, *43*
processor, *45*

random access memory (RAM), *45*
redundant array of independent drives (RAID), *53*
resolution, *51*
synthesizer, *50*
true color, *52*
Unicode, *41*
vector image, *43*
voice mail, *60*

Website References

Free News Sources

Associated Press	**wire.ap.org**
CNN	**www.cnn.com**
Ecola	**www.ecola.com**
ESPN	**espn.go.com**
Fox News	**www.foxnews.com**
Internet News	**www.internetnews.com**
MSNBC	**www.msnbc.com**
News.com	**www.news.com**
Newshare	**www.newshare.com**
USA Today	**www.usatoday.com**
United Press International	**www.upi.com**
Wired	**www.wired.com**
ZDNet	**www.zdnet.com**

Almost Any Magazine or Newspaper (many charge for access)

Business 2.0	**www.business2.com**
Fortune	**cgi.pathfinder.com/fortune**
The Economist	**www.economist.com**
Wall Street Journal	**wsj.com**
Washington Post	**www.washingtonpost.com**

Additional Reading

Adams, S., R. Rosemier, and P. Sleeman. "Readable Letter Size and Visibility for Overhead Projection Transparencies." *AV Communication Review,* 1965, 412–417. [An early discussion of creating good presentations.]
Bulkeley, William M. "NEC, Cray Reach Supercomputer Deal for Sales of Japanese Machines in U.S." *The Wall Street Journal,* February 28, 2001. [Analysis of the supercomputer market.]

"Science: The Numbers Game." *Time,* February 20, 1988, pp. 54–58. [Short history of computers.]

Simonds, D., and L. Reynolds. *Computer Presentation of Data in Science: A Do It Yourself Guide.* Boston: Kluwer Academic, 1989. [Ideas for presentations.]

Thibodeau, Patrick. "Mastering Babel." *Computerworld,* January 11, 2001. [Special report on global IT issues.]

Review Questions

1. List and describe the five basic types of data. How much space would it take to store a typical example of each type of data?

2. What are the primary hardware components in a computer?

3. How do the various computer components affect the speed of the computer?

4. What is multitasking? Give some advantages of multitasking. What are some potential problems of multitasking?

5. What hardware is currently used to run browsers capable of handling e-commerce?

6. What issues are important when selecting servers for e-business applications?

7. Identify at least three possible uses for a massively parallel processing supercomputer. Explain how the tasks can be split into the necessary pieces.

8. Briefly describe five tasks you expect to perform in your job as a manager and list the application tool you will use.

9. What will it take for people to adopt a paperless office?

10. How do computers improve productivity in communication? What is the difference between increased efficiency and effectiveness (better decisions)?

Exercises

1. What are the current prices of disk drives ($/GB) and RAM ($/MB)?

2. If you want to build a relatively high-level computer from parts, what parts would you buy and how much will they cost?

3. What current processor gives the best performance for the price? Explain your answer.

4. Investigate current speech recognition devices. How accurate are they and how much do they cost? Find at least two systems, including one high-end version.

5. Keep track of your printing for a week and estimate how many pages you print in one year.

6. A software package enables you to define rows of data, but it uses an integer to count the rows. This value is stored in 2 bytes. If half the values can be negative, what is the largest positive value that can be held in the 2 bytes? If the counter is increased to 4 bytes, what is the largest positive value?

7. Research state-of-the-art video displays. What are the best resolutions you can find? At what price? What additional capabilities exist (e.g., three-dimensional)?

8. Assume you wish to create a new e-business service, anticipating several thousand hits per day, potentially growing to tens of thousands per day. Research the hardware and software you could use to handle this business.

 CO2Ex09.txt

9. You are trying to decide on raises for your departmental employees. The accompanying table lists the performance evaluations they received along with an estimate of the percentage raises that you wish to give. To review your spreadsheet skills, enter the formulas necessary to complete the table, including the totals and averages. Also, create a graph that displays the percentage raise and the performance evaluation for each employee. (One extra credit point is given for identifying all of the employees.)

	A	B	C	D	E	F
1	Name	Salary	Evaluation	Raise%	Raise	New Salary
2	Mandelbrot	97600	5.8	12	11712	109312
3	Gardner	82000	6.5	9	7380	89380
4	Thom	61300	4.9	6	3678	64978
5	Russell	53200	5.2	5	2660	55860
6	Whitehead	45000	5.3	8	3600	48600
7	Goedel	39400	6.8	7	2758	42158
8	Hardy	38400	7.2	7	2688	41088
9	Cauchy	27600	4.5	5	1380	28980
10	Ramanujan	37500	7.8	11	4125	41625
11	Gauss	21300	8.9	10	2130	23430
12	Euler	16400	6.7	8	1312	17712
13		total	average	average	total	total

10. Estimate the storage space (number of bytes) required for each of the following items:

 a. A telephone book with 10,000 entries consisting of names, addresses, and phone numbers. Use your phonebook to estimate the average length of an entry.

 b. A fax transmission of a 30-page report at high resolution (200 by 200 bits per inch). What is the raw size? What is the size if you can use a compression algorithm that reduces each page to one-twentieth the original size?

 c. You have a 4- by 6-inch color photograph scanned in high resolution at 2,400 dots per inch and 16 million colors (24 bits for color). How far (percentage) would you have to compress this image to fit into 4 MB of available RAM?

 d. Kodak has a system that transfers photographs to a CD-ROM. Using the Base*16 resolution and the compression ratio described in the text, how many pictures can be stored on a CD-ROM that holds 650 MB? How many Base (TV) resolution pictures could be stored?

 e. If you wanted to store your favorite half-hour television show in digital form, how many bytes of storage would it take? Extra credit: How much space would it take if you remove the commercials? (Hint: time the commercials.)

11. To review your word processing skills: Create a short report on the current status of computer tablets. Define a set of styles for three different heading levels. Also, create a new style for BrandName and use it to highlight the brand names of the products you discuss.

12. A spreadsheet is an important tool that can be used to manage your personal finances. A simple plan that you can implement is a personal balance sheet. The top of the balance sheet includes your income. In it you can list all of the money that you have coming in each month. The bottom of the balance sheet is your expenses. Using it, you can list all the expenditures that you were required to make each month. Your instructor has a disk with a sample outline that you can fill in with your personal data. Of course, you can enter additional lines in each category.

 ## C02Ex12a.xls, C02Ex12b.xls

 a. An important part of financial analysis is the ability to compare your financial statement to those of others. Several sample worksheets are included on the sample disk. Examine several worksheets. They are each listed by student name. How do these worksheets compare to your income and expenses?

 b. Graph the most significant items in your worksheet. These would include those items that seem to have the most variance or the widest range of dispersion. What difficulties occur when you graph these items against the totals in each category?

Rolling Thunder Database

13. Using the Export Data form, copy the data to a spreadsheet and create graphs for the following situations. (Choose the type of graph you feel is best suited to present the data.)

   a. Sales by model type.
   b. Sales by month.
   c. Sales by model type for each month.
   d. Sales by state.
   e. Sales by employee by month.

14. Using the existing forms, enter data for a new bicycle order.

15. Design a small website (some forms and graphics) that could be used to advertise the products manufactured by Rolling Thunder Bicycles.

16. Find at least two other bicycles (e.g., on the Internet or from a dealer). Create a spreadsheet comparing the features and costs with a similar bicycle built by Rolling Thunder Bicycles.

17. Find at least five websites on which Rolling Thunder Bicycles might advertise their bicycles. Briefly describe the type of people who might see those ads, and why they would be interested in Rolling Thunder Bicycles.

Enterpreneurial Businesses

Introduction and Context

An entrepreneur is an individual who starts a business, usually with a new and different way of providing a service or making a new product. Entrepreneurship is the development of an innovative organization or network of organizations for the purpose of gain or growth under conditions of risk and uncertainty. It includes the following elements:

1. Creativity and innovation.

2. Resource gathering and the founding of an economic organization.

3. The chance for gain or increase under risk and uncertainty.

From a more personal standpoint, entrepreneurs are characterized by:

1. Compelling vision

2. Versatile planning

3. Driving passion

4. Confident execution

From an economic standpoint, the entrepreneurship industry should thrive most in times of economic slowdown and layoff. As opportunities in large corporations diminish, the attractiveness of the entrepreneurial opportunity increases.

Entrepreneurship is international in scope. Nothing has brought change faster than the rising ability of the countries in Asia to compete with the United States in productivity and ideas. Since these countries are beginning the process of change, they do not have to repeat the organizational and technological steps previously followed in other organizations. Adding the effectiveness of just-in-time inventories and manufacturing, the large capital investments in warehouses and inventories have been greatly reduced. In comparison, the larger corporations seemed to move too slowly. An entrepreneurship style of thinking was needed. As a result, large organizations began to teach and implement an entrepreneurial approach toward business.

Financial Analysis

During the rapid growth environment of the late 1990s, venture capitalists (companies that look for ideas in which to invest) poured millions of dollars into "an idea and a prototype" of the product or service. Today's environment is far different. The remaining venture capital firms are far more careful with their research and cautious with their investments.

Working capital is needed to get the production of products or the provision of services off the ground. Permanent working capital is the amount needed to produce goods and services at the lowest point of demand. Temporary working capital is the amount needed to meet seasonal or cyclical demand. When peak periods end, temporary working capital is returned to its source.

Financing is necessary across a new venture's lifecycle. This includes early-stage, expansion, and public financing. Early stage financing includes seed capital to prove the concept is viable and startup capital to bring the business into operation. Expansion financing supports the first commercial sales, expanding the product or service into new or broader markets. Public financing enables the firm to make the transition from being a private to a public company.

Stock/Investment Outlook

Investment in entrepreneurial firms is a risky proposition, to say the least. It is even more tenuous in today's cautious economic environment. The great majority of new businesses fail within the first five years. These businesses are usually small, not publicly traded, and financed by families or friends. Investing in them means contributing to the business directly in return for an equity stake in the company.

Entrepreneurially driven businesses can raise capital through debt and equity. Debt financing requires a fixed return over a stated period of time. It is borrowed capital and represents an agreement for repayment under a schedule at an interest rate. For investors in equity, the gains can be unlimited and the losses can include the full amount of capital invested. Private, or angel, investors are wealthy, risk-oriented individuals who are interested in capitalizing on the high-risk/high-reward opportunities that the new venture provides. Venture capital is outside equity that comes from professionally managed pools of investor money. Wealthy individuals and institutional investors pool their resources and hire professionals to make the investment and related decisions. Equity or public financing enables a firm to raise a much larger amount of equity capital than was previously possible. The initial public offering, or IPO, enables the entrepreneur, early investors, and top management team to price and sell some of their shares on the open marketplace.

Venture capitalists specialize in looking for good investment opportunities. Yet, with so much risk involved, the question remains, why invest in a startup? If the concept seems reasonable, usually the person trying to get the funding puts everything on the line, having already asked for money from everyone he or she knows. It follows that investors know that if the business fails, it will not be for a lack of trying. The involvement of the venture capitalists can provide general business guidance and advice so that the new business can avoid common problems. The payoff remains the incentive. If the business makes it, the return can be substantial. In return for the risk of the investment, venture capitalists receive the potential for a substantial reward.

A successful entrepreneurship can be quite profitable. Seventy-two percent of the 1997 Forbes Survey of the 400 richest Americans were first-generation entrepreneurs. This included Bill Gates and Michael Dell. Investing in entrepreneur-headed businesses should be carefully attempted and only done after extensive research and analysis. It should not be attempted on the spur of the moment or because this is the "last chance to get in on the ground floor." Personal investing in a small, entrepreneur company should only be done with resources you can afford to lose. You should enter these opportunities with the expectation that you will lose all the money.

Growth Potential

The growth in the entrepreneurship industry was unsurpassed in the late 1990s. The lure of big profits and the ability to be your own boss enticed a large number of people. Years of a healthy economy loosened the purse strings of many venture capitalists, making it is easier than ever before to get money for a new business venture.

All of this changed, of course, with the economic contraction of 2001. Even with greatly reduced interest rates, the resources have not surfaced to continue to fund the extensive number of opportunities that were formerly available. Assuming the business gets off the ground, the potential for growth depends on a number of factors, including the need for the new product or service, the state of the economy, how the product or service is priced, marketed, and delivered, and the customer service.

Today's technology makes it easier to compete with large companies offering similar services or products. Entrepreneurial and small business associations help entrepreneurs get business advice, find mentors, and make business contacts. Even in an economic downturn, the low cost of capital, the availability of labor and resources, the reduced competition for competitor's dollars, and the positive attitude toward entrepreneurs are available to help position for growth those who are willing to take advantage of the risk.

Competitive Structure

The competitive structure in the entrepreneurship industry is different from that in the longer established and more traditional industries. Since entrepreneurs do not all sell the same product or service, or even pursue the same type of client, the competitive structure of the entrepreneur's business depends mostly on the product or service they resemble most, or the one they are trying to replace. If this is a completely new product or service, which few are, there are no competitors. In that case, however, customers need to be convinced of the value of this new product or service. Store owners and buyers must also be convinced to give up some store shelf space for the new product.

Getting a new offering off the ground is a difficult endeavor, especially for entrepreneurs who lack the power (and money) of multinational corporations, which also come out with new products. This makes the process even more complicated.

Entrepreneurship is so well thought of that many major manufacturing companies, from drug to toy makers, have allowed and even encouraged entrepreneur-like behavior to develop and bring to market new products. Once a large company does have a new product, they have a lot more clout in stores than a small company in asking for shelf space. This further stacks the competitive environment against a new competitor. If the offer from the entrepreneur is a good idea and executed well, the product or service will easily sell itself once the company starts growing. Since the younger, smaller competitor can move so quickly, it usually takes time before the big companies come in to compete with a successful entrepreneur. This can result from believing that entering that market may not be worth it, to the internal delays faced by large companies.

Technological Investment and Analysis

Although the amount of technological investment in an entrepreneurial company depends on the main product of that business, there is no doubt technology and technological advancements have made being an entrepreneur easier and lowered the barriers to entry. Equally important, entrepreneurs in the field of technology have done extremely well. Companies such as Dell, Microsoft, and Netscape were all started as entrepreneurial businesses. In fact, Silicon Valley, where so many of the computer-related innovations have begun, is filled with venture capitalists looking for the next Netscape. While a person selling a service or a simple product might not need to keep abreast of the latest technology to survive originally, that business will need it down the road if the business grows.

It is easy to see that new technology is more than desirable for an entrepreneur—it can be critical to the success of a new entrepreneurial company. In fact, technology can deliver the competitive advantage that is driving the new business. Consider, for example, the Internet's leading compact disc and video store, CDNow. CDNow, which sells millions of dollars' worth of CDs each year, went public in 1998, yet was started less than five years earlier by twin brothers in their twenties. To this day, CDNow remains a virtual store, with no warehouse or inventory. It simply passes the order to the distributor, who ships it out. The people that work at CDNow work on customer service and Web page design, but do not have the overhead and lease costs of a normal record store. On the other hand, CDNow's business model changed radically when it ran out of cash. It was purchased by the media giant Bertelsmann and essentially became the e-commerce arm of that company.

At the very least, technology can help a small entrepreneurial company compete with the big company on many levels. Using technology such as websites, combined with software packages to do everything from the payroll to professional-looking presentations and proposals, a single person with a computer can appear as professional and competitive as a much larger company. A technology setup of this kind, while not cheap, is certainly within reach of most small businesses. This has lowered barriers to entry in many industries.

Role of Research and Analysis

Research and development is a critical part of an entrepreneurial environment. Entrepreneurs develop a vision for a product or service that is unique enough to warrant their full attention and financial support. The idea for a new product, for example, may come from simply asking, "Wouldn't it be great if something existed that . . . ?" In this case, follow-up research must be accomplished. This includes not only product research, but also market research. Would people be willing to pay for this concept? How much? How often would they buy it? As previously mentioned, some big companies make entrepreneur-like behavior a process. These companies realize that "thinking outside the box" means more than just addressing today's issue in the most efficient way.

For example, Merck and Company, the huge pharmaceutical company, has tried to standardize the invention process. The scientists who develop drugs in Merck's laboratories are encouraged to take a block of time and devote it to scouting for ideas outside the company. They can then conceptualize and follow up on drug projects of their choosing. They can make a case to a Merck board to finance the research or buy it from the outside. If successful, they are rewarded through stock options or salary bonuses.

Impact of the Internet

The Internet, of course, has lowered the startup costs and greatly reduced the technological barrier to entry for new companies. Companies can announce their presence and market their product far more broadly and target it more specifically than they ever could before. Providing information, enabling cost and product comparisons, and linking individuals to unique products of interest are all services enhanced by the Internet. The purchase and order fulfillment process can also be enhanced by the tracking capability of the Internet tools.

Recommendation for the Future

Entrepreneurs need to be prepared for the worst, but work hard to take advantage of the best. A good idea or product is not enough to make a successful business. Entrepreneurs need mentors. They need to be constantly thinking about their current and potential competitors. (If it was so easy for me to start this business, what stops others from starting their own business if mine becomes successful?). Entrepreneurs should look at technology to give them an edge, or at the very least, make their lives easier. Technology also helps because the never-ending barrage of technological advances constantly provides new entrepreneurial opportunities.

Entrepreneurs need to do their research and development to make sure that their concept is viable, one that consumers need or demand, and one that is not easily copied. One place to start looking is to use new technology to capitalize on current consumer (among other) trends. For example, the Internet has grown partly due to the fact that it makes data gathering so much faster in a time when people seem to have less and less spare time. With the realization that entrepreneurs play an increasingly important role in keeping the economy productive and innovative, it is important to continue to integrate these concepts into the business environment.

Case: Amazon.com

Short Description of the Company

Amazon.com opened its virtual doors in July 1995 with a mission to use the Internet to transform book buying into the fastest, easiest, and most enjoyable shopping experience possible. From the beginning, Amazon.com was committed to maintaining customer satisfaction and the delivery of an educational and inspiring shopping experience.

Today, millions of people in more than 220 countries use Amazon.com to find and discover anything they want to buy online, making Amazon.com the leading online shopping site. The site has the Earth's Biggest Selection™ of products, including free electronic greeting cards, online auctions, books, CDs, videos, DVDs, toys and games, electronics, kitchenware, and computers. Through their affiliations with Target, Toys-RUs, BabiesRUs, and Walmart, Amazon.com has leveraged its search and shopping cart technology to other stores and products.

Technology Innovations

Amazon.com uses its talented workforce to create its Web pages and to think of new ideas. Through developing the technology in-house, Amazon.com can control the programs more easily and keep its secrets from competitors. The disadvantage is that by keeping the technology development in-house, Amazon.com is limiting itself to the ingenuity of its small workforce in the development of its new products.

Networks

Online electric commerce has increased at a rapid pace due to its beneficial impact on the efficiency and competitiveness of service-orientated and sales companies. Amazon.com uses the Secure Netscape Commerce Server to handle online sales. Customers can enter their credit card number online using any computer network that supports the Secure Sockets Layer specification. Customers who do not have this technology can fax in their orders. Amazon's inventory system is run on separate computers and is not directly connected to the website.

With more businesses and households owning computers, the market segment for Amazon.com can only expand. Placing a credit card number on the Internet has been a stumbling block for some people. As a result, Amazon has developed, patented, and implemented One-Click Addresses & Settings. This technique enables users to enter their e-mail addresses and passwords and then click the "Sign in using our secure server" button.

Internet Applications

To be successful as an Internet company, "the lesson is be first, be dominant, and be the recognized leader," according to Bill Bumham, the e-commerce analyst for CS First Boston. Among cyber-merchants that offer recommendation services, Amazon.com has an edge over competitors because its service, though complex, can be accurate.

Web-based buying is particularly suited to products where instant access to updated pricing and configurations is advantageous. Sites can be expanded beyond the base information to provide a range of information, including special discounts, information on product availability, setup help, troubleshooting tips, driver updates, warranty information, comparisons to other products, and chat areas.

One of the more powerful features used by Amazon.com is affinity lists. When you look at a book, CD, or movie, the site automatically lists similar books that were purchased by people who bought the item you are looking at. These lists help consumers find similar items, and they encourage customers to purchase more items. Amazon.com is also promoting lists created by individuals—to encourage customers to consider related products.

Amazon.com also sells music on its website. The music section of the site uses the same theme as the book area, simplicity. Just as the book area allows users to search for the book they want to purchase, customers can search for the CD they want to buy. Navigation buttons are located in the same location as in the book area, allowing customers to easily access the sections. The Recommendation Center offers a computerized recommendation service that is based on the user's preferences and favorite artists.

Data

The growing reliance on shared databases and centralized information-collection systems has increased the need for conformity in the way data is collected, structured, and stored. While this uniformity can contribute to the more efficient operation of databases, it can also represent an inconvenience. Departments maintaining data that will be merged with data from other departments generally must adhere to companywide standards, whether they like it or not. That can be especially daunting in the case of a merger or acquisition. In these cases, information managers suddenly find themselves marching to a different drummer or, worse, multiple drummers. When it comes to extranets, on which companies share data with other companies, the issue can escalate from an inconvenience to a major stumbling block.

To address these issues, a number of Internet companies, including Junglee, owned by Amazon.com, and Jango, owned by Excite Inc., have developed technology to enable companies to collaborate over the Internet. Excite uses Jango's technology to develop a virtual online store that is an aggregation of multiple stores. Agent software resides on the main portal server and goes to a variety of Web sources to identify requested information. Based on rules guided by the source, the agents parse the resulting data to provide the key pieces of information needed by the user. This removes the need for all relevant information to reside on a single server.

The advantage of this technology is that it removes the necessity for an actual relationship to exist between the information provider and the information-retrieval system. Any change made by the information provider could cause the system to break down, depending on the accuracy of the technology that parses the Web pages.

A third approach, pioneered by Isadra Inc. in Palo Alto, California, is a two-part system that involves a cooperative relationship between the data source and the portal or information hub. One piece resides on the same server as the data source; the other is at the hub or portal. Working together, the two provide the conformity needed to find and parse information without requiring the source data to be the same.

Amazon.com announced the acquisition of Junglee and PlanetAll to diversify its electronic commerce offerings.

Junglee produces technology for aggregating job listings, retail product information, and other online data. It also manufactures Internet price-comparison software as well as comparison shopping services on various Internet sites. Amazon also acquired PlanetAll, which offers a Web-based calendar, address book, and reminder service that enables users to maintain contact with friends and associates. Amazon offered a total of $280 million in stock for both companies, of which about $185 million went to Junglee's management and investors and $93 million went to PlanetAll. These acquisitions enabled Amazon.com to expand its services by helping customers locate other Internet stores. Profit will come from Internet store commissions.

Junglee earned widespread praise when it introduced its JobCanopy service late in 2000. The system treats online information as a vast, distributed "virtual database" and applies a series of data wrappers that can gather information from a variety of sources, such as employers' recruiting sites. The technology formats the data in a uniform manner, enabling online publishers to reuse the aggregated information quickly and easily. A number of online newspapers, including the *Washington Post,* the *Boston Globe,* and *The Wall Street Journal* Interactive Edition, now use JobCanopy to supplement their employment listings.

Junglee exploited its potential by adapting its technology to allow comparison shopping for books, clothing, home electronics, and other product categories. Consumers can enter a book author and title and Junglee will return price, availability, and shipping information from a number of participating retailers. Yahoo, Snap, Go2net, and several other Web publishers currently use the Junglee system to supplement their e-commerce offerings.

Junglee is exploring XML as a means to aggregate this type of data and format it on the fly using tools such as Internet Explorer's client-side data-binding technology. Junglee's XMLizer, currently available as a demo on the company's site, delivers XML-formatted product information to an Internet Explorer 4.0 browser. Users can reformat the data to get the view they would find most convenient. As Web publishers and merchants adapt XML to structure their data, and as both Netscape and Microsoft deliver XML-compliant browsers, this approach will increase the power of Junglee and other comparison-shopping tools.

Once industries agree on specific tagsets for structuring their header data, Junglee will be able to automate the data-gathering process further. Currently, Junglee must build custom-designed data "wrappers" to analyze HTML-formatted data. This is a time-consuming, manual process that Junglee adapts for each participating retailer. Comparison-based services such as Junglee promise to be successful where "online malls" failed. In addition to aggregating price, availability, and other product information, the virtual database can provide views of the information not readily available in any other form. Differences in search interfaces can make it difficult to do straight-ahead comparisons. Junglee's technology irons out these incompatibilities, giving the consumer a single, coherent way to understand information. XML searching will enable Junglee to give customers more options regarding the best way to view products and speed up the process by doing more work on the client side.

Junglee technology could present problems for Amazon.com, however. Book selling is generally a commodity market. The Junglee technology can push prices down even further by giving consumers an easy way to find the lowest price for a given title. Jeff Bezos recently told *The New York Times* that Amazon would deemphasize price-based comparisons, claiming that "we don't think that customers find price comparisons very useful."

What this means is that if comparison-shopping services are successful, corporate publishers that publish catalogs will want their products to show up on the list that Junglee produces. Amazon.com has also acquired Bookpages Ltd., a U.K.-based online book retailer; Telebook, an online bookstore concern in Germany; and the Net-based Internet Movie Database directory site. The online retailers Bookpages and Telebook have become fundamental components of its expansion into the European marketplace. The Internet Movie Database supports Amazon.com's entry into online video sales.

The acquisition of Bookpages in the United Kingdom and Telebook in Germany provided distribution centers to enable Amazon to slash their shipping costs for their European customers. Currently it costs $30 per shipment plus $5.95 per book for a delivery time of one to four days between Amazon's U.S. operation and a customer on another continent. Bookpages ships books to any European destination for about $3.35 per book, with a maximum charge of $16.70 and a four-day delivery time. Bookpages' catalog offers all 1.2 million U.K. books currently in print.

Telebook operates not only in Germany, with 400,000 German titles, but also in Spain, where its subsidiary Libro Web offers a million titles in Spanish, German, English, and Dutch. Another Telebook subsidiary operates in South Africa. Amazon.com paid $55 million in cash and stock for the three companies, although the individual amounts were not broken out.

The movie database content will become the backbone for what Amazon.com CEO Jeff Bezos called a "best-of-breed video store." His goal is to add to the company's established franchise in books and music CDs. The movie database site will offer in greater detail the same kind of background and review material for movies as Amazon.com's site provides for books.

According to Colonel Needham, managing director of the Internet Movie Database, "The general direction of the database will remain unchanged. We will still be the most comprehensive movie information source on the Internet. However, we will be able to add new features as a result of having the resources of Amazon."

The Internet Movie Database is one of the 500 most visited sites on the Web, according to Media Matrix, and offers data on 140,000 movies. It began in 1990 as a Usenet newsgroup maintained entirely by volunteers. It was transferred to the Web in 1995 and became a business in 1996.

Amazon.com paid $55 million in cash and stock for the three companies, though the individual amounts were not broken out. Amazon.com's stock closed at $91.75 after the purchases, a jump of $9 over the price it commanded before the purchases and a smaller-than-expected first-quarter loss of 40 cents per share were reported.

Competition

In competition with the Internet site of Amazon.com, Barnesandnoble.com is expanding its offerings in the business-to-business environment. Barnesandnoble.com continues to upgrade its Internet bookselling service. The Barnesandnoble.com service includes subscriptions to more than 42,000 newspapers and magazines, in addition to the books already offered. The publications are sold through a partnership with electronic-commerce subscription vendor RoweCom in Cambridge, Massachusetts. RoweCom will also add direct account debiting and detailed financial reporting to corporate users. This will enable Barnesandnoble.com to better track company expenditures on books and publications.

According to Michael Donahue, director of business solutions, Barnesandnoble.com signed up 25 corporate customers in the service's first two months. Customers use specially developed tools to make links from their intranets to the Barnesandnoble.com business site. This enables them to put up specific titles for their employees to see.

Another alternative to simply buying books on a website is the opportunity normally linked to bookstores, that is the ability to browse and sample the books. Silicon Valley-based BookBrowse has launched a new website that publishes excerpts from popular U.S. bestsellers, as well as many top fiction and nonfiction titles. In addition to excerpts, book summaries, author biographies, and reviews help with the book-buying process. Amazon.com has expanded its use of browsing—now offering customers the ability to read several pages of a book online.

Recommendations for the Future

Amazon.com should continue to focus on increasing its market share in all areas. Amazon.com should also focus on a parallel business, online software sales. Software, like books, CDs, and videos, is an information-rich commodity. It is easy to order online and products can be shipped directly from the distributor to the customer.

Amazon.com's three most recent purchases indicate that it prefers to acquire best-of-breed companies with strong brand names rather than develop them internally. The leading brand names in Internet software sales are Software.net and Egghead.com. With current market valuations pushing half a billion dollars, these companies could be too expensive to acquire. Another possibility is the privately held startup Chumbo (http://www.chumbo.com). Like Amazon.com, Chumbo has many retail partnerships with other companies. It hosts a co-branded online software store and shares a percentage of the store's revenue, just as Amazon.com does with its Associates program.

The number one recommendation is to make a profit. Amazon.com's focus has shifted from the buoyant "get big fast" to the pedestrian "march to profitability." Instead of designing zippy new features for its website and plotting new industries to conquer, its employees are turning to the tedious work of ordinary companies: cutting costs and raising revenue. Amazon is seeking to accomplish this shift through improving its logistics and supply chain management. This parallels an effort to address the challenge of establishing a powerful, rapid supply-and-distribution network. Jimmy Wright, Wal-Mart's logistics chief, has been added as vice-president and chief logistics officer to provide access to logistics and supply-chain control techniques.

Dr. Russell Allgor has moved from Bayer Chemical and has built an 800,000-equation computer model of the company's sprawling operation. When implemented, the model is to help accomplish almost everything from scheduling Christmas overtime to rerouting trucks in a snowstorm. Allgor's preliminary work is focused on one of Amazon's most vexing problems. This is how to keep inventory at a minimum, while ensuring that when someone orders several products, they can be shipped in a single box, preferably from the warehouse—the company has six—that is nearest the customer [Hansell, 2001]. Dr. Allgor's analysis is simple, but heretical to Amazon veterans. Amazon should increase its holdings of best sellers and stop holding slow-selling titles. It would still sell these titles but order them after the customer does. Lyn Blake, a vice president who previously ran Amazon's book department and now oversees company relations with manufacturers, disagrees with this perspective. "I worry about the customer's perspective if we suddenly have a lot of items that are not available for quick delivery."

Driven by big dreams and seemingly endless cash from investors, Amazon.com provided an almost magical offering for its consumers. Tap into a website and buy any book, music, or other merchandise, at a low price, with responsive service and quick shipment. Now Amazon has assigned people like Allgor to analyze why it is losing money. What the company is finding throughout its operations is what many skeptics have long contended. It is finding that its magical offering is complicated, expensive, and inefficient.

According to Bezos, Amazon is right on target. The plan, which has been imitated by many other Internet companies, was to grow fast and to grow first and to figure out how to profit later. Amazon has accomplished all except the last part. It has opened outposts in four countries. It expanded to become a general store selling electronics, kitchen gadgets, and lawn furniture. Last year, 20 million customers bought $2.8 billion worth of merchandise—more revenue, Amazon says, than that of any 5-year-old company in history. But it also lost $1.4 billion in the process.

Nearly all its rivals have subsequently vanished or are just limping along, conserving their last drops of cash. And Amazon, with its head start and foresight to raise $2.1 billion, is one of the few dot-coms left. "We have been planning for a long time for this inflection point, after expanding geographically and our product categories in 1999," Mr. Bezos said. "This is the right time to focus on the fundamental economics of our business, even if it means sacrificing growth."

In contrast, critics argue that Amazon is at heart a mail-order merchant. Nearly every successful mail-order company has used a variation of the same formula—a limited selection of unique products. Only the high margins provided by such private-label goods can pay the costs of marketing, warehousing, and shipping. Amazon, instead, wants to be the online equivalent of Wal-Mart, with so much sales volume that it has the buying power and efficiency to sell the same products available everywhere, but at low prices, and still make money. To Amazon's critics, that is a recipe for mediocrity, if not total collapse.

Amazon is preparing to address its distribution problems by outsourcing this process to the Ingram Book Group. Besides having distributors supply books to its warehouses, Amazon is preparing to take the more radical step of hiring the Ingram Book Group, the book distribution giant, to mail books directly to customers.

According to analysts, this makes perfect sense. Why should Amazon unpack a book sent by a distributor, only to repack it and send it to a customer? But competitors argue, as had Amazon, that outside arrangements are too risky. According to Steve Riggio, the acting chief executive of Barnesandnoble.com, "I can't see entrusting our customer relationships to an outside company. If things go wrong you are in for a lot of trouble." Amazon's Blake argues, "You won't be able to tell if a book is sent from our center in Fernley, Nev., or Ingram in Laverne, Tenn." [Hansell 2001]

Today with Amazon, there is much discussion about using outside companies for service, for product shipping, and to sell products on its site. Amazon already sells Toys "R" Us products alongside its own. In that deal, Amazon handles toy shipping, but it may not do so with other companies. It may link with another big store chain to add an entirely new department, but it will also turn to smaller companies to fill in corners of its product line it doesn't want to handle.

One example [Hansell 2001], in particular, is quite telling. Amazon was selling a $9 candle holder. This was a large glass bowl containing rocks. It was meant to be filled with water that would float the candles. One customer returned the product four times because the rocks had shattered the glass during each shipment. That product is no longer part of "earth's biggest selection."

One question raised by this and many other examples, of course, is this: What was Amazon thinking to begin with? With hindsight, a glass bowl of rocks seems an unsuitable product for a mail-order company. Even more important is the question regarding why Amazon built five warehouses when it could have easily hired companies like Ingram Books to handle much of its shipping?

Bezos's response is that, yes, inefficiency was part of the plan. "We made a very deliberate decision to overbuild, although we hoped we were overbuilding by a little bit," he said. "If we hadn't done that, we would have disappointed customers, as a lot of Internet companies did, and we wouldn't be around anymore."

E-books are an interesting possibility for Amazon.com—they would substantially reduce costs; and Amazon.com would be in a unique position to benefit from increased e-book sales. However, although Amazon.com and Barnesandnoble.com both sell e-books, the prices tend to be the same or even higher than the same book printed on paper.

Questions

1. What forces are driving the strategic direction for Amazon.com?

2. Upon what technologies has Amazon.com relied?

3. How has Amazon.com financed its development efforts?

4. What alternatives exist for the service Amazon.com is providing?

5. What does the corporation's Web page present about their business?

6. How will technology continue to impact the book-selling industry?

7. How important is data to the corporation's continued success?

Additional Reading

"Amazon.Com: The Wild World of E-Commerce," *Business Week,* December 14, 1998, p. 106.

"Amazon.Com Turns to Sun," *InternetWeek,* August 3, 1998, p. 15.

Catchings, Bill, and Mark L. Van. "Abandoning Childish E-Commerce Myths," *PC Week,* December 21, 1998, p. 40.

Champy, Jim. "Why Web Won't Kill Middlemen," *Computerworld,* January 25, 1999, p. 54.

Hansell, Saul. "A Front-Row Seat as Amazon Gets Serious." *The New York Times,* May 20, 2001, http://www.nytimes.com/2001/05/20/technology/20AMAZ.html.

Karlgaard, Rich. "It's the Software, Stupid." *Forbes,* August 10, 1998, p. 37.

Koenig, Steve, and Aaron Ricadela. "Online Sales Hit Record Level." *Computer Retail Week,* December 7, 1998, p. 1.

Lombardi, Rosie. "Viable E-Business Model Is Still a Closed Book." *Computing Canada,* December 7, 1998, p. 34.

Nee, Eric. "Surf's Up." *Forbes,* July 27, 1998, pp. 106–114.

Perine, Keith, and Ben Hammer. "Bertelsmann Taps Joel Klein to Head U.S. Operations," *Computerworld,* January 31, 2001.

Rabinovitz, Jonathan. "E-Commerce Grows Up." *San Jose Mercury News,* October 25, 1998, pp. D1–D2.

Case: Peapod

Short Description of the Company

Thomas and Andrew Parkinson founded Peapod in the Technical Center/Classroom Building at Northwestern University in Evanston, Illinois, in 1989. Peapod was developed on the premise that people are too busy to spend hours each week in the grocery store. Peapod has since become the number-one online grocery shopping and delivery service in the world, with most of its recognition coming in the past two years.

The founders, with backgrounds in sales and brand and product management, saw a growing market consisting primarily of women in upper-middle class, dual-income families (with median income exceeding $60,000 per year), between the ages of 30 and 54. Many have children and are too busy living their lives to spend time each week on a little-favored task, grocery shopping.

The Parkinsons determined that this market would be willing to pay a premium for the time savings and convenience of having someone else do their grocery shopping for them, leaving them time for jobs, families, and other obligations. From this concept, the Peapod tagline developed: "Smart Shopping for Busy People." This business idea has continued to thrive. The response from a 1995 survey by Andersen Consulting (now Accenture) has shown that approximately 30 percent of consumers would pay a service fee for electronic ordering and grocery delivery services.

Technological Investment and Analysis

The Peapod consumer software is based on a three-tier architecture, which has positioned Peapod at the forefront of Internet computing. The first tier, the client layer, is located on the member's computer. The client layer utilizes instructions from the application server in order to create the user's interface, run the application, and return the input to the Peapod server. The two remaining tiers, the application and the database, are centrally maintained and manage all of the logic and data associated with the Peapod application.

Peapod believes that this "thin client" architecture has many advantages. The overall application performance is strong relative to other consumer network applications with comparable levels of interactivity. A major factor in the performance of a network application is the utilization of the narrow bandwidth connection between the consumer's computer and the server. Peapod makes efficient use of this bandwidth by performing certain processing on the member's computer and by exchanging only application-relevant information between a member's computer and the Peapod server (Prospectus).

It is also believed that this architectural structure offers a high degree of scalability. Efficient interaction between the Peapod server and the member's computer and the processing of certain application activities on the clients' side reduces the processing requirements of the Peapod server. The separation of the application and the database enables Peapod to isolate and optimize the different processing requirements of those layers. As the membership base expands and the number of simultaneous users increases, Peapod can integrate additional application servers without impacting the rest of the application architecture.

Another advantage is the functionality and flexibility of the application. Because the application logic and data is maintained centrally, Peapod can change much of the content and appearance of the software without having to modify or upgrade the software on the member's computer. For example, in 1996, Internet e-mail features were added to the application without any interruptions in client service or modifications to the customers' software. The centralized application logic also enables Peapod to present interactive marketing events and customize application appearances to individual members.

The new version of Peapod software, Version 5.0, will be based on Microsoft's ActiveX technology and will be designed to offer an even greater level of integration with the Web. Peapod will be able to incorporate website content, such as HTML documents or Shockwave animated images, into its consumer interface. With this new version, Peapod will be able to adapt its consumer software to support new technologies.

Peapod software is easily accessible via the Internet or from a Peapod diskette. Once the software is downloaded to the member's computer, members can then access the Peapod servers via direct dial-up or the Internet. The Peapod client software currently supports both Windows and Macintosh user platforms.

Peapod has designed and integrated several business support systems with its shopping application in order to facilitate the administration of services. The fulfillment management application, installed at each of Peapod's fulfillment centers, enables Peapod field operations managers to access and print member orders according to store layout, manage delivery time availability, and update store-specific product offerings. The Peapod accounting system provides the billing, processing, and collection functions, which include the electronic link of the processing of member credit card payments and funds transfer.

The next release of the fulfillment management applications will incorporate handheld scanning technology to enhance and streamline the order picking and packing functions and electronically integrate the actual member order with the Peapod accounting systems.

Peapod's services are vulnerable to weaknesses in the communications medium (the Internet), which may compromise the security of confidential electronic information exchanged with members. Disruptions of service or security breaches could cause losses to Peapod, reduce member satisfaction, and deter new members from joining as a result of lack of confidence in online commerce. Peapod has taken some steps to address these and other privacy concerns. It has restricted access to its database, limited the type of information it has made available to third parties, required each employee to sign a nondisclosure and confidentiality agreement, and implemented data security systems at the main data center.

Technological Innovations

Telecommunications

Peapod remodeled its website in 1998 so that a variety of Internet-accessible devices, besides the standard PC/Web browser combination, will be able to shop in Peapod's virtual supermarket. The new site complements its SuRF proprietary shopping system. SuRF combines the multimedia capabilities of the World Wide Web with Peapod's WinSurfer application controls. This integration enables Peapod to offer shopping functionality and performance that are superior to those available from standard Internet technologies. This is particularly true considering the Internet's narrow bandwidths and conventional modem speeds.

Data

Peapod developed a way to track how individuals respond to particular promotions, not just if they respond. The software is called Universal Event Processor (UEP). It not only knows that you buy diapers, but it also knows that you immediately used a two-for-one electronic coupon for raisin bagels even though you had never purchased bagels before, or that you ignore ads for cheese unless you're buying wine. "It's routine to search databases for people who conform to a specific profile. We wanted to create a system that automatically tracked the actual transactions that resulted," says Thomas Parkinson, Peapod's chief technology officer.

"We found, for example, that we could sell five times as much Keri hand lotion by running a banner ad whenever a customer clicked on bananas," Parkinson says. This may seem illogical but it is invaluable marketing information. Peapod says it's too early to tell whether this has made individual consumers more loyal to Peapod. Nonetheless, it helps Peapod sell more goods, and the UEP has led data-hungry consumer goods manufacturers to Peapod's door.

Kraft Foods, Bristol-Myers Squibb Co., and Kellogg Co. use Peapod to test consumer tastes and behavior. They have seen on average a 10 percent to 15 percent increase in sales when they run a targeted banner advertisement. This is twice as much as with targeted electronic coupons, Tim Dorgan said. He is an executive vice-president at Peapod, who oversees market research for consumer goods companies.

Recommendation for the Future

Peapod must build brand identity and awareness. This is to be accomplished by aggressively marketing its services, through promotion and advertising, to increase brand name recognition. Peapod will stress the functionality, quality, convenience, and value of its services in order to build on its brand identity.

Peapod must provide a superior member experience. Peapod is committed to providing its members with user friendly, highly functional, and cost-effective shopping tools, convenient delivery and pick-up service, and exceptional product quality, each of which ensures member satisfaction and loyalty. Peapod will continue to gather consumer preference information so it can introduce more personalized services to its members which will attract new members, retain existing members, increase member usage, and increase Peapod's share of members' household purchases.

Peapod must expand into new geographic markets and further penetrate existing markets. Peapod believes that it can achieve competitive advantages in various markets by being the first to build a substantial online membership base. Peapod is currently in talks with grocery retailers in a dozen new markets that could come online in 1997. To take advantage of economies in fulfillment and advertising, Peapod plans to penetrate these markets quickly by opening multiple fulfillment centers in each new market.

The company considers numerous factors when choosing new markets in which to expand. Factors include size, population density, prevalence of personal computer users, demographic composition, market conditions, availability of a high-quality grocer, and other general economic factors.

Peapod must build interactive marketing services and leverage its database. Peapod has pioneered, in partnership with consumer goods companies, innovative interactive marketing services consisting of advertising, promotion, and market research services. The company has a relationship with The M/A/R/C Group, a national marketing research organization, to develop and market custom and syndicated research applications that will bring the research benefits of Peapod to the marketplace.

Peapod plans to continue to use its database and online shopping channel to develop new services for its interactive marketing clients. As Peapod's membership increases, it is believed that consumer goods companies will find the interactive marketing services a more valuable and cost-effective research tool.

Peapod must work with retail partners in evolving the retail model. Peapod has been working closely with the retail partners to expand their roles in the fulfillment of member orders. This partnership has also been leveraged to improve product distribution and order fulfillment to reduce costs, improve quality and enhance scalability. Technological support for these goals includes the recent development of a handheld scanner which will be used to expedite the order-picking and packing functions. Peapod has recently initiated efforts to license its technology to retailers on an international basis and in select U.S. markets.

Peapod has also been developing new options for the customer in order to lower their costs. In Houston, Peapod and its retail partner, Randalls, have implemented a drive-through pick-up option. This option reduces the member's delivery fees and creates additional scheduling flexibility by allowing members to pick up their own orders at their convenience. Peapod plans to incorporate this option in existing and future markets.

Peapod must leverage its membership and technology into other online services. Peapod recently entered into agreements with Geerlings & Wade, Inc., a national direct marketer of premium wines, to offer an online wine store and Firefly Greetings, L.L.C., a provider of personal greeting cards and specialty products, to offer an online gift and specialty products center. Future plans include the partnership of Peapod with nongrocery retailers to offer additional online services that would appeal to the company's membership base. Peapod also plans to make its services accessible on a national basis via the Internet. These companies have agreed to pay Peapod development, management, and transactional fees so that these new services can be introduced in the next Peapod software version.

The next major step was to move online shopping from the computer to the television. Dispatch Interactive Television tested this system and hoped to introduce it sometime in 1997. Dispatch Interactive believed that this service should expand quickly once it was available in all households, not just the ones with home computers.

The lines between dot-com and brick-and-mortar stores has grown ever fuzzier, as traditional companies go online and Internet ones venture into traditional arenas. This requires new distribution centers separate from the restaurants that Peapod has built to handle the flow of goods.

In contrast, Value America has no inventory and relies completely on relationships with suppliers and distributors. NetGrocer does not see itself as a dot-com store, said Frederick Horowitz, president and chief executive officer of the company. [Hickey 2000] Because of its distribution model and nationwide network of nonperishable grocery delivery, "we look at ourselves as the ultimate brick store," he said. "Grocery stores will not disappear. The model will change, the format of the store will shrink as nonperishables are sold online." According to Horowitz, NetGrocer sees itself as a partner, not competitor, of grocery stores.

In 1999 Peapod had 1,400 employees, 150 delivery vans, and dedicated fulfillment centers in San Francisco and Chicago that stocked over 12,000 dry grocery, fresh, frozen and dairy products. [Biederman 1999] According to John Caltagirone, Peapod's logistics and operations chief, by the middle of 2002 there would be new facilities on New York's Long Island and near Seattle. The company plans to add one new facility per quarter in 24 selected markets. Caltagirone is a 25-year logistics veteran who has worked for Rand McNally, RR Donnelly, and Ryder Integrated Logistics. When Peapod considered outsourcing to 3PL providers it decided the best way to ensure top-to-bottom quality in its products and operations was to operate dedicated facilities. "We looked at third party but we felt that logistics was a core competency we needed to have. We want to control the three touchpoints with customers, which are the Internet, customer service and delivery." [Biederman 1999]

Like many online startups, Peapod had to merge the free-wheeling nature of Internet culture with the precise demands of the logistics world. Caltagirone said that required a change in the company's mindset. "What I am trying to do with Peapod is to help them think of themselves not just as an Internet company but as a distribution company that is using the Internet." [Biederman 1999]

Peapod follows logistics operations that are basic supply-chain management, except for the specialized pick-pack function that is unique to the grocery business. This is because there are so many "each picks" or items that have to be picked individually instead of by the pallet or case.

The online grocery environment presents routing challenges far different from those of other industries. Customers select delivery times within two-hour windows. The challenge is getting enough density on each route and time slot. The marketing challenge is to get others to fall into that delivery window.

In addition to delivering groceries, Peapod also delivers prescriptions for Walgreen's pharmacy and works with numerous local vendors and firms like Jewel/Osco to provide product replenishment services. When a store's shelves are empty, Peapod can provide a direct delivery from Frito Lay, Hostess, or from Jewel/Osco.

When Peapod started, it hired shoppers to pick groceries for customers. With the increased requirements for accuracy, quality, and speed in a JIT environment, they need logisticians to perform the pick and pack functions. According to Caltagirone, "We need people who understand work in a fulfillment center. The old logistics bill of rights hasn't gone away. You have to get the right products to the right place at the right time." [Biederman 1999]

Peapod plans to be a third-party deliverer for other retailers. While it always plans to make groceries the cornerstone, Peapod "ambassadors," as delivery drivers are called, will soon be carrying a wide range of products to the door. Peapod has funneled the consumer knowledge it gathers through fulfillment operations into a new division, Consumer Directions. This online research service provides companies with client-specific information related to the Internet grocery industry. Consumer Directions uses sophisticated Web technology to design and customize virtual stores and to design online promotions and test environments. The division's client list includes Coca-Cola, Colgate-Palmolive Co., Kraft Foods Inc., Nestle, and Hershey Foods Corp. [Biederman 1999]

As with other pure Internet-based firms, the success of Peapod remains a question. Although its chief competitor, Webvan, has failed, many customers still prefer to shop at grocery stores to see and touch and smell individual items. At the same time, grocery store giants like Albertson's are leveraging their buying power and efficient logistics by experimenting with individual order pick-up and even delivery services. To survive, Peapod sold a majority interest to the Dutch grocery giant Royal Ahold NV, who is funding Peapod with a $50 million credit line.

Questions

1. What forces are driving the strategic direction of Peapod?

2. To accomplish this service, upon what technologies must Peapod rely?

3. What has caused a change in the use of technology in the grocery industry?

4. An analysis of Peapod's financial information will produce what conclusions?

5. What does Peapod's Web page emphasize?

6. What role does data play in the future of the corporation?

Additional Reading

Bicknell, David. "Virtual Mall Is Master of the Aisles." *Computer Weekly,* October 1, 1998, p. 30.

Biederman, David. "Core Competency: Two E-Businesses that See Fulfillment as Integral to Identity." *Traffic World* 260, no. 1 (Oct. 4 1999) p. 26–27.

Dollinger, Marc J. *Entrepreneurship: Strategies and Sources.* Upper Saddle River, New Jersey: Prentice-Hall, 1999.

"Entrepreneurs: A Special Section." *New York Times,* September 23, 1998, pp. D1–D15.

"Food Delivery Services Look for Market to Peak by 2000." *Electronic Advertising & Marketplace Report,* September 23, 1997, p. 3.

Grover, Mary Beth. "Go Ahead: Buy the Dream." *Forbes,* June 15, 1998, pp. 146–150.

Hickey, Kathleen. "Web Sell." *Traffic World* 262, no. 4 (April 24, 2000) pp. 38–39.

Hof, Robert D. "Customizable Web Sites." *Business Week,* October 5, 1998, pp. 176–177.

Johnson, Andrew. "Peapod Launches Secure Firewall for Web Servers." *PC User,* February 21, 1996, p. 12.

Muchmore, Michael W. "Virtual Supermarkets." *PC Magazine,* November 18, 1997, p. 41.

"Peapod Expanding." *Computerworld,* August 17, 1998, p. 33.

"Peapod's Customer-Tracking System." *Computerworld,* August 10, 1998.

Useem, Jerry. "The New Entrepreneurial Elite." *Inc. Magazine,* December 1997, pp. 50–55.

Weiss, Todd R. "Struggling Online Grocer Webvan Shuts Down." *Computerworld,* July 9, 2001.

Appendix

Displaying Data

Computers make it easy to do certain things, such as writing reports and drawing charts. But conveying information and persuading people requires more than just writing a report and slapping in a chart. The purpose of a chart is to communicate ideas. Different types of charts exist to highlight different relationships. Your job is to choose the chart that most clearly describes the important concepts. You must also pay attention to the overall layout and style of the chart. For example, color, typeface, and white space all affect the viewer's perception of the graph.

Column or Bar Chart

One of the most important steps in presenting information is to choose the correct type of chart. Several common types exist that highlight typical business relationships. Choosing the wrong type may mislead the reader and will make it difficult for others to understand your comments.

The four most common chart types are column, line, pie, and scatter. The column or bar chart is used to compare values by categories. For example, Figure 2.1A shows the sales for the Rolling Thunder Bicycle company by the type of bicycle. The chart could have been drawn with horizontal bars, but charts that involve money typically place amounts on the vertical axis.

Every chart must have certain features. For example, it must have a title, and the axes must be labeled. If there are multiple categories of data, a legend will be used to identify each category. For instance, you could add another set of columns to Figure 2.1A to show sales for the next year. This additional set of bars would be marked with a different pattern and perhaps a different color.

Pie Chart

Pie charts are used to show how some total value is broken down into its constituent parts. For example, Figure 2.2A displays the same data that was shown in Figure 2.1A—the sales by type of bicycle. Although the two charts show the same type of data, they convey different information. The column chart focuses on the actual sales level for each model. The pie chart highlights the relationships across the model types. The emphasis is on the percentage contributed by each model as opposed to the total dollar level. Also note that pie charts can display only one set of data at a time.

Line Chart

Whenever you want to show how data changes over time you need to use a line chart. The horizontal axis displays time and the vertical axis displays the business data. As shown in Figure 2.3A, the different categories are shown with different markers or different line styles. Color can be used to differentiate the categories; however, you have to be careful to choose colors that people can see clearly. Each output device may display colors differently, so you will have to test your graph colors to be sure they come through correctly. Also, keep in mind that some people have difficulty distinguishing colors.

Scatter Chart

Scatter charts are particularly useful for examining the relationships between noncategorical variables. A noncategorical variable is one that can take on virtually any value. The example in Figure 2.4A compares the selling price of the bicycle to the number of days it took to build each one. As a manager, you might be interested to learn whether the company charges more money for bicycles that are harder to build. In this example, the results show virtually no correlation between price and time.

FIGURE 2.1A   Column chart. Column and bar charts are used to compare categories of data. In this case, sales by each type of bicycle.

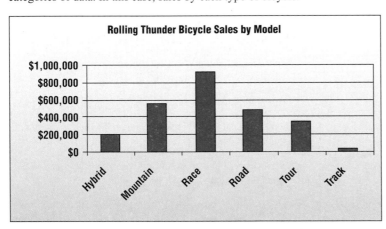

FIGURE 2.2A   Pie chart. This pie chart shows how the different bicycle models contribute to the overall sales.

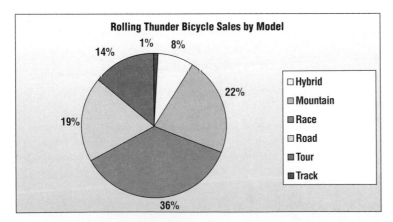

You can compare three variables using a surface chart in three dimensions. The control variables are generally placed on the *x* and *y* axes, while the dependent variable of interest rises from the page.

Style and Ornamentation

As Edward Tufte points out in his book *The Visual Display of Quantitative Information,* graphing software offers many temptations that should be avoided. Whenever you build the chart you should always first ask yourself: What is its purpose? You should then make sure that every option you choose highlights that purpose. Avoid cluttering your graph with excess lines, images, or garish color schemes. Although it is true that design requires some artistic creativity, in virtually every situation, conveying accurate information is far more important than splashy effects. The goal of any design is to strive for elegance.

Exercises

1. Create the graph in Figure 2.1A, and add another series for a second year of data.

2. Search the Internet and business publications and find an example of a chart that you believe conveys information easily and effectively. Find another example of a chart that does a poor job. Briefly explain what you like and dislike about each chart.

3. Use the export data form in Rolling Thunder bicycles to generate sales by state. Create a column chart and a pie chart for this data. Briefly explain why one chart is better than the other one.

4. Using Bureau of Labor Statistics data, plot the unemployment rate and the hourly wage rate over three years.

5. Find specifications for three storage devices (e.g., disk drives) on the Internet. Plot a set of features from the devices to compare them. Hint: Try C/net.

FIGURE 2.3A   Line chart. Time is displayed on the horizontal axis of a line chart. Categories are shown by different markers or different line styles.

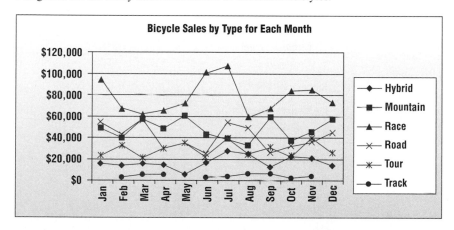

FIGURE 2.4A   Scatter chart. Scatter charts are useful for displaying relationships between noncategorical data. Randomly scattered results like those shown here indicate no correlation between the two variables.

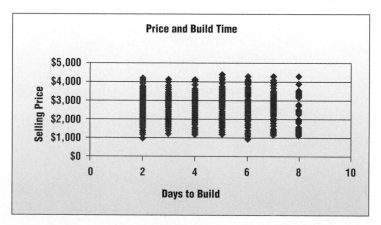

CHAPTER THREE

Networks and Telecommunications

What you will learn in this chapter

- How are networks used to solve business problems?

- What are the primary components of a network?

- Why are network standards necessary?

- How does the Internet work?

- What are the benefits of wireless networks?

- What telecommunications problems might you encounter in a global setting?

Unilever uses advertising and the Web to continue the image of Ben & Jerry's as a small, rural operation. Ben & Jerry's is also known for its commitment to social causes.

Ben & Jerry's Homemade, Inc.

Ben & Jerry's Homemade, Inc., the Vermont-based manufacturer of ice cream, frozen yogurt, and sorbet, was founded in 1978 in a renovated gas station in Burlington, Vermont, by childhood friends Ben Cohen and Jerry Greenfield, with a $12,000 investment ($4,000 of which was borrowed). Since then, Ben & Jerry's has grown into a multimillion-dollar powerhouse known worldwide for its plethora of frozen yogurt treats and ice cream in traditional and unique flavors. The company currently distributes ice cream, low-fat ice cream, frozen yogurt, sorbet, and novelty products nationwide as well as in selected foreign countries in supermarkets, grocery stores, convenience stores, franchised Ben & Jerry's Scoop Shops, restaurants, and other venues.

Overview

Richard:	Elaine, I'm in a hurry. When Larry brings the new data in, can you print out that last report and run it over to me at the client's office?
Elaine:	Sure, but how am I supposed to find you, and . . .
Ally:	Wait a second. Why not just bring the laptop with the wireless network. Then Elaine can just e-mail the documents. You'll get the documents faster, and you can make any changes while you're talking with the client.
Richard:	Hmmm. That sounds good. Does it really work?
Ally:	Sure, and you'll have full Internet access as well, so you can look up current data from our servers if anyone asks a question you're not ready for. But there is one catch: the microwave transmissions might be blocked in some rooms, so run this little meter to make sure you have a connection, and don't let them bury you in some back room.

Introduction

Communication is important to companies. There are two major categories of communication: internal and external. Internally, communication is used to keep the business running as one cohesive organization. Messages and data constantly travel among workers and managers. Workers collect data and share it with colleagues and summarize it for managers. Managers use the data to make decisions and change the organization. Changes are implemented as new policies and procedures, resulting in messages that are distributed throughout the company. External communications are important for many

Trends

The telephone system was originally designed to transmit sound by converting sound waves into electrical signals. Certain limitations were built into the system to keep costs down. An important feature of the phone system is its ability to handle multiple phone calls on one line. In the very early days of telephony, phone calls were connected by giant switchboards that required separate physical connections for each call. Over time, these switchboards were replaced with electronic switches. Today, the switches are the heart of the phone system network. Most of the switches in the United States are actually dedicated computers. To carry voice calls, the switches first convert the electrical signal into packets of digital data. These packets are then sent to the appropriate destination.

Another major change is the use of cellular telephones. In the 1980s, cellular telephone networks were installed in U.S. cities. By 2000, most of these systems were replaced with digital networks that could begin to handle data. The 3G system being built today will handle voice and high-speed data equally well.

A more recent trend that will affect personal communications is the rapid growth of cable television. Over 60 percent of U.S. households can receive cable television. In 1996, the government removed almost all barriers in the telecommunications industry. Cable providers are working on providing Internet access and more interactive features.

The late 1980s saw a significant increase in the number of companies connecting computers with local area networks (LANs).

The defining trend of the 1990s was the use of the Internet. From 1994, commercial use of the Internet grew exponentially. Substantial improvements were made in browsers, website capabilities, and transmission speed. Technologically, the Internet is simply a large global network created by the acceptance of standards. In practice, the Internet capabilities have the power to change society.

The next wave is wireless access—both high-speed connections within a company, and Internet access to cell phones and PDAs wherever you travel. These changes offer new ways of doing business and the potential to change society. Hundreds of opportunities exist in this new world, but the costs and complications can destroy a company.

FIGURE 3.1

Networks. Managing an organization requires communication and teamwork. Networks facilitate teamwork and create opportunities for new organizational structures. The Internet makes it easy to connect to customers and suppliers—creating new opportunities and new business relationships.

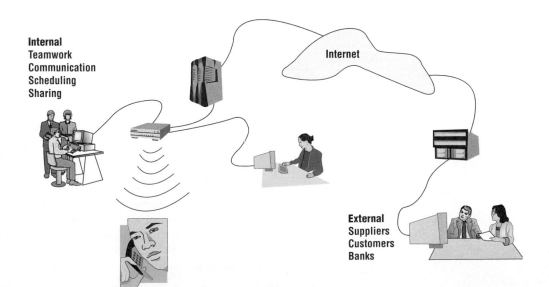

reasons including collecting data about customers and suppliers and providing information to shareholders and governmental agencies.

To understand the importance of telecommunications, note that AGS Information Services (a consulting firm) estimates that 48 percent to 68 percent of corporate technology budgets are spent on telecommunications. Some firms, like travel agents and brokerage firms, rely heavily on telecommunications and spend even more for them. Telecommunications expenses represent 2 percent to 7 percent of these businesses' total operating budgets—which amounts to more than $10 million a year for a $500-million firm.

Sharing data and resources can cause problems. For example, security must be addressed to determine who should be able to use and change the data. These concerns are multiplied in an international environment, because national governments may impose constraints on how companies can use the data they collect.

The objective of a network is to connect computers transparently, so that the users do not know the network exists. The network provides access to data on central computers, departmental computers, and sometimes on other workers' personal computers. Networks can create shared access to fax machines, modems, printers, scanners, and other specialized hardware. To the user, it does not matter where these devices are located. The network makes them work the same as if they were on any desktop.

Network Functions

Sharing Data

Sharing data is one of the most obvious uses of networks and it can make profound changes in the way an organization works. Managers can see customer and marketing data immediately as it is collected. Employees in one department can easily share data with other departments. A network facilitates the use of teams. In particular, it enables informal teams to spring up throughout the company to solve problems as they arise. Instead of waiting for a higher-level manager to appoint a team, employees can use the network to ask questions, notify others involved, and find in-house experts. A **local area network (LAN)** is commonly used to connect computers and share data within a company.

Transactions

One of the most important reasons for connecting computers is the ability to share data. Consider a retail store with five checkout registers. Each register is actually a computer. If these computers are not connected, it is difficult to compute the daily sales for the store. At the end of the day, someone would have to manually collect the data from each computer and enter it into another computer. Also, imagine what would happen if a customer asked a clerk to determine whether a product was sold out. The clerk would have to check with each of the other clerks or perhaps call the storeroom.

As shown in Figure 3.2, e-commerce consists of a transaction system with the Internet as the network and customer browsers as the client computers. The product data and sales transactions are stored in the central database connected to the Internet. Using a central database provides inventory data to customers. When a customer asks whether an item is in stock, the website can provide the answer. Managers can get daily sales figures from any location with a Web browser and an Internet connection. Payments and bills can also be handled directly online.

Decisions and Searches

Many types of data need to be shared in a company. Consider a situation in which a manager is told to close down 3 out of 200 stores. Selecting those stores can be a tough decision. It requires knowing sales volume for every store and projected future sales as well as operating costs. The manager will bring this basic information to a personal computer to create graphs and evaluate models. It is possible to collect all of the data from each store by hand and

FIGURE 3.2

Network for transaction processing. Networks are often used to collect data in a central database. From there, the data can be queried and analyzed by managers. E-commerce sales represent transactions across the Internet.

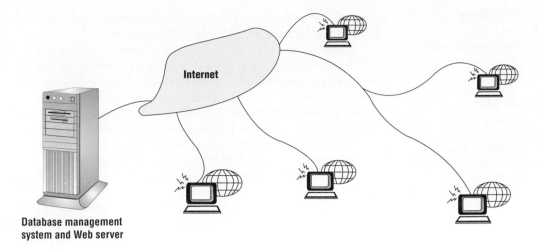

FIGURE 3.3

Network for decisions and collaboration. The file server holds basic data and software tools. Managers retrieve data and create reports. The reports can be shared with other managers. With collaborative software, revisions are automatically tracked and combined to form the final document.

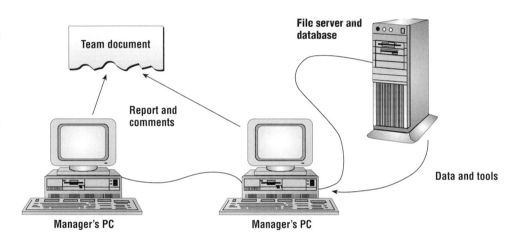

enter it into the computer. However, it would be much more efficient if the manager could simply transfer the data directly from the central database to the personal computer. Not only is this method faster, it prevents errors. The database should have the most recent information. Additionally, all managers will use the same data. A portion of a network for making decisions and sharing work with team members is illustrated in Figure 3.3. Without networks and centralized data sharing, many companies experience problems when managers have different versions of the data.

Messages

Most people are familiar with electronic mail, or **e-mail.** With e-mail, you can send a message to any person with a mail account. Many people have come to prefer e-mail contacts to phone calls. As shown in Figure 3.4, e-mail messages are asynchronous since the sender and recipient do not have to participate at the same time. A mail server holds the message until the user logs in and retrieves the e-mail. Additionally, users can create mailing lists and send a message to many people at one time. Messages can be stored, retrieved, and searched for later usage. In most systems, the computer can automatically notify you when the recipient reads your message. You never have to worry about whether your message was received. Voice mail systems, which resemble answering machines, have some of these same advantages. However, e-mail takes less space to store. More important, e-mail can be scanned electronically to search for key topics.

Junk e-mail, or spam, is an increasingly annoying problem. Many companies capture e-mail addresses and sell them to other companies that send out unwanted messages.

FIGURE 3.4

Networks for communication. With e-mail, a server holds the mail until the recipient logs on and can receive the message. Because several servers might be involved and each makes backup copies, e-mail messages are hard to delete.

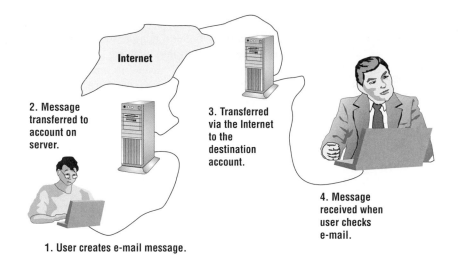

Internet

2. Message transferred to account on server.

3. Transferred via the Internet to the destination account.

4. Message received when user checks e-mail.

1. User creates e-mail message.

Reality Bytes   DoCoMo

DoCoMo is the leading wireless provider in Japan. From its first days, it has emphasized new technologies, and is now leading the way with 3G wireless services, spending over $10 billion to build a 3G network in Japan. Phones on the new system have built-in video cameras and can send and download video, photos, sound, animated cartoons, and e-mail. And they really are cell phones, so they can handle traditional voice calls. Despite the slightly higher monthly costs (increased from ¥7000 to ¥8000 or USD 83.72), DoCoMo's President Keiji Tachikawa predicts "We believe a lot of people are going to sign up." The company will also sell laptop wireless modem cards, enabling customers to download data at 384 kbps and upload at 64 kbps anywhere within range of a cell tower. Once the bugs are ironed out, it is possible that Japan's tech savvy customers will jump in. DoCoMo's earlier i-mode service is hugely popular. With 28 million subscribers, the service is a cash cow for the company, and brings in 30,000 new subscribers a day. The i-mode service offers e-mail and simplified Internet access.

Source: Adapted from Robert A. Guth, "DoCoMo Launches 3G Service; Industry Hopes for Recovery," *The Wall Street Journal,* October 1, 2001.

These messages take up space on company computers and make it more difficult for users to deal with legitimate messages. You should get in the habit of automatically deleting unsolicited messages—largely because the information they contain is highly unlikely to be true, and because they might contain viruses. Sometimes, you can set up e-mail filters that automatically read your mail and focus on the topics you have chosen. They cut down on the amount of junk e-mail messages, but they need more sophistication to be useful.

There are some drawbacks to e-mail. For one, some people are still reluctant to use computers, so they do not check the computer often enough to keep up with their mail. Another problem is that in 1991, the U.S. courts ruled that public transmission systems such as e-mail are not subject to the same legal protections for privacy as paper mail and phone calls. Unless the laws are rewritten, therefore, it is legal for employers (and almost anyone else) to read everyone's e-mail messages. Of course, the fact that it is legal does not make it ethical. The best solution to open communication systems is to encrypt the messages. Most word processors and spreadsheets make it easy to encrypt the files when they are saved. An interesting twist on this situation is that some courts have ruled that public officials *cannot* encrypt their messages; in fact, in some situations, it is illegal for public officials to communicate via e-mail at all.

Websites, Newsgroups, and Chat Rooms

Websites are essentially bulletin boards that are used to make information available to many people over the Internet. **Intranet** sites are similar in that they use Internet technologies but use security methods to restrict access to internal users. Websites can be interactive and retrieve customized information from a database.

Discussion sites and chat rooms allow users to post information as well as search for specific topics. Chat rooms do not usually store comments, but discussion sites provide databases and links so users can maintain a string of related messages. Discussion systems are generally more organized than simple e-mail, and store the data in one location to make it easier to find. Chat rooms are more interactive than e-mail, since they display messages as they are written.

A **newsgroup** is an Internet feature similar to a discussion site in that it carries comments from many people. It is designed to be copied from server to server so that the comments are available to a wide audience. Internet newsgroups are useful when you are searching for people with experiences similar to your own. However, they are a bad place to put company information.

Overall, the purpose of these systems is to enable people to send and retrieve electronic messages from others. The difference lies in the level of central control and monitoring. More highly monitored newsgroups are generally more accurate and more valuable in business. For example, the HRM department could run a newsgroup to provide information about benefits. Employee questions and answers could be posted in the newsgroup or on a website, because answers to one person might be valuable to many other employees.

Calendars and Scheduling

Managers spend a great deal of time in meetings. Yet, sometimes the greatest challenge with meetings is finding a time when everyone can get together. Several software packages use computer networks to solve this problem. As shown in Figure 3.5, managers enter planned meeting times and scheduled events into their personal electronic calendar file, where each event is assigned a priority number. For example, a time allotted for a haircut would be given a low priority; a meeting with a supervisor would receive a higher rating. If the CEO wants to set up a meeting, the CEO tells the computer which people are to be included, sets a priority level, and gives an approximate time. The computer then uses the network to check everyone else's schedule. When it finds an open time (overriding lower priority events if needed), it enters the meeting into each person's calendar. These systems can be useful when managers carry PDAs that are connected to a wireless network.

FIGURE 3.5

Sharing calendars. With the appropriate software, you can open your calendar to other members of your team. A team member can check the calendar and have the software find a common open time for a meeting.

8:00	Mgt meeting
8:30	(open)
9:00	Staff meeting
9:30	Staff meeting
10:00	New meeting

Teamwork and Joint Authorship

In any job, it is rare for one person to work alone. Most businesses are arranged as teams. Within the teams, individual people are given specific assignments, and each team member contributes to the final product. For instance, the marketing department might have to prepare a sales forecast for the next six months. Each person could work on a specific sales region or product category. These individual pieces would then be merged into a single document. If the computers are networked, the manager's computer can pull the individual pieces from each of the individual computers. Also, each team member can be given access to the others' work to ensure that the reports use the same data and assumptions.

Groupware is software that enables several people to work on the same document. Each individual computer has access to the master document. When one person makes a change to the document, the change is highlighted for everyone to read and approve. With existing international networks, each person might be located in a different country. Lotus Notes is a groupware product that makes it easy for employees to combine data and communicate interactively with each other. Microsoft distributes a product called NetMeeting, which combines several groupware tools and enables managers to participate in meetings across a network. It is described in more detail in the appendix to Chapter 7.

Backup

Another important reason for sharing data over computer networks is that most people are not very good at maintaining backup copies of their work—especially on personal computers. If each computer is attached to a network, there are two ways to set up an automatic backup system for individual personal computers. The older method relies on individual workers saving their data files to a central file server. The network manager then makes daily (or hourly) backups of the data on the central server. A few companies even provide this service over the Internet. For a monthly fee, you can transfer your files to their server, giving you a backup copy—plus they keep backup tapes for the server.

A newer method is significantly safer because it is virtually automatic and does not require users to remember to transfer their files. It does require users to leave their machines running. At a predetermined time, a central computer with a large backup capacity connects to the individual machines and copies the files that have changed. This data is then stored somewhere safe (such as a tape or optical disk). If a computer or a person accidentally deletes a file, the backup computer can restore the file and send it back to the personal computer. With the communication network, the backup process is almost completely automatic.

Sharing Hardware

Networks also enable workers to share expensive hardware. For example, networks are used to provide users access to special output devices, such as high-speed printers, plotters, or color printers. Networks can be used to give people access to special computers, such as when an engineer needs to use a high-speed supercomputer.

Printers

A common use of networks is to give users access to high-speed, high-quality printers. Even if each computer has a small personal printer attached, some jobs need to be handled by a high-speed laser printer. Many modern copiers now function as network printers and can collate and staple large quantities of documents. Similarly, at $3,000 each it would be expensive to buy color laser printers for everyone who might need one, yet it might be reasonable to buy one for a department to share. With a network, users can choose from among two or three different printers by selecting them on the screen. Figure 3.6 shows some of the hardware devices that are often shared.

Another advantage is that if one printer breaks down, users can send their jobs to another printer on the network. Think about what happens if there is no network and your printer breaks down. You have to copy the file to a floppy disk and interrupt someone else's work to borrow their computer to send the file to another printer. What happens if you are using a

FIGURE 3.6

Networks for sharing hardware. The workstations use the server to perform backups. Files are picked up by the server and transferred to tape. The LAN administrator can reload a tape and restore files as needed. Networks are often used to share printers and storage devices. Networks can be used to share access to supercomputers—even if they are in a different city or different country.

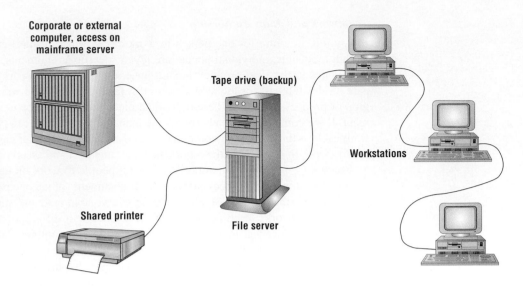

special software package that no one else has on his or her computer? You will probably have to physically move a printer from another computer desk to yours, connect the hardware, print your document, and return the printer. When you are on a network, you simply select a different printer from a list displayed on your computer and go pick up the output.

Several e-commerce printing companies enable you to send your large print jobs over the Internet and have the boxes of papers shipped to you. All of the setup, pricing, and payment can be handled over the Internet.

Storage Devices

The arguments used for network printer sharing can be applied to sharing storage devices. For instance, the firm's finance department may require access to large financial databases. Financial data and stock prices for most U.S. companies can be purchased on CD-ROM disks. It would be expensive to buy copies of the data disks for every person in the finance department. It makes more sense to connect the finance computers and the CD-ROM drive together on a network, then whenever someone wants to look up information in the database, the computer uses the network to transfer the information from the optical disk.

Special Processors

Special computers that are relatively expensive can be attached to a network to save costs and make it easier for users to access these machines. Parallel-processing computers and other supercomputers can perform calculations thousands of times faster than ordinary computers, but they are expensive. Consider a small engineering company. For the most part, the engineers use their workstations to develop their designs. They occasionally need to run simulations or produce detailed graphics images. Both of these tasks could take many hours to perform on individual client computers. The company can cable each engineer's workstation to a network that can access a supercomputer. When an engineer needs to perform high-speed calculations, the job is sent directly to the supercomputer. The results are returned via the network to the workstation so they can be added to the final report. More likely, a university could own the supercomputer, and the firm would lease time to run each job. If the network is designed properly, it makes no difference where the machine is located.

Sharing Software

Networks have been used at different times to share software. When disk space was expensive, it was cheaper to put one copy of the software on a server and download it to each computer as it was needed. Today, several firms have been working on a system that stores software on Internet servers, where client computers use Web browsers to connect to the server and run the software.

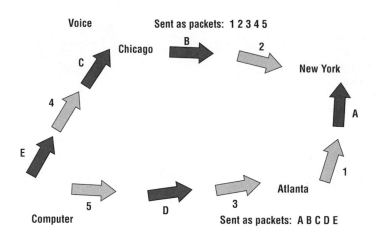

FIGURE 3.7
Packet-switched networks operate by partitioning all messages into small packets. Each packet contains a destination and source address, along with sequencing instructions. The packets can be separated and sent over different routes. At their destination, the original message is automatically restored by the network. Packets provide efficient use of transmission networks because they can mix packets and route transmissions over empty routes.

The main advantages of running software on a central server are (1) it is easier to install and update and (2) the client computers can be small and low cost, which makes it particularly useful for PDAs and cell phones. The main drawback is network performance and reliability. If the network is slow or the server crashes, no one can use the software.

Voice and Video Communication

A major cost of telecommunications in business is for telephone calls. Despite the total expenditures, there is little doubt about the value of communication and phones. Phone calls are almost always cheaper than in-person visits. With the rapidly declining costs of phone calls, cost is less of an issue. Even cellular phone costs are dropping rapidly; some experts predict that within a few years, almost all calls will be made over the cellular networks instead of traditional phone lines.

Newer technologies are emphasizing the value of routing all communication over a single Internet-based network, often called **voice over Internet protocol (VoIP)**. With this technology, your telephone becomes a device on the Internet and conversations are digitized and sent over the Internet along with all other traffic. Figure 3.7 illustrates the process. Your voice conversation is split into packets, mixed with other data traffic and routed to its destination over the Internet, where the computer/phone on the other end puts the packets in the proper order and recreates the conversation. **Packets** are a key feature of modern networks. A packet consists of a chunk of data, a destination address, and a source address. Additional data can be added by the network equipment to facilitate routing of the packets.

With improvements in technology and faster transmission of data at lower costs, it is becoming feasible to run full-service networks to each desk. These links enable workers to communicate with others using voice, pictures, computer data, or video across the same line. Although these links are technically feasible today, they are somewhat expensive. As Internet speeds improve and costs continue to decline, you will have more opportunities to use these technologies. Currently, one of the greatest difficulties with using these technologies over the Internet is that you may randomly experience delays from some link. But newer versions of the Internet protocols are being released that support guaranteed levels of service. Soon you will be able to conduct video meetings by reserving a certain level of speed at a set time.

Components of a Network

As networks have become more important, the components are increasingly built into the machines. However, you still face many decisions about which technologies to use and how to solve problems, so all managers should understand the basic elements of a network shown

FIGURE 3.8

Network components. Networks require a transmission medium and each device connected must have a network card to make the connection. Connecting to the Internet requires a router or switch and usually a firewall to block certain types of messages. Computers are often classified as workstations or servers. The distinction is blurring, but servers are dedicated to sharing data and files.

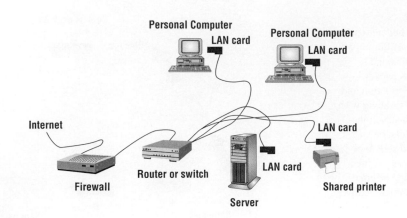

in Figure 3.8. Each of these components (computers, transmission medium, and connection devices) is discussed in greater detail in this section.

Computers

Virtually any type of computer device can be connected to a network. The earliest computer networks consisted of one computer with several terminals and printers attached to it. These networks were fairly simple, because the one computer performed all of the work. Substantially more problems are involved in connecting several computers together. For starters, each computer needs to know that the others exist and that they have a specific location (address) on the network. The computers need to know how to send and receive information from each other. To work together, they need connection devices (LAN cards) and special software.

Computers attached to networks tend to perform one of two functions: servers or clients. *Servers* are computers that store data to be used by other computers attached to the network. *Clients* are computers used by individual people. Sometimes a computer is used as both a client and a file server. Networks where many of the machines operate as both clients and servers are called **peer-to-peer networks.**

Servers

A wide range of servers exists today—from a simple PC to huge, expensive specialized computers. The main questions you face in choosing a server are the operating system and the issue of scalability, and the two questions are intertwined. **Scalability** is the ability to easily move up to greater performance—without having to rewrite all of your existing applications. Figure 3.9 shows two common methods used to provide scalability: (1) vendor-provided range of servers from low-cost machines to handle small loads, to mid-range, to high-capacity computers that can handle thousands of users simultaneously; and (2) integration technology that enables the workload to be distributed across hundreds or thousands of small servers, known as a **server farm.**

Both approaches have their benefits. The single server is easier to configure and administer. The server farm can be expanded easily and cheaply without disrupting the existing applications. The operating system software is crucial to making a server farm work efficiently. Several vendors sell enterprise versions of software that assigns applications to the least-busy server and makes it easier to manage the server farm.

Client Computers

The networked computers could be any type of machine. Because individual people at their own desks typically use these computers, they are often called *client computers*. These computers need to access the network and be able to send information to at least one other computer. A **network interface card (NIC)** (or LAN card) is installed in each computer.

FIGURE 3.9

Server scalability. Two common methods of providing easy expansion of performance are (1) to purchase a faster performance server within the same product family, and (2) to build a server farm where the workload is automatically distributed across machines and new low-cost servers can be added at any time.

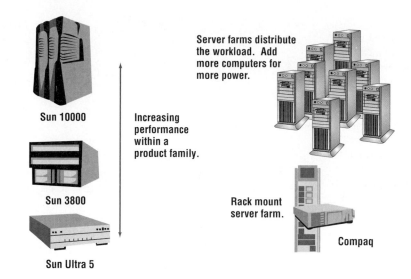

Sun 10000

Sun 3800

Sun Ultra 5

Increasing performance within a product family.

Server farms distribute the workload. Add more computers for more power.

Rack mount server farm.

Compaq

These cards are connected together by some transmission medium (e.g., cable). Additionally, these computers might have to be configured to connect to the network and set security parameters. Client computers today include laptops and PDAs that can be connected with wireless networks to enable workers to maintain connections and share data while they move around the building.

Many of the mobile devices have limited capabilities and essentially run browsers, e-mail, and calendars. Hence, more of the processing is done on the server, and the mobile device is only responsible for displaying data and basic user interface tasks. This type of environment is considerably different from the situation where all workers have desktop machines capable of handling large amounts of the processing. The thin-client PDAs rely on the server, while the desktop applications simply use the server for basic data sharing. Developing applications for this new environment requires some major changes in design, programming, and security—issues that will be explained in detail in other chapters.

Transmission Media

All communication requires a transmission medium. As illustrated in Figure 3.10, common methods include electric wires, light waves, and radio waves. Each method offers certain advantages and disadvantages, so they are designed for specific applications. Installation costs for all types of cables are high, and most organizations are unwilling to throw away old cable and install a totally new system.

Electric Cables

The two basic types of electric cables are twisted pair and coaxial. *Twisted pair* is the oldest form of electrical wiring. Since electricity must travel in a closed loop, electrical connections require at least two wires. Twisted-pair wires are simply pairs of plain copper wires. Telephone cables are the most common example of twisted-pair wires in households. Because of the cost, most businesses have already installed twisted-pair wires—typically a specific version known as Cat 5. Cat 5 wiring consists of four pairs of wires, and generally two pairs (4 wires) are used for most typical networks. Because of the extensive use of Cat 5 cables, the network industry has invested considerable research into maximizing the data that can be carried over that type of cable.

Twisted-pair wires have certain disadvantages. This type of cable cannot carry much information at one time. Plus, data transmitted on unshielded twisted-pair wires is subject to interference from other electrical devices. Interference can distort or damage a telecommunications signal. For instance, it is best to avoid running twisted-pair wires next to electric power lines and electric motors, because these devices produce electromagnetic radiation

FIGURE 3.10

Signals can be sent via several types of media. They can be carried by electricity, light waves, or radio waves. All of these methods have advantages and disadvantages. Fiber-optic cabling offers the fastest transmission rates with the least interference, but because it is relatively new, the initial cost tends to be higher.

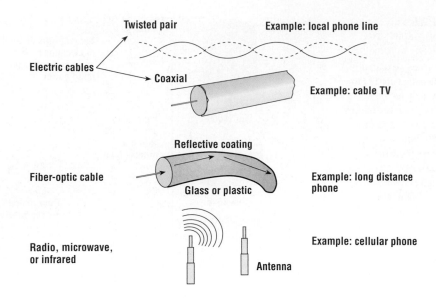

that can interfere with the signal. On the other hand, it is possible to put several twisted pairs into one cable at a relatively low cost. Sending portions of the message along each wire can increase the overall transmission speed.

Coaxial cables were designed to carry more information than twisted pairs, with lower chances of interference. *Coaxial cable* (often shortened to *coax*) consists of a central wire, surrounded by a nonconductive plastic, which is surrounded by a second wire. The second wire is actually a metallic foil or mesh that is wrapped around the entire cable. This shielding minimizes interference from outside sources. Cable television signals are transmitted on coaxial cables. Coax is capable of carrying more information for longer distances than twisted pair.

Fiber Optics

A relatively recent invention (early 1970s) in communication uses light instead of electricity. Because light generally travels in a straight line, it could be difficult to use for communication. Fiber-optic cable allows light to travel in straight lines but still be bent around corners. A fiber-optic cable consists of a glass or plastic core that is surrounded by a reflective material. A laser light (typically infrared) is sent down the cable. When the cable turns, the light is reflected around the corner and continues down the cable. Fiber-optic cable provides the advantages of high capacity with almost no interference. The limitation in using fiber is the higher cost of the cable and the cost of the connectors and interface cards that convert computer electrical signals into light. For example, NICs for coaxial or twisted-pair cables can be purchased for around $80, whereas NICs for fiber-optic lines that run directly to personal computers cost around $700 (in 2001). A study by Partha Mitttra and Jason Stark showed that even fiber-optic cables have limits. The theoretical capacity of a single fiber-optic cable is at least 100 terabits per second.[1]

Radio, Micro, and Infrared Waves

Radio, microwave, and infrared transmissions do not require cables. These communication methods are called **broadcasts**. Any receiver or antenna that lies in its path can pick up the signal. However, microwave and infrared transmissions require clear line-of-sight transmission. The major advantage of broadcast methods is portability. For example, computers can be installed in delivery vehicles to receive information from corporate headquarters. On a smaller scale, individuals can carry around laptops and PDAs and remain connected to the network. These computers can communicate with each other and with a central database via a broadcast network. For example, physicians in hospitals could carry small computers that would automatically receive information for each patient when the

[1] *The Economist,* June 28, 2001, or *Nature,* June 28, 2001.

A single fiber-optic line has thousands of times more capacity than an electrical line. Fiber connections are used for all long distance connections and connections between buildings.

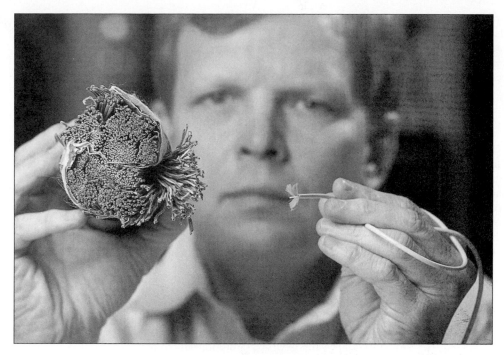

physician enters the room. Any instructions could be sent directly from the physician's computer to the nursing station. Commodity traders have also found portable computers and radio networks to be useful.

There are two potential drawbacks to broadcast media. First, it is more important to provide security for the transmissions. Second, broadcast transmissions carry a limited amount of data. The two problems are related. Because it is a broadcast method, the signals sent by one computer can be received by any other computer within range. There is no way to prevent other computers from physically receiving the signal.

The problem of limited capacity arises because only a small number of radio frequencies can be used to carry data. Most of the radio and television frequencies are already being used for other purposes. Figure 3.11 shows some of the major frequency allocations in the United States. The Federal Communications Commission (FCC) allocated the personal communication service (PCS) bands in late 1993 for use by personal communication devices such as laptop computers and personal digital assistants (PDAs). To provide these frequencies, the FCC had to take them away from existing users. Imagine what would happen if computers suddenly started sending information over the same radio frequency as that used by your favorite radio station. You would not be able to hear the voices on the radio, and the computers would miss most of their data because of the interference.

All governments allocate the frequency spectrum for various uses, such as radio, television, cellular phones, and garage door openers. The PCS frequencies were auctioned off to the highest bidders in 1994, raising more than $65 billion. The frequency problem is even more complicated when the signals might cross political boundaries. As a result, most broadcast telecommunications issues are established with international cooperation. Some of the overcrowding problems are being mitigated through the use of digital transmissions that cram more calls and more data into the same amount of frequency space.

Despite these problems, an increasing amount of business communication is being carried over radio networks. For example, from 1982 to 1993, the use of cellular (radio) phones expanded from almost zero to 13 million subscribers in the United States and 30 million worldwide in 70 countries. These numbers do not seem large compared to the worldwide estimate of 550 million telephone users, but the number of cellular phone users will undoubtedly increase. For starters, Motorola (a leader in radio communication) estimates that 40 million U.S. employees work away from the office for extended periods, as does 40 percent of

FIGURE 3.11

Electromagnetic frequency spectrum. Communication techniques are essentially the same for all media, because all waves physically have similar properties. However, the different frequencies affect the communication performance. Shorter wavelengths (higher frequencies) can carry more data. Some waves can travel longer distances. Others are more susceptible to interference. In any case, there are a finite number of frequencies available for communication. Hence, the frequency spectrum is allocated by governmental agencies.

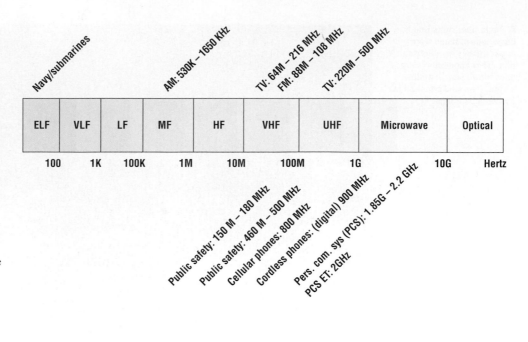

the global workforce. Additionally, in many cases, it is much easier to connect people over radio networks instead of installing cables.

Transmission Capacity

As shown in Figure 3.12, transmission capacity is often measured in millions of bits per second. Each transmission medium has a different maximum capacity. Twisted pair can be relatively fast for short distances, but fiber optic is substantially better for longer distances. Getting a faster Internet connection is primarily an issue of cost. Fiber-optic cable might also carry a high installation cost if there are no fiber optic connection points near your office.

The effect of the transmission capacity is shown in Figure 3.13. For small text and data files, the speed is not critical. Even slow dial-up lines can transfer a full page of text in a short time. The problem arises when you want to transfer more complex data like photos or even video. This figure shows why designing Web pages carefully is still so important. When over 75 percent of your clients are using dial-up lines, you need to limit pages to around 50,000 bytes, which takes at least 8 seconds to download. Most people will not wait more than 15 seconds for a page to load. Now you can see why Internet video is so bad. Even to handle video at broadband speeds of 1.5 mbps, site designers have to restrict the video to small sizes (one-fourth of a TV screen or smaller), and slower frame rates (as low as 15 frames per second). These two actions cut the video size by at least 1/8 (1/4 size * 1/2 frames). At that size, the 10 seconds of video could be sent in 10 seconds (80/8), which just barely matches the speed of the original video, and assumes that the viewer actually gets the full bandwidth.

Shared Connections

Figure 3.14 shows that transmission times become more important when more than two computers are involved, and when you want to send more than one item. For example, think about what will happen if you share a slow (2 mbps) wireless network with 10 other users—and everyone tries to retrieve a complex image at the same time. The networks are designed to handle multiple users, but heavy usage by a few people can slow down the connection for everyone.

Originally, most local area networks used shared lines; but as usage and data complexity have increased, firms have moved to switched networks. With a switched network, each

Managers are increasingly using wireless handhelds to communicate, share data, and access the Internet.

FIGURE 3.12

Transmission capacity. Fiber-optic cables have the greatest capacity and they are immune to most traditional interference. However, they are expensive to install and repair. Most firms use twisted-pair or wireless connections within buildings and fiber-optic cables to connect buildings. You can purchase almost any Internet connection speed that you are willing to pay for. Leased line rates are negotiable and depend on distance and degree of local competition.

Local Area Networks

Name	Format	Speed (mbps)
10Base-T	Twisted pair	10
100Base-T	Twisted pair	100
Gigabit Ethernet	Twisted pair	1,000
Wireless LAN	Wireless	11
Wireless LAN future	Wireless	54
LAN/fiber FDDI	Fiber optic	100
LAN/fiber ATM	Fiber optic	155
LAN/fiber future	Fiber optic	10,000

Internet Connections

Name	Format	Speed (mbps)	Estimated Cost
Dial-up	Twisted pair	0.05	$20/month
DSL	Twisted pair	1.5 down/0.13 up	$50/month
Cable modem	Coaxial	1.5 down/0.26 up	$50/month
Satellite	Microwave	1.5 down/0.05 up	$50/month
Wireless	Microwave	1.5	$70/month
Wireless/future	Microwave	20–50	
T1-lease	Twisted pair	1.544	$1,000–$2,000/month
T3-lease	Fiber optic	45	$10,000–$15,000/month
ATM	Fiber optic	155	negotiable
OC-3	Fiber optic	155	$72,000/month
OC-12	Fiber optic	622	
OC-48	Fiber optic	2,500	
OC-192/future	Fiber optic	10,000	

FIGURE 3.13

Importance of transmission capacity. Text is not a problem even for slow dial-up lines, but images and video can be slow even over relatively high-speed Internet connections.

	Text	Image	Video—10 sec
Bytes	10,000	500,000	15,000,000
Bits	80,000	4,000,000	120,000,000
	Seconds		
Dial-up 50 kbps	1.6	80	2400
DSL 1.5 mbps	0.05	2.67	80
LAN 10 mbps	0.008	0.4	12
LAN 100 mbps	0.0008	0.04	1.2
Gigabit 1 gbps	0.00008	0.004	0.12

FIGURE 3.14

Shared connections. Some networks rely on sharing the transmission medium with many users. Sharing means computers must take turns using the network. Sometimes one or two highly active users can slow down the network for everyone, so you will not really get the listed transmission capacity.

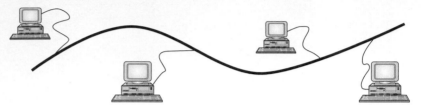

With shared connections, machines have to take turns, and congestion can slow down all connections.

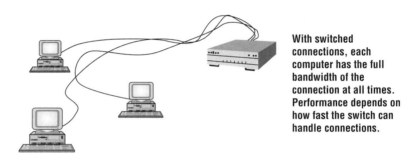

With switched connections, each computer has the full bandwidth of the connection at all times. Performance depends on how fast the switch can handle connections.

person has sole use of the wire run between the computer and the switch, providing faster throughput even for large numbers of users.

This issue can be particularly important for Internet connections. By nature, the Internet is a shared system—many links in the connections are shared lines. But consider two common broadband connections: DSL and cable modem. **Digital subscriber line (DSL)** is a system offered by phone companies, using the twisted-pair phone line into your house. **Cable modems** are shared Internet connections offered by the cable television company on a channel of the coaxial cable into your house. The DSL line is not shared between your house and the phone company. On the other hand, the cable modem connection between your house and the cable company is usually shared, so your performance might depend on the usage by your neighbors. Ultimately, the connections are shared once they reach the phone or cable company, so in a carefully designed network, there might not be much difference—since your ultimate performance will depend on all of the other connections on the Internet at that time.

Wireless radio connections always use a shared medium. Radio spectrum is very limited and it must be shared. In fact, advanced sharing techniques are responsible for the higher speeds that are available now. Figure 3.15 shows how modern wireless systems use spread spectrum techniques to utilize the available bandwidth as completely as possible for maximization of transmission capacity. All communications are broken into tiny packets that can be sent in a short time slot. At a given time, the transmitter searches for an open frequency. If all are being used, the transmitter waits for the next time slot and sends on an open frequency. The recipient monitors all allocated frequencies and identifies packets with its address.

FIGURE 3.15

Spread spectrum. Radio networks share the scarce airwaves by breaking communications into small packets that are sent at different frequencies and time slots. In a given time slot, if one frequency is not available, the transmitter shifts to the next frequency. If all frequencies are being used, the transmitter must wait for the next time slot.

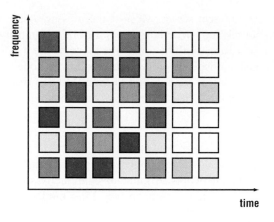

FIGURE 3.16

Connecting networks. Several challenges arise if you build an enterprise network. An enterprise network often connects many smaller networks established in different departments, buildings, or even nations. The hardware and software components must follow standards so they can communicate. An MIS team has to manage the overall structure to maximize efficiency, avoid duplication, and solve problems.

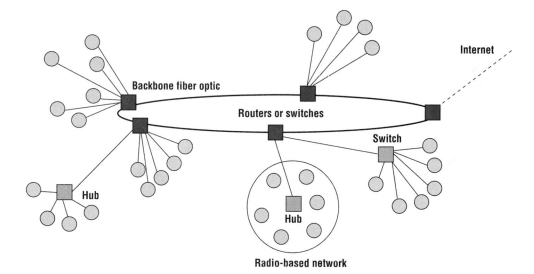

Connection Devices

To reduce overall traffic, larger organizations often find it beneficial to build the corporate network from a set of smaller networks. Both large and small companies use similar techniques to connect their networks to the Internet. Figure 3.16 shows a common configuration. Computers within a building or smaller area are linked into a hub, switch, or router. This interconnection device is then linked to the backbone, which is typically a fiber-optic line.

If you look at the physical box, it can be difficult to tell the difference between a hub, router, and switch. However, internally, they function quite differently, and you need to understand those differences to decide how a network should be configured. Hubs are the simplest connection devices. They essentially act like a giant junction box. Any device connected to a hub shares all of the lines with the other devices. It is just a mechanism to plug several computers together. Switches and routers actually examine every packet that passes through them and decide where to send each packet. They are actually specialized computers that can be programmed to identify network problems and intelligently route traffic to the fastest route.

Routers and switches are crucial to improving efficiency in large networks. In many respects, a router works like a post office. It examines the destination address of each packet of information and selects the best way to send that packet. Routers improve performance by choosing the path of the message and segmenting large networks into smaller pieces. For example, router segments might be assigned to each department of a large company, where each department has its own server. Most of the messages stay within the specific department, so they do not take up bandwidth across the entire company. Only messages that truly need to be sent to other areas will be transmitted outside the departmental segment. *Switches* perform a similar task but isolate communications down to one line. So your communication would have full use of a line for a period of time. Modern routers combine the function of both switching and routing to take advantage of both techniques.

Network Structure

Two primary methods are used to connect computers: shared-media networks and direct connections on switched networks. Arguments continually arise over which type of network is better, and often there is no one right answer. Most modern networks consist of both types of connections.

Shared-Media Networks

As shown in Figure 3.17, computers in a shared-media network can be connected to a common wire. They might also use the same radio frequency space. The main advantage of a shared-media network is that it is cheaper to install one wire (or share one frequency), than to run separate wires from each computer back to a central location. In many ways, a shared-media network is like a room full of people trying to talk to each other. The limitation of sharing the media (the air in the room) is that only one person or computer can talk at a time. As a result, *protocols* are needed to establish rules of behavior to avoid common problems. The protocols need to cover four situations: (1) providing a means to address each recipient and sender, (2) determining who is allowed to talk (initiate a conversation), (3) determining how long a single sender can talk at one time, and (4) specifying what to do if there is a *collision* when two machines (or people) try to talk at the same time.

Ethernet is one of the earliest protocols to resolve these problems. It has been standardized by several national and international standard-setting bodies so that a network can be built from equipment provided by different vendors. The Ethernet protocol is also known as CSMA/CD, which stands for *Carrier-Sense, Multiple-Access/Collision Detection.* In this system, any LAN card is allowed to transmit on the network, but first it must examine the media to see whether another card is currently transmitting (carrier-sense). If so, the second card must wait until the line is clear. Users are prevented from tying up the line for extended periods by restricting the length of time each card can transmit at any one time. One of the biggest drawbacks to CSMA/CD is that as the number of users increases, there will be more collisions. With many collisions, the computers end up spending more time detecting collisions and waiting than they do transmitting. It is also the reason why a high-speed medium is important to this method. The faster that every transmission can be sent, the sooner the line is clear and ready for the next user.

FIGURE 3.17

Shared-media (Ethernet) network. Each device is connected to a common transmission medium. Only one device can transmit at a time. Standards define when a device can transmit, how to specify a device, and how to tell whether the line is busy.

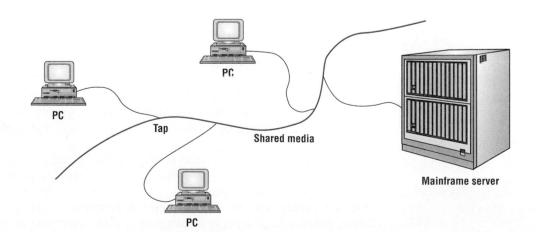

PC

PC

Tap

Shared media

Mainframe server

PC

Switched Networks

Switched networks originally evolved from the telephone system. Initially, each telephone had its own direct connection wire to the phone company switchboard. As shown in Figure 3.18, each computer has a connection to a switch. The switch is a specialized high-speed computer that examines each packet of data and transfers it to the appropriate destination. The performance of the network depends on the speed of the switch. In general, switches are faster than shared-media networks (such as those using hubs) because each computer gets full capacity on the line. But keep in mind that it often costs more money to install all of the cables.

Most modern networks are combinations of switched and shared-media. Within buildings and individual offices, where you have to run lines to each machine anyway, it makes sense to install a switch. Communications between buildings are carried over a shared-media connection—using fiber-optic cables.

Enterprise Networks

Many large companies have hundreds of local area networks. Connecting personal computers is only the first step in building a telecommunications system. The next step is to facilitate communication across the company and interconnect the LANs. A network that connects various subnetworks across a firm is called an *enterprise network.*

Several types of data need to be collected and shared throughout a company. Basic transaction-processing data such as accounting and HRM data need to be collected and aggregated for the firm. Management decisions and questions need to be communicated with all employees. Planning documents and forecasts are often prepared by interdisciplinary teams.

Although it is easy to agree that all computers in a company should be able to share data, several problems arise in practice. Various departments often use different hardware, software, and network protocols. It becomes more difficult to identify the cause of problems in a network as it becomes larger. Likewise, adding more components tends to slow down all transmissions. Network

FIGURE 3.18
Switched network. Each device is connected independently to a switch. The switch rapidly transfers each packet to the desired destination.

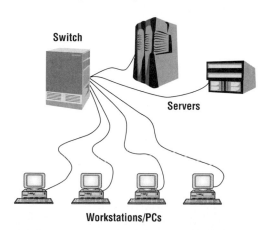

Switch

Servers

Workstations/PCs

Reality Bytes   DSL v Cable Modem

If you listen to the advertising, it sounds like you have many choices for high-speed Internet access. If you live in a major city, you might have two: cable modem from your local cable television company, or DSL from your local phone company. In many cases, you will have only one option. In many other cases, neither of these will be available. In these situations, you might consider the third choice: satellite. Older satellite connections only provided downloads; uploads ran through standard phone modems. Now, Starband provides bidirectional links, but with relatively low upload speeds. Satellite also has an inherent delay problem, known as latency, which is the time it takes for signals to travel the thousands of miles from earth to the satellite and back. This delay might not bother you—unless you play multiperson

online games. The cable companies and phone companies have been battling over mind share if not market share. Cable modem prices are generally lower and available in more locations. DSL speed is limited by distance from the main phone company connection. But DSL companies have been stressing that the last mile of cable is shared with your neighbors—with DSL that last mile is dedicated to your connection, so cable modem speeds can depend on the traffic of your neighbors. Of course, everyone shares all lines beyond either company, and the speed ultimately depends on the entire Internet and the sites being visited.

Source: Adapted from Shawn Young, "Choose a Cable Modem or DSL?" *The Wall Street Journal,* September 10, 2001.

FIGURE 3.19
Enterprise network. Switched networks within buildings are connected by shared-media fiber-optic cables. Distant offices and subsidiaries can be connected over the Internet.

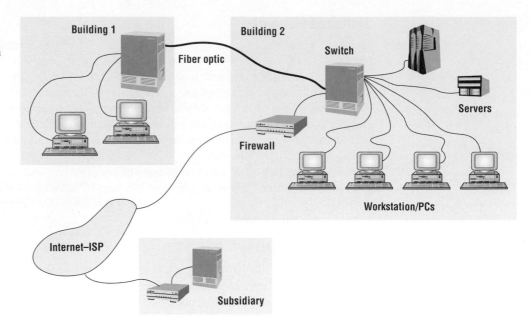

management issues multiply. Small tasks such as assigning usernames and maintaining passwords become major chores when there are thousands of users and hundreds of file servers. Security becomes increasingly complex, especially when corporate data is carried across public networks. Upgrading network components can become a nightmare, resulting in either complete replacement across the firm or incompatibilities between some divisions. Even simple network functions like e-mail can quickly bog down a system when there are 50,000 users.

Enterprise networking requires a combination of standards and special hardware and software to translate data from one system to another. It also requires investing in more network personnel to install, upgrade, and manage all of the components.

As shown in Figure 3.19, as enterprise networks spread across large distances, they tend to involve wide area networks. A *wide area network (WAN)* differs from a LAN because of the geographical distance that it covers. More specifically, a WAN involves links that are controlled by public carriers (e.g., telecommunication companies). Few individual firms can afford to build their own long-distance networks. Although some companies do have their own satellite connections, it is almost impossible for a company to install its own cables for any distance. Instead, you can lease lines from the phone company. It is possible, but expensive to lease point-to-point lines used only by your company. Today, it is often easier and cheaper to have each office connect to the Internet. The drawback is that data sent over the Internet is open and might be intercepted by others. In this case, you can install encryption software on each system to create a virtual private network (VPN). All of your Internet transmissions are automatically encrypted. Users see your network as one connected set of computers, regardless of their location.

Standards

The Need for Standards

Standards are important with networks. There are many different types of computers and various network types. Each computer and network company has its own idea of which methods are best. Without standards, there is no way to connect computers or networks produced by different vendors. Standards are also supposed to protect the buyers from obsolescence. If you install network equipment that meets existing standards, you should be able to buy products in the future that will work with it.

Unfortunately, there are many standard-setting organizations. Each major country has its own standards organization such as the American National Standards Institute (ANSI). There are several international organizations, such as ISO and the ITU (International Telecommunications Organization, renamed from CCITT) charged with defining computer and communication standards. Additionally, manufacturers of computers and telecommunications equipment try to define their own standards. If one company's products are chosen as a standard, they gain a slight advantage in design and production.

It is not likely that typical managers will be involved in the issues of setting and choosing communication standards. Yet, as a consumer, you need to be aware that there are many standards and sometimes variations on the standards. (In this industry, the word *standards* does not mean there is only one way to do something.) When you are buying telecommunications equipment, the goal is to purchase equipment that meets popular standards. It is not always easy to decide which standards will become popular and which ones will be abandoned.

A Changing Environment

Why are there so many standards? It would be far simpler if everyone could agree to use one standard and build products that are compatible. The problem with this concept is that technology is continually changing. Thirty years ago, phone companies never considered using digital transmission over fiber-optic cables, which is the dominant form of long-distance transmission used today.

As each technology is introduced, new standards are created. Yet, we cannot discard existing standards because it takes time for firms to convert to the new technology. Additionally, as manufacturers gain experience with a technology, they add features and find better ways to use the products. These alterations usually result in changes to the standards. An additional complication is that many companies are modifying their products at the same time. It is hard to determine in advance which changes are worthwhile and should be made standards.

The net result is that standards can be useful, but managers have to be careful not to rely too much on a standard. First, remember that even if two products support a standard, they still might not work together well. Second, if you choose a standard for your department or company, remember that technology changes. Corporate standards should be reevaluated every year or so to make sure they are still the best solution.

Internet TCP/IP Reference Model

If you want to understand the details of how the Internet works, it is best to begin with the TCP/IP reference model. As shown in Figure 3.20, the reference model breaks the process into four layers: application, transport, Internet, and subnet. Breaking the process into separate layers is critical to building large networks. Each layer can be handled independently of the others. For example, at the physical layer, replacing a wired connection with a wireless one should not affect any of the higher layers. The physical layer devices simply have to provide the same functionality to the Internet layer.

Notice that moving down, each layer takes the data from the prior layer and adds header and trailer information. This additional data is necessary for each layer to perform its function, but it means that more data must be transferred. For example, even if your physical connection can transmit data at 10 mbps, a 10-megabit file cannot be transferred in one second. Depending on the application and the network details, the overhead from the layers can be 20 percent or higher.

Subnet/Physical Layer

The purpose of the subnet or physical layer is to make the connection between two machines and physically transfer bits of data. It is directly related to hardware. There are standards to specify constraints on voltage, type of wire, frequency of signals, and sizes of physical connectors. Raw data bits are transferred at this stage. Many different technologies exist, including wireless, wired, and fiber-optic lines.

FIGURE 3.20
TCP/IP reference model. The model illustrates how data from an application like e-mail is turned into packet at the transport layer, routed to the destination at the IP layer, and physically transferred as bits at the physical layer.

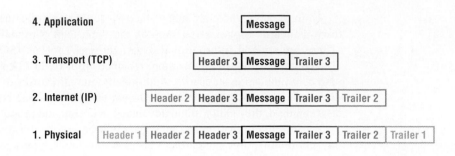

Internet/Network Layer

The Internet layer is concerned with routing messages to the appropriate location. In particular, it selects the appropriate path for a message in networks where there is a choice. Its main advantage is that it separates the higher layers from the physical transmission of data. The network layer handles connections across different machines and multiple networks. The Internet Protocol (IP) is the standard used in routing packets on the Internet network. With IP, each packet is treated independently of the others and each can follow a different route to the destination. Each machine must have a globally unique address, so a mechanism is established to assign numbers to machines. The current version of IP (IPv4) is creating problems because addresses are only 32 bits long—and the world is running out of numbers. The newer IPv6 standard supports 128-bit addresses, but it will take time to phase in the new system. Newer servers and hosts support the IPv6 protocol (e.g., Windows XP); but it will take time to update all of the routers on the Internet. In the meantime, most companies are using intermediate steps to allocate the IPv4 numbers.

Global standards are required to ensure compatibility of networks and efficient routing of data. The Internet Corporation for Assigned Names and Numbers (ICANN) and the Internet Engineering Task Force (IETF) are publicly run organizations in charge of establishing many of these standards. Both organizations are heavily dependent on volunteers and rely on public comments to design new standards.

Transport Layer

The transport layer is responsible for dividing the application data into packets and providing logical connections to the network. The transport control protocol (TCP) is commonly used on the Internet to handle these connections. TCP supports multiple applications at the same time by creating numbered ports. For example, e-mail is usually transferred through port 25, and Web data through port 80. TCP sends the data packet to the specified port on the desired machine. TCP on the host machine listens to these ports and sends the incoming data to the appropriate application server. TCP also monitors the packets to see if any are lost in transmission. If so, the recipient machine can request that the missing packet be resent, providing a highly reliable connection between two machines.

The Internet also supports the user datagram protocol (UDP) which is a highly simplified transport method. Most important, it does not guarantee that a packet will be transferred. Generally, users do not get to choose between TCP and UDP. This choice is made by the software developer at the network level. But why would anyone choose UDP when there is no assurance that the packets will be delivered? The main reason is speed. Because UDP is so simple, it adds only a tiny overhead to each packet, which makes it useful for large transfers of data, such as large files and streaming multimedia. If necessary, the application can check at the end to ensure that all data was transferred.

Application Layer

The application layer consists of tools and services for the user. Typical Internet applications include e-mail, file transfer (FTP), and Web browsing with the hypertext transfer protocol (HTTP). These systems work because developers have agreed to follow basic standards.

With the TCP/IP reference model, applications are responsible for incorporating authentication and compression. Not having a standard underlying method for handling security has caused some problems with TCP/IP. Few applications actually have any security, several incompatible variations of security systems have been created, and hackers have been able to write programs that attack the underlying, unprotected layers. Security is one of the main problems being addressed in IPv6 and Internet2.

The Internet

The Internet is a loose collection of computer networks throughout the world. It began as a means to exchange data among major U.S. universities (NSFnet of the National Science Foundation), and connections to various military organizations and U.S. defense suppliers (Arpanet of the Advanced Research Projects Agency). No one knows how many computers or networks are currently connected by the Internet. The numbers have been increasing exponentially since the early 1990s, so any number is likely to be wrong within a few days. To give you some idea of the Internet's astounding growth, in January 1993, there were 1.313 million host computers. In January 1994, there were 2.217 million hosts located in more than 70 countries. By January 1999, 4.757 million hosts were registered. In June 2001, 35.7 million domain names were registered. Current statistics are available at http://www.domainstats.com. Another 80 nations have e-mail access to the Internet. Remember that these are just registered servers. Millions more client computers are connected. In 1994, over 20 million people had access to at least e-mail services. As of mid-1994, commercial use (as opposed to university and government use) accounted for 50 percent of the Internet usage. International usage expanded so that since mid-1994, more than 50 percent of the networks on the Internet are located outside the United States. In 1998, Charles Lee from GTE estimated that by the year 2010 about 1 billion computers will be connected to the Internet. Increasingly, firms are talking about embedding Internet capabilities into common appliances.

Best estimates are that in 1998, consumers bought about $8 billion worth of goods over the Internet, which is a relatively small amount when compared to traditional sales. On the other hand, trade between businesses amounted to $43 billion.

What exactly is the Internet? At heart, the Internet is just a communication system for computers. It is defined by a set of standards that allow computers to exchange messages. The most amazing aspect of the Internet is that there really is no single person or group in charge. Anyone who wishes to connect a computer to the Internet simply agrees to pay for a communication link—via an Internet service provider (ISP), and to install communications hardware and software that supports the current Internet standard protocols. The person or company is given a base address that allows other computers to identify users on the new computer. Standards are defined by a loose committee, and addresses are controlled by another small committee. The committees are convened purely for the purpose of speeding the process; all decisions are up to the organizations connected to the network. Participation in the Internet is voluntary, and there are few rules, just standard practices and agreements. From a business or consumer viewpoint, there are two primary aspects to the Internet: establishing a connection and using the Internet.

How the Internet Works

The Internet is a communication system; it is a method of connecting computers together. So the first step in determining how the Internet works is to understand how your computer connects to others. As shown in Figure 3.21, the Internet has a hierarchy of service providers. Individuals pay a local **Internet service provider (ISP)** for access to the Internet. In turn, local ISPs pay an upstream *network service provider (NSP)* for access to their systems and features. Each connection must be made over a communication link. Local links are typically made over telephone wires, but cable companies also provide service over their coaxial lines. A few companies provide satellite connections. Most ISPs also utilize phone company lines to connect to their NSP, but they lease dedicated, full-time lines that provide

FIGURE 3.21

Internet connections. Each computer must be connected to others. The Internet has a connection hierarchy. Companies and individuals typically use phone company lines to connect to an ISP. The ISP connects to an NSP, which routes data over the high-speed backbone network to the destination NSP, down to the other ISP, and to the final computer. Each step may involve several computers.

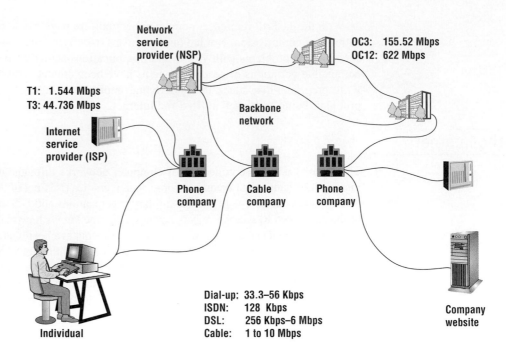

faster service. The largest NSPs also provide backbone service. That is, they route communications over their own fiber-optic lines that are installed across the United States. Increasingly, NSPs are also phone companies. Some started as phone companies and expanded into the Internet, others started with the Internet and gradually offered voice services.

You should understand the foundations of the Internet, because someone has to pay for each connection. Current pricing policies are to charge for the initial communication link and for the point-of-contact Internet service. For example, an individual pays the phone company for the local phone line and pays the ISP for basic services. The ISP pays the phone company for the next link and pays the NSP for access services. Figure 3.22 lists some of largest providers in each category. You can check with them for current prices and services.

The charging mechanism is similar for companies that wish to establish websites. The catch is that the costs are higher because the company needs faster communication services. The phone company charges more money for a faster link (e.g., $1,000–$2,000 per month for a T1 line). The ISP also charges more money for the increased traffic because it needs faster equipment and faster connections to the NSP.

The Internet service connection business is completely based on economies of scale. The high-speed fiber networks (OC3 and OC12) can handle a vast number of transmissions, but they carry a high fixed cost. The backbone providers make money by selling smaller increments of bandwidth to the ISPs, which incorporate a sufficient profit. Many of the NSPs are backbone providers and increasingly they also offer ISP services.

Internet Features

As a giant communication system, the Internet offers some advantages. But all features are available only because they are offered by the owners of the computers that are attached to the Internet. Some organizations offer free services; others charge for them. There are three basic types of services: (1) mail, (2) access to data and to computer time, and (3) electronic commerce.

Before you can use any of these services, you must be able to locate a particular computer. Technically, every computer is given a unique number, assigned by the ISP. Originally, the numbers were 32-bit numbers, typically written as four bytes separated by dots. For example, 161.6.28.18 was assigned to a specific machine. However, 32-bit numbers will identify a maximum of 4 billion machines, fewer in practice because some values cannot be

FIGURE 3.22

Leading Internet providers. There are thousands of ISPs and cable companies. This list provides only some of the large companies in each category.

Backbone Providers

AT&T	Sprint
GTE	Worldcom/MCI
Qwest	

Network Service Providers

AT&T	Qwest
Cable & Wireless	Sprint
IBM	UUNet

Phone Companies

Regional Bell operating companies (RBOCs)
Competitive local exchange carriers (CLECs)

Cable Companies

AT&T
Cablevision
Regional

Satellite

Direct Satellite
Starband

Leading Internet Service Providers

America Online
Microsoft Network
EarthLink
AT&T WorldNet

assigned. Hence, an Internet committee designed a new numbering system consisting of 128 bits, which allows for more than 1,000 numbers to be assigned to every person likely to live on the planet. The new system is known as IP v6 and will be phased in gradually. Every computer or device has a unique number. If you know its number, you can send e-mail or retrieve data—whatever the owner allows.

Of course, numbers are difficult for most people to remember. So, the Internet utilizes a system where a **domain name server (DNS)** converts names to numbers. Anyone can apply for a name and pay a nominal fee (e.g., $70 for two years) to use that name. Of course, names must be unique, so sometimes disagreements arise over popular names. Names are followed by a suffix such as .com, .edu, or .gov. Several organizations have suggested adding more suffixes, arguing that it would provide for more possible names. One interesting feature of the names is that each country is given a specific suffix. Some of the countries sell names using their unique suffix. For example, the small nation of Tuvalu allows companies to use its suffix (.tv) for a fee.

Internet Mail

One of the most popular features on the Internet is electronic mail. Virtually every machine on the Internet is capable of sending and receiving mail for registered users. As long as all participants have the appropriate software, they can send files, pictures, even sound as their message. One company even sells an Internet "phone" system that enables two people to talk to each other using the Internet links. Another sells a service that enables you to transfer real-time video images—as long as both sides have a video camera and appropriate software.

The Internet offers two other services similar to e-mail: discussion groups (listserv) and newsgroups (news). Discussion groups send electronic journals to anyone who "subscribes" to the list. Typically, there is no fee for subscribing. Editors control the "publication" of a group. Comments are sent first to the editor, who decides whether to include them. Newsgroups are similar, but more open. Anyone can submit a comment at any time to a newsgroup, which represents a giant, global bulletin board. There are thousands of established topics, ranging from science to alternative lifestyles to anything you can imagine. The comments are usually uncensored and might or might not be accurate. Some people have found newsgroups useful for addressing complex computer problems. With millions of people on the Internet, there is a good chance that someone else has already encountered your problem and might have a solution. Newsgroups and websites provide useful tools to managers, especially to small business managers who have limited resources.

Although messages on the Internet tend to be uncensored, be careful. If you somehow manage to insult a few thousand people, you could find yourself immersed in hundreds of thousands of mail messages that overwhelm your computer account. Also, avoid using the Internet for personal use while working for a company. In the United States, companies have the legal right to monitor your messages. In extreme situations, the computer manager can revoke accounts from people who abuse the system. Even more important, some hiring managers have been known to search the Internet for messages that you posted—to check you out before making a job offer.

Access to Data on the Internet

Anyone with a computer connected to the Internet has the ability to give other users access to data stored on that computer. Read that sentence again. The owner has control over the data. Unless someone specifically grants you access to data, it is basically illegal to try and get the data, or even to use the person's computer.

The World Wide Web is a first attempt to set up an international database of information. As discussed in the appendix to Chapter 1, today's challenge lies in finding the information you want. Sites are built as pages that contain links to other pages. Making a choice in one page will usually connect you to another computer on the Internet and bring up its WWW pages. From there you can look at library catalogs, pictures, or whatever information is provided by that Web server. The initial versions of the Web were developed at CERN, the European particle-physics laboratory, where the staff wanted to make it easier for researchers to share their work.

The easiest access to the Web is with a browser such as Internet Explorer or Netscape. Browsers present a page of information that contains links to other pages on the Web. The page can contain text, graphics, video, and sound clips. By selecting highlighted words, you can move to other systems, trace topics, and transfer data. Pictures are displayed automatically, and most operations can be completed by selecting items with a mouse.

Because the Internet is so large and is growing rapidly, it can be difficult to find useful data. Additionally, organizations are constantly changing the type of information they provide. The data available is constantly changing, making it impossible to provide an up-to-date listing. So how do you find anything on the Internet?

Search engines, offline advertising, and word-of-mouth are the most popular methods of finding information on the Internet. Several search engines exist, and new ones arrive every day. Most have their own quirks and strengths; but no engine indexes more than about 30 percent of the content on the Web.

Reality Bytes | Internet 2

Almost anyone who uses the Internet complains about the speed. As the number of users increases, and people use more audio and video, delays will get worse. The limited capacity of the current Internet also makes it difficult to display high-quality images of products. Universities are currently busy building a new Internet connecting the schools at much higher speeds; from 150 to 650 mbps. Technology companies are building routers and technologies to support this Internet II. While it is not yet available for commerce, the tools created will eventually be used to build a new network. The one catch is that these technologies will require more network capacity—particularly fiber-optic connections. Fortunately, firms installed huge amounts of capacity in the 1990s. The major cost is access to the land and digging the trenches. The marginal cost of additional fibers is low. Global Crossing, Level 3 communications, and 360Networks installed nearly 100 million miles of fiber. Consequently, as much as 90 percent of the fiber in the world is unused (dark). The biggest problem that remains is the last mile. The high-speed services will not be useful until better connections are available to individual houses. The current monopoly power maintained by the local phone companies has kept prices up and slowed the availability of high-speed services.

Source: Adapted from Michael S. Malone, "Internet II: Rebooting America," *Forbes,* September 10, 2001.

One of the biggest issues on the Internet is identifying reliable data. Anyone can say almost anything on a Web page, but that does not make it true. Problems tend to arise in areas like medicine and finance. A healthy dose of skepticism is required when retrieving information from an open network. Reputation of the source becomes an important factor.

Internet 2

Originally, the U.S. government funded much of the Internet design and development. By 1995, the U.S. government had discontinued almost all funding, and the Internet was largely financed and controlled by private organizations. From 1994, the commercial use of the Internet increased exponentially. In 1996, 34 university participants decided that they needed faster connections (the number of participants expanded to 100 in 1999). With the support of the government and industry, they began creating Internet 2 (http://www.internet2.edu). When the original Internet was developed, most traffic was simple text, and the bulk of the communications were via e-mail. There was little need for high-speed connections, and delays in delivering e-mail did not matter since most people did not read their mail immediately.

The two most important proposed features of Internet 2 are high-speed connections and quality-of-service provisions. The overall objective is to provide a transmission network that can support full-speed video and other high-bandwidth applications. To understand the change, consider that most existing "high-speed" Internet connections are in the range of 1 mbps to 50 mbps. The Internet 2 calls for gigabit connection points.

A related, but more fundamental change is the ability to specify a desired level-of-service quality. Currently, if traffic increases on the Internet, all communications slow down. This situation is annoying but not troublesome for simple tasks like sending e-mail. On the other hand, full video transfer requires a constant minimum level of transmission capacity. So participants need a mechanism to tell all components that a specific set of messages should take priority to receive a certain level of service. Some people have suggested that the system should enable participants to pay a fee to gain their desired levels of service, for each type of message. For example, basic e-mail messages would be free if there is no rush in delivering them. But to reserve a time slot for videoconferencing, participants would pay an additional fee. Then all of the Internet 2 components would give the video packets a higher priority. So far, there has been no agreement on whether additional fees should be charged, or on how the quality-of-service issues can be resolved. Although the system is being designed for academic and government users, the industry participants (e.g., Cisco) ultimately intend to transfer any useful technologies to the commercial Internet. Businesses could find many uses for high-speed connections and service-quality guarantees. For starters, better video transfer may finally open the way for desktop videoconferencing to replace travel to meetings.

FIGURE 3.23
Mobile commerce.
Wireless connections
offer new capabilities,
such as e-mail and
Internet browsers
on cell phones.

Wireless Networks and Mobile Commerce

Beginning with cell phones in the 1990s people and businesses have become fascinated with wireless communication. Wireless Internet and mobile commerce have the potential to revolutionize the Internet, business, and society. Technologically, wireless is different from the traditional Internet in only two ways: (1) the transmission medium is microwave radio, and (2) the client devices are smaller with smaller screens and less computing power. Yet, wireless connections open thousands of new possibilities. The client devices can consist of anything from enhanced cell phones, such as the device shown in Figure 3.23, to PDAs and digital tablets. It is highly likely that the functions of these devices will converge to form some type of digital notepad with Internet and cell phone capabilities. Some new cell phones even have digital cameras built in, offering the possibility that all of your data needs can be handled through one small device.

To date, the wireless communication presents the greatest challenges. The base cell phone network is too slow to support most applications. In most places, data transfers on cellular frequencies at the rate of 14.4 kbps. The 3G system (third generation cell phone) is being designed to handle data at speeds from 56 kbps to 2 mbps. The problem, as anyone with a cell phone knows, is the limited coverage area offered by wireless connections. Although major cities offer reasonable coverage, cell phones often have trouble deep within buildings, and in smaller cities and rural areas. While you might not be concerned about the need to establish a wireless Internet connection in the backwoods, what happens if you rely on the system for purchases, and you end up in a town that does not support your system?

Some of the more interesting possibilities of m-commerce come from the ability to use the phone to find and pay for virtually anything you might need. Rather than rely on credit cards or cash, your cell phone could record all of your transactions, and give you complete instantaneous access to your data. But an incredibly reliable and secure system must exist before consumers will trust it.

Another interesting possibility for m-commerce comes from the ability to use location to identify potential customers. Figure 3.24 shows that it is relatively easy to identify a person's location based on the way the cellular system works using signal strength and triangulation. In fact, the federal government requires that cell phone systems provide caller location within

Reality Bytes   **Third Generation (3G) Cell Phones**

First-generation cell phones were analog technology with limited features. The second generation switched to digital transmissions on the PCS wavelengths. But European nations used a different standard (GSM) than the United States. The third generation (3G) was designed to add substantially better data and Internet connections to cell phones. Speeds of 2G phones are often less than 20 kbps. Speeds for 3G are designed to be around 2 mbps. But 3G phones and networks have been delayed many times. In the meantime, several companies began shipping wireless products for local area networks. Following the 802.11b standard, the WiFi network hubs were designed for home or business use in small areas. The systems operate on a special frequency with limited power, so no communication license is needed to install an access point or hub that costs no more than a few hundred dollars. The systems nominally operate at 11 mbps. By installing a special antenna, the range of the hubs can be increased. Consequently,

people in the United States. and Europe are installing hubs in their homes. As the user moves, the system switches seamlessly to the next hub. If one of the hubs is connected to the Internet, then everyone within range of one of the hubs has access. The system works much like the cell phone system but in a much smaller area. Of course, if enough people have hubs, it is possible to cover a substantial area. Some sites offer suggestions on how to expand the range up to a kilometer using low-technology (cheap) devices like a Pringle's potato chip can. On the other hand, obtaining Internet access requires at least one hub-owner to pay for a permanent high-speed Internet connection. More advanced versions of the hubs can be configured to require a username and password, so people walking by do not automatically gain access to the network.

Source: Adapted from Robert S. Duncan, "The Skeptic: Is WiFi Why 3G Just Keeps Fading?" *The Wall Street Journal,* September 8, 2001.

FIGURE 3.24

Location knowledge in m-commerce. Businesses could contact potential customers on learning their location through the wireless system.

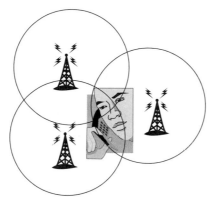

a couple hundred feet—primarily for use in 911 emergency calls. But the wireless providers can easily make this data available to anyone.

Think about the business opportunities that this system could provide, even from the perspective of a consumer. As you walk into a mall, you could enter your shopping list into a browser on your phone, which would contact all of the local stores for prices and availability and then provide a local map and directions to each item. You could enter notes and make your selection through the browser, then press a couple of keys and purchase the items. Similarly, some companies have proposed a system that would automatically notify you when a "buddy" is within a certain range of your phone, such as in the next store.

Businesses would have even more opportunities to collect data on customers, such as sending advertising to your phone and tracking the number of browsers versus buyers. But marketing systems would have greater knowledge of exactly what products and features each customer wants. For instance, the systems could offer a minisurvey to each customer who chooses to buy a competitor's product to find ways to improve products. Of course, the privacy aspects are scary. They will be examined in Chapter 5.

Global Telecommunications

Business firms in the 1990s are becoming more dependent on international markets. This internationalization increases the demands on the telecommunications system. The international transmission of data is becoming part of the daily business routine. A manufacturing company may have factories in several different countries, with the headquarters located in yet another country. Supplies have to be sent to factories. Finished and intermediate products have to be tracked. Customer demands have to be followed in each country. Quality control and warranty repair information have to be followed from the supplier through the factory and out to the customers. Financial investments have to be tracked on stock markets in many countries. Different accounting and payroll rules have to be provided for each country. Basic accounting and financial data have to be available to management at any time of day, in any part of the organization.

Creating networks across international boundaries creates many problems. Some of the complications are technical, some are political or legal, and others are cultural.

Technical Problems

The biggest technical complication is that each country may have its own telecommunications standards. For example, in the western European nations, the telephone systems are managed by governmental agencies called postal telephone (PTT) companies. Because PTTs are publicly run, national governments have a habit of insisting that communication equipment be purchased from manufacturers within their own nation. Despite the standards, there are still technical incompatibilities among the various nations.

In developing nations, the communications equipment may be antiquated. The older equipment will not be able to handle large amounts of data transfers, and there may be an unacceptable number of errors. Also, the government-controlled power supplies may not be reliable enough to run computers and network equipment.

One possible way to avoid the public telecommunications hassles is to use microwave transmissions through satellites. This approach can be more reliable but can be expensive unless you have huge amounts of data to transfer. For developing nations located in the southern hemisphere, there may not be adequate satellite coverage. Many of the satellite channels available to developing nations are used and controlled by the individual governments. It is generally not economically feasible to put up a new satellite, and most governments would object if you attempted to bypass their control.

To transmit more than simple text and numbers, there are more potential problems to consider. The United States, Europe, and Pacific Rim nations all have different video standards. Televisions made for the U.S. market, therefore, will not function in Europe. If a company creates a multimedia marketing presentation in the United States, it will probably be difficult to show it to clients in France. These incompatibilities are about to get worse with the introduction of high-definition television (HDTV) or digital television. Each of the national groups is working with a different technique.

Legal and Political Complications

Some important problems can be created when a firm wants to transmit information across national boundaries. These transfers are called **transborder data flows (TBDFs).** The problem arises because the information has value to the sender. Because it has value, some governments have suggested that they would like to impose a tariff or tax on that value. Besides the cost of the tariff, the issue raises the possibility that the national governments may want to monitor the amount and type of data being transferred. Most businesses are reluctant to allow anyone that much access to their information. Some countries go further—for example, France made it illegal to encrypt data.

Another important issue revolves around typical marketing data about customers. It is common for marketing departments to maintain huge databases. These databases contain customer names, addresses, phone numbers, estimated income levels, purchases, and other marketing data. Problems have arisen because the western European nations have much stricter laws concerning privacy than does the United States. In most European nations, it is illegal to sell or trade customer data to other companies. It must also be stored in protected files that cannot be seen by unauthorized employees or outsiders. In most cases, it is the responsibility of the company to prove it is meeting the requirements of the law. In many cases, this requirement means that customer data must be maintained on computers within the original nation. Also, this data cannot then be transmitted to computers in other countries. As a result, the multinational company may be forced to maintain computer facilities in each of the nations in which it does business. It also needs to impose security conditions that prevent the raw data from being transmitted from these computers.

There is one more important political issue involving international computer centers. Many nations, especially the developing nations, change governments quite often, as well as abruptly. There are many nations where terrorist activities are prevalent. Often times, large multinational companies present tempting targets. Because computer centers tend to be expensive, special security precautions need to be established in these countries. Probably the most important step is to keep the computer center away from public access. Several U.S. security specialists publish risk factors and suggested precautions for each country. They also provide security analysis and protection—for a fee.

A host of other political complications affect any multinational operation. For example, each nation has different employment laws, accounting rules, investment constraints, and local partnership requirements. Most of these can be surmounted, but they usually require the services of a local attorney.

Cultural Issues

All of the typical cultural issues can play a role in running multinational computer networks. The work habits of employees can vary in different nations. It may be difficult to obtain qualified service personnel at some times of day or night. These issues can be critical for computer networks that need to remain in operation 24 hours a day. In many nations, it is still considered inappropriate to have female managers when there are male subordinates. Collecting information may be exceedingly difficult or even culturally forbidden. In some countries, you will lose a customer if you try to obtain marketing data such as age and income.

In some nations, the connections between suppliers and customers are established by culture. For instance, in Japan, distribution of products is handled by only a few large firms. These companies have established relationships with the suppliers and retail outlets. In any country, it can be difficult for an outside firm to create a relationship between suppliers and customers. Trying to build computer networks with the various companies could cause severe repercussions. The established firms may think you are trying to steal their knowledge or information.

Comment

Creating international data networks can lead to many problems. There is no easy solution to many of these problems. However, international networks do exist and they will increase in the next few years. In many cases, firms have to operate in the international environment in order to succeed. There is no choice. The company must build international telecommunications networks.

As the European Union increases the amount of interdependence between western and eastern European nations, there will be even more reasons for companies to operate in many nations. The same holds true for the conversion of the Eastern European nations to market economies. The companies that take the lead in international computer networks will face many problems, but if they succeed, they will create the foundation necessary to be the leaders in their industry.

Summary

One of the most important concepts in MIS is the necessity of sharing data. Networks today are based on the Internet protocols, and provide data transfers as well as applications through Web browsers. Networks are used to send messages (e-mail), share experiences (discussion groups and Web sites), schedule meetings (electronic calendars), and share teamwork.

Advances in the cell phone and wireless industries are bringing a convergence of phones and data access through wireless network connections. Wired networks still form the backbone of our networks and provide better connections and faster data transfers. Internet costs are determined by the local phone companies that control the pricing of the last mile, and by the long-distance companies that own the nationwide fiber-optic network. To establish a business connection to the Internet (to run a server), you need to lease a communication line from a local provider (in most cases the phone company), and also pay an ISP for access to the Internet. Higher-capacity connections cost more money, but economies of scale make it profitable for the large providers to resell access to smaller businesses.

The telecommunications facilities and prices on which we rely in industrialized nations are not always available in other nations. Additionally, there are incompatibilities between equipment produced for various nations. Political restrictions are another source of complications when transferring data across international boundaries.

A Manager's View

All workers need to communicate, both through formal channels with reports and informal conversations with other workers throughout the company. Telecommunication systems are used to remove location as a factor in management and decisions.

As a manager, you need to understand several issues about how the Internet works. As the Internet and e-commerce mature, regulations are changing and businesses will be asked to create new services and provide more controls.

Key Words

broadcasts, *90*
cable modems, *94*
digital subscriber line (DSL), *94*
domain name server (DNS), *103*
e-mail, *82*
file transfer protocol (FTP), *121*
groupware, *85*
hypertext markup language (HTML), *119*

Internet service provider (ISP), *101*
intranet, *84*
local area networks (LANs), *81*
network interface card (NIC), *88*
newsgroup, *84*
packets, *87*
peer-to-peer networks, *88*
portable document format (pdf), *120*

scalability, *88*
server farm, *88*
standards, *98*
transborder data flows (TBDFs), *108*
voice over Internet protocol (VoIP), *87*

Website References

Financial News and Quotes

Big Charts	www.bigcharts.com
Bloomberg	www.bloomberg.com
Dun & Bradstreet	www.dnb.com
Dow Jones	www.dowjones.com
Financial Data Services	www.dataonfindata.com
Global Financial Data	www.globalfindata.com
Reuters	www.reuters.com
SEC Edgar	www.sec.gov/edgarhp.htm
StockPoint	investor.stockpoint.com
Thomson	www.thomsonfn.com
Wall Street Journal	wsj.com

Discount Online Trading

Ameritrade	www.ameritrade.com
CSFBdirect	www.csfbdirect.com
E*Trade	www.etrade.com
Datek	www.datek.com
Fidelity	www.fidelity.com
Quick & Reilly	www.quickandreilly.com
Charles Schwab	www.schwab.com
Fees and comments	www.sonic.net/donaldj

Additional Reading

Borzo, Jeanette. "At Last, European Telecom Gets Competitive." *Computerworld,* February 16, 1999. [Competition in telecommunications spreads to Europe.]

"The Capacity of Optical Fibre." *The Economist,* June 28, 2001. [Theoretical capacity of fiber-optic cables.]

"The Internet, Untethered." *The Economist,* October 13, 2001. [Special section on wireless issues with examples from Japan.]

Kahn, J.M., and K.P. Ito. "Communications Technology: A bottleneck for optical fibres." *Nature,* June 28, 2001, pp. 1007–1009. [Theoretical capacity of fiber-optic cables.]

Kahn, Robert E. "The Role of Government in the Evolution of the Internet." *Communications of the ACM,* August 1994, pp. 15–19. [Early days of the Internet.]

Kurose, James F., and Keith W. Ross, *Computer Networking: A Top-Down Approach Featuring the Internet.* Addison Wesley Longman: Boston, 2001. [Technical details on networking and TCP/IP.]

"Putting It in Its Place." *The Economist,* August 11, 2001. [Special report on how the Internet still depends on geography and location.]

Radding, A. "Leading the Way, the Wireless 25." *Computerworld ROI* 1, no. 4, September/October 2001. [Lead article in a special issue on wireless implementations in business.]

Wiggins, R. "How the Internet Works." *Internet World,* 8 (10), 1996. [Basic explanation of terms and connection points.]

Waltner, C. "Meet Your Connection." *Fortune Technology Review,* Summer 2001, pp. 59–66. [Discussion of business Internet connection costs and options.]

Review Questions

1. How are networks used to share data?
2. Why do businesses use networks to share hardware?
3. What is the value in sharing calendars electronically?
4. List the main components of a network.
5. List the types of transmission media that are available. How do they compare in transmission rates and cost?
6. What are the main advantages and drawbacks to wireless networks?
7. Explain the concept of an enterprise network.
8. Why are standards so important in networks?
9. In what way have phones and computers converged? Why is this convergence occurring?
10. How does the Internet work? What type of service do you need to set up a Web server and how much will it cost?
11. What applications might exist for mobile commerce? Why would people use Internet access instead of just a voice call?
12. Why is Internet service so slow at your house (apartment)?
13. What is the Internet 2 and how will it affect businesses?
14. What problems arise with global telecommunications?

Exercises

1. Find a hub or switch and build a small network. If available, connect it to the Internet. Keep notes on the steps you took to build the network.
2. Using the Internet, find at least two software packages that will back up data across a LAN. Briefly explain how the software functions and what components need to be installed. Estimate the price of the software for a network of four servers and 100 clients.
3. Find at least three e-mail packages and build a table that compares the features and costs of the packages. Try to include an estimate of the number of accounts the systems can realistically handle as well as the maintenance efforts involved.
4. Do some research on the current state-of-the-art in storage area networks (SANs). Briefly describe their purpose and how they work. What is the largest installation you can find? What are the data transfer rates on the network? What are the distance limits?

5. Research the current status of 3G for cellular phones. In what countries is 3G available? What features are provided? What are the data transfer rates?

6. Identify the primary organizations in charge of establishing standards for the Internet. Provide the name of the organization, its location, and its current president/leader.

7. Assume you want to start an e-business. What steps do you have to take to obtain and establish a domain name for the business? How much will it cost?

Rolling Thunder Database

8. Design a network for the Rolling Thunder Bicycle Company. Identify who will need access to the network; how many workstations you will need (and where to place them); and the data, input forms, and reports users will need. Using the existing data, estimate the storage requirements and transmission needs. Specify how changes and growth will affect the type of network needed.

9. Describe how the Internet could be used to increase sales at Rolling Thunder Bicycles.

10. Rolling Thunder Bicycles wants to expand international sales. What changes would need to be made to the application? What problems would you expect to encounter, and how would you overcome these potential problems?

11. What network problems would you encounter in a manufacturing environment?

Specialty Retail

Introduction and Context

The specialty retail industry consists of a group of companies focusing on a particular type of merchandise. Goods and products vary from casual apparel to cookware, and electronic high-tech merchandise. Because the industry is diverse, it generally has mixed operating prospects. Several well-managed retailers have posted solid gains in spite of the economic malaise that has punished the financial markets since 2000. However, the prospect of an economic recovery and growth has kept consumer confidence levels from plunging.

The 2001 recession made consumers more value-conscious. Hence, the successful specialty retailer must understand and cater to its customers' needs while maintaining competitive prices. Furthermore, specialty retailers must differentiate themselves from the competition. Typically, they promote the store name as a brand in itself in order to steal market share away from rivals. And several retailers have dropped all other brand names to launch their own private labels. For instance, Intimate Brands' Victoria's Secret offers its own perfume, and The Gap sells its own store music.

Many specialty retailers have entered the online market, though the industry is still in its infancy as far as the Internet is concerned. The jury is still out on which retail markets are most conducive to online shopping and which should be left for conventional methods. Costs for companies to enter the online market is high—many Internet ventures that have dipped into this medium have seen their business plans go belly up as the dot-com bubble burst in early 2000.

With the economy's descent into a recession, the reluctance of skittish consumers to spend money promises to intensify price competition that will likely accelerate changes to the retail landscape. Following the attacks of September 11, retailers saw their sales weaken amid uncertainty in the minds of consumers. A lot of the plans and purchases people were going to make without a second thought are now given a second thought. This decline in purchases was confirmed with the weakest holiday season in a decade.

Nevertheless, the nation's leading operators are expected to accelerate market share gains and those with a product mix of essentials such as food, pharmaceuticals, and other consumables will experience the greatest stability. Meanwhile, retailers whose product mix is weighted toward discretionary items will suffer. Other retailers, those in the midst of strategic repositioning efforts or addressing infrastructure flaws, have seen their prospects dim.

All retailers will suffer in a recession, but there is little concern about long-term prospects for Wal-Mart, Kroger, The Home Depot, Lowe's, Walgreens, Family Dollar, and others who lead their respective channels. Analysts upgraded several of these companies the week after the terrorist attacks.

One important trend affecting large specialty retailers looking to merge with each other comes from the federal government. The Federal Trade Commission has blocked two retail mergers in the past couple of years, one of which was the proposed merger of specialty retailer Office Depot with Staples. This type of restriction has helped keep specialty retailers from monopolizing the niche markets they serve.

Financial Analysis

Stock/Investment Outlook

Given the recession and rising unemployment, many retailers will likely experience near-term weakness, but things should start to look up starting in the second half of 2002 as the economic recovery kicks in. Economists forecast that 2002 will be marked by transition from a recession mode to a recovery mode. Since the September 11, 2001, terrorist attacks, specialty-retail stocks have rallied, registering a 32.45% gain (as of January 1, 2002) because of an anticipated economic recovery. For investors, the problem is that the corners of retailing that are likely to do best are already priced accordingly. The trick will be to wait for buying opportunities to come around, just as savvy bargain-hunters wait for big sales in the last few shopping days before Christmas.

Some specialty retail segments that performed well in 2001—home furnishing and consumer electronics—should also see decent sales, as shoppers continue to stay close to home. Investors should be keeping an eye on companies that dominate their retailing niche and are taking market share, as well as those that have a specific catalyst, like implementing a better distribution system or building an efficient logistic network, to improve operations.

The future looks brightest for those companies poised to take advantage of the recent trends in specialty retailing: superstores and "category killers." By attempting to stock every item in a certain line of merchandise, superstores/category killers gain the ability to charge really low prices. Office Depot is an example of a category killer in the office supply area. Other examples of category killers include Toys "R" Us and Circuit City.

Those large specialty retailers poised to become the leaders in their category have the best investment outlook. As far as small specialty retailers go, those with the best outlook are retailers who seem to be serving a new trend or increasing need.

Potential/Prospective for Growth

One advantage specialty retailers will always have is that their fortunes do not necessarily move in step with the overall economy. By definition, a specialty retailer sells products only in

Summary Valuation of the Special Retail Industry	
Stock market value as a multiple of revenue	1.02
Price/Earnings multiple	22.8
Price/Assets multiple	3.48
Stock market value as multiple of net worth	4.49
Revenue per employee	$258,800
Net profit per employee	13,600
Net after-tax profit	5.00%
EBITDA as a percent of revenue	10.20%
Assets needed to produce $1 of revenue	$0.37
Market value + total debt/revenue	1.44
Net profit as a percent of net worth	15.10%
Total debt as a percent of total assets	18.20%
Total debt as a percent of revenue	6.80%
Stock market value/EBITDA	13.36
P/E ratio relative to S&P 500	1.35
Average annual dividend yield	0.60%

specific categories serving niche markets. Therefore, a specialty retailer can make money as long as its niche market is profitable, regardless of the state of the economy as a whole. Likewise, a good economy is not enough to guarantee success for a specialty retailer.

Competitive Structure

Specialty retail stores are normally thought of as small stores competing for a small piece of the pie, the majority of which is owned by a few large players. While this statement is sometimes true, it depends on your definition of a specialty retailer. Certainly businesses such as Toys "R" Us, Staples, The Limited, and Radio Shack sell primarily one type of merchandise, yet they are large businesses. Therefore, specialty retailers can appear on both ends of the spectrum in size.

Consider the small specialty retailers. These can be either a national chain or mom-and-pop (or regional) stores. If it is a national chain, it is usually because there is a nationwide market for the niche products they sell. Generally, one or a few large specialty retailers have the lion's share of the market. An example might be the smaller FAO Schwartz stores competing against Toys "R" Us. Smaller retailers generally compete (especially against category killers) by focusing on something slightly different from the large category killer they are up against. For instance, they may have only high-end (or more expensive) merchandise. FAO Schwartz, for example, focuses on more expensive (and more profitable) merchandise, while Sharper Image's toys are geared toward adults.

The large retailers have found that they can only remain on top by never resting on their laurels and carefully following overall retail trends such as everyday value pricing (e.g., Home Depot). Some retailers seem happy to give up the leadership in order to retain their profitability. Borders Books and Music and Barnes and Noble are two examples of bookstore chains that are not trying to capture the other's customers by undercutting each other in prices. Therefore, the competitive structure depends on the niche market you are examining. In general, there are a few large players taking up a large share of the market, with the rest of the retailers fighting for the remainder, which often comprises more than half of the market.

Technological Investment and Analysis

Specialty retailers are poised to take advantage of technological improvements in different ways. For innovations in issues that all retailers face, such as inventory management, specialty retailers (especially the smaller ones) let the bigger, general retailers pay for research, and then the specialty retailers follow suit. Specialty retailers can be quick adopters of technological advancements and improvements, sometimes using new technology in innovative and unintended ways in order to gain a competitive advantage over their rivals.

For example, one small high-end men's apparel store in Washington, D.C., uses digital cameras to store pictures of outfits that clients purchase. That way, if a client needs to buy a new shirt to match a previously purchased set of pants, a simple call may be all that is needed. The salesperson will pull up pictures of outfits purchased in the computer and make recommendations. General retail innovations such as EDI or Internet shopping have been quickly accepted by specialty retailers.

According to Standard & Poor's, a commitment to information systems is emphasized in specialty retail, particularly the bigger chains. Information technology helps stores reduce and control costs and can provide key information about the business. For example, the use of point-of-sale data can tell retailers quickly what is selling and what isn't, allowing for better response time to trends.

The Internet

The Internet especially seems to be a powerful tool for specialty retailers. A specialty retailer on the Internet does not need a store or a catalog to present itself professionally to customers. The Web also allows customers from all over the world to shop at a store, even if the business has only a few locations. However, payment mechanisms need to be improved before worldwide shopping becomes a reality. Because of bad experiences with fraud, many U.S. companies will not ship overseas.

Role of Research and Development

Research and development has an important role in specialty retailing, although not in the traditional sense of R&D. Like all retailers, specialty retailers must do research regarding market conditions and keeping tabs on the competitors. Unlike general retailers, specialty retailers have to pay extremely close attention to trends within their niche. For example, a retailer that sold only typewriters and carbon paper would be hard-pressed if they did not plan adequately to change once personal computers started becoming popular in the 1980s. General retailers can afford to be slightly behind the trends and still survive, since they do not make their entire living from one smaller section of the population.

Development is similar. Specialty retailers need to develop new concepts and new ideas for growth to keep from being passed by or stagnating. Development of faster and cheaper ways of doing business can also help. Dell Computers (a direct computer retailer and manufacturer), for example, has reaped great profits from developing a fast assembly and delivery method in the time-sensitive market of home computers. The role of development in specialty retailing consists of refining the concept and shopping experience of customers to keep pace with changing demands.

Recommendation for the Future

Specialty retailers need to keep abreast of the latest market trends in the general economy, in retailing, and most important, in their niche. They must also exploit improvements in technology to keep up with their nimble competitors; even the large specialty retailers have smaller competitors who could turn operations around quickly. A more targeted and dedicated marketing approach seems to be the next trend in retail marketing, for example, and this is not lost in the least on specialty retailers. Standard & Poor's sees improvements in store design, customer service, merchandise quality, and technology innovation as coming trends. Some of these trends have already come to fruition. With increased usage of the Internet as a vehicle for shopping, specialty retailers will have to work hard to keep customers. Differentiated by their ability to gauge and quickly respond to the needs of customers, specialty retailers keen on maintaining and increasing market share should concentrate greater focus on brand-building efforts and offer unique customer-friendly services. With the Internet increasingly becoming the favored retail destination for business transactions, running a flawless website supported by bricks-and-mortar entities is a must-have. In addition, to cater to the varying lifestyle needs of customers, specialty retailers should expand their product offerings. In 2000, Gap expanded its Gap Body concept from 9 stores to 28 stores. Gap Body stores are typically freestanding shopping-mall units located next door to a Gap store and feature bodywear/intimate apparel.

Case: Ben & Jerry's

Short Description of the Company

Ben & Jerry's is one of corporate America's most generous donors, giving away 7.5% of pretax profits to philanthropic causes. The company operates in a socially conscious manner, supporting family farms and agriculture pro-environment policies, where the co-founders' values influence the corporate mission statement and strategy. It owns or franchises more than 230 Ben & Jerry's Scoop Shops and PartnerShops in the United States and Canada. Its other markets include Japan and Europe. Ben & Jerry's entire menu totals over 50 great ice cream, frozen yogurt, and sorbet products. Only about 34 of those are packaged in pints for sale in grocery stores—the rest are packaged in bulk tubs for sale to Scoop Shops and to restaurant and food service accounts.

In April 2000, Ben & Jerry's was acquired by Unilever, the European grocery products giant, for $326 million.

Unilever had agreed to let Ben & Jerry's remain somewhat autonomous with its own board of directors and Vermont headquarters.

Technological Investment and Analysis

Ben & Jerry's currently uses technology in the following areas: customer database management, manufacturing, website development, and multimedia. By examining each area individually, we can determine how the company should continue to invest in technology in the future.

Customer database management is a tool for satisfying customer needs and demands. The company currently uses its database for two primary reasons: (1) to discover what customers think of new product ideas and (2) to involve customers in social concerns.

Most of the database records are collected from the franchised Scoop Shops that send in the names of people who want to be placed on the Ben & Jerry's mailing list. When placed on the mailing list, customers are sent catalogues and newsworthy updates on company happenings. By using the customer databases, the company builds valuable relationships between people and products.

Ben & Jerry's uses a very advanced system in manufacturing to emphasize efficiency and productivity for the user. The system ultimately creates a better link between production and storage areas. The business planning and control groups use Ethernet and networking products.

The use of system architecture allows employees to exchange and analyze data. Through this system, the company allows its engineers and designers to share product development information so that the progress can be evaluated constantly. Systems architecture also offers pattern recognition and process learning. Thus, if employees spot inefficient trends during the manufacturing process, proper adjustments can be made that are more effective for the company.

Although the manufacturing process is constantly updated to improve efficiency, Ben & Jerry's also invests much time and effort into further website development. The website is an area of continual technological growth and investment. The company's current website features an interactive page with an animated tour guide helping visitors around the site in order to answer their questions. The range of interactive information that can be gathered on the site is useful in building long-term relationships with Ben & Jerry's customers.

Finally, the company focuses its resources equally on the expanded use of multimedia applications in its day-to-day operations. Specifically, Ben & Jerry's utilizes videoconferencing to maintain close teamwork and communications between employees who are more geographically scattered as the company expands into the worldwide market.

Recommendation for the Future

Since Ben & Jerry's manufactures products in the mature stage of the product life cycle, the company should now focus on strengthened market share and building brand loyalty.

Ben & Jerry's super premium ice cream product already has an established customer base. The company will gain new customers only if consumers choose to switch super premium brands. In this stage of the product life cycle, emphasis must be placed on customers by building brand loyalty and creating customer satisfaction through the use of technology.

The company might be able to build brand loyalty through the effective use of website development and database marketing. The Ben & Jerry's website currently uses several frames to encourage customer interaction with the product and the company. By increasing the number of interactive elements on their website, keeping the site current with product information, and most important, marketing their site among prospective clients, Ben & Jerry's should be able to maintain high customer loyalty among their target markets.

The real key to Ben & Jerry's future success lies in the company's ability to use and maintain customer databases effectively. Currently, Ben & Jerry's uses its customer databases to gather customer feedback and to introduce customers to social concerns and volunteer organizations. Although these are major current concerns of the company, Ben & Jerry's can use customer feedback in the future in other areas as well. For example, customers may recommend additional channels of distribution for the company, international opportunities, and new growth areas.

As technology grows, Ben & Jerry's should stay aware of increasingly new methods of adding to its customer database. In addition to Scoop Shops, sites such as grocery stores and restaurants where customers purchase the products, the company now has the opportunity to use the Internet to maintain contact with old and new customers alike. By expanding the method of creating additional customer databases, the company can find out more information about consumer habits and therefore gain more accurate marketing knowledge.

If Ben & Jerry's decides to focus on the customer first, super premium ice cream will not enter the declining stage of the product life cycle. The company must understand the importance of customer feedback and technology's role in using it appropriately.

Global giant Unilever acquired Ben & Jerry's in 2000. It remains to be seen how the buyout will affect the policies and operations. But there is already some conflict in the information systems. Unilever relies on purchased software including a global ERP system; Ben & Jerry's uses older custom-built software that is incompatible with other systems. Furthermore, corporate culture clash between executives of Ben & Jerry's and Unilever could undermine team cohesiveness. In May 2001, the quirky ice-cream maker's U.K. marketing chief resigned, citing disagreements about direction. Time will tell whether the brand can continue to hold its own against Häagen-Dazs and Wall's. The company's culture was reflected in the products it offered, and also in the way it chose to represent itself. Ultimately, Ben & Jerry's needs to reestablish a quirky image that differentiates it from the competition in order to leverage its branding power.

To regain its dominance, Ben & Jerry's should think beyond the confines of ice cream and desserts and pursue a more interactive brand experience for the consumer. It could refresh the brand through surprising new distribution outlets and generate excitement through innovative advertising campaigns.

Questions

1. What is the strategic direction for Ben & Jerry's ice cream?

2. What are the critical success factors and core competency factors for Ben & Jerry's ice cream?

3. What technologies has Ben & Jerry's relied on?

4. What has caused a change in the use of technology at Ben & Jerry's?

5. Are there replacement products for Ben & Jerry's ice cream?

6. What does the corporation's Web page present about its business directives?

7. Can Ben & Jerry's global brand which encompasses adult fun and rediscovering the child-in-you attitude, compete against the more sophisticated Häagen-Dazs?

Additional Reading

Arnold, Matthew. "Is Ben & Jerry's Losing Its Bohemian Appeal?" *Marketing* 17, May 3, 2001, p. 17.

"Raspberry Rebels." *The Economist,* September 6, 1997, pp. 61–62.

Goff, Leslie Jaye. "Summertime Heats Up IT at Ice Cream Maker Ben & Jerry's." *Computerworld,* July 2, 2001, p. 27.

Holland, Kelly. "Yummie!" *BusinessWeek,* November 3, 1997, p. 50.

"Ben & Jerry's Finds Buyer in European Food Giant Unilever." *Miami Herald,* April 13, 2000.

"Discovery Channel Multimedia Partners with Ben & Jerry's Team to Cross-Promote CD-ROMs." *Multimedia Business Report,* January 17, 1997, p. 4.

"Valuation of the Specialty Retail Industry." *Weekly Corporate Growth Report,* 9/20/99 Issue 1061, p. 10373.

Case: The Limited, Inc.

Short Description of the Company

On August 10, 1963, Leslie Wexner borrowed $5,000 from his aunt to finance the opening of a small women's clothing store in Columbus, Ohio. On his first day, Wexner sold $473 worth of merchandise. In the span of 34 years, Wexner's aunt's investment of $5,000 has become a multibillion-dollar company. One man's vision, perseverance, and business savvy have made The Limited a leading specialty retailer in the United States.

Growing from one store in the 1970s to a multistore, multibrand corporation has been the result of several strategic and operating efficiencies. Many new stores were opened in the

1970s. The Limited built a distribution facility in Ohio, next to the company headquarters. This allowed The Limited to have inventory shipped directly to the distribution center for prepackaging, price tagging, and store-order fulfillment. Additionally, the company acquired better control over inventory, storage, and shipping costs. The corporation has since opened additional distribution centers to accommodate the thousands of retail stores existing today.

Another strategic initiative that contributes to overall brand perception and success is storefront saturation. Whenever possible, The Limited will lease several contiguous spaces in new malls and act quickly to reposition their different stores in clusters in mall relocation and remodeling. This strategy causes the customer virtually to be surrounded with stores that are owned by The Limited. Otherwise, distractions like a cookie shop or a bookstore, for example, might flank a brand new Limited store. This retail space strategy leads to internal efficiencies also. Contiguous stores can share break rooms, inventory rooms, management, and other resources. Interior passages between stores (for instance, connecting a Structure and an Express) gives the customer the illusion of a much larger store, and keeps customers inside Limited stores and out of the rest of the mall.

Today, The Limited, Inc., through Express, Lerner New York, Lane Bryant, Limited Stores, Structure, and Henri Bendel, operates 2,049 specialty stores. The company also owns approximately 84 percent of Intimate Brands, Inc. (NYSE: IBI), the leading specialty retailer of intimate apparel, and beauty and personal care products, sold through 2,604 stores under the Victoria's Secret, Bath & Body Works, and White Barn Candle Co. brands. The company employs over 115,000 associates and has approximately 230,000 shareholders.

On September 14, 2001, The Limited, Inc. and Intimate Brands, Inc. donated $1 million to the September 11th Fund established by the United Way and the New York Community Trust. The contribution helped the families of the victims.

Technological Investment and Analysis

The Limited employs thousands of people, has almost 20 self-managing subsidiaries, and has managed to accumulate several billion dollars in assets. Technology has helped The Limited manage inventory, manage product lines, control day-to-day activities at the retail stores, and provide information to management enabling them to grow the business.

How can a retailer know each customer? Winners in the consumer information market will be expert managers of that data. Building upon the successes of data warehousing in other business fields, retailers will have to find data about customers, analyze it, and proactively use that knowledge to increase profitability and retain market share.

Also changing is retailers' use of the Internet to market goods, distribute corporate information, and attract customers. Specialty retailers like booksellers, wineries, T-shirt shops, and travel services have capitalized on doing business on the Internet. Technology will continue to play a vital role in determining the future of any retailing enterprise. The Limited is no excep-

tion. But being large and a market leader has led The Limited to take a somewhat conservative approach to technology.

Data, hardware, and software are the building blocks of information technology. The integration of these objects enables a company to work, predict results, and make money. Most sales and customer data is collected at the point of purchase. Hardware enables stores to scan inventory items into an IBM terminal-based cash register programmed with custom sales tracking routines and inventory modules. The sale is computed, payment is made, and the customer leaves. Nightly, store management closes the day's transactions, and enters cash and payment balancing information to reconcile the day's activity. Leased-line connections from the store to central data repositories in Columbus, Ohio, enable the transfer of sales data. Inventory levels are adjusted, shipping orders are formulated, and data is stored for management review. A warehousing strategy is used to store data. In turn, the data is mined to provide reports on store sales, product-line productivity, and patterns of consumer behavior.

The same principles are in operation in data warehousing. Intelligent handling systems track incoming goods, fill orders for stores, and monitor inventory levels. This hardware must be available to all levels of employees. Systems are also in place to automatically alert management of late shipments and deteriorating inventory levels. To make sure that the information stays current, custom software solutions track the flow of goods. Intranet-based database applications ensures smooth delivery to all warehouse personnel.

PC-based utilities are employed to manage employees, share information between store and corporate management, and facilitate client/server automation. These systems answer questions regarding future shipments and price and product availability. Home office users share information through local and wide area networks. The Limited's corporate campus is several blocks long and wide. Traditional memos and nonelectronic communication would be inefficient and costly.

The Internet plays a very important role in The Limited's information technology initiatives. In 1997, The Limited went online and started a website to supplement its bricks-and-mortar operations. The website initially was used primarily to distribute marketing and financial information. Newly developed commerce solutions could be plugged into the existing distribution channels with little infrastructure change.

Since The Limited, Inc. is aware of the importance of knowing its customers and their tastes, it has implemented Web-enabled questionnaires and marketing forms to gather critical information for evaluation. Management would then have the ability to peer through the data, and customers' feelings toward products could be analyzed. The company pilot tested an application from SAS that helped target 100,000 of the best potential customers for a cross-selling campaign. The targeted advertisements resulted in a 400 percent return on the marketing investment. Bill Lepler, vice president of CRM, noted that "The biggest challenge is that data is in silos, so it takes a lot of effort to take all that and get a single 360-degree view of the customer." [Songini 2001]

A virtual store on the Internet requires a fraction of the overhead required for a physical store. Once established, transaction processes would record the sale, produce entries in the data warehouse, and by default, collect marketing data. This same interactive information could be modified into back-end management applications to monitor and predict sales results. This would leverage The Limited, Inc.'s IT expenditure to gain sales insight. Because of the large-scale nature of the projects, The Limited outsources its Web servers to IBM. The Victoria's Secret online fashion webcast taxed the servers with 1.5 million viewers.

Over the last three years, developments in collaborative groupware and software have made sharing information across the enterprise less costly, more effective, and a valuable part of the information chain. A typical software suite like Lotus Notes could be used by all members of the information chain. Since an intranet-based information solution would be integrated into the supply chain, the same technology could be used to examine the front (marketing) and back (financial and operational) ends of the data. Employees would be able to share data, comment on contributions and new data, import and export raw data into other software application suites such as Microsoft Office, and generate variations of reporting for more departmental and personal uses.

Data models could be built to answer questions regarding the profitability of the Internet commerce project or any other business decision. External sources could supply the static inputs and industry paradigms. Internal data could be applied to the model logic, and the outflows would answer management hypotheses. Modeling enables companies to examine data through the use of constructed scenarios without actually executing the components of the model. As a testing ground for ideas, a model enables companies to query a set of data in countless ways not otherwise possible.

Technology will enable The Limited to answer questions regarding the profitability and effectiveness of the Internet. First, a descriptive model must be constructed to evaluate the effect of Internet commerce on supply and distribution chains, pricing, market segmentation, and information management. Assuming an enterprise information system has been installed, inputs from all aspects of this marketing channel could be considered. The model would evaluate the inputs and produce a set of descriptive outputs for management review. These sets of data would complement a decision support system designed to evaluate the effectiveness of the project.

One problem faced by The Limited's IT department is the multiple divisions and stores. The company formed Limited Technology Services as an IT subsidiary and moved all 700 IS employees into it. The goal was to centralize to improve integration and reduce costs.

Recommendation for the Future

The Limited must continue to refine its presence on the Internet. The younger, contemporary market is easily impressed with trends and marketing savvy. The Limited must act now to capture and maintain a sizable and influential market share. In 2001, The Limited invested in a customer relationship management package from SAS to help analyze sales data. The goal is to increase sales by cross-selling products to existing customers. The pilot test targeted 100,000 of the top customers for a special marketing campaign, resulting in a 400 percent return on investment.

As a company, The Limited, Inc. must implement strategies to capitalize on the huge business-casual trend. This means rolling out new sophisticated line of apparel for women and launching effective advertising campaigns that emphasize the message that The Limited, Inc., offers decent, fashionable clothes at value prices.

Questions

1. What is the strategic direction of the corporation, and who drives this direction?

2. Upon what technologies has the corporation relied?

3. How is customer data collected?

4. How successful has the technological change been?

5. What information does the corporation's Web page present about the business?

6. What role does data play in the future of the corporation?

Additional Reading

Goff, Leslie Jaye. "What It's Like to Work at . . . The Limited Inc." *Computerworld,* September 25, 2000.

Izmirlian, Robert J. "Retailing: Specialty; Industry Survey." *Standard and Poor's,* January 22, 1998.

"Limited Leans on NCR," *Computerworld,* December 15, 1997, p. 37.

"Limited Taps NCR," *Computerworld,* November 24, 1997, p. 37.

Newton, Nell. "Industry Snapshot: Retail & Wholesale." http://www.hoovers.com.

Shein, Esther. "Intranet Logistics Goes High Fashion." *PC Week,* September 8, 1997, pp. 29–30.

Sliwa, Carol. "Internet Outsourcing Increasingly Popular," *Computerworld,* October 8, 1999.

Songini, Marc. "Cost, Integration Top Analytical CRM Issues," *Computerworld,* July 23, 2001.

Creating Web Pages

One of the strengths of the Web is that it is easy to use. The user interface is straightforward. You see a page of text and graphics. Clicking a link brings up a new page. Search engines help you find additional pages. Anyone can learn to use the Web in a few minutes. The Web is a good method for presenting and sharing information with colleagues and other workers. Increasingly, most of the information you create as a manager will be shared through websites. Many companies set up servers that are accessible only to employees. These systems are called intranets to indicate that they contain information available only to insiders.

It is relatively easy to create Web pages. The basic steps are outlined in Figure 3.1A. The first two steps are perhaps the most difficult: determining content and defining a style. In a business situation, choosing content might be easy—creating it is what takes the time. For example, the accounting team might decide to create a website to post weekly financial data as common financial reports. The hardest part is collecting and formatting the data. The next step is to choose a style, which consists of the page layout and color scheme. Once you have the content and the layout, you can use a word processor or special Web page editor to create the text and tables and add graphics to each page. Each page is stored as a separate file. You can easily link pages together so users can jump to related information. Once you have tested your work, you can transfer the pages to a Web server.

Styles

Presentation is an important aspect to any job. When you make a presentation to the CEO, you want to look your best. When you build a website, you want to create a style that reflects the purpose of the site. Probably the two most important design issues are consistency and subtlety. Choose a color scheme, layout, and fonts that convey a specific image. Then apply that style to every page. You might want to hire a graphics artist to help you design the initial style.

FIGURE 3.1A   Steps to creating a website. The first two steps often require the most work. Many tools exist to help with the later steps.

Determine the content
Define a style
Create each page
  • Text
  • Graphics
Link the pages
Test your work
Transfer pages to a website

The best way to make sure that every page uses your style is to define a style sheet. A style sheet enables you to set every aspect of the page design, including margins, typefaces, colors, and backgrounds. The style sheet is saved as a separate (.css) file. Every page that contains a <LINK> tag with that file will use that style. When you want to change the style of your website, you simply change the style sheet and every page will automatically use the new settings.

Several Web development tools will help you define a style sheet. The alternative is to find a sample style sheet file and modify it to create your own style. The key to creating and using styles is that every element on your page must be named. You can create styles for any of the standard tags described in the next section, or you can create separate styles that you can apply to any text or section.

Creating Pages with HTML

Pages on the Web are created using a simplified page layout language: **hypertext markup language (HTML).** Several tools exist to help you create HTML documents, so you do not have to memorize the syntax. You can also use a word processor, but note that Microsoft Word has a habit of adding a huge overhead of extra material to the file. Word XP does allow you to save the file as "Web filtered" which deletes most of the unnecessary notes.

The main feature of HTML is that every element on your page is denoted with a tag. That is, each element is surrounded by a marker. For example, basic text is marked with the paragraph tags: <P>Sample paragraph.</P>. Other styles include headings, block quotes, and citations. With a word processor or other visual development tool, you simply type the text, then highlight it and select the appropriate style. When you save the document, the tool adds the necessary tags. Figure 3.2A shows a very basic HTML page. You can create text or edit the page with a simple editor (e.g., Notepad), but then you have to memorize the tags. It is generally easier to use a visual-editing tool. Many sources on the Internet provide information about the various HTML tags if you want to learn how to build a page by hand.

Graphics

For many years, graphics were a pain to share. Each software package defined a unique file format, so it was hard to share images unless your colleagues had the same hardware and software. The Web deals with this issue by defining three common types of graphic file formats: (1) graphics interchange format (GIF), (2) joint photographic experts group (JPEG), and (3) portable network graphics (PNG). Many systems now support a vector graphics format called *scalable*

FIGURE 3.2A   Basic HTML page. Each element is surrounded by tags. A word processor will insert the tags automatically—you simply mark the text and save the file as an HTML page.

```
<HTML>
<HEAD>
<TITLE>Sample HTML Page</TITLE>
</HEAD>
<BODY>
<H1>Section One</H1>
<P>This is a sample paragraph on a sample page.</P>
</BODY>
</HTML>
```

vector graphics (SVG). The earlier formats are bitmap images. JPEG and PNG files are designed for photos. GIF files are used for simple bitmap images and minor animations. To share images, your software must convert them into one of these four formats. The SVG format is relatively recent and supported only by the newer browsers. It is designed to speed up the transfer and quality of drawings and charts.

You can create your own image files—if you have the appropriate hardware and software. Scanners are used to convert photographs. Line art and icons can either be scanned or redrawn with a graphics package. Size is the most important issue with Web graphics. If your site will only be used in-house on a high-speed network, you can use large, fancy images. If people will access your pages across the Internet using phone lines, you need to keep image files to fewer than 50,000 bytes.

Images are placed on the HTML page with an <IMG> tag. For example: <IMG SRC="myfile.jpg" WIDTH=350 HEIGHT=200>. Again, the visual tools will help you place an image on a page, so you do not have to memorize the syntax of the tag.

Links

Links are one of the most useful features of the Web. Users can find related information by clicking on a link. Links are also used to download files. A link consists of two parts: the text displayed in the browser and the name of the new page/file. Visual page editors make it easy to create links. Just highlight the text in the browser, click a link icon, and enter the name of the new page or file. In HTML, links are marked with an anchor <A> tag. For example: <A HREF="annual.html">Annual Results</A>.

When you jump to a new page, you can also pick a specific location within that page. Simply add a marker <A NAME="sales"> within the new page, then specify the marker in the link reference: <A HREF="annual.htm#sales"> Annual Sales</A>. Again, visual tools make it easy to enter these items. The HTML is shown here to help you understand how the system works.

One problem with links is that if you delete or move a file, users may click on a link and receive an error message. If you

rename or delete a file, you need to find and update all of the references to that file in your other pages. Current visual editing tools help with this task by searching for broken links. Some tools will graphically portray your website by showing the links from each page. Even with these tools, it is time-consuming to change the files on your website.

Forms and e-Business

HTML also supports basic forms. It is relatively easy to create the forms. It is much more challenging to process the data from the forms. Handling forms and e-business requires custom programs written to run on the Web server. Several specialized systems exist to build server-side programs. The details depend on the computer, the operating system, and the particular software. This lack of standardization is both good and bad. The positive aspect is that competition leads to innovation and better prices. The drawback is that developers have time to learn only one system—and then they argue with everyone else over which system is best. So, once you commit to a particular technology, it is difficult to switch. Two leading Web server technologies are Microsoft's .NET and Sun's J2EE (also supported by Oracle).

Additional File Types

If you are building a website for internal use, you can use some additional features to provide more information to your colleagues. For example, you can include spreadsheets or slide shows on your website. When someone clicks on the file reference on your page, the file will be transferred to his or her machine and displayed in the browser. The file is easy to add with a standard link tag. For instance: <A HREF="myfile.xls"> Quarterly spreadsheet</A>.

Adobe has created the **portable document format (pdf)** type that is useful when you need precise control over the layout of your documents. Many governmental agencies (e.g., the IRS) use pdf to distribute electronic copies of common forms. Most browsers can display and print the documents exactly as they were created. You generally need Adobe Acrobat software to create the forms, and the browsers need Acrobat Reader to display them. The reader software is free, but you have to purchase the software to create the files. Once they are created, you link them into your website the same way you would any other file.

Publishing Documents on the Web

As indicated by Figure 3.3A, when you have created all of your pages and tested the links, you need to copy the files to a Web server. Many types of computers can function as Web servers, and they all have slightly different methods for accepting your pages and for assigning security permissions. If you are building a site for internal use, your MIS department will run a server and explain how to transfer the files. If you are publishing pages for external use, the server can be run by your company, or you can lease space on a server run by an ISP. The ISP will have its own rules and procedures for publishing Web pages.

Today, probably the easiest mechanism is if your server is set up to support the Microsoft Front Page publishing system. Several development tools can automatically communicate with the server using this system. Once you have the pages designed on your computer, you simply click an icon and enter the name of the server. Your PC then contacts the server and transfers the files automatically.

If the Front Page system is not available, you will generally use the Internet **file transfer protocol (FTP)** to transfer the files to the server. You need to know the Internet name of the server, an account name, and the corresponding password. The FTP software enables you to select the files and transfer them to the server. You might have to set security permissions so that the Web server can retrieve the pages (but not alter them). The details depend on the server.

If you have a powerful enough computer system on your desk (for example Windows XP or UNIX), you can run your own Web server. You simply set aside a directory for public access. Then to publish data, you copy the files into that public directory. This approach is generally used only for sharing files with co-workers. It requires someone (probably you) to manage the Web server and to maintain adequate security precautions. Security problems are minimized by allowing only internal workers to access the machine.

Exercises

1. Create three Web pages that are linked. Include at least one image.

2. Create a style sheet for your Web pages.

3. Create a website that will hold all of your assignments for this course. Create a main page with links to all of the future assignments.

4. Find an ISP and determine the costs of creating a website for a small business. List the additional features (and costs) that are available.

5. Create a basic promotional website for the Rolling Thunder Bicycles Company.

FIGURE 3.3A   Publishing Web pages. Files are created on your computer. They must then be transferred to a Web server. You can use FTP or Microsoft Front Page extensions if they are available.

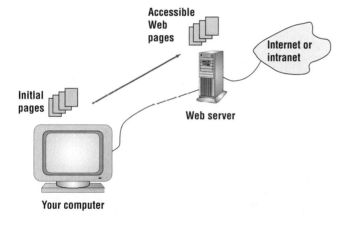

CHAPTER FOUR

Security, Privacy, and Anonymity

What you will learn in this chapter

- What are the security threats to information systems?

- What controls exist to protect the systems?

- How do computers identify users?

- What alternative security measures need to be taken?

- What is encryption and how does it solve several problems?

- What specific security problems does the Internet create?

- Can there be privacy with computers and the Internet?

- What are the advantages and problems with anonymity?

Fisher Scientific products are used by scientists throughout the world. Information technology and the Internet enable scientists to obtain up-to-date information on products, prices, and orders.

Fisher Scientific

In 1902, Chester G. Fisher, 22, of Western University of Pennsylvania opened his own business. He saw a need for someone to supply scientific laboratories so he purchased a local storeroom to begin a scientific supply business. Laboratory work was based on simple experiments involving solid, liquid, and gaseous measurement. Fisher's earliest products included microscopes, burettes, pipettes, litmus, balances, and calorimeters. In 1978, Fisher installed computer terminals at his major customers' sites, enabling them to place orders directly and receive immediate order verification. Customers were able to look up information on past purchases and other financial information. A year later, Fisher expanded this system to increase the speed and accessibility of the customers' terminals.

In 1994, Fisher Scientific became the first catalog distributor in the industry to have the majority of its product offering available to its customers on CD-ROM and for purchase on its website. Fisher's spending on computer technology has increased its efficiency and enabled it to win large preferred supplier agreements such as the Department of Defense for handling smaller instrumentation and operational products.

Overview

Ally:	Um, Richard, I think we have a problem.
Richard:	Relax Ally, it can't be that bad.
Ally:	Well, some FBI guy is outside. He says someone attacked a website and got away with thousands of credit card numbers.
Richard:	So . . .
Ally:	And that they traced the hacker back to our system, and it looks like the attack came from Elaine's computer.
Richard:	Oh, oh. Elaine! What's going on?!
Elaine:	What?

Richard: Have you been hacking other computers?

Elaine: What?

Ally: Wait a minute. That's not fair. Elaine. Didn't you lose your laptop last week?

Elaine: Yes, that's right. And it automatically logs into all of my accounts. Am I in trouble?

Richard: We don't know yet, but you need to talk to this FBI agent . . .

Introduction

There is little doubt that business use of computers is increasing—to the point where e-commerce businesses require all of the components to be functioning 24 hours a day. In this environment managers need to know what threats they face and what technologies exist to protect the systems. Figure 4.1 shows three aspects that affect all businesses, but are particularly important in e-commerce: (1) interception of transmissions, (2) attacks on servers, and (3) monitoring systems to identify attacks.

Encryption plays an important role in protecting systems. It can also be used to authenticate the sender of a message. A key aspect of security and encryption is the need to identify users. Consequently, the flip side of many security policies is the loss of privacy.

FIGURE 4.1

Security and privacy are important issues in the Internet era. People can intercept data and attack servers directly and indirectly, and companies routinely monitor all transactions.

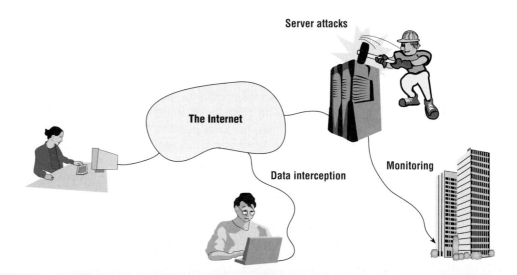

Trends

Security has been an issue for thousands of years, from the simple substitution ciphers of Caesar to the importance of codes and code breaking in World War II. As more data was moved to computers, several complications arose. One of the biggest obstacles has been the need to identify people. Passwords have been the most common method, but they cause many problems. Newer technologies are available, but they require standards and people will have to agree to use them. Since security requires identifying people, increased emphasis on security can result in a reduction in privacy. Firms have collected data on consumers for years, but only recently have technologies advanced to the point where it is relatively inexpensive and easy to collect and analyze data on millions of consumers.

Despite Hollywood's portrayals, the greatest security threats come from insiders. On the other hand, it used to be difficult to attack servers, and required programmers with a deep knowledge of the system. Today, with millions of computers connected to the Internet, it is relatively easy for beginners to download code from a site and run automated attacks against known bugs in operating systems. This technique is commonly used for creating denial of service attacks on websites. As e-commerce expands in importance, it becomes increasingly important to develop a more robust Internet protocol that can identify and stop denial of service attacks. Many security tools exist to protect servers and to encrypt data transmissions, but it is difficult to stop attacks that rely on flooding the server.

As more business data and more of our consumer lives go online, computer security and privacy become even more important to everyone. Hundreds of horror stories are created every year as unscrupulous people find new ways to steal or destroy data. To learn to protect computer data, you must first understand the threats. Encryption plays several important roles in protecting data and in identifying users. However, the newer systems require that people trust the companies creating the security systems.

The Internet and e-commerce add some challenging aspects to security. E-commerce requires that portions of the computer systems be available to consumers and other businesses. Greater business benefits are generated when websites are integrated with corporate data—such as inventory levels so customers can determine if an item is in stock. Yet, allowing public access to these systems creates greater security risks. Additionally, since the Internet is a shared public network, data needs to be protected in transmission—to ensure it is not intercepted or altered. Wireless networks are even more open to eavesdropping and interception. Because of the public nature of the Internet, even a well-protected system can be brought down with denial-of-service attacks.

In the last few years, consumers and workers have increasingly been asked to give up their privacy. With today's huge computer capacity, online sales, browsing, and even bar code scanners, it is now possible to track a large portion of a consumer's life. There are ways to restore some level of anonymity, but questions remain about the social effects of anonymous users on the Internet.

Threats to Information

Many potential threats exist to information systems and the data they hold. The complicated aspect is that the biggest information threat is from legitimate users and developers. Purely by accident, a user might enter incorrect data or delete important information. A designer might misunderstand an important function and the system will produce erroneous results. An innocent programming mistake could result in incorrect or destroyed data. Minor changes to a frail system could result in a cascading failure of the entire system.

We can detect and prevent some of these problems through careful design, testing, training, and backup provisions. However, modern information systems are extremely complex. We cannot guarantee they will work correctly all of the time. Plus, the world poses physical threats that cannot be avoided: hurricanes, earthquakes, floods, and so on. Often, the best we can do is build contingency plans that enable the company to recover as fast as possible. The most important aspect of any disaster plan is to maintain adequate backup copies. With careful planning, organization, and enough money, firms are able to provide virtually continuous information system support.

A second set of problems arises from the fact that as technology changes, so do criminals. Today, only a desperate person would rob a bank with a gun. The probability of being caught is high, and the amount of money stolen is low. Not that we wish to encourage anyone to become a thief, but the computer offers much easier ways to steal larger amounts of money.

It is important to determine the potential threats to computer security described by Figure 4.2. Some tools have made it easier for outsiders to attack companies over the Internet, but by far the biggest issues remain people inside the company and viruses.

Disasters

Fortunately, fires, floods, hurricanes, and other physical disasters do not happen too often. But when a disaster does hit a company's data center, it could destroy the company. Without advance preparations, the loss of a data center could shut down the operations. How long can a modern company survive without transaction processing?

Today, there are many ways to plan for and recover from disasters. A common method today is to contract with a disaster recovery services provider. Service providers like SunGard shown in Figure 4.3 provide access to their commercial recovery facilities and provide several levels of support for various fees. One common level of support, called a **hot site**, consists of a fully

FIGURE 4.2

Threats to information. By far, the most serious threats are from insiders—employees, mistakes, consultants, and partnerships. Businesses have to trust insiders to stay in operation, but you need to put limits on the access to data. It is possible for outsiders to break into most computer systems, but it is fairly difficult. Viruses are a serious threat both to data and security in general.

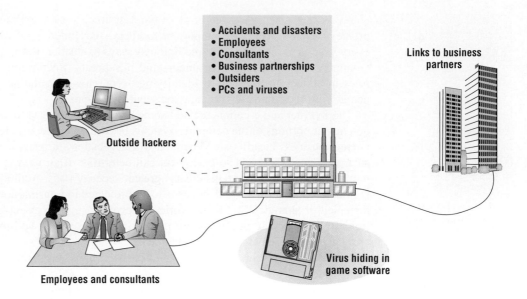

- Accidents and disasters
- Employees
- Consultants
- Business partnerships
- Outsiders
- PCs and viruses

Links to business partners

Outside hackers

Employees and consultants

Virus hiding in game software

FIGURE 4.3

Disaster planning. You can contract with a company like Sungard to provide backup computer facilities in the event of a disaster. For local problems with servers, you can run a backup server from a truck while your facilities are repaired.

configured computer center. Specific computer equipment is already installed and ready for immediate use. When the MIS staff declares a disaster, they install the backup tapes on the hot-site computers and use telecommunication lines to run the day-to-day operations. Another alternative is to contract for a **cold site,** which provides fully functional computer room space, without the computer equipment. If a disaster occurs, either the company or the disaster recovery services provider can arrange for the necessary equipment to be shipped to the cold site. However, there might be a delay of several days before the new data center will be operational, so a cold site is often used in conjunction with a hot site contract.

For computer operations that absolutely must never be interrupted, some firms utilize a backup computer that is continuously running to maintain a complete copy of the daily operations. All data is maintained simultaneously at both locations. If problems arise with one machine, the second one takes over automatically. Specialty firms are now offering these **data mirroring** facilities. The outside firm is sent copies of all of your data as it is generated. The firm makes backup copies and provides virtually instantaneous renewal of service if something interferes with your main computer.

Employees and Consultants

Employees are the heart of any company. Companies function and succeed by trusting their employees. Although almost all employees are honest and diligent, there is always the chance that one employee will use the company's knowledge, experience, and trust to misappropriate resources.

Reality Bytes   **September 11, 2001**

It might take months or even years for the people and companies to recover from the September 11 attack on the World Trade Center in New York. But businesses do not have months or years to restore networks and computers. Within hours of the destruction, communication firms and technology firms nationwide were busy rebuilding networks and computer systems in New York and Washington. Within minutes of the attack, businesses activated backup plans and rushed to SunGard backup data centers in Philadelphia. In many cases, systems were operational in a few hours. The morning after the attack, Sun loaded tons of equipment, including some from their own workers' offices, into a convoy of 10 trucks that drove to New York City. EDS helped American Express establish a new office with PCs and a new computer system to be operational within hours. HP provided computers and space for about 100 companies. One financial-services firm requested 400 servers and 4,000 PCs. Through these efforts and more, the stock markets were able to reopen on Monday, September 17.

Source: Adapted from Edward Iwata and Jon Swartz, "Tech Firms Jump in to Help Companies Mobilize to Rebuild Systems, Reclaim Lost Data," *USA Today,* September 19, 2001.

It can be difficult to identify people who might cause damage to the firm. Many companies today use psychological tests, background checks, and random drug tests to indicate potential problems. Most companies are wary of employees whose employment has been terminated. Businesses follow specific steps when employees leave, being particularly careful to remove the employees' access to company computers.

A more complicated problem arises with MIS employees. Programmers and analysts have to be trusted. Without them, there would be no software. However, it is generally best if the programmers are not the users of the program. Companies enforce a separation of duties among staff programmers and users. Think about what might happen if a bank teller was also responsible for writing the computer program used by tellers. It would be easy to use the computer to steal money from different accounts. Auditing transaction-processing systems is an important task for auditors.

Unscrupulous programmers have also been known to include "time bombs" in their software. Whenever the software runs, it checks a hidden file for a secret word. If the programmer leaves the company, the secret word does not get changed. When the program does not find the correct word, it starts deleting files. On large projects, these bombs can be impossible to spot (until they go off). Keeping good backups can usually minimize the damage. As a related side note, the software industry is pushing states to adopt a new set of laws (UCITA) that makes it legal to include a shutdown time bomb if a software company has a dispute with a business that uses its software.

Another danger area is that programmers might include a trap door or secret password that allows them to gain access to the software even if they leave the company. Sometimes these trap doors are installed innocently, to enable programmers to make corrections faster. The important point is to make sure they are removed when the system is permanently installed.

An interesting class of threats to securing your data arises from negligence instead of deliberate actions by the users. For instance, employees might accidentally delete data. Or, carrying disks, tapes, or even laptop computers past magnetic fields can sometimes damage the files. In these cases, the best bet is to have backups readily available. More complicated problems arise when laptop computers are lost or even stolen. In addition to the data stored on the machines, the files often hold passwords for corporate computers. Many laptops provide passwords and encrypt the data to minimize these problems. One other problem that falls into this category is a warning to be careful about how you dispose of old tapes, disks, and computer equipment. Businesses run similar risks when they send computer equipment out for repairs.

In general, the best way to minimize problems from employees stems from typical management techniques. Hire workers carefully, treat employees fairly, have separation of jobs, use teamwork, and maintain constant checks on their work. Consultants present the same potential problems as employees. However, consultants tend to be hired for a short time, so the firm knows even less about them than about regular employees. Consultants are generally used for specialized jobs, so there may not be any internal employees who can adequately monitor their work.

Business Partnerships

As computers spread throughout every aspect of business, many companies share their data. For example, General Motors asks its suppliers to provide all information electronically. This electronic data interchange (EDI) means that business information is processed faster and with fewer errors. The problem is that in many cases, it means GM gives other companies considerable access to GM's computer and vice versa. For instance, if GM is thinking about increasing production, the managers might want to check supplier production schedules to make sure the suppliers could provide enough parts. To do it electronically, GM needs access to the suppliers' computers. To participate in business today, you must trust your partners. However, you have limited ability to evaluate all of their employees.

The issue of partnerships becomes more important in an Internet world of software. Increasingly, firms are providing services over the Internet—where the software and your data reside on a service provider's website. A good example is NetLedger, which is an **application service provider (ASP)** that processes all of your accounting needs on its website. The main advantages of an ASP are (1) experts set up and run the site so you do not have to hire specialists, (2) storing the data on the Web means it is accessible to your employees wherever they have Web access, and (3) you can start small and scale up to a reasonable size without hassles. A potential drawback is that all of your financial data is stored on a site run by someone else. Of course, the reputation of the ASP depends on protecting your data and maintaining security, so it is probably safer than what a small business could handle independently; however, you should still investigate the ASP security procedures.

Outsiders

There is some threat from outsiders who might dial up your computer and guess a password. Using some common sense can minimize most of these threats. For example, in the 1980s, some groups gained access to computers because the operators never changed the default password that was shipped with the computer! The Internet causes additional problems because it was designed to give other people access to your machines. The key lies in providing people with just the level of access they need. The biggest problems today arise from a group labeled *script kiddies* who download system scanning/attack software from the Internet and randomly search computers for holes. Another major problem with passwords is a technique hackers call *social engineering.* A hacker calls up a victim (you), tells some story and convinces you to reveal your password. Never give your password to anyone.

In theory, modern computer security systems are effective and can prevent most outside attacks. The problem is that operating systems are complex software programs that have errors. Experts search these systems to find the errors, and ultimately, the vendor fixes the errors. However, this process can result in dozens of patches a year. Some businesses do not keep up with the patches, and some patches interfere with other programs and are not applied. Consequently, there can be thousands of systems connected to the Internet that suffer from published flaws. Software downloaded from the Internet can automatically search for these flaws and provide access even to inexperienced hackers. One key to protecting your servers is to make sure they have all current operating system patches.

Viruses

Microsoft Office software presents a major point of vulnerability because the tools support a macro programming language called Visual Basic for Applications. This language is a powerful feature that enables MIS departments and other software vendors to automate many tasks—such as synchronizing calendars and contact lists with multiple devices. The problem is that a programming language can also be used to create programs that steal or destroy data.

FIGURE 4.4

Virus activity. Once a virus is loaded on your machine, you will need an antivirus software package to remove the virus. Several versions are available at low cost. A virus can come from any software that supports executable code. Attachments sent through e-mail are currently the most common method of being infected.

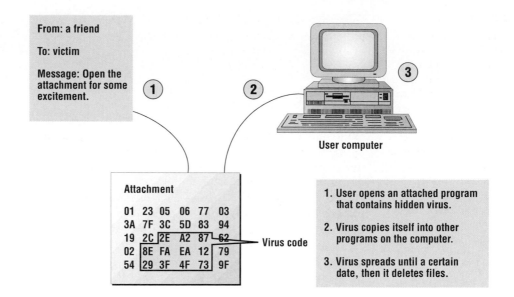

These programs can be hidden inside a document, slide show, database, or e-mail message. One particularly dangerous threat comes in the form of a software program called a **virus**. As illustrated in Figure 4.4, a computer virus is a small program that hides inside a program attached to an e-mail message. If you open the attachment, the macro program runs and the virus tends to do two things: (1) it sends itself to everyone in your contact list using your name, and (2) it attaches itself to other files in your computer. At some point, the nastier viruses then delete all of your files, or send your files to a Web server. Some writers make a distinction and call a program a worm if it simply replicates itself but is not designed to cause any damage.

A virus can be picked up from many sources, but e-mail attachments are the prevalent method today. Antivirus software will search your computer for known viruses. Even so, firms continue to experience problems with viruses. As shown in Figure 4.5, viruses and worms are the most common attack faced by companies today. Although the survey does not show it, virtually every company experiences several virus attacks every year. Antivirus software can help clean files once a virus is identified, but it has not proven very useful in stopping attacks—particularly since new viruses are created every day. In 1999, software virus costs were estimated to be slightly under $8 billion in the U.S. alone.

Today, it is easy to create a virus—simply find a virus software kit on the Web, make a few changes, and send it to someone. You would need only minimal technical skills. Of course, it is illegal to create and release viruses and other destructive software (in most nations).

The best way to stop a virus is to avoid running software acquired from the Internet and to never open script attachments sent to you by e-mail—even if they appear to come from a friend. Be cautious, because some attachments that appear to be pictures are actually virus scripts. Vendors are beginning to work on e-mail filters that can block script attachments, but they tend to be heavy-handed and also block useful files.

Ultimately, the most important step with viruses is to make certain that you always have current backup files. Then even if a virus deletes your files, you can recover the data, run an antivirus software package and remove the virus. It will cost you time, but at least you will save the data.

Computer Security Controls

Transaction and accounting data is clearly valuable to a company and needs to be protected. Computer security systems need to protect against three general problems: (1) unauthorized disclosure of information, (2) unauthorized modification, and (3) unauthorized withholding

FIGURE 4.5

Attacks on information systems. Percentage of firms reporting attacks. Despite safeguards, viruses and worms have been a growing threat to all companies. Even if the viruses cause no direct damage, recovering from the attacks can be expensive. Problems caused by insiders may be less prevalent, but potentially more damaging.

Source: Andy Briney, "2001 Industry Survey," *Information Security,* October 2001 (http://www.infosecuritymag.com/ articles/october01/images/ survey.pdf). Michael Alexander, "Infection Risk Not Spurring Use of Antivirus Software," *Computerworld,* December 16, 1991, p. 49. Gary H. Anthes, "Old, New Viruses Swarm PC Users," *Computerworld,* May 6, 1996, p. 55.

Attacks	1991	1996	2000	2001
Viruses/trojans/worms	62%	80%	80%	89%
Attacks on Web servers			24	48
Denial of service			37	39
Insider physical theft or damage of equipment			49	42
Insider electronic theft, destruction, or disclosure of data			24	22
Fraud			13	9

of information. As an example of the first problem, you would not want hackers to get access to your customer's credit card data. An example of the second problem would be employees' modifying their payroll records to change their pay rates. The third problem is less obvious, but just as important. Imagine what would happen if you needed to look at the latest inventory to decide how much to reorder, but the computer refused to give you access. This problem is often referred to as **denial of service (DoS),** and is a difficult problem faced by websites.

Manual and Electronic Information

Protection of information is a topic that has existed forever. Not surprisingly, the strongest developments in security have come from the military. The armed services lead the way both in manual and electronic security. Military funding has paid for much of the development of computer security. Because manual security precautions existed long before computers, the initial work in computer security focused on applying these older techniques. Nevertheless, some major differences arise from storing information electronically.

To see the complications added by electronic storage of information, consider a hypothetical case of two spies looking for a letter. Juan has gained access to a personal computer, but Mike is in a musty basement library full of paper files. Mike is not even sure he is in the right place. There are thousands of documents in the basement, and the letter might even be stored in some other building. The computer that Juan is searching is large enough to hold all of the company's information, so he only has to look in one place. For his search, Juan just uses the computer database. In seconds, he finds what he wants. He copies the letter to a disk, turns off the machine and walks out the door. Mike is still walking up and down aisles in the basement trying to read file tags with his flashlight. When he finally finds the letter, he uses his trusty spy camera to take pictures of the letter, hoping they will be legible. Now he has to put the letter back exactly as he found it so no one can tell he copied it.

Obviously it is much easier to locate and copy data stored on computers. Even more important, it is easier to change the data. In many cases, data on computers can be changed without anyone knowing that the file was altered. The Internet makes it even easier for people to steal huge amounts of electronic data.

Data Backup

The most important aspect of any security plan is to protect the data through formal backups. A company can recover from almost any problem—as long as the data is available. If you lose transactions data, you lose part of the company.

As shown in Figure 4.6, with a formal backup plan, data is transferred to a transportable format (usually tapes or DVD drives). The data must be stored offsite to protect it from local disasters. That means you need a plan to rotate the data so that the offsite backups remain up to date. One solution is to make complete backup tapes once a week, and then just send incremental change data over the Internet. Large organizations have several options because they probably have offices in many locations that can swap data. Smaller businesses can use commercial data storage facilities. Just remember to move the data far enough away so that

FIGURE 4.6

Data backup. Backup is critical to security. Offsite backups are needed to recover from disasters. Mirrored sites are used when extreme reliability is needed. PCs can be backed up over the network.

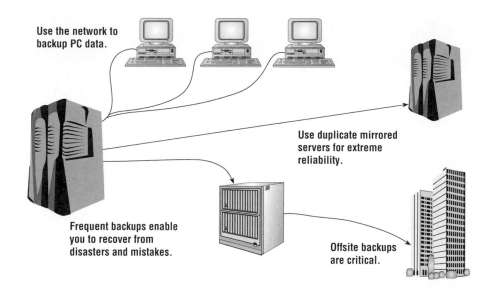

Use the network to backup PC data.

Use duplicate mirrored servers for extreme reliability.

Frequent backups enable you to recover from disasters and mistakes.

Offsite backups are critical.

Reality Bytes   Wang Wei

In 2001, a Chinese air force plane flown by Wang Wei crashed when it collided with a U.S. spy plane. In the ensuing diplomatic tension, Chinese hackers declared a cyberwar on the United States. U.S. hackers decided they would retaliate and attack Chinese sites. The Chinese hackers exploited operating system holes and defaced random U.S. websites—posting a photo of Wang Wei and anti-American messages. U.S. hackers performed similar, less publicized, changes on Chinese computers. In general, the attacks were minor and relatively harmless—although they did demonstrate the importance of security to many site administrators. A far more damaging attack came several months later from an unknown (and likely unrelated source), when the "Code Red" worm automatically attacked thousands of websites and used them to spread itself around the world. In both situations, the security problems arose because of the availability of automated tools that systematically search millions of machines for known problems. The main lesson from the attacks is the importance of installing current operating system patches.

Source: Adapted from Sam Costello, "What if They Waged a Cyberwar and Nobody Came?" *Computerworld*, May 11, 2001; and Jaikumar Vijayan, "Recent Hacker Attacks Demonstrate How Any Web Site Can Become Random Prey," *Computerworld*, May 14, 2001.

if a disaster hits the business, the backup data will not be affected. This rule is particularly important for areas subject to hurricanes and floods.

Data stored on personal computers is often difficult to back up. Users are not very conscientious about making copies, so few people have daily backups of their work. Networks can help, because users can store their data on network drives, which can be backed up on a regular schedule by the MIS department. Some software even automatically transfers data from personal computers to the network, so users do not need to remember to transfer it.

Along the same lines, if you want to keep your computer running—particularly servers—you need to install an **uninterruptible power supply (UPS).** A UPS is basically a large battery that is constantly recharged from the power outlet. The computer always runs off the battery, so if power fails, the computer keeps running. A UPS provides only a few minutes of power, but it protects the server during typical brownouts and short outages. If the power outage is extended, you will have time to shut down the machine safely or switch to auxiliary generators.

User Identification

One difficulty with providing computer security lies in identifying the user. In a manual security system, a guard can be used to physically identify each person by asking to see identification. There are few vision systems available for computers and they are expensive. The most common method of identifying users to computers is with a password.

Passwords

Each user is given an account name and a password that are known only to the computer and the user. If someone correctly enters both the name and the password, the computer assumes it must be the user. This method is cheap, fast, and does not require too much effort by the user. However, there are problems. The biggest difficulty is that users are afraid of forgetting their password, so they choose words that are easy to remember. Unfortunately, passwords that are easy to remember tend to be obvious to other people. For instance, *never* use the words *password* or *secret* as a password. Similarly, do not use the names of relatives, pets, or celebrities. Most of these can be obtained by looking in a phonebook or asking someone you know. In fact, you should not use any actual words. Most people use only a couple thousand words in typical conversation. The goal is to make it hard for someone to guess the password. You need to choose passwords from the largest possible set of characters and numbers. Two other rules about passwords: Change them often and never write them down. If you forget a password, the system administrator will let you create a new one. For additional security, many computer systems require users to change their passwords on a regular basis, such as every 30 or 60 days.

One drawback to passwords is that we need too many of them. Everything from ATM cards to phone calls to computer accounts uses passwords or *personal identification numbers (PINs).* It is difficult to remember several different passwords, especially if you choose random letters and numbers and change them often. With so many passwords, it is tempting to write them down, which defeats their purpose. Some computer network security systems use a **Kerberos** server. Users log in once and the security server provides authentication to all of the authorized servers. This system is built into the newer Windows servers and simplifies access to local computers. At this point in time, it is not used for access to Internet sites.

Passwords are not a perfect solution to identifying users. No matter how well they are chosen or how often they are changed, there is always a chance that someone could guess the password. They are so risky that U.S. government top-secret information is stored on computers that cannot be connected to phone lines or the Internet. By physically preventing outsiders from using the computers, there is a smaller chance that the information could be compromised.

Password Generators

Password generators are small electronic cards that users carry that generate new passwords every minute. The same system is embedded on the main computer. When you want to log in, you simply enter the number on the card. Since the password is changed every minute, you do not have to worry about anyone guessing it or intercepting it. On the other hand, you have to carry around the card.

FIGURE 4.7
Biometric devices. Several methods exist to identify a person based on biological characteristics. Common techniques include fingerprint or handprint readers, and retinal scanners. The iris scanner is a relatively useful technology since it requires only a camera and is noninvasive.

FIGURE 4.8
Access control. In Windows, right-click the folder or file to set its properties. Under the Security tab, you can set permissions to any person or group.

Biometrics

Biometrics is a field of study that attempts to identify people based on biological characteristics. The most promising devices are fingerprint and handprint readers. As shown in Figure 4.7, there are even devices that recognize the pattern of your iris (the colored ring surrounding the pupil of your eye). These systems work with a simple camera that can be installed cheaply. They are being tested now for identification at airports and in ATMs. The Canadian government is building a large-scale system to handle customs check-in for returning Canadian citizens.

As costs decline, the biggest drawback to biometric security devices is a lack of standards. In 2000, Microsoft bought a company to develop a set of standards to handle biometric devices within the Windows operating system. If this system gets implemented and accepted by the industry, it will be much easier to use biometric devices for all user identification needs.

Biometric security devices have some important advantages. The user does not have to remember anything or carry keys around. They are reasonably accurate and difficult to fool by an unauthorized person. But the industry still needs standards so that the security information can be transferred securely and validated by the final server.

Access Control

As long as the computer can identify each user, you can control access to any piece of data. As manager of the marketing department, you could allow other managers to read the sales data but not change it. Similarly, as shown in Figure 4.8, the accounting department could allow managers to see the accounts payable data, but only the accounting department would be able to modify the data and write new checks. With a good security system, it is possible for the human resources manager to allow employees to look up work phone numbers in the corporate database but not to see salaries or other confidential information.

The common access controls available are read, write, execute, and delete. With these security features, the owner of the information can give other users exactly the type of access they need.

As a creator of data, it is your responsibility to set the appropriate access permissions. Today, most of your files will be shared through a website. You can set aside different directories for each group of users and assign permissions to each directory. To avoid accidents, you generally do not give anyone delete permissions. Your main choice is which users should be able to read the data, and which ones need to be able to change it. Of course, if multiple people have permission to change a document, you should set the document to track changes so you can see who made each change.

Additional Security Measures

Audits

Accountants have long known that in order to maintain security over data, it is necessary to perform audits. There are too many ways for unscrupulous people to make changes to stored information. Audits are used to locate mistakes and to prevent fraud. Existing criminology practice states that in many cases, the threat of getting caught (by an audit) will convince most people to be more careful and to avoid fraudulent behavior. The same principles extend to security audits. By monitoring computer activity, auditing financial records, and periodically checking to see whether everyone is obeying security regulations, users are encouraged to follow the security guidelines of the company.

Of course, audits cost money and they interfere with the daily operations of the firm. As a result, it is important to schedule audits carefully and to keep an eye on the costs as well as the potential benefits. There are several professional organizations (such as the EDP Auditors Association) designed to help security employees learn more about the latest technologies and to teach them what to look for in audits. The American Institute of Certified Public Accountants (AICPA) also provides standards and audit guidelines that are useful at combating fraud.

Physical Access

Because it is so difficult to provide logical security to a computer, other mechanisms have been developed. Many of them rely on controlling physical access to the computer. For instance, computers and terminals should be kept in controlled areas. They must certainly be

Steganography

Today, when privacy has disappeared and the U.S. government monitors international calls, faxes and e-mails, and uses satellites to watch activities around the world, how could terrorists secretly set up the plan to hijack airplanes and crash them? By most accounts, those particular terrorists avoided using most electronic communication systems, relying on hand-to-hand messages among trusted members. Yet, encryption technologies today are readily available to anyone. Technologies that are difficult or impossible to break. Some experts speculate that terrorist organizations can use steganography, hiding secret messages within other communications. The British made use of these tricks in World War II. BBC public broadcasts often carried secret messages to agents, such as announcing a "secret" number within a weather forecast. Only the spies would know that the temperature for a certain town on a specific day would have a secret meaning. The huge volume of messages also makes it difficult to identify specific threats in advance. Scouring files stored on Internet servers, federal authorities have found copies of hundreds of e-mail messages sent over a month before the attack from personal and public library computers. The messages in Arabic and English indicate a plan for the attack. Modern steganography can hide messages inside images or other computer files. Free "stego-tools" can be found on the Internet. While bin Laden-funded terrorists have used this technique in the past, so far no one has found evidence of its use in the September 11 attacks.

Source: Adapted from Lisa M. Krieger, "How Technology Is Used to Mask Communications," *Mercury News,* October 1, 2001.

FIGURE 4.9
Employee background
checks are important. For
a fee, several websites
help small businesses
perform basic background
checks to verify SSNs and
check public criminal
records.

➤ **Audits**
➤ **Monitoring**
➤ **Background checks:**   http://www.casebreakers.com/

http://www.knowx.com/

http://www.publicdata.com/

kept away from visitors and delivery people. Many types of locks and keys can be used to protect terminals and personal computers. Similarly, all documents should be controlled. Paper copies of important reports should be shredded. All financial data is routinely audited by both internal and external auditors. Sometimes hidden control data is used to make sure procedures are followed.

Monitoring

Another effective security provision is to monitor access to all of the data. Most computers can keep track of every change to every file. They can keep a log of who accesses each file. They track every time someone incorrectly enters a password. An audit trail of every file change can be provided to management. That means it is possible to find out who changed the salary data, what time it was changed, and from which terminal.

Remember that every device connected to the Internet is given a unique number as an address. Every website that you visit can track this number. In some cases, you can only be identified down to the company your work for, but in many situations, companies can monitor exactly what each machine is doing at any time. Additional software can be installed on computers to provide even more detail—including storing all keystrokes.

Hiring and Employee Evaluation

Because insiders raise the greatest security issues, it makes sense to be careful when you hire employees. Employers should always check candidates' references. In more extreme situations, employers can check employee backgrounds for criminal records. There are several instances of disgruntled employees causing security problems. In many cases, the best security solution is to establish close relationships with your employees and encourage teamwork. Employees who work closely together can defuse potential problems and informally monitor the work of other employees. Figure 4.9 notes that several websites will search public records to perform basic background checks for small businesses. Validating social security numbers is an important step for many U.S. businesses.

Encryption

Encryption is the foundation of many aspects of security. For example, encryption protects messages sent across the Internet and protects files stored on servers. Cryptography has been around for thousands of years, but computers have radically altered the types of codes available. One important feature to remember in terms of cryptography and computers is the concept of **brute force** attacks. If a hacker knows the algorithm method used to encrypt a message, it might be conceivable to have a computer test every possible key to decode the message. The essence of stopping a brute force attack is to have a key that is so long that it would take hundreds of years to try every combination. The problem is that computers get faster every year. So encryption technologies that were secure 20 years ago can be broken in hours today.

FIGURE 4.10
Single key encryption.
Both the person who
encrypts the message and
the person who decrypts it
use the same key. The
systems are fast, but it is
difficult to safely
distribute the key.

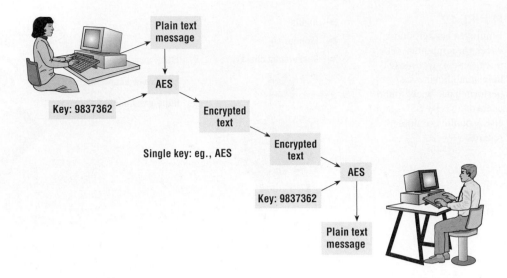

Encryption should be seriously considered for any communications that are sent between computers. Without encryption, it is relatively easy for unauthorized people to deliberately or accidentally read or change the messages. Encryption is available with many personal computer software packages. Almost all spreadsheets and word processors permit you to encrypt your file when you save it. To read it back, you have to enter the correct password. You also can find encryption packages on the Internet that will protect your e-mail messages.

Single Key

For many years, single-key encryption codes were the only systems available. Figure 4.10 shows the basic steps required to encrypt and decrypt a message with a single-key system. Both the sender and receiver have the software that handles the encryption and decryption. Both people also need to have the same key, which is the difficult part. How do you deliver a secret key to someone? And if you can deliver a secret key, you might as well send the message the same way.

On the other hand, single-key systems are fast. They can encrypt or decrypt a message with almost no delay. Since the late 1970s, most of the business world standardized on the **data encryption standard (DES)**. However, this system only supported keys of 56 bits, and by 2000, messages encrypted with DES were broken in about 24 hours by brute force attacks in various contests. Triple DES was popular for a while—essentially encrypting the message three times. But in 2001, the U.S. government chose a new method known as the **Advanced Encryption Standard (AES)** because it is fast and users have a choice of a key length of 128, 192, or 256 bits. Keep in mind that longer keys make the message more secure (harder to break by brute force), but increase the time it takes to encrypt and decrypt the message.

Public-Key Infrastructure

Public-key infrastructure (PKI) is a substantial leap in encryption technology. The method arose from a military-political question. Given a U.S. embassy in the middle of a foreign nation that can intercept all communications, how can a secret message be transmitted out of the embassy when there is no way to exchange a secret key? The answer was found by two mathematicians (Diffie and Hellman), and later refined into a system (and company) named after three other mathematicians (RSA: Rivest, Shamir, and Adleman). The solution is to create an encryption system that uses two keys: a **public key** and a **private key.**

Dual-Key Encryption

The essence of a dual-key system is that it takes both keys to encrypt and decrypt a message. Whichever key is used to encrypt the message, the other key must be used to decrypt it. Figure 4.11 illustrates the process. The beauty of the system is that anyone can be given your public

FIGURE 4.11

Dual-key encryption. Alice sends a message that only Bob can read. With a dual-key system, one key encrypts the message, the other decrypts it. Once Bob's public key is applied to the message, only Alice's private key will retrieve the message. Keys are usually very large prime numbers.

FIGURE 4.12

Dual-key encryption for message authentication. Bob sends a message to Alice at the bank. Using his private key ensures that the message must have come from him. Using Alice's public key prevents anyone else from reading the message.

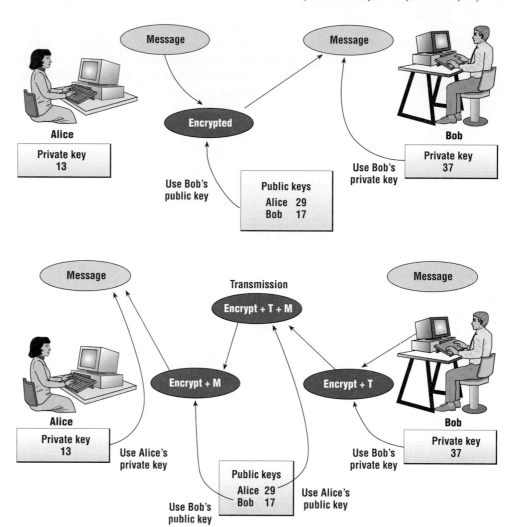

key—in fact, this key can be published in a directory. Then whenever someone wants to send you a secure message, he or she simply uses the RSA algorithm and your public key. At that point, the message is gibberish and can only be decrypted using your super secret private key. No one can read or alter the message. However, someone could destroy it before it reaches you.

Today's Web browsers use this method to encrypt credit-card transmissions. The Web server sends your browser a public key. The browser encrypts the content and sends it across the Internet. Only the Web server can decrypt the contents—using the private key. A similar system called **pretty good privacy (PGP)** is available on the Internet to encrypt e-mail messages.

The one drawback to dual-key encryption systems is that they tend to be slow—particularly for long messages. One common solution is to use dual-key encryption to establish the identity of the parties and to exchange a one-time secret key to be used for the rest of the transmissions. The single-key system is fast and protects the transmitted data, and the initial dual-key system makes it possible to distribute the secret key without anyone stealing it.

Authentication

A second aspect of dual keys has even more uses. PKI can be used for **authentication.** Consider the case where Alice works for a bank, and she receives a message that claims to be from Bob, and it says to pay you $1 million. How does Alice know that the message is authentic and not forged by you? Consider the case where Bob does want to pay you some money (but only $100).

Figure 4.12 shows the answer. To make sure that only Alice can read the message (and that no one else can modify it), Bob encrypts it with her public key. To ensure that the message is authentic, Bob also encrypts it with his private key. Remember that the keys always work in pairs. When Alice receives the message, she uses Bob's public key and her private key to decrypt it. If the message is decrypted correctly, then it was not modified in transit, and it could only have come from Bob. This process is used to create **digital signatures.** In 2000, the federal government passed a law declaring digital signatures to carry the same legal authority as a traditional signature for legal purposes.

Certificate Authorities

The proper name for dual-key encryption is public-key infrastructure (PKI). Why is the word *infrastructure* so important? Think about how a hacker might attack the system in Figure 4.12. What if Bob did not know much about technology and encryption? So, posing as Bob, you create a private key and publish the public key in a directory under Bob's name. Then you send your e-mail message to the bank pretending to be Bob, using "his" public key, and asking the bank to pay you $1 million. The message decrypts fine, and Alice believes the message is legitimate. Similar problems can arise by impersonating the bank.

To make the PKI system work, it is critical that the directory of public keys accurately represent the people indicated. So, some organization needs to be in charge of the public directory, and people who wish to use it need to verify their identity before registering a public key. At the moment, this task is handled only by Verisign, a public company—with virtually no regulation or rules. Verisign issues **digital certificates** that verify the identity of the person who generated the public key. Companies and individuals can purchase these certificates, and you are supposed to verify your identity before receiving the certificate. However, in 2001, Verisign announced that they accidentally issued a digital certificate to an imposter who claimed to be from Microsoft. Eventually Verisign caught the mistake and invalidated the certificate, but the incident points out that the process is far from foolproof. The troubling point is that for the PKI system to work, the certificates and keys must be controlled by a trusted organization. Other companies (including the U.S. Post Office) have attempted to become trusted **certificate authorities,** but so far none have been economically successful.

E-Commerce Security Issues

E-commerce uses the same security technologies available to any business. However, some aspects of e-commerce are more sensitive and require more careful security planning. These issues are highlighted in this section, with a discussion of the common solutions.

Data Transmission

Although security is an issue with all computer networks, the Internet presents a special challenge. In particular, the Internet is not owned by anyone and is really just a loose connection of computers. Virtually anyone can connect a computer to the Internet—even serving as a host computer or a router.

Because of the design and size of the network, messages are rarely sent directly from one computer to another. In almost all cases, messages are passed through several other computers or routers on the way to their destination. As indicated in Figure 4.13, it is possible for someone to join the Internet and spy on all conversations that pass through that section of the network. Unprotected credit card numbers sent over the Internet could be intercepted and used illegally.

Of course, with the huge volume of data on the Internet, there is probably only a slight chance that someone will notice one particular transaction. But, automated tools could be written to monitor all packets that transfer through one piece of the Internet; so the odds of someone stealing data are higher than they first appear.

Today, this aspect of Internet security is relatively easy to handle: simply encrypt your transmissions. Web transactions and e-mail can automatically be encrypted with a secure server. If you want to run an e-commerce site, you pay the money to Verisign for a digital certificate. Your Web server software has a special program to load the encryption identifiers. For

FIGURE 4.13

Internet security concerns. Data passes through many unknown servers. Any machine connected could read the data, destroy it, or fabricate a different message. Encryption techniques are available but not yet employed by the mainstream of Internet users. Rapidly changing automatic password generators are available for secure logins across insecure networks.

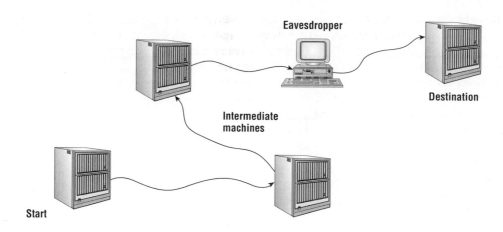

transmissions you wish to protect, you move the Web pages into a special directory. From that point, your Web server and the customer's browser automatically handle the data encryption.

To improve security for workers who need to connect to computers across the Internet, many companies have created a **virtual private network (VPN)**. A VPN encrypts all transmissions before they are sent across the Internet. Using this technology, it is safe for employees to work from home using high-speed Internet connection. The encryption protects the data just as securely as having a local wired connection.

Wireless Networks

Wireless networks add an extra challenge to security because the radio waves are accessible to anyone within a certain distance of the antenna. Two primary types of wireless systems exist today: (1) private LANs that you install at your company, and (2) public networks that offer shared access to millions of people (such as the cellular phone system). The public networks are similar to the Internet. If you want to protect your transmissions, you will have to encrypt your messages. Some of the digital phones offer encryption, but the systems are sometimes weak. But it is better than the old days of analog cell phones, where anyone with a scanner could eavesdrop on your phone calls.

Private wireless LANs can create more problems, because a stranger might sit outside your building and connect to your network. Early implementers of wireless LANs experienced these problems when they failed to activate all of the security features. Wireless LANs generally require a password to allow users to connect to the network. They can also encrypt all transmissions to prevent others from intercepting the transmissions. The only catch with encryption is that it slows down the transmission, and wireless networks are relatively slow already. So you have to make a tradeoff decision: do you want faster wireless communications or a more secure network?

Carnivore, Echelon, and Escrow Keys

An interesting twist to interception of data transmissions is government involvement. In the U.S., for years the government has had wiretap capabilities to force the phone company to intercept and record voice calls—with the permission of a judge. Digital and computer transmissions make this task more difficult. So, the federal government has been working on systems to intercept and decode data.

One public system revealed in 2000 is an FBI sponsored computer system known as Carnivore. (In 2001, it was renamed DCS-10000 but most people still call it by the more colorful name.) Essentially, it is a computer with special software that can be installed at an ISP to capture all Internet traffic from a specified person. The system is supposed to be used with the permission of a judge to reduce criminal activities, and it is supposed to only capture data from the alleged criminal.

Echelon is a more secret project run internationally by the NSA in cooperation with Canada, the United Kingdom, Australia, and New Zealand. The government has not officially

FIGURE 4.14

Escrow keys. The U.S. government is concerned that citizens and foreigners will use encryption for "undesirable" purposes, such as spying and committing crimes. The National Security Agency created a secret method of encrypting messages, including digital phone transmissions. Every encryption device can be broken with two special keys (numbers) that are held in escrow by judicial or governmental agencies. On receiving court permission, police would be able to decrypt any message or conversation.

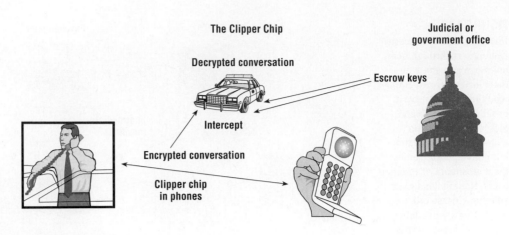

acknowledged its existence, but the foreign press (and several government committees) have investigated portions of it. It is a system that intercepts a variety of communications, including faxes, e-mail messages, international phone calls, and cellular phones in several nations (by law, it is not supposed to be used in the United States). Several powerful computers evaluate the intercepted data and search it for key words to search for terrorist and illegal drug activity.

Along the same lines and for the same reasons, the NSA created a special encryption system similar to dual-key encryption. However, it had a unique twist: every encryption key has two escrow keys that can be used to decrypt any message. The system was originally created for digital cell phones. The cell phones can automatically encrypt the transmissions. But the security organizations wanted the ability to get a wiretap authorization to intercept phone calls in certain cases. Figure 4.14 shows how the police would collect the escrow keys from a judge. Entering the key numbers into a special receiver would decrypt the conversation without the user's knowledge. For a short time, the U.S. government thought about requiring that only escrow-key encryption would be legal. But this requirement would have destroyed the international sales of most U.S. products, because businesses in other nations would not trust the U.S. government. The technology still exists and is used in some products, but most consumers would avoid it—if they knew it was being used.

Theft of Data from Servers

Because of the powerful encryption systems available, interception of transmissions is a relatively minor problem—as long as you use the encryption techniques. Instead, the servers connected to the Internet have become tempting targets. Several incidents have been reported of hackers stealing millions of records of customer credit card data from e-commerce firms. While credit laws protect consumers, the loss of a credit card is still painful and time consuming. Additionally, the e-commerce firm faces liability issues if it did not adequately secure the data.

Securing servers uses the same technologies as any computer system: (1) make sure the latest operating system patches have been applied, (2) set access control rights to the smallest number of people possible, (3) encrypt the sensitive data, (4) hire trusted employees, and (5) monitor access to the sensitive data. A sixth step (firewalls) is explained in a later section. In 2000, Visa added some details and expanded this list to 12 principles that all Internet firms are supposed to follow. At some point, the rules might become mandatory, but any e-commerce firm needs to be careful about protecting servers and customer data.

Denial of Service

Denial of service attacks have gained importance in the last few years. The essence of an e-commerce site is the ability to reach customers 24 hours a day. If someone floods the site with meaningless traffic, then no one can use the service, and the company may go out of

FIGURE 4.15

Denial of service attack. A bored hacker first breaks into weakly protected home and school systems and loads a hidden program on thousands of machines. At a signal, all of the zombie machines send messages to the server, preventing everyone else from using it.

FIGURE 4.16

Firewalls. Firewalls are packet analyzers that are used to keep local data from moving to the Internet and to limit the actions allowed in from the Internet. Firewalls examine each packet of data on the network and block certain types to limit the interaction of the company network with the Internet.

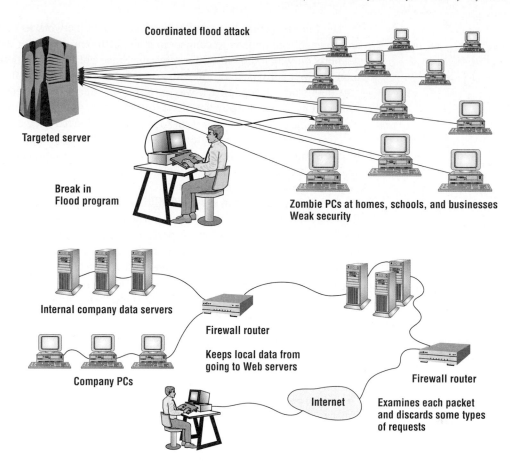

business. Several variations of DoS have been used in the past couple of years, sometimes dragging down large chunks of the Internet at one time. Most of the techniques take advantage of flaws in the Internet protocols or in their implementation on a particular type of server. Figure 4.15 illustrates the process. A hacker breaks into some weakly protected computers and loads a special program that is hidden. On a signal, the machines all send requests to the targeted server. With some known Internet design flaws, these messages can be multiplied so that a few thousand messages become millions and bog down the server. This type of attack is hard to trace to the original source unless investigators find monitor logs on the zombie machines. Several Internet sites provide simplified instructions on how to perform these attacks, so even weak hackers or "script kiddies" can create havoc.

Firewalls and Intrusion Detection

The Internet and e-commerce add some complications to protecting company data. You need to give customers access to some important company data to provide the best e-commerce site. For example, customers like to know if an item is in stock before they place an order. To offer this service, you need to connect your Web server to your company inventory system. But any time you open a connection from the Internet to your company data, you have to be extremely careful to control that interaction. Security access controls and database security controls are two important provisions.

Beyond access control, simply connecting your company computers to the Internet could cause problems within the network itself. You do not want company network traffic being sent to the Internet, and you do not want outsiders to be able to see your internal computers—giving them the chance to try and break into your servers. Figure 4.16 shows how firewalls are used to isolate sections of the network. **Firewalls** are essentially routers that examine each packet of network data passing through them and block certain types to limit the interaction of the company network with the Internet.

The Internet protocols were designed as an open network to transport many types of data and to enable computers to connect in many different ways. For example, servers have logical ports on which they listen for requests. Since only a few of these ports are used for common Internet activities, the firewall is configured to block all of the other ports, to prevent outsiders from finding a back way into one of your servers. Security experts configure the routers, but as a manager, you need to make sure your company is using them. Also, you will find that some tasks you want to do will be blocked by the firewalls. Usually, these restrictions are for your own safety, but sometimes security analysts go a little overboard and block useful features. This tradeoff between user access and company security is an ongoing problem. It often arises because the security tools are not sophisticated enough, so security personnel choose to block everything.

An **intrusion detection system (IDS)** is a combination of hardware and software that continuously monitors the network traffic. The hardware is similar to that used in a firewall, but instead of blocking the packets, it performs a more complex analysis. The systems use a set of rules to monitor all Internet traffic and search for patterns. For instance, a common attack often begins with a sweep of a target's network to look for open ports. The IDS observes this repeated scanning, blocks the requests, identifies the source, and sends a warning to the security manager. An IDS is an effective monitoring tool, but the cheaper ones tend to generate too many false warnings.

Privacy

Privacy is an increasingly important and controversial issue in our computer-driven society. As indicated in Figure 4.17, with increases in computing power and declining storage costs, it is becoming possible to keep and search records of almost all individual activities.

Marketers argue that increased knowledge of individual customers is critical to knowing exactly what items to provide and to market to each person. The basic argument is that if

FIGURE 4.17

Privacy. Many businesses and government agencies collect data. With increasing computer capabilities, it is becoming possible to collect and correlate this data to track many aspects of individual lives.

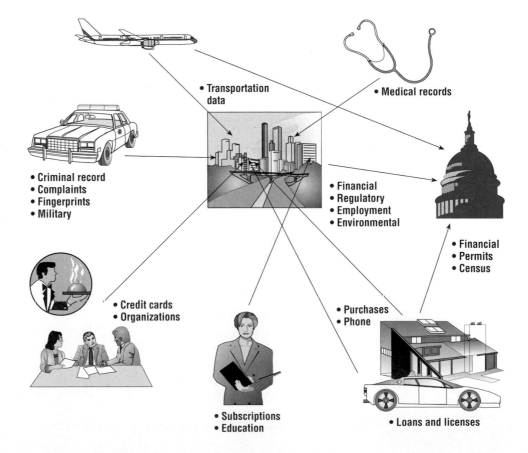

- Transportation data
- Medical records
- Criminal record
- Complaints
- Fingerprints
- Military
- Financial
- Regulatory
- Employment
- Environmental
- Financial
- Permits
- Census
- Credit cards
- Organizations
- Purchases
- Phone
- Subscriptions
- Education
- Loans and licenses

businesses know exactly what consumers want, then there will be fewer "junk" mail promotions, because each consumer will receive solicitations keyed to his or her lifestyle.

Of course, the potential for abuse is enormous. Several serious privacy violations have already been reported by government agencies. For example, IRS employees were accused of pulling records on their neighbors. Some law enforcement officers used the national computer systems to run background checks for private agencies. In response to these problems, the agencies increased their monitoring of worker activity to reduce the probability of future abuses.

Local and state governments collect a considerable amount of data for public records. This data includes real estate transactions, business licenses, marriages, divorces, and deaths and is open to public inspection at the county records office. In many cities, this data is published in local newspapers. Recently, several firms and some counties have been making this data available on websites, so everyone can check up on their neighbors. This situation illustrates the questions that society will eventually need to answer. This data has always been available publicly, but it has been difficult to obtain and hard to search and correlate. Placing it on the Internet makes it accessible to more people. For example, property taxes are based on real estate valuation, which depends on the prices of other houses in a neighborhood. Making data accessible to everyone makes it easier to find and correct inequities. But as the mass of online data increases, it becomes easier for people and businesses to learn more details about individuals.

Wireless and M-Commerce

Wireless devices offer even more potential invasions of privacy. Remember that radio devices remain in contact with the nearest cellular tower. Hence, the surrounding towers can be used to pinpoint the location of the device and the user—at any time. Additionally, many proposed m-commerce methods use the location of the consumer to offer information and advertisements. Some firms are already beginning to market tools to worried parents that can track the location of cell phones carried by their children. While this technology is probably useful to parents, it highlights the loss of privacy that can be applied to any person.

Consumer Privacy Statements

For some reason, people have been a little more wary of online privacy. Consumers who routinely give their names to grocery stores enabling them to track every purchase, are somehow concerned about privacy on the Internet. In response, e-commerce sites are encouraged to create privacy statements. Generally, privacy statements explain what data is collected and how it will be used. In the United States, there are no laws limiting how the data can be used, so companies are free to say almost anything in a privacy statement—particularly since few people actually wade through the thousands of words of legal text. Technically, there are no specific laws enforcing privacy statements, but in one case, the FTC did threaten to sue a bankrupt toy sales e-commerce company that publicly discussed selling its customer list, in contradiction to the privacy statement.

Cell Phone Location

Federal law now requires that cell-phone providers be able to locate customers placing emergency (911) calls from their cell phones. Sprint was the first to introduce a cell phone equipped with a GPS system. It is capable of locating the caller to within 50 meters. Sprint still needs to integrate the latitude and longitude data into its network so it can be passed to the emergency crews. Per FCC requirements, Sprint plans to sell only GPS-enabled phones after December 31, 2002. So far, AT&T and Cingular Wireless plan to offer location services with existing phones using triangulation from multiple towers.

Source: Adapted from Bob Brewin, "Spring PCS Debuts GPS-Equipped Wireless Phone for 911 Calls," *Computerworld*, October 1, 2001.

FIGURE 4.18
Web cookies. Cookies are used to keep track of the user across page requests. Each time the user PC requests a page, it returns a small text file (cookie) containing an identification number.

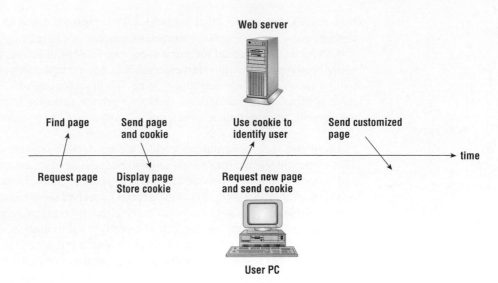

Worker Monitoring

According to one survey by IDG, 17 percent of the Fortune 1000 firms monitor their workers' use of the Internet and e-mail. Of those, 12 percent do not notify employees that they are being monitored. Some estimates predict that the majority of firms will be using surveillance software in the next few years. Some businesses are concerned about workers transferring confidential data. Others are attempting to avoid discrimination and harassment lawsuits arising from workers displaying objectionable content. A few managers have indicated they are trying to reduce the time employees "waste" on personal surfing. Given today's Internet technology, it is relatively easy to monitor computer usage by employees. These records are sometimes used to identify problems.

Most businesses today use electronic badges to control access to offices and other areas of the company. These badge systems are computer controlled and could be used to track the location of employees throughout the day. In a well-run organization, there would be little need to track employees; however, the point is that the capability exists.

Courts have repeatedly held that all of the technologies and monitoring are legal—because the equipment is owned and controlled by the company. Many companies do not actively use these records, but search them when a problem arises. This usage can be beneficial to employees. If a hacker breaks into the company system and takes over an employee's computer, the extensive records could be used to show the employee is innocent when the FBI comes knocking on the door.

E-Commerce, Cookies, and Third Parties

The technology for websites did not initially consider the demands of e-commerce. It was originally intended to simply display pages independently—every request for a page is independent of any other request. For e-commerce, the Web server needs to keep track of information about the person requesting a page. For instance, a shopping cart system needs to store items selected by the customer. Similarly, any site using security needs to track the user through a series of pages—otherwise it would force the user to log in for every new page. These problems were solved with the creation of "magic" **cookies**. A Web cookie is a small text file that the server asks the browser to store on the user's computer. As shown in Figure 4.18, whenever the browser requests another page from that server, it returns the cookie file containing an identification number. Hence, the server knows which user is returning. This use of cookies is common, and relatively benign. Yes, the cookie could be used to track visitors, but presumably the visitor is purchasing items and already willingly provides more detailed information to complete the transaction.

Figure 4.19 shows a more troublesome use of cookies. In 2000, it was revealed that Doubleclick.com, the leading Web advertisement-placing firm, was using cookies as a

FIGURE 4.19

Misuse of Web cookies. Doubleclick.com as a third party places cookies onto visitor PCs. Every time the visitor sees an ad delivered by Doubleclick, Doubleclick records the user, the date/time, and the site visited. Doubleclick attempted to market this huge database.

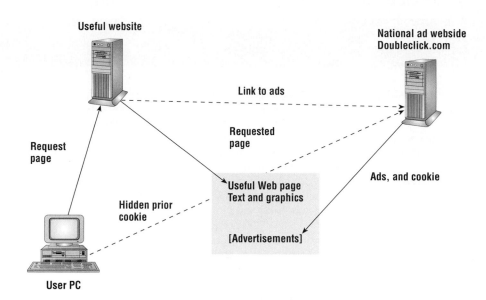

third party to track page visits by millions of people. Leading websites register with Doubleclick to carry advertising. Companies wishing to advertise on the Web create the ad and pay Doubleclick to carry it on its servers. The original website includes a link to Doubleclick software that delivers the ads and records page views so the site owners can be paid the correct fee. However, Doubleclick also includes a cookie that is sent to the visiting PC with each ad placement. Anytime the user visits a site that deals with Doubleclick, the identifying cookie, date/time, and site visited are stored on Doubleclick's servers. Web users were understandably upset when Doubleclick attempted to market this data collection—particularly when the company wanted to tie the online identities to real-world names and addresses.

To prevent this loss of privacy, browsers enable you to turn off cookies—but then you will not be able to use many secure sites, such those run by banks. With the XP release of Windows, Microsoft is offering another option: the ability to refuse third-party cookies, such as those placed by Doubleclick. The browser would still exchange the short-term cookies used to maintain identification across sessions, but it will not store or return cookies to any server that was a third party. This option is a useful compromise that allows customers to deal with one company and still maintain some control over privacy.

Privacy Laws and Rules

The U.S. has few laws regarding privacy, although a few states do offer some stronger protections. On the federal level, the Bork Bill states that video rental stores and libraries cannot release their rental data. It was passed by Congress when some overzealous reporters obtained the video rental records of a judge nominee (Bork). The 1974 Family Educational Privacy Act prohibits schools from releasing grade data without permission from the student. The Privacy Act of 1994 placed some minimal limits on the sales of state and local driver's license data. The Privacy Act of 1974 limits what data can be collected and shared by federal agencies. However, various rules, interpretations, and practices have created enough loopholes to circumvent most of the original provisions.

In terms of financial data, various laws give consumers the ability to obtain their credit records (for a fee), and the right to dispute items in the report and have the dispute resolved within 30 days. In 2001, a federal rule took effect that was initiated by former President Clinton, to provide some control over the use of medical data. Health care providers are already complaining about the high cost of implementing the provisions, and it will take years to establish an accepted interpretation of exactly what is allowed and disallowed under the rules. Nominally, the rules state that transfer of data (particularly prescription drug data) requires permission from the patient.

Reality Bytes   Locating the Internet

Many people perceive the Internet as being a cloud—companies and users simply connect machines to some point on the network, and data can be stored and transferred anywhere. Physical location and geography should not matter in this virtual world. Many people also picture servers as being the same as companies. A website is often assumed to be located in the corporate offices of some company. Users are seen as random people located anywhere in the world, but no one really cares where. Reality is somewhat different. Increasingly, servers need to be connected to high-speed fiber-optic lines. These lines are expensive to install and they terminate in only certain locations. Consequently, Exodus Communications hosts 49 of the top 100 websites in 35 server farms in strategic locations around the world. To improve user performance, another company (Akamai) runs 11,000 caching servers in 62 countries. These servers intercept requests for pages and hold copies of large content like graphics. By being located closer to customers, the servers can provide faster response times and can reduce the load on the primary servers. But, these locations also make it possible for Akamai to provide another service to companies: it can identify the location of the user requesting pages. Quova is a company that offers the GeoPoint location service. It continually tracks IP address by location. The company claims to be able to identify the user's country with 98 percent accuracy and for U.S. users 85 percent accuracy of the city. Of course, if users adopt Web-enabled cell phones with GPS locators, it will be possible to identify locations down to a few meters. Exodus filed for bankruptcy in 2001 and was acquired by Cable and Wireless in 2002.

Source: Adapted from *The Economist,* "Geography and the Net," August 11, 2001.

In contrast to the United States, the European Union has solid consumer privacy laws. Most EU nations have adopted the European Commission's 1995 Data Protection Directive. Since 1978, France has had its own strict Data Protection Act. The laws basically state that personal data can only be collected with the user's permission, the user must be clearly told how the data will be used, and the user has the right to see and to change any personal data. The laws have an additional important condition: personal consumer data cannot be moved to a nation with lesser privacy controls—notably the United States. The United States has negotiated a loose "safe harbor" provision, so that companies can bring European consumer data to the U.S. if the companies formally agree to abide by the EU directives and also agree not to resell the data. These provisions make it more expensive to collect data in Europe—sometimes beyond the price of small businesses. For example, in the United States, it is relatively easy to purchase e-mail lists of potential customers for a few hundred dollars. In Europe, these lists would generally be illegal to use, since the customer did not agree to the unsolicited use of his or her address.

Anonymity

Anonymity is the flip side of the privacy question. Until recently, it has been difficult or impossible to provide anonymous access to the Internet. Using advanced encryption, some firms now offer people the ability to use the Internet without revealing any data about themselves. For example, Zero Knowledge is a Canadian company that provides a proxy server that hides your IP address. Sites that you visit see only the address of the Canadian server. The server also intercepts all cookies and other files sent by some servers.

The ultimate question that you, as an important member of society, must answer is whether anonymity should be allowed, or how it should be controlled. Certainly it can be used to improve privacy. People who have a stronger belief in personal privacy will be willing to pay the fee—others will decide that privacy is not an issue. But, what about drug dealers, terrorists, child pornographers, and other illegal activities that society wishes to stop? Or what about anonymous harassment? Someone could use the technology to harass and intimidate people on the Internet. Perhaps society should not allow anonymity? On the flip side, who makes that decision? If some nation chooses to ban dissenting viewpoints, or if a government whistleblower needs to protect a career, anonymous sites can be valuable tools to increase information and open discussions. Keep in mind that existing servers are anonymous only up to a point. With a court order, it is possible for existing anonymity servers to log and trace all current communications back to the real user.

Reality Bytes   Employee Monitoring

Several software companies sell products to monitor employee Web and e-mail usage. Based on analysis of their financial reports the Internet usage of as many as 14 million U.S. workers is under continous surveillance. Companies such as American Express, Nike, and 20th Century Fox routinely monitor employees, as does the U.S. Army and the National Park Service. The most popular surveillance packages are Websense and MIMEsweeper. The Privacy Foundation notes that worldwide 100 million workers (about 27 percent of those who use the Internet) are being routinely monitored.

Source: Adapted from Stephen Shankland, "Web, E-Mail Monitoring Spreads," CNET, July 8, 2001.

A Manager's View

Computer security and privacy are critical issues for any company. For Web-based businesses, careful controls and continual vigilance are mandatory. Information systems have many potential weaknesses and threats. But overall, electronic security can be stronger than any other form—if it is maintained by experts. Encryption is a key component in securing systems, communications, and protecting privacy.

Privacy and anonymity are growing business and political issues on the Internet. Managers are increasingly being caught in the crossfire between marketing needs, consumer preferences and government regulations.

Summary

Companies have to trust employees, consultants, and business partners, but this group presents the greatest security threats. Natural disasters are a threat to the physical assets, but their business damage can be minimized by having up-to-date backups, and a disaster plan with arrangements to run operations offsite if a disaster strikes. The Internet provides more avenues of attack for outsiders—particularly from viruses spread through e-mail messages. The best defenses are to install all current operating system patches, to assign access rights carefully, and to monitor the computer usage with an intrusion detection system. However, denial of service attacks are particularly hard to prevent.

Encryption protects data during transmission. It is particularly useful for sending credit card data over the Internet. It can also be used to provide digital signatures that authenticate users to validate the source of messages.

The flip side of conducting more business on the Internet is a potential loss of privacy. Partly because of the way the Internet works, and partly because of the need for security, businesses track individual users. Some firms track people even further—to the point of recording most websites that they visit. With almost no laws, these companies are free to market this information to other companies. Some individuals may object to this loss of privacy. Without supervision, businesses have an obligation to establish clear and reasonable privacy policies—and to stick by those policies.

Encryption technology also makes it possible to have anonymity servers, so people can pay a fee to have an untraceable Internet presence. While it does protect privacy, this technology raises some unresolved societal issues in terms of the potential for harassment and criminal activities.

Key Words

Advanced Encryption Standard (AES), *136*	data encryption standard (DES), *136*	Kerberos, *132*
application service provider (ASP), *128*	data mirroring, *126*	pretty good privacy (PGP), *137*
authentication, *137*	denial of service (DoS), *130*	private key, *136*
biometrics, *133*	digital certificate, *138*	public key, *136*
brute force, *135*	digital signature, *138*	uninterruptible power supply (UPS), *131*
certificate authority, *138*	firewall, *141*	virtual private network (VPN), *139*
cold site, *126*	hot site, *125*	virus, *129*
cookies, *144*	intrusion detection system (IDS), *142*	

Website References

Computer Crime

CERT	**www.cert.org**
Computer Security Institute	**www.gocsi.com**
FBI: Internet Fraud Complaint Center	**www.ifccfbi.gov**
Hackers	**www.hackers.com**
Interpol	**www.interpol.int/Public/TechnologyCrime**
National Fraud Information	**www.fraud.org**
National Infrastructure Protection Center	**www.nipc.gov**
National Security Agency	**www.nsa.gov**
National White Collar Crime Center	**www.cybercrime.org**
SEC Internet enforcement	**www.sec.gov/divisions/enforce/internetenforce.htm**
Virtual Librarian crime links	**www.virtuallibrarian.com/legal/org.html**

Privacy

Electronic Frontier Foundation	**www.eff.com**
Electronic Privacy Information Center	**www.epic.org**
FTC advisory committee	**www.ftc.gov/acoas**
Kidz privacy	**www.ftc.gov/bcp/conline/edcams/kidzprivacy**
Platform for privacy preferences	**www.w3.org/p3p**
Privacy, ACM	**www.acm.org/usacm/privacy**
Privacy International	**www.privacyinternational.org**
Privacy Rights	**www.privacyrights.org**

Additional Reading

Bequai, August. *Technocrimes.* Lexington, MA: Lexington Books, 1989. [Security Pacific and other cases.]

Harriss, H. "Computer Virus Attacks Have Cost Businesses $7.6 Billion in 1999." *Computer Economics*, Report dated June 18, 1999. (http://www.infoec.com/viruses/99/viruses_062299a_j.shtml) [Increased costs of virus attacks.]

Faltermayer, Charlotte. "Cyberveillance." *Time*, August 14, 2000, p. B22. [Worker monitoring statistics.]

Forno, Richard, and William Feinbloom, "PKI: A Question of Trust and Value." *Communications of the ACM* 44, no. 6, June 2001. [A good summary of the difficulties of trusting public key certificate authorities.]

Feig, Christy. "Medical Privacy Rules to Take Effect." CNN, April 12, 2001. http://www.cnn.com/2001/HEALTH/04/12/medical.privacy/index.html?s=2 [Notice of new federal medical privacy rules.]

Oakes, Chris. "Privacy Laws Aim to Protect the Hunters as Well as the Hunted." *International Herald Tribune,* March 23, 2001. [Good analysis of European Union privacy controls.]

Thurman (pseudonym), Mathias. "What to Do When the Feds Come Knocking." *Computerworld,* June 4, 2001, p. 62. [Situation where hacker used a stolen laptop to attack other systems, and computer logs helped show the employee was innocent.]

Whiteside, Thomas. *Computer Capers: Tales of Electronic Thievery, Embezzlement and Fraud,* New York: Crowell, 1978. [Early cases of computer fraud and abuse.]

http://csrc.nist.gov/encryption/aes/ [Reference source for AES algorithm.]
http://www.visabrc.com/doc.phtml?2,64,932,932a_cisp.html [Reference to Visa CISP
security.]

Review Questions

1. What are primary threats to information processed by computers?
2. How do viruses spread over the Internet? How do you stop them?
3. What methods are available to identify computer users?
4. What are access controls and how are they used to protect information?
5. What threat are audits trying to protect against?
6. What are the advantages and disadvantages of dual-key encryption compared to single-key encryption?
7. How can dual-key encryption be used to authenticate a message?
8. Why are certificate authorities so important in a public key infrastructure?
9. Why are wireless transmissions more of a security problem than wired systems?
10. What is a denial of service attack? Why is it so important in e-commerce? Why is it so difficult to prevent?
11. What is a firewall and how does it protect a company from Internet attacks?
12. What capabilities do government agencies have to deal with crime and terrorism using electronic transmissions?
13. On the Web, what are cookies? Why are they necessary? How have some companies abused them?
14. What are the societal tradeoffs between privacy and anonymity?

Exercises

1. Should anonymity servers be allowed to exist? Is there a way to eliminate them?
2. Create a subdirectory on a computer that enables you to set access rights. Select a user or group and set permissions so members of that group can read the data but cannot change it. All other users (except yourself) cannot read the data.
3. Teamwork assignment. Get a copy of PGP (or sign up for a free e-mail encryption key at Thwate). Write an e-mail message and send an encrypted copy to the other members of your team.
4. Conduct a small survey of students (not in your MIS class). Find out how often they back up their data, the last time they updated their operating systems, and how many of them have been infected by a virus in the last 6, 12, and 24 months.
5. Find and download a free trial copy of a personal intrusion detection system, and install it on a PC connected to the Internet full time (school connection, DSL, or cable modem). Let the system run for a few days and record how many potential attacks it records.
6. Should government surveillance of electronic transmissions be increased or decreased? Defend your answer.
7. Based on past history (e.g., J. Edgar Hoover), who is most likely to be directly affected by excessive government surveillance?
8. Assume that you own a small business that is growing (e.g., 100 employees). Write a policy that details the use of e-mail and the Internet for your employees.
9. As manager in a Web-based B2C company, write a privacy policy for data collected on the site. Remember that if you violate the policy, you could be fined.
10. Find information on two biometric devices. Identify the costs and the steps required to install them. Can they be used for identification over the Internet?

Rolling Thunder Database

11. What privacy problems might exist at Rolling Thunder? What rules or procedures should we enact to avoid problems? Write a privacy statement for the company.

12. If Rolling Thunder Bicycles adds an Internet site to order bicycles and deal with customers, what security procedures should be implemented to protect the data?

13. Research the costs and steps involved in setting up a secure Web server for Rolling Thunder that can be used to sell bicycles over the Internet.

14. Write a disaster plan for Rolling Thunder. Identify how the backup tapes will be handled and the type of system you will need if a natural disaster hits.

Wholesale Trade

The wholesale industry is a broad and fragmented industry with multiple channels of distribution and more than $250 billion in annual sales. Wholesalers market to a number of distribution channels, including retail outlets; small distributorships; national, regional, and local distributors; direct mail suppliers; large warehouses; and manufacturers' direct sales force. The industry is focused primarily on the food, health, and industrial maintenance and repair sectors.

Industry and Market Analysis

The wholesale industry's customers have increasingly focused on reducing overall costs by dealing with fewer suppliers and maintaining relationships with those that can offer a broad product selection, automated order processing, and advanced services such as inventory management and nationwide support. To remain competitive, it has become increasingly important for distributors to provide customers with wider product selection, lower costs, and value-added service.

The principal means by which wholesalers compete with manufacturers and other distributors is by providing local stocks, efficient service, account managers, competitive prices, several catalogs, extensive technical and application data, procurement process consulting services, and other efforts to assist customers in lowering their total costs.

The wholesalers' advantage lies in their ability to supply products faster and allow smaller inventories to be held by the customer. Basically, wholesalers allow customers to have access to one-stop shopping, thereby reducing the number of suppliers and transactions required to obtain the supplies needed.

Financial Analysis

Since 2000, producer prices have been falling, limiting the wholesale industry's ability to increase prices. Since there has been very little price inflation, industry consolidation will likely continue as it did in the 1990s. Bottom-line gains in the industry come from increased productivity and logistic functionality, not from increased prices.

Stock/Investment Outlook

The investment outlook for the wholesale sector continues to be neutral. The lack of inflation continues to have a negative impact on profits given the companies' traditionally low profit margins. Only productivity gains and premiums paid for outright purchases are likely to influence the stock prices of wholesale companies.

Potential / Prospective for Growth

Growth in the wholesale industry is not expected to be strong. The industry is threatened by advances in communications and freight systems. Growth in individual companies will mostly be through acquisitions. Some overseas growth is possible since American companies are often at the forefront of utilizing new technologies to increase productivity.

Competitive Structure

The competitive structure of the industry has been changing. The wholesale industry now competes with more companies than ever before as manufacturers are able to reach more customers directly. Internally, competition has not allowed prices to rise and has focused on productivity gains and industry consolidation. One of the most consolidated areas is drug wholesalers, where three companies now account for over 50 percent of the industry's sales.

Technology Investment and Analysis

Wholesalers are using technology to provide many types of value-added services to the distribution of hard goods. Some of the services include sophisticated, continuous replenishment programs for customers, warehouse and inventory management, customized labeling, barcoding, and special packaging. All of these services are communications intensive, requiring powerful computer systems and data warehousing and management.

Role of Research and Development

The ability of wholesalers to succeed depends on their ability to increase productivity. Research and development to increase productivity depends on creative and thoughtful use of the many off-the-shelf products available. These technologies include bar-code scanners, wireless communications, data warehousing, and Internet communications.

The Internet

As highlighted by the Fisher Scientific case and by Baxter Healthcare, wholesale firms have a substantial advantage to tie in their customers with networks and information technology. So, the Internet is both good and bad. The Internet provides an inexpensive method to reach out to more customers, but it can also increase the competition within an industry. Several industries experimented with business-to-business auction websites. Wholesalers would offer products, tools, and raw materials for open bids. Companies that needed the specific product would place bids. The contracts and bids are all handled electronically. Few of these sites are currently profitable. Wholesalers see it as a means to drive down their prices and commissions. Buyers dislike having to pay commissions to the auction site.

Recommendation for the Future

The wholesale industry is under threat from the globalization of the world economy. Advances in communications, transportation, and data warehousing technology are decreasing the time and space that separate retailers and consumers from manufacturers. The speed with which these technological advances have been adopted varies from industry to industry. A definite trend toward the elimination of the middle person is in place. It is only by offering unique, value-added services in addition to the physical movement of goods that the wholesale industry will have opportunities for future success.

Case: Fisher Scientific International

Short Description of the Company

Fisher Scientific is best known as a manufacturer and distributor of scientific instruments, equipment, supplies, diagnostic instruments, workstations, and chemicals used by research and clinical laboratories. Fisher has been building a custom manufacturing business and, as a result, has been pursuing a path of information technology development. The strategic goal has been to maximize return on assets by increasing sales volume through all global trade channels. The Fisher Technology Group, dedicated to the development and support of advanced technology for businesses over computer networks, introduced developments to expand Internet services and develop other electronic solutions to increase business productivity.

Fisher's Acros Organics chemical business, originally acquired from the organic chemicals businesses from Eastman Kodak in 1993 and Janssen Chimica in 1994, offers custom chemical manufacturing services as well as 17,000 packaged and bulk chemicals from its catalog. In January 2000, Fisher acquired a reagent manufacturing facility in Middletown, Virginia, from Bayer Corporation. Fisher supplies reagents for Bayer diagnostic products and offers catalog and custom-manufactured reagents to biopharmaceutical companies. In March 2000, Fisher opened a CGMP kilolab facility in Loughborough, United Kingdom, to offer small-scale synthesis and process development services to the pharmaceutical industry.

Fisher's latest acquisition, Covance Pharmaceutical Packaging Services (CPPS), is one of the largest providers of contract clinical packaging services, with estimated sales of $50 million. In October 1999, CPPS opened a new 208,000-square-foot clinical packaging facility in Allentown, Pennsylvania. This represented an investment of $25 million and employed nearly 250 people. CPPS also has clinical packaging operations in Switzerland and the United Kingdom. Fisher expects to make additional pharmaceutical services acquisitions in the coming months. [Miller 2001]

Fisher was planning to merge with PSS World Medical. However, these plans were scuttled in the fall of 2000 when a drop in Fisher's stock cut the deal's value by 40 percent. Other concerns include regulatory issues and changing company financials. [Creswell 2001]

Technology Innovations

SupplyLink manages the entire product procurement process and centralizes all supplier information, making internal referencing of vendors' products more efficient. Integrated Supply-Net is a customer-specific electronic catalog that enables customers to maintain existing contracts with suppliers, including net prices.

Another leading-edge technology development of Fisher's Technology Group is ProcureNet, an online mall of more than 50 scientific suppliers run by Fisher. Even Fisher's competitors are lining up to participate. ProcureNet (www.procurenet.com) is the first public, business-to-business electronic mall that allows actual transactions to occur. ProcureNet enables vendors to create electronic storefronts to maximize exposure for their company and actually sell over the Internet. This site was developed by the Fisher Technology Group. Its main software product Cornerstone, on which ProcureNet is based, is available for sale to companies that need this technology function. Cornerstone operates much like its own catalog division. It includes online product descriptions and ordering and availability information.

The quality of this Internet commerce product has been so well received that IBM and Oracle plan to resell Fisher's software as part of their own Internet commerce products. This new business area will help Fisher offset downtrends in the laboratory markets and give Fisher a new area for future growth.

Given the high margins and after-sale consulting revenue that is involved with software licensing for Internet commerce products, this area could prove to be Fisher's most profitable area yet. The incentive for the Fisher Technology Group is that for every dollar of licensing products shipped, there are probably $10 of consulting and service revenue to follow. Given the alignment with IBM, Fisher has a high-profile distribution mechanism to launch its future marketing efforts. Fisher Technology Group's recent acquisition of UniKix will add to their expertise and capabilities in the electronic commerce area.

Internet Applications

Fisher Scientific Co. and VWR Scientific Products Corp. are working on overhauls of their business sales websites to support advanced processes such as real-time pricing and dynamic replenishment. VWR will spend at least $2 million, or about 40 percent of its annual Internet budget, on a pricing engine from Trilogy Development Corporation. The software went live in 2000, and calculates pricing and other negotiables for the company's 250,000 customers based on purchase volume and shipping logistics. Fisher has also launched a new Internet commerce site based on IBM's Net.Commerce server. The site performs real-time contract pricing, payment processing, and manages EDI transactions.

It accomplishes this by using the Trilogy and IBM servers to calculate pricing and other variables in real time in order to accommodate the nuances of business relationships. Variables include volume discounts, delivery logistics, multiple-supplier outsourcing, automated replenishment, sales forecasting, and reporting.

Telecommunications

Fisher Scientific launched a new Internet commerce site based on IBM's Net.Commerce server. It performs real-time contract pricing and payment processing, and manages EDI transactions, according to Mark Munson, general manager of Fisher Scientific's ProcureNet.

The Trilogy and IBM servers calculate pricing and other variables in real time in order to accommodate the nuances of business relationships. Variables include volume discounts, delivery logistics, multiple-supplier outsourcing, automated replenishment, sales forecasting, and reporting.

Cornerstone is Fisher's Web-based procurement software. ProcureNet is its electronic marketplace that matches buyers and sellers of business and scientific equipment. The latest version performs systems administration functions directly from the Web browser and provides improved navigation and management of product "hot lists." These are items that a company most commonly purchases from specified suppliers. ProcureNet currently lists scientific, laboratory, and electronic equipment from about 100 suppliers and receives about 500,000 inquiries per month. The service is free for buyers. Suppliers pay a setup fee of $3,500 and an annual fee of $3,900 in most cases. Fisher plans to license the ProcureNet technology to other Internet entrepreneurs who want to build electronic marketplaces or aggregate content of their own. Fisher has installed three additional upgrades to Cornerstone. These include application programming interfaces to SAP and Oracle ERP systems in version 4.4 in late summer. Customers are able to place product orders in Cornerstone that simultaneously update tables in SAP or Oracle.

On the other side, Fisher Scientific is turning to VerticalNet Inc. Internet-based industry exchanges to purchase items from smaller manufacturers. To cut costs, Fisher originally insisted on doing business only with vendors that supported EDI transactions—which ruled out most small manufacturers. With the Internet-based system, even smaller vendors can sell to Fisher Scientific.

Recommendation for the Future

The Fisher Technology Group has laid the groundwork for a promising start in the Internet commerce business. This approach should be developed further to help Fisher diversify its revenues across different industries and further focus on its competencies. Fisher has the jump on other business-to-business sites on the Web and should seize the opportunity to be the first to market a top-quality product. This focus will help Fisher stay close to its customers by making the procurement process the most convenient and efficient in the industry.

Questions

1. What are the core competencies for Fisher Scientific?

2. Upon what technologies has Fisher Scientific relied?

3. What has made Fischer so successful in developing changes in the use of advanced technology for the sales of its products?

4. What conclusions can be reached by analyzing Fisher's financial trends?

5. What does the corporation's Web page present about their business direction?

6. How is technology impacting the special parts industry?

Additional Reading

Creswell, Julie. "When a Merger Fails: Lessons from Sprint." *Fortune,* April 30, 2001, pp. 185–186.

Frook, John Evan. "E-Commerce Receives Real-Time Pricing Boost." *InternetWeek,* August 3, 1998, p. 8.

King, Julia. "Free Software Brings Small Suppliers Online," *Computerworld,* February 7, 2000.

Miller, Jim. "Outsourcing Outlook." *Pharmaceutical Technology,* March 2001, p. 158.

Case: W. W. Grainger Company

Short Description of the Company

When driving along the Edens Expressway just north of Chicago, a large sign spelling the name W. W. Grainger is visible. In fact, this name is visible no matter what state you live in. W. W. Grainger provides the products that keep the electricity flowing to all areas of America's buildings—hand and power tools, the lights that illuminate offices and classrooms, and cleaning, safety, and sanitary supplies.

Technology Innovations

In 1981, Grainger redefined their method of retrieving and replenishing inventory when they installed their Automated Storage and Retrieval System (AS/RS) at the Niles, Illinois-based RDC. This massive 10-aisle system was designed to supply over 60 percent of the replenishment stock to forward picking locations at a rate of 210 pallet loads an hour.

This AS/RS has greatly increased efficiencies in getting product to the customer as well as to the branches. Although the AS/RS helped in expediting inventory, this was only one component in improving customer service and efficiency. The other component was expediting information.

Information transmission has been enhanced through the use of satellite communications. Grainger utilizes a satellite communications network, which substantially reduces its reliance on phone lines by linking stores and other facilities together via a network control center. This was enhanced in 1995–96 when Grainger completed the installation of IBM minicomputers at each branch, office, and distribution center. The Grainger network enables all portions of the business to be linked by satellite network to provide the convenience of instant product availability information and real-time inventory management for more than $1 billion of inventory.

The network has decreased Grainger's response time through the almost instantaneous transmission of information. This expedites the completion of sales transactions and the initiation of stock replenishment, which, in turn, increases levels of customer satisfaction. It has also enabled Grainger to distribute software across the network with greater efficiency.

Grainger offers its general catalog on CD-ROM, free to Grainger customers. In 1996, the company introduced a website. With the introduction of its website, Grainger became one of the first business-to-business websites to accept orders over the Internet. Grainger's state-of-the-art technology helps Grainger customers to instantaneously look up products. When doing so, they use a guided interactive search engine, by description, brand name, specification, manufacturer's model number, and Grainger stock number to check the company-specific pricing.

Grainger has integrated the CD-ROM catalog version with Datastream products. Datastream is a leading manufacturer of computer software programs such as MRP2 and Maintain It (purchasing and preventive maintenance software programs). Now users of these Datastream products can click on an icon and immediately be transferred to the Grainger CD-ROM catalog—ECAT (electronic catalog).

By accessing Grainger's website (http://www.grainger.com), customers can now order online 24 hours a day, seven days a week to find more than 200,000 products quickly and easily. This provides the customer with fast and cost-effective paperless services. In addition, customers can use the website for inquiries and feedback. Grainger's Internet site has dramatically increased the number of companies using Grainger's distribution system.

Barbara M. Chilson, Grainger's vice president and general manager, electronic commerce, stated "Grainger's Internet commerce convenience was created in response to feedback received from our customers." Grainger's Online Catalog (Web Cat) also allows multiple users per account to order online. This provides a significant advantage to larger companies, which often give more than one employee purchasing responsibility.

Items such as the CD-ROM catalog and Web Cat give customers greater access to products in the general catalog. The CD-ROM version enables customers to access more than 500,000 product cross-references. The Internet provides over 1 million cross-references. Other electronic services include electronic data interchange (EDI), electronic funds transfer (EFT), and computerized maintenance management programs with built-in interface to the Grainger CD-ROM catalog.

According to James T. Ryan, Grainger's vice president of information services: "The company is continually upgrading its information systems to better serve its customers." In 1995, Grainger started moving major applications from the mainframe into a more distributed client-server network. Every branch now uses minicomputers and "intelligent" workstations. As a result, Grainger is now positioned to respond much faster to customer needs with more computing power resident at the branch level.

Technology has enabled increased products, services, and locations. Grainger's direct sales focus is shifting from servicing resellers, other distributors, and small customers to integrated supply chains, national accounts, and medium to large customers. Grainger has been careful not to make the critical mistake of ignoring its smaller customers, who up until the mid-1980s had been the largest source of Grainger's profit. To ensure that smaller customers were not neglected, Grainger piloted a telesales project in 1996. It was designed to further penetrate the accounts for whom direct mail alone was not sufficient.

Realizing that integrated supply was more than a fad, Grainger formalized a new division—Grainger Integrated Supply Operation (GISO). With GISO, a customer uses Grainger to supply some or all of its maintenance, repair, and operating supplies. According to Donald E. Bielinski, senior vice president of marketing and sales, "Most GISO customers are large corporations because GISO customers typically order about $1 million of product per location per year from Grainger. Currently, annual orders of less than $1 million are not cost effective for Grainger to fulfill within the GISO program."

As technology improves, Bielinski estimates it will become cost effective for the company to accept smaller orders. Bielinski estimates the national market for integrated supply to be around $2 to $3 billion. GISO is paying off. Grainger recently signed American Airlines at its Dallas-Fort Worth airport operation and Fel-Pro, out of Skokie, Illinois, as GISO customers. GISO currently has about 40 customers. Looking to the future, Bielinski adds that "Grainger will continue to work on the three major areas that any distributor must constantly strengthen. This includes continuing to improve the physical movement of products, the flow of information, and the efficiency of transactions." In keeping with Bielinski's iteration of the critical factors for future growth, it seems that technology has found a home with Grainger. The use of technology will allow Grainger to meet its customers' as well as its own internal goals.

One of the largest benefits to developing electronic mediums such as the Grainger website and CD-ROM catalog is to improve customer service and cut costs of producing catalogs. The website affords customers access to Grainger round the clock from all corners of the globe. In addition, the website and CD-ROM can help reduce the costs of catalog distribution. In 1995, more than 2 million copies of the general catalog were distributed to businesses nationwide. Given the freight charge to ship a catalog approximately five inches thick, the savings from shipping only a CD-ROM are substantial.

Not only do freight costs decrease when more users go online or use the CD-ROM catalog version, but costs are also saved on producing the catalog (paper version versus CD-ROM). Since 1995, Grainger has also produced the general catalog once a year instead of twice (spring and fall). This has also helped to reduce the cost of producing catalogs and to direct the money back to the company.

In late 1999, Grainger opened FindMRO.com and MROverstocks.com websites to help customers find and order specific products. In 2000, the company combined its OrderZone.com B2B site with Works.com, a leading Internet business purchasing service. The company is also consolidating its warehouses into two giant distribution centers to reduce costs and improve central control over inventory. In conjunction with the websites, the centralized system provides more products available to customers. Sales from Grainger's main website have increased from $13 million in 1999 to $267 million in 2000 (annual report). The FindMRO.com site is essentially a database of 14,000 suppliers and 5 million products. The Web-based search technologies enable customers to find products when they do not know who supplies them. The MROverstocks.com site is mainly an auction site to liquidate excess inventory from Grainger Industrial Supply. In January 2001, these two businesses were merged with TotalMRO.com into Material Logic. One of the goals is to convince other MRO suppliers and more purchasers to use the systems.

Telecommunications

W. W. Grainger is teaming with SAP to let customers use the R/3 application to buy products from Grainger via the Web. Grainger views the Web as a growth vehicle for business-to-business sales. The website accounts for less than 1 percent of Grainger's total sales but is growing as much as 100 percent per quarter. Grainger, like many other companies, faced difficulties installing and converting to R/3. The system was affecting profits because the inventory system was inaccurate—claiming more products in inventory than actually existed. Consequently, the firm lost $19 million in sales and $23 million in reduced earnings in 1999. One of the difficulties in dealing with the huge number of products Grainger sells was converting all of the inventory data to the new system.

Grainger will use electronic-catalog technology from Requisite Technology Inc. to provide the online content for all its Web initiatives. Requisite will also provide catalog technology to support Grainger's website and intranet, which sales representatives use to get information to fulfill orders and answer customers' questions.

One initiative includes a project with systems integrator Perot Systems to aggregate MRO products from Grainger and other distributors into a single Web portal for sales to small businesses. Grainger will form a subsidiary to manage the initiative, which should start early next year.

Data

Grainger gathers "basic registration information" from users who sign onto its website. The data includes whether the visitors are existing Grainger buyers. This helps to gauge overlap among the company's channels.

Recommendation for the Future

Grainger must continue to focus on technology to improve efficiencies, increase customer service levels, effectively manage inventory, and facilitate access to existing markets. In short, they must implement technology that will improve distribution processes as well as give them the upper hand against current and future competition. Technology is being used to align customer needs with the company vision. Technology has taken Grainger from 347 branches to the virtual store that can be accessed anytime from anyplace.

Grainger believes the key to integrating technology and the customers' needs lies in the ability to align investments in technology with the company's business objectives. In doing so, Grainger's success will be determined by how well it anticipates the needs of its customers and how well it responds to those needs. A key factor for Grainger's future is the decision to follow other companies and customers across national boundaries into the international marketplace.

MaterialLogic, one of Grainger's Web-based, analytical tools, added $20–$25 million in annual operating losses to the company. This caused a recently announced $38 million charge. Current estimates are that W.W. Grainger lost more than $125 million on its digital business since the first quarter of 1998. Quarterly losses peaked at $16 million in the second quarter of 2000.

Eliminating the MaterialLogic subsidiary will erase $20–25 million in annual operating losses. Ultimately, Grainger shut down all of MaterialLogic's branded e-commerce sites except FindMRO. FindMRO.com provides easy sourcing for hard-to-find, infrequently purchased items. It was recently expanded to filtration products, marine and electrical supplies. Areas shut down were TotalMRO.com, which aggregated catalogs from major suppliers and other MRO distributors. Also shut down was MROverstocks.com, which originated in 1999 and enabled firms to liquidate inventories of discontinued and surplus products through online bidding. In addition to these units, MaterialLogic included consulting and content development services that were focused on driving e-procurement adoption by end users.

Questions

1. What is W. W. Grainger's strategic direction and who or what forces are driving it?
2. What are the critical success factors and core competencies for Grainger?
3. What technologies have driven the process?
4. How has this technological change been implemented?
5. How successful has the technological change been?
6. What does Grainger's Web page present about its business direction?

Additional Reading

"E-Commerce Gains Ground with Purchasing Staff." *PC Week,* January 5, 1998, p. 69.

Frook, John Evan. "Blue-Collar Business on the Web." *InternetWeek.* September 14, 1998, p. 43.

Machlis, Sharon. "Supplier Seeks Sales via Web Searches." *Computerworld,* September 14, 1998, p. 20.

Stedman, Craig. "ERP Woes Cut Grainger Profits." *Computerworld,* January 7, 2000.

Tadjer, Rivka. "Purchasing Nirvana?" *InternetWeek,* September 22, 1997, pp. 55–58.

Wilder, Clinton. "Online Supplies Purchases via R/3 —W. W. Grainger Teams with SAP on Electronic-Commerce Initiative." *InformationWeek,* September 14, 1998, p. 32.

Appendix

Encrypting E-Mail

Most studies show that only a small percentage of e-mail messages sent over the Internet are encrypted. Yet, plain text messages can be intercepted and altered. It is also relatively easy for a hacker to forge a message—pretending to be from someone else. While you might not care about most of your e-mail messages, there will be times when you need to encrypt a message.

Despite the advances in technology, it is still somewhat challenging to set up e-mail encryption. Figure 4.1A outlines the major steps. A large part of the problem is that security companies need to make money from the process. Encryption and authentication generally require a trusted third party to validate users and issue secure certificates. VeriSign is currently the leading certificate authority—and it charges annual fees for

FIGURE 4.1A   Digital security certificates. Certificates are used to encrypt e-mail and to authenticate the sender. You obtain a certificate from a certificate authority, install it in your e-mail client, and then select option boxes to encrypt and authenticate messages.

Obtain a certificate from a certificate authority
- VeriSign
- Thawte (owned by VeriSign)
- Microsoft
- Your own company or agency

Install the certificate in Outlook
Select option boxes to encrypt or decrypt messages
Install certificates sent by your friends and co-workers

a variety of certificates. Personal e-mail certificates are about $15 per year. Thawte, a subsidiary of VeriSign, offers a free personal certificate, but it has a catch. Thawte has a complex process to verify your identity. So, you can encrypt e-mail messages, but it is difficult to authenticate a message. MIT offers a free version of Pretty Good Privacy (PGP) for personal encryption of e-mail. The system is available to U.S. and Canadian residents only. You can register with the MIT PGP key server to make it easier for others to obtain your public key to send you an encrypted message, but there is no method to verify your identity.

Obtaining a Security Certificate

Exactly what is a digital security certificate? Modern encryption systems use a dual-key system so a digital certificate consists primarily of a pair of very large numbers. Both numbers are stored in a special file on your computer. The private key is protected and not released to anyone. The public key is sent along with your signed e-mail messages. The certificate also includes data that tells the recipient when the key was issued and which company issued it. Once you obtain and install a digital key most of the encryption and validation process is automatic. The exact steps to obtain a certificate depend on your choice of the certificate authority.

It is relatively straightforward to apply for a certificate from VeriSign. You essentially go to its website and fill out a form. The company uses your credit card to verify your identity. This step makes the process easier, but it introduces an element of risk, because you can enter a nickname or pseudonym. Also, someone could steal your card and use it (and some personal data) to obtain a certificate and impersonate you online. Of course, if you see the charge on the credit card bill, you can call VeriSign and it will cancel the certificate. In 2001, this type of process was used by an imposter to falsely obtain a certificate to impersonate Microsoft. The process by Thawte is a little more involved. Anyone can obtain an ID, but that certificate will not be identified with any person until you prove your identity to Thawte by following a complex process—involving in-person signatures. Figure 4.2A shows one step in the process of obtaining a free Thawte certificate. Essentially, you enter your personal information and then select the default choices.

HOME	JOIN	BUY	TRACK STATUS	RENEW	MY ACCOUNT	GET SUPPORT
Hosting Partner		Starter PKI		Personal Certs		Web of Trust

You are about to request a certificate at the Freemail level of assurance. We can issue certificates in many different formats. Below you will see a list of each of the kinds of certificate we support. Remember, certs are FREE , so you can get as many or as few as you like now that you have come this far!

X.509 Format Certificates:

For an X.509 certificate, please choose your software from the list below:

- ○ Netscape Communicator or Messenger
- ⊙ Microsoft Internet Explorer, Outlook and Outlook Express
- ○ Lotus Notes R5
- ○ OperaSoftware Browser
- ○ C2Net SafePassage Web Proxy

[Get X.509 Certificate >]

FIGURE 4.2A   Obtain a digital security certificate. The Thawte certificate is relatively easy to obtain from the company's website. Its main advantage is that it is free. However, you will probably have to pay and contact other people to verify your identity to use it as an authentication certificate.

The interesting aspect to digital certificates is that it is relatively easy for any company to run a server that generates and validates its own certificates. Because of the cost and the complex process of obtaining certificates, some government agencies and large companies become their own certificate authorities. While this is a straightforward and inexpensive method to enable encryption, the certificates have to be trusted by other people. For example, you could run your own server and issue your own certificates. This method would work well to encrypt messages, but it is unlikely that anyone would accept them to verify your identity.

Installing a Certificate and Encrypting Messages

The steps used to encrypt an e-mail message depend on the e-mail client that you use. The steps outlined in Figure 4.3A are for the Microsoft Outlook client. Once the certificate has been installed in Outlook, the encryption and decryption process is relatively automatic. The main decision you have to make is whether you want to commonly encrypt and sign your messages. If so, be sure to check the boxes in the option tab. Why would you not want to encrypt and sign messages? First, encrypted messages are larger than plain-text messages and can take longer to transmit. Second, the message signature (or encryption) might not pass through some e-mail systems correctly. Third, your recipient might not know how to handle the signed or encrypted messages. Before you decide to sign every

message, picture your confused boss receiving "strange text" along with the message.

To encrypt messages to send to others, you also need to install the public keys from their security certificates. For PGP this key is sometimes sent separately, or possibly is available on a public server. Otherwise, it is sent along with the signed message. Before you try to exchange encrypted e-mail, you should send a plain-text message that contains your key in the signature. When you receive a signed message, you can install the key into your contact database. Simply right-click on the From line of the message and add the name to your contact list. In the Contacts database, you can open the person's entry and click the Certificate tab to see if you have the digital certificate. As shown in Figure 4.4A, once the certificates are installed, you simply use the Options and Security Settings button to encrypt or digitally sign a message. As long as the recipient has installed your certificate, he or she can simply open the encrypted message as usual.

Note that the digital certificates are tied to the specified e-mail account. If you have more than one e-mail account, or if you change your e-mail provider, you will have to obtain a new certificate and install it into Outlook. You will not have to change the encryption settings. Also, note that you should only install certificates on your own machine. For security reasons, never install them on shared (lab) computers. If someone obtains access to the machine you are using, he or she will be able to impersonate you and decrypt mail intended only for you.

FIGURE 4.3A   Installing a digital certificate in Outlook. Once you have obtained the certificate, use the Security option tab to tell Outlook to use the certificate Checking the Encrypt and Digital Signature boxes sets the default for future messages. You can change the settings for individual messages. From here, the encryption and decryption is relatively automatic.

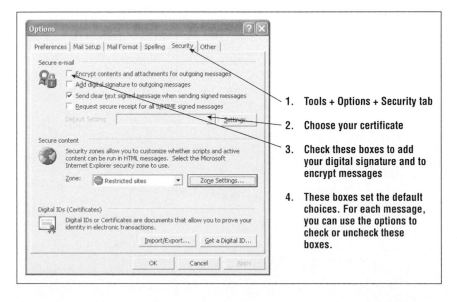

FIGURE 4.4A Encrypting and signing messages. Once you have installed your certificate, you should also install certificates from your co-workers. Then when you send a message, simply choose the Options, click the Security Settings button and check the Encrypt or Signature box.

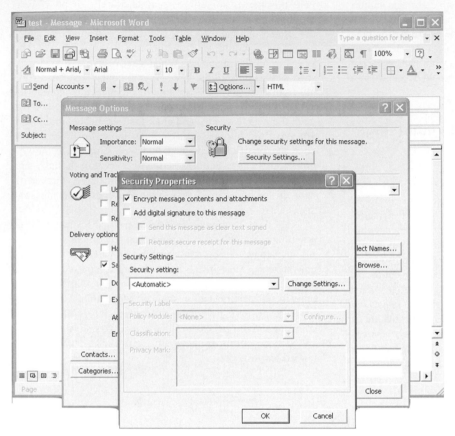

Exercises

1. On your own machine, go to one of the certificate authorities and obtain a digital certificate. Install the certificate, set up your mail client. Then send a signed message to a friend and install her or his certificate. Then send an encrypted message.

2. Do a Web search to obtain a list of certificate authorities who issue public security certificates.

3. For at least two major certificate authorities, outline the process needed to validate the identity of the applicant. Which method is the most secure or trustworthy?

4. Investigate the steps needed to set up a certificate authority within a company. What hardware and software are needed?

5. If your university set up a certificate authority, would you use it? Would the certificates be accepted by other people and companies?

CHAPTER FIVE

Transactions and Electronic Commerce

What you will learn in this chapter

- What are transactions?

- What difficulties arise in data capture and how do information system minimize the problems?

- What risks arise in transactions?

- How are transaction risks mitigated in electronic commerce?

- Why are new payment mechanisms needed?

- What are the major characteristics of data quality?

- What is the role of accounting in transactions?

- What are the operational elements in a human resources management system?

As a large retailer, Home Depot recognizes the importance of collecting quality data and automating the transaction-processing system.

Home Depot

Bryan Kahlow stepped back for a second to survey his work. He and his father-in-law had constructed a new deck. After receiving estimates in the $3,000 to $4,000 range, Bryan decided to investigate the possibility of completing the job himself. Of course, not being much of a handyman he knew that he needed a lot of help.

On a Saturday, the two men attended a short class at the neighborhood Home Depot store. There they learned all of the steps necessary to complete a deck. They were even given the name and phone number of their instructor, to call in case they ran into trouble along the way. After two days of diligent work, they constructed a new deck. This was made possible by the friendly and courteous staff at Bryan Kahlow's Home Depot.

A high level of customer service is what has helped Home Depot revolutionize the home improvement industry. Skilled contractors formerly dominated the industry. Now the industry includes many do-it-yourselfers eager to save time and money and achieve a sense of accomplishment.

Overview

Richard: Ally, I'm sure you've noticed the problems we're having with the billing system. It has always been a problem, but when clients start complaining, I guess we should spend some money and fix it.

Ally: Yeah. But I'm not sure it's a simple fix. Elaine screams every time I mention it, and clients have even been complaining to me about wrong bills. I think we need to throw it out and buy a new system.

Richard: Ohhh . . . That's going to be painful isn't it? OK. Ally, you're in charge. Just get it done fast. Wait. Let me negotiate the final contracts and prices.

Elaine:	Can we please set up an electronic presentation and payments system?
Richard:	A what?
Ally:	Sure. That way we get rid of most of the paperwork. Just record all of the charges in our system, once a month it can e-mail the bill to the client, and the clients can transfer funds directly from their accounts. The system tracks everything and feeds the data directly to the accounting system.

Introduction

Whenever two people make an exchange, it is called a *transaction*. Transactions are important events for a company, and collecting data about them is called transaction processing. Examples of transactions include making a purchase at a store, withdrawing money from a checking account, making a payment to a creditor, or paying an employee.

FIGURE 5.1

Transaction processing. Transaction processing involves collecting data from the business operations and from external partners. Electronic commerce can be used to handle consumer and business transactions over the Internet.

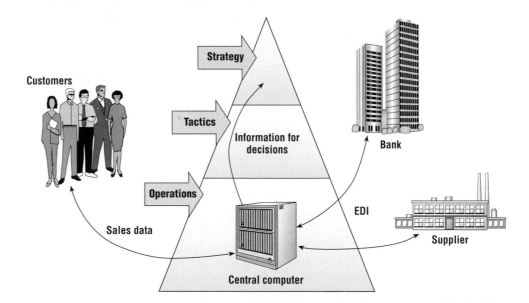

Trends

Because of legal ramifications, businesses have always collected data about transactions. Accounting systems play an important role in collecting and analyzing transaction data. Through the 1960s, most business computers were primarily producing basic accounting reports. Raw data was punched into the computer by hand, and the computer produced totals and updated the general ledger. In effect, the computer was used as a giant calculator to automate the production of printed reports that were structured as they were before the advent of computers. The primary reason for using the computer was speed and accuracy. It was justified because it was cheaper and less error-prone than hiring thousands of people to produce the reports.

As computer capabilities increased in the 1970s, the most important change was to use the computer to collect the raw data. In retail sales, the cash register was replaced with a computer terminal and a bar code scanner. Whenever a customer purchased an item, the transaction data was immediately sent to the main computer. This automation

eliminated the need to hire a person to enter the data at the end of the day. Together with fewer errors, these online transaction systems provided better service to the customer. Because sales were recorded immediately, the sales clerk could quickly determine whether an item was in stock. The systems also provided virtually instantaneous sales data to the managers. If some item was selling rapidly, the system could tell the employees to restock that item on the shelves.

The 1980s and 1990s resulted in more integration. Transaction data was made available to managers throughout the company. One goal was to combine the systems across the company into an enterprise system that enabled managers to examine all aspects of the business.

In many respects, electronic commerce and mobile commerce are simply new transaction systems. In these systems, the customer selects a product and enters purchase information directly into the vendor's computer system. Yet, new transaction systems can change the entire economy.

Because transactions generally involve an exchange of money, it is critical that the data be protected during transmission and stored carefully so that it cannot be altered. It is also critical that the data be saved so that managers can verify the data if any conflicts arise. Also, the sales and purchase data form the foundation of the accounting and financial systems of every company, so the system must be able to produce the standard reports.

Data Capture

The basic components of a transaction-processing system are illustrated in Figure 5.2. The focus is twofold: accomplishing the transaction and capturing data. Data capture consists of gathering or acquiring data from the firm's operations and storing data in the computer system. Entering data into the computer can be time consuming and difficult. For instance, banks have invested heavily in automating the collection and recording of transaction data. Yet, because many transactions are based on paper, clerks still spend considerable time entering data. First, tellers enter the data into their terminals. Then a bank staff reads the dollar value written on checks and deposit slips. The bank staff works through the night, typing the amount into a machine that codes the number on the bottom of the check so it can be read by other computers.

As the volume of transactions increased, businesses looked for faster and more accurate ways to get data into the computer. Four basic methods are used to collect data, depending on its source. The data-collection method consumers are most familiar with is **point of sale (POS)**, where the sales register is actually a computer terminal that sends all data to a central computer. On assembly lines, robots and manufacturing equipment can collect data, such as

FIGURE 5.2

Data that is captured at the operations level is used throughout the firm to make decisions. If there are problems in the data or in providing access to the data, all of the decisions will suffer.

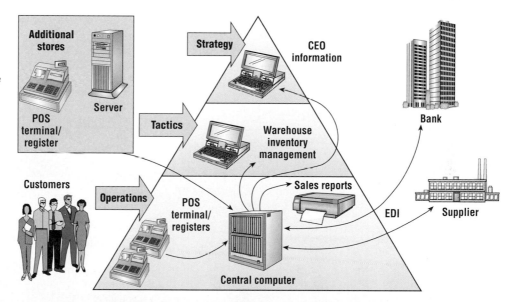

At least five cancer patients in Panama died and 23 others were injured when they were exposed to high levels of radiation as a result of data-entry errors in a radiation therapy program. The software written by Multidata Systems International is used throughout North America. David Kyd, a spokesman for the International Atomic Energy Agency, said that "had the instruction manual been followed to the letter, this wouldn't have happened. But this wasn't done." Additionally, there was no fail-safe mechanism in the software to prevent healthy tissue from being exposed to the radiation, so the software was unable to identify the data-entry errors.

Source: Adapted from Vanessa Gera, "Data-Entry Error Blamed for Cancer Deaths," *Seattle Times,* June 14, 2001.

quality control measures, and return it to a computer. Typically the computer also can send control instructions to these machines. This exchange of data between manufacturing machines and computers is known as **process control**. The third way to collect data automatically involves the exchange of information with organizations outside the firm, especially suppliers and customers. Instead of dealing with paper records such as purchase orders, it is possible to send orders electronically through a process called **electronic data interchange (EDI)**. The fourth method is to have the customers select products and enter data directly into the electronic commerce website. This fourth method offers the potential of reducing errors and costs—if the websites are built carefully, and if the customers are motivated and capable of selecting the products themselves.

Point of Sale

Several devices have been created to capture data at the point of the sale. Some companies rely on keyboards to enter data, but high-volume areas have switched to bar code scanners. All consumers are familiar with bar code scanners that read the universal product codes (UPCs). The scanner reads the code and sends it to the computer, which looks up the corresponding name and price. The computer prints the receipt, stores the sale information, and automatically decreases the inventory count.

Another type of scanner is used by the U.S. Postal System—**optical character recognition (OCR)**—to read handwritten zip codes, allowing mail to be processed and sorted faster. Even so, the post office hires thousands of workers to type in data that the scanners cannot read. Banks use a process called **magnetic ink character recognition (MICR)** to process checks and deposit slips. MICR readers are more accurate than straight OCR because they pick up a stronger signal from magnetic particles in the ink. A few companies are using speech recognition technology to enable workers to enter data by speaking to the computer. Speech recognition enables the users to enter data while leaving their hands free to do something else.

Several advantages arise from using automated data entry. Directly capturing data means fewer errors occur because the machines make fewer mistakes. However, sometimes it is not easy to collect data at the source.

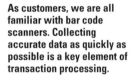

As customers, we are all familiar with bar code scanners. Collecting accurate data as quickly as possible is a key element of transaction processing.

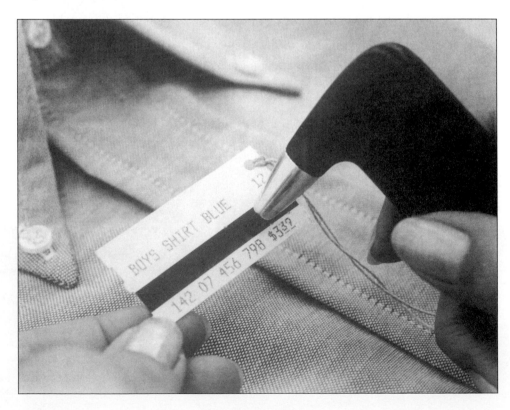

POS systems also have built-in error detection methods to make certain the numbers are read correctly. By collecting the data immediately, it is easier to find and correct mistakes. If a clerk using a POS system enters an incorrect product number (or the scanner reads it incorrectly), the error can be caught immediately.

With POS data collection, the computer performs all necessary computations immediately. Hence, the job is easier for clerks and fewer errors will occur. For example, a retail store might give discounts to certain customers. With a POS system, the employees do not have to keep track of the customers or discounts, because the computer can look up the discounts and apply them automatically. Similarly, prices are maintained and changed by the computer. To hold a sale, you simply change the price in the computer (one place) and put up a new sign. Of course, when there are thousands of items and prices, there are still plenty of opportunities for errors.

POS systems also can provide better service to customers. Because the sales data is captured immediately, the managers and clerks always know the inventory levels. If a customer calls to learn whether a product is in stock, the clerk can instantly determine the answer. With most systems, it is possible to tell the computer to hold that item until the customer picks it up. Some companies even connect their store computers together. If you find that one store has run out of a particular item, the clerk can quickly check the other stores in the area and tell one to hold the item for you.

Process Control

Manufacturing firms often deal with a different type of data. Most factories use machines that can be connected to each other and to computers. The computers can exchange data with the production machines. If you want to alter your product, you would need to change the manufacturing settings on several different machines. If the production line has 10 machines, each with five control items that need to be set, it could take several hours to reset the entire production line. Even a minor change in the product means that someone has to set each of the machines correctly. By connecting the machines to a computer, the computer can store the appropriate settings. When you make a change in the product, the computer sends the correct settings to all the machines. Computers are often used to monitor the progress of the production line. The data is used to identify problem spots and to help the firm meet production goals. Figure 5.3 illustrates the basic concept of individual machines controlled from one location.

Technology also can be used to collect data from manufacturing machines. With this communication, the computer can constantly monitor production levels. Managers can keep track of hourly and daily production, and even track individual products. If a customer wants

---

Reality Bytes   Data Entry Errors

Hilton Hotels Corp. has a minor problem with the Internet. At least three times in six months, employees incorrectly entered data into the reservation system, listing room prices at $0. Travelers using the online reservation systems were able to book free rooms at several hotels, including resort properties in Arizona, California, and Mexico City. Hilton spokeswoman Jeanne Datz noted: "What can I say—this is very embarrassing." We don't understand it. It obviously shows a terrible attention to detail." People who stumbled on the problem quickly booked free rooms. One person even booked 300 rooms. A few posted notices on the Web to tell other people. But, Hilton officials will not honor all fares. Some people were granted the free rate for the first night, but subsequent nights will be charged at a 50 percent discount from the best available rate. One traveler is not impressed with the offer, noting that Hilton is responsible for the mistake and that officials would not let him off the hook if he made a mistake when booking the room. After the first incident, Hilton sent memos to hotel employees to be more careful in entering rates; which, of course, did not solve the problem. Hilton began working on an electronic filter that prevents clerks from entering a rate of zero.

Source: Adapted from Jane Costello, "Hilton Hotels' Pricing Mistake Gives Free Rooms to Guests Booking Online," *The Wall Street Journal,* September 4, 2001.

FIGURE 5.3

Process control is the control of production machines from centralized computers. The computers monitor data from the machines and make continual adjustments. The central control enables designers to specify all production settings from one location.

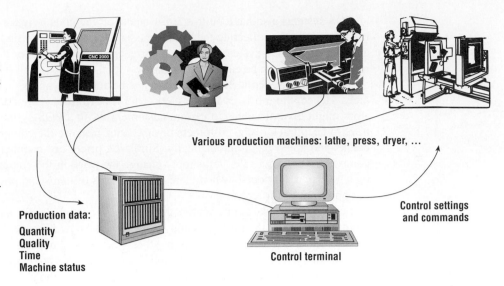

Various production machines: lathe, press, dryer, ...

Production data:

Quantity
Quality
Time
Machine status

Control terminal

Control settings
and commands

Reality Bytes   Shipping Automation

The Singapore port is one of the busiest in the world. To achieve this performance, it is also one of the most automated. For example, the crane operator at the Pasir Panjang ship terminal can move cargo containers from the terminal onto the ship by entering simple commands into the computer. The computer also schedules jobs and helps make sure the correct containers are loaded on trucks at the right time. The operator rarely leaves his air-conditioned control room. By comparison, workers at the port of Los Angeles have a crew of four people for each crane, including a clerk who writes container numbers by hand onto each truck with yellow chalk. The Dutch port of Rotterdam uses robotic cranes and unmanned vehicles to move cargo. The technology cut terminal employment in half. Of course, the technology is expensive. The Singapore crane system cost $200 million, but enables one operator to handle five or six cranes. But they also enable workers to unload and reload a large container ship in about 40 hours, compared to 76 hours at California ports. One complication in the United States is that labor union rules require that all shipping data be entered manually by a clerk instead of being scanned from bar codes.

Source: Adapted from Daniel Machalaba, "U.S. Ports Are Losing the Battle to Keep Up with Overseas Trade," *The Wall Street Journal*, July 9, 2001.

---

to check on the progress of a special order, the manager can determine how much of the product has been produced and when it is likely to be completed.

Process control computers can also be used to monitor quality in the manufacturing process. Sensors can automatically measure almost any characteristic. They can check for items such as thickness, weight, strength, color, and size. These measurements can then be passed to a computer. If the computer notices a trend or a major problem, it can notify the operators. In some operations, the computer can send messages to the machine causing the problem and reset its controls to correct the problem automatically.

Two basic difficulties exist with process control. First, the large number of machines makes it difficult to establish standards, making it harder to connect the various machines together. Second, production machines can produce an enormous amount of data. Some machines can generate billions of bytes of data per hour. This large amount of data requires efficient communication lines, high-speed computers, and a large storage capacity. Despite these complications, process control can provide enormous advantages. It enables companies to change production processes and alter products faster and more often. It provides better information and control over quality. It enables manufacturers to create products that match the needs of individual customers: mass customization.

Electronic Data Interchange (EDI)

EDI is a form of automated data entry that supports operations by transferring documents between firms electronically. The essence of EDI is the ability to transfer data among computers from different companies. The goal is to connect to suppliers so that production orders can be sent automatically at substantially lower cost than traditional paper-based systems. Two basic methods are used to accomplish the transfer: (1) send the data directly from one computer to the other or (2) send the data to a third party that consolidates the data and sends it to the proper location. Early EDI implementations were based on direct connections as individual firms experimented with the technology. In both methods, there are two important considerations: establishing the physical links and transferring data in a format compatible to all users.

For EDI to work, each company must translate its data into a form that can be used by the other companies. If one company like Sears or GM takes the lead and requires suppliers to send data via EDI, then they are free to define the base transaction objects. Suppliers must translate their objects into the appropriate EDI structure. Yet, a supplier might need links to several customers. If each customer used different EDI definitions, the supplier must have a conversion system for each link. Someday it might be possible to create standards for EDI connections, forcing everyone to conform to one type of data definition. Although there is some progress in this area, firms with existing EDI systems will be reluctant to spend the money to convert their data.

Data conversion might sound like an easy task, but it is complicated when the transaction systems were created over long periods of time and were poorly documented. In many cases, the programmer might have to search major portions of the corporate systems to find the appropriate data definitions. Once the appropriate data is found, it can be hard to modify. Existing programs might expect the data to maintain specific formats. Making changes to the data can require rewriting other programs.

Proprietary EDI

As displayed in Figure 5.4, most of the early EDI systems were created independently: one large company required suppliers to provide data and accept orders electronically. The goal was to cut the costs of transactions and speed up the ordering process. EDI arrangements also enabled manufacturers to improve quality control and to implement just-in-time inventory systems. Suppliers were "encouraged" to adopt the EDI systems by threatening a loss of sales if the vendors did not comply.

With proprietary systems, the lead firm establishes the standards in terms of the hardware and the types and format of data to be exchanged. From the standpoint of the lead firm, these controls ensure that they are able to connect to each supplier with one standard technique.

To a supplier, proprietary systems created by one company can lead to problems. Imagine what happens when the supplier sells to several firms, and each firm requires the use of a different EDI system. In addition to the hassles of providing data in the proper format for each customer, the supplier's employees would have to learn how to use several different systems. Purchasers face similar problems unless all of their suppliers follow a standard.

Commercial EDI Providers and Standards

Multiple proprietary systems lead to confusion and higher costs. Consequently, companies have formed groups to define common methods to exchange data among companies. As shown in Figure 5.5, third-party providers (such as banks) have begun operating as clearing-houses for EDI transactions. In both cases, the objective is to establish common hardware and software requirements so that any company following the standards can share data with other companies.

Communication standards enable firms to share the data and automate basic transactions. However, to provide useful information, companies need to integrate this data into their management information systems. Sending purchase orders over phone lines is faster than

FIGURE 5.4

EDI can be built from individual pair-wise links over proprietary connections. If the majority of transactions are between two companies, this method will work fine. If companies deal with many different suppliers or larger customers, this method can cause problems when each link requires conversion to a different format.

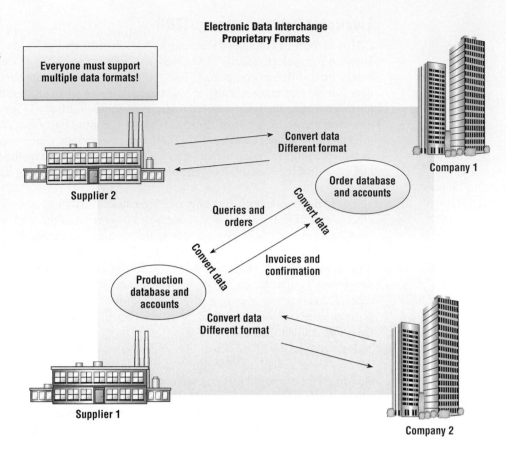

FIGURE 5.5

When many firms need to exchange data with several other firms, it is best if they can agree to a common EDI transaction format. In some cases, a central or regional firm can coordinate transfers among all parties. This method is especially beneficial to small firms.

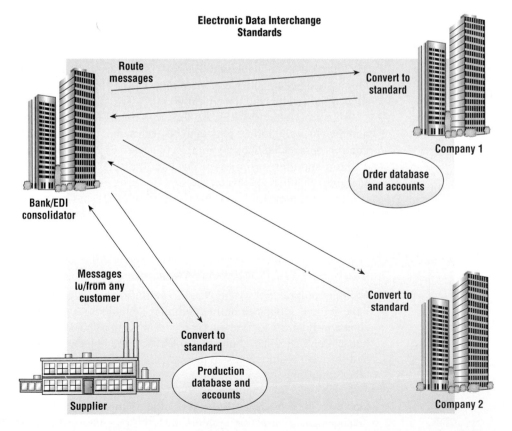

FIGURE 5.6

EDI standards. UN Edifact and U.S. ANSI X12 standards are similar in format; each message consists of segments and detailed data lists. Each message, segment and data element are defined by numbers from a predefined list of possible transactions. There are substantial differences in the numbering system used for the segments and data.

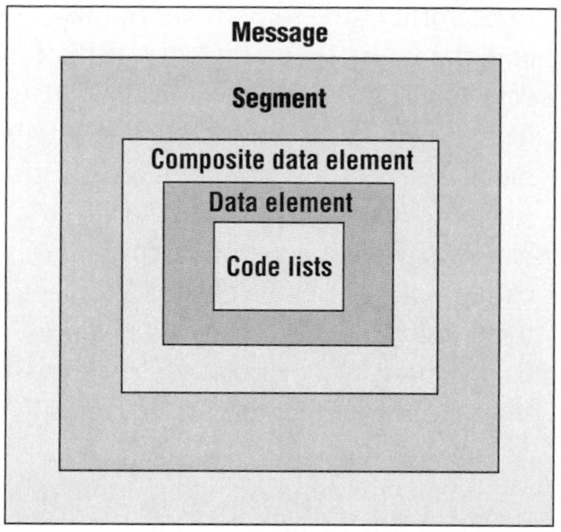

FIGURE 5.7

Sample segment codes for ANSI X12. A partial list of the codes used within X12 EDI messages. Only the number is transmitted. Each segment specifies the format of the additional data.

104	Air Shipment Information
110	Air Freight Details and Invoice
125	Multilevel Railcar Load Details
126	Vehicle Application Advice
127	Vehicle Baying Order
128	Dealer Information
129	Vehicle Carrier Rate Update
130	Student Educational Record (Transcript)
131	Student Educational Record (Transcript) Acknowledgment
135	Student Loan Application
139	Student Loan Guarantee Result
140	Product Registration
141	Product Service Claim Response
142	Product Service Claim
143	Product Service Notification
144	Student Loan Transfer and Status Verification
146	Request for Student Educational Record (Transcript)
147	Response to Request for Student Educational Record (Transcript)
148	Report of Injury or Illness
151	Electronic Filing of Tax Return Data Acknowledgment
152	Statistical Government Information
154	Uniform Commercial Code Filing
161	Train Sheet
170	Revenue Receipts Statement
180	Return Merchandise Authorization and Notification
186	Laboratory Reporting
190	Student Enrollment Verification

using traditional mail, but firms can gain more advantages if the resulting data can be tied directly to their internal accounting systems.

Two primary standards exist for EDI messages. The UN sponsors the Edifact standard; the United States defined the ANSI (American National Standards Institute) X12 definition. Figure 5.6 shows the overall structure of an EDI message. A significant difference between the standards is in the numbering system used to represent the types of messages, segments, and data elements. Figure 5.7 presents a partial list of the segment types available in the X12 standard. The standards also specify the exact format of the data required in each segment type.

Additional Features and Problems

Taken to its full capabilities, EDI enables firms to electronically handle all communications among other firms. It enables managers to create and review orders without relying on paper printouts. Having data available electronically means that several people can work with the same form at the same time. In most companies, purchase orders and invoices are examined and altered by several people. If the form is processed on the computer, each person has access to the data at the same time. It is also much easier to store and search the electronic data. Eventually, even prices and negotiations could be handled electronically, making it much easier to sort and compare bids from various suppliers.

Some unresolved issues with EDI's security and ethics need further consideration. What happens when a company denies that it placed an order? How do you protect the communication links so people cannot intercept orders? Reading, changing, or deleting your competitor's orders could destroy its business. Although these actions are illegal, they can be difficult to prevent or uncover. Privacy issues also arise in conjunction with EDI. If consumer transactions are captured electronically and stored, an enormous amount of personal information will be available. What will prevent a company from acquiring or selling a list of all the items you purchase along with your salary and your home address? These questions and solutions are addressed in more detail in Chapter 4.

Using the Internet for EDI

The entire purpose of EDI is to share data with business partners. Sharing data requires a communication link and standards that define how the data will be interpreted. The ANSI and Edifact definitions describe how the data should be organized. However, communication links are equally important. Increasingly, companies are using the Internet as a primary link to other firms. The main strength of the Internet is that it is widely available throughout the world. Standardization enables any firm to participate at a low cost.

Websites are used to advertise and display information about products and their availability. Search engines enable companies to find components and potential suppliers quickly. EDI transactions such as orders and request-for-prices can be handled over the Internet as e-mail messages. The Internet can also host secure communication channels between two partners. These links can be used for high-volume exchanges of data.

The one catch with the Internet is that currently there are no service guarantees. While messages are rarely lost, they might be delayed. Periodically, various segments of the Internet become overloaded and it can be difficult to transfer data. If these interruptions are infrequent, you could resort to manual methods such as fax machines and telephone calls. Plans for improving the Internet include the ability to specify (and purchase) dedicated bandwidth, so that companies can ensure a certain level of service. So far, the strengths of the Internet far outweigh the potential drawbacks. The newer version of the Internet protocol (IP.v6) is defined to have the ability to request a specified level of service, but firms have been reluctant to spend the money to upgrade to this system.

Electronic Commerce and Mobile Commerce

Electronic commerce consists of the ability to research, select, and purchase items on line. One of the primary goals of e-commerce is to support consumers 24 hours a day. Mobile commerce (m-commerce) has the additional goal of processing transactions regardless of location. M-commerce relies on the growth and acceptance of hand-held devices that are connected to the Internet by radio signals.

The foundation of e-commerce is driven by the wide acceptance of the Internet. Since more than 50 percent of U.S. households have access to the Internet, e-commerce gives them the ability to perform their own research and initiate their own transactions. The potential is even greater in business-to-business e-commerce, because vendors and purchasers have strong incentives to reduce costs.

Transactions play a critical role in e-commerce. In response to fraud, laws have been developed over hundreds of years to identify and enforce legitimate transactions. Yet, the interpretation of these laws and their application to e-commerce are not always clear. Situations that are covered under traditional transactions may carry unacceptable risk in an e-commerce setting.

Elements of a Transaction

Transactions are a critical foundation of modern economic societies. In many ways, transactions define and enable different types of societies and cultures. A transaction consists of an exchange of a product or service for money. Consequently, there is always a risk that something might go wrong in the exchange. Figure 5.8 summarizes the transaction risks that are borne by the vendor, the customer, and the government. The laws and culture determine how these risks are minimized.

Vendor Perspective

At heart, a vendor only cares about one fundamental aspect of transactions: receiving the money. This simple statement has several complicating factors: (1) the payment might never arrive, (2) the payment might be fraudulent, (3) the customer might repudiate the transaction and withhold the money, or (4) the government might invalidate the transaction.

In older times, these risks were minimized through personal reputation of the customer and money based on precious metals. More recently, in our mobile, anonymous society, credit card companies have stepped in to assume much of this vendor risk—for a price. The credit card companies and credit bureaus provide identification and personal reference services. Under the proper conditions, the card companies effectively guarantee payment to the merchant. The conditions primarily consist of (1) keeping good transaction records and (2) identifying the customer through either a magnetic swipe of the card or a signature.

Customer Perspective

In some ways, customers face a more complex set of risks. Their primary concern lies in receiving the identified value for their money. Specifically, they want to be sure that (1) they receive the product or service that they ordered, (2) they are charged only the amount they agreed to pay, and (3) the transaction is legal—for example, not stolen goods which could be confiscated.

In older times, these risks were small when customers shopped at local stores, could physically examine the goods, and paid in cash. Identification and reputation of the merchant were critical. Even so, fraud was a problem. Again, credit card companies stepped in to reduce much of this risk. Today, credit card companies warranty products, ensure delivery, and validate the merchants.

Transaction Fees

While often invisible to consumers, the fee for using a credit card consists of a percentage of the transaction cost paid by the merchant. Of course, economics shows that the price of the product reflects a portion of this fee, so the consumer and merchant both bear the cost. The

FIGURE 5.8

Transaction risk factors. Risk elements and causes vary depending on the transaction method. Laws and business procedures are created to minimize these risks, so new laws are needed when transaction methods change.

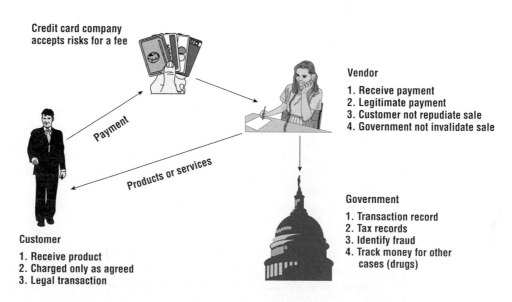

Credit card company accepts risks for a fee

Payment

Products or services

Customer
1. Receive product
2. Charged only as agreed
3. Legal transaction

Vendor
1. Receive payment
2. Legitimate payment
3. Customer not repudiate sale
4. Government not invalidate sale

Government
1. Transaction record
2. Tax records
3. Identify fraud
4. Track money for other cases (drugs)

cost depends on the size of the merchant, the card company, and the size of the transaction. Typical fees are 1.5 to 5 percent, with minimum costs of 1 to 2 dollars per transaction.

What about payments by check instead of credit card? In this case, the vendor bears a relatively high risk that the check is invalid or will be refused for insufficient funds. While there are laws against check fraud, the merchant would experience high costs to recover the money. Consequently, vendors generally contract with specialist firms to validate and process checks. Again, the merchant pays a fee to transfer this risk to another company.

Government Perspective

When discussing transactions, many people forget about the perspective of the government or society. Yet, several government organizations have a strong interest in transactions to protect various members of society. The primary interests include: (1) an auditable record of transactions and financial statements for the protection of investors, (2) a record of taxable transactions for the collection of sales tax, (3) identification and tracking of fraudulent transactions, and (4) general tracking of money used in transactions to monitor other types of crimes, such as drugs and terrorism.

Most government interests are established by laws and administrative rules that are enforced through manual audits of financial documents. Some data is collected from transaction partners, such as the $10,000 cash reporting-rule in the United States. On the other hand, governments are rapidly becoming aware of the jurisdictional problems inherent in electronic commerce. The most prominent issue is the inability of states to force out-of-state firms to collect sales taxes for them.

Risk Mitigation in E-Commerce

The transaction risks in e-commerce are similar to those of traditional commerce, but with a couple of twists because of the network connection. The Internet is an open network where messages can be intercepted and transferred at will. Consequently, it is challenging for the merchant and customer to verify the other's identity. Similarly, both merchant and vendor need to be concerned about the transfer of money and digital products. Because these two issues stem from the same cause (the insecure network), they have both been solved through the use of strong encryption methods. These techniques are described in Chapter 4, but they are commonplace on the Internet today and consumers and vendors face minimal risk from the interception of data. Figure 5.9 shows that encryption can protect the transmission and storage of credit card data, but vendors still assume several risks because the only method they have to identify customers is by the credit card data. Some vendors attempt to reduce this risk by only shipping products to the home address corresponding to the customer's credit file.

The risks of nonpayment or nondelivery are more difficult to solve. They have been particularly challenging in an international environment where governmental jurisdiction and enforcement are not effectively defined. For the most part, consumers are still protected if they use a credit card to pay for a product. However, the consumer may still find it hard to prove that a product was not received. On the other hand, e-commerce businesses have virtually no protection from fraud. The credit card rules specifically exclude mail orders, telephone orders (MOTO), and Internet orders. The card companies will assist merchants in identifying invalid cards, but will not guarantee the transaction. This issue is important because the Gartner Group (*Computerworld*, 8/11/2000) estimates that credit card fraud is 12 times higher for online merchants—with about 1.1 percent of all online transactions fraudulent.

Technically, it is relatively easy to use encryption to verify the identity of the merchant and the customer in any transaction. In fact, the common Web encryption system works because the merchant buys a digital certificate from an encryption company. Customers could obtain similar certificates or digital signatures, but they have little incentive to do so, since the credit card companies protect them.

With today's encryption systems, transmission risks are relatively minor. Two far more serious risks are: (1) theft of consumer data from the vendor's computer and (2) alteration of the purchase documents by either the merchant or the customer (repudiation).

FIGURE 5.9
Risk mitigation in e-commerce. Encryption verifies the identity of the vendor and protects the data in transmission. Credit card companies accept risks for the consumers but not for the vendors. Huge vendor databases of credit card data are tempting targets and need to be protected by the vendor.

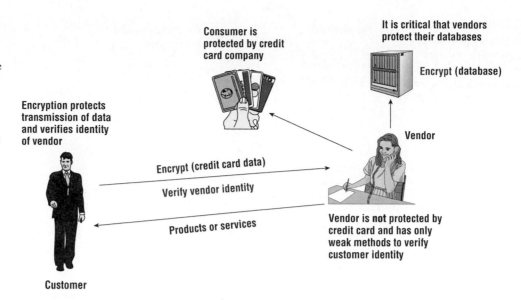

The risk of theft is real, and has happened to several vendors. The potential target is huge: thousands or millions of validated credit card numbers—all accessible via the Internet. The only effective solutions are for vendors to either keep the card numbers offline, or to encrypt them and bury the encryption key.

The second risk arises because digital orders are easy to alter. The solution is to create electronic orders that cannot be altered. Again, this solution requires encryption. In this case, the customer and the vendor both need a digital certificate. When both parties encrypt the order, it cannot be altered later.

Business to Consumer

As the percentage of U.S. households equipped with personal computers passed 50 percent, companies have become increasingly interested in using the Internet to sell products directly to consumers, known as **business to consumer (B2C)** e-commerce. The possibilities are enticing. The Internet gives companies the opportunity to save money by skipping the middle level of distributors and retailers. It also provides the ability to track customer preferences more closely and give them accurate and up-to-date information on products and options.

From a marketing perspective, the buying process has in three basic steps: (1) prepurchase information gathering, (2) the purchase itself, and (3) postpurchase support. These steps are listed with examples in Figure 5.10. The Internet can be used to support each of these areas. The level of support in each area depends on the industry, type of product, and capabilities of the customers. Note that the process differs depending on whether the customer is a retail consumer or another company. For example, sales to other companies are generally repetitive and typically require additional documentation and billing procedures.

Creating a website requires access to a server that has a full-time connection to the Internet. Initially, basic servers simply presented static pages, with text and limited graphics that rarely changed. Gradually, more sophisticated services have been introduced that add a higher degree of interactivity. One of the most important features is the ability of the website to connect to the corporate databases. In this situation, the Web simply becomes a front-end or client computer to the back-end database server. The strength of the Web is that it provides a standardized user interface that is accessible anywhere in the world.

Prepurchase Information

Prepurchase information is one of the easiest things to provide with a website. Whether supporting end consumers or other businesses, the information tends to be relatively static and can be stored on virtually any Web server. Common features include product specifications, pictures, schematics, and prices. For static sites, lists of frequently asked questions (FAQs)

FIGURE 5.10

Business to consumer electronic commerce. Websites are commonly used to support the three main phases of marketing.

Prepurchase	Purchase (requires interactive)	Postpurchase
Static data sites	Transmission security	Service
• Promotion	User identification	• Revenue generation
• Product specifications	Product selection	• Problem tracking
• Pictures	Payment validation	• Sales leads
• Schematics	Order confirmation	Resolve problems
• Pricing		Answer questions
• FAQs		Product evaluation
Interactive sites		• Modifications
• Configuration		• Tracking customers
• Compatibility		
• Complex pricing		

can provide additional information to prospective customers. More interactive sites provide configuration and compatibility data. Surveys and monitoring of website access provide data on customer preferences and activities.

Relatively static sites are easy to create and can be hosted on virtually any server. Today, many ISPs provide free basic website space. Because these sites are easy to create and to host, they are one of the most common elements of e-commerce.

One of the greatest strengths of using a website for prepurchase information is that it is relatively inexpensive. Additionally, the information is available worldwide 24 hours a day. It is also relatively easy to change the data, particularly since the data needs to be updated in only one location. For example, it is much cheaper to update a photo on a website than to reprint and ship an entire catalog.

The most challenging aspect to providing prepurchase information is getting customers to come to your site. Web search engines make it relatively easy for customers to find the site, so motivated customers may search you out. However, companies are increasingly trying to attract customers. Hence, website advertising is becoming more common—both on the Web and in more traditional media. Think about the number of advertisements you see that include a Web address. Today, it is difficult to find even a newspaper ad that does not have a Web address. Companies also advertise on other websites. For example, the big search engines are some of the most popular sites on the Internet—used daily by millions of people. These portal sites sell ad space to other companies, who hope that viewers will click-through to learn more about their products.

Purchase Mechanisms

Purchasing products over the Internet requires a substantially more interactive website. The purchase mechanism also varies depending on whether the customer is an end consumer or another company. Online purchase mechanisms need five basic elements: (1) transmission security, (2) user identification, (3) payment validation, (4) product selection, and (5) order confirmation. When the customer is another company, the steps are the same but can be more complicated. In this situation, the company generally wants the ordering to be more automatic (e.g., EDI), and requires automated notification of the order status and shipping times. Companies also want more sophisticated billing features such as itemized monthly bills, the ability to dispute individual items, and credit terms.

Transmission security is important on the Internet because unencrypted transmissions could be intercepted by thousands of people. Encryption is used to ensure that no one can intercept and read or change the order and financial data. Providing secure transmissions requires the use of a secure server. Browsers are already configured to accept the security conditions of the server. Server security is established by purchasing an authentication certificate from a security provider such as Verisign. The certificate ensures that your company exists and encrypts transmissions with the browser.

User identification depends on the type of customer. Commercial customers can also purchase authentication certificates, which provide a relatively strong means of identifying

Reality Bytes   Webvan versus Albertson's

Webvan was one of the early e-commerce firms that raised huge amounts of startup capital. When merged with HomeGrocer.com, the two firms combined had raised $1.2 billion in funding. Webvan founder Louis Borders had a grand vision, and he used press conferences to shout his plans to investors eager to believe in a new world. His plan was to change society by delivering products directly to homes—beginning with groceries and expanding to anything. The old bricks and mortar companies (like Albertson's) were out of date and would be replaced by Webvan's direct delivery. HomeGrocer was a smaller rival that was more cautious in its spending. Even then, sales were not high enough to support its costs, so they merged with Webvan in late 2000. At the time, the combined firm had $650 million in cash raised from IPOs. With the merger, Webvan's leaders increased their spending on expensive warehouses, employee salaries, and on repainting all of their vehicles. They also converted all of HomeGrocer's systems to Webvan's—confusing existing customers, so that orders fell by over 50 percent. Within nine months of the merger all of the cash was gone, and the company closed. Meanwhile, back in the real world, Albertson's—the second largest grocery chain—was testing an online ordering and delivery service in Seattle. When Webvan failed, Albertson's picked up many of its customers. Mike Muta, the vice president of Web technology notes "We don't really see this as a risky situation. We see this as a situation where we've been very methodical, we've been very quiet, we've been very smart." Instead of spending tens of millions of dollars on new warehouses, Albertson's uses its existing distribution centers and 2,500 U.S. stores. Electronic orders are compared against store inventories and grocery requests are routed to the nearest Albertson's store. Personal shoppers load the groceries into boxes that can be picked up or delivered for a small fee. The grocery industry is extremely competitive with low margins. Successful companies focus on reducing operating costs through economies of scale.

Sources: Adapted from Miguel Helft, "What a Long, Strange Trip It's Been for Webvan," *The Industry Standard,* July 23, 2001 "Webvan Shuts Down Operations, Plans to Seek Chapter 11 Protection," *The Wall Street Journal* July 9, 2001; and "An Online Grocer That's Not Rotten," *Tech Live,* September 6, 2001.

people and organizations on the Internet. Retail customers are generally identified by their credit card data. The credit card number, expiration date, and billing address must be provided and verified to minimize the possibility of fraud. For both personal and commercial customers, particularly for repeat customers, you can also establish usernames and passwords to identify the customers.

Currently, payment validation is straightforward but can be expensive. Commercial customers are generally billed on a monthly cycle. So once you identify the customer, the system simply adds the purchase data to the billing system. Payments can then be made directly to your firm, or to your bank through an EDI mechanism. The EDI systems are relatively fast and highly reliable. Individual consumer payments are generally made using credit cards, which must be processed through a bank or credit card agency. Banks typically collect fees based on the value of the transaction (e.g., 1 to 5 percent). Some companies are working on more direct payment methods that transfer money directly. Chapter 14 discusses some of the possibilities and issues related to these mechanisms.

Any transaction requires that your website identify the specific items and quantities being purchased. For retail consumers, the best method is to enable them to choose from a list. Virtual shopping carts are common: when customers see an item they wish to purchase, they click an icon and the ID number is added to the shopping cart. The most interactive sites enable customers to see if the item is in stock before they select it. Simpler systems are more static and require the customer to enter the product ID number directly. This method can lead to unacceptable errors, but might be faster for commercial customers who repeatedly purchase the same items. In both cases, the system needs to look up the current price of each item and compute the necessary taxes and shipping costs.

The actual purchase mechanisms are relatively complex, particularly since you must be careful to provide security and minimize errors. Consequently, it is often wiser to purchase software that runs your website somewhat automatically. Several companies sell servers specifically designed to generate interactive e-commerce sites: notably Microsoft and Netscape. For relatively uncomplicated sites, you can also lease space on a commercial mall site, which provides the underlying facilities. All you have to do is enter your database with product descriptions, images, and prices.

Order confirmation is related to the selection of the products. At a minimum, you should provide a list of the items purchased, the inventory status, the price, and the total value of the order. It is also helpful to provide an order number generated by the system. Then if questions arise, it is easy to locate the specific order. For many retail consumers, the order number is an important feedback mechanism that verifies the purchase was accepted. Order confirmation is generally more complex for commercial customers. They often need detailed information on each purchase and its current status. In these situations, many sellers provide the purchaser with direct access (read only) to the order database, so purchase managers can check status and billing amounts at any time.

Postpurchase Support

Postpurchase support consists of providing service, resolving problems, answering questions, and evaluating products. Some products require more service than others. In cases where the service generates continuous streams of revenue, a website can be useful at tracking customers, providing additional information, and generating leads for new sales. The resolution of complaints is an important part of service for any product. Some problems are relatively easy to solve and can be handled with a support database and perhaps an online expert system that walks the consumer through possible solutions. In more complex cases, the system can track complaints, identify causes, and rapidly inform engineers of potential problems. Similarly, the information obtained through the service site can be used to spot consumer trends and provide ideas for product improvements.

In general, a postpurchase website is relatively easy to create. Much of the content can be static—as long as there is an extensive, easy-to-use search system. Obtaining comments from consumers utilizes a straightforward, form-based site. About the only danger is that your competitors will have equal access to the information you provide. Most of the time, it will not be an issue, but you should be careful to protect comments and information returned by customers.

International Issues

In the early stages of e-commerce, several people suggested that the Internet's global reach would make it easy even for small businesses to sell products internationally. However, several factors interfere with international sales. Some are traditional (such as shipping and tariffs), others are unique to the Internet.

Figure 5.11 summarizes some of the major points involving sales into other nations. Jurisdiction for dispute resolution is a major issue. Nations have many different laws and cultures. Tactics (and content) that might be commonplace in one country could be illegal in another nation. Gambling is a classic example. The United States might ban gambling on the Internet, but how can it enforce that law? But if a U.S. citizen has a dispute with an overseas casino, there would be few options to protect the consumer. Similarly, fraud and Web attacks can easily originate from several different nations. Varying laws and lack of coordination make it difficult to identify and prosecute the perpetrators.

FIGURE 5.11

Some international issues in e-commerce. Jurisdiction is a big issue with different laws and cultures. Customers can use credit cards to mitigate risks, but people in many nations do not use them.

Jurisdiction questions for disputes
    Collection and payment for sales
        Currently rely on credit cards
        Many people do not use credit cards
        Does not protect vendor
    Coordinate and stop fraud
    Control harassment, spamming, and denial of service attacks
Encryption restrictions
    U.S. classifies as munitions
    France does not allow citizens to use encryption at all
Different privacy rules
Nations have differing perspectives of "offensive" content

Privacy and encryption present additional challenges. The European Union has privacy rules that are substantially higher than other nations, and it does not want international companies transferring personal data to computers outside of the Union. Likewise, governments sometimes control encryption, which makes it more difficult to prevent common transaction problems on the Internet. For many years, the United States forbade the export of strong encryption technology (even though similar technologies already existed worldwide). Only in 2001, did the United States begin to allow software to be shipped with strong encryption. Consequently, international customers could never be sure that their transactions were secure, since the weaker encryption systems could be broken in a matter of hours. On the other hand, France does not allow citizens to use encryption at all.

Business to Business

Business-to-business (B2B) e-commerce has the potential to vastly exceed business-to-consumer e-commerce. Consumers will always have a preference to see and touch the products they want to buy—and to take them home immediately. But businesses generally know exactly what products they want and they often buy in bulk. Businesses also need to hold costs down for repeat transactions. An important method of reducing costs is to reduce mistakes and minimize the use of people. When purchase orders cost $40–$50 in employee time, considerable money can be saved by using electronic transactions.

One question that remains to be answered in the industry is: How is B2B e-commerce different from EDI? On one hand, a basic B2B website set up by a vendor might simply be a proprietary version of EDI—using Web protocols and browsers. On the other hand, some B2B sites create an entirely new means of connecting businesses. The industry-specific auction sites are good examples of powerful new technologies to facilitate business transactions.

Repeat Transactions and Supply Chain Management

Businesses need a continual supply of products—both as raw materials and for support operations through office supplies and tools. In traditional environments, it would be prohibitively expensive to issue purchase orders for every individual item. Instead, most companies rely on long-term contracts with select vendors. This approach may not result in the most competitive pricing, but it controls transaction costs and makes it easier to monitor and improve quality.

In this situation, B2B e-commerce sites essentially become proprietary EDI channels. The office store websites (such as Office Depot) provide a good example. Once a business establishes an account, employees can find and order supplies directly through the website. Pricing and billing are handled electronically, and the purchasing manager can get detailed lists of all purchases. Payment can also be handled electronically, minimizing the involvement of expensive personnel for low-cost items.

Supply chain management revolves around purchasing, but also incorporates just-in-time delivery, searching for competitive pricing, and controlling and monitoring quality. Websites and search engines make it easier for businesses to find unique products and tools.

Auction Markets

In the last couple of years, several industries have established more powerful websites to facilitate business transactions. Auction sites have been created for specific products. Generally, these sites support sales of relatively generic products such as steel, oil, and paper. Generic products have standard definitions and quality measures, are used by many types of businesses, and can be traded on a long-term or short-term basis. As shown in Figure 5.12, the auction site is simply an electronic marketplace where suppliers list the item and quantity available, and buyers bid on the items.

Non-Internet spot auction markets have existed for many years in these commodities, but the Web versions open the markets to more participants and make it easier for firms to get information and make quick decisions. The auctions establish direct connections between the buying and selling firms instead of relying on an intermediary to handle the details of the transaction.

FIGURE 5.12
Online auction markets. Regardless of location, buyers and sellers can have instant access to information and can quickly and inexpensively negotiate a transaction.

Buyers and sellers connected through a website

The existence of these B2B sites provides additional options for firms. With low transaction costs (the sites do charge a transaction fee so it is not zero), firms can rethink their long-term/short-term purchasing strategies. For example, if a firm foresees uncertainty in production in the coming months, it can reduce its long-term contracts. If demand picks up unexpectedly, the firm can quickly pick up the additional materials at a spot auction site. Similarly, producers can use the auction sites to sell to new customers and level out the production cycles.

Payment Mechanisms

Payment mechanisms must change along with the changes in transactions. Years ago, when purchases were made locally, currency was the primary method of settling transactions. Eventually, as banks stabilized and gained respect (and government guarantees), transactions were settled by checks. Business transactions (particularly internationally) are often settled with letters of credit from banks. In the United States, many payments have migrated to credit cards.

From a consumer standpoint, credit cards are easy, available, provide short-term loans, and offer protection from fraud and errors. Figure 5.13 shows the drawbacks to credit cards and lists the characteristics desired from a new payment mechanism. From an e-commerce merchant perspective, credit cards offer only minimal support and are expensive. From the perspective of a mobile-commerce merchant, credit cards will be unacceptable because the transaction costs are too high to support small payments.

From a theoretical perspective, e-commerce payment mechanisms should be easy to create. In fact, dozens have been proposed or started in the past few years. None of them have garnered enough support to be successful.

Several companies have proposed alternative payment mechanisms. As illustrated in Figure 5.14, most involve the use of a trusted third party (like a bank). **Digital cash** is an example, where buyers can make anonymous purchases over a network, and sellers are assured of receiving payment. Consumers transfer real money to the third party and receive one-time-use digital cash numbers. These numbers can be given to a vendor, who returns them to the third party for an account credit. Other methods use the third party to verify the authenticity of the buyer and seller. The third party completes the transaction by transferring the money between accounts.

A few other payment mechanisms are used by customers that rely on e-mail messages to transfer money using traditional credit card or checking accounts. For example, PayPal (X.com corporation), Billpoint (Wells Fargo Bank), eMoneyMail (Bank One), and c2it (Citicorp). However, in most cases, the transaction costs for these mechanisms are still too high for low-price transactions.

FIGURE 5.13

Payment mechanisms. Credit cards do not protect merchants and have high transaction costs, so they cannot be used for low-price items. Several systems have been created to provide the desired characteristics, but customers have not yet been willing to adopt them.

Credit card drawbacks

    High transaction costs
    Not feasible for small payments
    Do not protect the merchant

Characteristics needed

    Low enough costs to support payments less that $1
    Secure transmission
    Secure storage
    Authentication mechanism
    Easy translation to traditional money

Alternatives

    Mobile phone bill
    Smart cards

FIGURE 5.14

Digital cash payment mechanism. Large payments or monthly payments can be made through most banks in the form of real money in checking accounts. These methods can be cumbersome and expensive for small transactions. Several companies have proposed standards for the creation of digital cash. The goal is to create an electronic form of money that can be verified, is inexpensive to use, can support anonymity, and cannot be easily counterfeited.

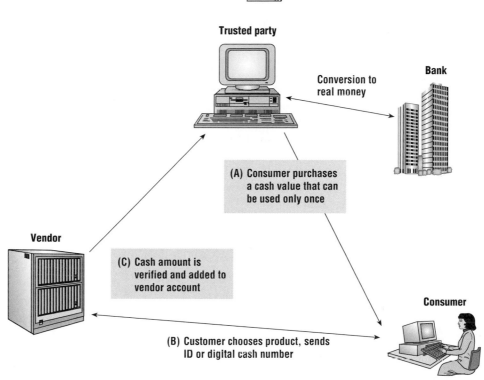

Mobile commerce offers one possibility for handling small transactions: put the cost on the customer's cell phone bill. Most phone bills already contain lists of small transactions, and the total monthly fee is high enough to pay using traditional mechanisms. As long as the vendor builds up enough credits with the phone company, the transaction costs on that side will be reasonable. Currently, the biggest potential drawback is the limited security. Phone numbers are easy to find, although a 4-digit PIN would improve security a little. Requiring physical access to the phone will provide more security, until the phone is lost or stolen.

At a minimum, encryption requires that the vendor obtain a digital certificate. The most secure systems require the consumer to obtain a digital certificate to authenticate the identity of the consumer. Most consumers are reluctant to pay the cost in money and time to obtain a personal digital certificate. As an alternative, credit card companies are pushing smart cards, which can contain customer authentication information. But these cards require new scanning hardware, and merchants and vendors are generally unwilling to pay for the new hardware.

In summary, electronic payment mechanisms are still in their infancy. It could take years for a standard to evolve and be accepted by enough merchants and customers to be important. In the past, governments have borne the costs of creating and printing money. Today,

FIGURE 5.15

Maintaining data quality is crucial to managing a firm. There are several problems that make it difficult to build good transaction processing systems.

Data Quality Attribute	Description and Problems
Integrity	Errors in data entry
	Missing data
	Failure to make updates
Multitasking—concurrency	Data altered by two people at the same time creating incorrect results
Volume	Cost, difficulty of searching, transmission costs, errors harder to find, system overload
Summaries	Too much detail is overkill when you only need summaries
	With only summaries, you cannot recover the details
Time	Many reports and decisions are subject to deadlines
	Different departments getting data at different times can cause sequencing errors and additional delays

most seem unwilling to become involved, and they have left the mechanisms to the private sector—which is more focused on developing a system that provides profits to the issuing authority, instead of developing a system that would be widely accepted.

Even for traditional businesses, **bill presentation and payment** mechanisms can make life easier and save money. Service businesses in particular can benefit because they tend to bill clients on a regular basis. The goal is to send all bills electronically and provide a simple method for clients to transfer funds to your account. If clients are large businesses, they may wish to use existing EDI or banking systems to transfer money. Smaller customers with smaller payments will generally prefer the newer online payment systems like BillPay because they have lower costs to the customers.

The electronic systems save time because the bills can be created automatically from the in-house billing system. They do not have to be printed or mailed. Customers can feed the data into their own accounts payable systems, and create electronic payments with only a few review steps. The payment data, and any disputes can be processed electronically and automated.

Data Quality

Transaction-processing systems can become quite complex. Problems are going to occur in any system—especially because all business organizations change over time. That means the computer system has to change to match the business. It is virtually impossible to change the system at exactly the same time as the business, so problems will occur. Other problems arise simply because the systems are so complex. Many processes involve humans who make mistakes. If you understand what types of problems might arise, they will be easier to solve.

The key to data quality is to focus on quality throughout the process. At input, data should be collected as close to the source as possible. For processing, data should be available to all users in a form they can use without having to reenter the data. In terms of output, reports should be linked to the databases so they always use the most recent data. Figure 5.15 lists the primary measures of data quality that you need to consider. In examining an information system, if you detect any of these problems, they are clues that you should search for ways to improve the transaction-processing system

Data Integrity

One of the most important concepts in information processing is the issue of data integrity. **Data integrity** means keeping data accurate and correct as it is gathered and stored in the computer system. There is little value in an information system that contains out-of-date or inaccurate data. A common complaint among shoppers today is that stores using bar-code scanners might have a different price in the computer than the amount displayed on the shelf. It is easy to change prices in the computer; it is more difficult to change the signs in the store. Shoppers will feel cheated if the computer tries to charge them a higher price than the amount listed on the shelf. Some states, such as Michigan, have passed laws requiring that the

Founded in Sweden in 1943, Ikea is a global furniture retailer based in the Netherlands. It has stores in 33 countries, with 1,960 suppliers in 53 nations, and 36 purchasing offices in 29 countries. In 1996, the company was forced to face the problems of Y2K and the introduction of the euro. The offices were using old software, and often different software in each location. So the company decided it needed to install a common, integrated system across the company. The company chose Coda-Financials from U.K.-based Coda. The international aspect of the company made the transition challenging. The company also had different needs for the different types of activities: wholesalers with few invoices and large flows of goods in multiple currencies; retailers with one currency by thousands of invoices; and service companies that handle treasury functions and real estate. Ulrika Martensson, project manager for the conversion, noted that some mistakes were made because the system allowed so much flexibility. The team was taking from 5 to 10 days for each implementation for customization. The European VAT system also proved challenging, because each nation had different rules. The Coda system handled most of the details, but a custom system was needed to deal with the Italian version. With the increasing importance of the euro, the financial data for the European nations is now being handled completely in euros—a switch that was easily facilitated in the new system.

Source: Adapted from Malcolm Wheatley, "Ikea's Financial Furnishings," *CIO Magazine,* September 1, 2001.

scanned price cannot be higher than the amount listed on the package or display. Similar errors cause problems when the computer shows more items in stock than actually exist.

The first step to ensure data integrity lies in its capture. Each item must be correctly entered and the complete information recorded. It is sometimes possible to check the data as it is entered. Item code numbers usually include a check number that is based on the other digits. In the item code 548737, the first five digits add up to 27, so the number 7 is included as the last digit. If the person or machine makes a mistake entering one of the digits, they will probably not add up to 7, so the computer can immediately determine that there is an error. Sophisticated methods exist to catch mistakes involving more than one digit.

Even with machine entry of data, validity problems can arise. What happens when a shipment arrives, but the receiving department forgets to record it? The same problem occurs when a clerk holds an item for a customer and does not record it in the computer. Data integrity can be destroyed by indiscriminately allowing people to change the numbers in the computer. It is one of the main reasons for creating secure computers and controlling access to each piece of information.

Multitasking, Concurrency, and Integrity

A useful feature offered by more sophisticated operating systems is the ability to perform more than one task at a time. In many situations it is useful to have several jobs running at the same time. What happens if you are searching a huge database and your boss calls and asks you for a sales figure? With a multitasking computer operating system, you could switch to a new program, look up the number, and allow the database to continue searching in the background.

If you use a multitasking operating system, it is important that your application software understand that other applications might be running at the same time. Each application needs to protect its data files from concurrency problems. **Concurrency** arises when applications attempt to modify the same piece of data at the same time. If two people are allowed to make changes to the same piece of data, the computer system must control the order in which it processes the two requests. Mixing the two tasks will result in the wrong data being stored in the computer. These problems can be avoided by only using software that was specifically written for multiuser (or multitasking) computers.

Consider the case of a mail-order firm shown in Figure 5.16. On the left side, customer Sanchez sent a payment on his account. At the same time the clerk begins to process the payment, Sanchez calls a second clerk and places a new order. The figure shows what

FIGURE 5.16

Concurrency and data integrity. Multiuser and multitasking systems can cause problems with concurrent changes to data. Two processes cannot be allowed to change the same data at the same time. Most systems will lock out transaction B until transaction A is completed. If a system becomes very busy, you can sometimes encounter delays while you wait for other users to finish their changes.

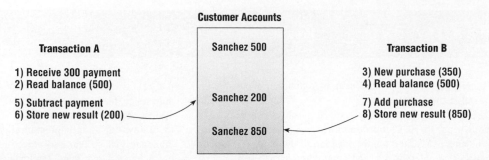

Customer Accounts

Transaction A

1) Receive 300 payment
2) Read balance (500)

5) Subtract payment
6) Store new result (200)

Sanchez 500

Sanchez 200

Sanchez 850

Transaction B

3) New purchase (350)
4) Read balance (500)

7) Add purchase
8) Store new result (850)

happens if both transactions continue and interfere with each other. What should the final balance be? Does the computer have the correct number?

To solve this problem, the application program must know that several people might try to access the same piece of data at the same time. The software locks out all users except one. When the first process is finished, the other users can try to gain access again. To keep data accurate, applications used by many people at the same time must be written to handle these concurrency problems. Early personal computers were designed for only one user, so much of the software did not prevent concurrency problems. Software designed for computer networks generally handles this issue. When you use this software, you will occasionally receive a message that says a piece of data you desire is currently being used by another person. If you get this message, simply wait for a few minutes and try again. When the first person is finished, you should be able to proceed.

Data Volume

A common problem experienced by a growing business is the increase in the amount of data or data volume. Consider the huge databases handled by Information Resources that processes data from supermarket checkouts, or United Parcel Service that tracks every package every day.

As the business grows, there will be an increase in the number of transactions. As the price of a computer drops, more applications are placed on the computer. Additional transactions become computerized. Several problems can be created from this increase: (1) processing overload or system slowdowns; (2) greater difficulty in making sure the data is accurate; (3) insufficient storage within the computer system; and (4) data not captured fast enough.

Visa International processes more than 6 billion electronic transactions a year. In the year 2000, the company expected to handle 15 billion annual transactions. There are 18,000 banks offering Visa cards, used by 10 million customers. So much data is generated on a daily basis that Visa cannot keep transaction data online beyond six months. All older records are moved to backup storage, making them inaccessible for additional research or decisions.

Sloppy practices and huge datasets can lead to inaccurate data. As the system slows down or the computer runs out of storage space, people avoid using it, so data is no longer up to date. With the increase in volume and the computerization of new types of data, it is more difficult for programmers and managers to check the data. If parts of the computer system are too slow, data may not be captured fast enough. As a result, some data might be lost. A tremendous amount of information is stored in raw data. The raw data could be analyzed to offer new services or improve the quality of existing services. However, the huge volumes require too much storage space and too much processing time.

Careful planning is required to avoid these problems. At best, new computers and storage usually take a month or two to purchase. It could take a year or more to evaluate and purchase a large, expensive central computer. The MIS department would like to forecast the demands that will be placed on the computers at least a year in advance.

Data Summaries

Another situation is commonly encountered in transaction-processing systems. In almost any company today, managers complain of having too much data. Consider the situation of a marketing manager who needs to determine the best way to increase sales for the next year. Think of the amount of data that is readily available. The firm's transaction-processing system can provide detailed records on sales of every item every day, by each salesperson, broken down by city, for at least the last five years. Scanner data from marketing research firms lists itemized sales by grocery store for every product. There is also internal data from consumer surveys, production, and responses to promotions. Demographic data is available from the government.

To deal with this much data, managers are forced to rely on summaries. The marketing manager may only see a list of sales totals by each salesperson. That total might or might not include merchandise that was returned. Imagine what happens if returns are *not* included in the totals, but the manager believes that they were included. An unethical salesperson could sell extra merchandise to a friend (boosting the totals), and then return the merchandise the same day (because the returns are not subtracted from the list).

The problem multiplies as the information travels through different levels in the organization. Higher-level managers in the firm deal with data that has gone through several types of summarizing at each lower level. By the time they finally receive the information, the reports might not contain the information that is needed. The details might have been deleted or the summaries might carry the wrong set of information.

Time

Time is another aspect of information quality in transaction-processing systems. The information system must furnish the information at the time it is needed for decision making. An information system that is overloaded or not producing properly summarized data will not be able to provide information at the right time. Consider the data needed to file tax forms. The government has a time limit for filing tax forms. Managers would be understandably upset if their computer system could not produce the annual accounting reports in time to calculate taxes. Similarly, it is difficult to place orders for new merchandise when the only available data is a three-month-old sales report.

Problems with timeliness generally arise because data is not captured early enough. The sales report might be delayed because too many people are needed to enter the data and make some of the computations. A POS system could provide a detailed sales list almost instantly. Other delays arise when the system cannot distribute data to everyone at the same time, so reports end up sitting on someone's desk.

The Role of Accounting

Accounting systems are important because they extend throughout the company and because they focus on money. They are used to collect data and evaluate performance. Accounting systems also enable managers to combine the many divisions into an integrated picture of the entire company. Accounting systems also provide controls over the data to ensure accuracy and to prevent fraud. The primary purpose of accounting is to collect the financial data of the firm, ensure that it is accurate, and create standard reports. It is hard to capture all of the elements of an accounting system in one illustration, but Figure 5.17 summarizes the essential components of an accounting system. The accounting transaction system can be examined in terms of inputs, outputs, and processes.

Input and Output: Financial Data and Reports

Raw financial data is collected by the accounting department and stored in an **accounting journal**. Modern accounting requires the use of a double-entry system to ensure accurate data. In a double-entry system, at least two entries must occur for every transaction. Generally, one entry records the effect of the money (e.g., cash, accounts payable, accounts receivable), and the other refers to a specific category (e.g., sales, office expenses, commissions). Each entry includes the date, amount of money, account number, the name of the person or firm involved, perhaps a comment, and the name of the person making the entry. The journal's purpose is to record all the transactions.

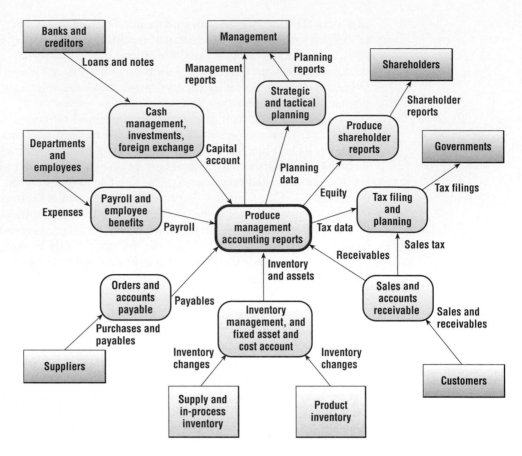

Journal entries represent raw data. To be useful, this data must be transformed into information. The first step is to categorize the data by *accounts* or categories, which is the purpose of the **general ledger**. The ledger is a collection of accounts that break the data into specific categories. Common categories include *accounts receivable, accounts payable, inventory,* and *cash.* Although there are some standards, each company can define its own **chart of accounts**, which allows owners and managers to examine data on whatever categories are important to their firm.

For managers to make comparisons between divisions and other firms, accounting systems produce standardized reports. Most companies produce *balance sheets, cash flow statements,* and *income statements* every quarter. These reports are produced following standard accounting rules to enable owners, managers, and investors to compare the financial positions of various companies over time.

Purchases, Sales, Loans, and Investments

One of the primary purposes of accounting is to record the financial transactions with external organizations. In addition to collecting the raw data, the accounting system contains controls that minimize fraud by limiting access to the data. The system also creates summary and detail reports to monitor key information.

Managers often build **exception reports** into the accounting system that are triggered when some event occurs. If sales in some region suddenly drop, if there is a major increase in the cash balance, or if inventories fall below a defined level, a message will be sent to the appropriate manager. The manager typically responds by searching the recent summary reports for a possible cause.

Inventory

Most organizations need to control inventory carefully. Retail stores find it hard to sell items that are not in stock. Manufacturing firms need to receive and process parts as cheaply as possible. Inventory control consists of knowing exactly what items are available and where they are located. The system also needs to determine when to place new orders. It must then track the orders to make sure each item is delivered to the appropriate location at the right time. With EDI, the inventory control system can monitor current sales and automatically place orders with the supplier.

Manufacturing firms use these systems to implement just-in-time inventory control. The computer system monitors the current production requirements, keeps track of deliveries, and electronically sends orders to the suppliers. The suppliers then deliver the parts just as they are needed on the production line.

Automated inventory control systems also help identify and prevent theft. By recording all movement of items from receipt to sales to shipping, management knows exactly how many items exist. Consider a retail store like a bicycle shop. The computerized inventory notes that there should be three *Sigma computers* in stock. Yet, when a customer asks to buy one, you notice there are only two left. If there is no mistake in your inventory report, you conclude that someone stole one of the items. Although the system did not prevent the speedometer from disappearing, it does show which items are susceptible to theft. It also helps control theft by employees, who will be less likely to steal if they know that the items are carefully monitored.

The Accounting Cycle

An important aspect of accounting systems is that they produce information in specific cycles. Firms are required to produce reports that reflect the financial condition of the firm at the end of every quarter. Accounting systems are based on these requirements. For the most part, managers operate from quarterly reports, with intermediate monthly reports for some items. Because of the volume of data in the detail, most companies only keep current statistics and summary reports on file. Older data is shuffled off the system to make room for the current numbers. As a result, managers may not have easy access to detailed data from prior years.

Process: Controls, Checks, and Balances

Double-Entry Systems

An important objective of accounting systems is to maintain the integrity of the financial data. The goal is to prevent mistakes and discourage fraud. Double-entry accounting provides a method to locate mistakes in data entry. If an amount is entered incorrectly, the account totals will not balance.

Because many transactions involve outside organizations, mistakes can be caught by sharing data. Every month firms receive a statement from the bank. The totals can be compared to changes in the firm's cash account. Similarly, companies typically send receipts when they receive payments from each other. Auditors periodically send verification requests to suppliers and customers to make sure the data was recorded correctly. EDI strengthens this approach, because transaction data is transmitted in computer form among the companies.

Separation of Duties

Another type of control is the separation of duties. A manager in the purchasing department might be responsible for choosing a supplier of parts. Only the accounting department can authorize the transfer of money to the supplier. The objective is to minimize fraud by requiring a potential thief to deal with multiple employees.

Many banks take this concept a step further. They require employees (especially tellers) to take their vacations every year. Several instances of fraud have been revealed when the employee was no longer at the job to keep the fraudulent mechanism running.

Audit Trails

An **audit trail** is important to accounting systems. It enables investigators to track backward through the data to the source. A cash-flow statement might indicate that the company has spent twice as much money this month as last. To find out why, trace backward

Reality Bytes — Features to Look for in Accounting Software

SMALL BUSINESS BASICS

General Ledger

Sample chart of accounts that can be modified.

Optional automatic posting to the ledger so you don't forget.

Automatic data entry for often-used vendor account numbers.

Define fiscal years instead of forcing calendar year.

How many months can be "open" at once?

Can entries be posted for prior months or prior years?

Audit trail.

Track expenses by departments and allocate portions of bills.

Accounts Receivable

Granting discounts for early payments.

Charging interest for late payments.

Multiple ship-to addresses.

Sales tax (by state and locality).

Automatic payment reminder notices.

Automatic entries for monthly maintenance fees.

The ability to add notes to invoices.

Carry invoice details month-to-month, not just total balance

Accounts Payable

Check reconciliation support.

Automatic recurring entries.

Monitoring and automatic notices of payment discounts.

Ability to select bills to be paid from the screen.

Ability to make payment by item, not just total bill, in case of dispute.

General Features

Support for printers.

Require special preprinted forms?

Custom reports.

Custom queries.

Security controls, access to various modules by password.

---

and find all of the raw entries that make up the number. Together with dates and amounts, the raw journal entries can contain the identity of the person responsible for the entry. By keeping this identification data, it is possible to list every article that affects an item on a report.

Human Resources and Transaction Processing

Every company has employees. Companies collect hundreds of pieces of data for each employee—some for management purposes, others because they are required by law. For years, the human resources (HR) department focused on filling out and storing forms. The enormous amount of paperwork alone begs for computerization just to cut down on storage space needed. Computerized databases also enable managers to find specific data on employees. Early HR software emphasized these two benefits. Modern HR software is expanding beyond simple forms to improving data collection and providing better analyses. To illustrate the problems presented by large-scale transaction processing systems, consider the three areas of input, output, and processing.

Input: Data Collection

Figure 5.18 illustrates the basic components of a human resource management (HRM) transaction-processing system. Note that the system is even more complex because the data comes from all areas of the company. To understand how the HRM systems became so complicated, begin with the obvious data that needs to be collected: numbers related to the payroll. For hourly workers, the system needs to collect and monitor hours worked. For many sales tasks, the system must compute sales by employee to determine commissions.

FIGURE 5.18

Most employees know that human resources management (HRM) deals with payroll and benefits. But HRM also collects data and produces reports for a myriad of government reports, oversees employee evaluations, and job applications. The department also handles training and education opportunities.

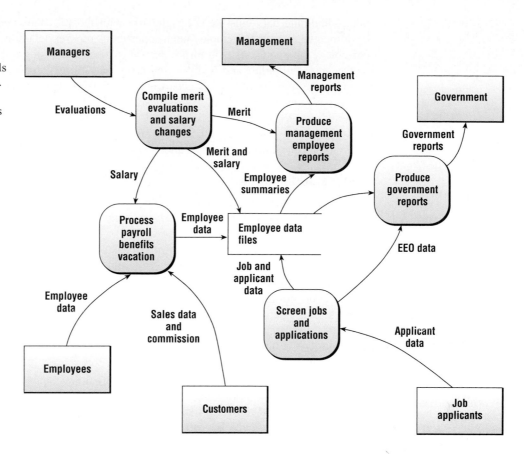

Professional service firms often ask employees to track their time in terms of billable hours for work that is charged back to clients. In all three situations, as the number of employees increases, it becomes increasingly difficult to collect all of these statistics and verify their accuracy. It also becomes harder to find specific pieces of data.

Think about paychecks you have received. In addition to the payment amount, there could be 10 to 20 other numbers on the pay stub. Companies monitor and report several types of payroll taxes, including federal, state, local, Social Security, and health. Also, firms monitor employee benefits, such as health care and retirement. Most firms also handle employee deductions for employee purchases, savings plans, stock purchases, parking, meal plans, and other options. In some situations, companies must garnishee wages and forward them to a third party.

Human resource departments also track days taken for vacations, personal time, and illness. In larger companies, HRM provides training courses and offers testing of critical skills. Employee attendance and performance data is stored and incorporated into evaluations.

With the increasing use of merit pay, the system must also track employee evaluations. Some performance measures are tied to productivity or output within the employee's department, so HR must relate employee work schedules to production and quality measures.

Most companies use a centralized HRM department to advertise job openings and to screen the initial applicants, verify credentials, and keep basic employment and hiring data.

Output: Reports

The human resources department also produces several reports related to payroll. Along with printing checks, HRM must provide expense reports and forecasts to the accounting system. Periodic reports are created for job vacancies and analyses of employee performance and morale.

HRM departments also spend a great deal of time creating reports for various government agencies. All companies must file various economic reports dealing with employment.

Tax-withholding data must be filed regularly with federal, state, and local agencies. HRM departments create equal employment opportunity reports detailing characteristics of their workforce, job applicants, and hiring decisions. Then there are various reports required by the Occupational Safety and Health Administration (OSHA) regarding injuries and exposure to various hazards. If employees need to be certified, companies file aggregate reports with the various regulatory agencies. All of these reports have deadlines.

In addition to the standard reports, the human resources department is responsible for maintaining compliance with all relevant employment laws. Hence, HRM staff must continually monitor the employment data and evaluate it for exceptions and problems.

Process: Automation

The human resources department is a busy place. Keep in mind that the data and reports apply to every branch of the company. Even standard items such as paychecks become complicated when the company is split into several divisions scattered across the country. Also, remember that accuracy is crucial. Employees can become upset if their paychecks are wrong. Errors with government reports can lead to fines and lawsuits. Equally important, companies with good HRM departments are able to offer additional benefits to employees. With a good information system, they can offer cafeteria-style benefits where each employee selects a personal combination of benefits.

Small businesses have long complained about the burdens imposed by government reports and data collection. To alleviate some of the hassles and expense, several companies specialize in automating the data collection and report writing. Consider payroll: Because of the constantly changing laws, many companies rely on an outside agency to collect data and print the paychecks. One of the largest providers is Automated Data Processing (ADP). Even if a company chooses to maintain its own payroll records, it typically purchases the software from a third party instead of trying to keep up with the annual changes using internal programmers.

Several companies sell software that automates HRM data handling and produces government-required reports. From economics to equal employment to OSHA reports, the basic HRM reports are being computerized. You still need to collect the data in the proper format and convert it to the purchased software. In addition to saving time in producing reports, the packages often contain the essential government rules and can analyze the data to spot potential problems.

Some newer technologies are being used to simplify data gathering. In particular, companies are searching for ways to make it easier for workers to deal with the HRM department. A system created by PRC, Inc., uses touchtone phones and a voice-response system to enable workers to make changes directly to their base information, like changing their address or tax withholding. Another approach is to install PC-based kiosks and use the Internet, so that employees can look up information, sign up for training classes, or modify their personal data whenever they wish. Other companies are using similar software and the corporate network to allow workers to perform basic HR tasks from their desks or from home using the Internet.

Summary

Every organization must perform certain basic operations: pay employees, pay bills, monitor revenue, and file government reports. Operations are relatively structured, short term, and easy to computerize. They form the foundation of the company. MIS supports operations by collecting data and helping to control the underlying processes.

Transaction-processing systems are responsible for capturing, storing, and providing access to the basic data of the organization. The goal is to capture the transaction data as soon as possible. Common collection methods include point-of-sale devices, process control, electronic data interchange, and electronic commerce websites. Because data is the foundation for all other decisions, transaction-processing systems must maintain data integrity and minimize the threats to the data.

A Manager's View

Transaction processing is a crucial task in any company. E-commerce makes transaction processing the heart of the business. The Internet provides many new methods of processing transactions electronically, and the success of the company will depend on how carefully managers establish these procedures.

Accounting and human resources management are two critical areas of transaction processing. They both highlight the importance of data quality and the difficulties of dealing with large quantities of data.

Financial data has always been important to any business organization. Accounting systems have been created over many years to help collect data, maintain its accuracy, and provide standardized reports to management. Financial checks and balances—such as double-entry accounting, separation of duties and audit trails—are used to maintain data integrity. Processing of accounting information leads to monthly, quarterly, and annual information cycles in most businesses.

Human resources systems illustrate the problems entailed in transaction processing: maintaining accurate databases and producing timely reports, and supporting employee and management needs at a low cost. They also show that good transaction-processing systems can provide additional benefits by offering new services.

Key Words

accounting journal, *183*
audit trail, *185*
bill presentation and payment, *180*
business-to-business (B2B), *177*
business-to-consumer (B2C), *173*

chart of accounts, *184*
concurrency, *181*
data integrity, *180*
digital cash, *178*
electronic data interchange (EDI), *164*
exception reports, *184*
general ledger, *184*

magnetic ink character recognition (MICR), *164*
optical character recognition (OCR), *164*
point of sale (POS), *163*
process control, *164*
supply chain management, *177*

Website References

General Travel Reservations

Microsoft Expedia	**www.expedia.com**
One Travel	**www.onetravel.com**
Orbitz	**www.orbitz.com**
Sabre Travelocity	**www.travelocity.com**

Discounts

Bestfares	**bestfares.com**
Priceline	**www.priceline.com**
The Trip	**www.thetrip.com**
TravelHUB	**www.travelhub.com**

Individual Airlines

American	**www.aa.com**
Delta	**www.delta.com**
Northwest	**www.nwa.com**
Southwest	**www.southwest.com**
United	**www.ual.com**

Additional Reading

Anthes, Gary H. "When Five 9s Aren't Enough." *Computerworld,* October 8, 2001. [Challenges of transaction processing at Visa.]

Bleakley, Fred. "Electronic Payments Now Supplant Checks at More Large Firms." *The Wall Street Journal,* April 13, 1994, p. A1, A9. [Costs of handling checks.]

Disabatino, Jennifer. "The Technology behind the Problem." *Computerworld,* October 22, 2001. [Transaction processing difficulties in providing airline passenger data to the FBI.]

Loshin, Pete. "Transaction Processing." *Computerworld,* October 1, 2001. [Basic concepts of transactions.]

Trombley, M. "Visa Issues 10 'Commandments' for Online Merchants." *Computerworld,* August 11, 2000. [Visa's attempt to get vendors to protect credit-card databases, and Gartner Group's estimate of online fraud.]

Winslow, Ron. "Four Hospital Suppliers Will Launch Common Electronic Ordering System." *The Wall Street Journal,* April 12, 1994, p. B8. [EDI for hospitals, including costs.]

Review Questions

1. Describe four methods of data capture.

2. What is electronic data interchange (EDI)? Why has EDI taken so long to catch on? Will businesses ever use EDI for all transactions?

3. What are the three phases of business-to-consumer e-commerce?

4. What risks are involved in transactions? How are these risks handled in electronic commerce?

5. What challenges have to be overcome to engage in international e-commerce?

6. How is business-to-business e-commerce different from business-to-consumer e-commerce?

7. What is the government's role in transactions?

8. Why has it taken so long for new payment mechanisms to be adopted?

9. What is meant by the term *data quality?* Give three examples of problems with data quality.

10. Why is data volume an important issue in transaction-processing systems? Will newer, faster machines automatically solve the problem?

11. What is meant by *concurrency,* and why is it a problem in a multiuser environment?

12. Why are so many transaction-processing systems based on accounting methods?

13. How does the accounting cycle affect decisions and operations in a typical firm?

14. What complications arise with transactions in human resources management?

Exercises

1. Choose an industry and research the use of EDI in that industry. Is it widely used? Explain the problems that exist. See if there is a B2B auction site for that industry. Has it been more successful than traditional EDI?

2. Find information on at least two accounting packages that could be used for a business with 100 to 150 employees. Identify the strengths and weaknesses of each package. Are the packages tailored to specific industries?

3. Visit at least three retail stores in your area and determine how they handle transaction processing for sales. How many checkout counters are available at each store? By counting the number of customers in a 10- to 15-minute time interval, estimate the total number of sales transactions occurring for a given day.

4. Find information on current proposals for at least three Internet-based payment mechanisms. Evaluate the strengths and weaknesses of the systems. Be sure to identify the transaction costs and who pays them.

5. From a list of at least 500 companies, randomly select five and examine their websites. Identify the elements of the site that fall into each of the three major categories (prepurchase, purchase, postpurchase). Does the overall emphasis of the site make sense for the particular industry?

6. Find at least three B2B sites. Hint: you will probably need to use a magazine or newspaper search. You will not have access to most of the sites. Identify the current status of the site and whether it is a common means of conducting business in that industry, or merely a secondary channel. Where possible, identify the costs and which participant pays them.

7. Because of the importance of transactions, there is a large number of cases involving fraud and other legal problems with sales and other transactions. Pick an industry and find articles in business and trade journals that identify problems of this nature. How will computerization of the transactions affect fraudulent transactions? Why would the computerization make it easier or harder to detect these problems?

8. Should consumers have the right to copy digital purchases (e.g., make backup copies of audio tracks)? If so, how can publishers and artists prevent people from sharing unlimited copies of their work?

Rolling Thunder Database

9. Identify the major transaction-processing components in the system.

10. What features are used in the database and the forms to ensure quality of transaction data?

11. What additional data quality features should be added?

12. Explain how additional data quality features can be provided with training, procedures, and manual controls.

13. For each major transaction type, identify the sequence of steps that are performed and determine which ones are time critical.

14. For each major transaction type, estimate the frequency of the transaction and the volume of data involved.

15. Identify any transaction forms that could be improved to make them easier for clerks and other users.

16. Using the existing forms, perform the following tasks for Rolling Thunder:

    a. Take a bicycle order.
    b. Assemble a bicycle.
    c. Create a new purchase order.
    d. Record the receipt of purchases.

Retail Sales

The retail sales industry encompasses all sales to end-product users—the consumers of the world. This industry is large and getting even larger as new and innovative means of reaching buyers continue to be developed. Although the media focuses on the Internet as a new medium for retail sales, the big question is whether people will buy over the Internet. Retail sales currently take place in department stores, warehouse stores, specialty stores, via mail-order, and in many other venues.

Financial Analysis

Retail sales have been robust for the past few years. Low inflation, rising income, falling unemployment rates, and an increase in consumer spending have led the drive in the retail sales industry bull market. In 1996, according to Reuters News Service, retail sales rose 5.3 percent, compared with 4.9 percent, 7.5 percent, and 5.6 percent for prior years. Using the returns of the Standard & Poor's 500 as a measure of performance, the general retail industry has recently shown return rates to be 21 percent higher on average over the S&P. Historically, normal valuation is only at 0.5 percent over the S&P 500.

Retail sales are generally cyclical in nature. Holiday sales are a significant measure of consumer sentiment. The National Retail Federation reports 1996 December holiday market sales posted a 0.6-percent increase, which was above industry expectations of a 0.4-percent increase. The 0.6 rise was a 2.5 percent increase relative to December 1995 sales.

Stock/Investment Outlook

Retailers were expected to have problems in 1997, despite high levels of consumer confidence, because of the high levels of consumer debt and personal bankruptcy. According to NatWest Securities group and historical benchmarks, the growth in retail sales would begin pulling back. It was likely that consumer demand for luxury items was at a peak. With a slowdown in the economy, consumers may not be willing to purchase many unnecessary items. To economists, the numbers tell an old story: too many stores, too few consumer dollars.

Most economic measures recognize that the United States entered a recession in 2001. Part of the decline was from the crash of the dot-coms, part from the decline in retail sales. Several retailers suffered declining sales and losses.

Potential/Prospective for Growth

The retail industry encompasses an extremely competitive and broad marketplace. The advancement in new retail avenues is ongoing. The up-and-coming Internet online retail industry grew by an estimated 50 percent in 1995, a rate much faster than the growth of retail in general. According to the Census Bureau, over $3 billion was spent in retail trade in 2000 and $27 million on Internet purchases, representing about 1 percent of the total retail sales.

The National Retail Federation believes that by the year 2005, 25 percent of basic merchandise could be bought on the Internet. While the use of online shopping will continue to increase, most retailers and consumers agree that online shopping will never be a complete replacement for the physical experience of browsing.

In addition to Internet access, there is competition among stores to develop the shopping environment for the future. An example of research at work is a present collaboration between JC Penney and Nordstrom. It proposes interactive home shopping through a consumer's television screen. This service would allow consumers to view merchandise on screen and make purchases through their television remote controls. Interactive home shopping networks are already in place; few allow the purchase of consumer goods through remote control.

Retailers who do not place information technology and research and development as top priorities will get squeezed out in the scramble to catch up. Retail industries must keep up with the changing demands, character, and demographics of their customers.

Competitive Structure

The retail sales industry is highly competitive in all areas. There are single store, franchise, and large retail outlets. Sandra Shaber of the WEPA group calls it either a "price business" or a "We've got a gimmick business." Barriers to entry are not always high. There are always many trials of new concepts in progress. Retailers must react quickly to consumer preferences in the industry.

Role of Research and Development

Much research and testing of Internet websites is presently underway. It is not clear which concepts will work and how consumers will respond. The use of data warehousing technologies to obtain, gather, and analyze customer data/purchasing habits is being developed to the fullest by Kmart Corporation. For example, in developing their idea of "Retail 2000," Kmart is researching cart scanning. With this process a whole cart is scanned at once to determine prices for checkout. Kiosks will allow customers to order products directly from a manufacturer. Marketing research and development is always underway in this industry.

Technological Investment and Analysis

Retailers have invested in many of the newest technologies. Technological improvements have allowed many retailers to thrive in this competitive industry. Tracking customer information via smart cards and computer programs designed for efficient stocking and warehousing has helped retailers cut costs and increase marketing capabilities. Websites with online shopping capabilities allow for an extension of the store hours to 24 hours. Information technology allows retailers to transact business deals around the clock and from any location on the globe.

Future Recommendations

Retailers must continue to take advantage of and innovate with the most up-to-date information technologies. They must seek ways to cut costs in a very competitive industry where much of the competition is based on overhead, inventory, and shipping costs.

Case: Home Depot

Short Description of the Company

Home Depot is a market leader that uses the right technology strategy to saturate its customers with information. Its unstated goal is to turn modestly competent amateurs into confident renovators. An examination of its website reminds one of the self-help section of a bookstore. The website and the associates within the store offer a wide array of instant advice and step-by-step guidelines.

Technology Innovations

Future growth for Home Depot will be contingent upon its ability to expand into new markets. The principles that built the company are the traits that will ensure its future success. Increased customer loyalty, expanding services within the store, and improving the product line will allow the company to operate more efficiently.

One of the ways Home Depot seeks to improve operating efficiency is through the implementation of a computer-assisted ordering system. This system reduces the time spent by associates ordering inventory and increases inventory availability. This leads to higher sales (the required items are in stock and on the shelves when the customers want them) and higher inventory turnover (inventory items that are not required are not sitting in a warehouse).

In order to provide better means of communication between individual stores and the home office in Atlanta, the company decided to move ahead quickly in the areas of communications and networking. In moving to a more open system, they installed HP9000 UNIX processors from Hewlett-Packard in the stores and connected them to headquarters using a TCP/IP (Transmission Control Protocol/Internet Protocol) connection.

The transition from in-store processors to a central TCP/IP hub was not terribly difficult, but the manager of network architecture at Home Depot ran into problems in finding an off-the-shelf package that would meet Home Depot's needs. To be effective, the package had to be capable of handling data transport to (and from) the stores since the file transfer application for the Data General proprietary environment was not suitable for the TCP/IP network. Additionally,

the package had to run in real time instead of processing in batch mode.

Corporate Microsystems (CMI) received the contract for its Mlink Advanced Communications Manager Software, which runs on a UNIX platform and delivers TCP/IP support. Mlink software offered capable data collection and downloading, connections for all the stores to the headquarters data, and coordination of e-mail between stores. By continually polling stores for updates in areas such as price or inventory, the system was continually updated instead of waiting until batch download was performed in the evening. Best of all, the system could run unattended and unobserved thereby minimizing operator interaction. The system has improved all levels of communication and information processing between the stores and headquarters and has improved inventory management.

Home Depot hopes to increase its customer base and improve customer service in its present markets. Implementing technological improvements in inventory management and improving its computer network will help keep inventory on hand and will reduce costs. Additionally, customer spending habits, rush orders, and general company information can be communicated between individual stores and the home office instantly.

Systems Development

In 1989, Home Depot was a $2 billion company with 35 people in its IT organization. Today, it is a $50 billion company with an IT organization of nearly 1,300 people and a greatly changed technology environment. In the past 12 years, almost every core IT system at Home Depot has been replaced or rebuilt from the ground up. This includes financial, order processing, supply chain, inventory management, and human resources applications. Home Depot stores that once averaged 25 to 30 IT devices such as scan guns and point-of-sale systems today routinely have more than 500 such devices feeding the company's databases. From 1997 to 2001, Home Depot has ranked number one in *Computerworld* magazine's listings of the 100 best places to work in IT.

According to Ron Griffin, former CIO, "From a technology perspective, things have gotten more complex by an order of magnitude." [Vijayan, 2001] Increasingly, the challenge for IT is to ensure that the infrastructure is scalable enough in years ahead to keep pace with enormous growth in transactions. According to Griffin, "The real challenge is to understand the implications of how to build something of industrial strength to [deal with this growth]." [Wiersema, 2001]

Updates and Control

In 2002, Home Depot is planning another major rebuild of several core systems, including its supply chain and inventory management systems. The system upgrades were supposed to occur earlier but did not get the necessary funding.

Home Depot is one of the few large companies that installed LAN cabling to every retail terminal. Now it wants to update the DOS-based systems in its 1,300 stores nationwide with a Windows 2000 inventory management system. It also is planning to update the workstations at corporate headquarters. But updating 17,000 PCs by sending out technicians and disk drives takes a huge amount of time. So the company is going to use On Technology's remote management software to remotely install and update the operating system and applications an all machines from the help center.

The Internet

Home Depot has managed to conquer most of its rivals—except Lowe's. The two chains battle head-to-head with large stores in major markets. But the recession of 2001 hurt both stores. Home Depot's earnings fell 20 percent in the first quarter—the first quarterly decline in more than a decade. Yet, in the middle of the downturn, Home Depot launched its e-commerce program, five months after Lowe's pushed its on-line shopping system. Both companies offer only a limited selection of products online—only 35–40 percent of the items available in the stores. But it makes sense for big items like washing machines that have to be delivered anyway. Even if the site does not generate huge amounts of revenue, managers see the importance of the advertising role and making information available to buyers who will come into the stores.

Recommendation for the Future

Home Depot focuses on sales growth and the stock reaction to its decisions. Home Depot sees its ability to establish and grow customer franchises as critical to its continuing in a market leadership position. Attracting customers is the key to overcoming customer scarcity. Several factors make sales growth the preferred indicator of Home Depot's competitive abilities. First, it assumes that customers are the ultimate arbiter of success. The only way to increase sales is to get customers to change and increase their buying decisions. Simply repeating the same purchases is not enough. Growing faster than the competition requires convincing customers to cast their votes for your company instead of the others. This approach keeps the gap between the top performers and their peers increasing. This sales-growth imperative suggests that unless a company is growing at twice the pace of its peers, it risks falling behind in the race for market leadership. [Wiersema, 2001]

This pace has been set by Cisco Systems, Wal-Mart, and Sony, each of which increased its sales in the past six years by more than its four closest competitors combined. Internet-driven markets that have doubled in size each year make it necessary for leaders such as Ariba (a developer of enterprise software) to grow at more than 200 percent annually just to secure their position. [Wiersema, 2001]

The stock market reaction to the decisions is also important. Sales growth indicates a company's ability to win customers but says little about continued growth and success. It is critical to evaluate the growth targets in consideration of the following points:

Whether growth has come at the expense of profitability?

Whether new customers were short-term buyers?

Whether the company converted its success with customers into solid and sustainable business results?

Questions

1. What forces are driving the strategic direction of the corporation/organization?

2. Upon what technologies has the corporation relied?

3. How did the corporation fund, purchase, and implement the technological program of advancement?

4. Are there replacement products for what Home Depot sells?

5. What can you learn from an examination of the corporation's Web page about their business direction of the organization?

6. What challenges and opportunities is the industry facing?

7. What role does data play in the future of the corporation?

Additional Reading

Dalton, Gregory. "Application Server Strategy Hits Bumps on Way to Lower Costs—Home Depot on Middle Road." *Computer Reseller News,* August 3, 1998, p. 42.

Hohman, Robin Schreir. "Marimba Solves Home Depot Dilemma." *Network World,* February 1, 1999, p. 29.

"Home and Garden Tips Focused for You." *Newsbytes,* January 4, 1999.

Karpinski, Richard. "Home Depot Picks Its Spots." *InternetWeek,* September 28, 1998, p. 13.

Litt, Mona R. "Solid Foundation for the Home Depot Network." *Network Computing,* January 15, 1997, pp. 88–91.

Meehan, Michael. "Home Depot Seeks Remote Control of the Desktop." *Computerworld,* January 7, 2002.

Sliwa, Carol. "Easing the 'Middle-Tier' Traffic Jam: Securities Firm Leads with Agent Technology." *Computerworld,* December 21, 1998, p. 14.

Stedman, Craig. "ERP with Fewer Consultants: Reebok, Home Depot Plan Bulk of Work In-House to Best Meet Business Needs." *Computerworld,* February 1, 1999, p. 40.

Stedman, Craig. "Retailers Adopt Different Strategies for Installing SAP R/3." *Computerworld,* January 25, 1999, p. 9.

Stein, Tom, and Jeff Sweat. "Focus Shifts from Technology to Managing Relationships—Supply Chains Emerge as Both a Tool, Philosophy." *Computer Reseller News,* November 16, 1998, p. 102.

Turek, Norbert. "Decision into Action—Closed-Loop Systems Are Making Retailers More Responsive to Inventory Adjustments." *InformationWeek,* October 26, 1998, p. 85.

Vijayan, Jainkumar. "Griffin Resigns as Home Depot CIO," *Computerworld* 1, 16 35, no. 48 (Nov 26, 2001): pp. 1,16.

Wiersema, Fred. "Customer Scarcity." *Executive Excellence* 6–7 18, no. 11 (Nov 2001): pp. 6–7.

Wilder, Clinton. "Consensus Builder—Ron Griffin Applies Technology to the Bottom Line, and Bottom-Line Thinking to the Retail Industry." *Information Week,* December 21, 1998, p. 38.

Young, Eric. "Home Improvement Chains Battle Online." *Computerworld,* May 14, 2001.

Case: Toys "R" Us

In 1957, Charles Lazarus saw the baby boom generation in the making. He observed that this was going to lead to a huge demand for baby products, in his mind, mainly furniture. The idea of selling just furniture did not last long. The furniture sold well, but Charles Lazarus got a lot of customers asking the same question, "Don't you stock any toys for my baby?" This led to the first "toy supermarket," which was also opened in 1957. In the mid–1970s, Toys "R" Us became a public company, and since that time has targeted other markets. These stores include Kids "R" Us, which concentrates mainly on kids' clothes, Babies "R" Us, which markets products for babies and younger toddlers, and Books "R" Us, which sells books.

Technology Innovations

The company's primary technology includes Unisys mainframes, IBM processors, and thousands of personal computers. Operating systems include DOS, Windows, and Windows 2000, all running under one protocol with IBM AS/400 midrange systems. Toys "R" Us uses a wide area network based on satellites, some local area networks, and third-party networks.

It is important for the company to keep in constant contact with all locations. At the same time, Toys "R" Us tries to maintain a decentralized focus, giving individual stores the autonomy needed to respond to local markets around the world.

Joseph Giamelli, vice president of information systems, international division, has decided to upgrade to Windows 2000 running on IBM AS/400 servers. This transition is intended to bring clients and distributed servers together under one standard open platform for Toys "R" Us stores around the world. With over 400,000 AS/400s in place, it is the largest installation of data warehouses. As far as training goes, Giamelli states that, "By going in with the AS/400, I just had to train people on the application, so I eliminated the technical knowledge required and focused on the business model."

Also involved in the upgraded system is a global data warehouse that will acknowledge 12 different languages and currencies. The length of time to remap data to the data warehouses in 12 languages and currencies was just six months.

This upgrade will allow all software from around the world to run on the same platform and still allow all activities to be analyzed by the head office. Toys "R" Us analysts will be able to run better reports on a global basis by item, vendor, and category.

Toys "R" Us hopes to expand its customer base with its website, which offers services that are not available in stores, such as the ability to search for gifts by age and price range. The website was put online in 1998. Purchases can be gift-wrapped and shipped with a personalized note.

Toys "R" Us is facing competition from Web startups E-Toys and Toys.com. By focusing on wrapping and other services, the company is looking to attract upscale consumers. The Toys "R" Us website is linked to the company's back-end inventory and fulfillment systems by commerce server software from InterWorld Corp. The Kmart system, which is also connected to back-end systems, uses Dell servers running IBM's Net.Commerce web server software.

In 1999, Toysrus.com was an online laughingstock. It led Toys "R" Us in losses and in customer complaints. In August 2000, ToysRUs linked to Amazon.com. Today, the Toys "R" Us website is the Internet's leading retailer of toys, video games, and baby products. Amazon.com took over the toy retailer's site operations and customer service. Toysrus.com takes advantage of Amazon's well-oiled fulfillment operation and sophisticated personalization technology. This outsourcing has enabled Toysrus.com to realize a 40 percent reduction in operating costs, largely by offloading fulfillment activities. Its conversion rate, the percentage of site visitors who make purchases, has doubled since the linkage to Amazon.com went into effect in August 2000. In the critical 2000 holiday season, Toysrus.com boasted 99 percent on-time delivery amid a huge volume of orders. Amazon's network of five U.S. distribution centers enabled Toysrus.com to defray the costs of building the infrastructure on its own. Amazon manages the holiday crush by moving its distribution centers to a 24/7 work schedule. The infrastructure proved to be robust enough to process a mass of orders. Sales volume more than tripled between 1999 and 2000 to $124 million. [Kemp, 2001]

Competition

E-Toys was hailed as one of the most promising online rivals. Yet it folded in January 2001. When it was established, the group estimated it would sell up to L150 million ($217 million) of toys in the United Kingdom and United States. The reality proved to be less than half that figure.

According to CFO Lipschitz, "E-Toys had no prayer of making money. They had a lot of suckers willing to put up a lot of money but they spent hundreds of millions of dollars building the infrastructure. The company had a lot of hype and got caught up in the dot-com surge but you can't do it as a stand-alone Internet site you've got to get the synergies from having both Internet and the bricks and mortar. We were doing the same thing—building distribution centres and Internet sites, which are not cheap. Now Amazon deals with all of that, with input from us." [Boyes, 2001]

Recommendation for the Future

Integrating the company's databases and yet putting decision-making power in the local store managers' hands gives Toys "R" Us a competitive edge. While operating locally, stores have the benefit of knowledge about the entire Toys "R" Us system. The company must expand into more countries, creating and expanding market share.

In the 1980s Toys "R" Us consistently produced annual returns of 30 percent. This level has declined due to the fact its market share has been attacked by discounters, most notably Wal-Mart, and there has been an economic downturn. Toys "R" Us also faces a growing reputation for having unhelpful, if not rude, staff in the stores.

According to CFO Louis Lipschitz, "The first thing we said is: 'how do we differentiate ourselves from our competition?' What we were doing was fighting them on their turf with price and letting everything else go. Then we realized that was not the way to win a battle, we should fight them where we're strong." [Boyes, 2001]

The company's new approach focuses on improving the shopping experience. Toys "R" Us has more than 1,200 stores worldwide and more than 1,500 in total, including Kids "R" Us and Babies "R" Us. Stores are being remodeled, shelves are being restocked, and staff are being trained to be efficient and friendly. Lipschitz believes this should help to encourage parents and kids back into the stores.

Questions

1. What has been the catalyst for change at Toys "R" Us?

2. What technologies have the corporation relied upon?

3. How has this technological change been implemented?

4. What is the financial ability of Toys "R" Us to embark on a major technological program of advancement?

5. What does the corporation's Web page present about its business?

6. Is the toy industry oligopolistic or competitive?

7. How important is data to the corporation's continued success?

Additional Reading

Boyes, Sara-Louise. "Reinventing Toys "R" Us." *Corporate Finance* 27–28 no. 202 (Sep 2001): pp. 27–28.

Dalton, Gregory, and Clinton Wilder. "Kmart, Toys "R" Us Turn to Internet for Sales Boost—Retailers Seek Larger Customer Base." *InformationWeek,* July 20, 1998, p. 30.

Garvey, Martin J. "AS/400 Gamble." *InformationWeek,* March 24, 1997, pp. 105–107.

Kemp, Ted. "Partnerships R Us—Toysrus.com Is Building a Sustainable E-Retail Business by Drawing on the Strengths of Its Two Giant Business Partners." *Internetweek*, October 15, 2001, pp. PG14–15.

LaMonica, Martin. "At Toys "R" Us, Help Desk Application Is No Plaything." *InfoWorld,* October 5, 1998, p. 60.

Leong, Kathy Chin. "Toys "R" Us Restructures for E-Comm." *InternetWeek,* June 8, 1998, pp. 47–49.

Musich, Paula. "Toy Story: Toys "R" Us Plays New Kind of Software Distribution Game." *PC Week,* October 21, 1996, pp. 1–3.

Orenstein, David. "Retailers Struggle to Keep Techs." *Computerworld,* November 2, 1998, p. 39.

"Transforming Toys "R" Us." *Computer Retail Week,* September 21, 1998, p. 3.

Case: Walgreens

Short Description of the Company

Walgreens is the largest and most visited drugstore chain in the United States. It provides most types of prescription and nonprescription drugs. Walgreens also has a large variety of items used on a day-to-day basis such as milk, film, soda, batteries, school supplies, bread, chips, bandages, toothpaste, deodorant, and chocolates. Walgreens' success can be attributed to convenience but also to its successful logistics, distribution, and inventory systems.

Technology Innovations

Inventory Management

Electronic data interchange (EDI) technology is used for the distribution/inventory system at Walgreens. The distribution/inventory system of Walgreens is the most automated in the industry, making heavy use of bar coding and radio frequency technology to track and transmit distribution/inventory information. Logistics, inventory, and distribution have always been important parts of the retail business. In the mid-1980s, many retailers discovered that the success factors for their businesses were logistics, inventory, and distribution.

One of the newer techniques used in retailing today is continuous replenishment. This technique focuses on eliminating duplicate inventory in the channel of distribution by increasing predictability and trust between buyer, seller, and any third-party support agencies. Continuous replenishment often hinges on moving from push strategies to pull strategies. Continuous replenishment applies the use of new information technology and new methods of materials handling designed to speed information and cut cycle times up and down the pipeline. This technique has been adopted not only by Walgreens but also by many of its competitors such as Wal-Mart and Target.

The thinking process for continuous replenishment starts at the planning and forecasting stage, which is done in conjunction with key vendors. The process requires the ongoing sharing of point-of-sale information. It concentrates on optimizing logistics planning to get shipping and receiving in sync with selling floor trends. The system targets reduction of time and inventory throughout the whole supply chain to realize cost savings and productivity gains for both the retailer and the supplier.

Managing distribution to get the right merchandise to the right stores at the right time in the right amount, makes a big difference. Cost and productivity benefits are realized by distributing lean up-front quantities to the stores, replenishing exactly and frequently based on SKU level sales.

A concept currently being used by Walgreens for the distribution of their products is that of cross-docking. In the cross-docking system, the product is not consigned to storage but rather continuously flows across the dock until it is resorted and moves to a store. In this system, the distribution center becomes a sorting rather than a holding area. In some cross-docking systems, the merchandise is held at the dock less than half the day before it is moved to the store. The tighter the window on cross-docking, the greater the inventory savings and the more careful the coordination between buyer, seller, and third party needs to be.

The process saves everyone money. Workers in the warehouses only touch the product once, to audit and move it from truck to truck. Communications technologies such as EDI are a critical link in this type of system.

Good asset management requires knowledge of what the company owns and where these assets are located. The inventory and tracking of data prevent property loss and theft. Asset management is made easier by technologies such as bar codes, radio frequency tagging, laser coding, and newly developed desired state software management. These technologies assign identification tags on company assets that are to be tracked, using relevant data in a central information system.

To speed the store checkout lane at Walgreens, bar-code technology is used. By moving bar coding into the warehouse, operations in the areas of receiving, stocking, and retrieval are now more efficient. Incorporation of bar codes with efficiency-driven programs like cross-docking and advanced use of EDI helps raise productivity levels. "It's a technology whose time has come," said Charlie Hunter, distribution center manager at Harvest Foods, Little Rock, Arkansas. For example, when the merchandise is taken out of the warehouse, the mainframe database is updated on a real-time basis.

Another tool used in the retailing industry for inventory control is laser technology. This tool is similar to bar coding. The laser produces a permanent code without the use of inks or solvents. They can be placed anywhere in the product. It is a low maintenance, inkless operation, with minimum downtime, maximum flexibility, and accurate, consistently reliable coding at high speeds.

The chief advantage of these types of systems is that there is a constant interactive flow of up-to-date inventory information. Any mistake is flagged immediately. If there is a discrepancy, it is known immediately rather than when a quarterly inventory review is done. Previously, everything was

---

Advantages of Bar Codes for Inventory Management

1. Improves inventory accuracy from receiving to shipping.
2. Provides immediate availability of inventory information.
3. Reduces the percentage of data entry errors.
4. Creates a permanent audit trail.
5. Reduces inventory levels previously inflated to compensate for errors.
6. Increases inventory turns.
7. Reduces shipment errors.
8. Improves relationships with customers and suppliers.
9. Reduces internal costs due to the elimination of errors, reduction of inventory levels, and accurate shipments.

---

reactive. Now, armed with up-to-the-minute information, product coding allows Walgreens to make timely and accurate decisions and become a more responsive partner to the customer. Using bar codes to identify inventory cuts distribution costs for Walgreens.

The company has also been successful at increasing the sales per employee and at reducing long-term debt to zero by 1995.

Networks

AT&T provides connections for companies like Walgreens to enable them to communicate instantaneously with their stores and pharmacists. In 1998, AT&T experienced a major T1 shortage. The shortage presented major problems since AT&T's standard frame relay backup options were rendered useless by the fact that the switches, rather than the physical routes, were out of service.

AT&T officials worked to discover the root cause of the failure. AT&T Chairman and CEO C. Michael Armstrong said in a briefing with reporters that the company would not charge customers for frame relay service until the network was restored and the root cause was identified and fixed.

Some users thought AT&T had an obligation to go even further. In January, AT&T announced service-level agreements (SLAs), which included 99.99 percent availability for the frame relay network. At the time, AT&T data services vice president Steve Hindman promised a four-hour mean-time-to-repair guarantee. If this failed, customers would receive free ports and permanent virtual circuits (PVCs) for a month.

An AT&T spokesperson said the SLAs had slipped past the scheduled March general availability date. He confirmed some larger customers had been given the guarantees anyway.

During this downtime, nearly all users reported that they did not have enough backup lines to keep their networks running. Many resorted to unusual measures. One giant pharmaceutical company called in a fleet of six jets to keep its networks of papers, services, and products working. Some of the pharmaceutical company's 80 sites had ISDN backup; others only had 9.6Kbps modems. Only half of the company's orders were able to get through via dial-up, so the company brought in the planes to fly paper orders to distribution centers. The company did not get its frame relay fully restored until Wednesday morning of the week of outage.

Walgreens does have financial protection because it contracted for a service-level agreement from AT&T. Ray Sheedy, Walgreens's director of corporate telecommunications, said 278 of the company's stores connected via AT&T were down for 24 hours. Walgreens' mailorder locations in Tempe, Arizona, and Orlando, Florida, which are ordinarily on the AT&T network, had backup frame relay capacity with MCI. Sheedy said Walgreens cannot afford dual networks in stores and indicated that ISDN is too expensive to run to individual stores and is not available everywhere.

Most analysts stressed the importance of discovering the root cause to prevent similar problems from occurring. Steve Sazegari, president of Tele.Mac, a Foster City, California, consulting firm, noted that data traffic typically spikes on Monday, the day this outage occurred, since this is the day order-entry systems accept weekend mail orders and transactions.

"These switches were never put under this kind of test in a public network before," Sazegari said. "Unlike a fiber cut, which could be avoided through rerouting, eliminating an impact on the rest of the network, this switching interruption had an impact upon the whole networking structure."

Internet Site

The Extensible Markup Language (XML) is a World Wide Web Consortium standard for tagging Web content to exchange data. The standard lets users make fields that name data. Search engines use those fields to make more accurate return lists.

This technology enables companies to attach data within a document, so internal users can find and share information easier by tagging each important data piece with a name. Pete Van Valin, team leader for Web systems at Walgreens, hopes to have XML up and running within 12 months on the company's website. Currently, employees must place meta tags in their HTML documents. The goal is to automate the process with XML. Van Valin is still evaluating tools.

Tagging is essential to get a hold of all the information generated from the intranet's 10,000 users. His team has developed a list of standards and best practices for intranet documents but has not completed formal training on tagging. "Tagging is all about precision. When that precision happens, it's ideal," Microsoft's Tuchen says.

In 2001, Walgreens concentrated on an e-business strategy largely focused on EDI. The goal was to make the pharmacists' jobs easier, simplifying the ordering process by integrating a supplier website with the existing distribution network. In late 2001, Walgreens announced a partnership with GE's Global eXchange Service (GXS) to tie into its 3,000 small suppliers. The GXS system is essentially a private EDI network. Walgreens is working hard to make its supply chain more efficient.

Search Tools

Walgreens uses several search tools to help employees find information faster. Autonomy uses Bayesian logic to track word patterns in documents. This is based on the relationship between multiple variables and includes the extent to which one variable impacts the other. Rather than searching for individual words, Autonomy's engine examines patterns of words within documents, marking their occurrence together. For example, if a user wants to search for information on Microsoft's Wolfpack, he or she is not interested in information about wolves in the wild. Because of the user's marked pattern, Autonomy's Agentware system will know that this request is dealing with software and Microsoft.

Semio uses visualization to help users understand their search options. It offers a search tool that indexes text, makes clusters of content, and then generates visual maps of those clusters for search results. For example, if a user searches on "NT," SemioMap will display the returns that directly pertain to that result, and then map out related concepts such as Windows, Microsoft, and operating systems. This gives users a sense of the hierarchy of their searches.

To be successful at companies like Walgreens, searching mechanisms will have to incorporate the following:

1. They will have to become more user-friendly and simplify search, extending beyond Boolean search mechanisms.

2. They will have to gather and process external information as well as they gather internal data.

3. Embedded agents will have to analyze search paths and offer other ways to find information. They will have to study data-gathering behavior, store that information, and be able to build suggested query lists based on that information.

4. They will have to incorporate standards such as XML.

Recommendations for the Future

One of the largest problems drug chains face is the attempt to navigate the category management maze. One of the biggest obstacles is the sheer volume of sales data. Walgreens recently became the first chain in its segment to formally partner with another company to solve that issue. It has joined retailers such as SuperValu, Meijer, and Hannaford Bros to use a new program from A.C. Nielsen called Category Business Planner (CBP). CBP is a Web-based category management tool that will be used throughout Walgreens' purchasing department.

Walgreens has also entered into a $5 million cross-network ad-sales partnership with Discovery Networks. The partnership revolves around Discovery Health's new Lifeline series. The yearlong agreement is the most expansive commitment Walgreens has made to the network group.

Questions

1. What forces are driving the strategic direction of the corporation/organization?

2. What technologies has the corporation relied upon?

3. What has caused a change in the use of technology in the corporation/organization?

4. How successful has the technological change been?

5. What challenges and opportunities is the industry facing?

6. What are some of the other services Intercom Plus's data can enable Walgreens to perform?

Additional Reading

Hoffman, Thomas. "Walgreens Heals Prescription Net." *Computerworld,* April 20, 1998, p. 43.

Schwartz, Ephraim. "GE GXS Brings Supply-Chain Medicine to Table." *Infoworld,* November 26, 2001.

Tadjer, Rivka. "Wanted: Technical Talent." *CommunicationsWeek,* June 2, 1997, p. 105.

"Walgreens Signs Deal to Simplify EDI with Vendors." *PC Week,* January 5, 1998, p. 69.

Watson, Sharon. "E-Commerce Architects." *Computerworld,* March 19, 2001.

Appendix

Accounting Review

The primary purpose of accounting is to track the financial transactions in an organization and provide reports that summarize the financial position of the organization. Standardization is a key aspect to modern accounting. To be able to compare financial statements from various firms, investors (owners) and managers need to know that each organization measures variables the same way. Consequently, the accounting profession has created a large set of rules for classifying transactions and for producing reports. Only the most elementary forms are reviewed here.

General Ledger

Every financial transaction is defined in two categories: money and a classification account. For example, if the firm purchases something, the accounting system records how it was bought (cash, credit, etc.) and the type of item (supplies, inventory, and so on). It is the classifications that provide the detailed information about the firm. All account classifications are defined in the general ledger.

Accounts are organized by the basic accounting equation: Assets = Liabilities + Owner's Equity. *Assets* are claims that the firm has on others. *Liabilities* are claims that others have the firm. *Owner's Equity* is the difference, which is owed to the owners or investors. These are the three primary classification accounts in the general ledger. The other accounts are simply increasing levels of detail within these three accounts. For example, assets are divided into current assets versus property, plant, and equipment. Similarly, liabilities are split into current liabilities and long-term debt. In general, current means items due within one year—although there are specific accounting rules for determining the classification of various items.

Although the primary categories are standardized, each firm will have a different set of accounts at the more detailed levels. In general, firms within an industry tend to have similar sets of accounts. For example, accounts in a retail firm focus on sales, purchases, and inventory. Whereas accounts in a manufacturing firm focus on production, capital costs (plant and equipment), and long-term contracts. In modern accounting systems, the general ledger is stored as a database. Each account classification is numbered, where detailed accounts have longer numbers. The numbers are used internally and do not appear on the financial statements.

Balance Sheet

The balance sheet is the standard method for presenting the current financial status of the firm. It is a report that summarizes the three basic account totals and shows the total values of the various accounts at a particular point in time. Figure 5.1A shows a typical balance sheet.

The balance sheet shows the totals for the primary account categories (assets, liabilities, and owner's equity), along with the totals for the first level of details. Balance sheets and other financial information are readily available for American firms through the SEC EDGAR files at http://www.sec.gov.

Earnings or Income Statement

Most firms are in business to make money. The amount earned is displayed on the earnings statement (sometimes called an income statement). Earnings are computed over a period of time (usually a year, a quarter, or a month). Generally, most earnings come from sales. The statement deducts the cost of goods sold, which usually consists of the purchase price of the items, shipping, and storage costs. Administrative expenses are listed separately. Additional revenue and costs arise from interest income and expense. Income taxes (federal and state) are always shown as a separate computation. Net earnings are useful, but for comparison, most investors are interested in earnings per share, which is computed by dividing net earnings by the number of outstanding shares. Figure 5.2A shows a typical earnings statement.

FIGURE 5.1A

Balance sheet for American Stores. It shows the primary account totals (assets, liabilities, and owners' equity); along with the first level of account detail.

Assets		
Current assets		
Cash and equivalent	$	57
Accounts and notes receivable, net		547
Inventories		3,364
Prepaid expenses		155
Property held for sale		71
Refundable income taxes		36
Deferred income taxes		70
Total current assets		4,300
Land, buildings, and equipment, net		9,622
Goodwill and intangibles, net		1,705
Other assets		451
Total assets		$16,078
Liabilities and Stockholders' Equity		
Current liabilities		
Accounts payable	$	2,163
Salaries		561
Taxes other than income taxes		141
Income taxes		
Self-insurance		218
Unearned income		112
Merger-related reserves		13
Current portion of lease obligations		20
Current maturities of long-term debt		62
Other		105
Total current liabilities		3,395
Long-term debt		5,715
Capitalized lease obligations		227
Self-insurance		216
Deferred income taxes		116
Other long-term liabilities		715
Total long-term liabilities		6,989
Stockholders' equity:		
Preferred + common stock		405
Capital in excess of par		48
Retained earnings		5,241
Total stockholders' equity		5,694
Total liabilities and stockholders' equity		$16,078

Cash Flow

The cash flow in an organization can be an early indicator of potential problems or future success. A troubled firm might be able to hold off problems by selling assets, not paying liabilities, or reducing the number of employees. However, the cash-flow statement shows the major sources and uses of cash. It will reveal all of these potential problems. The report is an ex-

FIGURE 5.2A

Earnings statement. Sales and cost of goods sold are generally the largest components. Investors often focus on the earnings per share.

Sales	$36,762
Cost of sales	26,336
Gross profit	10,426
Selling, general, and admin expenses	8,740
Merger-related costs	24
Operating profit	1,662
Interest expense, net	(385)
Other (expense) income, net	(3)
Earnings before income taxes	1,274
Income taxes	509
Net earning	$ 765

FIGURE 5.3A

Cash flow statement. By focusing on the sources and uses of cash, the report is a good indicator of current problems and successes.

Cash flows from operations		
Net earnings	$	765
Adjustments		
Depreciation and amortization		944
Goodwill		57
Merger-related charges		21
Net gain on assets sales		(4)
Net deferred income taxes		11
Other decrease (increases)		(14)
Net cash provided by operations		1,780
Cash flows from investments		
Capital expenditures		(1,771)
Disposal of land, buildings, equipment		189
Decrease (increase) in other assets		33
Net cash used in investing		(1,549)
Cash flows from financing		
Proceeds from long-term borrowing		1,232
Payments on long-term borrowing		(417)
Commercial paper and bank loans		(475)
Proceeds from stock options exercised		7
Cash dividends paid		(315)
Stock purchases and retirements		(451)
Net cash (used) provided by financing		(419)
Net (decrease) increase in cash		(188)
Cash at beginning of year		245
Cash at end of year	$	57

cellent source of information about the immediate financial problems or successes in the organization.

Figure 5.3A shows a cash flow statement. Notice the major categories: earnings, changes in assets, changes in liabilities,

FIGURE 5.4A   Equity statement. Amounts are in thousands. Note the effect of a major purchase of stock from one shareholder (in the notes, the company stated that they bought the stock from the founder).

	Common Stock	Capital over Par Value	Retained Earnings	Total
Balance at start	$ 424	$ 145	$ 5,133	$ 5,702
Net earnings			765	765
Deferred tax adj. on options		(12)		(12)
Exercise of stock options		6		6
Stock purchase and retirement	(19)	(92)	(340)	(451)
Deferred stock unit plan		1		1
Dividends			(317)	(317)
Balance at end	$ 405	$ 48	$ 5,241	$ 5,694

investments, and changes in financing. Increases in cash flow due to increases in net earnings are clearly a good sign. Increases due to changes in short-term assets usually arise from improved collection of accounts receivable. Changes due to liabilities, investments, or financing could signify problems within the firm. In particular, watch for one-time changes due to reorganizations or changes in tactics.

Equity Statement

Investors and owners are ultimately concerned about their equity. Over the last time period, how much did the firm add to its holdings? This information is displayed in the equity statement. Generally, the most important contribution is the retained earnings, which consists of the corporate profits (net earnings) that were not used for other purposes. Additionally, a firm may pay dividends, and it might repurchase stock. Treasury stock consists of stock held by the company—often as a result of a repurchase, but it is also used in director and employee compensation plans.

Figure 5.4A shows an equity statement. It is slightly more complex than those shown in introductory accounting textbooks because regulations require that firms disclose the effect of stock compensation plans. Hence, a modern equity statement shows the effect of the various stock option plans.

Accrual versus Cash Accounting

Accounting would be a fairly simple field if every business operated on a cash basis—where all revenues and costs were settled immediately at the time of a transaction. In reality, expenses and revenues rarely occur at the same time. To gain a fair picture of the firm's operations, the accounting system needs to match the expenses and revenues over a defined period of time. In a simple example, a firm might purchase supplies and pay employees to work on a project in December.

Yet the firm does not receive payment for the project until it is completed—in January. If we recorded the transactions on a cash basis as they were paid, it would appear that the firm lost money in the first year, and then earned a huge profit in the second year. It makes more sense to match the costs and revenue. In this case, the sales revenue would be counted in December when the contract was made and the work performed—even though the actual cash is not received until next year. As a result of the accrual basis, some costs and revenues are spread over multiple time periods. Accountants make adjusting entries at the end of every period to allocate these costs and revenues properly.

Exercises

1. Create an income statement, cash flow statement, and balance sheet using a spreadsheet.

2. Using the sales and cost data from Rolling Thunder along with bicycle industry averages, create a basic income statement and balance sheet for Rolling Thunder.

3. Using the SEC Edgar files on the Internet, find a balance sheet for a company that interests you. Copy it to a spreadsheet. Create an estimated balance sheet for the next year. Assume a 5 percent increase in sales, a 4 percent increase in costs, a 6 percent increase in receivables, the same tax rates, no increase in debt or stock, and a 1 percent increase in purchases of plant and equipment.

4. Find a balance sheet for a large manufacturing company (e.g., John Deere). Find a balance sheet for a similarly sized retail firm (e.g., CVS). Discuss the similarities and differences in the balance sheets.

5. Find an accounting textbook, or search the Internet, to describe three major changes that are made in accrual accounts at the end of a quarter.

Business Integration

HOW DO INFORMATION SYSTEMS HELP MANAGERS INTEGRATE BUSINESS TASKS?

A hundred years ago, there were very few large businesses. As firms became larger, owners needed a way to manage and control the huge number of employees. Managers needed assistance with hundreds of daily operational decisions. The primary approach was to build a hierarchical structure where each division was divided into ever-smaller departments. With guidelines and standard procedures, each department was independent and was responsible for its own operations.

Databases collect data from the whole organization, making it easy for managers to answer questions and make decisions. Additional tools improve communication and support teams of workers by making it easy to share all forms of data and projects. Companies can be managed with fewer workers, operating more efficiently to identify problems and make decisions.

CHAPTER SIX

Database Management

What you will learn in this chapter

- Why is a DBMS a good way to store data?

- How do you construct a query?

- What types of computation can a DBMS perform?

- How do you join multiple tables with a query?

- How are reports different from queries?

- What database administration tasks need to be performed?

- What tasks are better suited to a DBMS than to a spreadsheet?

- How are databases used in e-business?

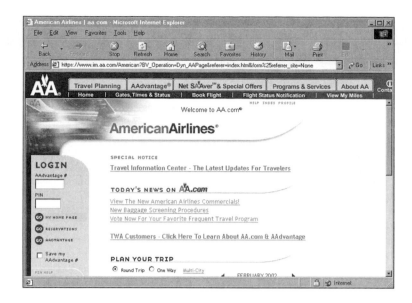

American Airlines was one of the first major companies to recognize the importance of databases. Today, the Internet makes it easy for travelers to interact with the databases for all their travel needs.

The Airline Industry

Running an airline was never easy, but in the days of heavy federal regulation, airline presidents simply focused on keeping costs low and slowly growing the industry. Changing technology, deregulation, and fierce competition eventually brought major changes to the industry. The early, world-dominating names like TWA and PanAm no longer exist. Even the major airlines like United, American, and Delta are struggling. And that was before the tragedy of September 11. But one airline has flourished, and even driven many of the changes: Southwest Airlines. Focusing on low-cost, no-frills, basic transportation, Southwest has been consistently profitable. Southwest was also the one major airline that resumed its full flight schedules immediately after September 11. Managers bet correctly that people still wanted and needed to fly.

It will take some time for the airlines to rebuild confidence and regain passenger traffic. Businesses in particular learned that technology is making it possible to avoid the costs of many trips. And since many of the large airlines made their profits by charging high fares to business travelers, it will take them time to reinvent their business model.

What the September 11 events really pointed out is the need to improve the airports. Security is the dominant issue, since it will require thousands of new employees, background checks, new scanners, and possibly airport redesign. In the meantime, passengers experience hours of delays and inconvenience. Airports and the air traffic control system present additional problems—most were built decades ago to handle a fraction of the current traffic. With congested skies, bad weather, or security alerts, travelers experience delays, which defeats the purpose of flying by air. While these items might be outside the control of the individual airlines, they are obstacles faced by passengers, who will always blame the airline.

FIGURE 6.19

The order form is used in almost any firm. We need to determine the best way to store the data that is collected by this form.

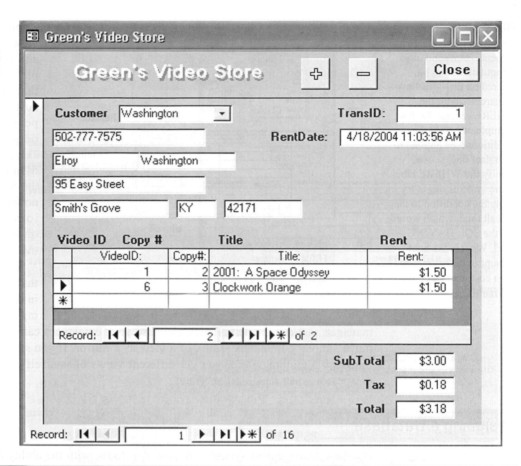

which identifies the transaction, the customer, and the date, and (2) a *repeating section* that lists the videos being rented. Each customer can rent several different videos at one time. We say there is a *one-to-many* relationship between the Rental and the VideosRented sections. As you will see, identifying one-to-many relationships is crucial to proper database design.

In some respects, designing databases is straightforward: There are only three basic rules. However, database design is often interrelated with systems analysis. In most cases, we are attempting to understand the business at the same time the database is being designed. One common problem that arises is that it is not always easy to see which relationships are one-to-many and which are one-to-one or many-to-many.

Notation

It would be cumbersome to draw pictures of every table that we use, so we usually write table definitions in a standard notation. The base customer table is shown in Figure 6.20, both in notational form and with sample data.

FIGURE 6.20

Notation for tables. Table definitions can often be written in one or two lines. Each table has a name and a list of columns. The column (or columns) that make up the primary key is underlined.

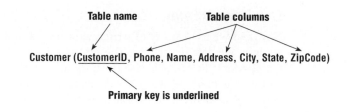

Customer (CustomerID, Phone, Name, Address, City, State, ZipCode)

Table name · Table columns · Primary key is underlined

CustomerID	Phone	LastName	FirstName	Address	City	State	ZipCode
1	502-666-7777	Johnson	Martha	125 Main Street	Alvaton	KY	42122
2	502-888-6464	Smith	Jack	873 Elm Street	Bowling Green	KY	42101
3	502-777-7575	Washington	Elroy	95 Easy Street	Smith's Grove	KY	42171
4	502-333-9494	Adams	Samuel	746 Brown Drive	Alvaton	KY	42122
5	502-474-4746	Rabitz	Victor	645 White Avenue	Bowling Green	KY	42102
6	615-373-4746	Steinmetz	Susan	15 Speedway Drive	Portland	TN	37148
7	615-888-4474	Lasater	Les	67 S. Ray Drive	Portland	TN	37148
8	615-452-1162	Jones	Charlie	867 Lakeside Drive	Castalian Springs	TN	37031
9	502-222-4351	Chavez	Juan	673 Industry Blvd.	Caneyville	KY	42721
10	502-444-2512	Rojo	Maria	88 Main Street	Cave City	KY	42127

FIGURE 6.21

Converting to notation. The basic rental form can be written in notational form. Notice that repeating sections are indicated by the inner parentheses. If we actually try to store the data this way, notice the problem created by the repeating section: Each time a customer checks out a video we have to reenter the phone and address.

RentalForm(TransID, RentDate, CustomerID, Phone, Name, Address, City, State, ZipCode, (VideoID, Copy#, Title, Rent))

Repeating section

Causes duplication

TransID	RentDate	CustomerID	LastName	Phone	Address	VideoID	Copy#	Title	Rent
1	4/18/04	3	Washington	502-777-7575	95 Easy Street	1	2	2001: A Space Odyssey	$1.50
1	4/18/04	3	Washington	502-777-7575	95 Easy Street	6	3	Clockwork Orange	$1.50
2	4/30/04	7	Lasater	615-888-4474	67 S. Ray Drive	8	1	Hopscotch	$1.50
2	4/30/04	7	Lasater	615-888-4474	67 S. Ray Drive	2	1	Apocalypse Now	$2.00
2	4/30/04	7	Lasater	615-888-4474	67 S. Ray Drive	6	1	Clockwork Orange	$1.50
3	4/18/04	8	Jones	615-452-1162	867 Lakeside Drive	9	1	Luggage Of The Gods	$2.50
3	4/18/04	8	Jones	615-452-1162	867 Lakeside Drive	15	1	Fabulous Baker Boys	$2.00
3	4/18/04	8	Jones	615-452-1162	867 Lakeside Drive	4	1	Boy And His Dog	$2.50
4	4/18/04	3	Washington	502-777-7575	95 Easy Street	3	1	Blues Brothers	$2.00
4	4/18/04	3	Washington	502-777-7575	95 Easy Street	8	1	Hopscotch	$1.50
4	4/18/04	3	Washington	502-777-7575	95 Easy Street	13	1	Surf Nazis Must Die	$2.50
4	4/18/04	3	Washington	502-777-7575	95 Easy Street	17	1	Witches of Eastwick	$2.00

Figure 6.21 illustrates another feature of the notation. We denote one-to-many or repeating relationships by placing parentheses around them. Figure 6.21 represents all the data shown in the input screen from Figure 6.19. The description is created by starting at the top of the form and writing down each element that you encounter. If a section contains repeating data, place parentheses around it. Preliminary keys are identified at this step by underlining them. However, we might have to add or change them at later steps. Notice that CustomerID is marked with a dashed line to indicate that in the RentalForm, it is not the primary key, but it might be used as a key in another table. Because TransID is unique for every transaction, there is no need to make CustomerID a key. We can already see some problems with trying to store data in this format. Notice that the same customer name, phone, and address would have to be entered several times.

Remember that some repeating sections are difficult to spot and might consist of only one column. For example, how many phone numbers can a customer have? Should the Phone column be repeating? In the case of the video store, probably not, because we most likely want to keep only one number per customer. In other businesses, we might want to keep several phone numbers for each client. Data normalization is directly related to the business processes. The tables you design depend on the way the business is organized.

First Normal Form

Now that we have a way of writing down our assumptions, it is relatively straightforward to separate the data into tables. The first step is to split out all repeating sections. Think about the problems that might arise if we try to keep the repeating VideosRented section with the customer data. If we design the database this way, we would have to know how many videos could be rented by each customer, because we would have to set aside space before hand. If we do not choose enough space, we will have to throw out transaction data. If we set aside too much, there will be wasted space. Figure 6.22 illustrates the problem.

The answer to this problem is to pull out the repeating section and form a new table. Then, each movie rented by a customer will fill a new row. Rows do not have to be preallocated, so there is no wasted space. Figure 6.23 uses the notation to show how the table will split. Notice that whenever we split a table this way, we have to bring along the key from the prior section. Hence, the new table will include the TransID key as well as the VideoID key.

When a table contains no repeating sections, we say that it is in *first normal form.*

FIGURE 6. 22

A table that contains repeating sections is not in first normal form. If we try to store data in this form, we are faced with the question of deciding how many videos might be rented at one time. We will waste a lot of space with missing data.

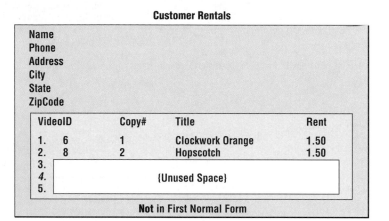

FIGURE 6.23

Splitting a table to solve problems. Problems with repeating sections are resolved by moving the repeating section into a new table. Be sure to include the old key in the new table so that you can connect the tables back together.

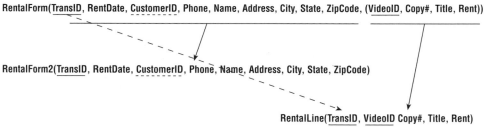

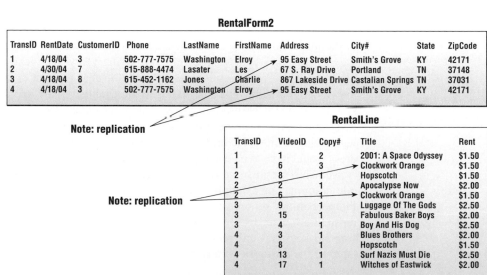

Second Normal Form

Even if a table is in first normal form, there can be additional problems. Consider the RentalLine table in Figure 6.23. Notice there are two components to the key: TransID and VideoID. The nonkey items consist of the Copy#, Title, and the Rental rate for the movie. If we leave the table in this form, consider the situation of renting a movie. Every time a movie is rented (new TransID), it will be necessary to enter the VideoID, Copy#, *and* the title and rental rate. It means that we will be storing the video title every time a video is rented. Popular movies might be rented thousands of times. Do we really want to store the title each time?

The reason we have this problem is that when the TransID changes, the movie title stays the same. The movie title depends only on the VideoID. It is tempting to say that the same problem arises with respect to the rental rate. Indeed, in some video stores, the rental rate might depend only on the VideoID. However, what if the store offers discounts on certain dates, or to specific customers? If the rental rate can vary with each transaction, the rate would have to be stored with the TransID. The final choice depends on the business rules and assumptions. For now, we will assume that rental rates are like the title and depend only on the VideoID.

When the nonkey items depend on only part of the key, we need to split them into their own table. Figure 6.24 shows the new tables.

When each nonkey column in a table depends on the entire key, we say that the table is in *second normal form.*

Third Normal Form

Examine the RentalForm2 table in Figure 6.23. Notice that because the primary key consists of only one column (TransID), the table must already be in second normal form. However, a different problem arises here. Again, consider what happens when we begin to collect data. Each time a customer comes to the store and rents videos, there will be a new transaction. In each case, we would have to record the customer name, address, phone, city, state, and zip code. Each entry in the transaction table for a customer would duplicate this data. In addition to the wasted space, imagine the problems that arise when a customer changes a phone number. You might have to update it in hundreds of rows.

The problem in this case is that the customer data does not depend on the primary key (TransID) at all. Instead, it depends only on the CustomerID column. Again, the solution is to place this data into its own table. Figure 6.25 shows the split.

FIGURE 6.24

Second normal form. Even though the repeating sections are gone, we have another problem. Every time we enter the VideoID, we have to reenter the title. That would waste a lot of space. There is a more serious problem: if no one has rented a video yet, we have no way to find its title since it is not yet stored in the database. Again, the solution is to split the table. In second normal form, all nonkey columns depend on the whole key (not just part of it).

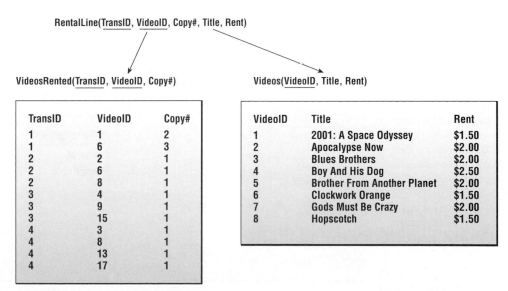

RentalLine(TransID, VideoID, Copy#, Title, Rent)

VideosRented(TransID, VideoID, Copy#)

TransID	VideoID	Copy#
1	1	2
1	6	3
2	2	1
2	6	1
2	8	1
3	4	1
3	9	1
3	15	1
4	3	1
4	8	1
4	13	1
4	17	1

Videos(VideoID, Title, Rent)

VideoID	Title	Rent
1	2001: A Space Odyssey	$1.50
2	Apocalypse Now	$2.00
3	Blues Brothers	$2.00
4	Boy And His Dog	$2.50
5	Brother From Another Planet	$2.00
6	Clockwork Orange	$1.50
7	Gods Must Be Crazy	$2.00
8	Hopscotch	$1.50

Splitting the table solves the problem. Customer data is now stored only one time for each customer. It is referenced back to the Rentals table through the CustomerID.

The four tables we created are listed in Figure 6.26. Each table is now in *third normal form*. It is easy to remember the conditions required for third normal form. First: There are no repeating groups in the tables. Second and third: Each nonkey column depends on the whole key and nothing but the key.

Note in Figure 6.26 that we could technically split the Customers table one more time. Because zip codes are uniquely assigned by the post office, the city and state could be determined directly from the zip code (they do not depend on the CustomerID). In fact, most mail

FIGURE 6.25

Third normal form. There is another problem with this definition. The customer name does not depend on the key (TransID) at all. Instead, it depends on the CustomerID. Because the name and address do not change for each different TransId, we need to put the customer data in a separate table. The Rentals table now contains only the CustomerID, which is used to link to the Customers table and collect the rest of the data.

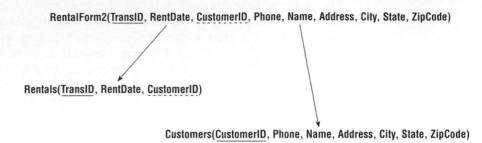

RentalForm2(<u>TransID</u>, RentDate, CustomerID, Phone, Name, Address, City, State, ZipCode)

Rentals(<u>TransID</u>, RentDate, CustomerID)

Customers(<u>CustomerID</u>, Phone, Name, Address, City, State, ZipCode)

Rentals

TransID	RentDate	CustomerID
1	4/18/04	3
2	4/30/04	7
3	4/18/04	8
4	4/18/04	3

Customers

CustomerID	Phone	LastName	FirstName	Address	City	State	ZipCode
1	502-666-7777	Johnson	Martha	125 Main Street	Alvaton	KY	42122
2	502-888-6464	Smith	Jack	873 Elm Street	Bowling Green	KY	42101
3	502-777-7575	Washington	Elroy	95 Easy Street	Smith's Grove	KY	42171
4	502-333-9494	Adams	Samuel	746 Brown Drive	Alvaton	KY	42122
5	502-474-4746	Rabitz	Victor	645 White Avenue	Bowling Green	KY	42102
6	615-373-4746	Steinmetz	Susan	15 Speedway Drive	Portland	TN	37148
7	615-888-4474	Lasater	Les	67 S. Ray Drive	Portland	TN	37148
8	615-452-1162	Jones	Charlie	867 Lakeside Drive	Castalian Springs	TN	37031
9	502-222-4351	Chavez	Juan	673 Industry Blvd.	Caneyville	KY	42721
10	502-444-2512	Rojo	Maria	88 Main Street	Cave City	KY	42127

FIGURE 6.26

Third normal form tables. There are no repeating sections and each nonkey column depends on the whole key and nothing but the key. This figure also shows the relationships between the tables that will be enforced by the DBMS. When referential integrity is properly defined, the DBMS will ensure that rentals can be made only to customers who are defined in the Customers table.

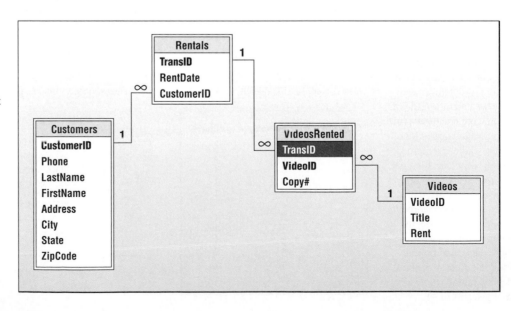

order companies today keep a separate Zip Code table for that very reason. For our small video firm, it might be more of a nuisance to split the table. Although we can purchase a complete zip code directory in computer form, it is a very large database table. For small cases, it is often easier to leave the three items in the customer table and use the database to assign default values so clerks can simply press ENTER and accept the common values.

Database Applications

Database systems typically have tools to help build applications. The tools make it relatively easy to create input forms and reports. Even if you never learn how to design a database, or become a programmer, you can learn to use these tools to build small applications and customized reports.

Data Input Forms

Rarely is data entered directly into the database's tables. Instead, input forms are used to enter some data automatically and to present a screen that is easier for users to understand. It is common to use colors and boxes to make the screen easier to read. Input screens can be used to perform calculations (such as taxes). Longer descriptions and help screens can be included to make it easier for the user to remember what goes in each column. A sample form is shown in Figure 6.27.

Many times, input screens look like existing paper forms. Consider a typical order form, which first collects customer information such as name and address. It also contains lines for items ordered, descriptions, and prices. These are usually followed by subtotals and totals. If these forms exist on paper, it is easy to create them as a DBMS input screen. If you are creating a completely new form, it helps to draw it on paper first to get a feel for what you want it to look like.

Most input forms begin as a screen that is empty except for a menu line or some other help message. Three types of information can be placed on an input screen: (1) simple text, (2) input blanks, or (3) data retrieved from the database. A Windows-based DBMS can also include pictures, graphs, sound, and video.

Paper forms have labels to tell the user what is supposed to be entered into each blank. For instance, many paper forms ask for a name: NAME _____. The label (NAME) tells you what you are supposed to enter on the blank line. A DBMS input form works much the same way. The first step is to type in the various labels. Move the cursor to a spot on the screen and type in a label or sentence that will tell the user what needs to be entered.

FIGURE 6.27
DBMS input forms. Input forms are used to collect data from the user and perform basic computations. Subforms or scrolling regions are used when there is a one-to-many relationship.

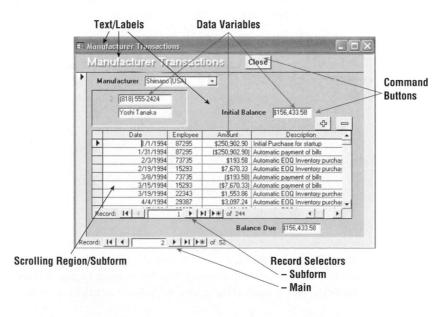

Renee Zaugg manages more than 174 terabytes of data on a daily basis for Aetna, the insurance company. Located in Hartford, the data is processed by 14 mainframe servers and more than 1,000 midrange servers—all running IBM's DB2 software. Physically, the data is stored on more than 4,100 different disk drives. Over 20 terabytes of the data are available to customers—mostly hospitals and other healthcare providers. The relational database consists of over 15,000 tables. The daily challenges Renee faces are data integrity, backup, security, and availability. Managers rely on accurate data to make decisions.

Mark Eimer of Atos Origin in Paris is responsible for 300 terabytes of data. The outsourcing company provides services to many large companies, so much of the data is stored in thousands of different file formats. Atos Origin has 22 data centers across the globe supporting hundreds of thousands of users in 31 countries. The systems run on 60 mainframe servers and about 5,000 midrange servers. Worldwide, Atos Origin employees 27,000 people.

Source: Adapted from Barry Nance, "How Much Data Do Large Corporations Manage?" *Computerworld,* April 23, 2001.

Most database systems automatically enter some types of data, such as the current date. If necessary, users can change the date, but it saves time by enabling them to press ENTER to accept the displayed value. The same situation holds for sequential items like order numbers, where the DBMS can automatically generate each unique order number.

After you have typed in the basic labels, the next step is to add the data-entry boxes. Just as you would type a blank line on a paper form, you need to tell the DBMS exactly what data will be entered by the user. For instance, move the screen cursor to a position next to the Date label, then tell the DBMS to enter data at that point. You will specify the name of the column where the data will be stored. You can also specify default values. A **default value** is a value that is automatically displayed by the computer. For the case of the date, the DBMS will let you enter a name like Date() that will display the current date.

When a DBMS prints out data, it can be formatted in different ways. You can control the way the data is displayed by using a format command. A date might be displayed as 10/24/2004 by entering the format MM/DD/YYYY. There are several common date formats; most firms tend to use one standard format. Note that many European firms use a format that is different from the common ones used in the United States.

The next section of the order form contains basic customer information. This data is stored in the Customer table, not the Orders table. When you select the Orders table, you might have to indicate that the Orders and Customer tables are connected to each other by the phone number. Now, place the text labels on the screen (customer name, address, etc.). Then place a data entry box after each label.

Next, you can add the Sales table; it is connected to the Orders table by the order number. Type in the column names for Item#, Description, Price, and Quantity. The DBMS input form will define this part of the table as a **scrolling region** or subform. To users, this subform will behave somewhat like a spreadsheet. They can see several rows at a time, and keys (or the mouse) will move the screen cursor up and down as users enter data into any row.

The only items entered in the sales table are the Item# and the Quantity ordered. The Description and Price can be found by creating a look-up in the items table. If the clerk using this screen types in the item number, the description and price will appear. With a good DBMS, it is possible to define a pop-up form or combo box in case the clerk does not know the number. This way, by pressing a certain key, a table listing each Item# and Description will be displayed in a window on the screen. The clerk can then scroll through the list to find the item.

Reports

Most of the time, the data listed in one table is not complete enough to help managers make decisions. For example, a listing of a Sales table might provide only phone numbers, item numbers, and the quantity ordered. A more useful report would print sales grouped by

FIGURE 6.28

DBMS report writers. Reports are created in sections. The report header is printed one time at the top of the report. Data in the page header section is printed at the top of every page. There are corresponding page footers and a report footer. Primary data is printed in the detail section. Data can be organized as groups by creating breaks. Titles are often printed in the break header with subtotals in the break footer.

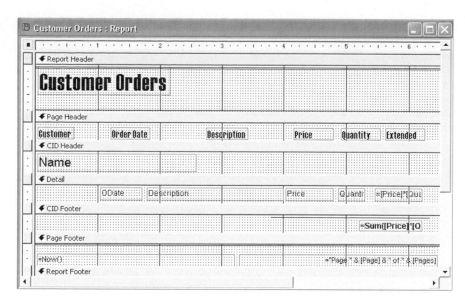

customer. It would also compute total sales for each customer. Because this report relies on data from several tables, it is best to base the report on a view.

The view for the sales report example needs four tables. An OrderReport view is created that joins the Customer table to Orders by C#, Orders to ItemSold by O#, and ItemsSold to Items by Item#. The DBMS will have a "create report" option to create the sales report. The report will be based on the OrderReport view. The report writer consists of a blank screen. You can put simple text statements anywhere on the page. You also can place data values on the page, and you can compute totals and make other calculations.

Most reports can be broken into categories. For example, there might be report titles that appear only at the front of the report (such as cover pages). Other information, such as the report title, date, and column labels, will be repeated at the top of each page. All of these items are called **page headers.** Similarly, there can be **page footers** at the bottom of each page. Reports may also contain **group breaks.** For instance, the sales report needs subtotals for each customer, so you need to break the report into subsections for each customer. Generally, you can specify several levels of breaks. For instance, you might break each customer order into totals by date. Each break can have a *break header,* a **detail section,** and a *break footer.* In the example shown in Figure 6.27, the customer name is printed on the break header. There is a detail line that lists the item information. The subtotals are displayed on the break footers. The report design or layout is illustrated in Figure 6.28. The report with sample data is printed in Figure 6.29.

To create this report, you first tell the DBMS that the report will contain one break based on customer phone number. You also define the variable *subtot,* which is price multiplied by quantity. Now you move the cursor to the top of the screen and type in the titles for the top of the page. Then place each column and variable on the report. You can format each item to make it look better. For example, you might want to format dates as MM/DD/YYYY so that all four digits of the year are displayed. Similarly, you can add dollar signs to the subtotals and totals.

When you have finished creating the report, you can print it. When you print this report, it should be sorted by customer name. The DBMS will also enable you to print the report so that it contains data just for one month. Notice that only five or six lines are needed to create a complex report. Without the DBMS report writer, it would take a programmer several hours to create this report, and it would be much harder to make changes to it in the future.

Putting It Together with Menus

If you are creating a database for yourself with just a couple of input screens and reports, you can probably quit at this point. On the other hand, for more complex databases or for projects other people will use, it would be wise to make the system easier to use. *Application*

FIGURE 6.29

Sample report. Reports are often printed by groups or breaks with subtotals for each group. With a report writer, the layout, typefaces, and computations are easy to change.

Orders by Customers

Name	ODate	Description	Price	Quantity	Extended
Adamz					
	5/6/99	Corn Broom	$1.00	2	$2.00
	6/27/99	Blue Jeans	$12.00	1	$12.00
	6/27/99	Paper Towels, 3 rolls	$1.00	3	$3.00
					$17.00
James					
	4/4/99	Corn Broom	$1.00	4	$4.00
	4/4/99	Men's Boots	$15.00	3	$45.00
	6/9/99	Blue Jeans	$12.00	1	$12.00
	6/9/99	Laundry Detergent	$2.00	1	$2.00
					$63.00
Jones					
	3/3/99	Corn Broom	$1.00	2	$2.00
	3/3/99	Laundry Detergent	$2.00	4	$8.00
	3/3/99	Paper Towels, 3 rolls	$1.00	1	$1.00
	4/9/99	Laundry Detergent	$2.00	2	$4.00
	5/23/99	Corn Broom	$1.00	1	$1.00
					$16.00
Kolke					
	5/1/99	Blue Jeans	$12.00	1	$12.00
	6/9/99	Blue Jeans	$12.00	1	$12.00
	6/9/99	Candy Popcorn	$0.50	5	$2.50
	6/9/99	Paper Towels, 3 rolls	$1.00	2	$2.00
					$28.50
Smitz					
	5/6/99	Candy Popcorn	$9.50	5	$2.50
	5/6/99	Paper Towels, 3 rolls	$1.00	1	$1.00
	5/8/99	Men's Boots	$15.00	1	$15.00
	5/8/99	Paper Towels, 3 rolls	$1.00	4	$4.00
					$22.50
				Grand Total	**$147.00**

generators are tools that enable you to combine the various features into a single application. The resulting application can be used by selecting choices from a menu, much like users do with commercial software. The important design feature is that you can create the entire application without writing any programming commands.

Consider a simple example. As a manager, you need a sales report printed every day that shows the best-selling items. Every week you want a list of total sales for each employee to bring to your sales meetings. You also send letters to your best customers every month offering them additional discounts. You want to put your secretary in charge of printing these reports, but you do not have time to explain all the details about how to use the database program. Instead, you create a simple menu that lists each report. The secretary chooses the desired report from the list. Some reports might ask questions, such as which week to use. The secretary enters the answers and the report is printed.

The first step in creating an application is to think about the people who will use it. How do they do their jobs? How do the database inputs and reports fit into their job? The goal is to devise a menu system that reflects the way they work. Two examples of a first menu are shown in Figure 6.30. Which menu is easier for a clerk to understand? The one that best relates to the job. Once you understand the basic tasks, write down a set of related menus.

FIGURE 6.30
Designing menus for
users. Which menu is
easier for a secretary to
understand? When
designing applications,
you should organize the
application to match the
processes users perform.

Main Menu

1. Setup Choices
2. Data Input
3. Print Reports
4. DOS Utilities
5. Backups

Customer Information

Daily Sales Reports
Friday Sales Meeting
Monthly Customer Letters

Quit

Some menu options will call up other menus. Some will print reports; others will activate the input screens you created.

Once you know how you want the menu structure to appear, you fill in the menu templates in the application generator. To create a menu, you type in a title and fill in the choices. Then you assign an action to each choice. Usually you just pick from a list of actions and type in specific data such as the name of the report and how you want it sorted. When you are finished, the application generator creates the application.

Database Administration

Managing a database can be a complex job. Often there are hundreds of choices that need to be made when the database is designed. Someone needs to be in charge of defining the data, making sure that all useful facts are captured, and managing security for this valuable asset. Databases have to be evaluated and fine-tuned on a regular basis. Someone has to keep track of these maintenance changes and decide when major updates should be installed. A **database administrator (DBA)** is usually appointed to manage the databases for the firm. The DBA needs to know the technical details of the DBMS and the computer system. The DBA also needs to understand the business operations of the firm.

The database administrator is responsible for all operations involving the database. These duties include coordinating users and designers, establishing standards, and defining the data characteristics. When new programs are created, the DBA makes sure they are tested and documented. The DBA also schedules backups and recovery, and establishes security controls.

In a few large companies, an additional person known as the *data administrator (DA)* is charged with overseeing all of the data definitions and data standards for the company. In this case, typically several DBAs are used to monitor and control various databases. The DA is responsible for making sure data can be shared throughout the company.

Standards and Documentation

In any company of moderate size, many different databases will be used by hundreds of workers. These databases were created at different points in time by teams of employees. If there are no standards, each piece will be unique, making it difficult to combine information from multiple databases or tables. The marketing department may refer to *customers,* whereas management calls them *clients.* The DBMS needs to know that both terms refer to the same set of data. Also, someone has to determine the key values for each table. Consider the Customer table. One department might assign identification numbers to each customer. Another department might use customers' phone numbers, and a third department might use the customer names. To prevent confusion and to be able to combine information, it is best for all users to use only one of these methods to identify the customers.

Many standards are related to the database process. It is easier to use a database if all input screens have similar characteristics. For instance, the base screen might use a blue background with white characters. Data that is entered by the user will be displayed in yellow. Similarly, certain function keys may be predefined. ESC might be used to cancel or escape from choices. F1 might be used for help and F3 to display a list of choices. If each application uses keys differently, the user will have a hard time remembering which keys do what with which database.

Likewise, it is helpful to standardize certain aspects of reports. It might be necessary to choose specific typefaces and fonts. Titles could be in an 18 point Helvetica font, whereas the body of reports could be printed in 11 point Palatino. To provide emphasis, subtotals and totals could be printed in boldface, with single and double underlining, respectively.

One of the crucial steps in creating a database is the definition of the data. Many important decisions have to be made at this point. Besides the issues of what to call each item, the DBMS has to be told how to store every item. For instance, are phone numbers stored as 7 digits, or should they be stored as 10 digits, or perhaps stored with the 3-digit international calling code? Postal zip codes pose similar problems. The United States uses either a five-digit or nine-digit zip code, but is considering adding two more digits. Other countries include alphabetic characters in their codes. Someone has to determine how to store this information in the manner that is best for the company.

There are many other aspects of database design that need standards to make life easier for the users. However, whenever there are standards, there should be a mechanism to change these standards. Technology always changes, so standards that were established five years ago are probably not relevant today. The DBA constantly reviews and updates the standards, and makes sure that employees follow them.

Even though databases are easy to use, they would be confusing if the designers did not document their work. Picture a situation where you want to find information about customers but the designers named the table *Patrons.* You might never find the information without documentation.

Documentation can assume many forms. Most DBMSs allow the designers to add comments to each table and column. This internal documentation can often be searched by the users. Many times it can be printed in different formats so that it can be distributed to users in manuals. Because it is maintained in the database along with the data, it is easy to find. It is also easy for the designers to add these comments as they create or change the database, so the documentation is more likely to be current. It is up to the DBA to ensure that all designers document their work.

Testing, Backup, and Recovery

One advantage of the DBMS approach is that it provides tools such as report writers and application generators that end users can employ to create their own systems. Although it is easier for users to create these programs than to start from scratch, the programs still need to be tested. Corporate databases are extremely valuable, but only if the information they contain is accurate. It is the responsibility of the DBA to keep the information accurate, which means that all software that changes data must be tested.

Most companies would not survive long if a disaster destroyed their databases. For this reason, all databases need to be backed up on a regular basis. How often this backup occurs depends on the importance and value of the data. It is possible to back up data continuously. With two identical computer systems, a change made to one can be automatically written to the other. If a fire destroys one system, the other one can be used to continue with no loss of information. Obviously, it is expensive to maintain duplicate facilities. Many organizations choose to back up their data less frequently.

The main point of backup and recovery is that someone has to be placed in charge. Especially in small businesses, there is a tendency to assume that someone else is responsible for making backups. Also, remember that at least one current copy of the database must be stored in a different location. A major disaster could easily wipe out everything stored in the same building. There are some private companies that for a fee will hold your backup data in a secure, fireproof building where you can access your data any time of the day.

Access Controls

Another important task in database administration is the establishment of security safeguards. The DBA has to determine which data needs to be protected. Once basic security conditions are established, the DBA is responsible for monitoring database activity. The DBA tracks security violation attempts and monitors who is using the database. Because there are always changes in employees, removing access for departed employees and entering new access levels and passwords can be a full-time job.

Databases and E-Business

Many people still think of websites as simple pages of text with a few images. But e-business requires interaction with customers and the company data. Consequently, most e-business websites are connected to databases. In e-commerce, customers want to know if a product is in stock—this information is in the database. Similarly, customer, order, and shipping data have to be maintained and shared throughout the company. Other e-business sites use databases to provide services, store transaction data, and provide search and matching capabilities.

Designing an e-business database is no different than traditional business applications. However, the technologies for building Web-based applications are still evolving. Currently, two leading systems are being developed: Sun is championing a Java-based approach known as J2EE and Microsoft is building the .NET platform. Databases are the heart of both systems, and both are server-based technologies designed to build interactive websites. Unfortunately, the two systems are completely independent and incompatible. If you build an application to run with one approach, you would have to completely rewrite it to use the other method.

Because the two approaches are so different, if you are building an e-business system, one of your first actions is to select one of these systems. In most cases, the J2EE approach runs on UNIX-based computers, but some versions exist for Microsoft-based systems. The Microsoft approach will probably only run on Microsoft servers, but some companies are experimenting with building versions that run on UNIX systems. Because the two systems are both new, it is difficult to evaluate them on technical grounds. The Microsoft approach offers a little more flexibility with its support for multiple languages. Microsoft .NET also provides a complete development environment with several easy-to-use tools that make it relatively easy for beginners to create database-oriented websites.

The basic approach is shown in Figure 6.31 Web developers create script pages that interact with the database. When customers request a page, the server executes the associated program script. The script sends queries to the database and retrieves the desired data. For example, the script might retrieve product descriptions, prices, and in-stock status. The data and images are added to the Web page and sent to the customer, who sees only the simple results.

Generally, the database runs on a separate server—which reduces the load on the Web server and makes it easier to handles backups and other database maintenance chores. However, with increasingly powerful servers, one server can handle smaller applications.

FIGURE 6.31

E-business database. When a customer requests a page, the server runs a script program that interacts with the database by sending queries and formatting the data to build a new Web page.

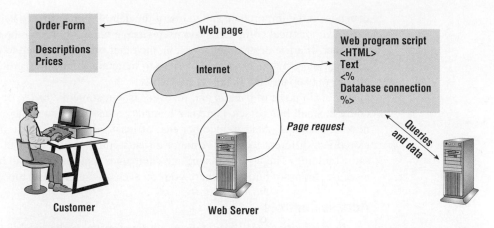

A Manager's View

Every manager needs to do research. Sometimes you will have to summarize and evaluate transaction data. Sometimes you will use external databases to evaluate the industry and your competitors.

Database management systems provide important capabilities to managers. One of the most useful is a query language, such as QBE or SQL, that enables you to answer questions without the need for hiring an MIS expert. A DBMS also speeds the development of new systems and provides basic features such as report writers and input forms.

Summary

Everyone needs to search for information. Computers make this job easier, but someone must set up and maintain the databases to ensure their integrity. There are many ways to search databases, and relational database management systems are a popular method. They are increasingly used as the foundation of the information system. They make it easy to share data among users while maintaining access controls. Equally importantly, the databases are easy to alter as the organization changes. Sophisticated databases can handle all the data types in use today, not just simple numbers and text.

It is relatively easy for users to obtain data using SQL or query-by-example tools. Because SQL is a recognized standard query language, it is worth remembering the basic elements of the SELECT command. The syntax is easy (SELECT columns, FROM tables, WHERE conditions, ORDER BY columns). Just remember that whenever you use more than one table, they must be joined by related columns.

An important step in databases is to design them correctly. The trick is to split the data into tables that refer to exactly one concept. Most organizations have a database administrator to help users create the initial database tables, define standards, establish access rights, and perform backups and testing. Once the tables have been defined, users can create input screens, reports, and views by using graphical tools to draw the desired items on the screen.

It is important to choose the right tool for each job. Databases excel at handling huge amounts of data and sharing it with other users. On the other hand, spreadsheets are designed to perform calculations and create graphs. One indication that a problem should be solved using a DBMS instead of a spreadsheet is that several tables of data are involved.

Every day, more information is stored in commercial databases. In many ways, they are becoming the libraries of the future. Almost any type of reference data you can imagine can be searched electronically. Just remember that you have to pay to access this data, so you have to design your search strategies carefully to save money.

Key Words

column, *208*	normalization, *219*	relational model, *207*
composite keys, *209*	object-oriented design, *207*	report, *207*
database administrator	page footers, *227*	row, *208*
(DBA), *229*	page headers, *227*	scrolling region, *226*
data independence, *209*	primary key, *208*	SQL, *211*
default value, *226*	query by example	table, *208*
detail section, *227*	(QBE), *211*	view, *218*
group breaks, *227*	query system, *207*	

Website References

Database References

Computerworld data management links	**www.computerworld.com/itresources/ rclinks/0,4167,KEY241_RLI142,00.html**
CIO data management	**www.cio.com/research/data/index.html**
September 11 Archive Project	**September11.archive.org**

Car Shopping Services

America's Automall	**ww.aautomall.com**
Autobytel	**www.autobytel.com**
Cars@Cost	**www.carscost.com**
Dealer Net	**www.dealernet.com**
Edmunds	**www.edmunds.com**
Kelley Blue Book	**www.kbb.com**
Microsoft Carpoint	**carpoint.msn.com**
Vehix	**www.vehix.com**

Additional Reading

Disabatino, Jennifer. "NHL Scores With Database on Draft Day." *Computerworld,* July 9, 2001. [NHL uses a database to provide more information and cut hours off the time to draft players.]

Fox, Prim. "Tax Filing Gets Connected to the Web." *Computerworld,* August 8, 2001. [The importance of connecting databases to the Web even for governments.]

Mayer, Merry. "New DNA Database Extends the Long Arm of Law Enforcement." *Government Computer News,* October 19, 1998, p. 47. [Government database to identify criminals.]

Post, Gerald. *Database Management Systems: Designing and Building Applications.* Burr Ridge, IL: McGraw-Hill/Irwin, 2002. [How to design databases and use them to build business applications.]

Sliwa, Carol; Lee Copeland; and Don Tennant. "Dead Voters in Florida?" *Computerworld,* November 13, 2000. [Only 10 states have an online central voter registration database, and 16 have no state database at all.]

Trombly, Maria. "Schwab Database Glitch Cuts Users Off from Some Information." *Computerworld,* February 13, 2001. [The importance of database availability and reliability.]

Tiboni, Frank. "FEMA Automates Property Inspection Scheduling." *Government Computer News,* November 9, 1998, p. 14. [Emergency agency uses telephone registration and database to help disaster victims in less time.]

Review Questions

1. How is data stored in a relational database?
2. How does data independence make it easier to design and maintain computer applications?
3. What four questions do you need to answer in order to create a database query?
4. How do you join tables with QBE? With SQL?
5. How do you enter restrictions or constraints with QBE? With SQL?
6. How do you perform computations with QBE? With SQL?
7. Would you prefer to use QBE or SQL to access a database? Why?
8. What tasks are performed by a database administrator?
9. Why are forms (input screens) important in a relational database?

10. Do you think users can create their own reports with a DBMS report writer? What limitations does it have?

11. Why are standards important in a database environment?

12. Why is a DBMS important for e-business?

Exercises

 C06Ex15.mdb

It is best to answer the first 15 exercise questions using a DBMS, but if one is not available, you can use the tables in the text and write your queries by hand. If you have a DBMS that handles both QBE and SQL, you should do the exercise with both methods.

1. List the customers who live on Main Street (in any city).

2. List the customers who have an account balance between $300 and $500, sorted by account balance in descending order.

3. What is the total amount of money owed us by customers who live in Miami?

4. How many orders have been placed by customers from Seattle after April?

5. What is the largest order ever placed (in terms of amount)?

6. Which item (ItemID and Description) had the most sales in terms of quantity?

7. What was the best day in terms of highest total value of orders?

8. Calculate the total commissions owed to salesperson Johnson. Hint: You need to compute the total of commission multiplied by order amount.

9. Get the name and phone number of customers who bought blue jeans in June 2004.

10. List all of the items sold in May.

11. Which salesperson sold jeans to a customer in Phoenix?

12. Create an input screen that enables a clerk to update information and add new customers to the database.

13. Using the tables in the chapter, create an order-entry input screen that can be used by a clerk who knows nothing about databases. Note: Depending on the DBMS, it might be difficult to compute the order amount total.

14. Create an inventory report that lists all of the products, group them by category, and within each category, sort them by ID number.

15. Create the customer order report that is described in the chapter. Hint: First create a view that joins the appropriate tables together.

16. For any business, choose five entities (objects) that might be used as database tables. Identify primary keys for each table.

17. Find at least five e-business websites that are connected to database management systems. Hint: look for something that indicates it is retrieving business data.

18. Assume that you need to buy a DBMS for a midsize company. Research the components needed and the approximate cost of at least two database management systems.

19. With the cooperation of a local small business, create a database for that company. Note that you should verify the initial layout of the tables with your instructor or someone who has studied database design.

20. A friend of yours has just opened a photofinishing operation. She wants you to create a database system to help her run the business. The basic processing is straightforward: A customer drops or mails in one or more rolls of film. A clerk records the basic data on the customer and the film. The rolls are assigned a number, sorted, and run through the processor. Processing varies slightly depending on the type of film, film speed, and processing options. Your friend wants to keep track of which clerk performed the processing and match the names with any complaints that might arise. She also wants to offer a frequent-buyer program to reward the most active customers. It is also important to track the chemical usage for the processing—both to keep track of orders and expenses, and to make sure the processors always have fresh chemicals. The clerks are also responsible for

cleaning the processing equipment. Create a set of normalized tables for this company. Identify attributes where possible. (Hint: Obtain a film mailer that lists various options.)

21. You have been hired by an environmental consulting company (ECC) that specializes in creating environmental impact statements (EISs) for large projects. It needs a database to track the progress of each EIS. The company is particularly concerned about tracking public comments, questions from state and federal officials, and the responses to all of these comments. All comments are scanned and stored as digital files. Create a list of normalized tables needed to build this database.

EIS Project #: Date initiated: Date ECC involved: Date ECC finished:	Client Principal contact Phone Contact address City, State, ZIP	Phone Billing address City, State, ZIP
Site location: Latitude Site address: Site description	Longitude City	State ZIP
Proposed development description	Proposed activities (standard list) Drain wetlands Fill Build roads Store waste	

		Comments and Responses				
Date Received	Category	Source	File	Response Date	Person	Title

 Rolling Thunder Database

Create queries to answer the following questions. *(Difficulty level: 1 = easiest.)*

22. How many customers are from California? *(1)*
23. Which customers currently owe more than $1,000? *(1)*
24. What is the most popular paint color for full-suspension mountain bikes? *(2)*
25. How many race bikes larger than 60 cm (FrameSize) were sold in New York in 2000? *(2)*
26. Which employee sold the most red mountain bikes in July 2001? *(3)*
27. What is the lightest weight rear derailleur for a mountain bike in production after 2000? *(2)*
28. What is the total salary cost? *(2)*
29. What is the average price we paid for Shimano XT derailleurs (rear)? *(4)*
30. On average, shipping costs are what percentage of the total order for merchandise purchased in March 2001? *(2)*
31. List the purchase orders where TotalList does *not* equal the computed total of the individual items. *(4)*
32. List the component items that had *no* sales in March. *(5)*
33. On average, which costs more, tires for road bikes or tires for mountain bikes? *(3)*
34. Compute the sales by model type by month for 2001. *(5 Hint: Crosstab)*
35. Compute total sales by month. *(2)*
36. Compute the total sales taxes we owe to each state (for 1999). *(2)*
37. List all of the employees hired before 1993. *(1)*
38. List all of the bicycles ordered in March 1999 that used the LetterStyle "Flash." *(1)*
39. What is the value of our current inventory of Shimano components? *(2)*
40. What percentage of sales came through retail stores in December 2001? Hint: Use two queries and compute the percentage with a calculator *(4)*
41. List all of the retail bicycle stores in your state. *(2)*

Airlines

Major Airlines
Annual revenues exceed $1 billion
American, United, Delta, Northwest, Southwest, and U.S. Airlines
Each has fleets of 300 or more aircraft
National Airlines
Annual revenues are between $100 million and $1 billion
More regional in focus with smaller seating capacities
Regional Airlines
Annual revenues are less than $100 million
Computer lines and startup carriers

The airline industry is an important component of today's global economy. Over 1.8 billion passengers in 2000 relied on the world's airlines for business and vacation travel. Approximately a quarter of the world's manufactured exports by value are transported by air. Since the first jet airliner flew in 1949, use of commercial aviation has expanded more than 65-fold.

The industry is mature but is still changing and growing. The passenger segment of the airline industry is the largest and in 2000 accounted for over $93 billion in revenues or 72.3 percent of the industry's total revenues. Other major segments include freight and express (9 percent), charter (3.4 percent), and mail (1.5 percent). Economically, the airline industry is an imperfect oligopoly, in which a few carriers dominate in long-haul passenger traffic, while several dozen small carriers compete for short-haul flights. The Department of Transportation classifies air carriers by the size of their revenue base. In the United States, 34 carriers have a fleet of 25 or more aircraft.

Airline industry demand is cyclical. Travel generally follows economic activity. Economic models for forecasting airline traffic are commonly based on projections for gross domestic product (GDP), disposable personal income, and consumer confidence levels. While air traffic volume reflects economic factors, the cost and convenience of alternative modes of transportation also impacts air traffic. Demand for discretionary travel, such as vacations, tends to be more price sensitive. In recent years, corporate travel budgets have also become price sensitive. Higher fares stifle air traffic demand, whereas low fares spur greater demand.

The federal government stopped regulating airlines in 1978. Since deregulation, the industry has grown significantly more concentrated. Since 1985, mergers have played a significant role in this concentration. Between 1986 and 1987, Texas Air merged with Eastern and People's Express, Northwest Airlines with Republic Airlines, and Delta with Western. Industry consolidation has resulted from slowing traffic growth and the exhaustion of conventional cost-cutting measures. Mergers offer savings opportunities through the consolidation of administrative, distribution, and mainte-

nance operations. Bankruptcies in the 1990s, most notably Pan American, Eastern, and TWA, have also led to the consolidation of the industry.

All major airlines with the exception of Southwest operate through hub-and-spoke networks. In this system, passengers are gathered from surrounding "spoke" cities to a central hub airport where they must transfer to the second leg of their flight. This system enables densities to be built for the longer portion of the flight, better matching equipment to demand. Because of the oligopoly, airlines rarely challenge each other within a hub, so airlines can usually count on stable airfares and profit margins in certain regions.

Despite deregulation, the Federal Aviation Administration (FAA) still imposes safety standards on carriers. It certifies aircraft and airlines and establishes age and medical requirements for pilots. A series of tragic airplane crashes in 1996 pushed air safety to the forefront. The crash of a ValuJet airplane in the Florida Everglades in May was followed in July by the mysterious explosion and crash of TWA's flight 800 over the Atlantic Ocean. The ValuJet crash prodded regulators to tighten their scrutiny of startup airlines and the practices of maintenance contractors. Certification of a new airline now takes twice as long as before. The number of aircraft that a new airline can operate is also limited based on the carrier's financial and managerial resources.

The Department of Transportation (DOT) levies civil penalties against airlines that engage in fraudulent marketing practices and violate code-sharing rules. It also decides airline ownership and control issues. Internationally, the DOT plays an important role by negotiating bilateral aviation treaties with foreign nations.

Financial Analysis

From 1997 to 2000, the growth rate in the airline industry averaged 5.6 percent per year. In 2000, the growth rate averaged 11.1 percent, with an average load factor of 72.4 percent. Compared to other transportation industries, this rate is high, due to the fact that regional and international airlines continue to increase their service to underserved destinations.

The airline industry includes high barriers to entry. It requires a huge capital investment, especially for purchasing aircraft but also for labor, gate fees, advertising, fuel, and so on. Nonetheless, the airline industry is easier to enter now than it was before 1978 when deregulation was passed. Flight equipment accounts for more than 62 percent of total airline assets.

A newer trend for startups, as well as major carriers, is to lease planes instead of buying them. If aircraft are purchased, tax implications occur such as charges for depreciation and financing costs such as interest or preferred dividend payments. Among major airlines, depreciation averages 4.7 percent. For Southwest Airlines, depreciation increased 4.9 percent compared to an increase in the percentage of owned aircraft.

An important measure is yield, or the revenue generated per passenger mile (RPM). Comparing the absolute yield level for different carriers is only useful if the carriers have a similar mix of flights. Another consideration is revenues from nonfare sources. Since these can account for as much as 10 percent of an airline's total revenues, this contribution can make the difference between an operating profit and loss.

Industry revenues are strongly linked to corporate earnings and disposable income. The second and third quarters, along with holidays, have commonly been the times when demand was highest and operating conditions most favorable. From 1990 to mid-1994, the industry suffered $12 billion in losses. From 1995 through 2000, the industry averaged over $3.8 billion of profit per year. In 2000, the yield ratio (cents/RPM) hit a record high of 13.51. However, in real terms, that value is substantially lower than it was in 1990. But the airlines managed to reduce costs and maintain substantially higher profit margins through 2000.

The events of September 11 caused a 25 percent reduction in passenger traffic. Even with a bailout of billions of dollars from the federal government, the airlines reported serious losses. In a related move, the reason for the U.S. government taking over airport security was to provide the capital costs to hire, check, and train employees, and to purchase new equipment. Costs that the airlines (and the airports) could not afford.

Ultimately, the airline industry is expected to continue to grow in pace with the U.S. economy. As the outlook for corporate profits and personal income growth improves, continued profits also appear likely. Forecasters warn, however, that this industry is highly cyclical, and thus is prone to overcapacity resulting in high levels of competition.

Stock/Investment Outlook

Airline stocks are the most cyclical on Wall Street. Investors tend to bid up shares of airlines when they look weakest and substantial losses are incurred. Once profits are returned, investors move on, dumping stocks with depressed price/earnings ratios. Investors tend to favor growth airlines with wide profit margins rather than those with a strong service performance and a young fleet. The biggest rally gains in equity airlines go to the "worst" airlines because investors anticipate a bigger gain from a depressed base in that carrier's bottom line.

Growth Potential

Once security has been improved and the delays reduced with new equipment, people will forget about the security threats, and the growth will continue. After all, the United States is a mobile society and few alternatives exist. By 2005, the number of people traveling by air could exceed 2.5 billion a year. Growth in air travel will be led by the Asia market. Demand for this region is anticipated to grow by an average of 8.6 percent annually between now and 2010.

Experts attribute the rapid rate of growth to the increasing disposable incomes of consumers and the decreasing fares being charged. Airfares today are 70 percent less after adjustment for inflation than they were in 1970. As world economic growth continues to accelerate, so should growth in the airline industry. A significant change in the structure of the industry is

"open skies." This term refers to the process of internationally deregulating air transportation services, an area of many regulations and restrictions.

For instance, the United States and Canada signed a bilateral air services agreement in February 1995. The deal allows for unlimited nonstop air services between two-thirds of the 100 largest U. S. cities and any major Canadian cities that previously did not have air services. This agreement should greatly expand air traffic between the two countries, with projections for growth to 20 million passengers annually. The United States has also been negotiating "open skies" agreements with several European nations, with discussions focused on initiating new transatlantic routes, increasing flight frequency on existing routes, and lifting pricing restrictions. Some airlines are also adding transarctic routes over newly opened Russian airspace, offering substantial time savings from the United States to Europe.

Another area for substantial growth is the regional airline market. Largely overlooked during deregulation, this market has become a bottom line profit booster for the national airlines, feeding passengers into their hubs. During the 1970s, the regional airline industry was made up of local commuter airlines serving local cities and connecting outlying communities to metropolitan areas.

Leading U.S. Airports in 2000		
City	Code	Passengers
Atlanta Hartsfield	ATL	80,162,407
Chicago O'Hare	ORD	72,144,244
Los Angeles	LAX	66,424,767
Dallas/Ft. Worth	DFW	60,687,122
San Francisco	SFO	41,040,995
Denver	DEN	38,751,687
Las Vegas	LAS	36,865,866
Minneapolis/St. Paul	MSP	36,751,632
Phoenix	PHX	36,040,469
Detroit	DTW	35,535,080

Source: www.airports.org/traffic/passengers.html

After deregulation, national and major airlines ended service to smaller communities, concentrating on higher-yield routes. The smaller commuter airlines began to acquire larger turboprop aircraft and replace the major airlines on these low-yield routes. In the 1980s, commuter airlines grew through industry consolidation and code sharing with larger airlines. In the 1990s, they grew into large regional carriers serving numerous cities and operating turbojet aircraft. This has enabled them to service new routes previously not possible without the longer-range regional jet aircraft.

Technological advancements have enabled code sharing, which is a major key to growth in the regional airlines. This enables them to take advantage of a single ticket source by using the ticket codes of the larger national airlines. This facilitates the coordination of schedules through a smooth transfer of passengers from one airline (regional) to another code-sharing partner (national). Code sharing has contributed to the consolidation of smaller commuter carriers into larger regional carriers. The number of regional carriers has decreased by

51 to 124 carriers in 1995. The average trip length has doubled from 121 miles in 1978 to 223 miles in 1995. The number of passengers has grown from 11.3 million in 1978 to 57.2 million in 1995.

In 1995, the two largest regional airlines were Simmons Airlines, Inc., an American Eagle carrier, and ComAir, Inc., a Delta Airlines carrier. Simmons flies a fleet of 92 turboprops out of Dallas/Fort Worth and Chicago O'Hare, serving more than 50 cities with 586 flights per day and carrying 4.98 million passengers. ComAir flies out of Cincinnati and Orlando, serving 79 cities with 680 flights per day.

Competitive Structure

Ten major airlines (each with annual revenues over $1 billion) currently account for more than 75 percent of all operating revenue and 90 percent of passenger revenue. The other 10 percent is made up of more than 100 airlines. The market share of other airlines has been increasing at the expense of the major ones.

The competitiveness in the airline industry was enhanced by the deregulation in 1978. Deregulation allowed airlines to fly wherever they wished. It also allowed new small airlines to compete with the existing major airlines. Some small airlines, such as Southwest, have done well with point-to-point, short-haul, and high-frequency operations.

Airlines do not sell a tangible product but simply supply transportation. Aside from offering certain frills, the service airlines provide is basically undifferentiated. Some of these frills include more legroom, better food, newer movies, telephone service, and most recently, hookups for fax and online communication. Frequent flier programs and rewards are also used to set airlines apart from their competitors.

Airlines use frequent-flyer programs to build brand loyalty and distinguish themselves from the competition. Frequent flyer programs have been developed in an attempt to gain customer loyalty and promote repeat business. Frequent flyers represent only 8 percent of the total number of passengers, but the miles they fly equal 45 percent of all miles flown. Satisfying these passengers can be key to an airline's success.

Passenger pricing is directly available to consumers and competitors, particularly due to consumer access to fares on the Internet. In sum, the airline industry is highly competitive. Airlines compete with each other on both service and price. For business travelers, the frequency of flights and the time of day is critical. Schedule reliability also influences airline selection. Smaller airlines unable to obtain gate space during peak travel times are unable to attract business travelers. Besides competing with each other, airlines compete with a variety of transportation modes, including automobiles, railroads, and buses.

James Goodwin, chairman and CEO of United Airlines, wrote a letter to his employees in October 2001. When the letter reached its intended audience far beyond United employees, it caused such an uproar that Goodwin was forced to resign. Goodwin asserted that the situation was dire and the airline was in deep trouble. Extraordinary cuts were needed or the airline would go bankrupt within a year. Employee costs were the largest component of the budget, the largest fixed costs, and potentially the easiest to cut substantially

Those who knew Goodwin were not surprised. He had not shied away from dramatic statements in the past. On the other hand, most market participants and commentators expressed some degree of shock. Some felt that the U.S. government's allocation of $15 billion of financial aid for the airline industry would prevent these dire consequences.

The cynics said Goodwin was trying to relieve the pressure caused by the large settlement with the pilots in 2000. Others said it was a legitimate bid for the survival of the airline.

United Airlines' balance sheet is one of the highest leveraged in the industry. The consequences of this leverage would be exacerbated as airline passengers and high-yield international and business class traffic would stay away from flying. If the costs were not brought down in some way and revenues did not recover, then servicing the outstanding debt would be difficult.

Role of Research and Development

Safety is an area the airline industry is always seeking to improve. The weakest link in air safety has been the human factor. Airlines continually seek advances in technology and training to help diminish this problem. In developing new, more reliable systems for aircraft and more advanced simulators for pilot training, the airlines can help the pilots identify and avoid problems before they become irreversible.

Airport capacity is another crucial issue facing the industry. It is usually cheaper to expand existing airports than to build new ones; thus it is crucial to squeeze more capacity out of existing airports. The FAA is responsible for making decisions regarding flight paths and determines when an airport is overcrowded. With the development of the global positioning system (GPS), a new system called *free flight* may reduce congestion and save time, energy, and the need for new airports.

Technological Investment and Analysis

Technology presents tremendous potential to cut costs and simplify the process of air travel. The airline industry has improved its operating efficiency by applying new information and communication technologies. Staffing levels can be cut because computers, modems, and ATM-like machines allow for fast and efficient communication and ticket distribution.

In 1995, airlines established home pages on the World Wide Web. These sites display information about schedules and fleets, contain financial and promotional material, give listings of in-flight movie offerings, and let travelers check the status of their frequent flyer accounts. Since 1996, because of ticketless travel, ticket purchases can be made on the Web. Once the reservation is paid for, passengers can board the airline by showing a valid driver's license. This eliminates the security surrounding ticketing stock as well as the accounting procedures required to track the used tickets.

In 1997, 2 percent of air travel was made through Internet bookings. As travelers use the Internet to obtain frequently sought information, airlines are cutting customer service operators. The Internet makes airfares publicly available and comparable on the World Wide Web. This enables consumers to compare and shop prices. Until the September 11 attack, several airlines were about to implement walk-on boarding for e-ticket passengers. Passengers would simply scan their frequent-flier cards in a terminal at the boarding door, and the system would verify the ticket. Now, you have to show your ID to a person at least three times before you can get on a plane. The government has discussed the idea of creating a database and using an iris scanner for frequent fliers. The system would be optional and would involve a simplified background check, but it would substantially improve security and reduce the lines for people who fly often.

Airlines are using technology to reduce operating costs. Early in 1995, for example, the airline industry realized the partial elimination of the traditional paper ticket. The "electronic ticket" was its replacement. It brings significant savings to airlines in ticket distribution costs. By the end of 1998, almost 40 percent of travel was booked on electronic tickets.

The airline smart card is another new product. It will provide frequent travelers with the ability to quickly identify themselves, board a flight, obtain a ticket, and pay for other products and services. It will also save airlines in ticket distribution costs, allow more passengers the use of self-service facilities, and provide better means of identification

It is predicted that most airline smart cards will eventually be cobranded cards. This means that they will be issued by banks or credit card companies and will also contain airline industry applications. The cards will have the capability to allow up to 10 airline applications. Space will also be allowed for immigration data for some governments.

All major airlines, with the exception of Southwest Airlines, are part of an intricate computer system that allows travel agents to book flights for customers. The nation's 30,000 travel agents sell 85 percent of the tickets. Major airlines are able to offer a high concentration and variety of flights along with the availability that makes it easier for agents to schedule. In addition, major airlines are able to offer more incentives to travel agents who sell the airlines seats. Earlier in 1995, most major airlines imposed a $50 cap on all seats over $500 sold by agents.

Many airlines form alliances through code sharing. Code sharing allows airlines with a market presence in one region to extend their services to those in another. This allows cost cutting through shared counters, gate space, noncompetitive computer software, and bulk purchases.

Recommendation for the Future

For airlines to survive in this highly competitive industry, they need to strive to become as cost efficient as possible. Only with low costs can airlines compete with low fares. Technology can cut costs and provide convenience as shown with the use of electronic tickets and smart cards.

In order to gain a competitive advantage in the industry, airlines should seek to gain access to emerging markets in Asia. As Asian countries such as China become more involved in the global marketplace, their rate of economic growth will rise, which will lead to a greater demand for air travel. For an airline that is able to capture this market, the returns will be considerable.

A method that could be used to capture this market is the smart card. If an airline introduces the card from the start, other airlines' procedures would seem tedious in comparison. Consumers would not want to switch from using the smart card due to the costs and inconvenience. Thus, the new market would be captured, at least, for a limited time.

Case: American Airlines

Short Description of the Company

In early 1977, hearings were held in Washington regarding airline deregulation. The hearings proceeded without event for much of the day. Phil Bakes, the legal counsel for Senator Ted Kennedy, remembers sitting in the hushed hearing room as a panel of airline witnesses finished testifying. As he glanced up from his seat, he noticed an unfamiliar, tough-looking man coming right at him. "You academic pinhead!" the man shouted, "You don't know anything. You can't deregulate this industry, you're going to wreck it. You don't know a thing!"

And so it was that this distinguished legal mind and other spectators got their first public introduction to Robert Crandall, vice president and future president and CEO of American Airlines.

While Crandall lost this initial fight over airline deregulation, from that day on, the rest of the airline industry knew he was a force to be reckoned with. Almost 20 years later, Crandall once again thrust himself into the spotlight, but this time with visions to change the airline industry forever. In the spring of 1996, Crandall announced that American Airlines and British Airways were pursuing an alliance. In a sense, it could be classified as an operational merger in that they would cooperate on pricing, sales, and marketing and share revenues, yet they would retain separate entities. The rest of the industry immediately protested in fury, claiming this would cause monopolylike conditions and shut almost everyone out of the U.S.-European gateways. Yet, Crandall, with his slicked-back hair and tireless spirit, decided he would take on government, his competitors, industry nay-sayers, and all others, to push through the merger.

As a leader in the development of the airline reservation systems, American Airlines was one of the first to take advantage of the Internet for booking flights. Access to the AA database provides consumers with more information and control.

Technology Innovations

The first move American Airlines Decision Technologies (AADT) Group made was to closely align itself with the SABRE Technologies group, to apply the expertise of the people already on that staff. As this newly defined group began to take shape, they realized their first hurdle would be to create the appropriate core modules in relational databases, and make sure the standalone systems could interact with the core. They settled on four core modules, which they felt would cover a larger percentage of the areas addressed by the decision support tools.

1. Aircraft records—As John Simmons, a director of the group explained, "it keeps track of hours, cycles, components, the airframe, the engines, and tells you exactly where you stand, whether a part is attached to an aircraft, or in a shop or a warehouse."

2. Materials—This module encompasses inventory, purchasing, warehousing, warranty tracking, and related activities.

3. Training Module—This system tracks mechanic and inspector licenses, as well as recurrent training requirements. The module provides a clear history of all personnel records.

4. Production Control—This module develops the package for a specific aircraft's base visit and then transfers the package electronically to mechanics anywhere in the world.

These modules were put into place in 1992 for American's own fleet. Sabre technologies built an interface that tied the module into mainframe applications as inventory control, flight scheduling, and financial analysis. Johnson explained the power of the tools when they are programmed to work as one:

> A mechanic can look up a part number at a terminal on the floor of the hangar and order the part; the front end interfaces with the mainframe to order the part, get it delivered to him, document the cost, assign the cost to the specific airplane he's working on, and change the decrement inventory. The inventory system then automatically reorders, to maintain current inventory levels.

Equally impressive are the labor reports, which allow a mechanic to log on to and off of a work card and indicate which piece of work is in process. This provides a real-time status of hours, materials, and labor for any ongoing project. The history database enables a mechanic to examine 20 to 30 airplanes and predict with a very large degree of certainty the exact parts that are going to be needed. This means that airlines do not have to stock everything needed for an airplane, which has a major impact on the levels of inventory that need to be maintained.

These technological strides keep American Airlines ahead of all the competitors. British Airways (BA) could not help but notice that the technologies that American was developing were those that directly addressed the main problems BA was facing. Areas like efficiency, usage, and maintenance were presenting serious problems for BA, while American was transforming itself into a technologically driven engine. If BA wanted to buy the technologies, not only would they have to make a major outlay of cash, but they would actually be supporting one of their competitors. This was due to the fact that BA would need to pay American personnel as consultants to get the systems running.

American has begun to develop technologies that would further implement the AA/BA concept of seamless travel through the alliance. Perhaps the program that promises the most obvious and appreciated results is American's newly developed AAccess electronic ticketing. Most of the major airlines went to the option of electronic ticketing in 1997. This means that the consumer does not need a hard copy or paper ticket but just has to check in at the gate with a picture ID to claim the boarding pass. American believes the AAccess program will take this concept to a new level, allowing travelers to go from their home computer to an airplane seat without any intervening stops inside the terminal.

The AAccess system combines online reservation and electronic ticketing with gate readers that allow e-ticketed passengers not checking bags to board their aircraft at 21 U.S. airports merely by inserting any credit card to identify themselves. This distinguishes the system as the only one that does not require the traveler to stop at a ticket or gate counter. American has begun testing airport kiosks that will be called AAccess self-service devices. At selected test airports, passengers will be able to change their seats, check their AAdvantage mileage, or make their own upgrades. These innovations make American more attractive as a potential partner with British Airways.

Telecommunications

American Airlines has leveraged Web technologies to reduce call center volume, sell vacant seats, and expand its affinity marketing programs. At the same time, the company is deploying intranet tools to knit together its distributed enterprise, which at any given time can have personnel spread across 115 different cities worldwide.

"What we've done is put the primary burden for developing the Internet strategy on the department heads," says Scott Nason, American's vice-president of information technology. "If you are running the operations department, it is your and your manager's job to figure out how to run your department better."

By pushing business managers to take responsibility, American has come up with solutions to difficult problems. An ever-increasing appetite for call center ticketing support has been satisfied through Internet electronic commerce. Dead inventory is being reduced through discount sales at its NetSavers site.

"The number of people buying online is still small, but there will be ongoing cost implications and broader marketing implications for the distribution of product from here on," said John Samuel, American's managing director of interactive marketing.

Data

American Airline's Revenue Accounting Data Access Resource (RADAR) started as a departmental data mart for use by 40 accountants in March 1997. It is now accessed by more than 100 users in diverse departments such as marketing and security. The data mart took about nine months to build.

RADAR consists of a Sybase IQ 11.5 running on a Sun Enterprise 5000 12-way server, which pulls data from a mainframe ticketing system that each year issues more than 125 million pieces of travel-related documents. The front end is IQ/Objects from IQ Software, which translates GUI-driven commands into valid SQL for custom, ad hoc queries.

RADAR development required several months of raking through data, looking for corrupted index. The finished data mart has 20 tables and completes the average query in seven minutes, with about 40 percent of queries being done in less than four minutes. The return on investment has exceeded expectation. During its first week RADAR saved $60,000 by spotting improper ticketing procedures. American Airlines says that the $400,000 project has paid for itself many times in straight cost savings.

Recommendation for the Future

In the fourth quarter of 1995, American placed sixth among all companies in World Wide Web advertising. The important thing is not just that American is reaching people on the Web, but that they are providing a service that the consumer wants. One example of this is Travelocity, American's consumer-oriented version of the reservation system that had previously been available only to travel agents. Consumers can now access this service online. In 1995 alone, American sold 1.6 million tickets through this medium. In addition, millions have signed up for NetSAAvers on the American Airlines website. Through this service, consumers are alerted to specials once a week via e-mail, helping to fill seats that would have otherwise remained empty. Also, by selling tickets directly to the consumer, American keeps the percentage that would otherwise go to a travel agent.

Questions

1. What is the strategic, future direction of the corporation/organization and what forces are driving this direction?

2. Upon what technologies has American Airlines relied?

3. What caused a change in the use of technology at American Airlines?

4. How successful has the technological change been?

5. What does the corporation's Web page present about its business directives?

6. How important is data to the corporation's continued success?

7. How will the capture and maintenance of customer data impact American Airlines' future?

Additional Reading

Adhikari, Richard. "E-Commerce Impact—Companies Are Finding New Ways for Web Technology to Expand Their Businesses." *InformationWeek* July 27, 1998, p. 77.

Air Transport Association, www.airlines.org/public/industry.

"American Taps Speech." *InformationWeek,* December 14, 1998, p. 34.

Cahlink, George. "From the Ground Up." *Government Executive,* January 2002, pp. 20–26.

Dwyer, Rob. "How Low and How Long?" *Airfinance Journal* 30–31 no. 244 (November 2001): pp. 30–31.

Frook, John Evan. "Future Trend: Getting Personal with Customers." *InternetWeek,* June 22, 1998, p. 11.

Furger, Roberta. "The Skies Just Got Friendlier." *PC World,* October 1996, p. 256.

Lasky, Michael S. "United versus American: Airline Software." *PC World,* November 1996, p. 104.

Manes, Stephen. "A Fatal Outcome from Misplaced Trust in 'Data'." *The New York Times,* September 17, 1996, pp. B11, C9.

Messmer, Ellen. "Revamped Web Site to Take Flight at American Airlines." *Network World,* June 15, 1998, p. 39.

Neil, Stephanie. "Airline Rides the Technology Tailwinds." *PC Week,* April 27, 1998, pp. 94–96.

Regional Airline Association, www.raa.org.

Sullivan, Kristina B. "Net to Help with In-Flight Emergencies." *PC Week,* April 21, 1997, p. 94.

"Surf to Fly." *Computerworld,* March 3, 1997, p. 59.

Tebbe, Mark. "American Airlines' Web Strategy." *PC Week,* September 30, 1996, p. N13.

Case: Southwest Airlines

Short Description of the Company

Look! Up in the sky! It's a bird. It's a plane. It's . . . Shamu? Sound crazy? If you have ever flown on Southwest Airlines, nothing seems more natural than munching peanuts inside a black-and-white painted killer whale. There's more: Imagine sitting in an aisle seat. Just as you lay your head back, a bunny-suited flight attendant pops out of the overhead bin and yells, "Surprise!" Or at the end of a trip, your flight attendant requests: "Please pass all the plastic cups to the center aisle so we can wash them and use them for the next group of passengers." These are examples of the unconventionality that characterizes Southwest Airlines. The unconventional approach carries over to the operations as well—making Southwest one of the most profitable airlines.

While most airlines rely on independent travel agents to write up a great majority of their tickets, Southwest has steadfastly refused to connect with the computer reservation system that the agents use. Agents who wish to book a Southwest flight have to pick up the phone like anyone else or go to the Southwest home page. Many try to persuade customers to pick another carrier or to make the call themselves. The result is that nearly half of all Southwest tickets are sold directly to passengers, with an annual savings to the airline of about $30 million. The percentage of Southwest tickets sold by agents is in the "mid-40s," which is far below the industry average.

Southwest Airlines, which only participates in the Sabre CRS, offers electronic booking options to agencies with more features than the website. Southwest's Direct Access software product, which enables non-Sabre agents to dial into the airline's computer system, gives an agent more information, and allows cancellations.

In 1996, Southwest Airlines became one of the first airlines on the Internet, offering "26 different types of information" from its own site, the Southwest Airlines Home Gate. The ultimate goal for the carrier was to add a booking capability so passengers could make ticketless reservations from their home personal computers. Southwest's strong customer orientation led them to invest in this customer-focused technology.

Once it added the option of bookings at the website, the company expected it to build gradually. The company advertised for the service, both online and in other media. So far it has proven to be very successful. As with other Web booking systems, Southwest's site accepts only bookings from a browser that can encrypt data.

Technology Innovations

In 1994, in a move that significantly improved the productivity of business travelers, Southwest Airlines and McCaw Cellular's Claircom Communications unveiled the world's first broadly available air-to-ground commercial fax and data service through the AirOne Communications Network. Prior to this, the wealth of data services accessible by computer on the ground were not available to the air traveler. Through the same AirOne system that delivers clear and reliable telephone calls from a plane, passengers can attach to electronic networks to get the latest news, weather, sports, and travel information or even play video games.

The AirOne system, installed throughout the Southwest fleet, provides high-quality, digital air-to-ground service using AT&T's long distance service. Passengers on all Southwest's planes can access electronic mail networks and information networks such as Compuserve, Prodigy, and Dow Jones. The AirOne System offers the most comprehensive fax and data services in the market. It can be used to send and retrieve faxes, data, and electronic mail through conventional laptop computers, portable fax machines, and personal data assistants such as the Palm Pilot.

In the above example, Southwest Airlines demonstrated that they recognized ahead of time the significant demand for this type of service because of the increased productivity and accessibility it provided to the business traveler. By providing this type of service, the airline has attracted the businessperson who does not pay out of his or her own pocket, and as a result, does not choose an airline based exclusively on low fares. This person was not exactly the company's target market before. Southwest was the first airline in the world to make this type of communication technology broadly available to its customers. This service is consistent with Southwest's history of providing POS (positively outrageous service).

The Internet

Previously, the airline had a vision that there would be a demand for ticketless travel. Their strong customer orientation, once again, led them to invest in something that would benefit the company as well. Electronic tickets provide a significant reduction of cost compared to printing, mailing, and processing paper tickets. Even more savings are generated from avoiding commissions. Before the introduction of electronic booking, approximately 40 percent of the airline's tickets were sold by agents. This is well below the industry average of 80 percent. Now that number is even smaller.

Southwest used Object Design, Inc.'s ObjectStore, an object database management system software to help build a ticketless reservation system into its Home Gate corporate website. The company was looking for a system that would make the online booking process easy to use, responsive, and quick to build. Object technology was quickly chosen and ObjectStore was selected after an exhaustive search, mainly due to the product's virtual memory mapping technology and the company's reputation. Southwest Airlines' 10 GB database stores passenger, fare, confirmation, and schedule data.

Home Gate is easy to use. Customers simply click on the departing location, their destination, travel date, and approximate departure time. Home Gate looks up the fare and schedule information and returns relevant information. The customer can then make a reservation, type in his or her credit card number, and purchase the ticket. The system provides a confirmation number. The passenger simply shows a driver's license at the gate to obtain a boarding pass. The purchasing process is secured through encryption technology. The ObjectStore database is designed specifically for building Internet and intranet applications. In the expanding Web environment, the product supports rapid development of applications, including those that call for extended data types such as image, free text, video, audio, HTML, and Java software objects.

Southwest's newest investment is shifting from Sabre Group's SAAS-hosted TPF reservation system to an in-house system developed in partnership with Hewlett-Packard. The system being developed is a hybrid of mainframe and client/server technology that combines a central inventory database with local schedules and fares databases using a proprietary operating system.

In January 2000, 25 percent of Southwest's revenue was generated from online sales. Southwest has always played games to avoid paying fees to the large reservation systems. Since the company did not rely on commissions paid to travel agents, Southwest was one of the first to seriously push customers to use its own Web-based reservation system. For example, passengers booking flights through the online system receive a free round-trip ticket after flying only four flights—compared to eight flights (per year) required for traditional reservations.

Network

Southwest migrated from a legacy multiprotocol network to a routed TCP/IP network in 1998. While the frame relay WAN is currently in its infancy phase and handles primarily operational traffic, it is eventually slated to handle passenger reservations and updates. The WAN currently transports traffic from operational applications such as e-mail, accounting, and procurement and links the check-in terminals at 51 airports, 9 reservations hubs, Southwest's headquarters, and 20 additional locations.

Questions

1. What is the strategic direction of Southwest Airlines?

2. What is causing a change in the use of technology at Southwest Airlines?

3. What does the corporation say about its financial ability to embark on a major technological program of advancement?

4. What does the corporation's Web page present about its business directives?

5. How will technology impact the industry?

6. What role does data play in the future of Southwest Airlines?

Additional Reading

Cravotta, Nicholas. "Network Health Remedies Frame Relay Bottlenecks." *Network,* April 1, 1998.

Dash, Julekha. "Soft Skills Soar at Southwest." *Software Magazine,* April 1998, p. 14.

Dryden, Patrick. "Airline's Network on Standby." *Computerworld,* November 24, 1997, pp. 53–55.

Garvey, Martin J. "RS/6000 Moves Up—S70 Line, Solutions Focus Make IBM More Attractive for New Users' ERP Apps." *InformationWeek,* December 21, 1998, p. 22.

Greenberg, Paul A. "Southwest Airlines Projects $1B in Online Sales," *E-Commerce Times,* February 29, 2000.

Hoffman, Thomas. "Airline Turbocharges Schedule Efficiency." *Computerworld,* March 25, 1996, pp. 1–3.

Karpain, Gregory. "Ticketless Travel Takes Off, Thanks to ODBMS Technology." *Databased Web Advisor,* August 1997, pp. 38–41.

Kathleen, Melymuka. "Sky King." *Computerworld,* September 28, 1998, p. 68.

"Middleware Deal." *Computerworld,* December 7, 1998, p. 51.

Shein, Esther. "Web Spinning New Help Desk Assistance." *PC Week,* September 1, 1997, pp. 85–87.

Appendix

Building Forms in Access

Database tables have to be designed carefully to store the data efficiently. But no one wants to enter data directly into the tables. Many of the tables consist of rows and columns of raw numbers—it is difficult to remember ID numbers and easy to make mistakes. Consider the tables needed for a simple Sale system: Customer, Item, Sale, and SaleItem. The SaleItem table lists items purchased on a given sale, one row (SaleID, ItemID, Quantity) might look like: 1, 15, 1. Picture hundreds of these rows and you quickly realize that a form is necessary. Instead, applications need to have data entry forms that resemble the paper forms that users understand. Microsoft Access has a form wizard that helps you build these forms.

The Form Wizard

To use the wizard to build a new form, click the Forms tab in Access, and select the option to create a new form using the wizard. As shown in Fig 6.1A, the most important step is to carefully choose the columns that will be used on the form. For the sales form, you first want to include all of the columns (SaleID, SaleDate, CustomerID) from the Sale table. Then, because it would be nice to see and be able to edit some customer data, select the Customer table and select LastName, FirstName, Phone, Address, City, State, ZIP—do not select the CustomerID column. Next, the Sales form needs a repeating list of items purchased, so choose the

SaleItem table and select the ItemID and Quantity columns. Finally, select the ListPrice column from the Item table.

The wizard will build the basic form shown in Fig 6.2A. Notice the subform and notice that the overall layout needs

FIGURE 6.1A
Access Form Wizard. To build a Sale form, begin by selecting all of the columns from the Sale table (click the >> button). The wizard will help build the form, but do not press Next or Finish just yet. You need to add columns from some other tables.

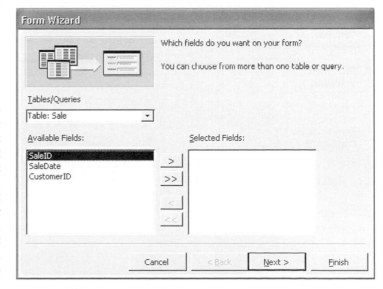

some work to make it easier to use. Design mode enables you to use mouse drag commands to change the size and location of the various text boxes.

More important, consider the CustomerID box. You cannot expect customers or sales clerks to memorize customer numbers. Instead, they should be able to select the appropriate customer from a list. So, as shown in Fig 6.3A, delete the CustomerID box and replace it with a Combo box. When the Combo box wizard asks you to select Lookup values, you choose the table (Customer), and the columns needed (CustomerID, LastName, FirstName, and Phone). When the form is run, the Combo box goes to the Customer table, gets the list of items you chose, and displays them as options. When the user selects a customer, the selected CustomerID (from the Customer table) is entered into the CustomerID column of the Sale table.

The final step is to clean up the subform—replacing the ItemID box with a combo box, and adding an ItemValue text box to multiply Quantity by ListPrice, and then adding up that subtotal. Figure 6.4A shows the properties needed to create the subtotal box. The main step is to enter the value of box as a formula: =Sum([Quantity]*[ListPrice]). Make sure you change the Name property to SubTotal—which tells us more than the default name of Text12.

The final form is shown in Figure 6.5A. It has one additional step on the main form. You need to add the Subtotal text box which copies the value computed on the subform. The formula is shown in Figure 6.4A. Copy it carefully because it is a little tricky. You should create and enter a few sample sales. Then go look at the data in the underlying tables to see what the form is doing. Notice how much easier it is to enter data on the form instead of directly into the tables.

FIGURE 6.2A

Form built by the wizard. It includes the selected elements, but needs some work to make it easier to read and use.

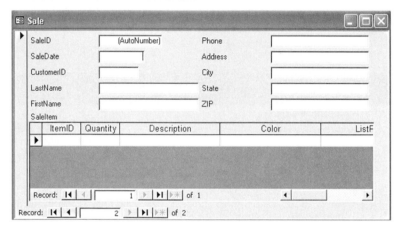

FIGURE 6.3A

Creating a Combo box. The Combo box wizard builds a selection list from the Customer table. Users choose one customer, and the matching CustomerID is entered into the Sale table. Users see only the names, and do not have to memorize ID numbers.

1. **Lookup values**

2. **Customer table**

3. **CustomerID, LastName, FirstName, Phone**

4. **Store value in: CustomerID**

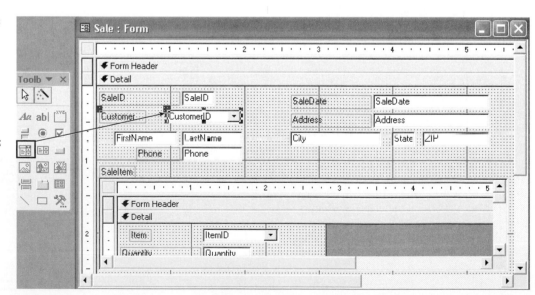

Similar wizards and a design view exist to create reports. In many ways, reports are easier than forms because you do not enter data. To create reports, you first build a query that contains all of the data you want to see. Then use the report wizard to set the main layout of the table. Finally, use design view to align items, set colors, and specify formats.

Exercises

1. Build the Sale form described in this appendix. The sample database with the tables is on the Student CD. [C06ApdxSaleForm.mdb]

2. Create additional forms for the sample database, including a simple form for adding customers and new items. Put a button on the Sales form that opens the Customer form and enables users to add new customers. [Hint: A command button wizard does most of the work.]

3. Create a report that prints a receipt for the individual sale. Put a button on the Sales form to print (preview) the report. Make sure you print only the receipt for the Sale being displayed. Hint: Build the report first, then use the command button wizard to specify that it should only be printed for the given SaleID.

FIGURE 6.4A

Creating a subtotal. Add a text box to the Form Footer, and enter the formula: =Sum([Quantity]*[ListPrice]). Be sure to set the Name property of SubTotal.

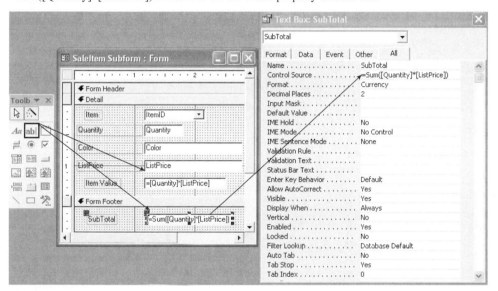

FIGURE 6.5A

The final form. The subtotal is a new box that simply copies the value computed on the subform with the formula: =[SaleItem Subform].[Form].[SubTotal]

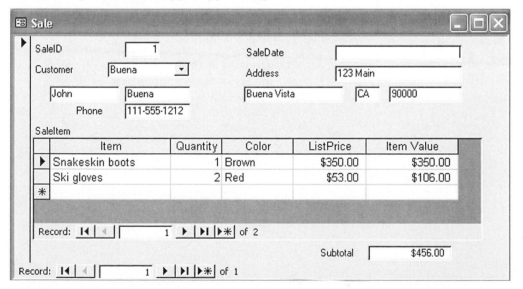

CHAPTER SEVEN

Integration of Information

What you will learn in this chapter

- Why is integration of data important in business?

- How do enterprise resource planning systems make businesses run better through integration of data?

- How do workgroup tools improve business integration?

- Why are data warehouses important in integrating data?

- How does the Internet help integrate data on different types of systems?

- How can a group decision support system help managers achieve a consensus?

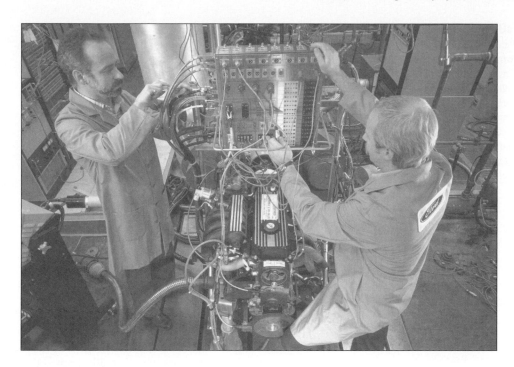

As a large manufacturer, Ford relies on integrating information to help design cars faster and with input from engineers around the world.

Ford Motor Company

In 1996, Alex Trotman, president, CEO, and chairman of the board of Ford Motor Company hosted a Ford family meeting. Trotman hosted the Ford family every year since his appointment to CEO in 1993. Approximately 20 Fords gathered to tour the facilities, drive new models on the test track, lunch with the board of directors, and drill Trotman on everything from sales in Latin America, productive capacity, and environmental issues to—important to the Fords—dividends.

The Ford family received roughly $88 million in dividends in 1995. Trotman knew the value of keeping on the good side of the Ford family. Although the company is publicly held, the family exerts significant influence on it. They are also protective of their investment. One outside director said, "With all this cash, if it weren't for the family, I'd take over this company." After former chairman and CEO Donald Petersen rubbed the family the wrong way, he retired prematurely. Trotman, however, hoped to retain the Ford family support.

On January 1, 1999, the disappointed Ford family replaced Trotman as CEO with Jacques Nasser. Nasser came from the international side of Ford which was experiencing strong sales. In 2001, a series of crises, capped by the Firestone tire recall on the Explorer led to high tensions in Ford and in the industry. On October 29, 2001, Bill Ford, Jr., fired Jacques Nasser and installed himself as CEO. Analysts agree that change was needed. Cash on hand at the conservatively run company had shrunk tremendously and Standard & Poor's had downgraded its credit rating. On the other hand, analysts are concerned that Bill and his top management have limited experience.

Overview

Richard: I'm sick of it.

Ally: What?

Richard: Every time I try to get information from the team in Japan, they send me the wrong data. And the accountant keeps complaining that they need to start

FIGURE 7.1

To simplify management, firms are often split into departments. Yet, they must be able to work as a single, integrated company. Information systems can help managers improve the integration and control of their firm.

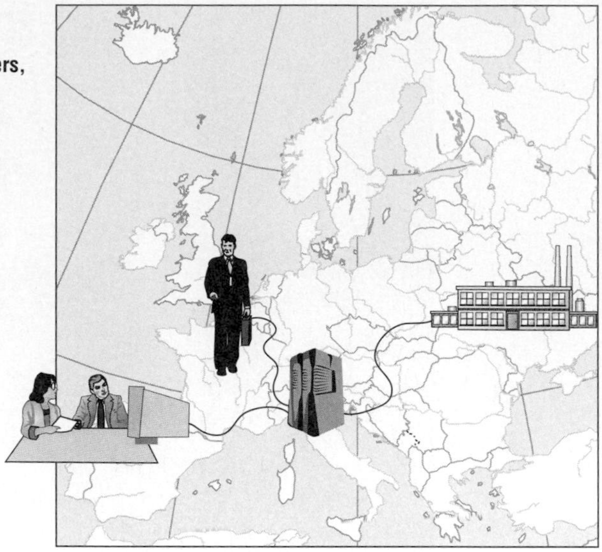

Everyone in the company including managers, salespeople, and engineers needs access to the same data across the organization.

using a different depreciation system. And then they complain that they have to use what they have, and that if I really wanted that data I should have asked for it . . .

Elaine: Calm down, you're creating too much stress.

Ally: Well, I've been having problems with them too. It's impossible to call them, and they aren't very good at replying to e-mail.

Elaine: Maybe we should try using some of those new groupware tools we saw at that demo last week. You know, where we can create a document on a website that everyone can use. And the software automatically keeps track of the changes and even makes it easy to get the older versions.

Ally: Hey, that's not bad. And we can use a Web discussion system so we track what everyone said. And maybe we can use Net Meeting when we need to discuss the complicated graphs.

Elaine: I just read about some ERP software that can handle all of the accounting problems—it produces reports using different rules for each country. But I heard it is expensive, so Richard will probably not buy it . . .

Richard: Hmmmm

Introduction

Coordinating the many aspects of business requires a wide variety of information from many sources. Perhaps you need to make a decision about how to market a new product. You would retrieve a variety of customer data from the sales database. You would use reports from the production team and a collection of graphs created from the initial marketing surveys. You could use a spreadsheet to analyze this information along with various marketing strategies. Along the way, you would probably use accounting data to create graphs to display costs and projected profits for the various cases. Finally, you would use a word processor to create a formal report for your supervisors that describes the choices and your analysis. The report would contain your writing along with the graphs, spreadsheet tables, and some of the data.

Trends

Consider a sample business decision where you are working as a manager at a department store. Three reports are produced by the central computer: the daily sales report (Figure 7.2), returned merchandise log (Figure 7.3), and a commission report (Figure 7.4). At the end of each week, you create a report that evaluates the profitability of each department. You also maintain a line graph that shows the net sales number for each week. At the end of the month, you write several pages of comments about the trends and the monthly activities. The report includes copies of the data and your graphs. It is sent to upper management. A small example is shown in Figure 7.5.

To see how the use of computers is changing, consider how this report might have been produced by managers at different points in time. As shown in Figure 7.6, in the 1970s, the central computer tracked all sales and printed the three reports. At the end of the week, a manager computed the net sales by hand and drew the graph on graph paper. A secretary would then type the report on a typewriter and staple the graph at the end of the document.

In the 1980s, personal computers with spreadsheets and word processors were introduced to the business world. At this point, the manager entered the numbers from the reports into a spreadsheet by hand. The spreadsheet did the calculations and created the graphs with only a few commands. A word processor was used to type the report. The spreadsheet printouts and the graphs were stapled into the final report.

In the 1990s, the process was simpler. First, a database management system held the sales data. Spreadsheet commands retrieved exactly the data needed, performed the calculations, and produced the graphs. The report was still typed on a word processor; however, the spreadsheets and graphs were automatically copied into the word processor document. This process was facilitated by software suites that consist of software packages designed to exchange data.

As shown in Figure 7.7, in the 2000s, managers can buy integrated software to instantly produce all of the reports and graphs, then click on items to obtain more detailed information.

Think about what happens if some of the original data is changed. Just before you send the report to management, someone calls and says that the sales figures for half the items in the housewares department are wrong. In the 1970s example, the manager had to recompute all of the totals, redraw the graphs, and rewrite the report. The 1980s manager had to change the numbers in the spreadsheet, rewrite sections of the report, and print the new graphs. The 1990s manager would simply tell the word processor to reprint the report. The word processor would automatically tell the spreadsheet to get the new data, update the graphs, and transfer the results to the final copy. With a truly integrated system, the data would always be correct, and reports and graphs would always have current values.

FIGURE 7.2

Sales Report. Businesses create many different reports. Begin with this small excerpt of the daily sales report. It itemizes sales for each department.

Daily Sales Report

February 7, 2004

Department	Item#	Q Sold	Price	Value
House	1153	52	2.95	153.40
	5543	13	0.59	7.67
W. Clothing	5563	1	87.32	87.32
	7765	4	54.89	219.56
	9986	2	15.69	31.38
Shoes	1553	2	65.79	131.58
	6673	1	29.39	29.39
Total sales:				**660.30**

FIGURE 7.3

Returned merchandise. To evaluate customer service and quality, the store tracks returned merchandise and produces a daily report by item number.

Returned Merchandise Log

February 7, 2004

Item#	Q	Price	Value
1153	3	2.95	8.85
3353	6	27.59	165.54
4453	2	15.95	31.90
8878	1	24.95	24.95
Total	**12**		**231.24**

FIGURE 7.4

Commissions. Managers compute daily sales by employee and determine the commission based on each employee's commission rate.

Commissions

February 7, 2004

Emp #	Name	Dept	Sales	Rate	Amount
1143	Jones	House	543.95	5%	27.20
2895	Brown	M.Clothing	775.35	4%	31.01
4462	Smith	W.Clothing	1,544.52	5%	77.23
7893	Torrez	Shoes	876.93	6%	52.62
9963	Cousco	M.Clothing	589.47	5%	29.47

FIGURE 7.5

Final report. The weekly sales analysis report requires selecting and aggregating data from each of the other reports. The text, data, and graph are combined into a final document.

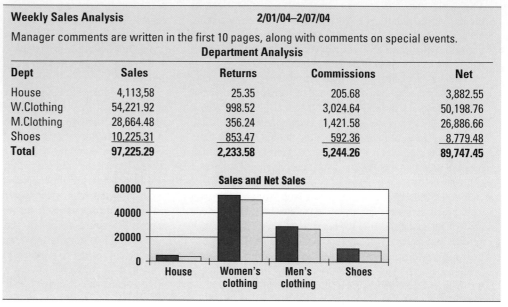

Weekly Sales Analysis   **2/01/04–2/07/04**

Manager comments are written in the first 10 pages, along with comments on special events.

Department Analysis

Dept	Sales	Returns	Commissions	Net
House	4,113,58	25.35	205.68	3,882.55
W.Clothing	54,221.92	998.52	3,024.64	50,198.76
M.Clothing	28,664.48	356.24	1,421.58	26,886.66
Shoes	10,225.31	853.47	592.36	8,779.48
Total	**97,225.29**	**2,233.58**	**5,244.26**	**89,747.45**

FIGURE 7.6

Middle management over time. The methods used to create integrated reports have changed over the past three decades. With simple transaction systems, managers computed the totals, drew graphs, and had secretaries type the report. With the adoption of personal computers, middle managers (or their secretaries) reentered the data into spreadsheets and used a word processor to print the final report. With an integrated system, top managers can use a personal computer to query the database, draw the graphs, and produce the final report.

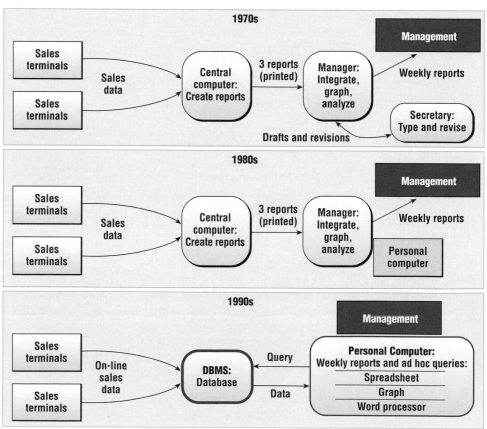

FIGURE 7.7

Integration with ERP. An ERP system can integrate almost all aspects of the company into one huge database. Either directly or through an executive information system, management can retrieve any report or piece of data by selecting options.

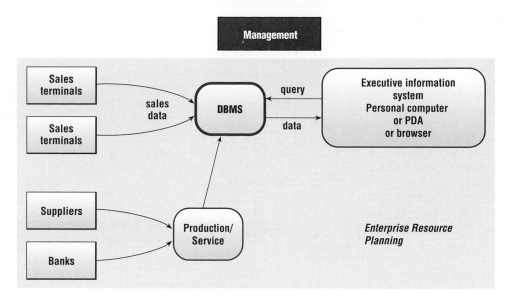

Integrating data is only the first step. Modern companies are increasingly based on teams, where individual employees from various departments are assigned to projects. Each person may be assigned separate tasks, but the work must be assembled into a final project evaluated and approved by the entire team. You need tools that track the progress of the group, let multiple people work on the same documents at the same time, and track the history of changes.

A difficulty that arises when you are trying to integrate information is the diversity in hardware and software. For example, each software package uses its own format to store data files. As a result, there are more than 50 different formats for word-processing documents. The problem multiplies rapidly when you consider that most of these formats change with each software revision. To integrate these different types of information, you need software that can read many different file types, or the software needs to use a common format.

One trend in software is the adoption of enterprise systems that are designed to hold data in a central database. These systems provide consistent data across the company. A trend in personal productivity software is toward packages that work together by sharing data through links. When the underlying data changes, the software automatically picks up the new data and updates the document. The concept is similar to a spreadsheet formula that refers to other cells. The key difference is that you can refer to data in different programs, such as transferring data from a spreadsheet into a word processor. With a network, the data can be located in different departments throughout the business.

Integration in Business

For a business to be successful, it needs to integrate information from all aspects of the organization. Figure 7.8 shows that modern management techniques of just-in-time production and mass customization require a high degree of internal integration, as well as strong links to suppliers and customers.

Most companies are split into functional departments, with varying degrees of independence. However, there are always pressures and decisions that affect the entire organization. For instance, changes in products or manufacturing schedules clearly affect the marketing department. Because these changes will probably alter the cash flows of the company, the accounting and finance departments also need to be aware of the changes.

In the 1960s and 1970s, computer systems were built for individual departments and areas within the company. In many companies, these systems became islands. They were focused on one task and did not share data with each other. For instance, the accounting department collected the basic transaction data and produced the necessary accounting reports.

FIGURE 7.8

Total data integration begins with the vendors, tracks data through all operations of the firm, and incorporates information from customers. Each area in the firm has easy access to data from any other location. This integrated data is used to make better decisions by enabling managers to focus on the big picture instead of on local solutions.

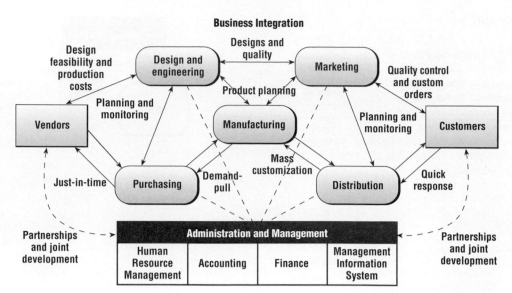

Anyone in the company who wanted to use this data relied on paper printouts of the standard reports. When spreadsheets arrived in the 1980s, the basic accounting numbers were often rekeyed into spreadsheets in other departments. Besides wasting employee time in retyping numbers that were already stored on a computer, this practice caused more errors from mistyping the data. Additionally, consider that when the accounting department changes the numbers, some users of the data might not get the updated versions, and people would attempt to make decisions on outdated data.

Computer use in most companies began with transaction-processing systems. Because transaction systems are structured and there is considerable experience at this level, it is a logical place to begin. However, it is also tempting to treat each transaction separately: (1) Payroll services can be purchased from a specialized data-processing company, so the data will be handled separately from the other corporate data. (2) A sales order-processing system might be constructed independently of the inventory control system. (3) Process control systems to handle manufacturing tend to be isolated because the data (e.g., robotic control signals) are different from the data used in the rest of the company. (4) Similarly, the corporate accounting system is often developed as a stand-alone product. Journal entries are created by copying data in reports produced by other systems. Although each of these transaction systems offers management advantages to their respective departments, it is difficult for managers to use data from other departments. Also, independent systems make it difficult for executives to share data and evaluate interrelationships between the departments.

The amount of data integration needed in a company often depends on the management structure of the firm. Some firms are highly decentralized, so that each business unit makes its own decisions and functions independently of the others. Typically in these situations, only accounting data (profit/loss) are integrated and reported to upper management.

On the other hand, some organizations are much more integrated. In your economics courses you were shown the difference between vertically and horizontally integrated firms. Consider a vertically integrated firm such as an oil company that functions at different levels of production (including oil exploration, drilling, transportation, storage, and retail sales). Although an oil exploration team may not need access to daily fuel sales in New York state, they do need to forecast future demand for oil. Likewise, the retail sales division does not need to know the daily costs associated with drilling for oil, yet they might need to track deliveries and communicate with the corporate office.

Consider a horizontally integrated firm such as Wal-Mart with retail stores in many different cities. It achieves lower costs by combining the buying power of all its stores. By coordinating sales, warehouses, and distribution, Wal-Mart can negotiate better prices with manufacturers. Additionally, Wal-Mart reduces operating costs by standardizing

Many organizations have experienced high costs and long implementation times when converting to ERP software. The challenges are great: you must replace the entire financial accounting system, reorganize the business operations, train everyone, and then learn to evaluate the data. ERP vendors responded to these problems by creating preconfigured versions of the tools—complete with implementation tools and templates to help quickly customize the systems. The systems are targeted at midsize firms ($100 million to $1 billion in revenue). Faster implementation means lower implementation and consulting costs, less disruption to the company, and quicker access to the benefits of the ERP software. Of course, "rapid" does not mean you can install a complete ERP system next week. The following table provides sample installation times:

Company	Vendor	Time
Cognex	PeopleSoft	6 months
Robinson Nugent	PeopleSoft	8 months
Imperial Holly	PeopleSoft	8 months
Dopaco	SAP	8 months
Borden	PeopleSoft	9 months
Rehrig	QAD	10 months
CIDCO	PeopleSoft	11 months
Yuwasa-Exide	Baan	11 months

Source: Adapted from Robert N. West and Murrell Shields, "Up and Running in Nine Months," *Management Accounting,* December 1998, pp. 20–24.

management practices (and information systems) across all the stores. By integrating information from all stores, it is easier for Wal-Mart to forecast customer demands. Also, by networking the store information systems, managers who experience higher sales of certain products can request shipments from stores that are not selling the item as rapidly.

Manufacturing firms can gain additional benefits from integrating data. Benefits like just-in-time inventory, total quality management, and mass customization can only exist with the tight integration of data. The National Bicycle Industrial Company of Japan illustrates how integrated data is used to provide customized products to mass markets.

Enterprise Resource Planning

Enterprise resource planning (ERP) is the current state-of-the-art in integrated information in business systems. The systems incorporate data from financial accounting, logistics, and human resource management. The field is dominated by large, expensive software packages from companies such as SAP, Peoplesoft, Oracle, Lawson, and J. D. Edwards. The systems use databases, processes, and rules to provide up-to-the-minute data on the major financial issues in a firm. One of the key points of ERP systems is that they run on top of a DBMS, hence, all of the data is centralized and accessible via DBMS queries and reports.

ERP systems handle all of the financial accounting systems. They also emphasize purchasing, human resource management, and investment management. The systems are tailored for specific businesses and can focus on areas such as manufacturing, research and development, and retail sales.

One of the primary strengths of the ERP systems is that they were designed to handle data for large companies operating in an international environment. In the late 1990s, many companies chose to install commercial ERP systems, instead of trying to modify their existing systems to handle the year 2000 problem.

International Environment

Several features are important to firms operating in an international environment. First, all menus and reports should be available in several languages, so clerks and managers can use the language they prefer. Second, the system should handle currency conversion automatically, so managers can view reports in any currency. Similarly, conversions should be capable of being fixed at a point in time, so that when items are transferred they can be valued at the exchange rate in effect at that time, even if the rate changes later.

Reality Bytes — Real Time Enterprise Computing

In 2000, Cisco was flying high. Based on stock valuation, briefly, it was the most valuable company in the world. With solid products and a substantial market share, it was widely admired. Cisco also touted its substantial information system—which was an advanced integrated system. In spring 2001, Cisco almost self-destructed. With the fallout in the telecommunications industry, orders evaporated and Cisco did not notice quickly enough. The company had to write off $1 billion in parts inventory that had been ordered to build products that were no longer needed. Despite increased sales for the year, Cisco lost another $2 billion in profits. Even the advanced, integrated information system was not sufficient. Companies are now talking about Real Time Enterprise Computing (RTEC) systems. RTEC systems not only integrate the internal systems, they tie to suppliers and customers; collecting and analyzing data in real time. All data is collected continuously and financial statements and analysis are created at any time and always up to date.

Source: Adapted from Michael S. Malone, "Internet II: Rebooting America," *Forbes,* September 10, 2001; and Scott Berinato, "What Went Wrong at Cisco?" *CIO Magazine,* August 1, 2001.

A more complex feature for the international environment is the ability to produce reports following the rules of individual nations. For example, a company with subsidiaries in many nations would need to produce reports that follow the rules (e.g., depreciation) for each specific nation, and then produce consolidated reports following the rules of the home nation.

A third complicating factor arises from taxes. In addition to the rates, the rules and procedures vary by nation. The rules are particularly important for payroll and benefit applications. A good enterprise application automatically incorporates the rules for each nation and state.

Financial Accounting

The accounting system is a core feature of an ERP. Eventually, all transactions must be recorded in the general ledger accounts. The accounts fulfill the standards required by each nation. They are used to create the standard accounting reports. The systems provide flexibility by enabling managers to create their own subaccounts and subledgers, which are used to create reports on additional topics. An important feature of the accounting system is that standard accounting reports can be generated at any time for any section of the company. The ERP system automatically uses the most up-to-date data.

In addition to standard financial accounting, the systems manage assets and provide common treasury functions such as cash management. The systems also provide basic audit trails and other accounting controls. To make them easier to use, most ERP systems provide enterprise (or executive) information system (EIS) capabilities. Managers can examine data at virtually any level of detail. From summary values, they can drill down to more detail.

Logistics

Logistics consists of the operations required to purchase materials, deliver them to the warehouses and factories, and sell and distribute products. It incorporates traditional MRP analysis, quality control, accounts payable, and accounts receivable.

In today's manufacturing companies, logistics is an important component of just-in-time inventory and demand-driven production. Using an integrated system, the marketing department gets up-to-the-minute data on customer demands. Marketers can cooperate with designers and engineers to develop new products. The specifications can be transferred to the production machines and raw material orders can be generated for vendors. Purchasing and payments can be tracked and generated over EDI networks—including the Internet. As orders are generated and inventory levels change, the accounting data is automatically updated—providing instant analysis of profitability.

For service-oriented companies, logistics involves service management tasks. The ERP systems can track customers, identify repeat customers, monitor service contracts, help salespeople with call management, and handle automatic billing and accounts receivable issues.

FIGURE 7.9

ERP integration. Although data can be distributed, it is still integrated across the organization. Changes in one item (inventory) cause changes in all related databases. Reports are generated from current data.

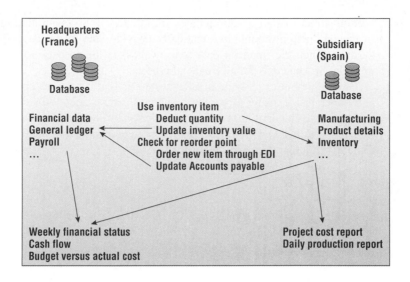

Human Resource Management

Payroll is a complicated function, particularly in a multinational environment involving different rules and currencies. Even in a single state, the issues of benefits, state and federal rules, and legal issues arising from child support make handling payroll a complex task.

Today's HRM departments handle such additional tasks as recruitment, training, travel, and organizational planning. Each step must be documented and requires a variety of federal and state reports. In addition to these basic tasks, most of the major ERP systems enable HRM departments to offer Web access to basic data. For example, employees can use the Web to check on their taxes, change their withholding status, and sign up for benefit plans and training sessions.

Integration

Integration is probably the most important feature of the ERP systems. All the data is stored in a central database; hence, data is entered only one time (but into a double-entry accounting system). All reports are generated from the base data. Custom queries and reports can be generated through the DBMS.

Consider a simple example. A manufacturing plant takes an item from inventory. The system instantly adjusts the inventory quantity on hand. It also updates the financial value of the inventory holdings on the general ledger and any subledgers that utilize that figure. New orders can be triggered automatically with the orders and payments sent through common EDI mechanisms. All of the changes are made automatically. When managers request reports, the new data is automatically incorporated and displayed using current currency conversions.

The key point to remember is that all of the transactions and accounts are integrated. Managers can request reports by using any combination of data at any time—and each report will use the most up-to-date information.

Most of the major ERP systems also utilize distributed hardware and software. Hence, the database can be split into many pieces stored in different locations. As changes occur in one location, they are automatically distributed across the network to the other locations. The company can add a subsidiary with its own processing support. Yet, all of the new data is readily accessible to managers throughout the company.

Figure 7.9 provides a simple example of data integration. When a factory uses an inventory item, the system reduces the current inventory count. It also changes the inventory valuation in the general ledger. The item usage might trigger a purchase through the EDI system, which must also be recorded—along with the accounts payable change. Since the databases are shared across the organization, all changes are automatically included when new reports are generated.

Remember that all of the modules are integrated. So manufacturing schedules developed in the production module automatically provide data to the payroll system and personnel systems. Then the financial data (e.g., wages) is linked back to the general ledger, which provides updated data for all financial reports.

One important catch with an ERP system is that it requires changes to the way the company operates. In many cases, these changes can be good—for example, it forces everyone to follow the standard accounting procedures. In other cases, the ERP is too inflexible and interferes with the way the company operates. Managers have to carefully evaluate the tradeoffs of integration and flexibility.

Customer Relationship Management

Although customers are important to all businesses, the Internet and wireless applications add new dimensions to managing customer relationships. One problem is the expanding number of customer contact points, from sales representatives, to call centers, to websites, and wireless connections. Customers expect merchants and suppliers to remember actions and decisions that were made earlier—regardless of the method of contact. Consequently, companies need integrated systems that instantly provide all details of customer contacts. The new technologies also provide innovative methods to keep in touch with customers and identify their specific needs to sell additional products and services. Several software tools have been developed to improve **customer relationship management (CRM)**.

Multiple Contact Points

One of the greatest challenges facing a company today is the multiple sources of contact points with customers. Most of the original systems designed to handle these interactions are separate. Salespeople often keep their own records; Internet support systems may not be totally connected to the sales fulfillment centers; faxes are rarely integrated into the online customer files. But customers assume that when they talk to one person, that person has records of all the prior interactions.

At first glance, it appears that it would be straightforward to build an integrated application to hold all customer interaction data. Of course, it would be a lot of data and would take time to build the application. But the real challenge lies in getting everyone to enter all of the data. Consider the situation of a salesperson who has invested time and collected substantial data on product preferences and customer work environments. That information gives an advantage to the salesperson. Why would the salesperson be willing to share it?

Customers with multiple divisions and many different product tracks also add complications to CRM. The system has to be able to track transactions, questions, and issues by a

Reality Bytes   CRM in a Crisis

On September 11, a Northwest Airlines flight from San Jose to Minneapolis aborted its takeoff after learning of the hijackings and crashes in New York, Washington, D.C., and Pennsylvania. Two Hewlett-Packard managers on that flight raced back to their offices and assembled crisis teams to track any employees and customers located near the crash sites. Within minutes, the team lead by Barbara Stinnett was able to retrieve names and contact numbers of every HP customer in the affected World Trade Center buildings. The list included details on every computer, server, and printer in those offices. Using this customer relationship management software, HP was able to immediately track replacement products and notify the nearest warehouses and resellers to provide the equipment. Similarly, the Chubb Corporation, an insurance company, used CRM software to quickly generate a list of all policyholders who lived within one mile of the disaster, and was able to contact the customers. Other companies, like State Farm and New York Life Insurance, did not have a CRM system in place and had no easy way to identify or contact customers. A State Farm spokeswoman notes "We had to wait for them to come to us."

Source: Adapted from Chris Gaither, "Software to Track Customers' Needs Helped Firms React," *New York Times,* October 1, 2001.

variety of factors (date, product, company, person, and so on). The system also needs a sophisticated search routine so users can find exactly the pieces of data required.

Feedback, Individual Needs, and Cross Selling

The main purpose of CRM systems is to provide individual attention to each customer to improve sales. By tracking prior purchases, you understand the status of your customers. By providing new channels of communication, you improve the ability of customers to provide feedback to comment on products and services and to make suggestions for improvements. By identifying patterns in purchases, you can develop new ideas for cross selling. If a group of customers tends to purchase several products, you can search the CRM database to find customers with only part of the solution, and have your salespeople demonstrate the advantages of the entire suite—using the other customers as examples and references.

The flip side to CRM is that collecting and coordinating substantial data about the customer can lead to privacy problems. As long as the data is secured and used internally, few problems arise. But firms still need to be sensitive to customer wishes about unsolicited contacts. In fact, customer privacy requests need to be part of the CRM system. The issues are more complex when the selling firm has multiple divisions, and each one wants to push new products to existing customers. The marketing staff needs to use the CRM system to coordinate and monitor all contacts.

Wireless applications provide even more options for CRM. Your salespeople can stay in constant contact with the corporate database. They can retrieve current shipping status, or detailed customer information during a sales call. They can forward questions or comments, which can be analyzed and answered immediately.

Workgroup Integration

Cooperation and teamwork have always been important in managing a company. Today, as firms remove layers of middle management and as they focus on teamwork, integration and sharing become crucial. Making decisions requires input from different people. Problems that arise are solved by creating a team of workers—often from different disciplines.

Picture yourself as a manager in a modern corporation. In addition to your day-to-day tasks, you will be asked to serve on various teams to solve problems. You could be working with three or four different groups simultaneously. How do you organize your work? How do you remember the status of each project? How do you keep in touch with the team members? How do you keep track of documents, comments, and revisions for each team? How do you know which team members are falling behind and need more help? Now assume that the team members are scattered across different locations. You cannot afford to schedule meetings every week. How do you keep the project moving and make sure that all important ideas are incorporated in the final decision?

Software tools known as **groupware** have been created to help answer these questions and make it easier for teams to work together. Groupware tools are designed to make it easy for several people to work on a document at the same time, regardless of where each one is located. Lotus (IBM) Notes and Microsoft Exchange are two tools based on e-mail that are often used as a foundation for groupware applications. Essentially all shared data is stored in a giant e-mail database with some links between related messages. Probably their strongest feature is the shared calendars that enable team members to schedule meetings.

On the other hand, Microsoft has slowly been integrating many of the features into the standard Office products (Word, Excel, PowerPoint). Microsoft Office XP did not change much in the way that components worked; however, it did add several Internet tools to facilitate teamwork. Most of the tools use standard Web protocols, so authorized users can use them even when they are traveling. A special website has to be created to support the tools. Generally, this website should be run on a company server, using standard security precautions. If you want higher security, you can run the website as a secure site and encrypt the data transmissions. Small companies might consider obtaining

Group decision support systems can be used to coordinate meetings, record notes, take votes, and encourage participation. As shown in this system by Ventana Corporation, each participant enters data in a PC, with summary results displayed on the central screen.

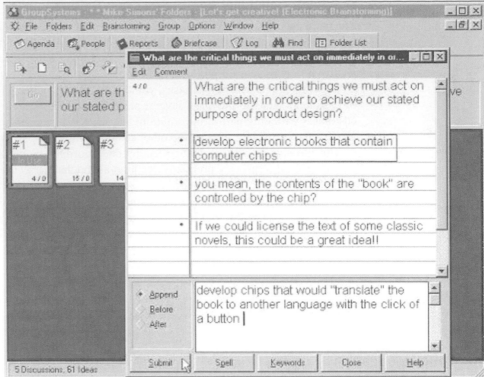

the service from their ISPs. The server technology is referred to as **SharePoint**. Participants are required to log in to the system, and security controls can specify detailed access rights.

Announcements and Lists

It is always amazing to learn how difficult it is to contact everyone on a team. People work on many projects, at different times, in different locations. Consequently, even simple information can be hard to share. Basic announcements are useful for these situations. Announcements are short messages that are displayed to everyone—generally they are displayed prominently on the first page. Lists can be created to display timetables for tasks, contact names, or any other category needed by the group.

The power of sharing lists through a website is that members of the team can see the lists at any time. As authorized members make changes, everyone has access to the current data. Additionally, the lists can be organized and searched by various categories, such as deadline, project sponsor, or participant. Some standard lists exist in SharePoint, such as contacts and schedules. Additional lists can be created at any time.

Web Discussions and Surveys

Most students are familiar with Web-based discussion groups. SharePoint implements a basic news-type service shown in Figure 7.10 where participants can post questions or reply to comments made by other members. Discussion administrators establish topics and can specify the roles of the other team members, such as the ability to read or reply to comments. Discussion groups are useful on team projects to discuss issues that arise. The

FIGURE 7.10

Discussion system. Team members can enter questions and reply to individual comments. Comments are stored in a database, making it easy to search for (filter) specific issues.

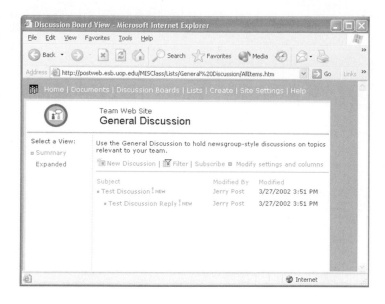

FIGURE 7.11

Create a survey. You add individual questions to the survey. They can have a variety of formats. After filling in the template for each question, users can enter data over the Web, and you can instantly see the responses on another Web page.

Team Web Site
Quality Survey: Add Question

Use this page to add a question to this survey.

Question and Type
Type your question and select the type of answer.

Question:
Service quality in the finance department can be improved

The type of answer to this question is:
- ◯ Single line of text
- ◯ Multiple lines of text
- ◯ Number (1, 1.0, 100)
- ◯ Currency ($, ¥, £)
- ◯ Date and Time (11/02/2001 12:15)
- ◯ Lookup (information already on this site)
- ◉ Choice (menu to choose from)
- ◯ Yes/No (check box)

Optional settings for your question
Specify detailed options for the type of answer you selected. Show me more information.

Require a response to this question:
◉ Yes   ◯ No

Type each choice on a separate line:
Strongly disagree
Disagree
Neutral
Agree

Display choices using:
◯ Drop-Down Menu   ◉ Radio Buttons

Default value:
Neutral

strength of the computer-assisted discussion is that everyone has access to the comments, and the entire record is available if questions arise later. It also makes it easy to search for specific problems. Discussions can be created on any topic. Common business uses include overall comments on scheduling, sharing research information, and discussing problems that arise.

Surveys are useful for some business applications. In particular, they come in handy when designing new systems. Generally they are used to obtain a quick perspective on individual opinions. Paper surveys are a pain. Web-based surveys are easy to change, easy to fill out, and can instantly report the data. As shown in Figure 7.11, SharePoint includes a basic survey-building tool. You simply write the questions by selecting a format, entering the question, and identifying the possible responses. When you post the survey to the SharePoint site, the other members of the team enter their selections. The results are immediately available. One advantage of the system is that the entire process is done through Web forms. Note that the surveys are not available to people unless they are registered in the group, so the technique does not work as well for public surveys. On the other hand, more sophisticated tools can be purchased from other companies to handle public surveys.

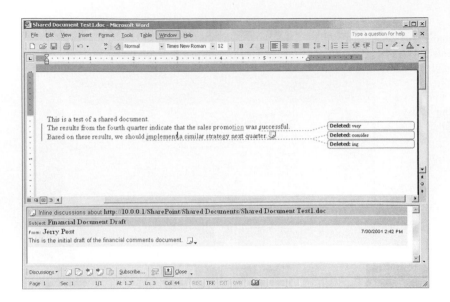

Document Libraries

Until recently, most organizations shared files through shared directories on LANs or via e-mail. Document libraries are simply Web-based folders that hold a related collection of documents—such as all work on a particular project. The files are accessed across the Web, so they are accessible to team members anywhere in the world. Additionally, the group leader can establish a template so that all documents have the same look.

Once the site is set up, accessing the documents is easy—through the familiar File and Open commands. Generally, you will create a link to the directory in "My Network Places" so you can find the documents with one click. In a team environment, it is important to store your files in a document library—instead of on your personal machine. That way, everyone in the group can read and contribute to the work. Once the documents are stored in the shared library, some other powerful tools and options can be used to coordinate the team, as described in the next sections.

Some versions of SharePoint can also handle version control. **Version control** consists of maintaining earlier copies of a document that can be retrieved if needed. Additionally, version control systems support check in and check out of documents, so that only one person can edit a document at a time—minimizing the problem of needing to determine which change to keep. It also tracks who made the changes and which team member is currently using the document. If you want complete version control including the ability to automatically track changes, you will also need Visual Source Safe, Microsoft's version control software.

Tracking Changes

Have you ever tried to write a document with two or three people? What happens when you have a draft that is passed around to the others for comment? If it is a paper document, odds are that each person starts marking changes on the document. Hopefully, each person uses a different color pen and records some notes about why the changes were made. Modern electronic documents can support the same type of editing electronically. Simply turn on electronic protection to enable the document to track changes. Then as each person deletes or adds items, the changes are marked in color. In the end, the person in charge of the document can unprotect the document and quickly go through and accept or reject the changes to produce the final version. Figure 7.12 shows a sample Word document with marked changes. It also shows how discussion comments can be added to the document.

FIGURE 7.13
Subscription form. You can select a document or folder to receive an e-mail message when it is changed. You can choose specific types of changes, and set the time interval (such as immediately or daily).

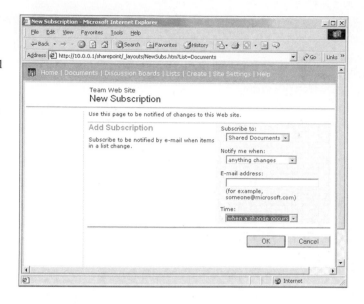

Subscriptions

As shown in Figure 7.13, individual team members can set a subscription to entire folders or to individual documents. Whenever a document is changed, the user is notified by e-mail. This feature has many uses for teams. Consider the situation when you need to wait for a team member to finish a section before adding your analysis. You could pester the team member with phone calls until he or she finishes; you could hope that the team member e-mails you directly; or now you can simply let the server notify you as soon as the file is updated. You can control how quickly the notification is sent; for example, immediately for critical items, or daily for minor items. Subscriptions also tie into the next topic of approvals and work flow control.

Approval Routing and Work Flow Control

Group members rarely work independently. Most businesses establish some type of control procedures. For example, your manager probably wants to review recommendations that you make; purchasing managers are responsible for approving the purchase of major items; and important documents have to be approved by the legal department. Projects tend to have discrete steps. Sometimes the steps are as simple as obtaining an approval and comments from someone before proceeding. Other times, complex business rules have to be followed to ensure the proper input and controls are followed. These more sophisticated systems are known as **work flow** procedures.

As shown in Figure 7.14, SharePoint makes it relatively easy to support routing documents and obtaining approvals. You can attach a routing list to any document when you send it. The system delivers it to the first person on the list. When done, he or she clicks a button and it is sent to the next person on the routing list. Along the way, each person can add comments. These comments are stored in a discussion board associated with the document. Additionally, the document can record changes and indicate who made them. Hence, everyone can see the final document, what changes were made, and comments on why the changes are important.

More complicated work flow rules can be created with lists and some minor programming. For example, a list can be created to describe the state of a document (draft, approved, final). Then various conditions and triggers can be applied to specify conditions for each state and how the document must be handled. For instance, two specific people must approve a document before it can leave the draft state and move to the next steps. Or, a document must have three completed and approved figures before it is considered to be complete. These rules require some effort to set up, but once established, the system

FIGURE 7.14

Routing slip. Much like a paper-based system, the routing slip e-mails the document in order to each person on the list. Any changes they make are highlighted. They can also add comments to the discussion list. Here, the altered document is returned to you at the end.

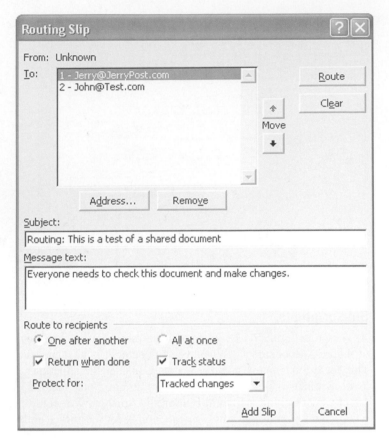

enforces the basic procedures of the business. Additionally, team members can check on the progress of a project to see what steps remain, or identify which team member is holding up a particular document.

Integrating with Legacy Systems: A Data Warehouse

In many ways, the design and implementation of an information system is easier if you are starting a new company or rebuilding one completely. With older (legacy) systems, existing data and software might be incomplete and inconsistent. Valuable information and processes are embedded in these systems; we cannot just throw them away and start over. Yet, it can be more difficult to retrieve data from these systems and integrate it into new management systems.

As business operations and management change, information systems need to be updated. Management emphasis on teamwork is a significant change in the last few years. The improved integration features of current software fit nicely with the changes in management toward teamwork and integration across the enterprise. The problem is that few companies have the opportunity or the money to completely redesign their information system to take advantage of these new features. As a result, they need to use the data stored in their **legacy systems**. This data must be made accessible to decision makers so it can be analyzed. To meet this need, some companies are creating a data warehouse. A **data warehouse** is a single consolidation point for enterprise data from diverse production systems. The data is typically stored in one large file server or a central computer.

Many older **online transaction processing (OLTP)** systems store data in their own files, without using a database management system. Although transaction systems produce standard reports, managers often need to use the base data to perform additional analyses or indepth searches. Before the widespread use of networks, managers often entered data from each report into their own spreadsheets. Installing a network offers the ability to share data

FIGURE 7.15

Data warehouse. A data warehouse is commonly used as a method to provide data to decision makers without interfering with the transaction-processing operations. Selected data items are regularly pulled from the transaction data files and stored in a central location. DSS tools query the data warehouse for analysis and reporting.

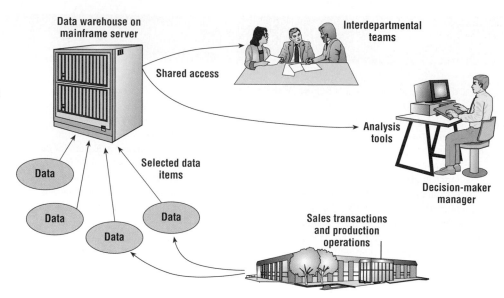

across the company. However, the data must be stored in a format that is accessible to the managers. The process shown in Figure 7.15 is known as **extraction, transformation, and transportation (ETT)**. Larger database management systems have specific tools and data storage methods to create data warehouses. Some companies also create specific **data marts** that are basically copies of a small portion of the data warehouse designed to feed a specific application. For instance, a financial data mart might be used by the accounting and finance department just to monitor investments and bank accounts.

Building a Data Warehouse

The goal of a data warehouse is to hold all of the data needed by managers to make decisions. Hence, the first step is to determine the data needs and models that managers use. The next step is to identify the data sources that are available in the company. This step can be difficult when the data is stored in hundreds of different files, scattered across many different machines. It requires analyzing company data sources in depth and documenting the business processes.

Once the data needs and data sources have been identified, the data must be transformed and integrated so that it can be searched and analyzed efficiently by the decision makers. In many cases, the data warehouse is created as a static copy of the original data. Instead of building a link to the original data files, it is easier to copy the data into new files. Special programs are run periodically to update the data warehouse from the original data.

The next step is to document the data warehouse. **Metadata** is used to describe the source data, identify the transformation and integration steps, and define the way the data warehouse is organized. This step is crucial to help decision makers understand what data elements are available. It also enables managers to find new data.

Once the data warehouse has been defined, programs are written to transfer the data from the legacy systems into the data warehouse. In some cases, managerial applications are created and distributed. Applications can be written for decisions that occur on a regular basis. For instance, finance decisions involving cash flow must be made every month or every week, and rely on standard data. On the other hand, applications for ad hoc decisions will have to be created as they are needed. U.S. West and Chase Manhattan Bank illustrate how a data warehouse can overcome problems with large, unconnected databases.

Limitations of a Data Warehouse

A data warehouse represents a subset of the total data in the company. In most cases, it is a static copy, not a dynamic link. Consequently, managers might not always have the most current data. Similarly, data not transferred to the data warehouse will still be difficult to

John I. Haas, Inc. is the largest U.S. grower and purchaser of hops and hop products—largely used in brewing beer. With 40 percent of the world's hop production in the United States, the company also has an important international presence. With widely dispersed customers (brewers) and growers, 20 percent of the company's employees work remotely and 10 percent are regular "road warriors." In June 2001, under the direction of Kyle Lambert, VP of information solutions at Haas, the company went live with Oracle E-Business Suite. The system is hosted by a third party, which solves all of the installation and daily management hassles, and provides Internet access to the data. The company uses Oracle financial management, procurement, process manufacturing, and manufacturing intelligence applications. The availability of the systems over the Internet is particularly valuable for the traveling and remote workers. Lambert noted that moving the system to an outside Web-hosted application "was actually a 20 percent cut in our Oracle application costs." Savings arise mainly in database administration, consulting costs, and software maintenance (upgrades). Additionally, employee productivity increased because employees are now able to focus on their jobs instead of the applications.

Source: Adapted from Heather Harreld, "Companies Report Growing Demand for Hosted E-Biz Apps," *Computerworld,* November 13, 2001.

find and use. Data warehouses are not always stored in relational database management systems. Instead, they are collections of files and the data items are extracted and transmitted to managers' personal computers. This type of system is relatively easy to use; managers do not have to learn data access commands (SQL or QBE). However, it is less flexible than using a database management system. Decision makers will be unable to get additional data or to compare the data in some previously unexpected way. The success of a data warehouse depends on how well the manager's needs have been anticipated.

The Internet: Integration of Different Systems

It is difficult to build systems that integrate data. Hundreds of problems arise even if all of the data lies within one company. The data is often pulled from different software packages running on diverse hardware. The data formats are rarely the same, so data has to be converted. For example, one system might use five-digit ZIP codes and a second might use nine digits. And dates are always a pain because every system stores and displays them differently.

Displaying data and documents developed by different people on many types of computers is exactly why Tim Berners-Lee developed the early Web browser. He was working with physicists at CERN and needed a method to help them share their data and research. The Web has come a long way since that time, but the emphasis on creating standards to share data is still paramount. Consequently, e-commerce is currently the hotbed for developments in integrating data.

EDI standards were originally developed to help companies share data with their partners, suppliers, and customers. But its progress stalled as firms found it difficult to build easy-to-use EDI systems that worked well with their internal systems and procedures. Initial EDI technologies also required that all transaction data be predefined and fit within the framework of the standards. Several firms began to realize that they needed a more flexible method of sharing data.

Technologists are working on systems to make it easier for companies to share data. One useful standard is the **extensible markup language (XML)**. XML is a method to define and transfer data between companies and applications. As shown in Figure 7.16, all of the data within an XML document is in a specified format and tagged so that a computer program can quickly read the file and identify the data and its purpose. Several companies, including IBM and Microsoft, are developing technologies to use XML to make it easier to share data across companies.

At its foundation, all data is transferred similarly to this example, but XML is considerably more powerful and more complex. Among other things, it supports a version of a style sheet to define and share the structure of the document (the tags). Several industry groups have created XML definitions for sharing data specific to their industry. These data templates make it

FIGURE 7.16

XML document. XML is designed to transfer data between companies and computers. You can define any type of tag to describe the data.

```
<?xml version="1.0"?>
<!DOCTYPE OrderList(View Source for full doctype...)>
- <OrderList>
  - <Order>
      <OrderID>1</OrderID>
      <OrderDate>3/6/2001</OrderDate>
      <ShippingCost>$33.54</ShippingCost>
      <Comment>Need immediately.</Comment>
    - <Items>
        <ItemID>30</ItemID>
        <Description>Flea Collar-Dog-Medium</Description>
        <Quantity>208</Quantity>
        <Cost>$4.42</Cost>
        <ItemID>27</ItemID>
        <Description>Aquarium Filter & Pump</Description>
        <Quantity>8</Quantity>
        <Cost>$24.65</Cost>
      </Items>
    </Order>
  + <Order>
  + <Order>
  </OrderList>
```

easier for you to share data, and easier for programmers to develop applications that automatically send and receive the data. The main advantage of XML is that each message contains a description of the purpose of the data as well as the data itself. Hence, the receiving program can evaluate and understand what was sent.

Standards are a critical process in sharing data. Hundreds of standards exist to enable computers to connect at a physical, electrical, and data level. New standards are being developed every day. Developing standards is not easy, and many arguments arise during the process. Each vendor wants specific protocols and methods in the standard, and many of them would give one vender an advantage over the competitors.

To a manager, the entire issue of computer standards can be confusing. The most basic issue is that it would be wonderful if everyone could immediately agree on a single standard for every definition. That way we could buy hardware and software from anyone and know that it would work together on any of our computers. This utopia will probably never exist because of changes in technology and the constant competition among manufacturers to gain an advantage. In reality, we are forced to guess which technology will succeed and which standard will eventually dominate the others. Choosing incorrectly can result in ownership of *orphaned* products that are no longer supported. You also end up changing hardware, software, and data more often, which results in expensive and disruptive conversions.

Unfortunately, there is no simple rule that will tell you how to choose a direction or standard. Some companies avoid the issue by avoiding new technology and waiting until it is clear which technology will win. Some managers simplify their choices by always buying from the market leader. Both strategies can cause problems: In particular it means that you will always be a follower instead of a leader. While there are advantages to being a follower, it makes it difficult to use technology to gain an advantage over your competition.

Group Decisions

A different type of groupware tool is designed specifically to help groups (or teams) make decisions. Many business decisions involve a group of people. Often, one person might be responsible for the final decision, but meetings are used to enable everyone to have a say, analyze the potential effects on each area, and persuade others to accept a decision. Decisions that involve groups of people have additional complications. Someone has to organize and control the meeting. During the meeting, people compete to make comments and get their opinions heard. Someone has to take notes of the meetings and votes have to be counted.

Information systems can help with group decisions. Groupware tools can be used to share data and documents. Message systems can be used to share comments and early drafts of work. Bulletin boards can be used to let everyone express opinions and evaluations. In the late 1980s, an additional tool known as a **group decision support system (GDSS)** was defined. A GDSS is designed to help managers reach a consensus during meetings.

Features of a GDSS

Most versions of a GDSS use a special meeting room like the one shown in Figure 7.17, where each participant is seated at a networked computer. A facilitator operates the network and keeps the discussion moving in the right direction. Before the meeting, the primary decision maker meets with the facilitator to establish the objective of the meeting. They set up sample questions and design the overall strategy.

Typical meetings begin with a brainstorming session, where participants are asked to think of ideas, problems, and potential solutions. They type each of these into categories on their computers. The basic ideas and suggestions are stored in a database and shared with the group through the networked computers.

In terms of discussion and comments, the facilitator can choose individual items and project them on a screen for the entire group to analyze. Participants can write comments or criticisms of any idea at any time. This system is particularly helpful if many participants come up with ideas and comments at the same time. The computer enables everyone to enter comments at the same time, which is faster than waiting for each person to finish speaking.

Another feature of using the computer for the entry of ideas and comments is that they can be anonymous. Although each comment is numbered, they are not traced back to the original author, so people are free to criticize their supervisor's ideas. Anonymity reduces embarrassment and encourages people to submit riskier ideas.

At various points, the facilitator can call for participants to vote on some of the ideas and concepts. Depending on the software package, there can be several ways to vote. In addition to traditional one-vote methods, there are several schemes where you place weights on your choices. The votes are done on the computer and results appear instantly. Because it is so easy to vote, the GDSS encourages the group to take several votes. This approach makes it easier to drop undesirable alternatives early in the discussion.

One useful feature of conducting the meeting over a computer network is that all of the comments, criticisms, and votes are recorded. They can all be printed at the end of the session. Managers can review all of the comments and add them to their reports.

In theory, a meeting could be conducted entirely on a computer network, saving costs and travel time if the participants are located in different cities. Also, if it is designed properly, a GDSS can give each participant access to the corporate data while he or she is in the meeting. If a question arises about various facts, the computer can find the answer without waiting for a second meeting.

Limitations of a GDSS

Perhaps the greatest drawback to a GDSS is that it requires participants to type in their ideas, comments, and criticisms. Most people are used to meetings based on oral discussions. Even if they have adequate typing skills, a GDSS can inhibit some managers.

Along the same lines, in a traditional meeting, only one person speaks at a time, and everyone concentrates on the same issues at the same time. With a GDSS, your focus is continually

FIGURE 7.17

Teamwork is an essential component of modern business. Software applications have developed to support communication, comments, and multiple authors.

drawn to the many different comments and discussions taking place at the same time. People who type rapidly and flit from topic to topic will find that they can dominate the discussions.

In terms of costs, maintaining a separate meeting room with its own network and several computers can be expensive. Unless the facility is used on a regular basis, the computers will be idle a great deal of the time. When you factor in the costs for network software, the GDSS software, and other utilities, the costs multiply. One way to minimize this problem is to lease the facilities that have been established by a couple of universities and some companies (e.g., IBM).

The use of a GDSS also requires a trained facilitator—someone who can lead discussions, help users, and control the GDSS software on the network. Hiring an in-house specialist can be very expensive if there are only a few meetings a year. Again, using facilities from an outside agency can reduce this cost, but it means that someone outside your company is watching and controlling your meeting. Although most facilitators are scrupulously honest, there might be some topics that you do not want to discuss with nonemployees.

One way to overcome these limitations is to alter the approach to meetings. Instead of requiring everyone to get together at the same time in one room, meetings could be held via network discussion groups. Each participant could read messages, add comments, and vote on issues electronically at any time from any location. Again, the Internet offers possibilities to provide these facilities, but it could be a few years before organizations and managers can accept the changes required.

Microsoft Pivot Tables

Microsoft **pivot tables** are the most advanced means of retrieving data and examining it in a spreadsheet. A pivot table is essentially a means of examining data from a variety of viewpoints. To use this program, you first set up a query to retrieve the detailed data you want to examine. The pivot table then provides several functions to help you define groups and examine subtotals.

On starting the pivot table wizard, your first step is to find your data. Typically, it will come from a database stored somewhere on the network. Then create a query to extract exactly the data you want. The query wizard uses QBE and SQL methods similar to those described in Chapter 5. In selecting data, look for natural groupings. In the Rolling Thunder example, you might want to examine sales by model type, by state, and by month. So from the Bicycle table, select the ModelType, SaleState, SaleDate, and SalePrice. You can use the Month( ) function to convert the SaleDate to a month number. You can also restrict the data to examine a single year.

Once the data is selected, set the basic structure of the pivot table by indicating which items are rows (ModelType and SaleState), columns (Month), and central data (SalePrice), which is automatically summed. Figure 7.18 shows the resulting pivot table. Notice that an additional group was created to display results by quarter instead of month. The groups were created by highlighting three months at a time and creating a new group. The strength of the pivot table is that the detail (e.g., monthly) data still exists and can be displayed quickly by selecting the "show detail" option.

FIGURE 7.18

Pivot table for Rolling Thunder sales. The detail is currently hidden. By clicking one of the title buttons (ModelType, SaleState, Quarter), you can select the option to display detail and the table will expand to show the individual items. Traditional spreadsheet functions can be used to format or graph this data.

Sum of Sale Price	Quarter	Month			
Model Type | SaleState	Quarter1	Quarter2	Quarter3	Quarter4	Grand Total
Hybrid	49,111.21	38,365.38	58,022.29	53,507.33	199,006.21
Mountain	138,419.65	150,297.45	133,240.00	141,669.80	563,626.90
Race	215,602.55	231,187.01	243,694.51	238,500.00	928,984.07
Road	145,108.33	112,108.20	111,749.85	120,901.80	489,868.18
Tour	79,222.71	89,869.80	81,602.01	95,506.07	346,200.59
Track	7,703.77	7,450.00	15,125.00	4,750.00	35,028.77
Grand total	635,168.22	629,277.84	643,433.66	654,835.00	2,562,714.72

Summary

Working together and sharing data are crucial in today's companies. MIS can help teams work better with tools designed to integrate data across an organization. Managers need to know how to use a variety of tools, from data sharing over networks, to dynamic linking, to groupware products.

Enterprise resource planning systems are commercial systems designed to collect and share data across the company. Most of them concentrate on transaction processing data with a special focus on accounting systems. However, the consistent data provides a solid foundation for additional analysis.

Workgroup software like Lotus Notes combines many features to facilitate work on group projects. It supports communication, document sharing, integration of data types, and tracking individual changes.

Group decisions can also be supported with GDSS software that is used to facilitate meetings. Its primary feature is that all managers can contribute at the same time. It also tracks comments for each idea and supports several types of votes and rankings.

Integration often requires combining data from many different locations. Networks enable you to dynamically link the work done by different people. However, if everyone in a company uses different software, it becomes difficult to combine the information because each software package stores data in a unique format. As a result, companies generally create standards for how the data will be stored and accessed. Although these standards are often necessary, several problems can arise when some users have special needs or the standards need to be changed.

At the personal computer level, software supports dynamic links that automatically update final documents as the underlying data changes. Microsoft pivot tables provide a flexible method of retrieving and examining data queries. Locking documents and tracking changes is useful to monitor the changes suggested by team members. Annotation facilities provide a mechanism to keep a log of changes and record the reason for the change.

A Manager's View

Teamwork is an increasingly important aspect of management. Integration of business units so they work together is another important issue. Effectively managed, the techniques can cut costs, improve quality, and improve response time.

Several tools will help you integrate data and share information. Enterprise systems collect and integrate transaction data across the organization. Workgroup software helps team members share documents. Group DSS software assists in meetings and discussions. Software suites enable users to integrate data and track changes.

Key Words

customer relationship management (CRM), *256*
data marts, *263*
data warehouse, *262*
enterprise resource planning (ERP), *253*
extensible markup language (XML), *264*

extraction, transformation, transportation (ETT), *263*
group decision support system (GDSS), *265*
groupware, *257*
legacy systems, *262*
metadata, *263*

online transaction processing (OLTP), *262*
pivot tables, *267*
SharePoint, *258*
version control, *260*
work flow, *261*

Website References

Common Statistics

Bureau of Labor Statistics   **www.bls.gov**
Census Bureau   **www.census.gov**
FedStats   **www.fedstats.gov**

General Reference Sites

Congress	**lcweb.loc.gov/global/legislative/congress.html**
Congressional Quarterly	**www.cq.com**
Copyright Office	**lcweb.loc.gov/copyright**
Executive Branch	**lcweb.loc.gov/global/executive/fed.html**
IRS	**www.irs.gov**
Judicial	**www.uscourts.gov**
Congress	**www.house.gov**
	www.senate.gov
Legislative votes	**www.vis.org/visweb/html/votes.htm**
Library of Congress	**thomas.loc.gov**
Patent Office	**www.uspto.gov**

Additional Reading

Harreld, Heather. "Extended ERP Reborn in B-to-B," *Infoworld,* August 27, 2001. [Updated perspective on ERP and new applications.]

Jones, Mark. "Ingram Micro: The Trouble with XML and Web Services." *Infoworld,* November 9, 2001. [The market penetration of proprietary EDI versus the uncertain future of open integration with Web services.]

Krill, Paul. "Data Analysis Redraws CRM Landscape." *Infoworld,* November 30, 2001. [CRM vendors and capabilities in sales analysis.]

"Never-Ending Story: Why ERP Projects Cause Panic Attacks." *Computerworld,* September 24, 2001. [ERP projects can cause problems when they are rushed.]

Schlender, Brent. "Microsoft: The Beast Is Back," *Fortune,* June 11, 2001, pp. 75–86. [Outline of Microsoft's new ideas for integrating data.]

Songini, Marc L. "PeopleSoft Project Ends in Court." *Computerworld,* September 10, 2001. [Serious problems with an ERP installation at Connecticut General.]

Weston, Randy. "ERP Users Find Competitive Advantages." *Computerworld,* January 19, 1998, p. 9. [Summary of ERP benefits.]

Review Questions

1. What is meant by the concept of integrating information in business? Give an example of problems that can arise if business information is not integrated.

2. How do enterprise resource planning systems integrate data across the company?

3. What are the primary features and capabilities of an enterprise resource planning system?

4. What tools exist to support workgroup coordination and teamwork?

5. Why are subscriptions to changes important with shared directories of files?

6. How does a *data warehouse* support integration? Why are they needed in many organizations?

7. What problems are you likely to encounter when attempting to integrate data across the entire company? How might you solve these problems?

8. How does the Internet facilitate integrating systems?

9. Describe three features of group decision support systems.

10. How do databases help integrate data and share data with team members?

Exercises

1. Create a spreadsheet and draw a graph. Now, copy them into a word processing system's document and dynamically link (embed) them. Make changes to the original spreadsheet to make sure the graph and the word processor's document are updated.

2. Research one of the enterprise resource planning systems. Identify the internationalization features available. If you are running a midsize company with offices and operations in several European nations, what benefits would be provided by these international features?

3. Research a company that recently installed an enterprise resource planning system. What problems did they encounter? What benefits did they gain? How long did it take?

 ## C07Ex04.mdb

4. Using the sample DBMS and a spreadsheet, create a sample report that computes net sales as sales minus returns for each region. Use the spreadsheet to import the data and graph the net sales by region.

5. As a group project, assume that each person in the group is a manager of a different department. Each person creates a spreadsheet to list the salespeople in his or her department (4–10), their hours worked, total sales, and commissions. Compute the totals for each column. Once the individual spreadsheets have been created and stored on separate computers, the group will create a composite spreadsheet that brings in the data from each individual spreadsheet. Compute the corporate total and draw pie charts for each column. If possible, use dynamic linking across the network to capture the data from the individual spreadsheets.

 ## DeptStor.mdb

6. Using a DBMS, spreadsheet, and word processor, create the four reports shown in the introduction: daily sales report, returned merchandise log, commissions report, and weekly sales analysis. If possible, use tools that support dynamic integration.

7. Using current business publications, find an example of a company that is experiencing problems with integrating data. Alternatively, find an example of a company that has an excellent system for integrating information. Identify data that is shared dynamically and data that is shared through static copies. (Hint: Companies are more likely to report successes than problems, and be sure to check the MIS publications.)

8. As a team project, if you have access to Office XP and SharePoint, have one member create a document with a paragraph reviewing some recent movie. Create a distribution list and send the review to each person on the list, who can make changes to the document and add discussion comments before sending it to the next person on the list.

9. As a team project, if you have access to a SharePoint server, have one person create a small document that describes a computer that he or she might wish to purchase. Set change subscriptions on the document for each team member. Then over the next few days, have members make changes to the document, with suggestions for different components. As team members are notified of changes, they should check the suggestions and either accept or reject them by adding additional comments.

10. Find a business situation that could benefit from the use of a groupware product. Describe the problems that exist and how they can be overcome with the groupware tools.

11. Using the small Department Store database, create a pivot table in Excel to extract the sales by category by month. Be sure to include a grouping to show sales by quarter.

12. Using the small Department Store database, create a pivot chart in Excel to graph the sales by category by month.

 ## Rolling Thunder Database

13. Extract sales and cost data by model type and create a spreadsheet to analyze it. (Hint: Use the Extract Data form.) Write a short report discussing profitability and any trends. Include graphs to illustrate your comments. Your spreadsheet should look at monthly sales by model and monthly material costs by model. Be sure to compute profit margins and examine percentages.

14. Assume that Rolling Thunder is experiencing problems with quality control. Suddenly there are several complaints about the components. Write a report describing all of the data and reports we would need to help us resolve these problems.

15. Top management needs an analysis of purchases and deliveries from vendors. Begin by using queries to extract the appropriate data to create a basic spreadsheet. Write a report analyzing the data; include graphs to illustrate your points.

Vendor	Purchases Order total $	Percent of vendor total	Received $	Receipts % of purchase	Avg. # days to deliver

16. Describe how an ERP solution could improve operations at Rolling Thunder. What operations would you implement first?

17. Using Microsoft Excel, build a query to get information about sales in November and December. Create a graph to compare the two months. Then using Microsoft Word, write a short report about your conclusions and link the graph dynamically.

18. Create a pivot table in Excel to dynamically extract the sales by month by bicycle type by sales state for three years. Be sure to build a grouping to show quarterly subtotals.

Automobile Industry

The automobile manufacturing industry is an increasingly competitive industry with respect to a number of factors. Automobile companies compete on quality, price, development, appearance, size, special options, safety, and financing terms.

Three types of automobile manufacturers dominate the industry:

1. Original equipment manufacturers (OEMs) supply such inputs as windshields, seats, and brake systems directly to another stage in the assembly process.

2. After-market/replacement parts manufacturers make parts such as brake pads and batteries supplied to assemblers and to the replacement market.

3. Capital goods tool manufacturers provide manufacturing and assembly-line equipment to the assemblers.

Financial Analysis

In the past few years, the automobile industry has benefited from certain factors. The first is the improved economic conditions in the United States. The second, a result mostly of favorable exchange rates, is a cost advantage in comparison to vehicles manufactured in Japan (or those vehicles containing significant amounts of parts manufactured in Japan).

Automakers and suppliers are also affected by the season. Operating results vary primarily because of the variability in types and numbers of vehicles sold in different seasons. In addition, results are affected by new product launches, sales incentives, and costs of materials and production changes.

Manufacturers have also benefited from the increased demand for trucks and sport utility vehicles (SUVs). The high-end models of these vehicles have substantially higher profit margins than basic cars. Sometimes as much as $10,000 profit for an SUV versus $500 for a car.

Stock / Investment Outlook

U.S. automobile manufacturers continue to struggle to come out on top in terms of quality and market share. In 1994 and 1995, operating revenues increased while net income decreased, lowering returns on investment.

Stock prices vary greatly in the auto industry. Stocks linked directly to the automotive industry fell out of favor in the late 1990s. The industry and stock prices tend to be highly dependent on the overall economy. The relatively lower prices in the late 1990s were an important factor in the worldwide industry consolidations.

Potential / Prospective for Growth

In the recent past, quality has become the main focus point in the domestic auto industry, and vast improvements have been made. Nonetheless, the perception persists that U.S. automobiles do not have the same high standard as certain foreign manufacturers.

Several trends in automotive manufacturing are setting the stage for future growth. As the industry responds to demands for safer vehicles and environmentally safe vehicles, emerging innovations are flourishing. A Dataquest report suggests three main sectors for growth:

1. Advanced driver information and communication systems. Examples include keyless entry, navigation systems, and near obstacle recognition. Such products will enhance the driver's awareness of his or her own personal safety as well as the safety of road conditions through power steering, electronic brakes, and collision avoidance.

2. Powertrain electronics. Examples include active suspension.

3. Body control electronics. This includes, for instance, "black boxes" for autos and security systems.

The next generation of smart cars will enable their passengers to automatically keep pace with the vehicle in front and signal emergency services to an exact location of an accident without driver action.

Moving past the year 2000, production capacity will likely continue to exceed demand. Europe has become the primary battleground for car manufacturers, with unified Germany now the biggest single market. Eastern Europe and South America offer limited growth as well as high risk during the late 1990s but will become significant markets in the years 2000 to 2010. China, India, and the Asian countries represent the greatest opportunities and challenges to Japanese, U.S., and European manufacturers.

Competitive Structure

Automobile manufacturing remains a highly competitive industry ranging from the big three automakers to a variety of suppliers. In addition, a number of foreign automotive companies are investing in North America. U.S. automakers are also taking advantage of new management tools and techniques.

One such trend is the just-in-time (JIT) manufacturing system, which essentially shifts inventory costs from the automakers down to the suppliers. Automakers are also using the system to reduce the number of suppliers. American automakers traditionally utilized thousands of different suppliers in short-term contract relationships, basing them on cost. Today, by implementing JIT, manufacturers reduce the number of suppliers by establishing long-term relationships with fewer suppliers.

Most European car manufacturers have significant positions only within Europe. U.S. companies tend to have major shares domestically and in Europe, while only two major Japanese companies can claim to be truly global. Although the industry is concentrating, no single company is close to dominating the market and in fact seven companies have between 10 percent and 15 percent. A variety of alliances and joint ventures have been utilized as a means of growth.

Consolidation will dramatically alter the profile of the entire industry over the next 10 to 15 years. Ford is trying to move further up-market with the acquisition of the Aston Martin, Jaguar, and Volvo brands. Facing tough Japanese competition in the U.S. market, Ford is set to challenge General Motors for second place in Europe with the purchase of 51 percent of Mazda. [PR Newswire 2001]

Consolidation in supplier relationships will also dramatically alter the profile of the that industry over the next 10 to 15 years. Ford had 2,300 direct suppliers in 1995 and expects to reduce this figure to 1,150 by the year 2000. Chrysler intends to reduce its direct suppliers from 2,000 to 1,500 over the same period. BMW recently announced its intention to reduce from its current figure of 1,400 line suppliers to just 200.

Role of Research and Development

Research and development in the domestic automobile manufacturing industry never ceases. Automakers and suppliers continually strive to improve their products to remain ahead of competition in the United States and in other countries.

Ford has a lofty goal: the global standardization of environmental systems and processes at all Ford facilities worldwide. Ford is standardizing its operational procedures while still striving for consistency and continuous improvement in their facilities. This program is called Ford 2000.

Automobile pollution is a worldwide problem. Automobiles currently have 80 percent of the global personal transport market and 55 percent of goods transportation. Their effect on the environment is large. Noise and solid waste also contribute to environmental deterioration. According to the study done by Harvard University, more than 500 kg of every car produced ends up in landfill sites, accounting for 4 percent of total rubbish weight.

Recycling is another way to deal with the pollution problems that cars pose. About 75 percent of current cars are steel and therefore are easily recyclable. The remaining 25 percent consist of plastic, glass, and rubber. Legislation will force reductions of the latter to 15 percent by 2002 and to 5 percent in the longer term. Alternatives to plastics include resin-bonded flax, which can be used as agricultural fertilizer when the car is eventually recycled. Green networks are being built to collect batteries, catalytic converters, and bumpers and recycle them directly in the production of new vehicles.

Reducing fuel consumption is a major research area. Engines are being developed with reduced friction, more efficient combustion, and better ignition. Diesel cars are an alternative; work also continues on small electric cars. Engines capable of using renewable fuels such as soya oil have been in existence since the 1970s. These renewable fuels will not become cost effective, however, unless there is a large change in oil prices or in the presence of government incentives.

Weight reduction is another area of research. In the future, car bodies may be composed of lighter, high-strength steels, alloys, polymers, and composites.

Technological Investment and Analysis

Motoman, Inc., Fanuc Robotics, and other robot manufacturing companies have been making sales to automobile manufacturers. Robots are capable of completing jobs humans have difficulty with or find tedious and boring and often make fewer errors. [PR Newswire, 2001] They are usually operated from familiar Windows-based PCs.

In order to speed up the design cycle, the big three U.S. automakers bring their electronics suppliers into the design cycle at much earlier junctures than in the past. According to Alex Popovic, automotive marketing manager at National Semiconductor Corp., "The sooner we [suppliers] get involved, the more cost-effective and better-performing system the customer gets." Early supplier involvement has another advantage in the automotive market. In advance, the system people can design diagnostic techniques that will help reduce the automaker's future warranty costs. Alex Popovic states, "We try to eliminate problems in silicon and increase the accuracy of the diagnosis of problems." [Financial Times, 2001]

Most of the 1.1 million employees working for Chrysler, Ford, and General Motors are expected to eventually use Web applications. The big three automakers are proving that intranets and extranets can open communications in the supply chain, improve international communications, and save money on support. The automakers are also looking to networking as a way to lower costs and improve profit margins. The big three are already among the leaders in providing Web access to their employees.

Members of the Automotive Industry Action Group trade association are working to help GM, Ford, and Chrysler overcome Year 2000 problems and problems at parts makers that threaten to disrupt the supply chain. A Year 2000 problem at even a small company could cripple a giant automaker because most companies tightly manage their business partners and use JIT inventory. These efforts are important because most of the automobile industry is running on old legacy computer systems and applications.

Recommendation for the Future

Although the automotive industry has had its ups and downs in the recent past, automakers and suppliers must continually improve their processes in order to survive in today's market. This means taking advantage of the latest technology to cut costs.

Quality control must also be a major goal of U.S. automobile manufacturers. This increasingly means providing customer service long after the completion of the sale.

Case: *Ford Motor Company*

In October 2001, William Clay Ford, the great-grandson of Henry Ford, fired Jacques Nasser, the chief executive, and took charge of the company himself. The Ford family still controls 40 percent of the company's voting rights, and has had a history of trouble with the "hired help." The relationship seems to work best with Brits: Alex (now Lord) Trotman, a Scot, retained the family's confidence; Sir Nick Scheele, the new chief operating officer, is thick with Mr. Ford; so is David Thursfield, chairman of Ford of Europe and maybe the company's next chief executive. But Nasser was not.

In late 1995, Elena Anne Ford, the great-great-granddaughter of Henry Ford, became the first member of the fifth generation to go to work for Ford. The event is a small reminder that the Ford family is a constant presence. The special Class B stock the Fords own gives them 40 percent of the shareholder votes.

The Fords also have a strong board of directors presence—with seats being held by Edsel B. Ford II, William Clay Ford, and William Clay Ford, Jr. Edsel and his cousin Bill, Jr., have also been mentioned as possible candidates to become CEO. However, Bill, Jr., resigned from the company in 1995 to succeed his father as chairman of the finance committee of the board, a position reserved for an outside director. In the 1920s, Henry Ford spoke of the opportunities available to young people if they work hard. It does not hurt, he should have added, if they answer to the name of Ford. Ford is still considered a family enterprise even though it is publicly held.

Technology Innovation

The global computer network, Global Studio, will allow team members throughout the world to work online with one another and effect changes in the design and manufacture of vehicles instantaneously. Coupled with other technology being implemented, the global network system will also help avoid lengthy and expensive product simulations, enable designers to view products being developed in other parts of the world, replace sketches and clay models as design tools and stages, and facilitate global communication. The Global Studio will allow teams to share data on a variety of subjects, including ergonomic studies, air-flow analyses, crash simulations, digital mockups, and general and group engineering review.

Ford has encountered difficulty in implementing the process. Information technology (IT) has more than 5,000 people who labor to support 7,000 engineering workstations and 85,000 PCs. Migration to the new system has been difficult, and convincing the system users of the advantages of Global Studio has been a laborious task. IT director Bill Powers has even encountered resistance from IT personnel.

To facilitate the retraining process and ensure further integration of the worldwide systems, Powers has permanently moved the head engineers from each of Ford's systems to the Systems Integration Center in Dearborn, Michigan, where they will work to establish the best infrastructure for the company. The integration issue is likely to become more difficult as employees are forced to work as a team and understand elements that previously did not fall into their jobs. Smaller teams may

be able to integrate faster, but as "larger units grapple with issues of time, costs, redundancy, and training, Powers is likely to discover many issues forming that could slow down the reengineering effort." [Bransten, 2000]

The implementation of the Global Studio is also severely limited by technological parameters such as bandwidth, which limits the amount of information that can be sent at once. Local communication laws define what can and cannot be done and the infrastructure and the capabilities of each country vary significantly.

In 1996, Ford launched a project called C3P, or CAD/CAM/CAE and Product Information Management. The system is intended to assist Ford in cutting prototype costs by 50 percent, improve efficiencies by 20 to 30 percent, and eliminate one-half of the company's costly late development design changes. Before C3P, "it used to take two to three months to build, assemble, and test a prototype of a car's chassis. Using the C3P technologies, Ford can do all that in less than two weeks," says Richard Riff, a C3P project officer. The system should help Ford reduce its product development lead time even further.

While developing the Global Studio, Ford has also had to contend with issues of security. Ford uses the Total Control Security Server, a system that manages sign-on requests originating from a SecureID card, a separate device from Security Dynamics. The SecureID card is a changing "lock and key" device that generates one-time passwords for user authentication. The credit card-sized device, which is synchronized with the security server, generates a new six-digit number every 60 seconds on a LCD display creating a cryptographic key. When an employee types in the number displayed and his or her unique PIN to request remote access, the security server runs an algorithm using the time and the cryptographic key, then matches up the number to the card it comes from. If all the pieces fit together, the server accepts the sign-on.

Network

Ford's intranet connects about 120,000 of Ford's computers around the world to websites containing proprietary company information such as market research, rankings of suppliers' parts, and analyses of competitors' components. The chief benefit of this network is that it has enabled Ford to bring new models into full production in 24 months compared with 36 months before.

The intranet is expected to save the company billions of dollars during the next few years. Ford plans to use its intranet to achieve manufacturing on demand. This would be a process that involves coordination of delivery and assembly of thousands of components. The company plans to manufacture most of its vehicles on a demand basis by 1999. This will require linking its 15,000 dealers around the world to the intranet.

Telecommunications

Ford has a pilot test in which consumers in Houston and Boston can use the Internet to buy used Fords, Mercurys, and Lincolns (www. fordpreowned.com).

Ford Motor Co. finds it far more difficult to sell those cars than new models. Many used cars come off multiyear leases and have up to 36,000 miles on the odometer.

Data

In 1998, Ford Motor Co. awarded an outsourcing contract to Ryder Integrated Logistics, Inc. to design and manage an integrated JIT supply-chain and transportation system for Ford's 20 North American manufacturing plants.

Ford is starting a project that will integrate its plants' individual supply-chain systems. It will connect them to suppliers for real-time information about component and part inventories, as well as real-time tracking of deliveries. The system will help Ford "squeeze out" the cost of transporting parts and components to its plants.

The consolidated system would let Ford managers monitor when plants in the same area need deliveries of similar auto parts. Currently, each plant's shipments are delivered individually by separate trucks. Managers will be able to coordinate parts transportation to multiple plants in the same region using just one truck.

Outsourcing of Technology

Ford licenses companies to produce dies, punches, and other tools by a thermal-spray process it developed. A ceramic master of the working die surface is spray-coated with molten wire, then backfilled with epoxy to create a working die. These dies hold production tolerances and be delivered in a fraction of the time and cost required for conventional dies. This means the dies can be constructed with no machining, heat-treating, or chips. These dies are not just used for prototypes. They also hold up well in production runs.

For more than a century, dies, punches, and tools have been made by the subtractive method. The forms work from a casting or block of steel which is chipped away until the desired net shape is achieved. The goal of technology in all these areas has been to make them faster and improve the length of time that they wear. This includes ballnut leadscrews, carbide tools, EDM, numerical control, and high-speed and five-axis machining.

Ford's thermal spray technology changes die making from a negative to an additive process. The spray-coating is based on knowledge from Sprayform Holdings, a small U.K.-based company, Ford acquired in the early 1990s. The part master comes from REN boards, stereolithography models, silicone rubber, or plaster. The part is cast in ceramic and frozen. This sets up a crystalline structure on the surface. Once the part master is separated from the ceramic mold, the mold is dried in an oven prior to spray-coating.

Supply Chain

To address its supply chain needs, Ford Motor Company purchased a minority stake in Executive Manufacturing Technologies Inc. The goal was to enable Ford to better see and analyze what was happening on the shop floor in terms of the development of supply chain management strategies. Ford had a successful enterprise resource planning (ERP) system and supply chain management solution already in place. However, it was still not able to evaluate critical data from the shop floor. EMT's Visual Plant software enabled Ford to track plant floor production in real-time over a Web browser. The technology,

known as *enterprise manufacturing intelligence,* is dedicated to executing production schedules. It identifies sources of production constraints and down time. Ford adopted Visual Plant to address this critical data need and save money through an increase in production efficiency.

The Internet

Like most other automobile manufacturers, Ford is wary of the Internet. Managers know that people need to touch and drive cars before they will buy one. The auto industry also lives on the premise that salespeople are a critical element—people need to be "talked into" buying a new car. The salesperson's job is to counter all of the little objections that people have and develop solutions that will sell the car. Manufacturers also rely heavily on dealerships to display, sell, and service the vehicles. In fact, some states (e.g., Texas) prohibit car manufacturers from selling directly to the public! Consequently, manufacturers are careful to keep this intermediary happy. So the use of the Internet is primarily to provide prepurchase information about vehicles, options, and pricing. On the other hand, Ford knows that it will always be difficult to produce customized vehicles. The company's approach to this problem has been to consolidate dealers into a few large regional dealerships—each carrying hundreds of versions. Consumers can then use the dealer network, or the Internet, to find a particular version of a car. Any one of the larger dealerships is more likely to carry the specific version—but if not, it can be found quickly and transferred to the closest dealer.

Questions

1. What is the strategic direction of Ford Motor Company?

2. What was the catalyst for change at Ford?

3. Upon what technologies has Ford relied?

4. How successful has Ford's technological change been?

5. What role does data play in the future of Ford Motor Company?

6. How will the capture and maintenance of customer data impact Ford's future?

Additional Reading

Bicknell, David. "Car Firms Test-Drive an Extranet." *Computer Weekly,* October 2, 1999, p. 32.

Bransten, Lisa, "E-Business: Starting Gate," *The Wall Street Journal,* August 28, 2000, p. B4.

Gartner Dataquest, "Worldwide Automotive Semiconductor Market Is Forecast to Grow 7 Percent in 2001," September 24, 2001.

Gouldson, Tim. "The Supply Chain Gang." *Computing Canada* 27, no. 22 (October 19, 2001): pp. 20–21.

"Power Shift." *Detroit News.* detnews.com/2001/autos/shakeup.htm.

"Essentials of Information Management," *Financial Times,* September 16, 2001.

PR Newswire. "FANUC Robotics Showcases Robotic Solutions at 21st International Die Casting Congress & Exposition," October 24, 2001.

PR Newswire. "Ford Motor Company Announces New Leadership Assignments," November 8, 2001.

Samson, Martin H. *Ford Motor Company v. Texas Department of Transportation, et al.,* www.phillipsnizer.com/int-art206.htm.

Taylor III, Alex, "Car Jacqued!" *Fortune,* November 26, 2001.

Case: General Motors Company

I ask you to think back to the 1980s for the moment. . . . GM was even called a dinosaur. We have since restructured our company, lowered our costs, improved our quality, wholeheartedly embraced lean manufacturing and common processes, and produced an entire new line of exciting cars and trucks.

John F. Smith, Jr., president and CEO of General Motors, in a speech delivered to The Executives Club of Chicago on April 17, 1997.

Obviously, information systems and computer services play a very important role in such processes. The push toward a consistent information system (IS) infrastructure has been a great challenge for GM since 1984 when GM bought EDS, a highly successful data-processing firm for $2.5 billion. After 12 controversial years, GM spun off EDS and started to look for a CIO to build an internal information strategy and management capability.

Effective June 28, 1996, GM named Ralf J. Szygenda, former CIO of Bell Atlantic, vice-president and CIO. Szygenda had to face two major challenges. One was to impose order on highly autonomous information systems groups within GM's operational units. The other was to ensure that outsourcing vendor EDS provides the best service at the best price as it seeks to build its non-GM business after being spun off from GM. Szygenda's main work was to develop and implement an information technology strategy that would help CEO Smith fully achieve his four top priority goals: getting common systems, running lean, competing on a global basis, and growing the business.

Technology Innovation

In the early 1980s, when GM owned 40 percent of the U.S. auto market with revenues exceeding $100 billion, the company did not have a unified information system that would satisfy its needs. Even though GM had used a scheme called electronic data interchange (EDI) to order parts automatically from suppliers since the concept was proposed in the early 1970s, different divisions and sections within divisions used different computers and software.

Thus, GM was forced to handle many tasks manually, whereas a unified computer system would prevent the need for much of that work. For instance, if two sets of engineers were not using the same computers to communicate with each other, they would often have to reenter the data and change their formats.

Roger Smith (GM's CEO from 1981 to 1991) envisioned a setup where everyone at GM would be connected to one network. Design, engineering, administration, payroll, health insurance, financing, the factories, and the telephones would all be integrated into one system. Smith thought that data processing was at the heart of General Motors and should be handled only by an internal group.

Since GM did not have strong IS capabilities, Smith decided to solve the problem by going outside of the company and hired Salomon Brothers to assist him with the acquisition of a computer services company. Out of several potential candidates, Smith chose Electronic Data Systems for several reasons. First, it was a highly successful (if small, by GM standards) data processing firm, and second, it had a corporate culture that minimized the red tape and bureaucracy that Smith hated so much. EDS merged with General Motors in 1984 and immediately assumed control of GM system and inventory. Overnight, thousands of GM workers became EDS workers.

The integration of EDS into General Motors turned out to be a painful and long-term process. Aside from the clash of cultures and resentment of EDS's intrusion into GM turf, there were professional complaints about GM's new subsidiary. When GM acquired EDS, the computer company had no automotive experience and little background in distributed systems. Also, EDS lacked experience in management control systems, robotics, computer-aided design, and manufacturing, which were all a large part of GM's computer systems. GM personnel complained that EDS mishandled parts supplying, often buying far too many or too few of an item, resulting either in overstock or factory delays.

However, EDS scored successes in consolidating purchases, improving payroll databases, and standardizing PC systems at GM. Ever since the merger, EDS tried to move to commercial packages. Automakers have been notorious for developing homegrown software, and GM led its competitors in this regard.

EDS coordinated the project for GM North American Operations called Consistent Office Environment (COE). COE was a three-year plan focused on replacing a hodgepodge of desktop models, network operating systems and application development tools with a shorter and hence more manageable list of vendors and technology platforms. COE represented the fastest and largest IS infrastructure upgrade in GM's history, which laid the foundation for the implementation of a common business communication strategy across General Motors. The goal was to change the way GM handled information on the desktop, in the workgroup, and across the enterprise. In 1993, GM had 27 e-mail systems, 10 word-processing programs, five spreadsheet applications, and seven business graphics packages.

All the contracts for COE were, by design, signed within 90 days of one another in mid-1993. The contracts were structured on a per-user/per-month basis, allowing GM to ramp up the new system without incurring capital spikes.

Obviously, COE was a landmark for the few lucky vendors tapped by GM/EDS to supply hardware and software components. For example, Lotus Development Corp., which supplied its Notes groupware platform, is said to have made its largest single Notes sale to date to EDS for the project. Similarly, Compaq Computer Corp., which got the nod to supply the desktop and laptop system, was believed to be looking at one of its largest nongovernment sales ever.

In June 1996, GM filled its top information systems job with Ralph Szygenda, former chief information officer at Bell Atlantic Corp. Before joining Bell Atlantic, Szygenda had been CIO at Texas Instruments. In his new job, Szygenda chairs GM's Corporate Information Council, which includes the IS heads from GM's business sectors. Szygenda reports to GM Vice Chairman Harry Pearce. Szygenda's job was to develop and manage GM's global information technology strategy as well as its relationship with outsourcers, most notably EDS.

Szygenda faced two major challenges. One was to impose order on the highly autonomous information systems groups within GM's operational units. The other challenge was to ensure that outsourcing vendor EDS provided the best service at the best price as it built its non-GM businesses. Szygenda had to rely on EDS for much of his IS needs, at a time when the newly liberated systems integrator was focused elsewhere.

Usually, getting a lower price from an outsourcer is good news for a CIO. But it could be more complicated for GM's CIO because lower earnings for EDS could drive down the value of EDS stock held by GM pension funds. That, in turn, could require GM to make special payments to those funds in compensation. The CIO is not responsible for the pension fund, but GM's contracts are important to the vitality of EDS. Therefore, GM has to phase in the shift of its business to EDS's competitors.

"Despite this semicaptive relationship, EDS is responding well to our cost-reduction effort. We need to align all of our investments in information systems with our business priorities [while] running information systems and services like a business," Szygenda said in late December 1996 [Caldwell, 1996].

Szygenda was pleasantly surprised to find 2,200 IS employees "hidden" within GM and not shipped off to EDS. Among the handful of corporate IS staff, he picked Raymond Kahn to head year 2000 compliance efforts for the company's 2 billion lines of code, a project estimated to cost hundreds of millions of dollars. But most of the new IS executives were to come from outside to assist Szygenda in accomplishing his mission.

Although GM management had been imposing tighter controls on IS for several years, Szygenda wanted to cut hundreds of millions of dollars more from GM's current information technology budget of more than $4 billion. To achieve this goal, he decided to hire 300 new CIOs who would help him in this effort by finding common software, processes, and expertise that can be reused across the company.

Integration and common global product development is critical to GM's prosperity. Because of EDS, GM's IT infrastructure was in relatively good shape, but applications were developed piecemeal by GM's units, leading to about 7,000 separate systems. Szygenda wanted to see at least half of GM's $4 billion IS budget go to developing applications. He wanted to finish GM's struggle to standardize and to collaborate globally.

GM took a step toward common systems in December 1996 when it announced it would standardize on EDS's Unigraphics CAD/CAM solid modeling software. Shortly after that, GM began automatic translations of solid model data with its suppliers, which use a variety of CAD/CAM systems, to cut costs and product development time. Another major step towards unified IS would be a complex business software system.

General Motors is thinking about purchasing R/3 from the German company SAP. R/3 ties together and automates the basic processes of accounting: taking orders, checking credit, verifying payments, and balancing the books. SAP's R/3 is becoming the new standard equipment of global big business.

An intranet is helping GM to develop products more efficiently. GM engineers need to share knowledge. If they do not, dozens of people end up writing the same bug fix or working with out-of-date versions of objects, simply because they do not know what their co-workers have done. Without a process for tracking changes and revisions, all large projects can get out of control.

GM's Powertrain Control Center uses its intranet to coordinate the work of more than 300 engineers all over the world. Prior to the intranet Web servers, GM engineers filed paper documents and distributed them via the internal mail system. In 1994, they installed a UNIX-based shared file server, but it lacked data organization, control, and file-naming standards. Now, using the Continuus/Web intranet solutions, instead of completing dozens of disjointed efforts, everyone works with consistent standards, procedures, documentation, and code.

Colleagues, whether in Michigan or Münich, can access this document with their Netscape Communications Corp. Netscape browsers. An e-mail notification system automatically sends users a message every time a document that concerns them changes.

They use a second intranet to deploy executable files—the code that runs the black boxes. Customers, including manufacturing companies, the GM service organization, auto dealers, and assembly plants, use the software to program the Powertrain and transmission controllers.

The intranet does not solve all of the problems, however. GM engineers still wrestle with incompatibility issues, such as reconciling the different UNIX and Windows file formats and tools. Nor does the intranet help them balance the need for security with the need for usability. So, the Continuus intranet solution has not yet helped GM to reach its ultimate objective: moving its "entire" software development process to a single database and communicating all that information through a Web server. But it accomplished an important interim goal: consistency.

Another area of GM's business that needed standardization and efficiency improvements was communication with the dealership network. GM has never had one common communications system in place for its dealerships. The old Dealer Communication System, which dated back to 1975, forced the dealers to take piecemeal technical downloads that took hours, and then cut and paste the messages into a cohesive format. To improve communications and information exchange between GM headquarters and its dealer network, the company asked EDS to introduce a new dealership automation program. The system was named GM Access.

EDS chose Novell rival Microsoft Corporation's Windows NT Server as the lynchpin of the program to link all the dealerships nationwide. This decision to deploy two network operating systems rather than standardize on one reflects industry-wide trends.

The main objective of the GM Access Program was to distribute data about the availability of new cars quickly to GM's car dealerships via a satellite network. The satellite network was supposed to replace the outdated X.25 network, which took hours to download information.

General Motors started to install Notes at its 8,500 U.S. dealerships as the platform for GM Access in the first half of 1996. Dealers will use Notes to check inventories, locate specific vehicles matching customer requirements, and find information on pricing, incentives, and service. Notes is estimated to help reduce by 30 percent the time it takes to get sales and service information to GM dealers.

The GM Access program allows dealers to access inventory data that is no more than 24 hours old, read service manuals and technical bulletins, and get recall notices and parts availability information. Access will also let dealers use an online search engine to find individual models or configurations. This information will be downloaded within 14 seconds to the dealerships to increase efficiency and get consumers the most up-to-date information. GM Access will also allow GM and its dealerships to standardize the entire system. Previously, Pontiac, Buick, and GMC all submitted their paperwork differently, which was an administrative nightmare.

In addition, to cut the time it takes to get information to its dealerships, General Motors decided to use an emerging technology called IP Multicasting. IP Multicasting, which broadcasts data from one main site to multiple receiving stations, was more efficient than creating an individual link from the central site to every remote location. "We went from transmitting a 1M-byte file to a very limited number of dealers in roughly 30 minutes to sending that same file to 500 dealers in three minutes," said Wayne Stein, a project manager at Electronic Data Systems. [Caldwell, 1996]

IP Multicasting lets GM provide dealerships with timely software updates, sales incentive data, service bulletins, and car availability information. In the past, this was done by numerous point-to-point transfers or by mailing diskettes to dealerships. All 8,500 GM dealerships nationwide were scheduled to be online by September 1997.

GM is using the Internet extensively in its advertising effort focused on increasing brand equity. GM was a true pioneer in the automotive industry when it started to broadcast its messages through the Back Web channel. GM first used "push" technology in the end of 1996 to send an animated advisory to subscribers of Back Web's GM Channel announcing the launch of the 1997 Buick Regal. A click on that notice sent users to the Regal's own website, which included video clips and chat areas. "We see a whole slew of different experiments to see how this aids the branding efforts for GM," said Larry Lozon, senior vice president and director of GM's new-media strategy arm. [PR Newswire, 2001]

While the Internet advertising succeeds in attracting new customers, GM is also using the Net to make it easier for its customers to get financing. GM's financial division, General Motors Acceptance Corporation, became the first automotive financial services company to offer an online credit application on the Internet in 1996.

In addition to promotion and customer services activities, the Internet is expected to be used extensively in areas such as market research and employee training. In the near future, by clicking on a picture of a red Corvette, a market analyst at General Motors might be able to call down a profile of red Corvette buyers. If he wants to break that up by region, he might circle and click on a map. All in the same motion, he might view a GM sales-training film to see whether the sales pitch is appropriate, given the most recent market trends.

Network

GM ran a two-year global rollout of an ambitious IT architecture that will provide up to 175,000 GM users with Web access. Called GM OnLine, the rollout includes new applications as well as Compaq Computer PCs.

"GM OnLine is a new integrated intranet infrastructure that gives our users access to the Internet," said GM CIO Ralph Szygenda. "It will be our platform for knowledge-sharing and collaboration, and will be the nucleus of a number of new applications in the future." [Caldwell, 1996] Besides the Compaq Windows NT-based desktops, GM OnLine includes Lotus Domino, Microsoft Office, and Tivoli Systems' TME 10 enterprise management system.

The Internet

GM has launched its response to websites such as Auto-by-Tel and Microsoft CarPoint, which let consumers shop for cars online. GM enables customers to configure and price GM cars and trucks on its corporate website (www.gm.com) and divisional sites such as www.buick.com and www.pontiac.com.

Dealers will still be utilized. Web users will be directed to the nearest GM dealer stocking the model in the desired color and with the desired options. The customer will receive online the manufacturer's suggested retail price and financing terms from General Motors Acceptance Corp., GM's credit unit.

Nevertheless, price negotiation, ordering, and payment will still be handled at the dealerships by traditional means. GM does have long-term plans to link from the Web into dealer inventory systems to enable online ordering, says Craig Norwood, interactive retail systems manager at GM in Warren, Michigan.

The configuration application will run on the Web-enabled version of Signature Plus interactive selling software from CWC, Inc., in Mankato, Minnesota. GM dealers in North America already use a customized client-server application from CWC called Prospec to configure, locate, and order cars from GM. The GM website application is the first customer deployment of the Web version of Signature Plus.

Data

GM is evaluating several data mining products for projects the company plans for this year and next, involving several GM divisions, including its GMAC loan division and its credit card division.

GM has experimented with data mining on a few scientific projects, but it is only recently that the automaker has tried to use data mining in production work to solve problems. Some of these problems are database marketing and using customer data and warranty information. For example, if GM can use warranty data to identify very specific problems, GM can fix those processes or parts and save on future warranty expenses.

Future Recommendations

GM and Ford both recognize the importance of reducing costs and improving quality. Both have suffered in the past few years. GM has continually lost market share since 1978 when 46 percent of all U.S. vehicles sold were made by GM. The company's share is now below 29 percent. [media.gm.com/uaw/mktshare.htm] Likewise, Ford's vaunted quality program has slipped in the past few years and has cost it sales.

One approach to improve quality and reduce costs is Covisint—an automotive procurement system designed to simplify purchasing in the industry. The B2B site was designed to share information and support electronic purchases across the industry. Automating the process should lead to reduced costs and better control over quality through tracking products. The system got off to a slow start when the U.S. and Germany challenged it on antitrust grounds. But in 2001 alone, GM used the system to purchase almost $100 billion in raw materials. Ford noted that the exchange has already saved it $70 million and anticipates saving $350 million for 2001 alone.

GM managers have also talked about being able to build custom automobiles in a short period of time. But most experts believe it will be years, and require a complete redesign of the automobile before that can happen. But it is not impossible. At the 2002 Detroit auto show, GM revealed a prototype shell consisting of four electric engines (one for each wheel) and a thin platform. The system is designed to enable different bodies to snap in—leaving the drivetrain untouched. GM engineers are contemplating selling interchangeable bodies that will snap onto the shell as the owner's needs change. The AUTOnomy system could also be used to quickly assemble customized vehicles. Even if the system is ever produced, it will not be viable for 15 or 20 years, in part because it requires a new national infrastructure to support the hydrogen fuel cell approach.

Questions

1. Where does General Motors see itself heading?

2. Who or what forces are driving this direction?

3. Upon what technologies has General Motors relied?

4. What has caused a change in GM's use of technology?

5. How has the technological change been implemented?

6. How successful has the technological change been?

7. What does General Motor's Web page present about its business directives?

8. How will the quality of the customer data impact the corporation's future?

Additional Reading

Adhikari, Richard. "Groupware to the Next Level—Collaboration with Customers and Suppliers Means Fewer Mistakes and Fast Turnarounds." *Information Week,* May 4, 1998, pp. 106–110.

Bicknell, David. "Car Firms Test-Drive an Extranet." *Computer Weekly,* October 2, 1999, p. 32.

Caldwell, Bruce, and Marianne Kolbasuk McGee. "Magnitude of Change." *Information Week,* August 11, 1997, pp. 2–48.

Caldwell, Bruce, Stuart J. Johnston, and Clinton Wilder. "NT Server Rollout: Two-Way Electronic Communications Will Link GM Dealerships and Divisions. "*Information Week,* May 2, 1996, pp. 15–17.

Copeland, Lee. "Covisint's Stalled Start." *Computerworld,* December 17, 2001.

"Disciplined Approach." *Information Week,* August 11, 1997, p. 56.

"Intra-National Intrigue." *Computerworld,* October 26, 1998, p. 72.

King, Julie. "The Challenge of a Lifetime." *Computerworld,* November 17, 1997, p. 12.

Konicki, Steve. "GM Buys $96 Billion in Materials via Covisint." *Informationweek,* August 16, 2001.

McGee, Marianne Kolbasuk. "GM Prepares Rollout of Integrated Intranet Platform—Plan Calls for Huge Desktop Procurement." *Information Week,* April 20, 1998, p. 26.

Miller, Joe. "GM Takes Another Step toward Fuel Cell Vehicle." *The Detroit News,* January 8, 2002.

PR Newswire, "Hughes Network Systems Merits Frost & Sullivan Market Engineering Leadership Award," June 26, 2001.

Schwartz, Jeffrey. "GM Taps Notes 4 for E-Mail and Groupware." *Communications Week,* January 8, 1996, p. 1.

Wallace, Bob. "GM Readies Fast Fiber Net." *Computerworld,* December 7, 1998, p. 4.

CHAPTER EIGHT

Models and Decision Support

What you will learn in this chapter

- Why is it hard for people to make good decisions?

- How do models help managers make better decisions?

- What are the key elements of decision support systems?

- How is data mining different from traditional statistical analysis?

- What is the purpose of OLAP?

- What is a digital dashboard?

- What are the advantages of an EIS?

- How can a GIS help managers make better decisions?

Chapter Outline

Overview

Introduction

It Is Hard to Make Good Decisions
Human Biases
Decision Tools

Decision Support Systems

Data: Data Mining

Models: Analytical Processing

Output: Digital Dashboard and EIS
How Does an EIS Work?
Advantages of an EIS
Limitations of an EIS

Decision Support Examples
Marketing
Human Resources Management
Finance
Accounting

Geographical Information Systems
Maps and Location Data
Example

Summary

Key Words

Website References

Additional Reading

Review Questions

Exercises

Cases: Computer Hardware Industry

Appendix: Forecasting
Structural Modeling
Time-Series Forecasts
Exponential Smoothing
Simple Linear Forecasts
Seasonal and Cyclical Components
Exercises

Dell Computer Corporation

Many people get a first job during high school, but few are as successful in high school as Michael Dell was. Dell made $18,000 selling newspapers in one year. He identified the newspaper most purchased by newlyweds and new families in the area, and targeted that particular segment.

He tracked this market segment via the city marriage license bureau, lists of new home purchases, and other sources. Later that year, he bought a BMW with $18,000 cash. The ingenuity and persistence Michael Dell demonstrated at an early age indicated a strong entrepreneurial spirit. The formation of Dell Computer occurred only two years later.

With competitors attempting to copy Dell's sales model, Dell focused on another direct route, the Internet. Compaq, Packard Bell, and other companies that sell through retailers allow "surfers" to browse through a product line catalog on the Internet. But while consumers look through Compaq's product line, others are purchasing PCs through Dell's homepage. Dell has revenues in excess of $1 million a day in Internet sales.

Michael Dell has used a made-to-order strategy to drive his company to the top of a highly competitive industry.

Overview

Elaine:	Ooh, my head hurts.
Ally:	I have some ibuprofen. Will that help?
Elaine:	I doubt it. I'm trying to figure out these price cuts.
Ally:	Oh, Richard was yelling about those yesterday. He said last year we cut prices two and three times on some things and ended up losing tons of money.
Elaine:	Yes, but if we don't cut prices we don't get the sale and we lose anyway. And that's what really happened last year. We made a bunch of small price cuts and none of them did much good. And if we cut prices too far, Richard will yell anyway, and we'll lose more revenue than we should.
Ally:	Sounds like you need a forecast system to estimate how clients will respond to the price changes, and then an optimizer to figure out the best price point.
Elaine:	I think we can buy software to do that, but I don't have time this year, and I need some help now.
Ally:	Well, I think we could pull sales data for the last couple of years and do some basic forecasts. If nothing else, we could build a spreadsheet and run some simple simulations to see the effect on revenue.

Introduction

What subjects are you required to study? Many of them are outside your major field; some may not seem relevant to the job you hope to have. Why do you think these subjects are required? One reason is to show you how various disciplines solve problems and make decisions. Every academic discipline has created models that describe an approach to problems and identify common solutions. Psychologists create models of how humans behave and interact. Sociologists concentrate on models of groups and societies. Economists have models that attempt to explain how people, firms, and governments interact using money and prices. Financial models help you evaluate various investments. Marketing models of consumer behavior help you decide how to promote and sell products and services. General management models examine the organization of firms and interactions between workers. The point of each subject is to learn these models and recognize the problems they solve. Regardless of the job you eventually perform, you will be amazed at the number of models that will prove useful.

FIGURE 8.1

Tactical decisions often require complicated analysis. Problems utilize forecasts, optimization, and in-depth analysis. Information systems provide support through data, modeling, and presentation tools. Managers use information system tools to build, evaluate, and maintain various models.

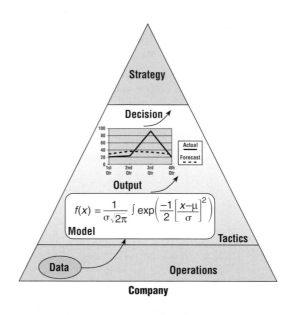

Trends

Through the 1970s, computers were largely used to assist with transaction processing. Support for making decisions was generally limited to the basic reports produced from the data. Computers were too expensive and programming too difficult to be used by every manager. As personal computers became commonplace through the 1980s, managers began transferring data from the corporate central computers to their personal computers.

Personal computers gave managers the ability to quickly examine the data from many different perspectives. They made it easy to compute totals and other statistics. Control over data on their personal machines also gave managers the ability to get reports and analyses faster. Spreadsheets gave managers the ability to create graphs quickly and easily. Managers now have the tools to evaluate data instantly and in detail. Combining basic statistics with graphs, it is easier to identify patterns and see trends. Spreadsheets also enable analysts to build models that can be used to examine the effects of changes using various assumptions and interrelationships between factors.

Another important trend that occurred during the 1980s and 1990s was the increased competitiveness experienced in most industries. Every decision became more important. Winning in business now requires that answers be more precise and decisions be made as rapidly as possible. More options need to be evaluated, and potential solutions have to be measured against corporate goals.

Our knowledge of business has also increased during the last decade. Academics and businesses have created more complex models or ways of approaching problems. Computers are used to analyze the corporate data using these models.

Information systems typically provide three levels of support for tactical decisions. First, they provide the data for the models. Second, technology provides support for building, evaluating, and analyzing models. Third, information systems provide the means to display the results in a variety of formats—especially graphs.

It Is Hard to Make Good Decisions

Most businesses have evolved over time. In many cases, their business processes have been built and patched in response to various changes in the industry. The firms that made better decisions and changes survived, the others failed. But the existing process might not be the most efficient. Consider the apparently simple process of farming. Farmers feed the animals and then sell them. The hard part is that the animals can be fed and housed many different ways—each with different costs. Should the animals be fed high-protein food that costs more and grows bigger animals faster, or should they be fed simple diets and take more time to mature? In the 1970s and 1980s, experts created software that analyzed these questions from the standpoint of minimizing the cost of feeding the animals. Using optimization methods, they were able to substantially reduce the production costs. But, some experts have found it is possible to do even better by focusing on profits across the entire industry chain.

Even if you do have a system for making a better decision, you need to convince managers to use it. Many managers distrust new technologies and different answers, because they see an element of risk. A few companies have established a culture that focuses on continual improvement and growth. In these companies, managers are encouraged to explore new ideas and replace the existing processes.

Human Biases

Assume you have money to invest in the stock market. Someone shows you two companies. As shown in Figure 8.2, Company A's share prices have risen by 2 percent per month for the last year. The other's share price was flat for five months but has increased by 3 percent per month since then. Which stock do you buy? But wait a minute. How can you possibly decide based on the little information you have? It sounds silly, but people make these decisions with minimal data and no logical analysis every single day. When people make decisions this way, the results are going to be inconsistent and dangerous. But it is so much easier to make a snap decision, and so much harder to do the research and complex analyses to make the right decision.

FIGURE 8.2

Sample decision. Do you invest your money in Company A or Company B? Be careful, it is a trick question.

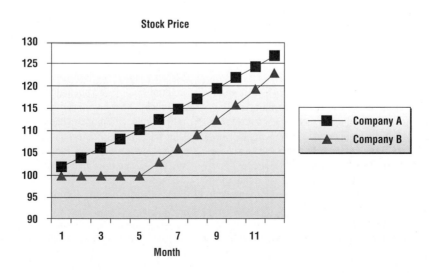

Consider a true example: designing a new automobile. Assuming you have money, what kind of car would you buy? Sporty, luxurious, flashy, utilitarian, big, small? What color? How many doors? Now ask a few friends or relatives what they would buy. Will all of the answers be the same? Not likely. Now think about the problem from the perspective of an automobile manufacturer such as General Motors. What features are car buyers going to demand in two or three years? This classic marketing problem is difficult to solve. For years, GM used its multiple divisions to create separate identities that appealed to different segments of the population. Designers within each division focused on the preferences and lifestyles of their specific target. Most of that structure fell apart in the mid-1980s with the introduction of a completely new line of cars. At that time, the GM divisions introduced a new car model from four main divisions. Somewhat surprisingly, all four cars (Oldsmobile Cutlass Ciera, Pontiac J2000, Chevrolet Celebrity, and Buick Century) were virtually identical—down to the color. In effect, GM was assuming that millions of customers all wanted the same car.

In response to these problems, Barabba and Zaltman, two marketing researchers working with GM, analyzed decision making at General Motors and noticed that several common problems arose. In summary, they found that people are weak at making decisions. For example, people place too much emphasis on recent events; they tend to discard data that does not fit their prior beliefs; they follow rules of thumb instead of statistical analysis; and they choose outcomes based on wishful thinking. As shown in Figure 8.3, all of these problems and more influenced the decisions of designers at GM. In particular, they found that the designers tended to discuss ideas with their bosses in an attempt to identify management preferences that would help get a particular design approved. So cars were designed to the preferences of a few managers, instead of to the needs of customers. Despite attempts to improve, the fiasco eventually forced GM to eliminate the Oldsmobile division. The books written by Barabba and Zaltman discuss even more examples and human biases in decision making.

The main point to remember is that making decisions without a good model and process leads to poor decisions. Sure, you might get lucky for awhile (like investors in the 1990s), but ultimately you need a solid decision making process.

Decision Tools

You understand the problems with making ad hoc decisions, but how do you make better decisions? What tools are available to help? Most realistic problems are hard to solve. They might have thousands of variables; it is never possible to collect all of the information you want; and the problems can be unstructured and hard to understand. Consequently, building a model of the problem is an important step in the analysis. A **model** is a simplified, abstract

---

Reality Bytes   **Dassault Systems CAD**

Dassault Systems developed the three-dimensional design software used to help design the Boeing 777—the most sophisticated commercial plane ever built. Bernard Charles, president of Dassault, notes that the software enabled the 777 to be the first airplane to fly with no physical mock-up. Additionally, it had fewer geometric errors than even the 747, which has been in production for 25 years. Mr. Charles notes "Now every new airplane on earth is made using our software." In addition to products, the software is also being used to design the factory layout. Today's CAD/CAM software does far more than build static models of the products. It creates dynamic models that obey the laws of physics, enabling designers to perform extensive

tests on ideas. Marketers are also using the tools to design product shapes and packaging, because they can see realistic views of the products even to the point of seeing how light will reflect under different conditions. For the future, Mr. Charles says "The next dream is to provide software that will enable our clients to simulate the entire life cycle of a product before it even exists. We are moving from digital mock-up to the digital life cycle." The digital lifecycle includes an analysis of the process and costs of dismantling the factory and reusing parts for future products.

Source: Adapted from "Lifelike Models that Leap off the Screen," *Financial Times,* December 23, 2001.

representation of some real-world system. It is simplified because we cannot handle all of the details of the real system.

Once the problem has been modeled, statistics can be used to estimate various components and responses and to forecast critical items. With estimates of the various model parameters, optimization tools can analyze the model and data to find the best solution. In complex cases, you can build simulations of various situations to see how the model will respond and evaluate possible options.

Models

Models are key aspects to any decision, but they are hard to create and difficult to validate. Many of the models you will use in business decisions were created by academics. You will be introduced to many of these models in other business courses. As a manager, you are responsible for knowing that hundreds of models are available to help you make decisions,

FIGURE 8.3

Biases in decision making. Without models, people tend to rely on simplistic "rules of thumb" and fall prey to a variety of common mistakes. These errors can be minimized with training and experience in a discipline. They can also be minimized by having computer systems perform much of the initial analysis.

Acquisition/Input		
Bias	**Description**	**Example**
Data availability	Ease with which specific instances can be recalled affects judgments of frequency	People overestimate the risk of dying due to homicides compared to heart disease
Illusory correlation	Belief that two variables are related when they are not	Ask any conspiracy buff about the death of JFK
Data presentation	Order effects	First (or last) items in a list are given more importance
Processing		
Inconsistency	Difficulty in being consistent for similar decisions	Judgments involving selection, such as personnel
Conservatism	Failure to completely use new information	Resistance to change
Stress	Stress causes people to make hasty decisions	Panic judgments and quick fixes
Social pressure	Social pressures cause people to alter their decisions and decision-making processes	Majority opinion can unduly influence everyone else: mob rule
Output		
Scale effects	The scale on which responses are recorded can affect responses	Ask a group of people to rate how they feel on a scale from 1 to 10. Ask a similar group to use a scale from 1 to 1,000
Wishful thinking	Preference for an outcome affects the assessment	People sometimes place a higher probability on events that they want to happen
Feedback		
Learning from irrelevant outcomes	People gain unrealistic expectations when they see incomplete or inaccurate data	In personnel selection you see how good your selection is for candidates you accepted; you do not receive data on candidates you rejected
Success/failure attributions	Tendency to attribute success to one's skill and failure to chance	Only taking credit for the successes in your job

FIGURE 8.4

The four primary reasons for building and using models. Descriptive, graphical, and mathematical models can be used for each of these purposes. However, mathematical models tend to be emphasized for optimization and simulation.

Model Building

Understand the Process

Models force us to define objects and specify relationships. Modeling is a first step in improving the business processes.

Optimization

Models are used to search for the best solutions: minimizing costs, improving efficiency, increasing profits, and so on.

Prediction

Model parameters can be estimated from prior data. Sample data is used to forecast future changes based on the model.

Simulation

Models are used to examine what might happen if we make changes to the process or to examine relationships in more detail.

and for knowing which model best applies to the problem you are facing. Understanding and evaluating models is an important aspect of a business education.

Models can be grouped into categories. Physical models are often used in design processes to make it easier to view and touch a proposed item. For instance, car manufacturers used to build full-size clay models of designs so people could get a better feel for the various features of the car. Today, designers increasingly rely on CAD/CAM systems to create realistic graphical displays. The electronic models are much easier to modify and share with other people.

Process models often use drawings and pictures to represent the various objects. However, at heart they typically use mathematical equations to represent the process and the various relationships. For example, an operations engineer would model a machine as a mathematical formula that converts raw materials and labor into products. Using equations for each step of the production process, the engineer could search for ways to reorganize production to make it more efficient or to improve quality.

We build models of a business or business process to help managers make decisions. Most businesses are far too complex for any single person to understand all of the details. Consequently, a variety of models may be created to present a simplified view of the business. In particular, one of the original purposes of accounting was to create a standardized model of the financial aspects of business. Another common model of business is the practice of dividing the company into functional areas. For example, a manager with experience in the finance department of one company can usually apply knowledge and problem-solving skills to finance departments in other companies and even other industries.

Of the thousands of models in business, some are simple rules-of-thumb that managers use to make quick decisions. Others are highly abstract, often expressed as detailed mathematical equations. Some models are incredibly detailed and require thousands of data variables, like economic forecasting models. Other models are descriptions of situations or behavior, such as motivational recommendations based on personality types. Why do we have so many different models?

The basic goals are summarized in Figure 8.4. The main reason we need models is because reality is too complex and hard to understand. Models help us simplify the world. They help us search for similarities in different situations. Models also enable managers to predict how changes might affect the business.

Consider a small example. You have an older car that has about 80,000 miles on it. You received a small raise in your job and are thinking about purchasing a newer car. Your initial impressions are swayed by the hundreds of automobile commercials you see and you would really like to buy a new car. You checked prices and dealer invoice costs using the Internet and are excited about buying a new car. On the other hand, you know that new cars lose

Reality Bytes   Building Quality Models in Spreadsheets

Many models are built using spreadsheets. In many respects, spreadsheets are similar to more traditional computer programs. Yet, designers rarely include comments that explain their intentions. Hence, when spreadsheets are passed to other users, there is enormous potential for mistakes and problems. You need to consider these problems when you create a spreadsheet and you should check other users' spreadsheets for them.

One common problem is the use or misuse of absolute and relative addresses (using the dollar sign to keep a cell reference from changing). Say that cell B1 holds the current hourly wage rate. Other cells can use that value to compute the cost of workers: =B1*C7. To be safe, the formula should be written as: =$B$1*C7. Without the absolute address, copying the formula to a new location will cause the B1 pointer to change, yielding incorrect results. These changes can be hard for later users to spot.

Be on the lookout for hidden columns, hidden rows, or hidden worksheets. Current spreadsheet software enables users to hide portions of the spreadsheet. There might be errors in these hidden segments—look for missing rows or columns. First save a backup copy, then "unhide" all of the rows and columns.

Beware of formulas in which the cell references have been changed to "hard" numbers or literals. Walter Schmidt, a CPA, recalls the time he gave a client a spreadsheet that computed the interest expense deduction for the client's taxes. At some point, the client discovered that the interest deduction was too low. On investigation, Schmidt learned that one of the client's employees had changed a cell reference to a constant value. When the spreadsheet was changed, the formula did not pick up the changes, leading to the wrong number.

Most current spreadsheets can present a "map view" of the spreadsheet, in which special characters indicate the purpose of each cell: value, formula, or label. These characters can help you spot formulas in which the entire cell has been accidentally replaced by a constant. You will still have to check individual formulas by hand. Other tools enable you to see how each cell depends on (or is used by) other cells. These tools are useful to spot cells that are no longer needed and to highlight circular references.

You can also protect spreadsheets by locking cells containing formulas. That way users will not accidentally overwrite your model.

Another useful trick is to make sure that any operations performed on columns have a "nice" starting and ending point. Place a line in the cell above the first row and after the last row. If the data range from B10 to B20, place a line in B9 and B21. Then any column operations should include the lines: SUM(B9:B21). The lines will not affect the computation. More important, if someone tries to insert a row before the first entry (B10), the new value will be included in the final total. If the original cell range only extended from B10 to B20, inserting a row before B10 would not update the total.

Cells and ranges should be given names. Then, instead of referring to a cell by its address, formulas will use the full name, making it easier to understand the purpose of the formula. Names are especially useful when you are linking spreadsheets.

Current spreadsheets make it easy to add notes to any cell. Use the notes to document the purpose of the cell and to answer questions that co-workers might have when they look at your spreadsheet. Be sure to reference the source of all equations and models.

10 to 15 percent of their value as soon as you drive them off the lot. A friend suggested that you should keep your old car for another year, but you are worried that it might lose too much value by next year.

You have just created a model. Part of the model is based on historical sales data that tells you how fast new cars depreciate in value. Another part of the model uses economic data to estimate the potential value of your used car if you keep it and add miles for another year. To make an informed decision, you could create a simple forecast of automobile prices to estimate what might happen to new car prices next year. You could then create a spreadsheet to analyze the cost of buying a new car. By using standard discount functions, you could compare the total cost of your choices.

As the decision maker, it is up to you to determine which models to use and to make sure they actually apply to the situation. Once you have selected the appropriate model, you apply whatever data you have, evaluate the results, and make the decision.

Understanding Processes

One of the primary reasons for building models is to help understand how the world behaves. Without a model or idea, how can you determine how things work? Citicorp uses a model to determine how well the banking firm is serving customers. By comparing the model results both to actual practice and to their corporate standards, Citicorp managers get

FIGURE 8.6

Prediction model. Several statistical techniques exist for analyzing data and making forecasts. Two common methods are regression and moving averages. Both methods require substantial amounts of data. Choosing between the two require some expertise in statistical analysis, but many times we display both methods show a range of possible outcomes.

FIGURE 8.11 Microsoft SQL Server cube browser. The location dimension is shown in the table of data, you can expand it or see subtotals by clicking on the grid. The other two dimensions (Category and SaleDate) are selected from the drop-down boxes at the top of the form. Here, the time dimension is expanded to show the selection of the second quarter. When values are changed, the new totals are displayed immediately.

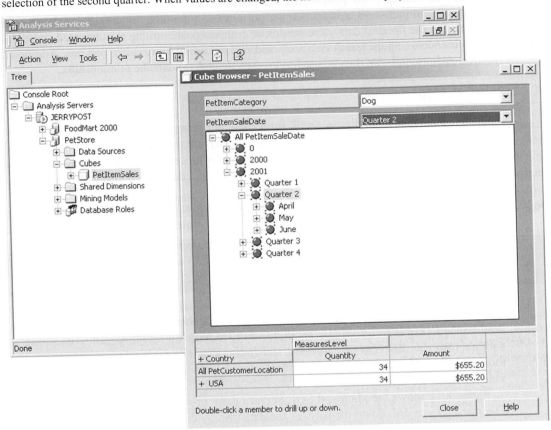

FIGURE 8.12 Microsoft pivot table report. Pivot tools make it easy for managers to examine cube data from any perspective, to select subsets of the data, to perform calculations, and to create charts.

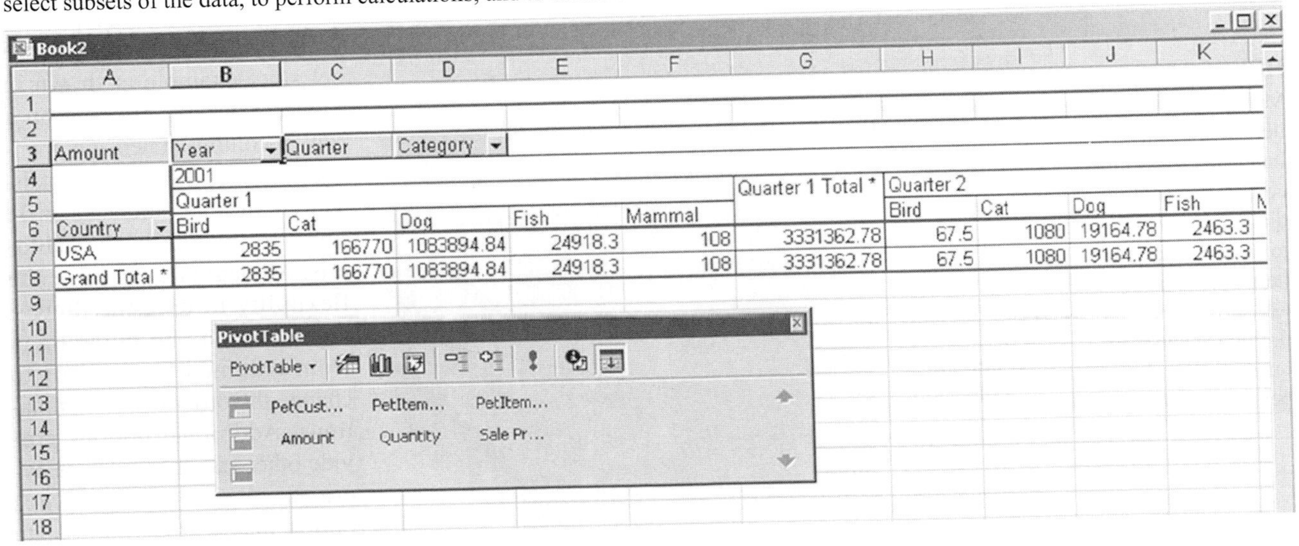

FIGURE 8.5

Optimization m
Optimization m
formed by ident
control variable
output or goals.
mathematical m
possible to locat
maximum or mi
point for the goa
problems are co
highly nonlinear
do not always ha
solution.

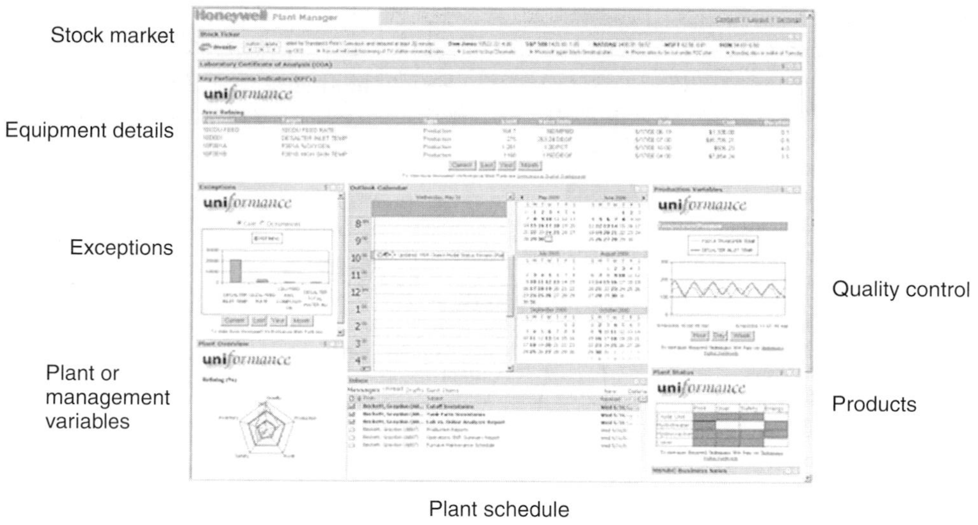

FIGURE 8.13

Digital dashboard example. Like the gauges on an automobile dashboard, the digital dashboard presents a top-level graphical representation of the status of various elements. It is particularly useful for manufacturing environments, but can also be used in more service-oriented industries.

Plant schedule

warehouses and pivot tables can also be used to create graphs and to feed data into other analytical software. For instance, once the pivot table data has been retrieved in Excel, it would be straightforward to add some financial calculations.

Output: Digital Dashboard and EIS

One of the major challenges to any information system is to make it easy to use. With DSSs this process is more complicated because the decisions need to be provided to upper-level managers who have little time to learn complex applications, yet deal with huge amounts of diverse data. One approach is to build a portal that displays key data and graphs on one page. The page retrieves data from a data warehouse, the Internet, even machines within a factory and displays graphs and warnings. Microsoft has developed a toolkit to help build this **digital dashboard**. The older term for this approach is an **executive information system (EIS)**. Figure 8.13 shows a sample digital dashboard that Honeywell is using to give plant managers a quick picture of the status of production lines.

Much like the dashboard on a car, the purpose of the main screen is to provide an overall picture of the status of the firm or a division or production plant. Managers can select the specific division and make comparisons to yesterday, last week, last month, or other locations. If there is a problem or a decision to be made, the executive can **drill down** to get more detailed data by pointing to another object. For example, if the main screen shows that current sales in the west region are low, the executive can focus on the west region and bring up the last few quarters of sales data. The EIS will graph the data to highlight trends. The manager can then dig deeper and bring up sales by departments or check the sales performance of each employee, highlighting unusually high or low sales figures. By pointing to customers, executives can get current profiles on the main customers and examine their recent purchases.

How Does an EIS Work?

For an EIS to work, it must be connected to the transaction processing system or data warehouse, since it is the source of the data. Many of these systems are created with special software that simply grabs data from the corporate databases. In one sense, the EIS is a complex model of the firm. Figure 8.14 illustrates how executives can "visit" different divisions on the computer and retrieve the data immediately. For the EIS to be useful, the computer model must be a faithful representation of the actual company.

As a model, the EIS display has inputs of raw materials and people. Outputs are typically measured by traditional accounting standards of profits, costs, and growth rates. The EIS

FIGURE 8.25

Geographic-based data. It is difficult to display this much data without overwhelming managers. Notice that the sales (radar) graphs use size and shape to highlight total sales, and the changing sales mix. Income is color-coded in a smaller graph. Notice in the sales graphs that the northern counties experienced a greater increase in sales in hard goods compared to the southern counties.

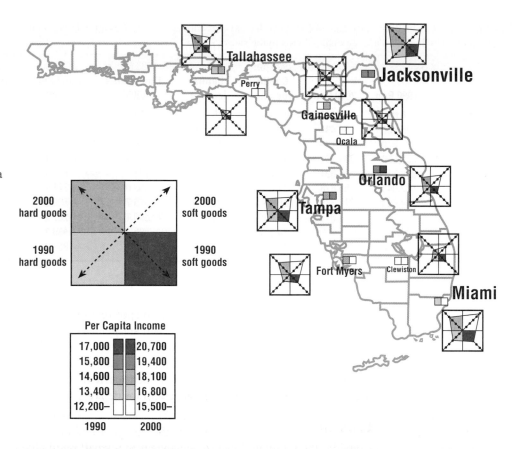

A Manager's View

Tactical-level decisions can be complex. Managers need to make forecasts, improve operations, and search for ways to reorganize the business. Making snap decisions based on "gut instinct" rarely leads to effective solutions. Rigorous analysis can involve mathematical and statistical evaluation of operations data. Models are tools that are used to make better decisions. Although they have limitations, models can provide insight into the business. Managers use decision support systems to collect data, evaluate models, present the results, and make better decisions.

It is unlikely that you will have to design your own theoretical models from scratch. On the other hand, you will be responsible for understanding the basic business models. You also will have to decide which model is needed to analyze and solve various problems. Once you have determined the appropriate model, a variety of software is available to help apply the model. Generic tools such as spreadsheets, statistics, and optimization packages rely on managers to supply the model. Some specific problems can be analyzed with prepackaged systems.

In many ways, executive information systems are models of the entire business. They are designed to make it easy for higher level managers to monitor the performance of the firm, identify problems, and retrieve data from the corporate databases. Digital dashboards can be used as the top-level interface to summarize current operations of the firm. For the many decisions related to location, a geographic information system helps highlight relationships that are hard to see within the data.

Key Words

circular reference, *309*	executive information	online analytical processing
converge, *309*	system (EIS), *299*	(OLAP), *297*
data mining, *297*	geographic information	optimization, *293*
descriptive models, *293*	system (GIS), *309*	parameter, *293*
digital dashboard, *299*	Global Positioning System	prediction, *293*
diverge, *309*	(GPS), *310*	simulation, *293*
drill down, *299*	model, *288*	unstable, *309*

Website References

Computer Manufacturers

Apple	**www.apple.com**
Compaq	**www.compaq.com**
Cray	**www.cray.com**
Dell	**www.dell.com**
Gateway 2000	**www.gateway.com**
IBM	**www.ibm.com**
Silicon Graphics	**www.sgi.com**
Sun	**www.sun.com**

Leading Software Companies

Microsoft	**www.microsoft.com**
Oracle	**www.oracle.com**
Computer Associates	**www.cai.com**
SAP	**www.sap.com**
Compuware	**www.compuware.com**
Siebel Systems	**www.siebel**
PeopleSoft	**www.peoplesoft.com**
BMC Software	**www.bmc.com**
Electronic Arts	**www.ea.com**
Cadence Design	**www.cadence.com**
Adobe	**www.adobe.com**

Additional Reading

Barabba, Vincent, and Gerald Zaltman. *Hearing the Voice of the Market.* Cambridge, MA: Harvard Business Press, 1991. [Overcoming design biases at GM.]

Dangermond, Jack, and Adena Schutzberg. "Engineering, Geographic Information Systems, and Databases: A New Frontier." *Journal of Computing in Civil Engineering,* July 1998, pp. 121–122. [Uses of GIS.]

Franses, Philip Hans. *Time Series Models for Business and Economic Forecasting.* Port Chester, NY: Cambridge University Press, 1998. [An introduction to forecasting.]

Krill, Paul. "Analytics Redraw CRM Lines." *Computerworld,* December 3, 2001. [A summary of vendors developing products to analyze customer data.]

Neil, Stephanie. "Blue Cross Dissects Data to Improve Care." *PC Week,* February 8, 1999. [BCBS uses data warehouse and online application processing DSS to improve service.]

Wilkinson, Stephanie. "PC Apps Help to Take a Byte Out of Crime." *PC Week,* February 23, 1998. [GIS and imaging tools help police predict and solve crimes.]

Review Questions

1. What are the primary reasons for creating business models?
2. What are three uses of models?
3. Describe three problems you might encounter when using models.
4. List the three major components of a DSS.
5. List the major steps involved in building or using a model to solve a problem.
6. What is the primary purpose of an executive information system?
7. List three advantages of an EIS.

8. What is a digital dashboard and how does it help executives manage a firm?

9. What is meant by the term *drill down* in an EIS?

10. How does a GIS help managers make better decisions?

Exercises

1. Find examples of five models. List the discipline (such as economics or marketing), give an example of how modeling is used and classify the use (optimization, prediction, simulation).

2. Find three software packages that would be useful for building decision support systems. Evaluate each in terms of the three DSS components. Are the packages generic or specific to some discipline?

3. Choose a local retail firm and identify three models that could be used by the manager to run the company. Which of these models is the most important to this firm? List the assumptions, input and output variables, and processes involved for this model.

4. Research software that can be used to create a digital dashboard. Assuming you are working for a midsized production firm, what data would you put on the dashboard? Sketch the screens you would like to see.

5. Interview a manager in your community to see what kinds of models he or she uses to make decisions. (Hint: Do *not* ask the manager to describe the models used.) Are the models mathematical, descriptive, or heuristic (rules of thumb)? Could some of the decisions be improved by using better models? How difficult would it be to create and use these models? Who selected and created the models currently being used?

6. A marketing manager has asked you to help design a DSS for the marketing department. Every month marketers need to evaluate the effectiveness of their advertising campaigns and decide how to allocate their budget for the next month. They advertise only in the local area and have four basic choices: radio, television, local newspapers, and direct mail. Each month, they conduct random phone interviews to find out who sees their advertisements. They can also purchase local scanner data to determine sales of related products. Each month, the media salespeople give them the Arbitron ratings that show the number of people (and demographics) who they believe saw each advertisement. They also receive a schedule of costs for the upcoming month. As a first step in creating the DSS, identify any relevant assumptions and input and output variables, along with any models that might be useful.

7. A government official recently noted that the government is having difficulty processing applications for assistance programs (welfare). Although most applications are legitimate, several facts they contain have to be checked. For instance, welfare workers have to check motor vehicle and real estate records to see whether the applicants own cars or property. The agency checks birth, death, and marriage records to verify the existence of dependents. They sometimes examine public health data and check criminal records. It takes time to check all of the records, plus the agency needs to keep track of the results of the searches. Additionally, a few applicants have applied multiple times—sometimes in different localities. The office needs to randomly check some applications to search for fraud. Every week, summary reports have to be sent to the state offices. A key feature of these reports is that they are used to convince politicians to increase funding for certain programs. Describe how a DSS could help this agency. Hint: Identify the decisions that need to be made.

8. From the marketing example, compute a new set of numbers and draw a similar graph given the costs of the promotions: Promo 1: $1,000 up front; Promo 2: $300 per week; Promo 3: $1,000 up front. (Advanced option: Use statistics to estimate the equations in the text.) Trivia question: What does inchiki mean?

9. Use a spreadsheet to create the example from the HRM section. Fill in the market adjustment column so that raises match the performance appraisals. Remember, total raises cannot exceed $10,000.

C08GIS.xls

10. Using the sample GIS data and the picture, can you identify any other potential relationships? What other information would you like to see? Can you measure how the different factors affect sales? (Hint: Use statistical techniques.)

 ## DeptStor.mdb

You are a midlevel manager for a small department store. You have collected a large amount of data on sales for 2001. Your transaction system kept track of every sale (order) by customer. Most customers paid by credit card or check, so you have complete customer data. Walk-in customers who paid cash are given a separate customer number, so you still have the sales data.

Department	Customers/month
Clothing—Children	180
Clothing—Men	150
Clothing—Women	180
Electronics	200
Furniture	150
Household	250
Linen	300
Shoes	300
Sports	400
Tools	340

You are trying to determine staffing levels for each department. You know that the store becomes much busier during the end-of-the-year holiday season. For summer months, you have thought about combining staff from the departments. From conversations with experienced workers, you have determined that there is a maximum number of customers that can be handled by one person in a department. These numbers are expressed as monthly averages in the table.

You are thinking about combining workers from some of the departments to save on staffing—especially over the spring and summer months. However, working multiple departments makes the sales staff less efficient. There are two considerations in combining staff members. First, if any of the departments are reduced to a staff of zero, sales in that department will drop by 10 percent for that month. Second, total staffing should be kept at the level defined by the monthly averages. If average staffing (total across all departments) falls below the total suggested, then sales in all departments will fall by 2 percent for each tenth of a percentage point below the suggested average.

11. Using the database and a spreadsheet, determine how many workers we need in each department for each month. Present a plan for combining departments if it can save the company money. Assume that sales members cost an average of $1,000 a month. Two queries have already been created by the MIS department and are stored in the database: SalesbyMonth and SalesCountByMonth. The first totals the dollar value; the second counts the number of transactions.

12. Write a report to upper management designating the appropriate sales staff levels for each department by month. Include data and graphs to support your position. (Hint: Use a spreadsheet that lets you enter various staffing levels in each department in each month, then calculate any sales declines.)

13. Find a financial model to evaluate investments. Apply the model to stock prices from at least five companies.

14. Describe five problems that could benefit from a GIS. Make sure it needs a GIS, not just a mapping system.

Rolling Thunder Database

15. Identify five models that could be used to improve the management of the Rolling Thunder Bicycle Company. What data would be needed to evaluate the models?

16. Identify shipments where receipts do not match the original order. Provide a count and value (and percentages) by supplier/manufacturer.

17. Using basic accounting, list costs and revenues by month. Provide any graphs and tables to illustrate trends or patterns.

18. Analyze sales and discounts by employee and by model type. Are some employees providing higher discounts than others? Are we discounting some models too much or not enough?

19. List a tactical-level decision in each of the main divisions of the company. How often is the decision made? Who makes it? What information is used? What types of analyses need to be performed?

20. Use an OLAP tool (Microsoft Pivot table if nothing else is available) to retrieve and organize sales data. Identify any patterns or potential problems in sales.

Cases

Computer Hardware Industry

The computer hardware industry is a maturing industry in rapid and constant transition. For example, in 2001, Intel had sales of about $28 billion. Yet, more than 90 percent of Intel's revenue came from products that did not even exist the previous year. This represents product life cycles at their shortest.

Growth in computer hardware spending has been largely driven by business purchases. The computer hardware industry can be divided into three segments: (1) systems and servers (including mainframes and supercomputers), (2) personal computers (PCs) and (3) workstations. Of the $800 billion spent on information technology in 2000, 40 percent was spent on hardware.

Financial Analysis

The significant growth of the computer hardware industry has dramatically increased revenues to companies in the industry. Profit margins are much slimmer in the United States due to fierce competition and the price wars waged for the sake of market share. Nonetheless, computer hardware companies are expanding internationally where profit margins are certainly higher.

Due to the extremely fast market cycle, inventory turnover is very high. Any company with lower inventory turnover than its competitors will quickly have balance sheet problems.

Stock/Investment Outlook

The outlook for the computer hardware industry, while not rosy, is positive. The continued build-out of LANs and WANs (also called *client-server computing*) in business settings creates a need for PCs. The increasing consumer interest in Web access is also very positive for the industry. Over 50 percent of U.S. households have a PC, but far fewer do worldwide. Thus, the PC market is nowhere near saturation on a global basis.

Stock in computer hardware companies will be volatile. Since the technologies involved are changing fast, hopes and fears will also be rising and falling in step. Expectations of future earnings and success will be difficult to gauge. Will Microsoft and Intel dominate the markets further? Will there be successful challenges to their hegemony? Will technological breakthroughs in other areas such as communications or physics change the industry? Computer hardware will never be as staid as breakfast cereals.

Growth Potential

The tremendous increases in PC power and flexibility and the ability to amplify PC strengths by networking, in local area networks (LANs) and wide area networks (WANs), has made the PC segment the largest. This segment is the biggest in both units and dollars. Between 1991 and 1995, PC shipments increased at 20 percent annually. However, that has since slowed considerably. Shipment growth of at least 5 percent annually should continue.

Large systems and services account for about 35 percent of the spending on computer hardware. Certainly mainframe sales have dropped, but sales of servers have increased. Servers are needed to enable the creation of LANs and WANs.

Workstations constitute only 5 percent of spending on computer hardware. Workstations combine powerful processors, networking, and graphical user interfaces. They are put together in packages aimed at certain intensive professions like engineering, 3-D animation, and scientific applications. The increasing power of PCs has infringed on the market segment where UNIX vendors dominate.

Competitive Structure

The top 10 PC suppliers control 65 percent of the market, and competition is fierce. In fact, the PC market in some ways resembles a commodity market; top vendors target market share over margins. Also, new entrants to the industry have slowed and the product offerings of existing vendors have widened.

"Wintel" is an acronym for the Microsoft Windows-Intel hegemony that dominates the PC market. Worldwide, 90 percent of PCs use the Windows operating systems and 80 percent of all PCs use an Intel microprocessor. This is a concern of many, including some at the U.S. Department of Justice. One feature of this market domination, unlike other monopoly situations, is constant innovation. Others see it as quite the opposite. In 2001, Microsoft was almost forced to split into two separate companies due to the ruling that it has engaged in anticompetitive behavior.

Intel and Microsoft spend 13 percent of their combined sales on R&D. This is far ahead of other computer hardware vendors, who only spend 3 to 5 percent of sales. Yet, with this constant innovation and improvement comes ever shorter product life cycles. In fact, the need or perceived need to upgrade PC systems has benefited the entire industry.

Declining sales in 2001 coupled with intense competitive pressure led by Dell forced significant restructuring in the personal computer industry. In January 2002, IBM announced that it would no longer manufacture personal computers—instead, the remaining production facilities would be transferred to Sanmina SCI. IBM will still put its name on the machines. However, IBM also announced that it would stop most of its direct sales, particularly to smaller businesses. Basically, IBM will continue to sell its branded desktops in bulk to large corporate customers. IBM will continue to make laptops. Similarly, in late 2001 and early 2002, Compaq Computer and Hewlett-Packard explored a merger. However, HP stockholders (led by the Hewlett and Packard children) were deeply concerned that the merger would be pointless. In the past few years, neither company was successful in the personal computer market, and many believed that a merger of two ineffective product lines would not improve sales or profits.

Technological Investment and Analysis

The investment in technology is particularly pronounced in the manufacturing aspect of computer hardware. Due to the fierce competition in the industry, cost control is very important. The price differentials between direct PC sellers and retail PC sellers have narrowed greatly because of the control of costs. The increased competition means there is less room for error by those in the industry.

The technical and scientific feats of further innovation in processor speeds and storage capabilities demands ever more complicated manufacturing constraints. Constant advantage must be gleaned from the latest technologies in manufacturing and research.

Recommendation for the Future

In the future, the computer hardware industry will have to broaden, in order to satisfy market needs. Presently, PCs fit this description: one type fits all. There is really only one type of PC with a few interchangeable parts of varying degrees of newness. Does one have a 700 MHz microprocessor or a 1300 MHz microprocessor? In many ways, it does not really matter.

Upgrading can be a costly endeavor. Who will design and create simpler, task-specific machines? Which companies will ensure that old software can talk to new software by making translators? The industry would do well to follow the auto industry. In the auto industry, it is no longer one car for all people but a different car for every individual.

Case: Dell Computer Corporation

Short Description of the Company

In 1997, Dell extended its use of technology by incorporating a service that electronically links Dell with several larger corporate customers. Purchases of Dell products can be made directly through corporate accounting systems of a suitably outfitted corporation or institution.

Dell Computer also focuses on the server market. Servers account for 6 percent of the company's system revenue. The company currently ranks fourth in server sales behind IBM. Beginning in 1997, Dell Computer made stronger efforts to move up in sales rank by cutting server prices by 16 percent on its midrange and high-end Pentium Pro processor-based Power Edge network servers. The price cuts positioned Dell Power Edge servers at prices 30 to 35 percent lower than comparable systems offered by Dell's major competitors.

Dell has been able to remain profitable and grow even during the most recent recession in 2001 due to its nimble and lean structure. Dell's "built to order" business model is the envy of the industry because it enables the company to keep inventory to a minimum. Dell keeps taking market share and profitability

from Gateway. Earnings have grown at more than 30 percent annually for the past five years as of the end of 2001. Dell overtook Compaq as the biggest manufacturer of PCs in 2001.

Dell Computer has also entered the international arena. In 1997, the company moved into 10 markets in Asia, enabling customers to purchase a computer online in Australia, the United States, Hong Kong, New Zealand, Thailand, Korea, Malaysia, Singapore, Taiwan, and Japan. Dell Computer has various Web pages for different countries, each developed in local languages and local currencies. The Dell website now has a different and customized page for over 80 different countries. To cut costs, computers are manufactured in foreign plants rather than in the United States.

Not everything that Dell has done has turned to gold, however. Around 1995, Dell attempted to expand its customer base by marketing PCs through discount retail electronic stores. This approach was a disaster for Dell. The biggest problem was that the computers sent to the stores quickly went out of date. Sales were low, and the stores wanted to return the old computers to Dell. After a short time, Dell backed out of the market and today focuses on selling customized systems, where each person can select the desired options, and the machine is custom-assembled.

In 2001, while competitors were losing money, Dell was busy cutting costs, making profits, and expanding its market share. During the last quarter of 2001, Dell's share of the world PC market increased by 2.5 percentage points to 14.2 percent. Dell's share of the U.S. PC market rose to 27.5 percent. This share exceeds the combined level of the number 2 and 3 manufacturers (H-P and Compaq).

Technology Innovations

Manufacturing

Dell has a significant advantage over other manufacturers. A computer is not built until the customer orders it. There is no middleman. The customer gets exactly what he or she wants at a cheaper price than anyone else can provide. Dell produces the machines so quickly that the company receives payment from the customer before Dell has to pay the suppliers. The system virtually guarantees a profit on every machine. In late 2000, Dell decided to use its strength and slashed prices on PCs, driving the other major manufacturers into red ink.

Network

Dell has not chosen the same strategy as Compaq for networks. Compaq markets components of networking that are tied to the server; these include the things that go in the box, the network adapters, and so on. Conceivably, things attached to the server could be sold easily. But Compaq must convince the reseller to sell the Compaq server and the Compaq router or the Compaq switch, rather than the Cisco or 3Com or Bay Networks product. That is not easy. Larger network users have already bought into architectures, and customers will need a compelling argument to switch vendors. Dell is therefore committed to pursuing only the server market.

CEO Michael Dell believes his company's strategy is appropriate and will be sufficient to make it the number-one server supplier. He asserts that Dell's own efforts have been helped by the move toward a standardization of products with the strength of sales of Microsoft-based servers. The company will continue to push for industry standards and does not see itself as a technology innovator.

Telecommunications

Dell's telecommunication plans are broad. They include customized websites for business customers. These let a company's employees buy computers directly over the Internet based on automated policies. Dell is also focusing on automated service and support based on the latest configuration information of a company. The vendor is currently designing a workflow capability that will automate the purchase-approval process within businesses.

Questions

1. Who or what forces are driving the strategic direction of Dell Computer?

2. What has been the catalyst for change at Dell Computer?

3. What caused a change in the use of technology at Dell Computer?

4. How successful has the use of technology been at Dell Computer?

5. Does Dell have the financial ability to embark on a major technological program of advancement?

6. What does the corporation's Web page present about their business directives?

7. How important is customer data to Dell's continued success?

Additional Reading

"The Billionares' Club." *PC Magazine,* December 1, 1998, p. 9.

"Breakfast with Michael Dell." *VAR Business,* September 28, 1998, p. 111.

Cullen, Drew. "IBM Outsources Netvista PC Production." *The Register,* January 9, 2002.

Darrow, Barbara. "Michael Dell—Dell Says He Still Enjoys Taking PCs Apart and Reassembling Them, Maintaining What Colleagues Say Is a Fascination with the Technology." *Computer Reseller News,* November 16, 1998, p. 126.

Davey, Tom. "Dell Turns to Servers—Chairman and CEO Michael Dell Discusses the Vendor's Plans for High-End Servers and Online." *Information Week,* April 27, 1998, p. 156.

"Dell Inks Big E-Commerce Deal." *InternetWeek,* February 15, 1999, p. 9.

"Dell Strengthens Server Leadership with Price Cuts of Up to 16 Percent." *The Wall Street Journal,* May 15, 1997.

"The Direct Route." *InfoWorld,* June 2, 1997, pp. 1, 19.

"The Entrepreneurial Bone." *PC Magazine,* February 23, 1999, p. 30.

Fisher, Andrew. "View from the Top: Michael Dell." *Financial Times,* September 05, 2001.

Gallant, John. "A Dollop of Michael Dell—on Servers and More." *Network World,* May 4, 1998, p. 20.

Girishanker, Saroja. "The InternetWeek Interview— Michael Dell, Chairman and CEO, Dell Computer." *InternetWeek,* April 13, 1998, p. 8.

McWilliams, Gary. "Michael Dell's Newest Role: Private Investor." *The New York Times,* December 16, 1998, p. B1.

McWilliams, Gary. "Dell Raises 4th-Quarter Profit Forecast As Its Share of World PC Market Grows." *The Wall Street Journal,* January 21, 2002.

Pendery, David, Dan Briody, and Ephraim Schwartz. "What Dell Does Best." *InfoWorld,* April 6, 1998, p. 1.

Serwer, Andy. "Dell Does Domination." *Fortune,* January 21, 2002.

Thurm, Scott. "H-P's Board Sends Letter Calling Deal Best Way to Increase Value of Company." *The Wall Street Journal,* January 18, 2002.

Trommer, Diane. "Michael S. Dell—Direct-Sales Mega-Maven Continues to Recast Biz Models." *Electronic Buyers' News,* December 21, 1998, p. 48.

Case: Gateway 2000, Inc.

Ted Waitt founded TIPC (Texas Instruments PCs) Network in August 1985 after dropping out of college. He brought in his friend Mike Hammond to work the technical side of the business. Contrary to popular belief, the pair started their business in an empty office on the Waitt cattle farm and not in a barn.

The company sold upgrades and accessories to owners of Texas Instruments (TI) PCs. Waitt's grandmother guaranteed the $10,000 loan that founded TIPC. Norm Waitt, Ted's older brother, joined the company in early 1986 to take care of the company's finances. In 1987, Texas Instruments reportedly offered its customers a chance to upgrade their old machines to IBM-compatible PCs for $3,500.

Waitt and Hammond saw this as a great opportunity, since they knew they could do the same for much less. The first Gateway computer had two floppy drives, a deluxe color monitor, and more memory than most PCs at the time. The $2,000 asking price was comparable to other models, but the Gateway PC offered far greater performance.

Gateway's marketing capitalized on a distinctive cow motif—which established an early brand identity in a market where PCs were typically seen as commodities.

Technology Innovations

The MMX processor was introduced in January 1997. Through diligent research, Gateway was able to capitalize on this new technology. Gateway was able to offer PCs with the new processor to consumers prior to many of its competitors. Consumer demand decreased in the fourth quarter of FY1996 in anticipation of the MMX introduction.

Gateway capitalized on the introduction of the MMX processor by immediately offering the new processor as soon as consumers demanded. Gateway experienced greater-than-expected demand in the first quarter of FY1997 for PCs with this new technology. This greater-than-expected demand was also a sign to the rest of the industry that there was strong demand for the new processor.

Gateway's strategic advantage over the competition is outstanding technical support. To ensure that the service levels remain high, Gateway continues to provide extensive training for its support staff with each new technological introduction. The support staff must be aware of each new product's capabilities and nuances in order to provide the most complete technological support available.

In 1998, Gateway created a new sales channel through retail stores. However, the stores carry only demonstration computers. Salespeople explain features and options and provide the customer with a hands-on experience. To purchase the computer, the clerks enter the specifications into the Gateway computer system. The customer's system is custom assembled at the factory and shipped to the customer.

Gateway was at the right place at the right time during the PC boom. However, slipping sales into 2000 convinced founder Ted Waitt to return as CEO. Even so, the recession of 2001 has proven to be difficult for Gateway. The company has lost significant market share to Dell and other competitors. Not only have profits shrunk, but so have revenues and units sold. The company is struggling to find a channel for growth in the slowing PC market. Analysts wonder how much longer the "Gateway country stores" will stay open in an era where most people who want a computer do not value a salesperson to hold their hand when buying one.

Recommendation for the Future

Gateway must continue monitoring the ever-changing technology environment to remain a step ahead of the competition. They must continue to offer consumers the latest new technology. Gateway must also continue to invest in the extensive training of their support staff to maintain their competitive advantage in customer support. A lapse of foresight could result in a serious setback to the company.

Gateway 2000, Inc., has displayed the ability to aggressively develop new PCs with the latest technology and pass along the savings resulting from improved technology directly to the consumer. This management style will enable Gateway

2000 to continue the growth the company has experienced. Gateway also must enter new areas where they can grow, since the PC business has slowed and is plagued by low margins.

The biggest question facing Gateway is the value of their retail stores. In early 2001, Gateway closed 10 percent of the U.S. stores, bringing the total to about 300 stores. Most stores were closed because there were too many stores in the same cities. Some analysts noted that the stores are providing an increasing level of revenue. During 2000, phone and e-commerce sales dropped from 76 percent to 65 percent of total revenue. The major strength of the stores is that they provide higher-profit items such as services and training.

Questions

1. What forces are driving the strategic direction for Gateway 2000, Inc.?

2. Upon what technologies has Gateway relied?

3. How has Gateway changed its use of technology over time?

4. What does Gateway's Web page present about its business directives?

5. What role does data play in the future of Gateway 2000?

6. How will the capture and maintenance of customer data, particularly from customer calls for support, impact the corporation's future?

7. How do the retail stores Gateway introduced in 1999 compare to Dell's failed retail attempt?

Additional Reading

Abel, Amee. "The Solo 2500SE Leads the Way for High-Value Notebooks." *Computer Shopper,* September 1998, p. 234.

Berlind, David. "Get Ready for Software with Cow Spots: Gateway Looks beyond Hardware." *Computer Shopper,* September 1998, p. 108.

"Gateway G6-333." *Computer Shopper,* September 1998, p. 181.

"New Gateway 2000 Customer Support Subsidiary Locating in Hampton; New Call Center Will Add 300 Jobs." *EDGE: Work-Group Computing Report,* December 30, 1996, p. 9.

Williams, Tish. "Gateway Struggles to Play Dell's Game." 01/08/2002, TheStreet.com.

Wolf, Marty. "Shopping Daze: Buying a Computer Led to an Epiphany." *Computer Reseller News,* January 25, 1999, p. 46.

Appendix

Forecasting

Think of what you could accomplish if you could see the future. Of course, no one can truly predict future events. However, in many situations a forecast can provide a good idea of the possibilities. Of course, forecasting patterns for the near future is much easier than predicting what might happen several years out.

Forecasting is used in many areas of business. Marketing forecasts future sales, the effect of various sales strategies, and changes in buyer preferences. Finance forecasts future cash flows, interest rate changes, and market conditions. The HRM department builds forecasts of various job markets, the amount of absenteeism, and labor turnover. Strategic managers forecast technological changes, actions by rivals, and various market conditions. Sometimes these forecasts are built on intuition and rules of thumb. But it is better to use statistical techniques whenever possible.

The science of forecasting is dominated by two major approaches: time-series forecasting that identifies trends over time, and structural modeling that identifies relationships among the underlying variables. Many forecasts require the use of both techniques.

As shown in Figure 8.1A, by focusing on the underlying model, structural modeling seeks to identify the cause of changes. For example, if consumer income increases, the demand for products shifts out, increasing sales. If you know the shapes of the supply and demand curves, it is straightforward to predict how sales will increase.

Figure 8.2A shows a time-series approach to the same issue of sales forecasting. In some ways it is simpler. We know nothing about the underlying model and have simply collected sales data for the past few months. The data is plotted over time. By fitting a trend line to the data, it is clear that sales are increasing. Assuming that this trend continues, it is easy to

forecast sales for the next period. Of course, without a structural model, you will not be able to identify the cause of the changes, and your forecast could be seriously wrong.

Structural Modeling

Modeling an underlying structure provides the most information and knowledge about a problem. Consider a simple physics problem: If you throw a ball at a certain angle, with a certain force, how far will it travel? You could try several experiments, timing each event and measuring the outcome. You could then use this data to make a forecast of future attempts. However, if you know the underlying model of gravity (e.g., Newton's equations), then it is easy to determine the outcome of any attempt.

Many economic models have been developed to determine relationships that apply to business decisions. For instance, cost models are used to determine supply relationships, and consumer preferences generate demand curves. Demand for a product can be expressed as a function of several variables: price, income, and prices of related products. These relationships can be estimated with common statistical techniques (e.g., multiple regression).

Figure 8.3A presents the basic steps in using a structural model to forecast sales demand. First you need a model—in this case, a basic economic model. Then you need to collect data for each of the variables in the model. It is best if the underlying variables change over time, and you will need observations from several points in time. It is best to have at least 40 observations, but you get better results with more data. Next you use regression analysis (in Excel: Tools + Data Analysis) to estimate the values of the model parameters. Finally, you plug in estimates of the independent variables to obtain a forecast of the future sales.

FIGURE 8.1A   Structural model forecast. The underlying model helps explain the causal relationships, making it easier to forecast the effect of changes. Here, an increase in income shifts the demand curve, which causes increased sales (Q) even at higher prices.

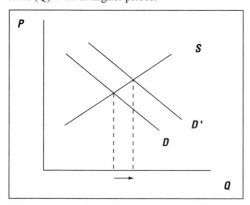

FIGURE 8.2A   Time series forecast. Sales change over time. The trend line provides a forecast of future values, but it assumes that underlying factors behave as they did in earlier times.

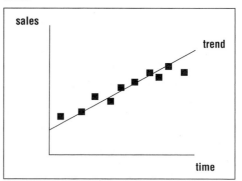

FIGURE 8.3A Forecasting process using a structural model. Collect data and use regression to estimate the underlying parameters. Then plug in estimates of the future values of the independent variables to forecast the value of the dependent variable (quantity).

Model	$Q_D = b0 + b1$ Price $+ b2$ Income $+ b3$ Substitute				
	Time	**Quantity**	**Price**	**Income**	**Substitute**
Data	1	24926	134	20000	155
	2	26112	150	21000	155
	3	27313	142	22000	135
	4	26143	141	21000	150
Estimate	$Q_D = 1114 - 0.1$ Price $+ 1.2$ Income $- 1.0$ Substitute				
Forecast	$33318 = 1114 - 0.1 (155) + 1.2 (20000) - 1.0 (160)$				

Time-Series Forecasts

When you do not have a structural model, or when you need to forecast the value of an underlying variable, you can use time-series techniques to examine how variables change over time. The basic process is to collect data over time, identify any patterns that exist, and then extrapolate this pattern for the future. The approach assumes that the underlying pattern will remain the same. For example, if income has been gradually increasing over time, it assumes that this increase will continue.

Figure 8.4A shows a time series consists of a number of observations made over a period of time. Four types of patterns often arise in time-series data: (1) trends, (2) cycles, (3) seasonal variations, and (4) random changes. A trend is a gradual increase or decrease over time. A cycle consists of up and down movements relative to the trend. Seasonal variations arise in many disciplines. For instance, agricultural production increases in the summer and fall seasons, and many industries experience an increase in sales in November and December due to holiday sales. Random components are variations that we cannot explain through other means. In some cases, the random component dominates the others, and forecasting is virtually impossible. For example, many people believe this situation exists for stock market prices.

Exponential Smoothing

Random variations make it difficult to see the underlying trend, seasonal, and cyclical components. One solution is to remove these variations with exponential smoothing. Exponential smoothing computes a new data point based on the previ-

FIGURE 8.4A Exponential smoothing. The smoothed data is computed by Excel by applying a smoothing factor to each new data point.

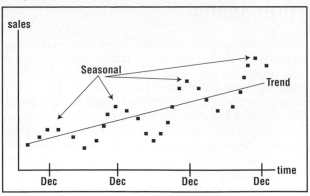

FIGURE 8.5A Time series components. A trend is a gradual change over time. Seasonal patterns show up as peaks and troughs at annual intervals. Other cycles are similar but cover longer time periods and are usually less regular. Random change is shown because the cycle and trend are not perfect.

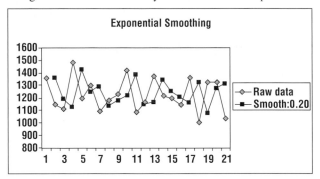

ously computed value and the newly observed data value. The weight given to each component is called the *smoothing factor*. The higher the smoothing factor, the more weight that is given to the new data point. Typical values range from 0.2 to 0.30, although it is possible to use factors up to 1.0 (which would consider only the new value and ignore the old ones). Lower values (down to 0.01) put more weight on previous computations and result in a smoother estimate.

Current spreadsheets (e.g., Microsoft Excel) have procedures that will quickly estimate the moving average for a range of data. You simply mark the range of data, highlight the output range, and supply the smoothing factor. As shown in Figure 8.5A, it is then easy to graph the original and the smoothed data.

How do you choose the smoothing factor? The best method is to apply several smoothing factors (start with 0.10, 0.20, and 0.30) and then examine the accuracy of the result. The accuracy is typically measured as the sum-of-squared errors. For each smoothed column of data, compute (actual − smoothed)*(actual − smoothed) to get the squared-error on

FIGURE 8.6A   Trend line in Excel. Right-click on the data points to add the trend line. It is also helpful to use the options to display the equation.

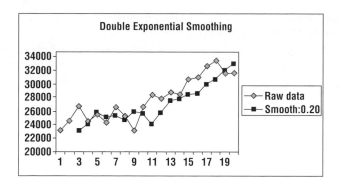

FIGURE 8.7A   Forecasting with linear trends. Use regression to estimate the two parameters. Then plug in the desired time value to obtain the predicted trend value for any new time period.

Time	Sales	Forecast	
9	22500	28703.41	=$F$20+$F$21*B6
10	28524	29215.04	
11	34600	29726.66	
12	29136	30238.29	
13	26000	30749.92	
14	30306	31261.55	*Coefficients*
15	32133	31773.18	Intercept 24098.7579
16	36200	32284.8	Time 511.62782
17	38300	32796.43	
18	35700	33308.06	
19	33355	33819.69	
20	29800	34331.31	*Tools + Data Analysis + Regression*
21		34842.94	*Dependent = Sales*
22		35354.57	*Independent = Time*
23		35866.2	
24		36377.83	
25		36889.45	

each row. Add these values to get the total. Now compare these totals for each of the smoothing factors. The smoothing factor with the smallest error is the one to use.

Simple Linear Forecasts

If you are only interested in the trend and not the cyclic components, you can use simple linear forecasts. A linear forecast statistically averages all of the elements and extends this line into the future. It can be relatively accurate as long as you do not try to predict too far out, and as long as there are no fundamental changes in the structure.

Microsoft Excel has three methods to create a linear forecast, (1) Mark a column of numbers, then drag the bottom corner down and Excel will generate the linear forecasts, (2) Graph the series using a line graph, then right-click the graphed points and Add a Trendline, (3) Use Tools + Data Analysis and Linear Regression to estimate the intercept and slope coefficients, then build the formula to predict the future values. The first method is so easy it is scary—because it automatically creates numbers that users probably do not know what they mean. Be sure to label your forecasted values or format them in a different color. Figure 8.6A shows the chart from the second method. It is relatively easy to create, and most people understand the purpose of the trend line.

If you just need the equation coefficients, you can obtain them from the linear regression tools in Excel (Tools + Data Analysis + Regression). The *y*-series is the column that you wish to forecast. The *x*-series is the time values (e.g., months). Figure 8.7A shows the partial results of the regression analysis. The analysis places the coefficients into the spreadsheet where they can be used to compute the forecasted values. The result is the prediction along the trend line, which ignores cyclical variations. If you want to see the cyclical, seasonal, and random factors, you can subtract the predicted values from the original series.

Seasonal and Cyclical Components

Two powerful methods exist to decompose time series data into its trend, seasonal, and cyclical components. They are Box-Jenkins and Fourier analysis. You can purchase tools that will perform the complex calculations for these methods. Unfortunately, it would take many pages to describe either one of these techniques, so they are beyond the scope of this appendix. Just remember that it is possible to perform much more detailed analyses (and forecasts) of time series data. If you need them, hire an expert, or take a separate class in time-series forecasting.

Exercises

1. Obtain a three-year set of monthly data from the Bureau of Labor Statistics website (http://stats.bls.gov) that is not seasonally adjusted (e.g., Producer Price Index). Transfer the data to a spreadsheet. Plot the data and include a trend line.

2. Plot the sales data from the table. Draw one graph with a trend line and a second chart with three-period moving average smoothing.

3. Using the regression functions in the spreadsheet, estimate the trend line and produce a forecast for four periods ahead.

4. Use the regression coefficients to create a predicted value for each month in the data. Create a new column by subtracting this predicted value from the actual sales. Graph the result and compute a moving average trend line.

Sales Data for Exercises 2, 3, and 4												
	Jan	**Feb**	**Mar**	**Apr**	**May**	**Jun**	**Jul**	**Aug**	**Sep**	**Oct**	**Nov**	**Dec**
2001	414	382	396	530	551	396	365	415	424	485	684	802
2002	457	432	465	598	632	424	392	476	489	555	768	883
2003	505	477	534	636	696	466	442	506	531	610	825	973

CHAPTER NINE

Complex Decisions and Expert Systems

What you will learn in this chapter

- How does information technology help solve certain complex problems?

- How do expert systems support managers?

- What are the limitations of expert systems?

- What functions do machines perform better than humans?

- How do computers solve pattern recognition problems?

- Can computers understand speech?

- How do you identify which technology to use on specific problems?

- Why is AI important in e-business?

Chapter Outline

Mrs. Fields is recognizable around the nation. Local franchises are supported by expert systems enabling the company to function with fewer expensive managers.

Mrs. Fields, Inc.

In 1977, Debbie Fields opened a small cookie store in Palo Alto, California, defying conventional wisdom that "No one will pay 75 cents for a cookie." The store specialized in chocolate chip cookies made from a recipe generous in chocolate chips. It became an overnight success. Mrs. Fields cookies struck a responsive chord in the taste buds of the Palo Alto residents. Today, these cookies are available nationwide at more than 635 licensed franchises.

Randy Fields, the "mister" in Mrs. Fields cookies, was a Stanford graduate with a great deal of programming experience. From the beginning, he insisted on the implementation of computers throughout the stores. Even so, problems began to develop in his efforts to keep track of the rapidly expanding chain of stores.

As the company continued to grow, more than 20 people were serving on the headquarters staff. The sales-tracking system required managers to key in sales information on Touch-Tone telephones. It worked fine with 25 locations. However, by 1985 it was falling apart under the burden of 136 stores. In addition, Mrs. Fields cookies had just bought a 70-store chain in the East that would have to be immediately integrated into the reporting system. Thus, Randy Fields made the timely decision to hire Paul Quinn, an expert in systems development, to head the MIS area.

The vision for Mrs. Fields cookies was to grow so quickly that no one would be able to catch up. With such an aggressive mission, the owners needed more than just an information management system to stay on top. Quinn had an idea. Because Mrs. Fields had started from an idea that defied conventional wisdom, why not remain innovative in the design of the new computer system? To answer this question, Randy Fields and Paul Quinn embarked on a program to develop an integrated store system that would use expert systems technology.

FIGURE 9.1

Computer analysis of data and models. Research into "intelligence" has led to some decisions that can be analyzed and "solved" by computers. Expert systems and neural networks are two tools that are being used to help make decisions. These tools are used to make faster, more consistent decisions.

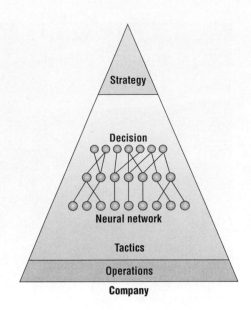

Overview

Richard:	Ally, what's going on with all of these client complaints?
Ally:	I don't know. Why?
Richard:	Well, I just got six e-mail messages saying they didn't get the right items. Most of the time the order is almost right, but the pieces don't fit together, and they have to keep calling back to get the right pieces.
Ally:	Let me look at the data and see if it's a serious problem or just a glitch . . . Ouch. Yes, returns and complaints do seem to be increasing. I guess we need to do something about it.
Richard:	So, go ahead. You and Elaine solve it. Let me know how it works out.
Elaine:	Oh thanks. What do you think, Ally? I know the salespeople are also complaining about the components being too complex and the ordering system is a pain because there are so many different combinations and the numbers are similar and . . .
Ally:	Hmmm. It seems like we need a system to analyze the orders to make sure everything works together and that all of the necessary pieces are included. If we can get the designers to set up a system of rules for each item, I'll bet we can build an expert system that automatically evaluates every order.
Elaine:	What do you mean "we" can build it?
Ally:	Well, OK, we'll start with an expert system shell, get the designers to enter the rules for us, and we might get the MIS department to connect it to the website, but sure, we can coordinate it.

Introduction

Some business problems are straightforward. In these cases, developers simply create a set of rules or procedures to follow that the computer can be programmed to follow. As long as the business behaves in a predictable manner, the rules apply and the computer can handle the details. However, many business problems are less structured and cannot be solved so easily. Additionally, problems often involve data that is not well defined. For example, it is

Trends

As businesses began to use computers, the easy problems were solved first, such as the highly structured transaction processing systems discussed in Chapter 4. But from the earliest days of computers, people have dreamed of machines that could solve more complex problems. One recurring question is whether or not machines can ever solve problems the same way as humans. Some of the earliest professional comments on artificial intelligence (AI) came from discussions by British mathematician Alan Turing and his co-workers in the 1940s. Books by Hubert Dreyfus provide a quick, critical review of the history of AI research.

At first (1957–1962), researchers tried to define intelligence and attempted to write programs that could solve general problems. In particular, a great deal of effort and money were expended on software that would automatically translate documents, especially from Russian to English. However, after spending about $20 million, the researchers gave up in 1966. Two additional groups of AI researchers were busy: Newell, Shaw, and Simon at Carnegie and Papert and Minsky at MIT. Newell, Shaw, and Simon created a "General Problem Solver" that could prove some basic theorems in mathematics, when it was given the basic assumptions and prior theorems.

When it became impossible to extend the early research into more general problems, AI research changed directions. From 1962 to 1967, research focused on "Semantic Information Processing" (which was the title of a book by Marvin Minsky). Researchers also began to suggest that to create intelligent machines, they first needed to understand how the human brain worked. So they began to build models of human thought. An interesting program called STUDENT was written by Brobow, a graduate student working under Minsky. STUDENT could solve basic algebra "story problems" by examining key words (*is* for *equals, into* for *divide,* etc.).

Research again changed from 1967 to1972 as workers focused on narrower subjects. Another MIT researcher (Weinograd) created a program called SHRDLU. SHRDLU displayed a set of geometric figures (boxes, pyramids, circles) and would answer questions or manipulate them in response to written commands. Within its limited area, it could understand fairly complex written statements.

From 1972 to 1977, research again narrowed its scope and focused on specific problems or "knowledge domains." The foundations of expert systems came from this early work. Feigenbaum at Stanford created Dendral, a system that contained rules and complex knowledge of chemical reactions.

The years from 1977 to 2000 and beyond have seen an expansion of research in AI, including robotics, pattern matching, language comprehension, and voice recognition. We have also seen the commercialization of many of the AI innovations, especially expert systems and speech recognition.

In the early years, researchers were optimistic about the possibilities presented by "thinking machines." In 1953, Turing suggested that by the end of the century, we would have "intelligent" machines. As technical advisor for the 1967 film *2001,* Marvin Minsky assured Kubrik that Turing was pessimistic, and we would see "intelligent" machines well before the end of the century. In 1957, Herbert Simon also suggested that his General Problem Solver would eventually show signs of intelligence. Although these predictions were overly optimistic, the ideas and results of this research have led to computer systems capable of solving more complex problems.

---

straightforward to create a computer system to handle inventory because the computer can easily keep track of item numbers and quantity sold. Consider the more difficult problem faced by a manager who has to decide where to locate a new plant. Some attributes are measurable, such as distance from suppliers, cost of land, and taxes. Other features are difficult to quantify: quality of the labor force, attitudes of government officials, and long-run political stability of the area.

Many problems involve nonnumeric data and complex interrelationships among the various factors. Without computers, businesses often call in experts or hire consultants to help solve these problems. Special software programs called expert systems (ESs) provide many of these features.

From the beginning, researchers and computer designers have known that humans perform some tasks much better than computers can. These differences led researchers to investigate how people solve problems and investigate how humans think. The research into techniques that might make computers "think" more like humans is known as **artificial intelligence (AI)**. There is some question as to whether it will ever be possible to build machines that can think the same way humans do. Nonetheless, the research has led to some useful tools that perform more complex analysis and can solve difficult problems. These tools attempt to mimic the processes used by humans in a simpler form that can be processed by a computer system.

For example, humans are very good at recognizing patterns, so techniques have been created to help machines identify patterns. Engineers are continuing to work on robots that can see, pick up diverse objects, and walk. Research continues into speech recognition and machine vision. In addition to application in manufacturing, these capabilities would make it easier for humans to communicate with machines.

Specialized Problems: Complex, Repetitive Decisions

Imagine your life as a top-notch manager. Co-workers perceive you as an expert and value your advice and problem-solving skills. You are constantly answering questions and there are always more problems than you can handle. You are using decision support systems and integrated information technology to perform your job better and more efficiently, but it is not enough. Can technology help you with more complex decisions and problem solving?

From another perspective, when you encounter new problems with different, complex models, it would be helpful to have an expert assist you with applying and understanding the models. Yet experts or consultants are expensive and not always available. Can you somehow capture the knowledge and methods of experts and use technology to make this knowledge available to workers throughout the company?

Expert systems have proven useful for many problems. The goal of an expert system is to enable novices to achieve results similar to those of an expert. The users need to understand the basic problem, learn the terminology, and be able to answer questions. For example, a typical patient would not be able to use a medical expert system because the questions and terms would not make any sense.

Think of an expert system as a consultant in a box. The consultant can only solve certain specific problems. For example, perhaps a retail store manager needs to estimate buying patterns for the next few months. The manager might call a marketing consultant to survey buyers and statistically search for patterns. The consultant will ask questions to determine the basic objectives and identify problems. Similarly, a production manager might be having problems with a certain machine. The manager might call a support line or a repair technician. The advice in this situation will be quite different from the marketing example, because the topics (or domains) of the two problems are different. It would be difficult to create one computer program that could help you with both types of problems. On the other hand, there are similarities in the approach to the two problems. Computerized expert systems are designed to solve narrow, specialized problems. Each problem can be relatively complex, but it must be reasonably well defined. Many business problems fall into this category, and expert systems can be built for each problem.

Diagnostic Problems

Several problems in the world can be classified as diagnostic situations. These problems arise when the decision maker is presented with a set of symptoms and is asked to find the cause of the problem, as well as solutions. Consider a firm that uses a complex machine. If the machine breaks down, production stops until it is fixed. Additionally, maintenance tasks have to be performed every day to keep the machine running. The company hires an engineer to perform these tasks. The engineer also knows which adjustments to make if various symptoms appear. This system has been working well, and the company wishes to expand to other locations with a franchise system. The problem is that there is only one engineer, and it would be too expensive to have a highly trained engineer at each location.

One possible solution would be to set up a phone link between the franchises and the engineer. One person at each franchise would be trained in the basics of the machine. If problems arise, the person could call the engineer. The engineer would ask specific questions, such as "What do the gauges show?" The answers will lead the engineer to ask other questions. Eventually, the engineer makes recommendations based on the answers.

Of course, if there are many franchises, the engineer will be too busy to solve all of the problems. Also, if the businesses are located in different countries, the time differences may

Expert Systems Applications

DIAGNOSTIC PROBLEMS

Many situations present a set of symptoms. Experts analyze these symptoms and search for a common cause. Interpretations are sometimes vague, use incomplete data, and can be hard to express in "rational" terms.

SPEED

Some decisions are only moderately complex but are made hundreds or thousands of times. The ability to make these decisions rapidly (and correctly) improves customer satisfaction and can lead to an advantage over the competition.

CONSISTENCY

From operational to legal consequences there are many advantages to making decisions consistently. Presented with the same basic inputs, the firm needs to reach the same conclusion, regardless of irrelevant factors.

TRAINING

Automated support for repetitive decisions can be useful for training new employees. As the workers use the system, they will learn the business rules that make up their job.

FIGURE 9.2

Expert System example from ExSys. This sample expert system acts as a knowledgeable salesperson and asks questions about how you intend to use a digital video camera. Based on your responses, it makes a recommendation from several cameras.

not allow everyone enough access to the engineer. A better solution is to create a computerized expert system. All the expert's questions, recommendations, and rules can be entered into a computer system that is distributed to each franchise. If there is a problem, the on-site person turns to the expert system. The system asks the same questions that the engineer would and arrives at the same recommendations.

As shown in Figure 9.2, expert systems also have the ability to explain their recommendations. In more complex examples, while running the ES, the user can ask it to explain why it asked a particular question or why it arrived at some conclusion. The ES traces through the answers it was given and explains its reasoning. This ability helps the user gain confidence in the decisions, allows mistakes to be corrected, and helps the users remember the answer for future reference.

The business world offers many examples of diagnostic situations, such as identifying causes of defects, finding the source of delays, and keeping complex equipment running. The common characteristic is that you are faced with a set of symptoms, and you need to find the cause.

Speedy Decisions

Other situations can benefit from the use of expert systems. Even if a problem is not exceedingly complex, you could use an expert system to provide faster responses or to provide more consistent recommendations. Several advantages can be gained from making decisions

Reality Bytes — NASA Goddard Space Flight Center

Satellites are expensive—typically worth between $50 and $100 million, plus the cost of launching them. And they are difficult to repair. Consequently, engineers build intensive diagnostic systems and redundant applications into the satellites. Even so, the satellites require constant monitoring; if some unit does fail, engineers have to solve the problems quickly before one minor problem cascades into major failures across the satellite. In 1996, NASA's Goddard Space Flight Center created the Spacecraft Emergency Response System (SERS) team to monitor and repair satellites. The system uses expert systems and software agents to monitor potential emergencies and failures. When it detects a problem, it consults its expert system to determine who should receive the notice. It then sends the appropriate data and initiates a two-way communication via a wireless device, such as a PDAs, Internet phone, or two-way pager. Julie Breed, branch head of the center notes that the main goal is to "reduce the cost of spacecraft mission operations without increasing the risk of losing the spacecraft or reducing the throughput of scientific data." Monitoring and repair used to require nine engineers taking turns around the clock. Now, only one engineer is needed from 9 A.M. to 5 P.M. Monday through Friday. The system monitors over 5,000 satellite parameters six times a day. All of the operations information is available to engineers through a Web-based interface. To save costs, SERS was built primarily on Lotus Domino—a database-driven groupware package.

Source: Adapted from "The List of Wireless 25 Innovators," *Computerworld*, September 24, 2001, and Julie Breed, Paul Baker, Kai-Dee Chu, Cynthhia Starr, Jeffrey Fox, and Mick Baitinger, "The Spacecraft Emergency Response System (SERS) for Autonomous Mission Operations," NASA, 1999, [http://isc.gsfc.nasa.gov/Papers/DOC/SERS_Taiwan.pdf].

faster than your competitors do. If you can identify a trend in stock prices before anyone else, you can make a higher profit. If you can answer customer questions faster, they will be more likely to shop with you in the future. If you can provide a loan to a customer sooner than anyone else, you will do more business.

Transaction-processing systems keep much of the basic data that you need to make decisions. Decision support systems help you analyze that raw data. Both of these tools enable you to make decisions faster than trying to make the decision without any computers. However, it still takes time for a human to analyze all of the information.

Consider the case of a bank loan. In order to get a loan, you go to the bank and fill out a loan application form. You tell the loan officer why you want the loan and provide basic data on income and expenses. Depending on the amount of money involved, the banker will probably check your credit history, get appraisals on any collateral, and perhaps get approval by a review officer or loan committee. All of these actions take time.

Now, consider the steps involved with a computerized process. First, you need to tell the bank that you want a loan. Instead of driving to the bank, you could use the telephone. With a touch-tone phone, you enter information directly into the bank's computer. The computer would give you a choice of loan types (car, boat, personal, etc.) and you push a button to select one. You enter the amount of money you want to borrow. The next step is to check your credit history. Your income, expenses, and credit record are available to the bank from national credit reporting agencies. The bank might also have its own database. The bank's computer could be connected to credit agency computers to collect additional data on your credit history.

To make the final decision, the bank needs a set of rules. These rules take into account the size of the loan, the value of the collateral, as well as your income, expenses, credit history, and existing loans. When the bank has determined the proper rules, the computer performs the analyses. If the bankers trust the rules, the computer could make the final decision. For example, there would be no need for a loan officer to be involved in simple decisions, such as making small car loans to customers with large savings accounts. With an expert system, a bank can cut the loan-approval period down to a few minutes on the phone.

Many other decisions need to be made rapidly. The first step in all of these cases is to make sure that the transaction-processing system provides the necessary raw data. The second step is to create a set of rules for making the decision. The difficulty lies in finding these rules. For some problems, there are well-defined rules that can be trusted. For other problems, the rules may not exist. In this case, the company will probably still need a human to make the final decision.

Consistency

The example of the bank loan demonstrates another advantage of expert systems. Business decisions are subject to a wide variety of nondiscrimination laws. An expert system can be used to provide consistent decisions. The rules followed by the ES can be set up to avoid illegal discrimination. Businesses also have credit ratings, which are often determined by Credit Clearing House (CCH). CCH uses an expert system to make the "easy" decisions, which speeds up the process by allowing humans to focus on the more complicated cases. It also leads to consistent application of the rules.

Consider the loan example. If each loan officer makes individual decisions, it is hard to determine whether they are consistent with corporate policy. Each individual decision would have to be checked to make sure it was nondiscriminatory. On the other hand, a committee could spend several weeks creating a set of lending rules that can be verified to be sure they are legal and ethical. As long as the bank employees follow the recommendations of the ES, the outcome should not be discriminatory. Because there should be few cases where the loan officer overrules the ES, managers will have more time to examine each of these circumstances.

Many business decisions need to be performed consistently to avoid bias and to treat people equally. Loans, pricing, raises, and promotions are some examples. However, there can be problems with using a computer system to enforce standards. The main difficulty lies in creating a set of rules that accurately describe the decisions and standards. For example, it might be useful to have a set of rules regarding raises and promotions, but think about what happens if an employee's job does not fit the basic rules. Organizations continually change, which means the rules have to be monitored and changed regularly.

Training

Training employees is closely associated with problems of consistency. All organizations must train employees. If the tasks are complex and the decisions highly unstructured, it can take years for employees to learn the rules and gain the experience needed to deal with problems. Two features of expert systems help employees learn. First, employees learn what questions need to be asked. In particular, after using the system for a while, certain groups of questions will occur together. Second, most expert systems have provisions for explaining their answers (and the motivation for each question). At any point, an employee can ask the expert system why it asked a certain question or why it reached a conclusion.

Decision Support Systems and Expert Systems

Consider a small example. You wish to fly from Miami to Phoenix for Thanksgiving. You go to a travel agent who uses a computer reservation system to display the basic flight information. If there are seats available on the flights that you prefer, the computer records your name and prints a ticket. But what happens if there are no open seats on the flights that you prefer? The computer system simply displays a message. You and the travel agent then have to find alternatives. The computer system is passive. It only provides basic information about schedules, availability, and prices.

Perhaps the computer designers have built a more sophisticated system that has decision support features. Now, when you have trouble finding a flight, the travel agent asks the computer to display a list of all open seats, sorted by price. It shows a graph of available seats arranged by price and departure times. A well-organized presentation of the data can make it easier for you to choose a flight.

Can the computer do even more? Look at the problem from another perspective. Why do we have travel agents? In the early days of flight reservation systems, the travel agent was necessary because passengers did not have access to computer terminals. Also, the agents needed special training to use the software. Today, it is easy to use the Internet to make your own reservations. Does that mean we do not need travel agents anymore? That's a question many people are asking. However, consider a situation when you want to book a vacation to

FIGURE 9.3
Expert systems are designed to help novices achieve the same results as experts. An expert uses symbolic and numeric knowledge along with rules to analyze a situation and make a decision. Knowledge engineers create a computerized knowledge base that is used to assist novices.

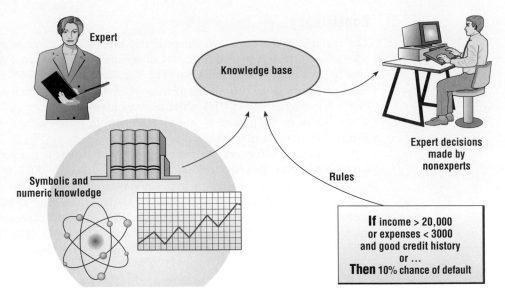

FIGURE 9.4
DSS versus ES. An expert system has a different goal and a different approach than a decision support system. A DSS is used by a trained decision maker to collect data, analyze models and produce output. An ES is built to provide advice to nonexperts and guide them to make a better decision.

	DSS	ES
Goal	Help user make decision	Provide expert advice
Method	Data—model—presentation	Ask questions, apply rules, explain
Type of problems	General, limited by user models	Narrow domain

a tropical island. Which resort should you choose? Does one offer better features? Is the food or service better at one? Which resort best fits the activities you prefer? You need the additional data and knowledge of someone who has been to the resorts. You need reliable information from someone that you trust.

Figure 9.3 indicates how the additional knowledge of the travel agent can make a difference in your decision. If this knowledge were incorporated into the computer system, it would become an expert system. Such a system would enable a novice traveler to make decisions as well as the experienced travel agent.

In practice, there is no solid line between decision support and expert systems, but Figure 9.4 highlights the primary differences. One of the most important differences is that the expert system evaluates rules and suggests a result or action. In the case of expert systems, users must always be careful to understand how the expert system is evaluating the choices. If the system is using short-term rules, but the users prefer to focus on the long term, use of the expert system can lead to problems.

Building Expert Systems

At first glance, you would suspect that expert systems are hard to create. However, except for one step, which is hard, tools exist to make the job easier. Expert system shells help nonprogrammers create a complete expert system. The area that causes the most problems when you are creating expert systems is finding a cooperative expert who fully understands and can explain the problem. Some problems are so complex that it is difficult to explain the reasoning process. Sometimes the expert may rely on vague descriptions and minor nuances that cannot be written down. Even though expert systems can deal with these types of problems, it might take too long to determine the entire process. Also, if you transfer the expert's knowledge to a computer, the expert might worry about losing his or her job.

Most expert systems are built as a knowledge base that is processed or analyzed by an inference engine. A **knowledge base** consists of basic data and a set of rules. In most situations, an *inference engine* applies new observations to the knowledge base and analyzes the rules to reach a conclusion.

FIGURE 9.5

Sample rules for the bank loan. A portion of the business rules that are used to determine whether a person should get a loan.

First, compute the monthly income before taxes.
Next, compute the monthly payment of the loan.
If the payment is greater than 5% of income:
　Compute total of other loans payments.
　Compute payments as percentage of monthly income.
　If this percentage is less than 25%:
　　If the new loan is less than 10%, make loan.
　　Else:
　　　If total monthly expenses are less than 40% of income, make the loan.
　　　Else:
　　　　If less than 50% and has been a customer for more than 5 years or if less than 60% and has been a customer for 10 years and has lived at the same address for 5 years, make the loan.

The basic steps to create an expert system are: (1) analyze the situation and identify needed data and possible outcomes, (2) determine relationships between data and rules that are followed in making the decision, (3) enter the data and rules into an expert system shell; and (4) design questions and responses. A **knowledge engineer** is often hired to organize the data, help devise the rules, and enter the criteria into the expert system shell, or supervise programmers as they create an expert system.

Knowledge Base

A knowledge base is more than a simple database. It consists of data but also contains rules, logic, and links among data elements. In most cases, it contains less structured and more descriptive data. For example, an ES for medicine might have a list of symptoms that contains items like "high temperature," and "intense muscle pain." This knowledge base is the reason why the problem must be narrow in scope. Even narrow, well-defined problems can require large amounts of information and thousands of rules or relationships. The real challenge in building expert systems is to devise the knowledge base with its associated rules.

There are three types of expert systems in use today. They are defined by how the knowledge base is organized: by rules, frames, or cases.

Rules

The heart of a rule-based ES is a set of logical rules. These **rules** are often complicated. Consider some of the rules that might be needed for an ES to evaluate bank loans, as shown in Figure 9.5. This example has been simplified to keep it short. There will usually be hundreds of rules or conditions to cover a wide variety of situations. Rules are often presented as *if . . . then . . . else . . .* statements. They can include Boolean conjunctions such as *and, or, not*. Figure 9.6 presents a portion of a **decision tree** that visually displays the rules.

The difficulty with any ES lies in determining these rules. Some of them will be easy. Others will be complex. Most of them will come from the expert. Unfortunately, most people do not usually express their thoughts in the form of these rules. Although we might follow rules of this sort, they can be difficult to express. It is even more difficult to remember all the rules at one time. For instance, say you have lived in the same place for five years and a new person moves into the neighborhood. She asks you to describe the best ways to get to school, the mall, and the grocery store. Then she asks you for the best shortcuts if one of the roads is closed. This problem is relatively simple, but can you sit down right now and provide a complete list of all the rules?

Knowledge Engineers

With the importance of descriptive data and complex rules, it can be difficult to determine how an expert system should function. In many cases, it is difficult for human experts to express how they make decisions. Once these obstacles are overcome, the data and rules need to be described in a form that the computer can understand and evaluate.

FIGURE 9.6

Decision tree for sample bank loan expert system. Parts of a knowledge base are often expressed as a decision tree. Each answer to a question leads to additional questions and eventually to a decision. Notice that questions sometimes require numeric answers but can also rely on subjective comments.

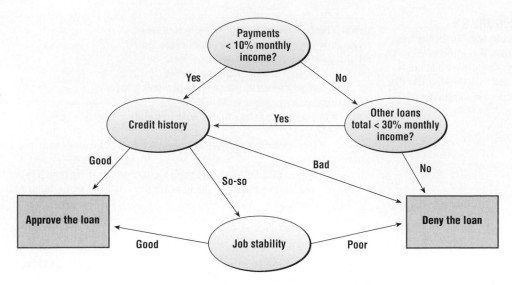

With the increasing use of expert systems, ES specialists have advanced during the last few years. Knowledge engineers are trained to deal with experts to derive the rules needed to create an expert system. The engineers also convert the data and rules into the format needed by the expert system. The format varies depending on the type of expert system being created. Some systems require a series of if-then rules, others operate from decision trees or tables, and some require the engineer to build and link frames.

When several experts are involved in a problem or when it will take considerable time to develop the system, it will be better to hire a knowledge engineer to design and build the expert system. When workers thoroughly understand the issues and are given some additional training, they can be the knowledge engineers and build their own system.

Creating an ES

There are two basic ways to create an expert system: (1) hire a programmer to write custom software or (2) use commercial ES shell software to evaluate rules. For some problems, you can also buy a prepackaged solution, but the system was originally created by one of these two basic methods.

Older expert systems were typically written using a special language such as LISP or Prolog. These languages work well with text data but require specially trained programmers, making it very expensive to create an ES this way. These two languages are still in use today, but programmers are also using object-oriented languages like C++ to build expert systems.

More commonly today, an ES is built from an **expert system shell**. This program provides a way to collect data, enter rules, talk to users, present results, and evaluate the rules. To create an ES, you must know what data you need and all of the rules. Once you express this knowledge base in the format used by the shell's inference engine, the shell takes care of the other problems. Many ES shells are available on a wide variety of computers.

To understand how to create an ES, consider the bank loan example. A typical dialogue with the user (the loan clerk) appears in Figure 9.7. Notice that the ES begins by asking some basic information-gathering questions. The responses of the user are underlined. Once the basic data is collected, the ES performs some computations and follows the built-in rules. Notice that the ES follows the rule that asks for the other loan payments. However, the loan clerk does not know about this rule, so he or she asks for clarification. This ability to ask questions is a powerful feature of expert systems.

Once you have collected all of the rules involved in the problem, you enter them into the ES shell. The shell lets you type in the questions you want to ask the user. You define the calculations and tell the shell how to look up any other information you need (e.g., the interest rates for auto loans). You then enter the conditions that tell the shell what questions to

FIGURE 9.7

Bank loan sample screen. An expert system carries on a dialog with the user. The ES asks questions and uses the answers to ask additional questions. The user can ask the ES to explain a decision or a question. Hence the ES can be used for training purposes.

Welcome to the Loan Evaluation System.

What is the purpose of the loan? *car*
How much money will be loaned? *10,000*
For how many years? *5*

The current interest rate is 10%.
The payment will be $212.47 per month.

What is the annual income? *24,000*

What is the total monthly payments of other loans? *Why?*

Because the payment is more than 10% of the monthly income. What is the total monthly payments of other loans? *50.00*

The loan should be approved, because there is only a 2% chance of default.

FIGURE 9.8

Expert system development. Once the knowledge is provided by an expert, there are two basic methods used to build an ES. One method is with an expert system shell, or software that already knows how to store and evaluate rules and handle the user interface. The other approach is to hire programmers and write the entire ES from scratch. Special-purpose languages like LISP and Prolog make the job a little easier, but custom programming is still expensive and time-consuming.

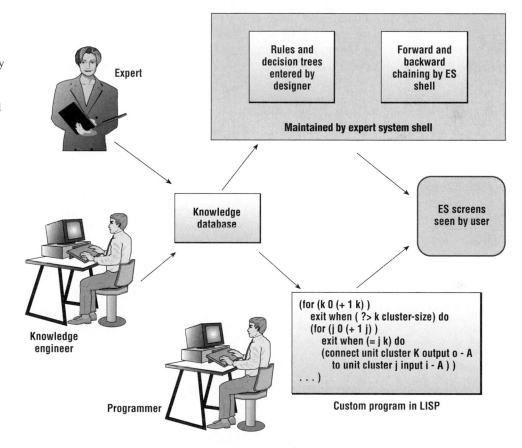

ask next. If there are many rules with complex interactions, it is more difficult to enter the rules into the shell. However, as illustrated in Figure 9.8, it is generally easier to use a shell than to have programmers create the system from scratch in LISP or Prolog.

One advantage of ES shells is that you generally have to enter only the basic rules and data. As the user enters the data, the shell performs the calculations and follows the rules. The shell also automatically answers the user questions. You do not have to be a computer programmer to create an ES with a shell. With training, many users can create their own expert systems using a shell. However, there are many dangers inherent in ES development, so it helps to have someone evaluate and test the resulting system.

Reality Bytes | **Common Limitations of Expert Systems**

- *Fragile systems:* If the underlying process changes or the environment generates changes, the rules need to be revised. Changes in one rule might force us to rebuild the entire system.

- *Mistakes:* Who is responsible when an expert system makes a mistake? The expert? Several experts? The novice operating the ES? The company that uses it? The company who created it? The knowledge engineers who built it?

- *Vague rules:* Many times the domain expert cannot completely describe the rules.

- *Conflicting experts:* If there are conflicting experts or rules, who will decide? Which one is right?

- *Unforeseen events:* What happens if the ES faces an unexpected problem or a new event? Experts solve these problems through creativity and learning. Expert systems cannot.

Reasoning

Expert systems usually perform two types of reasoning: forward chaining and backward chaining. **Forward chaining** is where the shell traces your rules from the data entry to a recommendation. In the bank example, forward chaining is used to display the questions and perform the calculations. For example, when the ES realizes that the payment amount is greater than 10 percent of the customer's monthly income, the corresponding rule is utilized. The ES works down the list of rules and evaluates each condition. If the condition is true, the ES does whatever the rule says, and we say that the rule has been fired or **triggered**. Eventually, if all the rules have been entered correctly, the system follows the rules and reaches a conclusion. Generally, the system will present some information indicating how sure it is of the decision. In the example, it uses historical data to indicate only a 2 percent chance of default on the loan.

With **backward chaining**, the user enters a "conclusion" and asks the expert system to see if the rules support that conclusion. Consider the lending example using the decision tree displayed in Figure 9.6. The bank is investigating the possibility of discrimination and has pulled representative applications from several categories of borrowers. For each of the applicants, the manager wants to determine whether that person should have been granted a loan. A backward chaining expert system begins with the hypothesized conclusion (e.g., that the applicant should have been granted the loan). It examines rules by looking at the conclusion and decides whether the premise supports the conclusion. For example, it might note that there is a poor credit history, hence the loan could not have been granted on the strength of past credit. So the ES next evaluates job stability. If job stability was "good," it traces back and reexamines the credit history. If it finds that credit history was "bad," it concludes that the applicant should not receive the loan. The backward chaining continues until the conclusion is found to be supported or rejected, or there is insufficient data to make a decision.

As you attempt to create an expert system, you should take a broad look at the rules before you begin. Some tasks and decisions simply cannot be described in enough detail to justify the use of an expert system.

Limitations of Expert Systems

Expert systems are useful tools that can be applied to several specialized problems. However, several important drawbacks arise in their design and use. First, they can only be created for specific, narrowly defined problems. Some complex problems contain too many rules with too many interactions. It quickly becomes impossible to express all of the interrelationships. For example, it is currently impossible to create a medical diagnostic system that covers all possible diseases. However, smaller systems are in use that help determine drug dosages and other treatments such as radiation levels for cancer patients.

Another problem that users and designers have encountered is that it can be difficult to modify the knowledge base in an expert system. As the environment or problem changes, the expert system needs to be updated. The changes are relatively easy to make if they affect only a few rules. However, many expert systems use hundreds of interrelated rules. It is not always clear which rules need to be altered, and changes to one rule can affect many of the others. In essence, as the situation changes, the company is forced to completely redesign the expert system. In fast-changing industries, it would cost too much to continually redesign an expert system. In the lending example, a policy change based on monthly income would be relatively easy to implement. On the other hand, some changes in policy would force a complete redesign of the expert system. For instance, a bank might decide to grant loans to almost everyone but charge riskier people higher interest rates.

Probably the greatest difficulty in creating an expert system is determining the logic rules or frames that will lead to the proper conclusions. It requires finding an expert who understands the process and can express the rules in a form that can be used by the expert system.

Management Issues of Expert Systems

Creating and building an expert system involve many of the same issues encountered in building any other information system. For instance, the problem must be well defined, the designers must communicate with the users, and management and financial controls must be in place to evaluate and control the project.

However, expert systems raise additional management issues. Two issues are particularly important: (1) if an expert transfers knowledge to an expert system, is there still a need for the expert, and (2) what happens when the expert system encounters an exception that it was not designed to solve?

The answer to the first question depends on the individual situation. In cases where the problem is relatively stable over time, it is possible to transfer expert knowledge to software—enabling the firm to reduce the number of experts needed. If this action results in layoffs, the experts will need additional incentives to cooperate with the development of the system. In other cases, the firm will continue to need the services of the experts, to make changes to the ES and to solve new problems. Before starting an ES project, managers need to determine which situation applies and negotiate appropriately with the experts.

The second problem can be more difficult to identify. Consider what happens when workers rely on an expert system to make decisions, and management then cuts costs by hiring less-skilled workers. The new workers do not understand the system or the procedures—they simply follow decisions made by the rules in the ES. If an exception arises, the ES may not know how to respond or it may respond inappropriately. A customer then would be left to deal with an underskilled worker who does not understand the process and cannot resolve the problem.

Knowledge Management

In many cases, decisions are too subjective or too large for an expert system. Yet, decision makers can still use some help. Many organizations make the same difficult decisions every month or every year. Difficult decisions can require the participation of dozens of employees and analysis of gigabytes of data. It would be nice if the organization could keep the knowledge gained from every decision and apply it to similar problems in the future. In the past, maintaining organizational knowledge was a key management factor in retaining and promoting key employees. But in medium and large organizations, turnover, distance, and the challenge of finding experts can make it difficult to maintain and share the knowledge. So, some companies have attempted to create **knowledge management (KM)** systems.

A KM system is different from an ES in that the KM is designed to store any type of data needed to convey the context of the decision and the discussion involved in making the decision. While the system might contain rules, it is primarily a giant database of easily accessible data for experts. KM systems are designed to organize information and to assist people

Reality Bytes — Knowledge Management in the Navy

Military commands represent some of the largest organizations in the world. Managing the details and responding to changes is a difficult business, and errors can cost lives. At any point in time, thousands of people within the Navy might need access to information to solve a problem. But, it can be difficult to find the appropriate expert. So the Navy created an online knowledge management system that links Navy personnel around the world. The U.S. Pacific Fleet's knowledge home portal provides knowledge links through more than 250 databases. The Navy reports that in use for only two years, it has saved over 18,000 staff hours per month. The system is designed for collaboration and can handle a broad array of data. For example, decision makers have created videos documenting important decisions in terms of the conditions, the criteria involved, and how the decision was made. Anyone facing a similar problem in the future can quickly find similar situations and use the prior discussions to save time and choose the best options. Providing the background context of the decision is an important part of the system. Larry Prusak, executive director of IBM's Institute for Knowledge Management, notes that the Navy's system is substantially better than an expert system because "One of the failings of expert systems is they don't capture context, just rules." Paul Strassmann, a professor of information warfare at the National Defense University notes the value of the knowledge management system because "The Defense Department is basically a learning institution; hardly anybody ever fires a gun. People spend more time learning than in any civilian organization."

Source: Adapted from Gary H. Anthes, "Charting a Knowledge Management Course," *Computerworld,* August 21, 2000.

in collaborative projects and research. The system can be relatively unstructured, and often consists of many individual cases. Decision makers can search the system for cases with features similar to their current issues. The cases are cross-referenced so that a decision maker might research one aspect of a case and find a related issue. The links make it easy to explore the related issues, tying together a variety of concepts and identifying related problems or consequences.

Because the field is relatively new, the definition of KM is somewhat nebulous and many software vendors promote tools as useful for KM. One of the difficulties is that the decisions and knowledge required can be different for each organization. And organizations may approach decisions differently, so it is unlikely that a single tool will be useful to every company. Instead, each company needs to evaluate specific decisions to determine whether it will be useful to explicitly collect the information and process knowledge that was involved in making the decision.

One of the biggest challenges with KM systems is creating an organizational environment that encourages decision makers to store their knowledge in the system. Initially, the system will have little data, and the early decision makers will have to spend a great deal of time organizing their discussions and creating the files and links necessary to make the system valuable in the future. Companies need to give managers enough time to consolidate their information and provide incentives to encourage them to help build the new system.

Additional Specialized Problems

Further research in artificial intelligence examined how humans are different from computers. This research led to tools that can be used for certain types of problems. Some of the ideas come from the early days of computers, but it has taken until now for machines to be developed that are fast enough to handle the sophisticated tasks. Ideas in AI have come from many disciplines, from biology to psychology to computer science and engineering.

Humans are noticeably better than computers in six broad areas: pattern recognition, performing multiple tasks at one time, movement, speech recognition, vision, and language comprehension. Some of these concepts are related, but they all represent features that would make machines much more useful. Even with current technological improvements, most observers agree that it will be several years before these features are available.

- *Expert systems:* Building systems that help novices achieve the results of experts.

- *Pattern recognition:* Identifying patterns in sound, vision, and data. Driven by neural network research.

- *Voice and speech recognition:* Recognizing users by voice, and converting spoken words into written text.

- *Language comprehension:* Understanding the meaning in written (or spoken) text.

- *Robotics and motion:* Building machines that have a high range of movement, physical sensitivity, and the ability to navigate.

- *Statistics, uncertainty, and fuzzy logic:* Finding ways to solve statistical problems easier. Dealing with associations and comparative data.

Pattern Recognition and Neural Networks

One of the early issues in AI research was the question of how human brains worked. Some people suggested that to make intelligent computers, the computers would have to work the same way as the human brain does. An important conclusion from this research is that humans are good at pattern recognition.

Humans use pattern recognition thousands of times a day. It enables people to recognize co-workers, to spot trends in data, to relate today's problems to last year's changes. Many problems in business could benefit from machines that could reliably recognize patterns. For example, what characteristics do "good" borrowers have in common? How will changes in the economy affect next year's sales? How are sales affected by management styles of the sales managers?

Pattern recognition is used by people to solve problems. It is one of the reasons teachers use cases to teach students to solve business problems. If you notice that a problem is similar to a case you have seen before, you can use your prior knowledge to solve the problem. Imagine how useful it would be if an expert system could recognize patterns automatically.

One current technique that is used to spot patterns is the use of neural networks. Initial study indicated that the brain is a collection of cells called *neurons* that have many connections to each other. Each of these cells is relatively simple, but there are approximately 100 million of them. In some respects, a neuron resembles a simple computer. It can be at rest (off), or it can fire a message (on). A neuron responds to other cells (input) to send messages to other neurons (output). A collection of these cells is called a **neural network.** Human neural cells are actually more complicated, but researchers have focused on this simplified form.

A common current example is a bank that uses neural network to spot credit card fraud. In some cases, Mellon Bank's neural network identified fraudulent patterns even before the human investigators spotted them. It is faster and more accurate than an earlier expert system. The original expert system looked at a limited number of variables and indicated 1,000 suspects a day, which was far more than actually existed and too many for the investigators to keep up with. The new neural network system examines more variables, lists fewer false suspects, and adjusts its methods on its own.

A finance manager might use a form of pattern recognition to search for patterns in the financial markets to forecast future movements. Of course, with thousands of other people searching for patterns, the patterns would not last very long. Similarly, a banker might use pattern recognition to classify loan prospects.

Neural networks can be built with software. Also, computer chips are available today that function as neural networks. Neural networks can be measured in two ways by (1) the number of neurons and (2) the number of interconnections between the individual cells. It is fairly easy to increase the number of cells, but the number of possible interconnections increases very rapidly. For instance, if there are four cells, there are six possible connections. With

Reality Bytes ShopKo

ShopKo is a discount chain headquartered in Green Bay, WI. Like many retailers, pricing merchandise is a delicate task. The difficult problems arise when items do not sell as well as anticipated. Then the individual stores need to markdown the price. While substantial markdowns would encourage customers to buy the items, it might also result in a loss on the sales. According to the National Retail Federation, sales of marked-down goods today account for 20 percent of sales—compared to only 8 percent in the 1970s. Like many retailers, ShopKo followed a strategy of using small markdowns. Generally once a month, the price of unsold items would be reduced by some percentage until all items were sold. In 2000, ShopKo tested and installed new software to analyze sales more carefully. It uses mathematical models similar to those used to price airline seats. With detailed data on past sales of similar items, the software from Spotlight Solutions Inc., predicts sales patterns and recommends the date and level of markdowns. In a test in 2000, the software predicted that sales of boys' fleece vests would peak in mid-August, so instead of continual markdowns, the system recommended a single 20 percent price cut in November. ShopKo ended up with a 30.2 percent gross profit margin on the vests—a substantial improvement over the prior years. In the total pilot test, sales for the 300 test products were 14 percent higher than the year earlier, while same-store sales of other products were flat. At the same time, the gross profit margins of the test products rose 24 percent. Managers are elated. Without the system, they were drowning in data and unable to spot trends and make accurate decisions. It also costs ShopKo 18 cents per garment to change the price of an item and 24 cents per shelf tag. Without the software, items were often repriced three or four times, now it is generally only one price cut. Some of the systems, such as software offered by ProfitLogic, incorporate unexpected events like snowstorms and automatically revise the forecasts. One interesting consequence of the software is that it sets prices for individual stores, so prices of the same items can vary by store. For example, at one ShopKo store in a Green Bay mall, a gas grill was listed at full price of $189.99. At a store across the river, 20 minutes away, the same item was going for $121.59. Initial surveys showed that employees and customers did not notice the difference. Yet, when Amazon.com ran price sensitivity tests—charging customers different prices for the same products—customers loudly complained when they learned that some people received lower prices.

Source: Adapted from: Amy Merrick, "Retailers Attempt to Get a Leg Up on Markdowns with New Software," *The Wall Street Journal,* August 7, 2001.

10 cells, there are 45 connections. With 1,000 cells, there are half a million connections. In general, if there are N cells, there are $N(N-1)/2$ possible connections. For many purposes, not every connection is needed, but with millions of cells, a neural network would incorporate a large number of connections. Most existing networks use only a few thousand cells.

Figure 9.9 presents a version of how a neural network converts an array of input sensors into a hidden layer and then stores patterns on an output layer. One useful feature of the neural network approach is that it is fairly good at identifying patterns even if some of the inputs are missing.

What can neural networks do that cannot be done with traditional computers? The basic answer is "nothing." However, they provide a new way of thinking about problems. More important, with hardware specifically designed to process neural networks, some difficult problems can be solved faster than with traditional computers. The primary objective of neural networks is the ability to store and recognize patterns. A well-designed network is capable of identifying patterns (such as faces or sounds) even if some of the data is missing or altered. The army has designed a neural network system to process visual data that can drive a vehicle at speeds up to 55 miles per hour.

Another advantage that researchers hope to achieve with neural networks is the ability to simplify training of the computer. The discussion of expert systems noted that changes in the business often mean that knowledge engineers have to redesign the entire expert system. A neural network has a limited ability to "learn" by examining past data. Feeding it proper examples establishes the interconnection weights that enable the network to identify patterns. In theory, neural networks have the ability to learn on their own. In practice, the learning stage is the most difficult component of building a neural network. Most times the designer has to understand the problem and provide hints to the network, along with good sample data. In many ways, training a neural network uses basic properties of statistics related to data sampling and regression.

FIGURE 9.9

Neural net for pattern matching. Input cells convert data to binary form. The required hidden layer recodes the inputs into a new internal representation. The connections represent outputs from the lower layers. When total input levels exceed some value, the receiving cell fires. Any cell can be connected to many other cells. Input weights are determined by training. The output cells are triggered when total input levels from the connections exceed some threshold. Note that a pattern can be recognized even if some input cells are wrong or not firing.

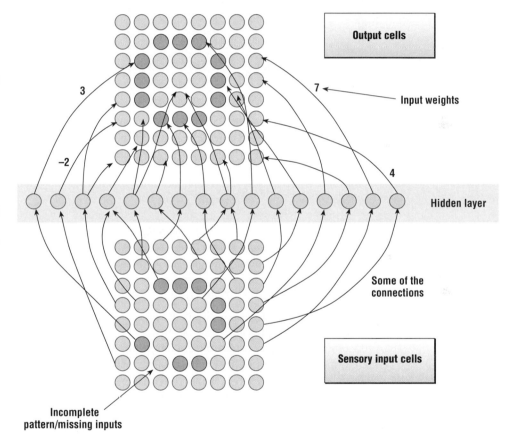

Machine Vision

Machine vision has many uses in manufacturing environments. Machines are used in optical character recognition, welding and assembly, and quality control. Mechanical sensors have several advantages over humans. They do not suffer from fatigue, they can examine a broader spectrum of light (including ultraviolet and infrared), and they can quickly focus at many different levels (including microscopic).

On the other hand, traditional computer systems are literal in their vision. It is hard for computers to compare objects of different sizes or to match mirror images. It is hard for machines to determine whether differences between objects are minor and should be ignored or if they are major distinguishing features.

Computers are better than humans at many repetitive tasks. Vision systems have been developed to help evaluate scans of baggage to search for dangerous cargo.

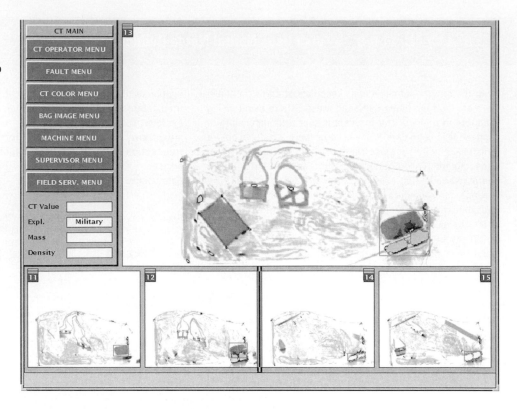

Say you are shown a picture of your instructor, and someone adds or subtracts features to it, such as bigger eyebrows, longer hair, or glasses. In most cases, you would still recognize the face. Computers would have difficulty with that problem because they see pictures as a collection of dots (or lines). How does the computer know which changes are important and which are minor?

Machine vision systems are improving rapidly but still have a way to go to become commonplace. For example, companies are working on applications in facial recognition and facial expressions, body tracking (so you can use your hand as a computer pointer), visual tracking of handwriting for use in computer tablets, product inspections for defects, and shape identification.

Voice and Speech Recognition

We hardly need to discuss the benefits of having a machine that can understand human speech. Most people can speak faster than they can type, so voice input to create and edit documents saves a considerable amount of time and money. Voice input is useful for hands-free operations. A quality control worker might need both hands to inspect a product. Speech recognition enables the worker to take notes that can be edited and printed later. Surgeons gain the same advantages. Additionally, voice input would eliminate the need for a keyboard, and possibly a monitor, making computers much more portable.

Two main types of speech recognition systems are available today. Both types are available on personal computers. The first type must be trained before it can be used. The user speaks a list of words and the computer stores the base patterns. With training, today's systems can recognize continuous speech with 90 to 95 percent accuracy.

A second form of speech recognition does not require training. Some systems can recognize a few words without additional training. For example, some phone systems recognize spoken numbers and a few key words.

Speech recognition is rapidly gaining acceptance as an input device. Modern systems examine pairs of words and sentence structure to reduce problems with homonyms. Punctuation is still a problem, but for data entry, the speaker simply inserts the correct punctuation by name. While speech recognition may never be *perfect,* it will be *acceptable.* The point is that because communication between humans is not perfect, we cannot expect communication between machines and humans to be perfect either.

FIGURE 9.10

There are inherent problems with voice recognition. Punctuation and implicit meaning are two difficult areas. Even communication between people has frequent misinterpretations.

Language Comprehension Example

See what happens when you give a computer the first set of instructions, but it does not hear the commas correctly and thinks you said the second line:

1. Copy the red, file the blue, delete the yellow mark.
2. Copy the red file, the blue delete, the yellow mark.

Consider the following sentence, which can be interpreted by humans, but would not make much sense to a computer that tries to interpret it literally.

"I saw the Grand Canyon flying to New York."

Language Comprehension

Related to voice recognition is the issue of language comprehension, or the ability of the computer to actually understand what we are saying. Technically the two topics are separate, since it might be possible to have a machine understand what we type onto a keyboard. Language comprehension exists when the machine actually understands what we mean. One test of comprehension would be the ability of the computer to carry on a conversation. In fact, Alan Turing, a British pioneer in the computer field suggested the **Turing test** for computer intelligence. In this test, a human judge communicates with a machine and another person in a separate room. If the judge cannot determine which user is the machine and which is a person, the machine should be considered to be intelligent. Some people have tested this concept (using specific topics). Other people have noted that perhaps you do not have to be intelligent to carry on a conversation.

Language comprehension would be useful because it would make it easier for humans to use computers. Instead of needing to learn a language such as SQL to access data, imagine being able to get answers to questions asked in English (or some other **natural language**). Of course, any natural language has its limitations. The greatest danger with language comprehension is that the machine will interpret your question incorrectly and give you the "right" answer to the "wrong" question. Figure 9.10 provides a simple illustration of the complexities of language comprehension. The first example involves the use of punctuation. A misinterpretation of the command can result in deleting the wrong file. Similarly, interpretation of a natural language involves understanding some basic concepts, such as the fact that the Grand Canyon cannot fly.

Robotics and Motion

Modern manufacturing relies heavily on robots, and the capabilities of robots continually increase. Most existing robots are specialized machines that perform a limited number of tasks, such as welding or painting. In many firms, there is little need for a general-purpose robot that can "do everything." However, one area that remains troublesome is the ability of machines to move. Making a machine that can navigate through an unknown or crowded area is especially difficult. Some work is being done in this area. Liability is a major problem when robots attempt to move among people.

Although science fiction writers have already devised thousands of uses for "intelligent" robots, there is still a long way to go. Part of the problem is that the concept of robots is closely tied to the issues of vision, pattern recognition, and intelligence. In order to navigate a crowded room, a robot needs to be able to see objects. It must also recognize each object and have a basic understanding of its characteristics. For instance, a robot needs to recognize and know the difference between a table and a wall to understand that it can go around a table but not a wall.

Statistics, Uncertainty, and Fuzzy Logic

Many situations can benefit from the use of applied statistics. Statistics enable us to examine large sets of data and spot patterns and relationships. It also enables us to define the concept of uncertainty. In life, we can rarely predict any outcome with complete certainty. There is

FIGURE 9.11

Subjective definitions. Many human tasks are characterized by subjectivity. When we say that the weather is "cold" we rarely specify an exact temperature. Instead, we are making a comparison to a reference point. Distances farther from the reference point provide a stronger impression of the change. Machine systems can be based on these principles using statistics or "fuzzy-logic" definitions. These interpretations often make it easier for people to deal with machines.

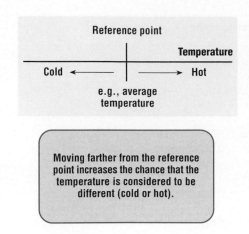

always a chance that some random event will arise, affecting our system and producing a different outcome. By assigning probabilities to various events, we can evaluate the effect of these random events.

The catch is that statistics is a relatively complex field, and it is often hard to apply in practice. Evaluating millions of data points, determining interactions, and estimating probabilities is not an easy task, even with top-of-the-line computer tools. These tasks often require the services of an expert in statistical analysis. Yet, people face uncertainty every day and manage to make decisions. Sometimes we might not make the "best" decision, but we have found ways to cope with the main issues. One common method of coping is our ability to use subjective and incomplete descriptions. When a person declares that "it is cold outside," listeners in the same area understand the statement. Yet, *cold* is a subjective term. Forty degrees can be cold to a resident of Arizona, but it would be considered pleasant to a resident of Wisconsin in mid-January.

It is possible to model these concepts with statistical definitions that involve means and standard deviations. However, it can be difficult to derive the underlying statistical functions and implement them for each situation. To overcome these limitations, Lofti Zadeh created a system that attempts to mimic the way humans perceive uncertainty. His definition of fuzzy sets and fuzzy logic use definitions of subjective terms such as *cold, hot, sometimes, fast,* and *slow.* The logic system defines a way to combine these terms to reach descriptive "conclusions." Figure 9.11 illustrates that the key is that each definition refers to a range.

In 1994, Charles Elkan showed that fuzzy logic is conceptually similar to more traditional methodologies. However, manufacturers (especially Japanese companies) have found it easier to design products using fuzzy logic. The fuzzy definitions also correspond with the way humans perceive the machine. Fuzzy logic is used in washing machine settings, elevator controls, and bullet train controllers (where operators can set controls like *hotter* or *faster).*

DSS, ES, and AI

The differences among decision support systems, expert systems, and artificial intelligence can be confusing at first. Take a simple problem and see how a computer system based on each method might operate. A common financial problem is to determine how much money to lend to customers. Any firm that grants terms to customers—not just financial institutions—must make this decision. Figure 9.12 discusses the differences among a DSS, ES, and AI approach to the inventory problem.

In a relatively simple system, the computer would retrieve data about the customer and the prior loans to that customer. Historically, loan officers used basic data and personal factors to make the lending decision. In some instances, these rules of thumb led to problems—with bad decisions and sometimes discrimination. The DSS could also be used to monitor existing loans and payments. As part of a transaction-processing system, it can notify managers when customers continually make late payments and help identify problem loans.

To improve consistency and reduce the decision time, many firms have moved to expert systems to help evaluate loans. Statistical analysis of prior loans is used to establish a set of rules that are coded into the ES. In some cases, the ES can then be operated with Touch-Tone phones or over the Internet. In straightforward cases, the ES can make the final decision and approve the loan. In more difficult situations, the preliminary results and data can be forwarded to a human loan officer to factor in personal judgment and factors not considered by the ES.

Of course, the value of the ES depends heavily on the accuracy of the underlying rules (and the supplied data). These rules might change over time or as economic conditions

FIGURE 9.12
Comparison of techniques for a loan. A DSS can display background data for a loan officer and can also monitor customer payments. An ES could help managers decide if they should make the loan by evaluating more complex rules. An AI such as a neural network can analyze past loans and determine the rules that should be used to grant or deny future loans.

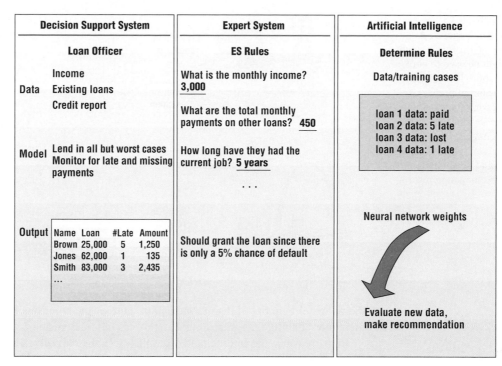

change. A neural network can be used to examine the prior loans automatically to identify the factors that predict successful and unsuccessful loans. Once these factors are identified, they can be coded into the ES to automate the decision process. In this situation, the AI/neural network takes the place of (or supplements) the decisions of the human expert.

Machine Intelligence

What would it take to convince you that a machine is intelligent? The Turing test has been proposed as one method. Many other tests have been proposed in the past. At one time, people suggested that a machine that could win at chess would be intelligent. Today's chess-playing computers have beaten even the top human players. Another test proposed was the ability to solve mathematical problems, in particular, the ability to write mathematical proofs. An early AI program created in the 1950s could do that. Today, for a few hundred dollars, you can buy programs that manipulate mathematical symbols to solve equations.

Some people have suggested that intelligence involves creativity. Creativity is probably as hard to measure as intelligence. Even so, there are examples of computer creativity. A few years ago, a programmer developed a system that created music. The interesting feature of the program was that it allowed people to call on the phone and vote on the music. The computer used this feedback to change its next composition. Not only was the computer creative, it was learning and adapting, albeit in a limited context.

Although there are limited business applications to much of this current research, there are two main reasons for staying abreast of the capabilities. First, anything that makes the computer easier to use will make it more useful, and these techniques continue to improve. Second, you need to understand the current limitations to avoid costly mistakes.

The Importance of Intelligent Systems in E-Business

Disintermediation is a primary aspect of e-business. Businesses can interact directly with customers, with less need for middle levels such as retail stores. However, these middle levels often existed because they provided more explanations and support to customers. If you remove that level, how are you going to deal with thousands or millions of customers? If you have to hire hundreds of workers to answer customer questions, you will lose most of

FIGURE 9.13
Software agents. A personal software agent might be used to book a vacation. It would take your initial preferences and communicate with other agents to find sites that matched your preferences. It might also be able to negotiate prices with competing resorts.

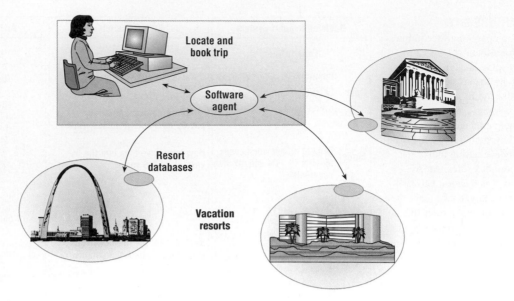

the potential benefits of disintermediation. One of the solutions to this problem is to implement more intelligent systems that can provide automated support to customers.

In many ways, the Internet adds complexity to the daily lives of customers and managers. The Internet provides access to huge amounts of data—and it is growing constantly. The growth adds more data, but it also means that the availability and use of information is constantly changing.

Agents

A recent application of AI techniques has arisen in the context of the Internet. A key issue of the Internet is searching for data. Although the Internet dramatically improves communication, there are problems with maintaining the "interpretation" of the information from various systems. Originally, most data on the Web was stored as standard pages of text using HTML. Search engines would simply scan these pages and build searchable indexes.

Increasingly the Internet is being used to store and transmit objects composed of data, pictures, spreadsheets, sounds, and video. From a pure transmission standpoint, any object can be decomposed into raw data bits and sent between computers. Where we run into problems is searching for the objects. Consider a simple example where you want to find a new printer, so you search the Internet for prices. Today, many vendors store the product descriptions and prices in a database, then build the HTML page on demand when you go to the site. Since the page is not static, the search engines do not index it.

One solution to this problem is to create software agents. **Agents** are object-oriented programs designed for networks that are written to perform specific tasks in response to user requests. The concept of object orientation is important because it means that agents know how to exchange object attributes, and they have the ability to activate object functions in other agents. The tasks could be simple, such as finding all files on a network that refer to a specific topic. One key feature of agents is that they are designed to communicate with each other. As long as your agent knows the abilities or functions of another agent, they can exchange messages and commands. General Magic is a pioneering company that created a standard programming language for agents. With this language, agents can transfer themselves and run on other computers. Agents also have a degree of "intelligence." They can be given relatively general commands, which the agents reinterpret and apply to each situation they encounter.

Consider an example illustrated by Figure 9.13. You have been working hard and decide to take a vacation. You want to go to a beach but do not have much money to spend. You are looking for a place where you can swim, scuba dive, and meet people at night. But you also want the place to have some secluded beaches where you can get away from the crowds and relax. You could call a travel agent and buy a package deal, but every agent you called just laughs and says that next time you should call three months ahead of time instead of only three days ahead. You suspect that a beach resort probably has last-minute cancellations and you could get in, but how do you find out? There are thousands of possibilities. If all of the resort computers had automatic reservation agents, the task would be fairly easy. You would start an agent on your computer and tell it the features you want. Your agent sends messages to all of the automated resort agents looking for open spots at places that matched your features. When your agent finds something close, it brings back details and pictures to display on your screen. When you decide on a resort, the agent automatically makes the reservations.

Notice three important features of software agents. First, the agents need to know how to communicate. It is not as simple as transmitting raw data. They must understand the data and respond to questions. Second, imagine the amount of network traffic involved. In the vacation search example, your agent might have to contact thousands of other computers. Now picture what happens when a thousand other people do the same thing! Third, all of the agents are independent. You, as well as other computer owners, are free to create or modify your own agent. As long as there are standard methods for agents to exchange attributes and activate functions, they can be modified and improved. For instance, you might program your agent to weight the vacation spots according to some system, or you might teach it to begin its search in specific locations.

Programmers have begun to incorporate expert system and other AI capabilities into these agents. By adding a set of rules, the agent becomes more than just a simple search mechanism. The more complex the rules, the more "intelligent" it becomes, which means you have to do less work. In fact, software agents have the potential to dramatically increase the research in AI. Currently, because of limited standards and the difficulty of creating them, there are few examples of useful agents. As increasing numbers of people use agents and begin demanding more intelligence, it will become profitable for researchers to work harder at building reliable, intelligent software.

Support and Problem-Solving Applications

Increasingly, your customers want personalized attention, to help in both selecting products and solving problems. Yet, it is expensive to provide individual personal support to every customer. Instead, firms are developing expert systems and other intelligent applications to help customers with a more personalized touch. For example, look at Amazon.com's recommendation system. It began with books, but has been expanded to most of their products. As you purchase items at Amazon.com, the system gives you a list of similar products that you might be interested in. For instance, if you purchase several science fiction books, it will suggest new releases of similar books. The system can increase sales because it helps show customers items that they might not have found otherwise.

More complex products can benefit from more sophisticated expert systems that help analyze customer needs and help configure the correct components. For example, a computer vendor could build a system that asks questions to help identify the applications that a customer will run. It could then suggest specific enhancements such as adding RAM or a second disk drive to improve performance.

Similarly, many firms are building expert systems to help customers with problems. If a customer has a problem installing a new product, he or she can turn to the website. The system asks questions to identify the problem and then make suggestions. The advantage of the expert system is that it is available 24 hours a day, can solve most of the easy problems, and is less embarrassing to customers who might think their questions are too "silly" to ask a human troubleshooter.

Intelligent systems can also be useful for B2B and other forms of e-business. The systems might analyze past purchases and suggest new products, or automatically analyze sales patterns and help managers develop new products and close out unprofitable lines. They can be used to develop automated ordering systems that predict customer demands, schedule production, and generate automated sales orders and payments.

It can be difficult to develop these applications, but firms that build powerful systems will attract customers and increase the level of sales to each customer. Ultimately, these systems could be the primary reason people switch to buying items over the Internet.

A Manager's View

Research in artificial intelligence has led to tools that are useful to managers. In particular, expert systems are used to make repetitive decisions rapidly and more consistently using novice employees. Although they are powerful, expert systems can only be used to solve problems in a narrow domain. Even then, they can be hard to modify as the business changes. Neural networks represent a new approach to using computers. They are much better than most other systems at recognizing patterns and have been applied in scanners, handwriting recognition, vision systems, and speech recognition. Advances in robotics, motion, and vision systems offer additional capabilities for specific problems.

Expert systems offer the ability to revolutionize customer service by providing personalized solutions to all customers.

Summary

Complex decisions, such as diagnostic problems, require more sophisticated computer tools. Expert systems can be used to solve complex problems if the problem can be narrowed down to a specific problem. Expert systems ask questions of the users and trace through rules to make recommendations. The systems can also trace backward through the rules to explain how they arrived at various questions or conclusions. Expert systems can be built using shells that contain the logic needed to process the rules.

Research into making machines more intelligent has led to several techniques and tools that can be useful in solving some problems. Pattern recognition is being studied with neural networks. Pattern recognition problems are involved in handwriting and voice recognition, vision systems, and in statistical applications. Researchers are also working on robotics and motion—especially combined with vision systems that will enable robots to navigate their way through new areas.

These techniques are still young and have many limitations. One of their most important uses will be the ability to improve the interaction between computers and humans. The better that computers can be adapted to humans, the easier it will be to use them. Voice recognition and language comprehension systems are important steps in that direction. Although current technology is still somewhat limited, considerable progress has been made over the last few years.

Key Words

agent, *348*

artificial intelligence (AI), 329

backward chaining, *338*

decision tree, *335*

expert system shell, *336*

forward chaining, *338*

knowledge base, *334*

knowledge engineer, *335*

knowledge management (KM), *339*

natural language, *345*

neural network, *341*

rules, *335*

triggered, *338*

Turing test, *345*

Website References

Expert Systems and AI Tools

A.L.I.C.E. conversation	**www.alicebot.org**
CLIPS (Started by NASA)	**www.ghg.net/clips/CLIPS.html**
ExSys (Commercial)	**www.exsys.com**
International Neural Network Society	**www.inns.org**
Jess (Java)	**Herzberg.ca.sandia.gov/jess/**
Mathworks neural network toolbox	**www.mathworks.com/producs/neuralnet**

Machine Vision

CalTech	**www.vision.caltech.edu/html-files/research.html**
Vision 1	**www.vision1.com/indapps.shtml**

Additional Reading

D'Inverno, Mark, (ed.) and Michael Luck (ed.). *Understanding Agent Systems,* New York: Springer Verlag, 2001. [Detailed description of software agents, somewhat technical.]

Dreyfus, Hubert L. *What Computers Still Can't Do.* Cambridge, MA: MIT Press, 1992. [Update of the 1972 and 1979 books on the difficulties of AI and the current limits of technology, including critical review of history of AI research.]

Genesereth, Michael, and S. Ketchpel. "Software Agents." *Communications of the ACM,* July 1994, pp. 48–53. [Software agents.]

Jackson, Peter. *Introduction to Expert Systems.* Boston: Addison-Wesley, 1999. [Detailed coverage of expert systems and AI technologies; somewhat technical but good references.]

Tiwana, Amrit. *The Knowledge Management Toolkit.* Old Tappan, NJ: Prentice Hall, 2000. [Basic concepts of creating a KM system.]

Review Questions

1. What types of problems are particularly well suited to expert systems?
2. What are the major differences between a decision support system and an expert system?
3. Do you think consumers would be happier if major decisions in banks were made by expert systems? Or would customers prefer to use a bank that advertised all decisions were made by humans?
4. What steps are involved in creating an expert system?
5. What research is being done in artificial intelligence?
6. Describe three situations that could benefit from the use of pattern recognition.
7. When will we have accurate speech recognition systems? What are the advantages of speech recognition?
8. What is the Turing test? Do you think it is a reasonable test?
9. How are expert systems used in e-business?

Exercises

1. Interview local managers or search the recent literature to find three diagnostic problems that could benefit from the use of expert systems. Where would you find an expert to assist with each of the situations?
2. What would it take to convince you that a computer system was intelligent? How close are existing computer systems to this standard? Do you think we might see intelligent machines within the next 5 or 10 years? Within your lifetime?
3. Interview an expert in some area and create an initial set of rules that you could use for an expert system. If you cannot find a cooperative expert, try researching one of the following topics in your library: fruit tree propagation and pruning (what trees are needed for cross-pollination, what varieties grow best in each region, what fertilizers are needed, when they should be pruned), requirements or qualifications for public assistance or some other governmental program (check government documents), legal requirements to determine whether a contract is in effect (check books on business law).
4. Obtain an expert system (e.g., Jess and CLIPS are free). Create a set of rules to evaluate a simple request for a car loan.
5. Identify a problem that would be well suited for a neural network. Explain how the system would be trained (e.g., what existing data can be used). Explain why you think the problem needs a neural network and what benefits can be gained.
6. For the following problems identify those that would be best suited for an expert system, decision support system, or a more advanced AI system. Explain why.
   - Helping students create a degree program.
   - Determining how many cooks are needed each night at a large restaurant.
   - Identifying potential criminals at an airport.
   - Investing in the stock market.
   - Hiring an employee for a technical job.
   - Troubleshooting the cause of power problems on a ship.
   - Predicting the impact of government economic policies.
   - Evaluating crime trends within a city.

7. Describe how artificial intelligence techniques could be used to enhance software agents. What additional capabilities could they be given? Give an example of the application of a "more intelligent" agent.

8. Assume that you have a software agent to handle your personal mail and other tasks on the Internet. Write a set of rules for your agent to follow.

9. Describe a situation, other than the vacation search example, where you would want to use software agents to perform some task. Describe the features of all agents, including attributes and functions that they can perform.

10. Who will pay for the creation of software agents? What about the use of the agents? Should (or could) users be charged every time their agent calls another one? What about network usage? What would happen if your agent used your telephone to connect to thousands of other agents?

11. In an e-business environment, will companies accept more automated purchasing systems? Research the topic in general, or choose a specific company, and identify the decisions made by humans. Are expert systems or AI systems commonly used? Why or why not?

12. Research the current state-of-the-art in intelligent systems used in automobiles. What features do they have? What benefits are provided? What risks are involved?

 ## Rolling Thunder Database

13. Identify an area in which an expert system could help. Be specific and explain the advantages of using an ES for that area. Where would you find an expert to assist with creating the knowledge domain?

14. Describe how new technologies might be used to improve decisions at the Rolling Thunder Bicycle company. What experimental and future technologies should we watch closely? If you could create an "intelligent" computer system for the company, what would it do and how would it be used to increase profits?

15. Do some research to identify complex decisions that are involved in designing and building bicycles.

16. What pattern-matching types of decisions arise at Rolling Thunder that could benefit from the use of neural networks?

17. What aspects of customer service might be automated with expert systems? What are the potential advantages and disadvantages?

Franchises

Franchising is a system in which a producer or marketer of a product or service, the franchisor, sells others, the franchisees, the right to duplicate a concept and use a trade name while providing sales support in a certain territory for an agreed-upon length of time. The location can involve the right to exclusivity. The amount of support varies from providing the product to resell, to extensive sales training, to control over business operations.

The first and simplest of three types of franchises involves a contract between a supplier and a business owner. The latter agrees to sell only one version of a particular product; for example, McDonald's sells only Coca-Cola soft drinks.

A second type of franchise, product trade name franchising, accounts for 52 percent of all franchise sales and 33 percent of all the franchise units in the United States. Product trade name franchising involves selling products to distributors who resell them.

Third, the fastest growing type of franchise is the prototype, or package, franchise in which a whole mode of business operations including the product or service, inventory system, sales and marketing methods, and record-keeping procedures are sold to the franchisee. Package franchising has grown 10 times faster than product-trade name franchising (11.1 percent versus 1.1 percent on average per year).

Financial Analysis

The franchisor's revenues are in the form of a startup fee, ranging from $10,000 to $600,000 depending on the size and market share of the franchise, the trade name, managerial training and support, and royalties that amount to 3 to 8 percent of gross sales.

For example, the startup fees for a McDonald's, Subway, and Domino's are $45,000, $10,000, and $1,300 respectively. Additional initial outlays include rent, inventory, legal fees, equipment, insurance, and licenses. These can amount to 10 times the startup fee, and in the case of McDonald's, can reach $500,000. The average initial cost is $330,000. There may be additional conditions before beginning; franchisers can require that purchasers have experience in the particular franchise or in the business segment it represents.

Besides covering the costs needed to acquire a franchise, the buyer needs to commit to making the system work. Franchisees who fail typically bypass immersing themselves in the business and instead attempt to be mere managers. The training program for McDonald's, for example, can take months and require a degree from Hamburger University for completion.

Financially, the outlook for investing in a startup franchise is modest profit and growth until market share increases. Due to substantial competition in low barrier-to-entry industries such as restaurants, cleaning services, and food delivery, franchise operators must keep their prices competitive. Therefore, in order to be profitable and generate a considerable return on assets, a large volume of sale must be generated. Market penetration is the goal.

Franchisors do not expect franchisees to produce substantial returns immediately. Because franchisees, as described above, face low profit margins due to stiff competition, they often experience salary decreases. On average, an owner's salary falls from $66,000 to $35,000 when leaving corporate America. Their workweek also increases.

Nevertheless, despite these statistics, franchising has continued to be a popular field, creating 170,000 new jobs in 1995. This can be attributed to the feeling of autonomy franchisees attain, which accounts for their high level of job satisfaction. Additional components include recent corporate layoffs, which have left many qualified middle managers ready to undertake new challenges.

Stock/Investment Outlook

Investing in franchise stocks gives the investor the ability to choose which industry to invest in and the desired levels of business maturity, ranging from new businesses to established, "graying" enterprises. Obviously, risk and, therefore, potential returns are higher on new ventures. Some of the risk is diversified because the investment represents a stake in a multitude of independent stores located in different areas of the country such that unfavorable economic conditions in a specific area will not be detrimental to franchisers in different territories.

Franchise stockholders need also to be aware that sometimes when a franchise is successful and the franchisor raises sufficient capital, he or she may begin repurchasing some of the business for slow growth. This is a long-term strategy for growing the franchise.

Growth Potential

Currently 8 million people are employed by franchises. Forty-one percent of retail sales are attributed to franchises. By franchising, a business can grow quickly and achieve higher market penetration that a sole proprietorship.

For the franchisee, who is often an entrepreneur lacking the knowledge of how to start a business, franchising provides an opportunity to adopt a business concept without having to start from scratch. The franchisee also faces less risk in starting a business because the concept behind the franchise has already proven to be profitable on a limited scale. Hence, the five-year survival rate for franchises is much higher than that startup businesses (85.7 percent versus 23 percent).

Competitive Structure

Franchises can achieve higher efficiency than individual small businesses and "mom and pop" stores. Franchisors do not have to be concerned with internal competition because the franchise contract stipulates how many units can coexist within a particular area. Additionally, franchise owners who leave to open a related business are often precluded from opening one within a specified vicinity of their former operations.

A liability of this form of business occurs when franchisees find a more efficient way to manage their businesses in their particular markets or feel a slightly altered product mix would be more profitable. They are often unable to implement these ideas due to the restrictions imposed by the franchiser who has a commitment to standardization within his franchise.

The amount of control that a franchisor can exert is stipulated in the contract; most franchisees are required to submit monthly, quarterly, and annual financial reports to the franchisor, while certain owners may be required to purchase supplies from a select list of vendors.

Role of Research and Development

Franchising has experienced considerable growth in the past two decades with currently 670,000 franchise units (5,000 franchises) operating in the United States. A new franchise opens every 6.5 minutes per business day.

According to the International Franchise Association, franchise sales are growing at 10 percent per year. Sales were expected to reach $1 trillion by 2000. The highest growth has been in the nonfood retail sectors, such as lodging and services. One reason for this growth has been the ability of franchisors to adapt their businesses to most effectively service emerging market trends.

Technological Investment and Analysis

Technology has also impacted the growth of the franchise industry. Improvements in the technology available to small business owners have been dramatic, including the development of comprehensive systems for tracking inventories and sales. Better and more varied communications tools have made the transmission of information between owner and franchisor much easier and more effective.

The wealth of information and services available to small business owners has also rapidly broadened. The Internet is a prime reason. The Internet also provides a means for small business to reach target customers regardless of location.

Recommendation for the Future

As many U.S. franchises, most notably in the food industry, have matured and reached market saturation, franchisors have expanded internationally. Besides international expansion continuing into the future, some other key trends are predicted for the franchise industry. Steady growth is expected to continue: retail sales from franchising will go from 41 percent to 50 percent, and sales are expected to reach $2.5 trillion by the year 2010. Franchises that are expected to thrive in the next 20 years are providers of home services such as cleaning, food delivery, and senior care services.

In conclusion, although franchising is a risky business venture for the franchisor as well as the franchisee, it has continued to expand. This can be attributed to the ability of franchisors to raise capital and replicate a business idea that has proven to be effective. Franchising has also benefited from international expansion, allowing it to continue its growth despite market saturation in certain industries. Last, technological advances have increased efficiency in the transfer of information, contributing to franchise growth while changing demographics and the current political situation have had offsetting effects on the industry.

Case: Mrs. Fields Cookies

In 1977, Debbie Fields's new husband, Randy, was hard at work giving financial advice to a client. Debbie had just returned from a history class that she was taking at a local community college. She had been wondering what impact her life would make. She decided to make another batch of her chocolate chip cookies. Because she had been doing this so long, she knew she was good at baking cookies. Furthermore, she enjoyed doing so. The light bulb in her head suddenly shone brightly. "Why not open a small cookie shop where she could bake and sell her cookies?" Since Randy's clients like them so much, she's sure that many others will, too. The first hurdle was to convince Randy that her idea would work.

Technological Investment and Analysis

To be successful, it was necessary to develop a system that would allow more control in a cost-effective environment. Approaching the sale of cookies with a new management system would enable Debbie to implement the control that she wanted, but with more cost efficiencies. Randy's philosophy was the best management structure should be built as flat as possible, meaning not too many people would involved, and not a great deal of paperwork would be necessary.

The early years of Randy's management information systems department were full of basic implementations that were very useful. The use of phone mail allowed Debbie to leave personal messages for each of the store managers at all of the stores. The form-mail program was an "e-mail" system created by the MIS department to allow personal messages to be typed up by store managers and sent to Debbie at corporate headquaters. Debbie promised a response to each message within 48 hours. Now she was able to communicate with each of her stores without actually visiting them. Visiting was time intensive; Debbie viewed it as important. She logged over 350,000 commercial air miles a year.

Improvements to the existing system included a corporate database that operated on IBM personal computers. IBM-compatible PCs, which interfaced with the cash registers, linked each store to corporate headquarters. The MIS group developed its own applications to perform various functions at the store level, such as production planning, staff scheduling, financial reporting, hiring practices, lease management, training, and baking schedules. This group of programs was labeled *retail operations intelligence (ROI)*. It was so successful within the company that Debbie and Randy decided to sell the software to the general public. The implementation of the ROI system gave Debbie the opportunity for the hands-on management that she wanted, allowing her to maintain control over individual store operations from one central office.

The ROI system simplified the role of the store managers to the point that they were told what, where, how, and when to do something. With the business focusing primarily on selling cookies, the new technology was able to tell a store manager how many cookies needed to be baked and sold at a certain time during the day. This eliminated a large amount of waste, further cutting cost. It also provided store managers with more time to focus on customer needs by alleviating administrative details.

The main strategy of the MIS department at Mrs. Fields Cookies was to assist in solving any business problems the company faced. The problem with this strategy was related to the rate at which the business was expanding. Focusing on current problems was not helpful in the prevention of new problems that might arise. Paul Quinn, the director of MIS, reported directly to Randy Fields. He was not concerned about problem prevention, but wanted to focus on the issues of cost efficiency. He was committed to using his department to provide benefits to the company. According to Quinn, problem solving was good for present situations. However, analyzing the big picture and the possibilities for the future were just as important, especially when it involved a business of the size and reputation of Mrs. Fields Cookies.

Quinn defined MIS strategy as anything that would promote sales and control food and labor costs. Quinn wanted to know not only how a new technique would cut costs and save money for the business, but also how it would develop new sales and put the company in a better position to take advantage of opportunities.

At the corporate level, Quinn implemented the ROI system for the business as it moved out of the 1980s into the 1990s. No longer was the company growing at such a fast rate and seemingly trying to flood the market. Many viewed the ROI system to be an expert system (ES).

Randy Fields made the following statement about his belief in the use of expert systems at Mrs. Fields Cookies:

> We couldn't run our business without information technology—not a single facet. Who we hire is determined by an expert system. What we make at each store is determined by an expert system. How we schedule our labor in each store is determined by an expert system. How we communicated internally is routed by an expert system. . . . What's left? At the store level, everything that the manager does that's related to control and administration has been 'offloaded' to a machine. So the manager's job is to think about people.

With the implementation of the ROI applications, control by one person was eliminated at the store level. Implementation of these applications took some of the burden off Debbie's shoulders as she tried to maintain control over everything for so long.

The ROI system included 12 applications, each with the purpose of decreasing the company's time and cost spent on each function. Four of the more important applications included interview, training and testing, automated trouble shooting, and form mail. These four applications helped to decrease the time managers spent completing these tasks. This, in turn, enabled them to offer better service to their customers.

The interview application process begins with the applicant sitting at the computer and filling out an application online on the computer. The basic questions give the company an understanding of the applicant's personality. The computer program asks why the applicant applied to work at Mrs. Fields. It pinpoints inconsistencies provided by an applicant such as a 17-year-old who lists an educational background up to graduate school. The expert system program produces a list of concerns about the candidate. Upon completion of the computer interview, it ranks the applicant in areas of education, honesty, and salesmanship, among others. After the computer interview, the applicant is given the opportunity to "audition" as a performer in front of customers. The manager then decides if the applicant will be hired.

Each employee, from manager to baker, engages in continual training and evaluation by using the training and testing systems application. Again, the system asks several questions based on experience and performance to test and evaluate individual skills learned, and to train in the development of new ones. Once employees complete a training module, their records in human resources are updated automatically at corporate headquarters.

Automated troubleshooting is a maintenance module used mainly by the store manager to deal with problems concerning faulty or broken store equipment. If the answers entered in the system do not lead to a solution for the problem, a function is added that requests an outside call for assistance. Each store has a file with the product service group at corporate headquarters, listing information about each piece of equipment at the store. This information is used to contact the product vendor to request any type of repair that is needed.

The form mail application enables store managers to maintain communication with corporate headquarters. Debbie is also able to send memos to each of the stores with the use of this application. It is built upon the basic e-mail system developed in the early 1980s.

Problems and Challenges

Maintaining Consistency

In 1980, Debbie Fields went to visit the company's first location outside her direct management control, a Mrs. Fields Cookies store in Hawaii. Until that store, maintaining a consistent set of standards and practices had been a fairly straightforward task. Debbie Fields would drive to her stores on a daily basis to review operations. As long as a location was under her direct span of control, there were few problems with replicating the concept, product offerings and practices that reflected company values and strategies. Product quality and Debbie's "hour by hour" management concept, in which managers work toward hourly sales and production goals, remained intact [Fields 1995].

The Hawaii store presented a new challenge. In spite of the fact that Steve, one of her best quality control managers, was assigned to the store, Debbie found that after four months the cookies bore little resemblance to her original product. In her opinion, "They looked like little cakes." [Fields 1995] Unknowingly, Steve had allowed the cookies to migrate a bit each day, in barely noticeable increments, from their original form and texture. This transition was unplanned and virtually undetectable by store employees, since each day's fare was compared with the previous day's altered version rather than the original. The unintended consequence was a product that was no longer consistent with company standards.

This management problem can be broken down into four problems.

1. **The Data Collection Problem.** A common administrative task is the collection of employee attendance data for use by payroll and human resources departments. At first glance, the collection process seems to be a reporting procedure that enforces company policies regarding employee pay for hours worked. Placed in the larger context of unit operations, inefficient data collection procedures result in a loss of consistency in overall performance.

2. **The Information Compilation Problem.** Reports collect, compile, and consolidate organizational information about sales, human resources, and operations. These reports can be misleading if the information contained is out-of-date. Subsequent decisions based upon where a company was 30, 60, or 90 days ago can result in inconsistent decisions and performance based on a zigzag course of constant catch-up and correction.

3. **The Analysis and Decision-Making Problem.** Increases in the integrity of information and the speed with which it is received leads to better analysis and decision making. Technology can be used to improve the consistency with which data is analyzed, including software that allows users to manipulate figures and develop multiple "what-if" scenarios.

4. **The Action Directive Problem.** Improvements in data collection, information compilation, and analysis and decision making can lead to better policy directives and increases in corporate intelligence. Executives must still disseminate directives to all employees to ensure that they are being followed. New procedures are distributed in the form of memos or manuals, with no way to measure whether or not the new policy was remembered or even read by an employee. This results in inconsistent performance and product quality since some employees follow the newest policies and some do not. [Fields 1995]

In an additional effort to improve service and to reduce theft, Mrs. Fields is installing closed-circuit cameras (CCTV) in all of its new and renovated stores and is working to install them in every store. The cameras primarily watch the cash register and sales area, storing data on videotapes. In a trial in 20 stores, the tapes were used for training and to improve customer service. After five months, sales increased by 6 percent. The tapes also helped catch an employee who stole more than $6,500 from the cash register.

Over Expansion

In March 1993, Mrs. Fields Cookies was forced to give its lenders, led by Prudential Insurance, nearly 80 percent of the company in exchange for writing off $94 million in debt. Debbie relinquished her posts as president and CEO and her

operational control to Thomas Fey, previously of Godiva and Pepperidge Farm. Fields remained the largest individual shareholder, with 8 percent. She took a $150,000 salary cut to $450,000 in 1993. In 1992, as bankers asserted themselves more and more, Field's husband, Randy, who had been chair, left to sell the financial software he developed for Mrs. Fields to franchised restaurants such as Burger King, National Pizza, and Skipper's Seafood. [Pogrebin 1993]

Expansion through Acquisitions

Mrs. Fields Cookies has been on a program of expansion and acquisition. Its new president, Larry Hodges, is determined to dominate the baked-snack segment. Under his direction, Mrs. Fields has aggregated the following name brands: Mrs. Fields Cookies, Great American Cookie Co., Hot Sam's Pretzel Bakery, Original Cookie Co., Pretzel Time, and Pretzelmaker. See table on page 358. Mrs. Fields continues to operate the stores under their original names. The company moved all the chain's administrative functions to the Mrs. Fields corporate offices in Salt Lake City. Mrs. Fields is seeking to solidify its position as the nation's leading retailer and franchiser of baked-on-premises snacks, with 1,411 outlets in the United States and 10 foreign countries. This breaks down to 526 Mrs. Fields cookie shops, 305 Great American Cookies stores, 213 Pretzelmaker sites, 245 Pretzel Time locations, 71 Original Cookie Co. branches, 43 Hot Sam Pretzel establishments, and eight Bakery Cafés. Franchisees or licensees operate nearly two-thirds of these units. In 2000, Mrs. Fields's, holding company purchased TCBY and all of its stores.

While Mrs. Fields's buying binge and restructuring strategy under Hodges has yielded higher earnings before interest, taxes, depreciation, and amortization, or EBITDA, which many investors consider a positive indication of a corporation's ability to pay down debt, the company is facing serious debt issues. Debt and capital lease obligations in 2000 rose to $188,069,000 with total stockholders' deficit of $24,932,000. Net loss in 2000 was $26,478,000 with net store and food sales of $144,156,000. Substantially higher interest expenses followed the issuance of $100 million in high-yield notes, which accounted for a significant portion of the company's losses. The bottom line was also impacted by rising general and administrative costs related to the acquisitions, higher unit level lease rates after renewals, and higher food costs that resulted from a nearly 400-percent increase in the price of butter since early 1997.

Future Strategy

Mrs. Fields Cookies has adopted the following future strategy.

Capitalize on Cross Selling and Cobranding Opportunities

The company wants to capitalize on cross selling and cobranding opportunities by offering multiple product lines in a single location, providing franchisees of one brand with the ability to become franchisees of the other brands, and marketing bundled brands to potential and existing licensees. An example of store-specific cross selling is Mrs. Fields's

Bakery Café, which sells each of the core brands in a single location. The company has a cobranding relationship with existing third-party partners, including Subway and Taco Bell.

Capitalize on the Strong Brand Names

The company believes its strongest brand identity is the Mrs. Fields brand name. As a result, it is converting its remaining company-owned Original Cookie stores to Mrs. Fields brand stores. Mrs. Fields achieved higher revenues than Original Cookie stores—$353,000 versus $255,000. Further development and expansion into kiosks and carts in malls, airports, convention centers, office buildings, storefronts, and sports complexes is planned. There will be an increasing emphasis on the catalog/e-tailing business, licensing opportunities, such as linking sales of Mrs. Fields with prominent names in the retailing and food service industry, expanding licensing agreements with the existing licensees, entering into new licensing agreements with food service operators; and developing product line extensions such as cocoa, chocolate chips, ice cream novelties, chocolates, and ready-to-eat cookies to be sold in supermarkets and other convenience locations.

Develop New Company-Owned and Franchised Stores

The company is building and franchising new stores, as well as carts and kiosks, in existing and new markets, including amusements parks and other entertainment centers.

Continue Development of New Products

The product development department continually researches and tests new products to attract new customers and revitalize the interest of current customers. After a trial period to evaluate both consumer response and store operation's ability to handle the new product, it is fully commercialized, modified, or discontinued.

Increase International Locations

As of February 24, 2001, there were 111 internationally franchised Mrs. Fields and Pretzelmaker brand stores.

Pursue Further Strategic Acquisitions of Related Businesses

The management intends to further identify and integrate new businesses through acquisitions like those of the cookie businesses of Original Cookie and Great American in 1996 and 1998, and the pretzel businesses of Hot Sam and Pretzel Time in 1997.

Further Systems Development

Today Randy Fields is divorced from Debbie and is the principal of the software firm Park City Group. According to Randy, "I'm built for big stuff." The Park City Group markets Action-Manager, an operations management software for foodservice operations and retailers.

In examining restaurant operations, Randy is focused on the automation of front- and back-office operations. In doing so, he focuses on these three straightforward questions.

How can we reduce turnover?

How can we get unit A to perform like unit B?

How can we move the unit manager from a back-of-the-house administrator to a front-of-the-house people person? [Rubinstein 1997]

Focusing on those questions, Fields extended the work he had done for Mrs. Fields to develop a line of rule-based software products for labor management, inventory, and profit and loss. The goal was to control costs through improved operational efficiency. The system alerts restaurant managers when there is preparation work to be done. It forecasts what needs to be prepared. If sales escalate beyond plan, the system applies predetermined rules to make sure the operator keeps inventories ample. Fields's goal is "Better technology models for operators to monitor all unit-level functions, alert managers to problems, and suggest the best practices for dealing with those problems." To address the home meal replacement business, Park City is working with supermarkets in the areas of forecasting and manufacturing resource planning. Fields remains convinced that the industry's chief concerns are the recruitment, retention, and utilization of the right people.

Questions

1. What is the strategic direction of Mrs. Fields Cookies?
2. Who or what forces are driving this direction?
3. What has been the catalyst for change for Mrs. Fields Cookies?
4. Upon what technologies has Mrs. Fields Cookies relied?
5. What caused a change in the use of technology in the corporation?
6. How has this change been implemented?
7. Who has driven this change throughout the organization?
8. How successful has the technological change been?

Additional Reading

Fields, Randall, and Nicholas Imparato. "Cost, Competition & Cookies." *Management Review* 84 no. 4, April 1995, pp. 57–61.

Pogrebin, Robin. "What Went Wrong with Mrs. Fields?" *Working Woman* 18 no. 7, July 1993, pp. 9, 11.

Prendergast, Alan. "Learning to Let Go." *Working Woman,* January 1992, pp. 42–44.

Rubinstein, Ed. "Randy Fields: Helping Operators Save More Than Just Cookie Dough." *Nation's Restaurant News* 31, no. 28, July 14, 1997, p. 80.

Sandberg, Jared. "At Thousands of Web Sites, Time Stands Still." *The Wall Street Journal,* March 11, 1997, p. B1.

	Company Owned	Domestic Franchised	International Franchised	Licensed	Total
Mrs. Fields	129	221	77	99	526
Great American	94	211	–	–	305
Original Cookie	71	–	–	–	71
Cookie Subtotal	294	432	77	99	902
Pretzel Time	95	138	–	12	245
Pretzelmaker	5	160	34	14	213
Hot Sam	43	–	–	–	43
Pretzel Subtotal	143	298	34	26	501
Bakery Café	8	–	–	–	8
Totals	445	730	111	125	1,411

Case: Blockbuster Video

On a typical night in America, if there is nothing to watch on regular television, people can simply switch among dozens of channels to watch a movie on cable or choose a pay-per-view movie. This does not mean leaving the house. Alternatively, improvements in video technology such as laser discs or digital videodiscs (DVDs) are beginning to provide other options. Running to the local video store has become less necessary than it used to be.

In today's society, going to the local video store to rent a movie with friends and family has been a source of entertainment. Video rental is still a relatively new technology. One of the pioneers in this key home entertainment industry is Blockbuster Entertainment Group.

Founded in 1985, Blockbuster Video is the world's number one video chain with more than 51 million U.S. and Canadian member accounts active during 2000, plus several million additional member accounts worldwide. In 2000, an estimated average of more than 3 million customers walked into U.S. Blockbuster stores every day. Blockbuster estimates that 70 percent of the U.S. population lives within a 10-minute drive of a store, which are generally open 365 days a year. Headquartered in Dallas, Texas, Blockbuster Inc. is a publicly traded subsidiary of Viacom Inc., with nearly 7,800 stores and approximately 95,000 employees throughout the Americas, Europe, Asia, and Australia.

Blockbuster is implementing ways to generate incremental profit through its store network. In September 2000, the company began marketing DirecTV System equipment in 3,800 of its U.S. stores. Through the success of this alliance, Blockbuster cobranded DirecTV's pay-per-view movie service in June 2001, establishing the Blockbuster brand in the pay-per-view segment of the home entertainment industry for the first time. In June 2001, the company entered a strategic alliance with RadioShack Corporation and began rolling out the RadioShack "Cool Things" store-in-store concept.

In 1998, Blockbuster opened a state-of-the-art distribution center in McKinney, Texas, just north of the company's Dallas headquarters. All company-operated stores in the United States are supported by this single 850,000-square-foot facility. During 2000, Blockbuster estimates that it processed more than 121 million units of its product from this distribution center.

Blockbuster sees a wide range of future opportunities presented by new media, home entertainment technologies. The company vision calls for moving from a retail-only power-house to a leading provider of multiple forms of home entertainment. Recently, the company introduced convenient online rental to a few selected markets through its website.

Technology Innovations

A partnership between the Blockbuster Entertainment Group and Sony Electronics, Park Ridge, New Jersey, to promote and demonstrate the new digital videodisc technology may portend how supermarkets can tie in to the product launch. Select Blockbuster stores in major markets installed in-store demonstration kiosks with Sony DVD players in April 1997. Meanwhile, purchasers of the Sony hardware units received coupons for free DVD rentals at Blockbusters. According to Benjamin S. Feingold, president of Columbia TriStar Home Video, Culver City, California, similar demonstration programs could be made available soon to supermarkets.

"Over time I'm sure we will develop various types of promotional programs for various accounts in conjunction with Sony Electronics," he said. "But in the beginning, there may be inventory issues about how much hardware and software is available. Over time we would expect that there would be promotional opportunities available for almost every class of trade that wants to be in the business." [Serwer, 1998]

The Blockbuster-Sony partnership is noteworthy because Viacom's ownership of Paramount Pictures is in direct competition with Sony's Columbia and TriStar units. "Blockbuster is committed to being a leader in developing the entertainment software experiences that exceed the expectations of our members." according to Tom Byrne, Blockbuster's vice chairman.

According to John Briesch, president of Sony's Consumer A/V Group, "We believe people already expect the latest in home video entertainment from Blockbuster, so it makes sense for them to be one of the first retailers in the country to demonstrate the incredible video and audio experiences only available from DVD. Once people have an opportunity to experience our new DVD video player, we believe they will immediately understand the excitement that DVD offers." he said. [Serwer, 1998]

Telecommunications

Modern audiences demand a technological touch in movies, advertising, and television. All of these enhancements are expensive to develop and to transmit. A company such as KWCC, the special-effects house behind the films *Clear and*

Present Danger and *Judge Dredd,* uses dedicated Silicon Graphics (SGI) workstations that run into the hundreds of thousands of dollars. These houses charge $2,000 to $12,000 per second of screen time for performing their digital special effects. To make waves with digital photos, Web graphics, or printed documents, eye-catching effects must be included. Everyday tasks look dull by comparison if some splash is not included, whether it is adding color to e-mail, animations to the home page, or a personal touch to photos and videos.

The Importance of Data

In 1990, Blockbuster planned to categorize its 30 million customers according to the types of movies they rented and to "sell information from the database . . . to direct mailers, for planning target-marketing campaigns." Blockbuster used sophisticated computer systems to keep records of each individual's transactions. The plans raised difficult privacy issues for the same reason it would prove to be a gold mine for direct mailers. Video choices are among the most revealing decisions a consumer makes. [*Wall Street Journal* 1990] While a federal law forbids video stores from disclosing the names of the movies it customers rent, it does not forbid stores from telling direct marketers "the subject matter" of the movies a customer has rented.

Blockbuster, whose members represent one out of six American households, says its database will be legal because it monitors video categories, not specific titles. In 1990, the chain organized its shelves by 37 categories, with plans to add 30 to 40 more.

The Internet

An agreement has been signed by General Electric's NBC and Intertainer, Inc. to enable individuals to request, on demand, rebroadcasts of NBC programming like *Late Night with Conan O'Brien* and *Dateline.* NBC said it will partner with Intertainer, Inc., to provide content from the programming it owns to Intertainer's on-demand broadband video entertainment and shopping service.

In the process, NBC and GE Capital's Equity Capital Group will pay $3 million in cash for 6 percent of privately held Intertainer. NBC and GE Capital will also have the option to purchase up to 19 percent of the Santa Monica, California-based company for about $75 million in the next 18 months. Details regarding the shows NBC will bring to the upcoming Intertainer service were not immediately finalized and were going to be subsequently revealed. Intertainer's service will be delivered through a high-speed cable or phone line and will provide movies, music, television programming, shopping, and informational programming to a user's personal computer or television set.

The Intertainer service is based on the concept of any on-demand video service. Customers will be given the ability to watch what they want, when they want. Intertainer's service is personalized, through intelligent agent technology from Firefly Networks. The agent "reads" user's preferences and provides prompts and suggestions leading them to personalized movie, music, television, or interactive shopping program options. Intertainer is available to consumers through their personal computers or televisions, initially through distribution provided by two of its original partners, Comcast and U.S. West.

Today, six mass media giants dominate the entertainment and information field. These companies are News Corp, Viacom, Seagram, Walt Disney, Time Warner, and Sony.

April 1997 was a low point for Viacom, Inc., and Sumner Redstone, its chairman. The stock price was down and the Blockbuster video retail chain was struggling. Since this time, Redstone has engineered a turnaround that has raised Viacom, Inc., to new heights.

According to Redstone, Blockbuster is fixed because he cut deals with the Hollywood studios that enable more hit movies to be in his stores. Still, Viacom remains a work in progress. Its UPN Network is losing money. Redstone says he would like to sell Blockbuster and Spelling Entertainment, and will likely make more acquisitions, too. "But we will not releverage," he concludes quickly. [Serwer, 1998]

Amid increasing concern at Viacom about reducing the company's $8 billion debt, rumors persist that Blockbuster Video will be sold. The success of *Titanic* helped to increase revenues by 12 percent at Viacom for the third quarter of 1998. However, profits from continuing operations were down 83 percent, due to the continuing losses at Blockbuster.

Redstone sold half of USANetworks to Seagram for $1.7 billion. The money went toward reducing Viacom's debt. Yet Viacom's stock did not move from the low 30s.

The logic for selling Blockbuster revolves around the commitment of Viacom's Paramount film subsidiary to embrace Divx, a new home video format for digital videodiscs. The format requires users to buy an encoded disc for about $5. After that, it is a pay-per-view deal. The disc player is hooked up to a phone line. The movie cannot be watched without dialing in. After a 48-hour viewing period, a charge is incurred for subsequent screenings. If the system catches on, the reduced likelihood that people will buy tapes will cut into rentals. Advanced an estimated $20 million by the format's developers, Paramount is already licensing films for production in the Divx format.

Competitor

The Hollywood Video rental chain paid $100 million to acquire the Internet-based video concern Reel.com, Inc. Wall Street responded favorably to Hollywood Video, increasing its stock price by 13.28 percent in one day of trading.

Hollywood Video is the second largest video store chain in the United States, with more than 1,000 superstores in 43 states. Each store carries about 10,000 titles and 16,000 videocassettes. Reel.com offers 85,000 VHS titles for sale, more than 1,200 DVD titles for sale, and 35,000 video titles for rent. The cyberstore is also the leading video-only store on the Internet.

The acquisition enables Hollywood Video to leverage its base of 25 million members, industry knowledge, and studio relationships to a new and rapidly growing distribution channel. Because of the uniqueness of an individual customer's taste in movies, the Internet together with the PC's information-processing capabilities are positioned to create a substantial increase in movie consumption through matching, collaborative filtering, and customized recommendations.

Recommendation for the Future

In its quest to become the neighborhood entertainment source, Blockbuster will use its extensive consumer database to select the product mix. "The goal is neighborhood retailing and the customization of each product for each store," says marketing manager, Baskin. "The key is to cater to the local market and service the local customer." [Desjar, 2001] Baskin says the chain has the "strategic advantage" of knowing the entertainment buying habits of half of the households in the United States. Managers at individual locations will have the most input on which products to stock. "Having unmatched demographic information is a great guide, but it's not a silver bullet," says Baskin.

Blockbuster tried to diversify by expanding into music stores. It even attempted to add book sales, tailoring the titles to specific locations. In 1999, after consistently losing money, Blockbuster sold all of the music stores.

Blockbuster's greatest strength in the last two years has been its unique association with Viacom, which enabled Blockbuster to change its purchase arrangement. The deal provides Blockbuster with thousands of copies of new releases at minimal cost, enabling the stores to guarantee hot titles will be in the store.

Blockbuster needs to continue to invest in technology. The demand for home entertainment will remain consistent. At this point in time, home entertainment includes television programming, movies, compact discs, and books. However, what is important today does not necessarily determine what will be important in the next two, five, or seven years.

On February 27, 2001, Blockbuster announced a partnership program in which RadioShack would open a store-within-a-store at all Blockbuster locations. In June 2001, Blockbuster entered a strategic alliance with RadioShack Corporation and began rolling out the RadioShack "Cool Things" store-in-store concept. A preliminary test of four markets—Austin, Texas; Las Vegas; Norfolk, Virginia; and Tulsa, Oklahoma—began in summer 2001.

The 600-square-foot space features 1,135 skus and is located at the rear of the store. The area is staffed by a RadioShack employee. The inventory is stocked behind the false walls backing the department. Nearly every product category is represented, even though the number of parts and accessories are pared back. Consumers can purchase a Compaq computer system, portable electronics, home audio and consumer electronics, and wireless communications, as well as pertinent batteries, parts, and accessories. Both Ultimate TV and DirecTV will be sold there.

The area facing the store interior and video rental area is designated the "Trend Zone." It will feature a rotating assortment of differentiated merchandise that includes gift items for upcoming holidays, licensed merchandise, and movie tie-ins. This area will be refreshed approximately every 30 days, due to the high frequency of visits Blockbuster customers typically make. In comparison, Best Buy is in the process of reworking more than 1,300 Musicland locations to better target women and younger shoppers. There is broad consensus among analysts that the adoption of broadband, both hardware and content, will largely be driven by entertainment products. By partnering together, Blockbuster and RadioShack are positioning themselves not only as a source for products and services, but also as leaders in the entertainment environment.

In July 2000, Blockbuster and Enron initiated a "20-year partnership." They indicated that they would develop a central platform to sell movies on demand over high-speed Internet systems. Blockbuster had the brand name and relationships with studios that wanted to move to home video. Enron had a high-speed backbone and could set up servers. Local DSL providers would connect customers to a special set-top box that would decrypt the movies. Plans called for the exclusive arrangement to offer consumers the ability to choose from among 400 to 500 movies and have the movie delivered to a set-top box on their televisions via DSL. At the time the deal was announced, Steve Pantelick, Blockbuster senior vice president of strategic planning, said talks with studios for content were under way.

The subsequent arrangements left Enron feeling less than satisfied and it broke off the relationship. "From Enron's standpoint, the main reason for discontinuing the relationship had to do with content," said Enron spokeswoman Shelly Mansfield. "We just felt that, through the exclusive relationship, we weren't able to attract the quality or quantity of movies that is necessary to really make this service thrive." According to media analyst Tom Wolzien, "Nobody has a network to the consumer here, and Blockbuster couldn't get the movies." [Kerschbaumer 2001] Blockbuster executives were probably happy the relationship fell apart before Enron's accounting scandal and collapse in 2002.

The Impact of Video on Demand

Blockbuster has improved its position from $7 per share in January 2001 to $21.80 in early September 2001. The drop in share price was the result of the pronouncement by dot-com companies in the late 1990s that the industry was dead. With the economic slowdown, investors were once again looking for recession-proof industries to invest in, especially low technology industry sectors.

The renewed interest in video retail was fueled by total rental spending at a record $12.4 billion in 2000 as compared to $11.2 billion in 1999. The surge was due in large part to the emergence of DVD, which accounted for $780 million in rental spending compared to $78 million in 1999. And even the threat of video-on-demand (VOD) did not diminish investor enthusiasm. In August 2001, five major movie studios announced plans to launch an Internet-based video-on-demand service in early 2002 that would pool the resources of Paramount Studios, Sony Pictures, MGM Studios, Universal Studios, and Warner Bros. While enthusiastic, the response of industry analysts has been lukewarm. Most feel that VOD will take years to make a significant impact on video retail.

"Until there is a direct route from broadband into the home and into the TV, it's going to be a niche market," said Tom Adams of Adams Media Research in Carmel, California. "There are only so many tech-savvy people who will want to watch movies on their PCs." [Desjar dins 2001]

While the movie studios periodically get interested in video on demand, the more immediate question is the issue of satellite movies. Satellites can beam hundreds of channels continuously, carrying hundreds of movies a week to your home. With the touch of a couple of buttons, digital recorders can capture dozens of these movies and instantly play them back whenever customers want. Premium movies require subscriptions to additional channels, but a properly programmed system can present dozens of movies on demand.

Questions

1. What is the strategic direction of the Blockbuster Entertainment Division of Viacom?

2. What are the critical success factors and core competencies for the Blockbuster organization?

3. Upon what technologies has Blockbuster relied?

4. What has caused a change in the direction of the use of technology at Blockbuster?

5. How successful has the technological change been?

6. What does the corporation's Web page present about its business directives?

7. How does technology impact the challenges and opportunities that the home video industry is facing?

8. How will the capture and maintenance of customer data impact Blockbuster's future?

Additional Reading

"Coming Soon to Your Local Video Store: Big Brother." *The Wall Street Journal,* December 26, 1990.

Desjardins, Doug. "Video Chains Experience Fast-Forward Growth." *Dsn Retailing Today* 40, no. 18 (September 17, 2001): pages 6 and 61.

Hamblen, Matt. "Web Site Gives Pay-per-View a Fighting Chance." *Computerworld,* June 30, 1997, p. 6.

Harrington, Mark. "Blockbuster Exits PC Business, Closes Stores." *Computer Retail Week,* October 13, 1997, pp. 1–2.

"Hollywood Video Reels Out $100Mil in Acquisition." *Newsbytes,* July 31, 1998, p. NEW07310025.

Kerschbaumer, Ken, and John M. Higgins. "Video No Demand." *Broadcasting & Cable* 131 no. 12, March 9, 2001, pp. 40–41.

Lewis, Peter. "Movie Madness." *Fortune,* September 17, 2001.

Marcus, Ann M. "Four on a Match." *PC Entertainment,* March 1996, p. 14.

"NBC: "Let Us Intertain You." *Newsbytes,* August 3, 1998, p. NEW08030032.

Pepper, Jon, and Cesar Alvarez. "Hollywood Comes Home." *Computer Life,* July 1998, p. 58.

Serwer, Andrew. "Viacom Wants an Oscar for Fixing Blockbuster." *Fortune,* April 27, 1998. p. 485.

"Wave Aims to Be Blockbuster Video of E-Commerce." *Newsbytes,* June 25, 1997, p. NEW06250072.

Appendix

E-Mail Rules

True expert systems can contain complex rules. Consequently they tend to use powerful expert system shells—like CLIPS. You can download the CLIPS software and documentation and learn the language, but it takes time to learn how to build the rules. On the other hand, you most likely already have a relatively simple expert system on your computer. Microsoft Outlook supports a rule-based system to help handle your incoming e-mail messages.

The volume of e-mail continually increases. It is not uncommon for some managers to receive a couple of hundred messages a day. Of course, some are more important than others: your client's request for a new sales quote is critical; the companywide notice about the new flower gardens is not. And then there are the spammers. Even reading through the subject text of a hundred messages and deleting the junk can be a

time-consuming task. Imagine what happens when you go on vacation. Now think about how the problem is going to multiply in the coming years.

Folders

One of the first steps in handling e-mail is to organize your Inbox as a collection of folders. Figure 9.1A shows a possible example, where corporate messages are separated from customer messages. The goal is to compartmentalize your mail so you can see the important items instantly, and save the less important items for later. It is also possible to attach categories to items (such as Expenses, Sales Leads, and VIP). Any item can be placed into any category (Edit + Categories). You can even define your own categories. The purpose of categories is to make it easy to group and find items even if they are in different folders. For example, you will generally view the Inbox organized by the subfolders. But you could just as easily use the View menu options to see all messages that you categorized by Expense—regardless of their current folder locations.

Simple Rules

Once you have created the folders, the most obvious question is how do you get new messages into the proper folder? You could read each subject or message and drag it to the right location. A better method is to use the Organize button and create a rule to move messages automatically. In the Organize box, simply choose the appropriate folder and any new messages from the same sender will be delivered to the specified folder.

If you have a large collection of messages, it will take awhile to create the rules for each sender. But the initial time investment is worthwhile because now all future messages will be placed in the appropriate folder. Keep in mind that you can also automatically move items directly to the Delete folder, where they will eventually be removed.

You can also use the Rules Wizard to create other simple types of rules. For example, you can have the system notify you with a pop-up message when an e-mail arrives from your boss, or flag messages as important. It can also automatically assign categories based on the sender or keywords.

Custom Rules

The Rules Wizard also has the ability to let you build relatively complex rules to handle mail. Begin by starting the wizard (Tools + Rules Wizard). Then add a new rule and select the

option to Start from a blank rule. A custom rule has three basic steps: (1) set a condition, (2) specify an action to take if the condition is true, and (3) specify an exception to the rule. The third step is optional.

Conditions

Figure 9.2A shows some of the conditions that you can monitor. Notice the two conditions that are checked: suspected junk mail and containing adult material. Outlook XP enables you to choose from 28 possible conditions, such as the sender; the words in the subject, body, addresses, or message header; categories; or importance level. You can select multiple conditions. The conditions are connected by Or clauses: if any of the selected conditions is true, then the rule triggers. You can establish relatively sophisticated rules by searching for key words within the subject or the text. The example searches for the phrase *credit card* or *Visa* in the subject—which are common solicitations for unwanted credit cards. You could keep building rules to block senders of junk e-mail, but the problem is that they continually switch accounts. So it is more effective to block based on content.

Actions

Each rule requires an action that will be executed when the condition is true. Figure 9.3A shows some of the actions available, with the delete option checked for our simple rule to handle unsolicited credit card offers. Note that you can check multiple actions, so your rule can perform multiple tasks with one message. Usually you want to focus on one action, but you might want to select multiple "mark" options, such as marking a message as important, marking it as read, and then forwarding it to someone else.

Most of the actions are straightforward, but four of them are relatively powerful: (1) stop processing rules, (2) run a script, (3) start an application, and (4) perform a custom action.

FIGURE 9.1A Inbox folder list. You need to create folders and subfolders to make it easier to find messages. It also makes it easier to see the important messages that must be handled first.

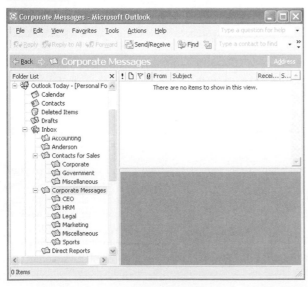

FIGURE 9.2A Rules wizard to set a condition. This example will be used to filter and delete a common form of junk mail: solicitations for credit cards.

You will see the value of the stop action in the next section. The other three actions make it possible to create powerful, complex actions in response to a message. But you will generally need a programmer to create the customized actions. For example, you could create an application that responds to e-mail messages from customers and automatically checks inventory, creates an order, and sends a reply to the customer.

After you establish an action, you can create an exception to the rule. For example, you might want to stash all general messages from HRM into a separate folder, unless they mention your name in the body of the newsletter.

FIGURE 9.3A Actions to take. You must specify at least one action for a rule, and sometimes you will want to add some additional actions, such as setting the importance level, copying it to a folder, and forwarding it to someone else.

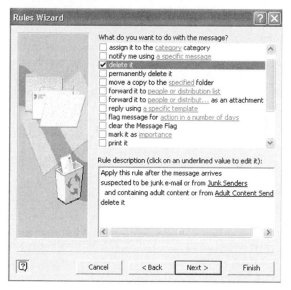

Sequence of Rules

An individual rule can be useful, but the system is even more powerful when you understand that multiple rules can be applied to any message. In fact, you need to think about the rules as a chain, where the first rule is run and tested against a message. If the message meets the rule's condition, then the specified actions are taken. Then the next rule is tested against the same message, and its actions taken if the conditions apply. Figure 9.4A shows how you can use this sequence to perform relatively complex analysis. The first two rules examine a message to determine that it relates to your expense account. Rule 1 automatically flags messages from the expense-account administrator, Rule 2 picks up messages from your manager with "expenses" in the subject. Messages are moved to the Expenses folder, but they are also marked by setting the Expenses category for that message. Then Rule 3 examines all new messages in the Expenses category and checks to see if they mention a payment. If so, the message is marked as important and an on-screen message pops up to let you know. Using the Expenses category as a flag enables you to split the rules. This way you can always add new rules to help determine if a message relates to your expense account, without having to change any of the other rules.

Remember that by default, all rules are applied sequentially to every incoming message. You can control the sequence by using the Rules Wizard to specify which rules are executed first. One other control you have is the stop action. Any rule can activate this action to stop further processing of a message. For example, think about what can happen if you get messages from friends or co-workers that contain key words like Visa or credit card. The antispam rule created earlier will also be applied to these messages and delete them. You could add all of your friends to the exception list on that rule, and every similar rule, but there is an easier way. When you create a rule to move messages from your friends and co-workers, include the

FIGURE 9.4A Rule sequence. Multiple rules can be applied to a given message. Build a decision tree to show the rule process. Here, messages from the expense accounting department or from your manager with a subject of expenses are moved to the expenses folder and the Expenses category is set. Then the third rule checks each new expenses item to see if the subject includes the word *payment*. If so, it highlights the e-mail and delivers an on-screen message.

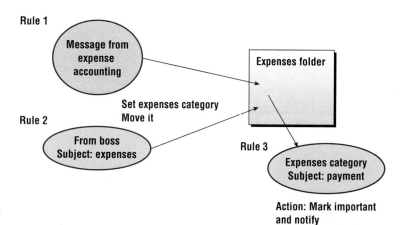

action to stop processing rules. Then make sure that these move rules are at the top of your list. This step is easy to set up and has the side benefit of making the rules processing faster.

Even with fairly simple rules, you can create a relatively powerful expert system to help handle your e-mail. If you have the time, you could create replies and custom actions to build an automated agent that handles common tasks. But even in a short time, with no programming, you can build a system that helps you wade through your daily e-mail more efficiently. One of the nice features is that you can add rules at any time, so you can start with a small system, and add more complex rules later. But as you get more complex, you should consider drawing a decision tree to help you understand the interactions of the rules.

Exercises

1. Create the set of e-mail folders shown in Figure 9.1A: Contacts for Sales (Corporate, Government, Miscellaneous), Corporate Messages (CEO, HRM, Legal, Marketing, Miscellaneous, Sports), and Direct Reports. Have someone send you a message and create a rule that directs future messages from that person into one of the subfolders.

2. Create a set of e-mail folders and subfolders for your own job. Create the rules that move messages into the appropriate folder. If you do not have a job that uses e-mail, consider a job that you want to obtain in a couple of years.

3. As shown in the example, create an e-mail rule from scratch that deletes messages mentioning credit card, Visa, or Mastercard.

4. Create the rules needed to handle the expense account messages discussed in the text.

5. You already have rules to organize messages into folders and categories based on the customer (corporate, government, or small business). Create a decision tree to organize messages from customers. If a corporate or government customer asks about a specific order (they have an order number), mark it as important and forward the message to shipping. If a small business customer sends a formal request for information (RFI in the subject), forward the message to engineering and add a To Do reminder to yourself to check in two days. In all cases, if the customer is on a special distribution list (created within your Contacts list), generate a pop-up message so you can check immediately. If they are not on the list, send an automated reply that you received the message and are investigating.

6. Build and test the rules for the problem in Exercise 5. You will probably want to have other students in your class or group send you mail that you can use as examples of different types of customers.

FIGURE 10.7

Value chain. The value chain illustrates the essential operations in a business. Every firm has operations for purchasing, production, shipping, marketing, and customer service. These processes are supported by the organization of the firm, human resources management, technology development, and procurement services. Providing services desired by customers contributes to the profit margin of the firm.

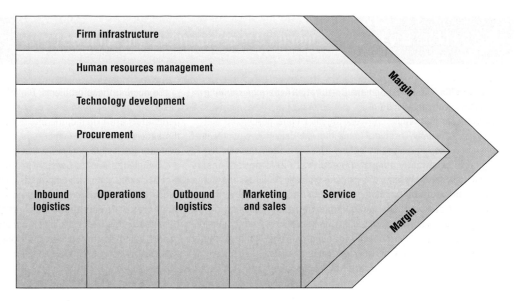

FIGURE 10.8

Process innovation. Production consists of the processes of supply logistics, manufacturing, and sales management. These processes are directly supported by design, engineering, and marketing. Research and customer service support all of the processes; top management organizes and controls the firm. Technology can provide innovations in all of these processes.

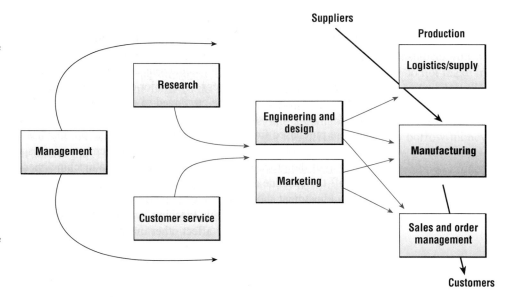

logistics and supply, marketing, sales and order management, service, and general management. Each of these processes has its own inputs, outputs, and objectives. Analyzing them in detail enables managers to spot problems and to search for innovative opportunities.

The following sections present general ideas for each of these processes that have generated interest and some success. Most of them use technology to improve the process or to help the processes work together better. Keep in mind that in any firm, there can be many ways of improving processes. Relying on information technology is not always the best answer.

Just coming up with a new corporate strategy is difficult, but it is not enough. As indicated by Figure 10.9, an effective strategic plan must also describe the changes in the process, identify the new data needs, and describe how the information system will be changed to support the new strategy. Figure 10.10 summarizes the capabilities of IT to support innovation.

Research

Research in firms varies enormously depending on the industry and the overall corporate strategy. At a minimum, most firms at least have a product development team that is constantly searching for new products or improvements in existing products. Some companies,

FIGURE 10.9
Developing strategies.
Market measures and firm
performance measures are
used to highlight
problems and
opportunities. Corporate
strategies are developed
from process
improvements and
innovations. Potential
strategies are evaluated
and prioritized. Processes
are reengineered and new
systems are designed and
implemented.

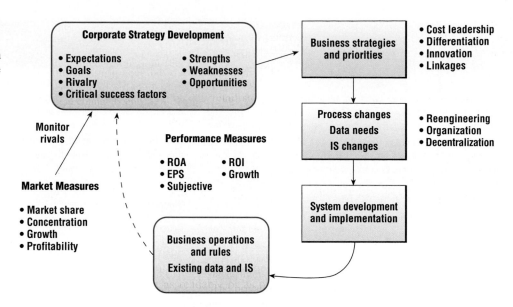

FIGURE 10.10
The search for innovation.
Information technology
provides many
opportunities for
improving the
fundamental business
processes. IT is used to
improve communication,
decrease costs, reduce
design times, monitor
customers and rivals, and
improve customer service.

Area	Information Technology Support
Research	Analysis and modeling, project management, workgroup support, databases, decision support
Engineering and design	CAD/CAM, testing, networks, workgroup support
Manufacturing	Mass customization, links from customers and suppliers, robotics, quality monitoring, expert systems for maintenance, production databases, business integration tools
Logistics and supply	Just-in-time linkages, forecasts, models, links for design, transaction processing
Marketing	Frequent buyer databases, target market and media analysis, survey design and analysis, multimedia promotion design, links between customers and design teams
Sales and orders	Portable computers for salesperson contact, expert systems for order customization and configuration, workgroup tools for customer support
Service	Phone support systems, location monitoring and scheduling of service people, expert system diagnostics, databases
Management	Enterprise information systems, links to service providers (accountants, consultants, etc.), e-mail, bulletin boards, decision support systems, personal productivity tools, workgroup support

like 3M, DuPont, AT&T, or Intel, spend considerable sums of money on basic research to create entirely new products. To these firms, strategic advantage comes from being the leader in the industry with a constant cycle of new products.

IT support for research takes the form of computer analysis and modeling, statistical analysis of data, project management and budgeting, and workgroup technologies that make it easy for researchers to collaborate and share information with each other and with managers throughout the company.

Engineering and Design

Engineering and design processes are responsible for converting theoretical research into new products. Engineers establish manufacturing procedures, design new equipment, and coordinate suppliers with production. In particular, the design process must optimize the production line to minimize costs and retain high quality.

Support for engineering and design takes the form of CAD/CAM systems that make it easy to create, modify, store, and share new designs. If these systems are coupled to integrated design databases, engineers can more easily reuse prior results. Tying into production databases enables the engineers to model and test various aspects of their designs. Engineers can also be supported with expert systems that help them analyze production aspects of their designs. As General Motors engineers design new cars, software helps them improve the layout to simplify production and to use existing components. Engineers are also being supported by workgroup technologies that make it easy to share designs and receive input from teams of workers throughout the company.

Manufacturing

There are four key features to production: costs, speed or timing, quality, and flexibility. Competing through lower costs and higher quality are time-honored means of gaining a competitive advantage. They might not be sufficient today. Increasingly, firms are turning to **mass customization** in an attempt to gain market share. Twenty or 30 years ago, the large firms in an industry were content to build huge plants, gain economies of scale, and aim at the mass market. This approach tended to leave niches open for competing firms. The problem with this strategy is that it allows rival firms to gain a toehold, which they might use to build market share and eventually compete directly against your primary market. Today's firms are trying to shift production fast enough so that they can cover virtually all of the niche markets.

Mass customization requires an IT system that links the sales system directly to the production line and through to supply. It also involves heavy use of robotics that are configurable directly from one computer. Other uses of IT include expert systems for maintenance and diagnostics. Japanese firms have long been proponents of preventive maintenance. If you wait until a machine breaks, it is too late. Expert systems can be used to schedule routine maintenance and spot problems before they cause problems. IT systems are also heavily used to monitor quality and suggest improvements.

Logistics and Supply

The implementation of just-in-time (JIT) inventory systems is largely credited to Japanese manufacturers. Today they are used by manufacturers worldwide. Manufacturers attempt to cut costs by holding minimal inventories. Instead, inventories are maintained by the suppliers, who deliver the products to the assembly line just as they are needed. The system can only work if the suppliers and factories are linked electronically—often there is only a one- or two-hour delay between ordering and delivery.

Suppliers are often involved in the design phase. Their knowledge is useful in identifying supply availability, costs, and substitutability of components. Sometimes, it is difficult to locate suppliers for equipment. Computer networks such as IndustryNet help firms connect with potential suppliers and identify equipment, parts, and prices.

Reality Bytes **Performance Measurement**

Most managers quickly learn the importance of strategy. With experience, they learn to formulate new ideas and focus on the search for competitive advantage. The ultimate challenge then lies in implementing and executing the strategy. An effective measure system is an important aspect of implementation that is often missing. The measurement system provides the link between the plan and the objectives. However, it is difficult for managers to absorb huge amounts of data from across the organization. Hence, a useful approach is to define critical measures for four areas: customer connectivity, internal process efficiency and effectiveness, individual and group innovation and learning, and financial data. Aspects of these four groups can be measured and presented on an information system in the form of gauges. By monitoring these areas, managers obtain an overview of how well the company is performing and how well it is moving to the new strategies.

Source: Adapted from Marla E. Hacker and Paul A. Brotherton, "Designing and Installing Effective Performance Measurement Systems," *IIE Solutions,* August 1998, pp. 18–23.

Marketing

A well-known application of IT to improve marketing is the use of frequent-buyer databases that identify major customers. More traditional point-of-sale transaction systems can be leveraged by identifying preferences and rapidly spotting patterns or trends. At the tactical level, expert systems are used to help analyze data and perform statistical trend analysis. Geographic information systems are being used by leading firms to identify patterns and possibilities for new sales. Information systems can also be used to link firms more closely to external marketing firms for research data, communication, and development of promotional materials.

Multimedia tools are being used by leading firms to develop initial ideas for advertising and promotional campaigns. Companies such as General Motors are also using video tools and computer dissemination of video to link customers and marketing departments closer to the design team.

Sales and Order Management

Sales and order management are often handled simply as an operations or transaction-processing area. However, in the last 10 years, several firms have used technology to gain a competitive advantage by improving the way they handle sales and orders. Frito-Lay's use of handheld computers is a classic example. The systems enable managers to more closely track their own sales, sales of competitors, and other external factors, because salespeople can enter data immediately. For certain industries, the concept can be extended further to installing workstations at the customer sites that tap into your central databases. Federal Express and Baxter Healthcare both used this technology to gain a leadership position.

Leading firms are also using expert systems to assist customers in choosing the products and options that best match their needs. These systems assist order-takers and improve sales by matching customer needs. Expert systems are similarly used to improve configuration and shipping.

Workgroup technologies, e-mail, and expert systems all combine to give more power to the frontline workers dealing directly with customers. Resolving problems and meeting customer needs faster improve customer satisfaction and cut costs.

Service

Service industries and service-based processes (like accounting, MIS, and law) have their own problems and opportunities. Technology is used to support services with on-site, portable computers. These systems enable workers to have complete access to information almost anywhere in the world. Leading companies are building specialized databases to support their service workers, such as the "answer line" databases that support General Electric and Whirlpool customer service representatives.

Systems are built that monitor locations of service personnel, enabling firms to identify the closest workers to problems and to fine-tune schedules throughout the day. Complex products are increasingly being sold with internal diagnostic systems that automatically notify service departments. Similarly, companies are cutting costs and reducing repair time by building expert systems to diagnose problems.

Management

One of the more dramatic IT support mechanisms for management is an executive information system. Giving top managers better access to data allows them to identify and correct problems faster. More sophisticated models can be built to examine alternatives—especially to analyze the potential reactions of rivals in a competitive situation.

Larger firms are building electronic links to their strategic partners, for instance, by providing electronic access to corporate data to accounting and legal firms. These links enable the external partners to keep a closer eye on the firm, speeding the identification of problems and assisting them in spotting broad patterns and opportunities.

Executives are also increasingly turning to electronic conferencing tools and workgroup software, even e-mail. Executives can cover more areas and deal with more people with these systems than they can by phone or through face-to-face contact. Some studies have shown that, in traditional conversations, managers spend as much as 50 percent of the time on personal chit-chat. Electronic systems (although they might be less personal) tend to be more efficient. On the other hand, some companies have been restricting employee access to electronic networks (especially the Internet) because they waste too much time on personal communications.

Another approach taken by management is the move toward standardization: the effort to make all jobs similar, routine, and interchangeable. By reducing jobs to their most basic level, they become easier to control and easier to support or replace with information technology. Franchises make good use of this concept. At the same time, management jobs in some companies are being reformulated as teams of knowledge workers. In the past, managers worked on fixed tasks within the corporate hierarchy. Today, you are more likely to be hired for your specific skills and knowledge. As the needs of the company change, you will work with different teams at solving problems and creating new products and services. Personal computers and client-server technologies are often used to support these management teams. Instead of relying on one central computing facility, each team has its own set of resources, which are shared over networks throughout the company.

Costs and Dangers of Strategies

Strategic uses of information systems can be seductive. There are many interesting cases in which companies have created innovative information systems. Inventing strategic alternatives requires a considerable amount of creativity. It is easy to get caught up in the excitement of designing new approaches and to forget about the risks. Evaluation of any project requires weighing the risks against the potential gains. Although it is often difficult to measure the potential gains and risks, it is important to consider all consequences. By their nature, strategic changes can alter the entire course of the firm. Figure 10.11 summarizes the skills, organizational effects, and risks involved with several strategies.

Robert Morison and Kirtland Mead ("A Hard Look at Strategic Systems") pointed out that it is easy to misinterpret the various classic cases regarding strategic use of technology. For example, in many cases, the true strategy does not lie in the computer system; instead, the gains came from changing the way the business operates. For instance, the gains experienced by American Hospital Supply (Baxter Healthcare) came about because they improved the way their customers (hospitals) handled supplies and inventory. The computer system facilitated this change but was not necessarily responsible for it. In other words, rather than search for a *killer* strategic computer system, it is wiser to identify ways to improve the overall business.

FIGURE 10.11

Implementing strategy can be difficult, costly, and time consuming. Firms generally choose one primary strategy and then build the resources and shape the organization to best support that strategy.

Strategy	Skills and Resources Required	Organizational Requirements	Risks
Differentiation	• Strong marketing • Product engineering • Basic research skills • Distribution channel acceptance and cooperation	• Internal coordination, R&D, production, and marketing • Incentives for innovation • Resources to attract creative and skilled labor	• Competitors imitate • Customers do not accept differences • Cost is too high
Cost leadership	• Continued capital investment • Process engineering • Continuous quality improvement • Tight supervision of labor and costs • Products designed for low-cost production • Low-cost distribution	• Tight cost control • Frequent, detailed control reports • Highly structured organization • Incentives based on quantitative measures	• Competitors imitate • Technology changes • Lose production or distribution advantage
Customer-supplier links	• Influence with partners • Communication channels • Standards or agreements	• Flexibility to respond to customers • Service culture • Ability to adapt to emergencies	• Security threats • Changing standards • Competitors copy with more links

High Capital Costs

One of the important considerations in strategic analysis is the cost. Strategic changes often involve implementing new technology before any of your competitors. Yet new technology tends to carry high costs. Manufacturers of technology may not have reached economies of scale, and they might have monopoly power over prices through patent rights. Additionally, the IS teams will have less experience with the technology, so it will take longer to implement and may result in missteps and require additional testing. For instance, Morison and Mead report, "It took six years and $350 million before American Airlines' Sabre travel agency reservation system started paying off." As Figure 10.12 implies, these costs might take away money from other projects (Morison and Mead, 1989).

It can be difficult to estimate the cost of major projects, especially when they involve new technologies. There are many examples of MIS projects going over budget and beyond deadlines. Additionally, strategic projects often require major capital outlays up front, but increased revenues do not appear until much later.

A big question with new technology is trying to decide when it should be implemented. There is an inherent conflict. If you offer an innovative service from the technology before your competitors, you can gain a competitive advantage. However, if you wait, the costs will be lower. In making this decision, you will also have to guess what action your competitors will take.

When the Competition Follows

Another difficulty with strategic systems is that much of the advantage comes from creating a service that is not offered by your rivals. Once you introduce the service, your rivals will watch the customer response closely. If the customers begin to switch to your firm, your rivals will undoubtedly create a system to offer the same services. At that point, you lose most of the competitive advantage. Even worse, you might end up with an escalating "war" of technology. Although the competition is good for the customer, the increased expenditures can cause problems for the company if the ideas do not work as well as you expected.

FIGURE 10.12

Dangers of strategy. When developing and choosing strategies, you must always remember that innovations can be risky and often carry high capital costs. Although it may be exciting to spend millions of dollars on technology, it can destroy the firm if you do not have enough resources to support research and operations.

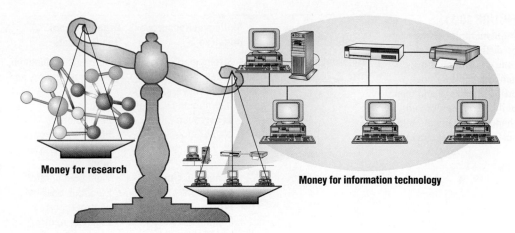

Money for research

Money for information technology

The gains to technology occur from when you first implement the strategy to the point that your rivals follow. For example, almost all of the major overnight delivery services now provide the ability to track shipments. If the system is easy to create, you may not gain much. However, it is likely that customers who switched to your firm will stay, so you can gain a larger share of the market.

On the other hand, if your strategic ideas do not pay off, your rivals will gain, because you will likely lose most of the money invested in the project. Some firms use this tactic to great advantage. They allow smaller firms to take the risk and experiment with new technologies. If the project succeeds, the large firm steps in with more money and more clout and creates its own, improved version. About the only risk it takes is that the smaller firm might become successful enough to grab a serious share of the market.

Changing Industry

An intriguing problem that can arise is that even if your strategic project succeeds, the company might lose because your project has changed the industry. Consider an insurance company that sells software to companies to allow them to track insurance deductions and payments to workers. The insurance company decides that it can add a program to compute payroll, so the companies could drop their existing payroll software. These features appear to give the company an edge over its rivals in the insurance industry. The problem is that there are many more companies that create payroll software, and it is very simple for these companies to add insurance capabilities to their existing software. The actions of the insurance company encourage the payroll software firms to move into the insurance market. Illustrated in Figure 10.13, the insurance company suddenly has hundreds of new competitors and could lose customers.

Sharing Data

One common technique in strategic systems is to share your data with customers and suppliers. Two questions arise from this situation. First, do you really want suppliers and customers to have access to the data? Second, can you control their access to protect other data? Security and control issues are examined in detail in Chapter 14. The main point to think about here is what might happen as your customers gain access to your data. Consider the situation of a supplier to General Motors. To save costs and improve communications, GM wants you to connect your computer to the GM factory computers. GM intends to use the links to place orders, monitor quality data, and track shipments. Are you willing to give GM access to your computer? Can you control the information that the large corporation is allowed to see? Maybe when checking on their orders, GM will also be able to determine how much you are producing for other companies. Or maybe GM will gain access to your supplier lists and raw material prices. Even if the GM managers are ethical and do not reveal this data to anyone else, you still might worry. What happens when you have to

FIGURE 10.13

Changing industry and government intervention. A complication with strategy is that it might alter the industry. A firm in Industry 1 might use IT to attract customers from a different industry. Because of this expansion, the firm gains new competitors (from Industry 2). While competition is often beneficial, you must thoroughly analyze the effect of the new competition before embarking on changing the industry. In a related manner, sometimes changes in government regulations alter relationships between industries, as in the telephone and cable TV markets.

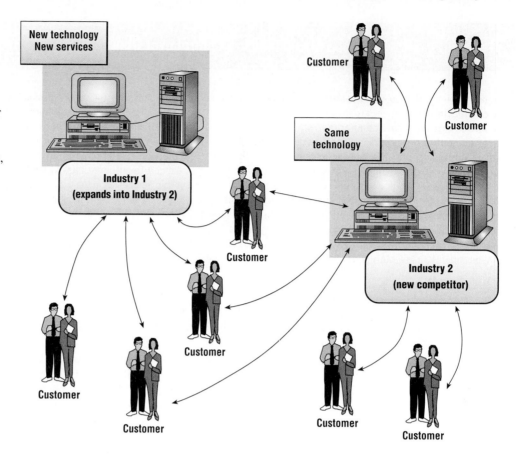

FIGURE 10.14

Security complications. Improving communication and sharing data are common themes in using technology for competitive advantage. This need to share data with "outsiders" makes it more difficult to protect your internal data. Some data you will want to share; other data must be kept secret. Security systems can provide some protections, but the more outsiders who are involved, the more difficult it is to provide adequate security.

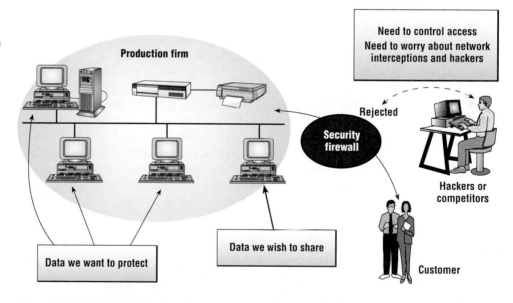

negotiate prices with GM the next time? If the corporation has access to your data, you might be concerned that it could influence the negotiations. Figure 10.14 illustrates the need for security systems that will enable you to control the access to your data.

Government Intervention

You have to be careful when considering strategic maneuvers. Many potential strategies violate **antitrust laws**. For example, many barriers to entry are illegal, as is price discrimination. In fact, attempts to monopolize a market are forbidden by the Sherman Antitrust Act. Price

Reality Bytes   Music Industry Control over Distribution

In late 2001, the U.S. Justice Department expanded its antitrust investigation of the music business. The department subpoenaed several companies on the grounds of "anticompetitive licensing of intellectual property rights associated with provision of music over the Internet." The heart of the issue is identifying why the music firms have been dragging their feet in providing online music—a format that is clearly being demanded by customers, but is not yet available. The basic complaint is that the major record labels colluded with each other in delaying services and in setting prices. The major companies have formed two joint ventures to provide online music. Judge Marilyn Hall Patel in the Napster case

questioned how they could possibly avoid collusion, noting the decision to use the joint venture "looks bad, sounds bad, and smells bad." Other online music firms have not been able to get licenses from the music labels to offer online services, while the labels quickly granted full rights to their joint ventures. The Justice Department has an additional complaint against the music companies in the way they set up an industrywide license rate for Internet radio companies.

Source: Adapted from Anna Wilde Mathews and John R. Wilke, "Probe of Online Music Business Expands as U.S. Reviews Licensing, Copyright Use," *The Wall Street Journal,* October 15, 2001.

fixing and other forms of collusion are also outlawed. Information system agreements between competitors could be scrutinized by the Justice Department or the Federal Trade Commission.

If government agents choose strict interpretations of the laws, it could complicate many information system issues. For instance, firms might be discouraged from forming consortiums that define standards. Agreements to share disaster backup facilities might be outlawed. Computer links to customers might be seen as limiting competition. So far, the U.S. agencies have allowed all of these activities to proceed without interference. However, there is always the chance that other nations or different political administrations will view the issues differently.

In the 1980s, the government was relatively lenient about antitrust issues, including those regarding information systems. However, one interesting case arose with the airline reservation systems. For many years, American Airlines and United Airlines had the leading reservation systems. Other airlines could list flights on the systems, but they had to pay money for each ticket sold through the system. A conflict eventually arose because the airlines that created the system programmed it to list their flights first. Flights from other airlines were often listed on separate screens, so travel agents and customers were encouraged to choose flights from the airline that built the system. Although this mechanism did not directly violate antitrust laws, Congress decided to pass a new law, making the practice illegal. Lawmakers decided that as long as the other airlines had to pay for access to the system, everyone should have an equal chance at being listed first. The point is that even though the initial action was not illegal, Congress has the ability to pass new laws and remove the advantages, so you cannot assume that the benefits will last.

Operations, Tactics, Strategy

Strategic plans involving information technology are not created from thin air. The systems are based on improved or expanded use of operations- and tactical-level systems. Consider the airline reservations systems, which began life as transaction-processing systems, reducing costs and making it easier for people to get the flights they want. Similarly, banking systems like ATMs and debit cards were targeted at improving transactions. Yet, these systems all had a strategic component: being the first organization to implement these systems led to better customer service and increased market share.

Tactical-level systems can also provide strategic advantages. Making better decisions faster creates improved products, more loyal customers, and lower costs. Building decision support systems, enterprise information systems, expert systems, and AI techniques helps to reduce the bureaucracy of middle management. Two important strategic consequences arise:

Reality Bytes   The New Economy?

In the late 1990s, particularly with the enormous growth and excitement generated by the Internet, many people were arguing that a new economy was being shaped. Some of their arguments were used to "explain" the sky-high prices being paid for Internet IPO stocks. Other people used the analysis to claim that business strategy needed to change. While there might have been some truth to the statements, it was dangerous to base your entire company on them—as some managers and entrepreneurs who followed the hype learned. The problem is that there are no easy answers to business success. The basic myths/statements were:

1. Grow or die.

2. You must be virtual.

3. Go global.

4. Capital is easy.

5. Everybody is an entrepreneur.

6. Technology makes life easier.

7. You must be on the Web in a big way.

The *Inc.* article presents many examples of managers who attempted to follow these ideas and encountered problems. For example, Jonathan Katz is CEO of Cinnabar, a $17 million company that creates scenery and special effects for movies, commercials, and theme parks. The company was enthusiastic about technology. Managers and employees quickly realized the value of cell phones and e-mail. Whenever a problem cropped up, employees used the electronic communication to contact clients and production studios to straighten it out. The problem is that at the start of 1997, Cinnabar's commercial and film business started to drop. After a great deal of thought, Katz realized that "my people had become complacent and too reliant on the conveniences of electronic communication like faxes, e-mail, and telephones. The real heart of our business, which came out of direct contact with our clients, was not happening." He told the employees to put away the cell phones and e-mail, and pay personal visits with directors, producers, and art directors. In the last quarter of 1998, Cinnabar's commercial business increased by 50 percent.

Source: Adapted from "Some of the Smartest CEOs Around Bought into the Myths of the New Economy," *Inc.,* February 1999.

(1) more control and authority are pushed down to customer service agents, enabling them to solve problems faster and meet the needs of the customer; and (2) top executives gain more information and control over the business—making it easier to identify problems, enact new strategies, and respond faster to changes in the business environment.

Overall, there are two important lessons to be learned regarding strategic uses of technology: (1) computer systems can provide value beyond simple cost cutting; and (2) strategic gains are often fleeting, requiring continual upgrades and investment in new technology. Because new technology is expensive and innovations do not always succeed, it can be risky being on the leading edge. Each firm needs to decide on *when* it should adopt new technology. Being first carries not only high costs and more risk but the opportunity for greater rewards, as well as a certain image. Being a technology follower has the advantage of reducing costs. Each industry contains both types of firms.

The Role of Economics

The main lesson from the failures of the early dot-com firms in 2000 and 2001 is that no matter what anyone tries to tell you, to succeed in business, you must make a profit on operations. The second lesson is that it takes time to acquire loyal customers—longer if you want to change the world. Many of the early e-commerce managers felt that to become the dominant player, they had to be the first and biggest firm. So their primary strategy was to sell products below cost and spend huge amounts of money on national advertising. The advertising was successful at attracting investors, whose cash kept the firms alive for a year or so. But when the sales failed to generate profits, there was no way to keep the companies running.

The advertising strategy also created an interesting domino effect in the early industry. By pushing the importance of name recognition (and a good domain name), many of the early firms were able to survive by attracting advertising money from other firms. For example, Excite was a leading Web-portal firm. With its easy name and relatively popular search engine, many people used the site on a regular basis. Based on the number of people visiting the site (known as eyeballs), Excite was able to sell advertising space on its pages to other Web firms. Over 80 percent of Excite's revenue came from advertising. As the other firms in the industry fell apart, they stopped their advertising spending, and Excite's revenue plummeted. Many other firms faced the same problem, and the chain reaction caused hundreds of firms to fail.

Despite the early setbacks, there is still uncertainty about what will become a successful Web strategy. Will consumers really buy enough products over the Internet to make e-commerce profitable? Should firms concentrate on publishing strategies—where they provide useful content for free or low cost, making profits by selling advertising space to other (preferably non-e-commerce) firms? Television stations and magazines survive under this model—is there room for Internet sites?

The strategic options in e-business are increasing as new tools are created, wireless capabilities improve, and people begin to adopt connectivity as a way of life. At this point, there is no single answer, which makes it even more important that you carefully define your goals, analyze the profits, evaluate your competition, and build a creative business plan.

Summary

Information systems can provide benefits beyond traditional cost saving. Competitive advantages can be gained by creating barriers to entry and gaining control over distribution channels. Using information systems to build ties to suppliers and customers can provide lower costs and better quality products. Computer systems also provide incentives for customers to remain with your company if they incur costs of learning new systems and transferring data when switching to a competitor. Information systems can also be used to differentiate your products from the others in the marketplace. Similarly, innovative services offered with the help of technology can entice customers and expand your market.

You can search for competitive advantages by examining Porter's external forces of rivals, customers, suppliers, substitute products, and new entrants. You can also search for strategies in research, engineering, and design. In manufacturing, you can look for ways to decrease costs and improve logistics. In marketing, potential gains can be found in better understanding of customer wants, as well as sales and order management. Services can be supported through better information flows and workgroup products. Management can be helped with better data and better decision tools.

Strategic systems face many risks. They tend to be expensive and difficult to create. Any gains created may disappear when competitors pick up the technology and imitate your offerings. Additionally, making strategic changes to your firm might alter the industry, which might adversely affect your firm. And if these problems are not enough to discourage you, remember that attempts to monopolize a market are illegal, so you have to make sure that your plans do not violate governmental regulations.

A Manager's View

With increased competition, every manager is being asked to identify ways to improve the company and find an advantage over the rivals. Gaining a competitive edge is not easy. Examining the entire value chain is a useful place to start. Information systems can provide data and evaluate models to help you identify strategic applications. Information systems can also provide direct advantages by creating a barrier to entry, gaining control over distribution, cutting costs, improving quality, and improving ties between suppliers and customers. Choosing an effective strategy is a critical task in e-business. Because of the risks, strategy requires flexibility and a willingness to experiment and change directions.

Key Words

Website References

Management Consulting

Accenture	**www.accenture.com**
Andersen	**www.andersen.com**
Bain & Company	**www.bain.com**
Boston Consulting Group	**www.bcg.com**
Booz Allen & Hamilton	**www.bah.com**
McKinsey & Company	**www.mckinsey.com**

Additional Reading

Applegate, Lynda M. and F. Warren McFarlan. *Creating Business Advantage in the Information Age.* New York: McGraw-Hill/Irwin, 2002. [Business strategy in information technology from a Harvard perspective.]

Melymuka, Kathleen. "State Street Bank's Change in Direction Required a New IT Approach." *Computerworld,* February 15, 1999. [Changing strategy with information technology.]

Porter, Michael. *Competitive Advantage: Creating and Sustaining Superior Performance.* New York: Free Press, 1985. [Early discussion of strategy and competitive advantage.]

Morison, Robert E. and Kirtland C. Mead, "A Hard Look at Strategic Systems," *Indications,* January 1989. [Myths and issues in IT strategy]

Porter, Michael E. "Strategy and the Internet." *Harvard Business Review* 79, Issue 3, March 2001.

Strassmann, Paul A. *The Squandered Computer: Evaluating the Business Alignment of Information Technologies.* New Canaan, CT: Information Economics Press, 1997. [A detailed, but controversial discussion of the value of information technology, with some excellent cases.]

Review Questions

1. Briefly describe four techniques that can be used to gain competitive advantage.
2. How is strategic analysis related to the environment aspect of the systems approach?
3. What are external agents?
4. What are the costs and dangers of strategic implementations?
5. For a large manufacturing firm, who are the customers? How many different types of customers can there be?
6. Why are barriers to entry important to gain a competitive advantage?
7. How does control over distribution channels give a firm a competitive advantage?
8. How can information systems be used to gain control over distribution channels?
9. How might EDI limit firms from gaining control over the distribution channels?
10. What are switching costs, and how can they give a company a competitive advantage?
11. How can information systems be used to enhance product differentiation and create new products?
12. What role is played by information systems in improving quality management?
13. What is the value chain and how is it used to search for competitive advantage?

Exercises

1. Consider a small service firm such as a physician, dentist, accountant, or lawyer. Is it possible for such an office to use computers to gain a competitive advantage? To start, identify the customers, suppliers, and rivals. Do you think the "natural" switching costs are high or low; that is, how often do customers switch to competitors? Which of the major techniques do you think would be the most successful (barriers to entry, switching costs, quality control, lower prices, ties to customers or suppliers, etc.)?

2. How long can firms maintain an advantage using an information system? Research one of the classic cases and find out how long it took for the competitors to implement a similar information system (for example, Merrill Lynch and its Cash-Management Account, American Airlines and the Sabre System, Levi-Strauss and its Levi-Link ordering system, or Federal Express and its tracking system). Find out when the system was implemented, identify the competitors, and find out when they implemented similar systems. Did the original company continue to update its strategy? Collect data on sales and profits for the firms to see whether there were major changes.

3. Choose a country other than the United States, Canada, Japan, or a Western European nation. (In particular, select a developing nation perhaps in South America, Africa, Eastern Europe, or Southeast Asia.) Research the communication and information system facilities available to firms in that country. Do you think firms in the United States have a competitive advantage over those firms? If so, what could the firms (or nations) do to overcome that advantage? How will the countries compare five years from now?

4. Read through the industry cases for each chapter in the book. Identify the firms that have chosen to be technology leaders and those that are followers. What other differences can you find between the firms (profits, sales, employees)?

5. Pick an industry. Find two firms in the industry—one a technology leader, the other a follower. Get the financial information on those firms for the last five years. Find analyst summaries of their operations. Compare the two firms. Are there differences in finances, operating methods, or customers?

6. Find information on two e-commerce firms in the same industry: one failing and one still operating. What differences are there between the firms? What strategies did the firms follow?

7. If you are managing one of many small suppliers building products for an industry dominated by a few large firms (for example, you run an auto parts supply company), what strategies do you have available? In particular, what can you do to protect yourself in a downturn that affects the parent industry?

8. In the case of digital products (for instance, books, music, and videos), why are the major publishers choosing a strategy to remain with physical-form items? Could a firm succeed with a digital strategy?

Rolling Thunder Database

9. Identify the competition in the industry. Who are existing rivals? Who are potential rivals? Be sure to define the industry carefully. Consider using NAICS codes.

10. Perform a value chain analysis of the company. Could they improve profits by expanding vertically or horizontally? Are there additional products we should consider offering?

11. What data do we collect? Can it be used to achieve greater value? Would other firms be interested in our data? Are there possibilities for alliances with other companies?

12. We have the opportunity to purchase a chain of retail bicycle stores. Evaluate the strategic aspects of this proposed acquisition. What will be the effect on the information systems? Can the existing information system be used to improve the operations of the retail stores? What additions and improvements would be needed?

13. Is there any way to increase ties to the customers using technology to gain a competitive advantage?

14. Examine the value chain in the bicycle industry. How many levels are there and which levels are the most profitable?

Travel Industry

The travel and tourism industry has been devastated by the terrorist attacks of September 11, 2001, and the fear that these attacks instilled. The winter of 2001–2002 saw drastic declines in travel and the related industries of hotels and motels, conventions, and restaurants.

The World Tourism Council projected that the terrorist attacks on the United States would result in a downward forecast of U.S. economic growth by 1/2 percent. The impact of the attacks on the confidence in the economy may have increased the risk of a recession to 35 percent compared to 20 percent before the attacks. [Oxford 2001]

The travel and tourism industry continues to face rapid change. This is due both to social factors that increase the demand for travel and to technological advances that make travel possible and less expensive. The swelling of the middle class in developing countries, years of prosperity in the United States, and lower prices had dramatically increased the ease and extent of travel domestically and worldwide.

While it is difficult to determine the economic impact of tourism, the World Travel and Tourism Council, an industry lobby group, placed it at $3.6 trillion in 1996. This was about 10 percent of the world's gross product. Falls in tourism arrivals between September 11 and November 20 were 10 percent in Singapore and 21 percent in Chinese Taipei.

Especially hot growth segments include package tours and cruises. Average tourist spending is expected to grow by 8 percent annually for the next five years, according to *The Economist.* This has led to demands from groups such as the World Travel and Tourism Council and local and national governments to spend money on improving infrastructures, which will support tourism. Some countries, such as Canada, have responded by increasing their spending on tourism dramatically.

With this fast growth, the hotel business has matured. Hotels, once mostly independent businesses, are quickly joining chains. They are, in effect, being branded. Information technology such as the Internet and electronic ticketing is also changing tourism by changing the way tourism is being sold. Nothing has made the globalization of travel and tourism grow faster than cheap airline tickets, however. It was less than 30 years ago that Pan Am flew the first 747 from New York to London.

Even with all these factors and trends, there are great risks. Hotels and airplanes are still big investments that can prove to be expensive failures. Also, the tourism part of travel (as opposed to business travel, a small but very profitable segment of the travel and hospitality industry) is basically a luxury. This means that a recession, especially if it affects a large area as does the one that began in Asia in 1998, can be devastating to the travel industry.

Surprisingly, the recession in the industrialized countries in the early 1990s only slowed down the growth of tourism, but did not stop it. Tourism is also highly sensitive to external shocks. Carribean islands are a paradise one day, but a hurricane can turn away tourists very quickly. Another example is the attacks suffered by European tourists in Miami in 1992. This hindered European visitors to South Florida for a few years.

One way to combat external dangers and to address the issue of depleting or destroying natural attractions is to create the tour environment from scratch. Theme parks are such places. These destinations are custom-built to entertain and delight visitors. As technology advances and popular destinations become more and more crowded, these artificial worlds may grow in their market share.

Stock/Investment Outlook

The outlook for companies in the travel and tourism industry is good. Certain companies positioned to take advantage of current trends in the travel and tourism industry will be star performers.

As far as airlines are concerned, those that look to be the best investment are those forming code-sharing alliances, which allow them to book travel on their partner's routes. This allows airlines to cover more territories by banding together. Thus, American Airlines' partnership with British Airways and other airlines seems to bode well for them; just like United Airlines' partnership with a handful of international airlines seems like a smart move.

Mergers and acquisitions in the hotel industry are frequent. Branding helps hotels smooth out demand. The recent spate of hotel mergers (especially outside the United States, where hotels are less likely to be part of a chain) is mostly a result of the overbuilding of hotels during the 1980s and technological improvements making economies of scale more significant.

Cruise-ship companies are also good investments, in light of their increasing popularity. Carnival Cruise Lines and Royal Caribbean, the two largest cruise companies, are both expanding and building larger ships to accommodate and take advantage of this boom in cruising.

Financial Analysis

The September 11 crisis forced airlines to rely even more heavily on their information systems. Right after the attacks, Southwest Airlines executives spent the weekend analyzing data in the airline's scheduling and logistics systems to determine where pilots, crew, and aircraft had ended up after the mandatory grounding. Then they repositioned the crews and planes as new flight trends emerged. "We had to make quick decisions, and we were able to do that," says Anne Murray, Southwest's senior director of interactive marketing. "It's a good feeling to know that you can move quickly when you have to." [Maselli 2001]

Throughout the crisis, airlines had to get the most value possible out of their IT systems—and some might say it is about time. "We're living on our systems and our people right now," said Larry Kellner, president of Continental Airlines Inc., which spends about $180 million a year on IT. [Maselli 2001] As consumers postponed flights and businesses restricted travel, airlines' IT staffs were enhancing scheduling and revenue-management systems to help their companies control costs and maximize revenue. Airlines also are accelerating planned IT projects, such as e-marketing, website, and customer service initiatives, to keep profitable customers happy and recruit new ones.

The outlook still remains uncertain for a troubled industry struggling to recover from the fallout from September's terrorist attacks. The nine largest airlines in the United States collectively reported net losses of $2.43 billion for the third quarter and operating losses of $3.65 billion. Before September 1, industry analysts were forecasting that U.S. airlines would have about $2 billion in losses this year; now the prediction for losses for the fourth quarter alone will be $3 billion to $4 billion.

Airplane manufacturing is also being impacted. Boeing Co. planned to deliver as many as 520 new aircraft next year; that number has dropped to the low 400s. Southwest Airlines said it filled only 63.7 percent of its seats in October, compared with 70 percent in October 2000. Northwest Airlines' load factor fell to 66.3 percent from 75.2 percent, and United Airlines' was down 7.7 percent to 63.4 percent. The 2000 figures are based on more flights.

United Airlines reported the worst results in its history in November 2001, with $542 million in net losses—after taking in half of the government's $5 billion bailout for the third quarter. Air Canada announced it may sell its 121 aircraft regional division to help erase some of its $6.3 billion debt. And America West was losing about $2 million a day.

As airlines were forced to reevaluate and change flights, logistics and scheduling systems were called upon to help them make decisions. Previously, Alaska Airlines had developed four flight schedules a year. In the days after September 11, it was forced to change its flight schedule two to three times a day. The airline, which spends less than $40 million annually on information technology, evaluated the frequency of flights and departure times at every airport. "It's something that usually took days, and we had to do it [more quickly], then balance all of that with costs," according to Robert Reeder, CIO. [Maselli 2001]

The airline also had to consider new security concerns when optimizing routes. Since passengers must now be at the airport at least two hours before a flight and a three-hour car trip can cover the same distance as a 45-minute flight, the willingness of passengers to fly might change. "We had a lot of smart people trying to sort out the best alternatives measured against a whole array of constraints." [Maselli 2001] Since more people needed access to the data to analyze it, Reeder developed Web interfaces to give the executives access to the company's Flight Times database. This pulled data from Alaska Airlines' Sabre reservations system, proprietary scheduling, and tactical operations applications. Meanwhile, scheduling personnel were given access to the company's Web-hosted crew-scheduling software.

Continental Airlines already had Web interfaces in place that enabled operations personnel and the executive team to see flight schedules, staffing, pilot qualifications, and more. After September 11, the airline relied on three applications originally developed to deal with the closing of a single airport. Operations Solver helps operations personnel reschedule flights when airports close; Manpower Solver helps pilots reschedule flights; and Crew Solver handles the flight crews.

Following the attacks, CIO and Senior Vice President Janet Wejman directed programmers to modify the applications to handle all airports simultaneously. This enabled schedulers to tell Operations Solver which aircraft are needed at what airports and when, enabling the application to map out a schedule. Manpower and Crew Solver match personnel to the new schedules. According to Wejman, "We saved several million dollars by being able to reschedule the airline so quickly after September 11." [Maselli 2001]

As schedules change, airlines are increasingly relying on revenue-management systems to analyze timetables, capacity, and passenger demand to determine ticket prices that maximize revenue. In boom times, if certain flights lost money, profitable flights could make up the difference. Now, every dollar on every flight must count. Revenue- and yield-management software have become increasingly important for the airline industry. For many airlines, they are the lifeline that determines whether the airlines stay in business. Before September 11, air traffic was predictable, and airlines typically stored three years' worth of data to project future business. The attacks have made it all but impossible to estimate how many ticketed passengers will show up. "Yield management basically went out the window," Reeder said. [Maselli 2001] In the weeks after the attacks, revenue-management analysts adjusted the predictive models on the basis that customers who bought tickets after September 11 would fly; those who purchased tickets before September 11 would be less likely. That let airlines sell more tickets without the fear of overbooking, Teradata's Pearce says.

At Frontier Airlines Inc., the terrorist attacks hurt demand for flights in and out of Boston, New York, and Washington worse than those in the western United States. Frontier adjusted its system in the East to use different models to predict demand and no-shows for each flight. "This isn't an exact science," said David Minnelli, director of pricing and revenue management for the Denver-based airline. [Maselli 2001] Like 35 other airlines, Alaska Airlines uses Sabre's AirMax revenue-management system, which combines data on fares that all airlines offer with a particular flight schedule to calculate ticket prices. After September 11, Sabre reprogrammed the system to reflect fluctuating demand and the fact that business travel has rebounded faster than leisure travel.

Growth Potential

Making an adjustment for the terrorist attacks, the next few years were supposed to be good ones for the travel and tourism industry. Depending on the market segment, the potential for growth ranges from moderate to high. The growth in the cruise ship segment looks to be very good, assuming companies can keep in mind why many people choose cruises: they are relatively inexpensive, all inclusive, (usually everything except liquor and gambling is included), and they provide a relaxing atmosphere with entertainment. Cruise ship operations are also more predictable than hotel operations, with generally higher occupancy rates, a captive audience, and more predictable costs. This bodes well for both the major cruise lines and smaller cruise lines that offer good alternatives.

The growth in the airline industry looks moderate. While airline travel is increasing and is expected to continue increasing, the market is saturated and mature in some areas (such as flying within the United States). Increased security regulations, newly formed alliances, deregulation abroad, and more foreign governments freeing up their airspace mean changes, challenges, and opportunities. Airlines that form alliances with international airlines seem to be the ones with the most to gain. The American-British Airways alliance is an example.

Hotels are also projected to be on a growth curve. Those hotels that are not part of major chains will need to identify special niches to do well in an era of branding, buyouts, mergers, and consolidation. There are, however, many aspects an independent hotel or small hotel chain can offer that would attract travelers, particularly if they market toward specific market segments.

Competitive Structure

For different reasons, most of the tourism and travel industry used to be fragmented. The airline industry was fragmented due to government regulations, the difficulty of growing in a less advanced technological age, and less powerful planes. The hotel industry was fragmented due to difficulties operating geographically dispersed properties in an efficient and consistent way. The cruise industry was first injured by the long-haul passenger jet, which all but replaced the cruises to Europe a few decades ago. However, once shorter-term and more affordable cruises were offered to the Caribbean from South Florida, the industry revived.

Currently, as the entire industry grows and matures, the competitive structure is moving toward an imperfect oligopoly. There will be a few major players in each segment of the travel and tourism industry, while there will be large numbers of small players fighting for the rest of the pie. The major players will offer competitive prices for their services, while the smaller players will offer a slightly different angle. This process can be slower in segments where government intervention is a significant factor, such as international flights.

Role of Research and Development

Research and development is an important component of this industry. R&D affects some segments more than others. Research and development has led to the realization by airlines, for example, that business travelers are less price-sensitive than leisure travelers. Hence, airlines have devised elaborate pricing strategies for available seats. R&D has led to technological advances like the jet airplane, hotel and airline reservation systems, jumbo cruise ships, and multiple kinds of rides in theme parks.

Research and development of a concept has allowed Las Vegas to develop from a place where only gamblers went, to a vacation mecca for the whole family. Developers in Las Vegas realized that the popularity of theme parks such as Disney World was not something that appealed only to children. By making each hotel almost its own theme park for adults, and placing all the hotels near each other, Las Vegas has been able to attract thousands of visitors to its city.

Airlines have used research to develop things such as frequent flyer programs to create loyalty, low weekend getaway fares to sell tickets on poorly sold routes, Saturday night requirements to differentiate passengers, and more fuel-efficient, longer-lasting, bigger, and safer planes.

By branding themselves, hotels can give a customer a familiar setting and a perception of quality, no matter where in the world the traveler is. Even the same hotel chain sometimes has different offerings, or subbrands. Each one is targeted and positioned to appeal to a different type of traveler; for example, a person that is looking only for the bare necessities and is very price sensitive, to the extended-stay business traveler that may be on a multimonth assignment outside his or her hometown. Another hotel innovation is the time-share business, which has slowly gained ground in acceptance.

Technological Investment and Analysis

Without technological advancement, the travel and tourism industry would still be mostly for the rich. The driving force behind industry growth has been the refinement of the jet airplane. Before the jet airplane, most vacations were either close to home or they required one of two things most people did not have or were not willing to part with: a lot of money or a lot of time. The jet airplane allowed prices to come down for flying, making faraway destinations more affordable for middle-class consumers. The newest revolution in technology with regard to tourism is the Internet.

Information technology is changing the way tourism is being sold. Travel agents find cheap tickets and package tours on their computer screens through one of the two major airline and tour reservation systems: Sabre or Galileo. Sabre is currently trying to expand beyond their core users of travel agents and have set up their own website for retail customers: http://www.travelocity.com. Galileo, meanwhile, has taken a different approach, concentrating on serving their main set of users: the travel agents that book most of the travel in this country. Now, with the Internet, customers can make their own searches and purchases directly through the computer, not only through Travelocity, but with a myriad of online travel agents as well. Sophisticated computer reservation systems help hotels track their customers' spending and preferences over time, giving the company a better idea of the lifetime value of the customer to that hotel chain.

The airlines use a yield-management formula to differentiate ticket prices for the same flight, thereby yielding what they hope will be the greatest amount of revenue per each flight. Without computers, calculating this in an efficient manner on a nationwide level would be impossible.

Theme parks are another development that would be impossible without the application of technology. These wonderlands of artificial reality are created solely for entertainment and leisure. Customers come back more than once, because the attractions change. Technology is used to find more and different ways to entertain and delight crowds. Technological developments will be one of the main avenues for developing new sources of revenues and profits.

Recommendation for the Future

Companies in the travel and tourism industry must look at current trends while keeping one eye on the future to remain competitive. When the industry was highly fragmented, complete information was harder to come by for travelers, sheltering many businesses from competition. Those days are gone. The technology is available now to take advantage of location, services, convenience, and value. An unaffiliated business with no apparent advantage is best served by affiliating themselves with a chain. For example, a nondescript hotel in North Miami Beach, in an area where hotel rooms are plentiful and many new ones are being built, will have difficulty thriving in the future. Even if the hotel does not become part of a chain, the least it might do would be to develop a Web page, list itself in as many search engines and Web directories as possible, and advertise in nontraditional (as well as traditional) channels where there is less competition.

Case: The Sabre Group

There is an underground complex of reinforced concrete surrounded by cement walls four-feet thick. It is fireproof, earthquake-proof, flood-proof, and blackout-proof. The roof is made up of three-and-a-half feet of reinforced concrete covered by five feet of hard packed dirt. The facility can withstand tornadoes and can operate for up to three days without outside electricity or water.

Such a place exists in Tulsa, Oklahoma, and it is home to the Sabre Secure Computer Center. Sabre is one of the largest real-time computer systems in the world, and its importance in the airline industry warrants such secured facilities.

Response to Terrorist Attacks

Currently, the Sabre Group is concentrating its programming efforts on meeting the U.S. Department of Transportation's recommendation that airlines start performing such functions as flagging the names of suspected terrorists in their reservations systems. This will impact Sabre's mainframe-based software, but it is not predicted to impact the responsiveness of the software in any unintended way. A capacity limit does exist on the Sabre core system. However, when actual demands on the system exceed capacity, the system does not seize. A long-standing operational process goes into a prioritized, partial shutdown and continues to process at or near the capacity of the system in a way predefined by a list of functions. A certain number of users will never be disconnected unless there is an unplanned outage, which is very rare. The airports are at the top of these must-complete users.

In conjunction with meeting this request, the Sabre System is working to move customer profiles to an open-systems technology. The goal of the new customer relationship management system is to replace activity-oriented access with customer-oriented access. The intention of the program is to link all the profiles, bookings, electronic tickets, loyalty programs, and credit references that are associated with a customer.

Technology Innovations

Currently, Sabre is concentrating on switching its reservations databases from IBM mainframes to Compaq's NonStop Himalaya servers. The Himalaya technology is slated to help in terms of quicker responsiveness through higher-level programming, increased standards, and better cost of ownership. Ultimately, the Himalaya project is about shopping, pricing, and fares, not check-in at the airport. The Himalaya project is only about shopping for tickets. The actual ticketing and check-in processes remain on the mainframe. In comparison, IBM's Transaction Processing Facility software is built on a lower-level programming and file system model. This model is very effective, but not as efficient as Sabre would like. Thus the change to the Himalaya system. The replacement of the Transaction Processing Facility provides opensystem characteristics and the reliability, operability, and scalability of the Himalaya servers.

The ticketing and check-in processes remain on the IBM mainframe, System/390 Parallel Enterprise Server. The reasons to keep these critical transactions on this computer include:

The cost of computing with S/390 CMOS processors is lower than the cost of using other processors.

Operating costs are reduced through the use of CMOS air-cooled processors; consumption of energy is lowered.

Maintenance costs are reduced.

The system powers Sabre's Internet location and makes possible the Internet accessibility. It uses powerful servers for network computing within the context of the client-server environments.

Telecommunications

The Sabre Group owns Travelocity, the successful Web-based travel agency. Travelocity runs with a three-tier architecture. The first tier includes the site's Web servers and uses Silicon Graphics' Origin 2000 servers. These servers run the Netscape Enterprise Server, which handles the static HTML pages.

The second tier consists of transaction-processing servers, which handle the dynamically generated HTML pages showing reservations and other information. These Silicon Graphics' Origin 2000 servers run proprietary software to access the third tier, the company's immense Sabre Reservations System, a 7-terabyte database that runs on eight IBM S1360 mainframes and is affectionately referred to as Mother Sabre. The Sabre Reservations System, which runs a proprietary transaction protocol, provides a response time no longer than three seconds anywhere in the world.

Even though bandwidth has not been a bottleneck, Travelocity added a new Internet connection in 1998, a T3 (45 Mbps) from UUNet Technologies. The site previously ran a 2-Mbps link from Sprint and a 10-Mbps connection from MCI.

Data

Sabre Technology was one of the first companies to adopt Informix's object-relational database for its data warehouse. Its object-relational technology speeds execution times for complex queries and makes the system easier to program, according to Sabre officials.

Sabre chose the Informix system because its DataBlade modules can execute in parallel and process many sources simultaneously. Its warehouse will eventually examine information from 80 sources ranging from passenger reservation to ticketing systems and will house up to 8 terabytes of data. Thirty developers are writing logic to clean the data and load it correctly.

The Informix data warehouse promises to be commercially significant for Sabre and its customers. By knowing who is flying where, when, and for what amount, Sabre can gather valuable data to sell to airlines and other businesses, such as travel agencies, hotels, an real estate firms.

The Informix relational database will enable Sabre to find who is flying to a specific city within a specific timeframe. This information could be very valuable to all kinds of associated industries, such as hotels, rental cars, and entertainment.

Sabre intends to consolidate on a single database for both transactional and warehouse purposes because maintaining two databases is cost prohibitive. Sabre's current 4-terabyte TPF database has the capacity to handle more than 1 billion transactions daily.

Sale of Sabre Logistics Group

Sabre sold its Sabre Logistics Group to the original founder of the area, Dr. Yossi Sheffi. The group will form the core of a new business venture, Logistics.com Inc. While the company is making a "clean break" with Sabre, it will continue to work with it as a partner and develop joint products in the future. The purchase included the decision support and optimization software, and about 80 people from Sabre. Currently, the software is used by more than 100 carriers and shippers, including Yellow Freight, Procter & Gamble, Kraft Foods, Ford Motor Co., and J.B. Hunt.

Logistics.com will continue to be geared toward trucking companies, with later expansion to other means of distribution. The goal is to integrate the site with vertical exchange sites such as e-Chemicals, an exchange under ICG. Future opportunities will include expansion into Europe and Latin America and the development of transportation exchanges specific to those markets. According to Sheffi, "It is not about saving money, it is about making money. By booking the right freight, which is revenue, the top line can be increased and the bottom line reduced." [Hickey 2000]

Sheffi realizes that for the idea to work, Logistics.com is coming into the exchange a little late and will really need to differentiate itself from other exchanges. Key differentiators could include its transportation expertise, logistics consultation services, and yield-management software to enable carriers to

determine whether the load offered on the exchange is the load they should be taking. The software would evaluate carrier capacity and profitability analysis.

Recommendation for the Future

Sabre has a number of opportunities for future revenue growth. These include an increase in the use of Sabre in foreign countries by both customers and transportation companies. In addition, Sabre can offer new products in emerging distribution channels, such as corporate direct distribution and the Internet, expand participation of travel providers in Sabre, and provide technology solutions products and services more broadly.

In terms of enhancing technology and operating capabilities, Sabre has budgeted approximately $100 million during the next five years to enhance Sabre's core operating capabilities. Sabre plans to use this development effort to accelerate new product development; increase flexibility, power, and functionality for subscribers and associates; improve data management capabilities; raise capacity levels; and lower operating costs.

Sabre is trying to increase its presence in the hotel and automobile rental market by making the reservation process for room or a car easier. Today, Sabre agencies worldwide with clients requesting a room with a participating chain can reserve the room electronically at any of the chain's properties. Agencies have the ability to access and request information on participating locations within preexisting formats. When a customer requests a room reservation, Sabre sends the appropriate hotel a message with all the booking information. Sabre then electronically reads information from the hotel's file and updates the reservation automatically.

Online systems raise the biggest question in the reservation industry. Sabre is competing with general reservation systems like Microsoft's Expedia, but it is also competing with individual firms. On the large-scale side, Sabre with Travelocity is now competing against Orbitz. Orbitz was formed by the leading airlines—including American. On the individual side, Southwest avoids paying fees to Sabre by running its own successful Web-based system. The question is whether customers want a general purpose system that searches multiple airlines, hotels, and car rental companies. Or do they prefer to choose their favorite companies and search there?

Questions

1. What forces are driving the strategic direction of Sabre?

2. What has been the catalyst for change at Sabre?

3. What are the critical success factors and core competencies of the Sabre group?

4. Upon which technologies is the Sabre System built?

5. What has caused a change in the use of technology at Sabre?

6. How successful has the technological change been?

Additional Reading

"Abacus, Sabre File IOPs; Wired Reduces Shares but Boosts Price." *Electronic Marketplace Report,* October 15, 1996, p. 5.

Anderson, Jennifer, Doug Beizer, and Trever Dawes. "Ticket to Ride." *PC Magazine,* April 21, 1998, p. 40.

Deck, Stewart. "Sabre in Privacy Hot Seat." *Computerworld,* July 13, 1998, p. 6.

Dillon, Nancy. ". . . While Climbing Storage Management Mountain." *Computerworld,* March 2, 1998, pp. 31–32.

Friedman, Matthew. "Mainframes Back in Mainstream." *InternetWeek,* September 15, 1997, p. 22.

Girard, Kim. "Storage Snafu Grounds Sabre for Three Hours." *Computerworld,* June 29, 1998, p. 16.

Hamblen, Matt. "Sabre Deems Outsourcing Deal a Success." *Computerworld,* December 1, 1997, p. 6.

Hickey, Kathleen. "It's Buy-Back TIme." *Traffic World* 261, no. 3, January 17, 2000, pp. 38–39.

Hoffman, Thomas. "Sabre Group Hastens Y2K Plans." *Computerworld,* March 2, 1998, pp. 31–32.

Joachim, David. "Travel Apps Branch Out to Internet." *InternetWeek,* April 20, 1998, p. 23.

Karpinski, Richard. "Commerce One Brings Aboard Travel Services." *InternetWeek,* February 15, 1999, p. 10.

Stephen, Klein. "Industry Surveys: Airlines." *Standard and Poor's,* May 14, 1998.

Madden, John. "Sabre Eyes Warehouse Space." *PC Week,* July 6, 1998, p. 10.

Maselli, Jennifer. "Can IT Keep Airlines Aloft?" *Information Week,* no. 863, November 12, 2001, pp. 22–24.

Ouellette, Tim. "Sabre Flies Big Iron in Heavy Traffic." *Computerworld,* March 10, 1997, pp. 43–44.

Oxford Economic Forecasting. "The Economic Impacts of the Terrorist Attacks in the US." September 12, 2001.

Palmeri, Christopher. "This Might Not Fly." *Forbes,* April 20, 1998, p. 200.

Roberts, Mark. "Dream Factories: A Survey of Travel and Tourism." *The Economist,* January 10, 1998.

Sandoval, Greg. "Orbitz Says Competitors Are Ganging Up." *News.com,* July 26, 2001.

Case: American Express

The American Express Company has long been the widely recognized leader in the worldwide travel and corporate financial services arena. Until 1995, American Express relied almost entirely on its strong brand name to maintain its position in the marketplace. The reality was that the company had been losing market share in the credit card business to Visa and Master-Card over the past 10 years. It had overexpanded into many different corporate divisions that did not provide adequate synergy for its core businesses.

The appointment of Harvey Golub to CEO in 1992 initiated a series of restructuring projects. Golub's objective was to strengthen the company's capital position, refocus on its core businesses, improve efficiency, and produce higher returns. Golub eliminated the brokerage, investment banking, and life insurance units and focused on the company's three principal operating divisions: (1) credit cards, (2) financial services, and (3) travel and entertainment.

Technological Investment and Analysis

The primary goal for American Express is to build long-term relationships with its customers through financial products and services that offer superior service and value. This enhances the value of the American Express brand name. The company has been successful on several fronts in the development of new and innovative technology that can be translated into legitimate products and services to upgrade the support and benefits given to customers. To a great extent, American Express has moved beyond simply using technology to improving its operations and services to the point where technology itself has become the product.

One change driver for the company is to find ways to strengthen the relationships with merchants and to increase the number of merchants that accept its card. Technology furnishes American Express with a mechanism to extend more assistance to merchants. This includes providing a low-cost way to set up Web storefronts for merchants, enabling merchants to access card-member spending information, and providing real-time authorization for American Express card purchases. Through these tools, American Express is able to offer a higher level of service than the merchants might receive from other vendors. It also helps justify the company's discount or per-transaction rate, which is higher than the industry average.

The goal is to leverage technology to establish a permanent link between the customer and American Express. Uniting customers with American Express systems and products prevents those customers from developing their own systems or using those of a competitor.

American Express, with Microsoft, has launched an online travel reservation system designed for corporate customers. Called American Express Interactive (AXI), the system is based primarily on Microsoft software, including the Internet Information Server, SQL Server, and Windows NT. The AXI software is aimed at companies that use American Express as their business travel agency. The software can be integrated with American Express's proprietary travel management software. This includes a low-fare search tool and an automated expense-reporting system.

AXI enables corporate employees to negotiate and book airfare, rental car rates, and hotel rates from their desktops. Data from computerized reservation systems can be loaded through the Internet or corporate intranets. The system can be customized for each company to reflect its individual travel policies and procedures. With travel generally being the third-highest controllable expense for a firm, the ability to control costs and enforce compliance with a stated corporate travel policy provides a significant benefit to customers. Chrysler is an early adopter of AXI. It projects a 50 percent savings in processing fees and transaction costs, and an increase in the number of people complying with the company policies through the use of the system.

At American Express's Smart Card Center of Excellence, the company is leveraging its technology and customer database to develop stored-value cards. The company is forging alliances and partnerships with other companies to market the cards. Unlike other debit cards, the transactions on American Express smart cards go through the company's central processing centers. These enable the company to collect its discount rate in exchange for transferring the credit risk from the merchant to American Express.

American Express had joined with Hilton Hotels and IBM Corporation to test the use of smart card technology to support ticketless travel. Customer information, as well as hotel and travel preferences and loyalty programs, are transferred to reside on a microchip. The microchip allows the cardholder to use a machine at the airport to immediately register for a flight. Information contained in the card is verified through electronic reservation. Traveler identification is confirmed, eliminating the need for a boarding pass. The card can also be used to register for a hotel room through the Internet. Subsequently, it will serve as the room key. It is capable of carrying stored value in multiple currencies and has the potential to be coded with the user's fingerprints. It can even be used as a passport.

By placing an early emphasis on the development of smart cards, American Express has positioned itself to reap the revenue rewards once the smart card market becomes viable. According to David Boyles of American Express, "Our goal is to give value and convenience through globally operable, multifunctioning cards." [Block, 1997]

American Express is implementing an innovative marketing program called CustomExtras. This program is designed to treat each card member as a "market of one," in which personalized offers are made to selected customers. One-to-one marketing requires system development efforts that include three technologies: (1) customer databases, (2) interactive media, and (3) mass customization.

Through the use of these technologies, American Express can learn specific details on customer spending patterns, from a deeper relationship with those customers, and provide them with customized products and services. Companies spend a great deal of time and money in the acquisition of new customers; one-to-one marketing solidifies that investment and more fully develops the amount of business that can be conducted with those customers.

Mass marketing is increasingly considered to be an inefficient approach (a 3 percent response rate is considered good in the industry). The goal of one-to-one marketing is to make more selective, cost-efficient solicitations that generate a much higher response rate. Within the industry, the market for products and services that support one-to-one marketing is pinpointed as one of the fastest growing uses of technology in the business.

The overall strategy for these initiatives is to define and maintain an ideal customer relationship. "All this enables us to follow our customers as they move from phone or paper-based customer support or transactions to the use of the Internet to handle their travel activities, all the way to the use of smart cards," according to Andrew Bartels, vice president of encrypted payments at American Express. [Gupta, 1986]

American Express is funding the technology expenditures through a combination of new business development and improved margins through improved processes. Under Golub, the company has focused on greatly reduced costs and the elimination of less profitable noncore divisions. Revenue has increased consistently over the past few years as a result of these and other efforts. The company is well capitalized and has the resources to support technology spending. As indicated in their 2000 annual report, American Express is focused on a cost structure that provides the initiative for company investment programs, product design, and pricing innovation.

With the primary objective of increasing customer card business with the company, American Express can measure its success based on levels of consumer spending using its card products. It can also measure the success of its one-to-one marketing strategy based on card member response rates to solicitations sent out by the company.

One of American Express's strategies has been to improve the technological support for its financial advisors division. The goal is to increase both productivity and the level of customer service. American Express intends to better utilize its advisors' laptops through remote access to the client and product data. It previously took from 50 to 60 days for a financial plan to be delivered to a prospective client; the increased technological support from the new systems should reduce the turnaround time to 24 hours. Prior to these improvements, 15 to 20 percent of the customers did not act on the plan or take the plan's recommendations to other product providers. Once the technological improvements are complete, American Express can measure the impact of the new programs on the number of customers accepting financial plans.

Another targeted use of data is the American Express Custom Extras one-to-one marketing program. This program begins with the company's collection of all card member purchase records and other information, which is stored in a marketing database. Proprietary software selects merchant offerings and other American Express promotions that fit the customer's unique profile. Those offerings and promotions are then printed as recommendations on the monthly bill. Through the use and evaluation of this stored data, American Express can tailor its marketing to the individual customer.

American Express has reinvented itself as a corporation that actively partners with other companies to develop new revenue opportunities. No longer the imperial standalone company it once was, American Express now engages in partnerships and cobranding efforts that are designed to increase the customer base in the United States and overseas. These partnerships are often with technology companies.

The tremendous amount of data from the high-profile client base maintained by American Express gives the company the ability to develop more effective marketing strategies. This information is used both to market its own products and services and to increase card member spending. By utilizing its database and a closed-loop network, American Express is able to store and use this information to identify customer spending patterns, assist in budget planning, and increase efficiency. One primary use of the data is for target marketing, in which specific merchant offers are targeted to those customers most likely to take advantage of them, based on their previous spending behavior. American Express also makes customer purchase data available to merchants through a Windows-based software product designed by the company.

Rather than simply relying on its own proprietary distribution systems, American Express uses many other types of distribution networks, including brokerage, direct marketing, and online systems to attract and service its customers. The company also uses a vast worldwide electronic network, which enables it to increase its charge volume, hold down fraud, and minimize bad debt. This network provides the infrastructure needed to access a multitude of markets, many of which provide opportunities for expansion.

American Express has two goals for its information technology area: (1) reengineer the company and (2) develop new products. American Express CIO Allan Loren notes that the new technologies can alter distribution channels. The Internet provides a mechanism to distribute new products and expand the transactional capabilities of the company. The overall goal is to better service the customer and maintain a solid relationship in a highly competitive business environment.

The most recent data for American Express identifies its allocation of IT expenditures as follows:

- Reengineering and new product development (50 percent).

- Maintaining existing technology (40 percent).

- Determining new directions for the company (10 percent).

American Express uses a closed-loop network to collect and process customer information for target marketing. Point-of-sale transactions feed a massively parallel database that collects data from across the organization. For the CustomExtras program, the company has deployed a second database, running on a mainframe with relational database software. This database draws data from the first database and uses it to track purchases, rewards, and promotions. It manages the printing of billing statements with customized offers and messages. As a follow-up, the American Express marketing database tracks customers' activities regarding offers and promotions. Whenever a customer acts on an offer, American Express shares the results with the merchant.

Teamed with Hewlett-Packard, American Express has introduced a new electronic commerce program (ExpressVault). This new program is designed to enable merchants to conduct business over the Internet quickly and securely. It combines HP's computing and security technologies with American Express's payment-processing system. ExpressVault enables merchants to add online commerce features to websites; it protects transaction, database, and website information against unauthorized access; and it provides real-time processing for American Express card transactions.

Network

Financial planning is an increasingly lucrative business for American Express. Its advisers work with individuals and families to develop long-range financial goals for retirement, education, illness, disability, or estate planning.

Employing 8,500 advisors, the IDS Division is at the core of the financial focus. These advisers are equally equipped so they can work out of their homes or remote field offices to sell a broad range of financial products and services to their clients.

As recently as five years ago, financial planning was a paper-intensive business. Advisers met with prospective clients, typically at the client's home or business location. They gathered relevant data on client assets, liabilities, and goals, and then reported back to the local regional office. At the regional office, a clerk entered information and uploaded it to the legacy mainframe-based application in Minneapolis. Weeks later, a rudimentary financial plan would be mailed to the adviser, who would go back to deliver it to the client and meet with him or her to tailor the plan to his or her precise needs. Depending on the client, this could go on for three or four iterations.

AdvisorLink has completely changed this process. This remote application encompasses a wide range of applications specifically designed for field advisers. Under its umbrella, new functionality is added either through in-house development projects or software purchased from third parties. AdvisorLink brings together internal "best practice" processes and technology that the firm believes will give its advisers a significant competitive edge over other financial services firms.

The internal proprietary adviser service software, written in Smalltalk, resides on advisers' laptops and processes client plans locally. Although client data is still uploaded to legacy systems, the turnaround time for completing sophisticated financial plans has been cut from weeks to days.

The adviser discusses the initial collection of data regarding the goals, income, assets, and debt from the client. The client then uses the new software to develop customized plans that specifically tie the client's long- and short-term goals to existing and future assets. Rather than relying on the boilerplate results that came from the previous legacy application, the new software gives the adviser the opportunity to more precisely focus the plan. When the plan is complete, the adviser meets with the client, validates the results, and conducts "what if" scenarios to ensure that the client is satisfied with the results. At any time, the client can request adjustments and the adviser can make them on the spot. AdvisorLink has dramatically shortened the processing time for sophisticated financial plans.

Telecommunications

On the consumer side, American Express promotes travel, dining, and entertainment. To do so, it has invested money in a company that is using the Internet to help consumers find places where they can do all of these things. American Express has entered an investment and joint marketing agreement with CitySearch Inc., the developer of online city guides. City-Search supplies maps and information for 16 cities, including New York, Portland, San Francisco, Washington, D.C., Chicago, Sydney, and Toronto. In doing so, it covers news about sports, the arts, entertainment, community activities, shopping, recreation, and weather. CitySearch also helps small and medium-size businesses develop websites. It can also serve as the host for those sites. It gathers this information from its newspaper partners in each city.

Security on the Internet. On May 31, 1997, Visa International, Mastercard, and American Express, with most of the major players in electronic commerce and internetworking, unveiled the Secure Electronic Transactions (SET) standard. SET promised to revolutionize online transactions and make the Internet safe for electronic commerce. Unfortunately, the implementation of this technology has moved more slowly than expected. Difficulties have come from both a business and technological perspective.

The goal of SET was to increase consumer confidence in the security of online transactions. Both credit card holders and merchants are issued digital certificates, which are verified by a certificate authority to make a transaction. Neither the merchant nor the consumer can be anyone other than who they purport to be. This emphasis greatly reduces the possibility of impersonation fraud.

The difficulty comes in the requirement that merchants using SET install expensive new software and build their businesses around a complex transaction infrastructure. These requirements have tempered merchants' interest in signing up for the SET program. In fact, one year later, the attempted standard still had not seen a single operational deployment. SET's biggest shortcoming is the client channel. Vendors like Veri-Fone and IBM have developed SET wallet plug-ins for the popular Web browsers. Yet, Internet users do not favor external plug-ins.

In the meantime, electronic commerce continues to grow on the Net, protected by Secure Sockets Layer encryption. While not as secure as SET, for many consumers, it is secure enough.

Free Internet e-mail. American Express introduced a free Internet e-mail service, AmExMail, in April 1998. The service, available only to American Express customers, was developed with the help of the Colorado Springs, Colorado-based electronic messaging firm, USA.Net. The new e-mail system uses USA.Net's mail engine architecture. This purchase makes American Express the first major business outside the Internet industry to offer free e-mail. Services such as AmExMail have become more common among companies seeking to build closer ties to their customers. This is an important mechanism for a credit card company to use to keep its customers active and to be able to share new information with them.

Other free e-mail services, such as Four11, Hotmail, and WhoWhere have been partnering with or purchased by larger companies, including Yahoo, Microsoft, and Qualcomm, respectively. These deals have linked free e-mail to already existing Internet products or services.

AmExMail will continue to be operated by USA.NET, a firm that will continue to offer free, ad-supported e-mail services. In April 1997, American Express announced the purchase of a minority interest in USA.NET, which is privately held. The AmExMail service is free to any Internet user. However, American Express cardholders will get toll-free customer service support and 10 Mbytes of mail storage space, compared to 5 Mbytes for noncardholders.

American Express Travel and Entertainment is a Web-based travel solution that integrates a company's travel policies and directives with the reservations system. Reservations that do not comply with policy directives are flagged, and "preferred supplier" services are emphasized. AXI's linkage to Microsoft's Expedia software means users can take advantage of added features such as airline seat maps for seat selection and access to international destination information. The travel system can operate in multiple environments, with multiple computer reservations systems and an Internet, intranet, or extranet connection.

American Express Travel online provides an easy-to-use reservation system, access to vacation and last-minute travel specials, and excellent customer service. As such, the service is good for travelers without a lot of special needs. It does not offer more specialized services such as the ability to book flights using frequent-flier miles or to book more than five legs of a business trip.

The AmEx reservations system is driven by Internet Travel Network (ITN). All reservations are sent to American Express Travel Related Services. This provides several advantages, including options to purchase tickets. AmEx provides the ability to change an itinerary worldwide through AmEx offices or through its toll-free number. Ticketing is available 24 hours a day, but customer service is available on a more limited basis.

To use the system, each user must register and establish a profile, which is identical to the ITN profile and stored for future use. For security reasons, the credit card number cannot be stored from one session to another.

The site's vacation packages, including many different suppliers and certified vacations, are guaranteed to be at the lowest prices available. The drawback of the vacation packages is that the prices quoted are for fixed tours; fares increase drastically when changes are made.

American Express Retirement Services. The American Express Retirement Services program has instituted natural language query software on its ExpressLink extranet to eliminate the need for retirement planners and benefits administrators to learn basic query software. The original query tool required users to download data to the desktop and to point and click on the data elements they wanted. This was enough to scare some users away. In its place, the natural language software returns an answer for queries typed in plain English or suggests alternatives to help the user find what they need. Some users accustomed to the older querying tools found the new option slow and awkward. They feel it would be most beneficial for those users who had not previously used a query tool. The ExpressLink service costs $2,500 plus a $1,500 annual support fee.

Amex used English Wizard, a natural language tool from Linguistic Technology Corporation in Littleton, Massachusetts, to develop the ExpressLink extranet. Many individuals use ExpressLink to work on their 401(k) plans. In addition to the query tool, ExpressLink provides users with monthly online reports, the ability to check call center statistics, and access to send electronic mail to reach their account managers.

American Express is working with Mercantec to further refine an economical and easy-to-use Web-based storefront. The companies will use Mercantec's SoftCart payment and virtual shopping software. American Express will handle the back-end processing and offer financial and marketing expertise. Soft-Cart offers companies a better way to utilize the possibilities of a Web store without making a major financial commitment. The partnership with Mercantec offers American Express a good entry point for offering Web-based services. American Express will use SoftCart and a network of payment gateways to provide Web merchants with authorization for American Express and bank card purchases.

Unlike many companies that act as Web commerce enablers, American Express already has strong relationships with both merchants and consumers. In comparison, Visa and MasterCard work through affiliate banks. Many of these have faltered in the area of electronic commerce.

SoftCart features a relatively low-cost entry point for Web merchants, with a onetime license fee of $1,800. Monthly licensing is also available. Merchants can purchase a solution directly from American Express or work with integration partners, including ISPs that will implement the software on their networks. The product has limited availability.

American Express is building a high-speed proprietary network, called TravelBahn, across the U.S. to connect travel agents and others who need direct access to reservation databases and travel inventory systems. The system will provide direct access to supplier (e.g., airline and hotel) databases. It will also improve security and support the transfer of detailed customer data without risk of interception on public (Internet) networks. The Customer Information Gateway will enable any Amex travel agent anywhere in the world to find and change customer reservations. Largely targeted at corporate travel, the system automates the negotiation process and provides access to corporate discount data along with customer details.

Data

American Express has enhanced an application for its corporate purchasing service. This enables customers' purchasing data to be fed directly into their back-end SAP systems. The interface with American Express's AccountingLink application eliminates any manual intervention. This is particularly important since large clients process more than 1 million purchasing documents a year.

The ultimate goal is to enable customers of American Express's purchasing service to outsource their accounts payable and purchasing operations to American Express. This business handled over $4 billion in invoices and 15 million transactions in 1998 alone.

Smart Card

American Express has formed a joint venture with Visa International to focus on developing applications for smart cards to spur the use of this technology in the United States. The companies hope that their smart-card applications will become the standard for the electronic-commerce industry. Their goal is to design open interfaces that will support competitor's systems as well.

Banksys SA in Belgium and ERG Ltd. in Australia are also partners in the venture, called Proton World International. The company will continue to develop and license smart-card applications that were originally developed by Banksys, including the Proton electronic purse application used by 30 million people worldwide.

Credit card companies have been reluctant to push multifunction smart cards because they fear that they will cannibalize the credit card company's brand by replacing traditional credit cards. The commitment of New York City-based American Express and Foster City, California-based Visa indicates that these firms believe they have more to gain than they have to lose through the implementation of smart cards.

"If you have a multifunction smart card, you can use it to gain entry to your office, take money out of the bank, and ride mass transit," according to Jim Balderston, an analyst at Zona Research, Inc., in Redwood City, California. [Cole-Gomolski, 1998]

In contrast, MasterCard International, Inc., supports the Mondex electronic purse system, which follows a different verification structure.

Recommendation for the Future

To be successful, American Express must meet the demands of its corporate customers to retain and grow in the more lucrative business marketplace. Industry observers expect the number of commercial cards and the charge volume to grow as much as 50 percent over the next few years. Some of that growth is expected to result from small businesses, which have limited technology to monitor and control expenses in-house. The ability of American Express, for instance, to develop an Internet system for purchasing cards ahead of its competitors is essential to capturing a large share of the small business marketplace.

Technology is enabling American Express to attempt to see whether it can sell additional financial services to its card members. Of American Express's 20.5 million customers, only 250,000 of them have accounts with American Express Financial Advisors. The company should be able to use its customer database to develop marketing strategies to expand the number of services that American Express provides to them. Technology can be put in place to evaluate the data of those customers who are both card members and financial service customers. These database tools could then extrapolate those patterns to identify other customers most likely to be interested in and responsive to proposals for financial services.

Given the intense competition in the industry, technology must keep American Express in the position of meeting customer needs. Management recognizes this fact in its effort to leverage technology to improve customer service and efficiency.

American Express has implemented a timely, detailed process to monitor both external business conditions, such as consumer spending, interest rates, and movements in the equity markets, and internal indicators, such as billings, mutual fund inflows and redemptions, and credit levels.

American Express believes its approach will be successful because it has set realistic goals for earnings per share at the low end of the targeted range. Its approach incorporates the following goals:

1. The businesses are diverse. The company's breadth provides business levers to adjust as the year progresses and circumstances change. Investment spending in one business can be reprioritized to counter weakness in another. The geographic scope allows the company to reallocate resources on a timely basis when certain markets slow, or others improve. The economic diversity provides the flexibility that is critical for success when the economic cycles change.

2. The core business remains strong. The company has made substantial investments within the United States and across international markets. It has launched new products, added a significant number of new card members, expanded merchant signings, and further strengthened the corporate and small business card bases.

3. The business is positioned for growth in a slow economy. The company believes that the breadth of its products and its reemphasis on financial planning will better position it for slowing economic times than its competitors. The downturn, then, will enable the company to capture market share in key business areas.

4. The fundamental business model is sound. American Express believes it will provide a number of significant advantages relative to their competitors and will position the company well for long-term future growth.

5. The experience with reengineering has been successful. The company has gone through three rounds of reengineering since 1990. This has removed more than $3 billion from the expense structure and base. During 2000 and 2001, the company turned up the level of intensity in reengineering, to better prepare itself for the slowing of the robust economy. Fiscal year 2002 will be no different. Specific reengineering targets are in place for each section of the company.

6. The investment opportunities have expanded. The investment opportunities have expanded in such a way that the company has the flexibility to take advantage of them. This has set in place a stronger competitive advantage from both a servicing and a margin perspective.

Questions

1. What has been the catalyst for change at American Express?

2. Upon which technologies does the corporation rely?

3. What has been the primary cause of change in the use of technology at American Express?

4. How successful has American Express been with this technological change?

5. How has American Express developed the financial ability to embark on a major technological program of advancement?

6. Are there long-term trends that seem to be problematic for American Express?

7. What does the corporation's Web page present about American Express's business directives?

8. How will technology impact the industry?

9. What role does data play in the future of the corporation?

Additional Reading

"American Express Links to Apps." *InternetWeek,* April 6, 1998, p. 7.

"Amex: Full Speed on Travel Network." *eWeek,* August 27, 2001, p. 39.

Block, Valerie. "Amex to Test Smart Cards with Hilton and IBM." *American Banker,* May 29, 1997, p. 1.

Cole-Gomolski, Barb. "Amex/Visa Deal to Push Smart-Card Technology." *Computerworld,* August 3, 1998, p. 6.

"EDS Inks Sale of ATMs." *PC Week,* February 1, 1999, p. 81.

Friedman, Matthew. "SET Standard not Exactly Hitting the Fast Lane." *Computing Canada,* June 15, 1998, p. 26.

Girishankar, Saroja. "American Express Online Travel Service Flies High." *Internet Week,* December. 1, 1997.

Gupta, Udayan. "Sharing Data to Get an Edge." *Information Week,* September 9, 1996.

Kestelyn, J. "Emerging Standard Gives Smart Card Players Hope." *Intelligent Enterprise,* October 1998, p. 10.

LaPlante, Alice. "Commanding a Mobile Army." *Computerworld,* July 20, 1998, p. 55.

Mulqueen, John T. "Big Business Remains Bullish on E-Commerce." *InternetWeek,* July 13, 1998, p. 48.

"Online Travel Group." *Computerworld,* June 22, 1998, p. 41.

Pike, Bill. "American Express Coins Its Euro Strategy." *Enterprise Systems Journal,* December 1998, p. 26.

Stedman, Craig. "Amex to Users: Speak English." *Computerworld,* December 15, 1997, pp. 57–59.

Sweat, Jeff. "American Express Upgrades SAP Links." *InformationWeek,* April 6, 1998, p. 40.

"Visa and Amex Start Smart Standard War." *Computer Weekly,* August 6, 1998, p. 6.

Appendix

Solving Business Problems and Cases

One of the goals of this text is to help you move a step closer to the business world and its unstructured problems. It takes time to develop your own approach to identify the important issues and search for alternative solutions with unstructured problems. Figure 10.1A illustrates one basic approach to solving problems. A useful way to learn how to solve business problems is to begin by working with smaller cases. These cases represent more compact, slightly better-defined business problems. Many business problems are loosely defined. You might be given a set of numbers and asked to create a report. In some cases, you will have to decide what problems need to be solved. Then you need to select appropriate tools to produce the report. Remember that in business, presentation is important because you will be judged both by the context and the appearance of your work, and you will often have to persuade decision makers that your decision is correct and appropriate.

Solve the Right Problem

One of the first complications you encounter with unstructured problems is that there are often many problems. It is not always clear which problem is the most important. You must be careful to identify causes instead of just symptoms. That is where systems theory is useful. It encourages you to look at all the components of the system. Keep in mind that almost no business runs perfectly. Some minor problems are not worth the cost to fix them. You will have to evaluate each problem and determine which ones are the most important. Remember that it is crucial to focus on the goals of the system. If there are multiple goals, you will have to assign priorities and determine

how your plans relate to the goals. Figure 10.2A provides some questions that you can ask to help you focus on the cause of the problem and the goals of the new system.

Choose the Right Tools

When the only tool you have is a hammer, everything looks like a nail. That is an old saying that has often been applied to MIS. Many students quickly see the value of spreadsheets, so they try to solve all their problems using a spreadsheet. Sometimes the exercise is easier to do with a database management system, or even a word processor. When you encounter a new business problem, stop for a minute and decide which tool is best for the job. Be open to new possibilities and consider combining tools. Remember that it is generally faster and less expensive to buy software and configure it to meet your needs, than it is to write a new system from scratch.

Divide the System: One Step at a Time

At first glance, many problems appear to be too difficult. Or you might have trouble finding a solution to a case. The trick is to split the problem into smaller pieces. For cases, use systems theory and data-flow diagrams to identify the components of the system. For exercises and problems, work one step at a time. Collect the data, perform computations, create graphs, and then create the final report. If the problem is structured appropriately, try to keep the individual components separate. If you need to make a change in one section, it should not interfere with the rest of the project.

FIGURE 10.1A
You should develop a systematic plan for solving problems. The steps outlined here provide a starting point. Each step leads to increasingly detailed analysis.

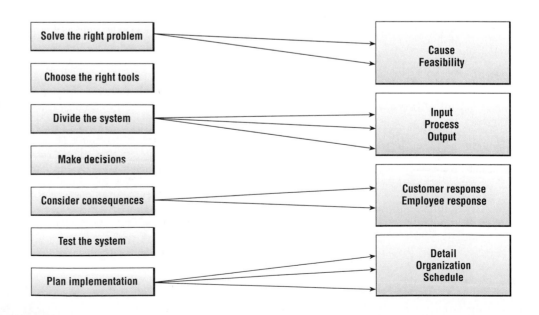

Making a Decision

Once you have evaluated the alternatives, you must make a decision. For most problems, you can only afford to pursue one option. Your choice should be clearly defined and the relative advantages and disadvantages spelled out in detail. You also need to include a solid action plan that describes each step of your proposal. If possible, you should estimate the potential costs. At least identify the items that must be purchased, even if you do not know the costs. Also, if it is relevant, you should identify the people who will be in charge of implementing your plan.

Consider the Consequences

Any time a system is changed, it is important to examine the participants to see who might be adversely affected and to identify how external agents might respond to the changes. For example, if you design a new system that alters the work flow within the company, some jobs and middle-level management tasks may be altered or eliminated. Although companies routinely alter jobs and occasionally reduce their workforce, a good plan will include a means to retrain workers for new jobs within the company whenever possible. Effects on external agents are more difficult to identify and harder to resolve. For example, a manufacturer might consider skipping over the retail channel and selling products directly to the final consumer. With this approach, the manufacturer could offer a lower price to consumers. However, the existing retail outlets would be upset at the additional level of competition. Many times the retailers add support through product demonstrations, comparisons with competitive products, training, and repair services. In these cases, a new system that irritates the retailers or skips them completely could be disastrous.

FIGURE 10.2A Initial questions for technology projects. All projects begin with a great deal of uncertainty. You need to begin with a high-level approach that helps define and structure the project. These initial questions help identify the main objectives.

- Does the project fit with the business goals and management style?
- Does the project improve the competitive position of the firm?
- How long will any competitive advantage last?
- What value or reward is created by the system?
- What level of technology is needed to create the system (experimental, leading edge, established, or old-hat)?
- What is the probability of technical success (actually building the system)?
- What is the probability of commercial success (making money once the project is technically successful)?
- What are the costs involved in creating the system: monetary? time? additional capital, marketing, and management?

Implementation

In business, creative ideas are always useful, but without a detailed implementation plan, the idea alone will not be used. Consider an idea for a new product. The idea itself is not worth much until you find a way to manufacture, market, and distribute the product. Similarly, in MIS it is easy to say that a company can achieve significant gains by installing a new computer system. However, the idea is more valuable and the project more likely to succeed if you include a detailed implementation plan. MIS implementation plans include hardware and software requirements, along with training, changes required in various departments, and timetables for installation.

Hints for Solving Business Problems and Cases

Cases are often used to illustrate business problems and to show the role played by information. As you progress in your business education, you will encounter more cases. The purpose of this section is to provide an approach to solving cases. Cases tend to be less structured than typical textbook exercises. With cases you not only have to solve the problem, you have to identify the cause of the problem, then decide what tools to use to address it. Figure 10.3A lists some of the elements that are required for a good analysis of business problems.

Treat cases as if they are real business situations. First, familiarize yourself with the situation and the symptoms (read the case). Next, create a system view of the organization (read the case again and take notes). Divide the system into components connected by data flows. Sketch the process. You do not always have to draw a complete data-flow diagram; any picture will make it easier for you to see the relationships between the components. Look for basic system problems such as defective subsystems, inputs not matching outputs, and weak interaction with the environment.

Remember that you are looking for causes of the problem. A symptom where reports contain errors could have many possible causes. Perhaps the system is not collecting accurate data. Maybe two departments are interfering with each other and

FIGURE 10.3A Elements of good business analysis. Because IT affects so many areas, it is important to identify the source of problems and how everyone will be affected by changes. Remember that projects are more likely to succeed if you can precisely identify the goals and requirements.

- Identification of the root causes of problems
- A solid grasp of the strategic components of the problem
- Identification of the critical success factors
- An evaluation of the financial implications
- Thorough discussion of implementation
- Realistic analysis of the expected results
- The effect on future growth and continued development
- The effect on the human resources
- An understanding of the target markets

altering the data. Possibly a clerk or a computer program is making the wrong computations. To find the cause in this case, you need to follow the data from the source to the final report and determine where the errors first arise. Most cases are complicated by the fact that there are many symptoms and sometimes more than one cause. A DFD can help you sort out the various relationships.

There are two difficult aspects to any business problem: identifying the true problem and trying to come up with a solution. With practice, you can learn to understand systems and determine causes. Solutions, however, often require creativity. There is no easy way to learn creativity. The best way is to examine what other companies have done to solve their problems. Often, problems that you encounter will be similar to those at other firms. Each chapter in this book carries cases of how actual companies have approached various problems. You can find more case situations in common business publications such as *Computerworld, Fortune, Business Week,* and *The Wall Street Journal.*

Finally, remember there can be many different answers to any case. You might find that it is easy to suggest that a company should "buy a new computer system." Although that statement is undoubtedly true, it is not very helpful. You really need to add more detail. The best answers describe the nature and cause of the problem, provide a detailed plan, and explain how the plan solves the problem and provides additional advantages.

A typical case will be written as a report to the managers of the company involved. Figure 10.4A shows a good way to organize your report. It is based on the elements of persuasion. First describe the need for a change, then present your plan, then show how your plan solves the problems and provides ad-

ditional advantages. The solution should be spelled out in detail. An implementation section should explain exactly how to arrive at the solution. This section includes a step-by-step plan of action that lists when to take each action, and specifies who is in charge. The report should also estimate the costs of the solution and describe the anticipated benefits. Some reports may need to include a contingency plan. If you make a risky suggestion that could backfire, it would be wise to give the company another option.

Exercises

1. Choose one of the cases in this book and write a short business report of three pages. The first page identifies the problems and cause of the problems. The second page presents your solution. The third page explains how your solution solves the problems and provides additional advantages.

2. Choose one of the cases in this book and draw a data-flow diagram. Highlight the main problems the company is experiencing.

3. Consider a small company that is growing rapidly. Employees want more options in terms of the payment methods and benefits. What choices does the company have to replace its payroll system? Do some research and be specific. How should the company evaluate the choices?

4. Interview faculty and staff at your school to find out what problems they have with the university information system. Summarize the comments and identify the possible causes of problems.

FIGURE 10.4A Proposal organization. When you write up a business analysis, it is helpful to use this format, which comes from formal debate methodologies developed over many years. Remember your role as a communicator is to be clear, precise, and persuasive.

Problem Description

State the facts and problems.
Identify the most important problems and causes.

Plan

Describe the new system.
Detail how to implement the plan.
Provide contingency plan for problems that might arise.

Advantages

Show how your plan will solve the problems.
List any additional opportunities that you might be able to pursue. In particular, look for new directions that might give your firm an advantage over your rivals.

Organizing Businesses and Systems

HOW DO MANAGERS ORGANIZE AND CONTROL BUSINESSES AND INFORMATION SYSTEMS?

Information technology provides new ways to organize businesses. In particular, the Internet makes it possible for firms of any size to conduct business around the world. But creating these new structures requires thought, effort, and time. Experience shows that it is easy to make mistakes and waste huge amounts of money. Organizing and planning are critical to avoiding these problems.

Because of their importance in a modern firm, information systems must be carefully planned, designed, and maintained. Business managers are increasingly involved in designing and organizing MIS resources. Managers need to understand the difficulties faced in systems development to understand the rules and processes. As technology changes, the organization of business operations and the MIS resources is changing. By identifying these changes, business managers can improve their operations and make better use of new information technologies.

Changes in technology and business cause fundamental changes in society. These changes affect everything from education to government to our daily lives as employees and citizens. Changing technology brings new responsibilities and problems. As managers and citizens we will face many new decisions. We must always remember our ethical responsibilities to other members of society.

CHAPTER ELEVEN

Electronic Business and Entrepreneurship

What you will learn in this chapter

- How does e-business fit into different levels in the production chain?

- What options are available for promoting websites?

- How does Internet technology improve customer relationship management?

- What options exist for building and hosting websites?

- What are the benefits to mobile commerce?

- Why did so many early EC firms fail?

- Why is entrepreneurship important to economies?

- What are the main steps to starting a new business?

The instant recognition of a FedEx delivery shows the dominance that FedEx has in the minds of consumers. Tracking packages over the Internet was just one in a series of innovations by FedEx.

Federal Express

Federal Express promises to deliver packages overnight absolutely and positively. Its extensive fleet of trucks and planes, Memphis distribution hub, and Cosmos II computer system enable it to accomplish these objectives. Cosmos II keeps track online of 14 million package deliveries every day. When a customer service representative keys in a package's registration number, the system can track the package from its dropoff at any Federal Express office to its ultimate destination. The advantages that this system provides have been indispensable in Federal Express's rise to be the leading provider of overnight package delivery around the world.

A key component of the system is the menu-driven Supertracker bar-code scanner. Worldwide, 60,000 Supertrackers scan packages every time a package changes hands. Data is stored in the Supertracker and relayed back to the minicomputers in the dispatch station when the Supertracker is replaced in its cradle in the van. At the end of the business day, the Supertracker is returned to a mechanical cradle in the dispatch station where its information is downloaded to the central computer. This transfer enables the master database to be automatically updated each night.

The Supertracker system provides more information than just the location of packages. Early access to the number of packages headed toward each destination enables management to allocate delivery personnel and trucks to each day's routes. Monitoring the number of pickups in a region also assists management in its efforts to evaluate advertising and other programs in an area. Quantitative measures of pickups and deliveries can also be used to evaluate offices and personnel against standards from other offices and areas.

FIGURE 11.1

Electronic commerce. The Internet is commonly used for sales from business-to-consumer and business-to-business. Salespeople can use it to collect data and communicate with clients and the main offices. New Web-based businesses are being created to provide data and services.

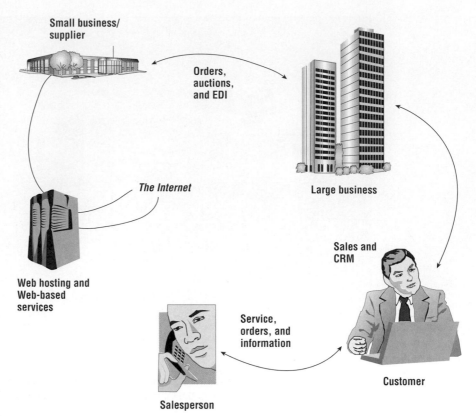

Overview

Ally:	Richard, I've been talking with some of our clients. And I think we need to get more involved in e-commerce.
Richard:	Why is that, Ally?
Ally:	Well, we can reach more people. We can sell products 24 hours a day. It doesn't cost much to set up and run the website. If it works, we can cut our sales staff, or use them more productively.
Richard:	Sure, sure, but we all know the dot-bombs crashed. Isn't this e-commerce stuff overrated?
Ally:	Not really. Some early companies were silly, but we have an established business, and we make a profit on all of our sales. Sure, we probably won't transfer all of our clients to the Web, but why not run the website at least for those who prefer it over our other sales channels?
Richard:	That makes sense.
Ally:	And while we're at it, we really need to build some decent ordering systems that tie to our suppliers over the Internet using XML. If we can integrate our systems to the Internet, we can cut all of our costs.

Introduction

What is electronic commerce? E-commerce, or EC, can be hard to define. On the one hand, it could be defined as doing business on the Internet. But there are many aspects to business and many ways of using Internet technologies. Some writers refer to the broader concept as

Trends

Largely because of transportation costs, consumers have been limited to purchasing products through local retail stores. Even for products produced elsewhere, it was generally cheaper to ship items in bulk to the retailer than to ship to individual customers. Plus, manufacturers and wholesalers did not want to deal with individual customers. They did not want to spend the money to create customer-service departments to handle thousands or millions of individual orders, returns, and complaints.

Eventually, shipping and transaction costs began to decline. Sears got its start and made its original reputation as a nationwide mail-order firm. Customers could order thousands of products from a catalog and have them delivered. Over time, Sears found it profitable to build stores in thousands of cities, and moved away from catalog sales. In the 1980s and 1990s, many other mail-order firms expanded to provide thousands of products direct from the manufacturer to the customer. While some people prefer shopping this way, only a fraction of total sales are made through mail-order companies. In 1998, mail-order sales were $356 billion, or slightly over 3 percent of GDP.

Around 1997, sales over the Internet started to become important, and by 1999, e-commerce was the hot topic in the nation. By 2001, over 50 percent of U.S. households had access to the Internet and e-commerce, promising access to millions of customers. Hundreds of dot-com firms were funded with venture capital and early IPOs to define new ways to interact with customers and businesses over the Internet. Hundreds of paper billionaires were created as stock prices were driven by expectations and hype. Some people were saying that bricks-and-mortar traditional firms were dead. But in late 2000 and early 2001, hundreds of the dot-com startups failed, laying off thousands of workers and crashing the technology sector of the stock market. Investors are wary, but the Internet continues.

Cell phones began with slow, poor quality analog signals that were gradually replaced with the second generation digital phones by 2000. The third generation wireless phone will handle data and Internet access as well as voice. Portable data access can create new opportunities in mobile commerce to improve contact with customers. Entirely new applications can evolve from virtually immediate contact.

e-business. The main point is that EC represents considerably more functions than just putting up a website to describe or sell products. The fundamental goal of EC is to increase sales and reduce costs by improving relationships with existing customers, and by reaching new customers and providing new services.

For at least the past 50 years, companies have followed and refined the modern business practices. These **business-to-consumer (B2C)** foundations were created to facilitate purchasing and distribution in a world with limited delivery systems and high communication costs. When the Internet changes these conditions, eventually the underlying structure will change. For example, retail stores for decades were small local firms where owners recognized customer trends and ordered a specific mix of products. Wal-Mart took advantage of size in purchasing and distribution to create giant retail stores with a relatively standard mix of products. Theoretically, the Internet could bypass the retail stores completely. Mobile commerce offers even more potential to alter our existing economic institutions. Who needs credit cards and banks when all transactions are handled through your cell phone?

On the business side, just-in-time inventory and EDI were only the beginning of a revolution in changing the ordering systems of manufacturers. Electronic marketplaces and auctions enable businesses to find new suppliers and obtain supplies on short notice. Sellers can find new customers and negotiate prices without expensive sales visits.

You should remember one important point: EC is not just an issue with new firms. In many ways, existing firms have the most to gain from EC, because they can leverage their existing strengths. **Business to business (B2B)** is also critical for existing firms because it can reduce costs and provide new options to managing purchases. Finally, the interactive aspects of EC will become increasingly useful for intranets to improve internal operations and facilitate human resources management.

Figure 11.2 shows a broader classification of e-commerce that includes B2B and B2C as well as consumer-led initiatives. The consumer issues C2B and C2C make up a minor portion of e-commerce. It is not even clear that good examples of these categories exist. Some (e.g., *The Economist*) have suggested that PriceLine might represent a C2B perspective

Reality Bytes   B2B E-Commerce

Business-to-business e-commerce (B2B) was supposed to be the next big thing on the Internet. After all, businesses spend billions of dollars per year buying everything from office supplies to raw materials. And businesses can afford advanced computer systems and high-speed access to the Internet. Many were also lured by the promise of reduced administrative costs. In this environment, several industries established B2B auction sites to market raw materials and other products. For example, MetalSite.com was established as an auction site to establish a spot market for surplus and scrap steel and other metals. But disputes over how the system should work, and how much of a commission MetalSite would capture prevented people from using it. Thomas J. Conarty from Bethlehem Steel notes that "Some people were worried that if I go out and bid for material, it's going to cost me more than if I just call you up and cut a deal." Of the 1,000 Internet companies attempting to operate industrial purchasing sites in 2000, half disappeared within 18 months. Deere & Company tried to establish a partnership with an appliance maker and two other manufacturers to create an auction site that would combine their buying power to obtain better prices. After several months, they gave it up. David F. Nelson in charge of supply management at Deere notes that "Each company had its own philosophy of how to do supply management. I won't say it's impossible, but it is virtually impossible to get companies working together unless you form

another company. Then it doesn't work very well." However, Deere did learn some lessons from the attempt and set up an internal system to simplify purchasing. The company found that its 72 worldwide plants differed considerably on standards and items. Consider only one item: work gloves. The company was purchasing 424 slightly different versions from 1,975 suppliers! Because of the confusion, in some cases suppliers were selling the exact same product to factories at different prices— sometimes twice as high. Consolidating the ordering system within the company, Deere was able to consolidate gloves to 30 kinds from 20 suppliers and obtain better prices. Other companies such as United Technologies and Chrysler Corporation have made similar gains through consolidating orders. When possible, the companies have turned to Internet purchases to coordinate the process and reduce the paperwork. However, both companies noted that the process did not reduce the number of workers needed. Kent L. Brittan from UTC notes that by using auctions on Freemarkets.com and buying in volume, "we save money, 6 to 8 percent on the low end, 20 to 30 percent on the high end." But many of the personnel positions have been upgraded and filled with engineers and business school graduates.

Source: Adapted from Joseph B. Treaster, "Goodbye to Grandiose, Hello to Nuts and Bolts," *The New York Times,* September 26, 2001.

FIGURE 11.2

E-commerce categories. E-commerce can be considered in the four categories shown. However, B2B and B2C are far more prevalent than consumer-led initiatives.

	Business	Consumer
Business	**B2B** EDI Commodity auctions	**B2C** Consumer-oriented Sales Support
Consumer	**C2B** Minimal examples, possibly reverse auctions like PriceLine	**C2C** Auction sites (eBay), but many of these are dominated by small business sales

because it relies on a reverse auction technique, where customers enter a price, and the "vendor" selects the highest offers. Although the auction method is slightly unusual, the effect of businesses offering products or services is not really any different from traditional commerce. C2C is slightly more likely, many writers place consumer auction sites like eBay in this category. While some of these auctions are consumer-to-consumer items, look carefully and you will see that many of the items are offered by small businesses or entrepreneurs. Many small firms, particularly those selling electronic items, use eBay to auction items in short supply, or to sell a few items on a regular basis.

The entire world changes when commerce systems change. But will the economy really change that far? Did the mass failure of the EC firms in 2000 and 2001 really mean that consumers prefer the traditional systems? These are the questions that make life fun and add the risk to entrepreneurship. You must understand the fundamentals before you can create your own answers to these puzzles and help shape the future of business.

FIGURE 11.3
Production chain. The production chain is important to EC because EC offers the ability to skip elements of the chain. It also makes it easier to reach new customers at any level in the chain.

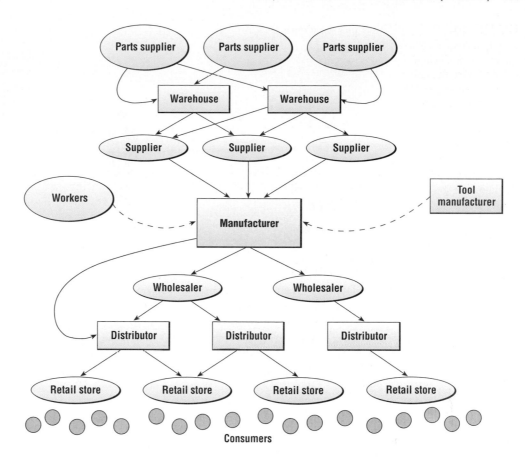

The Production Chain

To understand the issues in EC, you must first understand the production chain. Shown in Figure 11.3, this concept was described in more detail in Chapter 10, and its strategic effects are important to EC. One of the key aspects in B2C e-commerce is the ability to bypass entire sections of the production chain. Consider the situation of airlines. In the 1960s and 1970s, airlines created giant reservation systems to handle flight bookings. The system consisted of the airlines' massive central computers and databases and travel agent terminals connected by a custom network. It was too expensive for customers to connect directly. Also, the systems were hard to use and travel agents needed special training. Agents were paid a commission based on the value of the flights booked through the reservation system paid by the airlines. With the advent of frequent-flyer miles, airlines encouraged consumers to book flights with the airline itself, bypassing the travel agent and saving the cost of the commission. But it is difficult to search for flights using the telephone. The Internet changed everything. Several travel sites and the airline sites themselves make it easy to find flights, compare prices, and purchase a ticket any time of day without the assistance of an overworked travel agent or salesperson. Tickets are merely electronic reservation numbers, where you simply show appropriate identification at the gate. On the production chain, the airlines (as service providers) bypassed the intermediaries to sell directly to the consumer—a process known as **disintermediation.**

A similar process can occur on the supplier side. Instead of wholesalers, purchasing agents and suppliers are forming B2B auction sites. Companies can sell or buy products and materials on a variety of websites. Instead of searching out buyers or sellers, businesses simply submit a bid on a website that covers the desired product.

FIGURE 11.4

Disintermediation. The traditional production chain evolved because separate firms provided specialized functions more efficiently. E-commerce reduces costs and has the potential to circumvent various intermediaries. But disintermediation is a risky strategy.

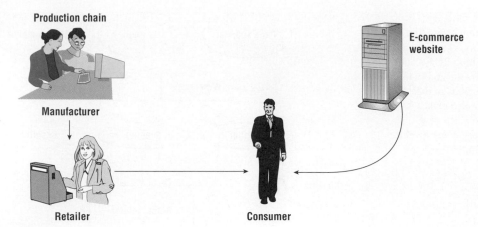

Disintermediation

Today, it is rare for a company to be vertically integrated across the production chain. For example, most manufacturers rely on other firms to handle distribution and retail sales. In a sense, they chose to outsource these functions because of the costs. Over the last 50 years or so, firms have worked to become more efficient within their niche. As shown in Figure 11.4, e-commerce has the potential to change these relationships. By reducing the costs of dealing with individual customers, it becomes possible for firms to circumvent the retailers and sell directly to the end consumer. Since retail price markups can be in the range of 100 percent, the manufacturer has a strong incentive to sell directly to the public to capture some of this additional profit.

However, particularly in these early days of e-commerce, many manufacturers are reluctant to remove the retail role. Taking sales away from the established retail channel could alienate the retailers, who are currently responsible for almost all of the sales. If retailers decide to drop your product, and consumers are slow to switch to direct purchases, you may lose the market.

Interrelationship with the existing retail distribution channel is a critical factor in any e-commerce strategy. Removing an intermediary can increase your profits and can be used to reduce prices to capture more market share. But is the intermediary a critical component? Will your sales remain if you remove it? Are customers ready to switch to direct purchases? Some firms attempt to do both: keep sales through traditional channels and also provide direct e-commerce sales through a website. But they minimize competition and appease the retailers by charging the suggested retail price on the website. So, consumers can often find the product cheaper at a local store—which is willing to offer a discount on the list price.

In some situations, the reliance on the retail channel leads to strange conclusions. In early 2001, Compaq was producing a popular PDA with a color screen. But Compaq had trouble with production and demand was substantially higher than supply. Consequently, few retailers carried the product. Some of the businesses that were able to obtain the product did not bother to sell it at their local stores. Instead, they auctioned the units individually on eBay for several hundred dollars over the list price. Would Compaq have been better off auctioning the PDAs directly to consumers?

Business to Consumer

When asked about e-commerce, most people think of B2C. We are all consumers, and it is easy to think about purchasing products and services over the Internet. But how is e-commerce different from traditional sales methods? And is it so different that consumers will not use it?

A couple of simple rules dominate marketing. First, consumers prefer instant gratification. Given a choice, with everything else equal, consumers will choose the product at hand over one that will be delivered later. Related to this rule, consumers will often buy items on

Reality Bytes   **Where Do You Want to Buy Jeans?**

In the early 1990s, Levi Strauss (Levi) captured the blue jean market with a new product (501 jeans) and bold advertising. But after peaking in 1996 at $7.1 billion, sales dropped significantly as teenagers switched to other designers. In 1998, leading the jump to e-commerce, Levi opened online stores to sell Levis and Dockers over the Web. One objective was to mix advertising with customer feedback to learn more about what styles the consumers preferred. At the same time, Levi's retail partners were forbidden from selling Levis and Dockers on their websites.

At the end of October 1999, Levis reversed its policies, stating "the cost of running a world class e-commerce business is unaffordable." Instead, Levi's site simply provided basic information on where to find retailers. Two major retailers (Macy's and J.C. Penney) were authorized to sell the jeans on their websites.

Levis was involved in another twist on retail distribution in a European lawsuit in 2001. The company sued Tesco, the large British-based grocery store chain. Tesco found that it could buy genuine Levis jeans from overseas suppliers and sell them in its grocery stores for about half the price traditional retail clothing stores could sell them. In an attempt to protect the traditional retail channel, Levis sued on the grounds that selling jeans in grocery stores "undermines the product experience," as noted by Gwyn Jones, the European advertising director for the jeans. Levis lost in some initial rulings, and it may take years to settle the dispute.

Sources: Adapted from "Levi Strauss to Stop Selling Merchandise on Its Web Sites," *The Wall Street Journal,* October 29, 1999, and A. Galloni, "Levi's Battles Supermarket Chain As It Struggles to Rebuild Brand," *The Wall Street Journal,* April 10, 2001.

impulse—simply because they are available and enticing. Second, consumers will prefer to pay a lower total price. While this rule seems obvious, it can be difficult in practice. Consumers need to know that the products being compared are equal. They need to know what other products or suppliers exist and their prices. And they need to be able to compare total prices (including taxes and transportation). Third, consumers prefer to see and touch many products before they buy them. The real challenge in marketing is analyzing the trade-offs when all conditions are not equal.

Ultimately, B2C e-commerce is relatively complex and needs to be evaluated in three major areas: (1) traditional products, (2) digital products, and (3) new services. Each of these issues has different features and different interactions with consumers and EC.

Products

In many ways, traditional products are the least likely to be successful in e-commerce—at least initially. Consider the four basic items on which people spend most of their income: food, clothing, shelter, and transportation. Distribution is the most critical issue with food. In the 1960s, when people lived closer together in central cities and small towns, neighborhood grocery stores provided basic food items within a short distance of many people. Yet, these stores were inefficient because they could stock only a limited number of common items; and the delivery and inventory costs were high. Ultimately, large grocery chains that used their size to hold down costs, provide a large selection, and negotiate favorable terms with suppliers replaced the local stores. Consumers had to travel farther to these new stores, but they were more than willing to accept the distance to reduce costs. Small local stores were driven out. The two initial leading firms to sell groceries over the Internet were Peapod and Webvan. Customers placed orders on the website, and drivers dropped off the purchases at a scheduled time, usually the next day. Customers paid a delivery charge for the service. Neither company was very successful in terms of profits. The increased costs, delivery time, and lack of ability to touch the items discourages customers.

A second way to look at EC and food is to realize that few families cook their own meals. Takeout from a variety of restaurants and even grocery stores is a popular substitute. Many restaurants—particularly pizza—deliver food on short notice with just a phone call. Would there be a reason to convert the phone system to an Internet connection? A few places do this, but many people still prefer phones. Theoretically, the Internet can provide menus and it is better at handling multiple customers at the same time. Additionally, it could be used to

Reality Bytes — Wal-Mart, Kmart, Target

The giant discounters Wal-Mart, Kmart, and Target were cautious in their approach to e-commerce. In the early days, startups were jumping onto the Internet, claiming squatters' rights, and crowing that the giants of bricks and mortar would never survive. Of course, the predictions were massively optimistic, and most of the startups failed. And the big discounters were still cautious and uncertain in creating websites. But, by 2001, both Wal-Mart and Target appear on the list of the 25 most visited retail sites that is published by Jupiter Media Metrix. While the online sales are trivial compared to the hundreds of billions sold through the stores, the companies are attempting to make the sites profitable. John Fleming, the senior vice president of Walmart.com notes "We need to run this thing like a real business and offer things online that we can actually make money with." Wal-Mart initially believed that it would have to offer the same items online as sold in the stores. But Mr. Fleming observes "If you go into a Wal-Mart store, you'll be blown away by how much they have for sale under $5. Once you put the real costs into shipping that product, there's no money for anybody." So, the low-priced items were removed; along with the apparel, because Wal-Mart had no way to handle it efficiently. Instead, Walmart.com began carrying higher-priced items like laptop computers that are actually difficult to sell in stores. Rather than focus on selling items, Target is focusing on marketing, and uses its website to build stronger ties to consumers. In fact, Target is forming an alliance with Amazon.com to handle order fulfillment and customer service. Gerald L. Storch, vice chairman of the Target Corporation summarizes the strategy: "In the early days of the Internet, people got confused and thought it was all about selling goods online, when it was really about deepening the relationship with the customer. But I like to say the stupid era of the Internet is over now."

Source: Adapted from Bob Tedeschi, "Discount Giants Learn Online Lessons: Film, Yes; Shampoo, No," *The New York Times,* September 26, 2001.

provide feedback to the consumer—in terms of status of the order and when it will be delivered. But most restaurants are small businesses, and they have resisted building the infrastructure to provide these features.

Clothing offers more prospects for e-commerce. Selection is always an issue with local stores. No matter how large the store, it can carry only a small, targeted selection of styles and sizes. And larger selection means greater inventory costs. So, there might be room for an EC firm to sell a wide selection of products across the nation. In fact, several catalog mail-order firms concentrate on these markets. These mail-order companies have also been relatively successful at e-commerce. The one problem is that clothing sizes are not quite standardized. Hence, many shoppers—particularly women—prefer to try on clothing before purchasing it. Some leading sites like Lands' End have implemented electronic virtual models that enable customers to select items and see how they might look. But many people prefer touching the individual garments first. In fact, some manufacturers have sophisticated websites to display products, but direct interested consumers to local merchants instead of trying to complete the sale online.

Finding a home is always a difficult task. A medium-size city might have thousands of homes for sale at one point in time. It is hard to find and compare all of the details. The Internet has helped in some respects. Searching is an important strength of the Internet. Several real estate databases exist online to retrieve house listings based on a variety of items. However, almost no one would buy a house without seeing it in person; so the role of the Internet is limited. At first glance, it would seem that real estate might be a prime opportunity for e-commerce. Real estate commissions are often priced at six percent of the sale price, which can be a high value for expensive houses. So there should be strong incentives for disintermediation—removing the commissioned agent from the middle of the transaction. But buyers often prefer to use agents, and agents control most of the existing online real estate search firms.

Transportation is more interesting because it can be a product (automobile) or a service (airplane or subway ticket). Airlines have done well with direct e-commerce sales. Yes, they have offended the traditional distribution channel (travel agents), but the people who travel the most have been willing to purchase tickets directly to save money and gain control over their choices.

Reality Bytes   International E-Commerce

Looking at traditional business, the fundamentals seem so easy: sell a product and take the money. What you do not see are the thousands of laws, rules, and court cases behind the scenes that establish the framework and rules to make it possible to conduct business. Most of these rules need to be reinterpreted for e-commerce. Most of them need to be rewritten to support international sales. For example, what happens if a German shopper is unsatisfied with a product he purchased online from a U.S. retailer—should he be allowed to sue the U.S. firm in a Munich court? The issue of jurisdiction is a critical question, and this provision was proposed by the European Union. In a similar vein, the music industry wants an international recognition of copyright laws, so that if a company wins a lawsuit against piracy in one country, all nations would accept the judgment of the court. Of course, that provision would enable the large companies to find the "easiest" judge possible and apply the rules everywhere. In 1999, delegations from 53 countries began working on a set of rules to answer these questions. By 2001, most had decided that the questions are too big, with too many opposing views. For the short term, it is likely that only simple rules will arise from the international treaties. But the problems will not disappear. At some point, representatives will have to sit down and work out the details necessary to protect consumers and businesses in an international environment.

Source: Adapted from Paul Hofheinz, "Cross-Border E-Commerce Continues to Raise Concerns," *The Wall Street Journal,* August 16, 2001.

Automobiles are more interesting. Few people are willing to buy new automobiles over the Internet, but websites offering searches for specific used automobiles are popular. Part of the difference is that consumers have greater bargaining power with used automobiles than with new ones, so the increased information on available cars gives them more leverage. If one owner or dealer offers a high price for a specific car, you can quickly find another one. New cars are more challenging because of the strong relationship between the few manufacturers and the dealers.

Most people want to test drive a car before they buy it, so the manufacturers have a strong incentive to keep the dealer network. Many insiders also believe that the salesperson is critical to selling cars by overcoming objections and talking people into buying cars when they hesitate. So, if dealers and showrooms are necessary, what is the value of e-commerce in selling a car? Both General Motors and Ford have experimented with online sales of new cars, with minimal success. Currently, the auto manufacturers prefer to sell through the dealers. A few states actually have laws that prohibit auto manufacturers from selling directly to the public. While the manufacturers want to keep the advantages of the dealers, they also want to find a more efficient method to distribute cars. Manufacturers have talked about an Internet-based build-to-order system, where customers could select options and cars would be made to order. A few larger regional dealers would maintain basic inventory to support test drives. The advantage of this system would be to reduce inventories and enable manufacturers to build only the number of cars that are needed. The main drawback is the difficulty in configuring assembly lines quickly enough to hold costs down.

On the other hand, used cars present a different situation. Buyers have embraced the Internet as a method to locate used cars and compare prices. Sellers find it a useful tool to avoid the high prices of newspaper advertising—particularly since it is inexpensive to place photos on websites.

The point of these examples is that without substantial changes in behavior, people will continue to prefer the traditional sales mechanisms. Particularly since these mechanisms have proven to be relatively efficient—or closely controlled by a group with a strong interest in maintaining the current system.

So, is the world really so bleak that B2C e-commerce is doomed to fail? What about Amazon.com, one of the larger retailers on the Internet? By selling commodities, they avoid the problem of choosing products. The latest best-selling novel is the same regardless of where it is purchased, so consumers do not need to see and touch it before purchasing it. Additionally, Amazon.com can offer a wide selection of titles. It can also make it easier to find books, and does a good job offering related products that might interest the consumer. But, the concept is still hobbled by the distribution problem—it takes time to deliver a book or CD to the customer. So, online vendors like Amazon.com compensate by offering lower base prices than those found at a traditional local store. Consumers then have the choice of paying a higher price to obtain an item immediately, or waiting and paying a slightly lower price through EC. But, can an EC firm make a profit with this model? To date, the answer has been no. Amazon.com, struggling to reduce costs, is slowly adopting many of the features of a traditional local store—minimize inventory by focusing on best sellers. And raise prices to a break-even point.

Internet EC Features

To find successful B2C strategies, you need to look at the features that the Internet provides that are superior to traditional stores. The most important ones are the: (1) search technologies, (2) ability to quickly compare multiple products and vendors, (3) low costs for large amounts of information, (4) ability to reach a wide audience, and (5) ability to tailor responses to individual customers.

The essence of a profitable website for products is to identify items that can benefit most from these features. For example, specialty products can be hard to find. A few firms could reach a national audience using EC and capture most of the market by being easy to find and offering competitive prices.

Another approach is to offer products with many options that require customization. Dell has been successful at selling computers over the Internet by making it easy to configure and compare prices, and by using modern production technologies to hold costs down so the EC solution highlights their prices.

Digital Products

Digital products are a field where e-commerce will eventually dominate. Already, many products are stored in digital format: music, news, books, movies, software, and games. In late 2000, many consumers found how easy it was to distribute digital music over the Internet using MP3 files and Napster—even though it was illegal. Digital content over EC meets two of the main consumer criteria: it is instantly available at any time, and costs should be lower since distribution costs are small. Additionally, digital content is more portable than traditional CDs, DVDs, and books.

The main challenge to digital content revolves around **intellectual property** rights and laws. Digital content can be easy to copy and redistribute—depriving the owners (artists) of any reward. The risk is that free distribution of digital content would remove all incentive for artists and authors to invest time for which they receive nothing.

Several companies (particularly Microsoft and RealNetworks) are working on **digital rights management** systems to prevent unauthorized copying. Microsoft and Adobe both have systems in place for books. Most systems take advantage of the Internet. When a consumer purchases a digital product online, the purchase is recorded in a digital rights management server and issued a unique ID. From this point, the systems vary. Some work by periodically checking the Internet server as the product is used to verify that it is an authorized copy. In some systems, the generated ID can only work on the computer for which it was first created, so giving the file to someone else does not allow it to be played or viewed. Some systems enable users to transfer rights to another person, others do not.

Another challenge with digital products is the payment mechanism. The transaction costs on credit cards and checks are too high to enable low-priced purchases, such as buying one song for a few cents. Until micro-payment systems become accepted, it is difficult for sites to charge for content. Currently, subscriptions are the common solution. One of the more successful sites is *The Wall Street Journal,* which charges an annual subscription fee to several hundred thousand subscribers. And even the *Journal* admits that it has difficulty controlling people from paying for one subscription and sharing it (although that would be in violation of the subscriber agreement.)

One difficulty with any protection system like the digital rights management schemes is that it is difficult to stop someone from breaking the system. Early software vendors in the

1980s learned the lesson that copy protection schemes were routinely defeated and removed. However, the digital millennium copyright act (DCMA) in the United States makes it illegal to break copy protection schemes. As a relatively new law, it remains to be seen whether this condition can be enforced. Also, the law does not apply to people outside the United States. DVD vendors pursued this issue in 2000 and 2001 when a group broke the encryption scheme used to slightly protect DVD movies. The Motion Picture Association of America (MPAA) has sued several companies in the United States for even linking to sites that list the decode algorithm, but the code remains on thousands of sites around the world. A major question exists in terms of whether copy protection schemes can survive.

New Services

Another way to look at e-commerce—particularly m-commerce—is to think about potentially new services that can only exist with the Internet or wireless technologies. For example, GM has been fairly successful with its OnStar system, which is essentially a wireless communication system from cars to a central service site. This new service helps sell cars and it could not exist without current technologies.

Some websites are actually services in disguise. For example, 1800flowers sells flowers, but the company does not grow or ship the flowers. It contracts all of the details to other firms. What the main site really does is keep track of special event days, like birthdays and anniversaries. It basically provides a reminder service and makes it easy to order products corresponding to those dates. Hundreds of other service-oriented sites exist, such as the ability to send greeting cards, share photographs, and file complaints about other companies.

The challenge with consumer-oriented service sites is to make money. The choices are: (1) charge for the service, (2) sell related products, (3) sell advertising space, and (4) sell the service to another company. Many of the failed dot-coms chose option three. When the advertising market crashed, they could not cover their costs and went out of business. Option four is discussed in the B2B section. Selling related products is probably the easiest solution today. In this case, the service is simply another feature that will attract customers to your site. But the additional costs can make it harder to compete on the basis of price, so you have to be certain that customers really do value the service. The ability to charge for services is a significant obstacle to this type of e-commerce. M-commerce offers a greater potential. People are accustomed to paying for usage of their cell phone time. Also, the billing system is in place to handle relatively small transactions (less than a dollar). So, as an example, it might be possible to have a restaurant reservation system on mobile phones. Customers select a range of restaurants—by location or type of food—and your system searches for the most available time slot. The restaurants might fund this service, or perhaps you could charge a fee to customers to move them higher onto a wait list if they are in a hurry.

Price Competition

A primary concern expressed by many firms investigating e-commerce is the issue of price. The Internet makes it easy for people to search vendors and compare prices. This process is particularly easy for products that are the same (such as books, videos, and electronic equipment). Consequently, merchants are concerned that people will only compare sites based on price. Availability of the item will also make a difference. For example, check out the search agent on CNET *(www.cnet.com)* that displays prices and availability for a variety of electronic products.

Why are merchants concerned about price competition? First, the existing retail product chain was originally created so that retail outlets could provide personalized service and product information to customers. Vendors survived and grew based on their ability to provide customized information and support to local areas. Competing purely on price and availability changes the rules and requires a different type of merchant system. Second, if customers look only at price and availability, it is easy for a new firm to enter the market. The new firm simply slashes prices and sells products at a loss to attract customers. Of course, in the long run, the firm will fail—but so will the other firms. We could be good economists and assume that managers and owners are intelligent and will eventually learn to charge a price that does provide a

FIGURE 11.5

Dynamic pricing. The ultimate goal is to set individual prices for each consumer to capture the maximum price each is willing to pay, as opposed to the perfect competition price, where everyone pays the same price, and some customers gain because they were willing to pay more.

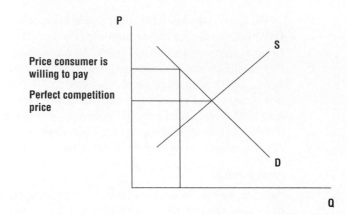

profit. But it might take time for this new economy to evolve. This fear of irrational firms does have an element of truth. Amazon gained its market position primarily by offering substantial discounts on books. In fact, Amazon's finance officer made the remark in 2000 that he was surprised people were criticizing Amazon for not making a profit. He said that Amazon never intended to make a profit on sales. However, after the crash in e-commerce stock prices, Amazon has worked harder to cut costs.

Initially, the largest impact of Internet price competition will be on the retail firms. By minimizing the aspect of location, the primary strength of local firms is eroded. If customers are willing to wait for products to be delivered, then there is no longer a point in having thousands of small local stores. But that "if" is huge. The ultimate economy will depend on consumer preferences between price and the ability to receive a product immediately.

A few e-commerce firms have attempted to use the interactive features of the Internet to set prices dynamically. In an experiment, Amazon.com charged different prices to different customers. It was a relatively standard attempt to statistically evaluate price sensitivity to various products. However, when customers learned that others had obtained the same product for a lower price, they complained. Yet, in traditional stores, customers routinely are charged different prices for the same items—for example, through coupons or negotiation. As shown in Figure 11.5, part of the fear is that the Internet might someday be used to force people to pay the highest amount they are willing to pay, as opposed to perfect competition price.

Business to Business

Business-to-business e-commerce has the potential to be substantially more important than B2C e-commerce. First, businesses tend to buy repeat items in bulk, so they do not need to test drive or touch every product. Second, medium and large businesses already have high-speed connections to the Internet and rely on computer systems in their daily operations. Third, costs are becoming a driving factor, and technology can reduce the transaction costs and the number of errors.

Extended EDI

By simply offering the ability to sell products to other businesses, the Internet can be used for EDI. For materials and components that are purchased on a regular basis, EDI software can connect across the Internet to automatically monitor inventory and send orders to the appropriate company. For less frequent purchases, a buying firm could set up software to scan servers for prices, select the appropriate items, and place orders automatically.

Currently, few systems work this efficiently. Most require a human to collect data and place orders. Websites make it easier to collect data on prices and availability, but every site has different search methods and different purchase screens. EDI software helps by following standards, but the companies involved must install and configure it.

XML is a more flexible method of sharing data with suppliers and customers. Eventually, the technology can be married with expert systems to provide more automated intelligence to handle ordering basic items and to monitor the progress of standard orders.

FIGURE 11.6

Distributed services. Firms can offer digital services over the Internet to other companies, such as document translation or reservation handling. With XML, the process is relatively automatic and can be billed for one-time and limited uses.

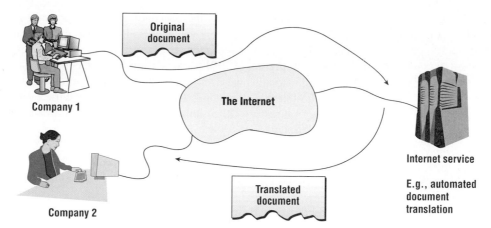

Auctions

From an economic perspective, B2B auctions are one of the most exciting tools created through e-commerce. In the past, companies purchased materials and supplies from a complex set of distributors and wholesalers, driven by in-person sales calls. Within this context, most manufacturers dealt with only one or two suppliers for each part. To hold down transaction costs, it was simpler to establish long-term relationships with a limited number of companies. Of course, it made it harder to ensure that the buyers were getting the best price. Competition helps hold down prices during the initial contract negotiations, but if anything changes in the ensuing year or two, it is difficult to renegotiate the contract. But in exchange, the buyer gains a more stable environment.

Economic theory shows that well-run auctions are the most efficient way to establish an efficient market price. To be well run, the auctions have to open to the widest range of participants, and everyone must have complete information on the items and prices. Several industry-specific auction sites have been established. One of the more successful sites involves the steel industry. Significant amounts of steel are still sold directly to manufacturers on long-term contracts. However, the auction sites make it easier for suppliers to unload specialty and overstocked inventory in a spot market. The auctions also give manufacturers the ability to monitor the spot market and availability of steel products, so that they can quickly pick up additional quantity.

For commodity items, auctions can hold down prices by improving competition and making price and quantity data available to all participants. Auctions are also useful for specialized products, when it is difficult to determine an asking price. Some companies have found that they can obtain higher prices for their products when they sell them at auction. Also, auction prices can change easily, so if there is a short-term jump in demand for your product, you will be able to capture the additional profit. Of course, you might have to accept lower prices the next day.

Distributed Services

XML is also creating opportunities for a new type of B2B e-commerce: websites that provide specific services that can be sold to other businesses. One example would be a website like Altavista *(babel.altavista.com)* that has an automated document translator. Figure 11.6 shows the basic concepts. The key is that the services are automated and simply called from your website. This arrangement is actually more of a peer-to-peer system than a client-server technology. You can create a website that uses services from many different companies. For example, you might create a website that pulls current stock price data from one site, performs some complex financial calculations on a second site, and converts currencies using a third site's exchange rates. All of these activities happen behind the page, so your users see only the final application.

The main advantage to this type of system is that experts can build objects and maintain and run the services on a website available to anyone willing to pay the service fee. In many cases, the service fee could be a small per-usage value. So you could build a composite application that has state-of-the-art features and only pay for the actual usage of these features. The other alternative would be to license these technologies on an annual basis for a higher fee, and run them on your own server, where you continually need to maintain and upgrade the services.

The technologies to support these services are still being developed. XML and the **simple object access protocol (SOAP)** are two important technologies. SOAP is a method of describing and activating services across the Internet. Ultimately, to make it easier to find services on the Internet, companies will want to register with a directory. IBM and Microsoft are pushing a directory called **universal description, discovery, and integration (UDDI).** Details can be found at the *www.uddi.org* website. Registering a service makes it easier for other companies to find the service and connect to it.

Increasing Sales and Reducing Costs

As noted in Chapter 4, from a marketing perspective, the buying process has been defined in three basic steps: (1) prepurchase information-gathering, (2) the purchase itself, and (3) postpurchase support. These steps are listed with examples in Figure 11.7. The Internet can be used to support each of these areas. The level of support in each area depends on the industry, type of product, and capabilities of the customers. Note that the process differs depending on whether the customer is a retail consumer or another company. For example, sales to other companies are generally repetitive and typically require additional documentation and billing procedures.

Initially, basic servers simply presented static pages, with text and limited graphics that rarely changed. Even now, Network Solutions, the division of Verisign that handles site registrations, reports that over 90 percent of existing sites are only in the prepurchase phase. Gradually, more sophisticated services have been introduced that add a higher degree of interactivity. One of the most important features is the ability of the website to connect to the corporate databases.

Prepurchase, Purchase, and Postpurchase Support

In many ways, the purchase issue is a minor component. EC purchases currently offer only minor benefits compared to traditional phone orders. The main benefit to EC lies in providing additional support to customers before and after the sale. In particular, intelligent websites supported by expert systems can help customers select options and products or solve problems. For fixed development costs and relatively low monthly fees, the online systems can provide 24-hour support. Sales can be increased by providing more detailed information, helping customers customize their selections, and using an expert system to build cross-sales. Costs are reduced because the system is automated. Sales and costs can be further improved by providing after-sale support. Expert-system guided support can help customers solve problems faster. Any product design or production problems can be reported directly, giving you the chance to fix the product before it ships to more people.

FIGURE 11.7

Electronic commerce. Websites are commonly used to support the three main phases of marketing.

Prepurchase	Purchase	Postpurchase
Static data sites	Transmission security	Service
Promotion	User identification	Problem tracking
Product specifications	Product selection	Sales leads
Pictures	Payment validation	Resolve problems
Schematics	Order confirmation	Answer questions
Pricing		Product evaluation
FAQs		Modifications
Interactive sites		Tracking customers
Configuration		
Compatibility		
Complex pricing		

Search Engines

Most people have used search engines to find information on the Internet. The searches are not always successful and tend to return a large number of sites unless the keywords are specific and relatively unique. Nonetheless, search engines are an important method for potential customers to find your site.

Search engines use different techniques to find sites and present the results to searchers. Yahoo is relatively unique in that it has humans evaluate the sites and place them into categories. Other engines, like Excite or Lycos, repeatedly track through Web pages following links and recording key words. Some are more selective in categorizing the Web pages. For example, Google concentrates on the text surrounding the links to identify the purpose of a site. All of the search engines have a Web page where you can register your website by entering the Internet address and a description of the purpose of the site. Eventually, your site will be added to the search engine list. Because of the human intervention, Yahoo is a minor exception. You can register with Yahoo, but it takes time for them to evaluate and classify your site. In some cases, they might choose to not list your site.

Some companies offer to register your website with the search engines for a fee. While this process might be convenient, it is rarely necessary. None of the search engines require a fee to register. The good search engines eventually find your site even if you do not register it at all. Some people claim to know tricks to make your page appear at the top of the search engine listings. Do not believe them. Read the website descriptions at the search sites for more useful advice. Basically, make sure your main page contains a precise description of the site's purpose. Include key words that consumers are likely to search for. Be as accurate as possible. Think like a customer and try searching for other sites. Look at the key words you used. Include them on your Web page.

In some cases, there is a way to get your site listed higher up in the search engine results. Many of the sites accept advertising payments to give higher priority to your site. You will have to carefully evaluate the costs and benefits of this approach compared to other advertising strategies.

Traditional Media and Name Recognition

To a consumer, name recognition of a company is an important element of buying products over the Internet. Trust is particularly critical when the consumer is not dealing face-to-face with the merchant. Depending on your target customers, it might be necessary to build this name recognition through advertising in traditional media (television, radio, or newspapers). Some early startups chose the splashy, but expensive, method of buying television spots during the Super Bowl to reach a large audience. If you do use traditional advertising, make sure that your website name is easy to remember and easy to type. Avoid words that are commonly misspelled.

Web Advertisements

Web advertising offers some potential advantages over traditional advertising. Ads can be delivered to specific audiences, and to some extent controlled so that people continually see new ads. An original promise of Web ads was the ability to track the **click-through rate,** or the percentage of people who actually clicked on an ad and came to your site to get additional information. Initial reports placed click-through rates around 2 to 3 percent. By 2001, this rate had dropped below 1 percent. In the early stages of e-commerce, some sites survived on advertising revenue. As people became disappointed with the advertising response, spending for ads declined, and the chain effect helped drive the EC crash.

Advertiser Perspective

Figure 11.8 summarizes the perspective of advertisers—the ones who pay for the ads. They generally want the ads to be seen and to generate click-through responses. There is some argument that click-through rates are not an effective measure of advertising. Possibly the

Reality Bytes   **EC Advertising**

Many early EC firms built sites on the basis of obtaining advertising revenue by selling banner ad space. But consumers quickly learned to tune out the ads. So, marketers got more aggressive—adding flashing objects, animation, pseudo games, and even ads that looked like system error messages. Then the newer browsers began supporting a feature that enables advertisers to open a new window and display larger ads. Anyone who clicks on an ad is brought to the marketer's site. Some people, like John Zuccarini, were overly aggressive. The FTC won a court order blocking his many different sites. He was charged with unfair and misleading business practices. One of his tricks was to register hundreds of variations of popular

names that are misspellings of legitimate sites (such as 41 variations of the name of Britney Spears). Any time someone goes to his site, the browser disables the Back button, making it more difficult for the visitor to leave. Users are also "bombarded with a rapid series of windows displaying ads for goods and service ranging from Internet gambling to pornography." It also hides a window beneath the system toolbar that periodically launches new attacks. FTC estimates indicate that Mr. Zuccarini earned up to $1 million a year in advertising revenue.

Source: Adapted from Mark Wigfield, "FTC Targets Web Practices that Divert, Trap Surfers," *The Wall Street Journal,* October 1, 2001.

FIGURE 11.8

Web advertiser perspective. Advertisers want the biggest target audience possible. They need demographics about the website visitors, and they monitor response rates.

- Want viewers to see the ad
- Want viewers to click through to the main site
- Need to match site demographics to target audience
- Monitor response rates
- Cost

---

effect of an ad is to build an image or a brand name. Consumers might not need to purchase something immediately, but they might remember the ads later and use them to accept the validity of the company.

Audience size and demographics are important to advertisers. In 1999 and 2000, according to the Interactive Advertising Bureau (www.iab.net), about 75 percent of online ad revenue went to the top 10 website publishers.

To facilitate the placement of ads, IAB has standardized several sizes, as described on their website. For example, a full banner ad is 468 pixels wide by 60 high. You can use animated GIFs to provide motion, but many sites limit the total ad size to 10 K bytes. Larger ads tend to slow the site down so much that it is abandoned by viewers.

Website Publisher Perspective

In 2000, according to IAB, Internet advertising spending for the year topped $8 billion. Many website publishers would like to get a share of that income. The first catch is that you need a substantial volume of visitors to get anyone to consider your site. Probably at least 25,000 unique visitors a month, and 1 million would be a more likely minimum—since advertisers prefer larger audiences. Figure 11.9 shows some of the key points from a publisher's perspective.

One of the most difficult issues is obtaining the demographic data. You need some mechanism to identify your Internet users and to obtain some personal data from them. Of course, this data raises many privacy questions. Most sites find that they have to reward customers in some fashion to get them to provide personal demographic data, but it is often amazing how little is required to get customers to respond. Common tactics include random drawings for prizes or free trinkets.

The daily issues of handling the ads, monitoring placements, finding clients, and billing can be time consuming and expensive. Most sites choose a third party to perform these tasks, and DoubleClick is by far the largest such company. Of course, DoubleClick takes a portion of the ad revenue for its services. The third party also simplifies the

FIGURE 11.9

Web publisher perspective. There is money being spent on advertising, but your rates depend on volume and the ability to provide detailed demographic data. The daily tasks of sales and providing the ads are often handled by a third party like DoubleClick.

Income
    Cost per thousand viewings ($1–$50)
    Need volume (25,000 or 1,000,000 per month)
    Need demographics
Tasks
    Ad rotation software
    Tracking and monitoring
    Ad sales staff
    Billing
    Third party: DoubleClick

FIGURE 11.10

Web log analyzer. SurfStats is one tool that analyzes and displays the data captured whenever someone views a page on the server. The graphs make it easy to monitor which pages and files are most requested, when they are viewed, the IP address of the requester, and which site directed the user to your server.

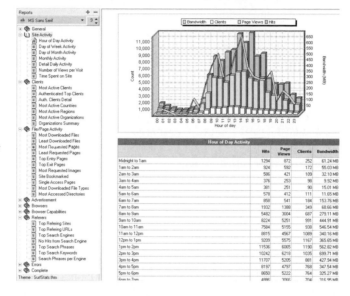

process for advertisers, since it would be difficult for a company to contract with hundreds of sites to place ads. On the other hand, software is now available to Web browsers that automatically block data being sent from third-party sites—intentionally stopping ads from being displayed.

Website Traffic Analysis

Analyzing traffic to your website is an important aspect of marketing. Among other questions, you want to know how many visitors arrive, what times the site is busy, which pages are most requested, and which outside sites commonly direct visitors to your site. All of this data and more is available by analyzing your server's Web logs. Most Web servers automatically maintain a detailed log of every single page request, the time it was requested, the amount of data transferred, and the IP address of the requesting user. These logs are stored as simple text files, but they are hard for people to read. Consequently, several companies, such as the one shown in Figure 11.10, sell software that retrieves the log, analyzes the data, and creates graphs to help managers understand the traffic.

The statistics generated from the Web logs are useful to identify the most popular sections of your server and to spot problems with certain pages. For instance, you might find that a large number of users get halfway through your purchasing process, but few of them complete the actual transaction. Then you need to make your purchasing system faster or easier to use. The logs are also good at identifying which other sites, particularly search engines, direct viewers to your site. You can use this information to target advertising to similar sites.

Privacy

Privacy is the important flip side of advertising. The more serious privacy problems that have arisen were due to issues with advertising. The problem is the trade-off faced by advertisers. Companies want to target ads as closely as possible to people who are likely to care about and purchase the product. Hence, advertisers want to know a considerable amount of information about current customers and viewers of various websites. Yet, collecting this data creates a loss of privacy for the customers.

DoubleClick has instigated one of the broader privacy problems. By routing so many ads through its servers, DoubleClick is able to track the Web pages visited by each of millions of Web browsers. At one point, DoubleClick wanted to sell this information along with demographic data on the individual consumers. Most consumers are not happy when a company tracks the sites they visit without informing them of the process. The basic premise of tracking demographic and customer data is that, by knowing more about the customer, it is easier to provide specific ads and data that might appeal to the customer, and, in essence, fewer "junk" ads the viewer does not want.

E-Commerce Options

In part because of the expense of maintaining a high-speed Internet connection, several companies have been created to provide alternative Web-hosting options. These hosting companies already have high-speed Internet connections, Web servers, databases, and management staff. They provide a variety of leasing options to host your site.

One of the most important decisions to make regarding the Internet is where to locate the Web files. A variety of choices exists, and each method has different advantages, costs, and drawbacks. The choice of Web-hosting method depends on several characteristics of your business. Companies will often start with one option and move to other selections as they expand—particularly small firms or startups.

Ultimately, a major factor in the Web-hosting decision is the degree of integration you want to establish between the website and your existing business applications. Tighter integration generally means that you will have to run the website on your own servers. For example, if you want a retail Web page to display the current inventory level (to indicate if an item is in stock), the Web server will need to access your inventory database. If you can live with a lower level of integration, several options exist for hosting your application on another company's server, sometimes at very low cost.

Simple Static HTML

The most basic website consists of simple HTML pages—text and some images. These pages are generally fast to load, require minimal support from the server, and are relatively easy and inexpensive to host. For example, many Web providers offer free Web space, generally around 5 MB. Most developers try to hold Web pages down to about 50KB per page, including graphics. The goal is to keep download times to an acceptable level even for dial-up users. A typical dial-up connection of 33 kbps will take about 12 seconds to download a 50KB page. That means a free website of 5 MB can hold about 100 pages of text and graphics. These basic websites cannot interact with the viewer. For example, you cannot accept form data or process credit cards. Similarly, the Web pages cannot interact with your internal databases. Generally, a single set of pages is made available to everyone, with little or no customization for individual users.

Although these relatively simple pages are easy to create, it is difficult to change them and keep them up to date. All changes must be made individually, and the developer must keep track of the details.

Consider the steps involved in creating a retail website with **static HTML** pages. You write a page that describes each product, including price and photo. You create a style for the site, adding fonts and colors. You can link the pages, probably using some type of index, or a start page that lists major categories. With free hosting, it is rare to have a personalized search engine, so customers will need an easy method to find the products you are selling.

FIGURE 11.11

Retail website with simple pages. Each product will generally be on a separate page, but each page must be created individually and linked by hand.

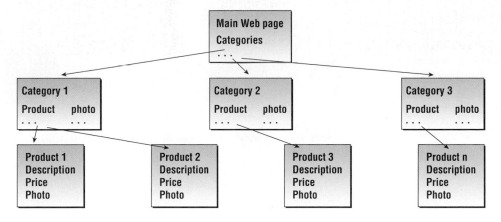

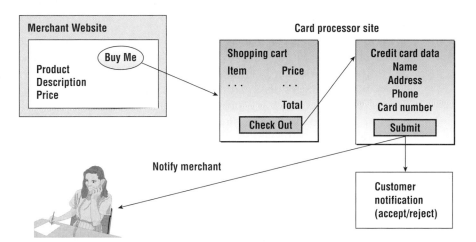

FIGURE 11.12

Order processing with static pages using a third-party processor. Clicking a link brings the customer to the card processor to enter card data and make the purchase.

Figure 11.11 shows the resulting hierarchical structure that you will have to follow. Each product will ultimately be displayed on a separate page. Each of these pages must be created individually, and links created by hand. To change any content, such as prices or descriptions, you must go to the desired page and make the change. This method may work for a small number of products, but as the number of products increases, it will become difficult for the developer to keep content and links up to date, and virtually impossible for users to find anything.

The other challenge with this Web structure is that the static Web server will not collect customer data, and because it cannot process form data, it is challenging to process a sale. One method is to use e-mail, where the customer enters product choices into a message that is e-mailed to your order-processing department.

Current technology offers a more sophisticated method to handle transactions. The EVS Holding Company *(http://www.goemerchant.com/buymebutton.htm)* offers a third-party order-processing system called the Buy-Me Button. As shown in Figure 11.12, any merchant can paste this image onto a Web page and enter the product's description and price. By clicking on the button, the user is directed to a website that creates an electronic shopping cart. When finished shopping, the user can enter a credit card number using secure processing, and the website validates the card and sends the order to the merchant. Because all of the interactive processing occurs on the third-party site, the merchant's site can be run from a set of simple static Web pages. The merchant pays $50 per month for the service.

Overall, the main advantage of this method is the price and simplicity of development. The static page site is often free. However, the merchant will have to pay for the credit-card processing site. The main drawback to this method is the difficulty in updating the data, and the related challenge for the customer in finding specific products. While it is possible to create these sites using a third-party credit-card processor, the method is realistic only if the merchant is selling a small number of products.

FIGURE 11.13
Auctions. Good for unique items where you do not know what price to set. Economic efficiency depends on the number of participants and full information.

Single-Unit Sales

Some companies are interested in selling only a few individual items. If you want to experiment with the Internet, have a few unique items, or need to clear out a couple of items, it usually does not pay to set up a separate website—primarily because it would be hard to attract customers on a part-time basis. Two Internet alternatives exist: online auctions and Web services that specialize in single-unit sales.

The two methods are similar in their ability to attract customers. The most obvious difference lies in setting the price. At the auction sites, you sell to the highest bidder, although you can specify a minimum acceptable (reserve price).

Auctions

EBay.com is the best-known general **auction** site. The system operates similarly to newspaper classified-advertising, but interactively enables potential buyers to bid on items. As highlighted in Figure 11.13, anyone can buy or sell products. The website lists the products and tracks the bids. At the end of the bidding period, the seller contacts the high bid and arranges shipment and payment.

One of the major difficulties with individual sales is authentication and ensuring that the transaction is handled properly. The buyer runs the risk that the seller is dishonest. If the seller ships the item before receiving payment, the buyer may never pay up. Most sellers are unwilling to accept this risk, so they generally require the seller to send payment before the item is shipped. However, the buyer runs the risk of fraud. In 2000, eBay recognized the importance of this problem, and added the ability for sellers to accept credit cards from any buyer (called Billpoint).

Several layers of pricing exist at auction sites. Generally, the seller must pay a fee to list the item, and a second fee once it sells. If the item does not sell, the seller pays the first fee. The fee amounts depend on the value of the item being sold and on the options you choose. Read the fee schedules closely. For an average, figure $1 to list an item, and about 3.5 percent of the value when it is sold. If you choose the credit-card billing option, the seller will generally pay another 3.5 percent of the selling price.

Several auction sites exist on the Internet. Some are general, others specialize in their choice of products. A special site even exists to list the auction sites *(http://www.internetauctionlist. com)*. For a small retailer, probably the most important feature in choosing an auction site is the number of potential consumers who use the site that will be interested in your product. Perform a wide Web search to identify potential auction sites. Not many of the sites keep demographic profiles of the buyers; so you will have to examine the existing sales carefully. Find some items similar to those that you want to sell and monitor the progress of the auctions.

Amazon.com zShops

Amazon.com was one of the early e-commerce sites to enable small merchants to start Internet sales. As shown in Figure 11.14, the system (**zShops**) enables merchants to sell items by setting a fixed price. Listing items for sale is similar to the auction process. The seller pays a

FIGURE 11.14

Amazon.com zShops. Vendors list individual items. Consumers see zShops as the store and search for a product. Amazon.com can process the credit card-based purchase, and the vendor ships the product to the consumer. Vendors pay fees for listing items, selling them, and using the credit card processing.

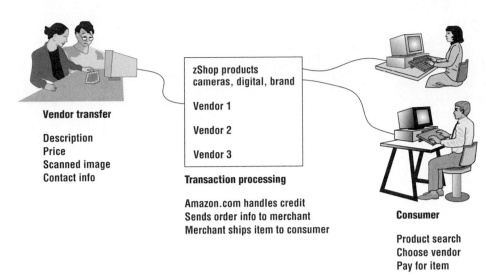

Vendor transfer

Description
Price
Scanned image
Contact info

zShop products
cameras, digital, brand

Vendor 1

Vendor 2

Vendor 3

Transaction processing

Amazon.com handles credit
Sends order info to merchant
Merchant ships item to consumer

Consumer

Product search
Choose vendor
Pay for item

fee for listing the item, and a fee based on the selling price when the item is sold. Amazon.com also offers to process credit cards, for approximately a 2.5 percent transaction fee. The basic listing fee at zShops is $0.10 per item, and the selling fee is about 2.5 percent of the value. Amazon.com offers a discount on listing fees for merchants who want to list up to 3,000 items: a flat rate of $10 per month. The company provides a bulk loading program to transfer all of the product descriptions and prices.

Auction versus zShops

If you wish to sell a small number of items, then auctions or the zShops are a good option. The transaction and shipping costs tend to rule out low-priced items. On the other hand, buyers are somewhat leery of high-priced items from unknown sellers. For example, most people might consider buying a rare coin from a dealer but would be more reluctant to deal with an unknown independent seller.

If you have a small number of intermediate-priced items to sell, should you choose an auction site or zShops? Auctions are particularly useful for unique items, or items where you are uncertain of the value. The zShops system has a good search engine and works well for small retailers who wish to maintain a continued presence on the Web. Auctions present a slight uncertainty in the final price. However, economic theory observes that an auction that is based on free information, and attracts all the relevant participants, will result in the highest price. One computer manufacturer that traditionally sold only through distributor channels tested this theory in 1999 by offering a limited number of machines at an auction site. All of them sold for higher prices than could have been obtained through traditional outlets. Keep in mind that if you have several products, you can always try multiple outlets and test the response.

Web Malls and ASPs

Does a traditional retail store have to construct its own building? No. Retail businesses often find benefits in locating in malls. The mall owner handles most physical details, and generally receives a portion of the retail store's revenue in exchange. Yet, the true reason for physical malls is to collect enough stores in one location to attract a mass of consumers. Since physical location of a website is irrelevant, do the same principles of malls apply to the Internet?

The Internet enables two types of retail mall perspectives: (1) virtual malls or directories that simply point consumers to a variety of businesses, whose sites could exist anywhere on the Internet; and (2) websites hosted on a shared set of servers, where the sites might have no other association.

FIGURE 11.15

Virtual malls. Essentially a marketing agreement, the mall is a directory listing of shopping sites. The merchant is responsible for providing the actual website and for processing all transactions.

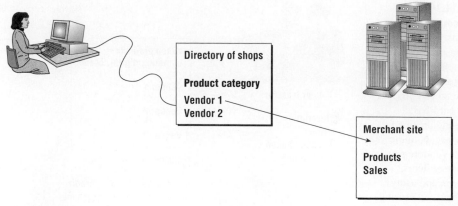

FIGURE 11.16

Web commerce servers. The Web hosting company provides the servers, Internet connection, and commerce software that processes transactions. The merchant loads the database with product descriptions, images, and prices. The commerce software provides a typical retail experience.

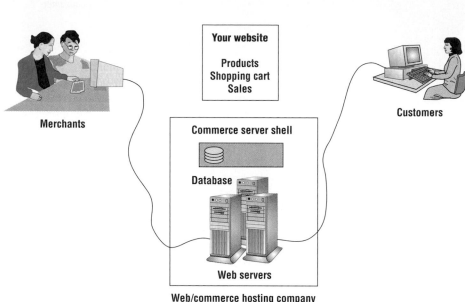

Virtual Malls or Marketing Agreements

Several organizations provide a virtual mall. A **virtual mall** becomes a pure marketing concept and decision. For example, the main portal websites like MSN.com and AOL.com provide a "shopping" section. As shown in Figure 11.15, these sections are directories to online merchants. In most cases, the merchants pay the portal site to get listed; or they pay for higher-priority listings. Sometimes, with large merchants, the payment is in the form of reciprocal advertising arrangements. The main point is that the virtual mall simply provides links to the merchant sites. The merchant site must be located on a different server.

Do companies gain by being associated with other stores? If so, then a Web business should consider associating with several virtual malls. Because a virtual mall is a Web link, the only costs are the advertising fees paid to the mall site owner. The decision reduces to a traditional marketing trade-off between increased customers (and sales) versus increased costs paid to the mall.

Web Commerce Servers

Many companies provide a more complete Web mall service, where they host your website, providing individual storefronts for each merchant, displaying products, and handling the transactions. Shown in Figure 11.16, these sites run a software application designed to automate all of these tasks. The capabilities of the site depend on the features available in the software. As a vendor, you should examine the features of different site products to see which ones you need. Common software systems are available from Microsoft, Netscape, IBM, Intershop, and OpenMarket.

FIGURE 11.17

Application service provider. The Web server runs an application that holds data for other businesses. The data may be exclusive to one business (e.g., accounting); it may be used to interact with other businesses (e.g., supplier auction site); or businesses may interact with consumers (e.g., real estate).

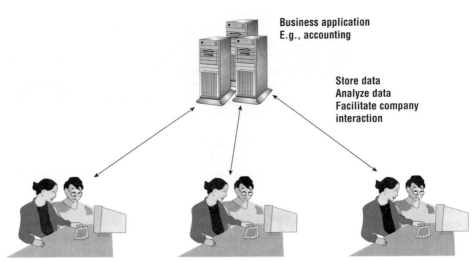

Business application
E.g., accounting

Store data
Analyze data
Facilitate company
interaction

Businesses that lease the use of the application

The Web hosting company provides a server, a connection to the Internet, an account for the hosting software, and credit-card processing. The Web **commerce server** hosting software provides displays of your products, the ability to customize your store's displays, a search engine for your products, and the ability to process transactions securely. Some of the hosting software packages offer detailed customization options, others are more restrictive; but all of them provide the basic elements you need to create and run a retail website. The Web hosting company generally charges the retailer a setup fee, a fixed monthly fee, and a transaction fee—particularly for processing credit cards. The fees are highly variable and each company bases them on different parameters (such as number of products versus number of transactions). Minimal fees for a site that processes credit card transactions is around $150 per month, plus about 5 percent of the transaction as a credit card fee.

A Web mall is different from the Amazon.com zShops model in several respects. The focus in zShops is on the individual items. There is minimal opportunity to create the image of an individual store. In this case, zShops is the store and thousands of merchants provide the products. With a Web mall, a business can establish a specific identity online and provide a collection of related products. In particular, you have the ability to obtain your own domain name. Customers can find your site directly as www.yourname.com, assuming that no one else is using yourname.com yet. Essentially, the Web mall approach makes it relatively easy for you to create a website that is independent and provides the basic functionality needed to sell products or services.

Application Service Providers

An **application service provider (ASP)** is a Web-based business that provides a specific service to other businesses. The service is very specific, and might or might not involve interactions with customers. For example, as shown in Figure 11.17, one company provides online accounting services for small businesses. For a monthly fee, you can enter all of your transaction data and generate standard reports. Other ASPs act as intermediaries in providing services. For instance, a few major companies provide Web-based real estate listing services. Other companies provide online reservations services for service businesses.

If you can find an ASP that provides the services you need, it will generally be easier and cheaper to use the services of the ASP than to create your own website. Competition should eventually give you greater choices in price and quality. Even if an ASP does not exist for the service you wish to provide, it might be possible to convince a firm to adapt their products or create a new service.

purchased. Since consumers are generally slow to volunteer payments, the states require businesses to collect the taxes and forward them to the appropriate agencies. This situation causes problems when the business is located in a different state. At various times, states have attempted to require out-of-state firms to collect the taxes, but the U.S. Supreme Court has always ruled that the U.S. Constitution clearly forbids the states from taxing interstate commerce. The fact that it is a constitutional issue is important, because it would require a constitutional amendment to change the situation. Congress has discussed creating a simpler tax system, but it is unlikely that it will pass as a constitutional amendment.

Local merchants often complain about the difficulty of competing with out-of-state firms that do not have to collect taxes. However, these same firms could sell into other states, so the issue could be neutral. Also, consumers who want to touch the product and bring it home immediately are still going to buy from local merchants. More important, state and local governments are concerned about losing their tax base. If consumers shift more of their purchases to e-commerce, the states will lose substantial revenue. For instance, consider the fact that Dell is one of the leading retailers of personal computers—relatively expensive items. Yet Dell has a physical presence in only a few states, so they do not collect taxes for most of the sales. This multibillion dollar industry represents hundreds of millions of dollars of annual tax revenue to the states. Ultimately, states will have to increase other taxes to compensate for this lost revenue. Since most economists consider an income tax to be more progressive than sales taxes, the effect is not all bad.

Global Economy

E-commerce has the potential to open up the global economy. Theoretically, anyone with access to the Internet can purchase products directly from anywhere in the world. However, actual practice cannot live up to the expectations of theory. Three major issues still limit international trade: (1) transportation costs, (2) national policies, and (3) payment and trust limitations.

Transportation costs will always exist, but they can be relatively high for individual orders. International bulk shipments are considerably more economical, so there will always be an incentive for retailers to purchase in bulk and resell individual items. Transportation companies consolidate shipments to reduce costs, but customers often want products relatively quickly, and shipping by air is more expensive than shipping by sea.

Nations have many different policies and taxes regarding imports and exports. Most shipments have to go through a customs agent. Even digital products carry restrictions. A few nations attempt to monitor and control all Internet usage—to the point of insisting that all Internet traffic be channeled through government computers. An interesting case arose in 2001, when France filed suit against Yahoo (a U.S. company) to force Yahoo to prevent French citizens from buying or selling Nazi-related items. By French law, French citizens are not allowed to buy and sell Nazi items. The Yahoo auction site would enable the French to circumvent the law, so a French court ordered Yahoo to block the French from any transactions. Keep in mind that it would be virtually impossible for Yahoo to identify which items are Nazi-related, particularly if sellers do not use the word Nazi in their descriptions. It would also be difficult for Yahoo to continually monitor each bidder on every auction to see if the bidder is French. Consequently, Yahoo eventually banned all sales of Nazi-related items on its auction sites. The point of this case is that Yahoo had no physical presence in France, and it is unlikely that the French court had the jurisdiction to order Yahoo to stop the sales. Yahoo most likely complied because the company might someday want to establish a presence in France, at which time the judgment could become an issue.

But think about the consequences if every nation imposed its will on Internet sales. While individual nations do have the right to control sales within their territory, it would destroy e-commerce if every nation imposed its control on all Internet sales. As e-commerce increases in importance, more of these issues are going to arise, and firms will need to have technology ready to handle them.

Reality Bytes   E-Commerce Sales

A 2001 study of pure-play Internet retailers revealed 123 firms that had raised at least $10 million. Of those, 43 had gone public and 80 remained private. Among the private firms, 35 (44 percent) had died; and 7 (16 percent) of the public firms had gone out of business. Several of the public firms (including Webvan) failed shortly after the study. Of the public companies still alive at the time of the study, 18 had stock valuations less than $500 million. At the same time the startup firms were failing, online sales were actually increasing by 66 percent in 2000 and an estimated 46 percent in 2001 to a total of $65 billion. Of course, most of this increase in sales was being captured by traditional firms. Yet, individuals and small businesses generate $8 billion in sales on eBay alone. Some specialty firms survive by selling low-volume high-priced items. A few have partnered with traditional firms, leveraging the technology and brand name they created into sales that are filled by traditional retailers.

Source: Adapted from Miguel Helft, "The E-Commerce Survivors," *The Industry Standard,* July 16, 2001.

Analysis of Dot-Com Failures

From about 1996 to 2000, hundreds of dot-com firms were created, many in the San Francisco area. The excitement of the Internet led people to believe that these firms were the start of a new economy. Overhyped statements were made about the death of the old economy, and that traditional bricks-and-mortar firms would soon fail, to be replaced by an online world of competitive prices and advertisements tailored to individual customers. Entrepreneurs believed that if they could be the first firm to break into a category, and if they advertised heavily enough, they would automatically become the dominant player in the new economy. Many investors felt it was important to get in on the ground floor of these firms. IPOs were released daily, stock prices soared. Newly minted paper billionaires graced the covers of business magazines. And then investors woke up and the market crashed. The NASDAQ market index that covered many of these technology firms dropped from over 5000 points to around 2000 in less than a year. Pundits whipsawed to the other end of the spectrum and proclaimed the end of e-commerce. Of course, reality lies between the two endpoints, but it is worth examining some of the concepts of the time to understand the role of e-commerce in the future.

Pure Internet Plays

One of the first types of firms to fail followed a strategy known as **pure Internet plays,** where the e-commerce firm relies entirely on Internet transactions for money—with no ties to real products. Examples include sites that provide services to other sites, such as the search engines and Web advertising sites. Closely related sites include some that advertised and sold products over the Internet, but relied on other traditional companies to produce and deliver the products to customers.

These firms were at risk because they depended almost completely on Internet traffic and funds. When a few of the firms failed, it set off a domino effect that reduced cash flow at many other firms. Many of the firms were interlocked with the others through service agreements and advertising relationships.

Profit Margins

Profit is an important issue for any firm. Yet, many managers claimed that there was no need for traditional profits. This belief was endorsed by a market where IPOs were celebrated and stock prices on new firms jumped over $100 per share in the first day. These IPOs provided the cash that firms used to fund operations. In many cases, the goal of the firm was to advertise heavily and undercut prices in an attempt to build name recognition and capture market share. Even Amazon.com, one of the early entrants and cheerleader for e-commerce, gained its prominence by offering products at 30, 40, and 50 percent discounts.

One of the challenges to measuring profits is that many different definitions of profit can be used, largely depending on which costs are included. But it is difficult to make a profit when products are sold for less than the cost of the item. It can be done, if additional revenue is received from other sources, such as advertising revenue, service contracts, or additional vendor payments. But, in the end, a firm must make a profit on operations or there is no point to continuing. In 2000, a McKinsey study revealed that only 20 percent of the e-commerce firms were making a profit on sales, and the top firms were actually traditional firms, such as mail-order companies.

Many of the early e-commerce firms attempted to establish market dominance through heavy advertising and large discounts. The plan was to use the name recognition to attract customers away from traditional firms, and eventually increase prices to make a profit. The problem was that these firms still had to compete with traditional firms that already face considerable competition. In this crucible, the existing firms learned to squeeze costs. These efficiencies enable them to sell products at a profit and to fend off competitors during short-term attacks.

Advertising Revenue

Internet advertising revenue was a dominant factor in the failure of many of the early e-commerce firms. For some, the Internet appeared to be a new educational medium—much like television. Websites would provide interesting or useful content that would attract viewers (often referred to as eyeballs). These sites would then sell screen space to other companies to use as advertising. The interactive nature of the Internet would also make it possible to track the effectiveness of the ads—both in terms of the number of times an ad was seen and in terms of the click-through rate for each ad.

This model does apply to some extent—the Interactive Advertising Board reported that U.S. Internet advertising revenue was $8.2 billion in 2000. However, only a handful of the top firms receive the lion's share of the revenue. Additionally, as click-through rates fell in 2000, advertisers began to believe that browsers no longer paid attention to the ads, so they began to question the value of advertising on the Internet, and became particularly leery of smaller sites.

The situation was compounded by the fact that many of the firms followed some shaky accounting practices. For instance, advertising exchange agreements were often counted as revenue. Firm A would agree to carry advertisements for firm B in exchange for similar ads on B's site. Both sites recorded revenue from the advertisements—but never received any cash.

With the declining emphasis on advertising revenue, content providers are increasing their attempts to charge consumers for the content. According to a study by Jupiter Media Metrix, one of the leading e-commerce monitoring firms, in 1999 the top 100 firms were charging for only 6 percent of their content. In 2000, that number almost doubled to 11 percent. Almost all of these firms anticipate charging for some content by 2003. Some of the content is paid with service agreements, some through micro-payments for individual pieces of data.

Entrepreneurship

Entrepreneurship is the act of building and running a business. The term is generally applied to new businesses, but it is becoming common for large businesses to encourage entrepreneurship within the main organization. For instance, a manager who comes up with an idea for a product might seek support to run a new project within the larger company.

Entrepreneurship is built on three broad fundamentals: (1) an idea, (2) a business plan, and (3) implementation. Risk is a fourth important element. You should not consider becoming an entrepreneur unless you are willing to accept a high risk of loss—loss of time and loss of money. However, having a good idea, building a solid business plan, and managing the implementation carefully can reduce risk.

Flexibility is another important characteristic of successful entrepreneurs. The problem with having a new idea is that it is difficult to forecast exactly how it will be received by customers. Hence, many ideas and plans began in one direction, and only succeeded when the managers used the information to change directions and find a more profitable solution. Along the same lines, a thousand unforeseen obstacles can leap into the path of any good plan; flexibility and perseverance are important to circumventing these problems.

Idea

Ideas are the foundation of entrepreneurship. There is little point in starting a business or project just to copy someone else. The idea could be a new product or service, or it could be a better method of production, or a better marketing or financial system.

Ideas are closely tied to strategy. As a startup firm, yours will be small and must have a clear focus. Are you trying to be the least-cost producer to attract customers from older firms? Or are you planning to offer radically new products and services that offer greater benefits than the competition? A successful strategy will depend on a careful analysis of the industry and your role within it.

Strategy

Chapter 10 discusses the details of strategic analysis. The key as an entrepreneur is to examine the many aspects of strategy to find and clarify an idea. For entrepreneurs, three key strategic issues are: (1) an understanding of where you will stand on the production chain, (2) identification of the competition and substitute products, and (3) barriers to entry.

As a new firm, yours will most likely be one of the smallest. Even if you start an entirely new concept or industry, you will be dealing with an entrenched base of suppliers and customers. As a newcomer, your business clout will be small, so you will not be able to count on discounts or goodwill from your suppliers.

Figure 11.3 showed the production chain that is described in Chapter 10. When you are looking for ideas, you should examine the production chain for various industries. Get information on the leading firms in each step of the chain. Determine the concentration ratios. Do four firms control 50 percent of the market at a given level, or are there many small firms with no dominant player? Look at the final price and profit of the product or service, then trace backwards and identify the various costs and profits at each level. Then combine your analyses. For example, if there is a reasonable profit at the consumer level, it might appear to be a good opportunity. But if only a few dominant firms supply the product, then these firms might be thinking about expanding into consumer sales—or they might make it difficult for you to create a new retail firm.

Even if you have an idea that creates an entirely new industry, your firm will face competition. You must carefully identify your closest competitors and also specify any potential substitute products. You can also use this analysis to generate new ideas. As a consumer, look at the products and services you buy and identify the main competitors and the potential substitutes. E-commerce specifically looks at the steps that consumers must go through to purchase an item. Can these steps be simplified? Can additional services or products be offered at the same time using information technology?

When searching for ideas, expand your focus to include different aspects of the problem. For instance, perhaps you can create an expert system to help customers select features of a product. You might think about creating a retail store or a website to sell that product. But, perhaps a few large firms dominate the retail side, or it requires expensive advertising to enter the market. In this situation, as shown in Figure 11.20, it might be more profitable to build your system and sell or lease it to the existing retail firms. Or you could create a service website that other sites can connect to and pay a fee for each use of your system.

FIGURE 11.20

Expand your focus. When searching for ideas, it might be better to partner with a large firm instead of competing head-on.

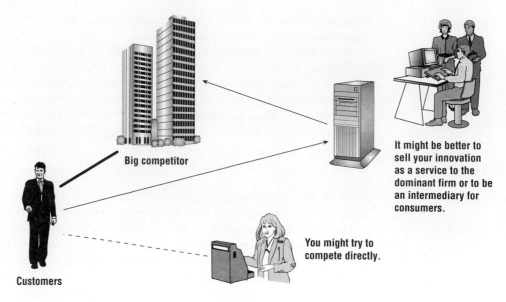

Big competitor

Customers

It might be better to sell your innovation as a service to the dominant firm or to be an intermediary for consumers.

You might try to compete directly.

FIGURE 11.21

Barriers to entry. If you cannot prevent others from entering your industry, prices will fall and your profits will suffer. Also, larger firms could enter and take over the market.

Economies of scale and scope
Capital requirements
Product differentiation (and patents)
Cost disadvantages (independent of size)
Distribution channel control
Relationships with customers
Relationships with suppliers
Government policy

When evaluating ideas, you must always consider the issue of barriers to entry. If you do have a great idea, and your company makes a profit, how are you going to keep rivals from entering your industry and taking away your customers? If you create a new business process or new software, what will stop others from emulating your system? Figure 11.21 lists some of the typical areas firms consider to create barriers to entry. As a new, small firm, the economies of scale, capital requirements, and control over distribution are not likely to apply to you, except negatively. Also, remember that there is a fine line between creating barriers to entry and violating antitrust laws. As explained in Chapter 10, technology can often help create these barriers legally.

In the United States it is still possible to obtain patents on business processes. These patents were popular in the early days of the dot-com expansion, but the patent office began to take a closer look and deny some obvious ideas. If you have a truly new process, you might be able to patent the concept—preventing anyone else from copying it for 20 years. Of course, a single patent can cost $10,000 to $30,000 or more to obtain.

Research

Research is closely tied to idea generation. As you evaluate alternatives, you need to obtain current data on several items. Figure 11.22 summarizes some of the basic data that you will need.

Broad industry information can be obtained from various government websites or publications. More specific data can be obtained from the companies themselves, if they are publicly traded. Sales data and more detailed comments on rivals can often be purchased from marketing companies. A few companies monitor website traffic, so you can obtain basic on-line activity data for some of the larger firms. Customer focus interviews are important. At some point, you need real world feedback on your ideas.

Production costs and other hints can be obtained from suppliers and salespeople. If you are serious about developing a presence in a particular area, scour the trade journals and

FIGURE 11.22

Business research. You
need to collect data on
competitors, the size of
the market and how it is
growing, production costs,
and the legal environment.

- **Competition**
  - **Number**
  - **Concentration ratios**
  - **Sales by firm**
  - **Technology plans**

- **Size of the market**
  - **Number of customers**
  - **Amount of revenue**
  - **Growth rate**
  - **Market comparison for substitute products**
  - **Consumer focus group interviews**

- **Production costs**
  - **Startup/fixed costs**
  - **Operating costs**

- **Legal environment**

find some of the leading suppliers. Call the regional sales representatives and they will provide detailed information on items that you will need. But be sure to compare prices from several firms.

Even for retail firms, several legal hurdles must be cleared. Some industries have more complications than others, so you need to carefully investigate all laws and rules that might apply to your business. Find out if there are restrictions on what you will be allowed to do. In terms of permits, identify the permits you need to obtain, exactly where to get them, how often they need to be renewed, the cost of the permits, and the time frames between application, inspection, and approval.

Plan

Once you have identified a reasonable idea and done the basic research so that you understand the industry, you need to write a business plan. The purpose of the plan is to create a roadmap that will help you set up, manage, and evaluate your progress. It is also critical to obtaining external financing. In 2000, the heyday of Web startups, there were stories of entrepreneurs obtaining financing on the basis of a short PowerPoint slide show. Those days are gone. A detailed business plan will convince prospective investors that you are serious and that you know what you are doing. It will also help them evaluate the true potential of your ideas.

You can purchase software that will help you organize the business plan, but you must still collect the data and write the descriptive sections. You must also be careful when using some software templates. When potential investors see plans that are simple fill-in-the-blank templates with little additional content, they do not believe you spent much time on the plan.

As shown in Figure 11.23, the goal of the plan is to precisely describe the business you wish to start (or expand), the market environment, and your strategy. You must also include financial analyses using forecasted sales and costs. You should also include a timetable that indicates how the company will need to grow. Based on these projections, you will be able to determine the amount of money you need to raise to run the company over the next three to five years. In terms of presentation, you must also include an executive summary that is a one-page review of the major points.

Strategy, Competition, and Market Analysis

The strategy section is based on your research of the market. It contains several subsections that describe exactly what products or services you will produce. It should identify the major competitors and estimate the size of the market and how it will change over time.

If you are creating or distributing products, you need to identify your suppliers, including backup suppliers if something happens to your primary source. For products, it is also

FIGURE 11.23

Business plan. A business plans helps you organize your ideas, provides a roadmap and schedule, and provides financial targets to use as benchmarks as you move forward. It is also critical for obtaining investment funding.

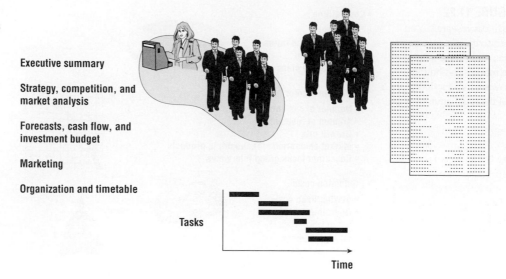

Executive summary

Strategy, competition, and market analysis

Forecasts, cash flow, and investment budget

Marketing

Organization and timetable

Tasks

Time

critical that you describe your distribution network. Will you distribute through standard retail stores? Ship products by UPS? If there are multiple layers, it is particularly critical that you identify how you will track shipments and sales through the process.

Forecasts, Cash Flow, and Investment Budget

The financial section is a primary component of the business plan. For a startup firm, it can also be one of the most difficult to create. This section includes estimates of sales and costs. You will have a separate section for startup costs and ongoing costs—this section is relatively straightforward, but you have to contact several suppliers and contractors to get good estimates of the costs.

The more challenging aspect of the financial section is the need to forecast sales by month for at least three years, and annual sales for five years. Figure 11.24 shows that the sales forecast is the foundation for the other financial data. The level of sales directly determines the revenue, the marketing costs, and the cost of goods sold. Once you know the sales level, you can determine the scale of the infrastructure needed to support those sales. For instance, the size of the Web server and Internet connection speeds in an e-commerce world, or size of distribution facilities in a traditional retail environment. The size of the firm also determines the number of employees needed, which identifies the cost of salaries. Salaries can be a significant component of some firms. Note that for e-commerce firms, you might require a larger number of contract employees to develop software in the beginning. Once the system is operational, you may be able to run with a smaller core group of employees. These costs should be recorded in a separate startup cost statement.

With sales, cost of goods sold, infrastructure costs (leases and so on), and salaries, you have estimated the primary costs and can create projected financial statements. You need to estimate a growth factor for each month or year. This growth factor is one of the most subjective elements in the projection. However, you should try to estimate growth rates of similar firms and keep your numbers in a reasonable range. Also, higher growth rates will mean that you need greater marketing expenses to obtain that increase in sales.

With the basic financial statements estimated, you can concentrate on cash flows. When will money arrive? Will there be delays in payments? Many of your costs occur up front or on a monthly basis, so calculate these and estimate the firm's cash position for each month. You will need a source of funds to cover times when the cash flow is negative. You should do the same for profit, so that you have an estimate of when the firm will become profitable.

Of course, you still face the problem of estimating the level of sales, which can be next to impossible for new products or services. If there is no way to generate a plausible sales forecast, it might be better to start with an estimate of the infrastructure size. From there it is generally easy to estimate the fixed costs. Now, examine various levels of sales to pick up revenue, cost of goods

FIGURE 11.24

Estimating financial statements. The estimate of sales determines the size of the infrastructure and the marketing and purchasing costs. The number of employees needed can be determined from the size of the firm and provides the estimate for salaries. With these major points, the financial statements can be projected to identify the cash flow and the amount of investment money needed.

FIGURE 11.25

Break-even analysis. If it is too hard to forecast sales, you can choose an infrastructure size and estimate fixed costs. Then estimate variable costs and revenue per unit sold. Compute total cost and total revenue for varying levels of sales. Look for the break-even point. That is the minimum level of sales you must be able to reach to be profitable.

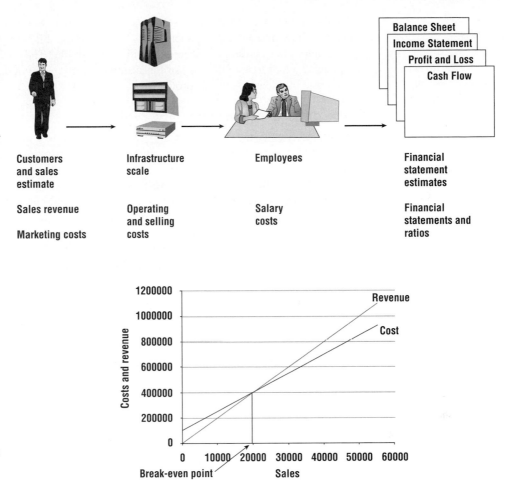

Customers and sales estimate — Sales revenue — Marketing costs

Infrastructure scale — Operating and selling costs

Employees — Salary costs

Financial statement estimates — Financial statements and ratios

Balance Sheet
Income Statement
Profit and Loss
Cash Flow

sold, and marketing costs. As shown in Figure 11.25, you can now compute total cost and revenue for varying levels of sales. The point where the two are equal (where the lines cross) is the break-even point. You must reach this level of sales before you can make a profit. Now, compare that sales number to similar firms. If the sales number is too high, it is unlikely that your venture will be profitable. Conversely, if it is substantially lower than for other firms, you are probably overestimating the price you can charge, or you are missing some costs. If the lines never cross—you have a major problem: the firm will never be profitable based on your estimates.

Marketing

As part of the business plan, you will have to create a marketing plan. The marketing plan will begin with the anticipated sales level. Then it will identify the target customers with as much demographic detail as you can obtain. Income level is critical. Regional location could be important for some businesses. It is also desirable to find out what magazines, newspapers, television shows, and radio programs the consumers prefer. If you are selling to other businesses, you should identify trade groups that are likely to represent the target businesses.

The marketing plan should contain an analysis of pricing. At a minimum, you should survey consumers, or create a focus group, and find out how much the potential customers are willing to pay for your product or service. You should also identify points for quantity discounts, particularly if you are selling to other businesses.

You then need to create an advertising plan. You need to find prices and viewer demographic data for newspapers, magazines, radio, television, and websites. You might also consider alternatives such as direct mail, billboards, and tie-ins with other products. For local promotions, you can contact advertising managers directly. For nationwide campaigns, you will want to hire an advertising design and placement firm. While it increases your costs, the experience and contacts of the firm will save you time and help focus your campaign.

You will also need to create a sales management plan where you focus on the internal structure of the marketing department. How many salespeople will you need? How will they be paid and what additional incentives will you provide? How will you handle customer complaints? What tools will you use for customer relationship management? How will you identify and build cross-sales of products?

Organization and Timetable

You need to specify the organizational structure and create a project timetable to provide a roadmap and benchmarks so that you can evaluate your progress. For the management, you need to identify who will fill each of the primary roles. If you are using the plan to raise money, you need to include a brief biography of each person. If there will be more than a handful of employees, you need to draw an organizational chart. You also need to indicate how the structure will change as the firm grows.

For complex startups, a project management timetable can be invaluable. The thousands of management tasks from government filings, construction, purchases, writing programs, hiring people, managing advertising, and dealing with suppliers can quickly bury you in details. You need a timetable to record when tasks should be started and which tasks depend on others, and to track which tasks have not been completed. A project management package is a useful tool to handle all of these details. It can also track assignments by employees and has tools to help you identify bottlenecks and times when you might need to hire additional people.

The timetable should also be integrated with the financial forecasts so that as the company moves forward, you can evaluate your progress. If you do not reach a certain sales level at the forecasted time, you can adjust your future growth rates and recalculate the amount of investment money you will need in the future.

Implementation

Ideas and planning are only the beginning of creating a business. The real work begins with implementation. Once the plans are in place and you know how much it is going to cost to get started, you need to form the legal company and obtain financing. You probably need to hire an initial staff, and you need to create an accounting system to record all transactions and monitor your progress.

Starting a firm requires a considerable amount of paperwork. Some of the basic steps are shown in Figure 11.26. Some types of firms require dozens of licenses, and if you need to construct or remodel facilities, you will need additional permits. One of the first decisions you must make is to choose a state in which to incorporate. Each state has different rules, procedures, and fees. Delaware is a popular choice because of the way its laws are written. But small businesses may find it easier to file with the state in which they are located. Then the company can be its own registered agent, and can avoid paying franchise fees to two states. Even if you incorporate in Delaware, you will still have to register in each state that you have a physical presence. A few companies specialize in helping you incorporate a new company for a fee. You answer a few basic questions, and the firm fills out boilerplate articles of incorporation and bylaws and files them with the state of your choice.

Ownership Structure

One of the more difficult decisions to make is the legal structure of the firm. Simple partnerships are relatively easy to create and to register with the state. However, partnerships generally cannot issue stock and it can be harder to protect the partners from lawsuits. Corporations stand as separate entities and can issue stock, but the accounting requirements are a little more time consuming, and you face a double-taxation issue. Any money the company makes is subject to corporate income taxes, and dividends that you pay to owners are subject to personal taxes. Most states enable you to create a **subchapter S corporation** or a **limited liability company (LLC)** to combine features of partnerships with those of corporations.

FIGURE 11.26
Primary forms to start a business. Companies are incorporated by the state, and states have different requirements and filing fees. Companies must also obtain an EIN from the IRS. The S corporation election is optional, but popular with small businesses.

```
State forms
    Articles of incorporation
    Corporate bylaws
    Registered agent (self)
    Business registration form
        State employer number
        Withholding ID
        Sales tax ID
    Additional licenses
Federal forms
    SS-4 Application for employer identification number
    2553 election by a small business corporation
```

Most small business startups choose one of these two structures. With both forms, income and losses flow directly to the owner's income statements and are only taxed once. Both protect the owners from lawsuits, as long as you keep a solid line between company business and personal funds. The primary difference between them is that the LLC is not a corporation and cannot sell stock. The S-corporation is also easier to convert into a standard (chapter C) corporation. States have different interpretations of the LLC, so your choice of structure depends on the state in which you incorporate.

Financing

Obtaining financing is related to the type of business structure and the size of your firm. The two choices are debt and equity (stock). However, as a startup, you will find it difficult to find a bank willing to lend you money. Banks will lend money for relatively liquid assets, such as inventory. But they will generally not lend over 80 percent of the value. Most startup businesses find investors and grant them partial ownership through shares of stock.

Debt

Firms can borrow money to finance certain things, but it is difficult to borrow money for a startup. Banks know that many small businesses fail within the first year, so they prefer to lend to an established business. Some banks specialize in merchant loans to cover some of the costs of buying products that will be sold at retail. But even in these cases, the company will have to provide cash to cover some of the costs. Larger firms can sell bonds on the market for long-term debt, but it is unlikely that anyone would be willing to buy bonds from an unknown startup company. Borrowing money also entails interest payments, so the cost can be relatively high.

Equity

Most entrepreneurs search for investors willing to provide startup capital in exchange for partial ownership in the form of shares of stock. Figure 11.27 shows that **venture capital (VC)** firms exist specifically to provide funding to startup firms. An entrepreneur generally presents the business plan to a VC firm, with a detailed budget and a request for the money to cover development and operating costs for the first year. VC firms evaluate hundreds or thousands of proposals in terms of the strength of the idea, the ability and track record of the management, and the potential profits. VC firms expect many of the small companies to fail, but to cover the losses by having a few firms with enormous returns.

Once the firm is established and potentially profitable, the managers take the firm public by issuing stock at an **initial public offering (IPO).** The public stock raises additional money, and eventually gives the entrepreneur and the VC firm an opportunity to sell some of their shares for a personal gain.

In a hot market, startup firms can often trade initial private shares of stock for many items they need. For example, many managers are willing to accept smaller salaries in exchange for stock options. **Stock options** are granted by the firm at a specific price. If the firm goes

FIGURE 11.27

Startup financing. Venture capital firms and partners are given ownership positions and sometimes provide management control in exchange for development funding. If the firm is successful, it issues an initial public offering of stock, which funds additional operations and rewards the original investors.

Venture capital
Angel investor
Partners

Funding for development and operations

Become owners with some control over management

Sucessful firm IPO:
Additional funds
Reward to original investors

public and the stock price increases, the employee buys the stock from the company at the option (low) price, and sells it for the higher public price. As an employee, keep in mind that this transaction is taxed as current income and can take one-third or more of the profit. But you need to offer stock options, because you need experienced employees willing to work for low pay in exchange for future rewards if the company succeeds.

Although equity has many advantages, remember that you give some control of the firm to the investors in exchange for their money. How much control depends on your negotiating skills, on the number of firms interested, and on the amount of money.

Accounting and Benchmarks

Careful accounting is an important requirement in a startup firm. You need to be particularly careful at tracking expenses. A good accounting system is important, but you must also establish procedures and policies. In the hectic day-to-day world of starting a firm, there is little time to stop and analyze every transaction. You need procedures in place so that everything gets recorded as soon as possible. If several managers have purchasing authority, a Web-based accounting system might be helpful to ensure that all items are recorded immediately—wherever the managers are located.

Your accounting system needs to run comparisons to benchmarks that you established in the business plan. For example, if your cash flow is running below projected levels, you will need to cut expenses or find additional funding. You need to closely monitor these numbers so you have more time to react and make corrections.

If your firm requires developing software, you need to track the development progress. Estimating design and programming time is notoriously difficult, but you should still track the progress because you will need to update your target completion dates. Project management software shows how each task depends on others, and it can identify bottlenecks and highlight which tasks need additional resources.

The entrepreneur also needs to provide feedback to investors. Beyond standard quarterly accounting reports, you will need to keep investors apprised of development progress, marketing campaigns, and sales data.

Flexibility

One theme repeatedly echoed by entrepreneurs is that you need to be flexible. Many times your initial idea just will not work. Perhaps consumers are not ready, or development costs are too high, or the competitors respond too quickly and take away the market. Whatever the cause, you need to constantly reevaluate the progress and be prepared to redirect your efforts to related areas.

FIGURE 11.28

Additional e-commerce startup tasks. An EC startup requires several tasks on top of the traditional steps. Developing software is difficult, time consuming, and unpredictable. Finding a Web hosting company can take several weeks. Processing credit cards is harder than it looks because many banks do not like dealing with small startup firms.

- Additional risk and challenge of obtaining funding
- Website development
    - Programming cost
    - Time and management
    - Purchase or lease merchant software if possible
- Find a Web hosting ISP
    - Site complexity
    - Internet connectivity
    - Costs
- Host site yourself
    - Time to get leased line
    - Choose site location based on Internet access

- Obtain digital security certificate (Verisign)
- Find bank that will provide merchant account services to accept credit card payments
    - Setup free
    - Monthly fee
    - Transaction fee
- Find a credit card processing firm that works with your bank and your software
    - Setup fee
    - Monthly fee
    - Transaction fee

For instance, in 1999, Nvest, a Boston investment firm, created a company around the URL mutalfunds.com. It began with a huge business plan to build the site as a portal for mutual fund companies, advisers, and investors. The ambitious plan was to make the site a central source for many aspects of mutual funds. By May 2000, the company realized that it would not be able to achieve all of its goals. The CFO went back to the investors to see if they could raise more money. But the plan was too aggressive (and the dot-com market was beginning to crash), so the firm filed for bankruptcy. However, several of the employees used the technology to get funding from a different set of investors to create a smaller site focused on providing online training for financial services professionals. Hundreds of similar stories exist. You must constantly reexamine your strategy, your performance, your rivals, and your customers—searching for an even better plan.

Starting an E-Commerce Firm

An EC startup faces the same paperwork, financing, and organizational issues as any other firm. However, it faces several additional hurdles. As shown in Figure 11.28, one of the biggest challenges is the innovation factor—few investors and managers have experience with EC firms. The problem is compounded since many EC firms are unique. It is even more complicated with the over 80 percent failure rate of the early EC firms in 2000/2001. All of these factors add to the risk and uncertainty. To attract funding and succeed, you will need a solid business plan that demonstrates traditional business emphasis on sales and profits.

Site development time and cost are important challenges. For simple retail sales, you can generally purchase software or lease a site that provides standard sales software. This approach is preferred for situations where you want to focus on marketing a new product, and the Web is simply the sales channel. You will still have to allocate time to customize the site and enter all of the product and pricing data; but the process is relatively organized and predictable. More complex EC service sites usually require custom software. And building custom software is still a time-consuming, somewhat unpredictable process. If you are not the lead programmer, you will have to find one willing to work with you, generally in exchange for money and stock.

You will also need to find a company to host your website. While there are many ISP hosting companies, you will have to talk to several to find one that can handle the complexity of your site and offer the bandwidth you need at reasonable rates. It can take several weeks to negotiate a contract, so you need to start early. On the other hand, if you need to host the site at your own facilities, you have even more hurdles to clear to obtain the leased line you will need from the phone company. In fact, if at all possible, you should probably avoid choosing a site for your company until after you contact the phone company and several ISPs. Some cities have firms that offer high-speed Internet connections at relatively low cost—as long as your offices are within certain buildings (sitting on top of existing fiber optic connections). If you do need to order a leased line, be prepared to wait six months or more for the installation.

To conduct business over the Internet, you will also have to obtain a digital security certificate. While this process is fairly easy, you need to budget for the annual cost and you might have to build your software to support the processing company's procedures. Likewise, you will have to contact a bank to establish a merchant account so that you can accept credit cards. Most banks price their services depending on the number and value of transactions you conduct monthly. They also tend to charge higher fees to startup firms, because the startup firms have no established credit rating. Note that to process transactions over the Internet, you will have to pay setup and monthly fees to the merchant bank and to the data processing company.

Summary

E-commerce is a complex topic. On one hand, the Internet and mobile commerce simply represent new ways to interact with customers and handle transactions. On the other hand, they have the potential to change the economy and society. The production chain is a key issue in e-commerce. Businesses must decide whether the advantages of selling directly to customers are worth the loss of goodwill from distributors and retailers. The production chain also provides the means to evaluate EC alternatives from business-to-business or business-to-consumer. EC also provides the ability to charge different prices to each customer through direct sales or auctions.

E-commerce can be analyzed in three phases: prepurchase, purchase, and postpurchase. The prepurchase phase consists primarily of advertising, providing specifications, and product configuration or selection. Purchase largely consists of handling the transactions, including verifying the customer, protecting the data transmissions, and handling the money transfer. Postpurchase support includes service, problem tracking, and cross-selling.

Promoting websites is increasingly important. Search engines are an important means for potential customers to find sites, but many sites also need to advertise on other websites and on more traditional media. It is also important to analyze the website's traffic patterns to find out what pages are in demand, and what sections do not work well.

Several types of e-commerce are in use, including simple static HTML pages to present information about products; single unit sales using low-volume payment systems and auction sites; and Web malls and commerce server software for large product catalogs. Many firms choose to outsource the website hosting to a specialty company, but hosting your own servers makes it easier to integrate the Internet data with the other corporate data.

Mobile commerce is similar to e-commerce, but the wireless capabilities can provide some interesting applications—particularly for B2B e-commerce. Sales taxes and the Internet are a challenging problem for states. Ultimately, states will have to alter their tax systems. Similar problems arise on a global scale. Many issues involving customer authentication, payment validation, and national control need to be resolved before global e-commerce can seriously expand.

A Manager's View

Despite the crash of the initial dot-com firms, e-commerce and e-business are going to remain important tools for every firm. As the technologies mature, existing firms will find ways to use the tools profitably. New services will be created, and the structure of many current businesses will change. M-commerce offers the potential to provide another shift in business and society—but it will be a while before the hardware, networks, and software become widespread enough to make a difference. You need to understand all of the aspects of e-commerce and m-commerce to make informed decisions and to choose technologies and processes that will succeed in the future. You should also examine some of the many dot-com failures to avoid making the same mistakes.

Early EC firms failed for many reasons, including unrealizable expectations by investors. Firms focused on pure Internet plays encountered many problems because they did not have ties to real sales. Other firms failed because they attempted to capture market share through heavy advertising and low prices, losing money on every sale. The slump in Internet advertising revenue contributed to the failure of many firms—particularly those offering free content and services. Despite the early problems, there is a strong future for e-commerce and m-commerce.

E-business and e-commerce mean more than just the dot-com firms that sell products. Many Internet-based business opportunities still exist, both within existing firms and for new companies. Joseph Schumpter, an economist, coined the term *creative destruction* to represent the dynamic changes required in a modern economy. A dynamic economy needs to have new firms to force the mainstream companies to respond to the pressure of new ideas. Firms that are set in their ways will ultimately fail. Entrepreneurs can work within larger organizations creating new products, but they generally choose to build entirely new firms. In any case, it takes solid ideas, good research, and an organized plan to succeed as an entrepreneur.

Key Words

application service provider (ASP), *431*
auction, *428*
business to business (B2B), *411*
business to consumer (B2C), *411*
click-through rate, *423*
commerce server, *431*
digital rights management, *418*

disintermediation, *413*
initial public offering (IPO), *443*
intellectual property, *418*
limited liability company (LLC), *442*
pure Internet plays, *435*
simple object access protocol (SOAP), *422*
static HTML, *426*
stock options, *443*

subchapter S corporation, *442*
universal description, discovery, and integration (UDDI), *422*
venture capital (VC), *443*
virtual mall, *430*
zShops, *428*

Website References

Angel Investors and Venture Capital

Angel Investor Magazine	**www.angelinvestormagazine.com**
Angel Investor Source	**www.angel-investor-source.com**
Inc angel investor list	**www2.inc.com/search/23461.html**
National Venture Capital Association	**www.nvca.org**
VCapital	**www.vcapital.com**
Venture Capital Resource Directory	**www.vfinance.com**

Additional Reading

Borzo, Jeanette. "Online Micropayment Systems See New Interest but Face Old Hurdles." *The Wall Street Journal,* April 3, 2001. [Decline of e-commerce advertising revenue and increase in selling of content.]

CNN. "Study: Four Sites Account for Half of Web Surfing," June 5, 2001. [Dominance of a few large firms in attracting users.]

Collett, Stacy. "Amid Turf Battle, Some Middlemen Call for Truce with Online Rivals." *Computerworld,* April 16, 2001. [Discussion of role of middlemen and disintermediation in e-commerce.]

Fireswick, Kris. "The E-Files." *CFO,* February 2001. [Comments and analysis of some lead managers of failed dot-coms.]

Matthews, Robert Guy. "Web Firm Lures Steel Giants," *The Wall Street Journal.* September 2, 1999. [Early auction site for the steel industry.]

Moss Kanter, Rosabeth, "The Ten Deadly Mistakes of Wanna-Dots," *Harvard Business Review,* January 2001. [Discussion of the e-Commerce failures.]

National Mail Order Association, 1998 Mail Order Sales Results, 1999, *http://www.nmoa.com/Library/1998sale.htm.* [Statistics on mail order sales.]

Regan, Keith. "Study: Era of E-Commerce Profits Underway." *EcommerceTimes,* June 20, 2001, *http://www.newsfactor.com/perl/story/11381.html.* [Summary of McKinsey study on e-commerce profits.]

"Shopping around the Web." *The Economist,* February 26, 2000. [Special section on e-commerce.]

Stone, Martha L. "U.S. cell phone technology lags Japan, Europe." *mediainfo,* June 7, 2000, *http://www.mediainfo.com/ephome/news/newshtm/stories/060700n2.htm.* [Statistics on cell phone usage in several nations.]

Swisher, Kara. "Web Retailers Faced Death; Now Can They Handle Taxes?" *The Wall Street Journal,* April 9, 2001. [Summary of issues on e-commerce sales taxes.]

Review Questions

1. How does e-business fit into different locations within the production chain?
2. What are the potential benefits and costs to disintermediation that can be accomplished with e-business?
3. How does EC differ in the three areas of prepurchase, purchase, and postpurchase?
4. What is CRM and why is it increasingly important—particularly in a world of wireless connections and the Internet?
5. What choices are available for promoting a website?
6. What standards exist in Web advertisements? How do Web advertisements affect customer privacy?
7. What options are available for building and hosting websites?
8. What will attract consumers to mobile commerce? What problems have to be overcome before it is successful?
9. Many people were concerned that by not requiring EC firms to collect sales taxes, traditional firms would eventually lose business, and the states would suffer large declines in tax collections. Why did this scenario not happen? Might it still happen in the future?
10. What problems make it difficult for EC to be global?
11. Why did so many early EC firms fail? Could the same problems affect EC firms now and in the future? Does it mean that EC is dead?
12. What are the primary steps in starting a new business?
13. What are the main elements of a business plan?
14. What additional steps are needed to start an e-commerce firm, or to expand a conventional firm into e-commerce?

Exercises

1. You are working for a small firm that wishes to sell products (B2C) on the Internet. Find three firms that could be used to host your website. Identify the features, tools, and costs of each firm. Which one would you recommend?
2. Find firms in three different industries that have used the Internet to disintermediate at least one level of the production chain. Were they successful? What problems did they encounter?
3. Choose one common product available for purchase on the Internet and from local retailers (for example, a specific book, CD, or toy). Find at least five sites and two retail stores that sell the product. Compare the price of the item, including shipping and taxes. Would you expect the prices to be the same? Explain any differences.
4. Find data on at least one B2B auction site. How long has the site been operational? What percentage of total industry sales are carried on the auction site? Do firms use the site for regular purchases, or only for special items? Who pays for the operating costs of the site?
5. Find at least five companies that are offering business Web services. What services do they provide? What do they charge? How long have they been in business? What technologies do they use (for example, SOAP or XML)?

6. Research the current standards for Internet ads (in terms of size). Check a few sites to see which size is the most common. Find a major site (newspapers are always good places to look) and identify how much it will cost to run a common ad.

7. Check with at least four major search engines. What do you need to do to get a page listed with the search service? How much does it cost? How can you prevent the search engine from searching a specified subdirectory?

8. Find software specifically designed for CRM. What features does it provide? How many customers can it handle? How much does it cost? What customer contact methods does it support?

9. Obtain a software package that analyzes Web logs (often you can get short-term demo versions for free). Using the software, examine a set of logs to identify the most popular pages. Using the additional analyses, can you find any problems with the website, or make any suggestions to the designers?

10. Find and compare at least two catalog management software packages. Which one seems easier to use? How many products can each one handle? Do they work with all websites, or only some commerce software packages?

11. Identify the current state-of-the-art in mobile commerce networks and handsets. What transmission speeds exist? What is the resolution on the video screens? What display languages do the leading devices support?

12. Write a business plan for a new company. Choose an existing small company if you do not have ideas for a new firm.

13. Research the detailed steps needed to start a Chapter S corporation in your state. Obtain the necessary forms (most states have them on websites).

Rolling Thunder Database

14. Identify at least three areas in which Rolling Thunder Bicycles could profit from e-business. Be specific and explain what technologies would have to be added (for instance, Web hosting).

15. Find at least five sites on which it would make sense to advertise Rolling Thunder Bicycles. As much as possible, identify the advertising costs and the demographics of the site visitors.

16. Develop a plan for expanding Rolling Thunder Bicycles into international sales. Be sure to identify any potential problems, and how you will deal with them.

17. Develop a plan for creating a Web-based system for connecting to suppliers. What software would you need? How can you convince the suppliers to cooperate?

18. Using the existing data, write a business plan to obtain venture capital to expand the operations of Rolling Thunder—focusing on the need to develop a marketing campaign and a Web-based ordering system.

19. Identify the steps needed to take Rolling Thunder public with an IPO.

Cases

Package Delivery

The secret to being a successful package delivery company is timeliness, efficiency, and affordability. In the last 30 years, guaranteed two-day and overnight delivery has made drastic changes in businesses' perceptions of *timely*. Pony Express delivered messages for several years, until the telegraph rendered it obsolete. Many thought that fax machines and e-mail would do the same thing to the overnight market. So far this has not been the case. The industry has continued to change nonetheless, hastened by the march of technology, a new set of customer needs, and a change in the way business is conducted.

Manufacturers and sellers had previously focused on reducing shipping costs and time to customers in a more competitive marketplace. The current marketplace now demands speed to market in order to reduce product cycle times. Many high-tech products are becoming obsolete in record times and the there is a need to provide fast-cycle logistics. Doing so adds enormous value to customers by compressing production and delivery cycles, particularly for time-sensitive products such as IT components, biotechnology and pharmaceutical products, or medical devices. Furthermore, it allows companies to reduce the carrying costs and lower their inventories levels.

Efficiency is also a critical element in the delivery industry. Companies in other industries are increasingly relying on UPS and FedEx to handle many common delivery tasks. Through efficiency, these companies can provide delivery services for lower costs than the other companies can match.

Financial Analysis

While moderate to high market growth continues in the industry, prices have declined because of fierce competition. Technological advances and efficiencies have enabled the industry to continually cut costs. United Parcel Service (UPS) and Federal Express (FedEx), the two most technologically advanced companies, have reported profit increases greater than yearly sales increases.

Stock/Investment Outlook

The stock projection for the package delivery industry is positive for the next few years. Most of the large delivery companies are rated a *buy* or *outperform* for the next three to four years.

Growth Potential

The package industry has shifted from providing delivery services to becoming integrators of customers' supply chain systems. FedEx and UPS have assisted companies with supply chain management by offering tools and consulting, and handling international shipment from end to end. One of the major areas for improvement that the package delivery must meet, particularly for express carriers, is that of free movement of packages through customs in order to meet global business demands for overnight delivery. Julian Oliver, the director general of the International Express Carriers Conference had the following figures to offer on the express carrier industry [Oliver]:

- 200 countries being serviced
- 650,000 people employed
- 1,200 aircraft
- 1,350 daily flights
- 175,000 trucks and vehicles
- 20 million daily shipments
- $50 billion in duties and taxes

In his presentation Oliver also points out that outside industry sources such as Boeing and Airbus predict prolonged growth in the industry. Both airline manufacturers predict double-digit growth rates for next 15 years for airfreight. According to estimates from the Colography Group, the global value of air-shipped goods approached $2.2 trillion in 2000, increasing by almost 7 percent over 1999. As in the United States, the express segment of international shipping is also growing twice as fast as the broad market in terms of tonnage. Globalization, just-in-time logistics, customized mass production, rapid customer response, and e-commerce, along with other trends, all point to greater use of parcel service in the future.

Market Share Competitive Structure

The U.S. market is made up of seven large companies, dozens of smaller entities, and the U.S. post office. The biggest shake-up in the package delivery industry occurred when UPS, the sleeping giant, awoke. For years, UPS was the industry cash cow. It owned the package delivery market and was a very staid company trying to do one thing well—mass-produced delivery. After the upstart FedEx began the new overnight market, UPS slowly began to transform itself to expand into that and other markets. One of the ways UPS transformed itself was to increase the marketing department from 7 to 600 people, in order to attract and keep corporate customers.

Given the high cost of entry, the oligopoly in the marketplace will continue. Billions are needed to develop facilities in trucking, delivery, computer, and air networks. These costs keep new companies from entering or becoming a dominant force in the marketplace. As time goes on, more buyouts, mergers, and alliances may further restrict the number of players.

Role of Research/Development

The role of research and development in the package delivery industry is to develop new technologies that will cut the cost of shipping, shorten delivery times, provide better services to customers, and integrate the supply chain between supplier and customer in order to reduce product cycle times. Wireless technologies and robust, Web-based applications that are accessible to customers, are key technologies and services that are being offered to customers today. Most of the focus lies in improving efficiency through distribution and planning. The use of mobile computers and transponders, as well as satellites, to monitor packages and vehicles is also increasing shipping efficiency. Other high-tech applications are on the horizon. One is an IT tool that allows shippers and intermodal operators to simulate flows of cargo, detect inefficiencies in combined transport operations, and search for alternative transportation scenarios.

Technological Investment and Analysis

FedEx and UPS are leading the industry in technological spending. They are attempting to integrate all facets of the delivery process so companies can eventually outsource their supply chain management to them. Eventually these delivery companies want to become the supply chain managers for corporations. Once FedEx and UPS have introduced their services into customers' routines, it is more difficult and troublesome for customers to switch to other delivery services.

Assets that provide the means to move goods physically are undifferentiated and generically available to all players. Technology has emerged as the method to distinguish a company's products, improve its service quality, and lower costs. As such, it has become increasingly important to manufacturers and sellers to be able to access real-time information about the status of parts, materials, and finished goods in a world of just-in-time inventory management. Furthermore, integration with suppliers' networks would provide a more accurate picture for managers to decide on production issues.

Recommendation for the Future

New economy dynamics have transformed the supply chain. Forced by the reality of competition, firms can no longer manage production, inventory control, transport, and sell and service as functions independent of one another. The new-economy supply chain is an entirely different animal, defined by its organic nature, whereby operational impacts of any part of the organism are keenly felt throughout the entire supply chain. Firms that want to compete and excel in the new economy need to integrate demand management, inventory management, distribution, and customer fulfillment with seamless information flows from the supplier level to the production level, and on to the customer level in real time. Each of the supply chain components must be supported by sophisticated information systems that provide the highest degree of visibility, precision, and efficiency. This is particularly true for companies engaged in electronic commerce.

Case: Federal Express

There was no such industry as express delivery of packages until FedEx started it in 1973. Not only did it create an industry, but it has also set the standard against which competitors

are measured. With annual revenues of $20 billion, FedEx Corp. is the premier global provider of transportation, e-commerce, and supply-chain management services. In order to gain a greater market, FedEx has expanded from its express delivery services to complete integrated business solutions through a network of subsidiaries operating independently, including FedEx Express, the world's largest express transportation company; FedEx Ground, North America's second largest provider of small-package ground delivery service; FedEx Freight, a leading provider of regional less-than-truckload freight services; FedEx Custom Critical, the world's largest provider of expedited, time-critical shipments; and FedEx Trade Networks, a provider of customs brokerage, consulting, information technology, and trade facilitation solutions. FedEx has grown from being a solely overnight express package-delivery service to a complete supply-chain management provider for any type of business need.

Technological Investment and Analysis

Despite the economic slowdown, FedEx has continued to invest in its IT infrastructure with a proposed $1.5 billion IT budget for 2002, unchanged from its 2001 IT budget. There are approximately 2.2 million unique visitors to the website each month. Approximately 69 million packages delivered by FedEx Express every month are either processed or prepared for delivery online. [Chen 2001] FedEx's website was the first to allow customers to track their shipments online and to also ship them.

While customer-interfacing technologies keep customers coming back, it is in back-end systems where the Internet has made the most impact at FedEx. FedEx offers multiple methods for customers to connect to its shipping, tracking, and logistics systems over leased lines, direct connections, private networks, and EDI (electronic data interchange). Now the company is actively pushing large and small customers alike onto the Internet through the use of XML. Today, the majority of large corporate customers continue to use private networks and leased lines to connect to FedEx's systems. But Robert Carter, executive vice president and CIO at FedEx, said he is optimistic that more and more blue-chip companies will begin to transact with FedEx using the Web and XML.

Technological Innovations

In 2002, FedEx launched online document completion to its customers that need to ship internationally. FedEx wants to enable its customers to complete documents online, therefore allowing them to export to more than 20 countries by completing the forms online and sending them directly to the appropriate customs officers over the Internet. The company currently provides customs forms that must be printed, filled out, and sent to customs by the customer.

Additionally FedEx's IT department began testing a number of additional wireless technologies, including Bluetooth on courier devices, which allow carriers to communicate in short-range with their offices. The technology upgrade provides FedEx Ground customers with the fastest signature proof of delivery and adds to the most detailed package-tracking information in the ground shipping market. [Transport News 2001] The company has also begun to wire its offices with WiFi wireless LANs that enable development groups to collaborate wirelessly in conference rooms. All of this is an effort to provide the latest technology to customers and help them become even more efficient.

Recommendation for the Future

FedEx should integrate as many tools to allow their customers to run their shipping departments if they wish to do so. However, FedEx has also recognized that there is a greater value to the customer in becoming involved in the many areas of supply-chain management in order to reduce product cycle times. This will allow major customers to concentrate on their core business and outsource the supply chain management aspect to FedEx. Furthermore, this move will allow FedEx to diversify and become a long-term partner of the company therefore ensuring future cash flows.

Questions

1. What has been the catalyst for change at Federal Express?

2. Upon which technologies has Federal Express relied?

3. How successful has technological change been at Federal Express?

4. What does the corporation say about its financial ability to embark on a major technological program of advancement?

5. What does Federal Express's Web page present about its business directives?

6. What challenges and opportunities is the package delivery industry facing?

7. How important is the collection and evaluation of data to the future of Federal Express?

Additional Reading

Chen, Anne. "#2: FedEx Delivers E-Biz Win,"
November 12, 2001,
http://www.eweek.com/article/0,3658,s%253D703%2526a
%253D18253,00.asp

Haddad, Charles. "Transportation: A Long Haul to
Recovery?" *Business Week Online.* January 14, 2002
http://www.businessweek.com/magazine/content/02_02/b3
765673.htm

"FedEx Ground Receives Wireless Industry Award for
New System that Captures Digital Signatures at Package
Delivery." Pittsburgh, December 10, 2001.
http://www.transportnews.com/Article/140271

"Global Impacts of FedEx in the New Economy."
http://www.sri.com/policy/csted/reports/economics/fedex/

Oliver, Julian. "Improving the Future Express Market."
Presentation http://www.postinsight.pb.com/files/
OliverWorldMailExpAmer.pdf

Sparks, Nancy S. "Recognizing the Importance of Air
Freight." *Understanding Aviation Economics.* London,
April 5, 2000.

Case: United Parcel Service

United Parcel Service, the world's largest package-delivery company, provides specialized transportation services through the pick-up and delivery of packages, primarily by air and ground transportation in the United States, as well as various logistics services. UPS is the leader in its industry for delivering 55 percent of merchandise sold online compared with FedEx's 10 percent, according to consultancy the Sageza Group Inc. The company, founded in 1907, now handles over 3 billion packages and documents per year and delivers to every address in the United States and in more than 200 countries and territories. Sales in FY 2000 totaled $29.771 billion, up 10.1 percent year-over-year.

New facilities in Georgia and New Jersey house what UPS claims is the largest database in the world, the DB2 database. The DB2 database has more than 7,000 gigabytes of records, the tracking information regarding all UPS packages shipped in an 18-month period. This kind of computing power translates into information regarding senders, receivers, billing, bar codes, time sent, estimated destinations, and other information for more than 4 billion packages.

The new Atlanta site is primarily backup for the New Jersey operations in case of disaster or expansion needs. Input into these new centralized computing facilities is through DIADs, or delivery information acquisition devices specially developed for UPS by Motorola. These devices are handheld by the delivery person and feature 1.5 MB of RAM, digital signature capability, and an optical coupler. The optical coupler is used to transfer information and signatures into the DVA or DIAD Vehicle Adapter, where data is then transferred via cellular phone or modem. UPSnet makes the transfer of data to the data facilities in New Jersey and Atlanta. UPSnet does this via a network of 500,000 miles of dedicated cables, more than 200 switching nodes, and a UPS satellite.

Outsourcing of certain functions needing expert advice and creating partnerships that support the needs of information systems are also underway. For example, to send all the information from the delivery trucks through the DVA using UPS TotalTrack, UPS has alliances with more than 90 local and regional cellular carriers including AT&T Wireless Communications, AirTouch Cellular, Southwestern Bell Mobile Systems, Pacific Telesis, GTE Mobilnet, and others. Northern Telecom switches provision UPSnet's dedicated cables directly linked to the central computing facilities. Several types of products from several companies result in a 100 percent uptime for the network.

Users of UPS MaxiTrac dial through lines provided by AT&T and Sprint. For data warehousing, UPS has chosen EMC Corp. and a system developed by Hewlett-Packard Co. and Oracle Corp. UPS's existing mainframes were not meeting the speed and availability needs required to service the vast amounts of data, but with the help of EMC, data warehousing will now be state of the art. These cooperative agreements have helped lessen UPS's technology-related-responsibilities and have focused UPS's energies on more core issues.

The final implementation of UPS's technological initiative is the development and upgrading of software application products. One of the results of this initiative is UPS Online. This service is a Windows-based system that lets customers manage finances related to the package, track the status of their package, and print out shipping summaries. This system will integrate UPS into the customers' daily operations while providing more valuable information, allowing the customer to react situations in real time.

Another new product is the UPS website. On the site, a browser can find information about the company, what is new in the company, employment information, news releases, and a host of other information related to UPS. The customer can also find on the site a service that will, using bar codes, locate where the package is in the delivery process. In this way, even the casual, noncompany-related customer could have access to most of the information that users of UPS Online would have. If all goes as planned, the Internet and the UPS website will also serve as a center where transactions will occur without the security hazards still present on the Web. The Internet potential is great and UPS wants to be one of the first companies capitalizing on its potential.

Another new product is the improved help desk that will service both internal users as well as external users in an attempt to "empower our [employees and customers] to become as independent as possible in using technology." The help desk function was not a formal organization five years ago, but as the volume and the sophistication of UPS and its software grew, and as the need for support for these new technologies grew, an operation was launched to service the need.

With the internal and external operations combined, the help desk receives approximately 70,000 calls a month, a dramatic increase compared to approximately 14,000 calls a month in 1991. The external operation is run by 130 front-line experts and the internal group is run by 65 first-line consultants in the Mahwah, New Jersey, campus.

The intimidating task of supporting all the software at UPS is, in turn, supported by Windows-based Expert Advisor from the Software Artistry company. Previously, the help desk function was supported by IBM's mainframe based Infoman, but its limitations became too apparent as the move to PC-based operations from mainframe operations came about.

Expert Advisor allows UPS to store more data online to assist helpers solve problems in a standardized manner quickly and efficiently. The help desk technicians no longer have to flip through binders full of information to solve an issue. Rather, they just have to type it into Expert Advisor. With its dynamic ability to constantly update and incorporate new diagnostic tools and solutions into the system, Expert Advisor has developed the help desk function into a real value-adding arm at UPS.

UPS has therefore taken steps to initiate and seek new technologies as well as react to industry forces. These technologies all have an element of risk involved as significant funds have been allocated for the acquisition of new equipment, new software, and new employees. However, it is clear that UPS is trying to innovate to keep its market share and profitability.

In an interesting twist, UPS acquired Mail Boxes Etc (MBE) in April 2001. MBE is the world's largest franchiser of local shipping centers. The transaction essentially gives UPS several thousand new customer counters, along with revenue from mail box rentals. More important, UPS extended its operations in the international area by purchasing Fritz Companies, which specializes in logistics, freight forwarding, and customs brokerage. In 2001, UPS also acquired First International Bancorp, which specializes in structuring international transactions. [Quarterly report]

Technological Innovations

Telecommunications

In 1998, UPS launched an Internet-based delivery service that the company says could make life a lot easier for firms wanting to send sensitive documents on tight deadlines. The service is called UPS Document Exchange. It is a suite of delivery and information management services that provides a choice of two Internet delivery services: UPS OnLine Courier and UPS OnLine Dossier.

UPS OnLine Courier uses either the UPS website or a separate software package and allows customers to send documents to anyone, regardless of the e-mail software package, operating system, or hardware being used on either side of the delivery process. UPS OnLine Courier is built on an open environment.

"It has a PDF (portable document format) and Adobe PDF built into it, so if the recipient doesn't have the same software as you do, it won't hinder their ability to read it. That's a benefit of the Courier," said Joan Schnorbus, a UPS spokesperson. [Press release]

UPS OnLine Dossier takes UPS OnLine Courier a step further by using a double-encryption process and offering insurance. The document will self-destruct if tampered with. UPS OnLine Dossier authenticates identities using digital certificates, which are required by both sender and receiver.

UPS is developing another service for corporate customers. This service integrates UPS package-tracking capabilities directly with the customers' websites. The move allows consumers to obtain tracking information for their orders from the site where they ordered rather than by jumping to UPS.

The Internet

Increasingly, UPS (and FedEx) are relying on the Internet to provide additional service to customers. For example, tracking packages through the company website is faster and substantially cheaper than the 800-number service using operators. For the 2001 holiday season, UPS extended the use of the Internet by offering a Web-based return service. Customers wishing to return a product simply click on a link to print a return shipping label. The service costs only 75 cents per transaction plus the shipping cost—making it substantially cheaper than other methods that require the help of a real person.

Questions

1. What has been the catalyst for change at United Parcel Service?

2. What are the critical success factors and core competencies for UPS?

3. Upon what technologies has UPS relied?

4. What caused a change in the way UPS used technology to meet the business needs of its customers?

5. How does the corporation's Web page support its business directives?

6. How important is the analysis of data to the corporation's continued success?

7. How will the capture and maintenance of customer data impact the corporation's future?

Additional Reading

Beizer, Doug. "When You Need It Now." *PC Magazine,* September 1, 1998, p. 40.

"Cyberscope: Tracking Santa's Helpers." *Newsbytes,* December 1998.

Enright, Greg. "UPS Ships Online Delivery System." *Computing Canada,* July 6, 1998, p. 29.

Gable, Gene. "Two Brilliant Ideas, or Two Megaflops?" *Publish,* May 1998, p. 26.

Holt, Stannie. "ERP Vendors to Boost Shipping: Companies Strive for 'Seamless, Paperless' Supply Chain." *InfoWorld,,* April 13, 1998, p. 19.

Kramer, Matt. "Web-Bound Attachments Remove Some Burden from E-Mail Servers." *PC Week,* November 23, 1998, p. 36.

Marlatt, Andrew. "Internet Emerges as Alternative to Overnight Mail, Faxes." *Internet World,* November 2, 1998, p. 54.

"Quality Stuff." *Computerworld,* July 27, 1998.

"UPS Buys Part of TanData." *InformationWeek,* October 19, 1998, p. 20.

"UPS Creates Wireless Industry Group." *Electronic Buyers' News,* September 28, 1998, p. 58.

"UPS Delivers a Lawsuit to Postal Service." *Network World,* October 12, 1998, p. 6.

"UPS E-Commerce; www.ec.ups.com." *Electronic Buyers' News,* June 8, 1998, p. 62.

Verton, Dan. "UPS: Many Easier Returns." *Computerworld,* December 26, 2001.

Williams, Paul. "The Virtual Receptionist." *Newmedia,* May 5, 1998, p. 22.

Winter, Richard, and Kathy Auerbach. "VLDB: The Big Time." *Database Programming & Design,* August 1998, pp. S2–S9.

Appendix

Creating a Business Plan

If you are starting a business, you need a plan—something that tells everyone the purpose of your company, how it will be organized and financed, and how you expect the business to progress over the next few years. Even existing businesses need a plan to help managers understand the strategies, goals, and trade-offs. Business plans are used internally to help guide the company, but they are also read by outsiders who might be interested in providing money to help finance your company.

You can hire experts, or buy software, to help organize and write a business plan, but with a little research, you will find that it is not that difficult to write your own business plan. Figure 11.1A shows a sample outline for a business plan. There are no fixed rules that specify the exact layout needed; however, some financers review hundreds of plans and often prefer them to be written in a specific style. In particular, if you are going to be dealing with a venture capitalist firm, you should find out any specific requirements or structure they recommend.

Marketing, Forecasting, and Financing

All firms need to sell something to make a profit. Whether you sell products or services, you will need a marketing plan. The marketing plan needs to identify the products or services and their prices and costs. While you might not need to specify exact prices on every item, you should identify a strategy, such as high prices with high service or low prices and minimal service. You also need to identify the potential customers and the existing competitors. Figure 11.2A shows the key points you need to include in the marketing plan. Most of the strategy and competitive analysis is straightforward—you just need to research the industry and identify the competitors. Study their websites, annual reports, and SEC filings to get as much information as possible. Several marketing firms will provide even more detailed data on sales—for a fee. For many firms, it is also critical to establish a plan for sales management (who is going to be in charge, how salespeople will be rewarded, how you will assign customers, and many other issues). For businesses selling products, you also need to identify how the products will be distributed to customers and how you will handle returns for service.

Figure 11.3A shows a key aspect of the marketing plan: estimating sales of the various products. The example represents the original business plan for the Rolling Thunder Bicycle Company. Note that rather than just invent a total sales figure, it is more reasonable to estimate the number of each bicycle type that the company anticipates selling in a given year. These numbers could be determined by looking at existing bicycle sales, interviewing prospective customers, and

guessing how many bicycles you think can be made and sold by a small company. Yes, there is a lot of guessing at this stage. The goal is to find a set of numbers that is reasonable and achievable. Two million dollars in sales for a startup bicycle company might be optimistic, but it should be possible to reach that level with reasonable prices and advertising.

Based on the sales data and a few other assumptions, it is now possible to project the standard financial statements. Figure 11.4A shows the estimated income statement data for the first three years. All of the financial data depend on assumptions that are detailed in the spreadsheet. Additionally, the financial statements are not yet complete—for example, there is no debt shown on the income statement. These preliminary statements are intentionally incomplete to highlight some of the decisions you will have to make. In practice, you will make the decisions and complete the statements.

The balance sheet is shown in Figure 11.5A. The first thing you see is that it does not balance. The educational

FIGURE 11.1A Business plan structure. You can choose alternative structures, but these are the common areas you need to include in any business plan.

- Introduction
    Outline and summary of the company and the plan
- Marketing
    Competitors
    Market analysis
    Advertising
    Sales management
    Product management: prices and costs
- Historic analysis
    Sales, profits, structural changes
- Organization
    Structure of the firm and management
- Financing
    Detailed cash needs
- Projections
    Estimates of sales, costs, growth with detailed data
    and forecasts

FIGURE 11.2A Marketing analysis. You can only succeed by selling, so it is critical to understand the market and the competition. You also need to set sales goals that will help define the size of your company.

- Products
    Costs
    Prices
    Profits
- Competition
- Strategy
- Sales goals and forecasts
- Promotional methods
- Sales management
- Distribution and service

FIGURE 11.3A Sample estimate of sales. Quantity estimates for the first year would be based on typical sales for a small company. The other years assume a 10 percent increase in sales. Average prices can be estimated fairly accurately from the industry data. The resulting $2 to $3 million in sales is probably reasonable for a small firm but will be affected by advertising and the economy.

Rolling Thunder Estimated Sales—Number of Bicycles								
Year	Increase	Hybrid	Mountain	Race	Road	Tour	Track	Annual Total
1		250	250	350	200	350	50	1,450
2	10%	275	275	385	220	385	55	1,595
3	10%	302	302	423	242	423	60	1,752
4	10%	332	332	465	266	465	66	1,926
5	10%	365	365	511	292	511	72	2,116
Average Sale Price of a Bicycle								
	$1,000	$1,500	$2,500	$2,000	$1,000	$2,000		
Estimated Sales Value								
Year	Hybrid	Mountain	Race	Road	Tour	Track	Annual Sales	
1	$250,000	$375,000	$ 875,000	$400,000	$350,000	$100,000	$2,350,000	
2	275,000	412,500	962,500	440,000	385,000	110,000	2,585,000	
3	302,000	453,000	1,057,500	484,000	423,000	120,000	2,839,500	
4	332,000	498,000	1,162,500	532,000	465,000	132,000	3,121,500	
5	365,000	547,500	1,277,500	584,000	511,000	144,000	3,429,000	

goal is to emphasize the fact that the company has a negative cash flow for the first year, and that it will need substantial financing for the first few years. This financing can be either as shareholder equity (venture capital, partnership funds, or sales of stock); or it can be long-term debt. Essentially, the company would need to borrow the money to purchase the tools needed in the production shop, unless it can be raised from investors or partners.

The cash flow statement in Figure 11.6A emphasizes the cash problems in the first year. Obviously the cash cannot be negative—it has to come from someplace. The statement simply demonstrates that the firm cannot even get started without a substantial amount of money. Even though the firm shows an operating profit in the first year (see the income statement), it will need investment money to purchase production tools, inventory, and fund the advertising campaign. Additional investment might be needed in subsequent years as well—but the actual numbers will change after you update the financing data for the first year. For example, if you elect to borrow money, the firm will incur interest expenses that will affect costs in the following years. As you enter the changes, you need to make sure the spreadsheet incorporates all of the impacts.

Management Structure

Starting a firm from scratch entails a tremendous amount of thought and effort. It is often tempting to skip a few details and jump right in to get the firm running. The problem is that once the company is operating, there is never enough time to sit down and solve all of the problems. Instead, you need to anticipate as many issues up front as possible. Then you build operating rules to guide the workers into making decisions autonomously. Essentially, you need to write the operating guidebook to identify who is in charge of each operation, and how the day-to-day decisions will be made. You should also identify who you will be using as a legal advisor and your accountants.

FIGURE 11.4A   Projected income statement. Estimates are based on several assumptions detailed in the spreadsheet.

Income Statement—Projected

	Year		
	1	2	3
Sales	$2,350,000	$2,585,000	$2,839,500
Material	822,500	904,750	993,825
Labor	550,000	550,000	550,000
Lease	60,000	60,000	60,000
Advertising/promotion	500,000	250,000	250,000
Tools depreciation	50,000	60,000	70,000
Cost of merchandise sold	1,932,500	1,764,750	1,853,825
Operating and admin expenses	100,000	100,000	100,000
Operating profit	317,500	720,250	885,675
Other income (expense)			
Interest Income	0	0	93
Interest expense	0	0	0
Shareholder related expense	(10,000)	(10,000)	(10,000)
Earnings before income taxes	307,500	710,250	875,768
Federal and state income taxes	(123,000)	(284,100)	(350,307)
Net earnings	$184,500	$426,150	$525,461

FIGURE 11.5A   Projected balance sheet. Notice that it does not balance yet. The purpose here is to show the negative cash flow problem in the first year and to highlight the need to obtain financing either through debt or equity.

Balance Sheet—Projected at Year-End

	Year		
	1	2	3
Assets			
Current assets			
Cash	$(193,550)	$ 3,095	$302,395
Receivables	235,000	258,500	283,950
Inventories	98,700	108,570	119,259
Prepaid expenses	1,000	1,000	1,000
Total current assets	141,150	371,165	706,604
Property, plant, and equipment			
Land	0	0	0
Buildings	0	0	0
Fixtures and equipment	250,000	50,000	50,000
Subtotal	250,000	50,000	50,000
Less accumulated depreciation	50,000	110,000	180,000
Net property, plant, and equipment	200,000	(60,000)	(130,000)
Total assets			
Liabilities and shareholders' equity			
Current liabilities			
Accounts payable	82,250	90,475	99,383
Accured payroll and benefits	0	0	0
Income taxes payable	(123,000)	(284,100)	(350,307)
Other current liabilities	0	0	0
Total current liabilities	(40,750)	(193,625)	(250,925)
Other liabilities	0	0	0
Long-term debt	0	0	0
Total liabilities	(40,750)	(193,625)	(250,925)
Shareholders' equity	0	0	0
Additional paid-in capital	0	0	0
Retained earnings	(193,550)	196,645	299,300
Total shareholders' equity	(193,550)	196,645	299,300
Total liabilities and shareholders' equity	$(243,300)	$ 3,020	$ 48,375
Money to be raised (equity or debt)	$ 575,450	$308,145	$528,229

FIGURE 11.6A Projected cash flow statement. Note the huge cash needs in the first year. Since cash on hand cannot be negative, the firm needs to obtain some type of financing.

Cash Flow—Projected

	Year		
	1	2	3
Net earnings	$ 184,500	$ 426,150	$525,461
Depreciation	50,000	110,000	180,000
Net (gain) loss on asset sales	0	0	0
Other	0	0	0
Subtotal from sales	50,000	110,000	180,000
(Increase) decrease in current assets:			
Receivables	(235,000)	(23,500)	(25,450)
Inventories	98,700	9,870	10,689
Prepaid expenses	(1,000)	0	0
Subtotal from assets	(137,300)	(13,630)	(14,761)
Increase (decrease) in current liabilities			
Accounts payable	82,250	8,225	8,908
Other current liabilities	0	0	0
Accrued payroll	0	0	0
Income taxes payable	(123,000)	(284,100)	(350,307)
Total change in current liabilities	(40,750)	(275,875)	(341,400)
Total adjustments	(128,050)	(179,505)	(176,161)
Net cash provided by operations	56,450	246,645	349,300
Cash flows from investing:			
Expended from property, plant, equipment	(250,000)	(50,000)	(50,000)
Proceeds from sales of assets	0	0	0
Net cash used in investing	(250,000)	(50,000)	(50,000)
Cash flows from financing:			
Proceeds (payments) from long-term debt	0	0	0
Stock or additional paid in capital	0	0	0
Cash dividends	0	0	0
Net cash provided by financing	0	0	0
Net increase (decrease) in cash	(193,550)	196,645	299,300
Cash and cash equivalents:			
Beginning of year	0	(193,550)	3,095
End of year	$(193,550)	$ 3,095	$302,395

Exercises

1. Using the spreadsheet for the Rolling Thunder Bicycle startup situation shown in the figures, choose a financing method and complete the projected accounting statements.

2. Choose a company that you would like to start, write the overall strategy section and build the projected accounting statements for the first three years.

3. Using queries, compare sales from the first three years at Rolling Thunder Bicycles to the projected sales. Use a graph to show the differences. What actions did the company take in response to the differences?

4. Assuming the salaries and capital costs are fixed to start Rolling Thunder Bicycles, and assuming the average price of a bicycle is $2,250, compute the break-even number of bicycles.

CHAPTER TWELVE

Systems Development

What you will learn in this chapter

- How are information systems built?

- What problems are encountered when you develop information systems?

- What are the strengths and weaknesses of development methodologies?

- How do you analyze systems and businesses?

Air traffic control is difficult job requiring intense concentration. Aging computer systems make the job more difficult, but the FAA has found it even more difficult to design and build a new air traffic control system.

The Federal Aviation Administration

Governmental control over aviation began in 1911, when Connecticut passed regulations governing the flights of planes. Although the federal government played an early role through the Department of Defense, control over civilians flights was not formalized until the creation of the Civil Aeronautics Board (CAB) in 1944 as a division of the Commerce Department. The Federal Aviation Administration (FAA) was created in 1958 and the CAB was merged into the new agency. In 1966, the FAA (and CAB) was made part of the Department of Transportation. The Airline Deregulation Act of 1978 effectively dismantled most functions of the CAB.

The FAA is charged with controlling civilian and military uses of U.S. airspace. The FAA is also responsible for modernizing the airways, installing radar, and training air traffic controllers. Probably their best-known function is control over commercial flights and routes to maintain safety and efficiency. With 50,000 flights a day among 300 major airports, the FAA has a huge task.

Several other governmental agencies are involved in aviation. The National Weather Service produces up-to-the-minute weather forecasts. The Federal Communication Commission allocates radio frequencies and rules. The National Ocean Survey creates the maps and charts used for navigation. The National Aeronautics and Space Administration supports aviation research. International flights are governed by the International Civil Aviation Organization formed in 1944 and moved under the aegis of the United Nations in 1947.

The FAA has a computer system to help it control the thousands of daily flights. However, the system was created in the early 1960s. It has been patched and upgraded, but most of the hardware and software are based on decades-old technology. On several occasions, the FAA attempted to upgrade the facilities, but complications have forced the agency back to the old technology.

Life for airlines and passengers became more complicated after September 11, 2001. Security screening was transferred from private companies hired by the airlines to the federal Department of Transportation (at least for several years). Some experts have suggested creating a large federal database to track and indentify potentially dangerous people. Others have suggested creating a national database of "safe" passengers with background checks. In both cases, the initial question is whether government agencies have the ability to create these large information systems and protect them.

FIGURE 12.1

It is not easy to create information systems to support business needs (strategy, tactics, and operations). Three basic development techniques are systems development life cycle, prototyping, and end-user development. As a manager, you will participate in each of these methods. You will sometimes have to choose which method to use.

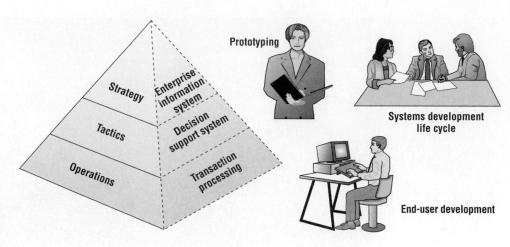

Overview

Elaine:	Richard, I agree we need all of these new systems, but where are we going to get them? I don't know how to build them.
Richard:	Well, I don't know. I hate to hire a bunch of people and then have to fire them.
Ally:	If we could find some prepackaged tools that came close, we could train some of the employees to build the applications.
Elaine:	I don't know. These problems seem pretty hard, and I don't think anyone else has the same type of issues.
Ally:	Well, then maybe we should outsource the development or hire some contract programmers.
Richard:	I don't know. I'm usually opposed to outside workers. It is too hard to control them, and how do we keep them from overcharging us?
Ally:	I agree, but I think it is the best choice. We will just have to define the projects carefully and then get the provider to commit to meeting a schedule and a price.

By now you should have some ideas of how MIS can help you in your job. Working as a manager, you will develop many ideas involving technology that you want to try. So how do you turn your ideas into an actual system? For complex systems, you will undoubtedly turn to experts for help: computer programmers and systems analysts. In order to communicate effectively with these people, you need to understand a little bit about how they do their jobs and the techniques that are available. Part of that understanding involves learning a little about the problems that are likely to arise when you develop computer systems. As illustrated in Figure 12.1, there are several different ways to create computer systems. Non-MIS managers are often involved in deciding which method to use, so you need to know the benefits, costs, and limitations of each method.

As a manager, you need to understand the problems and limitations facing MIS departments. You need to know why it can take MIS so long to create even small systems. Additionally, more and more often, managers and workers are expected to develop their own small systems (known as *end-user development*). The lessons learned from large MIS projects can help you create your own small system, particularly with implementation problems and solutions.

Trends

Internally, computer processors have limited capabilities. The processor has a set of a few hundred internal instructions that it knows how to perform, such as moving a number to a new place in memory or adding two numbers together. Initially, all computer programs were written at this low level; but writing programs at this level is difficult and time consuming. Over time, two major innovations were created to reduce the difficulty of programming at these low levels: (1) higher-level languages were created that handle many details automatically for the programmer, and (2) common algorithms used by many applications were created and sold as operating systems. These advances enable programmers to focus on the applications instead of machine-specific details.

Despite many advances, writing programs is still complex and time consuming. Large-scale applications require the teamwork of millions of hours of programmer time and cost hundreds of millions of dollars to build and maintain. These high, fixed, development costs underlie the growth of the commercial software industry. By making the software relatively generic and selling it to hundreds or thousands of firms, the development costs are spread over a wider group.

Increasingly, firms are moving away from custom-written software. They are purchasing packages and hiring outside programmers to develop many components. In these situations, design issues generally consist of choosing and customizing the software to meet the individual needs of the organization.

Introduction

There is a fundamental dilemma faced by anyone developing a computer application. Most problems are so large they have to be split into smaller pieces. The difficulty lies in combining the pieces back into a complete solution. Often each piece is assigned to a different team, and sometimes it takes months to complete each section. Without a solid plan and control, the entire system might collapse. Thousands of system development projects have failed or been canceled because of these complications.

Partly because of the problems that have been encountered in the past, and partly because of technological improvements, several techniques are available to develop computer systems. The most formal approach is known as the **systems development life cycle (SDLC)**. As indicated by the Reality Bytes, large organizations that develop several systems use this method to coordinate the teams, evaluate progress, and ensure quality development. Most organizations have created their own versions of SDLC. Any major company that uses SDLC also has a manual that is several inches thick (or comparable online documentation) that lays out the rules that MIS designers have to follow. Although these details vary from firm to firm, all of the methods have a common foundation. The goal is to build a system by analyzing the business processes and breaking the problem into smaller, more manageable pieces.

Improvements in technology improve the development process. The powerful features of commercial software make it easier to build new applications. Programmers and designers can work with larger, more powerful objects. For example, instead of programming each line in COBOL, a report can be created in a few minutes using a database management system or a spreadsheet. **Prototyping** is a design technique that takes advantage of these new tools. The main objective of prototyping is to create a working version of the system as quickly as possible, even if some components are not included in the early versions. The third method of creating systems, **end-user development** relies on users to create their own systems. This method typically uses advanced software (such as spreadsheets and database management systems) and requires users who have some computer skills.

It is important to be careful when you implement any new system. Case studies show that major problems have arisen during implementation of systems. In fact, some organizations have experienced so many problems that they will deliberately stick with older, less useful systems just to avoid the problems that occur during implementation. Although changes can cause problems, there are ways to deal with them during implementation.

There have been some spectacular failures in the development of computer systems. Projects always seem to be over budget and late. Worse, systems are sometimes developed

Accenture, a spin-off from Andersen, is the largest worldwide consulting firm in management information systems. It conducts major installations using a proprietary methodology called Method/1. Method/1 uses four phases in the development process: plan, design, implement, and maintain.

McKinsey and Co., a strategic consulting firm, examines organizations with a copyrighted "Seven S" model. The seven S's are structure, systems, style, staff, skills, strategy, and shared values.

Electronic Data Systems (EDS), started by Ross Perot, purchased by GM, and now independent, is the largest outsourcing company. It also develops systems using a traditional SDLC methodology. The detailed methodology has thousands of individual steps spelled out on separate pages that must be signed off at each step.

Rational Rose, a tool to support object-oriented development that was designed by the leading OO gurus. It is a graphical tool designed to show the object details and their relationships. It supports reverse engineering by reading existing code and converting it into the corresponding diagrams. The Rose tool can also generate the final code from the diagrams.

Microsoft, as a commercial software vendor developing highly complex systems used by millions of people, has developed its own methodologies for quickly creating code. The company has been a proponent of Rapid Application Development to reduce the time it takes to complete large projects. The methodology is designed to segment the code so hundreds of programmers can work on it simultaneously. The methodology also relies on creating code that can be modified later for improvements and patches.

Open Source, led by Richard Stallman and the GNU project, thousands of programmers around the globe are building complex projects in a loose-knit organization. Generally, one person is a project leader responsible for setting strategies and resolving disputes. All of the source code is publicly available to anyone (hence the name). Interested programmers suggest improvements and submit the modifications. Some complex systems have been built this way with minimal central control.

and never used because they did not solve the right problems or they are impossible to use. Several design methods have been created to help prevent these problems. All methods have advantages and drawbacks. As a result, they tend to be suitable for different types of problems.

Building Information Systems

Several methods exist to build information systems, but all of them can be challenging. The key to understanding the different methods is to realize that ultimately developers have to write detailed program code. The primary difference in the methods lies in who writes the code. The four basic methods are: (1) program the entire application from scratch, (2) pay an outside company to develop the application, (3) assemble an application by customizing various purchased components, or (4) purchase the entire application from another company. These methods apply to virtually any type of software development project, from small one-person applications to complex e-commerce solutions.

Custom Programming

Ultimately, all applications are created by teams of programmers writing detailed code. Writing your own custom program gives you complete control over the application. You can include any features, build in special routines unique to your company, and integrate the data with your existing systems. The problem with creating your own code is that programming is difficult, time consuming, hard to control, and expensive. Even when the application is completed, you will still need groups of programmers to fix problems, add new features, and develop future versions of the software.

Modern development tools make it easier to write programs today, but every application still requires intense development efforts and the tools never seem to provide all of the features you need.

The National Association of Software and Services Companies (NASSCOM) in India reported that export revenue in the second quarter of 2001 was Rs 86 billion ($1.8 billion) compared with 56.7 billion in the same period the prior year. Despite the economic slowdown, the United States accounted for 62 percent of the revenue. In many cases, the desire to reduce costs encouraged U.S. firms to outsource their software development to Indian firms. By October 2001, feeling the effects of the continuing economic slowdown and the September 11 attack, many firms were pushing back their development plans, including the use of programming companies in India. Indian companies like Aptech that provide programmers for on-site staff in the United States particularly noted a decline in the demand for programmers. Rama Raju, managing director of Satyam Computer Services Ltd in India, noted that in the past it was critical to get U.S. executives to travel to India to inspect the company's infrastructure and development facilities. But due to airline safety concerns, U.S. executives are reluctant to make the trip.

Source: Adapted from www.siliconindia.com, "India's Software, Services Exports Rise 52% in First Quarter," August 16, 2001. [http://www.siliconindia.com/tech/tech_pgtwo.asp?newsno=10784&newscat=Technology]

Outsourcing and Contract Programmers

One of the other problems with creating your own software is that you generally have to hire many programmers at some point in the development. But when the development is finished, you will rarely need all of these programmers. So, either you find new tasks for them or you have to release them to reduce your costs. But hiring and firing workers for a single project is frowned upon. Consequently, many firms use contract programmers, or even outsourcing, to handle system development.

With contract programming, you negotiate with a company to provide specialists for a given period of time. When their work on the project is complete, they move on to another job. The process saves you the problems of hiring and firing large numbers of employees. On the other hand, contractor salaries are usually higher than traditional employees. More important, several lawsuits have made it critical that you clarify the exact role of contractors—otherwise they can sue to be classified as regular employees to gain additional benefits such as stock options.

Outsourcing goes a step farther than contract programming. When you outsource project development, you transfer most responsibility to the outside firm. Typically, you negotiate a development price, provide detailed specifications, and the outsourcer hires workers and develops the system. A huge variety of outsourcing arrangements are available, including situations where the outsourcers run your entire MIS department or just your servers or networks, or handle PC maintenance.

The primary advantage of outsourcing is that the external company takes responsibility for managing the process and producing the application. You still have the responsibility to clearly define exactly how the application should work, but the outsourcer bears more of the risk—particularly with fixed-fee contracts. The one thing you want to avoid with contractors and outsourcers is uncontrolled hourly fees.

Assemble Applications from Components

A good way to reduce development time and costs is to buy portions of the system from other companies. Even if you need a custom solution, you can purchase a variety of software components that handle many of the difficult tasks for you. Components are a powerful feature of modern operating systems. They are blocks of code that are integrated into custom applications. For instance, you could purchase a security control to handle encryption on a website. Whenever your application needs to encrypt or decrypt some data, it simply calls the component's methods. Similarly, if you need to process a credit card application, you can install a component (or link to a Web service) that handles everything for you. Thousands of useful components are available for a few hundred dollars each, or less. You simply install the component on your server and your programmers can begin using the functions within their code. This approach relies on the capabilities of **commercial off-the-shelf software (COTS).** As the number and quality of software packages has increased, it has become easier to build a system based on COTS.

Increasingly, tasks currently performed by components will be offered as services over the Internet. The same principles will apply, but the external company will maintain the application, install upgrades, and add new features. Additionally, new services will become available. For example, services will provide instant exchange rate conversions so you can list prices in any currency. The conversion rates will always be current with no effort on your part.

Components have many substantial advantages and only minor drawbacks (primarily the price hassles with upgrades). They can significantly reduce development time and provide powerful features that are beyond the capabilities of many staff programmers. In fact, many outsource specialists develop their own collection of components to use in developing custom solutions. By integrating commonly used features, they can build new applications faster with fewer errors.

Purchase an External Solution

Taking the concept of components and outsourcing a step further, many commercial software companies sell prepackaged applications. Some are *turnkey* systems where you simply load your data, select a few preferences, and the system runs (much like buying an automobile, you turn the key and no assembly is needed). Other applications require detailed customization. The ERP packages (such as SAP) are classic examples. The system handles all of the basic operational data of the firm, including generation of financial reports. You purchase the software from the vendor and install it on top of a database management system. You still have to set up your accounts and some custom details for reports. The application can then be used by your company to track all financial and manufacturing data and produce standardized reports.

On the other hand, you can also customize most of the features. If you need unique manufacturing reports, you can write code to generate them. The degree of customization often depends on the attitude of management. The drawback to extensive customization is that it requires specially trained programmers and delays the entire project. Additionally, when the DBMS vendor or the ERP vendor upgrades the underlying software, you may have to rewrite all of your custom programs.

Prewritten packages can have high price tags (SAP costs can easily run into millions of dollars). But, it could take millions of hours of programmer time to create a custom system with the same functionality.

In general, it is almost always preferable to buy solutions, but keep a close eye on prices. The commercial software essentially spreads the development costs across thousands of firms. Unless you have a truly unique application and are willing to pay a staff of top-notch programmers, it is better to share the development costs. And if you do have a radically different application, you should consider packaging it and selling it to other firms to reduce your costs.

Systems Development Life Cycle

The Need for Control

Runaway projects are a substantial problem in any development effort, but they are particularly important for new designs. Since many e-commerce projects need to be developed from scratch, it is hard to estimate the amount of time and effort needed to build the system. As projects become larger, they become more difficult to monitor and control. Several e-commerce firms failed because they were unable to produce a working system.

A factor in many runaway projects is the concept of scope creep or expanding features. Once development starts, users and programmers start thinking of new ideas that they would

FIGURE 12.2

Runaway projects. Managers fear runaway projects, but they still occur. Some projects end up two to five times over budget and behind schedule. Some projects are canceled because they never meet their objectives. Some fail because of design problems and conflicts among users, management, and developers. An important step in managing projects is to identify when the project becomes a runaway project.

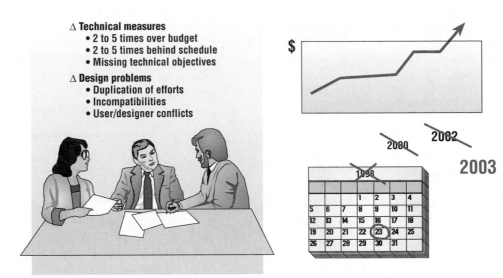

like to see in the project. So a simple, two-month project for one division suddenly expands into a two-year companywide project costing millions of dollars. A key role of any IT project manager is to politely avoid adding "features" that are not immediately necessary.

SDLC was designed to overcome the problems that arose with large projects that involve many users and require thousands of hours of development by multiple analysts and programmers. Difficulties with runaway projects are shown in Figure 12.2.

Before the use of the SDLC method, several related problems were common. It was hard to coordinate and control the various programmers and analysts, so there were duplicated efforts. Individual programmers created portions of a system that would not work together. Users did not always have much input into the process. When they did have input, there were conflicts between users, and analysts did not know which approach to use. With long-term projects, programmers were promoted to other areas or left for different companies. New employees had to learn the system and determine what others had done before they could proceed. Similarly, new users would appear (through promotions and transfers), and existing users would change the specifications of the system. These problems often lead to runaway projects—projects that are significantly late and over budget. Even today, there are many instances of runaway projects.

These problems are related through the issue of control. It is impossible to prevent users from changing the specifications and to prevent employees from taking other jobs. Likewise, large projects involving many analysts and programmers will always have problems with coordination and compatibility. The goal of SDLC was to design a system that can handle all of these problems.

A key value in SDLC is project management. As shown in the appendix to Chapter 13, an important aspect of project management consists of identifying the dependencies among the various tasks. Project management tools exist to help evaluate these dependencies and show how the overall schedule is affected by delays in individual tasks.

Introduction to SDLC

An important feature of the SDLC approach is that it is a comprehensive method. Some organizations (such as EDS) that specialize in systems development have hundreds of pages in manuals to detail all the steps and rules for using SDLC. Fortunately, it is possible to understand SDLC by looking at a smaller number of steps. As illustrated in Figure 12.3, the SDLC approach encompasses five basic stages: (1) feasibility and planning, (2) systems analysis, (3) systems design, (4) implementation, and (5) maintenance and review.

Actually, just about any systems-development methodology uses these five steps. They differ largely in how much time is spent in each section, who does the work, and in the

FIGURE 12.3

Systems development life cycle. Sometimes SDLC is known as the waterfall methodology because each step produces outputs that are used in the next step. The existing system is studied for problems and improvements. A new design is analyzed for feasibility. In-depth analysis generates the business requirements. Systems design turns them into a technical design that is implemented, creating a new system. This new system is analyzed and the process continues.

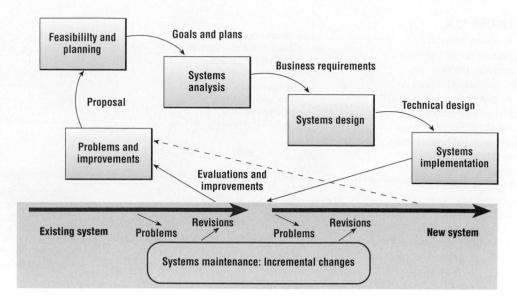

degree of formality involved. The SDLC is by far the most formal method, so it offers a good starting point in describing the various methodologies.

Feasibility and Planning

The primary goal of **systems analysis** is to identify problems and determine how they can be solved with a computer system. In formal SDLC methodologies, the first step in systems analysis is a **feasibility study**. A feasibility study is a quick examination of the problems, goals, and expected costs of the system. The objective is to determine whether the problem can reasonably be solved with a computer system. In some cases, maybe there is a better (or cheaper) alternative, or perhaps the problem is simply a short-term annoyance and will gradually disappear. In other cases, the problem may turn out to be more complex than was thought and to involve users across the company. Also, some problems may not be solvable with today's technology. It might be better to wait for improved technology or lower prices. In any case, you need to determine the scope of the project to gain a better idea of the costs, benefits, and objectives.

The feasibility study is typically written so that it can be easily understood by nonprogrammers. It is used to "sell" the project to upper management and as a starting point for the next step. Additionally, it is used as a reference to keep the project on track, and to evaluate the progress of the MIS team. Projects are typically evaluated in three areas of feasibility: economical, operational, and technical. Is the project cost effective or is there a cheaper solution? Will the proposed system improve the operations of the firm, or will complicating factors prevent it from achieving its goals? Does the technology exist, and does the firm have the staff to make the technology work?

When the proposal is determined to be feasible, the MIS team leaders are appointed, and a plan and schedule are created. The schedule contains a detailed listing of what parts of the project will be completed at each time. Of course, it is extremely difficult to estimate the true costs and completion dates. Nonetheless, the schedule is an important tool to evaluate the status of the project and the progress of the MIS teams. Figure 12.4 summarizes the role of planning and scheduling in providing control for projects.

Systems Analysis

Once a project has been shown to be feasible and is approved, work can begin on a full-fledged analysis. The first step is to determine how the existing system works and where the problems are located. The technique is to break the system into pieces. Smaller pieces are easier to understand and to explain to others. Also, each piece can be assigned to a different

FIGURE 12.4

Development controls. A complex system requires careful management. Without planning and control, any project will become a runaway. Control begins with a detailed plan and performance targets that enable managers to evaluate progress and identify problems. System control is provided by standardized practices and procedures to ensure that teams are producing compatible output. User input and control ensure that the final project will actually be useful.

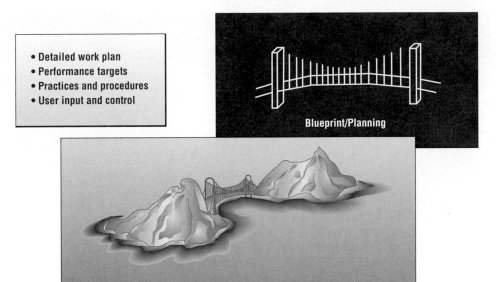

- Detailed work plan
- Performance targets
- Practices and procedures
- User input and control

Blueprint/Planning

MIS team. As long as they work from the same initial description and follow all of the standards, the resulting pieces should fit back together. Of course, it still takes time and effort to integrate all of the pieces.

Diagrams are often created to illustrate the system. The diagrams are used to communicate among analysts and users, other analysts, and eventually the programmers. Data flow diagrams are a common method to display the relationships that were determined during systems analysis. The diagrams represent a way to divide the system into smaller pieces.

Graphics tools provide a useful way to communicate with the user and to document the user requirements. However, they do not speed up the development process. Producing, changing, and storing documentation can be a significant problem. Yet these tools are necessary because they make it easier for the user to control the final result. One increasingly common solution is to keep all of the documentation on the computer. This method reduces the costs, makes it easier for everyone to share the documentation, and ensures that all users have up-to-date information for the system.

At the end of the analysis phase, the MIS team will have a complete description of the business requirements. The problems and needs are documented with text, data flow diagrams, and other figures depending on the methodology followed.

Systems Design

The third major step of the SDLC is to design the new system. During this step, the new system is typically designed on paper. The objective of systems design is to describe the new system as a collection of modules or subsystems. By subdividing the total project, each portion can be given to a single programmer to develop. As the pieces are completed, the overall design ensures that they will work together. Typically, the diagrams created during the analysis phase can be modified to indicate how the new system will work. The design will list all of the details, including data inputs, system outputs, processing steps, database designs, manual procedures, and feedback and control mechanisms. Backup and recovery plans along with security controls will be spelled out to ensure that the database is protected.

In traditional SDLC methods, managers and users will be shown various components of the system as they are completed. The managers will have to *sign off* on these sections to indicate that they meet the user needs. This signature is designed to ensure that users provide input to the system. If there are many diverse users, there can be major disagreements about how the system should function. Sign-offs require users to negotiate and formally agree to the design. It is relatively easy to make design changes at this stage. If everyone attempts to make changes at later stages, the cost increases dramatically.

Reality Bytes   PeopleSupport

Developing systems is a difficult task. Building new systems in other nations can be even more complex. In 2000, PeopleSupport, Inc., was developing a customer contact center in Manila when a typhoon took out the city's power facilities. But PeopleSupport's systems remained running because the company was located in a building that had its own power supply—capable of running the building for a month. Abby Hossein, CIO, notes "In Manila, the difference between being located in Building A or Building B could be the kiss of death." This local knowledge can be critical to the success of a project on international shores. Language issues are also important. Just because someone knows "English" does not mean that he or she understands all of the terms, or understands them to mean the same thing. Cultural

differences also present problems, particularly in terms of things like deadlines. Does everyone understand a deadline is critical, or do they just treat it as a guideline? Similarly, holidays and working hours vary around the world. If team members are working in different parts of the world, experts suggest you hang maps and clocks set to each time; so everyone can quickly identify the time at each location. In the end, local knowledge is critical, Hossein notes "Local people understand how things work in the country. They have contacts we can use, like a connection in an embassy to get a visa."

Source: Adapted from Kathleen Melymuka, "Projects across the Pond," *Computerworld,* October 8, 2001.

In terms of physical design, some of the hardware and software will be purchased. Programmers will write and test the program code. In most large projects, the actual coding takes only 15 to 30 percent of the total development time. Initial data will be collected or transferred from existing systems. Manuals and procedures will be written to instruct users and system operators on how to use the system.

Design tools can be used to create prototypes of major system elements. For example, a designer can quickly piece together displays that illustrate how each screen might look and how the user will see the system. These prototypes can be used to help users walk through aspects of the proposed system and make changes while it is easy and inexpensive. The walkthroughs also provide management with feedback regarding the time schedule and anticipated costs of the project, because they are often scheduled in the original feasibility study.

The output of the design stage consists of a complete technical specification of the new system. It includes as many details as possible, sometimes leading to thousands of pages (or computer files) of description.

One of the difficulties in the design stage is sometimes called *creeping elegance.* As the system is being built, analysts, programmers, and users all want to include additional features. Although many of the features are good ideas, the continual evolution of the system causes additional delays. It also complicates testing, because changes in one section can affect the rest of the system.

Systems Implementation

Systems implementation involves installation and changeover from the previous system to the new one, including training users and making adjustments to the system. Many nasty problems can arise at this stage. You have to be extremely careful in implementing new systems. First, users are probably nervous about the change already. If something goes wrong, they may never trust the new system. Second, if major errors occur, you could lose important business data.

A crucial stage in implementation is final testing. Testing and quality control must be performed at every stage of development, but a final systems test is needed before staff entrust the company's data to the new system. Occasionally, small problems will be noted, but their resolution will be left for later. In any large system, errors and changes will occur. The key is to identify them and determine which ones must be fixed immediately. Smaller problems are often left to the software maintenance staff.

Change is an important part of MIS. Designing and implementing new systems often causes changes in the business operations. Yet, many people do not like changes.

Changes require learning new methods, forging new relationships with people and managers, or perhaps even loss of jobs. Changes exist on many levels: in society, in business, and in information systems. Changes can occur because of shifts in the environment, or they can be introduced by internal **change agents**. Left to themselves, most organizations will resist even small changes. Change agents are objects or people who cause or facilitate changes. Sometimes it might be a new employee who brings fresh ideas; other times changes can be mandated by top-level management. Sometimes an outside event such as arrival of a new competitor or a natural disaster forces an organization to change. Whatever the cause, people tend to resist change. However, if organizations do not change, they cannot survive. The goal is to implement systems in a manner that recognizes resistance to change but encourages people to accept the new system. Effective implementation involves finding ways to reduce this resistance. Sometimes, implementation involves the cooperation of outsiders such as suppliers.

Because implementation is so important, several techniques have been developed to help implement new systems. Direct cutover is an obvious technique, where the old system is simply dropped and the new one started. If at all possible, it is best to avoid this technique, because it is the most dangerous to data. If anything goes wrong with the new system, you run the risk of losing valuable information because the old system is not available. The various methods are displayed in Figure 12.5.

In many ways, the safest choice is to use parallel implementation. In this case, the new system is introduced alongside the old one. Both systems are operated at the same time until you determine that the new system is acceptable. The main drawback to this method is that it can be expensive because data has to be entered twice. Additionally, if users are nervous about the new system, they might avoid the change and stick with the old method. In this case, the new system may never get a fair trial.

Several intermediate possibilities are called *phased implementation.* For example, if you design a system for a chain of retail stores, you could pilot test the first implementation in one store. By working with one store at a time, there are likely to be fewer problems. But if problems do arise, you will have more staff members around to overcome the obstacles. When the system is working well in one store, you can move to the next location. Similarly, even if there is only one store, you might be able to split the implementation into sections based on the area of business. You might install a set of computer cash registers first. When they work correctly, you can connect them to a central computer and produce daily reports. Next, you can move on to annual summaries and payroll. Eventually the entire system will be installed.

FIGURE 12.5

Conversion options. When you implement a new system, there are several possible conversion methods. In most cases, direct cutover should be avoided because of the disruptions and potential for lost data. Parallel conversion entails running both systems simultaneously, which is safe but can become expensive and time consuming. With multiple stores or business units, pilot introductions of phased implementations are common. For pilot testing, designers can bring extra workers, managers, and systems designers to one location and work out the problems with the system. Once the system is running well, it can be implemented at other locations. With a phased implementation, a system can be introduced slowly throughout the company (e.g., by department). Projects can also be phased in by modules.

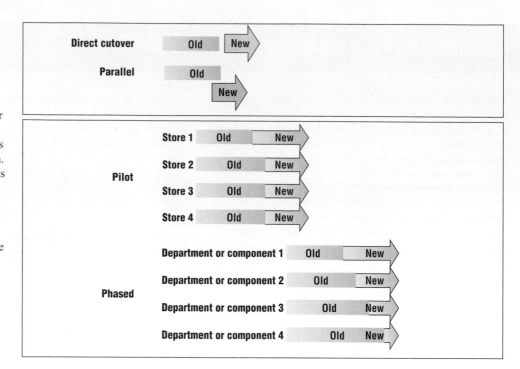

Maintenance

Once the system is installed, the MIS job has just begun. Computer systems are constantly changing. Hardware upgrades occur continually, and commercial software tools may change every year. Users change jobs. Errors may exist in the system. The business changes, and management and users demand new information and expansions. All of these actions mean the system needs to be modified. The job of overseeing and making these modifications is called **software maintenance**.

The pressures for change are so great that in most organizations today as much as 80 percent of the MIS staff is devoted to modifying existing programs. These changes can be time consuming and difficult. Most major systems were created by teams of programmers and analysts over a long period. In order to make a change to a program, the programmer has to understand how the current program works. Because the program was written by many different people with varying styles, it can be hard to understand. Finally, when a programmer makes a minor change in one location, it can affect another area of the program, which can cause additional errors or necessitate more changes.

One difficulty with software maintenance is that every time part of an application is modified, there is a risk of adding defects (bugs). Also, over time the application becomes less structured and more complex, making it harder to understand. These are some of the main reasons why the year 2000 alterations were so expensive and time consuming. At some point, a company may decide to replace or improve the heavily modified system. There are several techniques for improving an existing system, ranging from rewriting individual sections to restructuring the entire application. The difference lies in scope—how much of the application needs to be modified. Older applications that were subject to modifications over several years tend to contain code that is no longer used, poorly documented changes, and inconsistent naming conventions. These applications are prime candidates for restructuring, during which the entire code is analyzed and reorganized to make it more efficient. More important, the code is organized, standardized, and documented to make it easier to make changes in the future.

Evaluation

An important phase in any project is evaluating the resulting system. As part of this evaluation, it is also important to assess the effectiveness of the particular development process. There are several questions to ask. Were the initial cost estimates accurate? Was the project

FIGURE 12.6

Evaluation of completed projects. When projects are completed, the design team should evaluate the project and assess the development procedures. Cost and time estimates can be used to improve estimates for future projects. System performance issues can be addressed with future upgrades. It is important that the system achieve project goals and provide users with necessary tools and support.

Feasibility comparison	
Cost and budget	Compare actual costs to budget estimates
Time estimates	Was project completed on time?
Revenue effects	Does system produce additional revenue?
Maintenance costs	How much money and time are spent on changes?
Project goals	Does system meet the initial goals of the project?
User satisfaction	How do users (and management) evaluate the system?
System performance	
System reliability	Are the results accurate and on time?
System availability	Is the system available continually?
System security	Does the system provide access to authorized users?

completed on time? Did users have sufficient input? Are maintenance costs higher than expected? The assessment items are summarized in Figure 12.6.

Evaluation is a difficult issue. How can you as a manager tell the difference between a good system and a poor one? In some way, the system should decrease costs, increase revenue, or provide a competitive advantage. Although these effects are important, they are often subtle and difficult to measure. The system should also be easy to use and flexible enough to adapt to changes in the business. If employees or customers continue to complain about a system, it should be reexamined.

A system also needs to be *reliable.* It should be available when needed and should produce accurate output. Error detection can be provided in the system to recognize and avoid common problems. Similarly, some systems can be built to tolerate errors, so that when errors arise, the system recognizes the problem and works around it. For example, some computers exist today that automatically switch to backup components when one section fails, thereby exhibiting **fault tolerance.**

An important concept for managers to remember when dealing with new systems is that the evaluation mechanism should be determined at the start of the project. Far too often, the question of evaluation is ignored until someone questions the value of the finished product. It is a good design practice to ask what would make this system a good system when it is finished or how we can tell a good system from a bad one in this application. Even though these questions may be difficult to answer, they need to be asked. The answers, however incomplete, will provide valuable guidance during the design stage.

Recall that every system needs a goal, a way of measuring progress toward that goal, and a feedback mechanism. Traditionally, control of systems has been the task of the computer programming staff. Their primary goal was to create error-free code, and they used various testing techniques to find and correct errors in the code. Today, creating error-free code is not a sufficient goal.

We have all heard the phrase, "The customer is always right." The meaning behind this phrase is that sometimes people have different opinions on whether a system is behaving correctly. When there is a conflict, the opinion that is most important is that of the customer. In the final analysis, customers are in control because they can always take their business elsewhere. With information systems, the users are the customers and the users should be the ones in control. Users determine whether a system is good. If the users are not convinced that the system performs useful tasks, it is not a good system.

Strengths and Weaknesses of SDLC

The primary purpose of the SDLC method of designing systems is to provide guidance and control over the development process. As summarized in Figure 12.7, there are strengths and weaknesses to this methodology. SDLC management control is vital for large projects to ensure that the individual teams work together. There are also financial controls to keep track of the project expenses. The SDLC steps are often spelled out in great detail. The formality makes it easier to train employees and to evaluate the progress of the development. It also

FIGURE 12.7

Strengths and weaknesses of SDLC. The SDLC methodologies were created to control large, complex development projects. They work fairly well for those types of processes. They do not work as well for small projects that require rapid development or heavy user involvement with many changes.

Strengths	Weaknesses
Control	Increased development time
Monitor large projects	Increased development costs
Detailed steps	Systems must be defined up front
Evaluate costs and completion targets	Rigidity
Documentation	Hard to estimate costs, project overruns
Well-defined user input	User input sometimes limited
Ease of maintenance	
Development and design standards	
Tolerates changes in MIS staffing	

ensures that steps are not skipped, such as user approval, documentation, and testing. For large, complex projects, this degree of control is necessary to ensure the project can be completed. Another advantage of SDLC is that by adhering to standards while building the system, programmers will find the system easier to modify and maintain later. The internal consistency and documentation make it easier to modify. With 80 percent of MIS resources spent on maintenance, this advantage can be critical.

In some cases the formality of SDLC causes problems. Most important, it increases the cost of development and lengthens the development time. Remember that often less than 25 percent of the time is spent on actually writing programs. A great deal of the rest of the time is spent filling out forms and drawing diagrams.

The formality of the SDLC also causes problems with projects that are hard to define. SDLC works best if the entire system can be accurately specified in the beginning. That is, users and managers need to know *exactly* what the system should do long before the system is created. That is not a serious problem with transaction-processing systems. However, consider the development of a complex decision support system. Initially, the users may not know how the system can help. Only through working with the system on actual problems will they spot errors and identify enhancements.

Although some large projects could never have been completed without SDLC, its rigidity tends to make it difficult to develop many modern applications. Additionally, experience has shown that it has not really solved the problems of projects being over budget and late. As a result of this criticism, many people are searching for alternatives. One possibility is to keep the basic SDLC in place and use technology to make it more efficient. Other suggestions have been to replace the entire process with a more efficient development process, such as prototyping. Consider the assistance of technology first.

Alternatives to SDLC

The two primary drawbacks to SDLC are: (1) it takes a considerable amount of time, and (2) all of the system details have to be specified up front. The project management and control features add paperwork and delays, making SDLC unsuitable for small projects. SDLC worked reasonably well for transaction-processing systems that were well defined and the design elements could be specified up front. It does not work well for decision support systems particularly when users do not really know exactly what they want the system to do.

Prototyping

Prototyping has been proposed as a method to use for systems that are not overly complex and do not involve too many users or analysts. Just as automobile engineers design prototypes before attempting to build the final car, MIS programmers can build early versions of systems. These systems are then continually modified until the user is satisfied.

The first step in designing a system via prototyping is to talk with the user. The analyst then uses a fourth-generation language and a DBMS to create approximately what

FIGURE 12.8

Prototyping. Prototyping typically involves one user and one developer. The developer interviews the user and designs an initial system using a DBMS. The user works with the prototype and suggests changes. This process repeats until the user or developer is satisfied or gives up.

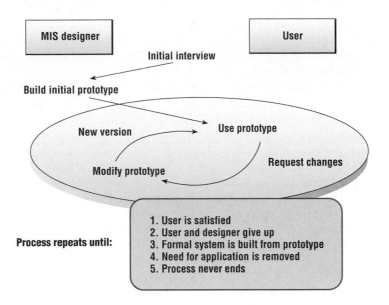

the user wants. This first step generally requires only a couple of weeks. The business user then works with the prototype and suggests changes. The analyst makes the changes and this cycle repeats until the user is satisfied or decides that the system is not worth pursuing. The emphasis is on getting a working version of the system to the user as fast as possible, even if it does not have all the details. Figure 12.8 illustrates the cycle involved in prototyping.

The major advantage of prototyping is that users receive a working system much sooner than they would with the SDLC method. Additionally, the users have more input so they are more likely to get what they wanted. Finally, remember that a large portion of MIS time is spent making changes. A system designed with the prototyping method is much easier to change because it was designed to be modified from the start.

Developing Systems Requires Teamwork: JAD and RAD

Designing and developing systems is much easier if the entire system can be built by one person. In fact, that is one of the strengths of recent tools—they enable a single person to build more complex systems. However, many information systems, especially those that affect the entire organization, require teams of IS workers. As soon as multiple designers, analysts, and programmers are involved, we encounter management and communication problems. MIS researchers have measured the effects of these problems. One study by DeMarco and Lister showed that on large projects, 70 percent of a developer's time is spent working with others. Jones noted that team activities accounted for 85 percent of the development costs. There seem to be substantial areas for improvement in systems development by focusing on teamwork.

One of the most difficult steps in creating any new system is determining the user requirements. What does the system need to do and how will it work? This step is crucial. If the designers make a mistake here, the system will either be useless or will need expensive modifications later. Prototyping and SDLC take different approaches to this problem. With SDLC, analysts talk with users and write reports that describe how the system will operate. Users examine the reports and make changes. This approach is time consuming and difficult for users because they only see paper notes of the proposed system. Prototyping overcomes some of the problems by letting users work with actual screens and reports. But use of prototyping is hard to expand beyond one or two users.

Some companies overcome the problems of SDLC by prototyping each input screen and report with one or two primary users. Once the main concepts have been designed, the analysts formalize the system and get approval from other users. The designs are then given to programmers to create with the traditional SDLC development methods.

Recall that an important reason for using SDLC is to obtain the views and agreement of many users. Using traditional interview methods and paper documentation, this process often takes several months. Each change has to be reexamined by other users, and disagreements have to be resolved.

A technique known as **joint application design (JAD)** was created to speed up the design stage. With JAD the main system is designed in an intense three- to five-day workshop. Users, managers, and systems analysts participate in a series of intense meetings to design the inputs (data and screens) and outputs (reports) needed by the new system.

By putting all of the decision makers in one room at the same time, conflicts are identified and resolved faster. Users and managers gain a better understanding of the problems and limitations of technology. The resulting system has greater value for users and managers because it more closely matches their needs. There is less need for changes later, when they become more expensive, so the system is cheaper to create.

The biggest drawback to JAD is that it requires getting everyone together at the same time for an extended period of time. Even for moderately complex systems, the meetings can run eight hours a day for three to five days. Most managers (and users) find it difficult to be away from their jobs for that length of time. Higher-level managers are also needed at these meetings to ensure the system provides the appropriate reports and information. Finally, the meetings can only succeed if they are led by a trained facilitator. The facilitator keeps the discussions moving in the right direction, minimizes conflicts, and encourages everyone to participate. At the end of the sessions, the systems development team should have a complete description of the proposed system.

Rapid application development (RAD) applies the value of teamwork to the developers. By providing advanced development tools, prebuilt objects, and collaboration tools, some companies have found it is possible to reduce the overall development time. The key is to target steps that can overlap and be performed by multiple teams. By improving the collaboration tools, more steps can be compressed. Many e-commerce projects were developed with RAD techniques. Firms were concerned about being the first in the market and felt they needed to develop software rapidly. The goal of being first was later shown to be pointless, but the techniques of using small groups of programmers using advanced tools, collaboration, and intense programming sessions was relatively successful at quickly producing thousands of new applications.

Extreme Programming

In some ways, **extreme programming (XP)** is a new concept; in other ways it is an extension of the earlier work in prototyping and RAD. The main premise of XP is that SDLC and its variants are too large and cumbersome. While they might provide control, they end up adding complexity, taking more time, and slowing down top programmers. XP simplifies the development process by focusing on small releases (similar to prototyping) that provide value to the customer. Note, Microsoft's Windows XP name is not related to extreme programming.

One new aspect to XP is paired programming, where two programmers work together constantly. Generally, one is the lead programmer and the other is responsible for testing, but the jobs can overlap and be defined by the team. Making testing a key element of programming is an important part of XP. However, paired programming is seen by many as an inefficient use of resources. The second programmer is often a less-experienced developer and can slow down an experienced developer. Additionally, it can be more efficient to have one person test large sections of code at a time, instead of multiple people testing separate pieces.

One of the most challenging aspects to development is that there is a tremendous difference between individual programmers—in subject area knowledge, speed of programming, number of defects, and code maintainability. Some methodologies work well when an organization has top-notch developers, but fall apart in other companies. In choosing a methodology, managers must be aware of the capabilities of the individual programmers—and beware of turnover.

End-User Development

The term *end-user development* simply means that users do all of the development work themselves. In many ways, it resembles prototyping, except that users (instead of analysts from the MIS department) create and modify the prototypes. Clearly the main advantage is that users get what they want without waiting for an MIS team to finish its other work and without the difficulty of trying to describe the business problems to someone else.

Two basic reasons explain why end-user development is increasingly popular. First, most MIS organizations are facing a two- or three-year backlog of projects. That means that if you bring a new project to MIS, the designers will not even start on it for at least two years (unless you give up some other project). In fact, with the Year 2000 changes, many MIS departments simply gave up on other modifications. The second reason is that software tools are getting more powerful and easier to use at the same time. Today it is possible for users to create systems with a spreadsheet in a few hours that 10 years ago would have taken MIS programmers a month to build with third-generation languages. As tools become more powerful and more integrated, it becomes possible to create even more complex systems. Reread the discussion of software integration in Chapter 7 and picture the reports you can create using off-the-shelf software. Five years ago, most users would not dream of being able to create these reports. Today, with windowing software you can build systems that share data with many users across the corporate networks, simply by pointing to items with a mouse. The advantages of end-user development are similar to those in prototyping. In particular, users get what they want, and they get working systems sooner.

The potential problems of end-user development are not always easy to see. Most of them arise from the fact that users generally lack the training and experience of MIS analysts and programmers. For instance, systems produced by end users tend to be written for only one person to use. They are oriented to working on stand-alone personal computers. The systems are often customized to fit the needs of the original users. Additionally, most users do not write documentation, so others will have difficulty using the products. Because of lack of training, users rarely perform as much testing as they should. The systems lack security controls and are hard to modify. Think about the problems you encounter when you are given a spreadsheet that was created by the person who held the job before you.

Other problems stem from the bottom-up approach inherent in end-user development. People in different areas of the company will wind up working on the same problem, when it could have been solved once by MIS. Data tends to be scattered throughout the company, making it hard to share and wasting space. Not following standards generates incompatibilities among systems, making it difficult to combine systems created by different departments or even by people within the same department.

End users are limited by the capabilities of commercial software. The initial systems may work fine, but as the company grows and changes, the commercial software might be unable to support the necessary changes. As a result, some users have created systems that produce incorrect answers, take too long to run, or lose data.

The last, and possibly most important, complication is that end-user development takes time away from the user's job. Some users spend months creating and modifying systems that might have been created by MIS programmers in a fraction of the time. One of the reasons for creating an MIS department is to gain efficiency from using specialists. If users are spending too much time creating and revising their own applications, the company needs to consider hiring more MIS personnel.

Analyzing Systems

To solve business problems, you first have to understand how the business operates. The basic idea is that systems consist of smaller, interdependent subsystems. Each subsystem can be broken into smaller sections with more details. By examining each piece and its interactions, it is easier to determine the cause of problems and to derive a solution.

Several techniques have been created to help analyze systems. A useful new method is based on the unified modeling language (UML). UML was designed to assist in creating object-oriented information systems. It asks you to identify the primary objects in the system in terms of their properties and the methods or functions that they can perform.

Most of today's information systems rely heavily on database management systems to collect and share the underlying data. An important strength of this approach is that you rarely need to worry about how data gets from one point in the company to another. Managers simply retrieve the data from the database as needed. The UML design techniques are useful in this environment because they focus on collecting and manipulating the data stored in each object.

Process Analysis

If you are examining a transaction-processing system or dealing with a system that is largely noncomputerized, you should consider creating a process diagram. The purpose of a process diagram is to describe how the individual processes interact with each other. It concentrates on the business activities instead of the objects.

A data flow diagram is a process-oriented technique used for investigating information systems. The method can be used to look at the "big picture" and see how a system works in total. It also can be used to examine the details that occur within each process. Examining organizations at both levels provides a relatively complete picture of the problems and potential solutions. The use of systems analysis is illustrated by evaluating a small system for a zoo.

Input, Process, Output

One useful approach to systems is to look at them as a collection of processes or activities. The most important step in solving problems is to find the cause of the problems. Identifying the major processes in a system will help you understand how the system works. Examining input and output objects helps you spot problems and trace them back to their source. As illustrated in Figure 12.9, systems receive *input* which is *processed* to produce *output*. The process could be mechanical, such as manufacturing using raw materials, workers, and power. Alternatively, it might be a process involving symbolic processing instead of physical activity. For example, accounting systems receive sales data and process it into cash-flow statements. In many cases, there are two types of input and output: physical and data. Physical flows are often accompanied by data. For instance, raw materials are shipped with an invoice that describes the products and the shipping information. Systems theory can be used to examine both types of flow. However, this is an MIS text, so most of the problems presented here deal with flows of data.

Systems are described by collections of these processes. Each system operates in an environment that is somewhat arbitrarily defined by the boundaries of the system. For most problems, anything directly controlled by the firm is considered part of the relevant system. Everything else exists in the environment outside of the firm. The environment typically includes at least the physical space, laws, customs, industry, society, and country in which the firm operates. The firm can influence the physical environment, laws, and customs, but it does not have direct control over them.

Consider the example of a zoo: input and output are less concrete because a zoo primarily produces services instead of products. Figure 12.10 shows the basic inputs of food, money, and health data for potential new animals. Output objects include education, educational materials, and baby animals for other zoos. For most purposes, the system boundary is relatively clear. Visitors, suppliers, and other zoos are outside the direct control of the zoo, so they are in the environment. If the zoo was operated by a governmental agency, it would be harder to identify the boundary. Government systems tend

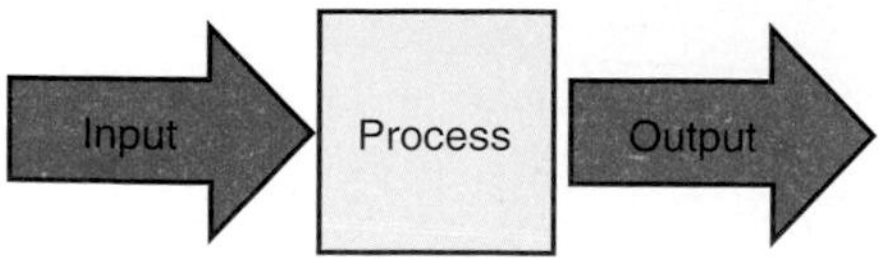

FIGURE 12.9

Each system can be decomposed into three major components: input, process, and output.

to reach into many different areas, and it can be hard to identify their exact limits, especially since they can be extended or contracted by political decisions.

If a system is entirely self-contained and does not respond to changes in the environment, it is called a *closed system.* An *open system* learns by altering itself as the environment changes. Systems are almost never completely closed because closed systems cannot survive for long. However, some systems (or companies) are more responsive to changes in the environment than others.

Most large firms face a certain amount of inertia. It is easier for these firms to keep operating the way they always have than to continually introduce changes. But if a firm becomes too static, it can no longer respond to changes in the environment. Much like the U.S. railroad companies in the 1960s, closed firms will lose ground to firms that are more open and responsive to the environment. Remember that a key component of strategy is to search the environment for potential advantages.

Divide and Conquer

Most problems are too complex and too large to deal with all at once. Even if you could remember all the details, it would be hard to see how everything was supposed to fit together. A crucial step in analyzing a system is to carefully break it into smaller pieces or a collection of subsystems. Each subsystem is separate from the others, but they are connected and interdependent.

Figure 12.11 shows the five primary subsystems within the zoo. Of course, there could be many possible subsystems for the zoo. The actual division depends on how the organization operates. Each subsystem is defined by identifying the input and output flows. How do you

FIGURE 12.10

System boundary at the zoo. As we build systems, we must identify the components that make up the primary system. There will be many other entities that interact with the system. However, these entities are beyond our control, so they are outside of the system.

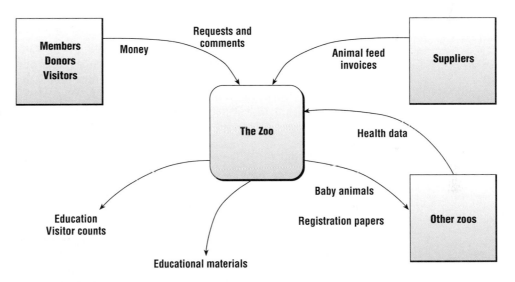

FIGURE 12.11

Primary subsystems of the zoo. The first step in analyzing a system is to identify the major subsystems. In most organizations, this step is relatively easy because the organization will consist of several departments or functions.

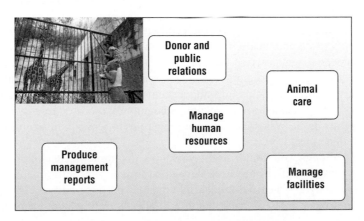

know how to divide a system into smaller parts? Fortunately, most complex systems have already been subdivided into different departments and tasks. Many companies are organized by business functions: accounting, finance, human resources, marketing, MIS, and production. Others are split into divisions according to the type of product.

Once you have determined the major components of the system, each subsystem can be divided into even smaller pieces. An accounting department, for example, might be split into management reporting, tax management, quarterly reporting, and internal auditing groups. Each of these areas might be split into even more levels of detail. At each step, the subsystems are defined by what they do (process), what inputs are used, and what outputs are produced.

There are some drawbacks to the divide-and-conquer approach. It is crucial that you understand how the components work together. If a project is split into small parts and given to independent teams, the teams might lose sight of the overall goals. Important components might not be completed, or the individual pieces might not meet the overall objectives of the system.

Goals and Objectives

Subsystems have goals or purposes. A goal of a manufacturing firm might be to sell more products than any rival (increasing sales). Or it might be to make as much money as possible for its owners (increasing revenues). Another goal might be to find an entirely new area in which to sell products (new market segments). The owners of the system should define its goals. If the system does not have a goal, it has no purpose, and there is no way to evaluate it. In fact, by definition, it would not be a system. When you observe a system, you will need to evaluate performance, which means you have to identify the goals.

Typical spreadsheets give us the ability to ask "what-if?" questions. For example, you might want to know what happens if you increase sales commissions by 10 percent. Goals help focus the answer by providing the ability to ask *Why?* and *So what?* The answer to the *What-if?* question involving commissions might be that revenue increases by 5 percent. But what does that result mean? If we also know that a goal of the company is to increase profits, we could look more carefully and find that increasing commissions by 10 percent leads to a 3 percent increase in profits. That result is important because it brings the system closer to one of its goals. Hence, it would make sense to increase the commissions.

It is clear that to solve business problems, you must first identify the organization's goals. The catch is that there are often conflicting ways to measure the goals. For instance, improved customer satisfaction or product quality might be useful goals. But how do we measure them? Managers who measure customer satisfaction by the number of complaints they receive will make different decisions than those who actively survey customers. In other words, the measurement of our performance with respect to the goals will depend on the data we collect.

Diagramming Systems

We often represent systems graphically to gain insights and spot problems. We also use diagrams to communicate. Communication is of critical importance in MIS and all areas of business. Users describe their problems to systems analysts, who design improvements and describe them to programmers. Ideas and comments can be misinterpreted at any step. We can minimize problems by using a standard diagramming technique. The data flow diagram approach presented in this section is commonly used because it focuses on the logical components of the system and there are few rules to remember, so almost anyone can understand the diagrams.

Although you could invent your own diagramming technique, a method called a **data flow diagram (DFD)** has been developed to represent information systems. It is designed to show how a system is divided into smaller portions and to highlight the flow of data between those parts. Because there are only three graphical elements (five if you count the

FIGURE 12.12

Only four or five objects are used to create a data flow diagram. External entities are objects that are independent and outside the system. Processes are functions and actions applied to data. A data store or file is a place to hold data. Data flows are shown as solid lines with arrows to indicate the data movement. Control flows are marked with dashed lines.

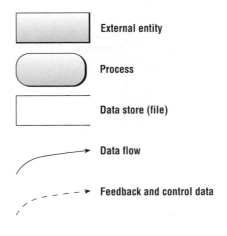

External entity

Process

Data store (file)

Data flow

Feedback and control data

dashed control flows separately), it is an easy technique to learn. The DFD illustrates the systems topics in this chapter.

The basic elements of a DFD are external entities (objects), processes, data stores (files), and data flows that connect the other items. Each element is drawn differently, as shown in Figure 12.12. For example, data flows are shown as arrows. Feedback and control data are usually drawn as dashed lines to show that they have a special purpose.

Figure 12.13 presents the main level of subsystems for the zoo. Notice that it contains external entities, processes, and data flows. This level generally does not show data files or control flows. They can be incorporated in more detailed presentations.

External Entity

When you identify the boundary of a system, you will find some components in the environment that communicate with your system. They are called *external entities*. Although each situation is different, common examples include customers, suppliers, and management. External entities are objects so they are labeled with nouns.

In the zoo example, the primary entities are management, certification agencies, other zoos, and members of the public (visitors, donors, and members). All relevant external entities need to be displayed on the first-level diagram.

Process

In a DFD, a process is an activity that involves data. Technically, DFDs are used to show systems that involve data, not products or other materials. However, in business today, virtually all physical processes have data-processing counterparts. When customers buy something, they get a receipt. In a manufacturing process, the amount of raw materials being put into a machine, measures of the volume of output, and quality control values are recorded. The DFD process is used to represent what happens to the data, not what occurs with the raw material.

Because processes represent actions, they are typically labeled with verbs, such as *sell products* or *create tax reports for management*. There are two important rules involving processes. First, a process cannot invent data. That means every process must have at least one flow of data entering it. Second, a process cannot be a black hole; every process must transfer data somewhere else. If you look at your DFD and find one of these two problems, it usually means that you missed a connection between the processes. On the other hand, processes that do not export data might be data stores or external entities.

Data Store

A data store or file is simply a place to hold data for a length of time. It might be a filing cabinet, reference book, or computer file. In a computerized system, data is likely to be stored in a database management system (DBMS). Chapter 5 provides more detail on the capabilities and uses of a DBMS. For now, it is important to note that data is a valuable resource to any company. In drawing a DFD, try to list exactly what needs to be stored, how long it should be held, and who should be able to read or change the data.

Data Flow

The data flows represent the inputs and outputs of each process or subsystem. The data flows are easy to draw. They are simply arrows that connect processes, entities, and data stores. Be sure to label every data flow. The diagram might seem obvious *now;* however, if someone else reads it or you put it away for several months, it can be hard to figure out what each flow represents.

FIGURE 12.13
The zoo: Level 0. The primary processes and data flows of the zoo.

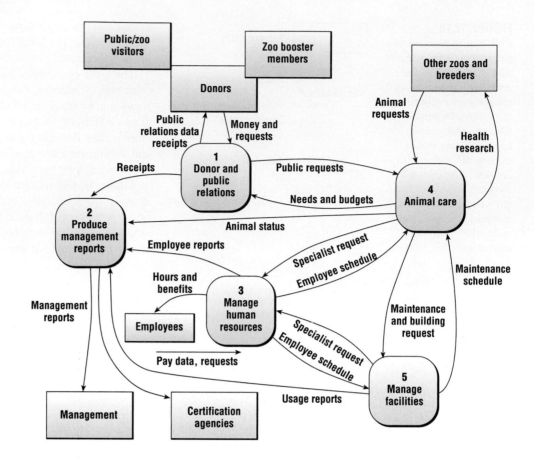

Division of the System

A DFD provides an excellent way to represent a system divided into smaller components. First, each task is shown as a separate process. The data flows between the processes represent the inputs and outputs of each subsystem. Second, the DFD for a complex system would be too large to fit on one page. Hence, the DFD is displayed on different pages or levels. The top level, or *context diagram,* acts as a title page and displays the boundaries of the system and the external entities that interact with the system. The next level (*level zero*) shows the primary subsystems. Figure 12.13 is an example of a level zero diagram. Each of these processes is then exploded into another level that shows more detail. Figure 12.14 is the exploded detail for the first process (donor and public relations). These explosions can continue to any depth until you have displayed all the detailed operations needed to explain the system.

Data Dictionary

In any project, you need to remember additional pieces of information about each object. You might want to keep a sample report for a *management tax report* data flow, along with any deadlines that must be met. For data stores, you need to record information such as who controls it, who needs access to the data, how often it should be backed up, and what elements it contains.

A **data dictionary,** or repository, contains all of the information that explains the terms you used to describe your system. A good computer added software engineering (CASE) tool will maintain the dictionary automatically and help you enter longer descriptions for each item. Without these tools, you will have to keep a notebook that contains the full descriptions. For convenience, the entries should be sorted alphabetically. A word processor can be used to hold and print the dictionary. Figure 12.15 shows sample entries for the zoo system.

FIGURE 12.14

Each process can be expanded into more detail. This diagram shows the interactions with various members of the public. Note that data flows from the higher level must appear on this level.

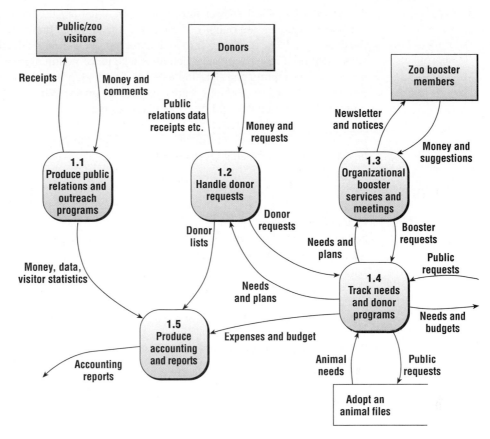

FIGURE 12.15

A few sample entries from the zoo's data dictionary. A data dictionary records details on all of the organization's objects. It is typically organized by type of object. It is easiest to maintain if it is stored in a computer database.

Processes	Description
Animal care	Feed, clean, and vet care
Donor & public relations	Handle public requests and provide educational information
Employee relations	Schedule employees, process benefits, handle government reports
Facility management	Handle maintenance, new construction, planning
Produce mgt. reports	Collect data and produce summary reports for management
Entities	
Certification agencies	Government and private agencies that create rules and regulate zoos
Donors	People and companies that donate money to the zoo
Employees	Primary (paid) workers, full-time and part-time
Other zoos and breeders	Zoos we trade with and share data with
Public/zoo visitors	Daily visits, we rarely keep data on individuals
Zoo booster members	Members who donate money and time for minor benefits
Data	
Accounting reports	Standard (GAAS) accounting reports for management
Certification reports	Reports for certification agencies; produced annually
Facility reports	Summaries of work done and plans, mostly weekly
Needs and budgets	Budgets and special requests from animal care
Public requests	Suggestions and comments from the public

Summary: How Do You Create a DFD?

The first step in creating a DFD is to identify the environment and boundaries of the system by asking the following questions. What problems do you need to solve? What areas do you want to avoid? What are the goals? What are the main external entities? The second step consists of identifying the primary processes that define the system. Keep the list short (fewer than 10). Then answer these questions: What are the main activities in the system? What are the inputs and outputs of each process? How are these processes interconnected by the data flows? The third step is to look at each process in more detail and draw an expanded subsystem on a new page. What activities take place within a given process? What detail is needed in the reports and data inputs? The fourth step is to build the control flows. What processes are used to monitor progress toward the goals? What additional data is collected to monitor the environment and the system's performance?

The key to analyzing systems is to start small. You can begin with one detailed subsystem and build your way up, or you can describe the general system processes and work down by adding increasing levels of detail.

Object-Oriented Design

One way to begin your analysis of a business is to focus on the business objects: what they are and what they do. Objects could be anything from people to raw materials to data files or schedules. The key to **object-oriented design** is to focus on defining what an object is and what it can do. A *class* is a generic description of a set of objects. This distinction is not crucial in this book, but you might want to know there is a difference. For example, the Bicycle class describes any bicycle that could be built by the company. A specific bicycle (e.g., serial number 15) is an object.

Properties and Functions

Objects are defined by a set of properties (or attributes). The properties define the object. They also represent data that will be collected for each object. Consider the small example of a banking system. One primary object will be Accounts. A generic account object would have basic properties such as: Account Number, Account Name, Client, Manager, Date Opened, Beginning Balance, Current Balance, and Interest Rate.

Each object also has functions which describe actions that can be performed by the objects and define how to alter the object. In the bank example, there would be functions to Open Account, Close Account, Accept Deposits, Pay Withdrawals, and Pay Interest. Note that each type of account could have a different method for computing interest payments. One account might compound them daily, another weekly, and so on. With the object-oriented approach, the properties and functions are combined into the definition of the object. The goal is to describe a system so that if you change a function, you only have to change one object. All of the other objects and processes remain the same.

Object Hierarchies

Objects are related to each other. Typically there is a base class of objects and other objects are *derived* from the base definitions by adding properties and altering functions. This process results in an **object hierarchy**, illustrated in Figure 12.16, that shows how the classes are derived from each other. The bank example has several types of accounts with each of these categories containing further subdivisions.

Figure 12.16 also shows detail in the classes by including some of the properties and member functions. The accounts have elements in common that are an **inheritance** from the base class (account), such as the balance attributes. Each level adds additional detail. Each account class also contains member functions to perform operations, such as paying interest. Because the interest computations can be different for each of the accounts, the method is stored with the original definition of each account.

Events

Another aspect of modeling objects is that they are often used in an **event-driven approach**. When some business event occurs, an object function is called or a property is modified. As a manager, you need to think about possible events and how they influence the objects you control. In the banking example, a customer's deposit triggers a credit to her account. This

FIGURE 12.16

Objects: encapsulation, hierarchy, inheritance, polymorphism. Object-oriented design focuses on individual objects and the data within the organization. Processes are secondary and they are usually embedded in the object. By encapsulating these definitions, the objects can be used to develop related systems with less effort. It is also easier to modify a system by making small changes to an object's behavior.

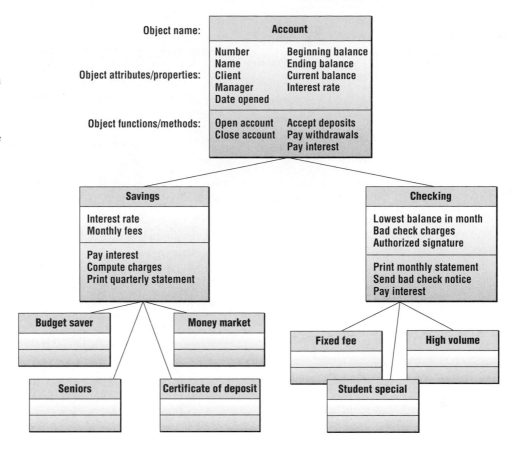

change might then force an update in a daily report object. This chain of events defines the business operations. As a manager, you are likely to be asked to identify the major objects and the events that affect your area of expertise in the company.

To see the usefulness of the object approach, consider what happens if the bank decides to collect additional data for the checking accounts. The only change needed is to add the new data items (and the associated functions) to the checking account class. All checking accounts will then inherit those properties and functions. None of the other operations are affected. Changes to the information system will only affect the specific accounts; the rest of the system will remain the same.

Object-Oriented and Event-Driven Development

The concept of object-oriented design has received considerable attention during the past few years. In some ways, the base design techniques are not much different from traditional SDLC techniques. In other ways, object orientation requires a completely new way of thinking about systems development. The ultimate goal of the object-oriented approach is to build a set of *reusable* objects and procedures. The idea is that eventually, it should be possible to create new systems or modify old ones simply by plugging in a new module or modifying an existing object.

One key difference between object orientation and other development methods is the way processes or functions are handled. With objects, all functions are embedded in the definition of the object—the object comes first. The object approach reverses the treatment of processes and data. With SDLC, illustrated by a data flow diagram, the emphasis is on processes, and data (attributes) is passed between processes.

One goal of an object-oriented approach is to create a set of information system building blocks. These objects and procedures could be purchased from commercial software companies (such as a spreadsheets from Microsoft or a database system from Oracle). MIS programmers or consultants can create additional objects tailored for your specific company or

FIGURE 12.17
SDLC versus object oriented. Initial design of an object-oriented approach takes more effort than an SDLC approach. However, once the objects are properly defined, it is much easier to create and implement a new system.

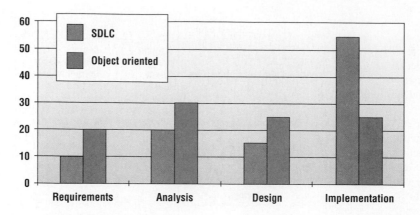

department. Once the basic blocks are in place, end users or MIS analysts can select the individual pieces to create a complete system. Hence, as Figure 12.17 indicates, less time is needed for implementation, as long as the analysis and design are performed carefully. On the other hand, the up-front costs of designing and building these objects can be quite high. Additionally, the tools and techniques tend to require substantial retraining of the existing MIS staff. Both of these types of costs have caused some companies to avoid object-oriented methods.

Summary

Systems development can be a difficult task. Many projects have failed because they cost much more than anticipated or they did not produce useful systems. Large projects are especially difficult to control because: there can be conflicting goals; it is hard to ensure that subsystems work together; business needs change during the development process; and there is turnover among the MIS employees. The systems development life cycle evolved as a means to deal with the complexity of large systems and provide the necessary controls to keep projects on track.

Systems analysis techniques are used to break projects into manageable pieces. Various graphing tools, such as data flow diagrams, are used to display the relationships between the components. Systems design techniques use the results of the analysis to create the new system. The new system consists of interconnected modules. Each module has inputs, outputs, processing steps, database requirements, manual procedures, and controls. At various stages in the design process, managers and users are asked to sign off on the proposed system, indicating that they will accept it with no further changes.

In contrast to the rigid control embodied in the SDLC method, the prototyping approach is iterative and creates an early working model of the system. Users and managers can see the proposed input screens and reports and make changes to them. As the project develops, the prototype goes from a simple mockup to a working system. Prototyping is sometimes used in conjunction with SDLC during the design phase to lay out input screens and reports.

A third way to build systems is for end users to develop their own projects using fourth-generation tools such as database management systems, spreadsheets, and other commercial software. As the capabilities of commercial software tools increase, users can develop more complex systems. The backlog facing MIS also encourages users to develop their own systems. The potential dangers of user development, such as lack of testing, incompatibilities, and unnecessary duplication, can be controlled by having MIS teams available to assist end users.

All three methods of developing systems involve five basic steps: feasibility and planning, systems analysis, design, implementation, and maintenance. Prototyping and end-user development typically focus on the design stage. However, managers need to remember that implementation problems can arise with any new system, regardless of how it was created. Similarly, there will always be a need to maintain and modify existing applications. It is easy to forget these steps when users develop their own software.

A Manager's View

As a manager in a large company, you will work closely with the MIS department to modify and build systems that support your operations. You need to be aware of the problems facing MIS staff to understand the reasons for their rules and methods. Managers are increasingly being asked to develop their own systems and to participate more heavily in the design of new reports and forms. The details of analysis, design, testing, and implementation will be useful regardless of the method used. As a manager, you also need to know the advantages and drawbacks of various development methods; you will often have to choose the method that is best suited to solving your problems.

Key Words

change agent, *469*
commercial off-the-shelf software (COTS), *464*
data flow diagram (DFD), *478*
data dictionary, *480*
end-user development, *461*
event-driven approach, *482*

extreme programming (XP), *474*
fault tolerance, *471*
feasibility study, *466*
inheritance, *482*
joint application design (JAD), *474*
object hierarchy, *482*

object-oriented design, *482*
prototyping, *461*
rapid application development (RAD), *474*
software maintenance, *470*
systems analysis, *466*
systems development life cycle (SDLC), *461*

Website References

Computer Industry News

ACM Digital Library Portal	**portal.acm.org/portal.cfm**
Computer Economics	**www.computereconomics.com**
Computerworld	**www.computerworld.com**
Domain Stats	**www.domainstats.com**
Federal Computer Weekly	**www.fcw.com**
Gartner Group	**www.gartner.com**
IDG	**www.idg.com**
IEEE	**www.ieee.org**
The Industry Standard	**www.thestandard.com**
Infoworld	**www.infoworld.com**
Internet.com	**www.internet.com**
Internet2	**www.internet2.org**
PC Week	**www.zdnet.com/pcweek**
PC World	**www.pcworld.com**

Additional Reading

Brooks, Frederick P. *The Mythical Man-Month,* Anniversary Edition. Boston: Addison-Wesley, 1995. [Classic book on software development problems and why adding people to a project often slows it down.]

Jeffries, Ronald, Ann Anderson, and Chet Hendrickson. *Extreme Programming Installed.* Boston: Addison-Wesley, 2001. [A detailed explanation of how to use extreme programming. Also look at other books in the series for theory.]

Naumann, Justus, and Milton Jenkins. "Prototyping: The New Paradigm for Systems Development." *MIS Quarterly,* Spring 1982. [Description, uses, and advantages of prototyping.]

McConnell, Steve. *Rapid Development: Taming Wild Software Schedules.* Redmond, W.A.: Microsoft Press, 1996.

Paulk, Mark C., Bill Curtis, Mary Beth Chrissis, and Charles V. Weber. *Capability Maturity Model for Software.* Carnegie-Mellon University, Software Engineering Institute, 1993. http://www.sei.cmu.edu/pub/documents/93.reports/pdf/tr24.93.pdf [Description of how to evaluate software development programs in terms of their capabilities on a relatively standardized maturity scale—essentially an evaluation of how well an organization follows the SDLC.]

Wallnau, Kurt, Scott Hissam, and Robert C. Seacord. *Building Systems from Commercial Components.* Boston: Addison-Wesley, 2002. [Description and cases of developing systems using commercial off-the-shelf software components, from the Carnegie Mellon Software Engineering Institute.]

Review Questions

1. What fundamental methods are available to build information systems?
2. What is the primary purpose of the systems development life cycle methodology?
3. What are the main steps in the systems development life cycle methodology?
4. What drawbacks are created with the systems development life cycle methodology?
5. What alternative methods are being used to develop information systems?
6. What is the role of a data flow diagram in analyzing systems?
7. What are the main components of a data flow diagram?
8. What is the role of object-oriented design, particularly class diagrams, in analyzing systems?
9. How do data flow diagrams and object-object oriented techniques differ in the way in which they divide systems?

Exercises

1. Interview a local manager to determine the requirements for a new system. Explain which method would be the best approach to develop the system. Estimate how long it would take to complete the project and how much it would cost. Advanced option: illustrate the new system with a data flow or object-oriented diagram. More advanced: create the system.

2. Consider an information system for a firm that manufactures furniture. Every day, production managers get shipping invoices that detail the supplies that were delivered that day. Production orders come in from the marketing department, listing each product and the options that need to be included. Once a week, the production team gets a quality report from sales outlets listing problems they have encountered with the products. Manufacturing is split into several component groups that are further split into teams. For instance, one component group makes sofas and recliners, another makes tables and chairs. Teams include frame groups, upholstery, wood working, and finishing. Once a week, each team creates a report that lists the products that were completed, the materials used in each product, the statistical quality measures on each component, and the amount of time spent on each step. Using an object-oriented approach and based on what you know (or can find out) about furniture, create a list of objects that might be used in building an information system for this company. Show the relationships among the objects. Hint: One important object is *reports.*

3. Interview computer users to determine how they feel about their current system. Do they like it? What are the major advantages and drawbacks? How long have they used it? When was it changed last? Are there changes users want to see? Are they willing to accept changes? How are relations with the MIS workers? Who initiates changes, users or MIS? If users proposed a new project, how long would it take for MIS to get to it (how long is the backlog)? Team approach: have each team member interview a different person (some users, some in MIS). Combine your results to get a picture of the entire company. Do users agree with each other? Does the MIS department agree with the users? Do they see the same problems? Hint: if you do not have access to another company, you can always find computer users in the university.

4. For each of the following information system projects, identify the method that would be the best approach for most companies.
   a. A new system to track customer requests and comments for the marketing department at a large ski manufacturer.
   b. A system to help managers evaluate regional sales data, from the existing sales system running on an Oracle database.

c. A system to track current location and maintenance status of thousands of baggage carts at an airport.

d. A website to sell "homemade" dog treats over the Internet for a small business.

e. A scientific system to help astronomers collect data from colleagues, track specific items (e.g., comets), and send announcements and questions over the Internet to a group of registered users.

f. A system to help a group of financial managers monitor client transactions and observe them for potentially illegal patterns such as insider trading.

g. A system running on one PC that connects to a truck scale and records incoming shipments of recyclable materials.

h. A system for a manager that pulls data on cell phone usage from all of her workers. It groups the calls and costs so she can see if workers are making too many personal phone calls.

 ## Rolling Thunder Database

5. Rolling Thunder Bicycles needs a new website to sell its custom bicycles. How should it be developed? What methodology could be used?

6. Using the help system and website description of Rolling Thunder, create a data flow diagram to show the main processes directly involved with the customers (taking orders, sending notices and bills, and receiving payments).

7. Rolling Thunder Bicycles needs a new system to generate and track electronic orders (EDI) to its suppliers. What methodology should be used to develop the system?

8. Assume that the managers of Rolling Thunder Bicycles have decided to purchase and implement an enterprise resource planning system. You have been selected to help determine which system the company should purchase. Outline the steps you will have to perform to select a vendor.

9. Assume that the managers of Rolling Thunder Bicycles have decided to purchase and implement an enterprise resource planning system. As the manager in charge of installing the system, outline the steps that need to be performed.

Some researchers note that reducing flight times will not be sufficient to speed up the system. Delays are also created by slow operations at the terminals, including refueling, baggage handling, and unscheduled gate changes. These researchers suggest that significant improvements are needed to improve communications among airport terminals. One possibility is wireless PDAs carried by all personnel and updated by the airlines.

The September 11 attacks caused the FAA to delay implementing some aspects of the free flight (CPDLC) deployment. A major reason for the delay was due to the costs that would be imposed on the airlines. The FAA was also not ready to implement the new technologies. [Vasishtha 2002]

Questions

1. What is the strategic direction of the Federal Aviation Administration?

2. What has been the catalyst for change at the Federal Aviation Administration?

3. With what technological changes has the FAA been forced to accommodate?

4. What has caused a focus on change in the use of technology at the FAA?

5. How has this technological change been implemented?

6. How successful has the technological change been?

7. Does the agency have the financial ability to embark on a major technological program of advancement?

8. How does the agency's representation of itself on its Web page compare to what is actually being done by the FAA?

Additional Reading

"Air Traffic Control—Good Progress on Interim Replacement for Outage-Plagued System, But Risks Can Be Further Reduced." *GAO Report,* October 17, 1996.

Bush, George. Office of the Press Secretary. Remarks by the President in Meeting with High-Tech Leaders, The East Room of the White House, March 28, 2001. http://www.whitehouse.gov/news/releases/2001/03/20010328-2.html.

Deck, Stewart. "Air-Traffic Union Puts Upgrades on Hold." *Computerworld,* February 1, 1999, p. 24.

Dorr, Les. "FAA Selects Raytheon for Next-Generation Air Traffic Control System Upgrade." *FAA News,* September 16, 1996.

"FAA Ready for Free Flight." *Advanced Transportation Technology News,* April 1996.

"FAA Radar Glitches Found." *Computerworld,* November 2, 1998, p. 12.

"FAA to Spend $65m on Stopgap Replacements for Old Computers." *Government Computer News,* August 7, 1995, p. 3.

"FAA's $500 Million Navigation Contract Takes Flight." *Federal Computer Week,* April 10, 1995.

Hasson, Judi. "Funding Bills Progress on Capitol Hill." *Federal Computer Week,* November 12, 2001.

Jackson, William. "FAA and GSA Renew Their Dogfight over Air Traffic Control Modernization." *Government Computer News,* September 18, 1995, p. 73.

Langlois, Greg. "Researchers: Don't Forget Airport Ops." *Federal Computer Week,* September 10, 2001.

Langlois, Greg. "Data Determining Free Flight Future." *Federal Computer Week,* October 2, 2001.

Langlois, Greg. "NASA: Simulation Proves Its Worth." *Federal Computer Week,* November 5, 2001.

Leopold, George. "Study: GPS Can Fly as Commercial Air Navigator." *Electronic Engineering Times,* February 8, 1999, p. 18.

Murray, Bill. "FAA Document Management System Helps Users Stay on Track." *Government Computer News,* December 14, 1998, p. 36.

O'Hara, Colleen. "FAA Kicks Off ATC Upgrade." *Federal Computer Week,* December 7, 1998, p. 1.

O'Hara, Colleen. "FAA Looks Abroad for Oceanic ATC Solution." *Federal Computer Week,* November 16, 1998, p. 6.

Ryan, Stephan M. "FAA's Bailout Betrays Citizens, Benefits Lawyers." *Government Computer News,* September 18, 1995, p. 29.

Slabodkin, Gregory, Florence Olsen, and Frank Tiboni. "Poll: FAA Lacks Good Systems." *Government Computer News,* January 25, 1999, p. 6.

Tiboni, Frank. "FAA Begins Upgrade Project on Its Controller-Pilot Comm System." *Government Computer News,* February 8, 1999, p. 8.

Tiboni, Frank. "FAA Names AT&T Exec Daniel Mehan to Become Its First Chief Information Officer." *Government Computer News,* January 25, 1999, p. 8.

Tiboni, Frank. "FAA Pulls Tracking App from Two Radar Centers." *Government Computer News,* November 23, 1998, p. 3.

Tiboni, Frank. "FAA Uses Patch to Prevent Air Traffic Lockups." *Government Computer News,* October 19, 1998, p. 46.

Tiboni, Frank. "Vendors Protest FAA Support Contract Award." *Government Computer News,* October 19, 1998, p. 49.

Vasishtha, Preeti. "FAA Defers CPDLC Deployment." *Government Computer News,* January 4, 2002.

Walker, Richard W. "Readying for 2000: One Agency Story. Federal Aviation Administration on Target." *Government Computer News,* December 14, 1998, p. 47.

Case: The Internal Revenue Service (IRS)

Counting both personal and business returns, the IRS processes more than 200 million tax returns a year. Many of the returns are simple one-page forms; others run to thousands of pages of supporting documents. Overall, the service handles more than 1 billion information documents a year. The IRS processes more than $1 trillion in tax revenue a year. The IRS has 10 regional service center that are responsible for processing and storing individual forms. In 1989, it cost the IRS $34 million just to store the paper documents.

Until 1990, all documents at the IRS were stored as paper records in a central warehouse. Documents were organized according to the year of filing. As a result, if a taxpayer had a problem or question that covered multiple years, the citizen had to schedule multiple meetings with IRS officials to correct problems for each of the years. In some cases, it could take weeks or months just to get the files. Occasionally, the IRS found it was faster to ask the taxpayer for a copy of the return. By the early 1990s, this problem was resolved by having each of the 10 service centers store digital images of the tax returns, making them available to agents on their terminals. While a step in the right direction, this approach did not give the IRS the flexibility it would receive from the ability to scan the returns directly into a computerized information system.

Automation sometimes causes problems in addition to solving them. Such was the case of Dickie Ann Conn. The IRS determined that she owed $67,714 in back taxes. She was sent a bill for more than $1 billion in interest and penalties. After being challeged, the IRS admitted that there was an error in the interest computation.

A History of Automation Problems

The IRS seems like a logical candidate for improved automation. The benefits of faster processing, fewer mistakes, and easier access to data ought to save a considerable amount of money. The computer's ability to search the data, automatically match transactions, and analyze each return presents several additional opportunities that can either cut costs or raise additional revenue. Managers at the IRS are fully aware of the potential, and they have proposed several systems over the years. The problem has been in implementation of the plans and in getting Congress to financially support the changes.

In the late 1960s, the IRS knew it needed to redesign its basic systems. In response, it began to plan for a system to be installed in the 1970s. The IRS did not get the needed support in Congress because of fears that it would be too expensive and too invasive into individual security and taxpayer privacy.

As a result of this lack of support, the IRS turned its attention toward keeping its existing computers running.

In 1982, the existing system was nearing capacity and the IRS established the Tax System Redesign program. It promised a complete redesign of the system. According to the GAO, changes in management resulted in the system never getting past the design stage. A new assistant commissioner in 1982 embarked on the design of a new system that promised to carry the IRS through the 1990s. Initial costs were estimated at $3 to $5 billion over the entire project. The primary objective was to replace the old central tape-based system with an online database. Eventually, optical technology would be used to scan the original documents and store the data in the database. A new communication system would carry the data to any agent's workstation. By 1989, initial planning had already cost the IRS more than $70 million, with no concrete proposal or results.

The main computer systems were replaced at the IRS service centers in 1985. The change in the systems was almost disastrous for the IRS. It delayed returns processing and led to delays in refunds that cost the IRS millions of dollars in interest payments. IRS employees worked overtime but still could not keep up. Rumors were flying that some employees were dumping returns to cut down their backlog. Because of the delays and backlogs, the IRS managed to audit only about half the usual number of returns on which it conducted audits.

In 1986, the IRS initiated a plan to provide 18,000 laptop computers to enable its field auditors to be more productive with its Automated Examination System (AES). Unfortunately, the service bought the Zenith laptops a full year before the software was ready. The system was written in Pascal and was delivered to agents in July 1986. It was designed to examine Form 1040 returns. The biggest drawback was that it used 18 different diskettes. This required agents to be constantly swapping disks. Based upon the privatization directives from the Reagan administration, the system was subcontracted to outside developers. As IRS funding was cut, programmers with experience in Pascal were cut. This led the system to be rewritten in C.

A survey in 1988 revealed that 77 percent of the agents were dissatisfied with the software. Only 33 percent said that they used it. By 1989, the IRS revised the software and managed to reduce it to eight disks. By this time, the AES project was more than six years behind schedule, and according to the GAO, was $800 million over the original budget. The IRS originally anticipated that the AES would produce $16.2 billion in additional revenue over nine years by making agents more productive. The GAO disputed those numbers, noting that "The IRS has been unable to verify that the use of laptops has actually resulted in the examination of additional returns or increased tax revenues." In 1990, the White House cut the funding for the program from $110 million to $20 million.

Technology Innovations

By 1989, the IRS knew that it desperately needed to redesign its entire system for collecting taxes and processing information. In hearings before Congress, Senator David Pryor

(D-Ark.) noted that the 1960s-era IRS computers were headed for a "train wreck" in the mid-1990s. The GAO estimated the total project would cost between $3 and $4 billion. The projected date for implementation slipped from 1995 to 1998.

The overall design for the Tax System Modernization Program (TSM) called for a centralized online database, smaller departmental systems containing local information, and linkage through a nationwide network. Tax return data would be entered through a combination of electronic filing and optical scanners.

By 1991, the estimated cost of the plan had expanded to $8 billion. Although the IRS projected that the system would cut $6 billion in costs, the plan was rapidly attacked by members of Congress. Three studies of the TSM plan by the GAO were released in early 1991:

1. The GAO was concerned that optical technology was not sufficiently advanced to perform the tasks demanded by the IRS. The GAO urged greater emphasis on electronic filing.

2. The GAO was concerned that management issues such as transition planning, progress measurement, and accountability were not sufficiently addressed by the plan.

3. The GAO and Sen. John Glenn (D-Ohio) voiced concerns about data security and integrity.

GAO official Howard Rhile noted, "This is a serious omission in view of the fact that the IRS intends to allow public access . . . to some of its systems and because concerns over the security of taxpayer information helped doom the first [IRS] modernization effort in the late 1970s."

Despite these misgivings, the IRS was committed to the TSM plan. Fred Goldberg, IRS commissioner, agreed with the GAO findings but observed that:

We have been running our business essentially the same way, using essentially the same computer and telecommunications systems design for 25 years. [Existing systems] will perform well and achieve incremental improvements for the next few years . . . Our best judgment is that [OCR] technology will be there when we need it, by the end of the decade.

By 1992, the situation grew worse. Shirley Peterson, the new commissioner of Internal Revenue, stated at a Congressional hearing that:

Our systems are so antiquated that we cannot adequately serve the public. The potential for breakdown during the filing season greatly exceeds acceptable business risk . . . Some components of these computers are so old and brittle that they literally crumble when removed for maintenance.

In December 1991, the IRS awarded a 12-year, $300-million contract to TRW to help manage the process and provide planning and system integration services.

The recommended system was ambitious. It called for 60 major projects, two dozen major purchases, 20 million lines of new software, and 308 people just to manage the purchasing process. Despite the best efforts of the administrators, elements of the IRS modernization plan were stalled because of purchas-

ing difficulties. In July 1991, the IRS awarded a billion-dollar Treasury Multiuser Acquisition Contract (TMAC) to AT&T. The goal was to standardize purchasing for the IRS and the Treasury Department by routing all purchases through one vendor. The contract was challenged by other vendors and overturned. The contract was rebid, and AT&T won the second time. IBM (one of the original protesters) again objected to the process, noting that the IBM bid of $708 million was less than the $1.4 billion bid by AT&T.

In 1993, the IRS acknowledged that the TSM design master plan needed to be rewritten. In particular, it had to focus on business aspects instead of technology elements. To better coordinate technical planning with IRS needs, the agency established a research and development center funded by $78.5 million of federal money but run by the private sector. The center was responsible for providing technical assistance and strategic planning for the TSM. The IRS also established a high-level "architect office" to evaluate technologies and direct their proposed uses.

Throughout calendar year 1992, the IRS spent $800 million on TSM. In 1993, new IRS estimates indicated that TSM would cost $7.8 billion above the $15.5 billion needed to keep existing systems running. The new system was projected to generate $12.6 billion in total benefits by 2008 through reduced costs, increased collections, and interest savings. Additionally, the improved processes was supposed to save taxpayers $5.4 billion and cut 1 billion hours from the collective time they needed to spend with the IRS.

In 1996, the IRS asked Congress for a $1.03 billion appropriation. This was a a substantial increase over the $622 million it spent on automation in 1995. Hazel Edwards from the General Accounting Office noted, "After eight years and an investment of almost $2 billion, the IRS's progress toward its vision has been minimal."

IRS Commissioner Margaret Milner Richardson denied the GAO claims. She noted, "I think we have made significant progress, not minimal progress . . . but we do know we can and must do more." [GAO, 1995]

The IRS situation represented a dilemma for Congress. The IRS claims that the only way to make a system that works is to spend more money. The GAO has set forth that it is impossible to complete the entire project envisioned by the IRS. The GAO believes the IRS should, instead, concentrate on smaller, more focused projects that can be completed in a one- to two-year timeframe.

In 2001, Congress passed tax-cut legislation and, to stimulate the economy, ordered the IRS to send "refund" checks to all taxpayers. It took several months to create and mail the tens of millions of checks, but most of them were correct. On the other hand, about 523,000 taxpayers received notices that they would be getting a check for the full refund amount, when they were actually eligible for only part of the refund. The mistake was attributed to a programmer error, and the final checks were correct; but some taxpayers were confused by the misleading letter.

Electronic Filing

The IRS introduced electronic filing in 1986, when 25,000 forms were filed electronically. By 1990, 4.2 million people filed for tax refunds electronically. In 1992, the number increased to 10 million filers.

The primary target for electronic filing is the millions of individual taxpayers who are slated to receive refunds. To control the process and ensure that documents are properly filed, electronic filing is only available through authorized tax preparers. The IRS is deliberately avoiding providing access to individual taxpayers. As a result, taxpayers who use the system pay an additional charge to the preparer. However, the electronic filing system provides refunds within a couple of weeks.

Forms that have been electronically filed cost the IRS one-tenth the processing cost of paper forms. This approach also eliminates the cost of paper storage. The IRS notes that it is able to store 800,000 returns on one side of a 12-inch optical disk.

For taxpayers with easy returns, the IRS is simplifying the process even further. Short forms can now be filed over the telephone. In a 1992 pilot, 117,000 Ohio taxpayers filed for refunds using Touch-Tone phone calls. The system was expanded nationwide in 1994. The Touch-Tone system can only be used by taxpayers who are able to use the 1040EZ form. A replacement form (1040-TEL) must still be signed and filed with the IRS, along with the W-2 (withholding) statements.

In the 1998 IRS Restructuring and Reform Act, Congress required the IRS to encourage the use of electronic filing. The IRS has made it easier for people to file electronically—particularly for those who use computer software to compute their taxes. In 1998, about 20 percent of individuals filed electronically; in 2000 the number was 28 percent; in 2001 about 32 percent (45 million). The IRS goal is to increase this number to 80 percent by 2007. For the 2001 tax year (filing in early 2002), the IRS used the Digital Signature law to send PINs to several million taxpayers, enabling them to legally sign their tax forms electronically. However, the one important catch is that taxpayers who file electronically must pay an additional fee to do so. Hence, only those who receive refunds (about 70 percent of the filers) are interested in paying the fee, because it enables them to get their money faster. Most experts believe it is unlikely that the IRS will meet the Congressional goal of 80 percent by 2007.

The Internet

In late 2001, the IRS announced plans to offer electronic payments by businesses over the Internet. A major portion of the money received by the IRS comes from withholdings collected by businesses. This money has to be forwarded to the IRS at regular intervals, so the IRS is trying to reduce handling costs by moving these transactions online. The Electronic Federal Tax Payment System (EFTPS) is a Web-based system that can also be used by small businesses. The system could also be used by taxpayers who make estimated quarterly payments. Using modern strong encryption technologies, the IRS is confident the system will be secure.

Relatively early in the dot-com and dot-gov restructuring, the IRS realized the importance of putting information on its website. In fact, a huge amount of information is available online. And that is a problem. In 2001, IRS executives were asked to search the site for common tax information. It generally took 20 or 30 clicks to find any piece of information. To improve its website, the IRS hired Greg Carson in 2001, a designer from private industry who helped to launch the Priceline.com website.

The IRS also signed a contract with the consulting group Accenture to redesign the IRS websites. In 2001, the site received 80 million hits a day. Gregory Carson, director of electronic tax administration modernization at the IRS notes that "The development of an intuitive, intentions-based design will make it considerably easier for taxpayers and tax preparers, who pull forms from the site, to obtain the information and documents they need to file tax returns." [Rosencrance 2001b] Accenture's goal is to make the site easier to use so that users can reach the desired information within three clicks. Additionally, Accenture will be hosting the site on its servers.

Automated Under-Reporter (AUR)

The Automated Under-Reporter (AUR) is another component of the TMS. The AUR is a system designed to monitor returns and identify people who are most likely to underpay their taxes. The system was first installed in 1992 at the Ogden, Utah, regional center. The system pulls data from the service center's Unisys 1180 mainframe. The data is downloaded across a local area network to a Sequent Computer System S-81 minicomputer. From there the information is sent to one of 240 networked UNIX workstations on the employees' desks.

The system automatically matches distribution documents (such as 1099s and W-2s) with the filings of individual taxpayers. Mark Cox, assistant IRS commissioner for information systems development, noted that in trials with the AUR, "We've been able to cut down the rework of cases from 25 percent to less than 5 percent. We see this type of work enabling us to share in more of a connectivity mode." [Quindlen, 1991]

The system uses an Oracle database running SQL to match data from various sources. It also performs basic tax computation and helps agents send notices to taxpayers. Managers have noted that even though the new system has not improved the speed of the agents, it has cut down on the error rates. As agents become familiar with the system, productivity is expected to improve.

In 1991, the Ogden center processed 26 million tax returns and collected $100 billion in tax payments. It processed $9 billion in refunds. In 1992, it won the Presidential Award for Quality for improved tax processing by saving the government $11 million over five years.

The Currency and Banking Retrieval System

In 1988, Congress passed a new law in an attempt to cut down on crime (notably drug dealing) and to provide leads to people who significantly underreport their income. Every cash transaction over $10,000 is required by federal law to be reported to the IRS on a Form 8300. The IRS created the Currency and Banking Retrieval System to match these forms against the filer's tax return. The system automatically identifies people who had large cash purchases but claimed little income. Because of a programming error, the system missed forms covering $15 million in cash transactions between 1989 and 1990.

The problem stemmed from the fact that the IRS used the same code number on the 8300 forms that it used on other cash transaction forms. The IRS later assigned separate codes for each form. When programmers wrote the new matching programs, they did not realize there were two codes for each transaction. The system was corrected in 1991. By 1992 it was used to process more than 1 million queries a year.

Jennie Stathis of the GAO noted there were additonal problems with Form 8300. In particular, the filings were incomplete or contained incorrect taxpayer identification numbers. The IRS is developing software to enable businesses to verify the taxpayer ID numbers automatically before the customer completes the purchase.

Document Processing System and Service Center Recognition/Image Processing System (SCRIPS)

In 1994, the IRS awarded a $1.3 billion contract to the IBM Federal Systems division to design a document processing system. The goal was that by the late 1990s, the system would convert virtually every tax return to a digital format. A day after the contract was awarded, IBM sold the Federal Systems division to Loral Corporation for $1.52 billion.

The 15-year systems integration contract was to have the system running online in 1996. The plan called for scanning incoming tax forms. Special software digitally removed the form layout and instructions, leaving just the taxpayer data. OCR software was to then convert the characters (including handwritten numbers) into computer data.

The system was scheduled for initial installation at the Austin, Texas, regional center in August 1995. Plans called for installing it at Ogden, Utah; Cincinnati, Ohio; Memphis, Tennessee; and Kansas City, Missouri, by 1998. Despite the popularity of electronic filing, the IRS still sees a need for the OCR system. The IRS anticipated receiving 252 million paper filings in the year 2001.

SCRIPS was the first scanning project. Presented at a cost of $17 million, it was approved to cost $88 million when it was awarded in 1993 to Grumman Corporation's Data Systems unit. SCRIPS was designed to capture data from four simple IRS forms that are single-sided. SCRIPS was supposed to be an interim solution that would support the IRS until DPS could be fully deployed. However, delays pushed back the delivery of the SCRIPS project. By the time it was declared finished, the project cost $200 million. [Birnbaum 1998]

DPS was the second scanning project. It has a projected cost of $1.3 billion. Interestingly, Grumman Data Systems was the loser in the contest for the DPS contract. The IRS noted that Grumman failed a key technical test. When completed, DPS was quite complicated to use. In this program, the IRS developed nine separate databases, most of which could not communicate with each other.

In 1996, Art Gross, a veteran of the New York State revenue department, was appointed to be IRS's new chief information officer. He stated that the IRS's computers didn't "work in the real world" and that its employees lacked the "intellectual capital" to transform them. When he arrived in 1996, the IRS's Year 2000 conversion project had a budget of $20 million and a staff of three; by 1998, it had grown to a $900 million project with 600 workers, many of them consultants. [Birnbaum 1998]

Gross tried to get control of the system. He ended the DPS or "Bubble Machine" project as being over budget and behind schedule. With help from TRW, he devised a new top-to-bottom computer architecture. The architecture was built around a centralized database that centralizes information at the IRS.

When Rossotti arrived as the new commissioner, he proposed an even more ambitious plan. In addition to Year 2000 changes, computer updates from the 1997 tax law, and the overall modernization, Rossotti proposed to restructure the entire organization. This proved to be too much for Gross, who resigned.

In 1998, Congress passed the Government Paperwork Elimination Act, part of which forces the IRS to move to more electronic transactions. Since then, the IRS has created electronic versions of its forms that can be downloaded from its servers. In 2001, the IRS signed a contract with ScanSoft Inc. for OmniPage Pro 11 for use in its federal tax offices around the nation. The goal is to convert the masses of paper files into electronic documents. Instead of taxpayer files, the system is designed more to convert internal forms and documents so that all employees will have immediate access to up-to-date forms and policies on the IRS intranet.

Customer Relationship Management

In late 2001, the IRS began installing customer relationship management (CRM) software that it purchased from PeopleSoft. A key element of the kinder, gentler approach is the ability to track customer issues. CRM software can collect all of the customer interactions into one location—making it easier for multiple agents to see the entire history of a particular problem. The system will also enable the agency to create Web portals for professional tax preparers, IRS employees, and taxpayers. The portals will securely provide individual information to these groups over the Web. In addition to faster service, the IRS hopes to reduce the costs of its call centers by moving more access online.

Security Breaches

In 1983, Sen. John Glenn (D-Ohio) released an IRS report indicating that 386 employees took advantage of "ineffective security controls" and looked through tax records of friends, neighbors, relatives, and celebrities at the Atlanta regional IRS office. Additionally, five employees used the system to create fraudulent returns, triggering more than 200 false tax refunds. Additional investigations turned up more than 100 other IRS employees nationwide with unauthorized access to records. Glenn observed that the IRS investigation examined only one region and looked at only one of 56 methods that have been identified to compromise security. Glenn expressed the concern that "this is just the tip of a very large iceberg."

The IRS noted that the TSM program "greatly increases the risk of employee browsing, disclosure, and fraud," because of the online access to the centralized databases.

Commissioner Margaret Richardson, of the Internal Revenue Service noted that the system used by the perpetrators was 20 years old and was used by 56,000 employees. It met all federal security standards, including the use of passwords and limited access based on job descriptions. The IRS found the problems in Atlanta by examining records of database access from 1990 to 1993. Because the system generates 100 million transactions a month, the data is stored on magnetic tape, making it difficult to search.

In 1989, the IRS arrested Alan N. Scott, of West Roxbury, Massachusetts, for allegedly submitting 45 fraudulent returns via the new electronic filing system. The IRS claims Scott received more than $325,000 in refunds.

The IRS requires tax return preparers to fill out an application before it issues an access code. Scott apparently used a fake taxpayer ID number and lied on the application form to gain the access number. The IRS claims he then submitted false returns using bogus names and taxpayer ID numbers to get refund checks ranging from $3,000 to $23,000.

IRS officials noted that the electronic filings actually made it easier to identify the problem, because the computer could scan the data earlier than the data would have been scanned if it would have been submitted by hand. Once the situation was identified, the IRS was able to immediately lock out further transactions from Mr. Scott's access number.

IRS Budget

Like any executive agency, the IRS budget is set by Congress and approved by the president. In 1995, the Clinton administration asked Congress to increase the IRS budget by 10 percent. The money was to be allocated to improving the information systems and procedures at the IRS in an effort to make them more effective. Congress responded by cutting the IRS budget by 2 percent. The Clinton budget called for $8.23 billion; the Congressional numbers cut the budget from $7.48 billion in 1995 to $7.35 billion in 1996. Congress did grant a slight increase in the budget for tax system modernization. Rep. Jim Lightfoot (R-Iowa) observed that "Without modernization, I think you're throwing good money after bad. The IRS is still working out of cardboard boxes. It's basically that bad."

Recommendation for the Future

In 1998, the message in Congressional hearings was to "Do something. Anything." The hearings into IRS dealings with the public revealed several problems within the IRS. They emphasized the negative perceptions the public has toward this important agency. After listening to these criticisms, the IRS eventually agreed to change some of its policies to improve its treatment of citizens. The 1998 IRS Restructuring and Reform Act was aimed at changing IRS attitudes and providing citizens with more control in the tax-collection process. Charles Rossotti, the new IRS commissioner, described the process of upgrading the vacuum tube-era technology as being "rebuilding Manhattan while we're still living in it." The $7 billion agency has attempted the same gargantuan task of modernizing its computers for 25 years and continues to fail. The total cost in the 1990s alone has been projected to be nearly $4 billion. [Birnbaum 1998]

Today the system includes 80 mainframes, 1,335 minicomputers, and 130,000 desktop boxes that are largely unable to communicate with each other. Before his appointment as Commissioner of the IRS in November 1997, Rossotti served as chairman of the computer consulting firm American Management Systems. In early 1998, Arthur Gross, the chief technology officer, who drafted the latest modernization blueprint, resigned in frustration. Shortly thereafter, Tony Musick, the chief financial officer, resigned to become deputy CFO at the Commerce Department. [Birnbaum 1998]

The IRS has 102,000 employees who collect $1.5 trillion annually. It is organized geographically into 33 districts that report to 10 regional offices. In 1997, it issued $107 billion in refunds to 68 percent of the taxpayers. The nation's 121.6 million taxpayers spend $8 billion a year to get help in preparing their returns. In 1996, the IRS collected nearly $29 billion in delinquencies, issued 750,000 liens, and seized 10,000 properties. The simplest form, the 1040EZ, has a 28-page instruction book. It takes an average of 10 hours to complete the regular 1040. In her 1998 book, *Unbridled Power,* Shelley L. Davis, the IRS's official historian from 1988 to 1995, described the agency as "secretive, paranoid, and arrogant."

In 1998, Congress passed the Taxpayer's Bill of Rights. The legislation promises some improvements. These include shielding divorced taxpayers from their ex-spouses' tax liabilities; reducing penalties and interest on overdue taxes; and reversing the burden of proof in court cases so the IRS will have to show that the taxpayer did wrong, not the other way around. The legislation also sets up an oversight board to see that the legislation is carried out.

Unfortunately, the IRS has been even less successful at implementing new technologies. By 1998, nearly all of the earlier systems-development efforts were canceled. In late 1998, the IRS signed a 15-year development contract with Computer Science Corporation (CSC) that was worth $5 billion. By contract, CSC is responsible for helping design new systems, indicating that the ultimate goal is still to be determined. Outside experts note that the contract does not necessarily solve all the IRS problems. The IRS must still deal with the contract management issues, which have proved difficult to the IRS in the past.

In the interim, the IRS still needs to process millions of forms. In 1999, the emphasis shifted to electronic scanning of payment forms. Tax form data will continue to be hand-entered by clerks. This cumbersome process requires two clerks to enter data from each form and check for errors.

Questions

1. What problems have been experienced by the IRS in developing its information systems?

2. How are these problems related to the service's systems-development methodologies?

3. The GAO thinks the IRS should place more emphasis on electronic filing. Is the GAO correct, or is the IRS approach better?

4. Are there any ways to speed up the development of systems for the IRS? What would be the costs and risks?

5. Are the IRS's problems the result of technology or management difficulties?

6. What are the advantages and drawbacks to outsourcing the IRS information systems?

7. Why did the IRS choose private banks to develop the Electronic Payments System? Could this technique be used for other systems?

Additional Reading

"All 208 Million Tax Returns Get Electronic Scrutiny on Arrival." *Government Computer News,* March 6, 1995.

"Automation Failed to Meet Requirements." *Government Computer News,* July 17, 1995, p. 6.

"Big Brother's Watching, but This Time It Could Be You." *Government Computer News,* December 12, 1994.

Birnbaum, Jeffrey H. "Unbelievable! The Mess at the IRS Is Worse than You Think." *Fortune,* April 13, 1998.

"CIO Says Goals Are Achievable." *Government Computer News,* January 25, 1999, p. 20.

Constance, Paul, James M. Smith, and Florence Olsen. "IRS RC Buy Is on Hold Yet Again." *Government Computer News,* July 3, 1995, p. 3.

Dorobek, Christopher J. "IRS: E-File Goal Is a Stretch." *Federal Computer Week,* April 9, 2001.

GAO. "Tax Systems Modernization—Management and Technical Weaknesses Must be Corrected if Modernization Is to Succeed." GAO/AIMD-95-156, July 1995.

Gleckman, Howard. "File Your Taxes—and Save a Tree." *Business Week,* February 1, 1999, p. 128.

Hasson, Judi. "IRS Takes on Old-Style Paperwork." *Federal Computer Week,* December 10, 2001.

"Intuit Joins IRS in Urging Taxpayers and Practitioners to E-File to Avoid Delays and Get Refunds Back Fast." *Yahoo,* January 11, 2002.

"IRS Beefs Up Its Phone Filing System." *Government Computer News,* July 17, 1995, p. 8.

Masud, Sam. "New Bells Are Ringing at IRS." *Government Computer News,* October 16, 1995, pp. 44–45.

Matthews, William. "Dot-Gov by Design." *Federal Computer Week,* December 10, 2001.

Mayer, Merry. "Interim Systems Will Tide IRS Over as It Modernizes." *Government Computer News,* January 25, 1999, p. 21.

McNamee, Mike. "A Kinder Gentler IRS?" *Business Week,* February 1, 1999, p. 128.

"Modernization." *Government Computer News,* January 25, 1999, p. 20.

Quindlen, Terrey Hatcher. "Recent IRS Award Puts TSM in Motion," *Government Computer News,* December 23, 1991, pp. 3–4.

Rosencrance, Linda. "IRS Sends Out 523,000 Incorrect Check Notices." *Computerworld,* July 17, 2001.

Rosencrance, Linda. "Accenture to Redesign, Host IRS Website." *Computerworld,* August 13, 2001.

Rosencrance, Linda. "IRS to Launch Online Tax Payment System for Businesses," *Computerworld,* September 5, 2001.

Rothfeder, Jeffrey. "Invasion of Privacy." *PC World,* November 1995, pp. 152–161.

Smith, James M. "IRS Spends $1b for Next Five Years of Systems Support." *Government Computer News,* July 17, 1995, p. 82.

Thibodeau, Patrick. "Private Sector to Tackle IRS Mess." *Computerworld,* January 4, 1999, p. 4.

Weiss, Todd R. "PeopleSoft Sells CRM Software to a Friendlier IRS." *Computerworld,* August 23, 2001.

"Where's AI Hiding?" *AI Expert,* April 1995.

Appendix

Visual Basic

As a manager, for most business applications, you will use existing software: spreadsheets, word processors, database management systems, and accounting systems. However, there will be times when you will want to customize some applications. Other times, you might hire someone to create small applications. In these situations, you might have to read some of the program code to make sure the computations are correct. In any case, it helps to have a basic understanding of computer programming.

Most modern computer languages perform a common set of elementary functions. When you learn a programming language, you focus on these primary features. Languages may differ in syntax (the name of a function, when to include parentheses, and so on). However, the logic is generally the same. Once you understand the logic of programming, it is relatively easy to read and understand a computer program. Learning to write your own code then requires practice. One of the easiest languages to use is Microsoft's Visual Basic (VB). It was designed to be readable and to minimize problems with syntax. It is a useful language to know because it is used in so many applications. All of the Microsoft software packages have a version available beneath the surface, which you can use to automate various tasks. It is also available as a stand-alone programming package.

Programming Logic

At heart, writing computer programs is an exercise in logic. At the high end, science and art become important issues, but the foundation of programming is logic and mathematics. When you write a program, simply think of the computer as a processor that executes each instruction that you give it. Unless you tell it otherwise, the processor examines each statement sequentially—performing the requested task and moving on to the next statement. Five primary types of statements are available: computations, conditions, loops, input, and output.

Computations usually involve numeric data. You can add (+), subtract (–), multiply (*), and divide (/) numbers. Standard algebraic rules apply, so computations are performed from left to right, and you can use parentheses to change to order of computations. Additionally, you can also manipulate string (text) data. For instance, you can append one string to another: "John" & " " & "Smith" yields "John Smith."

Computations, Variables, and Functions

Computations often involve variables. Think of a variable as a container that holds a value. For example, one statement might be $a = 32$, which assigns the value of 32 to the variable a. Then, a new statement could be $y = a/3 + 15$, which uses the value of a to compute the value of the new variable (y). To minimize mistakes, variables should be declared before they are used. VB uses the Dim statement to declare a variable. For example, Dim a as double. The main types of variables you will use are integer, double, string, and variant. An integer variable holds numeric data that does not contain fractions (1, 532, –2273, and so on.). A double variable holds numeric data that can contain fractions or digits to the right of the decimal point (3.14, –25.222, and so on). A string variable holds text ("John," "123 Maple Street," and so on). The variant data type is used when you do not know what type of data will be used, when you want to deal with special data (e.g., dates), or when you need to perform special tests, such as determining if the data is missing (null).

One important type of variable is called an *array*. An array is a variable that contains multiple values. For example, you might have an array that holds the sales for each month of the year. You could then obtain the values by number: SalesForMonth(1), SalesForMonth(2), up to SalesForMonth(12).

Every language has certain internal functions that perform common mathematical operations. For instance, VB uses the Sqr( ) function to compute the square root of a number. Additional functions manipulate string data, such as finding the number of characters in a string (Len) or converting a string to lowercase (LCase). Figure 12.1A lists the primary math and string functions that you might use. Additional functions, details, and examples are readily available from the VB Help system.

FIGURE 12.1A   Internal functions. Math and string functions are commonly used in programs. Additional functions and details are available from the Help system.

Math Functions	
Abs	Absolute value
Atn	Arc Tangent
Cos	Cosine
Exp	Exponential
Fix	Returns integer portion
Int	Converts to integer
Log	Logarithm
Rnd	Random number
Sgn	Signum (–1, 0, 1)
Sin	Sine
Sqr	Square root
Tan	Tangent

String Functions	
StrComp	Compare two strings
LCase, UCase	Convert to lowercase or uppercase
Len	Find length of a string
Format	Format a string
InStr, Left, L Trim	
Mid, Right, RTrim, Trim	Manipulate strings

FIGURE 12.2A   Conditions. One set of statements is executed depending on whether the condition is true or false.

```
If (Sales > 1000) Then
    Bonus = 100
Else
    Bonus = 0
End If
```

FIGURE 12.3A   Conditions with multiple values. The computer finds the matching value for the customer type, and computes the appropriate discount.

```
Select Case Customer
    Case Customer = 'Corporate'
        Discount = 0.05
    Case Customer = 'Government'
        Discount = 0.10
    Case Else
        Discount = 0.01
End Select
```

FIGURE 12.4A   Loops with For-Next. When you know how many times you want to execute the loop, you can use a For-Next statement.

```
total = 0
For month = 1 To 12
    total = total + SalesForMonth(month)
Next month
```

FIGURE 12.5A   A loop you do not know how many times to iterate. It repeats until some condition becomes true.

```
month = 0
sales = 0
Do Until (sales > 100000)
    sales = sales + SalesForMonth(month)
    month = month + 1
Loop
```

Conditions

Conditions are used to tell the processor to make a decision. The most common conditional statement is the If-Then-Else statement. If the condition is true, one set of instructions is executed. If it is false, a second set is executed instead. Figure 12.2A provides an example of a conditional statement that computes an employee bonus based on a level of sales. The actual condition can be relatively complex, containing Boolean expressions and multiple comparisons.

For situations when you have multiple values of one variable, it is easier to use a Select Case statement. As shown in Figure 12.3A, a business might give different discounts based on the type of customer. The same problem could be handled with multiple If-Then-Else statements, but the Select Case statement is much easier to read. Note the use of the Case Else statement to capture the values that are not predefined. Even if you think you know all possible values for customer type, it is wise to include the Else statement in case someone adds a new type later and forgets to alter the Select Case statement.

Loops

One of the strengths of a computer is that it can perform computations repeatedly. Loops are sections of code that can be performed more than once. Sometimes you know how many times you want to execute the loop. In this case, you can use a For-Next statement. The example in Figure 12.4A computes the total sales for the year. It assumes that an array (SalesForMonth) holds the sales for each month. Note the use of the total variable: total = total + SalesForMonth(month). It is known as an accumulator because each time the statement is executed, the computer takes the current value (on the right-hand side) and adds the new monthly

sales. The result is copied back to the total variable, providing a new total for the next time the statement is executed.

When you do not know how many times to iterate the loop, you can use a Do Until loop. Figure 12.5A provides an example that will tell you in which month the sales total reached 100,000. Notice the two accumulators: one for the sales total and one to count the months. Both of them have to be initialized (set to zero) before entering the loop. Failure to initialize accumulators is a common programming error. Also note that the increment statement (month = month + 1) inside the loop is crucial. If you forget this statement the loop will run forever—or until someone cancels your program.

Input and Output

Before Windows, input and output required special statements, and programmers spent a great deal of time learning them and writing them. With Windows, it is still possible to write traditional input and output commands (InputBox, MsgBox, and Printer object commands). However, these commands are rarely used. You can read the VB Help system documentation to learn more about these commands.

With Windows, it is easier to let the underlying application handle the input and output. For example, you can retrieve and store values in spreadsheet cells, or as lines in a word processor document, or in boxes on a database or Visual Basic form. Then your code simply reads the data from the application, performs the necessary computations, and stores the data back to the application. The user has complete control over the process and can use the application to format and print the results. This approach makes it easier to write programs and leaves the user in full control.

Retrieving and storing data within an application depends on the application. The easiest method arises with VB and database forms. Each form contains text boxes that are used to enter data and display results. The example in

FIGURE 12.6A   A VB form uses text boxes for input and output. The boxes leave the user with control over the form and make it easier to write the program.

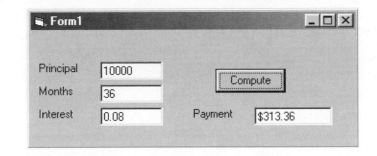

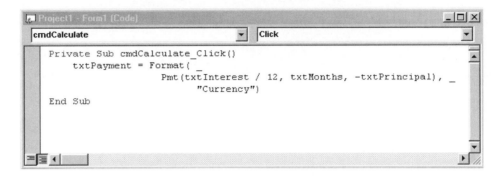

FIGURE 12.7A   Initial data from the Internet. You want to use proper case for the names to improve readability.

ALTA	143
SNOWBASIN	154
BRIGHTON	113
PARK CITY	115
DEER VALLEY	120
SOLITUDE	137

Figure 12.6A shows a simple form to compute the payment due on a loan. The user can enter the three items (principal, months, and interest rate) in any order. When they are ready, they click the Calculate button that executes your code. Your code stores the result in the Payment box. VB and Access forms make it easy to refer to textboxes: simply use the name that you gave the box (e.g., txtPayment) and treat it like a variable in your calculations. Spreadsheet cells and lines in a word processor are slightly more complex; the concept is the same, but the syntax is a little more complicated.

Visual Basic Example in Excel

Visual Basic runs as the macro programming language behind most Microsoft applications, including Excel. You can use it to write short programs that automate various tasks. Consider the example in Figure 12.7A. You obtained a data file from the Internet that contains a list of cities. Unfortunately, the cities were entered in uppercase. To make them easier to read, you want the names to be in proper case, where the first letter is capitalized. Also, when there are spaces in the name, the next letter should be capitalized as

well. You could just retype each name, but what if there are hundreds of them?

This type of repetitive task is what computer programs are designed to handle. With a few lines of code, you can fix the names. In fact, you can keep the program around in case you need it for similar problems in the future. As shown in Figure 12.8A, this program consists of two parts. The first part simply loops through the cells you select and passes the value to the PCase function, which is the second part. The PCase function first converts the entire name to lowercase. Then it makes the first letter uppercase. Next, it searches the name for a blank space. If it finds one, it converts the next letter to upper case. This search is repeated until there are no more spaces, or it reaches the end of the text.

The Macro1 routine is tied to an Excel keystroke combination: Ctrl+Shift+U. You convert the text by selecting the names in the spreadsheet and pressing the assigned keys. The names are converted to the proper case as shown in Figure 12.9A.

Even a few dozen names could take you a while to retype—and the retyping would probably introduce errors. These lines of code can be written in a few minutes, minimize errors, and be reused for other projects. Plus, it is a lot more interesting to write code than to retype names.

FIGURE 12.8A Code to convert text to proper case. The Macro1 routine gets each value from the spreadsheet and calls the PCase function to convert it.

```
Sub Macro 1()
' Keyboard Shortcut: Ctrl+Shift+U

  For Each c In Selection
      c.Value = PCase(c.Value)
  Next c

End Sub

Function PCase(txt)
' Convert a text value to proper case (first letter is capitalized)
  Dim i As Integer

  ' First make the entire string lower case
  txt = LCase(txt)
  '   Now capitalize the first letter
  Mid(txt, 1,1) = UCase(Mid(txt, 1, 1))
  ' Now search for a space
  i = 2
  Do While (i>0) And (i< Len(txt))
    i = InStr(i, txt,"")
    If (i > 0) And (i<Len(txt))Then
      Mid(txt, i + 1, 1) = UCase(Mid(txt, i +1, 1))
      i = i +1
    End if
  Loop

  PCase = txt
End Function
```

FIGURE 12.9A Results. Names are converted to initial capitals.

Alta	143
Snowbasin	154
Brighton	113
Park City	115
Deer Valley	120
Solitude	137

Exercises

1. Copy the code from Figure 12.8A into Excel and test the macro.

2. Write a short macro program in Excel that adds all of the numbers between the values in cell A1 and cell A2 and puts the result in cell A5. For example, if A1 = 1 and A2 = 5, then add 1 + 2 + 3 + 4 + 5 to get 15. Hint: You can read or write to a cell with the command Range("A1").

3. Write an Excel macro that looks at each item selected to see if any cells are blank. If any are blank, display a message notifying the user how many blank cells there are. Hint: Use the IsEmpty function to test and the MsgBox command to display a message.

4. Briefly describe an application that could benefit from the use of a macro (i.e., it cannot easily be solved with a built-in function).

5. Identify as many products as you can that use a version of Visual Basic as a programming language.

CHAPTER THIRTEEN

Organizing Information System Resources

What you will learn in this chapter

- What tasks are performed by MIS employees?

- What jobs are available in MIS?

- What methodologies are used to build information systems?

- How can systems be designed and built faster than before?

- What are the advantages and drawbacks of centralization versus decentralization in MIS?

- How do Internet technologies affect the flow and management of data in an organization?

Fidelity Investments runs some of the largest mutual funds in the world. Managing investments for millions of people requires good information systems and careful organization

Fidelity Investments

Edward Crosby Johnson III made the walk to 82 Devonshire with more on his mind than usual. It was the first day of winter in Boston, and he was evaluating his company's performance for the year. As the chairman of Fidelity Investments, the company was "his" because of his formal position of authority. It was also his because the Johnsons owned most of the privately held company, worth billions.

Most of all, Fidelity was Ned Johnson's because he had made the right decisions for Fidelity with remarkable regularity, building the firm into one of the world's most diversified and successful financial services companies, with over $800 billion in managed assets. As Ned made his way to the office, he began to think practically. What were the issues facing Fidelity over the long term?

Johnson's primary goal was to serve the customers, through high returns on their investment, quick access to information, and efficient administration of their accounts. Technology remained an important tool, perhaps the tool, for establishing a service edge over the competition. There was no widget-making flowchart that could guarantee Fidelity a good product in the investment sense. For Ned, the essential question became, how can Fidelity continue to satisfy and grow its customer base in the face of the volatility of financial markets and fierce competition?

Overview

Ally: Elaine, I don't understand it. I just tried to print this document three times. And I still can't get it.

Elaine: Maybe the printer's broken? Did you call MIS?

Ally: Maybe (sarcastically)? And yes, they are clueless. What am I supposed to do now?

Richard: Well, maybe we can call that repair shop for now. But we need to find a better solution. We pay good money for that IT group. They should be doing a better job.

Ally: I agree. Elaine, didn't you date one of those guys once? What do they do? On the job, I mean.

Elaine: Well, the guys I met all seemed really busy. Something about rewriting the billing system. There did seem to be a lot of people in their main office.

Ally: Then maybe we need to get a few of those guys over here. At least we'd be able to find them when we need them.

FIGURE 13.1

Organizing information system resources. Making effective use of information systems requires organizing the MIS resources: hardware, software, data, and personnel. A key decision involves positioning the resources in the organization, which revolves around decentralization versus centralization. The goal is to balance the need for central control with the value of decentralized decisions.

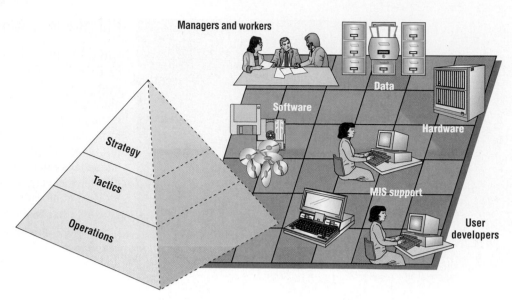

Introduction

The capabilities of application software are impressive. Because of these tools, businesspeople using personal computers are solving problems in a few hours that never would have been attempted five years ago. With these powerful tools available to the average businessperson, it is easy to wonder why a company needs an MIS department. That is a good question, and the answers keep changing through the years.

MIS departments provide many important services. For example, think about what happens when a new version of your word processor is released. Someone has to install the software, distribute the manuals, convert old document files to the new format, and show people how to use the new features. Now imagine the problems involved when there are 5,000 workers using this software.

According to statistics collected by *Computerworld,* large companies spend about 5 percent of their sales revenue on the MIS area. For a company with a billion dollars in sales, that amounts to $50 million a year spent on MIS. This money pays for personal computers, central computers, communications, software, and MIS personnel to manage it all. The primary tasks undertaken by the MIS department are software development, setting corporate computing standards, hardware administration, database administration, advocacy and planning, and end-user support.

Small businesses usually do not have a separate MIS department. That does not mean these duties are ignored. Even in small businesses, someone has to be responsible for these MIS functions. However, small businesses generally do not attempt to develop their own software. Even relying on commercial software requires that time be spent on determining data needs and evaluating software packages.

Probably the most important MIS decision facing business today is the issue of centralization. Because personal computers have a huge price/performance advantage over larger computers, there is a major incentive to decentralize the hardware. Yet, there are some serious complications with complete decentralization. Several strategies for organizing information resources provide the advantages of both centralization and decentralization. The management goal is to find the combination that works best for each situation. Before examining the alternatives, you need to understand the basic MIS roles.

Trends

In the early days, computers created few management issues. The large, expensive machines were placed in a central location and serviced by a centralized group of specialized employees. But as costs dropped over time, hardware spread throughout the organization. Soon, employees were collecting and creating data on hundreds or thousands of machines across the company. The local area networks of the late 1980s were installed in an effort to make it easier to share data and provide more centralized services.

But just connecting computers does not automatically improve data sharing. Companies need standards and management policies to make it easy to share data. Today, many of these standards come from the Internet side of computing. The Internet was originally designed to facilitate sharing data among researchers. The standards and tools also make it easy for individuals within companies to share data and resources. New collaboration systems are being created that make it easy for workers to access data and contribute to decisions from anywhere in the world.

Managing the Information Systems Function

Many times in your career you will find yourself heavily involved with members of the MIS department. In the case of a small business, you might be in charge of the one or two MIS personnel. At some time, you might be the company liaison to an outsourcing vendor, MIS contractor, or consultant. In all of these situations, you will be responsible for planning, monitoring, and evaluating the MIS organization. You will have to make decisions and answer questions like: Is the MIS department doing a good job? Should the company be spending more money on MIS? Is it getting a good value for its current spending? Are there other methods that would be more efficient or save money?

As many companies have found, it is difficult to evaluate the MIS function. There are few objective measures. Changes in technology make the process more difficult. Innovations in hardware and software often make it easier to build and maintain information systems. However, there is a cost to buying new equipment. There is also a cost to continually retraining workers and modifying databases and reports. The goal of management is to find the appropriate balance between the need to update and the costs.

Management of information systems begins by understanding the roles of MIS. The MIS function is responsible for hardware and software acquisition and support. The MIS staff provide access to corporate data and build applications. They support end-user development with training and help desks. MIS workers set corporate data standards and maintain the integrity of the company databases. All of these functions have to be organized, performed, and evaluated on a regular basis.

The issue of new technology points out the importance of planning. The only way to control costs and evaluate MIS benefits is to establish a plan. Plans need to be detailed so actual results can be compared to the plan. Yet plans need to be flexible enough to adapt to unexpected events and new technology. You also need to formulate contingency plans for events that might occur.

One key issue in managing information technology is organizing the MIS function so that it matches the structure of the firm. Centralization versus decentralization has been a key issue in the organization of MIS resources. Networks and powerful personal computers have led to more options supporting decentralization of information. The increased options are useful, but they create more issues managers must examine. To understand the advantages and drawbacks of MIS options, we must first examine the roles of MIS.

Managing the MIS functions is a difficult job. Leaders must always remain focused on the primary goals. The primary job of the MIS department is to support and enhance the

---

Reality Bytes   **The Changing Role of MIS**

The role of the MIS department has changed over time. In many respects, it is in the middle of a fundamental change. In the past, MIS departments focused on creating information systems and controlling data—particularly transaction data. Today, as explained by the Gartner Group (an IS consulting firm), the objectives of MIS are:

• Provide transparent access to corporate data.

• Optimize access to data stored on multiple platforms for many groups of users.

• Maximize the end-user's ability to be self-sufficient in meeting individual information needs.

These changes represent a shift in attitude. It moves toward the goal of increasing support for workers, not their replacement, so employees can do their jobs better on their own.

---

business. This mission is accomplished by enabling the sharing of data in a cost-effective manner but still providing adequate security controls to protect the information assets of the organization. An effective information system can create new methods of organizing and running the business. Of course, most of these goals are conflicting: security and sharing results in significant disagreements and trade-offs; holding down costs conflicts with just about everything.

MIS Roles

Good information systems do not simply materialize from thin air. Providing timely, accurate, and relevant information requires careful planning and support. Creating effective information involves maintaining hardware, providing software training and support, supporting end-user development, defining and controlling access to databases, establishing corporate standards, and researching the competitive advantages of new technologies. The basic roles of MIS are outlined in Figure 13.2.

Hardware Administration

In some respects, hardware administration has become a little easier in the last few years. Computers are more reliable, more standardized, and cheaper. It used to be difficult to accommodate users who needed slightly different hardware. Many companies still prefer to standardize PC hardware to simplify purchasing and asset tracking. But with common three-year support contracts, standardized hardware, and low prices, it is less and less important to require that all employees have the exact same computer. Instead, most companies need to choose a time frame for updating their computers. For most purposes, three years has been shown to be a productive length of time to hold a PC.

Mobility has become an increasingly important issue for many business computer users. More managers are requesting the use of laptops instead of (or along with) desktops. Mobile systems like the PDAs and Internet-accessible cell phones change the picture even more. Fortunately, the cost of most of these devices has dropped as well. Consequently, purchasing is less of an issue. Instead, mobile systems present more problems in terms of security—beginning with loss of the equipment.

Purchase costs do not represent the entire cost of hardware. In the mid-1990s, a few companies began pushing a concept they called **total cost of ownership (TCO).** The basic issue is that someone has to configure the PC, install software, and troubleshoot problems. At the time, most of these tasks required an onsite MIS support person, which was expensive. Various attempts were made to estimate these additional support costs and derive the TCO. The slightly hidden objective was to show that centralized computers were not really more expensive than personal computers. While most of the numbers from this process were unreliable, the process did highlight the difficulties of maintaining personal computers. Consequently, several firms created tools to install software and troubleshoot PCs from a central location over the LAN.

Just as in other areas of business, MIS jobs have become highly specialized. For instance, many advertisements for MIS jobs look like someone spilled a bowl of alphabet soup on the page. Companies often search for technical skills involving specific hardware and software.

Unfortunately, this approach to jobs causes problems for MIS personnel. In order to find other jobs or to advance in their current position, they have to acquire increasingly detailed knowledge of specific hardware and software packages. Yet,

with rapid changes in the industry, this knowledge can become obsolete in a year or two. These changes mean employees have to continually expand their knowledge and identify software and hardware approaches that are likely to succeed.

On the other hand, businesses need to keep their current applications running. With thousands of hours invested in current systems, companies cannot afford to discard their current practices and adopt every new hardware and software system that shows some promise.

FIGURE 13.2

MIS roles. The MIS department is responsible for hardware administration, software development, and training and support. MIS staff establish corporate computing standards, provide access to corporate data, and support end-user development. The MIS department also plays an advocacy role, presenting the IT benefits and strategies to the executive office.

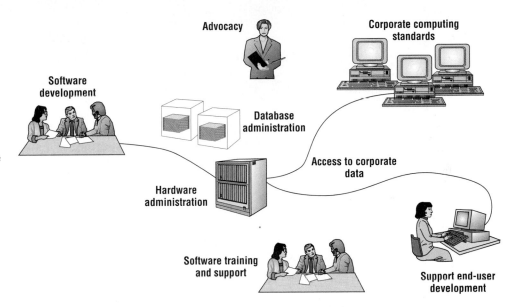

The move toward Internet-based applications removes many of the issues of managing personal computer hardware. As long as the systems support the Internet standards, and as long as they can be purchased inexpensively, there is little need for detailed MIS oversight. On the other hand, the central servers that run the websites, databases, and applications become more important. MIS personnel need to monitor the performance of the servers, provide backup plans, maintain security, and plan for capacity increases.

Capacity planning is a major factor in MIS organizations. Building scalable systems is an important goal for most organizations. The objective is to purchase only the level of hardware that is needed. Then, as demand increases, add more servers or larger servers to handle the increased load. This process holds down central hardware costs, but it means that MIS has to carefully design the systems and carefully monitor the usage and predict future demands.

Software Support

Software generally requires more support than hardware does. MIS staff can help users decide which software to purchase and then can install it. Users need to be trained to use various software features. Whenever workers change jobs or a company hires new workers, they need to be trained. Similarly, commercial software versions change almost every year, requiring more training for users. Additionally, someone has to install the new copies on the machines, distribute manuals, and convert data files.

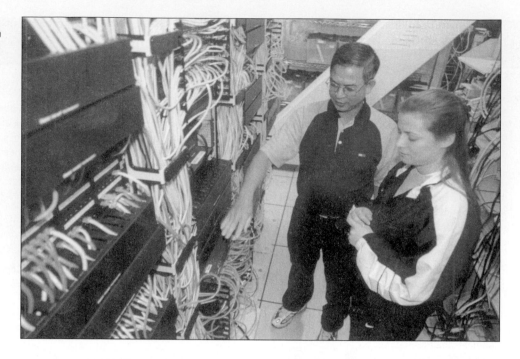

When users have difficulty getting the computer to do what they want, it saves time to have someone to call for help. Most commercial software companies provide telephone support for their products, although many of them charge extra for this support. In many cases, it is better for MIS to support users directly. Besides the possibility of lower costs, the MIS department has a better understanding of the business problems. Also, many users are now combining information from several packages. For example, you might put accounting data and a photograph into a word-processed document. If different companies created the three programs and you have trouble, which one of the three software companies do you call? Your own MIS department will have experience with all three packages and should be able to identify the cause of the problems.

Network Support

Both wired and wireless networks are critical to running a company. Managers rely on the networks being available 24 hours a day, 7 days a week. Fortunately, most modern network equipment is reliable and can run continuously for months. Additionally, network managers can build networks that can correct for failures and bottlenecks by routing traffic around a switch that has failed.

Network support becomes more complicated when managing Internet connections. Connecting to the Internet requires some specialized skills to configure the router. Once the connection is established, configuring the router for security becomes critical. Monitoring the connection and keeping up with current security advisories is even more challenging. Larger companies train specialized personnel to handle these tasks. Smaller companies often rely on consultants or contractors.

Wireless networks are relatively easy to install—several companies provide the hardware to install in your home. But, they are much more difficult to configure if you are concerned about security. Several true stories exist of people sitting in parking lots or even passing commuter trains and establishing a wireless connection into a company's network. Network specialists are trained to configure networks to minimize these problems.

Software Development

Developing software and business applications is difficult. Projects can require teams of hundreds of developers. Even smaller projects and purchases of larger software applications require devoted attention to detail. Managing software development and purchases is a critical role in MIS. Beginning with project evaluation and feasibility studies, through project management and tracking progress, to evaluating the team efforts, someone has to be in charge of the details.

These tasks are some of the more traditional roles in MIS. They are also the most difficult. Unfortunately, most companies have poor track records in managing software projects. Many development projects fail, and even more are behind schedule and over budget. Consequently, many firms choose to buy software or use outside companies to help in development projects. Even in these cases, someone in MIS has to be responsible for evaluating choices and monitoring progress.

Support for End-User Development

Many application packages include programming capabilities. For example, a manager may create a spreadsheet to calculate sales commissions. Each week, new sales data is entered and the spreadsheet automatically produces summary reports. It would be better to have a clerk rather than a manager enter this new data. To make the clerk's job easier, the manager uses the macro capabilities in the spreadsheet to create a set of menus and help messages. Similarly, using a word processor's macro facilities, a legal department can create standard paragraphs for various contracts. With them, an assistant can type one word to display a prewritten warranty paragraph. In theory, even complex applications traditionally provided by the MIS department, such as accounting systems, could be programmed by end users with prepackaged software.

Several problems can arise from these end-user applications. Techniques that are acceptable for small projects may lead to errors and delays with large systems. Programming major applications requires obtaining information from users and managers. Applications designed for corporate use require extensive checking of data and security provisions to ensure accuracy. The software often needs to run on different operating system and local networks.

The MIS department can provide assistance to minimize these problems. MIS personnel can assist end users in collecting ideas from other users. They can also help in testing the applications to verify the accuracy and make sure the software works with other applications. MIS can provide tools and help end users document their applications and move them to new operating systems or new hardware. Programmers can write special routines to overcome any limitations of commercial software that might arise. MIS staffs also maintain help desks or information centers to answer user questions and help users debug applications.

Corporate Computing Standards

Over time, MIS has learned that the firm gets into trouble if all of its people work independently. In the 1960s, applications such as payroll, accounting, and customer order processing were developed independently. During the 1970s, companies had to spend large amounts of money getting all of the pieces to work together. In the 1980s, personal computers arrived, and the problems got worse.

Reacting to the problems created by these incompatibilities, MIS professionals at different companies developed **standards.** If all vendors used standard formats for files, hardware connections, and commands, products from different vendors could be used together. Today, there are standards for everything: data, hardware, software, report layouts, and coffee pots.

It is unlikely that the computing world will ever see complete cooperation among vendors. Three factors prevent products from working together. First, standards are often ambiguous or incomplete. Human languages always have some ambiguity, and there is no way to determine whether the description actually covers every possible situation. A second problem is that standards incorporate what is known about a topic at the time the standard is developed. Computing technologies change rapidly. Often, vendors can produce better products by not following the standards. Then new standards have to be developed. A third problem occurs because vendors want to distinguish their products from the offerings of competitors. If there were standards that perfectly described a product, there would be only one way to compete: price. Many vendors find that it is more profitable to offer features beyond what is specified in the standards, enabling the developers to charge a higher price.

Training and education are increasingly important functions of the MIS department. With constant change in software applications, employees must constantly learn new tools and techniques.

Even though it is not possible to create perfect industry standards, there are advantages to creating companywide standards. They enable firms to buy products at lower prices. Most large businesses have special purchase agreements with hardware and software vendors. Buying in bulk allows them to obtain better prices. Similarly, it is easier to fix hardware if all the machines are the same. Likewise, it is much more convenient to upgrade just one word-processing package for 200 computers, instead of 20 different brands. Similarly, training is less expensive and time consuming if everyone uses the same software and hardware. Finally, standards make it easier for employees to share information across the company. The Internet and e-mail create additional demand for standards. To share a file on the Internet, you must store it in a standard format (e.g., HTML or PDF). People sometimes forget that a similar problem arises when attaching files to e-mail messages. Particularly when you send a file to someone in a different company, you need to remember that the recipient may not have the same version of software that you are using. If you attach a file in Word 2000 format, for example, the recipient needs to have Word 2000 to read it. Since some companies upgrade before others, it is generally safer to save attached files in either a standard format (HTML or RTF), or in a previous version.

Reality Bytes — Clueless Management

In the 1990s, a new system administrator was hired by a company having problems with its systems. At least one major system would crash every week, wiping out minutes or hours worth of data. The senior manager gave the new administrator one command: "Do whatever it takes to make sure people can do their jobs and that systems do not go down anymore." Over several months, the new worker improved security, created automated backups, and improved system monitoring. He also added some modifications that would let processes roll over to another system if hardware failed. He documented all of the changes and reasons and explained the systems to other IT managers running crash-prone systems in other divisions. One day he gets called to a meeting with all of the senior IT staff members. The head of the IT department says "All the departments are still having system problems, except for yours. In your area, the systems are always up, people are able to get on the systems anytime they need to, and the managers have no major complaints about the systems you're in charge of. It's like this little island that stands out." The system administrator is humble and explains he had help from many of the workers. He then offers to help the other administrators with their systems. Surprisingly, everyone is shocked. The head of IT breaks the silence, telling the administrator "I'm afraid you don't understand. You can't run your systems this way. They're not configured to company standards. Put everything back the way it was."

Source: Adapted from Sharky [The Shark Tank], "An Island of Sanity in a Sea of Confusion," *Computerworld,* January 2, 2002.

Some organizations forget that standards cannot be permanent. Hardware and software change almost continuously; new products arrive that are substantially better than existing standard items. Similarly, as the business changes, the standards often have to be revised. Also, there are exceptions to just about any policy. If one department cannot do its job with the standard equipment, MIS must make an exception and then figure out how to support this new equipment and software.

Data and Database Administration

Databases are crucial to the operation of any company. Keeping the databases up-to-date and accurate does not happen by chance. Larger organizations employ a **database administrator** (DBA) to be responsible for maintaining the corporate database. The DBA is responsible for maintaining the databases, monitoring performance of the database management system, and solving day-to-day problems that arise with the databases.

Companies also need someone to coordinate the definition of the data. Large organizations might hire a separate **data administrator** (DA), smaller companies will pass this role to the DBA. The DA is responsible for defining the structure of the databases. The DA has to make certain the data is stored in a form that can be used by all the applications and users. He or she is responsible for avoiding duplicate terms (e.g., customer instead of client). Additionally, the DA provides for **data integrity,** which means that the data must contain as few errors as possible.

The DA is also required to maintain security controls on the database. The DA has to determine who has access to each part of the data and specify what changes users are allowed to make. Along the same lines, companies and employees are required by law to meet certain privacy requirements. For instance, banks are not allowed to release data about customers except in certain cases. European nations have much stricter privacy rules. If a firm operates a computer facility in many European countries, the company must carefully control access to all customer data. Some nations prohibit the transfer of customer data out of the country. The DA is responsible for understanding these laws and making sure the company complies with them.

Finally, because today's databases are so crucial to the company, the business needs a carefully defined disaster and recovery policy. Typically that means the databases have to be backed up every day. Sometimes, a company might keep continuous backup copies of critical data on separate disk drives at all times. MIS has to plan for things that might go wrong (fires, viruses, floods, hackers, etc.). If something does affect the data or the computer system, MIS is responsible for restoring operations. For instance, an alternate computing site might be needed while the original facilities are being repaired. All of this planning requires considerable time.

Security

Since most of today's business data is stored in computers, computer security has become a critical role for the MIS department. Often this role is shared with the accounting department to establish standards and procedures to ensure the integrity of financial data. Medium and large organizations have full-time computer security officers to set policies, establish controls, and monitor systems for attacks. Because of the constant evolution of new threats and the large number of systems and employees, the task can be immense. Attackers often search for one little hole in one system or one mistake by an employee. Security managers have to keep up with hundreds of different systems and applications to make sure that all of the holes are plugged.

Advocacy Role

The MIS department is headed by a single manager, who often is called the chief information officer (CIO). The CIO position might be a vice president or one level below that. A major portion of this job involves searching for ways in which the information system can help the company. In particular, the CIO searches for and advocates strategic uses of MIS. The goal is to use the computer in some way that attracts customers to provide an advantage over the company's competitors.

Whenever a new technology is introduced, someone has to be responsible for deciding whether it will be worth the expense to make a change. If there is no one in this **advocacy role** who evaluates the existing systems and compares them to new products, an organization is probably not often going to get new equipment. Even when many users are dissatisfied with an existing system, they will have a better chance of acquiring new technology if they can voice their complaints through one highly placed person. Along these lines, the CIO is responsible for long-run planning in terms of information technology.

MIS Jobs

A wide variety of jobs is available in MIS. Some of the jobs require a technical education, such as that for programmers. Specialized positions are available in data communications and database management. On the other hand, **systems analysts** require an extensive knowledge of business problems and solutions. Some entry-level operator jobs require only minimal training. On the other end of the scale, analysts may eventually become team leaders or managers. The entire MIS function is coordinated by chief information officers.

As you might expect, salaries depend on experience, individual qualifications, industry, location, and current economic conditions. Six basic MIS job tracks are shown in Figure 13.3: systems development, networks, database, user support, operations, and other specialists. Systems development includes several levels of analysts and programmers. Network management involves installing network hardware and software, diagnosing problems, and designing new networks. Database management focuses on database design and administration. End-user support consists of training users, answering questions, and installing software. Operations consists of day-to-day tasks such as loading paper, mounting tapes, and starting long computer tasks. Many of these tasks are being automated. Entry-level operator jobs do not require a college degree, but there is little room for advancement without a degree. Specialist positions exist in larger companies and generally evolve from new technologies. For example, Web masters who would create and manage websites were in high demand for two or three years, then as the Internet became more important to companies, all of the workers were trained in Web development, so there was less need for specialists.

Every year, *Computerworld* surveys workers in the industry and publishes average salaries. Job placement firms such as Robert Half also collect data on salaries. This data can be useful if you are searching for a job or thinking about a career in MIS. As a business

FIGURE 13.3

IS salaries. As in any field, salaries depend on experience. However, in IS they also depend heavily on technical skills. Programmer/analysts with current skills and experience in new technologies find it easier to get jobs and obtain higher salaries. Note that there is a wide variety of jobs in IS, each requiring different types of skills.

IS Management

CIO/VP IS/CTO	$165,000

Systems Development

Director	$123,000
Manager	88,000
Project manager	85,000
System analyst	79,000
Senior developer	74,000
Programmer/analyst	55,000
Junior programmer	45,000

Networks

Director	$106,000
Manager	83,000
Administrator	60,000
Network analyst	40,000
Junior analyst	34,000

Database

Manager	$94,000
Administrator	89,000
Database analyst	67,000

User Support

Manager	$69,000
Help desk operator	40,000
PC technical support	43,000

Internet

Manager	$94,000
Webmaster	72,000
Application developer	70,000
EC specialist	74,000
EDI specialist	66,000

Security

Manager	$86,000
Administrator	72,000
Specialist	64,000
IS audit manager	81,000
IS audit staff	53,000

Operations

Director	$106,000
Manager	74,000
Lead operator	42,000
Computer operator	35,000

FIGURE 13.4

Internationalization. In the past few years, U.S. and European firms have turned to using programmers in other nations. For example, U.S. programmers are paid about 20 times as much as Indian and Russian programmers. Both India and Russia have extensive educational programs and few jobs for local programmers.

Sources: www.placementIndia.com; www.gojobsite.co.uk; www.auriga.com. Differences can be affected by other factors, including benefits, cost of living, productivity, access to equipment, and transportation and communication costs.

Nation	Programmer/Analyst Salary
United States	$ 55,000
Britain	57,000
Russia	10,800
India	2,508

Data in U.S. dollars.

manager, the numbers will give you an indication of the costs entailed in building and maintaining information systems. Basic averages are listed in Figure 13.3. As indicated by Figure 13.4, costs vary enormously by nation, which is leading some U.S. companies to use programmers from India and Russia.

One way to see the changes occurring in MIS is to look at the types of skills that businesses are looking for in MIS applicants. Figure 13.5 shows some of the top skills demanded in 1994, 1998, and 2001. Notice the high demand in new categories (ERP, groupware, and wireless/Internet skills). Note that COBOL was important for the year 2000 rewrites, but most firms can now find all the COBOL programmers they need. The continued high demand for ERP skills reflects the continued emphasis firms are placing on integrating their data, plus the fact that the task is difficult so it requires several MIS people.

Outsourcing

In the past 20 years, many businesses have noted that it has become difficult to terminate or lay off employees. In MIS, it has also been expensive for firms to hire the best people. Consequently, many firms have chosen to outsource various aspects of their MIS functions. The basic premise is that specialized firms can offer more efficient service at better prices. For example, EDS runs huge data centers, and it is relatively easy to add more

FIGURE 13.5
MIS skills in demand. At any given time, some skills are in demand— reflecting demand for applications and a shortage of workers for new technologies. Other skills are also in demand, but workers with the listed skills generally received premium wages and bonuses.

Sources: *Computerworld,* "In Demand: IT Starts Require Premium Pay," December 10, 2001; *Computerworld,* November 16, 1998; and Arnett and Litecky, *Journal of Systems Management,* February 1994.

Rank	2001	1998	1994
1	ERP	ERP	Networking
2	Object engineering	Groupware	Database
3	Data warehouse and data visualization	Database	UNIX
4	Groupware	Networking	Visual Basic
5	Wireless	COBOL	COBOL

clients with only minor increases in costs. As a huge MIS organization, EDS also hires and trains thousands of workers. Outsourcing also was attractive to firms as a temporary measure. For example, firms might outsource their old accounting systems while designing and installing a new ERP system. The old system will continue to function and be ably supported by an expert company. The internal employees can focus on designing and installing the new system.

Outsourcing can take many forms. Firms might sell their entire computer center to an outsource specialist—and all of the data, software, and employees would move to the new company. Other firms might contract out other MIS functions such as network management, PC repair, training, security, or development.

Two of the leading service providers are Electronic Data Systems (EDS) and Global Services, the IBM subsidiary. Some other leading outsourcing companies are listed in Figure 13.6. Note the huge growth in outsourcing in the 1990s. This trend was partly due to the desire to cut costs, the inability to hire IT workers, the increasing standardization of IT services, and the need to focus on core business management. In 1998, *Computerworld* reported that an average of 20 percent of IS budgets was spent on outsourcing. In 2001, IBM reported that 41 percent of IBM's total revenues were generated by the Global Services subsidiary.

Generally, a company signs an agreement to use the services of the outsourcing firm for a fixed number of years. Depending on the agreement, the outsourcing firm can be responsible for anything from machine operation and maintenance, to development of new systems, to telecommunication services.

Outsourcing has primarily been used to decrease operating costs or to get the initial money from the sale of the machines. In particular, the company gains an infusion of cash through the sale of the machines. Some firms have stated that they chose outsourcing because it enabled them to focus on their core business and not worry about maintaining computers and designing systems. Today, outsourcing website hosting and development are relatively common. Few firms have the expertise to securely configure the networks and servers required for e-businesses; so they pay outside firms to handle the technical details.

Figure 13.7 illustrates conditions under which it is useful to consider outsourcing. As you move away from the center of the diagram, outsourcing becomes less useful. The most common uses of outsourcing are for straightforward applications of technology, including personal computer installation and servicing, legacy system maintenance, and routine application development.

On the other hand, situations that are unique or require advanced uses of information technology are best handled internally. For example, complex markets that benefit from strategic applications require the knowledge and experience of employees who work for the company. Likewise, situations that require tight security are easier to control if they remain in-house. Also avoid outsourcing when the outsourcing firm will have to pay the same costs that you face—because they will charge for an additional profit margin, the final cost can be higher. Examples include applications with high fixed costs or those requiring high levels of expensive state-of-the-art equipment or specialized MIS talent.

Competitive pressures are also leading many managers to consider outsourcing their information systems. As technology continues to change, it becomes increasingly difficult for general business managers to keep up with the technology. Each change brings requests for new hardware and software, and the need to reevaluate the use of technology

FIGURE 13.6

Outsourcing revenue. In the latter half of the 1990s, outsourcing with the major providers accelerated as many companies chose to hire outside firms to run various MIS functions. For 2000 and beyond, much of the outsourcing is for ERP systems and Web hosting. Data is taken from annual reports and company websites.

Company	1991	1995	1997	1999	2000
IBM Global Services	0.4	17.7	24.6	35.0	37.0
EDS	1.2	12.4	15.2	18.7	19.2
CSC	0.4	4.2	6.6	9.4	10.5
Accenture	0.5	4.2	6.3	9.5	9.8
ADP	0.3	3.0	4.9	6.3	7.0
Affiliated Computer	0.16	0.4	1.2	2.0	2.1
Fiserv	0.23	0.7	1.0	1.4	1.7
Perot Systems	0.16	0.3	0.8	1.2	1.1
Total (billion dollars)	3.4	42.9	60.6	83.5	88.4

FIGURE 13.7

Outsourcing evaluation. Outsourcing entails many trade-offs. It means transferring control of a crucial resource to an outside company. If you are really interested in development of strategic applications and leading-edge applications, it is usually better to use an internal development team. If you are dealing with older technology used mostly for transaction processing, it can be cheaper to hire an outside firm to maintain your applications.

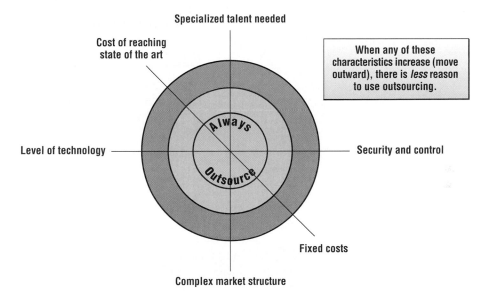

within the firm. Changing technology also requires continual retraining of the information systems staff. At the same time, middle-level management positions are being cut, and managers are asked to take on more tasks. Figure 13.8 shows why, in these circumstances, companies decide to transfer IS management to an expert through outsourcing.

There are drawbacks to outsourcing. First, there might be a slight increase in security risk because the MIS employees have weaker ties to the original company. On the other hand, outsourcing providers are likely to have stricter security provisions than an average firm does. A bigger question is the issue of who is responsible for identifying solutions and new uses of technology for the firm. If MIS workers are employed by an external firm, will it be their job to search for new applications? If not, who will?

In the past couple of years, some firms have begun to reconsider the costs of outsourcing. Although it results in a fixed charge for IS services, the hosting firm has little incentive to strive to reduce its prices. Additionally, it can be difficult to control the decisions of the outsourcing firm. Consequently, some firms have become more selective over which items are outsourced.

MIS Organization: Centralization and Decentralization

Two broad trends are slowly creating significant changes in the way we perceive and organize information: (1) declining sizes and prices of technology, and (2) expanding access to the Internet—particularly wireless connections. Internet sites are slowly becoming

FIGURE 13.8
Outsourcing forces. Firms are being pushed to cut margins. Many are focusing on their core competencies, leaving little time for wrestling with technology. At the same time, as the large outsourcing firms gain customers, their efficiency improves and they can offer more services and more specialists at better rates.

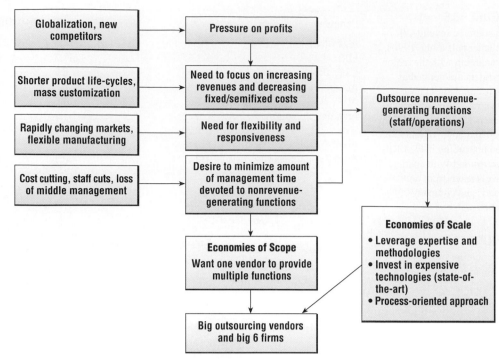

repositories of information that is accessible any time from almost any location. External data on the economy, news, financial markets, consumers, competitors, and more is readily available on the Internet. Increasingly, you will have to pay for this data but it is accessible. Advanced companies today are providing similar services in terms of internal organizational data. Data warehouses collect, clean, and present data to internal Web browsers. Ultimately, these databases will be integrated, so managers in a meeting can easily call up current sales data and combine it with economic forecasts on their handheld computers. The goal is to make integrated data available anywhere to authorized users. The question is: how should the MIS system be organized to provide these features?

When hardware was expensive, all data, software, and employees were centralized. As the use of midrange and personal computers expanded, hardware became decentralized and software and data began to follow it. For example, decision makers stored spreadsheets, analyses, and reports on their personal computers. But this decentralized data is more difficult to share, even with networks. This stage is where the Internet technologies become important—the search engines and browsers were designed to make it easier to find and view data in many forms. Applying these technologies within the company (called an *intranet*) provides easier access to corporate data.

Almost none of the issues of centralization and decentralization are new—politicians, economists, and organizational theorists have debated them for hundreds of years. The basic argument for **centralization** revolves around the need to coordinate activities and efficiencies that can be gained from large-scale operations. Proponents of **decentralization** argue that moving control to smaller units produces a more flexible system that can respond faster to market changes, encourage individual differences, and innovate. Figure 13.9 summarizes the arguments for centralization decentralization.

As with many arguments, there are different answers for different circumstances, and it is rare that the extreme choices are best. Wise managers will attempt to gain the advantages of both approaches. With information systems, four basic areas are subject to centralization or decentralization: hardware, software, data, and staffing. Determining the best way to organize information resources requires that managers understand the advantages and disadvantages for each of these areas.

FIGURE 13.9

Summary of benefits of centralization and decentralization. There are advantages to both centralization and decentralization of the MIS resources. The ultimate objective is to design an MIS organization to benefit from as many of the advantages as possible by combining both centralization and decentralization.

	Centralization	Decentralization
Hardware	Data sharing Purchases control Usage control Less duplication Efficient use of resources	Less chance of total breakdown Personalized machines for users
Software	Compatibility Bulk buying discounts Easier training Ease of maintenance	Different user preferences Easier access Customization
Data	Easy backup Easier to share Less duplication Security control and monitoring	Only transmit data that needs to be shared Keeps user control and politics
Personnel	Similar worker backgrounds Easier training Straightforward career path Specialized staff Easier to see and control costs	Faster response to users More time with users Better understanding and communication Different career path

FIGURE 13.10

Complete centralization. For many years, computers were expensive and there were few communication networks. Consequently, hardware, data, software, and MIS personnel were centrally located. Data was sent to the computer for processing and printed reports were distributed throughout the company. Users only dealt indirectly with MIS.

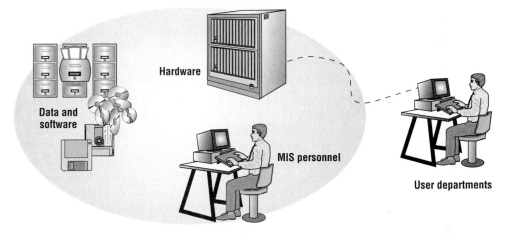

Hardware

Today, hardware is relatively inexpensive. Even centralized servers have come down in cost, often using systems based on server farms consisting of hundreds or thousands of inexpensive computers.

Similarly, on the user side, prices of personal computers have dropped substantially. Even portable devices are relatively inexpensive.

Centralization

The biggest advantage of centralized IS hardware is that it is easier to share hardware, software, and data with multiple users. Complete centralization is shown in Figure 13.10. Consider a simple example. If a company installs an expensive printer in one user's office, it will be difficult for other users to get access to the printer. On the other hand, with only one central computer, all of the hardware, software, and data will be located in one place. All users can be given equal access to these facilities. By keeping all hardware, software, and personnel in one location, it is easier to avoid duplication and keep costs down.

Along the same lines, centralized hardware also makes it easier to control user access to the information system. By storing all data on one machine, it is easy to monitor usage of the

R.R. Donnelley is one of the largest commercial printers in the United States. Headquartered in Chicago, the company has 300 printing plants around the world. Much of the growth came from acquiring other companies. But this strategy led to decentralization, since each plant ran independently. Customers were often frustrated when they had to deal with multiple plants—each with separate policies and schedules. Donnelley decided to move to a centralized system to manage everything from supplies to job scheduling. The system runs on a centralized Oracle database. It already saves time for employees.

Shift-change status reports used to take an hour, now they take five minutes. More important, customers can now turn to a website that shows them real-time reports on the status of their jobs—even if the jobs are scheduled across multiple plants. CIO Gary Sutula anticipates that the system will eventually shorten job cycle times from two or three months down to two or three weeks.

Source: Adapted from Tony Kontzer, "Centralization Redux for IT," *Information Week,* September 17, 2001.

data. In a sense, all user access to data must first be approved by the MIS department. Any data alteration or transfer is much easier to control if it takes place on one machine.

Centralized purchasing can also be used to save money. It is easier to standardize equipment if it is all located in one place. It is generally possible to obtain discounts from vendors by buying larger quantities. Centralized purchases also make it easier to keep track of the amount of money spent on information technology. When user departments are responsible for all IT purchases, the lack of centralized control can lead to duplication of hardware.

Decentralization

Decentralization of hardware carries its own advantages. First, there is less chance of a total breakdown. If your computer breaks, everyone else can continue working. You might even be able to borrow someone else's machine.

With decentralization, users can obtain personalized equipment. Perhaps a financial analyst needs an extremely fast machine to process complex equations. Or maybe a marketing representative needs a portable computer to collect data from clients. An advertising specialist could use high-resolution graphics to help design promotions. In each case, the company saves money by buying each user exactly what he or she needs, and not forcing everyone to use one standardized product.

Software and Data

Wherever there is hardware, it is also necessary to provide software. Nonetheless, it is possible to centralize some aspects of software, even though there are decentralized computers. The goal is to capture the advantages of both methods at the same time. Data files are similar to software files, but there are some additional features to consider when choosing where to store the data.

Software Centralization

If software applications are standardized and purchased centrally, it is possible to negotiate lower prices from software vendors. Additionally, if everyone uses the same basic software, fewer compatibility problems arise and it is easy for users to exchange data with co-workers. Similarly, upgrades, training, and assistance are much simpler if there is a limited number of packages to support. Imagine the time and effort involved if the company needs to upgrade different spreadsheets on 5,000 separate machines. Some companies have reported that by the time they managed to upgrade the entire company, an even newer version was released.

Software Decentralization

Forcing users to choose identical packages can lead to major arguments between users and the MIS department. Many times users have different requirements or perhaps they simply have different preferences. If one group of users prefers the software that is different from

Reality Bytes   Empire Blue Cross Blue Shield

Empire Blue Cross Blue Shield lost its headquarters in the terrorist attack on the World Trade Center towers. Yet, it was able to continue its services because the insurer had built a redundant IT facility to automatically pick up the operations. The company faced a different problem in restoring operations: relocating almost 2,000 employees and reconfiguring and connecting desktops. Consequently, David Snow Jr., Empire's president, is rethinking the benefits of decentralization. By placing workers in different locations, connected by networks, it will be less likely that everyone's work could be disrupted at the same time. Restoring a smaller office is much simpler than rebuilding everything at the same time. Other firms are considering similar moves. For example, the New York Board of Trade is planning to separate its data facilities from the trading operations. Smaller firms are pushing plans to move away from paper and into smaller offices using standardized technology—making it easier to back up data and to replace equipment.

Source: Adapted from Jaikumar Vijayan, "Sept. 11 Attacks Prompt Decentralization Moves," *Computerworld,* December 17, 2001.

the corporate standard, why should everyone in the company be forced to use the same tools? Cost becomes less of an issue as software prices drop. Support might be a problem, but major software packages today are similar. Data incompatibilities often can be resolved with conversion software.

To some extent, users should have the ability to customize their software to match their preferences. Today, most software packages enable users to choose colors, mouse or keyboard responsiveness, and locations to store personal files. If this software is moved to a centralized environment, you have to be careful to preserve this ability. One of the strengths of Windows XP is its ability to store individual user profiles on the server. Then from any machine, the desktop settings and preferences are retrieved from the server.

One complication with enabling users to choose different software is that it can be difficult to determine the configurations of each machine. If a user has a problem, the MIS support person needs to know what software is installed on the machine. When installing new hardware and software, the support team needs to know what software exists on each target machine. Managers also need to track software usage when they purchase upgrades and to verify compliance with software licenses. Several software tools exist to help the MIS department track software usage and report on the configuration of each computer. A small file is installed on each computer that reports on the software, hardware, and configuration of each machine.

Data Centralization

The most important feature of centralized data is the ability to share it with other users. Large central servers were designed from the ground up to share data. They were designed to solve the problems of allowing concurrent access and to protect the integrity of the data. Similarly, they have security facilities that enable owners of the data to specify which users can and cannot have access to the data. Centralized systems also monitor access and usage of the data to prevent problems.

Another important feature of centralized data is the ease of making backups. When all databases are stored on one machine, a single operator can be hired to maintain daily backups. If data files are lost, it is easy to restore them from the backups. With the data on one machine, it is easy to ensure that all files are regularly backed up. Contrast this situation with distributed personal computers, where users are generally responsible for making their own backup copies. How often do you personally make backups? Every night?

Data Decentralization

The strongest advantage to decentralizing data is that it gives ownership of the data to the group that creates and maintains it. Users also have complete control of the data and can prevent anyone else from even knowing that it exists. For data that does not need to be shared, this control presents no problems. However, scattered control of data can interfere with other

FIGURE 13.11

Complete decentralization. Each department maintains its own hardware, software, and data. Corporate standards and the network enable workers to utilize data across the company. MIS personnel are members of the user departments and support tasks within that department.

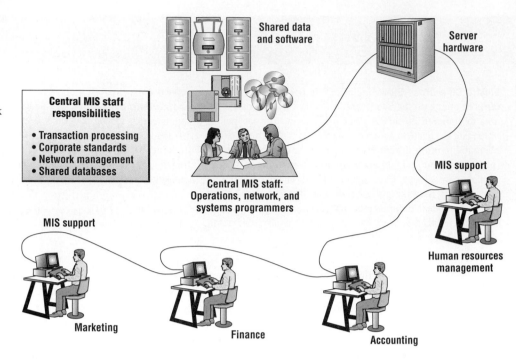

users when many people need access to the data. An example of complete decentralization—including data, hardware, and personnel—is displayed in Figure 13.11.

Data replication is sometimes used to provide the advantages of decentralized data—and still provide companywide access. With replication, the database is copied to multiple servers throughout the company. Users work on their local copies, which provide fast access to the data. The changes are copied to the other servers at regular intervals, so everyone has access to the latest data. This technique is often used with groupware products to distribute spreadsheets and word-processed documents.

Personnel

When most users think about decentralization, they often forget about the information systems personnel. Traditionally, the MIS roles have been performed by centralized MIS staffs. However, the increased decentralization of hardware increases pressures to decentralize the personnel by having them report directly to user departments.

Centralization

Most of the advantages of a centralized MIS staff accrue to the MIS workers. For example, MIS workers often feel more comfortable with other MIS specialists. Centralization creates a group of homogeneous workers who share the same education and experiences. Moving MIS workers to user departments places them in a minority position.

One implication of this situation is seen by looking at the career path of an MIS worker. In a centralized environment, workers are typically hired as programmers. They eventually become systems analysts. Some move on to become team or project leaders, and a few can look forward to becoming managers of IS departments and perhaps a CIO someday. If programmers are moved to user departments (say human resources), what career path do they have? Maybe they could become team leader or manager of the HRM department, but they would be competing with HRM specialists for those positions.

Centralization also makes it easier for the company to provide additional training to MIS staffers. Because hardware and software changes occur constantly, MIS employees need to continually learn new tools and techniques. If they are all located in a central facility, it is easy to set up training classes and informal meetings to discuss new technologies.

Centralization also gives the firm the ability to hire MIS specialists. If there are 50 positions available, two or three can be set aside for workers specializing in areas such as database administration or local area networks. If all workers are distributed to user areas, the individual departments will be less willing to pay for specialists.

Last, when the entire MIS staff is centralized, it is easier to see how much MIS is costing the firm. If the MIS functions are dispersed to user departments, they may be performed on a part-time basis by various employees. It is difficult to control the costs and evaluate alternatives when you do not know how much is being spent.

Decentralization

The primary advantage to decentralized MIS staffing is that the support is closer to the users. As a result, they receive faster responses to questions and problems. More important, as the MIS staffers spend more time with the users, they gain a better understanding of the problems facing the users' department. Communication improves and problems are easier to identify and correct. These are powerful advantages to the individual departments and have the potential to create much better development and use of information systems.

The Help Desk

One issue with decentralized MIS support is that it can be expensive to place MIS personnel in each department. Many companies compromise by creating a help desk that is staffed by MIS employees who specialize in helping business managers. When business managers have questions, workers at the help desk provide answers. Typical problems involve personal computers, networks, and access to corporate databases. One advantage for business managers is that they do not have to search for answers—they simply call one number. This system can also cut costs and ensure consistent support. The knowledge of the support workers is easily shared throughout the company. It is also easier to train and evaluate the workers.

To provide more decentralized support, some companies are using their networks to provide more detailed help to business departments. They set up a special program in the background on each personal computer. When someone calls for help, the microcomputer specialist can see the user's screen and take control of the user's machine. This method simplifies communication between the user and the specialist, making it easier to solve problems and make changes immediately. Of course, it also raises several security issues, because the help desk personnel could monitor any machine at any time.

Intranets

No organization is completely centralized or completely decentralized. The true challenge is to create a system that matches the needs of the organization. Networks are a critical part of the solution. With reliable high-speed networks, data can be stored anywhere. But most organizations do not yet have high-speed networks everywhere. In particular, connections to offices in other cities or nations can be expensive and relatively slow. Consequently, bandwidth is a crucial factor in deciding centralization issues. Web-based intranets provide a solution to many of these problems.

Networks

Web technologies are particularly good at handling low bandwidth connections to users. Web browsers are relatively efficient at displaying data. Many business pages contain only basic data and graphs, which can be easily and quickly sent to managers. Streaming media technologies can be used to send more complex data, such as speeches, to many users at the same time—even when the managers are connected through dial-up lines.

The capabilities of the Internet browser have led firms to consider a new approach to organizing the MIS resources. The **thin-client** approach, illustrated in Figure 13.12, uses a relatively simple computer to run a Web browser that is responsible for displaying data and getting input from the user. This approach recentralizes many of the MIS functions. All of the data and most of the applications reside on centralized servers. The use of Web standards simplifies many decisions. Users can choose almost any type of client hardware, including

FIGURE 13.12

Thin client. The thin client device is only responsible for displaying data and translating user input. The data and the application software reside on the central servers.

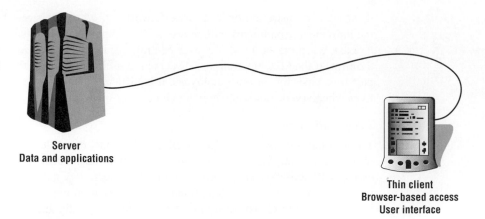

Server
Data and applications

Thin client
Browser-based access
User interface

laptops, tablets, and PDAs. As long as the system runs a browser, it can access the corporate data. Of course, some client computers will have more capabilities than others.

The browser client is becoming a user interface device, with responsibility for displaying data and translating input to a standard form. This approach simplifies the development of applications and provides more flexibility to users and organizations. For example, some users or entire organizations might stick with standard desktops for years to save money. Others might move to wireless-based PDAs or Web-enabled cell phones that rely on voice input instead of keyboards. The key point is that the choice of the user device should no longer matter to the application developer. Regardless of the user device, the back-end databases are the same, the Web servers are the same, and the applications are the same. Note that currently, it does take a middle-ware component to strip down websites so they are small enough for today's cell phones, but that limitation is likely to change in the near future. The simplicity of this approach is that it recentralizes the primary items that gain from centralization: the main business applications and the shared data. Users are free to use whatever devices they prefer, and to load additional software on their computers. A key benefit of the thin-client approach is that the clients can be built from relatively simple hardware and software, reducing the cost and improving the reliability of the clients. With fewer problems, user support becomes easier and cheaper.

Keep in mind that some tasks can still be too hard to perform using pure Web-based solutions. For instance, standard personal productivity tools like word processors need to be running on the individual client computers. Several years ago, Corel built a suite of Internet-based personal productivity applications but stopped work on them because they ran too slowly. As technologies change, it might eventually be possible to run even these highly interactive applications over the Internet.

Similarly, large data transfers require high-speed connections. For example, bulk data transfers from one division to another will suffer if sent over dial-up lines. Since high-bandwidth Internet connections are expensive, companies will cluster their servers in a few key locations. As shown in Figure 13.13, these server locations will be connected with high-speed lines, and everyone else will use lower-priced basic services to connect over the Internet.

The network personnel still have to decide where to locate the servers and which data should be stored on each server. Many systems use data **replication,** where each server location holds the same data. Data changes are exchanged on a regular basis, often overnight, so each server has a relatively up-to-date copy of the data. The MIS department is responsible for maintaining the servers and the networks.

Hardware

Companies have several choices for the central server hardware. But the software environment is more important than the specific hardware. The servers need to run software that generates the Web data while interacting with the database management system. Several companies offer competing technologies for these services that run on diverse hardware

FIGURE 13.13

Intranet networks. Server locations are connected by high-bandwidth networks to replicate data. Individual users obtain data using standard Internet connections.

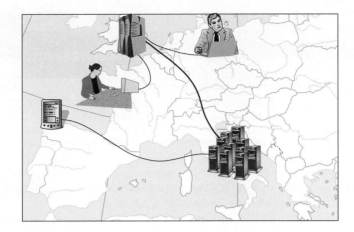

platforms. The main issues are (1) cost, (2) scalability of the servers so the system can be expanded without interfering with existing operations, and (3) reliability, maintainability, and backups to ensure the systems can remain operational at all times.

Data

Because of the challenges of running and securing servers, most companies lean toward centralizing the data. Certainly the basic financial data is consolidated in a data warehouse. This approach works well for managers retrieving data for analysis. The main problems arise in terms of creating or modifying the data. The workers who create and analyze the data to produce more useful information need more sophisticated tools. They also need greater access to the data, compared to users who simply view the data.

Giving users, even managers, the ability to create new data scares most MIS people. The security challenges are much greater when users need to add and change data. It is more difficult to control access and ensure that only authorized people can make the changes. Plus, if something goes wrong, the IS employee is the one who will be blamed. In the old days of simple transaction data, it was relatively straightforward to set up controls and procedures for the daily operations. And it was reasonably simple to keep transaction logs of all of the changes so errors could be corrected. But, in today's environment, teams of workers perform the analyses and information creation, so team members need access to work in progress. For instance, the financial budgeting team uses the marketing and production forecasts to generate estimates of future cash flows.

From the standpoint of data creation, the intranet approach requires two steps beyond traditional systems: (1) managers need tools that will create the final data and reports in a format suitable for the intranet browsers, and (2) managers need an easy method to securely transfer information to the intranet servers.

Better data creation tools have been created in the past few years, but in many cases they are still hard to use and can require specialized training. Likewise, several systems have been created to simplify transferring data to intranet servers. Some are relatively easy to use. As always, the challenge lies in providing security so that the transfer process is easy for authorized managers, but impossible (or exceedingly difficult) for unauthorized users. Both of these conditions require that managers have more powerful tools and often higher-speed data connections. Managers will also need more support and technical assistance. Hence, portions of the MIS organization must be decentralized to handle these issues.

Peer-to-Peer Communication

Increasingly, the Internet is adding support for **peer-to-peer communication,** which is substantially more decentralized than the traditional Web-server approach. In this situation, each department or even worker would have a computer that can function as a Web server as well as a browser. Each person would then be responsible for the content on his or her server.

Reality Bytes   Italcementi Group

Italcementi Group is a multinational company that produces cement and other building materials. With headquarters in Bergamo, Italy, and plants around the world, the firm has almost £4 billion in sales. In part because of the decentralized nature of the cement business (cement is generally produced near where it is needed to reduce the shipping costs), the company's divisions have been using intranets to share information. But each division tended to have separate, unrelated intranet sites. Italcementi needed to provide a more centralized site to direct internal users to the appropriate data. The company became a pilot user for a new portal product by Avanade—a joint venture

between Microsoft and Accenture. The system uses Microsoft's SharePoint portal server to provide a main intranet site in English. From there, employees are linked to data from the division intranets in different languages. The system provides search capabilities across the company, document management, and employee-collaboration applications. Italcementi is also planning to integrate sites from its operations in Morocco, Turkey, and Thailand.

Source: Adapted from Larry Greenemeier, "Taming Intranet Proliferation," *Information Week,* November 29, 2001.

In a business context, the main challenges with these systems are (1) it is more difficult for users to find data, (2) it is harder to establish and monitor security conditions, and (3) someone has to monitor and repair the servers scattered across the company. With the network, all of the data is available, but that does not mean it is easy to find. Everyone has encountered the challenge in finding data on the Internet. Searches have to be carefully written to obtain just the data you want. In a business intranet, the MIS department can establish central pages that point to the primary data used by most managers. But successful searches will depend on the ability of the data owner to accurately describe each page.

Security is always challenging, but it is even more difficult in a distributed environment. One of the primary requirements to security today is that server software must be constantly updated with security patches from the vendor. When all of the machines are in a single location, it is relatively straightforward for one person or team to be in charge of updates. When the servers are scattered across the company and run by general managers instead of IS professionals, it is difficult to ensure that all updates are applied. And once one of the decentralized servers is compromised, it is often easy for hackers to attack the other machines in the company.

Along the same lines, maintaining and upgrading hardware in many locations is more difficult. When the machines are just used by one person, it is not as critical if a machine breaks—the manager can simply find another computer. When the computer is a server that other people rely on for data, it is important that it be restored as quickly as possible.

Summary

Intranets and Web services are becoming an important method of providing data and information services throughout organizations. The standards for networks, hardware, and software make it easier to share and to find data. The ultimate goal is to enable managers to securely run their organizations from anywhere in the world—using standard, low-cost devices running Web browsers.

Object Orientation

Some new technologies offer the potential to expand the use of objects on the Internet and intranets. One of the primary technologies is the **simple object application protocol (SOAP).** It is a standard being pushed by several vendors to define how objects can be used across the Internet. It relies heavily on the **extensible markup language (XML)** to transfer data between diverse computers. As a general manager, you do not need to know the details of how these two technologies work, but you should remember their purpose. Ultimately, you will want to select applications that fully support these standards so that you can build and use systems that work transparently across the Internet.

FIGURE 13.14

Simple object application protocol. SOAP enables firms to offer application object services that other firms can use across the Internet. In this example, your application can call the bank's currency converter object to get the correct exchange rates.

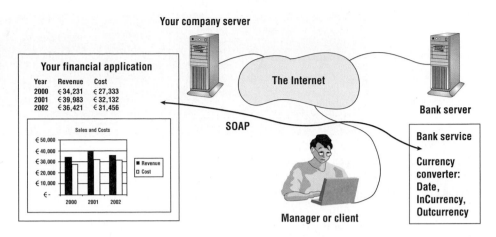

The purpose of SOAP is to enable firms to build application services that can be used by other organizations across the Internet. For instance, as shown in Figure 13.14, a bank (e.g., www.oanda.com) might offer a currency conversion application. Your company's accounting application could call the bank's program whenever it needed to convert money to a different currency.

Applications that use the SOAP and XML protocols will be able to interact with other services across the Internet. However, a big question that remains to be resolved is how firms will price their services. Firms that create service objects will ultimately be able to bill clients a usage fee or a monthly charge with unlimited access. But a standardized billing mechanism has not been implemented yet.

Summary

One of the more difficult problems facing MIS departments and company executives is the conflict between centralization and decentralization. These issues were involved in many decisions during the last 5 to 10 years, from politics to corporate organizations, to the way in which MIS fits into the organization. Although there is no single answer that applies to all situations, there has been a distinct trend during the last few years toward decentralization. In larger organizations, this propensity has been hampered by the highly centralized organizations and computer systems that have been in place for the last 30 years.

Decentralization of MIS can occur in any of four areas: hardware, software, data, and MIS personnel. Economics is driving the decentralization of hardware because of tremendous price performance values in personal computers. The challenge is to accommodate this decentralization without losing the benefits of centralization. One option would be a completely decentralized information system, where each user and department is responsible for its own information. Today, the Internet standards provide new technologies to gain the benefits of both centralization and decentralization. Applications running on Web servers can retrieve centralized data to be displayed and modified using thin-client browsers. The goal is to gain the economies of scale and improved control and ease of sharing offered by centralized servers, yet provide users with the individual tools needed to perform their jobs. The simpler client hardware and software platforms offer the promise of less user support.

Managing servers and networks, as well as building applications, can be difficult tasks for many companies. It is hard to find and reward good IS workers, and continually solving technical problems takes time away from the daily business tasks. So, many organizations have chosen to outsource various IS functions—from development to maintenance to development and operation of the servers. Outsourcing provides a short-term increase in cash for the company, access to computer specialists, and the ability to concentrate on the company's primary business. However, firms requiring specialized talent, high security and control, high levels of recent technology, new state-of-the-art information technology, or complex market structures should avoid outsourcing and retain in-house management of the information function.

A Manager's View

Centralization and decentralization are key issues in managing information systems. Many conflicts arise when the IS departments are not aligned with the business practices. New Web-based technologies offer new methods of maintaining the cost advantages of centralization while still providing decentralized user access and control. As a manager, you must be able to recognize organizational conflicts and understand how the new technologies can provide solutions.

Key Words

advocacy role, *516*
centralization, *520*
data administrator, *515*
database administrator, *515*
data integrity, *515*
decentralization, *520*
extensible markup language
(XML), *528*

outsourcing, *518*
peer-to-peer
communication, *527*
replication, *526*
simple object application
protocol (SOAP), *528*
standards, *513*
systems analysts, *516*

thin client, *525*
total cost of ownership
(TCO), *510*

Website References

Job Boards

Careerbuilder	**www.careerbuilder.com**
Computerworld	**www.computerworld.com/cwi/careers**
Dice	**www.dice.com**
Free Job	**www.freejob.com**
Information Week	**www.informationweek.com/career3**
Jobs.com	**www.jobs.com**
Kforce.com	**www.kforce.com**
Monster	**www.monster.com**
Riley Guide	**www.rileyguide.com**
Studentjobs.gov	**www.studentjobs.gov**
U.S. Government	**www.usajobs.opm.gov**
Wall Street Journal	**Careers.wsj.com**

Additional Reading

Arnett, Kirk P., and C.R. Litecky. "Career Path Development for the Most Wanted Skills in the MIS Job Market." *Journal of Systems Management,* February 1994, pp. 6–10. [Job skills.]

Arnold, David, and Fred Niederman. "The Global IT Workforce." *Communications of the ACM* 44, no. 7, July 2001. [A special section on global issues in IT management.]

Fryer, Bronwyn. "Difficult at Best." *Computerworld,* January 4, 1999, p. 38. [High demand for staff with ERP skills.]

"Managing Unruly Desktop Computers Costs Businesses Dearly." *The Wall Street Journal,* February 16, 1995, p. A1. [Maintenance costs of personal computers.]

York, Thomas. "Shift in IT Roles Ahead: Changes in Business and Technology Will Alter IT Careers." *Infoworld,* January 18, 1999, p. 75. [Predicting the future of IT jobs is hard, but useful.]

Review Questions

1. What are the basic roles of the MIS department?
2. What types of MIS jobs are available?
3. What methods exist to create information systems?
4. What are the potential advantages of outsourcing computer facilities? What are the drawbacks?
5. What is the systems development life cycle? What are its primary objectives?

6. Are there faster ways to build systems?

7. What are the advantages of centralizing computer hardware, software, and data? What are the advantages of decentralization?

8. How does the Internet/Web affect centralization and decentralization of information technology within a company?

Exercises

1. Interview computer users and managers in a local firm (or your university) and determine the degree of decentralization in their information system organization. Talk to several users and see whether their perceptions agree. Are they receiving all of the advantages of centralization and decentralization? If not, how could the system be modified to gain these benefits without significantly increasing the drawbacks? Be sure to analyze hardware, software, data, and personnel.

2. Interview some computer science majors to determine what types of jobs they are looking for. Also, interview some business-oriented MIS majors and compare the responses. Ask the subjects whether they would prefer working for a centralized IS department or within a decentralized department. What reasons do they give? Do they have a minor in a business discipline? (Team approach: Each team member should interview a different person, then combine the results and look for similarities and differences.)

3. Using salary surveys and local advertisements, find typical salaries for various MIS jobs in your area.

4. Make a list of symptoms you would expect to see in a company that has centralized databases and MIS personnel, but has just decentralized its departments and users have just bought hundreds of new personal computers in the last three years.

5. Identify the development methodology that would be best to use for designing and building the following applications. Explain your answer.
   a. A custom B2C website that handles several thousand products and thousands of sales per day.
   b. An intranet that enables employees to examine and modify benefit selections.
   c. An executive summary analysis of sales and profits by region by month by product.
   d. A complex website for displaying your products and assisting customers with prepurchase configuration.
   e. A mobile-commerce-based CRM system to collect data and improve communication with your sales representatives.

6. Make a list of symptoms you expect to see in a company that is "too decentralized." That is, company users are free to choose any hardware and software, and databases are maintained by each department. Data is shared through reports that are printed in each department and forwarded to other departments on paper. There is no central MIS staff and no CIO. Treat it as a company that started small using personal computers and grew but did not come up with a centralized information system approach.

7. Write a plan for moving a midsize service company to an intranet and mobile-commerce-based information system, where as many applications as possible will run through browsers, and data will be accessible from anywhere in the company. What technologies will you use? What functions will you centralize or decentralize? How will you provide adequate security?

Rolling Thunder Database

8. Describe the organization of the existing information system. What changes would enable the system to run better? If the company doubles in size in three years, what organizational changes do you recommend for the information system?

9. How should the company handle typical information system tasks such as backing up data, creating employee accounts, maintaining hardware, selecting new hardware and software, and so on?

10. Would you recommend a centralized or decentralized approach to information systems at the Rolling Thunder Bicycle Company? Who is currently in charge of the major components? What problems can we anticipate if we continue with the existing structure?

11. Assume users are complaining about lack of support from the MIS department. How can you improve MIS responsiveness? How can you do it without substantially raising costs?

Cases

Financial Services

The financial services industry is typically divided into banking and nonbanking organizations. Yet today, services overlap between these divisions in many different ways. Some of the services offered in this industry include, but are not limited to:

- Consumer loans such as home mortgages, home equity, and auto

- Personal and business lines of credit, especially profitable "subprime" credit risks

- Credit card and related credit (card) life insurance

- Purchase warranties and service guarantees generally offered with appliances and home electronics

- Equipment leases

- Investment management services

- Mutual fund management

- Multiple-line insurance

- Financial planning, including tax preparation and related services

Financial Analysis

The financial services industry, which had witnessed a decade of prosperity on the heels of a robust market and age of excess sparked by a global infatuation with the stock market, is officially entering into a recession. For now, the industry—humbled by the dramatic shakeout at the hands of the economic downturn—is in rebuilding mode, having seen many Wall Street giants implementing deep staff cuts. Faced with a severe economic environment only made worse by the September 11, 2001, terrorist attacks, investment and commercial banks have no choice but to slash costs to offset the drop in business.

With firms juggling fewer opportunities, power has shifted to clients, which have been asking investment banks for credit lines in exchange for retaining the business. Moreover, commercial banks, pushed by dwindling profits, have ventured into higher-margin businesses such as arranging IPOs and advising on mergers and acquisitions.

Growth of earnings at big banks has weakened amid fierce competition and macro-economic dynamics. Analysts forecast a 4 to 8 percent rise in profits in 2002, sharply down from the double-digit returns in 1999. Due to a higher frequency of bad loans, banks have had to increase their loan loss reserves, according to analysts.

As far as online brokers are concerned, ambitions to become one-stop shops for financial services have had to be put aside in the midst of fragile economic activity. Players such as Schwab and E*Trade have seen a significant drop in online trading and, as a result, have been forced to lay off thousands or employees.

Tough times on Wall Street have directly affected those in the mutual fund and investment management industries. Money managers have seen their fees fall along with the stock market and the value of assets they manage. Money has flowed out of equity mutual funds and into safe-haven investments. Big mutual-fund families have laid off staff and nixed underperforming funds.

To weather the economic storm, financial-services firms will have to reevaluate their business lines instead of taking on further risks in hopes of boosting returns.

Stock/Investment Outlook

Since the aftermath of the Sept. 11, 2001, terrorist attacks, the securities sectors has shown some impressive relative strength, easily outperforming the market with an average gain of 31 percent. Aggressive interest cuts at the hands of the Federal Reserve Board and the increased perception among the investment community that the market bottomed in late September has boosted investor confidence, culminating in the robust performance from the equity market in recent months. Hence, the brokerage industry has benefited from an advancing stock market as that typically translates into increased trading, IPO, and M&A activity—areas that have suffered considerably since the popping of the Internet bubble and current recession.

Optimism surrounding a rebound in the economy is rooted in several factors, namely the stimulative impact of the monetary and fiscal policies that have been implemented to resuscitate an ailing U.S. economy. Furthermore, coordinated easing on the part on central banks around the globe and a belief by many that the rally following the terrorist attacks will mark the start of a new bull market give bullish investors some assurance that stocks in general will stage a recovery.

Even though brokerage companies are still cutting their payrolls, the unemployment rate is a lagging indicator. For instance, companies were still hiring in the summer of 2000; at that time, the dot-coms and Internet plays were on the verge of crashing or had already gone under. Though, additional gains for the group may be harder to come by over the near-term due to valuation concerns and tentativeness on the part of investors who will be seeking more credible signs of economic, and earnings, recovery to confirm the validity of the recent rally.

On the whole, financial services stocks remain solid investment vehicles and should keep pace with the overall market as the federal stimulus and cyclical factors provide underlying support.

Growth Potential

The favorable interest rate environment, as well as low inflationary pressures, has positioned the financial services industry to rebound in the next few years. Although credit concerns could hurt some highly leveraged companies such as mortgage or credit card specialists, sizable spreads built into such subprime businesses make disastrous losses less likely.

Competitive Structure

The financial services industry is highly fragmented and competitive. Recently, there has been significant bank merger activity. Consolidation is a means of increasing efficiency, service levels, and product depth. It is also a means of spreading back-office costs over a larger product base. Not only do the money center banks compete with the growing super-regional and other large commercial banks, they compete with nonbank institutions providing financial services as well.

Commercial banks are now reaching out to offer mutual funds, annuities, and life insurance. With a substantial customer base and lending authority, banks have a market entree for financial advice. On the other hand, brokerage firms have moved in the direction of delivering more advice. Many are changing compensation emphasis from a transaction orientation to a fee-based asset management.

To stay competitive, mutual funds have bolstered direct relationships with the customer, instituting aggressive mailing campaigns and investing heavy capital in their website and customer service operations. The industry's innovations have threatened traditional banks, yet banks are far from relinquishing their market share to finance companies.

Competition is intense between the two leaders: Fidelity and Schwab. Both companies report over 4 million investors and handle hundreds of thousands of trades per day. Both create and run their own Web systems—enabling them to create new services. Fidelity was first with wireless access, but Schwab followed about a year later. Schwab's site is sometimes considered easier to use and offers personalized information. But both companies continually revise their sites. For awhile, Schwab was more expensive than Fidelity, but in early 2000, the company cut its fees in half for customers who make many trades.

Role of Research and Development

Research in the financial services industry is focused on product innovation and marketing. By researching new ways to market products, credit card issuers attempt to increase market share and develop new market niches. Many retail stores entering into the credit card business are utilizing cobranding to help increase market share. Cobranding strategies may allow smaller issuers to team up with larger organizations and obtain a competitive advantage.

The Internet has become another effective tool for marketing. Due to the high costs of current mass marketing campaigns, Internet marketing's value for financial services has soared. The challenge in this distribution channel is to remain innovative, effective, and targeted.

Technological Investment and Analysis

Strategic advances in this customer-service oriented industry are propelled by technological innovation. Technological improvements have aided banks in their efforts to control expenses while providing better customer service. Electronic banking through phone lines, automated teller machines (ATMs), and personal computers give customers improved levels of service by offering 24-hour banking at convenient locations.

Many financial services firms have utilized enormous phone banks to provide customer service. The customer service representatives often have instantaneous access to large customer databases with the ability to give credit approval, status, and balances, as well as account maintenance.

Generally, financial institutions have concentrated the technology on transactions—particularly aimed at cutting costs. With the advent of online usage and consumers becoming more technologically savvy, the Internet has emerged as a tool of convenience. Nevertheless, only 17 percent of households perform banking needs online, according to Tower Group; hence, banks are urged not to forget their roots.

Industry experts cite electronic bill presentments and account aggregation as prospective hot-tech investments in the financial sector. Some predict that wireless online bill payment will hit the consumer pavement in a couple of years. Wireless services would provide customers with faster access, however, mass acceptance of the technology could be hindered by security issues and insufficient bandwidth.

Recommendation for the Future

To get ahead in the competitive financial services industry, players must focus on leveraging technology and seizing opportunities that arise from regulation changes. It will also be important to consider strategies for a global market and for the consolidation and integration going on in the industry.

Technological and regulatory forces are moving the industry toward greater consolidation and product integration. Critical to financial firms' success will be their level of investment in technology and its ability to achieve cost savings. The reliability of instantaneous telecommunications and the converging of economies around the world increase the importance of a global focus for successful financial services firms.

The next step for financial services companies and brokerage firms could be to install online account aggregation technology, which would allow customers to see data from multiple accounts on a single screen. Companies that implement such a technology could boost client loyalty and enhance website "stickines." However, such investment is likely to cost in the millions and is not for the feeble-hearted. And it is uncertain how the technology will be received. Though, to recruit and retain online visitors and to cross-sell financial services products, this technology many be worth the investment. Some industry heavyweights have already launched aggregation services. Notables include Citibank, Chase Manhattan Corp, and Wells Fargo.

Case: Fidelity Investments

Founded in 1946 by Edward Johnson II, Fidelity Investments, through over five decades of growth and innovation, has maintained its status as an international provider of financial services and investment resources that help individuals and institutions meet their financial objectives.

Once known primarily as a mutual fund company, Fidelity has evolved over the years to meet the changing needs of its customers. That evolution is reflected in a diversified menu of products and services, which span over 300 Fidelity mutual funds, discount brokerage services, retirement services, estate planning, wealth management, securities execution and clearance, and life insurance.

The financial giant's philosophy centers around a commitment to continuous improvement, which applies state-of-the-art technology to provide customer service solutions, among others. Fidelity prides itself on its employees' focus on customer needs. In spite of its enormous success, the company has continually pushed the envelope of financial technology to sustain its dominance in the financial industry. Today, more than 15 million investors trust Fidelity with their money, and the company employs approximately 28,000 professionals around the globe.

Technology Innovations

Each year, Fidelity reinvests a portion of its revenues into technology to deliver new products and services to investors. For instance, in the span of a few months during 1997, the company completely revamped its Internet service to enhance the "customer experience." As a result, Fidelity's Web page made it easier for investors to navigate through the detailed site; yet it provided more information at the same time. Most important, the upgrade enabled customers to trade online and featured real-time access to stock and found quotes.

From 1992 to 1997, Fidelity delivered a 62.8 percent return on its technology expenditure. In doing so, Fidelity has looked beyond a temporary fix, employing a long-term technology strategy that directly and quickly benefits the company while adding value for the customers and distinguishing Fidelity from its competitors. Technology has allowed Fidelity to significantly reduce operational costs; by implementing a touch-tone system, the mutual fund giant's cost per customer interaction numbered approximately $0.70 compared with $11 if the communication required a "live" representative.

Another aspect of Fidelity's customer service and technological dominance lies in its Covington, Kentucky, mail distribution center. Fidelity treated the mundane activity of processing mail as a core part of its business. It gave "every ounce of its energy" to bettering rivals in this service-oriented end of the business. The investment was made to add as much predictability and efficiency as possible in a volatile business environment. High-investment returns cannot be achieved every year, but sending out a prospectus or a statement on time was an important step in maintaining customer satisfaction. Nevertheless, Fidelity's commitment to consistent service was pricey. The Kentucky operation cost $100 million, including a self-imposed testament to Fidelity's good corporate citizenship.

Another area in which Fidelity distinguished itself involved 401(k) plans. Fidelity viewed 401(k)s as a record-keeping business and strived to maintain the best-kept records in the business. While other competitors enjoyed the same technology, none had made such a long-standing commitment to continual change as Fidelity. By organizing all benefits administration around the same 800 number, Fidelity provided a one-stop shopping center for defined contributions, defined benefit plans, and health plans.

The Internet

In September 1999, Fidelity Investments launched a new set of financial planning and trading tools to make its investment services more accessible online. The service enabled customers to personalize their own Web start page through a new partnership with Lycos Inc. Hence, customers could control the flow of information as they see it. The company realized the importance of the "online experience" as its online trading business grew from 7 percent of commission trades in January 1997 to 79 percent of commission trades in August 1999.

Wireless

Fidelity was the first to implement wireless access to account information and trading. After only two years, by spring 2000, almost one-third of its online investors were using two-way pagers or wireless handheld computers to monitor investments. Almost 20 percent were placing actual trades. In a separate survey, Fidelity found that almost one-fourth of investors who owned Web-enabled phones were using them to monitor or trade stocks. Joseph Ferra, senior vice president at Fidelity's online division, notes that "Our mission statement is to enable wireless access to Fidelity enterprise data, anytime, anywhere, on any device." [Hamblen, October 2000]

In 2001, GM announced that its OnStar system would team up with Fidelity to offer stock trading with voice-activated commands within its vehicles. About 800,000 drivers subscribe to the general OnStar services. All of them will be able to get stock quotes. Only Fidelity customers will be able to place trades.

Despite the early responses, many people in the industry remain skeptical of the value of wireless access. Carl Zetie, a technology analyst, notes that "Once you get outside Wall Street and Silicon Valley, its hard to find people excited about trading stocks while riding the bus." [Hamblen, October 2000]

System Architecture

Like other firms, Fidelity runs its Web services and back-end databases on separate servers. Consequently, it needs software to convert data and exchange information between the two systems. In 1999, the company relied on proprietary system and middleware applications like EnterpriseConnect from Sybase.

In the fall of 2001, Fidelity sought to retrofit its internal communications, switching its data to an XML format. This move would simplify the company's communications between consumer Web applications and back-end systems. By implementing an XML format as its core communications connection, Fidelity would be able to eliminate translation protocols and message buffers, thereby allowing for a common language that would simplify the company's applications. Even at the start, the conversion enabled Fidelity to remove 75 of its 85 middle-tier servers, saving time and money by simplifying management of the systems.

Recommendation for the Future

Despite an impressive Internet presence, Fidelity Investments must remain alert to industry developments and continue its innovative approach that has reaped the mutual fund leader rich dividends. It remains to be seen whether Internet discount brokers will snatch market share away from more established, traditional brokerage companies.

When Edward Johnson II was at the helm, Fidelity was a successful but undistinguished mutual fund company. When Ned III took over, Fidelity made its name in customer service and technology. It became known as as investment powerhouse with a culture that bred brash, risk-taking managers whose investments always seemed to show the best returns. Today, Fidelity operates amid much uncertainty brought on by an economic recession that has seen many brokerage firms downsizing.

Nevertheless, since one of Fidelity's strengths lies in its commitment to excellent customer service, as recognized by industry surveys and publications, it would make sense for the company to pursue technologies that facilitate online navigation. Among technologies considered are wireless products that would function as personal digital assistants, enabling customers to make stock trades using voice commands. Furthermore, automated services could prove valuable; they range from instant messaging to help clients open new accounts online to software allowing customers to plug into financial plans data from various accounts over the Internet.

Questions

1. What forces are driving the strategic direction for Fidelity Investments?

2. What has been the catalyst for change at Fidelity Investment?

3. Upon what technologies has Fidelity Investment relied?

4. What caused Fidelity to adopt such an extensive use of technology?

5. How successful has the implementation of technology been for Fidelity?

6. What does Fidelity's Web page present about its business directives?

7. What challenges and opportunities is the industry facing?

8. How will technology impact the investment industry?

Additional Reading

Copeland, Lee. "GM's OnStar Adds Real-Time Stock Trading to In-Vehicle Service." *Computerworld,* February 14, 2001.

"Fidelity Investments (one million online customers)." *Wall Street & Technology,* July 1998, p. 30.

"Fidelity Unit Outsources Corporate Actions Data." *Wall Street & Technology,* August 1998, p. 17.

Gillin, Paul. "Schwab Impresses." *Computerworld,* October 20, 1997, pp. 49–50.

Hamblen, Matthew. "Online Investors Go Wireless." *Computerworld,* May 9, 2000.

Hamblen, Matthew. "Brokerages Put Plenty of Stock in Wireless Devices." *Computerworld,* October 23, 2000.

Hoffman, Thomas. "Fidelity Bolsters Online Investment Services." *Computerworld,* September 27, 1999.

Meehan, Michael. "Fidelity Swells to 4.22M Online Accounts." *Computerworld,* April 20, 2000.

Menagh, Melanie. "We're in the Money." *Computerworld,* November 23, 1998.

Mearian, Lucas. "Despite Growth in Online Usage, Banks Urged Not to Forget Their Roots." *Computerworld,* April 19, 2001.

Mearian, Lucas. "Fidelity Makes Big XML Conversion Investment." *Computerworld,* September 28, 2001.

Nash, Kim S. "The Competitive Heat between Fidelity Investment's Online Brokerage and Charles Schwab & Co. Just Got Hotter." *Computerworld,* February 2, 2000.

"Online Brokerage Arena to Explode with Services." *PC Week,* November 3, 1997, p. 90.

Schwartz, Jeffrey. "Fidelity's War Room—Brokerage Makes Sure It's the First to Know about Site Problems." *InternetWeek,* October 19, 1998, p. 1.

Schwartz, Mathew. "Battling for Web Investors." *Computerworld,* October 23, 2000.

Thornton, Emily. "Wall Street: The Big Chill." *BusinessWeek Online,* October 22, 2001.

Case: Charles Schwab & Co.

Charles Schwab & Co. was started in the early 1970s to capitalize on a particular investment philosophy: provide investors with the most useful and ethical brokerage services in America. Over the years, the company has championed and encouraged client empowerment, allowing the customer to manage her own assets decisions. Hence, Charles Schwab pioneered the practice of discount brokerage in the 1970s.

As to its commitment to technology, the company invested in centralized systems in the early 1980s. The systems enabled smooth automated transactions and resulted in an efficient record-keeping system, thereby proving management that technology can be a key growth driver.

In the 1980s, as mutual funds began emerging as the primary investing vehicles for investors seeking convenience and portfolio diversification, Schwab took the bold step in 1984 of creating the mutual fund supermarket concept: hundreds of funds available through the Schwab Mutual Fund Marketplace.

In the mid-1990s, Schwab anticipated the power of the Internet and invested heavily in online investing. Just as the company's move into discount trading 20 years earlier paid off, foresight in the mid-1990s earned Schwab an early and significant leadership position in online investing. From 1996 to 1998, online accounts grew to 2.2 million from 600,000, and online assets grew to $174 billion from $42 billion.

When the technology stock bubble burst in 2000 and 2001, investors left the market, and all brokerage firms suffered. In late August, Schwab reported a 50 percent drop in client activity. In March 2001, the firm laid off 3,400 employees (about 12 percent of its workforce), followed by another 2,400 employees in October. [Disabatino 2001]

Technology Innovations

Schwab's use of technology can be viewed as foreshadowing the future. In 1992, Schwab was one of three industry members that revolutionized the mutual fund industry by using information technology to offer a new distribution channel for mutual funds. Schwab called its mutual fund supermarket: OneSource. At the time it was introduced, OneSource provided a single point of purchase for more than 350 no-load mutual funds in 50 different fund families, allowing investors to switch between funds without a sales charge. Today, OneSource collects approximately 600 mutual funds from 70 fund families in one product, making Schwab one of the top three mutual fund distributors. Development of this product was innovative, breaking what was then an industry standard.

Until 1992, each mutual fund company serviced its own accounts. It was difficult for consumers to achieve both diversification and high performance in a single fund family. The result was consumers dealing with different firms, different statements, different rules, and different sales representatives. OneSource, through the use of technology, united Schwab with mutual fund providers to expand and diversify Schwab's product line. OneSource changed the mutual fund business by providing consumers with a choice of funds from a variety of fund providers, summarized in a single account with one monthly statement to track all their funds. No transaction fees are incurred on OneSource accounts, allowing customers to shift money to different fund families without charge

To implement OneSource, Schwab revamped its technology to a client-server platform. This system provides clients with the ability to download information on a daily basis for portfolio valuation. Technology also provided the Schwab customers with a variety of methods in which to conduct OneSource business: via a broker on an 800 line available 24 hours per day or without human contact via a touch-tone phone or computer keyboard.

Schwab was the first major brokerage to permit online trading via the World Wide Web. The success realized from the Internet pilot program resulted in Schwab offering Internet trading to all customers in May 1996. The cost savings Schwab realized from the increased percentage of trades executed electronically were passed on to its customers. And the technology Schwab implemented for its Internet trading was developed in-house.

Natural Language Interface

To improve site usability, Schwab recently installed a natural-language search technology—Iphrase technology—to facilitate customers' navigation on its website. This natural-language search could satisfy customers' appetite in obtaining efficient answers to their questions. The search engine uses an algorithm based on conversational phrases and takes into account spelling mistakes. Hence, a customer searching for a company's earnings estimates would get an answer in seconds.

Server Architecture

When Schwab originally built its system, the company followed common Web practices of using a multitier approach. The main trading is based on large IBM and Hitachi servers, designed to securely and safely handle heavy transaction loads. The Web servers were IBM RS/6000 computers running AIX (IBM's version of UNIX). In addition to creating the Web pages, these servers ran middleware software that converted the Internet protocols (TCP/IP) to IBM SNA communication protocols used on the big servers. On October 27, 1997, when the market crashed, Schwab's middle tier was almost overwhelmed because of the huge load on the limited number of machines. By 1999, the company rebuilt the middle tier, so that it was running 148 Web and middle-tier servers and 12 databases. In 2000, the system was handling an average of almost 300,000 trades per day.

Recommendation for the Future

Until recently, Schwab was regarded as one of the great stories—a lengthy record of product innovation capped by a great strategic initiative in offering online trading—however, the bear market that has mauled the financial markets since April 2000 has not spared the company from financial hardships. Commission revenues in June 2001 were off 57 percent from their peak 15 months earlier. Earnings for FY 2001 were down 51.67 percent from the year-earlier period, underscoring what Chairman and CEO Charles Schwab called "one of the most difficult market environments for the company."

On one level, what is happening at Schwab mirrors the carnage on Wall Street; Merrill Lynch, Morgan Stanley, Citigoup, among other firms, all have announced layoffs and other cost-cutting moves. Nevertheless, Schwab has been harder hit since it lacks alternative revenue streams, such as institutional trading, that typically help the Wall Street firms get through difficult times. Also, Schwab let its costs get out of control, having made significant capital investments to finance its growth at the height of the Internet bubble.

Technology has been and will remain an important part of Schwab's success. Top brass has reiterated that the company's diverse product lines and technological innovations will continue to deliver unique solutions tailored specifically to clients. Among the service options offered in 2001 is the CyberTrader Direct, which offers customers access to Schwab's state-of-the-art trading capabilities. In addition, through its SchwabPlan bundled 401(k) services, the company serves individuals through their workplace and has received top honors from *Plan*

Sponsor magazine. Schwab also introduced CDSource, a service that enables clients to research and purchase certificates of deposit from a variety of FDIC-insured depository institutions, including U.S. Trust, entirely online.

According to Charles Schwab, the company must continue to reduce costs quickly and support the reallocation of resources in order to execute its strategic objectives and to deliver superior client service in a tough market environment. With its 7.8 million active accounts and $846 billion in client assets, Schwab remains a force to be reckoned with in the financial services industry.

Questions

1. What is the catalyst for change at Charles Schwab?

2. What are the critical success factors and core competencies for this industry?

3. How successful has the technological change been at Schwab?

4. How does the corporation evaluate its financial ability to embark on a major technological program of advancement?

5. What does Schwab's Web page present about its business?

6. How has technology impacted the industry?

Additional Reading

Disabatino, Jennifer. "Schwab Announces More Layoffs." *Computerworld,* August 30, 2001.

Fletcher-MacDonald, Trina. "No. 7—Charles Schwab Extra Extranet Bonus." *InfoWorld,* October 5, 1998, p. 90.

Gaylord, Becky. "Schwab's Uphill Battle Down Under." *Business Week,* April 20, 2001.

Helenius, Tanya. "Acuity Delivers Real-Time, Online Interaction for Schwab." *Wall Street & Technology,* November 1998, p. 58.

Mearian, Lucas. "Schwab Taps Natural-Language Search Engine." *Computerworld,* July 16, 2001.

Musich, Paula. "How to Keep (E-) Business Humming." *PC Week,* September 28, 1998, p. 1.

"Reining in Stock Frenzy." *PC Magazine,* March 9, 1999, p. 10.

Schwartz, Jeffrey, and Richard Karpinski. "The Price of Success—Commerce Sites Scramble to Meet Unexpected Demand." *InternetWeek,* February 8, 1999, p. 1.

Smith, Laura B. "Schwab Puts Stock in Voice Recognition." *PC Week,* June 22, 1998, p. 95.

Sliwa, Carol. "Schwab Averts Disaster by Rewriting Middleware." *Computerworld,* August 30, 1999.

Trombly, Maria. "Schwab to Lay Off Up to 3,400." *Computerworld,* March 23, 2001.

Vogelstein, Fred. "Can Schwab Get Its Mojo Back?" *Fortune,* September 17, 2001.

Appendix

Project Management

Whether you work in information systems or any other discipline, project management is an important component of your job. Projects arise in many areas, examples include developing software, designing buildings, moving your operations to a larger building, developing a new advertising campaign, and organizing a fund-raising event.

Projects are defined in terms of a goal, the scope, a schedule, and the resources involved. Projects with precisely defined goals have a far better chance of succeeding. For example, a project goal of implementing a new general ledger system is easy to understand; a goal of "providing the best information to our employees" is next to impossible to understand, much less achieve. Well-defined goals have the advantage of keeping the project focused. For example, the 1960s U.S. goal of putting a man on the moon was a huge project, but the clearly defined goal made it easier to keep the project moving in the right direction. The 1980s and 1990s never-achieved goal of improving the IRS had little chance for success because no one knew what the end result should look like.

Scope is an issue of size and complexity, typically measured in terms of the number of tasks and the time frame involved. Projects can range anywhere from small to large. With only a few tasks and one or two people, you can afford to use informal project management techniques. As the project becomes larger or the tasks more complex, you will need a system to help you track the progress of each component. Be careful to match the management techniques to the scope of the project. Do not try to use informal techniques for large, complex projects; and do not try to impose rigid controls on short, simple projects.

A project ultimately must be divided into individual tasks. Some of the tasks depend on others. For example, when building a house you cannot paint the walls before they are constructed. A schedule shows the tasks, the time required to complete them (duration), and how they depend on other tasks.

Tasks are not accomplished by magic. They require resources. Generally, the most important resource consists of workers. Keeping costs under control is an important aspect of project management, so you need to assign workers to tasks. Sometimes you also need to schedule other resources, such as workrooms or machinery.

Project Management Steps

Project management involves four primary steps: (1) define the project, (2) create the plan, (3) track and manage the project as it proceeds, and (4) close the project when the goal is achieved or the project is canceled.

The project definition includes establishing the goal and identifying the major tasks. You must also identify your primary resources available and the major constraints. Finally, you should establish an initial timetable, including the final completion date and some of the major intermediate milestones.

The project plan is an important tool in managing the project. It outlines all of the tasks and the resources required to complete them. At the planning stage, you get time and resource estimates from the people who will perform the work on that stage. You must also identify the dependencies among the tasks. Which tasks can be performed independently? Which ones must wait for other tasks to finish?

Once the project is started, you need to monitor the progress and compare it to the plan. If some tasks take longer to complete, you must adjust the schedule. If some resources are overworked, you can decide if you want to add resources or accept the delays in the tasks. By constantly updating the project plan, you can identify potential problems and provide updated estimates of the completion date.

When the project is finished, review the original project plan and summarize the project. Were the original estimates accurate? What unexpected problems did you encounter? Were there sufficient resources for the project, or did you need to add more as the project evolved? These questions will help you generate better estimates on the next project.

Microsoft Project

It is impossible to memorize all the details involved in a project. You need to keep notes, and you need a system to track the progress, comparing actual values to the original estimates. Several project management tools exist to organize and help you analyze the data. The easiest way to use these tools is with an automated system like Microsoft Project.

In many ways, Microsoft Project is a specialized database. You enter data about the project, which is stored in a central database. The system then provides you with specialized views that help you see the relationships among the tasks, resources, and goals. By building on a DBMS, the system also allows you to retrieve data and create additional reports.

Gantt and PERT charts are standard project-planning tools for displaying and organizing tasks. The two provide similar types of information but in different formats. Some people prefer one method, other managers use both. The Tracking Gantt chart is used to compare estimates to the actual values while the project is in progress. The resource views provide details on how resources (e.g., workers) are assigned to tasks. The different views simply report the data from various perspectives (time, the resource, or tasks).

Sample Project

For a $20 fee, riders will also get a commemorative shirt. Profits from the ride will go to local charitable organizations. The date and general location of the ride have already been chosen. The ride will be called the Spring Forward Century. Organizing the ride requires several tasks. Volunteers from local bicycle clubs will help with some of the early tasks, and they will handle most of the tasks on the day of the ride.

Two projects have been set up to handle this example. The first project concentrates on tasks required to organize the ride. The tasks are grouped into the categories shown in Figure 13.1A. A few finishing tasks are required after the ride, such as sending thank-you notes, verifying the clean up, and writing final project notes. A second project is set up to handle day-of-the-ride tasks. These tasks involve more people and have a different time frame (hours instead of days), so it is easier to create separate projects.

It is possible to handle the planning using paper notes, but there are several advantages to using a tool like Microsoft Project to organize the preparations. One significant advantage is the ease of changing key factors and letting the system instantly display the new relationships. The first step in creating the project is to enter the finishing date (April 6, 2003) and tell the system to schedule backward from that date. The next step is to enter the task information. It is easiest to work with the Gantt chart view. A Gantt chart displays tasks down the left column and dates across the top of the screen. You enter each task by giving it a name and duration (length of time it requires). The Gantt chart displays the task as a horizontal bar, beginning on a certain date and extending for the specified duration. Initially, you do not care about the starting date. As you enter the tasks, you can group related tasks. Each of the groups in Figure 13.1A has a set of detailed tasks beneath it. You specify this hierarchical relationship by indenting (→) the detailed tasks. You can have multiple levels of groups, and the Gantt chart shows a summary bar for each group. If you want, you can roll up and hide the detail, enabling you to focus on the major groups.

Showing relationships among tasks is a critical step in project management. In particular, you need to link tasks that depend on each other. For example, the following tasks must be performed in order: create advertising poster, copy posters, distribute posters. We must complete the first task before beginning the next one. These relationships are created as links. In Microsoft Project, select two tasks and click the Link Tasks button (shown as a chain link). The Gantt chart will automatically move the earlier task to the left and connect the two with an arrow. You need to identify the relationships among all the tasks. Figure 13.2A shows that setting the dependencies establishes the main schedule of the tasks.

FIGURE 13.1A Primary tasks for organizing the Spring Forward Century ride. Each of these categories contains several detailed tasks.

- Choose starting point
- Legal paperwork
- Establish routes
- Create databases
- Create promotional materials
- Create commemorative shirts
- Register riders
- Organize volunteer groups
- Advertise ride
- Plan rest stops
- Plan registration

Resource Usage

You should also enter a list of resources, in this case the workers available for the project (yourself and a few volunteers). You can then assign workers to each task. The Resource graph shows you if the resources are overallocated (meaning that you either need to perform tasks earlier or find more resources). Microsoft Project has a tool for leveling the resources that will help arrange the tasks to allocate the resources better. However, you generally have to make adjustments to the schedule yourself.

Figure 13.3A shows the resource graphs for yourself and for the volunteers. The graph for the volunteers shows that they will not be able to complete all of the tasks scheduled for the Saturday before the ride. You will either have to get more volunteers or have them complete some of the tasks earlier. On examining the task list, you find several tasks that can be completed earlier; so you choose that solution.

Figure 13.3A also indicates two major time periods when you will be unable to complete the tasks assigned to you. Again, you either have to get volunteers to do more of the work, or you will have to perform some of the tasks earlier. The answer will depend on which is easier: finding more workers or taking more time off your normal job so you can begin earlier. The third possibility is to find a way to complete the tasks faster. However, you will already have to rely heavily on this prospect during most of the month of March. Most days are already allocated at 200 to 300 percent of your time. You can survive by being more efficient and working nights and weekends. However, you still have to find a way to handle the two major peaks.

Monitoring the Progress

Once you have established the detailed design, you should save a baseline of the project. The baseline is a saved version at a fixed point in time that you can keep for later reference. As each task is completed, you can mark its progress within the system. You can also track actual resource usage and costs by entering them into the appropriate worksheets. Then you can view charts or worksheets that compare the estimated (baseline) values to the actual data.

Additionally, if some tasks take longer than expected, you can enter the new data and the system will adjust the remaining tasks to show you the new completion times and resource requirements. If possible, you can add resources to put the project back on track. However, remember that adding more people to a complex project can just as easily cause more problems, because it is harder to manage the larger staff.

Day of the Ride

Figure 13.4A shows the Gantt chart for the day of the ride. Notice that tasks are scheduled by hours. Also notice that because of the advance planning, the day of the ride is relatively straightforward. Few of the tasks are linked, which makes it easier to adjust if something goes wrong. However, with more volunteers to coordinate, communication will be an important factor. Many ride organizers use cellular phones to stay in touch with the volunteer drivers and rest-stop workers.

One useful feature of this Gantt chart is that it highlights the number of volunteers that will be needed. For example, you will need only four SAG drivers, since they can loop the routes. The chart also shows that the driver from the 25-mile route can help out on the last sweep of the 100-mile route if there are delays or problems.

Likewise, you can get by with only five actual rest stops, since that is the most needed at one time. When the riders clear out from the first stops on the 25- and 50-mile routes, the workers can be moved to the ending stops of the 100-mile route.

When you enter the tasks for registration, rest stops, and SAG drivers, you should check the advanced options and set the task duration as fixed. These tasks will always take the same amount of time regardless of the amount of resources you assign to them. You should also assign two workers to each rest stop. One of them could be a mechanic, but you need two people at a stop so that one can run for refills if needed.

FIGURE 13.2A Gantt chart for Spring Forward Century ride. Dependence among the tasks is shown as lines. These links force some tasks to be completed first, which establishes the primary schedule.

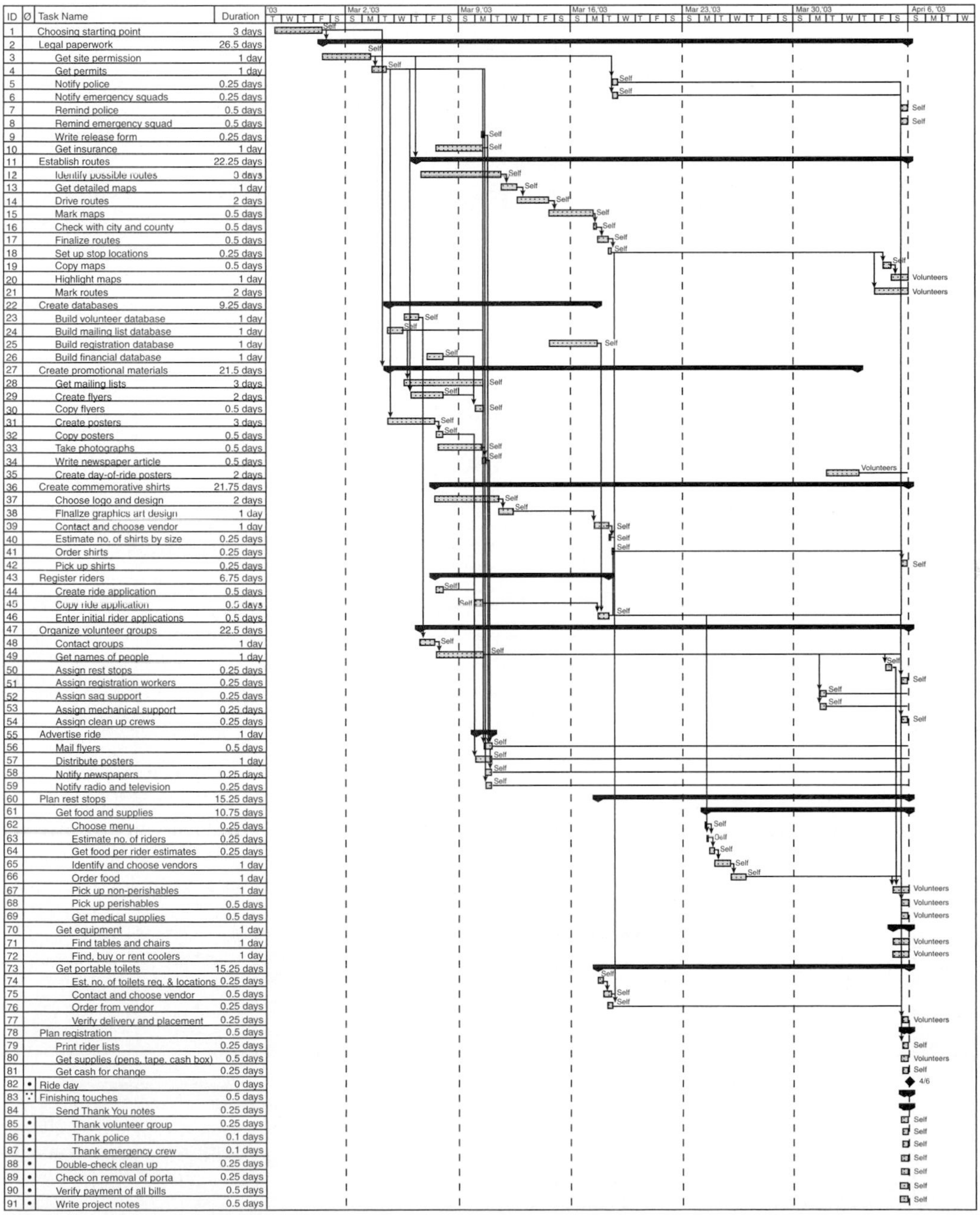

FIGURE 13.3A Resource needs for organizing the ride. You can probably solve the volunteer shortage by moving some of their tasks to Thursday and Friday. However, you will need additional volunteers to help with your two major peaks—or you will have to begin much earlier.

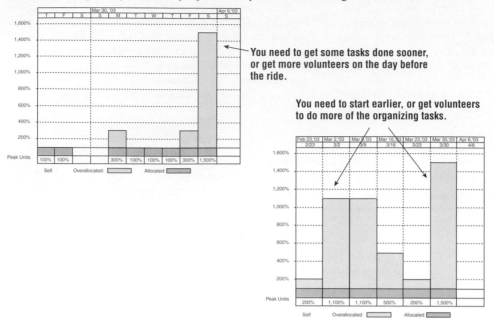

You need to get some tasks done sooner, or get more volunteers on the day before the ride.

You need to start earlier, or get volunteers to do more of the organizing tasks.

FIGURE 13.4A Gantt chart for the day of the ride. Most of the tasks are relatively independent, which makes it easier to adjust for problems. However, many tasks take place at the same time, requiring more workers and good communication.

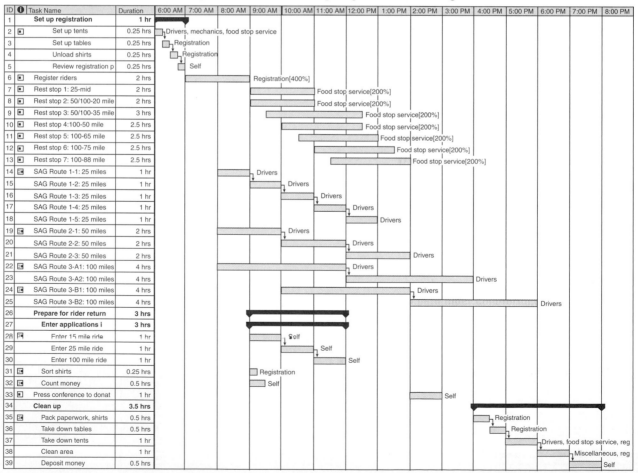

Summary

Overall, the project planning system makes it easy to enter your tasks. By defining the dependencies among the tasks, most of your schedule is automatically set. The schedule also helps you determine the resources needed. The system can display a variety of views, including resource lists and a calendar. Microsoft Project can also automatically generate reminder entries for your calendar system, or it can e-mail notices to various people involved in the project. Finally, by tracking actual time, resources, and costs, the system makes it easier to estimate and plan for the next project.

Exercises

1. Download a trial copy of Microsoft Project (if it is not available) and create the Bicycle Ride project. Print the Gantt chart.

Name	Duration	Depends on	Resources
1 Set up registration	1 hr		
2 Set up tents	0.25 hrs		Drivers, mechanics, food stop service
3 Set up tables	0.25 hrs	2	Registration
4 Unload shirts	0.25 hrs	3	Registration
5 Review registration procedures	0.25 hrs	4	Self
6 Register riders	2 hrs		Registration [400%]
7 Rest stop 1: 25-mid	2 hrs		Food stop service [200%]
8 Rest stop 2: 50/100-20 mile	2 hrs		Food stop service [200%]
9 Rest stop 3: 50/100-35 mile	3 hrs		Food stop service [200%]
10 Rest stop 4: 100-50 mile	2.5 hrs		Food stop service [200%]
11 Rest stop 5: 100-65 mile	2.5 hrs		Food stop service [200%]
12 Rest stop 6: 100-75 mile	2.5 hrs		Food stop service [200%]
13 Rest stop 7: 100-88 mile	2.5 hrs		Food stop service [200%]
14 SAG Route 1-1: 25 miles	1 hr		Drivers
15 SAG Route 1-2: 25 miles	1 hr	14	Drivers
16 SAG Route 1-3: 25 miles	1 hr	15	Drivers
17 SAG Route 1-4: 25 miles	1 hr	16	Drivers
18 SAG Route 1-5: 25 miles	1 hr	17	Drivers
19 SAG Route 2-1: 50 miles	2 hrs		Drivers
20 SAG Route 2-2: 50 miles	2 hrs	19	Drivers
21 SAG Route 2-3: 50 miles	2 hrs	20	Drivers
22 SAG Route 3-A1: 100 miles	4 hrs		Drivers
23 SAG Route 3-A2: 100 miles	4 hrs	22	Drivers
24 SAG Route 3-B1: 100 miles	4 hrs		Drivers
25 SAG Route 3-B2: 100 miles	4 hrs	24	Drivers
26 Prepare for rider return	3 hrs		
27 Enter application in database	3 hrs		
28 Enter 15-mile riders	1 hr		Self
29 Enter 25-mile riders	1 hr	28	Self
30 Enter 100-mile riders	1 hr	29	Self
31 Sort shirts	0.25 hrs		Registration
32 Count money	0.5 hrs		Self
33 Press conference to donate money	1 hr		Self
34 Clean up	3.5 hrs		
35 Pack paperwork, shirts, and material	0.5 hrs		Registration
36 Take down tables	0.5 hrs	35	Registration
37 Take down tents	1 hr	36	Drivers, food stop service, registration, miscellaneous
38 Clean area	1 hr	37	Miscellaneous, registration, food stop service
39 Deposit money	0.5 hrs	38	Self

2. By hand, draw a Gantt chart for the following project.

Name	Duration	Depends on	Resources
1 Feasibility statement	5 days		
2 Get hardware list and costs	1 day		Analyst
3 Count forms and reports	1 day		Analyst
4 Estimate development time	1 day		Analyst
5 Get benefits from user	1 day		Analyst
6 Create statement	1 day	2, 3, 4, 5	Analyst
7 Management approval	1 day	1	
8 Analysis	17 days	7	
9 Interview users	7 days		Analyst
10 Evaluate competition	3 days		Analyst
11 Search for existing software	3 days		Analyst
12 Evaluate options	4 days	9, 10, 11	Analyst
13 Management approval	1 day	8	
14 Design	15 days	13	
15 Design and create database	2 days		Analyst
16 Build forms	8 days	15	Programmer
17 Create reports	4 days	15	Programmer
18 Design application	3 days		Programmer
19 User approval	1 day	14	
20 Management approval	1 day	19	
21 Implementation	10 days	20	
22 Purchase hardware	2 days		Analyst
23 Transfer data	3 days	22	Programmer
24 Integration test	4 days	23	Programmer
25 Train users	1 day		Trainer
26 Write procedures	1 day		Analyst
27 Transfer operations	1 day	24	Analyst, programmer
28 Review	1 day		Analyst, programmer

3. Create the Gantt chart for exercise 2 using Microsoft Project. Assign resources at 100 percent as indicated and use resource leveling to determine the time it will take to complete the project.

4. For the project described in exercise 2, identify methods to reduce the overall project time.

5. For Rolling Thunder Bicycles, create a project analysis that describes the sequences and constraints of building a bicycle (from order through shipping).

CHAPTER FOURTEEN

Information Management and Society

What you will learn in this chapter

- How is information technology changing society?

- What impact does technology have on jobs?

- Do the intellectual property laws change the balance of power between business and consumers?

- How does information technology affect the power of small groups?

- What impact does information technology have on government?

- Do police agencies need new powers to deal with criminals using the Internet?

- What responsibilities do we have when collecting data or designing and using information systems?

Drug companies form an increasingly important share of health care dollars. Patents for designer drugs enable firms like Eli Lilly to fund new research.

Eli Lilly

With the expiration of Prozac's U.S. patent August 3, 2001, Eli Lilly's best-selling drug is no longer protected from cheaper generics. The Indianapolis-based pharmaceutical concern may not be able to depend solely on the antidepressant to provide a lift to its financial numbers. Prozac, with 40 million users, has accounted for a quarter of Lilly's $10.8 billion in sales and more than a third of its $3 billion profit last year.

Foreseeing the end of the Prozac monopoly, Eli Lilly has ramped up new-drug development and increased research and development budgets to more than $2.2 billion. Hence, Lilly's strategic positioning has involved two major steps: increasing its presence in rapidly growing new markets and aggressively introducing new drugs.

Overview

Richard:	I think I found a new line of work where we can make lots of money.
Elaine:	What's that?
Richard:	We'll become lawyers and specialize in the impact of technology on society. Think of the new criminal issues, the effect on education and government. And think of all the things that can go wrong.
Elaine:	We'll be rich!
Ally:	Well, there are a lot of issues to be resolved, but don't you think the government and companies can solve it on their own?
Richard and Elaine:	No!

FIGURE 14.1

Information management and society. Every organization and individual exists in a social environment. Changes in the firm and changes in technology affect the environment. Changes in the environment can affect the firm. An understanding of these interactions will make you a better manager.

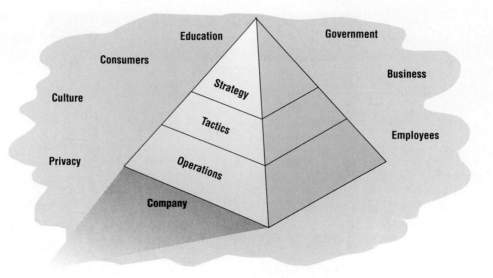

Ally: OK. Maybe you're right. But I still think managers and companies need to think about the interactions of technology with society.

Elaine: Sure, we can all hope that everyone acts responsibly. But we live in a capitalistic society, where self-interest does not always lead to the best decisions for everyone.

Introduction

If nothing else, history has shown that technological change is inevitable. Competitive economics virtually guarantees that the search for new products, new manufacturing techniques, and other ways to gain competitive advantage will continue.

Changes in technology often affect society. Technology can change individuals, jobs, education, governments, and social interactions. As components of society, each group has rights and responsibilities to others, such as a right to privacy and obligations regarding ethics.

Technology's effects on individuals can be beneficial or detrimental. Often a change in technology helps one set of individuals and harms another group. Typical problems include loss of privacy, depersonalization, and changing incentives or motivations. Advantages include lower prices and better products and service. The effect on jobs is hard to predict, but most observers conclude that workers will require more education and training. Most authorities think that increases in technology in the past generally led to an increase in the number of jobs. Now, however, many of the new jobs require higher levels of education, and the workers displaced by technology rarely have the qualifications needed for the new jobs. Technology also has an effect on crime. Technology creates new crimes, new ways to commit crimes, and new ways to catch criminals.

In addition to the increased demand, technology has provided new teaching methods. Although there is considerable debate over the costs and benefits of technology in education, there is usually a place for technology, even if only as a specialized technique. However, most educators remember the early claims of how television was going to revolutionize education. Fifty years later, television is beginning to play a role in education, but it is still hampered by the limited availability of two-way links.

Governments attempt to control these impacts of technology by creating laws, but laws often bring their own problems. Also, in times of rapid change, laws rarely keep up with the changes in technology. Governments are also directly affected by improved communication facilities. For example, technology makes it possible for governments to better understand the needs of the citizens and provide more avenues for communication.

Trends

The industrial revolution in the late 18th century caused many changes to society. Before the revolution, workers were predominantly employed as craftsmen, farmers, or lesser-skilled laborers. Mechanization brought standardization and assembly lines, for which jobs were reduced to simple, repetitive tasks.

As transportation improved, people moved from farms to cities, and cities spread to suburbs. Communication systems improved and linked the populations back together. Better product distribution mechanisms changed the way products are sold. Companies (such as Sears, through its catalogs) began to distribute products nationally instead of relying on small local stores. National and international markets developed with every change in the communication and transportation systems.

These changes were so strong that philosophers and writers began to take note of how technological changes can affect society. From the bleak pictures painted by Dickens, Marx, and Orwell, to the fantastic voyages of Verne, Heinlein, and Asimov, we can read thousands of opinions and predictions about how technology might affect the political, economic, and social environments.

Technology can alter any number of social interactions. Social groups can gain or lose power, and types or methods of criminals are altered. Additionally, society can become dependent on technology, which is not necessarily bad, but it causes problems if the technology is removed or substantially altered.

Individuals

Information technology plays an important role in the lives of most individuals. Many jobs are directly involved in the collection, processing, and evaluation of data. Performance of many workers is continually monitored by computers. As consumers, virtually our entire lives are recorded and analyzed. Governments maintain massive files on all public aspects of our lives.

Although data has been collected on citizens for many years, recent improvements in technology raise greater concerns about privacy. As computer capabilities increase, it becomes possible to collect, integrate, and analyze the huge volume of data. Using publicly available data, it is possible to collect an amazing amount of data on any person.

Privacy

As Figure 14.2 indicates, companies, governments, and employers collect data about many aspects of our lives. Recall the use of technology to improve marketing discussed in Chapter 8. Marketing and sales can be improved by maintaining databases of consumer information and tracking sales and preferences at the customer level. Combining government statistics and data from market research firms with geographical data can provide a precise picture of consumer demands. It also might represent an invasion of privacy for individuals. With databases available even to small companies, it is easy to acquire basic data on any individual. For instance, phone numbers and addresses for approximately 80 million U.S. households can be obtained for around $100 on CD-ROMs. Voter registration, motor vehicle, and property records are routinely sold by state and local governments. However, the omnibus crime bill of 1994 placed restrictions on the sales of some governmental data, especially to individuals.

It is easy to obtain lists from universities, clubs and social organizations, magazine subscriptions, and mail-order firms. Statistical data can be purchased from the U.S. government. Although most U.S. agencies are forbidden to release specific individual observations until 50 years after the collection date, statistical averages can be highly accurate. By combining the statistical averages with your address, your actual income might be estimated to within a few thousand dollars.

Because most people prefer to maintain their privacy, companies have an ethical (and sometimes legal) obligation to respect their wishes. Individuals can always ask companies not to distribute personal data. Companies should give consumers the option of protecting personal data by building the option into their databases and informing consumers whenever companies collect data.

Different countries have different laws regarding protection of consumer data. In particular, some European nations have stricter controls than the United States does. There has been some discussion among these nations (notably France) that firms should be forced to keep consumer data within the originating country; that way it is still subject to the local laws. If a U.S. firm transmits its local French database back to the United States, the data can no longer be controlled by French law. Although such restrictions would be difficult to enforce, companies have an ethical obligation to support the laws of the nation in which they operate.

The United Kingdom has a requirement that all databases involving personal data must be registered with the data protection agency.

The European Union in general has a restriction on trading data that states that personal data can only be transferred to another country if the nation supports "adequate" protection of personal data. According to *Network World,* the EU is considering a requirement that all businesses register databases containing personal data. Additionally, businesses would be required to obtain individuals' permission to collect or process the data. They would also have to notify the individual each time the data is reused or sold.

FIGURE 14.2

Privacy. Businesses, employers, and governments all have reasons to collect data on individuals. The challenge lies in balancing these needs with the privacy of the individuals. Historically, there have been many instances of abuse and fraud when this balance is not achieved.

The Internet elevates the issue of privacy. It is relatively easy for a website to track individual actions. Many sites closely track individual purchases. For instance, Amazon.com uses your prior purchases to suggest related books that might interest you. As of 1999, the U.S. government decided to allow the private sector to develop its own rules for dealing with privacy. However, several legislators have strongly suggested that at a minimum, websites should contain privacy statements so that visitors know how the company plans to use any personal data.

Employee Privacy

Computers have created other problems with respect to individual privacy. They are sometimes used to monitor employees. Computers can automatically track all of the work done by each person. Some employers post this data on public bulletin boards to encourage employees to work harder. Some software available for local area networks enables managers to see exactly what every employee is doing—without the employees knowing they are being watched. Some employers read their employees' electronic-mail messages. Currently, all of these activities are legal in the United States.

Many companies use electronic badges which employees use to unlock doors. The systems are run by a centralized computer that can be programmed to allow access to specific people only during certain hours. These systems enable employers to track the daily movements of all employees—including the amount of time spent in the restroom.

Courts have repeatedly held that property owned by the employer is completely within its control. Hence, employers have the right to impose any controls or monitoring they wish; as long as they do not violate other laws, such as the discrimination laws.

Reality Bytes   Surveillance

While most customers may not be aware of it, security is always a high priority at casinos. Most criminals are smart enough to eschew violent attacks, but many think they can devise methods to cheat at the games. In 1997, the Trump Marina casino in Atlantic City linked its network of video surveillance cameras to a mug-shot database of almost 10,000 known criminals. The database is linked to a biometric face-recognition system from Viisage Technologies. The system continuously scans faces in the casino, measuring key characteristics, such as the distance between the eyes and the length of the nose. When it finds a match against the database, it notifies security personnel. In four years, the system has identified hundreds of criminals who were ejected from the casino or arrested. The Mexican government used a similar system in the 2000 election to ensure that citizens voted only once. Following the terrorist attacks in the United States, some airports have begun installing a similar system from Visionics (for about $500,000 per installation). But it is unlikely that the systems would have stopped the September 11 hijackings—only two of the 19 terrorists were on CIA or FBI watch lists. Although the systems are relatively accurate, they are not perfect. As Bruce Schneier, a computer-security expert points out, if the system makes only one error in every 10,000 scans (99.99 percent accuracy), but you scan the 80 million passengers a year traveling through Atlanta's airport; there will be 8,000 mistakes, or 22 per day. The MIT Artificial Intelligence Lab (with 65 percent of its funding coming from the military) is working on more advanced systems. Professor Eric Grimson is developing a surveillance technology that uses an AI system to monitor activity in a given location. If something "unusual" happens, the software notifies security personnel. The system learns to identify "normal" behavior and flags actions that are different. In a test situation, it was able to identify a delivery truck backing across a sidewalk, and students pretending to case the parking lot. Several companies have been developing small, nearly invisible "planes" that can carry video cameras and broadcast back to a central monitoring facility. One company has a 2.5 ounce spy plane that can fly 30 miles per hour. Founder Paul MacCready notes that "The reason that we are pushing this area is that we think it's very important to monitor people without them knowing it. The government is interested in little things you can send up to do snooping. You want them to be so cheap they are expendable." Of course, there is an enormous tradeoff between surveillance and privacy. Do you really want to live in a world where every action is recorded and monitored to ensure that it is within the normal pattern of everyone else?

Sources: Adapted from Antonio Regalado and Rachel Zimmerman, "Terror Attack Accelerates Research into Surveillance," *The Wall Street Journal,* September 20, 2001, and John Simons, "Can Biometric Systems Foil Terrorists?" *Fortune,* October 29, 2001.

It is easy to question why employers might feel the need to monitor their employees. At some point, you have to trust your employees to do their jobs. If an employee has so little work to do that he or she can "waste time using the Internet for personal use," the bigger problem is money the company is wasting on an unneeded employee. On the other hand, most major financial losses come from insiders such as employees and consultants. Additionally, many companies have been burned by criminals when the companies were not careful enough in hiring and monitoring.

Government Privacy

Privacy from government agencies and their employees can be a touchy issue. As citizens, we agree to cooperate with government agencies to improve all of our lives. And to function properly, government agencies can require detailed personal data. For example, as shown in Figure 14.3, most governments collect health data, police records, driving records, international travel, and detailed financial data for taxes. Many people are also required to complete census surveys collecting detailed information about their lives. In the United States, much of this data is protected and can be shared or released only under specific conditions. But there have been several cases of government employees illegally browsing through records for their neighbors or even selling data. In 1991, 18 people were accused of selling social security information, including six government employees.

In the United States, few laws or regulations control the use of data held by private organizations. However, several federal laws control the use of data collected by government agencies. For example, federal agencies are restricted from sharing databases except in specific situations. In most cases the FBI cannot access the IRS data without special permits. In terms of collection and use of data by private companies, there are few restrictions. Contrary to popular belief, there is no "right to privacy" specified in federal law. However, an element of privacy is contained in a few scattered federal laws and some state laws. For

FIGURE 14.3

Government and privacy. Spying on "ordinary" people is not an issue. Spying on business and political leaders or journalists can cause problems. Collecting data on targeted individuals such as dissidents or minorities can stifle innovation.

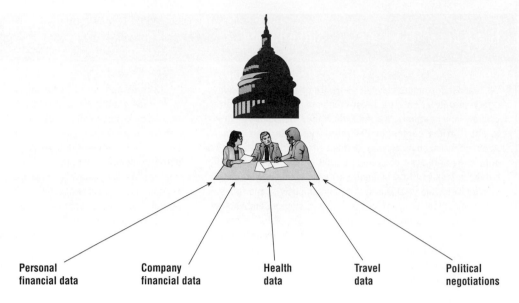

| Personal financial data | Company financial data | Health data | Travel data | Political negotiations |

example, one federal law prohibits movie rental stores (and libraries) from disclosing lists of items rented by individuals.

As everyone was reminded on September 11, 2001, the flip side to privacy is the need for governments to identify and track individuals to prevent crimes and terrorism. As an open society, the United States has chosen to lean toward individual rights and privacy; but many people have suggested that more control and less privacy would make it easier to stop potential terrorists and criminals. Because of the capabilities of modern information systems and networks, it is now possible to build powerful systems that identify and track individuals within the nation and around the world. Some people have suggested that the United States should establish national identity cards, as used in many European nations. A single, unified database would make it easier to track individual actions.

People tend to be split on the issues of government privacy. Some hate the fact that they have to provide data. Others wonder what the problem is: if you tell your friends how much money you make, why not tell the government? In one sense, public information keeps everyone honest. And for many people, it probably does not matter if various government agencies collect personal data. No one really cares about the personal details of most people. On the other hand, some people within governments have abused their positions in the past. Consider the tales of J. Edgar Hoover, long-time head of the FBI. He was obsessed with collecting data on people and built files on tens of thousands of people. Ostensibly he was attempting to remove "subversives" and was a leading cause of the McCarthy anticommunism hearings in the 1950s. He also collected thousands of secret files on politicians, journalists, and business leaders. He used these files to harass and blackmail leaders. Even if a modern-day data collector is not as blatant as Hoover, and even if modern politicians have fewer moral problems, there is still an important risk. What if a politician tries to spy on or interfere with political negotiations?

Protecting Your Privacy

Despite the shortage of laws, you can take several actions to protect your privacy and restrict access to personal data. First, it is your responsibility to direct employers and companies you deal with to not distribute your personal data. You can also ask them why they need personal data and whether it is optional or required. In particular, all federal agencies are required to explain why they need data from you and the purposes for which it will be used. You can also write to direct-marketing associations and file a request that your name not be included in general mailings or unsolicited phone calls. By using variations of your name or address, such as changing your middle initial, you can keep track of which organizations are selling personal data. In some cases, you can refuse to give out personal data (such as a social security or taxpayer identification number). If a private company insists, simply stop doing business with it. In a world where firms increasingly rely on a single number for identification, it is important that you protect that number.

With most government agencies and with banks, creditors, and credit-reporting agencies, you have the ability to check any data that refers to you. You have the right to disagree with any inaccurate data and request that it be changed. You can also file letters of explanation that are reported with the original data. In 1994, Congress updated the Fair Credit Reporting Act of 1970. The new version requires credit bureaus to verify disputed information within 30 days or delete it. Businesses that provide data to the credit agencies would also be required to investigate claims of incorrect information. The bill also limits who can have access to the data stored by the credit agencies and controls how it can be used in direct marketing campaigns. In 1994, according to the Associated Press, the bureaus processed 450 million files, selling 1.5 million records a day and handling almost 2 billion pieces of data every month.

Dehumanization

Companies should also be aware that many people find technology to be dehumanizing. Several years ago, Citicorp, a large bank based in New York, exhibited this **dehumanization** when it attempted to force people with small accounts to use automated teller machines instead of human tellers. The attempt lasted about a week and irritated many customers, because they preferred to deal with humans. Similarly, many people feel they should be recognized by their name and not have to rely on a number for identification. Companies can often minimize problems by using numbers only for internal identification and rely on a combination of name and address or phone number when they deal with customers.

Jobs

Loss of Jobs

There is no question that technology causes some workers to lose their jobs. In the 19th century, Luddites reacted to textile automation by destroying machines. Information technology is no exception. Norbert Weiner, a computer pioneer in the 1940s, predicted a major depression would result from computers replacing workers. Despite these predictions, during the last 100 years technology has increased the number of jobs and raised the standard of living of most workers. Since the introduction of computers in the 1950s, the world's economies have grown and incomes have increased. However, individual workers can lose jobs in the short run. Even in the long run, lower-skilled workers experience greater difficulty in finding new jobs. Compare the automated shipyards of Singapore to those in the United States. In Singapore, one man using computer screens and a joystick moves hundreds of containerized cargos without ever leaving his office. In the United States, each crane requires a crew of four workers, including one just to identify shipments and destinations that are handled by computer in Singapore. In Europe, the Dutch port in Rotterdam cut employment in half by installing robotic cranes and automated transfer vehicles.

The point is that some jobs will disappear, but others will take their place. In the shipyard example, more technical expertise will be needed to program and repair the equipment. Figure 14.4 shows the changes in jobs for the next few years that are anticipated by the Bureau of Labor Statistics. If you look at the jobs in terms of the greatest percentage growth rates (instead of total numbers), 8 of the 10 (and the top 7) fastest-growing jobs are computer-oriented.

Most economic experts believe that technology increases the total number of jobs. New technology creates demand for designers, manufacturing firms to produce it, and people to maintain and repair it. Computer hardware also creates demands for software programmers. More important, technology can cause the economy to grow, creating more jobs in all sectors. By most indications, new jobs created by technology tend to be higher paying,

FIGURE 14.4

Future jobs. Today there is no guarantee that your job will continue to exist. Demand for specialists changes constantly. Jobs that are well defined and require little innovation or thought can usually be performed easily by computers.

Source: U.S. Bureau of Labor Statistics.

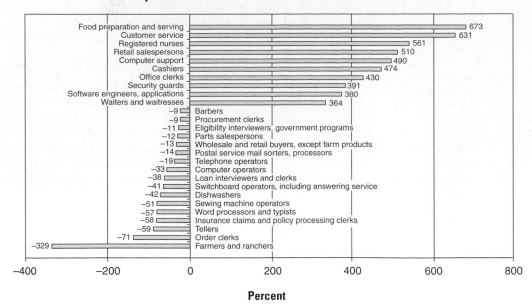

Occupations with Greatest Growth or Loss

physically safer, and less repetitive than those replaced by technology. Information technology can also reduce product prices, raising the standard of living by enabling people to buy more goods.

On the other hand, technology typically causes some workers to lose their jobs. Unfortunately, many of these displaced workers cannot be retrained for the new jobs created by the technology. Similarly, the new jobs might pay less money, have lower status, or might have less desirable work environments.

Governments have created several programs to provide benefits of money, retraining, and relocation to workers who lose their jobs. As managers, we need to understand the effects on employees when we introduce new technology. Many corporations provide ongoing educational payments and training classes to help workers improve their skills. Others provide out-placement services to help unemployed workers in their job search.

As individuals, we need to remember that changing technology can eliminate virtually any job. One of the best plans is to continue your education and learn new skills. Remember that technology continually changes. Some of the skills you learn today will be obsolete in a couple of years. We must all continually learn new skills and adapt to changes. Applying these skills in your current job adds experience that will help you find a new job. It also benefits your current employer and might help you keep your job or stay with the company if new technology makes your current job obsolete.

The concept of continually acquiring new skills sounds straightforward. However, many times you will have to choose among multiple technologies. Guessing wrong can lead you to invest time and money in a technology or skill that fades away. As you become more involved with technology, you will increasingly find it necessary to "predict" the future. Identifying trends and deciphering fact from rumor are important skills to learn.

Physical Disabilities

Technology offers many possibilities to provide jobs for workers with physical disabilities. In fact, in 1992, the U.S. Congress passed the Americans with Disabilities Act, stating that companies are not allowed to discriminate against disabled employees. Common uses of technology include the use of scanners and speech synthesizers for visually impaired workers; voice input devices and graphics displays for workers who cannot use keyboards; and telecommuting for those who work from home. In 2001, the U.S. government began requiring that all software it purchases must be accessible to users with disabilities. Since the fed-

FIGURE 14.5

Adaptive technology. This foot mouse (www.footmouse.com) uses one pedal to move the mouse, the other to click the button. It is useful for people who wish to keep their hands on the keyboard, or who have limited use of their hands. Other input and output devices exist for other purposes.

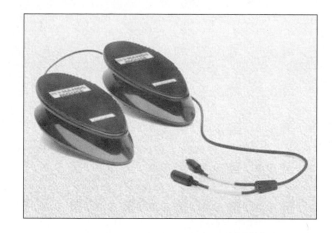

Telecommuting sounds appealing to those who spend hours in traffic. The computer and Internet connections are relatively straightforward. Security is more challenging. Workers also need self-motivation and organization.

eral government employs hundreds of thousands of workers, this order should encourage all software providers to improve their software.

Most Windows-based software contains features to facilitate usage by people with various physical challenges. In some cases, additional accessibility tools can be downloaded or purchased to provide more features. Speech recognition packages are useful for many applications. Sometimes devices like the mouse shown in Figure 14.5 are needed to provide alternative ways to enter data and obtain the results.

Websites still present accessibility problems, particularly for those with visual impairments. Many sites rely on color and graphics, which are difficult for the accessibility tools to interpret. These issues are being discussed by many vendors. Check Microsoft's accessibility site for more details.

Telecommuting

The fact that about 70 percent of U.S. jobs are service-based jobs raises interesting possibilities for workers. Many services like accounting, legal advice, education, insurance, investments, data analysis, computer programming, and consulting are not tied to a physical location. As a service provider, you could be located anywhere and still perform your job—as long as you have the appropriate telecommunications system. As communication improves to include video links and faster document transfer, even more jobs can be performed from remote locations.

FIGURE 14.6

Telecommuting. In the simplest form of telecommuting, individual workers connect to office computers from their homes. An intermediate method has been used to avoid the problems of distractions and the cost of creating a home office. Workers report to satellite centers in their suburban neighborhood. Workers retain a structured environment but reduce their travel time.

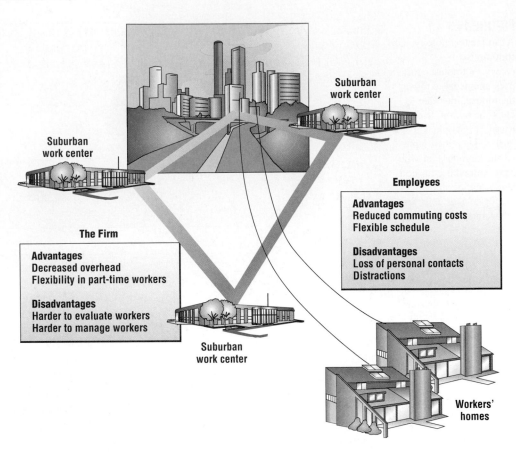

Some companies are experimenting with home-based workers, especially in cities such as Los Angeles and New York with long commute times. Some workers like the concept; others try it for a few months and return to a traditional workplace job. Several advantages and complications arise from the perspective of the worker, the firm, and society.

If a substantial number of workers choose to work from home, the firm gains two main advantages: (1) decreased costs through smaller offices, and (2) flexibility in hiring additional workers on a contract basis. Some people have predicted that companies might also gain from increased use of part-time workers, thus avoiding the cost of insurance and other benefits. The greatest complication to the firm is evaluating and managing employees. Without daily personal contact, including conversations, it is harder to spot problems and make informal suggestions as corrections.

To the worker, the most obvious benefit lies in reducing the time and expense of commuting to work. The biggest drawback lies in the loss of personal contact and daily ritual of a typical work schedule. Depending on your home environment, there can be substantially more interruptions and distractions at home. It is also more difficult to "get away" from your job. Working from home on a flexible schedule requires strong motivation and organization. Before you choose to work at home, talk to someone with experience.

A few firms have experimented with intermediate telecommuting options. As indicated in Figure 14.6, the firm leases smaller offices in city suburbs and workers operate from these satellite offices instead of one central location. The offices are linked by high-capacity telecommunication lines. Workers keep a traditional office environment but cut their commuting costs. Businesses maintain traditional management control but do not save as much money.

A few people have speculated about the effects on society if there is a large shift to telecommuting. At this point, there is not much evidence to support any of the hypotheses, but many of them focus on negative aspects. People could become isolated. Jobs could become highly competitive and short term. Firms could list projects on the network and workers would compete for every job. Workers would essentially become independent contractors and bear the responsibilities and costs of insurance, retirement, and other benefits, with little or no job security. They would also have no loyalty to any particular firm. Firms could become loose coalitions of workers and teams that are constantly changing, with little control over future directions. It is hard to predict what will really happen, but by understanding the negative effects, they become easier to avoid.

Business: Vendors and Consumers

Business consists of transactions. Changes in the way transactions are handled can alter society. In particular, as digital content becomes more important, can the existing laws created decades ago still be applied? And if the laws are replaced, will they affect the balance of power in the relationship between vendors and consumers?

Intellectual Property

Intellectual property is the general term to describe ownership of ideas (patents) and creative expressions (copyrights). For many years, there was a solid distinction between the two: ideas involving physical items (such as machines) could be patented. A **patent** essentially grants a monopoly to an inventor for a fixed period of time (originally 17 years in the United States but now 20 years). During that time, no other company can introduce a similar device—even if the second creator did not use any knowledge from the first inventor. A **copyright** is created for other creative works—traditionally writing and music. It protects the specific article from being copied and grants the owner the sole right to create derivative works (such as a sequel). But it does not prevent others from creating similar works. For example, one person could write a story about space explorers. Someone else could also write a story about space explorers, and it would not be an infringement on the first story. If the second story used the same characters and plot, it might be an infringement, but it might not, depending on the interpretation of the courts. In the mid-1990s, the U.S. patent office began granting patents for nonphysical items—specifically for business ideas. Patents were supposed to be granted only for nontrivial ideas, but for a while, the patent office got carried away and forgot that patents are only supposed to be granted for "nontrivial and nonobvious" inventions. For instance, it granted a business process patent to Amazon.com for one-click checkout of Web sales; so no other website was allowed to offer a checkout system with a single click without paying royalties to Amazon.

The goal of patents and copyrights is to encourage creativity by offering protected rewards to innovators. Remember from economics that without a barrier to entry, any firm that makes a profit will attract competitors. Patents and copyrights are designed to be barriers to entry for a limited time. But the laws were written in decades when the goal was to protect companies from other companies. For instance, before computers, only a large company would be able to copy a book and reprint it. The laws made it clear that this action was illegal, and the injured party could easily find and sue the single violator for damages. Several exemptions to the copyright law were specifically created to support important noninfringing uses that are considered valuable to society. For example, educational institutions can make limited copies of items for discussion and research.

Digital content changes most of the underlying assumptions of the intellectual property discussion. First, it is easy for anyone to make perfect copies. Second, it is equally easy for everyone to distribute those copies—at virtually no cost. Instead of a large competitor, now the threat is millions of your own customers. Some of these issues are cultural and economic. For example, some industry-sponsored reports indicate that software piracy in Southeast Asia is huge: over 90 percent of software in use is copied. Nations such as Vietnam do not have the tradition of paying for creative works, and do not have much money to pay for them.

The most famous case of these copyright issues involved the company called Napster. Napster was a pure Internet firm that ran a website to make it easy for consumers to find and share digital music files. In an attempt to stay within the copyright laws, Napster did not store any files and did not charge for its services. Instead, it was simply a giant directory.

Reality Bytes   Vivendi Universal

The Universal Music Group of Vivendi is the world's largest music company. In 2001, it announced that it would begin releasing CDs with a technology that prevents customers from making digital copies. Other companies have been testing similar technologies, but Vivendi's is the first widespread implementation. The company claims that the system "will not impede the consumer experience." Companies are largely concerned about customers converting the music to MP3 files and distributing them to their friends. Consumers in the United States (and some other nations) have long had a legal right to copy music to other formats for their own use. For example, if you buy a CD, it is legal to copy the songs to tape to play them in a car or portable device. In general, these court cases would also make it legal for a consumer to convert the CD songs to MP3 format—as long as the songs are not distributed to others. The new antipiracy measures would prevent consumers from making these copies. So far, the only recourse consumers have is to refuse to buy CDs that are copy-protected.

Source: Adapted from Anna Wilde Mathews and Martin Peers, "Vivendi to begin releasing music CDs equipped with antipiracy technology," *The Wall Street Journal,* September 26, 2001.

Individuals searching for specific songs went to the Napster site, found a fellow enthusiast with a desired file and copied the file from the other's machine. Napster lost the ensuing lawsuit from the music industry. But the battle is far from over. Napster made it easy by providing a single target to sue. What if there is no central company directing the copying?

In response to these problems, the United States passed the Digital Millennium Copyright Act (DMCA). One of the most important changes in the act, and the most contested today, is a provision that makes it illegal to circumvent any copyright protection scheme. In existing cases, this provision has been interpreted to mean that any discussion of how to circumvent protection is illegal. The first case pursued under this provision relates to DVD movie disks and the DeCSS program. DVD files are encrypted so that they can only be played on specific machines with authorized software. The files are only weakly protected. Direct from the manufacturer, the files can be copied to other computers, but can only be viewed with the special software. Since that software did not originally exist for some computer systems (notably Linux), a few experts found a way to defeat the encryption. They posted this method (known as DeCSS) on the Internet. The movie studios promptly sued every website that carried the program for violating the DMCA. Many people are concerned that these actions violate the spirit of free speech and open discussion. Of course, whether or not the movie industry wins the case is almost irrelevant. One key factor of the Internet is that it is impossible to destroy knowledge once it has been created. Several websites in foreign nations that do not support the DMCA carry the information.

Digital books are soon going to face similar issues. Even printed books can be copied relatively easily today. However, it is hard to distribute them so publishers have not been overly concerned. Digital books will exist online just as software and music files do today. To prevent mass copying, Microsoft and Adobe have created similar but incompatible systems utilizing a system known as **digital rights management (DRM).** Digital rights management systems provide copies over the Internet directly to the consumer and activate each copy for the specific machine. They also register the copy and the consumer with a central server. Ultimately, DRM could be used for any form of digital content. With DRM, the publisher can completely control the use and distribution of the copyrighted work, even to the point of specifying that the book cannot be loaned or even transferred to another person. These systems solve the problem from the perspective of the vendor—until someone breaks the protection system. Even though it would be illegal in the United States to break the system, many people will undoubtedly make the attempt. More important, will consumers accept the many restrictions and potential privacy invasion?

Figure 14.7 shows one of the DRM systems in use today. While Microsoft deliberately kept the traditional publisher, wholesaler, and retailer roles, it is possible for one firm to combine many of these steps. For example, a publisher could run the DAS as well as the e-commerce store and maintain complete control over distribution.

FIGURE 14.7

Digital rights management. Authors create manuscripts which the publisher converts into an e-book format and transfers to a company running a digital asset server. The customer finds the book and purchases it at an e-commerce vendor. The vendor uses a typical bank system to collect the retail price, and then sends the purchase information to the DAS. The DAS encrypts the book with the security specified by the publisher and transfers the book to the customer. The DAS keeps a percentage of the costs and settles the publisher account.

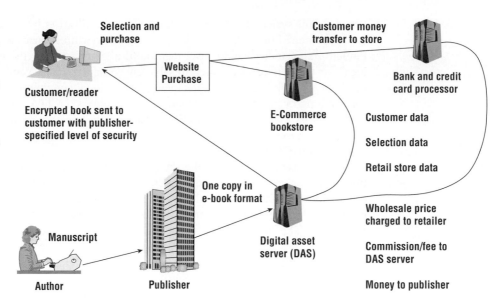

The real issue that consumers and society must eventually face is the level of security applied to the digital content. Microsoft's method supports three levels: (1) sealed with a base encryption that prevents the contents from being modified, (2) inscribed with the purchaser's username, making it possible to track the source of any pirated copies, and (3) *owner exclusive* books that are encrypted so they can only be read on machines activated by the specified owner. The book cannot be given to anyone else. Music publishers are evaluating even stronger security rules. For instance, it is possible to protect a song so that it can be played only one time—every time a customer wants to hear the song, he or she would have to pay an additional fee. Monthly subscription fees are a more common approach (e.g., www.pressplay.com). Customers pay a monthly fee that enables them to listen to a certain number of songs each month. If the customer drops the subscription service, he or she would no longer be able to play any of the downloaded material.

The flip side of copyrights is the argument that content should be free. But who would take the time to create useful content if it is free to everyone? Stephen King, the noted author ran an experiment in the late 1990s. He wrote a novella and began writing a novel in installments. He distributed them through his website. He attracted hundreds of thousands of visitors and free downloads. He ultimately stopped the projects because of lack of revenue (it was more profitable for him to devote his time to paying projects).

Balance of Power

Some of the issues with intellectual property arise because of questions of balance of power between the creator, the publisher, the retailer, and the consumers. For instance, the Internet, with its digital content, provides the opportunity for authors and creators to circumvent the traditional publishers. Currently, authors receive only a small portion of the list price of an item. Retailers, distributors, and publishers take the majority of the money. In a world that requires distribution of physical items, these are the costs you must pay to reach consumers. In a digital world, anyone can sell products directly to consumers. Of course, it will be simpler and more cost-effective when consumers adopt a small-payments mechanism. The point is that the few large publishers in each industry have a strong interest in maintaining control over the distribution system, so most proposals have catered to these large firms. For example, the DRM systems keep the role of the retailers and the publishers, so the costs to consumers are likely to remain high.

The changing laws offer even more potential to change the balance of power between vendors and consumers. In particular, many larger software vendors have been pushing states to adopt the Uniform Computer Information Transactions Act (UCITA). The laws based on this system dramatically alter the balance of power between digital content vendors and customers. For instance, the laws make shrink-wrap licenses binding agreements—even though the customer cannot read them until after purchasing the product. It also makes it legal for the vendor to remotely disable any products if the vendor suspects the customer might be in violation of the "agreements." Traditional commercial law provides due process for handling disputes between vendors and customers. UCITA throws these processes away and gives substantial control to the vendor, including the ability to disclaim warranties. Many businesses and individuals are concerned about these provisions and are fighting the adoption of UCITA.

All of these issues are challenging with multiple perspectives. There is no question that society needs to protect and encourage innovation. There is no doubt that technology makes it easier for individuals to copy and distribute protected works. And it is economically infeasible for an innovator to sue millions of people over patent or copyright violations. The issues also revolve around important economic issues. Digital content essentially has zero cost to copy and distribute (but high fixed costs to create). Some people are willing to pay higher prices for the content than others are. So it is difficult to set prices on these products. Setting high prices restricts the product to an elite group of wealthy consumers and tempts people to break the law and copy the item. Setting low prices may not attract enough revenue to cover the development costs. As shown in Figure 14.8, the concept of elasticity of demand is a useful tool for identifying the best price point for digital products. Digital products have no marginal cost to produce or distribute, and generally have a "monopoly" granted by copyright laws. No one else can legally distribute the exact same product. Economics shows that this type of company makes the most money by reducing prices to the point where the elasticity of demand is equal to –1. In comparison to traditional paper-based books (or CD-based music) that do have marginal costs of production, the more traditional products will carry a higher price and lower sales. So eventually, digital products should cost less than their traditional counterparts. However, the analysis does not consider the issue of illegal copying, and it would ultimately require elimination of the middle distribution layers (retail outlets).

FIGURE 14.8

Elasticity of demand. With zero marginal costs and a copyright "monopoly," firms can increase their revenue by reducing prices as long as the elasticity of demand is less than –1.

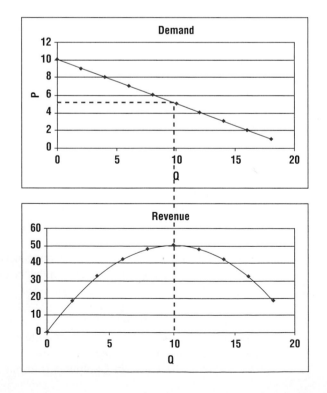

Education and Training

For hundreds of years, the principles and techniques of education have changed only slightly. As new technologies are introduced, people have often declared that the world of education would change markedly. Yet, few technologies have had a lasting impact on education. Television is a classic example. Although movies and news reports are sometimes used for teaching purposes, the role of television in formal education is minimal. However, it is used for informal education and for training, especially with the availability of videotapes for teaching specific tasks.

One of the drawbacks to video education is the lack of interaction and feedback. Multimedia tools that combine video, sound, and computer interaction represent one attempt to surmount this limitation. However, three basic problems arise when applying technology to education. First, technology is often expensive, especially compared to traditional methods. Second, it is time consuming to create lessons that generally are difficult to change. Third, there is little conclusive evidence that the techniques are equal to or superior to existing techniques. Especially in light of the first two problems, it is difficult to test the new technologies. In many cases, by the time prices have fallen and lessons are created, an even newer technology emerges.

Despite these obstacles, technological innovations are often used for specialized teaching purposes. For instance, interactive and multimedia computer tools can be used to provide more in-depth study for advanced students or to handle repetitive drills for those students needing extra work. Increasingly available two-way video links are used to connect teachers and students in remote locations.

The main questions regarding technology in education are summarized in Figure 14.9. Note that nontraditional areas have been faster to adopt the technologies, for example, business training classes—partly to reduce the cost of hiring instructors and partly because the lessons are available to workers at any time and can be studied at whatever speed the student desires.

The Internet is increasingly being pushed as a means to expand the reach of higher education. Several universities are experimenting with offering individual courses over the Internet. The early examples often consisted of simple e-mail-based systems where students worked on their own and occasionally sent messages to the instructor. A few organizations, such as the University of the South, currently offer complete programs over the Internet. Eventually, these programs will evolve, particularly as Internet transmission speeds improve to offer more interactive communication.

FIGURE 14.9

Information technology in education. The technology has the potential to change education, particularly in terms of individualized attention, course management, and distance. But it is expensive and time consuming to provide the infrastructure and create new applications. Nontraditional areas such as continuing professional education (CPE), employer training, and the military have found several benefits in the technologies.

Can technology change education?
- Computer-assisted instruction to provide individual attention
- Course management
- Distance learning

Do people want more technology in education?
- Teachers
- Students
- Employers

Lifelong learning
- Professionals
- Employers
- Military

The real key to online education is to use all of the power of the technology to develop entirely new applications. Communication is only one aspect of the Internet. Building more intelligence into the applications to create entirely new procedures will lead to more useful tools. Researchers have worked for years to develop computer-assisted instruction tools that will provide individualized attention to each student. While some individual products have been successful, these tools require considerable creativity and effort to create.

Social Interactions

As any good science fiction book illustrates, advances in technology can alter society in many different ways. Sometimes the responses are hard to predict, and they often occur gradually, so it can be difficult to spot patterns. At the moment, four patterns appear to be important: social group legitimacy, equal access to technology, e-mail freedom, and liability and control over data.

Social Group Legitimacy

One interesting feature of technology is that it has substantially lowered communication costs, including the costs of producing and distributing information to large public groups. For example, desktop publishing systems enable groups to create professional-quality documents at low cost. Additionally, video production facilities are easily affordable by any group, and access to mass markets is provided free through *public-access channels* on cable television. Websites can be created by anyone. These technologies enable small groups to reach a wider audience for minimal cost.

The only catch is that with growing professionalism of small-group productions, it becomes harder to distinguish fact from fiction, and it is harder for the public to tell the difference between mainstream, professional commentary and radical extremists. For example, do you believe stories that are printed in *The New York Times?* What about stories printed in supermarket tabloids that sport titles such as: "Space Alien Eats Movie Star"? Now consider the Internet and run some searches on medical questions. You will find hundreds of websites and comments. Which ones do you believe? Websites present the strongest challenge ever to trust and reliability issues. Literally anyone can create a site and say anything. Nonsensical comments will be found by the search engines and displayed along with accurate statements. Consider the examples in Figure 14.10 and see if you can determine which one to believe.

This issue has some interesting effects. For example, in several instances, disgruntled customers have created sites criticizing companies. If you search for a particular company, you are likely to encounter several of these sites. The Web makes it easy for people to criticize anyone—and the entire world can see the results. Of course, traditional defamation laws still apply, but in situations where there is an element of truth, companies will find it difficult to stop these activities.

The same issues can be applied to television broadcasts, except that for the moment, the high costs of broadcasts restrict this option to a few participants. With his "War of the Worlds" broadcast, Orson Welles shocked many listeners because they had come to accept radio broadcasts as fact. With existing technology, it is possible to create realistic-looking fictional broadcasts. It is not even necessary to resort to tricks such as hidden explosive charges. It is possible to create computer-generated images that exceed the quality of broadcast signals, so they appear to be realistic. Advertisers have made heavy use of these techniques. Every time you watch a commercial, you should remind yourself that a portion of what you are seeing is probably a computer-generated image. Now, imagine what would happen if an extremist organization used this same technology to create newscasts with altered pictures.

Access to Technology

Picture a world in which financial instruments are traded electronically, goods are purchased through computer-television systems, libraries are converted to electronic media, and businesses require suppliers to exchange data over computer links. Large portions of the United

FIGURE 14.10   A test of cynicism. Which website do you believe? Why? Would it help to know that the one on the left is from an independent chiropractor (ArthritisCure.com), and the one on the right from the BBC? With information technology, anyone can create a website. It can be difficult to determine the "truth." Of course, in many cases, truth may be only shades of gray, and there seldom are any "right" answers. All consumers must learn to challenge everything (even the report from the BBC).

| Home | Products | Ask the Doc | To Order |
| Testimonials | About Us | Reports | E-mail Us |

Long Lasting Arthritis Relief...Naturally!

Astounding All-Natural Arthritis Breakthrough Gives Joint Pain Relief to Millions!!

A local Doctor in Gaithersburg, Maryland has helped hundreds of his patients suffering with arthritis to drastically reduce (even eliminate in most cases!) their joint pain in 30 days or less! Here's his amazing secret weapon.. (Hint: It does not involve the use of arthritis medication!)

Dr. M. Kureshi, D.C.

- Clinical Director of Gaithersburg Pain Relief Center, P.A.
- Founder of Natural Medical Solutions, Inc.
- Has successfully helped thousands of Arthritis sufferers ease their pain naturally, without traditional arthritis medication.

Sunday, 29 October, 2000, 17:34 GMT
Scientists closer to arthritis 'cure'

There are 750,000 arthritis sufferers in Britain

A new arthritis treatment developed by British scientists may lead to a cure for the crippling disease.

Initial trials of the drug treatment have exceeded all expectations with only two out of 20 patients showing no benefits.

A team from University College in London announced details of their treatment method at an international medical conference on Monday.

But talk of a "cure" has been met with caution by leading experts in the field who say the new treatment is only in its infancy and far more tests are required.

States and Europe are getting closer to this scenario every day. Now, what happens to the individuals in poorer nations who can barely afford to eat, much less invest in personal and national information systems? If the means of production are based on technology and certain groups do not have access, the gap between those who have access and those who do not (the **digital divide**) will widen. Although some groups will be content to live without technology, some will become upset at the imbalance.

Figure 14.11 shows that access to the Internet requires more than simple PCs and software. Individuals need access to telecommunication lines. More important, nations need high-bandwidth connections to other nations. The figure shows the currently installed bandwidth between major world regions. Note the major connections between the United States and Europe, and the relatively small connections to Latin America and Africa. It takes time and money to install new fiber-optic connections across long distances. Telecommunication firms are reluctant to incur these high fixed costs until a region has enough paying customers to cover the costs with long-term usage.

Some companies have worked to give others access to technology. A few recycle older computers to libraries and citizen centers. On the international front, businesses can donate older personal computers to organizations for shipment to other countries. After three to five years, the technology is often out of date in the United States, but even old technology is better than nothing in some countries.

Wireless connections offer enormous potential to nations that cannot afford to install fiber-optic connections across their countryside. Wireless is particularly convenient and substantially cheaper to install in high-density areas.

FIGURE 14.11
International bandwidth. Access to the Internet requires more than computers; it requires high-speed communication lines between nations and continents. As noted by www.telegeography.com, most connections are between the United States and Europe.

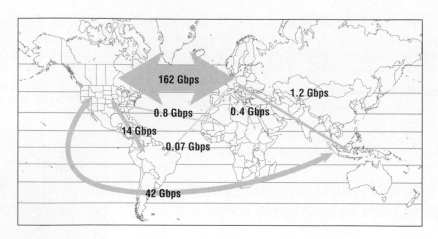

E-Mail Freedom

Some organizations have observed an interesting feature when they first replaced paper mail with electronic-mail systems. The first people to use the technology are generally younger, more likely to take risks, and bolder than the typical employee. If the top management levels accept and respond to electronic messages, they are likely to get a different perspective on the organization, its problems, and potential solutions. E-mail systems provide a means for employees (and sometimes customers) at the lower levels to bypass the hierarchy of middle management. A few directed comments and words of encouragement can enhance this effect, which is useful if managers are searching for new approaches to solving problems.

Liability and Control of Data

Virtually all of our legal structures and interpretations were created before the advent of a computerized society. Although federal and state governments have passed a few laws specifically to address problems with computer interaction, most legal systems still rely on laws and definitions created for a paper-based world. Sometimes these concepts do not fit well in a computerized environment. For example, how would you classify the operator of a website? Is that person a publisher of information, like a newspaper? Or is the operator merely a vendor offering disk space to anonymous writers? In particular, are the owners of websites responsible for the content of messages posted on their systems? To date, the court systems have tended to make the decision based on whether the owners exercise "editorial control." In 1995, the New York supreme court ruled that Prodigy could be sued for libel. An anonymous writer posted a message that was highly critical of the financial status of a certain firm. The firm claimed that the comments were false and sued Prodigy for publishing false information. Since its inception, Prodigy maintained a policy of forbidding people to post "profane" messages. The Prodigy staff used software to scan messages. The court noted that these actions constituted editorial control, so Prodigy could be treated as any other publisher of information (like a newspaper). These concepts were later clarified into law. Now, websites that do not exercise control over the content are merely distribution channels (like booksellers), and cannot be held liable for the content. However, many Web hosting companies place restrictions on content (such as pornography) and will remove a site that is reported to violate its policies.

Government

Government Representatives and Agencies

Governments can be slow to adopt new technologies. Typically, government agencies have limited budgets, long procurement cycles, and requirements for special allocations to acquire new technology. They tend to have smaller IS staffs, who also receive less pay than their counterparts in private business. Additionally, government projects tend to be large and involve thousands of people, which makes them expensive, harder to create, and more difficult to implement.

Reality Bytes   Dmitri Skylarov

When the U.S. Digital Millennium Copyright Act (DMCA) was passed in 1998, only a few people complained about its draconian policies regarding the publication and discussion of circumvention techniques for copyright technologies. The law makes it a federal crime to copy and distribute copyrighted material, particularly digitized information. But it also makes it a federal crime to distribute devices that circumvent copy protection technologies. Publishers of books, music, and movies have been reluctant to move to digital formats; partly because they did not believe customers were ready, partly because they were concerned that it would be too easy for people to freely distribute perfect digital copies, and partly because they would lose control over the distribution networks. In terms of text, Adobe and Microsoft have developed digital encryption techniques that are supposed to make it difficult for people to copy and distribute electronic books. In 2001, Dmitri Sklyarov, a Russian citizen working in Russia for a Russian company (ElcomSoft), wrote a dissertation that examined the security

technologies used to protect electronic books. In the process, he found that Adobe's protection system was weak, and he quickly developed a program that could decrypt any of the Adobe e-books; making it possible for anyone to copy them. For a short time, ElcomSoft sold the software over the Internet for a small fee. In July 2001, Dmitri gave a presentation of his ideas at an annual hackers' convention (Def Con) in Las Vegas. He was arrested by the FBI, charged with criminal violation of the DMCA, and held without bail. Ultimately, even Adobe officials admitted that the case was weak, but prosecution continues. In addition to the jurisdiction question and freedom of speech questions, it is helpful to know that Russian law specifically states that citizens cannot be prohibited from making backup copies of data and software they own.

Sources: Adapted from Jennifer Lee, "U.S. arrests Russian cryptographer as copyright violator," *New York Times,* July 18, 2001; and *CNN,* "Protestors seek release of hacker," July 24, 2001.

In the United States, the federal government has begun to provide information and responses to questions via the Internet. It is even possible to send electronic mail to the president—although the mail is actually read and answered by assistants. Almost all federal data is available in computer form. Many agencies are positioning themselves as providers of economic data to facilitate business decisions. Fedstats (www/fedstats.gov) is one of the best starting points for finding data produced by federal agencies. Even municipal governments are beginning to post notices and data on the Internet. Most government agencies are still nervous about electronic commerce. One of the main problems they face is the inability to positively identify consumers over the Internet. Of course, government agencies operate on government time. Little has been done to reduce the time it takes to release government data. For example, data reports from the 2000 census are being released over a five-year time period. Data from many agencies is months or years out of date when it is released. Additionally, many economic statistics are revised over time, so preliminary numbers you see one month may be replaced with different values several months later. Nonetheless, the government agencies are important sources for many types of data.

Politicians campaigning for office also use technology. For many years government officials have used databases to track letters and comments, solicit contributions, and tailor speeches to specific audiences. Politicians still rely on television to create images, but websites are commonly used to provide detailed position papers and background information that is too long to be covered in depth by traditional media.

Democracy and Participation

The U.S. Constitution and its amendments clearly recognize that democracy requires the participation of the citizens. And participation requires that citizens be informed—hence the importance of the press. Information is required to produce knowledge, which can lead to wisdom and better decisions. More important, it is not always clear exactly what information will be useful later. The Internet is a powerful source of information. Of course, distinguishing fact from fiction is critical. Yet, today it is still possible for a nation to control the content available within its borders. China maintains its hold by owning and controlling all routers that connect to the Internet. Ultimately, it may become impossible for a nation to control all information. Between the massive data flows, encryption, automated document translation, and wireless capabilities, it will become increasingly difficult to control data.

Reality Bytes — Information Control

Many people have suggested that the Internet can be a powerful force for democracy around the world. Information is critical to making decisions—particularly political decisions. In the cold war of the 1960s and 1970s, governments went to extensive lengths to control information. Nations like the Soviet Union controlled information to the point that they created false maps to misdirect people. The United States created Radio Free America to broadcast information (or propaganda depending on whose side you were on) to other nations. With the international reach of the Internet, it should be easy for citizens in any nation to obtain any information. However, some nations like China are still concerned about the need to control information. China maintains this control by owning all of the routers that connect to the Internet. Hence, the government can control and monitor the entire flow of data into and out of the country. For example, it can block access to any sites it deems offensive. A few companies have established servers inside China, but to maintain their position, they simply agree to do whatever the government asks, including not running certain stories. There is nothing wrong with companies protecting their self-interest—other media companies like satellite televisions have done the same thing for years. The point is that to some extent, it is still possible for a nation to control the Internet and regulate the information available within its borders.

Source: Adapted from Chen May Yee, "Big Internet Companies Often Censor Their Asian Sites to Please Local Officials, *The Wall Street Journal,* July 9, 2001.

FIGURE 14.12

Electronic voting requirements. Electronic voting sounds convenient and easy to set up—until you look at the detailed requirements. Many avenues for fraud exist. Additionally, complex systems are hard to create and susceptible to errors.

- Prevent fraud by voters (identify voters)
- Prevent fraud by counters
- Prevent fraud by application programmers
- Prevent fraud by operating system programmers
- Prevent attacks on servers
- Prevent attacks on clients
- Prevent loss of data
- Provide ability to recount ballots
- Ensure anonymity of votes
- Provide access to all voters
- Prevent denial of service attacks
- Prevent user interface errors
- Identify and let voters correct data entry errors
- Improve on existing 1 in 6,000 to 1 in 10,000 error rates

Voting

With the fiasco of the 2000 U.S. election, people began to realize the deplorable status of existing voting systems. The level of mistakes due to machine, user, and counter error is unacceptable in a modern society. Several people have mentioned the possibility of creating electronic voting systems to provide faster and more accurate tallies of votes. But many challenges exist as shown in Figure 14.12. Several experts have testified before Congress that they do not believe current technology is capable of surmounting all of the problems. But ultimately, the question comes down to whether a superior system can be developed, even though it may not be perfect; and whether it can prevent major problems. There is a long history of building and revising voting machines in an attempt to minimize fraud and abuse. But existing machines still miscount an average of one in 6,000 to 10,000 ballots. The other serious drawback to existing systems highlighted in the 2000 election was the usability issue, where thousands of ballots were disqualified and thousands more counted incorrectly because people did not understand them.

A few people have suggested that it would be nice to implement a voting system that works as easily as ATMs or even using their own PCs to connect over the Internet. But electronic voting has two main complications over traditional electronic commerce. First, it is critical to authenticate each voter. Current e-commerce handles this step with credit cards—which are not available to all voters, and not secure enough to use as a public voting identifier. (What would stop a business from assuming your identity?) Second, the votes have to

Reality Bytes — Cyberattacks or Random Hacks?

In April 2001, a U.S. spy plane crashed into a Chinese fighter jet and made an emergency landing at the Chinese air base. In the ensuing tension, hackers on both sides participated in an informal attack on computer servers in the other nation. Most of the attacks were simple defacements of random websites, and probably not sponsored by government agencies on either side. Chinese hackers claimed to have defaced 1,000 servers in the United States and U.S. hackers claimed even more hits. Overall, the attacks were relatively minor; but they begin to point out the possibilities of dedicated attacks on information systems. Of course, there was no war and both nations were working to defuse tensions. The incident also points out

another potential issue: Which is more dangerous—a group of trained government information security agents, or uncontrolled groups of bored hackers? Governments can negotiate a settlement. Decentralized attacks by hackers or terrorists are much harder to stop, but would probably be less damaging.

Sources: Adapted from Jaikumar Vijayan, "U.S.-China Cyberfeud Shows No Site Is Safe," *Computerworld*, May 14, 2001, Dan Verton, "U.S.-China Cyberwar: Fact or Fear-Mongering?" *Computerworld*, May 1, 2001; and Sam Costello, "U.S.-China Cyberwar a Dud, but Trouble Lingers," *Computerworld*, May 11, 2001.

be auditable, but anonymous so that no votes can be traced back to an individual. This second condition is even trickier if you are concerned about vote selling. Ideally, voters should not be able to show their final vote to anyone else. If they can, it opens the possibility of buying votes. Currently, there is little incentive to buy votes because there is no way to prove how someone voted, so no way to enforce the agreement.

Voting from your home over the Internet might take years to develop, largely because of the challenge of protecting the client computers and denial of service attacks. Security experts can protect the servers and data transmissions can be protected through encryption. But how can a government ensure the security of a PC in your house? Given the level of viruses, hoaxes, and false statements on websites, it would seem to be relatively easy to attack millions of home computers to control an election.

On the other hand, society has an additional critical objective in designing a new voting system: the need to make it easier for people to vote to increase participation rates. To combat this problem, several states have implemented paper-based ballots shipped to each person's home. Ultimately the point is that no system is perfect, so the question quickly becomes whether an electronic vote system is better than the existing methods, and whether it is possible to prevent significant fraud. In a test of electronic voting systems in the Georgia 2001 election, almost all said the system was easy to use and over 94 percent said the entire state should move to the electronic system.

Information Warfare

As firms and entire economies become more dependent on information systems, the underlying infrastructure becomes critical to the nation. Think about how the information society will work in 10 years or so. Communication will be based on Internet protocols. B2B e-commerce will take place over the Internet, with automated agents placing orders and handling most transactions. Private and government services will be provided through websites. Web services will be offered through interlinked sites.

Now, imagine what happens if some nation or group decides to attack this information system. Inexperienced people using software scripts found on various Internet sites have already attacked individual companies. These denial-of-service attacks can be mounted by anyone. If an experienced, dedicated group of experts attacked a nation, they could stop service to huge segments of the economy. This threat is one aspect of the Internet that scares many agencies.

The United States and other national defense departments have begun planning for **information warfare (IW)**—both in terms of potential defenses and attacks. The ultimate objective of information warfare is to control the information available to the other side so that you can encourage them to take certain actions. This definition includes the ability to intercept

Reality Bytes   France versus Yahoo!

Because of the memories of conflict and occupation of World War II, French law prohibits citizens from collecting and selling Nazi memorabilia. For many years, this law was only an issue to French citizens. The international expansion of the Internet changed everything. In particular, online personal auction sites like the one run by Yahoo! make it possible for anyone to sell virtually any item around the world. In response to this problem, the French government filed a lawsuit in French courts against Yahoo! requiring it to ban anyone from selling Nazi memorabilia to French citizens. The court order also required Yahoo! to block "any other site or service on Yahoo! that constituted an apology of Nazism or a contesting of a Nazi crime." The court also required Yahoo! to implement technology that would use IP addresses to identify French users. At the time of the ruling, Yahoo! had no assets or physical presence in France, which would make it difficult to enforce any fines against the company. Yahoo! protested that

it would not be technologically possible to be 100 percent accurate either in identifying the content or the users. Yet, in response to the court decision, Yahoo! now bans all Nazi-related items from its services worldwide. Other Internet companies such as e-Bay and Amazon have implemented policies to block French-language browsers from certain auction areas, and have not yet been sued by the French. Asian nations such as China and Singapore go a step further and control Internet access directly. In China, the routers that connect the nation to the Internet are run by the government, and entire sites are blocked by IP address.

Sources: Adapted from Mylene Mangalindan and Kevin Delaney, "Yahoo! Ordered to Bar the French from Nazi Items," *The Wall Street Journal*, November 21, 2000; and Chen May Yee, "Big Internet Companies Often Censor Their Asian Sites to Please Local Officials," *The Wall Street Journal*, July 9, 2001.

communications, as well as to provide new data that will be accepted as valid. IW goes way beyond hacking into a system or destroying enemy computers and networks. In many ways, IW has been a part of war and conquest for centuries. The increasing use of computers, both in the military and in economies, has made IW more important. IW has existed in many respects from the early centuries of warfare. Some aspects became prominent in WWII, such as code breaking, the Navajo code talkers, the use of the BBC to send coded signals, and misinformation. Misinformation and control of the press (domestic and worldwide) have become key aspects to IW; particularly given the worldwide reach of CNN.

Some U.S. reports indicate that the Chinese military is attempting to develop viruses that can be inserted into foreign networks to disrupt the flow of data or provide false information. Information attacks can be targeted against military or civilian objectives. Military uses of information warfare are common today. One of the first steps the U.S. Air Force takes is to disable the enemy's air defense systems to gain control over the enemy airspace.

Civilian attacks are still new, but the potential is huge. The military goal would be to destroy the economic ability of a nation to build and deploy weapons, but an attack would also destroy the underlying infrastructure. The Internet was originally designed to survive military attacks through decentralization and the ability to route around broken links. However, as e-commerce has evolved, several vulnerabilities have been created that would enable governments or terrorists to disrupt major sections of the Internet by attacking some critical points.

In general, the same security controls that businesses use to protect systems on a daily basis are important to defend against international attacks. Ultimately, many aspects of the Internet infrastructure need to be improved to prevent attacks by terrorists, since the underlying components were not designed with security in mind. Several Internet committees are working on these new standards.

Rise of the World-State?

In ancient history (literally), communities of people formed into city-states to share common resources and provide a common defense. Because communication was limited and transportation costs were high, the city-states were largely self-sufficient. However, merchants traveled among cities to barter products that were only available in some locations. Over many years, transportation and communication costs declined, giving rise to nation-states.

Through various battles and political arrangements, people accepted the role of the national governments, although some issues are still being fought.

For years, many writers have suggested that increasing international trade, declining transportation costs, and improving global communication will eventually lead to a world-state. National governments might still exist, but commerce would be more regional and global, and world laws would be more important than national policies. The rise of the European Union and other free trade areas (such as NAFTA) are sometimes seen as forerunners of this world.

International e-commerce provides some support for this hypothesis. In an environment where digital data and services can be transferred instantly around the world, it is easy to see the irrelevance of individual national laws. With encryption and a wireless (satellite) connection, how can a national government impose rules or taxes on the digital transfer? If a serious digital monetary system is developed and accepted, how will a nation impose its independent economic policies? Some of these issues are being addressed today by global political organizations. Nations are slowly learning to cooperate and create common procedures and laws.

On the other hand, a world-state would be a massively complex system that would undoubtedly be politically unstable. There are still many regional tensions and periodic fights over physical resources. It would take many years of prosperity and economic growth before nations were willing to accept a truly global government. However, in the meantime, many issues will need to be negotiated in a global setting because they are beyond the control of any national government. Some international organizations facilitate these discussions, but most are somewhat cumbersome.

Crime

Crime has many aspects—both in the Internet/information world and in the "real" world. Security issues related to protecting information systems and websites are discussed in detail in Chapter 5. The issues in this chapter refer to questions of how governments can combat crime in society. Criminals today have access to the same technologies as everyone else. Drug dealers and weapons merchants use encrypted spreadsheets to track their sales. Terrorists use encrypted e-mail to transfer information. Con artists use the Internet to steal money from victims. Entirely new forms of harassment and stalking have been created with chat rooms, e-mail, cell phones, and other electronic communication systems. Most people want the government to protect them from these many forms of crime. The complication is that the electronic tools make it more difficult for police to work. So you as a citizen need to identify the trade-offs you are willing to accept.

Police Powers

For years, politicians have used the threat of crime to argue for granting increased powers to police agencies. Interception and decryption of communications (wiretapping) is a classic example. The United States passed the *Communications Assistance for Law Enforcement Act* in 1994. It has taken effect and requires that when requested by the government, any telecommunication company must route any communication that passes through its facilities to an offsite U.S. government facility. The FBI similarly created the Carnivore system to monitor and record all Internet communications of a targeted person. On a global scale, the NSA in cooperation with other national partners routinely captures and monitors international communications. Under federal mandate, wireless providers are phasing in locater systems designed to route emergency crews to callers who use cell phones. Of course, these same locator systems could be used by police to monitor the locations of suspected criminals.

Two questions must always be addressed with each new technology: (1) Is the technology effective or are there other ways to accomplish the same result? (2) How can society control the use of the technology and is it worth the loss of privacy? The technology press contains many stories of abuses of power and information—including those by IRS agents and state and local police agencies. The police can also tell stories of how the criminals use modern technology to thwart investigations, and how additional police powers can be used to reduce crime.

Reality Bytes   Cyberwar

As businesses and economies become more reliant on computers and the Internet, they become more vulnerable to disruption if the computers are attacked. The world wars of the 20th century made it clear that economic production is an important element in fighting battles and winning wars. If businesses cannot produce war equipment or food, then a nation will find it difficult to win a battle. Consequently, an attack on the underlying computer or network infrastructure can be a major factor in a war. John Serabian, a CIA information operations issue manager, related a quote from an unnamed Chinese general: "We can make the enemy's command centers not work by changing their data system. We can cause the enemy's headquarters to make incorrect judgment(s) by sending disinformation. We can dominate the enemy's banking system and even its entire social order." Military analysts are particularly worried about cyberattacks from nations or terrorists that cannot match the United States in conventional weapons. Attacks on computers, networks, and power generators can be instigated relatively inexpensively.

Source: Adapted from Jack McCarthy, "CIA: China, Russia Develop Cyberattack Capability," *Computerworld,* February 24, 2000.

Privacy

Chapter 5 discusses **privacy** in more detail, but the subject is worth revisiting. Increasingly more data on our lives is placed online and accessible to companies, governments, and trial lawyers. Perhaps it should not matter. If you are a perfect citizen, you should have nothing to hide. If you are less than perfect, then the world should know so that your risk to society can be accurately assessed. But then, as George Orwell so clearly pointed out, there is little room left for individuals. And what happens when there are mistakes? Or if some official disagrees with your political views?

Freedom of Speech

As constitutional scholars have long known, freedom of speech is a difficult concept. In practice, many limits are placed on individual speech to protect society. The classic example: you are not allowed to yell "Fire!" in a crowded theater (when there is no fire) because the result is dangerous to many people. Similarly, there are restrictions on "speech" on the Internet. A big element is that you cannot defame or harass others. While this statement seems obvious, what happens when people sign up with an anonymity server? They could then use free e-mail services, chat rooms, and websites to attack other people or companies.

The flip side of this situation is the issue of how to control these problems. Should a police agency have the ability to routinely break the anonymity server to identify all people? But that raises the question of what constitutes defamation and harassment? It is legal for a person to report truthful information about a company or an individual, but sometimes marginal in whistleblower situations. But what if the person being criticized is a public official and uses the police power to retaliate and harass the original person? Of course that action would be illegal as well, but how do you prevent it?

The main thing to remember is that there are many sides to all of these discussions. Also remember that many people have strong personal preferences on each side, and debates are often filled with emotional and unsubstantiated claims. In the coming years, these topics will become increasingly important. It is critical that you form an educated opinion and make sure that your voice is heard.

Responsibility and Ethics

Users

Computer users have certain responsibilities in terms of computer security and privacy. First, they have an obligation to obey the laws that pertain to computers. The U.S. government and some states, along with other nations, have laws against computer crimes. Most

Reality Bytes   **Professor Edward Felten**

The music industry has been attempting to create a system to enable electronic distribution of music that cannot be copied and distributed to other users. They created several variations known as the Secure Digital Music Initiative (SDMI). As part of their development process, they issued a public challenge and offered a reward to anyone who could circumvent the copy-protection system. Princeton Professor Edward Felten and his graduate students accepted the challenge and broke the protection systems in a few days. Along with colleagues at Rice University and Xerox, Felten was going to present a scientific paper at a professional conference in April 2001 to discuss the flaws in the recording industry technologies. In phone calls and e-mail messages to the researchers, their universities, and the conference organizers, the Recording Industry Association of America (RIAA) threatened the

researchers with federal prosecution under the 1998 Digital Millennium Copyright Act (DMCA), intimidating the researchers into withdrawing their paper. While a version of the paper was eventually presented at a different conference, Felten is still concerned that he may be prosecuted for presenting additional research. Scientists from around the world are reluctant to attend conferences or publish research in the United States because of the threat of prosecution under the DMCA. The Electronic Frontier Foundation (EFF) is supporting Professor Felten and attempting to remove the dangerous provisions of the DMCA.

Source: Adapted from Scarlet Pruitt, "Scientists to Detail Controversial Research," *Infoworld*, August 14, 2001; and *www.eff.org/Legal/Cases/ Felten_v_RIAA.*

other traditional laws also apply to computer crimes. One law that has received much attention is the copyright law. European and U.S. copyright laws prohibit the copying of software except for necessary backup. It is the responsibility of users to keep up with the changes in the laws and to abide by them. In the last few years, software publishers have increased their efforts to stop illegal copying of software, called **software piracy.**

Although it might seem to be trivial, making illegal copies of software (or videotapes or other copyrighted works) can cause several problems. First, it takes money away from the legal owners of the software, which reduces their incentive to create new products. Second, you run the risk of hurting your employer. If employees illegally copy company-purchased software, the owners of the copyright can sue the employer. Third, copying software provides an illegal advantage over your competitors. A small design firm might decide to copy a $20,000 CAD design system instead of buying it. Consequently, honest firms are hurt because the original firm will be able to make lower bids on jobs because their costs are lower. Fourth, as an individual, you have a reputation to defend. If your friends, colleagues, or employers learn that you are willing to break the law by copying software, they can easily believe that you are willing to break other laws.

Users of computer systems also have an obligation as part of **computer ethics** to customers and clients. Most information in computer databases is confidential information. It should not be revealed to anyone except authorized employees. Some nations have laws to protect this privacy. If you find a company violating these laws, it is your responsibility to question the practice.

Users have an obligation to use the information provided by computer applications appropriately. When a user sets up calculations in a spreadsheet, the user must realize that those calculations might be wrong. The calculations must be tested and the information produced should always be checked for reasonableness. You should not believe information solely because it comes from a computer. All data should be verified.

Programmers and Developers

Programmers would never get jobs if they could not be trusted. This trust is one of the most crucial requirements to being a programmer. As a programmer or developer, not only do you have to be honest, you must also avoid any appearance of dishonesty. For example, practical jokes involving security violations can be dangerous to your career.

Programmers have more responsibilities than many other employees. Software is used in many critical areas. If a programmer attempts a job that is beyond his or her capabilities,

---

Reality Bytes   **Business Software Alliance**

For several years, the Business Software Alliance (BSA) has battled software piracy. It is an international organization that investigates companies and prosecutes them for using illegally copied software. When BSA receives a credible report of piracy (1-888-No Piracy or www.bsa.org), its lawyers attempt to settle out of court with the offending company, by asking it to perform an analysis of software usage. If it finds unlicensed copies, the firm is asked to purchase legal copies and pay a fine. If an offending company refuses to cooperate, BSA may file a lawsuit. In recent years, most of the piracy reports have been filed by employees—often systems administrators or programmers who have recently lost their jobs.

Source: Adapted from Michelle Delio, "Dumped Workers Find Revenge," *Wired,* July 3, 2001.

---

crucial errors can be introduced. For example, consider what might happen if an underqualified person took a job programming medical life-support systems. If he or she made a mistake, a person might die. Although mistakes can be made by anyone, they are more likely to arise when a programmer attempts too difficult of a job.

Along the same lines, programmers have an obligation to test everything they do. It also means that companies have the responsibility to provide adequate time for programmers to perform the tests. The important step is to identify components that are critical and to build in safeguards.

There have been enormous increases in the demand for software in the last decade. At the same time, new tools allow programmers to create much more complex applications. But our ability to create this new software has far outstripped our ability to ensure that it is error free. Even commercial programs, such as word processors and spreadsheets, still have errors that can cause problems. In spite of the best efforts of conscientious, talented people, software used appropriately can produce erroneous information.

Liability for erroneous information produced by software has not been fully established yet. Laws and court decisions during the next few years should settle many aspects of who is responsible when software makes mistakes or fails. A related issue is the extent to which the user is responsible for correctly entering information needed by the program and for using the information produced by the program appropriately.

Companies

Every company has obligations to society, customers, employees, and business partners. In terms of society, a firm must obey all relevant laws. For customers, firms must ensure privacy of data. That means companies will collect only the data that they truly need. The data must be safeguarded so that only those who need it for their jobs have access. If customer information is sold or distributed for other purposes, customers should be notified. Consumers must be allowed to remove their names from any distribution lists.

For employees, a company must provide training and monitoring (compliance programs) to ensure they understand the laws and are following them. Firms must provide sufficient funds to allow the employees to meet their individual responsibilities. Companies must provide enough time and money to test software adequately. Firms have an obligation to allow their employees a certain amount of privacy. For instance, companies have no reason to routinely monitor and read employees' electronic mail messages.

Companies are required to abide by all partnership agreements. In terms of computers, they must safeguard all data acquired from partners. They must not use the data in a manner that would injure the firms involved.

Governments

Federal, state, and local governments have obligations to establish laws that provide a means for those unfairly injured to allow them to gain compensation from those who did the damage. Until the 1980s, relatively few laws at any level were specifically directed at computer

Reality Bytes — Brain Waves P300 or 1984?

For years, researchers have studied EEG waves emanating from human brains. Small electrodes placed on the person record activity within the brain. Dr. Lawrence Farwell in Fairfield, Iowa, recognized that a certain pattern, called the P300 wave, can be seen only in specific circumstances. In particular, when people recognize a setting or phrase that they have seen before, their brain recalls the image and produces a specific pattern. People who have not seen or experienced the same scene do not produce the specific pattern. So, Dr. Farwell develops a test for specific cases that can be used to determine whether a person has experienced a particular event. He calls the system *brain fingerprinting*. For example, someone accused of a crime would have specific knowledge of the crime that an innocent person would not know. Suspects watch a computer screen while being monitored by an expert. Similar to standard polygraph tests, the screen displays three types of data: (1) irrelevant data as a control, (2) targets that the suspect would have seen during the police investigation, and (3) probes which are things only a culprit would know. The targets should generate a P300 wave for everyone, the irrelevant data for none, and the probes would generate P300 waves only for "guilty" people. Using the process in a 1993 test setting, Dr. Farwell was able to correctly identify 17 people who were new FBI agents versus 4 people who were not. The FBI agents recognized certain features from their training.

The system has been used in two real-world criminal cases. In one, Dr. Farwell concluded that James B. Grinder was guilty of a rape and murder charge. Previous evidence was contradictory and inconclusive. Dr. Farwell also used the test in an actual court case (but without a jury). Terry Harrington was convicted of murder in 1978 in Iowa. He has continued to profess his innocence. The results of the P300 test showed that Harrington had no memory of the crime details, but did have specific memories that matched his alibi. The judge ruled that the test was insufficient evidence to clear Harrington of the crime, and the decision is being appealed. Dr. Farwell is aggressively pushing the method as a possible means of identifying terrorists; suggesting that it be used on all people who apply for visas. Other researchers are more skeptical. Dr. Rosenfeld of Northwestern claims that he has trained students to beat the P300 test with several tricks. The test also raises the issue of self-incrimination. It is unlikely that law enforcement will ever be able to force defendants to take the test. The test bears a strong resemblance to the technologies hypothesized in George Orwell's *1984*.

Sources: Adapted from Clive Thompson. "The Lie Detector that Scans Your Brain," *The New York Times,* December 9, 2001; and Barnaby J. Feder, "Truth and Justice, by the Blip of a Brain Wave," *The New York Times,* October 9, 2001; and www.brainwavescience.com.

---

usage. Instead, laws intended for other purposes were stretched to cover computer crimes. Frequently, citing mail fraud laws was the only recourse. Some criminals were not convicted because the crime was considered "victimless" by the jury, or the injured corporation declined to prosecute.

Starting in the mid-1980s, the federal government and nearly every state passed new laws concerning computer crime. The 1984 Computer Fraud and Abuse Act outlawed unauthorized access to data stored in federal government computers. In 1986, the Computer Fraud and Abuse Act and the Electronic Communications Privacy Act were enacted. The Computer Fraud and Abuse Act makes it a federal crime to alter, copy, view, or damage data stored in computers subject to federal law. The law provides fines of up to $100,000 and up to 20 years in prison. The Computer Abuse Amendments Act of 1994 expanded the original definitions to include transmission of harmful code such as viruses. It also distinguishes between actions taken "with reckless disregard" for potential damages (misdemeanor) and intentionally harmful acts (felony). It also modified the language so that crimes causing damages of more than $1,000 or involving medical records are within federal jurisdiction. Additionally, it placed controls on states in terms of selling drivers' license records.

Most states have enacted similar laws for the few computers that might not be subject to federal law. European countries have been ahead of the United States in developing legislation to deal with computer crime.

Legislation, enforcement, and judicial interpretation have not kept up with changes in technology. A major question that is unresolved is the extent to which copyright law applies to the "look and feel" of software. For example, Lotus Corporation sued Borland because Borland's Quattro Pro spreadsheet used menu titles similar to those used by the Lotus 123 spreadsheet. Some people are calling for legislation making it illegal to *write* a computer virus program, although there is some question that such a law might be an unnecessary restriction on freedom of speech or freedom of the press. In fact, there is considerable

Reality Bytes **Public Data**

For decades, local governments have collected public records on citizens. Everything from birth, death, wedding, divorce, house purchase, business incorporation, voter registration is considered public information. Traditionally, this data was stored in paper files at county courthouses. Over time, some of the records were computerized. With the Internet, it becomes possible to put all of the public data online. In general, most governments have been unwilling to spend the money to place the records online. Several private firms have stepped into this vacuum. For instance, registeredtovoteornot.com copies all of the New York City voter registration lists and makes them available online. All you need is a last name and birth date to see if a person is registered—and obtain his or her home address. While you might argue about the loss of privacy, this data has always been provided to candidates to send campaign mail. An Internet system would make it easier for candidates with less money to reach voters. Nationwide, KnowX.com collects public data and makes it available for a fee. In Pittsburgh, Allegheny County placed all of the property value assessments online, so you can see how much your neighbor or favorite sports celebrity paid for his or her house. Should all public records really be publicly accessible? This question was initially raised in a Supreme Court case denying a reporter access to some FBI information on the grounds that it would be an invasion of privacy. Although the individual records were public, the FBI collection was protected by "practical obscurity" because it would be difficult for anyone to obtain all of the pieces—they were protected by barriers of time and the inconvenience of collecting the data. Governments (and citizens) at all levels need to think about the meaning and use of public data.

Sources: Adapted from Amy Harmon, "As Public Records Go Online, Some Say They're too Public," *The New York Times,* August 24, 2001, and www.knowx.com.

discussion over whether electronic mail and website operators should be treated as members of the press and receive first amendment protections.

In terms of enforcement, most federal, state, and local agencies have few, if any, officers devoted to solving computer crimes. In fact, many software piracy cases have been pursued by U.S. Secret Service agents. One complication is that most law enforcement agencies lack proper training in computer usage and investigation of computer crimes.

Summary

Technological change and increasingly aggressive use of information systems by businesses have several consequences. Technology affects individuals, their jobs, educational systems, governments, and society as a whole. Businesses have to be careful to protect the privacy of consumers and workers. Security provisions, disclosure policies, and audits are used to ensure that data is only used for authorized purposes. To ensure accuracy, it is crucial to allow customers (and workers) to examine relevant data and make changes.

Technology is generally believed to increase the total number of jobs available. However, the workers displaced by the introduction of technology are rarely qualified for the new jobs. Businesses and governments need to provide retraining and relocation to help those workers who lose their jobs. Sometimes technology allows physically disabled people to work in jobs they might not otherwise be able to perform.

Improved communication networks, huge databases, and multimedia tools provide possibilities for education and training in the public and business sectors. However, because of high development costs, technology tends to be used for specialized training.

Governments have long been involved in data collection, and technology enables them to work more efficiently. Of course, many political observers would argue that perhaps governments should not be *too* efficient. For example, it would be difficult for businesses to operate in an environment where the laws were changed every day. Technology also has the potential to improve communication between citizens and their representatives.

There are other interactions between technology and society. One feature is that lower prices, improved capabilities, and ease-of-use have made improved communication available to virtually any size group—providing a wider audience for small extremist groups. The new technologies also offer the ability to alter pictures, sound, and video; making it difficult to determine the difference between fact and fiction. Another important social issue is

Reality Bytes   e-Mexico

Mexico's President Vincente Fox established an "e-Mexico" plan to bring the Internet to Mexico's 100 million people. The main goal of e-Mexico is to improve education and health care through better communication and information sharing. The $4 billion initiative will require telecommunication connections to 10,000 cities by 2006. To date, no funding has been provided for the telecommunication lines or for the thousands of computers needed. As of 2001, only 250 cities had been connected. Since 1996, only 6.4 million PCs have been sold in Mexico. But Microsoft supports the project, and President Steve Ballmer pledged $58 million over five years to train thousands of teachers and software programmers.

Sources: Adapted from Chris Kraul and Aguirre Rafael, "Microsoft Pledges $58 Million to Get Mexicans Online," *Los Angeles Times*, August 24, 2001.

A Manager's View

As a manager, you need to understand how businesses, technology, and society interact. Dealing with changes in privacy and security threats will become increasingly important to managing a company. Evaluating changes in society will also give you an advantage in the marketplace; it is important to know your customers. As a citizen, you need to be aware of the negative and positive effects of technology. In particular, changes in technology often lead to changes in political power and control. As a manager and a citizen, you are obligated to make ethical decisions and to understand the consequences of your actions.

providing access to technology for everyone. It would be easy to create a world or nation consisting of *haves* and *have-nots* in terms of access to information. Those with information would be able to grow and earn more money, while those lacking the data continually lose ground.

Increasing dependence on technology brings with it new threats to the security of the firm. Managers need to recognize and evaluate these threats and understand some of the techniques used to minimize them. The most common threats come from inside the company, in terms of workers, consultants, and business partnerships. These threats are difficult to control, because firms have to trust these individuals to do their jobs. Training, oversight, audits, and separation of duties are common means to minimize threats. Depending on the communication systems used, there are threats from outsiders and viruses that can access computers with modems, over networks, or by intercepting communications. Dial-back modems, access controls, encryption, and antivirus software are common techniques to combat these threats.

Working in today's business environment means more than just doing your job. Each individual and firm has ethical obligations to consumers, workers, other companies, and society. In addition to obeying the laws, it is important for workers and companies to remember that the data in information systems refers to real people. The lives of people can be adversely affected by inaccurate data, poorly designed information systems, or abuse of the information.

Key Words

computer ethics, *571*	digital rights management	patent, *557*
copyright, *557*	(DRM), *558*	privacy, *570*
dehumanization, *553*	information warfare	software piracy, *571*
digital divide, *563*	(IW), *567*	

Website References

Technology and Society

ACM/society	**www.acm.org/usacm**
Center for democracy & technology	**www.cdt.org**
Center for information technology and society	**www.cits.ucsb.edu**
Center for the study of technology and society	**www.tecsoc.org**
Computer Professionals for Social Responsibility	**www.cpsr.org**
Information Technology Association of America	**www.itaa.org**
Internet Society	**www.isoc.org**
MassMed	**www.massmed.org**

Additional Reading

Arkin, William, and Robert Windrem. "The U.S.-China Information War." *MSNBC,* December 11, 2001. http://www.msnbc.com/news/607031.asp. [Description of some aspects of the U.S. information warfare preparations.]

Grosso, Andrew. "The Individual in the New Age." *Communications of the ACM,* July 2001 44(7), 17–20. [A readable legal perspective on individual versus society.]

Jones, Douglas W. "Problems with Voting Systems and the Applicable Standards." May 22, 2001. http://www.house.gov/science/full/may22/jones.htm [Issues on electronic voting systems.]

Machalaba, Daniel. "U.S. Ports Are Losing the Battle to Keep Up with Overseas Trade." *The Wall Street Journal,* July 9, 2001. [Effect of automation on jobs at the loading docks.]

Stoll, Clifford. *The Cuckoo's Egg: Tracking a Spy through a Maze of Computer Espionage,* New York: Doubleday, 1989. [Fascinating story of a spy searching US networks.]

Review Questions

1. Do employees need to worry about the data collected by their employers?

2. If everyone is identified by some biometric measure, will that cause more dehumanization? Will it reduce individual privacy?

3. Do you think increasing use of computers causes a loss of jobs? What about in the past or in the future?

4. How are computers helping disabled people to perform jobs?

5. Do computers and digital content change the balance of power relationship between consumers and businesses? Should consumers have a right to make personal (backup) copies of digital works?

6. How does information technology add legitimacy to fringe groups?

7. Do you think state, local, and federal governments are making efficient use of computers? Will citizens ever be able to vote online?

8. In what ways have computers affected society and organizations? Will these patterns continue? Are there other important patterns that might arise?

9. Should governments be granted more powers to monitor and investigate people and transactions on the Internet?

10. What are the ethical responsibilities of users in terms of information systems?

Exercises

1. Team project: Split into two groups. Individuals in each group will type a page of text into a word processor (pick any full page from the textbook). To start, everyone will work on the project independently, but there is a deadline of no more than two days. Second, team members will pair up and type the document a second time. This time, while one person types the document, the other one will time his or her performance and count mistakes at the end. The goal is to find the team member who is fastest and makes the fewest mistakes. The trick is that each person's work will be monitored at all times. Now, when all members of the team have completed their tasks, get the team back together and answer the following questions: Was there more pressure while you were being watched? Were you nervous? More attentive? Were you faster the second time? Did you make more mistakes? Would you object to working under these conditions on a daily basis?

2. Research the tools (hardware and software) available for a new employee of yours who is blind. List the sources, capabilities, and costs.

3. As a manager, you have an opening for a new employee. While checking the background of one applicant, you learn that two years ago he or she was fired from a job for deliberately accessing computer files of other employees and destroying data. One of your colleagues suggested that the incident means the person must know a lot about computers, which would be useful in your department. Are you willing to hire this person? Why or why not? If you are somewhat willing to hire the applicant, what questions would you ask in an interview, or what additional information would you want to see?

4. Imagine that a company develops a device that can drive a car, unassisted, on any major road. After the system is in use for two years, someone is killed in a car accident where one of the vehicles uses this new system. Should the injured people be allowed to sue the company that sells the system? What about the programmers who created it? What if the company knows that there is a 1 percent chance that an accident will occur while the system is being used? However, without the system, there is a 10 percent chance that you will be involved in an accident. Do these statistics change your answer? Do you think a system of this type should be required to have a 0 percent chance of error? Is such a level possible? Would you buy and use a system if these probabilities were true?

5. Do you think governmental agencies should share data about citizens? For example, should the FBI be able to access IRS records to locate suspected criminals? Should the FBI be allowed to access files from state and local governments? For instance, should all arrest records be automatically relayed to a central database? Should medical records be accessible to law enforcement agencies? Say that it is technically possible for the FBI to build a national database that contains DNA records for all citizens. If all medical records (from accidents, blood tests, and medical treatment) were computerized and automatically forwarded to the FBI, the agents could easily locate virtually any criminal.

6. Research the issues involved in electronic voting. What problems need to be overcome? What technologies could be useful? Does an electronic voting system have to be perfect, or simply better than the existing manual system?

7. Find at least five news sites on the Web. Evaluate them in terms of: (1) style/presentation, (2) accuracy, (3) believability, and (4) balanced news.

Rolling Thunder Database

8. What privacy problems might exist at Rolling Thunder? What rules or procedures should we enact to avoid problems?

9. Your boss says that, with the decline in sales, it would be wise to cut costs and suggests that you could buy only a single copy of some of the office software and install it on multiple machines. What do you do?

Health Care

The health care industry (NAIC 80) consists of public, private, and nonprofit institutions. Those institutions include hospitals, offices and clinics of medical doctors, nursing homes, and home health care facilities; other specialized healthcare facilities; and managed care organizations. These consist of prepaid plans, such as health maintenance organizations (HMOs), preferred provider organizations (PPOs), and independent practice associations (IPAs). The health care industry includes thousands of independent medical practices/partnerships, as well as public and nonprofit institutions, plus major private corporations that have assets of billions of dollars and are major employers in the U.S. economy.

Domestic spending on prescription drugs continues to expand at a compounded annual rate of 13 to 14 percent. However, due to patent expirations, the industry could see a setback over the next few years from drugs that had generated $40 billion. With fewer blockbuster drugs on the horizon and managed care firms focusing more on cost control, profit growth for pharmaceutical companies may be diminished. Furthermore, there are new federal and state regulations aimed at controlling drug costs and encouraging the use of less expensive generic drug offerings.

The health care and pharmaceutical industry is highly profitable because there is very little price elasticity associated with price increases. A patient will not change the demand for a product with a small change in price when there are no close or available substitutes. In fact, most patients are reimbursed for the bulk of their drug purchases by third parties. Therefore, price is not as big an issue to the end consumer. The industry is impacted by federal regulatory bodies and laws to a greater extent than by economic factors.

Financial Analysis

On the strength of stocks across the industry, health care funds return an amazing 51.9 percent in 2000. The group's record was unmatched by any other type of fund, beating the second-best performing sector—energy funds—by a wide margin. Of the top 15 mutual funds in 2000, 12 were focused on health care, with their performance far outpacing the technology-heavy Nasdaq in 2000.

Pharmaceutical companies have shined over the same period that has witnessed the demise of the Internet stocks. Investor enthusiasm toward health care concerns has rekindled as a result. Since the dot-com slump, drug companies have fared quite well. For instance, Pfizer reported third-quarter earnings for 2001 that were up 28 percent over the same period in 2000. Even though the stock is down 1 percent over the past 12 months, that small loss pales in comparison with a 15 percent slide in the S&P 500.

With the world's population still aging, drugs for previously untreatable conditions are constantly coming onto the market; and pharmaceutical companies are enjoying rare pricing power. Drugs are still a growth business.

Most pharmaceutical companies have stable, consistent, durable earnings growth. Companies that have lost patent protection on blockbuster drugs are working on new ones that should get their earnings back on track. Biotech outfits, once a sideshow, are delivering products that make money and have become mainstream holdings with big investors.

With Wall Street expecting annual earnings growth of as much as 20 percent, drug companies, which are supposed to be safe havens in a bear market, could be under pressure. Patent expirations, manufacturing setbacks, and government intervention in curbing prices contribute to the dilution of their earnings. However, computerized analyses of the human genome will increase the productivity of pharmaceutical companies. And advances in R&D methods could help drug makers meet their earnings goals in the long run.

Growth Potential

The long-term outlook is promising since the U.S. population is aging and will depend on a substantial amount of medicine as people enter their retirement years. Growth will also depend on the level of research and development expenditure, expansion of international markets, and the outcome of U.S. health care reform.

In recent years, pharmaceutical companies have witnessed a growing need to develop and market products in developing and emerging economies. In fact, a big chunk, as much as 40 percent, of all sales from U.S. companies come from international markets.

Competitive Structure

The health care industry has high barriers to entry for small firms. Substantial economic, regulatory, and legal obstacles present main hurdles for upstart firms. Heavy expenditures on research and development are required for the arduous processes of drug discovery, development, manufacturing, and approval through the Federal Drug Administration. Development of a new drug can take 10 to 15 years and cost over $500 million.

Manufacturers can recoup the cost of drug development and earn a normal return on investment by providing patent protection for new drugs. Patents can be issued on either a drug's chemical structure or its method of manufacturing or synthesis, and they enable the holder to manufacture and market the compound for specific therapeutic uses while preventing competitors from capitalizing on the "secret formula."

U.S. manufacturers account for nearly half of the major pharmaceuticals marketed worldwide. While consistently maintaining a positive trade balance, the industry also faces increasing international competition. Markets in Eastern Europe, China, Japan, Mexico, Canada, and the European Community (EC) offer mixed prospects for expanded pharmaceutical trade and investment.

Role of Research and Development

The pharmaceutical advances that have vastly improved life expectancy and health are the result of a steadily increasing investment in research.

Over the past two decades, the percentage of sales allocated to R&D has increased from 11.9 percent in 1980 to an estimated 20.3 percent in 2000. Based on corporate tax data compiled by Standard & Poor's Compustat, pharmaceutical manufacturers invest a higher percentage of sales in R&D than virtually any other industry, including high-tech industries.

Approximately one-third of company-financed R&D in the United States is devoted to evaluation of promising drug compounds in human clinical trials. Phase I, II, and III trials, required for drug approval, account for 28.3 percent of R&D. An additional 5.8 percent of R&D is allocated to Phase IV clinical trials, which may occur after the product has been approved by the FDA. In addition, stringent manufacturing standards require 9.9 percent of R&D for process-development and quality-control functions.

Nearly 82 percent of R&D in the United States is geared toward new products, while about 18.4 percent is devoted to significant improvement or modifications of existing products. About 67 percent of R&D is allocated to development. Development includes all technical activities related to translating research findings into products. Of the 33 percent of R&D allocated to research, most is applied research, including investigations directed toward discovery of new scientific knowledge that has specific commercial objectives.

Technological Investment and Analysis

Millions of dollars are spent each year in new health technology and procedures. Along with the advances in technology come better diagnosis, more accurate EKGs, and more accurate laser surgery.

Technology growth that emphasizes quality improvement may seem to increase costs. Other improvements to productivity may decrease costs. The continued shift in insurance coverage to lower-cost forms of managed care, primarily HMOs, will exert downward pressure on health care expenditures by enhancing cost-containment efforts.

Case: Eli Lilly & Company

Lilly is a leading innovation-driven pharmaceutical corporation. The company employs more the 35,000 people worldwide and markets medicines in 159 countries. Lilly has major research and development facilities in 9 countries and conducts clinical trials in more than 30 countries. Products are manufactured or distributed through owned or leased facilities in the United States, Puerto Rico, and other countries. Its products are sold in approximately 160 countries. Through its PCS Health Systems (PCS) business, which was sold in January 1999, the company provided health care management services in the United States. Research efforts are primarily directed toward discovering and developing products to diagnose and treat diseases in human beings and animals.

Technology Innovations

In 1998, Eli Lilly partnered with EDS, an information technology services provider, to provide a comprehensive health care electronic network for physicians and other health care professionals. The marriage produced a new company, Kinetra, which expanded connections among office-based physicians, health insurers, hospitals, and retail pharmacists.

Research and Development

Information technology (IT) plays a crucial role in the pharmaceutical industry; its goal is to speed up the research process that carries a drug through development, approval, and manufacturing. Today, PCs, server, and global networks shuttle data from research labs to clinical trials and to manufacturing plants. For Eli Lilly, IT's value stems not only from using software to speed regulatory approval but also in helping discovery researchers cope with more complex data. Hence, according to inside officials, Lilly Research Laboratories and IT work hand in hand. Eli Lilly is focusing on the emerging field of bioinformatics, which apply algorithms and databases to analyze the structure of genes. This analysis helps identify proteins that cause diseases.

Since patents on drugs last approximately 20 years, shortening time-to-market is a critical IT function. After that, generic drug makers can sell products for as much as 90 percent less than the brand names, eroding a chunk of the branded drug's market share within a year of a patent's expiration. With Eli Lilly's Prozac patent having expired, the company can expect to see its profits diminish on the top-selling drug. Hence, any extra time Prozac spent on the market before its patent expired helped Eli Lilly generate significant revenues.

Eli Lilly, along with other pharmaceutical firms, is interested in using information technology to speed up clinical trials. In particular, the firms are interested in collecting data electronically instead of requiring patients and physicians to enter data on lengthy forms. The main problems are lack of standards and the need to run the systems worldwide. For example, to share data, it is critical that all trials use the same basic patient information.

The Internet

Most doctors know that one of the biggest problems with medicines is that patients commonly forget to take them, or take the wrong dosage. To help patients, Eli Lilly created a website where patients could register. Patients could get more information about the drug. They could also sign up for a reminder service that would send them an e-mail message when it was time to take a specific drug. The site was largely marketed to users of the Prozac drug. Everything ran fine—until the company decided to redesign the site. In June 2001, the company sent an e-mail notice to registered customers that it was discontinuing the reminder service. Because of a "programming error," the e-mail was sent to 669 patients with all 669 e-mail addresses listed in the "to" field. So everyone on the list could see the e-mail addresses of other patients. Patients, the ACLU, and the FTC all jumped on Eli Lilly's violation of its privacy statement. Eli Lilly eventually settled with the FTC with no fines imposed, but required to improve its security and privacy program.

Financial Performance

For the third quarter of 2001, Eli Lilly saw its earnings per share decrease 7 percent from the year-earlier period even though sales were up 2 percent. The company cited the patent expiration of its best-selling drug, Prozac, as one of the culprits. In August 2001, Prozac faced generic competition in the market, which resulted in a severe erosion in sales for the blockbuster product. Foreseeing the end of the Prozac monopoly, Eli Lilly has put in a place a medicine cabinet full of promising new drugs. Provided that the company can handle daunting challenges from regulators, these new products could offset Prozac's loss.

To remain an industry giant, Eli Lilly plans to emphasize its new product pipeline, R&D capabilities, and sales and marketing expertise. Aside from its Prozac product, the company has seen newer growth products increase by 38 percent, fueling the revitalization of its product pipelines. Eli Lilly plans to increase its global sales force by 5,000 representatives in three years to spearhead its growth.

With nine potential first-in-class drug therapies in its late-stage pipeline, Eli Lilly has a powerful arsenal of weapons to use and, given its cutting-edge drug discovery programs, it is confident that projected growth and financial expectations will be met. Eli Lilly's product pipeline should position the company to remain a leading pharmaceutical company of the decade.

Questions

1. What is the source of the highest margin growth at Eli Lilly?

2. What has caused a change in the use of technology at Lilly?

3. Has technology improved productivity at Eli Lilly?

4. How successful has the technological change been?

5. How does Eli Lilly evaluate its financial ability to embark on a major technological program of advancement?

Additional Reading

Arndt, Michael. "Eli Lilly: Life after Prozac." *Business Week,* July 23, 2001.

Brown, Heidi. "Safe Haven." *Forbes,* December 10, 2001.

Dash, Julekha. "ACLU Knocks Eli Lilly for Divulging E-Mail Addresses." *Computerworld,* July 9, 2001.

Dash, Julekha. "Pharmaceutical Firms Face Tech Hurdles in Clinical Trials." *Computerworld*, July 16, 2001.

McGee, Marianne Kolbasuk, and Gregory Dalton. "Lilly Outsources to EDS." *InformationWeek,* February 23, 1998, p. 34.

PhRMA, PhRMA Annual Survey, 2000.

Thibodeau, Patrick, "FTC, Eli Lilly Settle Privacy Case." *Computerworld,* January 18, 2002.

Case: Owens & Minor, Inc.

Founded in 1882, Owens & Minor started as a wholesale drug company. Today, Owens & Minor is the nation's leading distributor of medical/surgical supplies. The Richmond-based Fortune 500 company manages distribution centers that serve hospitals, integrated health care systems, and group purchasing organizations. The company prides itself on delivering supply chain management solutions to selected segments of the health care industry, helping customers control health care costs and improve inventory management.

Technology Innovations

Owens & Minor Inc.'s business consists of delivering medical supplies to customers via warehouses. Through the use of technology, the distributor of medical and surgical supplies has evolved into a facilitator of critical information; information that its customers use to improve their businesses. Its technology-driven information services help manufacturers better manage their inventories and logistics. And even health care providers are implementing the company's IT to better manage costs related to their supply chains while avoiding significant in-house information tech investments.

Supply-Chain Management

The role Owens & Minor plays in the health care supply-chain process is invaluable. The company acts as an intermediary for health care manufacturers and providers, which typically do not share data on their own. Owens & Minor's star IT product is "Wisdom," a Web-based decision-support tool that details customers' supply-chain information according to their specific needs. Wisdom gives purchasing managers and health care executives a consolidated view of their information since it interfaces with health care companies' enterprise resource planning (ERP) and material management systems.

Owens & Minor's IT tools also free up administrative time for nurses, thereby allowing more time for patient care. Futhermore, the distributor offers a Web-based order-entry tracking system that gives customers real-time access to suppliers' pricing information, product availability, and order tracking. Its Cost Track service, which provides what-if cost scenarios to identify savings in a health care company's supply chain, has proved to be valuable for providers keen on tracking costs involved with the actual ordering, receiving, and delivery of supplies.

Given the company's use of IT to bolster the efficiencies of its business and customers, it is no surprise that Owens & Minor earned the top spot in 2001's Information Week 500 ranking.

New Health Exchange/HealthNexis/Global Healthcare Exchange

In April 2000, five major medical providers announced the establishment of a health care electronic marketplace. The primary partners are Owens & Minor, Cardinal Health, Inc., AmeriSource Health Corp., McKessonHBOC, Inc., and Fisher Scientific. Combined, the five companies already process

$80 billion in transactions each year. The goal is to offer a standardized neutral exchange to streamline the purchase of pharmaceuticals, medical supplies, and other health care products.

In July 2000, Owens & Minor backed out as a founder. Instead, the company agreed to continue as a supply-chain partner. The company's announcement indicates that Owens & Minor will pursue relationships with competitor exchanges as well as continue its own systems.

In 2001, the company was renamed HealthNexis to emphasize that the purpose of the company is to provide centralized information to manufacturers, distributors, and purchasing organizations.

In late 2001, Global Healthcare Exchange LLC acquired HealthNexis. HealthNexis was founded by distributors of health care products, and Global was founded by manufacturers (Abbott Laboratories, Baxter International, Boston Scientific, GE Medical Systems, Guidant, Johnson & Johnson, and Medtronic). Global Healthcare is developing e-commerce front-end software to enable hospitals and other health care providers to order supplies over the Internet. HealthNexis is building back-end B2B e-commerce services to exchange data between manufacturers and distributors. The new system will combine catalogs from the companies and attempt to handle manufacturer rebates (to providers) and charge backs (from manufacturers to distributors).

Despite the mergers, Owens & Minor continues to develop and sell its own services. The company emphasizes its ability to control all aspects of health care supply-chain management. In particular, in 2002, the company is selling systems and services to outsource logistics management at health care providers. Essentially, Owens & Minor manages all aspects of negotiation, purchasing, and delivery of supplies.

Recommendations for the Future

Technology will continue to be the topic du jour at Owens & Minor. Company management envisions Owens & Minor becoming more of a third-party logistics provider that handles product warehousing for supply manufacturers. In order to maintain its competitive edge, Owens & Minor must continue to capitalize on its award-winning supply-chain product lines to customers.

For the third quarter of 2001, Owens & Minor reported earnings of $0.27 per diluted share, reflecting an increase of 12.5 percent over the comparable quarter in 2000. Sales

jumped 11 percent to $968.2 million. The solid third-quarter and year-to-date operating performance is indicative of the company's ability to gain business by employing innovative technology, increasing account penetration, and providing superior service in the industry.

Questions

1. What forces are driving the strategic direction for Owen & Minor?

2. Upon which technologies have Owen & Minor relied?

3. What has caused a change in the use of technology at O&M?

4. Is Owen & Minor financially able to continue to embark on a major technological program of advancement?

5. What does Owen & Minor's Web page present about its business directives?

6. What type of Web page does the company have (promotional/transactional/informative)?

Additional Reading

"Electronic Purchasing Vendors to Merge." *Health Data Management,* November 26, 2001.

McGee, Marianne. "Owens & Minor Ranks Number One in the 13th Annual Information Week 500 Survey." *InformationWeek,* September 17, 2001.

"New Health Exchange Changes Name to HealthNexis." *PR Newswire,* March 26, 2001.

"Owens & Minor Changes Its Relationship with New Health Exchange." Press Release, July 18, 2000 [http://www.owens-minor.com/newreleases/20000718.asp]

Robinson, Robin A. "Business Objects Offers Extranet Version of Tool." *Computerworld,* January 17, 2000.

"Tenet Awards Owens & Minor $2 Billion Contract." *The New York Times,* October 29, 1998, p. C4.

Weston, Rusty. "Mark Growing Pains." *PC Week,* February 5, 1996, p. E1. July 9, 2001.

Appendix

Computer-Related Laws

Laws form the foundation of society. They provide the structure that enables businesses to exist. As society changes the laws must also be changed. Hence, as the use of computers grows, we can expect to see more laws governing their use. Existing laws will be extended, and new ones created. To date, computer laws have been concerned with three primary areas: property rights, privacy, and crime. These areas overlap, and they cannot cover all possible issues. As information technology and robotics become entwined into all our activities, virtually any law can be applied or interpreted to the situation.

Laws continually change and new interpretations and applications regularly arise. You will generally need a lawyer to help you understand and apply the current laws. This short appendix can only provide you with a limited background. You can find additional information in many places on the Web. This information will help you identify problems and generally enable you to obey the laws. However, a lawyer is still the best source of information—particularly if you anticipate problems or conflicts.

Property Rights

A property right gives you ownership and control over an object. While the term originated with physical property, the more important issues now involve intellectual property. If you write a book, a song, or a computer program, you should be able to receive money from sales of that item. Copyright, patent, trademark, and trade secret laws provide definitions of ownership and control transfer of these rights. They provide you with the opportunity to prevent others from using or stealing your work. Each of the four types of property-rights laws applies to different material.

Copyrights are used for books, songs, and computer software. The laws apply to the specific item, such as a book. You cannot copyright a general concept. For example, you can obtain a copyright for a specific word-processing application. But other people are free to write similar applications, as long as they do not utilize your specific code or text. Copyrights generally last for 50 years after the death of the writer. In the case of a work produced by a group of workers in a company, the copyright lasts for 75 years after the publication of the work. After that time, the work falls into the public domain, where anyone can use or copy it with no restraints.

Patents were originally designed for mechanical devices, although today you can receive a patent for any device that is innovative and useful. For many years, computer software applications could not receive patents because "laws of nature" including mathematical algorithms were specifically excluded. In the last few years, the U.S. Patent Office has changed this interpretation and now grants patents for computer software. A U.S. patent right exists for 20 years from the date the application was filed. The strength of a patent is that it prevents other people from creating a similar product, even if they do not directly copy your work. Consequently, a patent is much more difficult to obtain than a copyright.

Trademarks are used to create a unique name. Once you find and trademark a name (or logo), no one else can use that name without your permission. It is relatively easy to obtain a trademark, except that you must find a name that no one else has already chosen.

Trade secret laws provide you with the ability to seek damages if someone steals your secret information. The catch is that you are responsible for protecting the information. The laws are generally used to enforce a nondisclosure agreement (NDA). If a company wants to work with another company or a consultant, it is a good idea to have the outsiders sign an NDA, in which they agree not to reveal any information you share. If you forget to have them sign an NDA and they release your "secret" information, you will have few options. It is your responsibility to protect the data.

These four basic protections have different purposes and different strengths and weaknesses. Copyrights and trademarks are relatively easy and inexpensive to obtain. You simply fill out a form, submit the material, and wait a few months for the agency to process the request. Actually, a copyright exists as soon as you create the material. You do not need to file the registration form. However, there are some legal and monetary advantages to registering the copyright. Patents require considerable documentation, and a formal review to identify prior and related patents and to determine the legitimacy of the innovation. They usually require the help of a specialized law firm, take at least a year to obtain, and will probably cost about $10,000 in legal and processing fees. Trade secret protection requires no registration with the government, but requires you to create and enforce a security policy to ensure that your information is adequately protected.

In a digital age, copyright law is the most challenging to apply and to enforce. The first question is identifying ownership. Who owns a particular item? If you write a book on your own time with your own resources, then generally you own the rights. If you write a computer program for your employer as part of your job, the employer owns the copyright. Interestingly, if you are an outside contractor and create a program for a company, it is more likely that you own the copyright, unless you agree to transfer the rights.

There is an interesting exception to copyright law: mere collections of data cannot be copyrighted. Consider the example of *Feist Publications v. Rural Telephone Service* [499 U.S. 340 (1991)]. Feist wanted to publish a telephone directory, but Rural would not provide the data. So Feist copied much of the data from Rural's printed directory. The U.S. Supreme Court eventually ruled that Feist's action was not a copyright infringement because the directory contained only data, which is not sufficiently original to obtain a copyright. Now consider the case of *ProCD, Inc. v. Zeidenberg* [86 F3d 1447 (7th Cir. 1996)]. ProCD collects and publishes a CD-based list of phone numbers and addresses, which they generally obtain from printed phone directories. Zeidenberg purchased a copy of the CDs and transferred them to his website. He then charged people to access the site. ProCD sued for violating the copyright laws. Based on the Feist case, Zeidenberg was found innocent of copyright infringement. However, he was guilty of violating the shrinkwrap license agreement. Note that the data collection argument probably applies to most data collected by federal and state agencies.

Copyright protection gives you the ability to stop others from profiting from your work. There are a few minor exceptions—such as parody, excerpting short quotations, and educational "fair use," which allows educational institutions very limited provisions to make a limited number of copies for teaching purposes. A more interesting, unanticipated exception involves money. Consider the 1994 case of *U.S. v. LaMacchia,* who was a student running a bulletin board system on university computers. He routinely placed commercial software on the site and allowed people to download (steal) the software for their own use. The catch is that he did not charge access to the system and made no money from the process. Without this profit motive, the court ruled that LaMacchia could not be convicted on charges of criminal violation of the copyright laws. Of course, the commercial software vendors could sue him on civil grounds, but unless he was an unusually wealthy student, there would be little gain. On the other hand, the university could throw him out for violating university policy. Congress has proposed a law to modify the copyright provisions to cover this situation in the future.

Copying becomes a more serious problem every day. As more works are created and distributed in digital form, it becomes more difficult to protect them. Even though you might have a legal right to prevent copying, it becomes increasingly difficult to prevent the distribution of your work, particularly if individual ethics are weak. For example, say that you write a story and sell it through your website. Once the first few people have read the story, they could copy it and e-mail it to their friends. What are you going to do? Arrest and sue your customers who first read the story? On the other hand, if a publisher took your story, printed it, and sold it, you clearly have the legal authority and monetary incentive to seek compensation. Consider a similar example. You build a website and create some interesting graphics and sound effects. Over time, other people routinely download your objects and use them on their own sites. Have they violated copyright laws? Can you stop them? Can you even find them? Would it be economically worthwhile to pursue them?

It is unlikely that individual motivations and ethics will improve. That is, despite the laws, many people will still copy anything they can (software, art, text, photos, video clips, and so on). Whatever technology might be applied, it is unlikely to be economically feasible to pursue them. Yet, without incentive why should you create and distribute new works? One possible outcome is that large, expensive content will disappear. Why should you write and distribute an entire book in one piece, when most people would steal it instead of paying $20 a copy? Instead, you could sell the book a section at a time, for a few cents per section. By releasing the sections over time, people would have to pay to receive the most recent (and organized) sections. Yes, some people might wait and have a friend pay for the section and e-mail

it, but it is a question of economics. If the price is low enough, more people will opt to get the data earlier and directly from the source.

The federal white paper ("Intellectual Property and the National Information Infrastructure") contains an extended discussion of copyright issues and possible federal solutions. It is available online from the Information Infrastructure Task Force (IITF) bulletin board. You should also read Pamela Samuelson's criticism of the white paper proposal, which points out that the discussion strongly favors copyright holders as opposed to the public, particularly since the primary author (Bruce Lehman) was a lobbyist for the copyright industry.

Privacy

Privacy is an intriguing concept. Humans are a social group: we can accomplish far more by living in communities and sharing our talents. Yet, individuals have a desire to keep some things private. More to the point, we have a desire to control what information we wish to share. For example, you might not want everyone to know exactly how old you are or how many times you were sick last year, but it is okay if your mother knows these things, and possibly essential that your doctor knows them.

Society has a vested interest in knowing some things about you and your life. For example, communities need to know how much you paid for your car and your house so they can fairly assess taxes. Society needs to track criminal behavior to help identify antisocial people who might harm us. Medical researchers need to track diseases to identify trends, causes, and potential solutions.

Businesses have an incentive to obtain considerable amounts of data on groups and individuals. And individuals have an incentive to provide some information to businesses. Whenever you make a purchase, you need information, and businesses are generally happy to provide you that information. The problem is how do you find the business or company that best matches your needs? Conversely, how can a company identify its potential customers? With no information, companies might resort to mass e-mail (spam) that clogs networks and irritates people who have no use for the services advertised.

The catch is that we do need to share information about ourselves, with government agencies, researchers in various disciplines, and with businesses. Yet, there is no reason that everyone in the world should be able to obtain every detail of our lives. The difficulty lies in determining where to draw this line. It is further complicated by the fact that every person (and social group) has different preferences.

First, it is important to realize that there is no constitutionally defined "right to privacy," especially with respect to data. A few laws have been enacted in the United States to provide minimal restrictions on the use and sharing of personal data. The most notable are the following:

- Freedom of Information Act

- Family Educational Rights and Privacy Act

- Fair Credit Reporting Act

- Privacy Act of 1974

- Privacy Protection Act of 1980

- Electronic Communications Privacy Act of 1986

- Video Privacy Act of 1988

- Driver's Privacy Protection Act of 1994

- Graham-Leach-Bliley Act of 1999

The Freedom of Information Act generally provides people with the ability to obtain information held by governmental agencies. There are limits for national security and on the release of data relating to individual personal data. For example, you cannot ask the IRS for personal information about your neighbor.

The most important feature of the Family Educational Rights and Privacy Act is that it limits the release of educational data. Institutions can release basic information such as the names of students (commonly sold to businesses), but they cannot release grades without the students' express written permission.

The primary purpose of the Electronic Communications Privacy Act was to extend traditional wiretap provisions to "electronic communication," which includes cellular phone and e-mail transmissions. Essentially, the law makes it illegal for individuals to intercept these conversations, and requires law enforcement agencies to obtain court permission to intercept and record the conversations. On the other hand, it is specifically legal for an individual to record his or her transmissions (although a few states limit this right). Consequently, employers generally have the legal right (since they own the equipment) to monitor most communications by employees. Note that there may be some exceptions and an honest employer will always notify employees first.

The Fair Credit Reporting Act primarily gives consumers the right to inspect credit records—and it gives them the right to correct errors. The Driver's Privacy Act limits the use and release of state motor vehicle data. Its primary purpose was to prevent release of specific data to individual requesters. However, it has generous exceptions for insurance companies, research, and business use. The Video Privacy Act was created to limit the release of rental records from video stores and libraries.

The Privacy Protection Act of 1980 is primarily concerned with law enforcement investigations. It provides some definitions for when police searches are legitimate and when they are an invasion of privacy. The act predates the advances in information technology, so it is generally silent on the issue of privacy in terms of electronic data.

On the other hand, the Privacy Act of 1974 deals more directly with the collection and dissemination of information by the federal government. It specifically limits the collection of data by an agency to information that is relevant to its work. It provides citizens with the ability to examine and contest the data. The act initially limited agencies from sharing and matching data with other agencies, but most of these restraints have been removed by subsequent amendments.

For example, the postal service is generally not permitted to disclose data on individual addresses. However, it does release data to a few large commercial service bureaus. Companies can submit address lists to these bureaus for correction of their mailing lists.

The Graham-Leach-Bliley Act of 1999 primarily deregulated some financial services. In exchange, it imposed some trivial privacy clauses. In particular, it requires financial institutions to notify customers that they have the right to opt out of (1) selling their names to other companies and (2) marketing requests from the institution. Institutions reportedly spent hundreds of millions of dollars sending notices to customers, but many feel they deliberately made the process obscure and few consumers replied to the mass mailings. Consequently, businesses are basically free to continue using consumer data in any manner they want.

The bottom line is that this piecemeal approach to privacy means that it is difficult for consumers to determine their rights and for businesses to identify their responsibilities. Consequently, except for the few specific limitations (e.g., credit and educational records), most businesses are free to collect and share information. On the other hand, you can improve relationships with customers by always asking them for permission to use and share personal data.

Information Era Crimes

As commerce moves to digital form, existing crime laws need to be extended and new ones need to be created. The biggest concerns are fraud, theft, and destruction of property. To understand the complications, consider what happens if someone steals your car. Why is that bad? Largely because you no longer have the use of the car. Now, what if someone steals your company's marketing plan? Why is that bad? You still have the use of the plan. Similarly, what if someone deleted your computerized customer database? Assuming that you are smart enough to keep a backup, what have you lost? The point of these questions is to show you that our traditional views on crime may not apply to crime-related information. Additionally, computers create the prospect of new types of crime. For instance, what happens if someone writes a program that prevents you from obtaining access to your financial records? The alleged criminal did not steal or destroy anything, so what crime has been committed?

The Computer Fraud and Abuse Act of 1986 provides answers to many of the questions regarding crime in the digital realm. In particular, it outlaws (1) access to computers without authorization; (2) damage to computers, networks, data, and so on, (3) actions that lead to denial of service; and (4) interference with medical care. Interestingly, the act charged the U.S. Secret Service with enforcement.

Enforcement of the act has been challenging. It has been difficult to find qualified law enforcement personnel, including prosecutors. Additionally, many businesses are reluctant to prosecute cases because they do not want competitors or shareholders to learn the details. On the other hand, sometimes companies and the Secret Service are too enthusiastic in their pursuit of alleged criminals. For example, one of the first cases supported by the Electronic Frontier Foundation (EFF) involved a BBS that supplied a document obtained from the telephone company that detailed information about the 911 system. The phone company complained that the document was stolen and that hackers might use it to break into its system. The Secret Service confiscated the BBS computer equipment and arrested the teenage owner. In court, with the help of the EFF, it was shown the document could be purchased from the phone company for a few dollars.

If we examine crime historically, we see the same problems in preventing more traditional crime and enforcing the laws. In the United States, it was the introduction of the FBI and their professional investigative techniques that improved law enforcement and the detection of various crimes. In the digital arena, until we gain more experience and improve training of police, attorneys, and judges, we will face the same problems of weak laws, difficulty in prosecution, and variable enforcement.

The Digital Millennium Copyright Act (DMCA) of 1998 changed some copyright provisions to synchronize the U.S. laws with the European laws. It also included a controversial provision that makes it a federal crime to create or to distribute devices that circumvent copy protection schemes. Part of its original purpose was to prevent people from advertising and selling black boxes to decode scrambled satellite TV signals. Many people believe that these provisions are too strict and they infringe on the free speech rights in the Constitution. For instance, some researchers have been threatened with prosecution under the DMCA if they attempted to publish their work. The problem with copyright laws is that they can provide only limited legal protection. To enforce these laws, a copyright holder generally has to prosecute violators. But as the record industry was aware in the Napster case, it is virtually impossible to find everyone who copies a song—even more impossible to take them all to court. So, property owners are searching for ways to prevent casual theft. The problem is that in theory, it is impossible to completely prevent the copying of a digital work. So, portions of the DMCA are required to make it difficult for people to sell circumvention technology. By making it more difficult for people to copy a work, the laws essentially raise the cost of stealing. But there are fine lines between protecting copyright holders, protecting consumers' rights to use a work, and protecting everyone's right to study new ideas. It will take time and discussion to draw these lines.

Driven by the September 11 attack on the World Trade Center in New York, the U.S.A. Patriot Act (antiterrorism bill) of 2001 provides considerable new powers to federal, state, and local police agencies. Some of these provisions reduce privacy by making it easier for police agencies to monitor conversations, intercept e-mail and Internet messages, and detain people without cause. Law enforcement agencies are asking for even more flexibility to investigate people. These provisions do have some justifiable uses, and there are times when enforcement agencies have to jump through too many hoops to perform their jobs effectively. However, as J. Edgar Hoover proved, the challenge lies in preventing abuse of the laws, particularly preventing people from using them as political tools.

Online Resources

http://fedlaw.gsa.gov/
Good overall links, but too much reliance on outside providers.

http://www4.law.cornell.edu/uscode/
http://www.access.gpo.gov/nara/cfr/cfr-table-search.html
Searchable listings of the U.S. Code and Code of Federal Regulations.

http://www.loc.gov/copyright/
U.S. copyright office.

http://www.uspto.gov/
U.S. patent office.

http://www.copyright.com/
U.S. copyright clearinghouse. You can pay here to make legal copies of documents for distribution within your company or school.

http://www.eff.org/
The Electronic Frontier Foundation. A private organization to influence legislation related to computers. Largely created by Mitch Kapor who founded Lotus.

http://www.epic.org/
Electronic privacy information center.

http://www.uspto.gov/web/offices/com/doc/ipnii/
The IITF white paper and proposal for copyright law modifications.

http://www.wired.com
The Copyright Grab, Pamela Samuelson, issue 4(1). A lawyer's perspective on the IITF white paper.

Exercises

1. Explain what you would do if your employer asks you to use illegally copied software.

2. What laws does your state have that apply specifically to computer-related crimes?

3. You downloaded some data from a federal agency. Is it legal to sell that data as part of a software package you wrote?

4. How should U.S. police forces prepare for a probable increase in computer crimes?

5. Should new privacy laws be enacted to handle Internet and Web data? What aspects should they cover?

10Base-T: A system of connecting computers on a LAN using twisted-pair cable. The method relies on compression to increase raw transfer rates to 10 megabits per second.

Access speed: A measure of disk drive speed. Loosely, the time it takes a disk drive to move to a particular piece of data.

Accounting journal: Raw financial transaction data are collected by the accounting department and stored in a journal. Modern accounting requires the use of a double-entry system to ensure accurate data.

Activity-based costing (ABC): ABC allocates costs by examining a detailed breakdown of the production activities. The cost of each process is computed for each different product. The detail provides a better picture of the production cost for each item.

Advanced encryption standard (AES): A new U.S. standard for single-key encryption; approved in 2001 by the government to replace DES and triple DES. With 128 bit keys, it is substantially more difficult to break, but still very fast to encrypt and decrypt.

Advocacy role: Someone in MIS, usually the chief information officer, who bears responsibility for exploring and presenting new applications and uses of MIS within the company.

Agent: An object-oriented program designed for networks that is written to preform specific tasks in response to user requests. Agents are designed to automatically communicate with other agents to search for data and make decisions.

American National Standards Institute (ANSI): An organization responsible for defining many standards, including several useful information technology standards.

American Standard Code for Information Interchange (ASCII): A common method of numbering characters so they can be processed. For instance, the letter A is number 65. It is slowly being replaced by the ANSI character set table and the use of international code pages that can display foreign characters.

Angel investor: An individual who provides a limited amount of funding to startup firms. Unlike a partner, the investor is rarely involved in management. The amount of funding is generally small—$25,000 to $100,000.

Antitrust laws: A variety of laws that make it illegal to use monopoly power. Some basic (economic) actions to achieve a competitive advantage are illegal. Strategic plans must be evaluated carefully to avoid violating these laws.

Application service provider (ASP): A specialized Internet firm that provides an individual application to other businesses. For example, a reservation system can be run by an ASP to provide services to other companies.

Artificial intelligence (AI): An attempt to build machines that can think like humans. Techniques evolved from this research help solve more complex problems. Useful techniques include expert systems, neural networks, massively parallel computers, and robotics.

Assumptions: Models are simplifications of real life, so they require assumptions about various events or conditions.

Asynchronous Transfer Mode (ATM): A packet-based network system that uses high-speed transmission lines (150 megabits and over) and routers to maximize network efficiency and throughput.

Attributes: Descriptions of an object or entity. For example, a customer object would at least have attributes for name, phone number, and address.

Auction: In an e-commerce context, a Web-based system where individuals bid for items. Useful when you do not know the exact value of an item, or have only a few items to sell. The auction site helps handle payments but charges a percentage fee.

Audit trail: The ability to trace any transaction back to its source. In accounting, transaction values are accumulated on the general ledger and used to create reports. An audit trail is a set of marks or records to point back to the original transaction.

Authentication: The ability to verify the source of a message. Dual-key systems are a useful technique. The sender uses a private key to encrypt the message. The recipient applies the sender's public key. If the decrypted message is readable, it had to have come from the alleged sender, because the keys always work in pairs.

Backbone: A high-speed communication line that links multiple subnetworks. It is usually a fiber-optic line.

Backward chaining: In an expert system, the user enters a "conclusion" and asks to see whether the rules support that conclusion.

Barriers to entry: Anything that makes it more difficult for new firms to enter an industry. Several possibilities would violate antitrust laws. An acceptable barrier is the increased use of information systems, which raises the cost of entering an industry because a rival would have to spend additional money on information technology.

Beginners All-purpose Symbolic Instruction Code (BASIC):   An early computer programming language designed to be easy to program and to teach. Visual Basic is a current version for Windows programming.

Benchmark: A set of routines or actions used to evaluate computer performance. By performing the same basic tasks on several machines, you can compare their relative speeds. Benchmarks are especially useful when the machines use different processors and different input and output devices.

Bill presentation and payment: Web-based software that automatically displays bills and invoices for customers. The payment side accepts various forms of payment including credit cards and electronic checks. Generally run as a Web service.

Binary data: A collection of ones and zeros called bits. Computer processors operate only on binary data. All data forms are first converted to binary.

Biometrics: A field of study that is trying to determine how to identify people based on biological characteristics. The most common devices are fingerprint and handprint readers.

Bit: The smallest unit of data in a computer. All data is converted to bits or binary data. Each bit can be in one of two states: on or off. Bits are generally aggregated into collections called a byte.

Bitmap image: A method of storing images. The picture is converted to individual dots that are stored as bits. Once a picture is stored in bitmap form, it is difficult to resize. However, bitmaps are good for displaying photographic images with subtle color shading.

Board of directors: A group of people paid to oversee and evaluate the decisions of the company. Technically the CEO reports to the board of directors, but they are charged more with reviewing the CEO's decisions. Most boards have the authority to remove a CEO, but many board members are selected by the CEO.

Boolean search: Searching for data by using the logic operators AND, OR, and NOT conditions in a WHERE statement, for example, find a list of customers where city = "Detroit" and age >50 and do not own a car.

Bottom-up development: An approach to designing and building systems in which workers build system components to solve each problem as it arises. Eventually the pieces are combined to create an integrated system. The method relies on standards and controls to facilitate cooperation and integration. *See also* Top-down development.

Brainstorming: A group technique in which each individual is asked to come up with possible suggestions to a problem. Any ideas are useful, regardless of how wild they are. Even fanciful ideas could stimulate someone else to improve it or to explore a related area.

Broadcasts: A technique of transmitting messages using radio, micro, or infrared waves. Broadcast messages are sent to all devices in a certain area. Others in the vicinity can also receive the messages.

Browser: A software tool that converts World Wide Web data into a graphical page with hypertext links. Using standard (HTML) commands, companies can offer data and additional links to users. Users simply click on individual words and pictures to retrieve additional data and move to other network sites.

Brute force: An attack on encrypted data that attempts to use every possible key. Can be stopped by using very long keys. For example, using a key or password of only three letters means there are only 26*26*26 = 17,576 possible values. Even a slow computer can test all combinations in a few seconds.

Bulletin board system (BBS):   Similar to a typical bulletin board, except that people access it from computers. The BBS enables users to store comments, pictures, and files for other people to retrieve. Bulletin boards are usually organized by topics and can be searched for specific phrases or comments. They are useful way to disseminate information that is of interest to many different people.

Bus: Most computers have special slots called a bus to provide high-speed connections to other devices. Various manufacturers make boards that fit into these slots. The processor can exchange data with these other devices, but performance is sometimes constrained by the design of the bus.

Business to business (B2B):   Business-to-business electronic commerce; sales by suppliers to other businesses over the Internet; often long-term relationships. See B2C and EDI.

Business to consumer (B2C):   Business-to-consumer electronic commerce, purchases by individual consumers similar to traditional mail-order systems, but conducted on secure websites over the Internet.

Bus network: A network organizing scheme in which each computer is attached to a common transmission medium. Protocols are needed to determine when a machine can transmit and to recover from collisions.

Byte: A collection of bits. Traditionally, 8 bits make up one byte. From binary arithmetic, an 8-bit byte can hold 2 to the 8th power, or 256, possible numbers. In many systems a byte is used to hold one character.

C: A powerful programming language that is flexible and creates efficient code. A language commonly used to build complex applications, and to create commercial software products.

C++:   An object-oriented extension of the C programming language. It is commonly used to build commercial software. It produces efficient code and supports the development of reusable objects.

Cable modem: An Internet connection device that translates local area network protocols to turn over a television cable line. It can provide transmission speeds around 3 Mpbs. But the communication line is shared with other users.

Cache: A buffer between the processor and a slower device such as a printer, disk drive, or memory chips. The cache generally consists of high-speed memory. Data is transferred in bulk to the cache. It is then pulled out as it is needed, freeing up the processor to work on other jobs instead of waiting for the slower device to finish.

Carrier-Sense, Multiple-Access/Collision Detection (CSMA/CD): A communications protocol that determines how computers will behave on a shared-medium network. Ethernet protocols rely on CSMA/CD. Other alternatives are Token Ring and packet switching.

Case-based reasoning: An expert system approach that records information in the form of situations and cases. Users search for cases similar to their current problem and adapt the original solution.

CD-ROM: Compact disk-read only memory. Data is stored and retrieved with a laser. A special machine is required to create data on a CD-ROM. Used to hold data that does not change very often. Useful for multimedia applications because a disk can hold about 650 megabytes of data. The format used to store music CDs.

Centralization: A business scheme for performing most operations and making management decisions from one location in an organization. MIS organization can be examined in four areas: hardware, software, data, and personnel. *See also* Decentralization.

Certificate authority (CA): Dual-key encryption and authentication require that the public key be published and available to others. A certificate authority is an organization that validates the owner's identity, issues the keys, and runs the public directory. Almost anyone can run the software to be a CA, but others must trust that host.

Change agents: Objects or people who cause or facilitate changes. Sometimes the change agent might be a new employee who brings fresh ideas, other times change can be mandated by top-level management. Sometimes an outside event such as a competitor or a hurricane forces an organization to change.

Change drivers: Concepts or products that have altered the way businesses operate. Classic examples include: bar-code scanners in retail stores, handheld miniterminals or notebooks by delivery firms and salespeople, and reservation systems by travel and entertainment industries.

Charge-back system: A scheme for charging other internal departments for services. For example, some firms charge departments a fee based on how often they use the central computer. The goal was to ration a limited resource by avoiding free use.

Chart of accounts: A listing of all of the accounts and subaccounts in the general ledger. It must be defined ahead of time for each business.

Chief executive officer (CEO): The head of a company. The person ultimately responsible for setting the direction and policies of the firm. Usually the CEO is also the chairperson of the board of directors.

Chief information officer (CIO): The person who is in charge of the MIS organization within a firm, charged with overseeing operations, setting MIS priorities, and being a top-level advocate for MIS. Also develops and supports strategy for the firm.

Circular reference: In a spreadsheet, a set of cells that eventually refer to each other. In the simplest example, cell A1 would use values stored in cell A2, but cell A2 uses the value stored in A1. This technique is sometimes used to create an iterative solution to a model.

Classes: Base descriptions of objects. Technically, classes describe generic attributes and methods. Objects are a specific instance of a class.

Click-through rate: Used in Web advertising, the percentage of people viewing an online ad who actually click it to see the details on the advertised product or service. By 2000, the average click-through rates had declined to less than 1 percent. But it is not necessarily a good measure of advertising effectiveness.

Client-server network: A network configuration in which a few machines are used as file servers and the others (clients) are independent workstations. Shared data is first sent to a file server where it can be examined or transferred by another client.

Client-server organization: A method of organizing the MIS function so that some operations are centralized while others are decentralized. The client-server model separates all of the components into two categories: servers or clients. The functions associated with the server tend to be centralized, whereas the client components and tasks are dispersed among the users.

Clip art: Artwork created and sold to be used by nonartists. Hundreds of collections are available of people, places, buildings, and other objects. Clip art images are often used to create presentations and illustrate reports.

Clipboard: The method used to transfer data between software packages in windows-oriented operating environments. All objects that are cut or copied are placed onto the clipboard, ready to be pasted to another location or another package. Clipboard viewers exist to show the current contents of the clipboard. Some software systems allow a clipboard to hold several cuttings. Many automatically delete the older cuts—keeping only the most recent.

Clipper chip: An encryption method created by the U.S. top-secret National Security Agency (NSA). It uses a secret algorithm to encrypt and decrypt digital messages. It was particularly designed for digital voice communication. Its key feature is the use of two escrow keys assigned to each chip. If the police decide they want to listen to a conversation between two suspects, they can get a court order, collect the escrow keys and instantly decrypt the call.

Closed loop: A system or piece of computer code in which every step in a control mechanism is contained inside the system, and does not utilize external input. *See also* Feedback.

Closed system: A system that is entirely self-contained and does not respond to changes in the environment. Most closed systems eventually fail due to entropy.

Coaxial cable: A cable used to transmit data. Cable television is a widespread application. The inner cable is surrounded by a plastic insulator, which is surrounded by a wire mesh conductor and an outer casing. The wire mesh insulates the internal signal wire from external interference.

Cold site: A facility that can be leased from a disaster backup specialist. A cold site contains power and telecommunication lines but no computer. In the event of a disaster, a company calls the computer vendor and begs for the first available machine to be sent to the cold site.

Collision: In networks, a collision arises when two computers attempt to broadcast messages at the same time. The network protocols need to identify the situation and determine which machine will go first.

Column: A vertical part of a table that holds data for one attribute of an entity in a database or spreadsheet. For example, a table to describe automobiles will have columns for make, model, and color.

Command-line interface: A method of controlling the computer by typing commands. The user must generally memorize specific commands. Older machines still use them because GUI systems require too much overhead. Some people prefer command lines, because it is faster to type one or two commands than to manipulate an image on the screen.

Commerce server: A software system that runs an e-commerce Web server. It handles the product catalog, searching, a shopping cart, and the payment mechanism. Several vendors sell versions to be run on your own server, or you can lease space on a hosting company.

Commercial off-the-shelf software (COTS):   Purchased software for building applications. Relatively popular because it is faster than building from scratch.

Common Business-Oriented Language (COBOL):   An early programming language designed to handle typical transaction processing tasks. Its death has been predicted for years, but it is hard to throw away billions of lines of code.

Common Object Request Broker Architecture (CORBA):   A model largely developed in the UNIX community that will enable objects to communicate with each other across networks. In particular, it is designed to enable users to combine different data types from various software vendors into a single compound document. The data could reside on any server on the network.

Competitive advantage: Something that makes your company better or stronger than your rivals. Examples include lower costs, higher quality, strong ties to loyal customers, and control over distribution channels.

Composite key: In relational databases, a key that consists of more than one column. The columns are combined to yield a unique primary key.

Compound document: A document that incorporates different types of data: text, graphics, sound, and video. The different objects might be transmitted across a network to be included in a final document.

Computer-aided design (CAD):   Programs that are used to create engineering drawings. CAD programs make it easy to modify drawings. They also make it easier to keep track of material specifications. They can perform spatial and engineering estimates on the designs, such as surface or volume calculations.

Computer-aided software engineering (CASE):   Computer programs that are designed to support the analysis development of computer systems. They make it easier to create, store, and share diagrams and data definitions. Some versions even generate code. There are two categories of CASE tools: software development and maintenance of existing systems.

Computer ethics: The concept that all of us have an obligation with respect to data. For example, managers have a responsibility to customers to protect personal data, to collect only data that is truly needed, and to give customers the ability to correct errors in personal data.

Computer information system (CIS):   *See* Management information system (MIS).

Computer-integrated manufacturing (CIM):   Using a computer to control most of the production equipment in a manufacturing environment. The computer can monitor the production statistics. It is also used to set individual machine controls.

Concurrency: A situation that arises when applications attempt to modify the same piece of data at the same time. If two people are allowed to make changes to the same piece of data, the computer system must control the order in which it processes the two requests. Mixing the two tasks will result in the wrong data being stored in the computer.

Context diagram: The top level of data flow diagram that acts as a title page and displays the boundaries of the system and displays the external entities that interact with the system.

Converge: The ability of an iterative model to stabilize on a fixed solution. The alternative is that values continually increase and never reach a solution.

Cookies: Small test files that a Web server sends to client computers. When the user returns to a site, the browser automatically returns the cookie file. Servers use them to keep track of transactions—so they know when the same user has returned. Marketers have used them to track individual users on the Web.

Copyright: A legal ownership right granted to the creators of intellectual property. All works are automatically copyrighted. Registering with the copyright office is not required but grants additional protection to the owner.

Critical success factors: A limited number of concrete goals that must be met for the organization to be successful. Identifying these key factors helps determine the strategic directions and highlights the areas that can benefit from improved information systems.

Customer relationship management (CRM): A system for tracking and integrating all customer data. Salespeople, managers, and clerks all have access to the same data, so everyone has the same consolidated view of all customer interactions.

Cut, copy, paste: A common mechanism used to transfer and link data between different software packages. The data to be transferred is marked. When it is cut or copied, it is placed on the clipboard. Switching to the second package, the object is pasted into the appropriate location. Dynamic and static links are specified through options in the "paste special" menu. With the cut option, the original object is deleted. With copy, the original is unchanged.

Data: Consists of factual elements (or opinions or comments) that describe some object or event. Data can be thought of as raw numbers.

Data administrator: MIS manager who is charged with overseeing all of the data definitions and data standards for the company to ensure that applications can share data throughout the company.

Database: A collection of related data that can be retrieved easily and processed by computers; a collection of data tables.

Database administrator (DBA): (1) A person appointed to manage the databases for the firm. The DBA needs to know the technical details of the DBMS and the computer system. The DBA also needs to understand the business operations of the firm. (2) A management person in the MIS department charged with defining and maintaining the corporate databases. Maintaining data integrity is a key component of the job.

Database management system (DBMS): Software that defines a database, stores the data, supports a query language, produces, reports, and creates data-entry screens.

Data dictionary: Contains all of the information to explain the terms used to define a system. Often includes report descriptions, business rules, and security considerations.

Data encryption standard (DES): An older method of encrypting data was commonly used by financial institutions. With current computer capabilities that can break a DES-encrypted message, DES is no longer considered a secure encryption system.

Data flow diagram (DFD): A diagramming technique used to analyze and design systems. It shows how a system is divided into subsystems and highlights the flow of data between the processes and subsystems. It displays processes, external entities, files, data flows, and control flows.

Data independence: Separating programs from their data definition and storage. The main advantage is that it is possible to change the data without having to change the programs.

Data integrity: (1) A concept that implies data is as accurate as possible. It means the database contains few errors. (2) Keeping data accurate and correct as it is gathered and stored in the computer system.

Data mart: A small version of a data warehouse. A database designed to hold concise collections of data for retrieval and analysis by managers.

Data mining: An automated system that examines data for patterns and relationships. Partly based on statistics, but it also searches for more specific associations. The results are not always applicable to other situations.

Data mirroring: The ultimate backup technique where all data that is stored on one machine is automatically transferred and stored on a second computer. Useful to prevent loss of data and recover from disasters—particularly when the second computer is located many miles away.

Data store: A file or place where data is stored. In a realistic setting, a data store could be a computer file, file cabinet, or even a reference book.

Data types: To humans, there are four basic types of data: text and numbers, images, sound, and video. Each data type must be converted to binary form for computer processing.

Data warehouse: A single consolidation point for enterprise data from diverse production systems. The data is typically stored in one large file server or a central computer. Because legacy systems are difficult to replace, some data is copied into a data warehouse, where it is available for management queries and analysis.

Decentralization: Moving the major operations and decisions out to lower levels within the firm. In MIS, decentralization has largely been led by the declining cost and improved capabilities of personal computers. *See also* Centralization.

Decision biases: Without models and careful analysis, decisions made by people tend to be biased. There are several biases in each of the four systems categories: data acquisition, processing, output, and feedback.

Decision support system (DSS): System to use data collected by transaction-processing systems to evaluate business models and assist managers in making tactical decisions. There are three major components: data collection, analysis of models, and presentation.

Decision tree: A graphical representation of logic rules. Each possible answer to a question or situation leads to a new branch of the tree.

Decision process: The steps required to make a decision. It includes problem indentification, research, specification of choices, and the final selection. Midlevel managers are often involved in the initial stages and affect the outcome, even though they may not make the final decision.

Default value: A value that is automatically displayed by the computer. Users can often override the default by deleting the old value and entering a new one. The goal is to choose a value that will almost always be entered, so the user can skip that item.

Dehumanization: Some people feel that technology isolates people and decreases our contact with other members of society. Treating people as identification numbers and summary statistics can lead managers to forget the human consequences of their decisions.

Denial of service (DoS):   Preventing legitimate users access to systems and networks. A common Internet trick is to force thousands of zombie computers to flood a server with millions of meaningless messages—preventing anyone else from using the system.

Descriptive model: A model that is defined in words and perhaps pictures. Relationships between objects and variables tend to be subjective. Useful for an initial understanding of a system but difficult to evaluate by computer.

Desktop publishing (DTP):   The art of creating professional documents with personal computers and small laser printers. Beyond basic word processing, DTP software provides controls to standardize pages, improve the page layout, and establish styles.

Detail section: The section in a report that is repeated for every row in the associated tables. It is often used for itemized values, whereas group and page footers are used for subtotals.

Diagnostic situations: Spotting problems, searching for the cause, and implementing corrections. Examples include responding to exception reports to identify problems and potential solutions and determining why the latest approach did not perform as well as expected.

Dial-back modem: A special modem placed on a central computer. When a user attempts to log in, the dial-back modem breaks the connection and calls back a predefined phone number. Its use minimizes the threat of outsiders gaining access to the central computer.

Digital cash: An electronic version of money that is provided and verified by a trusted third party. It consists of an encrypted number for a specified value that can only be used one time. It provides for verifiable and anonymous purchases using networks.

Digital certificate: Part of an authentication mechanism used with dual-key encryption. Companies that host servers need to encrypt transactions over the Internet. They purchase a digital certificate from a certificate authority and install it on the Web server. The client browser recognizes the certificate key and encrypts the data.

Digital dashboard: A visual presentation of broad measures of current activity in an organization. The data is generally displayed as gauges, and the system must be customized for each organization. As part of an executive information system, managers can drill down to get more data.

Digital divide: The distance between those—individuals or nations—who have network capabilities and those who do not. Despite declining costs, many people and many nations cannot afford the hardware and software. If a large portion of the economy moves online, it could alienate those who cannot afford the network connection.

Digital rights management (DRM):   A combination of encryption and Internet validation for protecting vendor copyrights to prevent unauthorized copying of digital content (software, music, books, movies, and so on).

Digital signature: Any electronic signature technology that verifies the user. U.S. law now recognizes digital signatures as equivalent to handwritten ones. The most secure system is to obtain a digital certificate from a public company that verifies each person's identity. But, the IRS accepts a simple PIN issued by the agency as a digital signature.

Digital subscriber line (DSL):   A special phone service connection available to customers within three miles of the phone company's switch. It provides about 1 Mbps transmission speed for Internet connections.

Digital video/versatile disk (DVD):   A digital format primarily used for storing video and movies. However, it can also hold audio and traditional computer data. One side of the disk can hold over 3 gigabytes of data.

Disintermediation: In an e-commerce context, using a Web-based system to skip over sections of the production chain, such as manufacturers selling directly to consumers. The approach can give the manufacturer a higher percentage of the sale price, but risks alienating retailers, resulting in lost sales.

Distribution channel: The layers of distributors in between the manufacturer to the final customer. If a producer can gain control over this means of getting the product to consumers, the producer can prevent new rivals from entering the industry. Improved communication systems offer the possibility of eroding control over some distribution channels.

Diverge: The property of an iterative model where successive computations keep leading to larger values (in magnitude). The model never reaches a stable solution. Generally due to insufficient or incorrect feedback mechanisms.

Documentation: Descriptions of a system, its components, the data, and records of changes made to the system.

Domain name server (DNS):   A computer on the Internet that converts mnemonic names into numeric Internet addresses. The names are easier for humans to remember, but the computers rely on the numeric addresses.

Dot-com: Abbreviation given to the many Internet firms formed in the late 1990s because their Internet names ended with the .com suffix. For a couple of years, having a dot-com name was prestigious and attracted funding. When hundreds of these firms failed in 2000 and 2001, they became known as dot-bombs.

Download: To transfer files from a remote computer to a local computer (usually a personal computer). *See also* Upload.

Drill down: To use an information system to get increasingly detailed data about a company. In an enterprise information system, the ability to look at overall company data, then select breakdowns by regions, departments, or smaller levels.

Dual-key encryption: A method of encrypting a message that requires two keys: one to encrypt and one to decrypt. One of the keys is a public key that is available to anyone. The other key is private and must never be revealed to other people. RSA is a popular dual-key encryption system. Dual-key systems can also be used to authenticate the users.

Dynamic data exchange: An early method of linking data from multiple sources with the Windows operating system. The software packages literally send messages to other software packages, which enables them to combine and update data. *See also* dynamic integration and Object Linking and Embedding (OLE).

Dynamic integration: A means of linking data from multiple documents. One compound document (or container) can hold data objects created by other software. As the original data is changed, it is automatically updated in the container document. *See also* Static integration.

EBCDIC: Extended Binary Coded Decimal Interchange Code. A method of numbering characters so they can be processed by machines. Used exclusively by large IBM and compatible computers. *See also* ASCII.

E-business: Electronic business. The process of conducting any type of business over the Internet. It includes all forms of e-commerce and m-commerce, as well as internal processes and Web services.

E-commerce: Electronic commerce. The process of selling items over the Internet. The most familiar form is business-to-consumer, but it includes business-to-business and auction sites like eBay.

Electronic data interchange (EDI): Exchanging transaction data with entities outside the control of your firm. Private connections can be established directly between two firms. Public networks are also being formed where one provider collects data and routes it to the appropriate client.

E-mail: Electronic mail, or messages that are transmitted from one computer user to another. Networks transfer messages between the computers. Users can send or retrieve messages at any time. The computer holds the message until the recipient checks in.

Encryption: A method of modifying the original information according to some code, so that it can only be read if the user knows the decryption key. It is used to safely transmit data between computers.

End-user development: Managers and workers are to develop their own small systems using database management systems, spreadsheets, and other high-level tools.

Enterprise network: A network that connects multiple subnetworks across an entire firm. Often, the networks use different protocols and different computer types, which complicates transmitting messages.

Enterprise resource planning (ERP): An integrated computer system running on top of a DBMS. It is designed to collect and organize data from all operations in an organization. Existing systems are strong in accounting, purchasing, and HRM.

Ergonomics: The study of how machines can be made to fit humans better. One of the main conclusions of this research in the computer area is that individuals need to be able to adjust input (and output) devices to their own preferences.

Escrow key: In an encryption system, it is a special key that can be used by government officials to decrypt a secret conversation. The Clipper chip uses escrow keys.

Ethernet: A network communications protocol that specifies how machines will exchange data. It uses a broadcast system in which one machine transmits its message on the communication medium. The other machines listen for messages directed to them.

Ethics: The concept that various elements of society have obligations to the others. In IT, it focuses on the roles of users, developers, and vendors.

Event-driven approach: (1) A user-interface approach where the user controls the sequence or operations and the software responds to these events. Events can range from a simple key-press to a voice command. (2) Modern, window-based software does not follow a sequential process. Instead, actions by users generate events. The programs respond to these events and alter data or offer additional choices. Typical events include mouse clicks pointing to items on the screen, keystrokes, changes to values, or transmissions from other systems.

Exception report: Report that is triggered by some event to signify a condition that is unusual and needs to be handled immediately.

Executive information system (EIS): A type of decision support system that collects, analyzes, and presents data in a format that is easy to use by top executives. To achieve this objective, the EIS is based on a model of the entire company. In most cases the model is presented graphically and the executives retrieve information by pointing to objects on the screen.

Exhaustive testing: Testing every possible combination of inputs to search for errors. Generally not a feasible option, so most computer systems will always contain errors.

Expert system (ES): A system with the goal of helping a novice achieve the same results as an expert. They can handle ill-structured and missing data. Current expert systems can only be applied to narrowly defined problems. Diagnostic problems are common applications for expert systems.

Expert system shell: A program that provides a way to collect data, enter rules, talk to users, present results, and evaluate the rules for an expert system.

Export: An older method of exchanging data among various software packages. One package exports the data by storing it in a format that can be read by other software. Object Linking and Embedding is a more powerful way to exchange data.

Extensible markup language (XML): A tag-based notation system that is used to assign names and structure to data. It was mainly designed for transferring data among diverse systems.

External agents: Entities that are outside the direct control of your company. Typical external agents are customers, suppliers, rivals, and governments. Competitive advantages can be found by producing better-quality items or services at a lower cost than your rivals. Also, many firms have strengthened their positions by building closer ties with their suppliers and customers.

External entity: Objects outside the boundary of a system that communicate with the system. Common business examples include suppliers, customers, government agencies, and management.

Extraction, transformation, and transportation (ETT): The process in data warehouses that involves taking data from existing systems, cleaning it up, and moving it into the data warehouse.

Extreme programming (XP): A new version of development loosely based on prototyping. Pairs of developers rapidly build and simultaneously test applications. The goal is to build releases and then modify them to meet the changing needs of the users.

Facsimile (Fax): A combination scanner, transmitter, and receiver that digitizes an image, compresses it, and transmits it over phone lines to another facsimile machine.

Fault-tolerance: The ability of a computer or a system to continue functioning properly even if some of the components fail. Fault-tolerant machines rely on duplication of subsystems with continuous monitoring and automatic maintenance calls.

Feasibility study: A quick examination of the problems, goals, and expected costs of a proposed system. The objective is to determine whether the problem can reasonably be solved with a computer system.

Feedback: Well-designed systems have controls that monitor how well they meet their goal. The information

measuring the goals and providing control to the system is known as feedback.

Fiber-optic cable: A thin glass or plastic cable that is internally reflective. It carries a light wave for extended distances and around corners.

File server: Computer on a network that is used to hold data and program files for users to share. To be effective, it should use a multitasking operating system.

File transfer protocol (FTP): A standard method of transferring files on the Internet. If you control a computer, you can give other users access to specific files on your computer without having to provide an account and password for every possible user.

Firewall: A small, fast network computer device that examines every packet entering a company. Rules or filters can be created that will reject certain packets that are known to be dangerous to the network.

Five forces model: Michael Porter's model used to search for competitive advantage. The five forces are: rivals, customers, suppliers, potential competitors, and substitute products.

Floating point operations per second (FLOPS): The number of mathematical calculations a processor can perform in one second. Typically measured in millions (mega-FLOPS) or billions (giga-FLOPS). Bigger numbers represent faster processors.

Flow chart: An old pictorial method for describing the logic of a computer program. It has largely been replaced by pseudocode.

Font size: An important characteristic of text is its size. Size of type is typically measured in points. For reference, a capital letter in a 72-point font will be approximately 1 inch high.

Forward chaining: In an expert system, the ES traces your rules from the data entry to a recommendation. Forward chaining is used to display questions, perform calculations, and apply rules.

Frame: A related set of information that humans group together. Sometimes groupings can be arbitrary. A concept used in discussing AI applications and human cognition.

Frame relay: A network communication system that uses variable-length packets. It is useful for high-speed, large bursts of data. It is being used for long-distance network communications.

Franchise: A means of organizing companies. Independent operators pay a franchise fee to use the company name. They receive training and benefit from the name and advertising of the parent company. They purchase supplies from the parent company and follow the franchise rules.

Front-end processor: A simple communications device for large central computers that accepted all of the terminal wires and then assigned each user to an open communications port on the computer. This device decreased the number of physical access ports required on the computer.

Functions: *See* Methods.

Fuzzy logic: A way of presenting and analyzing logic problems that is designed to handle subjective descriptions (e.g., hot and cold).

General ledger: A collection of accounts that break financial data into specific categories. Common categories include accounts receivable, accounts payable, inventory, and cash.

Geographic information system (GIS): Designed to identify and display relationships among business data and locations. Used to display geographical relationships. Also used to plot delivery routes and create maps.

Gigabyte: Approximately 1 billion bytes of data. Technically, 1,024 to the third power (or 2 to the thirtieth), which is 1,073,741,824. The next highest increment is the terabyte.

Global positioning system (GPS): A system of 24 satellites created by the U.S. Department of Defense. The civilian receivers will identify a location to within about 50 feet. Used for navigation, tracking vehicles, and plotting delivery routes.

Graphical user interface (GUI): A system based on a graphics screen instead of simple text. Users perform tasks by clicking a mouse button on or manipulating objects on the screen. For example, copies are made by dragging an item from one location on the screen to another. Pronounced as "gooey."

Group breaks: Reports are often broken into subsections so that data in each section is grouped together by some common feature. For example, a sales report might group items by department, with subtotals for each department.

Group decision support system (GDSS): A type of groupware that is designed to facilitate meeting and help groups reach a decision. Each participant uses a networked computer to enter ideas and comments. Votes can be recorded and analyzed instantly. Comments and discussion are automatically saved for the further study.

Groupware: Software designed to assist teams of workers. There are four basic types: communication, workflow, meeting, and scheduling. The most common is communication software that supports messages, bulletin boards, and data file transfers and sharing.

Hacker: Primarily used to indicate a person who devotes a great deal of time trying to break into computer systems.

Hardware: The physical equipment used in computing.

High-Definition Television (HDTV): Transmission of television signals in digital form. It provides clearer reception. It also supports encrypted transmissions so broadcasters can control who receives the images. HDTV also supports compression, so more data (better pictures or more channels) can be transmitted in the same frequency space.

Hot links: *See* Dynamic integration.

Hot site: A facility that can be leased from a disaster backup specialist. A hot site contains all the power, telecommunication facilities, and computers necessary to run a company. In the event of a disaster, a company collects its backup data tapes, notifies workers, and moves operations to the hot site.

Hub: A network device used to connect several computers to a network. Commonly used in a twisted-pair LAN. A cable runs from each computer's NIC to the hub. The hub is often connected to a router.

Hypertext markup language (HTML): The standard formatting system used to display pages on the Internet. Special tags (commands inside angle braces, e.g., <HTML>) provide formatting capabilities. Several software packages automatically store text in this format, so users do not have to memorize the tags.

Icon: A small picture on a computer screen that is used to represent some object or indicate a command. A classic example is the trash can used to delete files on the Apple Macintosh.

Image: A graphic representation that can be described by its resolution and the number of colors. They can be stored as bit-mapped or vector images.

Import: An older method of exchanging data among various software packages. Most software (e.g., a database management system) can export or store data in a text file format. Another software package (e.g., a spreadsheet) can import or retrieve this data. Object Linking and Embedding is a more powerful way to exchange data.

Inference engine: Within an expert system, the inference engine applies new observations to the knowledge base and analyzes the rules to reach a conclusion.

Information: Data that has been processed, organized, and integrated to provide insight. The distinction between data and information is that information carries meaning and is used to make decisions.

Information center: An MIS group responsible for supporting end users. It typically provides a help desk to answer questions, programmers who provide access to corporate databases, training classes, and network support people to install and maintain networks.

Information system: A collection of hardware, software, data, and people designed to collect, process, and distribute data throughout an organization.

Information technology: The hardware and software used to create an information system. Sometimes used as an abbreviation for management information systems.

Information threats: There are two classes of threats to information: (1) physical, in the form of disasters; and (2) logical, which consists of unauthorized disclosure, unauthorized modification, and unauthorized withholding of data. The primary source of danger lies with insiders: employees, ex-employees, partners, or consultants.

Information warfare: The use of information in a conflict setting. It includes protecting your own information, providing misinformation to the enemy, and monitoring and disrupting the enemy's information.

Inheritance: Creation or derivation of classes of objects from other object classes. Each derived class inherits the attributes and methods of the prior class. For example, a savings account object can be derived from an account object. The savings account object will automatically have the same attributes and methods. Attributes and methods specific to the savings account can be added.

Initial public offering (IPO): The step when firms sell stock to the public. A method of raising additional funds and a major step for most startup firms.

Input devices: People do not deal very well with binary data, so all data forms must be converted into binary form for the computer. Input devices—for example, keyboards, microphones, and bar-code readers—make the conversion.

Input-Process-Output: A shorthand description of a subsystem. Each subsystem receives inputs and performs some process. The output is passed to another subsystem.

Integrated data: The practice of combining data from many sources to make a decision. Data can come from different department throughout the business, and it can come in many different forms. Networks, groupware, and products that support dynamic linking are all useful tools to integrate data to make better decisions.

Integrated Services Digital Network (ISDN): A set of services, and a transmission and control system, offered by telephone companies. It uses complete digital transmission of signals to improve transmission speed and quality.

Intellectual property: As defined by copyright laws, the concept that property like music, books, software, and movies can be protected. The laws clearly define the owners of the property and specify that the owners can establish any type of copy protections they desire.

Internet: A collection of computers loosely connected to exchange information worldwide. Owners of the computers make files and information available to other users. Common tools on the Internet include e-mail, ftp, telnet, and the World Wide Web.

Internet service provider (ISP): A private company that provides connections to the Internet. Individuals pay a fee to the ISP. The ISP pays a fee to a higher-level provider (e.g., NSP) to pass all communications onto the Internet.

Intranet: A network within an organization that utilizes standard Internet protocols and services. Essentially, this includes websites that are accessible only for internal use.

Intrusion detection system (IDS): A combination of hardware and software that monitors packets and operations on the network and computers. It watches for suspicious patterns that might indicate an attack.

Iterative solution: Building a model and evaluating it until the parameter values converge to a fixed solution. Sometimes an iterative model will diverge and never reach an acceptable solution. *See also* Circular reference.

Joint application design (JAD): A method to reduce design time by putting everyone in development sessions until the system is designed. Users, managers, and systems analysts participate in a series of intense meetings to design the inputs (data and screens), and outputs (reports) needed by the new system.

Just-in-time (JIT) inventory: A production system that relies on suppliers delivering components just as they are needed in production, instead of relying on inventory stocks. JIT requires close communication between manufacturers and suppliers.

Kerberos: A security system created at MIT that enables systems to have a single sign-on. Users log into the Kerberos server and other systems can validate the user's identity from that server; much simpler than requiring users to log-in multiple times. Named after the hound that guards the gates of Hades (spelled Cerberus in Latin).

Kilobyte: Approximately one thousand bytes of data. Technically it is 2 to the tenth, or 1,024.

Knowledge: A higher level of understanding, including rules, patterns, and decisions. Knowledge-based systems are built to automatically analyze data, identify patterns, and recommend decisions.

Knowledge base: Within an expert system, the knowledge base consists of basic data and a set of rules.

Knowledge engineer: A person who helps build an expert system by organizing the data, devising the rules, and entering the criteria into the expert system shell; trained to deal with experts to derive the rules needed to create an expert system. The engineer also converts the data and rules into the format needed by the expert system.

Knowledge Management (KM): A system that stores information in the context of a set of decisions. It contains cross-references and search methods to make it easy for workers to understand how and why decisions were made.

Legacy systems: Information systems that were created over several years and are now crucial to operating the company. They probably use older technology, and the software is difficult to modify. However, replacing them is difficult and likely to interfere with day-to-day operations. Any changes or new systems must be able to work with the older components.

Limited liability company: A legal variation of organizing a company. It protects the owners with the same separation of funds offered to corporations, but because it does not allow it to issue stock, the record keeping is somewhat easier.

Local area network (LAN): A collection of personal computers within a small geographical area, connected by a network. All of the components are owned or controlled by one company.

Magnetic hard drives: Magnetic hard drives (or disk drives) consist of rigid platters that store data with magnetic particles. Data is accessed by spinning the platters and moving a drive head across the platters to access various tracks.

Magnetic ink character recognition (MICR): A special typeface printed with ink containing magnetic particles. It can be read rapidly and reliably by computers. Banks are the primary users of MICR. Checks are imprinted with MICR routing numbers. MICR readers are more accurate than straight OCR because they pick up a stronger signal from magnetic particles in the ink.

Mail filters: Programs that automatically read e-mail and sort the messages according to whatever criteria the manager prefers. Junk mail can be discarded automatically.

Management information system (MIS): Consists of five related components: hardware, software, people, procedures, and databases. The goal of management information systems is to enable managers to make better decisions by providing quality information.

Manufacturing Resource Planning (MRP II): An integrated approach to manufacturing. Beginning with the desired production levels, we work backward to determine the processing time, materials, and labor needed at each step. These results generate schedules and inventory needs. Sometimes known as a demand-pull system.

Mass customization: The ability to modify the production line often enough to produce more variations of the main product. The goal is to cover virtually all of the niche markets.

Materials requirements planning (MRP): An early production system, where at each stage of production, we evaluate the usage of materials to determine the optimal inventory levels.

Mathematical model: A model that is defined by mathematical equations. This format is easy to use for forecasts and for simulation analyses on the computer. Be careful not to confuse precision with accuracy. A model might forecast some value with great precision (e.g., 15.9371), but the accuracy could be quite less (e.g., actual values between 12 and 18).

Media: For the means of transmissions, connecting computers in a network. Common methods include twisted-pair and coaxial cable; fiber-optic lines; and radio, micro, and infrared waves.

Megabyte: Loosely, 1 million bytes of data. Technically, it is 1,048,576 bytes of data, which is 2 raised to the 20th power.

Megaflops: Millions of floating-point operations per second. A measure of the processor speed, it counts the number of common arithmetical operations that can be performed in one second.

Megahertz: One million cycles per second, a measure of the clock chip in a computer, which establishes how fast a processor can operate.

Menu tree: A graphical depiction of the menu choices available to users in a system.

Metadata: Describes the source data, and the transformation and integration steps, and defines the way the database or data warehouse is organized.

Methods: Descriptions of actions that an object can perform. For example, an employee object could be hired, promoted, or released. Each of these functions would necessitate changes in the employee attributes and in other objects. The methods carry out these changes.

Microsecond: One-millionth of a second. Few computer components are measured in microseconds, but some electrical devices and controllers operate in that range. One microsecond compared to one second is the same as comparing one second to 11.6 days.

Million instructions per second (MIPS): A measure of computer processor speed. Higher numbers represent a faster processor. However, different brands of processors use different instruction sets, so numbers are not always comparable.

Millisecond: One-thousandth of a second. Disk drives and some other input and output devices perform operations measured in milliseconds. One millisecond compared to one second is the same as comparing 1 second to 16.7 minutes.

Mirror drive: A backup system where data is automatically written to a second disk drive. If the primary drive fails, operations can be switched instantaneously to the mirror drive.

Model: A simplified, abstract representation of some real-world system. Some models can be written as mathematical equations or graphs, others are subjective descriptions. Models help managers visualize physical objects and business processes. Information systems help you build models, evaluate them, and organize and display the output.

Modem: Modulator-demodulator. A device that converts computer signals into sounds that can be transmitted (and received) across phone lines.

Morphing: Digital conversion of one image into another. The term is an abbreviation of *metamorphosis*. True morphing is done with digital video sequences, where the computer modifies each frame until the image converts to a new form.

Multimedia: The combination of the four basic data types: text, sound, video, and images (animation). In its broadest definition, multimedia encompasses virtually any combination of data types. Today, it typically refers to the use of sound, text, and video clips in digitized form that are controlled by the computer user.

Multitasking: A feature of operating systems that enables you to run more than one task or application at the same time. Technically, they do not run at exactly the same time. The processor divides its time and works on several tasks at once.

Musical Instrument Data Interchange (MIDI): A collection of standards that define how musical instruments communicate with each other. Sounds are stored by musical notation and re-created by synthesizers that play the notes.

Nanosecond: One-billionth of a second. Computer processors and memory chips operate at times measured in nanoseconds. One nanosecond compared to 1 second is the same as comparing 1 second to 31.7 years.

Natural language: A human language used for communication with other humans, as opposed to a computer programming language or some other artificial language created for limited communication.

Network interface card (NIC): The communication card that plugs into a computer and attaches to the network communication medium. It translates computer commands into network messages and server commands.

Network operating system (NOS): A special operating system installed on a file server, with portions loaded to the client machines. It enables the machines to communicate and share files.

Network service provider (NSP): A high-level Internet service provider offering connections to ISPs. The NSP leases high-speed, high-capacity lines to handle the communication traffic from hundreds of ISPs.

Neural network: A collection of artificial neurons loosely designed to mimic the way the human brain operates; especially useful for tasks that involve pattern recognition.

Neuron: The fundamental cell of human brains and nerves. Each of these cells is relatively simple, but there are approximately 100 million of them.

Newsgroups: A set of electronic bulletin boards available on the Internet. Postings are continuously circulated around the network as people add comments.

Normalization: A set of rules for creating tables in a relational database. The primary rules are that there can be no repeating elements and every nonkey column must depend on the whole key and nothing but the key. Roughly, it means that each table should refer to only one object or concept.

Numbers: One of the basic data types, similar to text on input and output. Attributes include precision and a scaling factor that defines the true size or dimension of the number.

Object: A software description of some entity. It consists of attributes that describe the object, and functions (or methods) that describe the actions that can be taken by the object. Objects are generally related to other objects through an object hierarchy.

Object hierarchy: Objects are defined from other base objects. The new objects inherit the properties and functions of the prior objects.

Object Linking and Embedding (OLE): A standard created by Microsoft for its Windows operating system to create compound documents and dynamically link data objects from multiple software packages. You begin with a compound document or container that holds data from other software packages. These data objects can be edited directly (embedded). Most OLE software also supports dynamic linking.

Object orientation: An approach to systems and programming that classifies data as various objects. Objects have attributes or properties that can be set by the programmer or by users. Objects also have methods or functions that define the actions they can take. Objects can be defined from other objects, so most are derived from the four basic data types.

Object-oriented DBMS: A database system specifically created to hold custom objects. Generally supports developer-defined data types and hierarchical relationships.

Object-oriented design: The ultimate goal of the object-oriented approach is to build a set of reusable objects and procedures. The idea is that eventually, it should be possible to create new systems or modify old ones simply by plugging in a new module or modifying an existing object.

One-to-many relationship: Some object or task that can be repeated. For instance, a customer can place many orders. In database normalization, we search for one-to-many relationships and split them into two tables.

Online analytical processing (OLAP): A computer system designed to help managers retrieve and analyze data. The systems are optimized to rapidly integrate and retrieve data. The storage system is generally incompatible with transaction processing, so it is stored in a data warehouse.

Online transaction processing (OLTP): A computer system designed to handle daily transactions. It is optimized to record and protect multiple transactions. Because it is generally not compatible with managerial retrieval of data, data is extracted from these systems into a data warehouse.

Open operating system: An operating system that is supposed to be vendor neutral. It should run on hardware from several different vendors. When a buyer upgrades to a new machine, the operating system and software should function the same as before.

Open system: An open system learns by altering itself as the environment changes.

Operating system: A basic collection of software that handles jobs common to all users and programmers. It is responsible for connecting the hardware devices, such as terminals, disk drives, and printers. It also provides the environment for other software, as well as the user interface that affects how people use the machine.

Operations level: Day-to-day operations and decisions. In a manufacturing firm, machine settings, worker schedules, and maintenance requirements would represent management decisions at the operations level. Information systems are used at this level to collect data and perform well-defined computations.

Optical character recognition (OCR): The ability to convert images of characters (bitmaps) into computer text that can be stored, searched, and edited. Software examines a picture and looks for text. The software checks each line, deciphers one character at a time, and stores the result as text.

Optimization: The use of models to search for the best solutions: minimizing costs, improving efficiency, or increasing profits.

Output devices: Data stored in binary form on the computer must be converted to a format people understand. Output devices—for example, display screens, printers, and synthesizers—make the conversion.

Outsourcing: The act of transferring ownership or management of MIS resources (hardware, software, and personnel) to an outside MIS specialist.

Packets: Network messages are split into packets for transmission. Each packet contains a destination and source address as well as a portion of the message.

Packet switching network: A communications protocol in which each message is placed into smaller packets. These packets contain a destination and source address. The packets are switched (or routed) to the appropriate computer. With high-speed switches, this protocol offers speeds in excess of 150 megabits per second.

Page footer: Data that is placed at the bottom of each page in a report. Common items include page totals and page numbers.

Page header: Data that is placed at the top of every page in a report. Common items include the report title, date, and column labels.

Parallel processing: Using several processors in the same computer. Each processor can be assigned different tasks, or jobs can be split into separate pieces and given to each processor. There are a few massively parallel machines that utilize several thousand processors.

Parameter: Variables in a model that can be controlled or set by managers. They are used to examine different situations or to tailor the model to fit a specific problem.

Patent: Legal protection for products (and sometimes business processes). It grants the owner sole right to sell or create modifications of the product for 20 years. No one can create the same product unless approved by the patent owner.

Peer-to-peer communication: A method of sharing data and information directly with colleagues and peers, instead of transferring data through a shared central server.

Peer-to-peer network: A network configuration in which each machine is considered to be an equal. Messages and data are shared directly between individual computers. Each machine continuously operates as both a client and a server.

Personal digital assistant (PDA): A small portable, handheld computer designed primarily to handle contacts, schedules, e-mail, and short notes. Some models have more advanced features to support documents, spreadsheets, photos, and music. A few have wireless connections, others have to be synchronized with desktops to transfer e-mail and update schedules.

Photo-CD: A standardized system created by Kodak to convert photographs to digital (bitmap) form and store them on optical disks.

Pivot table: A tool within Microsoft Excel used to extract and organize data. It enables users to examine aggregated data and quickly see the accompanying detail.

Pixel: Picture element, or a single dot on an image or video screen.

Point-of-sale (POS) system: A means of collecting data immediately when items are sold. Cash registers are actually data terminals that look up prices and instantly transmit sales data to a central computer.

Polymorphism: In an object design, different objects can have methods that have the same name but operate slightly differently. For example, a checking account object and a savings account object could each have a method called pay interest. The checking account might pay interest monthly, whereas the savings account pays it quarterly.

Portable document format (PDF): A file format often used on the Internet. It can display documents with detailed precision, including special fonts and shading. Defined by Adobe, readers are freely available for many machines. Special software must be purchased to create the files.

Precision (numeric): In computers, numeric precision represents the number of digits stored to the right of the decimal point. So, 10.1234 is more precise than 10.12, however, it is not necessarily more accurate. The original value might not have been measured beyond two digits.

Prediction: Model parameters can be estimated from prior data. Sample data is used to forecast future changes based on the model.

Pretty good privacy (PGP): A dual-key encryption system based on the Diffie-Hellman approach similar to RSA. Created by Philip Zimmermann and commonly used to encrypt e-mail. Free copies for noncommercial use are still available from MIT.

Primary key: A column or set of columns that contains data to uniquely identify each row in a relational database table. For example, each customer must have a unique identifier, possibly a phone number or an internally generated customer number.

Privacy: (1) The concept that people should be able to go about their lives without constant surveillance, that personal information about people should not be shared without their permission. (2) Collecting personal data only when you have a legitimate use for it, allowing customers to correct and remove personal data. Protecting confidential data so that it is not released to anyone. Giving customers the option so you do not sell or lease their personal data.

Private key: In a dual-key encryption system, the key that is protected by the owner and never revealed. It is generally a very large number.

Problem boundary: The line that identifies the primary components of the system that are creating a specific problem. Subsystems inside the boundary can be modified to solve the problem or enhance the system. Subsystems outside the boundary cannot be altered at this time.

Procedures: Instructions that help people use the systems. They include items such as user manuals, documentation, and procedures to ensure that backups are made regularly.

Process: An activity that is part of a data flow diagram. Systems can be built to process goods or to process data. Most information system work focuses on processes that alter data.

Process control: The use of computers to monitor and control the production machines and robots. Production lines generally use many different machines, each requiring several adjustments or settings. Computer control simplifies and speeds the setup.

Process control system: A computerized system that monitors and controls a production line. Some systems are completely linked so that a central computer can set up machines on an entire assembly line.

Process innovation: Evaluating the entire firm to improve individual processes, and to search for integrated solutions that will reduce costs, improve quality, or boost sales to gain a competitive advantage. *See also* Re-engineering.

Processor: The heart of a computer. It carries out the instructions of the operating system and the application programs.

Product differentiation: The ability to make your products appear different from those of your rivals, thus attracting more customers. Information systems have been used to alter products and provide new services.

Properties: *See* Attributes.

Protocols: A set of definitions and standards that establish the communication links on a network. Networks are often classified by their choice of protocol. Common protocols include Ethernet, Token Ring, and TCP/IP.

Prototyping: An iterative system design technique that takes advantage of high-level tools to rapidly create working systems. The main objective of prototyping is to create a working version of the system as quickly as possible, even if some components are not included in the early versions.

Pseudocode: A loosely structured method to describe the logic of a program or outline a system. It uses basic programming techniques but ignores issues of syntax and relies on verbal descriptions.

Public key: In a dual-key encryption system, the key that is given to the public. Each person wishing to use dual-key encryption must have a different public key. The key works only in tandem with the user's private key.

Pure Internet plays: Dot-com firms that have no direct tie to traditional business. Firms that make all their revenue from Internet sales or other Internet firms. A popular concept in 1999, but most pure Internet firms failed in 2000 and 2001.

Query by example (QBE): A visual method of examining data stored in a relational database. You ask questions and examine the data by pointing to tables on the screen and filling in templates.

Query system: A method of retrieving data in a DBMS. It generally uses a formal process to pose the questions: (1) what columns should be displayed? (2) what conditions are given? (3) what tables are involved? And (4) how are the tables connected? See Query by example and SQL.

Random access memory (RAM): High-speed memory chips that hold data for immediate processing. On most computers, data held in RAM is lost when the power is removed, so data must be moved to secondary storage.

Rapid application development (RAD): The goal of building a system much faster than with traditional SDLC methods. Using powerful tools (database management system, high-level languages, graphical toolkits, and objects), highly trained programmers can build systems in a matter of weeks or months. Using workgroups, communication networks, and CASE tools, small teams can speed up the development and design steps.

Read Only Memory (ROM): A type of memory on which data can be stored only one time. It can be read as often as needed but cannot be changed. ROM keeps its data when power is removed, so it is used to hold certain core programs and system data that is rarely changed.

Reduced instruction set computer (RISC): When designing a RISC processor, the manufacturer deliberately limits the number of circuits and instructions on the chip. The goal is to create a processor that performs a few simple tasks very fast. More complex problems are solved in software. Because RISC processors require fewer circuits, they are easier to produce.

Redundant array of independent disks (RAID): A system consisting of several smaller drives instead of one large one. Large files are split into pieces stored on several different physical drives. The data pieces can be duplicated and stored in more than one location for backup. RAID systems also provide faster access to the data, because each of the drives can be searching through their part of the file at the same time.

Re-engineering: A complete reorganization of a company. Beginning from scratch, you identify goals, along with the most efficient means of attaining those goals, and create new processes that change the company to meet the new goals. The term *re-engineering* and its current usage were made popular in 1990 by management consultants James Champy and Michael Hammer.

Relational database: A database in which all data is stored in flat tables that meet the normalization rules. Tables are logically connected by matching columns of data. System data, such as access rights, descriptions, and data definitions are also stored in tables.

Repetitive stress injury (RSI): An injury that occurs from repeating a stressful action. For instance, several people have complained that constant typing damages their wrists. Ergonomic design, adjusting your workspace, and taking breaks are common recommendations to avoid repetitive stress.

Report: A printed summary or screen display that is produced on a regular basis by a database management system. The main sections of a report are: report header, page header, group/break header, detail, group/break footer, page footer, and report footer.

Request for proposal (RFP): A list of specifications and questions sent to vendors asking them to propose (sell) a product that might fill those needs.

Resolution: The number of dots or pixels displayed per inch of horizontal or vertical space. Input and output devices, as well as images and video, are measured by their resolution. Higher values of dots-per-inch yield more detailed images.

Reverse engineering: The process of taking older software and rewriting it to modernize it and make it easier to modify and enhance. Reverse engineering tools consist of software that reads the program code from the original software and converts it to a form that is easier to modify.

Rivals: Any group of firms that are competing for customers and sales. Similar to competitors, but "competition" carries an economic definition involving many firms. Even an industry with two firms can experience rivalry.

Rivest-Shamir-Adelman (RSA): Three mathematicians who developed and patented a dual-key encryption system. The term often refers to the encryption technique. It is based on the computational difficulty of factoring very large numbers into their prime components.

Rocket scientists: Mathematically trained financial analysts who build complex mathematical models of the stock market and help create and price new securities.

Router: A communication device that connects subnetworks together. Local messages remain within each subnetwork. Messages between subnetworks are sent to the proper location through the router.

Row: A horizontal element that contains all of the data to describe an entity or object in a relational database or spreadsheet.

Rules: A set of conditions that describe a problem or a potential response. Generally expressed as "If . . . Then" conditions. Used by expert systems to analyze new problems and suggest alternatives.

Sampler: An input device that reads electrical signals from a microphone and stores the sound as a collection of numbers. It measures the frequency and amplitude of the sound waves thousands of times per second.

Scalability: The ability to buy a faster computer as needed and transfer all software and data without modification. True scalability enables users to buy a smaller computer today and upgrade later without incurring huge conversion costs.

Scrolling region: On a data entry form, a subform or section that is designed to collect multiple rows of data. Much like a spreadsheet, the user can move back and forth to alter or examine prior entries.

Secondary storage: Data storage devices that hold data even if they lose power. Typically cheaper than RAM, but slower. Disk drives are common secondary storage devices.

Serifs: The small lines, curlicues, and ornamentation on many typefaces. They generally make it easier for people to read words and sentences on printed output. Sans serif typefaces have more white space between characters and are often used for signs and displays that must be read from a longer distance.

Server farm: A collection of dozens or hundreds of smaller servers. Software allocates tasks to whichever server is the least busy. This approach to scalability is fault-tolerant and easy to expand, but can be difficult to manage.

SharePoint: Microsoft's Web-based tool for teamwork. It supports file sharing, version control, discussion groups, and surveys.

Sign-off: In a systems development life-cycle approach, the approval that managers must give to forms, reports, and computations at various stages of the development. This approval is given when they sign the appropriate documents.

Simple object access protocol (SOAP): A standard, easy-to-implement method of exchanging information and messages among different computers on the Internet. A protocol that works with XML to support Web-based services.

Simulation: Models are used to examine what might happen if we decide to make changes to the process, to see how the system will react to external events, or to examine relationships in more detail.

Social legitimacy: At one time, mainstream organizations were identified by the quality of their presentation and their image. Large firms spend millions of dollars on graphic artists, professional designers, and professional printing. The decreasing cost of computers enables even small organizations to create an image that is hard to distinguish from large organizations.

Software: A collection of computer programs that are algorithms or logical statements that control the hardware.

Software maintenance: The act of fixing problems, altering reports, or extending an existing system to improve it. It refers to changes in the software, not to hardware tasks such as cleaning printers.

Software piracy: The act of copying software without paying the copyright owner. With few exceptions (e.g., backup), copying software is illegal. Companies and individuals who are caught have to pay thousands of dollars in penalties and risk going to jail. It is commonly accepted that piracy takes money away from the development of improved software.

Software suites: Collections of software packages that are designed to operate together. Theoretically, data from each package can be easily shared with data from the others. So word processors can incorporate graphics, and spreadsheets can retrieve data from the database management system. Suites are often sold at a substantial discount compared to buying each package separately.

Sound: One of the basic data types. There are two methods to describe sound: samples or MIDI. Digitized (sampled) sound is based on a specified sampling and playback rate, and fits into frequency and amplitude (volume) ranges.

Speech recognition: The ability of a computer to capture spoken words, convert them into text, and then take some action based on the command.

SQL: A structured query language supported by most major database management systems. The most common command is of the form: SELECT *column list* FROM *table list* JOIN *how tables are related* WHERE *condition* ORDER BY *columns.*

Standard operating procedures: A set of procedures that define how employees and managers should deal with certain situations.

Standards: An agreement that specifies certain technical definitions. Standards can be established by committees or evolve over time through market pressures. As technology changes, new standards are created.

Static HTML: Simple HTML pages that are changed only by humans, so they are rarely changed. Generally used only for the prepurchase information stage of e-commerce.

Static integration: A means of combining data from two documents. A copy of the original is placed into the new document. Because it is static, changes made to the original document are not automatically updated. *See also* Dynamic integration.

Statistical quality control (SQC): The statistical analysis of measurement data to improve quality. Several statistical calculations and graphs are used to determine whether fluctuations are purely random or represent major changes that need to be corrected.

Stock options: A right to purchase a specific stock at a given price. Often granted to workers and managers in startup companies. If the company grows rapidly, its stock price should increase. The option owner can cash in the options and receive the difference between the current price and the option price.

Strategic decisions: Decisions that involve changing the overall structure of the firm. They are long-term decisions and are unstructured. They represent an attempt to gain a competitive advantage over your rivals. They are usually difficult and risky decisions. MIS support for strategic decisions typically consists of gathering, analyzing, and presenting data on rivals, customers, and suppliers.

Structured decisions: Decisions that can be defined by a set of rules or procedures. They can be highly detailed, but they are defined without resorting to vague definitions.

Structured walkthrough: A review process in which the objective is to reveal problems, inaccuracies, ambiguities, and omissions in the systems design before the program code is finalized. The users are presented with a prototype or mockup of the proposed system.

Subchapter S corporation: A legal variation of a corporation that can be chosen by the owners. The IRS and some states impose limits on the type of company that can elect this option. It avoids the problem of double taxation by passing income and losses directly to the owners' personal income tax statements.

Supply chain management (SCM): Organizing the entire supply process including vendor selection, parts management, ordering, payment, and quality control.

Switch: A network device used to connect machines. Unlike a router, a switch creates a virtual circuit that is used by a single machine at a time.

Switching costs: The costs incurred in creating a similar information system when a customer switches to a rival firm. Information technology creates switching costs because customers would have to convert data, re-create reports, and retrain users.

Synthesizer: An electronic device to convert electrical signals into sound. One basic technique is FM synthesis, which generates and combines fixed waves to achieve the desired sound. A newer method combines short digitized samples of various instruments with waveforms to create more realistic sounds.

Sysop: System operator. Person in charge of an electronic bulletin board who organizes files and controls access and privileges.

System: A collection of interrelated objects that work toward some goal.

Systems analysis and design: A refinement of the scientific method that is used to analyze and build information systems.

Systems analyst: A common job in MIS. The analyst is responsible for designing new systems. Analysts must understand the business application and be able to communicate with users. Analysts must also understand technical specifications and programming details.

Systems development life cycle (SDLC): A formal method of designing and building information systems. There are five basic phases: (1) feasibility and planning, (2) systems analysis, (3) systems design, (4) implementation, and (5) maintenance and review.

T1, T3: An older communication link provided by phone companies. Used to carry digitized analog signals, it is being replaced with ISDN links. T1 refers to a group of 24 voice-grade lines and can carry 1.544 megabits per second (Mbps). A T2 trunk line is equivalent to 96 voice circuits providing 6.312 Mbps. T3 provides 44.736 Mbps, and T4 can carry 139,264 Mbps. Services can be leased at any of these levels, where greater bandwidth carries higher costs.

Table: A method of storing data in a relational database. Tables contain data for one entity or object. The columns represent attributes, and data for each item is stored in a single row. Each table must have a primary key.

Tactical decisions: Tactical decisions typically involve time frames of less than a year. They usually result in making relatively major changes to operations but staying within the existing structure of the organization. MIS support consists of databases, networks, integration, decision support systems, and expert systems.

Telnet: A method supported on the Internet that enables users of one computer to log on to a different computer. Once logged on to the new system, the user is treated as any other user on the system.

Terabyte: Approximately 1 trillion bytes of data. Technically, it is 2 to the 40th power.

Text: The simplest of the four basic data types, it also includes numbers. In its most basic form, text is made up of individual characters, which are stored in the computer as numbers. More sophisticated text is described by its typeface, font size, color, and orientation (rotation).

Thin client: Simpler hardware than a full-blown personal computer, with minimal software. It is generally used to display applications running on the server and accept input from the user.

Token Ring: A communications protocol that describes when each machine can send messages. A machine can only transmit when it receives a special message called a token. When the message is finished or a time limit is reached, the token is passed to the next machine.

Top-down development: An approach to designing and building systems that begins with an analysis of the entire company and works down to increasing detail. A complete top-down approach is usually impossible because it takes too long to analyze everything. *See also* Bottom-up development.

Total cost of ownership (TCO): The cost of purchasing and running a client computer (personal computer). A highly subjective number, it typically includes the hardware cost, the software license fees, maintenance costs, and training costs.

Total quality management (TQM): A management doctrine that states that quality must be built into every process and item. Every step and each person must be dedicated to producing quality products and services.

Transaction-processing system: A system that records and collects data related to exchanges between two parties. This data forms the foundation for all other information system capabilities. MIS support typically consists of databases, communication networks, and security controls.

Transborder data flow (TBDF): The transfer of data across national boundaries. Some countries place restrictions on the transfer of data, especially data that relates to citizens (and of course, data related to "national security"). Some people have discussed taxing the flow of data.

Triggered rule: In an expert system, if a rule is used in an application, it is said to have been triggered or fired.

Trojan horse: A special program that hides inside another program. Eventually, when the main program is run, the Trojan horse program might delete files, display a message, or copy data to an external computer.

True color: Humans can distinguish about 16 million colors. Devices that can display that many colors are said to display true color. It requires the device to use 3 bytes (24 bits) for each pixel.

Turing test: A test proposed by Alan Turing in which a machine would be judged "intelligent" if the software could use conversation to fool a human into thinking it was talking with a person instead of a machine.

Twisted-pair cable: Common dual-line wire. Often packaged as three or four pairs of wires. The cable can be run for only a limited distance, and the signal is subject to interference.

Typeface: A defined way to draw a set of text characters. Several thousand typefaces have been created to meet different artistic and communication needs. A common characterization is serif and sans serif typefaces.

Unicode: An international standard that defines character sets for every modern (living) language and many extinct languages (e.g., Latin).

Uninterruptable power supply (UPS): A large battery and special circuitry that provides a buffer between the computer and the power supply. It protects the computer from spikes and brownouts.

Universal description discovery, and integration (UDDI): A public Web-based directory system designed to enable computers to find and use Web services offered by other companies. For example, someday your computer could automatically find all companies that can use current exchange rates to convert prices.

UNIX: A popular operating system created by Bell Labs. It is designed to operate the same on hardware from several different vendors. Unfortunately, there are several varieties of UNIX, and software that operates on one version often must be modified to function on other machines.

Unstable model: A model that cannot be solved for a single solution. The solution might continually diverge, or it could oscillate between several alternatives. Generally due to insufficient or incorrect feedback mechanisms.

Upload: To transfer files from a local computer (usually a personal computer) to a distant computer. *See also* Download.

Usenet: *See* News groups.

User resistance: People often resist change. Implementation of a new system highlights this resistance. Managers and developers must prepare for this resistance and encourage users to change. Education and training are common techniques.

Value chain: A description of the many steps involved in creating a product or service. Each step adds value to the product or service. Managers need to evaluate the chain to find opportunities to expand the firm and gain more sales and profits.

Vector image: A stored collection of mathematical equations, representing lines, circles, and points. These equations can be rescaled to fit any output device or to any desired size. Users deal with the base objects, not the mathematical definitions.

Venture capital: Money offered by specialized firms to startup companies. Banks rarely give money to startups, so venture capitalists finance risky ventures in the hope of high profits when the company goes public. Many strings can be attached to the money—including a loss of control.

Version control: Software that tracks changes made to other documents. Often used in software development to enable developers to go back to prior version.

Video: One of the basic data types. Video combines the attributes of images and sound. An important attribute is the frames-per-second definition. U.S. standard video operates at 30 frames-per-second, movie films run at 24 frames-per-second. Digitizing video requires capturing and playing back the frames at the appropriate speed.

View: A stored query. If you have a complex query that you have to run every week, you (or a database specialist) could create the query and save it as a view with its own name. It is then treated much like a simple table.

Virtual mall: A collection of Web-based merchants who join together for marketing purposes. Generally they share a common Web host and the same commerce server software. By sharing costs, they can survive without a huge amount of sales.

Virtual private network (VPN): Software installed on a company network and on each client that automatically encrypts all communications between the two; useful when workers travel or need to reach the company servers from home using the Internet.

Virtual reality (VR): Virtual reality describes computer displays and techniques that are designed to provide a realistic image to user senses, including three-dimensional video, three-dimensional sound, and sensors that detect user movement that is translated to on-screen action.

Virus: A malicious program that hides inside another program. As the main program runs, the virus copies itself into other programs. At some point, the virus displays a message, shuts down the machine, or deletes all of the files.

Visual BASIC: A modern variation of the BASIC programming language created by Microsoft for application programming in Windows. A variation resides inside many of the Microsoft applications, enabling programmers to manipulate and exchange data among the database, spreadsheet, and word processor.

Visual table of contents: A graphical design method that shows how modules of a system are related. Versions of the technique are also used to display menu trees.

Voice mail: A messaging system similar to telephone answering machines but with additional features like message store and forward. You can use your computer to send messages to co-workers. There are tools that will read e-mail and fax messages over the phone, so managers can stay in touch while they are away from the computer.

Voice over Internet protocol (VoIP): Connecting telephones to the network and using the Internet to transfer phone conversations—instead of traditional phone lines.

Voice recognition: The ability of a computer to capture spoken words and convert them into text.

Webmaster: Specialized IS worker who is responsible for creating, maintaining, and revising a company's World Wide Web site. Webmasters use technical and artistic skills to create sites that attract browsers.

Wide area network (WAN): A network that is spread across a larger geographic area. In most cases, parts of the network are outside the control of a single firm. Long-distance connections often use public carriers.

Window: A portion of the computer screen. You can move each window or change its size. Windows enable you to display and use several applications on the screen at one time.

Wisdom: A level above knowledge. Wisdom represents intelligence, or the ability to analyze, learn, adapt to changing conditions, and create knowledge.

Workflow software: A type of groupware that is designed to automate forms handling and the flow of data in a company. Forms and reports are automatically routed to a list of users on the network. When each person adds comments or makes changes, it is routed to the next process.

Workstations: Computers attached to a network, designed for individual use. Typically, personal computers.

World Wide Web (WWW): A first attempt to set up an international database of information. Web browsers display graphical pages of information, including pictures. Hypertext connections enable you to get related information by clicking highlighted words.

WORM (Write Once, Read Many) disk: Similar to a CD-ROM, but it is easier to store data. Once data is written on the disk, it cannot be changed. Early WORM drives were superseded by lower-cost drives that can store data in standard CD-ROM format.

WYSIWYG: What you see is what you get. With a true WYSIWYG system, documents will look exactly the same on the screen as they do when printed. In addition to format, it means that the printer must have the same typefaces as the video display. Color printers use a system to match the colors on the monitor.

zShops: Amazon.com offers small companies a relatively inexpensive e-commerce solution with little or no fixed costs. Useful for small firms, the system provides marketing, visibility, and a payment mechanism.

PHOTO CREDITS

1.1	Courtesy of McDonald's Corporation
1.2	David Young-Wolff/PhotoEdit
2.1	Andreas Pollok/Getty Images
3.1	Stephen Swinburne/Stock Boston
3.2	Rob Crandall/Rainbow
3.3	Courtesy of Ericsson
3.4	Courtesy of Nokia
4.1	Courtesy of Fisher Scientific
4.2	Courtesy of Sungard
4.7	Courtesy of EyeTicket
5.1	Courtesy of the Home Depot
5.2	Bettmann/Corbis
7.1	Courtesy of Ford Motor Company
7.2	Mark Scott/Getty Images
7.3	Courtesy of GroupSystems.com
8.1	Reuters NewMedia/Corbis
8.2	Darryl Bush/The Liaison Agency
9.1	Nubar Alexanian/Stock Boston
9.2	Courtesy of InVision Technologies
11.1	AFP/Corbis
11.2a	Courtesy of Fujitsu Corp.
11.2b	Courtesy of Nokia
11.2c	Courtesy of Ericsson
12.1	V.C.L./FPG/Getty Images
13.1	Courtesy of Fidelity Investments
13.2	Courtesy of Sun Microsystems
13.3	Fisher/Thatcher/Getty Images
14.1	Courtesy of Eli Lilly and Company
14.2	Gary Buss/Getty Images

STRIKE
BEYOND TOP GUN

WRITTEN AND PHOTOGRAPHED BY
RICK LLINARES

ZENITH PRESS

This book is dedicated to my wife, Susan, who supports, encourages, believes in, and tolerates me and my lifelong passion for military aviation. I also dedicate this book to my two children, Sam and Nicole, with one piece of wisdom to be passed on— believe in your dreams, nurture them, work tirelessly and patiently on their fulfillment, for they really can come true.

First published in 2006 by Zenith Press, an imprint of MBI Publishing Company, Galtier Plaza, Suite 200, 380 Jackson Street, St. Paul, MN 55101-3885 USA

MBI Publishing Company titles are also available at discounts in bulk quantity for industrial or sales-promotional use. For details write to Special Sales Manager at MBI Publishing Company, Galtier Plaza, Suite 200, 380 Jackson Street, St. Paul, MN 55101-3885 USA

Library of Congress Cataloging-in-Publication Data
Llinares, Rick
    Strike: from the air and sea : the U.S. Naval Strike and Air Warfare Center / written and photographed by Rick Llinares.
        p. cm.
Striking power from the air and sea—Transitions—Farewell to the Big Cat—NSAWC, the center of exellence—Beyond TOPGUN—Electronic warriors and Seahawk Weapons School—Red Air.
    ISBN-13: 978-0-7603-2525-4 (hardback)
    ISBN-10: 0-7603-2525-1 (hardback)
    1. Navel Strike and Air Warfare Center (U.S.) 2. Air warfare—Study and teaching—United States. 3. United States. Navy—Tactical aviation—Study and teaching. I. Title.
    VG94.6.N385L56 2006
    359.9'45—dc22
                                                    2006001464

On the cover: The U.S. Naval Strike and Air Warfare Center (NSAWC) operates both the F/A-18 Hornet and F-16 Fighting Falcon as dedicated adversary tactics simulators during Top Gun and air wing training exercises. In aircraft sporting some of the most dazzling camouflage paint schemes of any American warplanes, NSAWC pilots are the finest fighter pilots in the world.

On the endpapers: NSAWC relies on F/A-18As, F/A-18Bs, and F-16s to meet its training commitments. The size of the range complex and the number of NSAWC aircraft allows for realistic threat scenario simulations. This trio is returning from an area defense mission. Mission objective (formally stated): attrit enemy aircraft inbound to carrier battle group; (informally stated) destroy the bad guys before they get to any of our ships.

On the frontispiece: The F-16 Fighting Falcon offers superb unrestricted visibility from its single-piece teardrop canopy, a crucial attribute for modern fighters. The F-16 is extremely maneuverable, and the pilot sits slightly reclined in the ejection seat in order to provide additional tolerance to the high g forces that the aircraft experiences in dogfights.

On the title page: The aircraft carrier is the centerpiece of American naval power projection. The carrier is the center of the carrier strike group (CSG), which includes numerous support ships. The CSG is the most flexible weapons system in the American arsenal and can project immense power with its complement of air wing aircraft.

On the back cover, left: The Bounty Hunters of VFA-2 transitioned to the F/A-18F after trading in their F-14D Tomcats in July 2003. Each fighter unit paints one aircraft in a high-visibility scheme as well as the standard low-visibility fleet gray. **Right:** The E-2C variant of the aircraft made its initial flight in January 1971 with the APS-120 family of radar systems and a new airborne early warning antenna system. Ongoing enhancements provided an increase in the quality of the radar system and the range with which it could detect targets.

Editors: Lindsay Hitch and Steve Gansen
Designer: Kou Lor

Printed in China

CONTENTS

Acknowledgments

I first developed the concept for this book in 1998, when the U.S. Naval Strike and Air Warfare Center (NSAWC) was still a relatively new command. It is many years in the making! Over the years, I have written numerous magazine articles on the command and witnessed its growth and maturity, as well as its ongoing evolution. Many different people lent their time, skills, and effort to help me make this book a reality. Some have moved up and on with their Navy careers, and, as is often the case, they have been difficult to keep in touch with. Nonetheless, I am very grateful to all for their support of my efforts and would like to thank them for their assistance: Admiral Andrew Moffit, Admiral Bernard Smith, Admiral Timothy R. Beard, Admiral H. Denby Starling, Captain John "Jocko" Worthington, Captain Jim "Mean Jim" Greene, Captain Roy Rogers, Commander Tom "Scrote" Lang, Commander Greg "Shifty" Peairs (U.S. Navy, retired), Captain Rolland "Dawg" Thompson, Commander Roe "Skid" Massey, Commander Dan "Bat" Masterson, Lieutenant Commander Chad Mingo, Lieutenant Commander David Goodman, Lieutenant Commander Steve Hartung, Lieutenant Commander Otto "Lechter" Streiber, Lieutenant Commander Steve "Caz" McCazlin (U.S. Navy, retired), Lieutenant Commander Pete "Skids" Matthews, Lieutenant Matt Conliffe, Lieutenant Greg Hicks, Lieutenant Joseph Alden, Lieutenant Rob Woods, Lieutenant Natalie Caruso, Chief Petty Officer Jason Tross, Lieutenant Jeremy Clark, Lieutenant Ross Drenning, Lieutenant Commander William Yates, Lieutenant Shawn Bailey, Lieutenant Joshua Bohach, Senior Chief Aviation ASW Operator Mark Jones, Aviation ASW Operator First Class Jeremey Howsere, Lieutenant Dan Bense, and Lieutenant Steven Groves.

Special thanks need to be extended to certain individuals who worked tirelessly with me: Captain Kevin Wensing and Commander John T. Fleming, great friends, supporters, and the hardest-working people in the U.S. Navy; and to Mike Maus, AIRLANT Public Affairs, the hardest-working civilian in the Navy! At NSAWC, Captain Eamon Storrs, Lieutenant Commander Karla Olsen, Commander Kevin Kenney, and Commander Vic Weber for all the help and patience with my never-ending requests.

A note of thanks to my friends at the "Jolly Rogers" and Air Wing Seven, specifically Lieutenant Commander Len "Sieg" Haidl and Commander Brian "Bear" Koehr.

Special thanks to the Public Affairs officers and individuals of the following squadrons and ships: VF/VFA-103 Jolly Rogers, VF/VFA-2 Bounty Hunters, VFA-122 Flying Eagles, VFA-154, VFC-13 Fighting Saints, VAQ-209, VAW-120, VRC-40, USS *George Washington*, USS *John F. Kennedy*, USS *Dwight D. Eisenhower*, Naval Air Station Fallon—Mr. Zip Upham, Aviation Survival Training Center—Master Chief Jill Aniolek-Maners.

I would also like to thank my friends at MBI Publishing for their support. Both Richard Kane and Steve Gansen believed in the *Strike* book and lent their full support. Very special thanks to Lindsay Hitch for her wonderful efforts and expertise in the editing of the book. Final thanks to Hans Halberstadt for all of his advice and guidance.

A Navy Flyer's Creed

I am a United States Navy Flyer.

My countrymen built the best airplane in the world and entrusted it to me. They train me to fly it. I will use it to the utmost of my ability.

With my fellow pilots, air crews, maintenance, and deck crews my plane and I will do anything necessary to carry out our tremendous responsibilities. I will always remember we are part of an unbeatable combat team—the United States Navy.

When the going is fast and rough, I will not falter. I will be uncompromising in every blow I strike. I will be humble in victory.

I am a United States Navy Flyer.

I have dedicated myself to my country, with its many millions of all races, colors, and creeds. They and their way of life are worthy of my greatest protective effort.

I ask the help of God in making that effort great enough.

The birth of military aviation is virtually synonymous with the birth of strike and air warfare, and brings to mind the very first dogfights, aerial observer flights, and bombing missions in biplanes over Europe during the First World War. Naval aviation was launched a few years later and has grown tremendously from its humble beginnings due in large part to its integration with the world's premier sea-going Navy.

Strike warfare has evolved as the technology of warfare has become more complex and sophisticated. The traditional way of thinking about war—in which we fought heavy armor against heavy armor, battleships against battleships, and massed soldiers against massed soldiers—is less relevant. Current threats are more sophisticated and less defined, creating a joint service response to an asymmetric threat. Today, we need to be as swift as we are strong, as flexible as we are deadly.

The history of strike and air warfare is punctuated by events that led to changes in direction. One of those events brought about the Ault report. During the early years of the Vietnam conflict, the United States was not achieving the level of superiority in air-to-air warfare that it had enjoyed in previous conflicts, and Navy leadership directed corrective action. In 1969, Top Gun was formally commissioned in Miramar, California, to train a nucleus of fighter crews who would be the best in the world in aerial combat maneuvering and weapons employment. In the mid-1970s, the need for advanced training in the area of fleet air defense was recognized, so November 1976 saw the beginning of a training course to focus on defining the threat to U.S. carrier task groups and teaching how fighter aircraft could best be used to counter this threat. With that, the Carrier Airborne Early Warning Weapons School (CAEWWS), or Top Dome, was born.

An adversary instructor course was established in 1982, designed to teach pilots the skills required to become a realistic opponent, simulating the air combat maneuvering techniques

of potential threats. In 1983, the Navy formed the embryo of what became known as the Naval Strike Warfare Center (NSWC, Strike University) at Naval Air Station Fallon. This was a direct result of the strike warfare combat performance of naval aviation in action over Lebanon.

On July 11, 1996, Strike U, Top Gun, and Top Dome were consolidated into a single organization—the Naval Strike and Air Warfare Center (NSAWC)—creating a center of excellence to enhance naval aviation combat training effectiveness.

The consolidation of these training programs has had a synergistic effect on naval aviation's ability to perform in peacetime and in combat. From its earliest days, the story of

Naval Air Station (NAS) Fallon, Nevada, is one of the most critical facilities in all of naval aviation. In an age in which many military facilities are encroaching on expanding civilian populations, NAS Fallon remains one of the most remote in the entire military. In addition to having the advantage of its location on the sparsely populated high desert of western Nevada, the base has massive unrestricted instrumented ranges that allow realistic training of high-performance jet aircraft.

Two Navy Strike and Air Warfare Center (NSAWC) instructors turn their F/A-18 Hornet strike fighters toward home, Naval Air Station Fallon, Nevada, after a late-afternoon Top Gun mission. The NSAWC instructors are some of the most experienced aviators in the entire U. S. Navy.

A VFA-131 F/A-18C Hornet cruises back to NAS Fallon after a late-afternoon strike fighter advanced readiness planning (SFARP) mission in December 2005. The unit deployed with its sister squadrons assigned to Carrier Air Wing Seven (CWW-7) for the air wing's precruise training.

naval strike and air warfare has been a saga of continuous growth, change, adaptation, and advancement. There has been nothing static about naval strike and air warfare capability.

At this very moment, and as you read this, somewhere in the world naval aviators are flying in support of national policies and objectives. Highly skilled and among the best in the world at their chosen profession, they are America's maritime tactical aviators, and this book is designed to showcase the arena in which they train.

—M. G. MOFFIT
Rear Admiral, United States Navy Commander,
Naval Strike and Air Warfare Center

The SH-60 Seahawk has had its mission expanded to include more than the antisubmarine warfare role it filled initially. The NSAWC's N8 department stood up to provide specific training in the full range of Seahawk missions to pilots and air crews.

CHAPTER 1

STRIKING POWER FROM THE SEA

In times of national emergency, the first question usually asked by the U.S. commander-in-chief, civilian command authority, and senior military officers is "Where are the carriers?" And for good reason—there is no weapons system in the history of modern warfare that provides the firepower, flexibility, and freedom of movement that the modern U.S. Navy aircraft carriers and their support ships provide. This has been demonstrated time and again in conflicts dating back well over fifty years.

The aircraft carrier gives American military planners a fearsome weapons platform when they may not have the assets on hand in various flashpoints around the world, or when they don't have access to secure bases and air fields needed to project air power. With over 70 percent of the earth's surface made up of water, the U.S. Navy's fleet of twelve aircraft carriers and their supporting ships represents a floating mass of sovereign American soil. Able to operate unfettered in international waters, the carrier strike group (CSG) does not concern itself with obtaining permission from uncooperative foreign countries for aircraft basing or for over-flight rights.

With the simple motto of 90,000 tons of American diplomacy, as needed, where needed, the USS *George Washington* (CVN-73) is the sixth *Nimitz*-class nuclear-powered aircraft carrier in the U.S. Navy. The powerful aircraft carrier can carry up to eighty aircraft, including a mix of strike fighters, electronic warfare, and airborne early warning aircraft, as well as helicopters.

A brown shirt connects the holdback bar in place and the nose tow bar of this F/A-18 Hornet to the catapult shuttle. The sheer force of the catapult will snap the holdback bar and drag the shuttle and Hornet down the catapult track and off into the air. The jet will accelerate from zero to 130 knots in under three seconds.

Right: The F/A-18 Hornet—and its variants—is the mainstay of U.S. naval carrier aviation. The first two versions of the Hornet to enter Navy air wings in 1983 were the single-seat A and two-seat B models. Enhancements in avionics led to the more capable F/A-18C version, which entered service in 1987. These two aircraft are assigned to the "Blue Blasters" of VFA-34 and the "Rampagers" of VFA-83.

The aircraft carriers and their complement of Fleet Marine Forces can be a show of force, a forward presence used by the President to support allies in time of need. They can also be a power projection instrument to insert and support ground forces where needed. When former President Theodore Roosevelt spoke those famous words, "speak softly and carry a big stick," he could never have imagined the impression a carrier would make.

A QUICK LOOK BACK

The years following the first Gulf War were busy ones for naval aviation, as Navy carriers supported the enforcement of "no-fly zones" over Iraq with Operation Southern Watch. Flights were conducted from both the Mediterranean and Red Seas. Operation Provide Comfort saw Navy aircraft providing support for U.S. and allied ground forces working to assist and protect the Kurdish people in the northern section of Iraq from Saddam Hussein's forces. Flare-ups on the African continent also saw Navy carriers respond as a show of force on numerous occasions.

Navy aircraft helped put some teeth into the United Nations (UN) sanctions against Iraq and also the crumbling situation within the former Yugoslavia with the onset of a

The aircraft carrier is the centerpiece of American naval power projection. The carrier is the center of the carrier strike group (CSG), which includes numerous support ships. The CSG is the most flexible weapons system in the American arsenal and can project immense power with its complement of air wing aircraft.

brutal civil war. The UN recognized the new Muslim state, and Navy carrier aircraft began flying missions to prevent Bosnian Serb air forces from conducting combat operations in the UN-mandated no-fly zone. Carrier-based F-14s began flying close air support and combat air patrols around the clock. As the combat operations' tempo increased, Navy aircraft expanded the full scope of their capabilities. EA-6B and ES-3 electronic warfare aircraft suppressed Serbian air defense systems and communications. F/A-18 and F-14 strike fighters conducted precision strike, close air support, combat air patrol, reconnaissance, and forward air control missions. E-2C Hawkeyes served as airborne controllers handling the high volume of combat activity. There was always an American carrier on call in the Adriatic Sea supporting Operation Deny Flight. The USS *John F. Kennedy* (CV-67), USS *Saratoga* (CV-60), USS *America* (CV-66), USS *George Washington* (CVN-73), and USS *Theodore Roosevelt* (CVN-71) all saw action.

On September 11, 2001, the USS *Enterprise* (CVN-65) had been relieved from its duties in support of Operation Southern Watch in the Iraqi theater of operations. The ship was heading back to Norfolk when it made a hard rudder over-180-degree turn and headed back to the waters of southwest Asia. It became clear that the Islamic fundamentalist govern-

ment led by the Taliban in Afghanistan had provided a safe haven for Osama bin Laden and al Qaeda. The *Enterprise* and her air wing were immediately available for Operation Enduring Freedom and began launching the first of over seven hundred missions against the Taliban and targets throughout Afghanistan. The war on terror would test the Navy and its fleet of aircraft carriers and once again prove their value.

Geography posed unique challenges to American military planners, as Afghanistan was surrounded by countries that did not house American military assets or were not predisposed to cooperating with the United States. Estimates placed Taliban and al Qaeda forces at over fifty thousand strong in a desolate and forbidding country. Navy carrier aircraft had to traverse 700 miles of ocean and inhospitable territory to get to their designated target areas. This made for some very long and demanding flights on the part of Navy F-14 and F/A-18 air crews that would spend upward of seven hours in their cockpits.

The USS *Enterprise* (CVN-65) was joined by additional carriers, including the USS *Carl Vinson* (CVN-70), USS *Theodore Roosevelt* (CVN-71), and USS *Kitty Hawk* (CV-63), which all took part in Operation Enduring Freedom. U.S. special forces played a visible and crucial role in supporting the Northern Alliance fighters in striking the Taliban and al Qaeda

The E-2C Hawkeye serves as the eyes and ears of the fleet. The aircraft is the dedicated carrier-based airborne early warning aircraft capable of scanning thousands of miles of airspace in search of airborne threats. Using secure data link communications, the Hawkeye can direct fighter aircraft to meet any potential airborne threat.

forces. The USS *Kitty Hawk* replaced all of its aircraft with special operations helicopters to support their efforts.

Navy carriers worked in concert with each other, acting as a force multiplier to allow for the highest number of sorties possible. Navy aircraft flew more than half of the total number of air sorties and well over 60 percent of the strike sorties. (An air sortie could be any mission, including a support mission such as aerial refueling. A strike mission is a dedicated ground-attack mission.) Unlike the first Gulf War, Navy strike aircraft delivered greater numbers of precision-guided munitions, which dramatically increase target destruction. Aircraft would deploy as the war went on without specific target information and would receive real-time information from ground controllers. Navy strike fighters would take up station and await specific attack instructions. The special

operations forces throughout Afghanistan provided precise, real-time targeting information. With the support of carrier-based strike fighters, as well as U.S. Air Force aircraft, the Northern Alliance was able to drive south and capture Kabul, forcing the routed remnants of the Taliban and al Qaeda into remote sections in the south.

The war on terror continued. In March 2003, President George W. Bush authorized the use of force to remove Saddam Hussein and his two sons from Iraq when they refused to relinquish power. This set the stage for Operation Iraqi Freedom (OIF). Once again, Navy carrier air power was called upon. A total of five carrier battle groups deployed in support of the operation. The USS *Harry S. Truman* (CVN-75) and USS *Theodore Roosevelt* (CVN-71) took up stations in the Mediterranean, while the USS *Kitty Hawk* (CV-63), USS

Constellation (CV-64), and USS *Abraham Lincoln* (CVN-72) steamed in the Persian Gulf. The Iraqi theater of operations represented a large number of air defense systems, both surface-to-air missiles and antiaircraft artillery. Navy F-14s, F/A-18s, EA-6Bs, and S-3s conducted around-the-clock operations, running the gamut from close air support, forward air controller, deep strike, aerial refueling, suppression of enemy air defense, and antishipping missions. The brand-new F/A-18E/F Super Hornet made its first combat deployment during OIF.

CARRIER STRIKE GROUPS

The ability to quickly deploy the necessary naval forces needed for the task at hand is a key component of today's Sea Power 21 doctrine. This represented a broad, wide-ranging organizational change. Sea Strike, Sea Shield, and Sea Basing are the three main concepts within Sea Power 21. Sea Strike is the ability of the U.S. Navy to decisively project offensive power. Sea Shield entails forward-deploying forces that more easily detect and deal with threats as far away from American soil as possible. Similarly, Sea Basing is the concept of utilizing the flexibility that naval forces offer to stage and deploy striking power where needed.

To implement this plan properly, the Navy reorganized itself and developed a more agile structure. The carrier strike group (CSG) is the result. The CSG replaced the carrier battle group (CVBG) and amphibious battle group (ABG). A typical CSG will include a single aircraft carrier and its complement of seventy-plus aircraft, a guided-missile cruiser, two guided-missile destroyers, an attack submarine, and a combination of logistical support ships such as supply, oiler, and ammunition ships. The CSG has a three-fold mission: to protect economic and military shipping, protect U.S. Marine amphibious forces, and establish a naval presence in support of national interests.

The CSGs have been renumbered in the Navy tradition with even numbers on the East Coast and odd numbers on the West Coast. During the summer of 2004, the Navy conducted its first exercise under the fleet response plan (FRP) with Operation Summer Pulse. Under the FRP, the Navy needs to be able to deploy, or "surge," six CSGs in less than thirty days anywhere they are needed in the world. Furthermore, two more CSGs must be ready within three months to reinforce or rotate in support of the six deployed CSGs.

THE MODERN AIRCRAFT CARRIER

Standing over twenty stories above the ocean with a flight deck that could equal several football fields, the carrier is as long as the Empire State Building is tall. These amazing warships are the centerpiece of the CSG.

The future of naval aviation has arrived in the form of the advanced fifth-generation F/A-18 Super Hornet, which is rapidly joining carrier air wings. This Super Hornet is assigned to the "Black Aces" of VFA-41, a former F-14 Tomcat squadron. Most F-14 units are converting to the two-seat F model Super Hornet.

CURRENT ACTIVE U.S. NAVY AIRCRAFT CARRIERS

CARRIER	DESIGNATION
USS *Dwight D. Eisenhower*	CVN-69
USS *Enterprise*	CVN-65
USS *John F. Kennedy*	CV-67
USS *Kitty Hawk*	CV-63
USS *Abraham Lincoln*	CVN-72
USS *Harry S. Truman*	CVN-75
USS *Nimitz*	CVN-68
USS *Theodore Roosevelt*	CVN-71
USS *John C. Stennis*	CVN-74
USS *Carl Vinson*	CVN-70
USS *George Washington*	CVN-73
USS *Ronald Reagan*	CVN-76

CARRIER SNAPSHOT: USS *GEORGE WASHINGTON* (CVN-73) "THE SPIRIT OF FREEDOM"

The "Spirit of Freedom" is the sixth *Nimitz*-class carrier to be built, and its keel was laid in August 1986 with the carrier being commissioned on July 4, 1992.

SPEED	30 knots
LENGTH	1,094 feet
WIDTH	257 feet
HEIGHT	244 feet (equal to a 24-story building)
AIR WING SIZE	70-plus aircraft
FLIGHT DECK AREA	4.5 acres
NUMBER OF ELEVATORS	Four
DISPLACEMENT	97,000 tons
CREW	5,500 with air wing
MEALS SERVED	18,000 daily
COMPARTMENTS	over 2,500
WEIGHT OF TWO ANCHORS	30 tons each
NUMBER OF CATAPULTS	Four
ARRESTING WIRES	Four
DISTILLATION CAPABILITY	400,000 gallons daily
PROPULSION	Two nuclear reactors, allowing the ship to steam for one million miles before fueling
COST	$3.5 billion

As amazing as the machinery is on the carrier, the really impressive part is the interaction of the flight deck crew, pilots, officers, and sailors throughout the ship, enabling each floating city of 5,000 people to function. The flight deck is a hot, noisy, crowded environment. Modern combat aircraft engines produce furnacelike temperatures, as well as wind blasts that can send a person rolling down the flight deck and off the side of the ship. The large intakes and spinning propellers of the various aircraft on deck represent significant hazards. Discipline, training, and courage are all required to do the job, and the flight deck is not for the faint of heart. Flight operations take place in all types of weather, day and night, and it is easy to see why the flight deck is considered the most dangerous place onboard to work.

By far the most amazing aspect of the carrier is the intricate, dangerous, and well-choreographed ballet that takes place on the "roof," or flight deck, to launch and recover high-performance aircraft. As massive as the ship is, its flight deck fills up fast with the seventy or so air wing aircraft. Directly underneath the flight deck is a massive hangar bay. Aircraft that require maintenance are brought down on any one of four elevators from the flight deck to the hangar bay where air wing maintenance personnel can work on the aircraft. Those not in the hangar deck are parked, or "spotted," usually in the bow or along the sides of the carrier and are secured to the deck with chains.

To the uninitiated, the frenzied activity on the deck would be confusing. In fact, it is very well orchestrated. Each person has a specific job and wears a unique colored jersey to identify them and their role. Official Navy websites call this the rainbow wardrobe. The noise on deck can be ear-shattering, and communication is largely done via hand signals. Every person on the flight deck must wear a life preserver in their jacket, also known as a float coat, along with a cranial, which protects their head and contains ear muffs to dampen the noise.

While on deck, the brown shirts usually secure the aircraft, and each unit has individual aircraft plane captains assigned to specific aircraft. Modern combat aircraft have a ravenous appetite for fuel. Purple shirts, also known as "grapes," handle the highly flammable jet fuel. Once the pilots are secured in the aircraft by the plane captains, and the grapes have refueled the aircraft, the brown shirts unchain the aircraft, or "break it down," so it can be maneuvered to the catapults.

The aircraft are taxied from the position on the flight deck to the catapult by yellow-shirted flight deck directors. There are numerous flight directors located around the ship, and they act as traffic cops, moving aircraft from one section of the flight deck to the next, safely handing them off to one another. During the launch, the flight directors maneuver the aircraft in sequence to the various catapults. During normal operations,

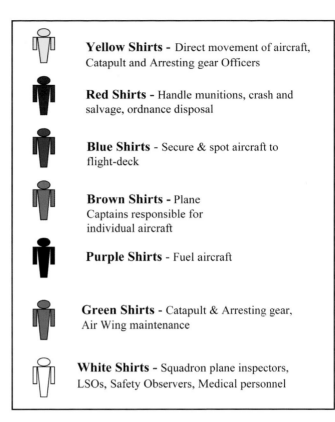

Yellow Shirts - Direct movement of aircraft, Catapult and Arresting gear Officers

Red Shirts - Handle munitions, crash and salvage, ordnance disposal

Blue Shirts - Secure & spot aircraft to flight-deck

Brown Shirts - Plane Captains responsible for individual aircraft

Purple Shirts - Fuel aircraft

Green Shirts - Catapult & Arresting gear, Air Wing maintenance

White Shirts - Squadron plane inspectors, LSOs, Safety Observers, Medical personnel

the SH-60 Seahawk Plane Guard helicopter takes off first and hovers alongside the carrier. If a jet crashes on either takeoff or landing, the Plane Guard will recover the air crew that would have ejected from their stricken aircraft. Next, the E-2C Hawkeye surveillance aircraft will take up its station, flying a large orbit many miles from the carrier in search of threats. Dedicated refueling aircraft, such as specially configured F/A-18 Super Hornets, will go next. From there, the strike package of F/A-18 fighters and EA-6B electronic warfare will be launched.

Each carrier is outfitted with four catapults that take steam generated by the ship's engines and hurl the thirty-ton aircraft into the air in less than 150 feet and less than three seconds. Two catapults, or "cats" as they are referred to, are positioned on the forward section, or bow, of the carrier. Two are located amidships on the left, or port, side, and are called waist cats. When operating at full strength, the four catapults can launch one aircraft every thirty seconds. Though massive, carriers lack sufficient length for normal takeoff and landing operations. The catapults solve the first part of the problem. Essentially, the catapult is a huge slingshot. A pair of large pistons below the flight deck is connected to a single shuttle that protrudes up through the flight deck. The flight director lines up the aircraft precisely on the catapult. Green shirts connect the tow bar of the nose landing gear assembly on the aircraft to the shuttle. A holdback bar is also placed behind

the nose landing gear and secured to the deck, and, as its name implies, it keeps the aircraft in position while its engines are brought up to full power; this is also known as "going into tension." Behind each catapult is a large steel wall called a jet blast deflector (JBD), which is raised behind the aircraft once it is secured to the catapult. The water-cooled JBD protects flight crew and aircraft behind the launching aircraft from the wind blast and heat created by the aircraft's jet engines and turboprops. It is raised and lowered for each launch.

Once the flight deck crew is comfortable that the aircraft is secured to the shuttle and the holdback bar is in place, a series of signals are exchanged between the pilot, flight director, and catapult officer, also known as the shooter, who is positioned below deck. The catapults need to maintain the correct pressure, which is unique for each aircraft based on its individual weight and flight characteristics. The flight deck crew will confirm the weight of the aircraft with the pilot using a weight board, which is also confirmed with the catapult officer. Final visual checks are done by squadron inspectors and safety officers. With a crisp salute during daytime operations, the pilot lets the flight deck crew know the aircraft is ready for launch. At night, the lights will be flashed to confirm all is okay.

The yellow shirt signals that the aircraft is ready for launch by touching the flight deck and pointing down the deck. Many have been known to do this with dramatic style and flair, adding to the excitement and drama of the impending cat shot. The pilot and weapons systems officer brace themselves for the ride of their lives The catapult officer fires the catapult, releasing the steam into the catapult pistons, which will move forward to hurl the shuttle and the attached aircraft down the track. At the end of the catapult, there are a series of brakes that absorb and stop the movement of the piston and shuttle; the aircraft is released from the shuttle and becomes airborne. The shuttle is retracted back into position so the process can start all over again.

LANDING AND THE LSO

One of the unsung heroes of carrier aviation is the landing signal officer (LSO), who works closely with the pilots during the recovery process. These highly experienced naval aviators carry the responsibility of safely recovering aircraft aboard the carrier. During the recovery phases of flight operations, the LSOs stand out on a platform alongside the aft end of the ship just off the port side of the landing area. The LSOs ensure that the complex process of recovering the air wing's aircraft is done as quickly and safely as possible.

The LSO, also known as paddles—a term that dates back to the early days of carrier aviation when LSOs used a set of

hand-held paddles to guide landing aircraft onto the ship—is a key link in the recovery of aircraft. While the pilot is ultimately responsible for landing the aircraft, it could not be done without the guidance of the LSO. Not only does the LSO assist the pilot in landing aboard ship, but they also grade every landing. On this grading, their word is final. To a naval aviator, the running grade point is a source of great pride and is the barometer by which much of their capability as a pilot is measured. Since landing on a ship is what separates American naval aviators from all other military pilots, how well they do it is what separates them from one another. You can be the hottest stick in the air wing, besting all comers in air combat maneuvering, or perhaps accuracy in bombing, but if you cannot land in a consistently safe manner on the carrier, you will not be flying Navy aircraft for very long. The LSOs go through extensive training to learn how to instruct, or wave, the aircraft. They will observe hundreds of landings, perfecting their art on land during field carrier landing practice (FCLP) as well as aboard ship.

The venerable EA-6B Prowler is the sole tactical electronic warfare aircraft in the entire American military. The Prowler is crewed by a pilot and three electronic warfare officers (ECMOs) who handle the various communications and jamming systems. The Prowler has served the Navy since 1971.

CARRIER LANDING GRADING SYSTEM

GRADE/ DESIGNATION	NAME	COMMENTS
5.0/OK	Perfect landing	No deviations or problems
4.0/OK	Okay landing	Slight deviations, good corrections
3.0/OK	Fair landing	Slight deviations, average corrections
2.5/B	Bolter	Safe approach, no wire engaged
2.0/ -	No grade	Safe approach, below standard
2.0/-B	No grade bolter	Below average approach, no wire engaged
2.0/PWO	Pattern waveoff	Poor start position on approach, waved off
1.0/WO	Waveoff	Below average approach, unsafe corrections
0.0/P	Cut Pass	Unsafe, excessive deviations inside waveoff envelope

The catapult officer's office is below deck, where he can communicate from the safety of his bubble with flight deck personnel as aircraft are taxied and launched just overhead. There are two bubbles, one in between the front catapults and one on the side for the waist catapults. Each can be lowered when not in use.

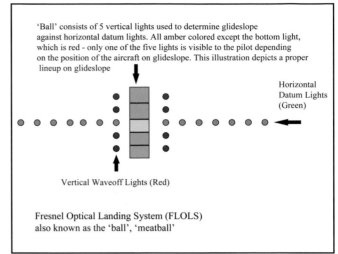

'Ball' consists of 5 vertical lights used to determine glideslope against horizontal datum lights. All amber colored except the bottom light, which is red - only one of the five lights is visible to the pilot depending on the position of the aircraft on glideslope. This illustration depicts a proper lineup on glideslope

Horizontal Datum Lights (Green)

Vertical Waveoff Lights (Red)

Fresnel Optical Landing System (FLOLS) also known as the 'ball', 'meatball'

Landing aircraft aboard a ship at sea is both an art and a science. It is without question the most dangerous and demanding aspect of military aviation. There is almost no room for error, and should a pilot not maintain an acceptable proficiency in carrier landing as judged by the grading system, that pilot will not be permitted or qualified to continue to fly from the ship. Rarely are the LSOs' grades changed, and each squadron aboard ship maintains the landing performance standings of its pilots for all to see. The goal on every landing is to fly a safe approach and achieve the 4.0 okay grade by snagging the number-three arresting cable. The pilots must have a 3.0 average to maintain flight status.

The recovery of air wing aircraft can take place in any weather, day or night. This is possible through use of the Fresnel lens optical landing system (FLOLS), the modern angled-deck design of today's carriers and arresting gear, pilot skill levels, and, of course, the LSO.

The FLOLS is an automated device that sits at the midpoint of the port-side angled deck edge, providing a visual cue to the pilot relative to the glide slope of the aircraft. Its primary purpose is to provide the pilot with a precise reading as to the

position of his aircraft relative to the correct path needed to ensure a safe, arrested landing. Basically, the FLOLS is a mirror that points upward from the side of the flight deck aft to the area that the aircraft approach from. The viewing path of the system takes a conical form outward to get the tail hook of each aircraft type to follow the same exact glide path and to hit the ideal spot on the deck if the pilot flies properly.

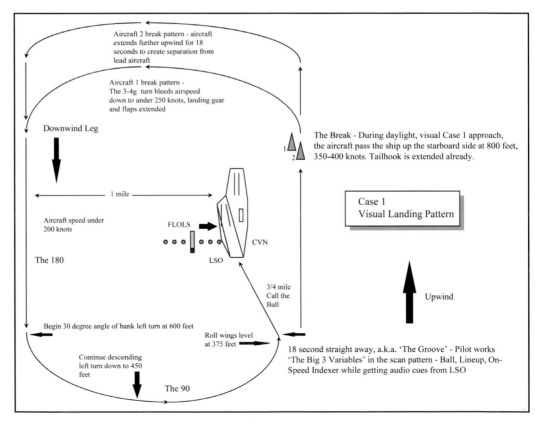

Aircraft 2 break pattern - aircraft extends further upwind for 18 seconds to create separation from lead aircraft

Aircraft 1 break pattern - The 3-4g turn bleeds airspeed down to under 250 knots, landing gear and flaps extended

Downwind Leg

The Break - During daylight, visual Case 1 approach, the aircraft pass the ship up the starboard side at 800 feet, 350-400 knots. Tailhook is extended already.

1 mile

Case 1
Visual Landing Pattern

Aircraft speed under 200 knots

FLOLS

CVN

The 180

LSO

3/4 mile
Call the Ball

Upwind

Begin 30 degree angle of bank left turn at 600 feet

Roll wings level at 375 feet

Continue descending left turn down to 450 feet

18 second straight away, a.k.a. 'The Groove' - Pilot works 'The Big 3 Variables' in the scan pattern - Ball, Lineup, On-Speed Indexer while getting audio cues from LSO

The 90

The most important components of the system are the lights. They consist of two sets of four outboard and three inboard green horizontal datum lights. A vertical row of five larger amber lights intersect these datum lights. The top two are above the horizontal datum lights, one is centered with it, and two are below. If the amber ball, or meatball, is centered on the horizontal row of lights, the aircraft is on the proper glide slope. If the aircraft is high, the pilot will see the amber ball above the horizontal lights; if the pilot is low on approach, he will see the ball below the intersecting green lights. If the approach is too low, the red ball will be visible. The pilot calls the ball within three quarters of a mile before touchdown, confirming to the LSO that he has picked up the FLOLS, specifically, the position of the vertical light in relation to the horizontal lights.

A proper approach will have the aircraft touch down eighteen seconds after entering the groove. The LSO will call directions to the pilot. This is the most demanding part of the landing process. The pilot will move his visual scan pattern to monitor three variables—glide slope, lineup, and speed. Once the aircraft hits the deck, the pilot will advance the throttles to full power. If the tail hook engages one of the four arresting cables, the aircraft will come to an abrupt stop. If not, the aircraft will fly off the angled deck into what is called the "bolter pattern," which sets the aircraft up for a safe reentry into the landing pattern.

Fire is always the greatest threat to any warship, and this is no exception with the aircraft carrier. The flight deck is hazardous, with jet fuel and ordnance handled on deck. The red-shirted fire crews are always on alert and available to deal with any potential fire, and also handle all ordnance.

Navy aircraft are designed in large part to handle the arrested landing. Unlike their air force brethren that have several miles of steady runway to land on, the Navy pilots have a very small area on which they are required to touch. Their runway—the ship—is moving away from them at a constant speed and may not always cooperate if the seas are rough. The landing area may pitch and roll quite a bit. In carrier landing, even a good one is often referred to as a "controlled crash" and for good reason. The landings are violent events that require a sturdy design to withstand the forces. Navy aircraft designers usually engineer very strong landing gear to absorb the punishment of getting slammed onto a steel deck at one hundred

As large as the aircraft carriers are, space is still at a premium, and the flight deck is some pretty expensive real estate. Aircraft can be parked, or spotted, on the main flight deck, as well as in the cavernous main hangar bay just below the flight deck. Aircraft are immediately chained to the flight deck once in place.

Planning and skill are required in moving the aircraft around the flight deck. It is part art and part science. Here, the specific aircraft are identified on this table by the aircraft handling officer and his team. The small, simple aircraft models are an easy way to visually display each aircraft location.

The Fresnel lens optical landing system (FLOLS) was one of the major innovations that make carrier operations efficient. This, along with the angled deck, increased the safety of carrier operations. The lights provide a visual reference to the pilots on their proper glide slope. The amber light, or meatball, needs to be centered across the row of green lights for the correct landing.

and thirty miles an hour. The wings need to be strong and large enough to withstand the stress and to allow the plane to fly slowly enough, with sufficient maneuverability, to land precisely on target. Finally, the ten-foot arresting hook needs to be secured to the lower rear fuselage of the aircraft to catch the arresting wires and slow the aircraft.

Four steel cables roughly two inches in diameter are strung across the rear flight deck area at fifty-foot intervals. They are raised several inches above the deck and are connected to the arresting gear system. There is a dedicated system for each of the four cables that absorbs the forward momentum of the aircraft and safely slows it upon landing. The pilots will snag the third wire if they fly a near-perfect approach. Slightly short or long and they end up in any of the other three wires.

AIR WING

As amazing as modern aircraft carriers are, they depend on their air wings for the real firepower. The air wing includes a mix of many different aircraft that perform a variety of missions. The air wing consists of much more than just airplanes, however. The individual squadrons that operate each different aircraft are also accompanied by thousands of officers and sailors who make the wing a fully functional, highly lethal instrument of war.

The air wing is the air component of the aircraft carrier and its battle group. It is comprised of up to eight squadrons of different aircraft types, squadron personnel (pilots, naval flight officers, officers, and sailors), spare parts, and assorted materials. The Navy splits its air wings between the Atlantic and Pacific Fleets and assigns them to specific carriers, whether the ship is on deployment or not. Upon returning from a cruise, and during activities such as workups that lead up to deployment, the air wings' squadrons will be home based at a number of different naval air stations. It makes more sense from a logistical, maintenance, and training standpoint to segment aircraft communities by facility as opposed to mixing all air wing aircraft across many air stations. The air wing will visit Naval Air Station Fallon in preparation for deployment and work on integrating as a team. The ranges and good weather make Fallon the ideal spot for this preparatory training. Individual squadrons conduct mission-specific training and detachments as required, including carrier qualifications for all air wing pilots. The U.S. Naval Strike and Air Warfare Center (NSAWC) works closely with air wings, preparing them for their upcoming deployments. This training, conducted at Naval Air Station Fallon, Nevada, is an integral part of their training cycle and is referred to as a "workup." NSAWC instructors and aircraft conduct advanced training to prepare the entire air wing for the rigors of combat.

The EA-6B Prowler is a specialized variant of the Grumman A-6 Intruder attack aircraft. The jet has been in service since the early 1970s and is set to be replaced by the new Boeing EA-18G Growler aircraft, a specialized version of the Super Hornet.

The requirements dictated by the offensive and defensive missions are the driving forces in selecting the aircraft that comprise the air wing. Over the last twenty-five years, a number of changes within naval aviation have had a major impact on the makeup of the air wing.

The future portends more change that will impact the air wings and their composition. The naval aviation plan for the twenty-first century, as defined by the Director of Air Warfare (N88) Office, follows the necking-down strategy of minimizing the number of single-mission aircraft. The direction of naval aviation and the air wing is toward multi-mission war fighting. This extends beyond the fighters to helicopters and support aircraft as well. The cost savings of this strategy are significant as the Navy faces budgetary challenges. No longer can the Navy afford to operate many different mission-specific airframes.

The introduction of the F/A-18E/F Super Hornet to the fleet and the future introductions of the Joint Strike Fighter (JSF) and Common Support Aircraft (CSA), expected between 2010 and 2015, will change the face of the air wing. The necking-down policy will reduce the inventory of airframes to primarily the E/F and JSF for the fighter and attack roles. The

Left: It takes the coordination of a great many flight deck personnel to safely launch modern combat aircraft from the deck of an aircraft carrier. The flight deck is a busy, dangerous place to work.

Pri-Fly is the home of the air boss, who rules the flight deck and air operations around the ship. The air boss is part of the carrier's air department, which is the largest department on the ship, with more than 600 men and women assigned. The air department ensures the safe and efficient launch and recovery of aircraft. The air boss' word is law, and he is a highly experienced naval aviator. Pri-Fly is located on the aircraft carrier's island and provides a "god's-eye" view of all flight-deck activity.

Head-on view of the massive USS *John F. Kennedy* (CV-67) as it heads into New York Harbor for the beginning of the annual Fleet Week celebration. "Big John," as it is referred to, was first commissioned in September 1968. The carrier's mission is to provide a credible, sustainable, independent forward presence and conventional deterrence. The *Kennedy* and its complement of aircraft, officers, and sailors do just that.

Super Hornet is well on its way to replacing all F-14 Tomcat units, and the big cat will be phased out completely by 2007. The EA-6B and E-2C, as well as the SH-60, will remain for some time. The Prowler will be replaced by the EA-18G Growler, and the E-2C/C-2/S-3/ES-3 will be replaced by the CSA at some distant point in the future.

Each air wing is commanded by the commander air group (CAG), which is a throwback to the days when the air wing was named carrier air group. The CAG is responsible for the entire air wing's functional capability and is checked out in all the various aircraft that are in the air wing. The CAG is a peer to the commander of the carrier, and both officers report to the battle group commander that is a flag rank position. The aircraft carrier commander is responsible for the ship, the CAG for the air wing. Typically, the CAG holds the rank of captain and has fifteen to twenty years of experience as a naval aviator. He typically served as a squadron commanding officer before rising to this prestigious assignment.

Continued on page 37

The E-2C Hawkeye provides an over-the-horizon view for the carrier strike group and is capable of scanning many thousands of miles of airspace for any and all airborne threats. This Hawkeye is assigned to the "Tigertails" of VAW-125. E-2Cs can communicate with *Aegis*-class cruisers, ensuring that no threats can strike the carrier.

Behind each catapult is a Mk.7 jet blast deflector (JBD) that protects the aircraft and flight deck personnel from the exhaust of the launching aircraft. The JBD is raised and lowered for each aircraft and is water cooled to dissipate the extreme heat generated by the jet engines. The JBD is a massive structure and is flush with the flight deck when not in use.

The landing signal officer (LSO) is responsible for safely landing air wing aircraft aboard ship. An LSO from each squadron will serve as part of a team and help land, or wave, the aircraft. LSOs go to a dedicated school at NAS Oceana to learn the trade, and a typical LSO will wave hundreds of practice landings before doing them aboard ship. *Photo by Chuck Lloyd*

An F/A-18 Hornet with the "Gunslingers" of VFA-105 goes into tension. The pilot will wipe out, or cycle, the flaps and ailerons to ensure they work properly before saluting that the aircraft is ready for the cat shot. The tailplanes of the Hornet are deflected downward so the nose of the aircraft rotates properly upon launch.

An F/A-18C Hornet is photographed halfway through the catapult stroke. Unlike previous carrier aircraft, the Hornet uses advanced digital flight controls to handle the takeoff. The pilot actually places his hand on what's known as the "towel rack" during the stroke and then takes control immediately after the jet leaves the deck.

A yellow-shirted flight director motions for this F/A-18 Hornet pilot to slowly move forward from where the aircraft is parked, or spotted, on the bow to one of the four catapults. Each yellow shirt is responsible for a certain area of the flight deck and will pass the jet off to another yellow shirt farther down the deck.

Right: An F/A-18 Hornet is photographed moments before slamming down onto the deck for landing. This position is a bit tricky as the airflow is slightly disrupted by the wake of the ship's island and is referred to as the "burble" by carrier aviators. Note the large flaps and extended tail hook of the Hornet.

Left: The future of carrier-based aviation in the first decade of this century is represented in this photograph. A pair of CVW-11 Super Hornets with VFA-14 and VFA-41 flanks a VAW-117 E-2C Hawkeye 2000. Each of the squadron aircraft represented is wearing the higher-visibility paint schemes indicative of the commander air group (CAG) aircraft.

Below: The Hawkeye carries more than 12,000 pounds of advanced electronics equipment. The aircraft can monitor six million cubic miles of airspace and in excess of 150,000 square miles of ocean surface. The Hawkeye can detect enemy missiles, ships, and aircraft and is operated by a crew of five.

CHAPTER 2

TRANSITIONS

U.S. Navy carrier-based aviation is currently undergoing a significant transformation. Air wings are in the midst of retiring the F-14 Tomcat—the long-standing fleet air defense strike fighter—and upgrading to the new F/A-18E/F Super Hornet. The Navy fighter squadron community (VF) is quickly becoming a memory, and the strike fighter (VFA) community is rapidly expanding. The Super Hornet is not only replacing the Tomcat but also older-legacy F/A-18A and C Hornets as well. With a few exceptions, the units flying the F-14 Tomcats will upgrade to the two-seat F/A-18F, and the legacy F/A-18C Hornet units will upgrade to the single-seat F/A-18E Super Hornet. Soon, the carrier decks will be dominated by F/A-18E/F Super Hornets handling a wide variety of missions.

Shown here is a brand-new F/A-18F Super Hornet with the "Black Knights" of VFA-154 on a training mission outside its home at NAS Lemoore, California. The unit upgraded from the F-14 Tomcat and moved across the country from its previous home at NAS Oceana, Virginia. This jet is slick, carrying only a single fuel tank under the fuselage and no other ordnance or avionics pods.

A VFA-94 "Mighty Shrikes" F/A-18 pulls into the vertical during an air combat training mission out of its home at NAS Lemoore, California. The Hornet is particularly adept at slow-speed, high-angle-of-attack dogfighting. Unlike other fighter aircraft, the Hornet can move its nose around in a slow fight to gain the advantage.

THE WORKHORSE OF NAVY CARRIER AVIATION: THE LEGACY F/A-18 HORNET

The versatile F/A-18 Hornet has been the premier multirole aircraft flying from Navy aircraft carriers. The F/A-18 (and its variants, A–F) will ultimately replace five separate aircraft types for the Navy. Initially, the Hornet replaced the F-4 Phantom and A-7 Corsair. The Navy's primary all-weather, precision night-attack aircraft, the A-6 Intruder, was also retired. The role that the Intruder handled so ably will be filled by the F/A-18E/F. Plans are also in place for a modified version of the Super Hornet, called the EA-18G Growler, which would replace the EA-6B Prowler as the dedicated carrier-based electronic warfare aircraft. The S-3 Viking, which handled aerial refueling, is also being removed from active service; the Super Hornet will fill that role as well.

The F/A-18A and C aircraft (now considered the legacy Hornets) first brought fourth-generation technology to naval aviation with their advanced avionics and superb maneuverability. The Hornet is the mainstay of the Navy's fighter attack squadrons, which were designated with the VFA (fighter attack) prefix. Prior to the Hornet's entrance into active service, the Navy carrier wing strike aircraft were single-role, dedicated ground-attack aircraft in VA-designated (attack) units. When the new Super Hornet came on the scene, F-14 units that converted went from fighter (VF) to strike fighter (VFA) designations.

Two of the recently retired aircraft from Navy carrier air wings are the F-14 Tomcat and S-3 Viking. The antisubmarine warfare role has been taken over by the SH-60 Seahawk and P-3 Orion. The aerial refueling mission that the S-3 handled, as well as the strike fighter F-14 mission, is now done by the F/A-18 Super Hornet.

The venerable A-6E Intruder served as the primary all-weather night-attack aircraft until its retirement from active service in February 1998. The A-6 utilized a side-by-side seating arrangement in the cockpit with the pilot in the left seat and the bombardier/navigator in the right seat. This unique design was rarely used in modern combat aircraft.

The Hornet also serves naval aviation in a number of other units and capacities. The Navy's aerial demonstration team, the famous Blue Angels, chose the Hornet in 1986 to replace their A-4F Skyhawk. The combination of power, maneuverability, and reliability make the Hornet a superb aircraft for the team. The Hornet also serves as a fourth-generation adversary tactics trainer with NSAWC and with the "Omars" of Fighter Squadron Composite Twelve, Naval Reserve Forces (VFC-12).

SUPER HORNET ORIGINS

The Navy leadership saw a drastically changing environment as they looked at challenges posed in the early twenty-first century. The end of the Cold War and the realities of political and financial constraints impacted the decisions the Navy made. The dismantling of the former Soviet Union and its air forces meant a reduced threat to the American carrier strike group posed by air-launched cruise missiles and manned bombers. The idea of transforming the U.S. Air Force's new F-22 fighter to replace the F-14, as well as the dedicated A-12 attack aircraft to replace the A-6E Intruder, was under consideration. As

A VFA-37 F/A-18 Hornet cruises in the Whiskey 72 range off the coast of NAS Oceana. NAS Oceana is a master jet base that is home to Atlantic Fleet legacy and Super Hornet squadrons, as well as the few remaining F-14 Tomcat units. This jet is carrying a fuel tank on the single station under the fuselage.

an interim solution, to meet needs until the F-22 and A-12 were fielded, McDonnell Douglas (now part of Boeing) proposed the Hornet 2000 in early January 1988. The end of the Cold War and the associated arms race forced the Pentagon and Navy planners to accept the realities imposed by a drastically reduced defense budget. Neither the A-12 nor the Navy F-22 came to fruition. The Navy's strategy shifted significantly with the end of the former Soviet Union.

The strategy statement set forth in the 1992 white paper "From the Sea: Preparing the Naval Service for the Twenty-first Century" stressed the changing environment and the Navy's vision for the future. The Navy needed to be able to quickly react to local and regional conflicts as opposed to global conflicts. Quoting the document: "Focusing on the littoral area, the Navy and Marine Corps can seize and defend an adversary's port, naval base, or coastal air base to allow the entry of heavy army or air forces." Without the need for a dedicated long-range strike aircraft or fleet air-defense fighter, the Navy selected a single platform that could protect the carrier from airborne threats as well as conduct strike missions. The Super Hornet was born, and the initial engineering and manufacturing development (EMD) contract was signed with Boeing in December 1992. The first flight of the single-seat prototype took place three years later, in 1995, followed by the first flight of the two-seat version in the spring of 1996.

THE F/A-18E/F SUPER HORNET: FIFTH-GENERATION FIGHTER FOR THE FUTURE

The Super Hornet looks enough like the legacy F/A-18C to see the basic family resemblance, but it actually is a completely different airplane. The big gray aircraft has already earned the nickname "Rhino" in the fleet. The E model is the single-seat variant and the F is the two-seat model. The first Super Hornet was unveiled in September 1995. The primary contractor for the aircraft is Boeing, with major subcontractors, including Northrop Grumman Corp. as the principal maker of the airframe (center and aft fuselage) and Raytheon, makers of the APG-73 radar.

The Super Hornet is slightly longer than the first-generation Hornets, but it is significantly stockier in the midsection. The most noticeable differences on the outside are the larger square engine intakes and wings. The Super Hornet is 20 percent larger than the F/A-18C. The biggest rap against the earlier Hornet is that it has always suffered from range and endurance limitations. The new jet has a 40 percent greater range and 80 percent greater time on station than the F/A-18C. Its new General Electric F414 engines provide 35 percent more thrust. The Super Hornet has 40 percent fewer moving parts than the F/A-18C, making it more reliable and easier to maintain.

Like that on all Navy carrier–based aircraft, the landing gear of the Super Hornet is very sturdy and built to withstand the rigors of punishing carrier landings. This single-seat F/A-18E is assigned to VFA-122 and was photographed on final approach to NAS Lemoore, California, home to the Pacific Fleet Hornet community.

The fleet replacement training squadron for the East Coast Hornet community is VFA-106, based at NAS Oceana, Virginia. The unit trains pilots, naval flight officers, and maintainers in both the legacy F/A-18 and the new F/A-18 Super Hornet. This jet was photographed during landing practice.

Unlike the F-117 and newer F-22, the F/A-18E/F is not a pure stealth aircraft. Certain accommodations had to be made within the context of financial limitations. The Super Hornet designers needed to deal with the aircraft's vulnerability while enhancing its overall survivability. Compared to the fourth-generation aircraft it replaced, the Super Hornet is stealthier. It achieves its enhanced stealth through a blend of standoff precision weapons that minimize the Hornet to ground threats directly over the target, radar-reducing materials, and enhanced avionics systems. Self-defense systems, ranging from the flare and chaff systems to electronic countermeasures receivers and warning avionics, greatly enhance the Super Hornet's survivability.

A U.S. Air Force exchange pilot and instructor pilot with VFA-122 who flew both the Super Hornet and F-16 Fighting Falcon compared the two aircraft: "The F-16 and the F/A-18E/F have similar missions but go about meeting them in different ways. The Super Hornet was built for carrier operations, which require certain trade-offs. The large wings and flaps of the Hornet allow better slow-speed performance and handling, which is so important to landing aboard an aircraft carrier. The F/A-18E/F is a superb aircraft, and, while it bleeds energy faster than the F-16, it is much better at slow speeds. The Hornet has a much greater ability to maneuver the nose at high angles of attack at slow speeds. If the fight gets slow, the Hornet can point the nose at the opponent, which is a nice benefit in combat. The smaller F-16 has a slight advantage in a faster

The Super Hornet has a much larger wing than the legacy Hornet, which allows it to carry more fuel and ordnance. This jet belongs to the Jolly Rogers of VFA-103 and is carrying a pair of AGM-88 HARM and AGM-45 Maverick missiles on its wing stations. The Super Hornet can carry ordnance on a total of eleven stations.

53

The clean lines of the Super Hornet are evident in this photo of a VFA-103 aircraft in the understated fleet-gray paint scheme. The new General Electric F414-GE-400 engines on the F/A-18E/F provide a combined thrust of 44,000 pounds. The more powerful engines require a larger intake, which was redesigned on the Super Hornet.

VFA-122, based at Naval Air Station Lemoore in the San Joaquin valley of central California, make up the West Coast fleet replacement squadron (FRS). The "Gladiators" of VFA-106, based at Naval Air Station Oceana in Virginia Beach, Virginia, is the East Coast Super Hornet FRS. Both units provide training for the new Super Hornet community. The units' singular mission is the same: "To train Super Hornet aviators and maintainers to conduct prompt and sustained combat operations from the sea, putting fused ordnance on target, on time, first pass . . . anytime, anywhere."

TRAINING CURRICULUM
VFA-122 conducts five training classes per year and has turned out hundreds of qualified Super Hornet pilots and weapons systems officers (WSO) to date. Lieutenant Dave

Aamodt, a former instructor WSO with VFA-122 and former F-14 radar intercept officer, describes the training curriculum for pilots and WSOs: "There are nine stages that use a building-block approach. Things start simple; there is dedicated classroom time on the basic aircraft systems, such as fuel, hydraulics, flight controls, etc. Much of the learning takes place individually using computer-aided instruction (CAI). There are about forty computers in the learning center where students learn the basics. One of the nice things about the CAIs is that they are interactive."

The Super Hornet training curriculum is broken down as follows:

Familiarization (FAM/FORM)—Basic orientation in the aircraft. There is extensive simulator work before the crews actually begin flying the jets.

NAS Lemoore, California, is the West Coast home of the Super Hornet. This quartet of aircraft that includes single-seat and two-seat versions assigned to VFA-122, VFA-154, VFA-41, and VFA-14 (from bottom to top), lines up in a perfect echelon formation over the nearby Sierra Nevada mountain range.

An F/A-18F with VFA-41 hits the hot pits at NAS Lemoore after a mission to refuel. Intrepid ground crew personnel connect the refueling equipment to the still-running aircraft to top off the Super Hornet's tanks so it is ready for the next mission. This jet is carrying a pair of AIM-120 AMRAAM missiles on its wing stations.

All-Weather Intercept (AWI)—Students learn how to operate the radar. The emphasis of this phase is to have the students get comfortable using the radar and employing missiles. It is typical during AWI (and the rest of the syllabus) to place a student WSO in the back seat of the (flight lead) instructor pilot. The student pilot flies wing with an instructor WSO in the back seat. Some flights in the F/A-18E instruction take place with a WSO in the back seat (as a silent observer), while others take place in a single-seat F/A-18E or an F/A-18F with the back seat empty.

Section Radar Attacks (SRA)—The student pilots know how to use the radar, but they have to do it while flying formation (pilots) or leading a section (WSO).

Basic Fighter Maneuvers (BFM)—Basic dogfighting begins with a one versus zero (1V0), in which students learn how to maximize the jet's performance. A building-block approach is used. Students learn how to fight when they are in an offensive position initially, as it is easier to fight when you have the advantage. The pilots are then allowed to try to tackle defensive maneuvering before putting it all together with neu-

tral setups, in which the challenge for the students is to realize when they are offensive or defensive and to act accordingly using the skills they learned on previous flights.

Fighter Weapons (Fighter Weps)—This phase strings all the air-to-air training together, including radar intercepts taken to the merge (the point in which two or more opposing fighter aircraft meet during a head-on engagement), which involves close-in dogfighting.

Air-to-ground (Strike)—The Super Hornet students train in the Superior Valley in R-2508 within the Fallon ranges and occasionally a detachment to Naval Air Station El Centro, California. Students drop live high-drag practice bombs and more involved joint direct-attack munition (JDAM) and joint standoff weapon (JSOW) tactics.

Carrier Qualification (CQ)—The pilots practice landings a great deal at Naval Air Station Lemoore, which leads up to them going to the boat.

Strike Fighter—This combines the air-to-air training with the air-to-ground training, and the students practice self-escort strike tactics. The students have to fight their way into a target, attack it, and fight their way out again.

Instructor Under Training (IUT)—When air crews have completed their transition syllabus, they go through a brief syllabus to ensure they have the knowledge and briefing skills required to effectively teach students.

TOMCATS TO SUPER HORNETS: A TALE OF TWO UNITS

The Jolly Rogers of VFA-103

The Tomcat community has undergone drastic downsizing as the F-14 is phased out with the introduction of the F/A-18E/F Super Hornet. One of the units cut was VF-84, which had first received the F-14A in 1976. Not wanting the skull-and-crossbones logo of VF-84 to disappear forever, the Navy decided to change the name of VF-103 from "Sluggers" to the "Jolly Rogers" name and symbol in late 1995 to keep the tradition alive. Few squadrons in American military aviation have the proud history, color, and flare of the Navy's Jolly Rogers of Strike Fighter Squadron 103 (VFA-103). The Jolly Rogers are based at Naval Air Station Oceana and now operate twelve F/A-18F Super Hornets, having traded in their F-14B Tomcats. They completed Super Hornet training and received the necessary certifications on July 15, 2005.

In describing some of the challenges of the transition, VFA-103 maintenance officer and Top Gun graduate Lieutenant Commander Raymond Drake recalls: "Taking the F-14s and transporting them to the bone yard in Davis-Monthan Air Base, Arizona, was a challenge. We did this in January of 2005.

The Flying Eagles of VFA-122 are the West Coast fleet replacement squadron (FRS) for the Super Hornet. All Super Hornets on the West Coast are assigned to the Strike Fighter Wing Pacific. VFA-122 was the first air crew training unit in the Navy for the Super Hornet and operates a mix of single-seat E and two-seat F model Super Hornets.

We came off of our final cruise the second week of December, and in January we flew two aircraft out to the desert per week for four weeks. Two other aircraft were inducted by the wing for other things. The biggest challenge was getting all the maintenance guys into school and trained on the other aircraft and getting them proficient so we could launch and recover airplanes and achieve our 'safe for flight' status. We also had to get the air crew through the FRS at VFA-106 and get them ready to fly the aircraft.

"The maintenance guys went through two training programs in the Super Hornet. Initial training involves a great deal of class work on the systems they specialize in, be that avionics, powerplants, electronics, ordnance, etc. After that, they go over to VFA-106 and do on-the-job training on the aircraft for about sixty days. They work in the shop with experienced guys, receive their certifications, and then come back to the unit. The classroom work is done here at the unit and depends on their specific rating and specialty and usually runs between thirty and sixty days. We have about two hundred and fifteen maintenance people in the unit, all enlisted, and fourteen officers. My job as the maintenance officer has the primary responsibility of managing and directing all the personnel to ensure that the aircraft undergo their scheduled and unscheduled maintenance and that we provide the required aircraft ready

A pair of VFA-94 Mighty Shrikes Hornets rolls in on a target during an air wing training mission over the Fallon ranges. The Hornet is a highly capable multirole fighter that is equally adept at air-to-air and air-to-ground missions. These jets are assigned to Air Wing Eleven (CVW-11).

for flight as the squadron needs. I am directly responsible to the squadron's commanding officer.

"We had very good luck with our Tomcats on our final cruise and had roughly thirty-five to forty maintenance hours per flight hour. With the Super Hornet, it's down to about ten maintenance hours per flight hour. One of the key factors is that it is a brand-new aircraft. Mission availability is much higher, which is expected when going from a thirty-year-old airplane to a new one. One of the key differences is that the Super Hornet is a digital airplane with very advanced diagnostics. When we return from a flight, the maintainers plug into a code panel and, with the self-diagnostics, the airplane tells them what failed and needs to be repaired quite precisely."

Tomcat versus Super Hornet: The View from the Cockpit

When comparing the two aircraft—the F-14 and F/A-18F— Lieutenant Commander Drake says, "The F-14 is a bigger aircraft, and it carried a great deal more fuel, which gave it a robust range and endurance. It is a very fast airplane, and I don't think we will have one that fast in the inventory for a long time. It was very versatile. We could get where we needed to be quickly and loiter as needed. It was also a pretty good dogfighter. One of the challenges with the Tomcat was that it was an older airplane that had some newer technologies integrated into it. You still had to look at numerous instruments, for example, to get a clear picture as to situational awareness. The Super Hornet, a fifth-generation airplane, is much more user friendly. Situational awareness is much greater from an air crew perspective; the information is collated for you and displayed on the moving map and other digital displays within the 'glass' cockpit. The radar and data-link information is overlaid on the displays, making it a very easy airplane to assimilate mission status with. The Super Hornet is a phenomenal dogfighter and very maneuverable. It has the joint helmet-mounted cueing system and the AIM-9X all-aspect Sidewinder missile; the newer models will have the electronically scanned radar, making it a very versatile airplane. It does have less speed and less range than the F-14, but it has a very versatile weapons payload with the eleven weapons pylons. We can carry a very robust mix of weapons. The Tomcat's strengths were that it had very good sustained energy performance, had a lower bleed rate, and good energy addition. It did

Marine Corps F/A-18 Hornets like this F/A-18C with the "Red Devils" of VMFA-232 regularly deploy within Navy air wings during deployments at sea. Displaying the Hornet's versatility, this jet is carrying a mix of AIM-9 and AIM-7 air-to-air missiles under one wing and AGM-65 Maverick air-to-ground missiles under the other.

not possess the same abilities as the Super Hornet in high-angle-of-attack regimes. The B and D model F-14s did not have the engine challenges the A model did. With the Super Hornet, I feel more comfortable in a slow-speed or positional fight, due to the aircraft's strong nose authority. In the Super Hornet, I am not afraid to get the fight slow, and I can influence an opponent's maneuvering."

Lieutenant Commander Drake adds, "My mindset going into a dogfight with the Super Hornet, using the joint helmet-mounted cueing system and the AIM-9X, is that this fight is going to be over quickly. The Super Hornet was designed to use the helmet system, and the higher-lot jets have the ability to support this built in. It works with all the sensors, so whichever direction your head looks, the sensors follow. If you can put your eyeballs on another airplane, you can also now have the FLIR [forward-looking infrared], the radar, the missile on it as well. You can also look at a target on the ground

and have it designated by your weapons systems. With the helmet, you are looking to get the nose of the aircraft around to get bore sight on the target so you can engage it. You are not thinking about a protracted engagement but rather just making an aggressive first move so you can get your helmet on him and shoot him. Nine times out of ten this will be successful."

When asked which aircraft they'd rather take to a fight, the Navy fighter pilots who have had experience in the F-14 and the F/A-18E/F invariably respond with a question of their own: "What kind of fight?" The F-14 Tomcat, though thirty years old, was very well designed for its primary role, unlike the Super Hornet, which is tasked with fulfilling many different missions. Lieutenant Commander Drake says, "If I am going to do strictly fleet defense, where I have to go four hundred miles away from the carrier and be expected to shoot down incoming airplanes at long ranges, then I want the F-14. If I am going to conduct a high-speed strike mission, I would

prefer the F-14. If it's a forward air controller airborne (FACA) mission, it's a toss-up since both airplanes have their strengths and weaknesses. The Super Hornet has the advantage with the integrated cockpit, but it has a little less on-station time than the Tomcat. The newer advanced-targeting forward-looking infrared (ATFLIR) pod in the Super Hornet would make it a slightly better precision night-strike aircraft than the Tomcat."

When comparing the two aircraft around the aircraft carrier, Lieutenant Commander Drake says, "The F-14 is a handful around the ship, especially during landings at night. It was a difficult airplane to land well aboard the ship. Since it was so big, taxiing was different than the Super Hornet, especially with respect to when you spread the Tomcat's wings and hydraulics for this. The catapult shot is different between both airplanes. The F-14 has a much higher weight than the Super Hornet. The Super Hornet is all digital, fly by wire, so it is very stable. Around the ship, the Super Hornet is much easier to handle. The one thing us former Tomcat guys had to get used to with the Super Hornet is during the cat shot, you don't touch the stick. You keep your right hand up on the canopy rail and let the airplane fly itself away from the ship. That takes some getting used to. On the catapult itself, the nose strut of the F-14 would compress slightly, and then upon leaving the deck, it would uncompress, and I would have to set the attitude of the airplane a little bit. Not so with the Super Hornet, since the flight control computers actually handle this. It would be fair to say that you fly the Tomcat off the cat [catapult] but not the Super Hornet. The computers in the Super Hornet handle the first few seconds of flight. Once the attitude is set, I will take over and bring up the landing gear and take control. This can be a little different for us Tomcat guys, especially at night when everything is unsettling. You do a lot of things at night on pure faith."

Drake continues, "The F-14 is a bit more work during the landing process aboard ship; you have to manually sweep the wings forward after the break over the ship, the gear and then the flaps. You would then engage the direct lift control (DLC), and you trim the stick and rudder to horse the F-14 around to land aboard ship. With the Super Hornet, it's different and easier since the aircraft does not have any pitch transients when you put the flaps down with the flight control computers taking care of this. The aircraft is very stable with the gear and flap transitions. It does not require any real trim adjustments or experience any pitch changes. You set a digital trim number on a display, and the aircraft is perfectly trimmed up. It flies really crisply, even during the transitions, unlike the F-14. The Super Hornet is a smaller airplane; it's more crisp and stable. The Tomcat had a lot more inertia between the larger wings and the different motors. The F110 engines in the B and D

Many F-14 squadrons have been disestablished as the Tomcat community draws down. The remaining units have transitioned to the Super Hornet. The Jolly Rogers of VFA-103 are one such unit, having handed in their beloved F-14s for the newer F/A-18F Super Hornets. Tomcat air crews are fiercely loyal to the F-14 and grudgingly concede that the newer Super Hornet is a highly capable fifth-generation fighter.

model were larger and spaced further apart than the 414's in the Super Hornet. In the Tomcat, when you wanted more power, you had to wait for it to spool up, and the same for slowing and taking power off. Landing aboard ship is not easy, but the Super Hornet makes a lot of the administrative tasks much easier and does a lot of the work for you."

The Bounty Hunters of VFA-2

Few squadrons faced a series of challenges and met them head-on like the VFA-2 "Bounty Hunters" did upon transitioning from the F-14 to F/A-18F. The squadron came off combat operations in Iraq, handed in their venerable F-14 Tomcats, and moved across the country to a new home at Naval Air Station Lemoore and into the Navy's new fearsome F/A-18F Super Hornet—all in less than one year's time!

Former public affairs officer for the Bounty Hunters, Lieutenant (jg) Ryan Fulwider explains, "VF-2 was deployed aboard the USS *Constellation* (CV-64) with Carrier Air Wing Two (CVW-2) from October 14, 2002, to June 2, 2003. The Bounty Hunters participated in Enduring Freedom, Southern

The F/A-18 Hornet possesses eye-watering 9-g maneuvering and is a fearsome dogfighter. The Hornet is a more forgiving fighter than the F-14, which the Hornet was introduced to complement upon its entry into the fleet in 1981. Over one thousand F/A-18 Hornets were built in numerous variants for the Navy and Marine Corps.

Watch, and Iraqi Freedom (OIF), flying over two thousand combat hours and four hundred eighty-three sorties. The challenge of keeping the squadron's ten aging F-14Ds ready for all tasking was met by the dedication and effort of the Bullet sailors and chiefs. [Bullet is an in-flight call sign for VFA-2 squadron aircraft.] It cost nearly sixty maintenance man hours per flight hour, but the effort paid off in a 98 percent sortie completion rate during OIF and the dropping of three hundred twenty thousand pounds of ordnance with 100 percent weapons system reliability."

"We began our transition on July 1, after we completed our home port change from Oceana," says VFA-2's former commanding officer, Commander Doug "Boog" Denney. "In reality, our transition began about a year before that, when we were given the word that the music was stopping at Oceana and we were missing a chair. I appointed a very capable transition officer; you can imagine the multitude of challenges and the hundreds of decisions that he and I made. We, as well as our department heads and senior enlisted, worked very hard to make personnel decisions early on so sailors and families could prepare for the move that would happen right after our return from cruise."

One of the sharpest-looking Super Hornets in the skies today is the CAG bird with VFA-2. The squadron is one of the oldest in the Navy and was the first to land aboard a Navy ship, the USS *Langley* in 1922. The squadron adorned its aircraft with red, white, and blue stripes, referred to as "Langley stripes." Paying homage to the unit's lineage, the brand-new Super Hornets of VFA-2 wear their Langley stripes proudly.

A rapidly disappearing sight in naval aviation is the swept-wing F-14. The Tomcat is ending its thirty-year career of service and fading into history as one of the most capable carrier-based multirole aircraft ever produced. The Bounty Hunters received the F-14A Tomcat in 1973 and operated the jet until 2003.

Commander Denney continues, "Because our deployment was extended for Operation Iraqi Freedom, we had to slide some of our transition dates to the right. It was a moving target. We got everybody across the country safely, and passed our 'safe for flight' inspection from the wing. This inspection will allow us to release our jets safe for flight and, for the first time, write and fly our own flight schedule."

On July 1, 2003, VF-2 was officially recommissioned as VFA-2, thus beginning transition training to the F/A-18F Super Hornet. In the morning hours of October 6, 2003, the VFA-2 Bounty Hunters took delivery of their first F/A-18F. Bullet 102 is just one of the first twelve Super Hornets that will eventually wear the traditional Langley stripe of the Navy's first carrier-based squadron.

While the new Super Hornet represents the cutting edge of naval aviation technology, the transition has not been as dramatic as one would think. Lieutenant (jg) Fulwider says, "For the VF-2 air crew, we had the luxury of flying the F-14D previously, which had a glass [digital display] cockpit, unlike the other Tomcats. This has made the change to the Super Hornet glass cockpit a lot easier. Initially, the transition was tougher

The EA-6B Prowler is flanked by a pair of F/A-18F Super Hornets. The replacement for the Prowler is the two-seat EA-18G Growler, a derivative of the Super Hornet. The Growler will carry specialized electronics but will be able to travel much faster than the EA-6B Prowler and will retain a viable self-defense capability.

Shown here is the view from the rear seat of a CVW-7 F/A-18F during an air-to-air refueling operation. The Super Hornet replaces the recently retired S-3 Viking. The large colored multifunction displays dominate the rear cockpit of the Super Hornet. The displays in this photo are intentionally left off for security reasons at the pilot's request.

Victory 200, one of the two Jolly Rogers F/A-18F Super Hornets adorned in high-visibility paint, forms up on a squadron mate during an SFARP (strike fighter advanced readiness program) mission. The newest versions of the Hornet are the single-seat E and two-seat F models, which made their first appearance in 1995. The Super Hornet can quickly be configured for a wide variety of air-to-air and air-to-ground roles.

for the maintainers, going from an aircraft built on Cold War technology to an aircraft built with next-generation systems."

Lieutenant (jg) Fulwider outlines the training process VFA-2 has been involved in since transitioning to the F/A-18F. "The squadron was split up into two classes at the fleet replacement squadron (FRS) VFA-122. The first started on July 7, and the second class on August 18. The majority of their training has been done here at Naval Air Station Lemoore in the provided military working areas. The first class did a fighter weapons detachment to Naval Air Facility Key West for two weeks, from September 13 to September 27, and just returned from a week on the USS *John C. Stennis* (CVN-74), getting their carrier qualifications and completing their FRS instruction. The second class left yesterday for Naval Air Station El Centro, California, for a strike detachment and will be going out for their carrier qualifications in about a month."

The air crew's syllabus at the FRS includes forty-one flights for about sixty-one flight hours, forty simulators for about fifty hours, and roughly 215 hours of either classroom or computer-aided instruction. The maintainers had to endure months of classes and training to recertify and qualify fourteen shops to work on the Super Hornet. Commander Denney, a WSO, speaks of the transition training: "The RAG [replacement air group] is incredibly efficient, and I was very pleased with the high quality of the syllabus. To give you an idea of how good these new airplanes are, I've flown about thirty times, and I've never gone down, and I've never written a gripe."

A former operations officer with VFA-2, Lieutenant Commander Mike Peterson, a WSO in the Super Hornet, described the transition to the new jet: "As Tomcat guys, we are familiar with the Hornet, having had three F/A-18 units in the air wing. As an F-14 strike fighter unit, we had many similarities to the Super Hornet units. We generally do the same missions. It's similar to a football team in some ways. One team might run the run-and-gun offense, another might use the West Coast offense, but they both do the same basics—blocking,

The cockpit of the F/A-18 Super Hornet is definitely high tech. The rear cockpit of the F model is dominated by several programmable color displays. The weapons systems officer interfaces with the systems via a pair of side stick controllers and the multifunction displays.

tackling, passing. For the F-14 crews, we are familiar with offensive counter-air, air-to-ground strike, and forward air control missions. With standardized procedures, we had an easier time than you might think moving to the new Hornet."

Lieutenant Commander Peterson commented on the value of the two-seat community to naval aviation: "One of the most important aspects of the F-14 to F/A-18F transition is the continuation of the two-seat strike fighter community. The F/A-18F allows us to fulfill several missions that are simply too complex for a single person to fulfill. The forward air controller (FAC) mission and the electronic warfare mission, with the eventual replacement of the EA-6B Prowler, are two examples."

A Jolly Rogers F/A-18F rotates off runway 31 right at NAS Fallon during an air wing training mission. NAS Fallon is a sprawling air base that contains superb training facilities, four dedicated bombing ranges, an electronic warfare range, 14,000-foot runways, and clear weather over three hundred days per year.

CHAPTER 3

FAREWELL TO THE BIG CAT

With the proliferation of the new F/A-18E/F Super Hornet into Navy carrier air wings, the last chapter in the long career of the F-14 Tomcat is being written. The F-14 nobly served for over thirty years and leaves a résumé of great accomplishments. The big Grumman cat served in three wars, countless skirmishes, appeared in numerous movies in supporting roles, and was the star of a blockbuster (albeit factually challenged) motion picture.

The Tomcat's beginnings were among the most turbulent of any modern military aircraft program. The Navy developed a requirement called the "VFX specification" in 1969 for a dedicated air-superiority fighter. The specification described a twin-engine, tandem two-seat fleet air defense fighter for combat patrols more than 200 miles from the carrier, with a two-hour loiter time and a weapons payload of more than 14,000 pounds.

In September 2003, the last Top Gun class to fly the F-14 Tomcat graduated, marking the end of an era. The Tomcat is quickly disappearing from the active duty force and will soon be seen only on static display or at the bone yard in Arizona, the final resting place for all retired combat aircraft. It will also, sadly, mark the end of the great line of Grumman fighters.

Here an F-14A radar intercept officer (RIO) is captured on the turn away from NAS Fallon during a Top Gun mission. The second crewman in the Tomcat was indispensable and handled the radios and the complex radar system. Tomcat RIOs are highly experienced and well-trained naval flight officers.

Shown here is a pair of Jolly Rogers F-14 Tomcats from what was once Fighter Squadron 103 (VF-103). The unit flew ten F-14B aircraft before transitioning to the Super Hornet. The unit changed its designation to VFA-103, signifying the attack mission, upon receiving the new Super Hornets.

This specification was born out of a failure several years earlier with the General Dynamics F-111B as a naval fighter jet. At that time, Defense Secretary Robert S. McNamara insisted that the Navy take the U.S. Air Force's strike fighter, the F-111. The Navy version, the F-111B, was a fiasco. It was far too heavy and nowhere near maneuverable enough to ever fly off a carrier flight deck. A bitter political fight ensued. In one memorable moment, former Deputy Chief of Naval Operations (Air Warfare) Vice Admiral Tom Connolly stood up under significant political pressure during hearings on the F-111B and declared it would never do the job. This act of courage and honesty doomed the F-111B as a Navy fighter and opened the door for Grumman Aerospace to provide a solution.

Thus, the VFX specification was born. Several manufacturers responded, but only two made the short list, and Grumman Aerospace's design was selected in January 1969. With its combination of AWG-9 radar and Phoenix missiles, variable-geometry sweep wings, and twin tails, the F-14A ushered in a new era in air combat capability for the U.S. Navy. The fleet

NSAWC painted a single F-14 in this desert scheme to simulate adversaries flying former Soviet Union MiG-23 strike fighter aircraft. This jet was photographed on the NSAWC ramp in 2000. Most of the NSAWC stable of Tomcats were decked out in the standard fleet-gray scheme.

had gained a weapons system that could strike at multiple airborne threats from sea level to more than 50,000 feet at ranges in excess of 100 miles. In naval terms, that mission is described as fleet air defense. This is the singular role that the Tomcat was designed to fill and one in which it had no peer.

The Tomcat was unique among fighter aircraft in that it could handle three different air-to-air missiles as well as the internal Vulcan 20mm M61 cannon equipped with 675 rounds of ammunition. The AIM-9 Sidewinder heat-seeking missile is carried on the outboard wing pylons, along with AIM-7 Sparrow radar-guided, medium-range missiles. The AIM-54, with its 100-mile-plus range, is normally carried under the fuselage on special pallets, as well as on the wing stations. Few aircraft can attack from such extreme ranges or with as deadly a mix.

Shown here is a section of VF-143 "Pukin' Dogs" F-14s on the NAS Oceana flight line prior to a midday flight. The air crews are seen strapping in and preparing the Tomcats for the upcoming flight. The Pukin' Dogs have subsequently upgraded to the single-seat F/A-18E Super Hornet and are still based at NAS Oceana.

An F-14A with the "Tophatters" of VF-14 peels away, displaying the immense size of the Tomcat. The A model suffered from temperamental TF-30 engines that did not provide sufficient thrust to properly power the heavy F-14. They were also prone to compressor stalls in high-angle-of-attack maneuvers, which often led to the aircraft departing controlled flight and heading into a flat spin.

The complex AIM-54 missile/AWG-9 radar system necessitated a dedicated second crewman (the radar intercept officer, or RIO) to operate. The F-14 is definitely a two-person fighter; without the RIO (a naval flight officer, or NFO) in the rear seat, the F-14 doesn't leave the ground.

The wings of the Tomcat are configurable based on the different flight regimes the aircraft can fly within. Besides moving forward (20 degrees) and aft (68 degrees), generally for slow- and high-speed flight, respectively, the wing can be brought back (72 degrees) to the over-sweep position for storage on the carrier. The benefits of the swing-wing design are numerous. The Tomcat is surprisingly agile at slow speeds with the wings out, and with them swept back it is able to fly well at high speeds. The large wings also store fuel that is segmented in the Tomcat between the two wings and several fuselage tanks.

F-14A+/B: POTENTIAL REALIZED

As potent as the initial F-14A variant is, it is still nagged by problems with the troublesome Pratt & Whitney TF-30 power-plant. At the time of the cancellation of the F-111B (the

A VF-31 F-14 Tomcat carrying just a pair of AIM-9 Sidewinder and single AIM-54 Phoenix air-to-air missiles on underwing stations cruises over the Atlantic Ocean. The Tomcat was huge for a fighter and not the most forgiving aircraft. It possessed superior range and, in the hands of an experienced, aggressive pilot, could give a good account for itself in air combat.

Three major variants of the F-14 were built: the F-14A, F-14B, and F-14D in quantities of 712, 38, and 37, respectively. The A model was underpowered and used the Pratt & Whitney TF-30P-414A turbofans. Both the F-14B and F-14D used the much-improved General Electric F-110-GE-400 turbofans.

The complex AIM-54/AWG-9 system necessitated a dedicated second crewman (the RIO) seated in the rear cockpit. The F-14 is definitely a two-man fighter; without the RIO (a naval flight officer, or NFO), the F-14 doesn't leave the ground. The new F/A-18F Super Hornet maintains the two-person-crew concept.

The VFX specification demanded an aircraft capable of combat air patrols in excess of two hundred miles from the carrier, a two-hour loiter time, the ability to carry 14,500 pounds of ordnance, and support of the AWG-9 radar and AIM-54 Phoenix missile. The VFX aircraft needed to be large to handle these requirements; the F-14 is over sixty feet in length.

The long line of magnificent Grumman Cats will, sadly, end with the Tomcat. The continuing consolidation within the American industrial military complex claimed the finest manufacturer of naval aircraft, Grumman Aerospace, when it was merged with the Northrop Corporation in the early 1990s.

aircraft that the F-14 would ultimately replace), the Tomcat had to use the only available powerplant at the time, which was the TF-30. Because of budgetary constraints, the A model would remain the primary production variant with the TF-30 engine. Compressor-blade failures and excessive in-flight stalls resulted in the loss of several F-14As. The A model of the Tomcat had a tendency to depart from controlled flight and enter a flat spin after the onset of a stall in one of the two engines. Thus, the TF-30 was only used until the F-14B and its F110-GE-400 engines arrived.

In air combat maneuvering, the underpowered F-14A could be at a distinct disadvantage against more maneuverable and powerful adversaries. In visual, close-in fight, especially in the vertical-flight regime, the F-14A was in a less-than-ideal position. The pilot had to mentally stay ahead of the aircraft, wary of placing the jet in a condition that could lead to a stall. To make matters worse, the TF-30 did not immediately respond to engine inputs. The constant adjustments needed during a dogfight could also lead to stalls. It should be mentioned, however, that in the hands of an experienced F-14A crew, the Tomcat can fight very effectively in the basic fighter maneuvers

The F-14D, arguably the finest long-range fighter ever produced, was capable of handling a wide range of strike fighter missions. This has to be the sharpest-looking F-14 ever flown, the black *Vandy-1*, with the "Vampires" of VX-9. Located at NAS Point Mugu, California, VX-9 handled various flight testing for the Tomcat.

The F-14 first arrived at the Navy Fighter Weapons School (Top Gun) in 1973 as the hottest fighter to grace the skies above Naval Air Station Miramar. The Tomcat had been part of the Navy Strike and Air Warfare Center (NSAWC) since it stood up, and served until the command retired the F-14 in 2003 after the last F-14 Top Gun class graduated.

(BFM) arena. But it takes a great deal of skill and training to get to that point as compared to other communities, such as the F/A-18 air crews who operate a more forgiving aircraft.

Without a new engine, the true potential of the Tomcat was yet to be realized. In the early 1980s, Grumman awarded a contract to General Electric to develop a new powerplant for the Tomcat. The engine manufacturer introduced the F110-GE-400, rated at 23,100 pounds of thrust with afterburner. The engines offered unrestricted throttle movement, far fewer engine stalls in high angle of attack aspect flight, and better fuel economy. For catapult shots, the pilot did not need to go to full afterburner. The Tomcat does not need the thrust for a cat shot, and the afterburner is not used. A test-bed F-14A was fitted with the new engines and began flight testing. The most distinguishing aspect of the A+/B model is the exhaust nozzle (also called an afterburner can) of the new F110 engine.

THE FIERCEST CAT, THE F-14D

The ultimate Tomcat is the F-14D. The D incorporates a digital data bus and a digital architecture for the integration of more

The Jolly Rogers of VF-103 enjoyed a long history with the Tomcat. Initially, the unit flew the F-14A when they were designated VF-84 in the mid-1970s. The Jolly Rogers of VF-84 were disestablished for a time as the F-14 community shrank in the 1990s. In order to keep the history of the famed Jolly Rogers, the Sluggers of VF-103 changed their name and the rich history of the Jolly Rogers continued.

Another of the well-known units to transition from the F-14 to the F/A-18F is the "Diamondbacks" of Strike Fighter Squadron 102 (VFA-102). The true multirole capability of the Super Hornet has necessitated the change in unit designation from "VF" for fighter to "VFA" for fighter attack.

advanced displays, avionics, and weapons capability. Further improvements were made to the main radar system, designated APG-71. The enhanced computer capability afforded significant processing improvements over the previous system. It also extended the detection and firing range of the AIM-54. Avionics and defensive electronic countermeasures (DECM) systems improvements were also made. One of the distinguishing aspects of the F-14D relates to the dual sensor pods underneath the nose. Whereas the A and A+ utilized a simple ALQ-100 radar warning receiver, an infrared search and track (IRST) system, or the Northrop television camera set (TCS), the F-14D uses the General Electric/Martin Marietta twin side-by-side sensor pods.

A VF-102 Diamondbacks F-14B undergoes final systems checks prior to being broken down, or unchained from the flight deck. For safety reasons, the flight deck personnel do not unchain parked aircraft aboard ship until they are ready to taxi to the catapult. Space is tight on the flight deck, and the aircraft are parked perilously close to the edge of the flight deck to save space.

The starboard pod holds the Northrop TCS, while the port-side pod houses the GE IRST. The IRST is a passive sensor that greatly enhances the F-14's ability to track stealthy opponents.

The joint tactical information distribution system (JTIDS) was incorporated and allows the Tomcat to effectively communicate with other F-14s. With the D model, the Tomcat entered the digital world. Both the front and rear cockpits were revamped to include multi-function displays (MFDs) and hands-on throttle and stick (HOTAS) systems. One of the changes made in the F-14D was the replacement of the older Martin Baker GRU/7A ejection seat with the Martin Baker naval air common ejection seat (NACES) system.

An NSAWC F-14 pilot scans the skies during a Top Gun mission prior to the final F-14 SFTI class. Visibility out of the Tomcat was fair. The RIO in the back seat served as a second set of eyes for visual scans. The fourth-generation F-16 and F/A-18 fighters addressed this problem and have superb visibility.

The large intakes of the F-14 are evident in this photo of a VF-31 F-14 over the Atlantic Ocean. As a swing-wing fighter, the F-14 carried all of its ordnance and fuel tanks on stations under the fuselage. The typical configuration during local training sorties may not have included any missiles, just a pair of fuel tanks.

The Jolly Rogers celebrated sixty years flying Navy fighter aircraft in 2003. The first unit to bear the Jolly Rogers name was VF-17, established in 1943. From 1948 to 1959, the Jolly Rogers were assigned to VF-61, flying jet aircraft. VF-84 was next, and the unit operated the F-4 Phantom, then the F-14A Tomcat. VF-103 flew the F-14B, and the current VFA-103 flies the F/A-18F.

Soon to be a sight gone forever over Navy air stations, a trio of F-14s enters the break. The F-14's swing-wing design and immense size and power guaranteed that every return from a mission was made in impressive style. The lead jet is pitching away ninety degrees to begin the landing process; the two wingmen will follow shortly.

NIGHT-ATTACK TOMCAT

In June 1996, the Jolly Rogers of VF-103 took their F-14Bs to sea aboard the USS *Enterprise* (CVN-65) and wrote a new chapter in the tale of the Tomcat. In fact, nine of the squadron's fourteen F-14s were fitted with the proven Lockheed Martin low-altitude navigation and targeting for night (LANTIRN) system. This advanced system, similar to what has been used within the U.S. Air Force F-15E Strike Eagle and F-16 Falcon, provides a devastating precision day-and-night-attack capability to the Tomcat community.

The primary element of the LANTIRN system is the AN/ALQ-14 pod, which is carried on the right wing station. The pod is modified to include a global positioning system (GPS) and inertial unit that affords improved target location and acquisition. The main computer system carries all the necessary ballistics data for the precision-guided munitions (PGM) that the Tomcat carries underneath the fuselage between both engines. The LANTIRN system is not exactly

Fledgling F-14 Tomcat pilots and RIOs received their initial training at two fleet replacement squadrons (FRS). The East Coast–based FRS was the Grim Reapers of VF-101, based at NAS Oceana, Virginia. With the impending retirement of the Tomcat, the need to train new air crews is gone and the Reapers were disestablished in the summer of 2005.

Squadron maintenance personnel tend to a VF-32 F-14 aboard the USS *Dwight D. Eisenhower* (CVN-69) for the evening's upcoming flight. One of the challenges for F-14 squadrons toward the end of the aircraft's operational career was keeping it maintained despite the aging airframes.

the same as the system used by the U.S. Air Force. The current naval configuration is tightly linked to the Tomcat's AWG-15 fire control system and AWG-9 radar. The Navy and Marine Corps make greater use of night-vision goggles (NVGs), and these were added to the VF-103 F-14s (also a first for the squadron).

Other modifications to the Tomcat that support LAN-TIRN include changes to the aft cockpit. A LANTIRN panel and a hand controller allow the RIO the ability to control the system. The hand controller contains several buttons that handle target search, acquisition, and attack functions while also supporting magnification of the FLIR display by either 4X, 10X, or 20X.

The other important aspect of the system is, of course, the precision-guided munitions that deliver the actual punch. The current weapon of choice is the GBU-16 or GBU-12 laser-guided bomb. The GBU-16 is a 1,000-pound Mk.83 general-purpose bomb married to a laser-guided seeker in the nose; the GBU-12 is the 500-pound Mk.82 bomb.

The F-14 Tomcat served Top Gun for thirty years and has seen the program grow from its inception at NAS Miramar to its current dedicated department within NSAWC. Initially, the syllabus focused on the air-to-air role, which was the Tomcat's specialty. As the strike mission was added to the F-14, so was the ground attack role added to the Top Gun curriculum.

FLYING THE TOMCAT IN COMBAT

Commander Paul Haas, the outgoing commanding officer of the Grim Reapers of VF-101, describes combat operations with the Tomcat during Operation Iraqi Freedom: "The Tomcats, even the newer D models, were getting old, and there was some difficulty in getting certain parts we needed. About the time I took over VF-31, we went through a particularly tough time with maintenance. The CAG supported me because he knew that he had VF-31 and twelve F-14 Tomcats able to protect us with AIM-54 Phoenix missiles and also able to drop JDAMs. It was very reassuring to have him support us through our peaks and valleys based on his comfort with our ability to do all the missions asked of us, even with the readiness challenges. The F-14 represented an immensely valuable tool for his air wing. He was insistent that we train our FACAs and give them all the opportunities they needed in order to do what they needed to do in combat. I can't help but think that in some small way the Tomcat helped us end the Cold War." The former Soviet Union relied on its long-range TU-95 Bear bombers to threaten U.S. carrier fleets. The F-14 countered this threat by finding and intercepting Bear aircraft many miles from the carriers. It became too expensive for the Soviets to operate this aircraft and it was rendered ineffective thanks to the F-14.

"When you talk with the folks that built the F-14, they remind you that they built the airplane to be a swing-wing fighter that was designed to be both a fighter and attack aircraft. The decision was made by some senior officers that the aircraft was going to just be a fighter. I remember being a junior officer, thinking about being just a fighter guy and leaving the mud-pounding mission to the other guys that will fly low and slow. We were going to concentrate on flying at mach two and shooting other guys down, pulling high g's and all that. It is remarkable that, in the twilight of its career, the F-14 went on to become such a versatile aircraft and superb bomber."

Commander Haas recalls his first combat mission during Iraqi Freedom: "On the 22nd of March, I launched with the CAG on a mission on the second full night of the war. The entire shock and awe thing occurred the first night, and we were a fairly small strike package. We had U.S. Air Force F-16CJs and a Marine Corps EA-6B Prowler, along with our two Tomcats. We were scheduled to hit a target well south of Baghdad, out of range of active SAMs [surface-to-air missiles]. As we were heading to the target, we got a call to reroll and hit a new target, an air field on the western side of Baghdad. It was a small target of opportunity, and we needed to engage it quickly. My CAG and his Super Hornets went on to engage the original targets, and my wingman and I were to hit the new target. So now it was down to just two airplanes, me and my young wingman. The funny thing was, I planned for an attack mission in the same area the night before but ended up breaking two airplanes on the deck of the carrier and could not go. (I had a generator failure while on the catapult of my primary jet. I then went to the spare aircraft and had a nose strut problem while taxiing to the catapult, so the jet kneeled as it would for the catapult shot but would not come back into place. We missed our tanking window and could not go on the mission.)

"Since I did the mission planning for the same area for the previous night's mission, I was familiar with the targets, the threats, and the ingress and egress routes. I got to thinking that, when we planned this originally, it did not seem so bad since we were going to overwhelm the Iraqi air defense system with between one and two hundred aircraft in the sky; now, it was just me, my RIO, and the two guys in the other F-14. Our chance of being engaged by a SAM the first night was small; but now I was one of two airplanes flying into downtown Baghdad with nothing but me and one other jet for them to look at. Sure enough, we came around the target and we got lit up by SAM radar. Our prebriefed abort criteria dictated that if we got engaged by a SAM or detected a tracking radar, we would jettison our weapons and fight to survive. With as much ordnance as we were carrying, we would not be maneuverable and it would not have made sense to press on and risk losing a couple of jets on the second night of the war. So we started out doing our defensive maneuvers, and I was thinking, 'Well, that's it.' My wingman, who was a nugget, and his experienced backseater, a real level-headed guy, who were following behind us, said, 'Roger that, we're pressing on.' They continued. I could not let him go in on his own. At that time, our defensive measures worked and we turned back into the target. Due to our defensive maneuvers, we were then behind our wingman by a couple of miles as he was going through a series of defensive maneuvers. I was watching him from the best seat in the house, and he was my missile sponge. He was first, so I was watching this wall of SAMs coming up ahead of us and also to the north of us. I was thinking that he trusts his airplane, his instincts, and his training, and he's just slalom skiing through these SAMs.

One of the SAMs we didn't see came up between the two jets about a half mile away. It had to be fired ballistically, because I did not get a spike on my warning receiver. We were carrying JDAMs, and we agreed on the launch point called the 'chicken range,' which would give us a fifty-fifty chance of striking the target from a further distance if we were heavily engaged by SAMs. It's also known as the maximum employment range of the weapon. As we were going in to the target and getting closer, we approached the agreed-upon chicken line, and I was thinking, 'Okay, he's going to drop the weapon.' But bless his heart, he kept pressing on right to the target. We were dodg-ing the air defenses and looking down and saw all these angry red bursts coming up at us from the ground antiaircraft guns, and we were going as fast as we could, leaving it all behind us. So then we were thinking, 'Okay, no kidding, they know we are here.' My wingman dropped his weapons at the perfect range. Since he had been doing so much maneuvering, I was abeam of him and dropped my weapons just after he did. We both made a hard turn out, and I continued the maneuvering since they were still shooting at us. All of our weapons hit this target simultaneously and made a spectacular explosion and fireball that could be seen from fifty miles away."

An F-14B Tomcat with the Jolly Rogers of VF-103 departs NAS Oceana. The F-14B entered service in the late 1980s. Forty older F-14A Tomcats were retrofitted to the new model, along with thirty-eight newly built aircraft. The more-capable F-14D followed the B model into service in 1984.

Perhaps the most impressive-looking Tomcat to ever grace the skies is this splinter-style, camouflaged F-14A previously flown by the NSAWC. The aircraft simulated the massive former Soviet Union SU-27 Flanker fighter aircraft. NSAWC adorned several of its Tomcats in different camouflage schemes. *Photo by Chuck Lloyd*

CHAPTER 4

NSAWC—THE CENTER OF EXCELLENCE

T he Naval Strike and Air Warfare Center (NSAWC), located at Naval Air Station Fallon, is the center of excellence for naval aviation training and tactics development. NSAWC provides expert services to air crews, squadrons, and air wings throughout the U.S. Navy in the form of flight training, academic instructional classes, and direct operational and intelligence support. NSAWC flies and maintains a fleet of F/A-18 Hornets, F-16 Fighting Falcons, and SH-60 Seahawk helicopters.

Shown here is a section of NSAWC Hornets photographed on one of the initial BFM phase flights in the Top Gun SFTI syllabus. This flight, called "Tac 1," usually lasts just over an hour and is intended to provide the student with advanced handling familiarity of the Hornet.

Before NSAWC created a uniform single command, there were three independent commands—Strike U handled air-to-ground strike training, Top Gun air-to-air combat, and Top Dome airborne early warning. NSAWC was officially formed on July 11, 1996, and is the center of excellence for naval aviation training and tactics development.

THE HISTORY OF TOP GUN AND STRIKE U

The roots of NSAWC can be traced back to combat operations over Vietnam, in which the Navy played a significant role, and the hard lessons learned from these operations. The idea to create the Navy Fighter Weapons School (Top Gun) dates back to the Vietnam War. The Strike Warfare Center, a.k.a. Strike University—the air-to-ground equivalent of Top Gun—dates back to the 1980s. There are many direct similarities between the former Naval Strike Warfare Center (NSWC) and today's NSAWC command. The mission of NSWC included serving as the primary authority for strike warfare tactics and developments, improving strike and war-at-sea tactics development, working with other commands on air wing training, and advising the deputy chief of naval operations on strike warfare research. NSAWC brings together all of these aspects and expands on them to include Top Gun, Top Dome (the E-2C Hawkeye training program), and other newer elements, such as SH-60 Seahawk training operations, all in one place.

During the Vietnam era, the U.S. Navy saw its win-to-loss ratio in air combat sink to an unacceptably low level. The reality was that Navy air crews lacked the proper equipment and, more important, the proper training to maintain the level

All Navy carrier-based aircraft, as well as a selection of NSAWC aircraft, sport the drab fleet-gray paint scheme worn on this NSAWC Hornet. As a sign of respect to the original Strike University program, this bird has the former Strike U emblem on its tail. This has been retained on NSAWC aircraft.

Currently, NSAWC operates three platforms: the Hornet, Fighting Falcon, and Seahawk. There are twenty F/A-18 Hornets (two two-seaters), thirteen F-16s (nine single-seaters and four two-seaters), and four SH-60 Seahawks.

of proficiency needed to achieve air superiority. The situation had deteriorated significantly since World War II, in which Navy air crews enjoyed a commanding 10:1 advantage. The Korean War saw the ratio drop to just about 4:1. By 1968, with the U.S. Navy embroiled in the Vietnam War, the ratio dropped to 2.9:1.

Senior naval officers took note of the decline and reacted by appointing the former commanding officer of the USS

Coral Sea (CVA-43), Captain Frank W. Ault, to conduct a sweeping analysis of the situation and make specific recommendations to remedy the problems. The captain received a very straightforward mandate to determine why the Navy wasn't shooting down more enemy MiGs. Ault was given the authority to conduct the study as he needed to in order to increase the kill ratio by a factor of three at the very least. The result was a

A sinister-looking NSAWC SH-60 hovers near the Edwards South section of the massive Fallon range complex. NSAWC operates four SH-60s under the Seahawk Weapons School, which first stood up in 1998 to become the focal point for all tactics, techniques, and procedures for the SH-60 community.

480-page report officially titled "Air-to-Air Missile System Capability Review" and later called simply the "Ault Report." It listed five areas of inquiry that warranted further study. The fourth point posed this question: "What is the combat performance of the Navy fighter weapons systems, and what are the principal factors influencing it?" That question would ultimately begin the genesis of the NFWS.

The Navy was flying primarily the missile-toting F-4 Phantom during most of the Vietnam War, along with a small number of older F-8 Crusaders. The F-8 carried an internal gun and a pair of AIM-9 Sidewinder missiles. The larger, twin-crewed F-4 Phantom II was strictly armed with missiles, using the AIM-9 and the AIM-7 Sparrow radar-guided missile. It became apparent to Captain Ault that the Navy crews did not

The Search and Rescue (SAR) unit located at NAS Fallon operates the UH-1. This photo has a Huey chasing an NSAWC SH-60. Operating modern high-performance jet and rotary-wing aircraft is not without its element of risk, and there are accidents that will cause the SAR crews to jump in their trusty Hueys and head out to retrieve downed airmen.

The camouflage tail of an NSAWC F/A-18 also includes the Top Gun logo. Proud traditions run deep throughout the U.S. Navy, and NSAWC is no exception. The Top Gun logo, which is worn proudly as a patch on the flight suits of SFTI graduates, is superimposed over the lighting-bolt design that was used by the former Strike University program of the original Navy Weapons Tactics Center.

possess sufficient knowledge of the weapons systems, specifically the AIM-7 missile, nor had they been exposed to the proper training to employ them with real success. The problem was not unique to Navy crews. Between the U.S. Air Force and the Navy, over 600 air-to-air missiles had been fired during 360 engagements in an eighteen-month period leading up to September 1968. These engagements had a one-in-ten chance of killing the adversary. The Navy Phantom crews spent too much time with their heads down in the cockpit, managing the radar and missile systems. The Crusader had more luck in the war and confirmed the need for an internal gun to complement the missiles. It was also apparent that there was a need for an air combat maneuvering range in which to train air crews with the missile systems and their optimal employment parameters. The Ault Report issued 242 recommendations, of which two principal directives led to the formation of the NFWS in order to provide the required training and the establishment of dedicated, instrumented ranges in which to conduct the training. Initially, a fleet air gunnery unit was formed on an experimental basis embedded within VF-121, the F-4 fleet replacement training squadron. An air combat

A pair of NSAWC F-16 Vipers crosses over NAS Fallon after an SFTI mission. This photo was taken from 8,000 feet above the NAS Fallon complex. The two main runways are 31L and 31R, which are 14,000 and 11,000 feet long, respectively. NSAWC and VFC-13 have their own dedicated ramps.

maneuvering (ACM) syllabus was incorporated into the training program. VF-126 provided adversary support with their nimble A-4E Skyhawk aircraft. The first class began in March 1969.

The results of these efforts became apparent with the success of Navy air crews in combat over Vietnam. The air crews that returned to the fleet from Top Gun spread the knowledge they had gained quickly. Kill ratios began to swing back in favor of the Navy.

By January 1972, Top Gun became a detachment of VF-121, and on July 21, 1972, it became a separate command based at Naval Air Station Miramar, California, dubbed "Fightertown." It was officially named the Navy Fighter Weapons School. As we look at NSAWC and the Fallon Range Training Complex (FTRC) today, we can see the results of the far-reaching 1969 Ault Report.

In October 1985, Top Gun became an Echelon II shore command, reporting directly to the chief of naval operations. Prior to its incorporation into NSAWC, Top Gun steadily improved upon its mission and evolved to include training intercept controllers and began to emphasize the air-to-ground mission in 1994. This was a major change to the program, as it had previously focused specifically on the air-to-air mission. The F/A-18 Hornet brought its multirole capability to the

An NSAWC F/A-18B basks on the flight line just after a late-afternoon rain shower. NSAWC aircraft are parked outside hangar five. There is a predetermined scheme to parking the aircraft. Each of the four rows facilitates the placement of NSAWC's inventory of F/A-18As, SH-60s, and F-16s.

NSAWC instructors are an elite cadre of naval aviators. All instructors are handpicked to serve at NSAWC or the two Strike Fighter Weapons Schools (Atlantic and Pacific Fleets). All are previous Top Gun graduates who undergo additional training while at NSAWC to hone their instructional skills.

101

NSAWC's mission as officially stated is as follows: The premier aviation center of excellence, and the primary authority on training and tactics development. NSAWC is broken up into nine departments: personnel resources; intelligence; operations; maintenance; plans, programs, and tactics development (Strike); Carrier Airborne Early Warning Weapons School/Electronic Reconnaissance Weapons School; Strike Fighter Weapons School (Top Gun); Seahawk Weapons School; and operational risk management/safety.

forefront of Navy air wings. The F-14 was also evolving into a respectable attack platform. The scope and length of the course expanded with the multirole Hornet and the ground-attack role of the F-14 and was changed from the power projection course to the strike fighter tactics instructor (SFTI) course. Top Gun conducted four SFTI courses per year, each nine weeks in duration, with up to a dozen F-14 and F/A-18 air crews.

The NSWC was developed after a failed strike mission in 1983 against targets in Lebanon. Navy Secretary John Lehman, an A-6 bombardier/navigator, was convinced that something had to be done to improve tactics training and procedures, and he supported the development of what became the NSWC. The lore around the command's origins is linked to the Lebanon mission, but in reality, support had already existed at Lehman's level for the warfare center. Lehman had quite a bit of experience with the U.S. Marine Corps Marine Aviation Weapons and Tactics Squadron One (MAWTS-1), located at Marine Corps Air Station Yuma, Arizona. He believed the Navy needed an equivalent, and the NSWC was developed. Lehman selected Captain Joe W. Prueher to lead the development of the center and get it off the ground.

The NSWC was a unique organization dedicated solely to the study and development of carrier aviation power projection. Strike's mission formally stated that it was to serve as the primary authority for integrated strike warfare tactical development and training. From humble beginnings in a single former U.S. Air Force barracks at Naval Air Station Lemoore, California, the initial cadre of officers under Captain Prueher created Strike University on September 15, 1984. The last commander of Strike, prior to its integration into NSAWC, was Rear Admiral David C. Nichols Jr., who recalls: "When we first stood Strike up, we had two things in mind: We were going to train strike leaders in a classroom course that included practical exercises aimed at senior air wing strike leaders. We envisioned a two-week course called the strike leader attack training syllabus (SLATS). SLATS dealt with five main areas of study: planning, tools, factors, execution, and tactics.

"Our plan was to teach integrated air wing tactics and provide input to the assistant chief of naval operations for air warfare on programmatic and procurement issues. We would focus on what kind of bombs to use, airplane performance, and missile requirements.

"That changed slightly in the fall of 1984 for several reasons. Shortly after Strike stood up, the tactical air crew combat training system (TACTS) range also stood up at NAS Fallon. We immediately saw what a tremendous tool this was, but there really wasn't a plan for how this was going to be used in the air wing training business. At the time, the Naval Strike Warfare Center was not supposed to be involved in air wing

In addition to combat search and rescue, plane guard, and antisubmarine warfare, the SH-60 conducts special operations missions with Navy SEAL teams. The black paint scheme is used for night operations and forms its own version of low-technology stealth. The inaugural class of the Seahawk Weapons School graduated in September 1998.

NSAWC relies on F/A-18As, F/A-18Bs, and F-16s to meet its training commitments. The size of the range complex and the number of NSAWC aircraft allows for realistic threat scenario simulations. This trio is returning from an area defense mission. Mission objective (formally stated): attrit enemy aircraft inbound to carrier battle group; (informally stated) destroy the bad guys before they get to any of our ships.

training. But after we saw a couple of wings come through there, it was clear that there needed to be a more formal and controlled process to ensure the Navy got the most out of the money it spent to send the air wings to Fallon. It made sense for Strike to pick up that role, as we then described it as 'facilitating' air wing training at Fallon. We also took on the role of managing the TACTS range."

Strike U was organized into five departments: tactics, operations, intelligence, administration, and maintenance. NSWC operated a small collection of the three strike aircraft in the Navy's inventory at the time: the A-6E Intruder, A-7 Corsair, and F/A-18 Hornet. Like NSAWC today, the NSWC instructors flew their own aircraft.

During the first two years, air wing training support was in its infancy, and Strike U's major contribution was to fly with the air wing on major coordinated strikes and offer a postmission evaluation during extensive debriefs. The command also provided the air wing commander with a complete

The range complex used by NSAWC is a key ingredient to the success of the command, allowing for the realistic training that modern combat air crews need. This section of NSAWC fighters appears to get lost in the vast expanse of the ranges.

NSAWC Hornet in the break over NAS Fallon. The biggest advantage NAS Fallon has is its massive ranges. These highly instrumented ranges permit the highest degree of realistic combat training for Navy fixed- and rotary-wing air crews. The close proximity of the ranges to NAS Fallon also conserves fuel and allows the jet air crews to fly all out, even supersonically.

postdetachment assessment of the air wing's strike capabilities. This changed by the mid-1980s, when Strike was directed to act as the central coordinator for the development and execution of a comprehensive air wing detachment training program. Strike personnel began to liaison with each air wing to develop and execute a deployment training plan tailored to each air wing's specific needs. To accomplish this, scenarios were developed to support strike tasking, and strike planning assistance was provided for debrief and mission reconstruction. Strike intelligence personnel assisted air wing planning efforts by supplying real-world intelligence and making available a rapidly expanding intelligence library.

The school's move to Naval Air Station Fallon in 1984 allowed the program to take advantage of the bombing ranges surrounding the sprawling base. The Navy noticed the success of the U.S. Air Force's Red Flag exercises at Nellis Air Force Base, Nevada. Of particular importance was the air force's use of instrumented ranges that allowed for postflight analysis of the missions. This allowed the instructors to see specifically what was and was not working. The key to the NSWC air wing training program was the integration of air wing tactical capabilities. A building-block approach was used, moving

The hills around Pyramid Lake form the backdrop against which these NSAWC Hornets roam during a demo area defense hop. This mission is designed to train the fleet pilots in protecting the carrier strike group (CSG). The scenario developed involves the use of the CSG to project power against a hostile country that has invaded an ally of the United States. Enforcement of a no-fly zone is considered a littoral operation, and the NSAWC aircraft will simulate both the Mirage F-1 and MiG-29.

from basic to more complex scenarios. The availability of the TACTS system and the expansive Fallon ranges were a cornerstone to the air wing training. The training events could be monitored in real time, and information from each aircraft could be displayed on the large screens and displays.

NSAWC

On July 11, 1996, NSAWC merged three commands into a single command structure. The Navy needed to evolve its combat aviation training programs to address new generations of fighters and threats, joint fighting strategies, and the realities of reductions in the country's defense budget. A concept was developed in 1992 to create a center for naval tactical air warfare to deal with these challenges.

Vice Chief of Naval Operations Admiral Jay Johnson formalized the Naval Strike and Air Warfare Center on June 4, 1996. Naval aviation's three centers of excellence—Strike University (fighter/strike), Top Gun (Fighter Weapons School), and the carrier airborne early warning weapons school (CAEWWS)—were combined under one organization with a mission to focus on aviation tactical training enhancements. The objective of NSAWC is to maximize the capabilities of the carrier battle groups (CVBGs). NSAWC would be tasked with air crew postgraduate training, producing tactics instructors, and providing carrier air wing (CVW) workups.

NSAWC personnel describe their mission in its simplest terms as a training mission that is focused on the individual, the squadron, and the air wing. The end goal is to develop and grow the world's finest tactical aviation war fighters.

At the core of NSAWC's success and efficacy is the cadre of superb instructors. Most NSAWC instructors are handpicked from previous classes. After a successful tour with NSAWC, the instructors will usually return to the fleet to manage the tactical training program within their respective squadrons, while acting as liaisons to NSAWC and providing feedback on the effectiveness of the training and tactics refinement.

NSAWC's first commander, Rear Admiral Bernard J. "Hawk" Smith, arrived in Fallon in August 1995 to begin a year of staff preparation and new facilities construction. His task was by no means a small one, and bringing all the people and equipment together under one unified command would require the skills of a credible and knowledgeable officer. The admiral, a naval academy graduate, spent his career as an attack pilot and flew over 400 combat missions during three Vietnam deployments. He served as an air group commander with Air Wing Three in 1981 and as commanding officer of the USS *Midway* (CV-41) in 1989. Rear Admiral Smith was chief of staff to the commander of U.S. naval forces during Operations Desert Shield and Desert Storm. With combat and battle

Shown here is a section of Naval Strike and Air Warfare Center F/A-18 Hornets on a late-afternoon patrol. The command provides service to air crews, squadrons, and air wings throughout the Navy in the form of flight training, instructional classes, and direct operational and intelligence support.

group command experience to serve and guide him, Rear Admiral Smith commissioned NSAWC on July 11, 1996. NSAWC stood up with approximately 500 personnel, including 130 officers, 230 enlisted, 89 civilians, 12 Marine Corps officers, and representatives of the U.S. Air Force and British Royal Navy.

For sheer remoteness, Naval Air Station Fallon can't be beat. Located roughly an hour's drive east of Reno, Nevada, Naval Air Station Fallon was the perfect location for NSAWC. The excellent weather and open space of the Nevada high desert region offers obvious advantages for tactical training flight operations. Rear Admiral Smith cites the Base Realignment and Closure Act as another reason for concentrating the three aviation schools at Fallon. "We can concentrate air wing training in one place, and that's more economical," Smith says. The original concept saw a one-star admiral supervising three separate organizations; the original NSWC would have become an Echelon III command reporting to either a theater commander in chief or warfare commander. Rear Admiral Smith believed that there would be enormous benefits in creating

Shown here is a section of NSAWC F-16 Vipers over the Carson Sink section of the Fallon range. The range complex is divided into two main areas, NSAWC 1 and NSAWC 2, and encompasses over 10,200 square miles. Although the range is mostly desolate, there are some inhabitants. The Navy tries very hard to minimize any disturbances to the population by posting notices to air crews on noise-sensitive areas. These are typically over wildlife refuge and populated areas. As a rule, the aircraft are kept above 3,000 feet above ground level (AGL) and/or five miles from these areas.

an Echelon II command, which would eliminate the layers between the NSAWC command and the chief of naval operations (CNO) by reporting directly to the CNO's office. The advantage to this type of command relationship, as described by Rear Admiral Smith: "NSAWC is like the hub of a wagon wheel, supporting and supported by the many spokes of different commands on both coasts. This new structure will enhance and improve the naval aviation training continuum."

The transition process began with Strike U, which had been moved to Fallon in 1984, and moving the CAEWWS to Naval Air Station Fallon from Naval Air Station Miramar at the end of 1995. The NFWS (Top Gun), established in 1969, arrived from Naval Air Station Miramar in June 1996.

The original goals of the schools that now serve NSAWC are well established, and the command's mission remains true to its historical origins and combat experiences: teaching naval aviators to fly and fight. The ultimate goal of NSAWC is to ensure that excellence in training will lead to victory in battle.

NSAWC OVERVIEW AND MISSION

Four carrier air wings matriculate at NSAWC annually to hone skills in preparation for major deployments. Air wings spend three and a half weeks of intensive training at NSAWC, operating in tactical environments nearly as realistic as those that they might encounter in true combat engagements. The air wings reach the pinnacle of combat readiness at NSAWC as the final phase of air wing preparation prior to deployment. NSAWC does a lot more than train carrier air wings for front-line duty.

"NSAWC is the prime authority for air wing battle group tactics," says Captain John Worthington, former CAG of CVW-9 and former deputy commander of NSAWC. "As the single point of contact for strike warfare, we strive to increase the standardization of basic combat tactics, providing a unity of purpose and efficiency in the graduate-level flight training which we manage. We have great connectivity with deployed carrier battle groups to provide them operational support. We liaison directly with the unified CINCs [commanders in chief] and fleet commanders. Our instructors are pack-plus types—experienced, well motivated, and work well with their fleet counterparts."

Currently, NSAWC operates three platforms: the Hornet, Fighting Falcon, and Seahawk. There are twenty F/A-18 Hornets (two of which are two-seaters), thirteen F-16s (nine single-seaters and four two-seaters), and four SH-60 Seahawks.

NSAWC is broken up into nine departments: personnel resources; intelligence; operations; maintenance; plans and programs; command, control, communications, computers, and intelligence (C4I)/command and control warfare (C2W); training and standardization; range; and safety.

NSAWC MISSION

NSAWC is the premier aviation center of excellence and the primary authority on training and tactics development. NSAWC provides training, assessment, aviation requirements recommendations, and research and development priorities for integrated strike warfare, maritime/overland air superiority strike fighter employment, airborne battle management, combat search and rescue (CSAR), close air support (CAS), and associated planning support systems. The command is also responsible for the development, implementation, and administration of several courses of instruction, while functioning as the Navy point of contact for all issues relating to the air combat training continuum (ACTC). Additionally, NSAWC is the Navy point of contact for all issues related to the Fallon Range Training Complex (FRTC).

TRAINING

In addition to extensive classroom academic training, there are two distinctly different areas of NSAWC training that utilize the Fallon Range Training Complex (FRTC)—the carrier air wing (CAW) course and the SFTI course. Air wing training brings together all the squadrons of an air wing for approximately four weeks and provides a strike planning and execution training opportunity in a dynamic, realistic scenario driven in a simulated wartime environment. This typically takes place prior to the air wing's joint war fighting exercises and is usually three months before they deploy at sea. This training is crucial to honing the air wing's readiness as a team and vital in its preparation. The training represents one of the most important contributions NSAWC makes to the Navy's war-making capability.

NSAWC conducts a variety of training programs, including the Top Gun SFTI program, which is nine weeks long for Navy and Marine Corps strike fighter air crews. The training is a graduate-level program, specializing in advanced strike fighter weapons and tactics instruction. The adversary tactics instructor course is six weeks long and is designed for Navy adversary Red Air pilots. Like Top Gun SFTI, the course is a graduate-level program that specializes in advanced adversary instructor training.

The SFTI course trains individuals in the arts of air-to-air and air-to-ground superiority, providing highly advanced tactical training in the F/A-18 and previously in the F-14.

An NSAWC Hornet in a wraparound brown paint scheme is heading out to engage a fleet F/A-18 out of view during an offensive basic fighter maneuver (BFM) mission. NSAWC is the primary authority on naval aviation training and tactics development. The command incorporates all of the previous elements of the former Top Gun syllabus.

Numerous paint schemes are employed on NSAWC Hornets in addition to the standard fleet-gray design. To enhance the realism of the adversary aircraft, a wide variety of paint schemes are utilized on Top Gun aircraft. This aircraft takes the runway for a late-afternoon mission.

Shown here is the premier issue of the *NSAWC Journal* Volume 1, Issue 1, Fall 1996. The *Journal* is a secret document covering weapons, tactics, and training. The *Journal* combines the newsletters previously published by Top Gun, Strike University, and the Carrier Airborne Early Warning Weapons School.

An important aspect of NSAWC's mission involves preparing visiting air wings for their impending deployments at sea. All departments within NSAWC participate in the training; the N5 department, also known as Strike, takes the lead. It's been over twenty years since the original Strike University first opened its doors to improve the war-fighting ability of carrier air wings.

The splinter-style paint scheme on this NSAWC F/A-18A adds to the realistic Red Air presentation for Top Gun students. This scheme is found on former Soviet Union SU-27 fighters. This jet was captured while trying to make an unnoticed entry into a fight against a pair of Top Gun Hornet students.

program. The Seahawk weapons and tactics instructor course is nine weeks long and intended for SH-60 Seahawk air crews. Advanced training for helicopter air crews in aerial gunnery, close air support, surface-to-air counter tactics, and maritime air support is all part of the Seahawk Weapons School (SWS) instructor course.

NSAWC STRUCTURE

NSAWC is segmented into nine distinct departments, numbered N1 through N9.

N1: Personnel Resources
N2: Intelligence
N3: Operations
N4: Maintenance
N5: Plans, Programs, and Tactics Development (Strike)
N6: Carrier Airborne Early Warning Weapons School/ Electronic Reconnaissance Weapons School
N7: Strike Fighter Weapons School (Top Gun)
N8: Seahawk Weapons School
N9: Operational Risk Management/Safety

N1: *Personnel Resources*

N1 oversees the command's administrative functions, supply, security, and automated information systems. This is a vital link to the fleet in managing all of the details for student and air wing participation, as well as staffing the NSAWC departments.

N2: *Intelligence*

N2 provides support to air wing training in Fallon, as well as to fleets and battle groups globally. N2 is one of NSAWC's most interactive departments. Within this department, there are target and weaponeering experts, assisted by enlisted intelligence specialists who gather data on potential trouble areas around the globe where deployed naval forces might be called upon to establish a naval presence or initiate action. Inherent in the intelligence mission is preparation of air crews for all circumstances they may face in combat. During air wing training, the intelligence department presents tailored scenarios in which the levels of enemy sophistication and intensity are controlled. Air wing intelligence officers are evaluated in their ability to efficiently disseminate intelligence information to the air crews. In addition to air wing training, another function of the NSAWC's intelligence department is to prepare for contingencies.

When called upon, members of the N2 department can rapidly deploy, armed with the latest intelligence gathered by the department to directly advise commanders in any theater of operation. The intelligence and cryptology officers and enlisted specialists contribute to NSAWC academic programs, the new *NSAWC Journal* (combining Top Gun's *Journal,* Strike U's *Aimpoint,* and Top Dome's *Vector*), and virtually every other program.

The NSAWC N2 department offers a full curriculum designed to train junior intelligence personnel to perform the tactical intelligence missions in support of integrated strike warfare. Modern strike warfare requires the fusion of accurate intelligence with effective operational doctrine. The goal is to promote a close working relationship between the air wing's intelligence team and air wing strike planners. NSAWC pursues this goal by teaching intelligence concepts in the classroom, offering hands-on training on the automated intelligence and mission planning systems currently employed in the fleet, and by exercising intelligence fusion and teamwork during a rigorous and realistic contingency strike simulation.

N3: *Operations*

N3 manages scheduling for aircraft and air crews, the training ranges, and keeps air crew log books and records. N3's primary role is to ensure that the NSAWC command has all of the required assets in place for the dutiful execution of NSAWC's mission.

The operations officer is among the hardest-working individuals within NSAWC, managing tight coordination between all of the departments and the NSAWC commanders. Daily tasks include oversight of the daily execution of flight schedule, producing the daily flight schedule for deputy commander approval, oversight of the Fallon Tactical Training Range scheduling, providing required flight planning materials, working with the Naval Air Station Fallon operations department regarding base scheduling issues, and monitoring air crew qualifications and qualifications currencies. Operations oversees more than seventy-five air crews, thirty-seven aircraft, five weapons schools courses and lectures, as well as air wing detachments.

N4: *Maintenance*

N4 maintains all NSAWC aircraft, including parts and supplies for F/A-18s, F-16s, and SH-60 helicopters; manages the loading, unloading, and storage of ordnance; and maintains air crew flight equipment. The N4 department has one of the most demanding jobs in the command, keeping the air assets ready to go. Prior to the F-14 Tomcat's retirement, the N4 department had to keep the rapidly aging F-14 Tomcats flying; all older F-14A models had been flying for over twenty-five years. Aircraft maintenance is done under a seven-year multi-million-dollar contract with Boeing Aerospace Operations.

N5: *Plans, Programs, and Tactics Development (Strike)*

N5 is involved in tactics development and assessment for tactical aircraft and SH-60 helicopters, program management and participation, mission planning, and inter/intraservice liaison. Combining the three commands of excellence expanded the original Strike U mission. The focus has grown into addressing the future vision for naval aviation with the creation of the N5 Plans, Programs, and Tactics Development division. NSAWC's original commander, Admiral Bernard Smith, was careful to describe the integration of the VF/VA worlds in today's Hornet Navy, with F-14s also performing attack missions before their retirement. "We need to establish a strike fighter mindset with attack and fighter attitudes," he commented. "Our goal is unity of purpose with excellence in training and tactics development." Toward that end, NSAWC has a full plate of responsibilities with connections throughout the Navy and to other branches of the U.S. military. NSAWC also interacts with the Nellis Air Force Base Weapons School, Red Flag, and range operations. Naval Air Station Fallon's NSAWC and Nellis Air Force Base ranges are being electronically linked to enhance joint tactics development. Additionally, Admiral Smith highlighted that fiscal savings can be achieved by using Fallon

The SWS, the N8 department of NSAWC, trains SH-60 air crews and pilots in mountain flying. The terrain within the NAS Fallon ranges provides ample opportunities for Seahawk crews to master this demanding and dangerous flying. The training is done during the day as well as at night with night-vision goggles. This aircraft skirts by a ridge in the B-16 portion of the ranges.

ranges for test and evaluation projects, which sometimes are difficult to do elsewhere.

N5 is staffed with aviators in the strike cell who support the five unified commanders in chief with contingency planning. N5 also studies plans and works on tactics development and evaluation. One of N5's main assets is the Top Scene digital 3-D imagery system, which can provide a very detailed look at any potential target or point of interest on the surface of the earth.

Air wings complete their training at NSAWC and leave Fallon roughly six months before a deployment, but the relationship with NSAWC doesn't end there. N5 remains in touch with each air wing's CAG staff, providing updated information on tactics development so that deploying air wings have the benefit of timely data. N5 is constantly involved in formulating integrated tactics. N5 produces the "Standardized Power Projection Tactical Notes," distributed to all aviation commands in the fleet and provides updates to

these notes every six months. Whatever the nature of the enemy, ashore or afloat, N5 has the responsibility of devising tactics to eliminate any enemy threat. N5 personnel advise fleet force command staffs on requirements and program issues and lend support as weapons experts to real-world operations to provide liaison and standardization to other naval and joint training organizations.

N5 oversees and manages the use, maintenance, and operation of equipment in the Fallon Range Training Complex (FRTC), including the Advance Data Display System (ADDS), which provides computerized replication of each completed aircraft training mission for review by student and instructor air crews.

The FRTC encompasses over 10,200 square miles of airspace that lies east of Naval Air Station Fallon. NSAWC has a vast array of threat systems throughout the FRTC that support squadron, air wing, and SFTI training. The heart of this program is the TACTS. This computer-supported real-time digital display

monitors each training event as it occurs on the ranges. Information is transmitted from each aircraft to the TACTS large-screen displays in the headquarters building of NSAWC and is recorded for playback to the air crews for postflight analysis of procedures and tactics. The system allows controllers and air crews a view from several different aspects in three dimensions.

N6: Carrier Airborne Early Warning Weapons School/Electronic Reconnaissance Weapons School

N6 provides graduate-level command, control, communication, computer intelligence (C4I), and battle management training to E-2 and EP-3 air crews. N6 also provides joint interoperability training to naval warfare communities, the U.S. Air Force, and NATO commands. N6 focuses on all aspects of tactical command and control.

The CAEWWS, or Top Dome, became the nucleus of the N6 department. The department has approximately twenty-five officers comprised of air crew from the carrier airborne early warning (VAW), carrier tactical electronic warfare squadron (VAQ), and fleet air reconnaissance squadron (VQ) communities. These officers train and serve as the subject-matter experts for airborne command, control, and communications (C3), signal intelligence, and electronic warfare.

In the information age of technological advances, C4I/C2W, the military implementation of information warfare, is becoming one of two fastest-growing areas of naval aviation. The second is airborne signal intelligence. N6 has an integral role in defining the requirements for future war fighting platforms and systems.

N6 is responsible for three primary functions related to C4I/C2W: subject matter expertise, training and systems architecture, and coordination and management. N6 works closely with N7 training programs for curriculum development, squadron-level advanced readiness programs, and counter-drug interdiction training. Academics include the advanced mission commanders' course, as well as joint interoperability courses

The Fallon Range Training Complex (FRTC) is the linchpin of the NSAWC training program. Without the FRTC, NSAWC would not be able to fulfill its mission. The FRTC encompasses over 130,000 acres and includes five air-to-ground training ranges (Bravo 16, 17, 19, and 20, as well as the electronic warfare range).

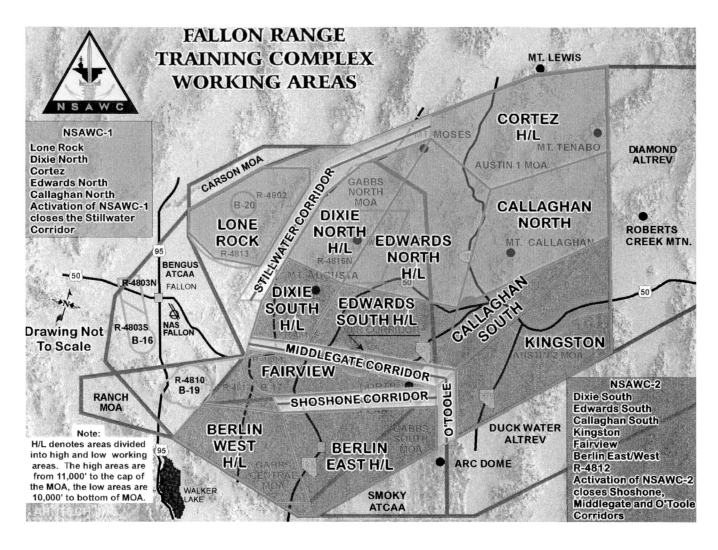

directed at surface ships and staffs, and other U.S. and NATO forces. The department also contributes a number of C4I/C2W-related briefings for the NSAWC senior officer course for carrier task group commanders and other senior officers. Additionally, N6 is deeply involved in predeployment briefings for squadrons and air wings, as well as lessons learned in discussions with C4I/C2W warriors who return to Fallon from theaters as diverse as the Adriatic, the Persian Gulf, and the Caribbean. N6's charter is to provide the expertise and training to ensure that the aviators, surface warriors, and operators in the other services can join together in a theater and fight as one force. The only item missing from N6 is airplanes, as none of the valuable E-2C Hawkeye and EP-3 aircraft have been permanently assigned to NSAWC.

N7: Strike Fighter Weapons School (Top Gun)

N7 instructs in graduate-level strike fighter employment, including tactics, hardware, and threats through the Top Gun SFTI course. N7 conducts the SLATS, which addresses all aspects of air wing, battle group, and joint force tactics, planning, and hardware. N7 also conducts the SOC to address broader battle group commander issues and manages air wing power projection training, including strike warfare, amphibious operations, joint battlefield operations, close air support (CAS), and CSAR.

The N7 department retained the entire Top Gun training syllabus and has assumed the task of training air wings during a three-and-one-half-week air wing deployment. Training is the primary role for N7, requiring twenty-four Top Gun instructors and eleven dedicated air wing training officers to accomplish its mission. A major responsibility of N7 is the ten-week SFTI course, aimed at producing junior officers who ultimately return to a fleet squadron and pass along their cultivated teaching skills with little or no loss in translation.

Concurrent with each SFTI course, NSAWC conducts an adversary training course to qualify adversary air crew for each Navy adversary squadron and NSAWC. These pilots receive individual instruction in threat simulation, effective threat

presentation, and adversary tactics. With each class, NSAWC also trains five or six air intercept controllers (AIC) in effective strike fighter command and control.

Aside from its training programs, many N7 officers also serve as subject-matter experts for the Navy. NSAWC's instructors seek not only to impart knowledge, but a conceptual understanding of their subjects as well. NSAWC's famous (some would say infamous) murder boards remain a source of pride. The instructors are merciless in their critiques, often down to the tone and inflection of voice, with brutal, yet constructive, assessments of flight performance. The quality of the instructors is phenomenal; they are the elite naval aviators, and only the best need apply. This is an essential element in NSAWC staffing. NSAWC also requires a three-year extended commitment from SFTI graduates to maximize the return on their investment in the students.

N8: Seahawk Weapons School

Established in 1998, the Seahawk Weapons School (SWS) is the focal point for Navy helicopter tactics, techniques, and procedures. When NSAWC stood up in 1996, the SWS didn't yet exist, although a plan for it had been created. Since N6 was the Top Dome/CAEWWS group and N7 was Top Gun, it was natural for the SWS to become the N8 department.

The N8 staff plays several important roles, from graduating Seahawk weapons and tactics instructor (SWTI) pilots and air crews to training air wing pilots in search and rescue (SAR) and CSAR operations. N8 also trains helicopter pilots in high-altitude/high-elevation operations during the mountain-flying course, which has been very important in the ongoing war on terror in operations in Afghanistan. N8 operates four SH-60 aircraft decked out in a variety of camouflage schemes.

N9: Operational Risk Management/Safety

N9 manages air- and ground-related safety programs, as well as medical training programs. N9 has department members who have attended the Aviation Safety School in Monterey, California. The school includes thirty-nine days of instruction in several areas, including mishap investigation and tactics, reporting procedures, aero-medical aspects, seventy-two-hour histories, nutrition, stress levels, and aerodynamics. N9 members have also studied material diagnosis, which is the process of analyzing metals and their reaction to stress, torsion, fracture, melting points, etc. This expertise helps N9 determine if certain metal parts failed in flight, whether or not the engines were running, whether or not parts burned in flight, and whether parts failed due to torsion, stress, or corrosion.

CHAPTER 5

BEYOND TOP GUN

Although a primary intention and benefit of creating NSAWC was to enhance the integration of training and expertise, the Top Gun program and the Strike U and Top Dome curriculums have largely stayed consistent and intact. Within Top Gun, there are two primary courses given: the SFTI and the adversary tactics (ADTAC) instructor courses. In the past, Top Gun courses were segmented for Navy pilots and Marine Corps pilots, but they are now combined.

The AGM-62 Walleye is a large weapon, weighing in at over 1,100 pounds. Over 130 Walleyes were fired during the first Gulf War, many by the Hornet's predecessor in the light attack role, the A-7 Corsair. The Hornet brought a true multirole capability to naval aviation without having to make the performance sacrifices that often accompany aircraft required to fill a variety of roles.

An NSAWC Hornet turns hard into a Top Gun student (out of view) during a mission. In fighter pilot lingo, this is known as "the merge," the point at which opposing aircraft pass each other head-on. Closure rates can exceed 800 knots—definitely not for the faint of heart! Fleet aviators benefit greatly from mixing it up with the highly trained NSAWC instructors, who are arguably among the best fighter pilots in the world.

The former Strike U program provided specific air wing training and support as part of the standard workup cycle that each air wing undergoes before deployment at sea. Air wings typically operate in an eighteen- to twenty-four-month cycle that usually ends with a six- to eight-month deployment at sea. Usually, upon returning from sea, the various squadrons and their personnel will return to their respective air stations and get reacquainted with their families after being away for such a long period of time. After a month or so, it is back to business. The squadrons will replace departing officers and sailors and

begin the process of training all personnel to get back into the required state of proficiency. The air crews will undergo specific training and qualifications at the squadron or unit level, including FCLP and detachments to build basic air-to-air and air-to-ground skills before moving to more integrated training with the air wing.

F/A-18 units will undergo strike fighter advanced readiness program (SFARP) training. The SFARP is a training program administered by the Strike Fighter Weapons School Pacific and Strike Weapons and Tactics School Atlantic. Typically, the

This is a frequent view for Top Gun students "checking their six," which means looking back to see if an opponent is sneaking up on them from behind. In reality, Top Gun instructors seek to teach the SFTI students during missions, not just wax them in dogfights. The goal is to learn the difficult and demanding art of air combat, and NSAWC instructors are specifically trained to properly impart their knowledge to the students.

SFARP will be taught at Naval Air Station Fallon, but it could be completed at other facilities. Top Gun, and specifically the N7 department at NSAWC, is the model manager for SFARPs; N7 is responsible for the course curriculum but doesn't actually have its instructors run the SFARP. This is handled by the weapons schools. The SFARP training bridges unit-level training that the squadron completes independently with the more involved strike training at NS AWC, which incorporates an entire air wing and is handled by NSAWC's N5 department. The unit-level work builds up to the more involved deployments

that test the integration of the air wing as a cohesive fighting force as well as with the carrier strike group.

TOP GUN

Major Dirk Cooper, a Top Gun graduate and former Marine Corps F/A-18 Hornet pilot, is now the deputy department head for N7 (Top Gun). He says of the Top Gun class: "We alternated the classes between Navy and Marine Corps students. We ran five courses a year, three Navy courses that were nine weeks long and two Marine courses that were six weeks

Shown here is the famous hangar of the original Top Gun and Fightertown USA, a.k.a. NAS Miramar. The early Top Gun program represents an important part of NSAWC's heritage. The current strike fighter tactics instructor (SFTI) course was developed from the Top Gun program and has been modified to include the air-to-ground mission that is so integral to the Navy strike fighter community.

long. The Navy classes had eight air crews per class, which could be either single- or two-seat crews, depending on which platform was coming through at that time. The Marine Corps classes were typically six crews, four or five single-seat crews or maybe one or two of the two-seat crews. The Navy crews were either Tomcat or Hornet crews, and the marines were strictly Hornets." That changed in early 2004 when the F-14 was retired. Subsequent classes have all been Hornet based and mixed Navy and Marine Corps students.

Major Cooper continues, "The current SFTI course is nine weeks long, and the adversary course is five weeks long. The curriculum for the nine-week course starts with a full week of academics. We focus on employment and threat lectures. We will generally follow this up with a training detachment away from NAS Fallon that focuses on basic fighter maneuvering (BFM). It's a 1V1 det [one-versus-one detachment] to a fleet location, which is typically near the coast so we can fight over the water. The advantage to this is we can fight down to a hard deck of 5,000 feet as opposed to over the mountains here at Fallon, which is 9,000 to 10,000 feet because of the high terrain. This gives us better performance out of the airplanes for more realistic training. We take all the instructors with us so we get

The tranquility of the snow-covered Sierra Nevadas is momentarily interrupted by a pair of NSAWC Hornets during a sweep versus SU-27 mission. The trio of NSAWC Hornets will act like a flight of SU-27 flankers. The flight, call sign Sundown, will be engaged by students that are tasked with destroying the threatening SU-27s, thereby establishing air superiority for the air wing strike package that will hit the target area thirty minutes later.

An important element of the NSAWC syllabus is the section phase that is designed to introduce the basics of multiplane employment with emphasis on formation, radar, and communication. This flight, call sign Shamrock 11 and 12, was photographed during an intercept basics hop.

fleet support at the same time. We usually got to MCAS Miramar, MCAS Beaufort, or NAS Oceana."

N7 conducts four SFTI classes each year with eight air crews with call signs Top Gun One through Eight, two to three of which are two-seat crews. All crews arrive with their own aircraft, although the aircraft may not be from their specific squadron. Major Cooper says, "We will send our NSAWC aircraft, usually eight to ten birds. When we return from the detachment [det], we will go back into another one to two weeks of lectures interspersed with air-to-ground training during the fourth week of the program. We will do several missions, including close air support, armed reconnaissance, and strike coordination and reconnaissance (SCAR). We will then go

down on another det, which is only two days down to NAS China Lake, which is an electronic combat range.

"After this detachment, we will return to NAS Fallon and hit the section phase, which is two aircraft versus many, in which we fly missions such as self-escort strike or sweep missions. The final portion of the phase is the division phase, which is four aircraft versus many opponents. With even more aircraft, the missions get more complicated and realistic."

The training the students receive while going through the SFTI program is best described as intense, challenging, and at times outright grueling. Lectures, complex briefs, physically demanding flights followed by detailed postflight debriefs and analysis make for very long days for both students and

The division phase of the training curriculum is designed to build upon the basics of multiplane employment. A division consists of four aircraft, like these F/A-18s and F-14. Here, call sign Sundown was photographed conducting a sweep mission before the Tomcat's retirement from NSAWC.

instructors. Throw in numerous self-paced exams that follow lectures, and the students face a challenging program unlike any they have experienced before. It's a high-energy, fast-paced environment that can be very stressful. Failing more than one self-paced exam, including a failure of the same exam twice, will land the student in a meeting with the training officer and standardization officer to discuss specific problem areas before the student can continue. The typical students are senior lieutenants who have completed their first tours. They are generally strong people within their squadrons, recommended by their squadron commanders. They will usually have completed one or two boat cruises with between eight hundred and one thousand hours in their aircraft.

The ADTAC syllabus is designed to ensure the adversary student can fly the requisite level to fly as a dedicated Red Air opponent. Since the ability to teach is one of the main parts of the job description for an adversary pilot, the student must be able to master the instructional tools and techniques. As is the case with SFTI students, adversary students must exhibit flight leadership and BFM skills. The adversary tactics syllabus has some similarities to the SFTI syllabus in how the information

is provided, but the adversary student does differ from Top Gun students. The intent of the ADTAC program is to create a fully qualified adversary pilot, not a strike fighter pilot. The curriculum is more heavily weighted toward basic fighter maneuvers as they relate to threat presentations. The ADTAC does not worry about area defense, protecting aircraft carriers, or the subtleties of close air support. The adversary's world is more specific to shooting down other fighter aircraft.

Top Gun covers ACM, as well as a variety of more involved missions. In a 2VX area defense, two students are pitted against an unknown number of adversaries and the students need to protect a particular area. Self-escort strike missions are also part of this and have a section of (two) friendly aircraft (2VX) and a division (four) of friendly aircraft (4VX). Top Gun students are involved in missions that pit a division against as many as twelve adversaries.

The BFM phase of the Top Gun curriculum is designed to teach the student to fly at the requisite level and to introduce the instructional tools required to in turn teach BFM to future students. Through a combination of lectures, simulator work, planning labs, and actual flights, the BFM phase teaches flight

Several NSAWC Hornets take it down low during a self-escort strike (low-altitude) mission that is part of Top Gun's SFTI section phase. The training objectives of the mission are to conduct effective section target area tactics that include target acquisition and precise, accurate weapons delivery. *Photo by Chuck Lloyd*

There are real benefits to fighting against an airplane that's different from yours, especially one as capable of replicating fourth-generation capabilities as the F-16. Fleet aviators in the strike fighter community spend most of their time fighting other Hornets. NSAWC's stable of Vipers presents a different set of challenges to SFTI and air wing jocks.

Marine Corps F/A-18 Hornet pilots now attend joint SFTI classes with Navy air crews, as opposed to the separate programs previously run at NSAWC. This snapshot was taken from the rear seat of a Marine F/A-18B in a tight section formation as the students head out into the ranges during a mission.

leadership. The lecture's syllabus is extensive and covers a multitude of topics. Basic radar theory, as well as every aspect of the friendly aircraft's weapons and systems, is covered in detail and is referred to as "blue hardware." The blue hardware includes the AIM-9, AIM-120 air-to-air missiles, and the APG-73 radar system, as well as expendables like chaff and flares. Threat material from the opposing red side is included, and that includes adversary pilot tactics, aircraft, missile systems, radar, and bandit presentations. The next phase includes tactics and begins with one-versus-one (1V1) basic combat. Air-to-air mission planning, close air support, and intercept control are also part of the tactics section.

In total, the students spend approximately ninety-three hours in academic instruction, along with an additional ten hours of planning labs for mission planning, etc. In terms of flight hours, the students conduct thirty hours of syllabus flights, some of which will be reflown for performance issues as the students need to retake certain missions. On average, each flying event will require six to eight hours of detailed briefing

from the start of the prebrief to the end of the postflight debrief. These are much more thorough and detailed than a typical brief that would accompany a standard fleet hop.

Every phase of the Top Gun program begins with a demonstration flight that is briefed before and after the mission by a Top Gun instructor pilot (IP). The students will then have the opportunity to do their own. Major Cooper believes the division phase is the most challenging aspect of the Top Gun program. He says, "The division phase is probably the most difficult; that's when we start ramping it up. The bandit presentations start getting more dynamic and more complicated. It is a crawl-walk-run mindset. It is full bore and very challenging. We also take them down to the echo ranges (electronic ranges), where they train in surface-to-air countertactics against air-to-air threats simultaneously. Those are very challenging hops."

It is not uncommon for Top Gun students to fail, or bust, a flight. Major Cooper says, "There could be many reasons they do not pass a flight. Generally, when a student busts a flight, it does not mean they necessarily did poorly. It might just be they have one area of difficulty and we think they can do better. We build time into the syllabus for this. We don't want them to move on to the next section unless they feel they have mastered the particular phase. It can be for small performance items, such as flight leadership, decision making in the air, or maintaining situation awareness. This could come down to radar mechanics, for example."

Major Cooper describes a Top Gun student's typical day: "If they have the first go of the day, then their first brief will be 5:15 in the morning. They will have finished their three or so hours of premission planning the evening before. We will start the day with a mass brief with all the bandits and fighters in the same room. We will split up, and the bandits will conduct their brief, which lasts maybe twenty minutes, and the students (fighters) will prebrief for about an hour. It takes about forty-five minutes to an hour for all the students to walk, preflight, and taxi out for the flight.

"The typical mission is roughly one to one-point-two hours long. We don't have to hold back or waste time since the airspace is right next to NAS Fallon. We don't worry too much about the throttles and fuel consumption, and we can do the

The F/A-18 Hornet is the most widely used aircraft at NSAWC. The command operates a mix of single-seat and two-seat versions of the original F/A-18 Hornet, the first variant to enter service. Further improvements to the Hornet have led to the newer C model as well as the fifth-generation Super Hornet.

This camouflaged NSAWC Hornet, armed with the AIM-9 Sidewinder carried on the wingtip rails, sweeps by a ridge at low level using terrain masking to sneak up on some unsuspecting Top Gun students. Put this jet in the hands of one of the qualified NSAWC pilots and you have one tough adversary, as some visiting SFTI students will soon learn.

NSAWC welcomed back the F-16 Viper after its absence of many years. Top Gun operated a fair number of F-16s many years ago, but they were retired due to a high cost of operation and fatigue on the airframes. The benefit of fighting dissimilar aircraft remains high, and NSAWC received a new batch of Vipers.

In addition to the single-seat F-16, NSAWC operates several two-seat aircraft. The primary benefit of the two-seater is to assist in the training of naval flight officers, who are a critical component within the strike fighter community with the proliferation of the F/A-18F Super Hornet.

training at realistic air speeds. The hop actually goes pretty fast, and we are quickly back on deck. From the last 'knock it off' call, ending the training flight, until we are down and back in the debrief, is roughly fifty minutes. The Red Air guys will rehash their brief by themselves, then the Red Air leads will go to the mass debrief with the students. If it is not the first demo brief, the students will be leading the debrief. If it is a division phase mission, it will be done on TACTS. This will take about forty-five minutes. The students then go off to their own separate fighter debrief, which will cover flight communications, decision making, and overall mission objectives attainment. This can take from ninety minutes to almost three hours.

"We are pretty far into our day now. The instructors will then debrief the student on his individual performance, which could add another one to two hours. For the division phase, they will get one flight in per day. They might get a day off after this mission. It all boils down to a long work week with twelve- to fourteen-hour days."

As difficult as the program is on the students, it is not much easier for the instructors. It is not enough to be a good stick or a decent teacher; the instructors need to be experts in specific areas. A new instructor to Top Gun is usually given three to six months to become an expert on a specific area.

The murder board process used at NSAWC is designed to test the subject-matter expertise of each instructor. Major

Within the Strike Fighter Weapons School (N5 department) there are two primary courses: the strike fighter tactics instructor (SFTI) and the adversary tactics instructor (ADTAC) courses. In the past, Top Gun courses were segmented for Navy pilots and Marine Corps pilots but are now combined.

Cooper explains, "It is our process for standardizing our lecture series. Each instructor owns a lecture that will become their subject-matter expert (SME) area. By using the murder board process, we make certain the instructor is a master of the material. Before the actual murder board process, the instructor will give the lecture to everyone on the staff at least once, where everyone gives their input as to the content to make sure that when he gives the final lecture during the murder board, it is correct. If it is up to par, then he is the SME on the topic. We have SMEs on tactics like close air support, for example, as well as the weapons, such as the AMRAAM (AIM-120 advanced medium-range air-to-air missile). The lecture is just what he presents to the students; the actual scope of knowledge on the subject has to be much wider.

"We use the instructor under training, or IUT, process to train instructors. There is a flying aspect to this, in which they work their way up to become a Red Air instructor capable of leading the Red Air presentation during the classes. Initially, the new instructors start out as 1V1 instructors, then move up to section and then division phase instructors. The flying qualifications are developed in conjunction with the SME training throughout the IUT process. The instructors come to Top Gun for a three-year tour, and generally by the final year of their tour, they have hit all their wickets and they are fully qualified.

"Within N7, there are thirty instructors, including enlisted air intercept controllers and twenty-six strike fighter air crews. In any given year, 30 percent of the instructors rotate out of Top Gun and are replaced. The selection process for

new instructors includes an application process that is done on a biannual basis. Message traffic goes out to the fleet for instructors for us, as well as the weapons schools on the East and West Coasts."

NSAWC VIPER: THE RETURN OF THE NAVY F-16

When NSAWC first stood up, the command operated a cadre of F/A-18 Hornets and F-14A Tomcats, along with several SH-60 Seahawks. Since that time, NSAWC has retired its aging Tomcats and replaced them with F-16 Fighting Falcons. The Navy has brought back into its adversary community the superb F-16, also known by its more menacing nickname, the Viper.

VFC-13 Red Air adversary pilot Lieutenant Commander Chad "Cooch" Mingo flies both the F-5E and F-16, and he was an F-14 Tomcat pilot with over eleven hundred hours in the F-14 with VF-102 and three hundred carrier traps. Lieutenant Commander Mingo had extensive combat experience in the Tomcat while deployed with VF-102 during Operation

Initially, Top Gun trained F-4 Phantom air crews when the command first stood up. As the F-4 was phased out and replaced with the F-14, the mighty Tomcat was the primary aircraft at Top Gun, joined by the F/A-18. Soon, the new Super Hornet will be seen over the skies of NAS Fallon during SFTI courses.

An NSAWC two-seat Hornet turns in to engage an SFTI student. The SFTI course covers a wide range of subjects, including the aircraft weapons systems, the full spectrum of threat material of potential opponents, and tactics. A building-block approach is taken, and the missions get more complex as the course goes on.

A pair of NSAWC instructors heads out over the ranges looking for some trouble during a Top Gun class. The Top Gun instructor position is highly sought after. The tour is typically three years in duration and is enjoyable and demanding. Instructors are required to become subject-matter experts in a specific aspect of the program and undergo rigorous training.

An NSAWC F-16 Viper in full burner rotates up and away from NAS Fallon for the start of a training mission. The F-16 has many attributes that make it a great asset to NSAWC. It is dissimilar to the fleet aircraft the Navy flies, namely the F/A-18, and the F-16 offers a near-perfect mix of power and maneuverability.

Enduring Freedom, and he comments on the return of the Navy Viper: "NSAWC received F-16A Block 15 aircraft that were initially intended for Pakistan but were never shipped. The F-16 uses the Pratt & Whitney 220 engines and is just a great adversary aircraft. The heads-up display (HUD) and hands-on throttle and stick (HOTAS) are great attributes of the F-16.

"I think the HUD and HOTAS on the F/A-18 are better than the F-16, but the Viper is still a big step up from the F-5 Tiger. Hornet guys are going to argue a lot with this statement, feeling that the flight control system on the F-16 lacks desirable slow-speed handling qualities. While the Viper has great energy addition, a Hornet should beat the F-16. New F-16s (Block 52 and 60) are very advanced, but our Block 15s have not been upgraded and have no new technology and can't really be described as sophisticated. We cannot accurately simulate the radars in former Soviet Union advanced fighters with any of our planes, but the capabilities of the F-16 radar are similar."

The F-16, which is arguably the finest close-in air combat fighter ever built, is a valuable addition to NSAWC. With the legacy Hornet and newer Super Hornet quickly becoming the only fighter aircraft in Navy air wings, the F-16 offers a uniquely different, highly sophisticated, and capable platform in which to train and test fleet aviators. Nothing beats dissimilar air combat training. The F-16 gives NSAWC this capability.

The F-16N first entered the Navy in the late 1980s, when the much larger adversary program flew the jets at Naval Air Station Miramar with Top Gun, and other dedicated adversary units were stationed at Naval Air Station Oceana and Naval Air Station Key West. The fighter jocks in the adversary units knew they had a great deal and had literally flown their Vipers to the breaking point, stressing the airframes and leading to the F-16s' removal from service. In the 1990s, the Navy drastically reduced its number of adversary units. This, and the increasing operating costs for the adversary units, led to the removal of the F-16N from Navy service. After operating lean for some time, the Navy spun up NSAWC, and the value of its training has reinvigorated the adversary program and led to the Viper taking to the skies in Navy colors.

Lieutenant Commander Mingo says, "The Viper allows NSAWC to make advanced learning points against fleet aviators based on the jets' capabilities. For example, the Viper is extremely fast and accelerates quickly compared to the F-5 Tiger. A fleet pilot that attempts to flee a fight, especially after a mistake, will not be able to run from the Viper. The better radar in the F-16 allows us to try and simulate as best we can the more advanced former Soviet Union fighters. It is far easier to tone down the threat profile and simulated capabilities with

An EA-6B with VAQ-140 cruises over the Dixie North section of the Fallon ranges during an air wing deployment training exercise. The N5 department of NSAWC manages all the air wing training, which is one of NSAWC's major contributions to naval aviation preparedness.

NSAWC operates a significant number of aircraft, including the F-16 and F/A-18 Hornet pictured here. The command has the assets to put up a large force of adversary Red Air fighters and simulate a variety of bandit presentations. For major exercises, NSAWC aircraft are supplemented with fighters from the Saints of VFC-13.

a superior aircraft like the F-16 than to take the less-capable third-generation F-5 and ask it to simulate more advanced aircraft." Against the Hornet, the Viper is especially dangerous in a close-in knife fight where its tremendous thrust and maneuverability come into play.

AIR WING TRAINING: STRIKE U

Air wing training is one of the critical activities covered at NSAWC. It involves resources from every department and division within NSAWC, including N2 intelligence, N3 operations, N5 tactics, plans, and programs, and N7 fleet training.

Approximately four air wings deploy to NAS Fallon each year for four weeks at a time. Like many aspects of NSAWC training, a building-block approach is taken. Academic work is first and typically lasts the first week, followed by academic and flight training broken down as follows:

First week: academics for the air interdiction mission commander (strike leader) course, the air wing SLATS, and the intelligence predeployment course

Second week: mission-level training (MLT)

Third week: integrated training phase (ITP)

Fourth week: advance training phase (ATP)

Training air wing strike leaders in all facets of power projection strike planning, briefing, and execution is the primary objective of the air interdiction mission commander (AIMC) course. Upon completion of the course, the air wing commander designates eight to ten air interdiction mission commanders who will be well versed in understanding fighter responsibilities, the weaponeering process, and the development of target area tactics. The AIMC course also ensures the student can demonstrate large-force airborne leadership and decision making and can adequately debrief and analyze the strike event.

The SLATS program includes over thirty hours of specific lectures within its course catalog and covers such topics as suppression of enemy air defenses (SEAD), integration with all air wing squadron types, CSAR, joint operations, and all aspects of strike mission planning. Surface warfare, Tomahawk, and rules of engagement are also covered.

Mission-level training (MLT) is designed to bridge the gap between unit-level training at the squadron and the fully integrated air wing training done during the third and fourth weeks of the deployment to Fallon. MLT focuses on six mission areas, including CSAR to rescue downed airmen, suppression of enemy defenses, and close air support. MLT takes place over six days and culminates with a dedicated Navy SEAL CSAR event that includes a night extraction and high-threat insertion. The building-block approach is used, as the initial CSAR missions are stand-alone, low- to medium-threat scenarios. The training seeks to be as realistic as possible. A pair of air wing personnel is selected to serve as downed airmen, and they are placed in a field for extraction. The aviators need to be trained to be saved, as well as to have air wing assets learn to properly recover them.

NSAWC's CSAR program is designed to provide the air wing with ground and airborne CSAR training. The program includes SAR mission-level training as stand-alone events, as well as more involved integrated CSAR training and advanced CSAR training. NSAWC will designate two air wing survivors who are actually taught how to be survivors in case they are shot down.

The final two elements of the training for the air wing during the four-week deployment are integrated training (ITP) and advanced training (ATP) phases. ITP emphasizes air wing integration in both strike planning and execution. The number of sorties for this phase may total as many as thirty-five over the six daytime and five nighttime scenarios.

The advanced training phase (ATP) simulates an air warfare battlefield preparation campaign. The scenario has the carrier strike group leave port and conduct an air warfare campaign in response to an immediate national emergency. The overall objective is to suppress the enemy country's advancement and then to begin preparing the battlefield for an eventual Allied landing. The air wing assets need to deal with a simulated enemy air defense environment. The ATP is designed to simulate air wing support of a marine air ground task force (MAGTF) operating under a combined joint task force structure.

CHAPTER 6

ELECTRONIC WARRIORS AND THE SEAHAWK WEAPONS SCHOOL

The success of the Top Gun program permeated other communities that sought to develop successful, advanced training programs for their own aviators. While less glamorous, the E-2C Hawkeye and SH-60 Seahawk communities provide increasingly important support to carrier aviation operations.

Information management and warfare is one of the fastest-growing aspects in modern combat and is an important aspect within NSAWC's training. The N6 department's mission covers all aspects of command and control, and provides advanced tactical training for VAW and VQ air crews.

The Hawkeye is the largest aircraft in the air wing, and its massive rotodome is evident in this photo. The other unique feature of the design was the tail structure. The strange airflow over and behind the new rotodome necessitated the use of a multiple-surface tail unit. The aircraft has four tail fins, of which three contain actual double-hinged rudders, with one, the inside port-side rudder, being a fixed single-piece unit.

The E-2C uses two Allison T56-A-427 engines, replacing the T56-425. They each use a Hamilton Sundstrand standard four-blade, reverse-pitch, constant-speed propeller. The engines provide over 5,000 horsepower each, roughly 600 more horsepower than the previous engine. The engines also have a unique sound. This humming sound is what gives the Hawkeye its nickname, "the Hummer."

Rotary-wing operations have come to the forefront in recent combat operations, particularly in support of the war on terror. With the demise of the S-3 Viking, the SH-60 Seahawk helicopter community has taken on expanding roles, including antisubmarine warfare. NSAWC has evolved since its inception to handle the changing and expanding requirements of the electronic warfare and rotary-wing communities of the N6 and N8 departments, respectively.

N6: CAEWWS

The N6 department includes the Carrier Airborne Early Warning Weapons School (CAEWWS). Founded in 1988, and originally located at Naval Air Station Miramar, the CAEWWS was chartered with providing E-2C Hawkeye air crews with a focused academic regimen in an effort to broaden their knowledge of current tactics, techniques, and procedures used by the various communities throughout naval aviation.

The E-2C Hawkeye is responsible for airborne command and control in nearly every facet of naval surface, subsurface, amphibious, and air warfare. The ability of U.S. naval forces to integrate successfully into a joint/combined operations area frequently hinges on the ability of Hawkeye crews to adapt to operational situations that can literally change minute by

During typical flight deck operations, the Hawkeye is the first aircraft to launch and the last to recover. Normally, aircraft are launched and recovered in cycles. With the shorter range and loiter time of most jet-powered aircraft, the E-2C can leave the deck early, take up its station, and then return once all other aircraft have already landed.

The Hawkeye is fully capable of fulfilling several secondary missions: surface surveillance, search and rescue, air traffic control, and strike control for multiship strike packages. For a short time, the Navy loaned several Hawkeyes to the U.S. Coast Guard for drug interdiction requirements. Small, low-flying aircraft, in addition to small boats, can be tracked by the Hawkeye's powerful radar systems.

minute and to facilitate the application of the full force of Navy carrier and expeditionary strike groups. This unique role makes the advanced training of Hawkeye crews a crucial element in combat readiness for the entire joint force. CAEWWS provides that training and serves as a central bastion of knowledge and leadership to assist deployed forces in responding to new challenges in air combat.

In the years since its founding, the principal role of CAEWWS has changed very little. It is designed to develop the most highly trained, flexible, and aggressive leaders of air combat in the world. The training program, however, continues to adapt to the dynamic nature of air combat. To foster a more effective environment for training, CAEWWS relocated to Naval Air Station Fallon, Nevada, in 1996. Naval Air Station Fallon provides the ideal setting for students and instructors to focus on refining their war-fighting skills while working alongside tactical experts from the strike fighter, electronic reconnaissance, and rotary-wing communities.

Like the Top Gun students, candidates are nominated for CAEWWS attendance by their commanding officers based on demonstrated proficiency and knowledge in both the employment of the platform and its integration into naval and joint warfare environments. These candidates arrive at Fallon and complete the Hawkeye AMCC, including two weeks of demanding ten-hour academic days at NSAWC, followed by three weeks of intense simulator instruction at the Pacific Fleet E-2C Hawkeye simulator complex onboard Naval Base Ventura County in Point Mugu, California. During the simulator phase, students are subjected to detailed mission planning exercises, followed by complex simulator scenarios where their success or failure as a crew hinges upon their ability to brief, plan, and execute a tactical mission at an extremely high level of performance.

The elite cadre of instructors at CAEWWS is individually selected by the Hawkeye community leadership from the nine active-duty squadrons home ported in Norfolk, Virginia; Point

The Navy decided in the late 1950s to seek a replacement for the aging Grumman E-1B Tracer in the airborne early warning role. The winner for the program was Grumman, with its G-123 entry selected on March 5, 1957. In the fall of 1960, the first Hawkeye prototype, initially designated W2F-1, made its maiden flight. The aircraft was redesignated as the E-2 and was complete aerodynamically— but not from an avionics standpoint.

The E-2C variant of the aircraft made its initial flight in January 1971 with the APS-120 family of radar systems and a new airborne early warning antenna system. Orders for the new aircraft totaled 144 by 1988, in addition to the first overseas contracts for the aircraft. Ongoing enhancements provided the same end result, an increase in the quality of the radar system and the range with which it could detect targets. The radar antenna, main system computers, and communications systems also increased in capability with the growth in their associated technologies, but not at the same frequency.

Mugu, California; and Atsugi, Japan. These instructors are subjected to a four-month training program to refine their tactical expertise and instructional skills prior to qualifying as a Hawkeye weapons and tactics instructor (WTI). WTIs are also trained to serve in select billets at the East and West Coast weapons training units, the Hawkeye fleet replacement squadron, and as liaison officers in air force units at Nellis and Tinker Air Force Bases.

The role of the staff at CAEWWS is not limited to the production of highly trained E-2C mission commanders. The WTIs at CAEWWS serve the Hawkeye community in many other important capacities. Most notably, these WTIs

are continually sought out by civilian contractors to provide input into future Hawkeye systems and versions of the aircraft. The ability to directly affect the research and design of the Hawkeye has enabled the staff at CAEWWS to focus the effort of those responsible for providing the U.S. Navy with the best possible product, and to ensure that the product received gives Hawkeye air crews the tools they need to succeed in combat.

The EP-3 airborne reconnaissance integrated electronics suite II (ARIES II) aircraft is a shore-based, long-range, fixed-wing aircraft that provides near-real-time electronic reconnaissance to tactical commanders through detection and identification of tactically significant electronic signals.

The aircraft are operated by Fleet Air Reconnaissance Squadrons One and Two, co-located at Naval Air Station Whidbey Island, Washington. The EP-3 is operated by a multidisciplinary air crew of twenty-four highly skilled officers and enlisted personnel, providing full mission capability for the reconnaissance platform.

In an effort to better integrate EP-3 and ES-3 crews into standardized CVW training and to improve VQ/CVW interoperability, NSAWC stood up the VQ tactical training cell (TTC) in 1998. When the carrier air wing's indigenous reconnaissance capability was lost due to the decommissioning of the ES-3s in 2000, it became increasingly important to integrate the EP-3 within the air wing.

In September 2000, the VQ TTC was renamed the Electronic Reconnaissance Weapons School (ERWS) and realigned in function and focus with the CAEWWS. ERWS is the Navy's airborne signals intelligence (SIGINT) center of excellence and acts as a clearinghouse for tactics, techniques, and procedures (TTP) and cross-community interaction for the VQ (electronic warfare) community. Additionally, ERWS provides air combat training continuum (ACTC) level three, VQ advanced readiness program (ARP) training, ACTC level four, joint advanced tactical SIGINT training program (JATSTP), ACTC level five, and VQ weapons tactics instructor (WTI) course.

VQ ARP is a two-week course that consists of academics and fly events. During VQ ARP, students participate in CVW strike planning and fly events during the ITP and ATP of Air Wing Fallon. The students employ an actual EP-3 or the mission avionics system trainer (MAST) virtual EP-3 during fly events to refine EP-3/CVW integration.

JATSTP is a three-week course of integrated academic and practical programs designed to produce VQ ACTC level-four positional instructors. Simulator and out-of-area-range training events provide EP-3 air crews with realistic, hands-on training on effective tactical SIGINT platform employment.

The VQ WTI course is designed to provide graduate ACTC level-five training, standardized unit-level training, crew certification training, and increased readiness and warfighting capability. Particular emphasis is placed on training students to become proficient tactics instructors. This intensive eight-week course is offered every ten to twelve months for EP-3 officers and enlisted air crews with orders to ERWS or wing training unit (WTU).

The EP-3 community leadership individually selects the instructors at ERWS. These instructors are subjected to a two-month training program to refine tactical expertise and instructional skills prior to qualifying as an ERWS WTI. WTIs are also trained to serve in select billets at the WTU, located in Whidbey Island, Washington.

The massive 24-foot rotating rotodome is the most prominent feature of the E-2C Hawkeye. The dome sits on a series of metal spars that can be raised and lowered when the aircraft is brought below deck into the carrier hangar deck for storage or maintenance.

A VAW-117 Hawkeye 2000 decked out in CAG bird colors cruises over the Sierra Nevada mountain range. Upgrades to the primary mission computer and the cooperative engagement capability are major aspects of the Hawkeye 2000 (H2K). This will further enhance the Hawkeye's ability to communicate with other fleet assets, such as *Aegis*-class cruisers.

In September 2000, the VQ tactical training cell at NSAWC was renamed the Electronic Reconnaissance Weapons School (ERWS) and realigned in function and focus with Carrier Airborne Early Warning Weapons School (CAEWWS), the N6 department. In 2000, the ES-3 was retired and the carrier air wings no longer had a carrier-based reconnaissance capability.

In addition to providing highly trained operators to the fleet, the ERWS staff also provides tremendous input into the development of training courseware and new systems integration to the fleet.

E-2C HAWKEYE: EYES OF THE FLEET

The Northrop Grumman E-2C Hawkeye is the most advanced surveillance and airborne early-warning aircraft operating from U.S. Navy carriers. Its primary mission is airborne early warning (AEW), providing over-the-horizon threat detection for the carrier battle fleet. The E-2C Hawkeye detects, identifies, and prioritizes airborne threats from sea level to over 50,000 feet through the use of its advanced radar and avionics systems. The E-2C operates at high altitudes, usually over 25,000 feet, monitoring over three million cubic miles of airspace. The aircraft can detect and track at ranges of over 200 miles, and it stores memory tracks on over 2,000 targets. The new engines on the E-2C allow the Hawkeye to loiter at altitude, hundreds of miles from the carrier, for up to six hours.

The Hawkeye is able to fulfill various mission profiles through a combination of advanced avionics and radar systems and a five-person flight crew. The crew consists of a pilot and

The ES-3A Shadow was a dedicated electronic reconnaissance version of the S-3 Viking antisubmarine warfare aircraft. Both aircraft have been retired from active service. The ES-3 used the same ARIES II avionics suite as the EP-3 Orion, which is now the primary aircraft within the Electronic Reconnaissance Weapons School at NSAWC.

co-pilot seated up front in the cockpit, a combat information center officer, an air control officer, and a radar operator seated in the fuselage.

The Hawkeye has a unique appearance similar to its predecessor, the E-1B, thanks to its large radar system carried over the middle of the airframe. The twenty-four-foot-diameter Randtron APN-171 rotodome revolves at six revolutions per minute, and the antenna array group contained within the dome is linked to the various avionics systems onboard the aircraft. The rotodome sits on top of a pylon with a retractable upper section that can be lowered hydraulically to stow the aircraft on the carrier.

There are several minor differences in the airframe between variants, including the enlarged over-fuselage radiator vent that dissipates heat generated from the radar systems. The E-2C Group II variant had enhancements across almost every system, particularly the radar, identification of friend or foe (IFF), and display and communications subsystems. At the heart of the Group II's avionics is the Grumman/General Electric APS-145 radar system. This latest system provides greater levels of threat detection and processing capabilities, along with an enhanced ability to detect targets at extreme ranges.

The latest version of the E-2C Hawkeye, the Hawkeye 2000, fitted with an eight-bladed composite propeller. The NP2000 propeller system is an electronically controlled, all-composite propeller system being retrofitted to all new Hawkeyes. The system reduces maintenance, reduces noise and vibration, and enhances performance.

The N8 department focuses on several areas of emphasis in its training of Seahawk weapons and tactics instructors (SWTIs), including advanced aircraft handling, defensive maneuvering, aerial gunnery, surface-to-air counter tactics, close air support, and naval surface fire support.

An SH-60 Seahawk with HS-15 maintains patrol as the plane guard during carrier air operations. The Seahawk operates in several variants and from both large-deck aircraft carriers as well as smaller surface ships. The SH-60B first entered service in 1979 and replaced the SH-2, which operated aboard cruisers, destroyers, and frigates.

Advancements in communications, both voice and digital, allow for secure bidirectional communications between the E-2C and either fighter escorts or ground-based control stations. In a high-threat environment, the carrier battle group relies on the E-2C to extend its eyes and ears. The E-2C can transmit critical information to the carrier's combat information center (CIC) through this secure data link facility. With fighter aircraft operating in front of the E-2Cs, threat data can be transmitted from the Super Hornet to the E-2C. In addition, the vectoring intercept data provided by the Hawkeye can go to the fighters.

Enhancements to the mission computer with the E-2C Hawkeye 2000 variant in 1998 extended the aircraft's role as the airborne communications hub for the carrier strike group. The increased computing power through a cooperative engagement capability upgrade affords the Hawkeye 2000 the ability to bring together information from other sources, such as satellites and surface ships, and make this available throughout the network. The Hawkeye will provide a more complete picture of the battle space and enhance overall situational awareness through enhanced detection, identification, processing, and communications capabilities.

The most recent variant, the E-2D Advanced Hawkeye (AHE), is scheduled to be introduced to the fleet in 2011. The E-2D will include enhanced battle space target detection and situational awareness. An important component of the Advance Hawkeye is the support of theater air and missile defense (TAMD) operations. The AHE is intended to meet airborne early warning surveillance, battle management, and TAMD needs as the Navy develops its Sea Power 21 vision. Significant advancements in the radar and antenna systems will provide even greater threat-detection capabilities. The Hawkeye will continue to be the critical airborne component in fusing all the data that comes from its sensors and those of other assets, making this information available throughout the network.

One of the more obvious new features of the latest Hawkeye is the addition of the Hamilton Sundstrand NP2000 composite eight-bladed propellers. The new propellers will improve performance for the aircraft and decrease noise. Less obvious features of the newer Hawkeyes will be more modern glass cockpits, allowing the pilot or co-pilot to work more closely with the systems operators in the back of the E-2.

N8: THE SEAHAWK WEAPONS SCHOOL

Simply stated in its mission statement, the NSAWC N8 department is in place to "train Seahawk pilots and air crew in the skills and techniques required for advanced performance as weapons and tactics instructors (WTI)." Like the other WTI

An NSAWC SH-60 painted like a former Soviet Union Hind gunship rests on the Fallon flight line. The Seahawk and its missions are vital to naval aviation and are therefore a major part of NSAWC and the N8 department. N8 operates four Seahawks painted in a variety of schemes.

programs, the Seahawk Weapons School (SWS), also known as the N8 department, has two primary goals. The first goal is to provide exposure and thereby develop subject-matter expertise in the deployment of the SH-60's varied missions, which include CAS, maritime air control, defensive maneuvering, antisubmarine warfare, surface-to-air countertactics, and air-craft systems such as the Hellfire missile and FLIR. The second main goal is to develop instructional techniques, briefing skills, and flight discipline. The SWS and the ranges at Fallon also allow for training of SH-60 air crews in the rigors of mountain flying, both daytime and at night.

"The new expanding mission sets of the SH-60 is largely what brought about the creation of the SWS," says Deputy Department Head Lieutenant Commander Shane "Rowdy" Yates. "Our most important job, like the other programs at

One of the NSAWC Seahawks is painted in a colorful desert camouflage that is all the more striking against the backdrop of Walker Lake and the Wassuk mountain range. The high-altitude performance course teaches Seahawk students to fly in mountains, and the N8 department has a dedicated mountain-flying program manager.

NSAWC's Seahawk Weapons School (SWS) has as part of its curriculum a dedicated overwater training segment. The students will travel from NAS Fallon to fleet areas for five days of simulator work and six days of dedicated overwater flights. Two of these are dedicated to antisubmarine warfare, two are for visitor board search and seizure, and two for maritime air support.

NSAWC, is to train the trainer. The guys we get coming into the program typically are coming off their first tour and know the aircraft systems well. Our job is to make them excellent trainers so when they are instructors they can teach effectively. This can be challenging for the NSAWC instructors in that we have great familiarity with the systems and the aircraft and have to be able to impart this knowledge effectively. We focus on teaching the students the proper techniques to get the teaching points across. One of the other challenging aspects of

our job here is to know when a student is properly picking up the information we are teaching."

To date, the SWS has graduated over four hundred Seahawk weapons and tactics instructors. Typically, the program conducts two classes per year, each with thirty-two students; sixteen are pilots, sixteen are air crew. The SWS curriculum has over one hundred and fifty hours of classroom work, as well as thirteen flight and simulator events. Most of the training is done at Fallon; however, the students will deploy to Naval Air Station

Navy Seahawk pilots can be called on to work with SEAL special forces teams. Part of this includes very dangerous day and night flying in rugged terrain. SEALs may call for Seahawk crews to deliver and retrieve them from very specific and inaccessible locations. As part of the Seahawk weapons and tactics instructor course, NSAWC trains Seahawk pilots and air crews to land on one wheel on a mountain to support SEAL teams.

Jacksonville at the Atlantic Undersea Test and Evaluation Center to conduct the undersea warfare portion of their training.

Commander Kevin Kenney is the current department head for the N8 department and is a twenty-year veteran of the Navy. He has 5,200 hours in many different aircraft models, both fixed-wing and helicopters, and served as a test pilot as well. Kenney describes the creation of the Seahawk Weapons School: "Top Gun was so successful that all the other communities said, 'We would like to have SFTI-like people in our respective communities.' The first to copy were the E-2 guys. The SWTI guys in my program have been around for seven years or so. We train both pilots and air crews to be Seahawk weapons and tactics instructors. The students have to be nominated by their chain of command to come here. We have helicopter Wing Weapons School, which takes a look at the list and ranks them as to who will eventually come to the course. We have the first right of refusal, although we have never exercised that.

"We would like to run the course four times per year with a smaller class size of sixteen students per class. Because we need fleet airplanes to support the class, and there are so few of specific types like the HH-60 Combat SAR bird, and they are in such high demand, asking for them four times per year is difficult. This year, we went to two classes per year with twice the number of students. We have thirty-two students, plus six attendees just going through the course academics. The current course runs for nine and a half weeks."

The first six and a half weeks of the class, including classroom work, are conducted at Fallon. The water portion of the curriculum is taught during the last three weeks, at Naval Air Station Jacksonville or another such fleet area. Kenney explains, "We are a bit different from the Top Gun guys in that they are fairly pure in what they do. They come here [NSAWC] and learn how to do air-to-air and air-to-ground missions exclusively. The Seahawk weapons and tactics instructors have nine different mission areas they need to address. This includes special operations support, antisubmarine warfare, surface warfare, and others. We have to cover a lot more ground. We teach according to what we term 'areas of

The Navy's Seahawk is a mission-specific "navalized" version of the basic H-60, first developed by the U.S. Army. The army first fielded the UH-60 Black Hawk in 1979. The aircraft has found a home with every branch of the U.S. military. This aircraft is attached to the U.S. Air Force search-and-rescue unit based in New York.

emphasis,' such as aerial gunnery, advanced aircraft handling, defensive maneuvering, close air support, and combat search and rescue. We are the jack-of-all-trades."

The SWS takes a building-block approach to the course and uses simulators at other facilities, combined with classroom work and actual flying throughout the course. The simulators at Naval Air Station Jacksonville help to base line everyone. All the students are supposed to be good at what they do when they arrive at NSAWC. The Seahawk Weapons School verifies their competence through the use of simulators.

The N8 department and Seahawk Weapons School is able to provide WTIs with the opportunity to become proficient in areas that they would not typically be exposed to, many of which are of increasing importance. For example, students are often not taught CAS until their training at SWS. "The Navy SH-60 helicopter community traditionally did not get a lot of exposure to this [CAS], but we teach it here and it is one of the areas the students find most challenging. We do it not because we expect to provide close air support in the traditional sense but because it leads to maritime

air superiority (MAS), which we do often provide," Kenney says. "This involves protecting surface assets from threats such as terrorist attacks launched from small craft. We begin with CAS and master this first, then go over water to practice MAS, and they are involved missions."

THE SH-60 SEAHAWK

There are few aircraft in the American military inventory that fill as many different roles as the Sikorsky-built H-60-series helicopter. The H-60, in its different variants, is operated by every branch of the U.S. military. With specific mission-related modifications, the H-60 can provide SAR and combat SAR for the Navy, as well as for antisubmarine and Navy SEAL special operations missions. The U.S. Air Force uses the H-60 for CSAR and special forces operations. The U.S. Army employs the UH-60 for troop transport, medevac, and utility missions. The helicopter community lacks the glamour of the tactical jets, but the missions fulfilled by the SH-60 are as critical to naval aviation as any aircraft. This is evident in the emphasis placed by NSAWC on SH-60 operations.

The Seahawk Weapons School (SWS) graduated its first class in September 1998 with twelve students and a limited curriculum focused on combat search and rescue and antisubmarine warfare. Since then, the SWS has graduated over four hundred Seahawk weapons and tactics instructors (WTIs) and has expanded the curriculum to cover all Seahawk missions.

H-60 Variants

VARIANT NAME	OPERATOR	MISSION
HH-60 Seahawk	U.S. Navy	SAR, antisubmarine
SH-60 Seahawk	U.S. Navy	SAR, antisubmarine
HH-60J Jay Hawk	U.S. Coast Guard	SAR
MH-60G/K Pave Hawk	U.S. Air Force	CSAR, special operations
S/70/UH-60L Fire Hawk	Civilian	Firefighting
UH-60 Black Hawk	U.S. Army	Utility/troop transport
UH-60Q Black Hawk	U.S. Army	Medevac
VH-60N Marine One	U.S. Marine Corps	Vice Presidential transport

The aircraft was initially developed and put in service with the U.S. Army under the UH-60 Blackhawk designation. The Navy selected the Sikorsky S-70 (SH-60B designation) as the air vehicle for its Light Airborne Multipurpose System Mk.III (LAMPS III). This system provides Navy surface combatants, such as frigates and destroyers, with an airborne antisubmarine capability. The Seahawk is capable of carrying Mk.46 and/or 50 torpedoes. The SH-60B first entered service with the Navy in 1983, replacing the SH-2.

The SH-60B retained many of the UH-60's characteristics, and there was little change to the basic airframe. The major changes were a result of the specific needs of the Navy and the aircraft's requirements in filling antisubmarine missions. An in-flight refueling system was added, allowing the SH-60B to refuel from a ship while in a hover. The SH-60B aircraft includes folding blades and tail rotor, increased fuel load, and modifications to the landing gear. Changes to the avionics include the use of the chin-mounted APS-124 search radar that is used for surveillance. The Seahawk is operated by a crew of three: pilot, co-pilot, and crew chief. For antisubmarine missions, an air tactical officer and sensor operator are used as well. Further variants of the Seahawk have entered service with the Navy, including the SH-60F with additional weapons stations and support for special operations. The multirole capabilities of the Seahawk have led to the latest variant, the MH-60R/S, which has improvements to the LAMPS, an AGM-114 Hellfire capability, and other improvements to the avionics system.

The EP-3E ARIES II (Airborne Reconnaissance Integrated Electronic System II) is the Navy's only land-based signals intelligence (SIGINT) reconnaissance aircraft. The EP-3 is a specialized variant of the Lockheed P-3 ORION antisubmarine warfare aircraft. The EP-3 uses sensitive receivers and antennas to fill the (SIGINT) gathering role. There are eleven aircraft within two fleet air reconnaissance squadrons. *Photo courtesy of U.S. Navy/NSAWC*

CHAPTER 7

RED AIR

A ir combat proficiency is an acquired skill and one that is highly perishable. The ability to suc-ceed in the demanding world of modern aerial combat is in direct proportion to the effort expended in preparing for it. It's basically a use-it-or-lose-it situation. NSAWC is the center of all tactics training and is assisted in its training role by a cadre of pilots in two naval reserve squadrons. The "Fighting Omars" of Fighter Squadron Composite VFC-12 and the "Fighting Saints" of VFC-13 are dedicated training units that are key players in sharpening the tip of the spear of naval aviation.

Both squadrons fulfill a two-part mission. The first, to provide air combat training for fleet fighter squadrons, includes the advanced training for air wing SFARP and supporting NSAWC with air wing and SFTI training. The second mission is basic air combat training for fleet replacement squadrons (FRS) that train new air crews in the F/A-18 Hornet.

The F-16 Fighting Falcon was added to the NSAWC fleet; the airframes were originally destined for the Pakistani Air Force but were embargoed for political reasons. They are stripped-down Block 15 models compared to frontline U.S. Air Force F-16s and spent a fair amount of time in storage at Davis-Monthan Air Force Base before being sent to NSAWC.

Red Air pilots, like those with reserve unit VFC-13, are among the most skilled practitioners of air combat maneuvering (ACM). Unlike fleet aviators, who need to practice and master numerous types of missions, the adversary pilots with VFC-13 are highly skilled in the air-to-air arena and are very difficult to beat.

VFC-12 and VFC-13 are part of Carrier Air Wing Reserve 20 under the Naval Reserve Forces Command, based in New Orleans, Louisiana. Both units were established on September 1, 1973, as composite squadrons and were redesignated VFCs on April 22, 1988. They both flew the A-4 Skyhawk, the agile single-engine jet that was a staple within the Navy's adversary program for many years.

Based at Naval Air Station Oceana, Virginia, the Omars fly ten F/A-18As and a pair of two-seat F/A-18B Hornets. In 1994, the Omars traded in their Skyhawks for the upgraded F/A-18 Hornet, a more capable threat replicator of the MiG-28 and SU-27 fighters being built by the former Soviet Union.

A rigorous in-house training program is maintained by both VFC units in order to teach their pilots to be experts in adversary tactics simulation and training. The focus of the units is to teach student and fleet aviators and to prepare them for real combat operations. A combination of academic syllabus and proficiency check flights builds the adversary pilots' body of knowledge. The building-block approach allows them to control increasingly more complex scenarios or threat presentations. It

can take up to a year for a VFC pilot to go from a level one to level four Red Air qualification.

A level one adversary is a bandit wingman playing the role of a junior threat pilot. An adversary level two pilot represents a threat country that is able to lead two airplanes into battle. A level three is an adversary division leader of a four-plane group of Red Air fighters. The level four bandit is an overall bandit lead for large force exercises. More than stick and rudder skills are needed to be an effective Red Air pilot. For example, a single SFARP flight will require a six- to eight-hour evolution with the briefing, flight, and postmission analysis. It's an intense, graduate-level training program in which the Red Air pilots pick apart the smallest details in an effort to make the pilots better.

The Fighting Saints trace their beginnings back to 1973, when they were established at Naval Air Station New Orleans. They were first designated VC-13 and flew the F-8 Crusader. The squadron initially consisted of 17 officers and 127 enlisted personnel. The unit would transition to the A-4L Skyhawk in the spring of 1974, and the increase in their workload dictated

A VFC-13 F-5 sporting a North Korean Air Force paint scheme crosses over NAS Fallon after a mission. The unit is swapping out its inventory of aging F-5E Tigers for newer F-5 aircraft previously flown by the Swiss Air Force. It is more economical to buy the Swiss jets, which have far fewer flight hours.

A VFC-13 F-5 banks against the stunning backdrop of the mountains rimming picturesque Lake Tahoe, roughly fifty miles west of NAS Fallon. The two primary dedicated adversary tactics training units in the Navy are both full-time reserve squadrons and include VFC-13 located at NAS Fallon and VFC-12 based at NAS Oceana.

a move to Naval Air Station Miramar, California. The squadron has operated a number of different variants of the Skyhawk, including the two-seat TA-4J model. In 1983, the unit returned to single-seat aircraft with the A-4E. The squadron received its current VFC-13 designation on April 22, 1988, in recognition of its evolving mission. That same year, the Fighting Saints received the A-4F Super Fox, a more powerful and capable variant. The Saints upgraded to the Hornet from the Skyhawk in 1993, but subsequent force structure alignments forced the unit to give back the Hornet. In exchange, VFC-13 received the F-5 Tiger II in 1996.

VFC-13 is the largest operator of the F-5 Tiger in the U.S. armed forces with twenty-three aircraft of which ten are single-seat F-5Es, three are two-seat F-5Fs, and seven are F-5N aircraft. The N variant aircraft were previously operated by the Swiss Air Force.

Eventually, all single-seat E models will be replaced by the N variant. Lieutenant Commander Chad Mingo, VFC-13 pilot, notes, "The Swiss aircraft have lower hours and are still relatively inexpensive to operate, which has always been a key advantage of the F-5. The N model is a little heavier than the E and has several improvements, including RWR gear [radar warning receiver] and enhanced radars, as well as antiskid systems, which provide enhanced handling on wet runways. The

The F-16 Fighting Falcon offers superb unrestricted visibility from its single-piece teardrop canopy, a crucial attribute for modern fighters. The F-16 is extremely maneuverable, and the pilot sits slightly reclined in the ejection seat in order to provide additional tolerance to the high-g forces experienced in dogfights.

Shown here is an NSAWC Hornet driver in the break under some bad weather. This is the most common recovery pattern, as the Hornet pilot flies 1,500 feet above the main runways 31L and 31R. The Hornet will roll out 180 degrees to the downwind heading, then turn 90 degrees to line up on runway 31L.

Red Air pilots with VFC-13 are some of the toughest adversaries in the air and can be especially difficult to fight in their small F-5 Tigers. Even though the F-5 is a simple, third-generation fighter, it can make a respectable account for itself in a dogfight. Its greatest attribute is its small size, which makes it tough for an opponent to spot.

F-5N is distinguishable with its squashed, platypus nose and extended leading-edge extensions, which provide enhanced maneuverability. The F-5 is a solid simulator of third-generation threats and has good speed, although it takes a while to get up to it. The IHQ [improved handling quality] upgrade has enhanced the jet's ability."

The aircraft on the VFC-13 flight line are painted in a wide variety of striking camouflage schemes to match the different potential adversaries they must simulate. When coupled with some of the most experienced and finest fighter pilots anywhere, the Fighting Saints pose a very credible adversary force. Lieutenant Commander Mingo says, "While VFC-13 is not part of NSAWC officially, we do support each other mutually and work together quite a bit, which is how I was able to get checked out to fly the F-16 as well as the F-5. During the SFARP, NSAWC assists VFC-13 in providing fourth-generation threat aircraft with their Hornets and Falcons. During air wing training, we reciprocate by providing third-generation threat aircraft with our F-5s. With specific Top Gun classes, we also support NSAWC with dedicated Red Air adversary support."

Lieutenant Commander Mingo details the training required of Red Air pilots: "Both NSAWC and VFC-13 Red Air pilots are highly trained, experienced fighter pilots when they arrive at NAS Fallon. They all go through a rigorous

This unique jet-black paint scheme contrasts sharply against the high desert scrub around Naval Air Station Fallon. This Tiger is carrying an inert AIM-9 Sidewinder on its starboard wingtip rail and the important air combat maneuvering instrumentation (ACMI) pod on its port wingtip pod. The ACMI pod provides positional data back to the TACTS range for postmission debriefs.

training program to become dedicated Red Air pilots. The pilots are fleet division leads with no Red Air experience, however. The first syllabus is simply to get them checked out in the new aircraft, be that the F-16 or, as is the case with VFC-13 pilots, the F-5. Level one training includes eleven hops, which culminate in the pilot being a Red Air wingman. Level two has the pilot undergoing another twenty hops, resulting in Red Air element lead status. These pilots usually fight against fleet readiness squadron (FRS) students typically new to the Hornet. Level three Red Air pilots go through an additional five hops and can then act as an SFARP lead. Level four is the highest classification, and the pilot is designated an SFARP air wing lead."

"We represent third-generation aircraft of the former Soviet Union. One of the best things about the F-5 is that it is very hard to see," adds Lieutenant Michael "Physco" Picciano,

a former F-14 pilot with 1,300 hours in Navy fighters. "This is one of the biggest learning objectives for the missions we fly—to show just how easily we can obtain unobserved entry onto the fighters. It is interesting for the student pilots from the FRS, as well as the fleet pilots, because they often spend their time fighting against similar aircraft, and their eyes almost get trained to look for the same-size opponent. They look for the same color and size aircraft. When you throw an F-5 into the mix, it makes it more difficult for them. We are so much smaller than what they are used to; we look different, and our paint schemes blend in, especially against the desert or against the overcast. That becomes one of the biggest learning objectives—they need to be able to see all of us at the merge and not allow us unobserved entry. This is a unique thing we can do with the F-5. Another interesting thing with the F-5 is that we are a simple, less advanced aircraft, and when you kill a

For most of its operational career, the F-5E Tiger II fighter was the aircraft of choice for the Fighting Saints of VFC-13. The constant high-g maneuvers of mock dogfights stress the airframes of all adversary aircraft. The decision was made to replace the F-5E with newer airframes previously flown by the Swiss Air Force.

In addition to the nine F-16 single-seat fighters, NSAWC flies four two-seat variants as well. This bird was photographed returning to NAS Fallon after an SFTI mission and is carrying a single underbelly fuel tank. The F-16 has superb range for a modern fighter; typically, the second ejection seat comes at the expense of almost one thousand pounds of fuel.

The F/A-18 Hornet is a superbly maneuverable adversary threat aircraft and is flown by both NSAWC as well as the Fighting Omars of VFC-12. Prior to VFC-13 standing up a permanent detachment at NAS Key West, the Omars often detached aircraft down to Key West to support initial air combat training for F/A-18 training squadrons.

fighter like an F/A-18 it definitely gets their attention. Losing against the F-16 seems less personal, as though they lost against a superb aircraft, whereas against the F-5, it's against an older, less capable fighter.

"I love flying the F-5," says Lieutenant Picciano, who has had quite a bit of stick time in the F-14 Tomcat previously. "It's obviously less capable than a Tomcat or Hornet, but it is very simple and easy to fly. It's less forgiving and fun to fight in. Since we do so much 1V1 [one versus one] training, I have done more dogfighting in one year with VFC-13 than I did in four years in a fleet F-14 unit. With the F/A-18 and the F-14 you have so many missions that you have to train to, like air-to-ground, it takes away from basic air-to-air work. With the F-5 here at VFC-13, we get to really focus on this one mission, primarily 1V1 and 1V2 [one versus two] dogfighting. Everyone here at the unit is well above average with proficiency and knowledge of BFM.

"As far as an F-5 against a Super Hornet or legacy Hornet with pilots of equal skill, the F-5 would not stand a chance. If you get to a neutral merge and both guys have equal sight of each other, the Hornet or Tomcat would own an F-5. What we do here at VFC-13 is try to fly fundamentally sound BFM and either capitalize on any mistakes the other guy makes or try to present them with a situation they haven't seen and try to force a mistake out of them we could take advantage of," Lieutenant Picciano explains.

The Saints transitioned to the F/A-18 with the disestablishment of the other West Coast adversary units, although the change was short lived. The decision was made to send all of the F/A-18As from the "Desert Bogies" of VFA-127 to VFC-12 at Naval Air Station Oceana. The Navy's inventory of F-5s from VF-43, VF-45, VF-126, and VFA-127 were sent to VFC-13.

Lieutenant Picciano adds, "We have a unique situation here in the squadron in that as a reserve composite unit we have a mix of full-time pilots, full-time reservists, and also part-time reservists. For me, it is considered the same type of tour as a full-time Navy pilot, as if I served in one of the RAGs [replacement air groups] still on my initial commitment. Currently, we have between six and eight full-time guys, the five or six full-time reservists, and roughly twenty-five part-time reservists, although a bunch of these guys are down in our Key West detachment. All of the squadron's maintenance is handled by Sikorsky on a contract basis, so there are no enlisted maintenance people with the unit. The unit is currently outfitted with twenty-eight aircraft in total. Initially, eight will be sent permanently to the NAS Key West detachment, then another four will be sent."

The detachment will support VFA-106, VFA-125, and VFA-122 primarily. The units are the Navy's F/A-18

The F-16 is arguably the best all-around Red Air fighter. The F-16 has the important distinction of being a truly dissimilar aircraft, which benefits Navy F/A-18 pilots in presenting them with a unique fighter. This aircraft is wearing a paint scheme designed to mimic the former Soviet Union's Sukhoi SU-27 flanker fighter.

A two-seat NSAWC F-16 taxis back to the NSAWC flight line postmission. The F-16 is perhaps the most successful aircraft program of the modern era. The Fighting Falcon is flown within the air forces of dozens of countries in addition to the U.S. Air Force, air national guard, reserves, and the Navy.

Hornet/Super Hornet FRS, which train new aviators in the aircraft. Picciano continues, "We had been doing eight to ten individual dets per year from NAS Fallon to NAS Key West, which is involved when you consider we have to fly the aircraft there for two weeks at a time. It's much easier than having us or VFC-12 sending down aircraft. We do place an officer in charge (OIC) down in Key West and the det acts almost like its own separate squadron, with dedicated pilots that stay down there with part-time reservists supplementing them when needed. Things are pretty slow when there is no RAG in town, but it can get quite busy with up to sixteen sorties a day when they are in town."

At the time of publication, only Hornet fleet replacement squadrons are sending students and instructors down to Key West. The last F-14 air crews with VF-101 completed the final training with the Tomcat in 2005. Even though the Hornet and Super Hornet are relatively similar when it comes to the basic introductory training at the FRS level, the syllabus does differ slightly.

The basic FRS detachment lasts for two weeks. Like most other training, it employs a building-block approach. The first week concentrates on basic one versus one (1V1) and two versus one (2V1). For the 1V1, the RAG starts in-house with similar training, meaning a Hornet or Super Hornet versus another Hornet or Super Hornet. Toward the end of the 1V1 syllabus, they will fly dissimilar missions with a Hornet fighting against an F-5 Tiger. Lieutenant Picciano says, "We do a handful of 1V1 missions during the early part of the first week, then move to 2V1s, which is a section-engaged maneuvering hop. We, as the adversary, will be the single aircraft and provide some visual sets with the students as a single bandit, getting them to work together to kill us. This usually completes the first week. We will then move to 2V2 hops the second week of the training. This includes basic section intercepts with canned maneuvers. The emphasis is on BVR [beyond visual range] radar work, not so much on the merge and engaged maneuvering. As we get toward the middle of the second week, we will begin doing mission-specific hops like OCA [offensive counter air] or DCA [defensive counter air]. These are a bit more involved and will be two versus an unknown number of adversaries [2VX] missions. These missions will involve more maneuvering and are less canned that the earlier missions. It is still a much more tame presentation compared to what we do for an SFARP or air wing training. We don't go full out and try to kill the students, but rather give them a problem that makes them work hard but is appropriate for their skill level. At this point in the students' training, they are still new to their aircraft and it is important to get them to nail down the fundamentals. We try to keep it a simple and solvable problem for them."

It is this strict intent to teach that separates skilled adversary pilots from other fighter pilots. Simply going up and killing the students quickly serves no purpose. The student learns nothing and it becomes a waste of time for all involved. The adversary pilot is a teacher who maintains discipline and uses his skill to underfly in the aircraft so as to present the student with a scenario that fosters learning. That is, until they get into knife fighting at close-in range when their fangs come out.

Lieutenant Picciano describes the attitude of the adversary pilot during the close-in dogfight: "One thing we don't do is intentionally underfly our aircraft once we do the head-on pass, which is called the 'merge.' We maneuver full up at this point every time. Assuming the safety rules are met, we never fly stupid just to let the student get a kill. We will provide positional problems for them to solve during their radar training missions that exceed beyond-visual-range engagements; but once we get into the second week of FRS training, we get into ACM [air combat maneuvering] missions where we fight pretty hard. The missions will be more real-world like and

Decked out to simulate the impressive former Soviet Union SU-27 flanker, this NSAWC F/A-18A Hornet cruises over the Carson Sink area of the range complex. The Hornet can offer a fair representation of the highly maneuverable SU-27 and is particularly adept at slow-speed, high-angle-of-attack dogfighting.

Two NSAWC Hornets, each dressed in a different paint scheme, make a strong argument for the benefit of camouflage. These aircraft are tough to pick up visually, especially during the winter, which is exactly the intent of the paint scheme. Each scheme mimics one worn by potential adversaries.

might include protecting the ship, for example, which is not covered during the first week of training."

Picciano continues, "Any time you are working with the RAG, you always have safety in your mind. We are responsible for all of the aircraft out there and for the training rules. As bandits we want to be aggressive but err on the side of safety. We will pass on taking a shot or take being shot ourselves as opposed to pushing a situation and doing something unsafe. Everything is exaggerated when working with the RAG; you tend to be more conservative. On a 2V1 against a student, you will spend a lot more time watching altitude and air speeds for him to keep him safe than you would if you were fighting a fleet pilot. For example, we would want to make sure he does not make an aggressive nose-low maneuver below the soft deck. He may be flying with his own instructor, who could have as much as or more experience than we do, but as an adversary pilot you do spend more time trying to keep him out of trouble.

"From their perspective, BFM is tricky; it takes a long time to get good at it. It's not something they can master in a

few weeks at the RAG. It is expected and normal for them to make basic mistakes, which we try to highlight and bring to their attention during the debrief so they learn something on every flight. Showing the student as many problems and having them make mistakes is the best approach to learning. After they see enough situations, they begin to learn what to do properly."

For the most part, the Saints conduct largely FRS training during the detachments to Key West and support air wings from Naval Air Station Fallon, working in concert with NSAWC. On some occasions, VFA-122, the Super Hornet FRS based at Naval Air Station Lemoore, will have students fly against VFC-13 pilots; this represents 15 percent of their work. The majority of the time, the unit supports fleet unit activities, such as SFARPs and Top Gun. Lieutenant Picciano says, "We all work together; NSAWC actually runs the air wing training, leading the Red Air support for those exercises. During the SFARP, we run the Red Air, and the Top Gun instructors lead Red Air for the SFTI course. "

Interview with Former VFC-13 Commanding Officer and Top Gun Graduate Commander Dan "Bat" Masterson

Commander Dan "Bat" Masterson, the former VFC-13 commanding officer, has amassed a total of 3,500 hours in the A-6, F-14, F/A-18, and F-5. Bat went through the adversary instructor course at Top Gun in September 1990, flying the F-5. In September 1996, he went through the adversary training course again, this time in the F/A-18. His recollections of going through Top Gun as a student are unique: "It is a different program now compared to when I went through it. Back then, it was strictly air-to-air and now, of course, it is air-to-ground with the strike fighter emphasis. I went through it as a lieutenant flying F-5s in VFA-127 here at Fallon. I went through the initial adversary syllabus here at the squadron first, and then went down to Miramar for the Top Gun syllabus. It was an awesome opportunity for a pilot to be trained by the guys that train the trainers. The SFTI, after all, are the guys going back out into the fleet, spreading the information on a daily basis. It was incredibly exciting to be given a chance to go to NAS Miramar and fly against the Top Gun instructors in their A-4 Super Foxes and F-16N.

"Going through and getting the adversary qual was tough, but the squadron prepared me for it. I would say going through the SFTI class now is a lot more work; it's a longer class. Back then, it was a six-week class in total, with the adversary portion just four of those weeks. Now it's at least an eight-week class for SFTIs and six weeks for the adversary. As the tactics and threats change, along with the newer airplanes and an expanded mission, Top Gun has evolved. Back in the 1990s, the lecture syllabus on everything that involved fighter aviation for the Navy was very in-depth. We started out with about a week and a half of lectures; then you go flying as well. Toward the end of the course, it's strictly flying. As an adversary pilot going through it, I flew strictly as Red Air and flew as part of the presentations for the SFTI students. We started out flying 1V1 against Top Gun instructors in either A-4s or F-16s to practice our briefing and debriefing skills, as well as our flying skills. Flying an F-5 against either of those aircraft was not easy. We were the only guys in the Navy flying the F-5 at the time, so we took our airplanes with us. The most challenging part was the level of expertise that they were trying to get me to as an instructor. We were going to be wearing the patch and training the RAG students, as well as supplementing the Strike University pilots before it was integrated into NSAWC.

"The most difficult portion was making sure you briefed the hop completely and correctly to the level of detail involved. In reality, it is more than the flying that is challenging. The book portion is as well—learning the threat, the numbers, everything involved in fighting various types of airplanes, was very comprehensive and challenging. How are we going to fight them, how do they turn, how to fight this other platform, involves a tremendous amount of book work. It's not good enough to just be good in the airplane; you have to be able to brief it, and, more importantly, you have to be able to sit with that pilot after the flight and debrief it. We had to be able to tell him why he either did well or why he did not so that he can become a better pilot the next time he goes out to fight. It's one thing to go out and be the master of the platform you are flying; it's an entirely different thing to take what you do in the three-dimensional world of air combat, recall the fight, and be able to tell the student when he started losing. There are no magic moves out there; at every merge and with every turn, you need to be able to show the student where you got an advantage on him, or conversely where he got the advantage on the instructor, so that he can learn that on the ground and take that into the next fight so he gets better.

"Week one was mostly book work and lectures. We did a warm-up flight at the end of the first week. Then we went right into the 1V1 missions, briefs, etc. When you showed up, you were expected to be up to date on the Top Gun material in advance. The unit I was with, VFA-127, prepared me quite well for the Top Gun course. It was expected that once I went down to Miramar and into the Top Gun course itself, they would take me to the next level as an adversary instructor pilot. By the second week of the course, we started flying twice a day, which built up our experience level and allowed us to learn how to fly these missions more safely. Most of the times, we briefed at NAS Miramar early in the morning, then flew the missions over the Yuma, Arizona, ranges, landed at MCAS Yuma, where we debriefed the first flight, and then took a break for lunch. We would brief the second mission, go fly it, and then return to Miramar, where we would debrief again. It turns into a very long day. It all has to happen in the air; you have to prove you are making the right decisions, making the right presentations in the dynamic ACM environment.

Continued on page 184

"The hardest part for me during the Top Gun course was having to fight in the F-5 and trying to take advantage of its attributes, such as small size, and making it a viable adversary platform. The F-16 or A-4 were advanced enough that you could make a mistake as an adversary against F-14s or F/A-18s and still fight, whereas in the F-5, that is much harder to do based on its limitations. A properly flown F/A-18 or F-14 will beat the F-5 no matter what we do. Remember, the Top Gun instructors are very good at their craft. It's something they work on every day; their murder board lectures and briefs and debriefs are at a level you just will not see anywhere else, including when we went to the USAF Fighter Weapons School at Nellis AFB, Nevada, to fight against them.

"One thing to remember is, unlike the SFTI students, the adversary students are there to be a tool used by the Top Gun instructors to help train the SFTI students going through the class. We were with the SFTI students through the lectures, but remember, the SFTI students are the good guys and we are the bad guys. This is a big distinction. When we launch, we are supposed to give the SFTI students a very good threat presentation, but ultimately we are supposed to die. We are supposed to get shot, as opposed to the fighters who are out there expected to win. Needless to say, when you have Top Gun–trained instructors in F-16s, A-4s, and F-5s, it is a difficult process for the SFTI students to go through. The students often die during the learning process. That added pressure on them of having come back from a mission after getting killed is tougher than on us, and we are not held to the same level of scrutiny that the SFTI students are. Top Gun did not have enough adversary assets to be able to fly against the students, so having us there as adversary assets, even under training, is a win-win for everyone.

"One of our biggest goals is to ensure we are doing things safely. ACM fighting is certainly the most dynamic type of fighting out there, and once you put the patch on your shoulder, you are expected to be able to lead an event someday and do it safely. We can't afford to lose assets while training and being able to handle things at the merge and not hurting anybody, while maintaining SA [situational awareness]. Flying in an F-5, which did not have a radar, meant that all of my SA came from my experience and training because I am flying against guys with better airplanes and better radar. We found that due to our experience and training, we had much better awareness of the fight than the guys with the better equipment. The Top Gun guys take this to the highest degree; they do this every day and hold themselves to an even higher standard. When I went through the Top Gun program, I found that I had to fight the Top Gun instructors to the very best of my ability every time just to have a chance. They are that good at what they do.

"You have to be able to step away, especially during 1V1, from the personal nature of the fight. As an instructor, I am not supposed to think in terms of defeating another person. It's not personal; I have to step away from getting my personality into the mix. I am fighting a guy with a better airplane, but the goal is to teach."

The F-5E Tiger evolved from the Northrop F-5A Freedom Fighter, which enjoyed wide success as a low-cost fighter in the export market. Neither version served extensively as a front-line fighter with American forces but did find a long and useful career as a dedicated adversary tactics training aircraft.

Looking rather sinister in a North Korean Air Force–styled paint scheme, this VFC-13 F-5 Tiger was photographed near NAS Fallon. The Fighting Saints trace their beginnings back to 1973, when they were established at NAS New Orleans. They were first designated VC-13 and flew the F-8 Crusader.

This F/A-18 Hornet with the Omars of VFC-12 rockets across the Atlantic Ocean in the Whiskey 72 range area off the coast of Norfolk, Virginia. VFC-12 pilots are Red Air threat experts, offering graduate-level training in enemy threat simulations and in-depth lectures to fleet and training Hornet units.

A Top Gun F-16 spins up for a mission. The Navy initially used twenty-two single-seat and four two-seat F-16N aircraft within Top Gun and other adversary units back in 1988. The continuous high-g maneuvers rapidly fatigued the airframes, and they were subsequently removed from service.

VFC-12 flies a dozen early-model F/A-18A Hornet aircraft. VFC-12 provides direct fleet support, especially with participation in the strike fighter advanced readiness program (SFARP). This intense three-week training exercise is geared toward F/A-18 Hornet units to refine their skills prior to deployment. VFC-12 will conduct the SFARP training at NAS Oceana as well as at other locations.

The F-5 is simple to maintain and easy to fly. While it cannot replicate fourth-generation fighter aircraft, it does a solid job representing third-generation former Soviet Union aircraft still operated in wide numbers throughout the world. The Tiger is powered by a pair of J85 engines and has a top speed of over 1,000 miles per hour.

The current fixed-wing adversary aircraft operated by NSAWC are the F-16 and F/A-18, both pictured here. The NSAWC maintenance department, along with contractor Sikorsky, is responsible for keeping the twenty F/A-18s and thirteen F-16s available and ready for flight.

The F-5N variant previously flown by the Swiss Air Force is now coming into service with the VFC-13. It has several improvements, such as a radar warning receiver and an antiskid system, to provide enhanced handling on wet runways. The F-5N is distinguishable by its squashed, platypus nose.

For most of its career, the F-5 has simulated the MiG-21, flown by the former Soviet Union Air Force and satellite communist countries. The Tiger is operated by VFC-13 as well as the U.S. Marine Corps' dedicated adversary tactics squadron, VMFT-401, based at Marine Corps Air Station Yuma, Arizona.

GLOSSARY

ACLS: automated carrier landing system

ACM: air combat maneuvering

ADTAC: adversary tactics

AEW: airborne early warning

AGM: air-to-ground missile

AIM: air intercept missile

AMCC: advanced mission commanders' course

AMRAAM: advanced medium-range air-to-air missile (AIM-120)

ARIES II: airborne reconnaissance integrated electronics suite II (EP-3)

ASW: antisubmarine warfare

ATP: advanced training phase

AWACS: airborne warning and control system

AWI: all-weather intercepts

BARCAP: barrier combat air patrol

BFM: basic fighter maneuvers

BVR: beyond visual range

CAEWWS: Carrier Airborne Early Warning Weapons School

CAG: commander air group

CATCC: carrier air traffic control center

CIC: combat information center

CINC: commander in chief

CNO: chief of naval operations

COD: carrier onboard delivery (C-2 Greyhound)

CQ: carrier qualifications

CSAR: combat search and rescue

CV: carrier (non-nuclear)

CVN: carrier (nuclear)

CVW: carrier air wing

C3: command, control, and communications

DCA: defensive counter air

DDI: digital display indicators

DECM: defensive electronic countermeasures

ECM: electronic countermeasures

ECMO: electronic countermeasures officer (EA-6B)

ERWS: Electronic Reconnaissance Weapons School

FLIR: forward-looking infrared

FRS: fleet replacement squadron, also known as replacement air group (RAG)

FRTC: Fallon Range Training Complex

HARM: High-speed antiradiation missile (AGM-88)

HMP: helicopter master plan

HOTAS: hands-on throttle and stick

HUD: heads-up display

HVUCAP: high-value combat air patrol

ICAP: improved capabilities (EA-6B)

IFF: identification, friend or foe

ITP: integrated training phase

IUT: instructor under training

JDAM: joint direct-attack munitions

JHMCS: joint helmet-mounted cueing system (F/A-18 Super Hornet)

JSF: joint strike fighter (F-35)

JSOW: joint stand-off weapon

JTIDS: joint tactical information distribution system (E-2C)

LAMPS: light airborne multipurpose system (SH-60)

LANTIRN: low-altitude navigation and targeting infrared for night system

LEX: leading-edge extension (F/A-18)

LLD: light landing device, a.k.a. Fresnel optical landing system, meatball

MCAS: Marine Corps Air Station

MFD: multi-function display

MIGCAP: MiG combat air patrol

MLT: mission-level training

MPCD: Multipurpose color displays (F/A-18 Super Hornet)

N1: NSAWC personnel resources department

N2: NSAWC intelligence department

N3: NSAWC operations department

N4: NSAWC maintenance department

N5: NSAWC Strike plans, programs, and tactics development department

N6: NSAWC Carrier Airborne Early Warning Weapons School/Electronic Reconnaissance Weapons School

N7: NSAWC Top Gun training and standardization department

N8: NSAWC Seahawk Weapons School

N88: director air warfare (U.S. Navy)

N9: NSAWC operational risk management and safety department

NAS: Naval Air Station

NATF: naval air tactical fighter

NFO: naval flight officer

NSAWC: Naval Strike and Air Warfare Center

NSWC: Naval Strike Warfare Center

NVG: night-vision goggles

OCA: offensive counter air

PGM: precision-guided munitions

RIO: radar intercept officer (F-14)

RWR: radar warning receiver

SAR: search and rescue

SEAD: suppression enemy air defenses

SEAL: SEa, Air, Land (U.S. Navy SEAL team)

SECNAV: secretary of the navy

SFARP: strike fighter advanced readiness planning

SFTI: strike fighter tactics instructor

SLATS: strike leader attack training syllabus

SME: subject-matter experts

SRA: section radar attacks

TACTS: tactical air crew combat training system

TALD: tactical air-launched decoy

TARCAP: target air combat patrol

TARPS: tactical air reconnaissance pod system (F-14)

TJS: tactical jamming system (EA-6B)

TLAM: Tomahawk land attack missile

TTC: tactical training cell

TTP: tactics, techniques, and procedures

VA: naval attack squadron

VAQ: naval electronic warfare squadron (EA-6B)

VAW: naval airborne early warning squadron (E-2C)

VFA: naval fighter/attack squadron (F/A-18)

VFAX: lightweight multi-mission fighter

VF: naval fighter squadron (F-14)

VFC: composite fighter squadron reserves

VQ ARP: fleet air reconnaissance advanced readiness program

VS: naval antisubmarine warfare squadron (S-3)

XO: executive officer

INDEX